Lecture Notes in Computer Science 13536

Shiqi Yu · Zhaoxiang Zhang · Pong C. Yuen ·
Junwei Han · Tieniu Tan · Yike Guo ·
Jianhuang Lai · Jianguo Zhang (Eds.)

Pattern Recognition and Computer Vision

5th Chinese Conference, PRCV 2022
Shenzhen, China, November 4–7, 2022
Proceedings, Part III

Editors
Shiqi Yu 🆔
Southern University of Science
and Technology
Shenzhen, China

Pong C. Yuen 🆔
Hong Kong Baptist University
Hong Kong, China

Tieniu Tan
Institute of Automation
Chinese Academy of Sciences
Beijing, China

Jianhuang Lai
Sun Yat-sen University
Guangzhou, China

Zhaoxiang Zhang
Institute of Automation
Chinese Academy of Sciences
Beijing, China

Junwei Han
Northwestern Polytechnical University
Xi'an, China

Yike Guo
Hong Kong Baptist University
Hong Kong, China

Jianguo Zhang 🆔
Southern University of Science
and Technology
Shenzhen, China

ISSN 0302-9743   ISSN 1611-3349 (electronic)
Lecture Notes in Computer Science
ISBN 978-3-031-18912-8   ISBN 978-3-031-18913-5 (eBook)
https://doi.org/10.1007/978-3-031-18913-5

This Springer imprint is published by the registered company Springer Nature Switzerland AG
The registered company address is: Gewerbestrasse 11, 6330 Cham, Switzerland

Preface

Welcome to the proceedings of the 5th Chinese Conference on Pattern Recognition and Computer Vision (PRCV 2022) held in Shenzhen, China!

PRCV was established to further boost the impact of the Chinese community in pattern recognition and computer vision, which are two core areas of artificial intelligence, and further improve the quality of academic communication. Accordingly, PRCV is co-sponsored by four major academic societies of China: the China Society of Image and Graphics (CSIG), the Chinese Association for Artificial Intelligence (CAAI), the China Computer Federation (CCF), and the Chinese Association of Automation (CAA).

PRCV aims at providing an interactive communication platform for researchers from academia and from industry. It promotes not only academic exchange but also communication between academia and industry. In order to keep track of the frontier of academic trends and share the latest research achievements, innovative ideas, and scientific methods, international and local leading experts and professors are invited to deliver keynote speeches, introducing the latest advances in theories and methods in the fields of pattern recognition and computer vision.

PRCV 2022 was hosted by the Southern University of Science and Technology and Shenzhen Polytechnic. We received 564 full submissions. Each submission was reviewed by at least three reviewers selected from the Program Committee and other qualified researchers. Based on the reviewers' reports, 233 papers were finally accepted for presentation at the conference, comprising 40 oral presentations and 193 posters. The acceptance rate was 41%. The conference took place during November 4–7, 2022, and the proceedings are published in this volume in Springer's Lecture Notes in Computer Science (LNCS) series.

We are grateful to the keynote speakers, Alan Yuille from Johns Hopkins University, USA, Kyoung Mu Lee from the Korea National Open University, South Korea, Zhengyou Zhang from the Tencent AI Lab, China, Yaonan Wang from Hunan University, China, Wen Gao from the Pengcheng Laboratory and Peking University, China, Hong Qiao from the Institute of Automation, Chinese Academy of Sciences, China, and Muming Poo from the Institute of Neuroscience, Chinese Academy of Sciences, China.

We give sincere thanks to the authors of all submitted papers, the Program Committee members and the reviewers, and the Organizing Committee. Without their contributions, this conference would not have been possible. Special thanks also go to all of the sponsors.

October 2022

Tieniu Tan
Yike Guo
Jianhuang Lai
Jianguo Zhang
Shiqi Yu
Zhaoxiang Zhang
Pong C. Yuen
Junwei Han

Organization

Steering Committee Chair

Tieniu Tan Institute of Automation, Chinese Academy of
Sciences, China

Steering Committee

Xilin Chen Institute of Computing Technology, Chinese
Academy of Sciences, China

Chenglin Liu Institute of Automation, Chinese Academy of
Sciences, China

Yong Rui Lenovo, China

Hongbing Zha Peking University, China

Nanning Zheng Xi'an Jiaotong University, China

Jie Zhou Tsinghua University, China

Steering Committee Secretariat

Liang Wang Institute of Automation, Chinese Academy of
Sciences, China

General Chairs

Tieniu Tan Institute of Automation, Chinese Academy of
Sciences, China

Yike Guo Hong Kong Baptist University, Hong Kong, China

Jianhuang Lai Sun Yat-sen University, China

Jianguo Zhang Southern University of Science and Technology,
China

Program Chairs

Shiqi Yu Southern University of Science and Technology,
China

Zhaoxiang Zhang Institute of Automation, Chinese Academy of
Sciences, China

Pong C. Yuen Hong Kong Baptist University, Hong Kong, China

Junwei Han Northwest Polytechnic University, China

Organizing Committee Chairs

Jinfeng Yang   Shenzhen Polytechnic, China
Guangming Lu   Harbin Institute of Technology, Shenzhen, China
Baoyuan Wu   The Chinese University of Hong Kong, Shenzhen,
                                  China
Feng Zheng   Northwest Polytechnic University, China

Sponsorship Chairs

Liqiang Nie   Harbin Institute of Technology, Shenzhen, China
Yu Qiao   Shenzhen Institute of Advanced Technology,
                                  Chinese Academy of Sciences, China
Zhenan Sun   Institute of Automation, Chinese Academy of
                                  Sciences, China
Xiaochun Cao   Sun Yat-sen University, China

Publicity Chairs

Weishi Zheng   Sun Yat-sen University, China
Wei Jia   Hefei University of Technology, China
Lifang Wu   Beijing University of Technology, China
Junping Zhang   Fudan University, China

Local Arrangement Chairs

Yujiu Yang   Tsinghua Shenzhen International Graduate
                                  School, China
Yanjie Wei   Shenzhen Institute of Advanced Technology,
                                  Chinese Academy of Sciences, China

International Liaison Chairs

Jingyi Yu   ShanghaiTech University, China
Qifeng Liu   Shenzhen Polytechnic, China
Song Guo   Hong Kong Polytechnic University, Hong Kong,
                                  China

Competition Chairs

Wangmeng Zuo   Harbin Institute of Technology, China
Di Huang   Beihang University, China
Bin Fan   University of Science and Technology Beijing,
                                  China

Tutorial Chairs

Jiwen Lu   Tsinghua University, China
Ran He   Institute of Automation, Chinese Academy of
                          Sciences, China
Xi Li   Zhejiang University, China
Jiaying Liu   Peking University, China

Special Session Chairs

Jing Dong   Institute of Automation, Chinese Academy of
                          Sciences, China
Zhouchen Lin   Peking University, China
Xin Geng   Southeast University, China
Yong Xia   Northwest Polytechnic University, China

Doctoral Forum Chairs

Tianzhu Zhang   University of Science and Technology of China,
                          China
Shanshan Zhang   Nanjing University of Science and Technology,
                          China
Changdong Wang   Sun Yat-sen University, China

Publication Chairs

Kui Jia   South China University of Technology, China
Yang Cong   Institute of Automation, Chinese Academy of
                          Sciences, China
Cewu Lu   Shanghai Jiao Tong University, China

Registration Chairs

Weihong Deng   Beijing University of Posts and
                          Telecommunications, China
Wenxiong Kang   South China University of Technology, China
Xiaohu Yan   Shenzhen Polytechnic, China

Exhibition Chairs

Hongmin Liu   University of Science and Technology Beijing,
                          China
Rui Huang   The Chinese University of Hong Kong, Shenzhen,
                          China

Kai Lei   Peking University Shenzhen Graduate School,
                                   China
Zechao Li   Nanjing University of Science and Technology,
                                   China

Finance Chairs

Xu Wang   Shenzhen Polytechnic, China
Li Liu   Southern University of Science and Technology,
                                   China

Website Chairs

Zhaofeng He   Beijing University of Posts and
                                   Telecommunications, China
Mengyuan Liu   Sun Yat-sen University, China
Hanyang Peng   Pengcheng Laboratory, China

Program Committee

Yuntao Chen   TuSimple, China
Gong Cheng   Northwest Polytechnic University, China
Runmin Cong   Beijing Jiaotong University, China
Bin Fan   University of Science and Technology Beijing,
                                   China
Chen Gong   Nanjing University of Science and Technology,
                                   China
Fuyuan Hu   Suzhou University of Science and Technology,
                                   China
Huaibo Huang   Institute of Automation, Chinese Academy of
                                   Sciences, China
Sheng Huang   Chongqing University, China
Du Huynh   University of Western Australia, Australia
Sen Jia   Shenzhen University, China
Baiying Lei   Shenzhen University, China
Changsheng Li   Beijing Institute of Technology, China
Haibo Liu   Harbin Engineering University, China
Chao Ma   Shanghai Jiao Tong University, China
Vishal M. Patel   Johns Hopkins University, USA
Hanyang Peng   Pengcheng Laboratory, China
Manivannan Siyamalan   University of Jaffna, Sri Lanka
Anwaar Ulhaq   Charles Sturt University, Australia
Changdong Wang   Sun Yat-sen University, China

Dong Wang	Dalian University of Technology, China
Jinjia Wang	Yanshan University, China
Xiwen Yao	Northwest Polytechnic University, China
Mang Ye	Wuhan University, China
Dingwen Zhang	Northwest Polytechnic University, China
Ke Zhang	North China Electric Power University, China
Man Zhang	Beijing University of Posts and Telecommunications, China
Qieshi Zhang	Shenzhen Institute of Advanced Technology, Chinese Academy of Sciences, China
Xuyao Zhang	Institute of Automation, Chinese Academy of Sciences, China
Bineng Zhong	Guangxi Normal University, China
Quan Zhou	Nanjing University of Posts and Telecommunications, China

Contents – Part III

Recognition, Remote Sensing

Vision Analysis and Understanding

3D Computer Vision
and Reconstruction, Robots
and Autonomous Driving

Locally Geometry-Aware Improvements of LOP for Efficient Skeleton Extraction

Xianyong Fang[✉][iD], Lingzhi Hu, Fan Ye, and Linbo Wang

School of Computer Science and Technology, Anhui University, Hefei 230601, China
fangxianyong@ahu.edu.cn

Abstract. The skeletons extracted from 3D point clouds depict the general distributions of the mesh surfaces, which are affected by the local geometrical relations embedded in the neighboring points. However, the local mesh geometry is still not effectively utilized by the popular contraction based skeleton extraction method LOP and its variants. Therefore, this paper improves LOP from two aspects based on the local geometrical distributions. One is the bilateral filter based weighting scheme which additionally takes curvature similarities between neighboring points to better distribute the samples and the other is the eigenvalue based adaptive radius scheme which makes the contraction area varied according to the local shape. These two updates combine together so that an effective contraction of samples during optimization can be obtained. The experiments demonstrate that the improved LOP can obtain more efficient skeleton extractions than existing methods.

Keywords: Skeleton extraction · LOP · Local geometry

1 Introduction

Skeleton extraction has been studied for a long time and can be applied to various areas [4,8,11,13,21,24,26,37,43], such as computer graphics, computer vision and image processing. We are interested in the contraction based methods [7, 17,22,35,36,39,44] which gradually shrink the clouds to obtain the skeleton.

In particular, we are interested in the Locally Optimal Projection (LOP) [25] based methods [17,23,32] among the contraction oriented ideas. LOP was originally for computing the geometry surfaces of raw scans, which projects each point to its nearby local center according to a support radius. It was recruited by Hang *et al.* [17] to compute L_1-medial skeletons of 3D point clouds. However, this method is not stable because it does not consider the local geometrical structure when doing the contraction. In addition, its contraction can be very inefficient without discriminating the surface variations of the local shapes.

Supported by the Natural Science Foundation of Anhui Province (2108085MF210, 1908085MF187).

S. Yu et al. (Eds.): PRCV 2022, LNCS 13536, pp. 3–14, 2022.
https://doi.org/10.1007/978-3-031-18913-5_1

Existing improvements [23,32] either rely on an additional local medial surface for effective contraction [23] or take a mixture model for fast computation [32]. However, their performances are still limited. The local distribution of points reflects the shape of the object and thus plays an important role in the skeleton estimation during the contraction process However, it is not explicitly considered in these methods.

Therefore, this paper takes the local geometrical distribution as the starting point and revises LOP from two aspects for better skeleton estimation. One is a bilateral filter [3,38] based idea adopted in the contraction process so that the geometrical similarity in curvature is additionally considered for better shape consensus. The other is an eigenvalue based radius estimation so that adaptive radii reflecting the variations of the local surface can be used for effcient contraction of different object parts. These two combine together so that an improved LOP algorithm incorporating local geometrical distributions are proposed.

2   Related Work

Skeleton extraction has been studied for a long time [11,37]. One popular type of methods for curve extraction is the contraction based method [1] which, however, cannot ensure a central skeleton because of the varying contraction speeds [7,36,39]. Therefore, some studies [17,22] focus on generating the centered curves, which is interesting to us. Especially Huang *et al.* [17] adopted locally optimal projection (LOP) [25] for extracting the skeletons from raw scanned data. They adopted L1-medians locally for 1D based L_1-medial skeletons, which is also used by [35,44] through iteratively contracting sample points while gradually increasing their neighborhood sizes.

There are also variants of LOP [16,23,32]. Huang *et al.* [16] extended LOP to cope with non-uniform distributions by a weighted locally optimal projection operator, which was later improved by Preiner *et al.* [32] with a Gaussian mixture model for fast computation. Wang [23] extended LOP for 3D curve skeletons by two ideas, constraining the LOP operator applied on the medial surface and adaptively computing variable support radii, and fulfilled fast computation and accurate localization without interference.

There have been other non-contraction based methods, such as image based [27], medial surface based [10,40], graph based [2,9,28] and geodesic distance based methods [18,19,41]. Qin *et al.* [33] took the mass transport view and estimated the skeleton with the minimization of Wasserstein distance between mass distributions of point clouds and curve skeletons. Jiang *et al.* [20] even combined the contraction and graph based ideas together and proposed a graph contraction method, including a contraction term in graph geodesic distances and a topology-preserving term by the local principal direction. Similar compound way is taken by Fu *et al.* [14]. However our focus here is on the contraction based methods, especially on LOP and its variants.

Deep learning based methods [12,15,29–31,42] become popular nowadays. For example, Panichev *et al.* [31] took an U-Net based approach for direct skeleton extraction; Luo *et al.* [29] included an encoder-decoder network to fulfill hierarchical skeleton extraction. Deep learning techniques are attractive, however, they generally require skillful training with large data for high performance.

Some studies also extend skeleton extraction to structure or outline estimation from point sets [8,34], whose foci are on fitting outer structure lines but not the skeletons.

3   The Improved LOP

This section introduces the proposed LOP method, where the general idea of LOP and its two proposed local geometry based improvements are presented in succession.

3.1   Overview

Generally, LOP is to find the set I representing the L_1-medial skeleton point set $X = \{\boldsymbol{x}_{i_{i \in I}}\}$ of an unorganized and unoriented set J of points $P = \{\boldsymbol{p}_{j_{j \in J}}\} \subset \mathbb{R}^3$.

$$\arg \min_X G(X) + R(X), \tag{1}$$

where $G(X)$ keeps the geometry of J in I and $R(X)$ lets points in I evenly distributed.

$$G(X) = \sum_{i \in I} \sum_{j \in J} \|\boldsymbol{x}_i - \boldsymbol{p}_j\| \theta(\|\boldsymbol{x}_i - \boldsymbol{p}_j\|), \tag{2}$$

where

$$\theta(r) = e^{-r^2/(h/4)^2} \tag{3}$$

is a fast-decreasing smooth weighting function with the compact support radius h defining the size of the influence radius [25].

$$R(X) = \sum_{i \in I} \lambda_i \sum_{i' \in I \backslash i} \eta(\|\boldsymbol{x}_i - \boldsymbol{x}_{i'}\|) \theta(\|\boldsymbol{x}_i - \boldsymbol{x}_{i'}\|), \tag{4}$$

where: λ_i represents the balancing term; and $\eta(r)$ is another decreasing function penalizing $\boldsymbol{x}_i$ too close to each other, which is generally set to be $1/3r^3$, or $-r$ for slow decreasing of large contraction radii.

Accordingly, I is generated as follows. First the input cloud is down sampled to obtain the sampling points evenly. These sampled points are the future source points of the estimated skeleton. Then the displacement of each sampling point $\boldsymbol{x}_i$ is estimated recursively till convergence, which is based on the eigen decomposition with the neighboring points. Here, weighted principal components analysis (PCA) is used to compute the eigenvalues in decreasing order $\lambda_i^m (m \in \{0, 1, 2\})$ and their corresponding eigenvectors $\boldsymbol{v}_i^m$ from the covariance matrix C_i,

$$C_i = \sum_{i' \in I \backslash i} \theta(\|\boldsymbol{x}_i - \boldsymbol{x}_{i'}\|)(\boldsymbol{x}_i - \boldsymbol{x}_{i'})^T (\boldsymbol{x}_i - \boldsymbol{x}_{i'}). \tag{5}$$

These values will guide the update of x_i according to Eq. 1 [17, 25].

As can be seen, the contraction process relies heavily on the distances of points between I and J. However, it only considers the spatial distances, which can mislead the process to wrong positions without considering the local geometrical relationships. In addition, the decay weight relies on a fixed radius for contraction which also omits the differences of local shapes of the cloud object, i.e., a wide and flat shape can have a big radius for robust contraction and vice versa. Apparently, local geometrical distributions should be considered when doing the contraction. Therefore, two geometry based improvements are proposed to update the optimization process for more robust contraction, which will be discussed in details in the following.

3.2   Bilateral Filter Based Weighting

The weighting function (Eq. 3) computes the weights by the spatial distance only, which may overlooks the importance of the geometrical similarities. Therefore, local geometrical similarities should also be considered in weighting the contributions. Therefore, the bilateral filter [38] based weighting scheme which takes these two properties together is proposed.

Traditional, the bilateral filter aims at replacing the intensity of the central pixel, u_c, at c with a weighted average of the intensities of the neighboring pixels $\{u_{c_1}, u_{c_2}, \ldots, u_{c_N}\}$, $\hat{u}_c$. These weights are estimated by both Euclidean distances and radiometric differences between the central pixel and its neighbors.

$$\hat{u}_c = \frac{1}{W_c} \sum_{i=1}^{N} f_g(\|u_c - u_{c_i}\|) f_r(c - c_i) u_{c_i}. \tag{6}$$

Here, W_c is a normalization term, and f_g and f_r are the spatial and range weighting kernels for the Euclidean and radiometric distances respectively.

For the skeleton estimation of 3D clouds, the Euclidean distance for the spatial difference measurement is kept. But the radiometric difference can be substituted with geometrical similarity, where curve distance of two points is adopted. Consequently, a bilateral filter based on the spatial and geometrical distances can be superimposed to the neighboring points by the following equation:

$$\rho(x_i, p_j) = \omega_s(\hat{s}(x_i, p_j)) \omega_g(\hat{g}(x_i, p_j) h(x_i, p_j), \tag{7}$$

where standard Gaussian filters represent $\omega_s(x)$ and $\omega_g(t)$ respectively, i.e., $\omega_s(x) = e^{-x^2/2\sigma_s^2}$ and $\omega_g(t) = e^{-t^2/2\sigma_g^2}$ with σ_s and σ_g being the variances. Here $\hat{s}$ and $\hat{g}$ targets at spatial and geometrical distances and measure the Euclidean distances and the curvature distances between x_i and p_j respectively:

$$\hat{s}(x_i, p_j) = \|x_i - p_j\| \tag{8}$$

and

$$\hat{g}(x_i, p_j) = \|\delta(x_i) - \delta(p_j)\|, \tag{9}$$

where $\delta(\cdot)$ computes the curvatures. Note that in Eq. 7, to effectively capture the local geometrical variance, the weights are superimposed on the sample points according to their distanaces projected to the tangent plane, $i.e.$,

$$h(\boldsymbol{x}_i, \boldsymbol{p}_j) = <\boldsymbol{n}_i, \boldsymbol{x}_i - \boldsymbol{p}_j > . \tag{10}$$

To constraint the contraction process, σ_s is chosen according to the standard deviation among neighboring points and σ_g is defined to be the radius of the neighboring set, $i.e.$, $\sigma_g = \|\boldsymbol{x}_i - \boldsymbol{m}_i\|$ with $\boldsymbol{m}_i$ being the fartherest point in the neighbors of $\boldsymbol{x}_i$. Consequently, the following updated version for the contraction (Eq. 2) is obtained based on Eq. 7,

$$G(X) = \sum_{i \in I} \sum_{j \in J} \|\boldsymbol{x}_i - \boldsymbol{p}_j\| \rho(\boldsymbol{x}_i, \boldsymbol{p}_j) \tag{11}$$

Figure 1 shows the effects before (Fig. 1b) and after (Fig. 1c) applying the bilateral filter based weights. There are more stray samples shown in the traditional LOP than the proposed method. This experiment shows that the additionally bilateral filter based weighting scheme makes the samples distributed more conformal and consistent with the object shape than the original LOP.

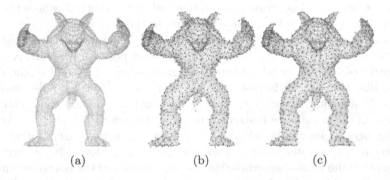

(a)   (b)   (c)

Fig. 1. Color figure onlinetracted samples by LOP or the bilateral filtering updated LOP. The sample points are shown in red. (a) Source cloud; (b): samples contracted by LOP; and (c): samples contracted by the bilateral filter based LOP. (Color figure online)

3.3 Adaptive Radius

The contraction radius is also very important because it decides the contraction scale and affects the areas to be contracted. Intuitively, the wide and flat area can have a bigger contraction scale while the narrow area should be with a smaller one. Figure 2a demonstrates this observation, where the belly should have a bigger radius than the arm for an efficient contraction. However the traditional one is fixed and thus cannot cope with the contraction efficiently and may lead

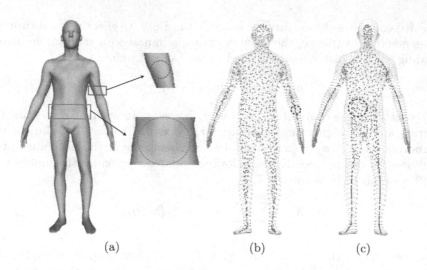

Fig. 2. Illustration of the adaptive contraction radius and its working examples. The dashed circus show the sizes of radii for the principle (a), and the sample contraction in the intermediate (b) and 5 more iteration steps (c) during the optimization.

to wrong estimation. Therefore, an adaptive radius is expected, where the local geometrical property can be taken as the clue to the solution.

However, it is difficult to directly capture the relationship between the local geometry and radius. Luckily, the covariance matrix points a way out. A covariance matrix of a point cloud captures the distribution or spread of the cloud, *e.g.*, the direction of the largest variance represents the largest dimension of the data. In addition, these directions can be computed as the eignevectors by decomposing the covariance matrix of the cloud through PCA (Fig. 3). Accordingly, the eigenvalues can be adopted to measure the extensions of clouds in all directions and, therefore, taken as a measurement of the local shape variation.

To capture the local shape variation, the eigenvalues of the covariance matrix of the local neighbors (Eq. 5) which reflects the local geometrical distributions are adopted to define a gradually increasing contraction radius. First, the directionality degree [17] defining the shape spreading feature of x_i, d_i, is adopted

$$d_i = \frac{\lambda_i^2}{\sum_{m=0}^{2} \lambda_i^m}. \tag{12}$$

Fig. 3. Illustration of the directions of a point cloud estimated by PCA with the covariance matrix of a 2D cloud. The red and blue arrows represent the major and minor directions respectively. (Color figure online)

It can be seen that the shape turns narrow as d_i approaches 1. Clearly, it is expected that the radius used in the narrow part to be also small for an effective contraction. Therefore, the following adaptive radius $h(i)^{(t)}$ for t-th iteration of x_i can be obtained.

$$h(i)^{(t)} = h(i)^{(t-1)} + e^{\frac{1}{d_i}}, \tag{13}$$

where $h(i)^{(0)} = 0$. Accordingly, the contraction radius h in Eq. 3 is replaced with Eq. 13 during the iterations.

The contraction happens first in narrow parts such as arms and legs with small radii and then gradually find the correct position with big radii for the wide parts, such as torso. Figure 2 gives the example of the adaptive radii during the contraction process. It can be seen that the narrow parts are contracted significantly first with smaller radii (Fig. 2b) and then gradually the wide parts are contracted apparently with bigger radii (Fig. 2c). These varying radii can help obtain a geometrically consistent skeleton.

The geometrically updated contraction weights and radii are incorporated into the traditional LOP algorithm and then an improved method is resulted. For more details on how to iteratively implement the algorithm, please check [17,25].

4   Experimental Results

Experiments are undertaken with two human and animal mesh datasets: TOSCA [6] and FAUST [5]. Two related improvements of LOP are considered for performance comparison: the L_1 medial skeleton based method [17] (L1) and the KNN based method [44] (KNN).

Figure 4 shows the results of our method on four clouds consisting of different object shapes. They show that our method can contract the sample points successfully to be the central skeleton points.

Fig. 4. Example results of our method

Figure 5 shows the experimental results on TOSCA. Here performance comparisons with L1 and CNN are taken. There are apparent unconnected and uncontracted samples for L1 and KNN, with L1 being generally worse. Ours, on the other hand, obtains the best performances among all methods, even though there are a few unconnected joints between some skeleton parts.

Figure 6 shows the performance comparisons on FAUST. The same observations about the three methods can be found, where ours still achieves the best performaces among all methods.

Statistical evaluation of the proposed method are also undertaken. Generally all skeleton points should be close to the neutral axis of the skeleton for a compact skeleton generation. However, the true neutral axis may not be easy to localize for each mesh. Here the max distance among all skeleton points to the center axis of the skeleton bounding box is taken as the metric. The smaller the distance, the better accuracy is. Figure 7 visualizes the max distances of different methods for 14 meshes from the two sets. Our method almost always the best one for all meshes among all methods, which further demonstrates the merits of our method.

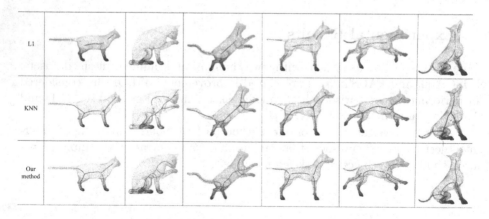

Fig. 5. Skeleton estimation by different methods for TOSCA.

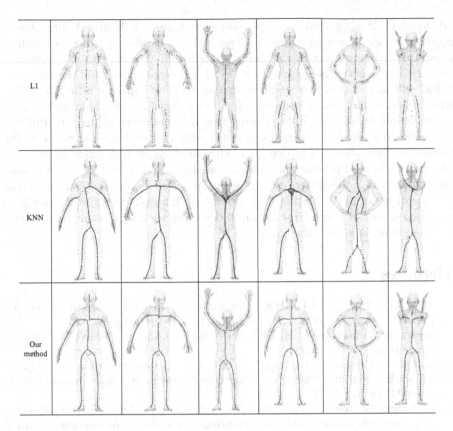

Fig. 6. Skeleton estimation by different methods for FAUST.

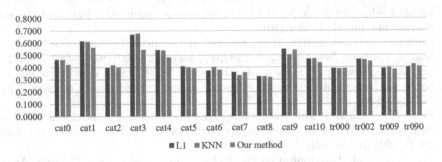

Fig. 7. Statistical comparisons of the max distance of each estimated skeleton for 14 meshes by different methods.

5   Conclusions

This paper proposed an improved LOP algorithm for skeleton extraction. Building on closely capturing the local geometrical variations, we update the traditional LOP algorithm from two aspects: One is a bilateral filter based weighting scheme where additional local geometrical similarities are used to make the contraction consensus to the mesh surface; and the other is an eigenvalue based varying radius scheme where the local geometrical distributions are used produce efficient contraction radii according to the shapes of different object parts. Experimental results demonstrate the merits of the proposed method.

The estimated skeleton in the contraction oriented methods may be difficult to converge to a skeleton keypoint connecting different skeleton segments, as the experiments have shown. The density of the clouds is often different in different part, which can lead to different contraction speed and, therefore, the common joint is sometimes difficult to get. In addition, more samples will improve the accuracy of skeleton estimation experimentally, however, this also incurs high computation load. Those two shortcomings will be the focus of our future work for more robust skeleton extraction.

References

1. Au, O.K.C., Tai, C.L., Chu, H.K., Cohen-Or, D., Lee, T.Y.: Skeleton extraction by mesh contraction. ACM Trans. Graph. **27**(3), 1–10 (2008)
2. Bærentzen, A., Rotenberg, E.: Skeletonization via local separators. ACM Trans. Graph. **40**(5), 1–18 (2021)
3. Banterle, F., Corsini, M., Cignoni, P., Scopigno, R.: A low-memory, straightforward and fast bilateral filter through subsampling in spatial domain. Comput. Graph. Forum **31**, 19–32 (2012)
4. Batchuluun, G., Kang, J.K., Nguyen, D.T., Pham, T.D., Arsalan, M., Park, K.R.: Action recognition from thermal videos using joint and skeleton information. IEEE Access **9**, 11716–11733 (2021)
5. Bogo, F., Romero, J., Loper, M., Black, M.J.: FAUST: dataset and evaluation for 3D mesh registration. In: IEEE Conference on Computer Vision and Pattern Recognition, pp. 3794–3801 (2014)
6. Bronstein, A.M., Bronstein, M.M., Kimmel, R.: Numerical Geometry of Non-rigid Shapes. Springer, New York (2008). https://doi.org/10.1007/978-0-387-73301-2
7. Cao, J., Tagliasacchi, A., Olson, M., Zhang, H., Su, Z.: Point cloud skeletons via Laplacian based contraction. In: Shape Modeling International Conference, pp. 187–197. IEEE (2010)
8. Chen, R., et al.: Multiscale feature line extraction from raw point clouds based on local surface variation and anisotropic contraction. IEEE Trans. Autom. Sci. Eng. **19**(2), 1003–2022 (2021)
9. Cheng, J., et al.: Skeletonization via dual of shape segmentation. Comput. Aided Geomet. Design **80**, 101856 (2020)
10. Chu, Y., Wang, W., Li, L.: Robustly extracting concise 3D curve skeletons by enhancing the capture of prominent features. IEEE Trans. Visual. Comput. Graph, pp. 1–1 (2022)
11. Cornea, N.D., Silver, D., Min, P.: Curve-skeleton properties, applications, and algorithms. IEEE Trans. Visual Comput. Graph. **13**(3), 530 (2007)
12. Dey, S.: Subpixel dense refinement network for skeletonization. In: IEEE/CVF Conference on Computer Vision and Pattern Recognition Workshops, pp. 258–259 (2020)

13. Fang, X., Zhou, Q., Shen, J., Jacquemin, C., Shao, L.: Text image deblurring using kernel sparsity prior. IEEE Trans. Cybernet. **50**(3), 997–1008 (2018)
14. Fu, L., Liu, J., Zhou, J., Zhang, M., Lin, Y.: Tree skeletonization for raw point cloud exploiting cylindrical shape prior. IEEE Access **8**, 27327–27341 (2020)
15. Ghanem, M.A., Anani, A.A.: Binary image skeletonization using 2-stage U-Net. arXiv preprint arXiv:2112.11824 (2021)
16. Huang, H., Li, D., Zhang, H., Ascher, U., Cohen-Or, D.: Consolidation of unorganized point clouds for surface reconstruction. ACM Trans. Graph. **28**(5), 1–7 (2009)
17. Huang, H., Wu, S., Cohen-Or, D., Gong, M., Zhang, H., Li, G., Chen, B.: L1-medial skeleton of point cloud. ACM Trans. Graph. **32**(4), 1–8 (2013)
18. Jalba, A.C., Kustra, J., Telea, A.C.: Surface and curve skeletonization of large 3D models on the GPU. IEEE Trans. Pattern Anal. Mach. Intell. **35**(6), 1495–1508 (2012)
19. Jalba, A.C., Sobiecki, A., Telea, A.C.: An unified multiscale framework for planar, surface, and curve skeletonization. IEEE Trans. Pattern Anal. Mach. Intell. **38**(1), 30–45 (2015)
20. Jiang, A., Liu, J., Zhou, J., Zhang, M.: Skeleton extraction from point clouds of trees with complex branches via graph contraction. Vis. Comput. **37**(8), 2235–2251 (2020). https://doi.org/10.1007/s00371-020-01983-6
21. Ko, D.H., Hassan, A.U., Suk, J., Choi, J.: SKFont: Skeleton-driven Korean font generator with conditional deep adversarial networks. Int. J. Doc. Anal. Recogn. **24**(4), 325–337 (2021)
22. Li, L., Wang, W.: Contracting medial surfaces isotropically for fast extraction of centred curve skeletons. In: Computer Graphics Forum, vol. 36, pp. 529–539 (2017)
23. Li, L., Wang, W.: Improved use of LOP for curve skeleton extraction. In: Computer Graphics Forum, vol. 37, pp. 313–323 (2018)
24. Lin, C., Li, C., Liu, Y., Chen, N., Choi, Y.K., Wang, W.: Point2Skeleton: learning skeletal representations from point clouds. In: IEEE/CVF Conference on Computer Vision and Pattern Recognition, pp. 4277–4286 (2021)
25. Lipman, Y., Cohen-Or, D., Levin, D., Tal-Ezer, H.: Parameterization-free projection for geometry reconstruction. ACM Trans. Graph. **26**(3), 22-es (2007)
26. Liu, Y., Guo, J., Benes, B., Deussen, O., Zhang, X., Huang, H.: TreePartNet: neural decomposition of point clouds for 3D tree reconstruction. ACM Trans. Graph. **40**(6) (2021)
27. Livesu, M., Guggeri, F., Scateni, R.: Reconstructing the curve-skeletons of 3D shapes using the visual hull. IEEE Trans. Visual Comput. Graph. **18**(11), 1891–1901 (2012)
28. Lu, L., Lévy, B., Wang, W.: Centroidal Voronoi tessellation of line segments and graphs. Comput. Graph. Forum **31**, 775–784 (2012)
29. Luo, S., et al.: Laser curve extraction of wheelset based on deep learning skeleton extraction network. Sensors **22**(3), 859 (2022)
30. Nathan, S., Kansal, P.: SkeletonNetV2: a dense channel attention blocks for skeleton extraction. In: IEEE/CVF International Conference on Computer Vision, pp. 2142–2149 (2021)
31. Panichev, O., Voloshyna, A.: U-Net based convolutional neural network for skeleton extraction. In: IEEE/CVF Conference on Computer Vision and Pattern Recognition Workshops, pp. 1186–1189 (2019)
32. Preiner, R., Mattausch, O., Arikan, M., Pajarola, R., Wimmer, M.: Continuous projection for fast L1 reconstruction. ACM Trans. Graph. **33**(4), 1–13 (2014)

33. Qin, H., Han, J., Li, N., Huang, H., Chen, B.: Mass-driven topology-aware curve skeleton extraction from incomplete point clouds. IEEE Trans. Visual Comput. Graph. **26**(9), 2805–2817 (2019)
34. Ritter, M., Schiffner, D., Harders, M.: Robust reconstruction of curved line structures in noisy point clouds. Visual Inform. **5**(3), 1–14 (2021)
35. Song, C., Pang, Z., Jing, X., Xiao, C.: Distance field guided l_1-median skeleton extraction. Vis. Comput. **34**(2), 243–255 (2018)
36. Tagliasacchi, A., Alhashim, I., Olson, M., Zhang, H.: Mean curvature skeletons. Comput. Graphics Forum **31**, 1735–1744 (2012)
37. Tagliasacchi, A., Delame, T., Spagnuolo, M., Amenta, N., Telea, A.: 3D skeletons: a state-of-the-art report. Compu. Graph. Forum **35**, 573–597 (2016)
38. Tomasi, C., Manduchi, R.: Bilateral filtering for gray and color images. In: International Conference on Computer Vision, pp. 839–846 (1998)
39. Wang, Y.S., Lee, T.Y.: Curve-skeleton extraction using iterative least squares optimization. IEEE Trans. Visual Comput. Graphics **14**(4), 926–936 (2008)
40. Yan, Y., Letscher, D., Ju, T.: Voxel cores: efficient, robust, and provably good approximation of 3D medial axes. ACM Trans. Graphics **37**(4), 1–13 (2018)
41. Yan, Y., Sykes, K., Chambers, E., Letscher, D., Ju, T.: Erosion thickness on medial axes of 3D shapes. ACM Trans. Graph. **35**(4), 1–12 (2016)
42. Yang, L., Oyen, D., Wohlberg, B.: A novel algorithm for skeleton extraction from images using topological graph analysis. In: IEEE/CVF Conference on Computer Vision and Pattern Recognition Workshops, pp. 1162–1166 (2019)
43. Zhang, L., Hu, F., Chu, Z., Bentley, E., Kumar, S.: 3D transformative routing for UAV swarming networks: a skeleton-guided, GPS-free approach. IEEE Trans. Veh. Technol. **70**(4), 3685–3701 (2021)
44. Zhou, J., Liu, J., Zhang, M.: Curve skeleton extraction via k-nearest-neighbors based contraction. Int. J. Appl. Math. Comput. Sci. **30**(1), 123–132 (2020)

Spherical Transformer: Adapting Spherical Signal to Convolutional Networks

Yuqi Liu[1], Yin Wang[1], Haikuan Du[2], and Shen Cai[2(✉)]

[1] School of Electronics and Information Engineering, Tongji University, Shanghai, China
yinw@tongji.edu.cn
[2] Visual and Geometric Perception Lab, Donghua University, Shanghai, China
hammer_cai@163.com

Abstract. Convolutional neural networks (CNNs) have been widely used in various vision tasks, e.g. image classification, semantic segmentation, etc. Unfortunately, standard 2D CNNs are not well suited for spherical signals such as panorama images or spherical projections, as the sphere is an unstructured grid. In this paper, we present Spherical Transformer which can transform spherical signals into vectors that can be directly processed by standard CNNs such that many well-designed CNNs architectures can be reused across tasks and datasets by pretraining. To this end, the proposed method first uses local structured sampling methods such as HEALPix to construct a transformer grid by using the information of spherical points and its adjacent points, and then transforms the spherical signals to the vectors through the grid. By building the Spherical Transformer module, we can use multiple CNN architectures directly. We evaluate our approach on the tasks of spherical MNIST recognition, 3D object classification and omnidirectional image semantic segmentation. For 3D object classification, we further propose a rendering-based projection method to improve the performance and a rotational-equivariant model to improve the anti-rotation ability. Experimental results on three tasks show that our approach achieves superior performance over state-of-the-art methods.

Keywords: Spherical transformer · 3D object classification · Omnidirectional image semantic segmentation

1 Introduction

Recently, with the increasing availability and popularity of omnidirectional sensors, a wide range of learning problems in computer vision and related areas require processing signals in spherical domain. For instance, for omnidirectional images and 3D models, standard CNNs working with structured data are not perfectly applicable to them. This limitation is especially pronounced for 3D models, which provides accurate encoding of 3D objects. In recent years, various methods have been proposed to deal with 3D objects for different data representations, such as voxelization, point cloud, multi-view

This work is supported by the Foundation of Key Laboratory of Artificial Intelligence, Ministry of Education, P.R. China (AI2020003).

images and spherical images. Recent works [6,8] propose different network architectures that achieve rotation invariance and direct operation in spherical domain. However, the sampling method in these networks is preliminary, which only maps spherical signals to local-distorted planar domains. This will result in undesirable distortions and loss of information. The work [13] presents a new convolutional kernel to apply CNNs on unstructured grids, and overcomes the above shortcomings. However, it does not contain the standard convolutional operation which shows strong capabilities in 2D image classification and semantic segmentation tasks. Seeing the rich asset of existing CNNs modules for traditional image data, we are motivated to devise a mechanism to bridge the mainstream standard CNNs to spherical signals. One particular challenge is how to express spherical signal in a structured manner.

Classic deep neural networks take structured vectors as input. How to encode the input vectors is crucial to the performance. Spatial Transformer Networks (STN) [12] are commonly used to learn spatial transformations on the input image to enhance the geometric invariance of the model. Inspired by STN, we present a spherical transformer method to transform the spherical signals to structured vectors that can be directly processed by standard CNNs. Therefore, it is able to deal with different tasks of spherical signals. In this paper, we focus on three typical applications: spherical MNIST recognition, 3D model classification and omnidirectional images semantic segmentation. In detail, we employ the popular VGG-11 [24] and U-Net [22] for 3D model classification and semantic segmentation separately. For MNIST recognition on sphere, we use a simple CNN with 5 layers to accomplish this task.

In summary, this paper makes the following contributions:

- We devise a spherical transformer module which can transform spherical signals into vectors friendly to standard CNNs. We can easily reuse the VGG-11 [24] and U-Net [22] architecture for spherical data. Moreover, our seamless use of standard CNNs enables the benefit of pretraining (transfer learning) across different datasets.
- We propose a novel rendering-based projection method which can project the local shading of the internal object points to the spherical image. This rendering method can enrich the spherical features and improve the classification performance of 3D objects.
- Our spherical CNNs achieve superior performance on spherical MNIST recognition, 3D object classification and spherical image semantic segmentation, compared to state-of-the-art networks [6, 13]

2   Related Work

3D-based methods. 3D-based methods are mainly designated for voxel grids or point clouds as input data format. Like 2D images, voxels can be directly processed by using 3D convolution operations. However, due to memory and computational restrictions, the voxel-based methods are often limited to small voxel resolution. This will result in the loss of many details. Although this issue has been recently alleviated by Octree-based representations such as OctNet [21], the cost of 3D CNNs is still distinctly higher than 2D neural networks of the same resolution.

Table 1. Features of 3D object recognition networks.

Method	Input	Convolution feature
Voxnet [16]	Voxels	3D CNNs
OctNet [21]		
PointNet [18]	Points	MLP implemented by 1×1 conv kernel
PointNet++ [19]		
DGCNN [28]		
SFCNN [20]		
MVCNN [25]	Images	2D CNNs
MVCNN-NEW [26]		
S2CNN [6]	Spherical	FFT of spherical non-uniform points
SphericalCNN [8]		
UGSCNN [13]		Parameterized differential operators to replace 2D conv
DeepSphere [17]	Spherical	GNNs implemented by 1×1 conv kernel
STM (Ours)	Spherical	2D CNNs

Alternative approaches have been recently explored to handle 3D points, such as PointNet [18]. It proposes a novel network architecture that operates directly on point clouds. Moreover, PointNet uses the global max pooling to solve the disorder of the point cloud input. However, PointNet cannot capture the local structure, which limits its ability to identify fine scenes and generalize complex scenes. PointNet++ [19] and DGCNN [28] alleviate this problem and achieve improved performance. SubdivNet [11] also adopts 2D CNN to process 3D Mesh by exploiting an analogy between mesh faces and 2D images, which is similar to our idea. Despite this, our method is proposed earlier, although it uses specific Spherical data.

Planar-Image-Based Methods. One advantage of 3D based technology is that 3D objects can be accurately described by the corresponding 3D representations. However, the network architecture applying to 3D representations is (arguably) still in its open stage. As standard CNNs have achieved great success in the field of planar images, there exist methods using 3D object's multi-view images to classify the object. The two prevailing methods are MVCNN [25] and MVCNN-new [26]. They produce 12-view images of a 3D model and classify the rendered images through standard convolutional neural network architectures such as VGG [24] and ResNet [10] which can be pre-trained on ImageNet dataset. Although image-based technology can take advantage of the pre-trained parameters of classification networks and achieve superb results, object projection inevitably leads to information loss in theory.

For semantic segmentation, there have been recently proposed many methods, such as U-Net [22] and deeplab [4] etc. Nevertheless, these methods are all devised for 2D images. Converting a spherical panorama directly into a equirectangular image leads to severe distortion, especially near the pole, which makes these methods less effective.

Spherical-Image-Based Methods. Several other works e.g. spherical CNNs [6] seek to combine 3D-based techniques and image-based techniques. In the work [1,3], the authors provide benchmarks for semantic segmentation of 360 panorama images.

For 3D object classification, several classification networks based on spherical depth projection are proposed in recent years. [6] proposes spherical convolutions that are rotational-equivariant. And spherical harmonic basis is used in [8] to obtain similar results. The above methods have achieved good results on 3D object classification through depth-based spherical projection. However, they often have restrictive applicability and can only be used for a specific task, mainly due to the inflexibility of the adopted sampling method. More recently, convolution is achieved on unstructured grids by replacing the standard convolution with a differential operation [13]. While this kind of pseudo convolution lacks the ability to reuse standard CNNs. SFCNN [20] proposes a spherical fractal CNNs for point cloud analysis. It first projects the point cloud with extracting features onto the corresponding spherical points, and then uses the graph convolution for classification and object segmentation.

For equirectangular image segmentation, [27] proposes spherical convolution by changing the convolution kernel through equirectangular projection. SphereNet [7] introduces a framework for learning spherical image representations by encoding distortion invariance into convolutional filters. But this method only supports 3×3 convolution kernel and max pool, and it needs bilinear interpolation to index the adjacent points of spherical points while we are directly looking for them.

In recent studies, DeepSphere [17] proposes a spherical CNNs by using graph neural networks for cosmological data analysis. Table 1 briefly summaries the convolution characteristics of common 3D object recognition networks.

3 The Proposed Approach

3.1 Spherical Sampling

The major concern for processing spherical signals is distortion introduced by projecting signals on other formats, such as projecting panorama image to planar image. Thus the best way to process spherical signals is finding a spherical uniform sampling method. We find HEALPix spherical grid [9] (as shown in Fig. 1) and icosahedral spherical grid [2] methods are able to achieve this goal. Here we adopt HEALPix sampling in the proposed method, mainly because most spherical points on HEALPix grid have 8 neighbor points. It can form 3×3 transformer grid and then convert to vectors to be processed by 3×3 convolution kernels. But for icosahedral grid, all spherical points has 6 neighbors, which means they can only be processed by 1×7 convolution kernels. HEALPix grid starts with 12 points as the level-0 resolution. Each progressive level resolution after is 4 times the previous number of points. Hence, the number of sampling points on the sphere n_p^l with level-l is:

$$n_p^l = 12 \cdot 4^l \tag{1}$$

It can be clearly discovered that the resolution changing process perfectly matches the 2×2 pooling layer.

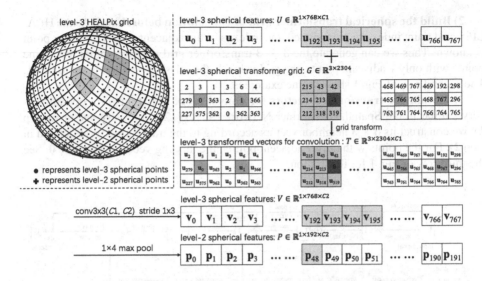

Fig. 1. Sketch for how the spherical transformer works. The left side shows the level-*3* HEALPix grid; the right and bottom show how we use the transformer grids to process spherical signals. For example, the four yellow dots in level-3 grid with index 192–195 will be transformed to the yellow cross with index 48 in level-2 grid after 1×4 max pool; For the green dot with eight adjacent points, such as index 0, 1, 766 and 767, the 3×3 spherical transformer grid can be constructed directly; While for the blue dot with seven adjacent points, such as index 213, the missing purple element is set to −1 in transformer grid and set to **0** in transformed vectors. (Color figure online)

3.2 Spherical Transformer Module

Sphere is local planar and a few of spherical grids in local region are structured, such as HEALPix spherical grid [9] as adopted in the paper. Thus the next key step is to conduct a transformer grid by using the location information of spherical points and their neighbors. Specifically, our proposed spherical transformer module (STM) includes two layers: spherical convolution layer and spherical pooling layer, as will be described in detail.

Spherical Convolution Layer. Standard convolution layer needs structured grid such as image data. As shown in Fig. 1, the local points are structured in HEALPix spherical grid. It can be seen that most of the spherical points have eight adjacent points, one of which is depicted with green in Fig. 1. For level-l $(l \geq 1)$, there are always 24 points with the number of the adjacent points being 7. For specific examples, see the blue part of Fig. 1. For every point on HEALPix grid, the spherical convolution operation includes the following steps, as shown in Fig. 1 for level-*3* HEALPix grid:

1) Determine the point index and extract the corresponding feature vectors. Here we adopt the nested scheme which arranges the point index hierarchically (see [9] for detail). 768 points in level-*3* HEALPix grid are arranged from small to large as the first row of Fig. 1 whose element is the feature vector of the current index point.

2) Build the spherical transformer grid of convolution beforehand. As the HEA-LPix grid point index are preassigned, the indexes of the adjacent points for every point is known. Thus we can generate the 3 × 3 transformer grid for every point. For some points with only 7 adjacent points, the grid value of the missing position is set to be −1. The second row of Fig. 1 shows some examples.

3) Obtain the transformed vectors for convolution. This transform operation is very similar to the Spatial Transformer Network (STN) [12]. For every vector in step **1)**, we construct its 3 × 3 neighbor vectors according to the transformer grid defined in step **2)**. For the points with only 7 adjacent points, the missing vector is set to be **0**. See the third row of Fig. 1 for illustration.

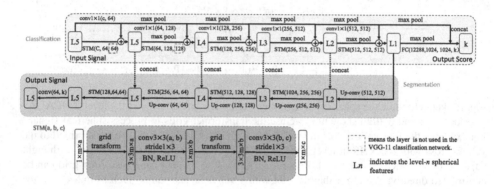

Fig. 2. Overview of the model architecture for classification and segmentation. Our spherical transformer module is implemented according to Fig. 1. Up-conv uses standard 2 × 2 deconvolution function. For classification, we change the basic VGG-11 model and add 1 × 1 convolution kernel to improve the anti-rotation ability. For fully connected layer in classification compared to it in standard VGG-11 architecture, we use 1024 dimensions rather than 4096. And for segmentation, we use the U-Net architecture without the 1 × 1 convolution.

4) Run the standard 3 × 3 convolution. Since the transformed vectors have been obtained in the above step, we can use standard 3×3, stride 1×3 convolution kernels to process it directly. For example, for the feature vectors $U \in \mathbb{R}^{1 \times 768 \times C1}$ in level-3, it is transformed to the vectors $V \in \mathbb{R}^{1 \times 768 \times C2}$ after the processing of $conv3 \times 3(C1, C2)$ with stride 1×3.

Spherical Pooling Layer. In HEALPix spherical grid, the distribution of spherical points for each level resolution is fixed. For example, in Fig. 1, the level-2 spherical points are marked as plus sign. Its four nearest points in level-3 grid are marked as dots. In the yellow area in HEALPix gird, these four points are adjacent to each other. See the last row of Fig. 1. The nested points index has defined a natural pooling way that four successive vectors of level-3 are pooled to form a vector p of level-2. Thus we can use 1×4 max pooling layer directly instead of building spherical transformer grid for spherical pooling layer. Consequently, the spherical features in level-l are straightforward pooled to the features in level-l-1 as they are coded in proper order in HEALPix grid.

3.3   Network Architecture

As described in Fig. 1, we have constructed our spherical convolution layer and spherical pooling layer by using the proposed spherical transformer method. By doing this, we can directly use the classical CNN architectures as we originally designed. For 3D object classification, we adopt VGG-11 network architecture but replace its convolution layer and pooling layer with our proposed spherical convolution and pooling layer. And to get rotational-equivariant, we change the basic VGG-11 model and more details are described in next section. For semantic segmentation, we similarly construct a novel network which combines the U-Net architecture with the proposed STM. Detailed schematic for these two architectures is shown in Fig. 2. Moreover, both the classification and segmentation networks share a common encoder architecture. Since these architectures have been verified in various vision tasks, it is reasonable to apply them to the proposed spherical structured grids.

Table 2. Classification accuracy on the spherical MNIST dataset for validating STM.

Method	Acc (%)	Parameter #
S2CNN [6]	96.00	58 k
UGSCNN [13]	99.23	62 k
STM (Ours)	99.36	32 k

Anti-rotation Model. As previous studies e.g. S2CNN [6] and SphericalCNN [8] propose spherical convolutions that are rotational-equivariant, in order to improve the anti-rotation ability of our 3D object classification model, we modify our VGG-11 liked model architecture as shown in Fig. 2. It is well known that convolutional neural networks implement translation-equivariant by construction, for other transformations such as rotations, however, they are ineffective. Though recently some convolution kernels are proposed for rotation-equivariant such as G-CNNs [5] and SFCNNs [29], here we resort to the simple 1×1 convolution kernel which is naturally rotation-equivariant. For its simplicity, we add 1×1 convolution kernel to our basic model. To find features that are sensitive to these two convolutions, for every 3×3 convolution layer before max pooling, we sum these two features. Certainly, to preserve most rotation-equivariant features, we concatenate these two features before the first full-connected layer. More details can be seen in Fig. 2.

4   Experiments

4.1   Spherical MNIST

To verify its efficiency, we first use our method on classic digital recognition.

Experiment Setup. To project digits onto the surface of the sphere, we follow the projection method of S2CNN [6] and UGSCNN [13]. We benchmark our method with the above two spherical CNNs. All models are trained and tested on data that has not been rotated. In this experiment, we use a 5 layers CNN architecture with 4 conv-pool-BN-ReLU and 1 FC-softmax.

Results and Discussion. Table 2 shows the classification accuracy on spherical MNIST. It shows that our method outperforms S2CNN and UGSCNN. In particular, the number of parameters of our model is about only half of that of the above models. We attribute our success to the seamless reuse of 2D CNNs which has been dominant in wide range of vision tasks.

4.2   3D Object Classification

The benchmark dataset used in this task is ModelNet40 [30]. It contains 12,311 shapes across 40 categories, which is used to illustrate the applicability of our approach in 3D deep learning. For this study, we focus on classification accuracy and rotational-equivariant. Two types of spherical projection in our experiments are used: depth-based projection and rendering-based projection.

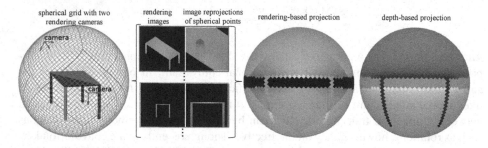

Fig. 3. Two projection methods used in our experiments, including the proposed rendering-based one. This special rendering-based projection allows to directly combine the two methods' features. (Color figure online)

Depth-Based Projection. For depth-based projection, we follow the processing protocol of [6]. Specifically, as shown in Fig. 3, we first move the model to the origin and then normalize it. Then we calculate level-5 resolution spherical points and send a ray towards the origin for each point. Three kinds of information from the intersection are obtained: ray length, *sin* and *cos* values of the angle between the surface normal of the intersected object point and the ray. The data is further augmented by using the convex hull of the input model, finally forming spherical signals with 6 input channels. The rightmost plot in Fig. 3 shows the visualized depth-based spherical signals. Even if spherical image is one kind of feature representation from 3D to 2D, we can clearly see the various parts of the table, just like a distorted image.

Rendering-Based Projection. Motivated by the multi-view based method [14] that has achieved the best performance on ModelNet40 dataset, we explore and propose a rendering-based spherical projection method. However, such rendering-based methods have difficulty in stitching multi-view images to a spherical image directly. This is because the projections of multi-view images on spherical image are not aligned. One 3D object point can even appear multiple times in stitched spherical image. Therefore, we propose a novel projection strategy to separately obtain projections of 12 regions whose inner points correspond to different parts of the object, while boundary points correspond to the same part. For example, in Fig. 3, the red and green regions are 2 of 12 regions divided by HEALPix grid, respectively. We put the virtual camera on the ray of the origin and the center of this region which captures the image of the model from the current perspective. By adding six fixed point light sources on $+-x, +-y, +-z$ axes, 12 gray images can be rendered. Through the depth-based projections, we already know the point at which the model intersects the spherical ray. Hence, the gray value of one spherical point can be obtained by re-projecting the corresponding object point back to the rendered image of each region. It can be found that our rendering-based method only uses the internal points of the object, which contains the local shading of the object surface, without contour information. The third sub-figure from left to right in Fig. 3 shows the rendering-based spherical images from the view of the camera of the green region. Although the rendering spherical image is not visually straightforward, it indeed provides alternative feature that improves the performance.

Table 3. Classification accuracy (Acc (%) and SO(3)/SO(3) Acc (%)) on ModelNet40.

Method	Input	Acc	SO(3)/SO(3)
MVCNN 12x [25]	images	89.5	77.6
3D Shapenets [30]	voxels	84.7	-
Voxnet [16]	voxels	83.0	87.3
PointNet [18]	points	89.2	83.6
PointNet++ [19]	points	91.9	85.0
DGCNN [28]	points	92.2	-
SFCNN [20]	points	92.3	91.0
S2CNN [6]	spherical	85.0	-
SphericalCNN [8]	spherical	88.9	86.9
UGSCNN [13]	spherical	90.5	-
Ours-VGG11 (depth)	spherical	92.3	87.7
Ours-rot (depth)	spherical	92.7	91.3
Ours-VGG11 (rendering, w/o pre-training)	spherical	86.2	-
Ours-VGG11 (rendering, w/ pre-training)	spherical	91.1	-
Ours (overall)	spherical	93.0	-

Experiment Setup. For this task, the level-5 spherical resolution is used. We use two spherical inputs to train the network separately. For classification accuracy, we use the aligned ModelNet40 data [23]. While SO(3)/SO(3) means trained and tested with arbitrary rotations. Our rendering-based projection method can use the VGG-11 model parameters pre-trained on the ImageNet data. For classification accuracy, we compare the best result of our method with other 3D deep learning methods. The baseline algorithms we choose include UGSCNN [13], PointNet++ [19], VoxNet [16], S2CNN [6], SphericalCNN [8], SFCNN [20] and MVCNN [25].

Results and Discussion. Table 3 shows the classification accuracy on ModelNet40. The proposed spherical depth feature based model is superior to the above existing methods. And our rotational-equivariant model shows better performance in both the best classification accuracy and SO(3)/SO(3) classification accuracy. Our rendering-based approach also achieves promising results after using pre-trained parameters. The overall model means we combine the features of the penultimate full-connection layer of the two methods and that we retrain the last fully connection layer. When combining depth-based projection and rendering-based projection, our overall method achieves the highest accuracy. This also suggests that our devised rendering-based projection is effective and complementary to depth-based projection method.

4.3 Spherical Image Semantic Segmentation

We demonstrate the semantic segmentation capability of the proposed spherical transformer module on the spherical image semantic segmentation task. We use the Stanford 2D3DS dataset [1] for comparison with the state-of-the-art UGSCNN [13]. The 2D3DS dataset contains a total of 1,413 equirectangular RGB images, along with their corresponding depths, and semantic annotations across 13 different classes. Except compared with UGSCNN that is aimed to segment spherical image, we also include classic 2D image semantic segmentation networks for more comprehensive comparison.

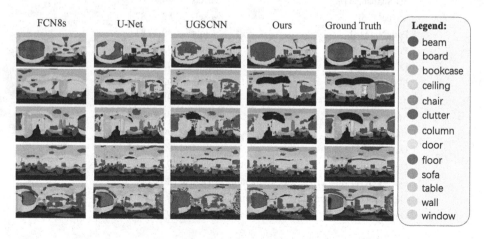

Fig. 4. Semantic segmentation results on Stanford 2D3DS test dataset. Our results are generated on a level-5 HEALPix grid and mapped to the planar image by using nearest neighbor sampling for visualization. Each row shows the results of different methods including ground truth for a specific scene. Note that only our method well captures the beam structure.

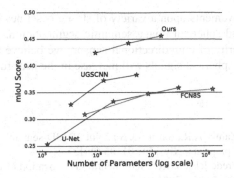

Fig. 5. Parameter efficiency study on 2D3DS for semantic segmentation. Our proposed spherical segmentation model outperforms UGSCNN and two planar-based methods by notable margin across all parameter regimes.

Experiment Setup. To apply our method on semantic segmentation tasks, the first thing is sampling on the original rectangular images to obtain spherical signals. To make a fair comparison with UGSCNN [13], we follow the interpolation method of UGSCNN. The input RGB-D channels are interpolated using bilinear interpolation, while semantic segmentation labels are acquired using nearest-neighbor interpolation. We use level-5 resolution and the official 3-fold cross validation to train and evaluate the experimental results. For this task, we benchmark our semantic segmentation results against the spherical semantic segmentation architecture UGSCNN and two classic semantic segmentation networks: U-Net [22] and FCN8s [15]. We evaluate the performance under two standard metrics: mean Intersection-over-Union (mIoU), and pixel-accuracy. These methods are compared under two settings: peak performance and parameter efficiency study by varying model parameters. For parameter efficiency study, we change the number of parameters by reducing the dimension of the convolution layer. The only difference between our network and the standard U-Net is the dimension of the last layer of our model encoder is 512, rather than 1024, as the ladder case does not have obvious improvement.

Results and Discussion. Figure 5 compares our model performance against state-of-the-art baselines. Our proposed spherical segmentation network significantly outperforms UGSCNN and two planar baselines over the whole parameter range. Here three different parameter numbers for each method denote the reduction of feature dimensionality, in line with the setting in UGSCNN. Figure 4 shows a visualization of our semantic segmentation results compared to the ground truth, UGSCNN and two planar baselines. It can be seen that our method clearly achieves the best accuracy and the results are also visually appealing.

5   Conclusion

In this paper, we present a novel method to transform the spherical signals to structured vectors that can be processed through standard CNNs directly. Experimental results show significant improvements upon a variety of strong baselines in both tasks for 3D object classification and spherical image semantic segmentation. With the increasing availability and popularity of omnidirectional sensors we believe that the demand for specialized models for spherical signals will increase in the near future.

References

1. Armeni, I., Sax, S., Zamir, A.R., Savarese, S.: Joint 2D–3D-semantic data for indoor scene understanding. arXiv preprint arXiv:1702.01105 (2017)
2. Baumgardner, J.R., Frederickson, P.O.: Icosahedral discretization of the two-sphere. SIAM J. Num. Anal. **22**, 1107–1115 (1985)
3. Chang, A., et al.: Matterport3d: Learning from RGB-D data in indoor environments. arXiv preprint arXiv:1709.06158 (2017)
4. Chen, L.C., Papandreou, G., Kokkinos, I., Murphy, K., Yuille, A.L.: DeepLab: semantic image segmentation with deep convolutional nets, Atrous convolution, and fully connected CRFs. IEEE Trans. Pattern Anal. Mach. Intell. **40**, 834–848 (2018)
5. Cohen, T., Welling, M.: Group equivariant convolutional networks. In: International Conference on Machine Learning, pp. 2990–2999 (2016)
6. Cohen, T.S., Geiger, M., Köhler, J., Welling, M.: Spherical CNNs. In: International Conference on Learning Representations (2018)
7. Coors, B., Paul Condurache, A., Geiger, A.: SphereNet: learning spherical representations for detection and classification in omnidirectional images. In: European Conference on Computer Vision, pp. 518–533 (2018)
8. Esteves, C., Allen-Blanchette, C., Makadia, A., Daniilidis, K.: Learning SO(3) equivariant representations with spherical CNNs. In: Ferrari, V., Hebert, M., Sminchisescu, C., Weiss, Y. (eds.) ECCV 2018. LNCS, vol. 11217, pp. 54–70. Springer, Cham (2018). https://doi.org/10.1007/978-3-030-01261-8_4
9. Gorski, K.M., et al.: HEALPix: a framework for high-resolution discretization and fast analysis of data distributed on the sphere. Astrophys. J. **622**(2), 759 (2005)
10. He, K., Zhang, X., Ren, S., Sun, J.: Deep residual learning for image recognition. In: IEEE/CVF Conference on Computer Vision and Pattern Recognition, pp. 770–778 (2016)
11. Hu, S.M., et al.: Subdivision-based mesh convolution networks. ACM Trans. Graphics **41**(3), 1–16 (2022)
12. Jaderberg, M., Simonyan, K., Zisserman, A., et al.: Spatial transformer networks. In: Advances in Neural Information Processing Systems, pp. 2017–2025 (2015)
13. Jiang, C.M., Huang, J., Kashinath, K., Prabhat, Marcus, P., Niessner, M.: Spherical CNNs on unstructured grids. In: International Conference on Learning Representations (2019)
14. Kanezaki, A., Matsushita, Y., Nishida, Y.: RotationNet: joint object categorization and pose estimation using multiviews from unsupervised viewpoints. In: IEEE/CVF Conference on Computer Vision and Pattern Recognition, pp. 5010–5019 (2018)
15. Long, J., Shelhamer, E., Darrell, T.: Fully convolutional networks for semantic segmentation. In: IEEE/CVF Conference on Computer Vision and Pattern Recognition, pp. 3431–3440 (2015)
16. Maturana, D., Scherer, S.: Voxnet: A 3D convolutional neural network for real-time object recognition. In: International Conference on Intelligent Robots and Systems, pp. 922–928. IEEE (2015)
17. Perraudin, N., Defferrard, M., Kacprzak, T., Sgier, R.: DeepSphere: efficient spherical convolutional neural network with HEALPix sampling for cosmological applications. Astron. Computi. **27**, 130–146 (2019)

18. Qi, C.R., Su, H., Mo, K., Guibas, L.J.: PointNet: deep learning on point sets for 3D classification and segmentation. In: IEEE/CVF Conference on Computer Vision and Pattern Recognition, pp. 652–660 (2017)

19. Qi, C.R., Yi, L., Su, H., Guibas, L.J.: Pointnet++: deep hierarchical feature learning on point sets in a metric space. In: Advances in Neural Information Processing Systems (NIPS), pp. 5099–5108 (2017)

20. Rao, Y., Lu, J., Zhou, J.: Spherical fractal convolutional neural networks for point cloud recognition. In: IEEE/CVF Conference on Computer Vision and Pattern Recognition, pp. 452–460 (2019)

21. Riegler, G., Ulusoy, A.O., Geiger, A.: OctNet: learning deep 3D representations at high resolutions. In: IEEE/CVF Conference on Computer Vision and Pattern Recognition (2017)

22. Ronneberger, O., Fischer, P., Brox, T.: U-Net: convolutional networks for biomedical image segmentation. In: Navab, N., Hornegger, J., Wells, W.M., Frangi, A.F. (eds.) MICCAI 2015. LNCS, vol. 9351, pp. 234–241. Springer, Cham (2015). https://doi.org/10.1007/978-3-319-24574-4_28

23. Sedaghat, N., Zolfaghari, M., Amiri, E., Brox, T.: Orientation-boosted voxel nets for 3D object recognition. arXiv preprint arXiv:1604.03351 (2016)

24. Simonyan, K., Zisserman, A.: Very deep convolutional networks for large-scale image recognition. arXiv preprint arXiv:1409.1556 (2014)

25. Su, H., Maji, S., Kalogerakis, E., Learned-Miller, E.G.: Multi-view convolutional neural networks for 3D shape recognition. In: IEEE/CVF Conference on Computer Vision (2015)

26. Su, J.C., Gadelha, M., Wang, R., Maji, S.: A deeper look at 3D shape classifiers. In: European Conference on Computer Vision Workshop (2018)

27. Su, Y.C., Grauman, K.: Learning spherical convolution for fast features from 360 imagery. In: Advances in Neural Information Processing Systems, pp. 529–539 (2017)

28. Wang, Y., Sun, Y., Liu, Z., Sarma, S.E., Bronstein, M.M., Solomon, J.M.: Dynamic graph CNN for learning on point clouds. arXiv preprint arXiv:1801.07829 (2018)

29. Weiler, M., Hamprecht, F.A., Storath, M.: Learning steerable filters for rotation equivariant CNNs. In: IEEE/CVF Conference on Computer Vision and Pattern Recognition, pp. 849–858 (2018)

30. Wu, Z., Song, S., Khosla, A., Yu, F., Zhang, L., Tang, X., Xiao, J.: 3D shapeNets: a deep representation for volumetric shapes. In: IEEE/CVF Conference on Computer Vision and Pattern Recognition, pp. 1912–1920 (2015)

Waterfall-Net: Waterfall Feature Aggregation for Point Cloud Semantic Segmentation

Hui Shuai(✉)[iD], Xiang Xu[iD], and Qingshan Liu[iD]

Engineering Research Center of Digital Forensics, Ministry of Education,
School of Computer and Software, Nanjing University of Information Science,
Nanjing 210044, China
`huishuai13@nuist.eud.cn, qsliu@nuist.edu.com`

Abstract. In this paper, we observe that the point cloud density affects the performance of different categories in 3D point cloud semantic segmentation. Most existing point-based methods implicitly deal with this density issue via extracting multi-scale features in a single forward path. Instead, we propose a Waterfall-Net that explicitly utilizes the density property via cross-connected cascaded sub-networks. In Waterfall-Net, three sub-networks successively process the input point cloud. Each sub-network handles the point features sampled at different densities, obtaining the information at various densities. The output features of one sub-network are up-sampled via a learnable up-sample method and fed into the next sub-network. This Sub-Network Fusing aligns the density of two sub-networks and maintains the contextual information. Meanwhile, Sub-Stage Fusing fuses the sub-stage features between successive sub-networks according to the density. Such waterfall-like feature aggregation ensembles all the features from different densities and enhances the model learning ability. We empirically demonstrate the effectiveness of the Waterfall-Net on two benchmarks. Specifically, it achieves 72.2% mIoU on S3DIS and 55.7% mIoU on SemanticKitti.

Keywords: Point cloud semantic segmentation · Density property · Feature aggregation

1 Introduction

Point cloud semantic segmentation is a fundamental task in 3D scene analysis. It plays a vital role in many applications, such as autonomous driving and robotics. Recently, many methods have obtained promising performance on several benchmarks [2,3]. In this paper, we focus on the point-based methods [7,13,19,31] directly processing the 3D points as no information conversion occurs.

For point-based methods, we observe that the density of the input points can significantly affect the performance of different categories. As shown in Fig. 1, we feed the point cloud of S3DIS randomly sampled at different densities into the

S. Yu et al. (Eds.): PRCV 2022, LNCS 13536, pp. 28–40, 2022.
https://doi.org/10.1007/978-3-031-18913-5_3

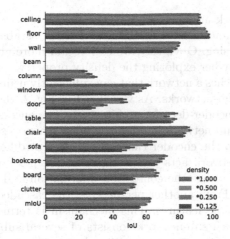

Fig. 1. The performance of RandLA-Net on S3DIS at different input densities. Different categories achieve the best performance at different densities.

RandLA-Net and evaluate the IoU of all the categories. The results demonstrate that a particular category is better resolved at a certain density. Some categories are better predicted at high resolution while some other categories achieve the best performance at lower densities. The reasons for this phenomenon are twofold. First, points sampled at different densities can reflect the geometric property of the objects. For example, when points are sampled at low density, the performance of ceiling and floor increases because low density can smooth the noise on these large planes. On the contrary, the performance of the window and clutter decreases as these objects need more detailed geometric information for accurate prediction. Second, the density of the sampling procedure affects the receptive field of the sampled points. At different densities, the K nearest neighbor points of a point will provide contextual information of different scopes. So, how can we take advantage of all the superiority of different densities?

The naive idea to utilize multiple densities is to combine the results predicted at a range of densities, but we do not know the best density for each category. An alternative is to aggregate the feature arising from various densities. Some previous works utilize points sampled via various rules or features with different receptive fields intuitively. PointNet++ [17] employs the density adaptive layer to aggregate multi-scale features from the neighborhood of different scopes, dealing with the non-uniform sampling density in the point cloud. JSNet [33] fuses the features from multi-layers with concatenating and adding operations at the end of the backbone. RandLA-Net [7] and KPConv [19] et al. both use a U-shape encoder-decoder structure, in which features with different receptive fields are fused via skip connections between the encoder and decoder. These methods extract multi-scale features in a single "funnel" forward path, and the density of the point decreases as the depth of the layer increases. The features from early layers are detailed features at high density and the features from layers in the back are abstract features at low density, but some features of various semantics-and-density combinations (such as abstract features with high density) are missing. Obviously, we can obtain more abundant features in different states via further exploring the density property.

This paper establishes a network that can sufficiently utilize the density property with cascaded sub-networks. As visualized in Fig. 2, the proposed method employs a U-shape encoder-decoder architecture. The encoder consists of three sub-networks. Each sub-network handles the point features sampled at different densities. In this way, the encoder can extract clues at different densities. The output of one sub-network acts as the input of the next one via a learnable up-sampling, to fully utilize the contextual information and provide features of multiple granularity. From another perspective, the cascaded sub-networks is a polishing process for the features. This mechanism is termed as sub-networks fusing. Meanwhile, each sub-network consists of several sub-stages. The corresponding sub-stage features from adjacent sub-networks are fused according to the same density, and we term this mechanism as sub-stage fusing. Overall, the features from different layers are cross-connected like a waterfall. Such waterfall feature aggregation assembles features at different states and enhances the model learning ability. Thus, we name the proposed method as Waterfall-Net. We evaluate the Waterfall-Net on two standard benchmarks, S3DIS and SemanticKitti, and the results demonstrate that the proposed method can significantly improve the baseline's performance. Our main contributions are summarized as follows:

1. We observe that the density of input point cloud can significantly affect the performance of different categories.
2. We propose a Waterfall-Net to take advantage of the density property. It extracts abundant features at different densities and aggregate them in an waterfall-like manner for better prediction.
3. We propose a learnable up-sampling method for point cloud feature interpolation. It can adaptively incorporate the contextual clues for interpolation and outperforms the rule-based methods.

2   Related Work

Point-Based Point Cloud Semantic Segmentation: Point-based methods process the raw point cloud directly. PointNet [16] is the first method to employ point-wise MLP and symmetry function for point cloud analysis. Based on Point-Net, PointNet++ [17] and PointSIFT [8] use shared point-wise MLPs for point-wise manipulation and adopt aggregate modules to capture the context information. Subsequently, Francis et al. [6] further utilizes K-means and KNN in both the world space and the latent feature space to regularize feature learning. To overcome the drawback that MLPs only process points individually, PointWeb [30] and RSCNN [13] design some measurements to explore the relationship between the point pairs in a local region. Besides, PCCN [23] and KP-FCNN [19] explore effective convolution operations for point clouds. Along with the rise

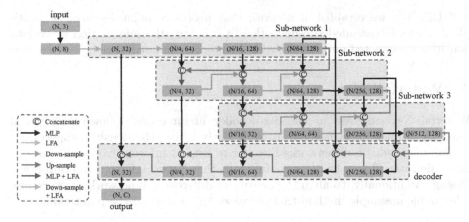

Fig. 2. The overview architecture of Waterfall-Net. The Waterfall-Net employs an encoder-decoder architecture. The encoder consists of three sub-networks, each sub-network handles point features sampled at a certain density. These sub-networks are cross-connected via Sub-Network Fusing and Sub-Stage Fusing mechanisms.

of Graph Neural Networks, PyramNet [34] and GAC [22] use graph-based networks to model point clouds and capture the underlying shapes and geometric structures. DGCNN [24] proposes an Edge-Conv based on a graph to recover the topological information of the point cloud. Beyond that, RandLA-Net [7] employs a local feature aggregation module on randomly sampled points to progressively increase the receptive field. These methods process the point cloud in a single forward path, and the density of the points decreases as the depth increase. However, the density property we observed is not explicitly considered by previous methods. In this paper, we take full use of the density property through several cascaded sub-networks.

Multi-scale Feature Fusing: In image analysis methods, the multi-scale feature is very important to deal with the scale space. The straightforward method is using image pyramid [1] to feed multi-resolution images into multiple networks and aggregate the output [20]. To improve efficiency, PSPNet [32] and Deeplab series [4] aggregate features from different scales. Hourglass [15] and its extension [9] combine the low-level and high-level features with short-cut connections. HRNet [21] and DFANet [11] construct several subnetworks for different resolution and conduct multi-scale fusion repeatedly. For the 3D point cloud, the multi-scale feature fusing methods are relatively few. PointNet++ [17] employs the density adaptive layer to aggregate multi-scale features from the neighborhood of different scopes like PSPNet. JSNet [33] fuses the features from multi-layers with concatenating and adding operations at the end of the backbone. RandLA-Net [7], KPConv [19], and GAC [22] et al. fuse features with different receptive fields via skip connections between the encoder and decoder. These methods extract multi-scale features in a single forward path, but the density property of the point cloud is not fully utilized. Inspired by the idea of HRNet and DFANet, we establish a network that processes point features at multiple densities in cascaded sub-networks. In this way, the information at various densities is extracted and the network architecture is not bloated.

3   Waterfall-Net

Waterfall-Net employs an encoder-decoder architecture, following a typical semantic segmentation fashion. To sufficiently utilize the density property, we design a Cascaded Sub-networks Encoder to extract informative features at different densities. These features are fused via Sub-Network Fusing and Sub-Stage Fusing. Additionally, to align the density of different sub-networks, we propose a learnable upsample method that increases the density of the point cloud.

3.1   Cascaded Sub-Networks Encoder

The Cascaded Sub-networks Encoder transforms the input point cloud $\mathbf{P}$ into latent features via stacked sub-networks. Each sub-network consists of 4 sub-stages, it decreases the number of points via Random Sample (RS) and expands the dimension of per-point feature via the Local Feature Aggregate (LFA) module inherited from RandLA-Net [7]. We represent the feature of j-th stage in i-th sub-network as $\mathbf{F}_i^j$, $i \in \{1,2,3\}$ and $j \in \{1,2,3,4\}$. The multiple sub-networks are cross-connected via Sub-Network Fusing and Sub-Stage Fusing mechanisms.

Sub-Network Fusing joins successive sub-networks via transmitting the features in a cascaded manner. The output of the i-th sub-network acts as the input of the $(i+1)$-th sub-network. Each sub-network's input is formulated as:

$$\mathbf{F}_i^1 = \begin{cases} \mathrm{LFA}(\mathcal{M}(\mathbf{P})) & \text{if } i = 1 \\ \mathrm{LFA}(\mathcal{M}(\mathbf{F}_{i-1}^2 \oplus \mathrm{UP}(\mathbf{F}_{i-1}^4))) & \text{otherwise} \end{cases} \tag{1}$$

where $\mathcal{M}$ represents the MLP, $\oplus$ is the concatenation operation, and UP is the upsample operation will be introduced in the next subsection. Note that $\mathbf{F}_{i-1}^4$ has a sparser density than $\mathbf{F}_{i-1}^2$, so the upsample operation is necessary to align their density. The preceding sub-network extracts features with high semantic awareness but at low density. With the interpolation of upsample operation, the Sub-Network Fusing inherits the semantic awareness from the previous sub-network and retains structure details at high density. Thus, this mechanism provides semantics-and-density combined features of more variety.

Sub-Stage Fusing establishes connections between sub-stages in adjacent sub-networks. The feature F_{i-1}^j and F_i^{j-1} contribute to the feature F_i^j together. The intermediate feature of each sub-stage in different sub-network is:

$$\mathbf{F}_i^j = \begin{cases} \mathrm{LFA}(\mathrm{RS}(\mathbf{F}_i^{j-1})) & \text{if } i = 1 \\ \mathrm{LFA}(\mathcal{M}(\mathrm{RS}(\mathbf{F}_i^{j-1}) \oplus \mathbf{F}_{i-1}^{j+1})) & \text{otherwise} \end{cases} \tag{2}$$

where $j > 1$. We first decrease the density of $\mathbf{F}_i^{j-1}$. Then, $\mathbf{F}_{i-1}^{j+1}$ and $\mathbf{F}_i^{j-1}$ are concatenated and fed to LAF. This mechanism constructs more informative features via aggregating features with different information granularity.

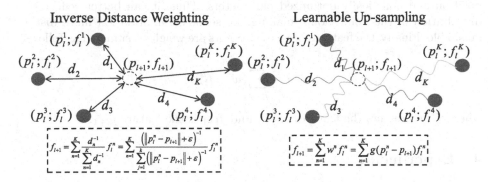

Fig. 3. IDW interpolates the features of the target point via weighting the surrounding points with inverse distance as weighing coefficients. The learnable up-sampling employs a network to estimate the weighting coefficients.

With these fusing methods, named waterfall feature aggregation, the multiple sub-networks work in a complementary manner. The feature of various semantic-and-density combinations is abstracted and fused. Through the waterfall-like cross connections in sub-networks, the information flow can be transferred through an arbitrary network pipeline.

3.2   Learn to Upsample

In the Cascaded Sub-network Encoder, the point cloud is randomly down-sampled. However, point cloud semantic segmentation aims to assign a semantic label for each point, which needs to propagate features from down-sampled points to the original points. RandLA-Net [7] employs the nearest interpolation that simply duplicates the features, making the interpolated features undistinguishable. More works, such as PointNet++ [17], uses Inverse Distance Weighted (IDW) average on k nearest neighbours. However, IDW only considers the distance between points while missing the needed semantic clues of the point cloud.

We propose a learnable up-sampling that can better capture the semantic clues of point cloud with a data-driven network. As shown in Fig. 3, given the point cloud $\mathbf{P}_l$ and its feature $\mathbf{F}_l$, the learnable up-sampling propagates $\mathbf{F}_l$ to $\mathbf{F}_{i+1}$, i.e. the feature of $\mathbf{P}_{l+1}$ ($\mathbf{P}_i \subset \mathbf{P}_{l+1}$). For one point p_{l+1} in $\mathbf{P}_{l+1}$, the nearest K points of it, i.e. $\{p_l^n\}_{n=1}^K$, are firstly selected from P_l. Then, a shared MLP is designed to encode the relative position between p_{l+1} and $\{p_l^n\}_{n=1}^K$ into weights, followed by a softmax function for normalization:

$$w^n = g(p_l^n - p_{l+1}; \mathbf{W}) \tag{3}$$

where p_{l+1} and p_l^n are the three-dimensional coordinates of points, $\mathbf{W}$ is the parameters in MLP, and $g()$ represents the MLP followed by softmax function. $w^n \in \mathbb{R}^1$ represents the weight between p_{l+1} and p_l^n. Compared with the distance-based weight in [7,17], the learned weight derives from the relative position and holistically optimized parameters. Thus, it can better reflect the distribution of the point cloud, making the semantic information more distinguishable. Finally, the features of nearest points are weighted summed as follows:

$$f_{l+1} = \sum_{n=1}^{K}(w^n \cdot f_l^n) \tag{4}$$

where f_l^n represents the features of p_l^n, and f_{l+1} is the feature p_{l+1}.

4   Experiments

In this section, we first conduct ablation studies to verify the effectiveness of our design on area 5 in S3DIS. Then, the results of Waterfall-Net in three popular datasets are reported, including S3DIS and SemanticKITTI.

4.1   Analysis of Waterfall-Net Architecture

We verify the effect of each design, including the Sub-network Fusing, Sub-stage Fusing, and Learnable upsampling. The quantitative results are reported on area5 in S3DIS.

Waterfall Feature Aggregation: In this part, we set RandLA-Net as the baseline. Then, a multi-scale block that extracts features from three parallel branches with various densities is embedded between the encoder and decoder. For Sub-Network Fusion verification, we remove the horizontal connection in the Waterfall-Net (marked as purple arrows between the sub-networks). For Sub-Stage Fusion verification, we remove the vertical connection between the stages (marked as black arrows between the stages), and the encoder acts as a forward network that consists of three cascaded subnetworks. The results of all the above-mentioned modules and Waterfall-Net are shown in Table 1. The RandLA-Net obtains mIoU of 62.8% in area5. However, embedding a multi-scale

Table 1. Performance of different modules on S3DIS area5

RandLA-Net	Multi-scale block	Sub-network fusing	Sub-stage fusing	mIoU(%)
✓				62.8
✓	✓			62.3
✓		✓		64.3
✓			✓	64.4
✓		✓	✓	66.1

block into RandLA-Net decreases the mIoU by 0.5%. The features at the end of the encoder are all derived from the same forward path. Thus, the multi-scale block is hard to introduce more abundant features but causes extra parameters, leading to over-fitting. When we only employ Sub-Network Fusing, our method obtains the mIoU of 64.3%, improving the baseline by 1.5%. When we only employ Sub-Stage Fusing, the performance of the baseline is improved by 1.6%, to 64.4%. It means that both the Sub-Network Fusing and Sub-Stage Fusing are beneficial for the discriminative feature extracting. Finally, combining the Sub-Network Fusing and Sub-stage Fusing into the waterfall feature aggregation, Waterfall-Net obtains the mIoU of 66.1%, by 3.3%. The improvement is larger than the sum of the gain arising from Sub-Network Fusing and Sub-Stage Fusing individually. That is to say, the Sub-Network Fusing and the Sub-Stage Fusing are complementary to each other.

Up-Sampling Method: The up-sampling method bridges the density gap between successive sub-networks in Waterfall-Net. It should increase the density of the point cloud and keep the contextual information simultaneously. For comparison, we implement the nearest-neighbor interpolation, inverse distance interpolation, and the learnable up-sampling as the up-sampling method. Their results are shown in Table 2. The nearest neighbor interpolation replicates the feature of the nearest point but the contextual information of other surroundings is not considered. Eventually, it achieves a performance of 64.3%. The inverse distance interpolation exploits all the surrounding points and uses the inverse of distance as the weighting coefficients. It outperforms the nearest neighbor interpolation by 0.6% and achieves the mIoU of 64.9%. However, its weighting coefficients are based on geometrical prior but what we need is the semantic information. Our proposed learnable up-sampling also uses all the surrounding points, and the weighting coefficients are inferred by a neural network. It explores the semantic relation in a data-driven manner and achieves the mIoU of 66.1%, outperforming the inverse distance interpolate by 1.2%.

Table 2. Performance of different up-sample methods on S3DIS area5

Method	mIoU(%)
Nearest neighbor interpolate	64.3
Inverse distance interpolate	64.9
Learnable up-sampling	**66.1**

Other Basic Block: Waterfall-Net is implemented based on the Local Feature Aggregation module proposed in RandLA-Net. To verify the general applicability of waterfall feature aggregation, we also implemented the Waterfall-Net based on the hierarchical point set feature learning layer proposed in PointNet++. The result of the PointNet++ based Waterfall-Net in S3DIS area5 is presented in Table 3. The waterfall-Net improves the performance of PointNet++ to 54.1%, by 3.2%. It demonstrates that the waterfall feature aggregation can generally improve the performance of point-based methods for point cloud semantic segmentation.

Table 3. Quantitative results of different basic block on S3DIS (area 5)

Method	mIoU (%)	Ceil.	Floor	Wall	Beam	Col.	Wind.	Door	Table	Chair	Sofa	Book.	Board	Clut.
PointNet [16]	41.1	88.8	97.3	69.8	0.1	3.9	46.3	10.8	52.6	58.9	5.9	40.3	26.4	33.2
PointNet++ [17]	50.9	90.7	98.1	75.5	0.0	2.7	35.8	31.9	70.8	73.9	25.7	54.1	42.5	49.8
PointNet++ & Waterfall-Net	54.1	90.9	98.3	79.8	0.0	10.3	38.4	30.8	74.5	77.2	47.3	59.3	40.2	55.7
RandLA-Net [7]	62.8	91.5	96.0	80.6	0.0	26.1	62.5	47.6	76.4	84.1	60.7	71.3	65.5	54.1
RandLA-Net & Waterfall-Net	66.1	92.9	97.8	83.3	0.0	30.8	61.5	54.5	77.6	89.4	79.9	72.1	63.9	55.7

Table 4. Quantitative results of different approaches on S3DIS (6-fold cross validation)

Method	OA (%)	mACC (%)	mIoU (%)	Ceil.	Floor	Wall	Beam	Col.	Wind.	Door	Table	Chair	Sofa	Book.	Board.	Clut.
PointNet [16]	78.6	66.2	47.6	88.0	88.7	69.3	42.4	23.1	47.5	51.6	54.1	42.0	9.6	38.2	29.4	35.2
SPG [10]	85.5	73.0	62.1	89.9	95.1	76.4	62.8	47.1	55.3	68.4	73.5	69.2	63.2	45.9	8.7	52.9
PointCNN [12]	88.1	75.6	65.4	94.8	97.3	75.8	63.3	51.7	58.4	57.2	71.6	69.1	39.1	61.2	52.2	58.6
PointWeb [30]	87.3	76.2	66.7	93.5	94.2	80.8	52.4	41.3	64.9	68.1	71.4	67.1	50.3	62.7	62.2	58.5
ShellNet [29]	87.1	-	66.8	90.2	93.6	79.9	60.4	44.1	64.9	52.9	71.6	**84.7**	53.8	64.6	48.6	59.4
PointASNL [27]	**88.8**	79.0	68.7	**95.3**	**97.9**	81.9	47.0	48.0	**67.3**	70.5	71.3	77.8	50.7	60.4	63.0	**62.8**
KPConv [19]	-	79.1	70.6	93.6	92.4	**83.1**	63.9	**54.3**	66.1	**76.6**	57.8	64.0	**69.3**	**74.9**	61.3	60.3
RandLA-Net [7]	88.0	82.0	70.0	93.1	96.1	80.6	62.4	48.0	64.4	69.4	69.4	76.4	60.0	64.2	65.9	60.1
Waterfall-Net	88.5	**82.4**	**72.2**	94.7	97.8	82.8	**64.2**	53.9	64.8	70.5	**74.2**	78.3	66.0	65.3	**66.7**	60.0

Input	GT	RandLA-Net	Ours

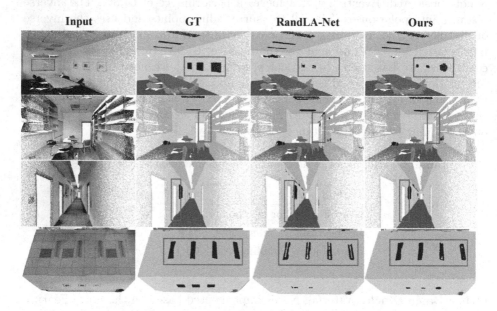

Fig. 4. Qualitative results of Waterfall-Net on S3DIS.

4.2   Results and Visualization

To verify the effectiveness of Waterfall-Net, we conduct it in two benchmarks: S3DIS and SemanticKitti, both indoor and outdoor scenarios.

Table 5. Quantitative results of different approaches on SemanticKITTI

Method	Size	mIoU(%)	road	sidewalk	parking	other-ground	building	car	truck	bicycle	motorcycle	other-vehicle	vegetation	trunk	terrain	person	bicyclist	motorcyclist	fence	pole	traffic-sign
PointNet [16]	50K pts	14.6	61.6	35.7	15.8	1.4	41.4	46.3	0.1	1.3	0.3	0.8	31.0	4.6	17.6	0.2	0.2	0.0	12.9	2.4	3.7
SPG [10]		17.4	45.0	28.5	0.6	0.6	64.3	49.3	0.1	0.2	0.2	0.8	48.9	27.2	24.6	0.3	2.7	0.1	20.8	15.9	0.8
PointNet++ [17]		20.1	72.0	41.8	18.7	5.6	62.3	53.7	0.9	1.9	0.2	0.2	46.5	13.8	30.0	0.9	1.0	0.0	16.9	6.0	8.9
TangentConv [18]		40.9	83.9	63.9	33.4	15.4	83.4	90.8	15.2	2.7	16.5	12.1	79.5	49.3	58.1	23.0	28.4	8.1	49.0	35.8	28.5
PointASNL [27]		46.8	87.4	74.3	24.3	1.8	83.1	87.9	39.0	0.0	25.1	29.2	84.1	52.2	70.6	34.2	57.6	0.0	43.9	**57.8**	36.9
PointNL [5]		52.2	90.5	72.5	48.3	19.0	81.6	92.1	9.8	**42.6**	37.4	20.0	78.5	54.5	62.7	49.2	**57.8**	**28.3**	50.2	41.7	55.8
RandLA-Net [7]		53.9	90.7	73.7	60.3	20.4	86.9	**94.2**	**40.1**	26.0	25.8	**38.9**	81.4	61.3	66.8	49.2	48.2	7.2	56.3	49.2	47.7
SqueezeSeg [25]	64×2048 pixels	29.5	85.4	54.3	26.9	4.5	57.4	68.8	3.3	16.0	4.1	3.6	60.0	24.3	53.7	12.9	13.1	0.9	29.0	17.5	24.5
SqueezeSegV2 [26]		39.7	88.6	67.6	45.8	17.7	73.7	81.8	13.4	18.5	17.9	14.0	71.8	35.8	60.2	20.1	25.1	3.9	41.1	20.2	36.3
DarkNet53Seg [3]		49.9	91.8	74.6	64.8	**27.9**	84.1	86.4	25.5	24.5	32.7	22.6	78.3	50.1	64.0	36.2	33.6	4.7	55.0	38.9	52.2
RangeNet53++ [14]		52.2	91.8	**75.2**	**65.0**	27.8	87.4	91.4	25.7	25.7	34.4	23.0	80.5	55.1	64.6	38.3	38.8	4.8	58.6	47.9	55.9
PolarNet [28]		54.3	90.8	74.4	61.7	21.7	90.0	92.9	22.9	40.3	30.1	28.5	**84.0**	**65.5**	67.8	43.2	40.2	5.6	61.3	51.8	**57.5**
Waterfall-Net	50K pts	**55.7**	91.0	75.0	63.0	23.4	**90.4**	93.0	30.8	40.5	**38.6**	30.0	82.3	58.2	**68.0**	**49.9**	47.6	5.6	**63.9**	49.6	57.1

S3DIS: We use the 6-fold cross-validation for fair comparison, following previous methods [7,16,17]. Results are reported in Table 4. Waterfall-Net outperforms RandLA-Net in all criteria and achieves superior results over previous point-based methods on mACC and mIoU. Compared with RandLA-Net, Waterfall-Net obtains obvious improvements in a large plane (ceil, floor, wall) and complex geometry (table, chair). It means waterfall feature aggregation can improve the categories that need clues of different granularity. In other words, the multiple density property is more sufficiently utilized in Waterfall-Net. Figure 4 displays some results in S3DIS. Some elaborate objects surrounded by large objects are misclassified by RandLA-Net, while the Waterfall-Net can handle these issues properly.

SemanticKitti: We follow the official split of training and testing set and evaluate the results in the competition server. Results are presented in Table 5. The Waterfall-Net outperforms all the point-based methods and improves the performance of RandLA-Net in most categories. It is inferior to RandLA-Net in the categories that have few samples as the number of samples in SemanicKitti is unbalanced. The topic of unbalance sample is another tough issue in point cloud analysis but out of the scope of our research.

5   Conclusion

In this paper, we present a Waterfall-Net to take advantage of the density property of different categories. It extracts more informative features with cascaded sub-networks. The sub-networks are connected via Sub-Network Fusing and the sub-stages in sub-networks are connected via Sub-Stage Fusing. Such a waterfall feature aggregation strategy provides more abundant semantics-and-density feature combinations. Quantitative experimental results and analysis on S3DIS and SemanticKitti demonstrate the effectiveness of our method.

References

1. Adelson, E.H., Anderson, C.H., Bergen, J.R., Burt, P.J., Ogden, J.M.: Pyramid methods in image processing. RCA Eng. **29**(6), 33–41 (1984)
2. Armeni, I., et al.: 3d semantic parsing of large-scale indoor spaces. In: Proceedings of the IEEE Conference on Computer Vision and Pattern Recognition, pp. 1534–1543 (2016)
3. Behley, J., et al.: Semantickitti: A dataset for semantic scene understanding of lidar sequences. In: Proceedings of the IEEE/CVF International Conference on Computer Vision, pp. 9297–9307 (2019)
4. Chen, L.C., Zhu, Y., Papandreou, G., Schroff, F., Adam, H.: Encoder-decoder with atrous separable convolution for semantic image segmentation. In: Proceedings of the European conference on computer vision (ECCV). pp. 801–818 (2018)
5. Cheng, M., Hui, L., Xie, J., Yang, J., Kong, H.: Cascaded non-local neural network for point cloud semantic segmentation. In: 2020 IEEE/RSJ International Conference on Intelligent Robots and Systems (IROS). pp. 8447–8452. IEEE (2020)

6. Engelmann, F., Kontogianni, T., Schult, J., Leibe, B.: Know what your neighbors do: 3d semantic segmentation of point clouds. In: Leal-Taixé, L., Roth, S. (eds.) ECCV 2018. LNCS, vol. 11131, pp. 395–409. Springer, Cham (2019). https://doi.org/10.1007/978-3-030-11015-4_29

7. Hu, Q., et al.: RandLA-Net: efficient semantic segmentation of large-scale point clouds. In: Proceedings of the IEEE/CVF Conference on Computer Vision and Pattern Recognition, pp. 11108–11117 (2020)

8. Jiang, M., Wu, Y., Zhao, T., Zhao, Z., Lu, C.: PointSIFT: a sift-like network module for 3d point cloud semantic segmentation. arXiv preprint arXiv:1807.00652 (2018)

9. Ke, L., Chang, M.-C., Qi, H., Lyu, S.: Multi-scale structure-aware network for human pose estimation. In: Ferrari, V., Hebert, M., Sminchisescu, C., Weiss, Y. (eds.) ECCV 2018. LNCS, vol. 11206, pp. 731–746. Springer, Cham (2018). https://doi.org/10.1007/978-3-030-01216-8_44

10. Landrieu, L., Simonovsky, M.: Large-scale point cloud semantic segmentation with superpoint graphs. In: Proceedings of the IEEE Conference on Computer Vision and Pattern Recognition, pp. 4558–4567 (2018)

11. Li, H., Xiong, P., Fan, H., Sun, J.: DFANet: deep feature aggregation for real-time semantic segmentation. In: Proceedings of the IEEE/CVF Conference on Computer Vision and Pattern Recognition, pp. 9522–9531 (2019)

12. Li, Y., Bu, R., Sun, M., Wu, W., Di, X., Chen, B.: PointCNN: convolution on χ-transformed points. In: Proceedings of the 32nd International Conference on Neural Information Processing Systems, pp. 828–838 (2018)

13. Liu, Y., Fan, B., Xiang, S., Pan, C.: Relation-shape convolutional neural network for point cloud analysis. In: Proceedings of the IEEE/CVF Conference on Computer Vision and Pattern Recognition, pp. 8895–8904 (2019)

14. Milioto, A., Vizzo, I., Behley, J., Stachniss, C.: Rangenet++: fast and accurate lidar semantic segmentation. In: 2019 IEEE/RSJ International Conference on Intelligent Robots and Systems (IROS), pp. 4213–4220. IEEE (2019)

15. Newell, A., Yang, K., Deng, J.: Stacked hourglass networks for human pose estimation. In: Leibe, B., Matas, J., Sebe, N., Welling, M. (eds.) ECCV 2016. LNCS, vol. 9912, pp. 483–499. Springer, Cham (2016). https://doi.org/10.1007/978-3-319-46484-8_29

16. Qi, C.R., Su, H., Mo, K., Guibas, L.J.: PointNet: deep learning on point sets for 3d classification and segmentation. In: Proceedings of the IEEE Conference on Computer Vision and Pattern Recognition, pp. 652–660 (2017)

17. Qi, C.R., Yi, L., Su, H., Guibas, L.J.: PointNet++: deep hierarchical feature learning on point sets in a metric space. Adv. Neural Inf. Process. Syst. **30**, 1–10 (2017)

18. Tatarchenko, M., Park, J., Koltun, V., Zhou, Q.Y.: Tangent convolutions for dense prediction in 3d. In: Proceedings of the IEEE Conference on Computer Vision and Pattern Recognition, pp. 3887–3896 (2018)

19. Thomas, H., Qi, C.R., Deschaud, J.E., Marcotegui, B., Goulette, F., Guibas, L.J.: KPConv: flexible and deformable convolution for point clouds. In: Proceedings of the IEEE/CVF International Conference on Computer Vision, pp. 6411–6420 (2019)

20. Tompson, J., Goroshin, R., Jain, A., LeCun, Y., Bregler, C.: Efficient object localization using convolutional networks. In: Proceedings of the IEEE Conference on Computer Vision and Pattern Recognition, pp. 648–656 (2015)

21. Wang, J., et al.: Deep high-resolution representation learning for visual recognition. IEEE Trans. Pattern Anal. Mach. Intell. **43**, 3349–3364 (2020)

22. Wang, L., Huang, Y., Hou, Y., Zhang, S., Shan, J.: Graph attention convolution for point cloud semantic segmentation. In: Proceedings of the IEEE/CVF Conference on Computer Vision and Pattern Recognition. pp. 10296–10305 (2019)
23. Wang, S., Suo, S., Ma, W.C., Pokrovsky, A., Urtasun, R.: Deep parametric continuous convolutional neural networks. In: Proceedings of the IEEE Conference on Computer Vision and Pattern Recognition, pp. 2589–2597 (2018)
24. Wang, Y., Sun, Y., Liu, Z., Sarma, S.E., Bronstein, M.M., Solomon, J.M.: Dynamic graph CNN for learning on point clouds. ACM Trans. Graph. (TOG) **38**(5), 1–12 (2019)
25. Wu, B., Wan, A., Yue, X., Keutzer, K.: SqueezeSeg: convolutional neural nets with recurrent CRF for real-time road-object segmentation from 3d lidar point cloud. In: 2018 IEEE International Conference on Robotics and Automation (ICRA), pp. 1887–1893. IEEE (2018)
26. Wu, B., Zhou, X., Zhao, S., Yue, X., Keutzer, K.: SqueezeSegv2: Improved model structure and unsupervised domain adaptation for road-object segmentation from a lidar point cloud. In: 2019 International Conference on Robotics and Automation (ICRA), pp. 4376–4382. IEEE (2019)
27. Yan, X., Zheng, C., Li, Z., Wang, S., Cui, S.: PointaSNL: robust point clouds processing using nonlocal neural networks with adaptive sampling. In: Proceedings of the IEEE/CVF Conference on Computer Vision and Pattern Recognition, pp. 5589–5598 (2020)
28. Zhang, Y., et al.: PolarNet: an improved grid representation for online lidar point clouds semantic segmentation. In: Proceedings of the IEEE/CVF Conference on Computer Vision and Pattern Recognition, pp. 9601–9610 (2020)
29. Zhang, Z., Hua, B.S., Yeung, S.K.: ShellNet: efficient point cloud convolutional neural networks using concentric shells statistics. In: Proceedings of the IEEE/CVF International Conference on Computer Vision, pp. 1607–1616 (2019)
30. Zhao, H., Jiang, L., Fu, C.W., Jia, J.: PointWeb: enhancing local neighborhood features for point cloud processing. In: Proceedings of the IEEE/CVF Conference on Computer Vision and Pattern Recognition, pp. 5565–5573 (2019)
31. Zhao, H., Jiang, L., Jia, J., Torr, P.H., Koltun, V.: Point transformer. In: Proceedings of the IEEE/CVF International Conference on Computer Vision, pp. 16259–16268 (2021)
32. Zhao, H., Shi, J., Qi, X., Wang, X., Jia, J.: Pyramid scene parsing network. In: Proceedings of the IEEE/CVF Conference on Computer Vision and Pattern Recognition, pp. 2881–2890 (2017)
33. Zhao, L., Tao, W.: JSNet: joint instance and semantic segmentation of 3d point clouds. In: Proceedings of the AAAI Conference on Artificial Intelligence, vol. 34, pp. 12951–12958 (2020)
34. Zhiheng, K., Ning, L.: PyramNet: point cloud pyramid attention network and graph embedding module for classification and segmentation. arXiv preprint arXiv:1906.03299 (2019)

Sparse LiDAR and Binocular Stereo Fusion Network for 3D Object Detection

Weiqing Yan[1], Kaiqi Su[1], Jinlai Ren[1(✉)], Runmin Cong[2], Shuai Li[3], and Shuigen Wang[4]

[1] Yantai University, Yantai 264005, Shandong, China
qfrenjinlai@126.com
[2] Beijing Jiaotong University, Beijing 100044, China
[3] Shandong University, Jinan 250100, Shandong, China
[4] Yantai IRay Technologies Ltd., Co., Yantai 264006, China

Abstract. 3D object detection is an essential task in autonomous driving and virtual reality. Existing approaches largely rely on expensive LiDAR sensors for accurate depth information to have high performance. While much lower-cost stereo cameras have been introduced as a promising alternative, there is still a notable performance gap. In this paper, we explore the idea to leverage sparse LiDAR and stereo images obtained by low-cost sensors for 3D object detection. We propose a novel multi-modal attention fusion end-to-end learning framework for 3D object detection, which effectively integrate the complementarities of sparse LiDAR and stereo images. Instead of directly fusing LiDAR and stereo modalities, we introduce a deep attention feature fusion module, which enables interactions between intermediate layers of LiDAR and stereo image paths by exploring the interdependencies of channel features. These fused features connect higher layer features after upsampling and lower layer features from the stereo image pathway and sparse LiDAR pathway. Hence, the fused features have high-level semantics with higher resolution, which is beneficial for the following object detection network. We provide detailed experiments on KITTI benchmark and achieve state-of-the-art performance compared with the low-cost based methods.

Keywords: 3D object detection · Sparse LiDAR · Stereo images · Low cost

1 Introduction

Autonomous driving is receiving more and more attention from the industry and the research community, the requirements for 3D object detection are also getting more and higher. Besides autonomous driving, 3d object detection has

This work was supported by the National Natural Science Foundation of China under Grants 61801414, 62072391, Natural Science Foundation of Shandong Province under Grants ZR2020QF108.

been applied to many other fields, such as virtual reality and medical simulation. It is one of the most important tasks in the field of computer vision.

Different from 2D object detection, 3D object detection can estimate depth and orientation of bounding boxes of objects by input sensor data. Depending on the different type of sensor, 3D object detection can be divided into LiDAR-based methods(point cloud-based methods) [6,9,12,16,20,36,40] , monocular image-based methods [1,18,21,27,32], and binocular stereo image-based methods [5,17,24,30,31,35,39]. Existing LiDAR-based methods provide accurate depth information by 3D point clouds. Although highly precise and reliable, LiDAR sensors are notoriously expensive: a 64-beam model can cost around $75,000 (USD). Compared with LiDAR and binocular stereo cameras, monocular cameras provide the cheapest data for 3D detection. However, a single image lacks reliable depth information, which results in low precision for 3D detection. Compared to monocular cameras, binocular stereo cameras can provide absolute depth information. And it is not expensive and can provide denser image information for small objects. While much lower-cost stereo cameras have been introduced as a promising alternative, there is still a notable performance gap compared with the results of LiDAR. All these sensors have their own advantage and disadvantage, in which none of them complete well on all practical scenarios. Some works [7,19,25,33,37] have researched how to fuse multiple sensors information so that improve the performance of 3D object detection. However, these methods take LiDAR data with 32 or 64 beams as input, which are very expensive. LiDAR sensors with 4 beams are cheaper compared with 64 beams and thus it is easily affordable. However, it cannot be used to detect small 3D object only by themselves, since 4 beams LiDAR data are very sparse. As aforementioned, stereo images can provide denser information for small objects. Therefore, we consider the fusion of binocular stereo camera and 4 beams LiDAR sensor for 3D object detection, which is a more practical choice. Depending on sparse LiDAR and stereo images, You et al. [41] proposed Pseudo-LiDAR++ method for 3D object detection. In this method, they first generate a dense depth map by stereo images, and then correct depth map by using sparse LiDAR information. However, in process of generating depth map, they need 64-beams LiDAR supervision.

In this paper, we propose a novel multi-modal fusion architecture that make full use of the advantages from both sparse LiDAR and stereo image feature fusion. It is worth noting that our proposed architecture is designed from low-cost sensors. Since 4-beam LiDAR information is extremely sparse, the fusion is from LiDAR feature to image feature, which augments image features with information accuracy of LiDAR features.

Different from the previous fusion methods based on LiDAR and images, we take a sparse 4-beam LiDAR and stereo images to detect 3D object by using the complementary information between both. In the proposed framework, we first take a sparse 4-beam LiDAR and make it dense image coordinate by using a simple and fast depth completion method. And then, the feature of stereo images and sparse LiDAR depth maps is extracted respectively, an feature attention fusion module is proposed to integrate the feature information from two pathways. Next, this network takes Stereo RPN [17] to output corresponding left and right RoI proposals. Left and right feature maps are fed into two different branches. One is the stereo regression branch to regress accurate 2D stereo boxes, dimensions, viewpoint angle and 2D center. Another is the depth prediction branch employed to predict the single-variable depth z of the 3D bounding box's center.

Our main contributions of this paper are summarized as follows:

- We propose a novel multi-modal fusion end-to-end learning framework for 3D object detection, which effectively integrate the complementarities of sparse LiDAR and stereo images.
- An deep attention feature fusion module is proposed to explore the interdependencies of channel features in the sparse LiDAR and stereo images while fusing the significant multi-modality spatial features.
- The proposed method achieves state-of-the-art performance compared with the low-cost sensor based methods without depth map supervision.

2 Related Work

2.1 LiDAR-Based 3D Object Detection

Since LiDAR sensors can provide the more accurate 3D information, most 3D detection approaches [6,9,12,16,20,36,40] utilize LiDAR data as input to obtain the best performance. Current LiDAR data can be processed into different representations for input to 3D object detection, including raw point clouds [20,36], volumetric forms [9,40], and 2D projection [16]. The representations of raw point clouds and volumetric forms can make full use of the 3D information of the object. However, they improve the computation cost drastically, especially for large-scale datasets. To improve the efficiency of 3D representations, the 3D point clouds are projected into a 2D image to utilize standard 2D object detection networks for predicting 3D bounding boxes.

2.2 Monocular-Based 3D Object Detection

Some works focus on 3D object detection using monocular cameras due to its low cost and convenient use. MonoGRNet [27] utilizes instance-level depth estimation to obtain a coarse 3D location, which is then refined by combining early features. M3D-RPN [1] proposes a standalone 3D region proposal network for joint prediction of 2D and 3D boxes. RTM3D [18] first predicts nine perspective keypoints of the 3D bounding box and then leverages geometric constraints of perspective projection to optimize 3D object information. SMOKE [21] uses the prediction information of a single key point paired with each object and the 3D regression information to predict a 3D bounding box. M3DSSD [22] solves the feature mismatching problem based on anchor-based methods by feature alignment and extracts depth-wise features for accurate depth prediction.

2.3   Stereo-Based 3D Object Detection

With the improvement of 3D object detection performance based on stereo vision, the gap with LiDAR-based methods is narrowing. Stereo-RCNN [17] extends Faster RCNN [29] to match objects in stereo images and utilizes dense alignment to refine the center depth of 3D bounding boxes. Disp R-CNN [31] and ZoomNet [39] share a similar idea that constructing the instance point cloud to improve detection quality. Pseudo-LiDAR [35] first converts the depth map from stereo vision to pseudo-LiDAR representation and then applies existing LiDAR-based algorithms to detect 3D bounding boxes. DSGN [5] transforms 2D feature to differentiable volumetric representation for encoding 3D geometry structure in 3D regular space. IDA-3D [24] proposes an IDA module for accurate the depth predicted of objects center to have high performance.

2.4   Multi-modal 3D Object Detection

Recently, some techniques [7,19,25,33,37] are proposed to improve 3D object detection performance by exploiting multiple sensors(e.g. 64 beams LiDAR and camera). Though LiDAR sensors with 64 beams are notoriously expensive, LiDAR sensors with only 4 beams are cheaper and easily affordable. In this respect, Pseudo-LiDAR++ [41] proposes a propagation algorithm to integrate the two data modalities, which takes advantage of sparse LiDAR to de-bias the 3D point cloud converted by the depth map from stereo vision. It is complex since it incorporates several independent networks. SLS-Fusion [23] proposes a approach to fuse sparse LiDAR and stereo camera for depth estimation, which is then converted to Pseudo-LiDAR for 3D object detection. However, it fuse the two data modalities by adding directly, not a weighted, which may lead to non-discriminative depth estimation. Inspired by the above approaches, we propose a novel attention network with fusing sparse LiDAR and binocular stereo images to accurately predict the information of 3D bounding box.

3   Proposed Method

In this section, we introduce the proposed 3D object detection architecture by using binocular stereo images and 4-beam sparse LiDAR information in detail. Our detection architecture consists of three stages: we first extract feature for input binocular stereo images respectively by weight-shared Resnet network and extract feature for sparse LiDAR in the same way as stereo images. And then different modal features are fused by attention fusion module. Finally, stereo information and single depth is obtained by regression network to predict 3D bounding boxes. Our architecture is shown in Fig. 1. In this architecture, we fuse LiDAR point cloud information to stereo images feature to augment image features with geometry information accuracy of LiDAR features. However, instead of directly using a 3D point cloud from 4-beam LiDAR, we form two sparse LiDAR depth maps corresponding to stereo images by reprojecting the 4-beam

LiDAR to both left and right image coordinates using the calibration parameters. LiDAR can provide accurate 3D information for 3D object detection. However, the observation is sparse, especially 4-beam LiDAR. Here, we perform depth completion of sparse LiDAR depth maps to produce dense depth maps, similar to the approach in [14]. The holes in the sparse LiDAR depth image are filled by morphological operations and Gaussian blurring operations using nearby valid depth values. The filled depth image is then normalized by the maximum depth value in the dataset, resulting in depth values between 0 and 1. Next, we present each component in detail.

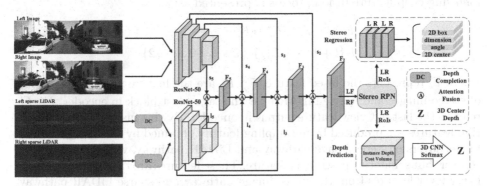

Fig. 1. Network architecture. Our network has three stages. First, sparse LiDAR and stereo RGB images use ResNet-50 as encoder to extract features respectively. Next, stereo images features and their corresponding sparse LiDAR features are fused by attention mechanism. After left and right features (LF,RF) passed through Stereo RPN, we obtain rough alignment region of interest of left and right view (LR RoIs). Finally, we predict position, dimensions and orientation of 3D bounding box.

3.1   Feature Extraction

The stereo images and sparse LiDAR use identical feature encoder architectures, one for each input sensor information. Both encoders for stereo images and sparse LiDAR consist of a series of ResNet blocks. By convolution with stride and downsampling operation, the feature resolution eventually is 1/16 of the input. Each feature encoder weight are shared with left and right input.

We propose a deep fusion approach to fuse sparse LiDAR and stereo image features hierarchically. Specifically, we fuse left sparse LiDAR with corresponding left feature maps in this module, which is the same way for the right. For a network with L layers in encoder stage, early fusion [15,34] combines features from multiple views in the input stage:

$$F_L = D_L(D_{L-1}(\cdots D_l(D_1(F_0^s \oplus F_0^l)))) \tag{1}$$

where D_l is feature transformation function, $\oplus$ is a join operation (e.g., summation [15], concatenation [34]), F_0^s, F_0^l are the input information of stereo images and sparse LiDAR data respectively. Recently, [26] uses separate subnetworks to learn feature transformation independently and combines their outputs in the prediction stage:

$$
\begin{aligned}
F_L = D_L^s(D_{L-1}^s(\cdots D_1^s(F_0^s))) \\
\oplus D_L^l(D_{L-1}^l(\cdots D_1^l(F_0^l)))
\end{aligned}
\tag{2}
$$

where D^s, D^l are the separate feature transformation function of stereo images and LiDAR data respectively.

To make more interactions among features from different modalities, the following deep feature fusion process is presented as:

$$
\begin{aligned}
F_{i+1} = F_i \oplus F_j^s \oplus F_j^l \\
i\epsilon\{l+1,\cdots,L\}; j\epsilon\{L-l+1,\cdots,2\}
\end{aligned}
\tag{3}
$$

where F_i represents the fused feature, F_g^s, F_g^l are the feature activations output of stereo images and sparse LiDAR by each stage's last block in encoder, F_l^s, F_l^l refer to the last left view feature output in encoder. By this fusion, higher resolution features are produced by upsampling feature obtained by Resnet network in higher layers of stereo image pathway and LiDAR pathway, which are spatially coarser, but semantically stronger feature. These features are then enhanced with lower layer features from the stereo image pathway and sparse LiDAR pathway via connections. Moreover, These lower layer features from the stereo image pathway and LiDAR pathway are of lower-level semantics, but its activations are more accurately localized due to its higher resolution. Therefore, the fused features have high-level semantics with higher resolution, which is beneficial for object detection. In our network, F_1^r and F_1^s aren't added to the fusion module due to its large memory footprint.

Since the input sparse depth is strongly related with the decoder output(the prediction depth of object Z), features from the sparse depth should contribute more in the decoder. As such, we add the features from the sparse depth onto the stereo features in decoder instead of concatenation. As the summation favors the features on both sides in the same domain [4], the decoder is encouraged to learn features more related to depth, which keep consistent with the feature from the sparse depth. However, the 4 laser beams LiDAR are too sparse to alone provide sufficient information for 3D detection. Therefore, the fusion is directed from LiDAR steam to image steam to augment image features.

3.2   Attention Fusion

As Eq. 3 indicates that features of different models are fused equally, not a weighted, which may lead to the different importance of each models cannot be correctly reflected. To solve this problem, we employ an attention mechanism to add sparse LiDAR feature into image feature, which sets the weight w_i for each feature level. Since the depth information in sparse LiDAR is accurate, we hope to capture the depth information from sparse LiDAR map to stereo

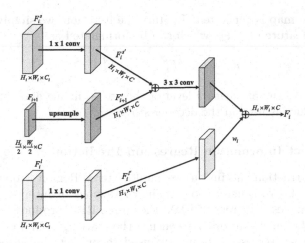

Fig. 2. Illustration of attention fusion module.

images. Therefore, the w_i is obtained by calculating the correlation between sparse LiDAR and corresponding stereo feature maps on each level. It is defined as:

$$w_i = \cos < F_i^s, F_i^l > = \frac{F_i^{s\top} \cdot F_i^l}{\| F_i^s \| \cdot \| F_i^l \|}, i = 2 \ldots, 5 \tag{4}$$

where $F_i^s, F_i^l \in \mathbb{R}^{(H_i \times W_i \times C_i) \times 1}$ are the ith stereo images and sparse LiDAR feature maps in the feature extraction. Technically, as shown in Fig. 2, we first upsample F_{i+1} by a factor of 2 into $F_{i+1}' \in R^{H_i \times W_i \times C}$ (using nearest neighbor upsampling for simplicity). Next, we apply 1×1 convolution operation to F_i^s and F_i^l to reduce channel dimensions. The process can be described as:

$$
\begin{aligned}
F_{i+1}' &= upsample(F_{i+1}) \\
F_i^{s'} &= f_{1\times1}(F_i^s) \\
F_i^{l'} &= f_{1\times1}(F_i^l)
\end{aligned}
\tag{5}
$$

where *upsample* is the up-sampling operation via nearest neighbor interpolation, and $f_{1\times1}$ refers to the 1×1 convolution layer.

Further, we fuse the upsampled feature map F_{i+1}' and the corresponding $F_i^{s'}$ feature map by element-wise addition. Here, a 3×3 convolution is appended on each merged feature map to reduce the aliasing effect of upsampling. Finally, the merged feature is added to the sparse LiDAR feature $F_i^{l'}$, which applies the w_i. The output feature is computed as follow:

$$F_i = f_{3\times3}(F_i^{s'} + F_{i+1}') + w_i \cdot F_i^{l'} \tag{6}$$

where $f_{3\times3}$ represent the 3×3 convolution layer. The fusion result F_i is exactly the higher level feature of the next fusion stage. This process is iterated until the final feature map is generated. To start the iteration, we simply to produce the init fusion feature map F_5, which can be formulated as:

$$F_5 = f_{3\times3}(F_i^{s'} + w_5 \cdot F_i^{l'}) \tag{7}$$

where $F_i^{s'}, F_i^{l'}$ are the 5th feature level of the stereo image and sparse LiDAR, respectively, which is used in the decoder stage.

3.3   3D Object Information Regression Prediction

After feature extraction and fusion, we employ stereo Region Proposal Network (RPN) module [17] to generate some pairs of Regions of Interest (RoI) in the left and right images. Different of RPN, the stereo RPN produces an union RoI for left and right images in order to ensure the starting points of each pair of RoIs, and then six regressing terms are used to predict the offsets of anchor box in left and right images. The six regressing terms include the offsets of horizontal and vertical coordinates, the offsets of width and height of the 2D box in left image, and the offsets of horizontal coordinate and width in right image. After stereo RPN, we can obtain corresponding feature maps in left-right proposal pairs by applying RoI Align [10] on the left and right feature maps respectively at appropriate pyramid level. The left and right RoI features are concatenated and fed into the stereo regression branch, which includes four sub-branches to predict 2D box, dimension, and viewpoint angle, 2D center respectively. In addition to the stereo regression branch, we predict the 3D depth of object center in the depth prediction branch. Instead of predicting the depth information of each pixel, we only compute the depth of instance object between left and right images. In our network, we takes Instance-Depth-Aware (IDA) module [24] to predict the depth of instance object center.

Finally, 3D bounding box can be represented by 2D box, dimension, orientation, and depth information.

3.4   Implementation Details

Our loss function can be formulated as:

$$L = w_1 L_{cls}^s + w_2 L_{reg}^s + w_3 L_{box}^r + w_4 L_{dim}^r$$
$$+ w_5 L_\alpha^r + w_6 L_{ctr}^r + w_7 L_z^d \tag{8}$$

where we use $(\cdot)^s, (\cdot)^r$ and $(\cdot)^d$ for representing the loss in Stereo RPN module [17], Stereo Regression module [10], and Depth Prediction module [24] respectively. L_{cls}^s and L_{reg}^s denote the loss of classification and regression on stereo RPN module respectively. $L_{box}^r, L_{dim}^r, L_\alpha^r, L_{ctr}^r$ are the loss of stereo boxes, dimension, viewpoint, 2D center on stereo Regression respectively. L_z^d is the loss of depth on Depth Precision module. Each loss is weighted to balance the whole loss following [13]. In our experiment, the weight is 1,1,1,3,0.1,2,0.2 separately.

Two weight-shared ResNet-50 [11] architecture are treated as the feature encoder for stereo images and sparse LiDAR, respectively. For data augmentation, we flip and exchange the left and right image in the training set and mirror the image information. For sparse LiDAR information, we first project it on image planes using the calibration parameters and then apply the same flipping strategy as previous stereo images. Our model is implemented under PyTorch 1.1.0, CUDA 10.0. By default, we train our network with batch-size 4 on 4 NVIDIA Tesla V100 GPUs for 65000 iterations, and the overall training time is about 26 h. We apply stochastic gradient descent(SGD) optimizer with initial learning rate 0.02.

4 Experiments

Table 1. 3D object detection results evaluated on the KITTI object validation set. We report average precision of bird's eye view (AP_{bev}) and 3D boxes (AP_{3d}) for the car category. PL(AVOD) is reported by [5] without LiDAR supervision. We use original KITTI evaluation metric here.

Method	AP_{bev}(IoU = 0.5)			AP_{3d}(IoU = 0.5)		
	Easy	Moderate	Hard	Easy	Moderate	Hard
MonoGRNet [27]	54.21	39.69	33.06	50.51	36.97	30.82
M3D-RPN [1]	55.37	42.49	35.29	48.96	39.57	33.01
RTM-3D [18]	57.47	44.16	42.31	54.36	41.90	35.84
Decoupled-3D [2]	73.22	54.31	45.97	69.40	50.50	42.46
MLF [38]	-	53.56	-	-	19.54	-
3DOP [3]	55.04	41.25	34.55	46.04	34.63	30.09
TL-Net [28]	62.46	45.99	41.92	59.51	43.71	37.99
PL(AVOD) [35]	76.8	65.1	56.6	75.6	57.9	49.3
Stereo R-CNN [17]	87.13	74.11	58.93	85.84	66.28	57.24
IDA-3D [24]	88.05	76.69	67.29	87.08	74.57	60.01
Ours	88.58	77.70	68.15	87.92	75.32	66.27

4.1 KITTI Dataset

Our method is evaluated on the challenging KITTI object detection dataset [8], which provides 7481 training images and 7581 testing images. In this paper, the 4-beam LiDAR signal on KITTI benchmark is simulated by sparsifying the original 64-beam signal as the way of [8]. Following [3], the training data is divided into roughly the same amount of training set and validation set. The ground-truth of Car, Pedestrian and Cyclist is provided by annotations in the training set. Following the KITTI settings, each category is divided into three regimes: easy, moderate, and hard, depending on the occlusion/truncation and the size of 2D box height.

Table 2. 3D object detection results evaluated on the KITTI object validation set. We report average precision of bird's eye view (AP_{bev}) and 3D boxes (AP_{3d}) for the car category. PL(AVOD) is reported by [5] without LiDAR supervision. We use original KITTI evaluation metric here.

Method	AP_{bev}(IoU$=0.7$)			AP_{3d}(IoU$=0.7$)		
	Easy	Moderate	Hard	Easy	Moderate	Hard
MonoGRNet [27]	24.97	19.44	16.30	13.88	10.19	7.62
M3D-RPN [1]	25.94	21.18	17.90	20.27	17.06	15.21
RTM-3D [18]	25.56	22.12	20.91	20.77	16.86	16.63
Decoupled-3D [2]	44.42	29.69	24.60	26.95	18.68	15.82
MLF [38]	-	47.42	-	-	9.80	-
3DOP [3]	12.63	9.49	7.59	6.55	5.07	4.10
TL-Net [28]	29.22	21.88	18.83	18.15	14.26	13.72
PL(AVOD) [35]	60.7	39.2	37.0	40.0	27.4	25.3
Stereo R-CNN [17]	68.50	48.30	41.47	54.11	36.69	31.07
IDA-3D [24]	70.68	50.21	42.93	54.97	37.45	32.23
Ours	71.62	52.15	44.6	56.00	39.77	33.64

4.2 Evaluation Metrics

We use average precision of 3D detection (AP_{3d}) and average precision of bird's-eye-view (BEV) detection (AP_{bev}) to evaluate the performance of our method. The results of AP_{3d} and AP_{bev} on the validation set are reported on the car's category. It is worth noting that the Intersection over Union (IoU) thresholds are set at 0.5 and 0.7, following previous works [17,24]. In order to compare with previous approaches fairly, our validation results are evaluated using the original evaluation code, which calculates AP with 11 recall positions instead of 40 recall positions.

4.3 Main Results

The main results as shown in Table 1, 2 (IoU $=0.5,0.7$), where we compare the proposed method with previous state-of-the-art approaches from low-cost sensors (monocular to binocular). Our method obtains a significant improvement in comparison to previous monocular-based methods in all cases across all IoU thresholds. Comparing with binocular-based methods, our method gains the highest performance at 0.5 IoU and 0.7 IoU. Specifically, our approach outperforms previous state-of-art IDA-3D [24] by 1.94% and 1.67% in AP_{bev} across moderate and hard sets at 0.7 IoU, respectively. The similar improvement trends can be obverse in AP_{3d}, which manifest that our approach achieves consistent improvement compared with other approaches. The results of our approach in the moderate and hard set on the most metric AP_{3d} (IoU $=0.7$) outperform

IDA-3D by over 2.32% and 1.41%. Although only a small margin of our approach outperforms IDA-3D (IoU = 0.7) in the easy set,the proposed method gain significant improvement over 6.26% on AP_{3d} (IoU = 0.5) in the hard set. The reason is that our method fuses sparse LiDAR information to extract feature, which provides more accurate depth.

In addition to the aforementioned comparison methods, we also compare with the current multi-modality based method. Since these methods [19,25,33,37] use 64-beams LiDAR information as input or intermediate supervision, we only compare the proposed method to the Pseudo-LiDAR++ (PL++) [41], which takes L#+S as input. PL++ produced dense depth map with 64-beams LiDAR supervision, however, the proposed method only use 4-beam LiDAR. We show the reproduced result of PL++ without 64-beam LiDAR supervision (PL++ * (AVOD)) in Table 3. The experimental results in Table 3 demonstrate that our approach outperforms PL++ * (AVOD) approach on some metrics. Specifically, we achieve 11.3% improvement for AP_{3d} using IoU = 0.7 in the easy set. For AP_{bev}, our method gains over 7.82% improvements. The reason is the proposed network pays more attention to nearby objects, while the 3D point cloud is projected onto the front-viewing image. In addition, Table 3 also reports the running time comparison between PL++ * (AVOD) method and the proposed method. Our approach has a high speed of 0.116 s per frame at inference time, which far exceeds PL++ * (AVOD) method. The efficiency is attributed to our network, which is an end-to-end architecture with light weight modules compared to the network of PL++ method.

Table 3. AP_{bev} and AP_{3d} of IoU = 0.7 on KITTI validation set.

Method	Running time (s/frame)	AP_{bev}		AP_{3d}	
		Easy	Moderate	Easy	Moderate
PL++ * (AVOD) [41]	0.519	63.8	57.2	44.7	38.9
Ours	0.116	71.62	52.15	56	39.77

In addition to the above quantitative analysis, we also show the qualitative detection results of several scenarios in the KITTI validation set in Fig. 3. It can be observed that the proposed method can accurately detect objects in these scenarios, and the detected 3D box are well aligned on the vertical view and front view point cloud.

4.4 Ablation Study

In this section, we analyze the effectiveness of Sparse LiDAR, Depth Completion, and Attention Fusion components in our method. Results are shown in Table 4. In condition of just using Sparse LiDAR, we directly add the sparse LiDAR features into their corresponding stereo images features at appropriate level in

Fig. 3. 3D object detection results on the KITTI validation set. The predicted results are shown in green box and the ground truth are shown in red box. In order to facilitate observation, the detection results are shown on the vertical and front view point cloud. (Color figure online)

the decoder. In condition of not using Depth Completion, we regard the sparse LiDAR depth maps as the depth feature extractor input. In condition of not using Attention Fusion module, the sparse LiDAR feature maps are added directly to their corresponding image feature maps.

From Table 4, we can see that the performance achieves significant improvement, when sparse LiDAR is only applied, which demonstrates that sparse LiDAR is crucial for high-quality 3D detection. The absence of Depth Completion makes the percentage drop from 38.83% to 37.31% on AP_{3d} with a threshold IoU $= 0.7$ in the moderate set. Besides, the performance of our AP_{bev} has a drop of 1.87% at 0.7 IoU in the easy set when Attention Fusion is removed. Large improvements can be observed on all metrics by using these three key components together, and results surpass almost all prior low-cost based methods.

Table 4. Ablation studies on the KITTI validation set.

Sparse LiDAR	Attention fusion	Depth completion	AP_{bev}(IoU $= 0.7$)			AP_{3d}(IoU $= 0.7$)		
			Easy	Moderate	Hard	Easy	Moderate	Hard
			67.66	48.74	41.73	53.35	36.49	31.26
✓			70.06	50.47	42.86	55.77	37.31	31.6
✓		✓	69.75	51.52	44.22	55.93	38.83	33.05
✓	✓		71.35	51.46	43.87	55.8	37.91	32.7
✓	✓	✓	71.62	52.15	44.6	56	39.77	33.64

5   Conclusion

In this paper, we take 4-beam sparse LiDAR and stereo images as input for 3D object detection. The key idea is that a deep fusion module combines features across multiple modalities by utilizing an attention mechanism. Our deep attention feature fusion module explores the interdependencies of channel features in the sparse LiDAR and stereo images while fusing the significant multi-modality spatial features. Experimental results show higher 3D detection performance of our proposed method compared with other low-cost sensor based method.

References

1. Brazil, G., Liu, X.: M3d-RPN: Monocular 3d region proposal network for object detection. In: Proceedings of the IEEE International Conference on Computer Vision, pp. 9287–9296 (2019)
2. Cai, Y., Li, B., Jiao, Z., Li, H., Zeng, X., Wang, X.: Monocular 3d object detection with decoupled structured polygon estimation and height-guided depth estimation. In: Proceedings of the AAAI Conference on Artificial Intelligence, vol. 34, pp. 10478–10485 (2020)
3. Chen, X., Kundu, K., Zhu, Y., Ma, H., Fidler, S., Urtasun, R.: 3d object proposals using stereo imagery for accurate object class detection. IEEE Trans. Pattern Anal. Mach. Intell. **40**(5), 1259–1272 (2017)
4. Chen, X., Ma, H., Wan, J., Li, B., Xia, T.: Multi-view 3d object detection network for autonomous driving. In: Proceedings of the IEEE Conference on Computer Vision and Pattern Recognition, pp. 1907–1915 (2017)
5. Chen, Y., Liu, S., Shen, X., Jia, J.: DSGN: deep stereo geometry network for 3d object detection. In: Proceedings of the IEEE/CVF Conference on Computer Vision and Pattern Recognition, pp. 12536–12545 (2020)
6. Cheng, B., Sheng, L., Shi, S., Yang, M., Xu, D.: Back-tracing representative points for voting-based 3d object detection in point clouds. In: Proceedings of the IEEE/CVF Conference on Computer Vision and Pattern Recognition, pp. 8963–8972 (2021)
7. Choi, C., Choi, J.H., Li, J., Malla, S.: Shared cross-modal trajectory prediction for autonomous driving. In: Proceedings of the IEEE/CVF Conference on Computer Vision and Pattern Recognition, pp. 244–253 (2021)
8. Geiger, A., Lenz, P., Urtasun, R.: Are we ready for autonomous driving? the kitti vision benchmark suite. In: 2012 IEEE Conference on Computer Vision and Pattern Recognition, pp. 3354–3361. IEEE (2012)
9. He, C., Zeng, H., Huang, J., Hua, X.S., Zhang, L.: Structure aware single-stage 3d object detection from point cloud. In: Proceedings of the IEEE/CVF Conference on Computer Vision and Pattern Recognition, pp. 11873–11882 (2020)
10. He, K., Gkioxari, G., Dollár, P., Girshick, R.: Mask R-CNN. In: Proceedings of the IEEE International Conference on Computer Vision, pp. 2961–2969 (2017)
11. He, K., Zhang, X., Ren, S., Sun, J.: Deep residual learning for image recognition. In: Proceedings of the IEEE Conference on Computer Vision and Pattern Recognition, pp. 770–778 (2016)
12. He, Y., et al.: DVFENet: dual-branch voxel feature extraction network for 3d object detection. Neurocomputing **459**, 201–211 (2021)
13. Kendall, A., Gal, Y., Cipolla, R.: Multi-task learning using uncertainty to weigh losses for scene geometry and semantics. In: Proceedings of the IEEE Conference on Computer Vision and Pattern Recognition, pp. 7482–7491 (2018)
14. Ku, J., Harakeh, A., Waslander, S.L.: In defense of classical image processing: fast depth completion on the CPU. In: 2018 15th Conference on Computer and Robot Vision (CRV), pp. 16–22. IEEE (2018)

15. Ku, J., Mozifian, M., Lee, J., Harakeh, A., Waslander, S.L.: Joint 3d proposal generation and object detection from view aggregation. In: 2018 IEEE/RSJ International Conference on Intelligent Robots and Systems (IROS), pp. 1–8. IEEE (2018)
16. Lang, A.H., Vora, S., Caesar, H., Zhou, L., Yang, J., Beijbom, O.: Pointpillars: fast encoders for object detection from point clouds. In: Proceedings of the IEEE/CVF Conference on Computer Vision and Pattern Recognition, pp. 12697–12705 (2019)
17. Li, P., Chen, X., Shen, S.: Stereo R-CNN based 3d object detection for autonomous driving. In: Proceedings of the IEEE Conference on Computer Vision and Pattern Recognition, pp. 7644–7652 (2019)
18. Li, P., Zhao, H., Liu, P., Cao, F.: RTM3D: real-time monocular 3d detection from object keypoints for autonomous driving. In: Vedaldi, A., Bischof, H., Brox, T., Frahm, J.-M. (eds.) ECCV 2020. LNCS, vol. 12348, pp. 644–660. Springer, Cham (2020). https://doi.org/10.1007/978-3-030-58580-8_38
19. Liang, M., Yang, B., Chen, Y., Hu, R., Urtasun, R.: Multi-task multi-sensor fusion for 3d object detection. In: Proceedings of the IEEE/CVF Conference on Computer Vision and Pattern Recognition, pp. 7345–7353 (2019)
20. Liu, Y., Fan, B., Xiang, S., Pan, C.: Relation-shape convolutional neural network for point cloud analysis. In: Proceedings of the IEEE/CVF Conference on Computer Vision and Pattern Recognition, pp. 8895–8904 (2019)
21. Liu, Z., Wu, Z., Tóth, R.: Smoke: Single-stage monocular 3d object detection via keypoint estimation. In: Proceedings of the IEEE/CVF Conference on Computer Vision and Pattern Recognition Workshops, pp. 996–997 (2020)
22. Luo, S., Dai, H., Shao, L., Ding, Y.: M3DSSD: monocular 3d single stage object detector. In: Proceedings of the IEEE/CVF Conference on Computer Vision and Pattern Recognition, pp. 6145–6154 (2021)
23. Mai, N.A.M., Duthon, P., Khoudour, L., Crouzil, A., Velastin, S.A.: Sparse lidar and stereo fusion (SLS-fusion) for depth estimation and 3d object detection. arXiv preprint arXiv:2103.03977 (2021)
24. Peng, W., Pan, H., Liu, H., Sun, Y.: IDA-3D: instance-depth-aware 3d object detection from stereo vision for autonomous driving. In: Proceedings of the IEEE/CVF Conference on Computer Vision and Pattern Recognition, pp. 13015–13024 (2020)
25. Prakash, A., Chitta, K., Geiger, A.: Multi-modal fusion transformer for end-to-end autonomous driving. In: Proceedings of the IEEE/CVF Conference on Computer Vision and Pattern Recognition, pp. 7077–7087 (2021)
26. Qi, C.R., Liu, W., Wu, C., Su, H., Guibas, L.J.: Frustum PointNets for 3d object detection from RGB-D data. In: Proceedings of the IEEE Conference on Computer Vision and Pattern Recognition, pp. 918–927 (2018)
27. Qin, Z., Wang, J., Lu, Y.: MonoGRNet: a geometric reasoning network for monocular 3d object localization. In: Proceedings of the AAAI Conference on Artificial Intelligence, vol. 33, pp. 8851–8858 (2019)
28. Qin, Z., Wang, J., Lu, Y.: Triangulation learning network: from monocular to stereo 3d object detection. In: 2019 IEEE/CVF Conference on Computer Vision and Pattern Recognition (CVPR), pp. 7607–7615. IEEE (2019)
29. Ren, S., He, K., Girshick, R., Sun, J.: Faster R-CNN: Towards real-time object detection with region proposal networks. Adv. Neural. Inf. Process. Syst. **28**, 91–99 (2015)
30. Shi, Y., Guo, Y., Mi, Z., Li, X.: Stereo centerNet-based 3d object detection for autonomous driving. Neurocomputing **471**, 219–229 (2022)

31. Sun, J., Chen, L., Xie, Y., Zhang, S., Jiang, Q., Zhou, X., Bao, H.: DISP R-CNN: stereo 3d object detection via shape prior guided instance disparity estimation. In: Proceedings of the IEEE/CVF Conference on Computer Vision and Pattern Recognition, pp. 10548–10557 (2020)

32. Tang, Y., Dorn, S., Savani, C.: Center3D: Center-based monocular 3d object detection with joint depth understanding. In: Akata, Z., Geiger, A., Sattler, T. (eds.) DAGM GCPR 2020. LNCS, vol. 12544, pp. 289–302. Springer, Cham (2021). https://doi.org/10.1007/978-3-030-71278-5_21

33. Vora, S., Lang, A.H., Helou, B., Beijbom, O.: Pointpainting: Sequential fusion for 3d object detection. In: Proceedings of the IEEE/CVF Conference on Computer Vision and Pattern Recognition, pp. 4604–4612 (2020)

34. Wang, T.H., Hu, H.N., Lin, C.H., Tsai, Y.H., Chiu, W.C., Sun, M.: 3d lidar and stereo fusion using stereo matching network with conditional cost volume normalization. In: 2019 IEEE/RSJ International Conference on Intelligent Robots and Systems (IROS), pp. 5895–5902. IEEE (2019)

35. Wang, Y., Chao, W.L., Garg, D., Hariharan, B., Campbell, M., Weinberger, K.Q.: Pseudo-lidar from visual depth estimation: Bridging the gap in 3d object detection for autonomous driving. In: Proceedings of the IEEE/CVF Conference on Computer Vision and Pattern Recognition, pp. 8445–8453 (2019)

36. Wang, Y., Sun, Y., Liu, Z., Sarma, S.E., Bronstein, M.M., Solomon, J.M.: Dynamic graph CNN for learning on point clouds. ACM Trans. Graph. (TOG) 38(5), 1–12 (2019)

37. Xiao, Y., Codevilla, F., Gurram, A., Urfalioglu, O., López, A.M.: Multimodal end-to-end autonomous driving. IEEE Trans. Intell. Transp. Syst. (2020)

38. Xu, B., Chen, Z.: Multi-level fusion based 3d object detection from monocular images. In: Proceedings of the IEEE Conference on Computer Vision and Pattern Recognition, pp. 2345–2353 (2018)

39. Xu, Z., et al.: ZoomNet: part-aware adaptive zooming neural network for 3d object detection. In: Proceedings of the AAAI Conference on Artificial Intelligence, vol. 34, pp. 12557–12564 (2020)

40. Yin, T., Zhou, X., Krahenbuhl, P.: Center-based 3d object detection and tracking. In: Proceedings of the IEEE/CVF Conference on Computer Vision and Pattern Recognition, pp. 11784–11793 (2021)

41. You, Y., et al.: Pseudo-lidar++: accurate depth for 3d object detection in autonomous driving. In: ICLR (2020)

Full Head Performance Capture Using Multi-scale Mesh Propagation

Hanchao Li, Yizhu Lin, and Xinguo Liu[✉]

State Key Lab of CAD and CG, Zhejiang University, Hangzhou 310000, China
{hanson_li,bemfoo}@zju.edu.cn, xgliu@cad.zju.edu.cn

Abstract. We present a template fitting based method for efficient markerless full head performance capture. Our method starts with high-resolution multi-view videos and efficiently outputs high-fidelity full head mesh sequences with the same topology of a common template model. A GPU accelerated stereo reconstruction firstly computes a high-quality point cloud at each frame. Then the template model is warped and fitted to the reconstructed geometries using a combination of detected landmarks constraint, nearest neighbor constraint, and volumetric regularization. Additionally, we reconstruct the detailed ear structures at the initialization frame and track the movement with a global rigid transformation assumption in the following frames. To solve the error accumulation problem when dealing with long sequences, the method updates the positions of mesh vertices using priors from the previous and initial frames in a coarse to fine manner. Summing up the above technical innovations, our method can significantly reduce the whole processing time for reconstructing topology consistent full head meshes with fine details. We conduct several experiments and demonstrate the efficiency and outperformance of the proposed method compared to previous methods.

Keywords: Facial performance capture · Full head reconstruction · Space-time geometry reconstruction · Template fitting

1   Introduction

3D/4D face modeling has been a popular research topic in recent decades with tremendous applications in movies, games, and virtual reality systems. 4D facial modeling, also called *dynamic* facial performance capturing, usually takes videos as input and seeks to reconstruct facial models with a consistent mesh topology. It requires a great deal of spatial fidelity and temporal correspondence accuracy to reproduce an authentic output.

Classic marker-based approaches draw markers uniformly distributed over the whole face and track these points manually or automatically to recover the accurate facial geometry movement. These techniques require time-consuming

Supplementary Information The online version contains supplementary material available at https://doi.org/10.1007/978-3-031-18913-5_5.

and expensive artist input to fine-tune the marker tracking results and remove unseen markers when extreme expressions occur. On the contrary, markerless methods are more friendly to subjects and significantly reduce the data acquisition procedure. Recent advances in facial landmark detection can provide an initial mesh deformation and sparse tracking across different expressions. Then the dense correspondence between frames can be computed using optical flow or scene flow. Though many methods are proposed, there still exists room for improvement such as the quality of reconstructed models, and the robustness and efficiency when dealing with long sequences.

In this paper, we propose an efficient facial performance capture method using hybrid multi-scale mesh propagation. The term of *mesh propagation* is firstly introduced in [4] and means the update of the positions in space of the reference template mesh. We follow the classic two-stage framework: individual per-frame multi-view scan reconstruction and across-frame facial tracking. In the first stage, the method reconstructs a dense point cloud of each frame from the multi-view imaging data. In the next stage, a reference template mesh is firstly registered to a neural 3D scan at the beginning. Then the subject-specific template mesh is propagated to the following frames. We use the detected landmarks and image-space pixel matching to guide the mesh deformation and fit the template mesh toward the target point cloud from coarse to fine. We also recover the ear structure to provide a full head performance capture. In consideration of the rigidity of the ears in the presence of any expressions, we treat the ear region as a whole and only compute the global rigid transformation using visible ear landmarks in the facial tracking stage. We propose a multi-scale hybrid mesh propagation scheme combining the priors from both the initial frame and the previous frame. A base mesh is computed using the between-frame movement and then progressively refined to capture the finer-scale details. To evaluate the efficiency and accuracy of our methods, we build a passive multi-cameras system and conduct several experiments showing the advancement of our method in terms of both temporal consistency and spatial fitting accuracy. We report the timings of the main modules of our method and the acceleration compared to state-of-the-art methods.

In summary, our contributions include:

- a template fitting based facial performance capture method that efficiently reconstructs high-quality meshes with a consistent mesh topology.
- a template warping algorithm for the registration of the full head geometry including ears.
- a multi-scale mesh propagation scheme that propagates a base mesh incorporating the priors from both the initial and the previous frame and then progressively refines the base mesh to a detailed mesh.

2 Related Work

The objective of dynamic performance capture is to compute temporal correspondence for a sequence and deform a template geometry to match the video

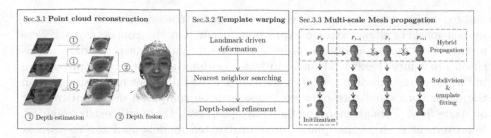

Fig. 1. Overview of the full pipeline. The input video sequences are divided into synchronized multi-view frames. The pyramid-based depth estimation module reconstructs a colored dense point cloud at each frame (Sect. 3.1). A shared template shape is then warped and fitted toward the target point cloud from coarse to fine (Sect. 3.2) at the initial frame. In the following frames, the person-specific mesh is propagated and progressively refined for finer details (Sect. 3.3).

input. Derek et.al [5] proposed to obtain an initial geometry as the template geometry at the beginning frame. The motion between the initial and every subsequent frame was computed using dense optical flow in the texture domain. And the template was deformed and updated with as-rigid-as-possible [26] constraint. Beeler et.al [4] further added anchor frames dividing the long sequences into small clips and tracking the performance between anchor frames to reduce the error accumulation. Fyffe et.al [13] proposed a fully parallelizable framework that jointly optimized stereo constraints and consistent mesh parameterization. They skipped the multi-view stereo step at each frame and directly computed the dense multi-view optical flow on imaging data to guide the deformation of a common template model. The volumetric Lapalacian regularization was employed to better constraint 3D vertex estimates.

Other methods leveraged facial priors such as user-specific expression (blendshape) models to enable real-time performance capture. Weise et.al [2] formulated the deformation as a maximum posterior estimation in a reduced blendshape space. The user-specific blendshape model was automatically generated in an offline pre-processing. In the online stage, the blendshape weights were estimated given the acquired 2D imaging and 3D depth input in real-time. However, the quality of the reconstructed 3D facial dynamics is directly restricted to the blendshape model. Fyffe et.al [12] argued that the combination of static facial scans and dynamic video frames could create animated performance geometry with high-resolution detail and relightable reflectance properties. Recent work paid more attention on statistical morphable models such as FaceWareHouse [6], FLAME [14] and FaceScape [21]. The coefficients of each components were estimated in an optimization-based or learning-based framework [8–10].

3   Template Fitting Based Dynamic Full Head Performance Capture

Figure 1 shows the processing pipeline from multi-view video sequences to a set of parameterized face meshes with the same topology. Firstly, at each frame,

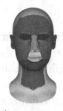   

(a)segments map   (b)facial landmarks   (c)ear landmarks   (d)tetrahedral mesh

Fig. 2. The template setup.

a colored dense point cloud is reconstructed from multi-view images using a pyramid-based depth estimation method. Then in the facial tracking stage, a generic full head template model is registered at the initial frame and the person-specific mesh is propagated to the following frames. The output contains a sequence of facial scans with consistent topology and can be directly used in production like virtual avatar animation.

We choose the freely available *Louise*[1] model as the generic head template mesh. The necessary pre-processing includes: subdivision of the template mesh to better represent the face structure, labeling the corresponding landmark vertex indexes, generation of the mesh segments map along the landmark vertices, and the tetrahedral mesh structure using TetGen [28]. The segments map and landmark diagram are shown in Fig. 2. Note that the support structures (such as the inner mouth cavity and the backside of the head) as annotated as OTHER and deformed without finding the corresponding vertices in the target point cloud. Also, the template mesh can be replaced with any other models as long as the above pre-processing is provided.

3.1   Per-frame Multi-view Scan Reconstruction

Given the synchronized multi-view video data, a GPU accelerated stereo matching method [22] is applied to generate per-frame 3D facial geometries from the pyramidal imaging data. For each view, the plane map is firstly initialized from the previous frame and then estimated in a coarse to fine manner. Inspired by [23], we further refine the estimated plane maps by re-projecting good estimates from neighbor views. Then the plane maps of all views are fused into a single consisted point cloud using consistent check [22]. The fused point cloud is simplified using RANSAC to reduce the ambiguousness in the following template fitting stage when searching for the best correspondences. The RANSAC-based simplification finds the most representative vertex within a small sphere and excludes the other redundant vertices.

---

[1] https://www.eisko.com/louise/virtual-model.

3.2 Template Warping

After computing the multi-view scan of each frame, we track the movement between frames and generate every topology consistent mesh aligned to the corresponding scan. We firstly describe the method used to deform a template mesh S toward the target point cloud Γ. We use the popular As-Rigid-As-Possible (ARAP) mesh deformation [26] as the backbone framework. ARAP formalizes an energy function that measures the deviation from the rigid transformation of two connected vertices. The current position x_i and the local rotation matrix R_i are iteratively updated by optimizing the following energy function:

$$E(x_i, R_i|_{i=1}^n) = E_{data} + E_{shape} + E_{land} \tag{1}$$

where,

$$E_{data} = \sum_{i=1}^n \|x_i - \Gamma(x_i)\|^2, E_{land} = \sum_{i=1}^k \|x_i - \mathcal{L}(x_i)\|^2$$

$$E_{shape} = \sum_{i=1}^n w_i \sum_{j \in \mathcal{N}(i)} w_{ij} \|(x_i - x_j) - R_i(p_i - p_j)\|^2$$

$$+ \sum_{i=1}^n \delta_i \sum_{j \in \mathcal{N}_v(i)} \delta_{ij} \|(x_i - x_j) - R_i(p_i - p_j)\|^2$$

In the above, the matching term E_{data} measures the point distance between the mesh vertices and the point cloud. $\Gamma(x_i)$ is the target position of current vertex x_i using the nearest neighbor searching in the point cloud Γ. E_{shape} combines the Lapalacian and Volumetric regularization. w_i, w_{ij} are the per-cell and per-edge Lapalacian weights, δ_i, δ_{ij} are the volumetric weights, $\mathcal{N}(i)$ is the neighboring vertices defined through the surface and $\mathcal{N}_v(i)$ is defined by the tetrahedral mesh. E_{land} denotes the landmark term with pre-computed 3D landmarks. The weights of each term are set respectively at each fitting stage and for different mesh regions.

The deformation of the template mesh is computed in three steps:

Step 1: Landmark Driven Deformation. Firstly, we leverage the detected 3D landmarks. The optimizing energy function consists of $\{E_{shape}, E_{land}\}$ and the landmark term is given a relatively bigger weight. The facial and ear landmarks of each view are provided by open-source deep-learning based methods. We exclude some ambiguous landmarks (e.g. facial outline points) and occluded landmarks (mainly in the ear region). Moreover, we extend the sparse landmarks to all the vertices belonging to the contour lines defined by landmark (e.g. eye and mouth). To be more specifically, for a template shape S and its corresponding landmark vertices $\{v_k\}$, we get the contour vertices $\mathcal{L} = \{v_i | v_i \in line(v_k, v_{k+1})\}$. v_k and v_{k+1} are two ends of a contour line. Compared to sparse discrete landmarks, continuous contour vertices constraint gives improves the smoothness in feature sections, especially for the rim of the eye region.

Step 2: Nearest Neighbor Searching. The next step finds the best matching positions in the target point cloud Γ and updates the template mesh by minimizing the *scan-to-mesh* distance. The optimizing energy function now consists of $\{E_{data}, E_{shape}, E_{land}\}$ and the data term is given a higher weight while the landmark term is lower. An error function combining point distance, color, and the normal difference is used to search the corresponding nearest neighbor(NN) on Γ. However, in complicated regions like the mouth, mismatching regularly happens resulting in a locally optimal solution. We propose the max overlap searching to close the gap in regions like the mouth. More specifically, all vertices of Γ are divided based on the location inner or outer of the current mesh S. For a vertex $p_i \in S$, the target position is calculated as the weighted sum of all outer vertices in Γ. The weight function takes into account point distance, color, and normal difference. If there do not exist outer vertices within a certain radius, the target position falls into the regular nearest neighbor in Γ.

Step 3: Depth Based Refinement. After the above two steps, we get a mesh aligned to the target point cloud but lacks the fine-scale detail. The mesh can be further refined by minimizing the reprojections onto the estimated depth maps in the per-frame model building stage. We first determine the most frontal view for each vertex given its normal and update the position by minimizing the energy function $\{E_{data} + E_{shape} + E_{land}\}$. The target position $\Gamma(x_i)$ is computed with the corresponding depth in the most frontal depth map.

3.3 Multi-scale Mesh Propagation

We now describe the proposed multi-scale mesh propagation scheme in the facial tracking stage. The generic *Louise* template mesh is firstly warped to the captured subject in the initial frame. Then we propagate this person-specific mesh to the following frames. The propagation is achieved through computing the new positions of the mesh using multiple cues including between-frame optical flow, new landmarks, and the new multi-view scan. Also, the propagation scheme itself varies. For example, you can compute the new mesh based on the finished previous frame. Also, you can always compute the new mesh based on a fixed frame

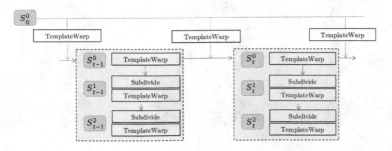

Fig. 3. The personalized template mesh is propagated in a hybrid manner at the coarsest mesh level and refined progressively to the finest mesh level.

like the initial frame or an anchored frame [4,13]. As a matter of convenience, we call the first the sequential propagation scheme and the second the parallel propagation scheme. The sequential propagation scheme is hardly used due to the severe error accumulation. The parallel propagation scheme may fail to capture the very fine details due to the large difference between the initial frame and the current frame. We combine both schemes and propose a multi-scale hybrid propagation scheme. For a new frame F_t, the new shape S_t is the weighted sum of deformation from the previous frame F_{t-1} and from the initial frame F_0:

$$S_t = \zeta_{t-1} \cdot S_{t \leftarrow (t-1)} + \zeta_0 \cdot S_{t \leftarrow 0} \tag{2}$$

$S_{t \leftarrow (t-1)}, S_{t \leftarrow 0}$ are the deformed shapes from previous frame F_0 and F_{t-1} respectively. ζ is the error function of each vertex in the deformed shape combing multi-view re-projection error and local Gaussian curvature:

$$\zeta(p_i) = 1/(\sum_{j=1}^{m} \| I_j(T_j(p_i)) - I_r(T_r(p_i)) \|^2 + \| \kappa(p_i) \|^2) \tag{3}$$

where r is the reference view index, I_j, I_r are the reference and neighbor image, T_j, T_r are the corresponding projection matrix, κ is the Gaussian curvature.

A brief diagram of the propagation procedure is shown in Fig. 3. In our experiments, the hybrid propagation scheme is proven efficient to reduce the error accumulation making it possible to capture in long sequences.

3.4   Ear Reconstruction

As the facial landmarks in the lower jawbone near the ear part are too ambiguous to find the real physical points in the face. In regions like cheeks, due to the lack of landmark regularization, the reconstructed meshes fail to keep the fine-scale consistency in the UV domain. We improve the overall accuracy of the mesh reconstruction including cheeks by adding the ear regularization.

In the initialization stage, we deform the template ear structure toward the target point cloud using the method described in Sect. 3.2 During the deformation, we set a higher volumetric regularization weight to retain a smoother

 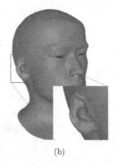 

(a)   (b)   (c)

Fig. 4. Ear reconstruction with symmetry regularization.(a) is mvs scan with occluded ear part. (b) and (c) are the reconstructed results without/with symmetry regularization.

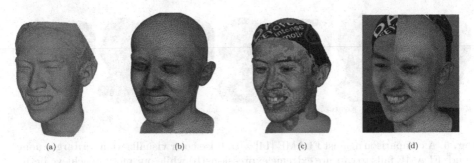

(a)   (b)   (c)   (d)

Fig. 5. One example frame. (a)reconstructed point cloud; (b)topology consistent mesh; (c)overlay with the point cloud; (d)*half-face* overlay.

result and set the back ear region as OTHER to ignore the nearest neighbor correspondence. Also, we add a symmetry regularization to further improve the reconstruction. In the extreme case as shown in Fig. 4, the symmetry regularization ensures the right reconstruction given an incomplete mvs scan. In the facial tracking stage, the ear part allows for only rigid transformation computed from visible landmarks. A multi-view consistency check is performed to choose reliable ear landmarks.

4 Experimental Results

Acquisition Setup. We build a multi-camera system to test the presented method and capture the 4D data. The system consists of 24 Canon 800D digital cameras (25fps, 1920×1080) around the actor's head and 6 LED lights providing uniform illumination. The cameras are synchronized and pre-calibrated using a spherical checkerboard. We captured ten subjects with one minute length performance each, where five of them are shown in Figs. 5, 8.

Table 1. Mean per frame run time of each module.

		$N_{view} = 8$	$N_{view} = 24$	Fyffe [13]
Point cloud estimation		31.79 s	127.25 s	
Template warping ($\Gamma_{size} = 250,000$)	S^0	3.82 s	7.17 s	
	S^1	4.93 s	8.44 s	>25 mins
	S^2	20.48 s	34.96 s	
Overall		61.02 s	177.82 s	>35 mins

Run Time. We evaluate the mean run times of each module based on computers with Intel Core i7-7700 K processors and an NVIDIA GeForce GTX 1080 Ti graphics card. Two different settings are recorded: all 24 views are used or a

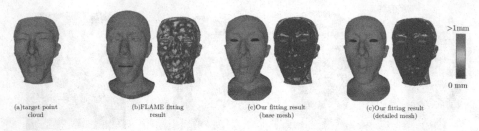

Fig. 6. A comparison against FLAME [14] with false color visualization. (a)target point cloud; FLAME fails to capture extreme expressions(b) while our method achieve better fitting results((c) and (d)).

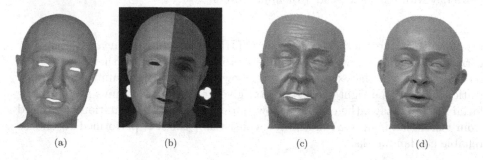

Fig. 7. A comparison against [13] using publicly available examples in [4]. (a)our fitting result; (b)*half-face* overlay shows the accurate capture; (c)result of [4] and (d)result of [13].

small subset with 8 views. The mean vertical size of the point cloud is 250,000. In the setting of $N_{view} = 8$, the overall timing is nearly 1 min per frame. Compared to the method proposed in [13], though the hardware is different, our method costs much more time. The detailed timing of each stage is shown in Table 1.

Qualitative Comparison. Figure 5 shows an example of the reconstructed full head geometry at a certain frame. Our method can recover the finer facial detail and the accurate ear structure. We compute the *scan-to-mesh* error with comparison using a morphable model FLAME [14] based on our own acquired examples. The *scan-to-mesh* error function describes the smallest euclidean distance of each vertex in the point cloud to the registered mesh. For the sake of fairness, we demonstrate our fitting result in the coarsest scale close to the FLAME model. As illustrated in Fig. 6, our method achieves a much lower fitting error indicating the high accuracy of our performance capture in even extreme expressions. Figure 7 shows the comparison with previous methods [4,13] based on publicly available datasets. Our method can recover more details in the eye and forehead region compared to [13]. In Fig. 8, we show several frames with challenging expressions. The reconstructed meshes shown in wireframe indicate the well-distributed triangle structure.

Quantitative Analysis. We also conduct some experiments to quantitatively analyze the topology consistency across frames. A special marker-based sequence is captured and processed as usual without extra steps like recognizing and tracking the markers. After acquiring the 4D mesh sequences, an albedo texture map in each frame is computed from the multi-view imagery using the corresponding recovered mesh. We then calculate the mean marker mismatching error between each frame and the initial frame in the UV domain. We compare our hybrid propagation method with a baseline method using parallel propagation (similar to the method proposed in [13]) that always deforms from the neural template mesh at the initial frame. As illustrated in Fig. 9, despite small fluctuations,

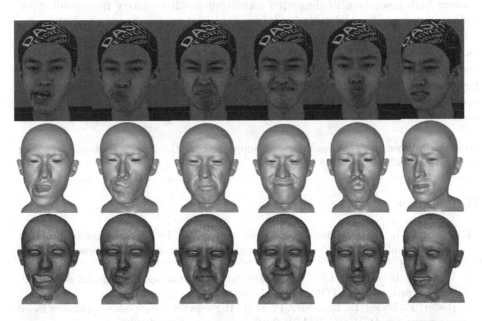

Fig. 8. Example frames of a subject. Top row: the images from one frontal view. Middle row: registered topology consistent meshes. Bottom row: geometries rendered with wireframe.

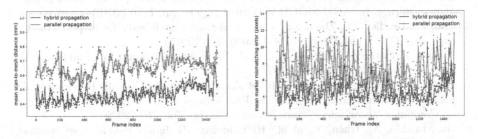

Fig. 9. Left: We track the painted markers in the UV domain across frames to evaluate the topology consistency. Right: Scan fitting accuracy along frames. (Red)parallel propagation; (Blue)our hybrid propagation scheme. (Color figure online)

our hybrid propagation scheme reduces the marker mismatching error indicating well topology consistency of reconstructed meshes across frames. We also evaluate the scan-fitting accuracy of our proposed pipeline by computing the mean scan-to-mesh distance across frames. Compared to the baseline method, the proposed method achieves the higher scan-fitting accuracy.

5 Conclusion

In conclusion, we propose a template fitting based dynamic full head performance capture method. The proposed method can efficiently and robustly recover high-resolution models with consistent mesh topology from multi-view video sequences. Several techniques are proposed to accelerate the processing and reduce the error accumulation. Experiments demonstrate that our method can handle even extreme expressions and shows good performance both in accuracy and efficiency. In the future, we would continue to improve our dynamic performance capture method and build a 4D facial database for many other applications. For example, the avatar creation from a single image or multi-view images.

Acknowledgment. This research was supported by the National Natural Science Foundation of China (No. 61872317).

References

1. Williams, L.: Performance-driven facial animation. In: Proceedings of the 17th Annual Conference on Computer Graphics and Interactive Techniques, pp. 235–242 (1990)
2. Weise, T., Bouaziz, S., Li, H., et al.: Realtime performance-based facial animation. ACM Trans. Graph. (TOG) **30**(4), 1–10 (2011)
3. Beeler, T., Bickel, B., Beardsley, P., et al.: High-quality single-shot capture of facial geometry. In: ACM SIGGRAPH 2010 papers, pp. 1–9 (2010)
4. Beeler, T., Hahn, F., Bradley, D., et al.: High-quality passive facial performance capture using anchor frames. In: ACM SIGGRAPH 2011 papers, pp. 1–10 (2011)
5. Bradley, D., Heidrich, W., Popa, T., et al.: High resolution passive facial performance capture. In: ACM SIGGRAPH 2010 papers, pp. 1–10 (2010)
6. Cao, C., Bradley, D., Zhou, K., et al.: Real-time high-fidelity facial performance capture. ACM Trans. Graph. (ToG) **34**(4), 1–9 (2015)
7. Riviere, J., Gotardo, P., Bradley, D., et al.: Single-shot high-quality facial geometry and skin appearance capture (2020)
8. Lattas, A., Moschoglou, S., Gecer, B., et al.: AvatarMe: Realistically Renderable 3D Facial Reconstruction in-the-wild. In: Proceedings of the IEEE/CVF Conference on Computer Vision and Pattern Recognition, pp. 760–769 (2020)
9. Bao, L., Lin, X., Chen, Y., et al.: High-fidelity 3D digital human head creation from RGB-D selfies. ACM Trans. Graph. (TOG) **41**(1), 1–21 (2021)
10. Li, T., Liu, S., Bolkart, T., et al.: Topologically Consistent Multi-View Face Inference Using Volumetric Sampling. In: Proceedings of the IEEE/CVF International Conference on Computer Vision, pp. 3824–3834 (2021)

11. Fyffe, G., Graham, P., Tunwattanapong, B., et al.: Near-Instant Capture of High-Resolution Facial Geometry and Reflectance. Comput. Graph. Forum **35**(2), 353–363 (2016)
12. Fyffe, G., Jones, A., Alexander, O., et al.: Driving high-resolution facial scans with video performance capture. In: University of Southern California Los Angeles (2014)
13. Fyffe, G., Nagano, K., Huynh, L., et al.: Multi-View Stereo on Consistent Face Topology. Comput. Graph. Forum **36**(2): 295–309 (2017)
14. Li, T., Bolkart, T., Black, M.J., et al.: Learning a model of facial shape and expression from 4D scans. ACM Trans. Graph. **36**(6), 194:1–194:17 (2017)
15. Fanelli, G., Gall, J., Romsdorfer, H., et al.: A 3D audio-visual corpus of affective communication. IEEE Trans. Multimedia **12**(6), 591–598 (2010)
16. Zhang, X., Yin, L., Cohn, J.F., et al.: Bp4D-spontaneous: a high-resolution spontaneous 3D dynamic facial expression database. Image Vis. Comput. **32**(10), 692–706 (2014)
17. Zhang, Z., Girard, J.M., Wu, Y., et al.: Multimodal spontaneous emotion corpus for human behavior analysis. In: Proceedings of the IEEE Conference on Computer Vision and Pattern Recognition, pp. 3438–3446 (2016)
18. Weyrich, T., Matusik, W., Pfister, H., et al.: Analysis of human faces using a measurement-based skin reflectance model. ACM Trans. Graph. (ToG) **25**(3), 1013–1024 (2006)
19. Ma, W.C., Hawkins, T., Peers, P., et al.: Rapid acquisition of specular and diffuse normal maps from polarized spherical gradient illumination. Rendering Tech. **2007**(9), 10 (2007)
20. Cheng, S., Kotsia, I., Pantic, M., et al.: 4dfab: A large scale 4D database for facial expression analysis and biometric applications. In: Proceedings of the IEEE Conference on Computer Vision and Pattern Recognition, pp. 5117–5126 (2018)
21. Yang, H., Zhu, H., Wang, Y., et al.: Facescape: a large-scale high quality 3D face dataset and detailed riggable 3D face prediction. In: Proceedings of the IEEE/CVF Conference on Computer Vision and Pattern Recognition, pp. 601–610 (2020)
22. Galliani, S., Lasinger, K., Schindler, K.: Massively parallel multiview stereopsis by surface normal diffusion. In: Proceedings of the IEEE International Conference on Computer Vision, pp. 873–881 (2015)
23. Donne, S., Geiger, A.: Learning non-volumetric depth fusion using successive reprojections. In: Proceedings of the IEEE/CVF Conference on Computer Vision and Pattern Recognition, pp. 7634–7643 (2019)
24. Tai, Y., Liang, Y., Liu, X., et al.: Towards highly accurate and stable face alignment for high-resolution videos. In: Proceedings of the AAAI Conference on Artificial Intelligence, vol. 33(01), 8893–8900 (2019)
25. Zhou, Y., Zaferiou, S.: Deformable models of ears in-the-wild for alignment and recognition. In: 2017 12th IEEE International Conference on Automatic Face and Gesture Recognition (FG 2017). IEEE, 626–633 (2017)
26. Sorkine, O., Alexa, M.: As-rigid-as-possible surface modeling. In: Symposium on Geometry Processing, vol. 4, pp. 109–116 (2007)
27. Kwok, T.H., Yeung, K.Y., Wang, C.C.L.: Volumetric template fitting for human body reconstruction from incomplete data. J. Manuf. Syst. **33**(4), 678–689 (2014)
28. Hang, S.: TetGen, a Delaunay-based quality tetrahedral mesh generator. ACM Trans. Math. Softw **41**(2), 11 (2015)

Learning Cross-Domain Features for Domain Generalization on Point Clouds

Hang Xiao, Ming Cheng$^{(\boxtimes)}$, and Liangwei Shi

School of Informatics, Xiamen University, Xiamen 361005, China
`chm99@xmu.edu.cn`

Abstract. Modern deep neural networks trained on a set of source domains are generally difficult to perform well on an unseen target domain with different data statistics. Domain generalization (DG) aims to learn a generalized model that performs well on the unseen target domain. Currently, most DG approaches are applied to images, and there is less related research in the field of point cloud. In this paper, we propose a novel cross-domain feature learning network architecture for DG on 3D object point clouds, which learns domain invariant representation via data augmentation and hierarchical features alignment (HFA). The data augmentation is empowered by two subtasks: (1) A point set mask on source data such that some parts of the point cloud are removed randomly, to capture domain-shared representation of semantic categories; (2) A linear mixup of different source domain point cloud samples, to address the large domain gap between different domains. HFA is used to align multi-level local features and narrow the distribution distance between different domains. Since there is no common evaluation benchmark for 3D point cloud DG scenario, we experiment on the PointDA-10 and PointSegDA datasets, and extend point cloud domain adaptation (DA) methods to DG for comparison. Our method exhibits superiority in classification and segmentation accuracy over state-of-the-art general-purpose DA methods.

Keywords: Domain generalization · Domain-invariant representation · Hierarchical feature alignment

1 Introduction

Point cloud is a common 3D data representation widely used in computer vision tasks, owing to its rich spatial geometric information and easy acquisition. In recent years, deep neural networks running directly on point cloud have greatly boosted the performance of 3D vision understanding tasks including detection, tracking, and segmentation [9,23]. With the rapid development of depth camera and LiDAR, we can capture large amounts of 3D point cloud data conveniently. However, just a bunch of unlabeled point cloud data cannot train a reliable

© The Author(s), under exclusive license to Springer Nature Switzerland AG 2022
S. Yu et al. (Eds.): PRCV 2022, LNCS 13536, pp. 68–81, 2022.
https://doi.org/10.1007/978-3-031-18913-5_6

model. Although a large amount of label-rich synthetic point cloud data can be generated from 3D computer-aided design (CAD) models, it is time-consuming and expensive to obtain enough labeled real-world data in practical applications [5]. Recent studies have shown that trained models generally perform well on test/validation datasets that follow similar feature distribution to the training data, but suffer significant performance degradation on unseen datasets that may present different styles, which is called domain gap/shift [15]. This issue significantly limits the generalization of deep models in the real world, especially when we want the models to recognize unseen objects.

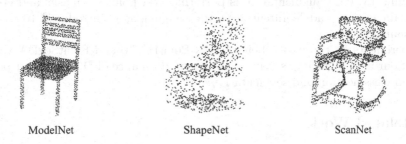

ModelNet   ShapeNet   ScanNet

Fig. 1. Examples from PointDA-10 [18], a general DA benchmark containing samples of 10 overlapped categories from three popular 3D object/scene datasets, among which ModelNet [19] and ShapeNet [3] are generated from 3D CAD models, and ScanNet [5] is scanned and reconstructed from real-world indoor scenes.

Domain generalization (DG) aim to make a model trained on single or multiple different but related source domains generalize well on completely unseen target domains. As shown in Fig. 1, given a training set containing two of the datasets, DG requires training a good learning model that performs well on the remaining completely unseen dataset which clearly has distinct distributions. Over the past years, DG has made some progresses on image [28] while there is less related research in the field of point cloud [7]. Unsupervised domain adaptation (UDA) on point cloud is somewhat similar to our work, which aims to train a model that can perform well on the target domain with a labeled source domain and an unlabeled target domain.

In this paper, we propose a novel cross-domain feature learning network for DG on object point cloud. We design three simple yet effective modules to learn domain invariant features and approximately narrow the feature distribution distance between the multiple source domains in the training set. Specifically, this paper introduces: (1) Using point set masks to randomly mask some structures in the original point cloud to learn domain-shared features of semantic categories; (2) Cross-domain mixup of point clouds for data augmentation. Only samples from separate domains are not sufficient to ensure domain-invariance at most part of latent space, and we propose to use linear mixup of cross-domain point clouds to expand the domain diversity of the training set and thus increase the generalization of the trained model; (3) Hierarchical feature alignment (HFA) using maximum mean discrepancy (MMD) [2] to align the feature distributions of source domains at each feature layer. As there is currently no DG benchmark for object point clouds, we experiment on the 3D UDA benchmarks PointDA-10 [18] and PointSegDA [1]. The results show the superiority of our proposed method over state-of-the-art 3D UDA methods in classification and segmentation accuracy. In summary, our contributions are summarized as follows.

- This paper proposes a novel 3D point-based DG method to extract and align features across different domains by constructing a domain-shared feature space.
- Technically, data augmentation is performed via point set masks and cross-domain mixup, and hierarchical feature alignment is introduced to bridge domain gaps.
- Experiments on the public benchmarks PointDA-10 and PointSegDA verify that our method achieves state-of-the-art performance of DG on object point cloud classification and segmentation.

2   Related Work

2.1   Deep Learning on Point Cloud

Typical deep learning methods for 2D image cannot be directly applied to point cloud due to the irregularity and permutation-invariance. PointNet [16] is the first deep neural network to directly deal with point cloud, which uses shared multi-layer perceptrons (MLPs) and max-pooling as a permutation-invariant feature extractor. However, local geometric information is omitted in PointNet which is significant for describing object in 3D space. The follow-up work Point-Net++ [17] gathers local features in a hierarchical way. DGCNN [20] builds a feature space graph and dynamically updates the graph to aggregate features. Point Transformer [25] adopts transformer as feature extractor.

2.2   Unsupervised Domain Adaptation

UDA is a branch of transfer learning whose purpose is to alleviate the dependence of traditional deep learning on labels. The main challenge of UDA is that domain gap exists between the source and target domains. Based on the strategy to bridge domain gap, UDA methods on 2D images are mainly divided into two categories. Methods in the first category align the feature distributions of the source and target domains via generative adversarial networks (GANs) to obtain domain-invariant representations [6,22]. The second category matches either the marginal or conditional distributions between domains via feature alignment, in order to maximize the inter-class differences while minimizing the intra-class distances in the subspace [2,4]. However, DA methods on 2D images cannot be directly extend to 3D point clouds.

In 3D UDA, the learning of local geometric information is essential to achieve good performance. PointDAN [18] aligns the distribution of 3D objects across different domains both locally and globally, but its performance on PointDA-10 is not very good. DefRec [1] proposes deformation reconstructions as a self-supervised task, and Luo et al. [12] extend it to a learnable deformation task to further improve the performance. GAST [30] proposes geometry-aware self-training to align features at both local and global levels.

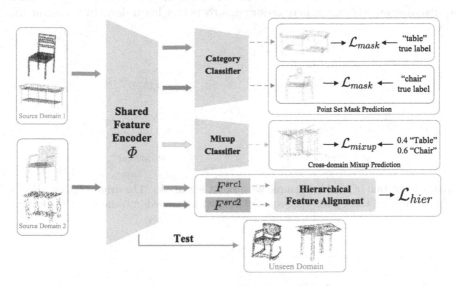

Fig. 2. Overview of our network architecture, which includes three key components: point set mask, cross-domain mixup, and hierarchical feature alignment. The two individual classifiers take the features from the shared feature encoder as their input. Data flows and features from different source domains are marked with different colors. Note that the grey arrow indicates cross-domain point clouds input and the small black arrow indicates the direction of optimization. (Color figure online)

2.3   Domain Generalization

The difference between DG and UDA is that UDA can access unlabeled target domain data, while DG cannot see target domain data at all during training. This makes DG more challenging and more valuable in practical applications. Since there is no target domain data for the model to analyze the negative effects of domain gap, DG model must rely on the source domains and focus on learning domain invariant feature representations in order to remain discriminative on unseen target domain. Many DG methods are currently proposed for 2D images. Some methods follow the distribution alignment idea in domain adaptation by learning domain invariant features via domain-adversarial learning [11,15]. There are also meta-learning based DG methods that improve the performance of model generalization by simulating meta-training and meta-testing tasks in training

domain [10]. Another popular way to address DG problem is data augmentation [26,27]. In contrast to images, there is less DG method applied to 3D point
clouds. MetaSets [7] focuses on the single-source DG problem and prevents the
model from overfitting the source dataset through meta-learning strategies and
point cloud transformation methods. In this paper, we propose a point-based
multi-source DG framework. It adopts two ideas including data augmentation
and distribution alignment across domains to better learn domain invariant features.

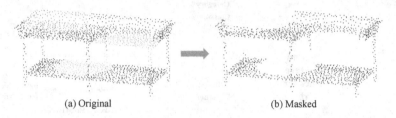

(a) Original   (b) Masked

Fig. 3. Illustration of a table example with point set masks. The original point cloud is
randomly masked three parts (the colorful points) before fed into the feature extractor.

3   Network Architecture

In typical DG settings, given a training set of multiple source domains $\mathcal{D}^s =$
$\{\mathcal{D}^1, \cdots, \mathcal{D}^M\}$ with n^m labeled point clouds $\{(P_i^m, y_i^m)\}_{i=1}^{n^m}$ in the m-th domain
$\mathcal{D}^m$, where $P_i^m \in \chi \subset \mathbb{R}^{N \times 3}$ is represented by 3D coordinates (x, y, z), N is
the number of sampling points of a 3D object, and $y_i^m \in \{1, \cdots, C\}$, C is the
number of classes. The goal of DG is to learn a domain-agnostic mapping function
$\Phi : \chi \rightarrow \mathcal{H}$ on source domains that projects source point clouds into a shared
feature space $\mathcal{H}$ for cross domains.

We propose a DG network structure consisting of three modules. The pipeline
of our approach is shown in Fig. 2. In the following subsections, we introduce our
point set mask (Fig. 3), cross-domain mixup, and hierarchical feature alignment
(Fig. 4) strategies respectively.

3.1   Point Set Mask

Augmentation and transformation based on input data is commonly used in
DG problems. A single input point cloud is typically sampled to 1024 or 2048
points during training. With such point densities, synthetic point cloud generated from 3D CAD models (e.g., ModelNet or ShapeNet) can roughly represent
the complete object. However, point cloud obtained from the real world (e.g.,
ScanNet) usually appears in a mutilated form due to sampling methods and

occlusion issues, and cannot fully express an object. In this case, we hope that the unknown data of the complex environment can be simulated by the source domain data.

Intuitively, the real world data can be simulated by randomly masking some structures of the synthetic point cloud. Thus we adopt masking as a data augmentation technique to help the model capture domain-shared features and improve DG ability. During training, we randomly select 3 points with equal probability in the original point cloud P and discard a certain number of points closest to each point. The generated point cloud $\hat{P}$ will lose some local structures, as shown in Fig. 3. In general, using multiple masks on each point cloud may lead to more effective data augmentation for generalization in real environment. DefRec [1] suggests to focus on the mesoscale features and capture information at the scale of regions or parts. Inspired by this, we set each mask to one eighth of the input points, hoping that a mask can completely remove a certain local structure of the point cloud.

In this way, the point cloud classification is carried out after data augmentation with point set mask. Specifically, the masked point cloud $\hat{P}_i^m$ is projected into a shared feature space by the mapping function Φ, and then fed into the category classifier. The classifier is trained in a supervised manner with feature input $\Phi(\hat{P}_i^m)$ and the corresponding label y_i^m, and generates the classification result $\hat{y}_i^m$. The classification task uses a cross-entropy loss, which is formulated as:

$$\min \mathcal{L}_{mask} = -\frac{1}{M} \sum_{m=1}^{M} \frac{1}{n^m} \sum_{i=1}^{n^m} \sum_{c=1}^{C} y_{i,c}^m \log(\hat{y}_{i,c}^m), \tag{1}$$

where M is the number of source domains, n^m is the number of point clouds in the m-th domain $\mathcal{D}^m$, C is the number of classes, $y_{i,c}^m$ and $\hat{y}_{i,c}^m$ are the true and predicted probabilities that point cloud P_i^m belongs to class c.

3.2   Cross-Domain Mixup

Mixup [24] is a data generation idea that generates a new labeled sample by performing linear interpolation between any two instances x and x', and their labels y and y'. The newly generated sample and its label can be represented as $(\gamma x + (1 - \gamma)x', \gamma y + (1 - \gamma)y')$, where γ is sampled from a *Beta* distribution. Mixup can be performed in the original space [21] to generate new samples, or in the feature space [28].

We introduce this idea into point cloud DG. In 3D UDA methods, both of the point clouds for mixup come from the same source domain [1,30]. We hope that the two point clouds are from different domains as mixup of samples with different feature distributions may better explore the domain invariance of the latent space. Therefore, we chose cross-domain mixup. Given two point clouds P, $P' \in \mathbb{R}^{N \times 3}$ and the corresponding labels y, y' from different source domains, we first sample a mixup coefficient $\gamma \in (0, 1)$, then form a new shape $\tilde{P}$ by farthest point sampling (FPS) γN points from P and $(1 - \gamma)N$ points from P'. Following the normal mixup method, the mixup label is a convex combination of the one-hot labels of the two point clouds, i.e., $\gamma y + (1 - \gamma)y'$. Considering that the number of point cloud samples in the two domains may be inconsistent, we take the smaller value as the number of mixed point clouds, denoted as $\tilde{n}$. After that, the mixup point cloud $\tilde{P}$ is projected into a shared feature space by the mapping function Φ, and then fed into the mixup classifier. The classifier generates the classification result $\tilde{y}$, and is trained using a cross-entropy loss:

$$\min \mathcal{L}_{mixup} = -\frac{1}{\tilde{n}} \sum_{i=1}^{\tilde{n}} \sum_{c=1}^{C} \left(\gamma y_{i,c} + (1 - \gamma)y'_{i,c} \right) \log(\tilde{y}_{i,c}), \qquad (2)$$

where $\tilde{y}_{i,c}$ is the predicted probability that the mixed point cloud $\tilde{P}_i$ belongs to class c. Optimizing objective (2) enables the model to explore the domain invariant features of point clouds from two source domains. See Fig. 2 (Cross-domain Mixup Prediction) for illustration

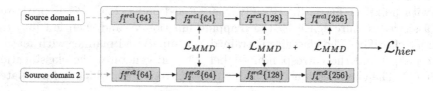

Fig. 4. Hierarchical feature alignment between two source domains. DGCNN is used as shared feature encoder which has 4 EdgeConv layers to dynamically aggregate edge features of 20 adjacent points at each point. We choose to compute the MMD loss between the two domain features in the last three layers.

3.3   Hierarchical Feature Alignment

As a nonparametric distance estimation between two distributions, MMD [2] is often used to minimize the distribution difference between two domains and learn a general representation. Traditional MMD method generally uses single-layer adaptation, which aligns the last global features. PointDAN [18] adopts this single-layer adaption idea but the effect in 3D UDA is not good. The main reason is that the global scale is too broad for point cloud. In fact, each local structure in the point cloud has its specific geometric meaning, and the overall semantic category is determined by the combination of multiple local structures. Therefore, local information is significant for distinguishing a 3D object. When applying MMD for feature alignment, it is crucial to align the discrepancy between feature distributions at multiple scales instead of restricting to global features. Inspired by DSAN [29], we choose to align the feature distributions of different domains in the shared encoder on multi-scale feature layers.

The EdgeConv module designed by DGCNN [20] can dynamically extract the features of local point cloud shape, and can be applied in stack to learn the global shape properties. We use DGCNN as the shared feature extractor of the model, with a total of 4 EdgeConv layers. In the first layer, the features gathered at each point are not enough to express a complete local structure. We find that this layer is heavily influenced by parts unique to the object, which negatively affects domain alignment, and we hope to pay more attention to the common structures of the point clouds at regional scale. As shown in Fig. 4, the MMD loss is minimized for the last three layers to align the cross-domain multi-scale local feature distributions as:

$$\min \mathcal{L}_{hier} = \sum_{l=2}^{L} \mathcal{L}_{MMD}(f_l^{src1}, f_l^{src2}), \tag{3}$$

where $L = 4$ is the number of EdgeConv layers and f_l is the local feature at the l-th level. The calculation process of $\mathcal{L}_{MMD}$ is as follows:

$$\mathcal{L}_{MMD}(X,Y) = \frac{1}{m^2} \sum_{i,j}^{m} \kappa(x_i, x_j) + \frac{1}{n^2} \sum_{i,j}^{n} \kappa(y_i, y_j) - \frac{2}{mn} \sum_{i,j}^{m,n} \kappa(x_i, y_j), \tag{4}$$

where κ is a kernel function obtained by applying the radial basis function (RBF) to map the features to higher dimensions, X and Y are two feature spaces generated from two source domains in the shared feature encoder, m and n are the number of samples in the two feature spaces.

(a) ADOBE   (b) FAUST   (c) MIT   (d) SCAPE

Fig. 5. Examples from the dataset PointSegDA. (a) from ADOBE, (b) from FAUST, (c) from MIT, and (d) from SCAPE

3.4   Overall Loss

The overall training loss of our method is a linear combination of the three parts:

$$\mathcal{L} = \alpha \mathcal{L}_{mask} + \beta \mathcal{L}_{mixup} + \mu \mathcal{L}_{hier}, \tag{5}$$

where α, β, μ are trade-off hyper-parameters. All parameters in the model are simultaneously learned in an end-to-end manner. Note that the classification loss of the original point cloud is not added to our method as we believe that the point set mask module can provide a good substitute for the original classification loss, by avoiding overfit to source domains and getting closer to the domain-shared feature space.

4   Experiments and Results

In this section, we first introduce the PointDA-10 and PointSegDA datasets used in this paper. Then we show the state-of-the-art performance of our method on the DG task of 3D object classification and part segmentation. As no multi-source DG method for object point cloud classification appears before, we migrate the 3D UDA methods to these tasks for comparison.

4.1   Dataset

PointDA-10 [18] extracts subsets from three widely used point cloud classification datasets: ModelNet40 [19], ShapeNet [3], and ScanNet [5]. All three subsets share the same 10 categories (bed, chair, table, etc.). ModelNet-10 (M) and ShapeNet-10 (S) are sampled from clean 3D CAD model surfaces. But ShapeNet-10 has more object instances than ModelNet-10, among which a larger structure variance exists. ScanNet-10 (S*) is an RGB-D video dataset of scanned real-world indoor scenes. Point clouds in ScanNet are usually incomplete in view of missing and occlusion with objects in the scenes. The data preparation procedure in our experiments follows the general method settings in 3D UDA [18] [30].

Table 1. Comparative evaluation in classification accuracy (%) on the PointDA-10 dataset.

Method	Mask	Mixup	HFA	M, S* → S	M, S → S*	S, S* → M	Avg.
DGCNN(w/o) [20]				80.46	47.26	83.53	70.42
PointDAN [18]				79.17	39.51	79.56	66.08
DefRec [1]				79.61	45.34	86.21	70.39
DefRec+PCM [1]				82.34	52.57	84.93	73.28
GAST [30]				80.74	50.08	82.36	71.06
Ours	✓			83.23	47.54	84.35	71.71
		✓		83.55	49.29	82.71	71.85
			✓	84.79	52.01	82.71	72.76
	✓	✓		84.79	48.84	84.35	72.66
	✓	✓	✓	**85.67**	**53.19**	**86.92**	**75.26**

PointSegDA [1] is based on a dataset of meshes of human models proposed by [14] containing 8 shared classes of human body parts, which consists of four subsets: ADOBE (A), FAUST (F), MIT (M), and SCAPE (S). They are differ in point distribution, pose, and scanned humans. Point clouds is sampled to 2048 points through the FPS method. We follow the official train and test split in DefRec [1]. Some samples are shown in Fig. 5.

4.2 Comparative Methods

We transfer the following 3D UDA methods to DG problem for comparison: (1) PointDAN [18], (2) DefRec+PCM [1], and (3) GAST [30]. PointDAN suggests to align features both locally and globally. Alignment with target domain features is omitted as target domain data are not available in DG. DefRec+PCM proposes two self-supervised tasks, and we combine the tasks on the two source domains for comparative experiments. GAST proposes a new method of geometry-aware self-training. We combine the two self-supervised tasks on the source domains, while the self-paced self-training for target domain pseudo-label generation cannot be used. In addition, DGCNN(w/o), which refers to the model trained only by labeled source samples but without DG, is also evaluated as references of the lower performance bounds.

Table 2. The mean IoU (%) on the PointSegDA dataset

Method	DGCNN(w/o)	DefRec	DefRec+PCM	Ours
A,M → F	62.96	60.88	54.13	**66.18**
A,M → S	**68.47**	66.19	59.44	67.49
A,F → S	59.20	61.03	56.54	**62.83**
A,F → M	51.95	53.58	55.41	**62.61**
A,S → F	**65.78**	61.15	63.47	65.25
A,S → M	54.89	52.07	50.17	**61.86**
M,F → S	**78.05**	75.78	73.32	74.32
M,F → A	79.67	80.05	72.81	**80.27**
M,S → F	64.18	63.44	61.95	**67.97**
M,S → A	66.90	64.48	63.75	**71.85**
S,F → A	78.11	77.51	76.32	**81.18**
S,F → M	60.25	64.47	63.13	**64.74**
Avg.	65.86	65.05	62.53	**68.88**

4.3 Implementation Details

In our implementation, we choose DGCNN [20] as the backbone of the feature encoder Φ, and the configurations of DGCNN is the same as DefRec. The task head of classification is based on MLPs with three fully connected layers of [512, 256, 10]. The task head of semantic segmentation is derived from the feature propagation module in PointNet++ with MLPs of [256,256,128]. The size of the mask is 128 and 256 points in the classification and part segmentation tasks, respectively. The Adam optimizer [8] is utilized with initial learning rate 0.001, weight decay 0.00005, and an epoch-wise cosine annealing learning rate scheduler. We train the classification network for 150 epochs and the segmentation network for 200 epochs with batch size 32 on single NVIDIA RTX 3090 GPU. The hyperparameters α, β, μ are set to 1.0, 1.0, and 0.4.

4.4 Results

Point Clouds Classification DG: Table 1 presents comparisons between our method and other competing 3D UDA methods on the PointDA-10 dataset. Evidently, our method outperforms all other methods on average and all individual terms. Compared with the DGCNN(w/o), our approach improves 4.84% on average. It is noteworthy that for the challenging and realistically significant synthetic-to-real task M, S → S*, our approach acquires a remarkable enhancement over DGCNN(w/o) by 5.93%. We utilize t-SNE [13] to visualize the feature distribution on the unseen target domain. As seen in Fig. 6 top, features of different classes in the target domain are mixed without DG. After generalization, features of different classes become more discriminative, and the same class features are clustered together. The confusion matrices of class-wise classification accuracy achieved by the DGCNN without generalization and ours are shown in Fig. 6 bottom.

Point Clouds Segmentation DG: We compare our method with DGCNN(w/o), DefRec, and DefRec+PCM. PointDAN and GAST are specialized for classification and are not considered in this part segmentation task. The results are shown in Table 2, in which the performance is measured in mean intersection over union (mIoU). The table shows that our method outperforms all baselines on mIoU and improves by 3.02% compared to DGCNN (w/o).

4.5 Ablation Study

We examine the effects of the three modules in our method, i.e., point set mask (Mask), cross-domain mixup (Mixup), and hierarchical feature alignment (HFA). The results are summarized in Table 1, which contains five different combinations: (1) Mask only, (2) Mixup only, (3) HFA only, (4) Mask + Mixup, and (5) Mask + Mixup + HFA. As can be seen, each module has a positive impact, surpassing the DGCNN(w/o) method on average. Combinations (1), (2), and (4) demonstrate that data augmentation on the training set is beneficial to the model performance in unseen domain. Combination (5) with all modules achieves the best performance, verifying that all modules are complementary.

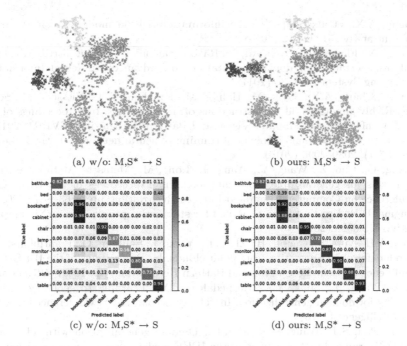

(a) w/o: M,S* → S   (b) ours: M,S* → S

(c) w/o: M,S* → S   (d) ours: M,S* → S

Fig. 6. Top: The t-SNE visualization of feature distribution on the target domain in PointDA-10 dataset. Colors indicate different classes. Bottom: The confusion matrices of classifying testing samples on target domain in PointDA-10 dataset.

5   Conclusion

In this paper, we propose a cross-domain feature learning network for DG on point cloud. Specifically, we combine three simple but effective modules to help the network learn domain invariant features. Point set mask and cross-domain mixup are used to increase the diversity of training set data, and hierarchical feature alignment is proposed to align the diverse feature distributions at multiple scales. Ablation experiments show that the three modules can complement each other well. We demonstrate the superiority of our method for DG on object point cloud classification and part segmentation, achieving state-of-the-art performances.

References

1. Achituve, I., Maron, H., Chechik, G.: Self-supervised learning for domain adaptation on point clouds. In: Proceedings of the IEEE/CVF Winter Conference on Applications of Computer Vision, pp. 123–133 (2021)
2. Borgwardt, K.M., Gretton, A., Rasch, M.J., Kriegel, H.P., Schölkopf, B., Smola, A.J.: Integrating structured biological data by kernel maximum mean discrepancy. Bioinformatics **22**(14), e49–e57 (2006)

3. Chang, A.X., et al.: ShapeNet: An information-rich 3d model repository. arXiv preprint arXiv:1512.03012 (2015)
4. Courty, N., Flamary, R., Habrard, A., Rakotomamonjy, A.: Joint distribution optimal transportation for domain adaptation. In: Advances in Neural Information Processing Systems, vol. 30 (2017)
5. Dai, A., Chang, A.X., Savva, M., Halber, M., Funkhouser, T., Niessner, M.: ScanNet: Richly-annotated 3d reconstructions of indoor scenes. In: Proceedings of the IEEE Conference on Computer Vision and Pattern Recognition (CVPR) (2017)
6. Ganin, Y., et al.: Domain-adversarial training of neural networks. J. Mach. Learn. Res. **17**(1), 2030–2096 (2016)
7. Huang, C., Cao, Z., Wang, Y., Wang, J., Long, M.: Metasets: Meta-learning on point sets for generalizable representations. In: Proceedings of the IEEE/CVF Conference on Computer Vision and Pattern Recognition, pp. 8863–8872 (2021)
8. Kingma, D.P., Ba, J.: Adam: A method for stochastic optimization. arXiv preprint arXiv:1412.6980 (2014)
9. Lang, A.H., Vora, S., Caesar, H., Zhou, L., Yang, J., Beijbom, O.: Pointpillars: Fast encoders for object detection from point clouds. In: Proceedings of the IEEE/CVF Conference on Computer Vision and Pattern Recognition, pp. 12697–12705 (2019)
10. Li, D., Yang, Y., Song, Y.Z., Hospedales, T.M.: Learning to generalize: Meta-learning for domain generalization. In: Thirty-Second AAAI Conference on Artificial Intelligence (2018)
11. Li, H., Pan, S.J., Wang, S., Kot, A.C.: Domain generalization with adversarial feature learning. In: Proceedings of the IEEE conference on computer vision and pattern recognition, pp. 5400–5409 (2018)
12. Luo, X., Liu, S., Fu, K., Wang, M., Song, Z.: A learnable self-supervised task for unsupervised domain adaptation on point clouds. arXiv preprint arXiv:2104.05164 (2021)
13. Van der Maaten, L., Hinton, G.: Visualizing data using t-sne. J. Mach. Learn. Res. **9**(11), 2579–2605 (2008)
14. Maron, H., et al.: Convolutional neural networks on surfaces via seamless toric covers. ACM Trans. Graph. **36**(4), 71–1 (2017)
15. Muandet, K., Balduzzi, D., Schölkopf, B.: Domain generalization via invariant feature representation. In: International Conference on Machine Learning, pp. 10–18. PMLR (2013)
16. Qi, C.R., Su, H., Mo, K., Guibas, L.J.: PointNet: deep learning on point sets for 3D classification and segmentation. In: Proceedings of the IEEE Conference on Computer Vision and Pattern Recognition, pp. 652–660 (2017)
17. Qi, C.R., Yi, L., Su, H., Guibas, L.J.: PointNet++: deep hierarchical feature learning on point sets in a metric space. Adv. Neural. Inf. Process. Syst. **30**, 5099–5108 (2017)
18. Qin, C., You, H., Wang, L., Kuo, C.C.J., Fu, Y.: PointDAN: A multi-scale 3D domain adaption network for point cloud representation. In: Advances in Neural Information Processing Systems, vol. 32 (2019)
19. Vishwanath, K.V., Gupta, D., Vahdat, A., Yocum, K.: ModelNet: Towards a datacenter emulation environment. In: 2009 IEEE Ninth International Conference on Peer-to-Peer Computing, pp. 81–82. IEEE (2009)
20. Wang, Y., Sun, Y., Liu, Z., Sarma, S.E., Bronstein, M.M., Solomon, J.M.: Dynamic graph CNN for learning on point clouds. ACM Transactions On Graphics (tog) **38**(5), 1–12 (2019)

21. Wang, Y., Li, H., Kot, A.C.: Heterogeneous domain generalization via domain mixup. In: ICASSP 2020–2020 IEEE International Conference on Acoustics, Speech and Signal Processing (ICASSP), pp. 3622–3626. IEEE (2020)

22. Xu, M., et al.: Adversarial domain adaptation with domain mixup. In: Proceedings of the AAAI Conference on Artificial Intelligence, vol. 34, pp. 6502–6509 (2020)

23. Yin, T., Zhou, X., Krahenbuhl, P.: Center-based 3D object detection and tracking. In: Proceedings of the IEEE/CVF conference on computer vision and pattern recognition, pp. 11784–11793 (2021)

24. Zhang, H., Cisse, M., Dauphin, Y.N., Lopez-Paz, D.: mixup: Beyond empirical risk minimization. arXiv preprint arXiv:1710.09412 (2017)

25. Zhao, H., Jiang, L., Jia, J., Torr, P.H., Koltun, V.: Point transformer. In: Proceedings of the IEEE/CVF International Conference on Computer Vision, pp. 16259–16268 (2021)

26. Zhou, K., Yang, Y., Hospedales, T., Xiang, T.: Deep domain-adversarial image generation for domain generalisation. In: Proceedings of the AAAI Conference on Artificial Intelligence, vol. 34, pp. 13025–13032 (2020)

27. Zhou, K., Yang, Y., Hospedales, T., Xiang, T.: Learning to generate novel domains for domain generalization. In: Vedaldi, A., Bischof, H., Brox, T., Frahm, J.-M. (eds.) ECCV 2020. LNCS, vol. 12361, pp. 561–578. Springer, Cham (2020). https://doi.org/10.1007/978-3-030-58517-4_33

28. Zhou, K., Yang, Y., Qiao, Y., Xiang, T.: Domain generalization with mixstyle. arXiv preprint arXiv:2104.02008 (2021)

29. Zhu, Y., et al.: Deep subdomain adaptation network for image classification. IEEE Trans. Neural Netw. Learn. Syst. **32**(4), 1713–1722 (2020)

30. Zou, L., Tang, H., Chen, K., Jia, K.: Geometry-aware self-training for unsupervised domain adaptation on object point clouds. In: Proceedings of the IEEE/CVF International Conference on Computer Vision, pp. 6403–6412 (2021)

Unsupervised Pre-training for 3D Object Detection with Transformer

Maosheng Sun[1], Xiaoshui Huang[2], Zeren Sun[1], Qiong Wang[1], and Yazhou Yao[1(✉)]

[1] Nanjing University of Science and Technology, Nanjing 210094, China
{maosheng,zerens,wangq,yazhou.yao}@njust.edu.cn
[2] Shanghai AI Laboratory, Shanghai 200232, China

Abstract. Transformer improve the performance of 3D object detection with few hyperparameters. Inspired by the recent success of the pre-training Transformer in 2D object detection and natural language processing, we propose a pretext task named random block detection to unsupervisedly pre-train 3DETR (UP3DETR). Specifically, we sample random blocks from original point clouds and feed them into the Transformer decoder. Then, the whole Transformer is trained by detecting the locations of these blocks. The pretext task can pre-train the Transformer-based 3D object detector without any manual annotations. In our experiments, UP3DETR performs 6.2% better than 3DETR baseline on challenging ScanNetV2 datasets and has a faster convergence speed on object detection tasks.

Keywords: Unsupervised pre-training · Transformer · 3D object detection

1 Introduction

3D object detection is the task of detecting objects from 3D data and is one of the most fundamental tasks in the computer vision community [39, 40, 48, 54, 60, 61]. In the past few years, object detection has achieved significant progress with recent development of deep neural networks [22, 29, 42, 50, 56, 62]. However, the current 3D object detection accuracy is still low.

Object detection with Transformer [44] (3DETR) [26] is a novel framework, an end-to-end object detection model with Transformer for 3D point clouds. 3DETR needs only a few hyperparameters to compete with the 3D object detection algorithm that needs to adjust many hyperparameters manually. However, the performance of 3DETR is still low due to the challenges in network training and optimization.

To solve the training and optimization issues, many pre-trained methods are proposed in 3D object detection, the number of pre-training methods is increasing [9, 14, 17, 33, 63]. [16, 45, 63, 64] take the unsupervised contrastive learning of point clouds as a pretext task to improve the performance of 3D object detection.

S. Yu et al. (Eds.): PRCV 2022, LNCS 13536, pp. 82–95, 2022.
https://doi.org/10.1007/978-3-031-18913-5_7

4DContrast [9] and CrossPoint [1] are cross-modal contrastive learning methods that learn the representation of transferable 3D point clouds and 2D images during pre-training, significantly improving the performance of 3D object detection.

In 3DETR [26], the CNN backbone (PointNet [32]) is pre-trained and can extract good visual representation, the Transformer module weights is not pre-trained. Although significant progress has been made in 3D pre-train, the existing pretext tasks can not be applied to pre-training the Transformer of 3DETR. The existing pretext tasks focus on representation learning, while 3DETR needs to improve the location ability. Location learning has been overlooked in the existing methods while it plays an important role in object detection.

Inspired by the great success of unsupervised pre-training in 2D object detection [12,37,38,41,51–53,55,58,59], our goal is to unsupervisedly pre-train Transformer in 3DETR on SUN RGB-D-v1 [36]. The most important procedure here is to design a reasonable pretext task and unsupervised construct a label from the point clouds, so as to pre-train the model and improve the performance of object detection. However, none of the existing pre-training tasks are suitable for 3DETR transformers [3–5,23,42,49,57].

To overcome this problem, We propose a new unsupervised pretext task called random block detection. This pretext task can pre-train the detector without any human annotation. We name the model obtained by unsupervised pre-training of 3DETR as UP3DETR. Specifically, we sample multiple random blocks from the point clouds and input them into the decoder, while the original point clouds are fed into the encoder. Then the whole task turns into providing multiple random blocks, and the detector finds their location in the point clouds. From the perspective of this pretext task, random blocks do not need to have physical meaning. Before pre-training, we solve the following three key problems:

(1) To improve the detection performance of the model, the randomly sampled blocks need to be kept loose, and the points in a single block should be as close as possible. We randomly sample N points. To make the random block more compact, we calculate the Euclidean distance between all points in the point clouds and sample the nearest K points to form the random blocks.

(2) We can unpack 3D object detection tasks into localization and classification tasks, while 3DETR uses the same branch for localization and classification. Thus, we introduce Frozen PointNet Weights to avoid affecting the classification ability of the Transformer in the pre-training.

(3) In 3DETR [26], the decoder has query points, representing the points close to objects in 3D space. We take the center points of the random blocks as part of the query points. If all the query points use the points of the random blocks, it will lead to the loss of background information. To address the lack of background information, we employ the farthest point sampling (FPS) [32] and combine these points with the center points of the random block as the query points in the encoder for pre-training.

In our experiment, UP3DETR performs better than 3DETR in object detection and has faster convergence and higher average accuracy on the ScanNetV2 [11] and SUN RGB-D-v1 [36]. Our extensive ablation study demonstrates that freezing backbone weights is the key to advancing feature learning in pre-training.

2   Related Work

2.1   Object Detection on Point Clouds

Recently, significant progress has been made in 3D object detection. 3D object detectors can be divided into 3D convolution-based and Transformer-based methods.

3D Convolution-Based. 3D convolution-based methods can be divided into two directions: Point-based method and Voxel-based method. The pioneering work of the point-based 3D object detection method is the PointNet [31], which used invariant displacement operation to aggregate point features. PointR-CNN [35] proposed a Region Proposal Network (RPN) to generate proposals and applied a refined module to predict the bounding box and class label. VoteNet [30] grouped the points according to the voting center and extracted the object features from the grouped points through PointNet [32]. VoteNet mainly solved the problem of 3D object detection and feature extraction in some indoor scenes. The main difference between Voxel-based methods is the initialization of voxel features. The pioneering work of the 3D object detection method based on voxel detection [7] encoded the point clouds into a bird-eye view feature map. It has triggered many methods based on bird-eye view representation [20, 21, 47] and significantly improved the accuracy. Some methods [7, 46] project the point clouds to the front view and apply the 2D object detection method.

Transformer-Based. Transformer plays a significant role in 3D object detection. The current methods have discussed the use of Transformer for object detection [13, 24–26, 34]. For example, Groupfree3d [24] uses Transformer to calculate object features from the point clouds, and the contribution of each point to the object is automatically learned through network training. 3DETR [26] is an end-to-end Transformer object detector, which redefines the difficulty of 3D object detection. The method based on Transformer has a more straightforward structure and has achieved impressive detection results. However, due to the Transformer fitting difficulty, we use 3DETR as the prototype to pre-train the Transformer to improve the spatial localization ability of the Transformer to speed up the model fit speed.

2.2   Unsupervised Representation Learning on Point Clouds

Inspired by the success of 2D representation learning, especially the use of case discrimination and comparative learning [6, 8, 15], people have great interest in unsupervised tasks to find the best pretext task [10, 12, 27, 28]. The point clouds are more difficult to annotate than an image, so unsupervised representation learning is more beneficial to 3D tasks. Recent studies have explored unsupervised learning of 3D pretext tasks, which can be used to fine-tune downstream reconstruction, classification, and partial segmentation tasks [1,9,14,45,63,64].

4DContrast [9] instills 4D dynamic object priors into learned 3D representations through unsupervised pre-training. CrossPoint [1] is a simple cross-modal contrastive learning approach. That ensemble a rich learning signal from both 3D point clouds and 2D image modalities in a self-supervised fashion. Depth-Contrast [64] only uses single-view 3D data is enough to learn state-of-the-art representations. PointContrast [45] used a unified triplet of architecture for pre-training, demonstrating that the learned representation can generalize across domains. These methods focus on feature representation learning. In contrast, our method focuses on learning transferable spatial localization abilities without using any annotation.

3   UP3DETR

UP3DETR consists of two steps. The first step is unsupervised pre-training. We conduct unsupervised pre-training on SUN RGB-D-v1 [36] without using any human-labeled information. The next step is fine-tuning. We use the weights of unsupervised pre-training to fine-tune the model on ScanNetV2 and SUN RGB-D. This section mainly introduces how to pre-train the Transformer in 3DETR to improve the spatial localization ability in 3D object detection.

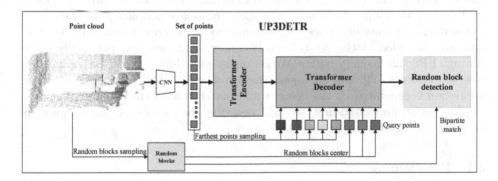

Fig. 1. UP3DETR is an unsupervised pre-training network for 3DETR. It takes the original point clouds as the input and outputs the prediction box of random blocks. We sample 20 random blocks and take their center as part of the query points. The farthest point sampling (FPS) algorithm generates other query points on the downsampling point clouds through CNN. We use binary matching to match the prediction frame with random blocks.

As shown in Fig. 1, we design a pretext task called random block detection. The main idea of random block detection is to sample random blocks

---

Algorithm 1: Framework of UP3DETR

Input: Pre-training architecture UP3DETR; Dataset $P = \{\mathbf{p}_i \in \mathbb{R}^{X \times 3}\}$;
Number of random blocks N; Number of random block points M;
Number of predicted boxes Q; Encoder feature dimension D; Number of
background point N_b; Number of downsampling points X';

Output: Pre-trained weights for Transformer.

for *each point clouds p in P* **do**

> ;
> - From p, generate N random blocks $P_R = \{\mathbf{b}_i \in \mathbb{R}^{M \times 3}\}$ and compute
>   bounding box $B_R = \{\mathbf{b}_i \in \mathbb{R}^{N \times 8}\}$.
> - Compute encoder features $F_e \in \mathbb{R}^{X' \times D}$ by $F_e = UP3DETR_{encode}(p)$.
> - From p, generate background points $P_{background} \in \mathbb{R}^{N_b \times 3}$.
> - Generate query points $P_{query} \in \mathbb{R}^{(N+N_b) \times 3}$.
>   by combining random blocks center points $P_{blocks} \in \mathbb{R}^{N \times 3}$ and $P_{background}$.
> - Compute query embeddings $Q_e \in \mathbb{R}^{D \times X'}$ by Fourier positional
>   embeddings $Q_e = F_e (P_{query})$.
> - Compute predicted boxes $B_P = \{\hat{\mathbf{b}}_i \in \mathbb{R}^{Q \times 8}\}$
>   by $B_P = UP3DETR_{decode}(Q_e, F_e)$.
> - Backprop. to update UP3DETR with bipartite matching loss $L_m(B_R, B_P)$.

end

---

from the point clouds and let the pre-trained model predict the location and size of random blocks to improve the spatial localization ability of the Transformer. Firstly, the frozen PointNet downsamples the point clouds composed of X points to obtain X' points, and then the down-sampled points are projected to X'−dim feature space and transmitted to the Transformer encoder. For randomly sampled blocks, we take their center points and the points obtained through FPS [32] as query points. We get query embeddings through Fourier positive embeddings [43], and then pass them to the encoder of Transformer. The prediction is generated by the decoder and matched with the sampled blocks.

For better understanding, we will describe the details of pre-training in Sect. 3.1 and fine-tuning in Sect. 3.2.

3.1   Pre-training

In Algorithm 1, we summarize the whole pretext task framework named UP3DETR explored in this work. In general, we sample random blocks on the original point clouds and detect random blocks to improve the performance of object detection.

By providing the center points of the random blocks as part of the query points for the decoder, the decoder generates predicted boxes $\hat{\mathbf{b}}_i$. The predicted boxes $\hat{\mathbf{b}}_i = \left(\hat{\mathbf{c}} \in \mathbb{R}^3, \hat{\mathbf{d}} \in \mathbb{R}^3, \hat{\mathbf{a}} \in \mathbb{R}^2, \hat{\mathbf{s}} \in \mathbb{R}^2\right)$ consists of four elements: $\hat{\mathbf{c}}$ is the box center and $\hat{\mathbf{d}}$ is the box size, $\hat{\mathbf{a}}$ defines the quantized class and residual for

---

Algorithm 2: Process of Sampling Random Blocks

Input: Dataset $P = \{\mathbf{p}_i \in \mathbb{R}^{X \times 3}\}$; Number of random blocks N; Number of random block points M;

Output: N random blocks and bounding boxes.

for *each point clouds p in P* **do**

> ;
> - From p, randomly sample N points as the first point of N random blocks.
> - Generate random blocks $P_R = \{\mathbf{b}_i \in \mathbb{R}^{M \times 3}\}$ by computing the Euclidean distance between all points in the point clouds and these points, and take the nearest (M-1) points to form a random block for each point.
> - Compute Axis Aligned Bounding Box $B_R = \{\mathbf{b}_i \in \mathbb{R}^{N \times 8}\}$ by P_R.

end

---

the angle, $\hat{\mathbf{s}}$ represents the object class, including the block class and background class. The ground truth box $\mathbf{b}_i$ has the same parameters.

Following 3DETR [26], we use the Hungarian algorithm [2] to calculate the matching cost of the predicted boxes $\hat{\mathbf{b}}_i$ and the ground truth boxes $\mathbf{b}_i$. We use ℓ_1 regression loss as the loss function, including the box center loss and the box size loss. Huber regression loss is employed as the angular residual loss. Cross entropy loss is adopted for the angle classification loss and semantic classification loss. Accordingly, the final loss function is defined as:

$$\mathcal{L}(b, \hat{b}) = \lambda_c \|\hat{\mathbf{c}} - \mathbf{c}\|_1 + \lambda_d \|\hat{\mathbf{d}} - \mathbf{d}\|_1 + \lambda_{ar} \|\hat{\mathbf{a}}_r - \mathbf{a}_r\|_{\text{huber}} \\ -\lambda_{ac} \mathbf{a}_c^\top \log \hat{\mathbf{a}}_c - \lambda_s \mathbf{s}_c^\top \log \hat{\mathbf{s}}_c \tag{1}$$

Here, the loss of the prediction box matched with the sampled block is calculated by the above loss function. For the prediction box matched with the background class, we only calculate the semantic classification loss.

Sampling Random Block. In Algorithm 2, we summarize the method for sampling the random blocks. We randomly select N points from the original point clouds and use them as initial points. Then calculate the Euclidean distance from all points in the point clouds to the initial points [18]. We take the nearest $(M - 1)$ points for each initial point to form random blocks, where N takes 20 and M takes 2048. Then we calculate their axis-aligned bounding boxes, set their classes to 1 and set the heading to 10^{-7}. The object classes in the bounding box include background and sampled blocks, noted as 0 and 1, respectively.

Query Points Setting. To enable UP3DETR to predict sampled blocks, we provide the decoder of Transformer with the center points of the blocks in advance. We take the center points of the blocks as part of query points. The number of query points N_{query} is 128. In our implementation, we only set 20 random blocks. If all query points use the center points information of the sampled blocks, Transformer will lose the background point information.

Therefore, we add background points to the query points. We sample $N_{query} - N$ background points from the point clouds through FPS [32] as query points. Then query embeddings are obtained by encoding query points through Fourier positive embeddings [43]. Finally, the decoder generates prediction boxes to detect the bounding box $B_P = \left\{ \hat{b}_i \in \mathbb{R}^{Q \times 8} \right\}$ of sampled blocks in the input point clouds [19].

Frozen Pre-trained Backbone. In the pre-training process, the goal of the random block detection is to improve the spatial localization ability of the Transformer. Pre-training Transfomer needs the stable point clouds feature. However, the disorder of sampled blocks is not suitable for pre-training PointNet [32] to improve the ability to extract features.

As mentioned above, we propose to freeze PointNet weights to maintain the ability to extract features from the point clouds. In Sect. 4.3, we will analyze and verify their necessity through experiments.

3.2 Fine-tuning

In the process of fine-tuning, we fine-tune 3DETR on SUN RGB-D and ScanNetV2.

The object class only has random blocks and background in the pre-training process, so the learned semantic classification module has no practical significance. Therefore, in fine-tuning, we abandon the prediction head weights of pre-training. Our parameter setting follows 3DETR.

In Sects. 4.1 and 4.2, we will fine-tune 3DETR on SUN RGB-D and ScanNetV2 to verify the effect of pre-training.

4 Experiments

We use the point clouds data from SUN RGB-D to pre-train UP3DETR. In the pre-training process, no human annotation information is employed. We fine-tune network parameters on ScanNetV2 [11] and SUN RGB-D-v1 [36]. We pre-train the model with 2 V100 GPUs for 200 epochs with a batch size of 8. Our UP3DETR model is equipped with PointNet backbone, three Transformer encoder layers, eight Transformer decoder layers, and five attention headers.

Dataset and Metrics. The ScanNetV2 contains 1513 reconstructed 3D indoor scans. Each scan has 18 object categories and axis-aligned bounding box labels. The training subset consists of 1201 scans, and the remaining 312 scans are reserved for verification.

The SUN RGB-D contains 10335 monocular point clouds, of which 5285 are used for training, and 5050 are used for verification. The annotation of SUN RGB-D consists of per-point semantic labels and oriented bounding boxes of 37 object categories.

Table 1. Evaluating UP3DETR on ScanNetV2 and SUN RGB-D.

Method	ScanNetV2		SUN RGB-D	
	AP_{25}	AP_{50}	AP_{25}	AP_{50}
BoxNet	49.0	21.1	52.4	25.1
VoteNet	60.4	37.5	58.3	33.4
3DETR	62.7	37.5	56.2	29.7
UP3DETR	63.1(+0.4)	43.7(+6.2)	56.6(+0.4)	32.5(+2.8)

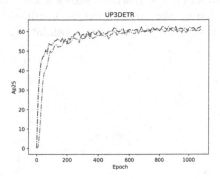

Fig. 2. AP_{25} learning curve of 3DETR and UP3DETR on scanner.

Our experiments follow the experimental protocol from [30]. We use the average accuracy (mAP) to evaluate the detection performance under two different IOU thresholds (i.e., 0.25 and 0.5, expressed as AP_{25} and AP_{50}).

4.1 ScanNetV2 Object Detection

In this section, we verify the pre-training ability of UP3DETR. The model is fine-tuned on ScanNetV2. We use the same settings as 3DETR in the fine-tuning process for a fair comparison.

Experimental results are shown in Table 1. We compare UP3DETR with 3DETR, BoxNet, and VoteNet. UP3DETR achieves comparable or better performance than other methods. The values in the brackets are the gaps compared to 3DETR with the same training setting. Compared with the original 3DETR, AP_{50} is improved by 6.2%. UP3DETR significantly improves the detection and localization performance of 3DETR.

Figure 2 shows the AP_{25} learning curve on ScanNetV2. UP3DETR significantly accelerates the convergence speed, and AP_{25} has been greatly improved. The figure shows that UP3DETR outperforms 3DETR, especially in the early stage. After converging, UP3DETR still achieves better performance.

4.2 SUN RGB-D Object Detection

We also fine-tune UP3DETR on SUN RGB-D using the same settings as 3DETR.

Table 2. Object detection results of UP3DETR and 3DETR on ScanNetV2.

Method	Frozen-CNN	Pre-trained	AP_{25}	AP_{50}
3DETR			62.7	37.5
UP3DETR		✓	63.2	42.2
UP3DETR	✓	✓	63.1	43.7

We present the results in Table 1, which shows a 2.8% improvement in AP_{50} compared to 3DETR. Even with large datasets, unsupervised pre-training has played a considerable role. These experiments validate the effectiveness of our method.

4.3   Ablations

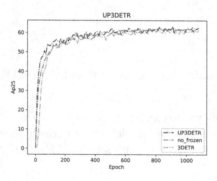

Fig. 3. AP_{25} learning curve of 3DETR, UP3DETR(no frozen), and UP3DETR.

Frozen PointNet Weights. To illustrate the importance of freezing PointNet weights in UP3DETR, we pre-train models with frozen PointNet weights and unfrozen PointNet weights.

Table 2 shows AP_{25} and AP_{50} results on ScanNetV2. All pre-trained models are better than 3DETR. The performance with frozen PointNet weights is better, which proves the importance of freezing PointNet.

Figure 3 shows the AP_{25} learning curves of two different pre-trained models and 3DETR. The model with frozen PointNet weights converges faster, proving the importance of freezing PointNet weights. Experiments show that random block detection is an effective representation learning method, which can be extended to more 3D object detection networks and improve the ability of spatial localization through pre-training.

UP3DETR vs Fine-Tuning with the Supervised Fashion Weights. To illustrate the effectiveness of unsupervised training, we compare our unsupervised UP3DETR with supervised 3DETR (Supervised training weights for 1080 epochs on SUN RGB-D-v1).

Table 3. Object detection results of two pre-training models and 3DETR on Scan-NetV2.

Method	Initialization	AP_{25}	AP_{50}
3DETR	Scratch	62.7	37.5
3DETR	Supervised	59.3	40.9
UP3DETR	Unsupervised	63.1	43.7

Table 3 shows the comparison of different methods. We can observe that the supervised pre-training method hinders the learning of downstream tasks. We believe that there is a gap between source data and object data. Simple supervised pre-training on different datasets tends to have a negative effect.

5   Conclusion

We propose a random block sampling method and a new pretext task called random block detection, which can pre-train the Transformer in 3DETR to improve the localization ability of the Transformer. By performing unsupervised pre-training, UP3DETR is significantly better than 3DETR in object detection tasks. UP3DETR is a flexible framework that can be easily integrated with 3D Transformer-based models to improve the 3D detection performance.

Acknowledgments. This work was supported by the pre-research project of the Equipment Development Department of the Central Military Commission (No. 31514020205).

References

1. Afham, M., Dissanayake, I., Dissanayake, D., Dharmasiri, A., Thilakarathna, K., Rodrigo, R.: Crosspoint: Self-supervised cross-modal contrastive learning for 3D point cloud understanding. arXiv preprint arXiv:2203.00680 (2022)
2. Carion, N., Massa, F., Synnaeve, G., Usunier, N., Kirillov, A., Zagoruyko, S.: End-to-end object detection with transformers. In: Vedaldi, A., Bischof, H., Brox, T., Frahm, J.-M. (eds.) ECCV 2020. LNCS, vol. 12346, pp. 213–229. Springer, Cham (2020). https://doi.org/10.1007/978-3-030-58452-8_13
3. Chen, T., Wang, S.H., Wang, Q., Zhang, Z., Xie, G.S., Tang, Z.: Enhanced feature alignment for unsupervised domain adaptation of semantic segmentation. IEEE Trans. Multimedia (TMM) **24**, 1042–1054 (2022)

4. Chen, T., et al.: Semantically meaningful class prototype learning for one-shot image segmentation. IEEE Trans. Multimedia (TMM) **24**, 968–980 (2022)
5. Chen, T., Yao, Y., Zhang, L., Wang, Q., Xie, G., Shen, F.: Saliency guided inter-and intra-class relation constraints for weakly supervised semantic segmentation. IEEE Trans. Multimedia (TMM) (2022). https://doi.org/10.1109/TMM.2022.3157481
6. Chen, T., Kornblith, S., Norouzi, M., Hinton, G.: A simple framework for contrastive learning of visual representations. In: International Conference on Machine Learning, pp. 1597–1607. PMLR (2020)
7. Chen, X., Ma, H., Wan, J., Li, B., Xia, T.: Multi-view 3D object detection network for autonomous driving. In: Proceedings of the IEEE conference on Computer Vision and Pattern Recognition, pp. 1907–1915 (2017)
8. Chen, X., Fan, H., Girshick, R., He, K.: Improved baselines with momentum contrastive learning. arXiv preprint arXiv:2003.04297 (2020)
9. Chen, Y., Nießner, M., Dai, A.: 4Dcontrast: Contrastive learning with dynamic correspondences for 3d scene understanding. arXiv preprint arXiv:2112.02990 (2021)
10. Choy, C., Park, J., Koltun, V.: Fully convolutional geometric features. In: Proceedings of the IEEE/CVF International Conference on Computer Vision, pp. 8958–8966 (2019)
11. Dai, A., Chang, A.X., Savva, M., Halber, M., Funkhouser, T., Nießner, M.: ScanNet: Richly-annotated 3D reconstructions of indoor scenes. In: Proceedings of the IEEE Conference on Computer Vision and Pattern Recognition, pp. 5828–5839 (2017)
12. Dai, Z., Cai, B., Lin, Y., Chen, J.: UP-DETR: Unsupervised pre-training for object detection with transformers. In: Proceedings of the IEEE/CVF Conference on Computer Vision and Pattern Recognition, pp. 1601–1610 (2021)
13. Guan, T., et al.: M3DETR: Multi-representation, multi-scale, mutual-relation 3d object detection with transformers. In: Proceedings of the IEEE/CVF Winter Conference on Applications of Computer Vision. pp. 772–782 (2022)
14. Hassani, K., Haley, M.: Unsupervised multi-task feature learning on point clouds. In: Proceedings of the IEEE/CVF International Conference on Computer Vision, pp. 8160–8171 (2019)
15. He, K., Fan, H., Wu, Y., Xie, S., Girshick, R.: Momentum contrast for unsupervised visual representation learning. In: Proceedings of the IEEE/CVF Conference on Computer Vision and Pattern Recognition, pp. 9729–9738 (2020)
16. Hou, J., Graham, B., Nießner, M., Xie, S.: Exploring data-efficient 3d scene understanding with contrastive scene contexts. In: Proceedings of the IEEE/CVF Conference on Computer Vision and Pattern Recognition, pp. 15587–15597 (2021)
17. Huang, S., Xie, Y., Zhu, S.C., Zhu, Y.: Spatio-temporal self-supervised representation learning for 3d point clouds. In: Proceedings of the IEEE/CVF International Conference on Computer Vision, pp. 6535–6545 (2021)
18. Huang, X., Fan, L., Wu, Q., Zhang, J., Yuan, C.: Fast registration for cross-source point clouds by using weak regional affinity and pixel-wise refinement. In: 2019 IEEE International Conference on Multimedia and Expo (ICME), pp. 1552–1557. IEEE (2019)
19. Huang, X., Fan, L., Zhang, J., Wu, Q., Yuan, C.: Real time complete dense depth reconstruction for a monocular camera. In: Proceedings of the IEEE Conference on Computer Vision and Pattern Recognition Workshops, pp. 32–37 (2016)
20. Ku, J., Mozifian, M., Lee, J., Harakeh, A., Waslander, S.L.: Joint 3D proposal generation and object detection from view aggregation. In: 2018 IEEE/RSJ International Conference on Intelligent Robots and Systems (IROS), pp. 1–8. IEEE (2018)

21. Liang, M., Yang, B., Wang, S., Urtasun, R.: Deep continuous fusion for multi-sensor 3d object detection. In: Proceedings of the European Conference on Computer Vision (ECCV), pp. 641–656 (2018)

22. Liu, H., et al.: Exploiting web images for fine-grained visual recognition by eliminating open-set noise and utilizing hard examples. IEEE Trans. Multimedia (TMM) **24**, 546–557 (2022)

23. Liu, H., Zhang, H., Lu, J., Tang, Z.: Exploiting web images for fine-grained visual recognition via dynamic loss correction and global sample selection. IEEE Trans. Multimedia (TMM) **24**, 1105–1115 (2022)

24. Liu, Z., Zhang, Z., Cao, Y., Hu, H., Tong, X.: Group-free 3D object detection via transformers. In: Proceedings of the IEEE/CVF International Conference on Computer Vision, pp. 2949–2958 (2021)

25. Mao, J., et al.: Voxel transformer for 3D object detection. In: Proceedings of the IEEE/CVF International Conference on Computer Vision, pp. 3164–3173 (2021)

26. Misra, I., Girdhar, R., Joulin, A.: An end-to-end transformer model for 3d object detection. In: Proceedings of the IEEE/CVF International Conference on Computer Vision, pp. 2906–2917 (2021)

27. Noroozi, M., Favaro, P.: Unsupervised learning of visual representations by solving jigsaw puzzles. In: Leibe, B., Matas, J., Sebe, N., Welling, M. (eds.) ECCV 2016. LNCS, vol. 9910, pp. 69–84. Springer, Cham (2016). https://doi.org/10.1007/978-3-319-46466-4_5

28. Pathak, D., Krahenbuhl, P., Donahue, J., Darrell, T., Efros, A.A.: Context encoders: Feature learning by inpainting. In: Proceedings of the IEEE Conference on Computer Vision and Pattern Recognition, pp. 2536–2544 (2016)

29. Pei, G., Shen, F., Yao, Y., Xie, G.S., Tang, Z., Tang, J.: Hierarchical feature alignment network for unsupervised video object segmentation. In: Proceedings of the European Conference on Computer Vision (ECCV) (2022)

30. Qi, C.R., Litany, O., He, K., Guibas, L.J.: Deep hough voting for 3d object detection in point clouds. In: proceedings of the IEEE/CVF International Conference on Computer Vision, pp. 9277–9286 (2019)

31. Qi, C.R., Su, H., Mo, K., Guibas, L.J.: PointNet: Deep learning on point sets for 3D classification and segmentation. In: Proceedings of the IEEE Conference on Computer Vision and Pattern Recognition, pp. 652–660 (2017)

32. Qi, C.R., Yi, L., Su, H., Guibas, L.J.: PointNet++: Deep hierarchical feature learning on point sets in a metric space. In: Advances in Neural Information Processing Systems, vol. 30 (2017)

33. Sauder, J., Sievers, B.: Self-supervised deep learning on point clouds by reconstructing space. In: Advances in Neural Information Processing Systems, vol. 32 (2019)

34. Sheng, H., et al.: Improving 3D object detection with channel-wise transformer. In: Proceedings of the IEEE/CVF International Conference on Computer Vision, pp. 2743–2752 (2021)

35. Shi, S., Wang, X., Li, H.: PointrCNN: 3D object proposal generation and detection from point cloud. In: Proceedings of the IEEE/CVF Conference on Computer Vision and Pattern Recognition, pp. 770–779 (2019)

36. Song, S., Lichtenberg, S.P., Xiao, J.: SUN RGB-D: A RGB-D scene understanding benchmark suite. In: Proceedings of the IEEE Conference on Computer Vision and Pattern Recognition, pp. 567–576 (2015)

37. Sun, Z., Hua, X.S., Yao, Y., Wei, X.S., Hu, G., Zhang, J.: CRSSC: salvage reusable samples from noisy data for robust learning. In: Proceedings of the ACM International Conference on Multimedia (ACMMM), pp. 92–101 (2020)

38. Sun, Z., Liu, H., Wang, Q., Zhou, T., Wu, Q., Tang, Z.: Co-LDL: a co-training-based label distribution learning method for tackling label noise. IEEE Trans. Multimedia (TMM) **24**, 1093–1104 (2022)
39. Sun, Z., et al.: PNP: Robust learning from noisy labels by probabilistic noise prediction. In: Proceedings of the IEEE Conference on Computer Vision and Pattern Recognition (CVPR), pp. 5311–5320 (2022)
40. Sun, Z., et al.: Webly supervised fine-grained recognition: Benchmark datasets and an approach. In: Proceedings of the IEEE International Conference on Computer Vision (ICCV), pp. 10602–10611 (2021)
41. Sun, Z., Yao, Y., Wei, X., Shen, F., Liu, H., Hua, X.S.: Boosting robust learning via leveraging reusable samples in noisy web data. IEEE Trans. Multimedia (TMM) (2022). https://doi.org/10.1109/TMM.2022.3158001
42. Sun, Z., Yao, Y., Xiao, J., Zhang, L., Zhang, J., Tang, Z.: Exploiting textual queries for dynamically visual disambiguation. Pattern Recogn. **110**, 107620 (2021)
43. Tancik, M., et al.: Fourier features let networks learn high frequency functions in low dimensional domains. Adv. Neural. Inf. Process. Syst. **33**, 7537–7547 (2020)
44. Vaswani, A., et al.: Attention is all you need. In: Advances in Neural Information Processing Systems, vol. 30 (2017)
45. Xie, S., Gu, J., Guo, D., Qi, C.R., Guibas, L., Litany, O.: PointContrast: unsupervised pre-training for 3D point cloud understanding. In: Vedaldi, A., Bischof, H., Brox, T., Frahm, J.-M. (eds.) ECCV 2020. LNCS, vol. 12348, pp. 574–591. Springer, Cham (2020). https://doi.org/10.1007/978-3-030-58580-8_34
46. Xu, B., Chen, Z.: Multi-level fusion based 3D object detection from monocular images. In: Proceedings of the IEEE Conference on Computer Vision and Pattern Recognition, pp. 2345–2353 (2018)
47. Yang, B., Luo, W., Urtasun, R.: Pixor: Real-time 3D object detection from point clouds. In: Proceedings of the IEEE Conference on Computer Vision and Pattern Recognition, pp. 7652–7660 (2018)
48. Yao, Y., et al.: Non-salient region object mining for weakly supervised semantic segmentation. In: Proceedings of the IEEE Conference on Computer Vision and Pattern Recognition (CVPR), pp. 2623–2632 (2021)
49. Yao, Y., Hua, X.S., Shen, F., Zhang, J., Tang, Z.: A domain robust approach for image dataset construction. In: Proceedings of the ACM International Conference on Multimedia (ACMMM), pp. 212–216 (2016)
50. Yao, Y., Hua, X., Gao, G., Sun, Z., Li, Z., Zhang, J.: Bridging the web data and fine-grained visual recognition via alleviating label noise and domain mismatch. In: Proceedings of the ACM International Conference on Multimedia (ACMMM), pp. 1735–1744 (2020)
51. Yao, Y., et al.: Exploiting web images for multi-output classification: from category to subcategories. IEEE Trans. Neural Netw. Learn. Syst. (TNNLS) **31**(7), 2348–2360 (2020)
52. Yao, Y., Shen, F., Zhang, J., Liu, L., Tang, Z., Shao, L.: Extracting multiple visual senses for web learning. IEEE Trans. Multimedia (TMM) **21**(1), 184–196 (2019)
53. Yao, Y., Shen, F., Zhang, J., Liu, L., Tang, Z., Shao, L.: Extracting privileged information for enhancing classifier learning. IEEE Trans. Image Process. (TIP) **28**(1), 436–450 (2019)
54. Yao, Y., Sun, Z., Zhang, C., Shen, F., Wu, Q., Zhang, J., Tang, Z.: Jo-SRC: A contrastive approach for combating noisy labels. In: Proceedings of the IEEE Conference on Computer Vision and Pattern Recognition (CVPR), pp. 5192–5201 (2021)

55. Yao, Y., Zhang, J., Shen, F., Hua, X., Xu, J., Tang, Z.: Exploiting web images for dataset construction: a domain robust approach. IEEE Trans. Multimedia (TMM) **19**(8), 1771–1784 (2017)
56. Yao, Y., et al.: Towards automatic construction of diverse, high-quality image datasets. IEEE Trans. Knowl. Data Eng. (TKDE) **32**(6), 1199–1211 (2020)
57. Yao, Y., Zhang, J., Shen, F., Yang, W., Huang, P., Tang, Z.: Discovering and distinguishing multiple visual senses for polysemous words. In: Proceedings of the AAAI Conference on Artificial Intelligence (AAAI), pp. 523–530 (2018)
58. Zhang, C., Lin, G., Wang, Q., Shen, F., Yao, Y., Tang, Z.: Guided by meta-set: a data-driven method for fine-grained visual recognition. IEEE Trans. Multimedia (TMM) (2022). https://doi.org/10.1109/TMM.2022.3181439
59. Zhang, C., Wang, Q., Xie, G., Wu, Q., Shen, F., Tang, Z.: Robust learning from noisy web images via data purification for fine-grained recognition. IEEE Trans. Multimedia (TMM) **24**, 1198–1209 (2022)
60. Zhang, C.,et al.: Web-supervised network with softly update-drop training for fine-grained visual classification. In: Proceedings of the AAAI Conference on Artificial Intelligence (AAAI), pp. 12781–12788 (2020)
61. Zhang, C., Yao, Y., Shu, X., Li, Z., Tang, Z., Wu, Q.: Data-driven meta-set based fine-grained visual recognition. In: Proceedings of the ACM International Conference on Multimedia (ACMMM), pp. 2372–2381 (2020)
62. Zhang, C., et al.: Extracting useful knowledge from noisy web images via data purification for fine-grained recognition. In: Proceedings of the ACM International Conference on Multimedia (ACMMM), pp. 4063–4072 (2021)
63. Zhang, Z., Girdhar, R., Joulin, A., Misra, I.: Self-supervised pretraining of 3d features on any point-cloud. In: Proceedings of the IEEE/CVF International Conference on Computer Vision, pp. 10252–10263 (2021)
64. Zhang, Z., Girdhar, R., Joulin, A., Misra, I.: Self-supervised pretraining of 3D features on any point-cloud. In: Proceedings of the IEEE/CVF International Conference on Computer Vision, pp. 10252–10263 (2021)

Global Patch Cross-Attention for Point Cloud Analysis

Manli Tao[1,2](✉) ⓘ, Chaoyang Zhao[2], Jinqiao Wang[1,2], and Ming Tang[1,2]

[1] University of Chinese Academy of Sciences, No.19(A) Yuquan Road,
Shijingshan District, Beijing 100049, China
{manli.tao,jqwang,tangm}@nlpr.ia.ac.cn
[2] Institute of Automation Chinese Academy of Sciences,
95 Zhongguancun East Road, Beijing 100190, China
chaoyang.zhao@nlpr.ia.ac.cn

Abstract. Despite the great achievement on 3D point cloud analysis with deep learning methods, the insufficiency of contextual semantic description, and misidentification of confusing objects remain tricky problems. To address these challenges, we propose a novel approach, Global Patch Cross-Attention Network (GPCAN), to learn more discriminative point cloud features effectively. Specifically, a global patch construction module is developed to generate global patches which share holistic shape similarity but hold diversity in local structure. Then the local features are extracted from both the original point cloud and these global patches. Further, a transformer-style cross-attention module is designed to model cross-object relations, which are all point-pair attentions between the original point cloud and each global patch, for learning the context-dependent features of each global patch. In this way, our method can integrate the features of original point cloud with both the local features and global contexts in each global patch for enhancing the discriminative power of the model. Extensive experiments on challenging point cloud classification and part segmentation benchmarks verify that our GPCAN achieves the state-of-the-arts on both synthetic and real-world datasets.

Keywords: Global patch · Cross-attention · Contextual description · Point cloud analysis

1 Introduction

The task of processing and analyzing 3D point cloud has drawn a lot of attention in the computer vision community due to its wide applications such as autonomous driving and robot manipulation. However, different from the regular and density image, the difficulty of extracting comprehensive information directly from irregular and discrete point cloud keeps it a challenging problem.

This work was supported by Key-Area Research and Development Program of Guangdong Province (No. 2021B0101410003), National Natural Science Foundation of China under Grants 61976210, 62176254, 62006230, 62002357 and 61876086.

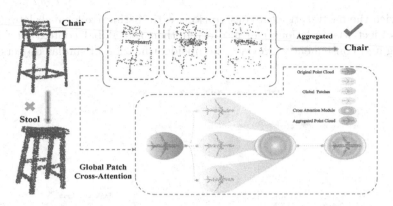

Fig. 1. Motivation: Sufficiently contextual semantic grasp is crucial for the shape understanding of point cloud. The "chair" is prone to be misidentified as the "stool" by only operating on the original point cloud. With diverse features of each global patch aggregated, the contextual semantic description is enhanced and correspondingly makes a meaningful contribution to the accurate recognition. The red dotted lines represent the underlying point cloud skeleton [15], which enriches the structural diversity of the target. Here, we only use the airplane instead of chair in the"Global Patch Cross-Attention" for the visual clearness of structural diversity. (Colour figure online)

To address this issue, the pioneer PointNet [20] directly processes the point cloud by using the Multi-layer-Perceptions (MLPs) [8] and aggregates all the point features to a global point cloud representation. Though impressive, this design only independently learns each point feature and ignores the local geometric structure information which is indispensable to the description of 3D shape. To remedy this defect, some local-patch-based schemes [33,43] construct a local group to learn relations between the center point and its neighbors. To some extent, these methods can leverage local structure information to strengthen partial geometric description, however, they neglect the long-distance point relations that are advantageous to overall shape recognition of the target. To capture global context, PCT [7] designs a transformer-style network, which extremely relies on specially designed local neighbor embedding to achieve prominent performance.

Most of the previous methods excessively focus on enhancing the local feature and inevitably fall into just locally internal geometric interaction. Moreover, different from clean synthetic datasets, the real-world objects generally appear together with background noise and suffer from local geometric deficiency due to partial observation or clutter, which weakens the effectiveness of the local feature. Besides, some similar objects (e.g., chair and stool in Fig. 1) are prone to be misidentified without the assistance of holistically contextual interactions.

Based on the above analysis, we aim to address these problems from a global patch perspective, which is defined as a group of points that are originated from the input point cloud but maintain similar shape contours. These global patches can be regarded as a lightweight representation of the original object and enrich the partial structure descriptions with distinctive local skeletons [15]. Then, object-wise relations can also strengthen the global contextual feature learning and consequently alleviate the misidentification of similar objects.

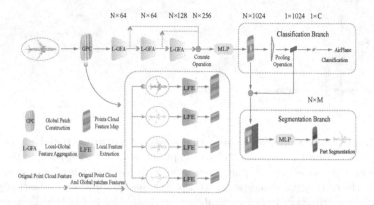

Fig. 2. GPCAN architecture for point cloud classification and segmentation. We design a hierarchical structure to learn multi-level features of the input points. Classification network concatenates the features of each level and pools it to a 1D global vector for classification scores generating. The segmentation network is an extension of the classification net. It outputs per-point part segmentation scores.

To this end, we propose a global patch cross-attention network (GPCAN) for point cloud analysis. Firstly, global patches are generated through the global patch construction module (GPC in Fig. 2). Then, inside the original point cloud and each global patch, the local features of diverse local skeletons are encoded with the support of the nearest neighbor search. Further, we develop a cross-attention model (CAM in Fig. 3) to model object-wise relations for learning context-dependent features in each global patch. By respectively fusing features in these global patches with the original point cloud features instead of only operating on the original point cloud, we get the "Aggregated Point Cloud" (painted with various colors in Fig. 1) boosting the discriminative performance of the network on different tasks.

Extensive experiments have been conducted on point cloud classification and part segmentation benchmarks to verify the effectiveness of our approach. Experimental results on widely used synthetic datasets ModelNet40 [34], ShapeNet, [41] and more challenging real-world dataset ScanObjectNN [29] demonstrate that our GPCAN achieves state-of-the-art performances and is more robust to background perturbation and object rotation. In summary, the key contributions of our method are summarized as follows:

1. We extend the point cloud study to a novel global patch perspective. By introducing global patches, our approach is able to enrich the local geometry diversity and further enhance local feature expression ability.

2. We design a transformer-style cross-attention module to learn object-level representation with object-wise relations. Furthermore, a cascade feature fusion strategy is employed to obtain sufficiently contextual semantic information for boosting the power of the model inference.
3. Our model achieves state-of-the-art performances on both synthetic and real-world datasets for different point cloud tasks.

2   Related Work

2.1   Multi-view Based and Voxelized Methods

Convolutional Neural Networks (CNNs) have obtained remarkable success for various 2D vision tasks. However, it consumes regular data and is incapable of the 3D point cloud. In order to take advantage of well-engineered CNN's style network, some works convert irregular points into a regular presentation. There are two main processing directions: view-based and voxelized methods.

Multi-view based methods render 3D points into multi-view 2D images [3, 6,21,26,35] and then apply 2D convolution to process them. Though easy to apply, this line of methods often demands a huge number of views for decent performance. What's more, 2D projections also draw into incidental defects such as the loss of shape information due to self-occlusions.

Voxelized methods [4,34] convert the input point cloud into regular 3D grids and apply a 3D convolutional neural network on the voxelized shape. However, the vast computation cost of 3D convolution and the loss of 3D geometric shape information due to low resolution enforced by 3D voxel constrain its application space. In contrast to these methods, our work aims to process 3D points directly.

2.2   Point Based Method

PointNet [20] is the pioneering network that directly processes point cloud. It independently learns on each point with shared MLPs and aggregates all individual point features to a holistic signature with the max-pooling operation. Yet, this design can't capture local structure information. To remedy the above defect, PointNet++ [22] proposes a hierarchical application of the PointNet combined with query ball grouping operation to capture the local context. Some local structure exploitations with the PointNet are also investigated in [5,25]. Other approaches [10,13,27,31] suggest a graph-convolution-based scheme to study point cloud processing, these methods aim to capture local spatial relations by aggregating point features through local graph operations. Commonly, each point is regarded as a graph vertex and the point's relative positions correspond to edge relations in the graph. Therefore, graph convolution can capture the surface presented by the graph and then aggregate features on local patches. However, graph convolution pays excessive attention to local context and ignores long-distance point relations. Unlike the above methods, our GPCAN attempts to study point relations from a global patch view rather than only capture spatial relations within a local space.

2.3   Attention Based Method

The attention mechanism is first introduced in natural language processing (NLP) for machine translation tasks and achieves remarkable success. There are many different forms of attention, e.g., self-attention, also known as inner-attention, is the aggregation of attention towards itself. Multi-head attention jointly attends to the information from different representations. Over the last few years, many excellent works [1,24,32,42] combining CNNs with different forms of self-attention have also emerged in 2D image tasks. The goal of these vision attention methods is to focus on the key parts of input data and enhance feature representation. All of the above methods achieve impressive results in different image tasks. Recently, inspired by the success of attention-based methods in 2D image processing, some works attempt to introduce the attention mechanism for 3D point cloud analysis. PATs [40] designs self-attention layers to capture the relations between points and develops a parameter-efficient Group Shuffle Attention to replace the costly Multi-Head Attention. Set Transformer [11] models interactions among points in the input sets through a specially designed encoder and decoder, both of which rely on attention mechanisms. PCT [7] is a transformer-based framework, which makes it suitable for globally long-range point relations learning with the support of self-attention. The excellent achievements of previous approaches show that self-attention has an intrinsical advantage in global feature capture.

Though self-attention can learn long-distance global context, it is also subjected to considering point relations within the object. In this paper, we attempt to aggregate global context from different global patches through the cross-attention operation.

3   Method

In this section, we first introduce the framework of our GPCAN approach and demonstrate how it can be used in the point cloud classification and the part segmentation tasks. Thereafter we introduce our global patch construction procedure. Finally, we present cross-attention operation on point cloud and elaborate on how it learns local features and global contexts for point cloud processing.

3.1   Overview

As shown in Fig. 2, given a d-dimensional point cloud with N points, denoted by $\mathcal{P} = \{x_1, x_2, \cdots, x_N\} \in \mathcal{R}^{N \times d}$. A set of global patches are firstly obtained via the GPC module. After that, both original point cloud and derived global patches are consumed by L-GFA (Local-Global Feature Aggregation) module, whose key component is CAM (Cross-Attention Module, details see Fig. 3). LFE module (Fig. 2) aims to learn point-wise local features of both the original point cloud and the corresponding global patches. Thereafter, all these point clouds with local features embedded are fed into CAM for capturing object-wise relations and further boosting the original point cloud feature representation ability.

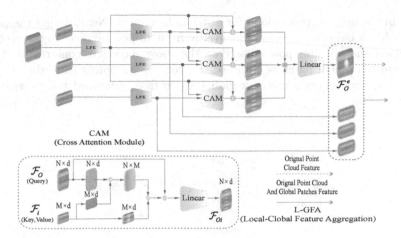

Fig. 3. The architecture of Local-global feature aggregation

As for the classification branch, we concatenate all levels of features together and then deploy the max-pooling to extract the holistic feature, which encodes the overall shape information, for classification. Finally, the probabilities of each category are obtained with the following Multi-layer-Perceptions and the category with the greatest probability is regarded as the classification result.

The part segmentation network architecture is similar to the above classification network. The only difference is the components of the ultimate feature. Unlike the classification network, there are three components for the segmentation head. The first one is a 64-dimensional label feature, which is obtained by operating the MLPs on a one-hot category vector. The second one is the concatenation of multiple-level features. The last component is the result of max pooling on the second one. Each point segmentation scores $S \in \mathcal{R}^{1 \times m}$ are predicted by MLPs. Finally, we regard the category corresponding to the maximal score as the predicted part label.

3.2 Global Patch Construction

The GPC module aims to split the original point cloud $\mathcal{P} \in \mathcal{R}^{N \times d}$ into a set of sub patches $\Phi = \{\mathcal{P}_1, \mathcal{P}_2, \cdots, \mathcal{P}_S\}, \mathcal{P}_i \in \mathcal{R}^{M \times d}$, S is the size of global patches, which have holistically similar shape but tiny distinction in local structure. There are two requirements for global patch construction: (1) how to ensure that each patch has a similar shape representation with the original point cloud; (2) how to produce the unique part distinction of each patch. In this work, we employ an easy sampling strategy to achieve the above goals. Firstly, we shuffle all point indices in the original point cloud for order-independent. Next, we get the point indices of a global patch by sampling evenly from all point indices in the original point cloud and selecting points based on the above indices to construct a global patch. Once a global patch is obtained, we remove its points from the original point cloud and generate the next global patch from remained points with the same operation.

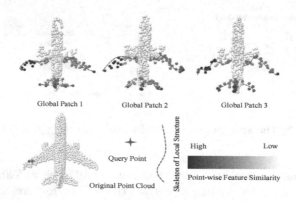

Fig. 4. Visualization of global patches and point-wise feature similarity. The red curve denotes the skeleton of the local structure, which shows the local diversity. Colors from white to blue indicate the point-wise similarity degree from low to high (Color figure online)

This no-repeat sampling can ensure each global patch has no overlap points, which brings the patches unique local structures (the skeleton of local structure in Fig. 4).

3.3   Local-Global Feature Aggregation

Local Feature Extractor. As for local feature capture, we use a graph convolution [33] based method, denoted as LFE (local feature extractor), to learn local features for both the original point cloud and its global patches. Here we use the global patch to illustrate this process. Given a point cloud feature map $\mathcal{F}_i = \{x_1, x_2, \cdots, x_M\} \in \mathcal{R}^{M \times d}$, $i \in [1, S]$, M is the point number of each global patch, S is the number of global patch. The local region $\mathcal{G}_j = \{x_{j1}, x_{j2}, \cdots, x_{jk-1}, x_j\} \in \mathcal{R}^{k \times d}, j \in [1, M]$ is constructed by the k-nearest neighbors of x_j. Then, we compute the Euclidean distances of each neighbor point towards x_j and descript local region $\mathcal{G}_j$ with all point-pair distances. Finally, the convolution operation and max-pooling are applied on $\mathcal{G}_j$ to extract the local feature of point x_j. After all points are processed, the point cloud feature map updating is completed. The above process can be summarized as follows:

$$\mathcal{G}_j = knn(x_j) \tag{1}$$

$$x_j^{'} = MaxPooling(Conv(\mathcal{G}_j)) \tag{2}$$

$$\mathcal{F}_i^{'} = \left\{ x_1^{'}, x_2^{'}, \cdots, x_M^{'} \right\} \tag{3}$$

where $x_j^{'}$ indicates the updated feature of x_j; $\mathcal{F}_i^{'}$ denotes updated feature map.

Cross-Attention Module. Self-attention can capture long-range relations among points within the object. In contrast, we design a cross-attention module to learn cross-object point relations about original point cloud and global patches, which are called object-wise relations in this work. The formulation of query, key, and value are from transformer [30], which is used for allocating different attentions for different parts according to corresponding attention weights and makes it naturally suitable for global context capturing. As shown in the lower left of Fig. 3, given the feature map of the original point cloud, which we denote as $\mathcal{F}_O \in \mathcal{R}^{N \times d}$, and the feature map of global patch i, which we denote as $\mathcal{F}_i \in \mathcal{R}^{M \times d}$, i = $\{1, 2, \cdots, S\}$ and S is the size of global patches. Then query, key, and value matrices (denoted as Q, K, V) can be obtained by applying linear transforms on the above feature map.

$$Q_i = \mathcal{F}_O \cdot \mathcal{W}_q \tag{4}$$

$$K_i, V_i = \mathcal{F}_i \cdot (\mathcal{W}_k, \mathcal{W}_v) \tag{5}$$

where $K_i, V_i \in \mathcal{R}^{M \times d}; Q_i \in \mathcal{R}^{N \times d}; \mathcal{W}_q, \mathcal{W}_k, \mathcal{W}_v \in \mathcal{R}^{d \times d}$.

Then, we use the dot-product of query and key matrices as object-wise attention weights matric. The pseudo feature representation of the original point cloud (denoted as $\mathcal{F}_{pse_i}$) can be obtained by calculating the dot-product of attention weights and the value matric. Finally, the output feature of the cross-attention module can be generated by differencing the original point cloud feature map to each pseudo feature representation and applying linear transform on the above result, which indicates the supplementary feature information from these global patches.

$$\mathcal{A}_i = Q_i \cdot K_i^T \tag{6}$$

$$\mathcal{F}_{pse_i} = \mathcal{A}_i \cdot V_i \tag{7}$$

$$\mathcal{F}_{Oi} = Linear \left(\mathcal{F}_O - \mathcal{F}_{pse_i} \right) \tag{8}$$

where $\mathcal{A}_i \in \mathcal{R}^{N \times M}; \mathcal{F}_{pse_i} \in \mathcal{R}^{N \times d}; \mathcal{F}_{Oi} \in \mathcal{R}^{N \times d}$.

Feature Aggregation. Both local and global features are indispensable for the point cloud representation. We design an L-GFA (Local-Global Feature Aggregation) module to effectively aggregate them. As shown in Fig. 3, The CAM consumes updated $\mathcal{F}_O'$ and $\mathcal{F}_i'$ to obtain global-patch-based original point cloud representation $\mathcal{F}_{Oi}$, which encodes the distinction information about each global patch towards the original point cloud. Since each global patch is originated from the original point cloud and globally similar to it, we argue that they can be regarded as a light representation of the original point cloud. Therefore, they can provide different supplementary geometry description information for the original point cloud. Then we add $\mathcal{F}_{Oi}$ to each $\mathcal{F}_O'$ and add them all up for global feature embedding. Finally, linear transform operation is applied on the above collection result to strengthen the original point cloud feature representation, and the output is called enhanced feature, denoted as $\mathcal{F}_O^e$.

$$\mathcal{F}_O^e = L(\sum_{i=1}^{S}(\mathcal{F}_O' + \mathcal{F}_{Oi})) \tag{9}$$

The output of L-GFA module contain two branches: the original point cloud feature branch $\mathcal{F}_O^e$ and overall feature branch $\mathcal{O} = \left\{\mathcal{F}_O^e, \mathcal{F}_1', \mathcal{F}_2', \cdots, \mathcal{F}_S'\right\}$. The first branch is used for multiple-level feature concatenating. And the second branch is used as the input of the next L-GFA layer.

4   Experiment

In this section, we arrange comprehensive experiments to validate the proposed GPCAN. We separately evaluate GPCAN on classification and part segmentation benchmarks for point cloud analysis (Sect., 4.1). In Sect. 4.2, we perform different analyses to verify the rationality of our network design.

4.1   Point Cloud Analysis

Shape Classification on ModelNet40 Dataset. We evaluate our GPCAN on synthetic ModelNet40 [34] for point cloud classification. It contains 12,311 CAD models in 40 categories. Following PointNet [20], we uniformly sample 1024 points with (x, y, z) coordinates as the initial feature of each point. The classification branch of GPCAN, which contains 6 global patches with 170 points within each patch, is used for this shape classification task. Table 1 summarizes some quantitative comparison results with the state-of-the-art methods. Our GPCAN achieves superior performance (93.7%) compared with the local-patch-based method DGCNN (92.9%) and the self-attention method PCT (93.2%). All of these verify the effectiveness of our GPCAN.

Table 1. Shape classification ModelNet40

Method	Input	#Points	Accuracy (%)
PointNet [20]	xyz	1 k	89.2
A-SCN [36]	xyz	1 k	89.8
So-Net [12]	xyz	2 k	90.9
Kd-Net(depth=15) [9]	xyz	32 k	91.8
PointNet++ [22]	xyz	1 k	90.7
PointNet++ [22]	xyz, nor	5 k	91.9
3D-GCN [16]	xyz	1 k	92.1
PointWeb [43]	xyz	1 k	92.3
Point2Sequence [17]	xyz	1 k	92.6
DGCNN [33]	xyz	1 k	92.9
KPConv [28]	xyz	1 k	92.9
GS-Net [37]	xyz	1 k	92.9
GS-Net [37]	xyz	2 k	93.3
InterpCNN [19]	xyz	1 k	93.0
DRNet [23]	xyz	1 k	93.1
PCT [7]	xyz	1 k	93.2
GPCAN(ours)	**xyz**	**1 k**	**93.7**

Table 2. Overall and average class accuracy (%) on ScanObjectNN's most challenging variant PB_T50_RS. The PB indicates perturbations while the suffix R and S denote rotation and scaling respectively.

Methods	Overall acc	Avg class acc
3DmFV [2]	63.0	58.1
PointNet [20]	68.2	63.4
SpiderCNN [38]	73.7	69.8
PointNet++ [22]	77.9	75.4
DGCNN [33]	78.1	73.6
PointCNN [14]	78.5	75.1
BGA-PN+ [29]	80.2	77.5
BGA-DGCN [29]	79.7	75.7
GPCAN(ours)	**80.7**	**77.9**

Shape Classification on ScanObjectNN Dataset. ScanObjectNN [29] is a real-world object dataset with about 15 k objects in 15 categories. We test our model on its most challenging variant PB_T50_RS. The results are summarized in Table 2. Even with background element and rotation perturbation, our model can still achieve fine performance compared with previous methods.

Table 3. Shape part segmentation results (%) on the ShapeNet part benchmark.

Method	InstancemIoU	Airplane	Bag	Cap	Car	Chair	Earphone	Guitar	Knife	Lamp	Laptop	Motorbike	Mug	Pistol	Rocket	Skateboard	Table
PointNet [20]	83.7	83.4	78.7	82.5	74.9	89.6	73.0	91.5	85.9	80.8	95.3	65.2	93.0	81.2	57.9	72.8	80.6
PointNet++ [22]	85.1	82.4	79.0	87.7	77.3	90.8	71.8	91.0	85.9	83.7	95.3	71.6	94.1	81.3	58.7	76.4	82.6
Kd-Net [9]	82.3	80.1	74.6	74.3	70.3	88.6	73.5	90.2	87.2	81.0	94.9	57.4	86.7	78.1	51.8	69.9	80.3
SO-Net [12]	84.9	82.8	77.8	88.0	77.3	90.6	73.5	90.7	83.9	82.8	94.8	69.1	94.2	80.9	53.1	72.9	83.0
DGCNN [33]	85.2	84.0	83.4	86.7	77.8	90.6	74.7	91.2	87.5	82.8	95.7	66.3	94.9	81.1	63.5	74.5	82.6
P2Sequence [17]	85.2	82.6	81.8	87.5	77.3	90.8	77.1	91.1	86.9	83.9	95.7	70.8	94.6	79.3	58.1	75.2	82.8
GS-Net [37]	85.3	82.9	84.3	88.6	78.4	89.7	**78.3**	**91.7**	86.7	81.2	95.6	72.8	94.7	83.1	62.3	81.5	83.8
PCT [7]	86.4	**85.0**	82.4	**89.0**	**81.2**	91.9	71.5	91.3	88.1	86.3	95.8	64.6	**95.8**	**83.6**	62.2	77.6	83.7
RS-CNN [18]	86.2	83.5	**84.8**	88.8	79.6	91.2	81.1	91.6	88.4	86.0	**96.0**	**73.7**	94.1	83.4	60.5	77.7	83.6
3D-GCN [16]	85.3	82.9	84.3	88.6	78.4	89.7	**78.3**	**91.7**	86.7	81.2	95.6	72.8	94.7	83.1	62.3	**81.5**	83.8
PointASNL [39]	86.1	84.1	84.7	87.9	79.7	**92.2**	73.7	91.0	87.2	84.2	95.8	74.4	95.2	81.0	63.0	76.3	83.2
GPCAN(ours)	**86.6**	84.3	82.2	88.6	78.2	91.8	75.4	91.1	**89.3**	**87.0**	**96.0**	69.6	94.0	81.4	**66.9**	73.3	**85.2**

Shape Part Segmentation on ShapeNet. ShapeNet-Part dataset [41] contains 16881 shapes with 16 categories and is labeled in 50 parts. We choose the instance mIoU as the evaluation metric which is averaged across all instances. Table 3 shows that our GPCAN achieves the best performance with mIoU of 86.6%. Figure 5 shows that our GPCAN owns strong discriminative ability in the part structure recognition.

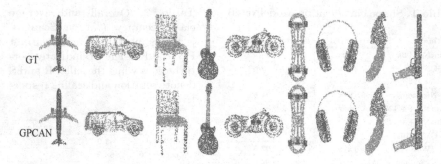

Fig. 5. Segmentation examples on the ShapeNet part benchmark. "GT" denotes the ground truth. "GPCAN" indicates the part segmentation result based on our method.

4.2   Analysis of GPCAN

Components Analysis. We analyze the effectiveness of our method's components on the ModelNet40 for classification. "knn" indicates use KNN for feature aggregation. The results in Table 4 show that cross-attention coupled with global patches can boost object recognition.

Robustness Analysis of Background Noise. We also train and evaluate our method on the variant PB_T50_RS (without background point). The results are summarized in Table 5, our method achieves not only the highest accuracy on both with and without BG but also the lowest accuracy drop (2%) from without BG to BG. All of the above results and analyses show the applicability of our model in the real world.

Table 4. Ablation study of GPCAN.

Knn	Self-attention	Cross-attention	Global patch size	Accuracy (%)
-	✓	-	-	90.3
✓	✓	-	-	92.4
✓	✓	-	4	93.1
-	-	✓	2	90.6
✓	-	✓	2	93.2
✓	-	✓	4	93.4
✓	-	✓	6	**93.7**
✓	-	✓	8	93.2
✓	-	✓	10	92.8

Table 5. Overall and average class accuracy (%) on the ScanObjectNN's.

Method	W/o BG	W/BG	Acc Drop
3DmFV [2]	69.8	63.0	↓ 6.8
PointNet [20]	74.4	68.2	↓ 6.2
SpiderCNN [38]	76.9	73.7	↓ 3.2
DGCNN [33]	81.5	78.1	↓ 3.4
GPCAN(ours)	**82.7**	**80.7**	↓ **2.0**

Misidentification Analysis of Confusing Classes. To further explore the recognition ability of the model, we visualize the confusion matrixes generated by our GPCAN, PCT, and DGCNN respectively. As illustrated in Fig. 6, the top row shows some examples with contour similarity and the bottom row shows the confusion matrices of different methods, which only show the mainly misidentified classes for clear visualization. Compared with the self-attention-based method PCT and the local-patch-based method DGCNN, our GPCAN has better performance on samples that are prone to be misidentified.

Density Robustness Analysis. Sensor data directly captured from the real world usually suffer from a sparse issue. We randomly drop the input points during test time to validate the network's robustness to sparse data (Fig. 7 left). As Fig. 7 right illustrated, even 384 points are given, our model can still obtain 89.9% accuracy compared with PointNet's 89.2% with 1024 points as input.

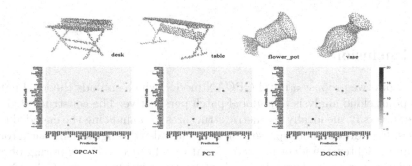

Fig. 6. Visualization of the confusing examples and confusion matrixes

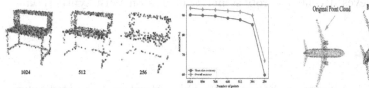
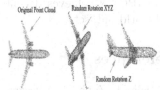

Fig. 7. Visualization of the density robustness. Left: point cloud with different densities. Right: test accuracy of using sparser points as the input.

Fig. 8. Visualization of the point cloud with random rotation around Z or XYZ axes

Rotation Robustness Analysis. We evaluate rotation robustness on ModelNet40. The results are summarized in Table 6 with two scenarios (Fig. 8): (1) both training and test datasets are augmented by rotating random angles around z axes (denoted as z/z); (2) both training and test dataset are augmented by rotating random angle around all three axes (s/s). GPCAN achieves decent robustness with the lowest accuracy drop (0.4%) from the z to all three axes rotation.

Complexity Analysis. Table 7 shows that the GACAN can achieve fine accuracy result with only 1.07 M parameters and 2.04G FLOPs.

Table 6. Accuracy (%) comparisons of rotation robustness on the ModelNet40 classification task.

Method	Z/z	S/s	Acc drop
DGCNN [33]	90.4	82.6	↓ 7.8
PointNet [20]	81.6	66.3	↓ 15.3
PointNet++ [22]	90.1	87.8	↓ 2.3
SpiderCNN [38]	83.5	69.6	↓ 13.9
GS-Net [37]	89.8	87.9	↓ 1.9
GPCAN(ours)	**92.5**	**92.1**	↓ **0.4**

Table 7. Comparisons of the model complexity on the ModelNet40 classification task.

Methods	Params(M)	FLOPs(G)	Acc (%)
PointNet [20]	3.47	**0.45**	89.2
PointNet++(SSG) [22]	1.48	1.68	90.7
PointNet++(MSG) [22]	1.74	4.09	91.9
DGCNN [33]	1.81	2.43	92.9
PCT [7]	2.88	2.32	93.2
GPCAN(ours)	**1.07**	2.04	**93.7**

5   Conclusion

In this work, we propose a novel GPCAN model, which extends the local patch-based point cloud analysis to a global patch perspective. The constructed global patches diversify the locally geometric structures for enhancing the encoded local features. In addition, more sparse global patches also downgrade the background noise and heighten the identification of real-world objects. By exploring object-wise relations instead of just internal interactions inside objects, GPCAN can achieve contextual shape-aware learning and simultaneously improve identification performance on confusing classes. Extensive experiments have demonstrated that GPCAN achieves decent and robust performances on both synthetic and real-world datasets.

References

1. Bello, I., Zoph, B., Vaswani, A., Shlens, J., Le, Q.V.: Attention augmented convolutional networks. In: Proceedings of the IEEE/CVF International Conference on Computer Vision, pp. 3286–3295 (2019)
2. Ben-Shabat, Y., Lindenbaum, M., Fischer, A.: 3DmFV: three-dimensional point cloud classification in real-time using convolutional neural networks. IEEE Robot. Autom. Lett. **3**(4), 3145–3152 (2018)
3. Feng, Y., Zhang, Z., Zhao, X., Ji, R., Gao, Y.: GVCNN: Group-view convolutional neural networks for 3d shape recognition. In: Proceedings of the IEEE Conference on Computer Vision and Pattern Recognition, pp. 264–272 (2018)
4. Gadelha, M., Wang, R., Maji, S.: Multiresolution tree networks for 3D point cloud processing. In: Proceedings of the European Conference on Computer Vision (ECCV), pp. 103–118 (2018)
5. Guerrero, P., Kleiman, Y., Ovsjanikov, M., Mitra, N.J.: PCPNet learning local shape properties from raw point clouds. In: Computer Graphics Forum, vol. 37, pp. 75–85. Wiley Online Library (2018)
6. Guo, H., Wang, J., Gao, Y., Li, J., Lu, H.: Multi-view 3D object retrieval with deep embedding network. IEEE Trans. Image Process. **25**(12), 5526–5537 (2016)
7. Guo, M.H., Cai, J.X., Liu, Z.N., Mu, T.J., Martin, R.R., Hu, S.M.: PCT: Point cloud transformer. Computational Visual Media **7**(2), 187–199 (2021)

8. Hornik, K.: Approximation capabilities of multilayer feedforward networks. Neural Netw. **4**(2), 251–257 (1991)
9. Klokov, R., Lempitsky, V.: Escape from cells: Deep Kd-networks for the recognition of 3d point cloud models. In: Proceedings of the IEEE International Conference on Computer Vision, pp. 863–872 (2017)
10. Landrieu, L., Simonovsky, M.: Large-scale point cloud semantic segmentation with superpoint graphs. In: Proceedings of the IEEE Conference on Computer Vision and Pattern Recognition, pp. 4558–4567 (2018)
11. Lee, J., Lee, Y., Kim, J., Kosiorek, A., Choi, S., Teh, Y.W.: Set transformer: A framework for attention-based permutation-invariant neural networks. In: International Conference on Machine Learning, pp. 3744–3753. PMLR (2019)
12. Li, J., Chen, B.M., Lee, G.H.: So-Net: Self-organizing network for point cloud analysis. In: Proceedings of the IEEE Conference on Computer Vision and Pattern Recognition, pp. 9397–9406 (2018)
13. Li, R., Wang, S., Zhu, F., Huang, J.: Adaptive graph convolutional neural networks. In: Proceedings of the AAAI Conference on Artificial Intelligence, vol. 32 (2018)
14. Li, Y., Bu, R., Sun, M., Wu, W., Di, X., Chen, B.: PointCNN: Convolution on x-transformed points. Adv. Neural. Inf. Process. Syst. **31**, 820–830 (2018)
15. Lin, C., Li, C., Liu, Y., Chen, N., Choi, Y.K., Wang, W.: Point2skeleton: Learning skeletal representations from point clouds. In: Proceedings of the IEEE/CVF Conference on Computer Vision and Pattern Recognition, pp. 4277–4286 (2021)
16. Lin, Z.H., Huang, S.Y., Wang, Y.C.F.: Convolution in the cloud: Learning deformable kernels in 3D graph convolution networks for point cloud analysis. In: 2020 IEEE/CVF Conference on Computer Vision and Pattern Recognition (CVPR), pp. 1797–1806. IEEE (2020)
17. Liu, X., Han, Z., Liu, Y.S., Zwicker, M.: Point2sequence: Learning the shape representation of 3D point clouds with an attention-based sequence to sequence network. In: Proceedings of the AAAI Conference on Artificial Intelligence, vol. 33, pp. 8778–8785 (2019)
18. Liu, Y., Fan, B., Xiang, S., Pan, C.: Relation-shape convolutional neural network for point cloud analysis. In: Proceedings of the IEEE/CVF Conference on Computer Vision and Pattern Recognition, pp. 8895–8904 (2019)
19. Mao, J., Wang, X., Li, H.: Interpolated convolutional networks for 3d point cloud understanding. In: 2019 IEEE/CVF International Conference on Computer Vision (ICCV), pp. 1578–1587. IEEE Computer Society (2019)
20. Qi, C.R., Su, H., Mo, K., Guibas, L.J.: PointNet: Deep learning on point sets for 3D classification and segmentation. In: Proceedings of the IEEE Conference on Computer Vision and Pattern Recognition, pp. 652–660 (2017)
21. Qi, C.R., Su, H., Nießner, M., Dai, A., Yan, M., Guibas, L.J.: Volumetric and multi-view cnns for object classification on 3D data. In: Proceedings of the IEEE Conference on Computer Vision and Pattern Recognition, pp. 5648–5656 (2016)
22. Qi, C.R., Yi, L., Su, H., Guibas, L.J.: PointNet++: Deep hierarchical feature learning on point sets in a metric space. Adv. Neural Inform. Process. Syst. **30** 5104–5144 (2017)
23. Qiu, S., Anwar, S., Barnes, N.: Dense-resolution network for point cloud classification and segmentation. In: 2021 IEEE Winter Conference on Applications of Computer Vision (WACV), pp. 3812–3821. IEEE (2021)
24. Ramachandran, P., Parmar, N., Vaswani, A., Bello, I., Levskaya, A., Shlens, J.: Stand-alone self-attention in vision models. Adv. Neural Inform. Process. Syst. **32** 68–80 (2019)

25. Shen, Y., Feng, C., Yang, Y., Tian, D.: Mining point cloud local structures by kernel correlation and graph pooling. In: Proceedings of the IEEE Conference on Computer Vision and Pattern Recognition, pp. 4548–4557 (2018)
26. Su, H., Maji, S., Kalogerakis, E., Learned-Miller, E.: Multi-view convolutional neural networks for 3d shape recognition. In: Proceedings of the IEEE International Conference on Computer Vision, pp. 945–953 (2015)
27. Te, G., Hu, W., Zheng, A., Guo, Z.: RGCNN: Regularized graph CNN for point cloud segmentation. In: Proceedings of the 26th ACM International Conference on Multimedia, pp. 746–754 (2018)
28. Thomas, H., Qi, C.R., Deschaud, J.E., Marcotegui, B., Goulette, F., Guibas, L.: KPConv: Flexible and deformable convolution for point clouds. In: 2019 IEEE/CVF International Conference on Computer Vision (ICCV), pp. 6410–6419. IEEE Computer Society (2019)
29. Uy, M.A., Pham, Q.H., Hua, B.S., Nguyen, T., Yeung, S.K.: Revisiting point cloud classification: A new benchmark dataset and classification model on real-world data. In: Proceedings of the IEEE/CVF International Conference on Computer Vision. pp. 1588–1597 (2019)
30. Vaswani, A., Shazeer, N., Parmar, N., Uszkoreit, J., Jones, L., Gomez, A.N., Kaiser, L., Polosukhin, I.: Attention is all you need. In: Advances in Neural Information Processing Systems, pp. 5998–6008 (2017)
31. Wang, C., Samari, B., Siddiqi, K.: Local spectral graph convolution for point set feature learning. In: Proceedings of the European Conference on Computer Vision (ECCV), pp. 52–66 (2018)
32. Wang, X., Girshick, R., Gupta, A., He, K.: Non-local neural networks. In: Proceedings of the IEEE Conference on Computer Vision and Pattern Recognition, pp. 7794–7803 (2018)
33. Wang, Y., Sun, Y., Liu, Z., Sarma, S.E., Bronstein, M.M., Solomon, J.M.: Dynamic graph CNN for learning on point clouds. ACM Transactions On Graphics (tog) **38**(5), 1–12 (2019)
34. Wu, Z., Song, S., Khosla, A., Yu, F., Zhang, L., Tang, X., Xiao, J.: 3D shapenets: A deep representation for volumetric shapes. In: Proceedings of the IEEE Conference on Computer Vision and Pattern Recognition, pp. 1912–1920 (2015)
35. Xie, J., Dai, G., Zhu, F., Wong, E.K., Fang, Y.: Deepshape: deep-learned shape descriptor for 3D shape retrieval. IEEE Trans. Pattern Anal. Mach. Intell. **39**(7), 1335–1345 (2016)
36. Xie, S., Liu, S., Chen, Z., Tu, Z.: Attentional shapecontextnet for point cloud recognition. In: Proceedings of the IEEE Conference on Computer Vision and Pattern Recognition, pp. 4606–4615 (2018)
37. Xu, M., Zhou, Z., Qiao, Y.: Geometry sharing network for 3D point cloud classification and segmentation. In: Proceedings of the AAAI Conference on Artificial Intelligence, vol. 34, pp. 12500–12507 (2020)
38. Xu, Y., Fan, T., Xu, M., Zeng, L., Qiao, Y.: Spidercnn: Deep learning on point sets with parameterized convolutional filters. In: Proceedings of the European Conference on Computer Vision (ECCV), pp. 87–102 (2018)
39. Yan, X., Zheng, C., Li, Z., Wang, S., Cui, S.: PointASNL: Robust point clouds processing using nonlocal neural networks with adaptive sampling. In: Proceedings of the IEEE/CVF Conference on Computer Vision and Pattern Recognition, pp. 5589–5598 (2020)
40. Yang, J., et al.: Modeling point clouds with self-attention and gumbel subset sampling. In: Proceedings of the IEEE/CVF Conference on Computer Vision and Pattern Recognition, pp. 3323–3332 (2019)

41. Yi, L., et al.: A scalable active framework for region annotation in 3D shape collections. ACM Transactions on Graphics (ToG) **35**(6), 1–12 (2016)
42. Zhao, H., Jia, J., Koltun, V.: Exploring self-attention for image recognition. In: Proceedings of the IEEE/CVF Conference on Computer Vision and Pattern Recognition, pp. 10076–10085 (2020)
43. Zhao, H., Jiang, L., Fu, C.W., Jia, J.: PointWeb: Enhancing local neighborhood features for point cloud processing. In: Proceedings of the IEEE/CVF Conference on Computer Vision and Pattern Recognition, pp. 5565–5573 (2019)

EEP-Net: Enhancing Local Neighborhood Features and Efficient Semantic Segmentation of Scale Point Clouds

Yicheng Liu[1], Fuxiang Wu[1,2,3], Qieshi Zhang[1,2,3]([⊠]), Ziliang Ren[4], and Jun Chen[1,2,3]

[1] Shenzhen Institute of Advanced Technology, Chinese Academy of Sciences, Shenzhen, China
qs.zhang@siat.ac.cn
[2] Shenzhen College of Advanced Technology, University of Chinese Academy of Sciences, Beijing, China
[3] The Chinese University of Hong Kong, Hong Kong, China
[4] DongGuan University of Technology, Dongguan, China

Abstract. Semantic segmentation of point clouds at the scene level is a challenging task. Most existing work relies on expensive sampling techniques and tedious pre- and post-processing steps, which are often time-consuming and laborious. To solve this problem, we propose a new module for extracting contextual features from local regions of point clouds, called EEP module in this paper, which converts point clouds from Cartesian coordinates to polar coordinates of local regions, thereby Fade out the geometric representation with rotation invariance in the three directions of XYZ, and the new geometric representation is connected with the position code to form a new spatial representation. It can preserve geometric details and learn local features to a greater extent while improving computational and storage efficiency. This is beneficial for the segmentation task of point clouds. To validate the performance of our method, we conducted experiments on the publicly available standard dataset S3DIS, and the experimental results show that our method achieves competitive results compared to existing methods.

Keywords: Semantic segmentation · Scale point clouds · Rotational invariance

1 Introduction

In recent years, image recognition technology has developed rapidly relying on deep learning. In addition to 2D image recognition, people are increasingly interested in 3D vision, because directly learning 3D tasks from acquired 2D images always has certain limitations. With the rapid development of 3D acquisition technology, the availability and value of 3D sensors are increasing, including various types of 3D scanners, lidar, and RGB-D cameras. The advent of large-scale

S. Yu et al. (Eds.): PRCV 2022, LNCS 13536, pp. 112–123, 2022.
https://doi.org/10.1007/978-3-031-18913-5_9

high-resolution 3D datasets with scale information has also brought about the context of using deep neural networks to reason about 3D data. As a common 3D data format, the point cloud retains the original geometric information in three-dimensional space, so the point cloud is called the preferred data form for scene understanding. Efficient semantic segmentation of scene-level 3D point clouds has important applications in areas such as autonomous driving and robotics. In recent years, the pioneering work PointNet has become the most popular method for directly processing 3D point clouds. The PointNet [1] architecture directly processes point clouds through a shared MltiLayer Perceptron (MLP), using the MLP layer to learn the features of each point independently, using maximum pooling to obtain global features. On the other hand, since PointNet learns the features of each point individually, it ignores the local structure between points. Therefore, to improve this, the team introduced PointNet++ [2], as the core of this network hierarchy, with an ensemble abstraction layer consisting of three layers: a sampling layer, a grouping layer, and a PointNet-based learning layer. By overlaying several ensemble abstraction layers, this network learns features from local geometric structures and abstracts local features layer by layer. PointWeb [3] connects all local point pairs using local geographical context, and finally forms a local fully connected network, and then adjusts point features by learning point-to-point features. This strategy can enrich the point features of the local region and form aggregated features, which can better describe the local region and perform 3D recognition.

The effect of these methods in processing small-scale point clouds is gratifying, but it will bring some limitations to processing scene-level point clouds, mainly because: 1) High computational volume and low storage efficiency caused by the sampling method. 2) Most existing local feature learners usually rely on computationally expensive kernelization or graph construction, and thus cannot handle large numbers of points. 3) Existing learners have limited acceptance and size to effectively capture complex structures, and do not capture enough local area features for large-scale point clouds, RandLA-Net [4] provides us with a solution to these problems. RandLA-Net [4] based on the principle of simple random sampling and effective local feature aggregator, can increase the sampling rate while gradually increasing the receptive field of each neural layer through the feature aggregation module to help effectively learn complex local structures. However, after research, it was found that RandLA-Net [4] did not pay attention to the relationship between each point and point in a neighborhood when learning the local structure.

Our main contributions are as follows:

- As the input point cloud is direction-sensitive, we propose a new local space representation that is rotationally invariant in the X-Y-Z axis, which can effectively improve the performance of point cloud segmentation.
- We propose a new local feature aggregation module, Local Representation of Rotation Invariance (LRRI) , which connects the spatial representation with rotation invariance in X-Y-Z axis to the local relative point position

representation to form a new local geometric representation that effectively preserves local geometric details.

– We perform experimental validation on a representative S3DIS dataset, and our method is compared with state-of-the-art methods and achieves good performance.

2 Related Work

The goal of point cloud semantic segmentation is to give a point cloud and divide it into subsets according to the semantics of the points. There are three paradigms for semantic segmentation: projection-based, discretization-based and point-based.

2.1 Projection-Based Methods

To leverage the 2D segmentation methods, many existing works aim to project 3D point clouds into 2D images and then process 2D semantic segmentation. By which conventional convolution of 2D images can be used to process point cloud data, to solve target detection and semantic segmentation tasks. There are two main categories of such methods: (1) multi-viewpoint representation [5–8]. (2) spherical representation [9–12]. In general, the performance of multi-viewpoint segmentation methods is sensitive to viewpoint selection and occlusion. In addition, these methods do not fully utilize the underlying geometric and structural information because the projection step inevitably introduces information loss; the spherical projection representation retains more information than the single-view projection and is suitable for LiDAR point cloud labeling, however, this intermediate representation also inevitably introduces problems such as dispersion errors and occlusion.

2.2 Discretization-Based Methods

Discretization-based methods, which voxelized point clouds into 3D meshes and then apply the powerful 3D CNN in [13–17]. But the performance of these methods is sensitive to the granularity of voxels, and voxelization itself introduces discretization artifacts. On the other hand, the main limitation of such methods is their large computational size when dealing with large-scale point clouds. This method is very important in practical applications when choosing a suitable grid resolution.

2.3 Point-Based Methods

Different with the first two methods, point-based networks act directly on irregular point clouds. However, point clouds are disordered and unstructured, so standard CNNs cannot be used directly. For this reason, the paper [1] proposes the pioneering network PointNet. The irregular format and envelope invariance of the point set are discussed, and a network that uses point clouds directly is proposed. The method uses a shared MLP as the basic unit of its network. however, the point-like features extracted by the shared MLP cannot capture the local geometric structure and interactions between points in the point cloud. So PointNet++ [2] not only considers global information, but also extends Point-Net [1] with local details of the farthest sampling and grouping layers. Although PointNet++ [2] makes use of the local environment, using only maximum pooling may not aggregate information from local regions well. For better access to contextual features and geometric structures, some works try to use graph networks [18–20] and Recurrent Neural Networks (RNN) [21–23] to implement segmentation. The article [4] proposes an efficient lightweight network Rand-LA for large-scale point cloud segmentation, which utilizes random sampling and achieves very high efficiency in terms of memory and computation, and proposes a local feature aggregation module to capture and preserve geometric features.

3   EEP-Net

In this section, we discuss the EEP module for large-scale point cloud segmentation, which mainly consists of two blocks: Local Representation of Rotation Invariance (LRRI), Attentive Pooling (AP). Then we introduce EEP-Net, which is an encoder-decoder network structure with EEP modules.

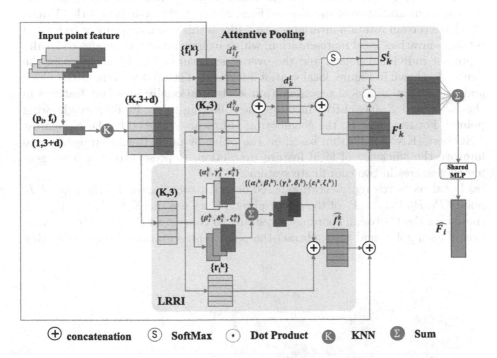

Fig. 1. Architecture of the EEP module.

3.1   Architecture of EEP Module

The architecture of the EEP module is shown in Fig. 1. Given a point cloud P and the features of each point (including spatial information and intermediate learned features), the local features of each point can be learned efficiently using two blocks, LPPR and AP, as shown in Fig. 1. It shows how the local features of a point are learned and applied to each point in parallel. The local space representation constructed by LPPR with XYZ axis rotation invariance is automatically integrated by AP, and we perform LPPR/AP operation twice for the same point to obtain the information of K-squared neighboring points, which can significantly increase the perceptual field of each point and obtain more information. The final output of this module learns the local features with XYZ axis rotation invariance.

Local Representation of Rotation Invariance (LRRI). As a geometric object, the learned representation of a point set should be invariant to rotation transformations. Points rotated together should not modify the global point cloud category, nor the segmentation of points. In many real scenes, such as the common chairs in indoor scenes as shown in the figure below, the orientations of objects belonging to the same category are usually different. Further, it can be clearly understood that the same object is not only represented by the rotation invariance of the Z-axis (Figs. 2(d)(e)), the X-axis and the Y-axis also have certain rotation invariance. To address this issue, we propose to learn a rotation-invariant local representation, which utilizes polar coordinates to locally represent individual points, and the overall structure of LRRI is shown in the figure. As shown in Figure, local spatial information is input into the LRRI block and the output is a local representation with rotationally invariant features in the X, Y, and Z axes. LRRI includes the following steps: Finding neighboring points: For the point P_i, the neighboring points are collected by the K-Nearest Neighbors (KNN) algorithm based on the point-by-point Euclidean distance to improve the efficiency of local feature extraction. Representation of local geometric features in two coordinate systems:
(a) Local geometric representation based on polar coordinates: for the nearest K points $P_1, P_2, P_3, \ldots, P_k$ of the center point P_i, we use the X, Y, Z of each point (based on the Cartesian coordinate system) to convert to the polar representation of each point, and then subtract the polar representation of the neighboring

(a)   (b)   (c)   (d)   (e)   (f)

Fig. 2. Pictures of the same chair from different angles.

points and the center point to obtain the local geometric representation based on polar coordinates, the specific operation is as follows:

1) Local representation is constant for Z-axis rotation:

$$\alpha_i^k = \arctan\left(\frac{y_i^k}{x_i^k}\right) - \arctan\left(\frac{y_{im}}{x_{im}}\right), \tag{1}$$

$$\beta_i^k = \arctan\left(\frac{z_i^k}{\sqrt{x_i^{k^2} + y_i^{k^2}}}\right) - \arctan\left(\frac{z_{im}}{\sqrt{x_{im}^2 + y_{im}^2}}\right). \tag{2}$$

2) Local representation is constant for X-axis rotation:

$$\gamma_i^k = \arctan\left(\frac{z_i^k}{y_i^k}\right) - \arctan\left(\frac{z_{im}}{y_{im}}\right), \tag{3}$$

$$\delta_i^k = \arctan\left(\frac{x_i^k}{\sqrt{z_i^{k^2} + y_i^{k^2}}}\right) - \arctan\left(\frac{x_{im}}{\sqrt{z_{im}^2 + y_{im}^2}}\right). \tag{4}$$

3) Local representation is constant for Y-axis rotation:

$$\epsilon_i^k = \arctan\left(\frac{x_i^k}{z_i^k}\right) - \arctan\left(\frac{x_{im}}{z_{im}}\right), \tag{5}$$

$$\zeta_i^k = \arctan\left(\frac{y_i^k}{\sqrt{x_i^{k^2} + z_i^{k^2}}}\right) - \arctan\left(\frac{y_{im}}{\sqrt{x_{im}^2 + z_{im}^2}}\right). \tag{6}$$

(b) Relative point position encoding: For each of the nearest K points of the centroid P_i, we encode the location of the points as follows:

$$r_i^k = MLP\left(P_i \oplus P_i^k \oplus \left(P_i - P_i^k\right) \oplus \|P_i - P_i^k\|\right). \tag{7}$$

(c) Point Feature Augmentation: The enhanced local geometric representation of a point can be obtained by concatenating the relative position codes of adjacent points and the representation of local geometric features in their corresponding two coordinate systems.

$$\widehat{f_i^k} = MLP\left(\alpha \oplus \beta \oplus \gamma \oplus \delta \oplus \zeta \oplus r_i^k\right). \tag{8}$$

Attentive Pooling (AP). In the previous section, we have given the point cloud local geometric feature representation, most of the existing work for aggregating neighboring features uses max/mean pooing, but this approach leads to most of the information loss, we are inspired by SCF-Net [29] network, our attention pooling consists of the following steps:

(a) Calculate the distance: point features and local geometric features generated by the LRRI block, and neighboring point geometric distances are input to the AP module to learn the contextual features of the local region. We want to express the correlation between points by distance, the closer the distance, the stronger the correlation. Two distances are calculated: geometric distance between points and feature distance between point features:

$$d_{if}^k = \text{mean}(|v(i) - v(k)|), \tag{9}$$

$$\mathbf{d_i^k} = \exp\left(-d_{ig}^k\right) \oplus \lambda \exp\left(-d_{if}^k\right). \tag{10}$$

(b) Calculate the attention score: use a shared MLP to learn the attention score of each feature:

$$\mathbf{A_i^k} = \text{softmax}\left(MLP\left(\mathbf{d_i^k} \oplus \mathbf{f_i^k}\right)\right). \tag{11}$$

(c) Weighted sum: use the learned attention scores to calculate the weighted sum of neighboring point features to learn important local features:

$$F_i^k = MLP\left(f_i^k \oplus \hat{f}_i^k\right), \tag{12}$$

$$\hat{F}_i = \sum_{k=1}^{K} \left(F_i^k \cdot A_i^k\right). \tag{13}$$

To summarize: given the input point cloud, for the i-th point P_i, we learn to aggregate the local features of its K nearest points through two blocks LPPI and AP, and generate a feature vector.

3.2 Global Feature (GF)

To improve the reliability of segmentation, in addition to learning locally relevant features, we borrowed the GF module from SCF-Net to complement the global features. The relationship between position and volume ratio is used.

$$B_i = \frac{V_i}{V_g} \tag{14}$$

where B_i is the volume of the neighborhood's bounding sphere corresponding to P_i, and is the volume of the bounding sphere of the point cloud.

$$\mathbf{f_{iG}} = MLP\left((x_i, y_i, z_i) \oplus B_i\right) \tag{15}$$

The x-y-z coordinate of P_i is used to represent the location of the local neighborhood. Therefore, the global contextual features are defined as f_{iG}.

3.3 Architecture of EEP-Net

In this section, we embed the proposed EEP module into the widely used encoder-decoder architecture, resulting in a new network we named EEP-Net, as shown in Fig. 3. The input of the network is a point cloud of size $N \times d$, where N is the number of points and d is the input feature dimension. The point cloud is first fed to a shared MLP layer to extract the features of each point, and the feature dimension is uniformly set to 8. We use five encoder-decoder layers to learn the features of each point, and finally three consecutive fully connected layers and an exit layer are used to predict the semantic label of each point.

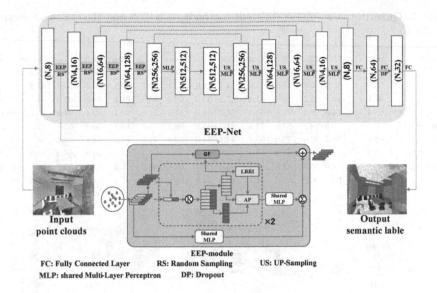

Fig. 3. Architecture of the EEP-Net and the EEP module

4   Experiments

In this section, we evaluate our EEP-Net on a typical indoor field attraction cloud benchmark dataset S3DIS. S3DIS is a large-scale indoor point cloud dataset, which consists of point clouds of 6 areas including 271 rooms. Each point cloud is a medium-sized room, and each point is annotated with one of the semantic labels from 13 classes. Our experiments are performed on Tensorflow (2.1.0). We also report the corresponding results of 8 methods on S3DIS. In addition, after verifying the effectiveness of each module, we focus on ablation experiments on Area 5 of S3DIS.

4.1   Evalution on S3DIS Dataset

We performed six cross-validations to evaluate our method, using mIoU as the criterion, the quantitative results of all reference methods are shown in Table 1, our method mIoU outperforms all other methods on this metric, and achieves the best performance on 2 categories, including clut and sofa. Also near the best performance in other categories. Figure 4 shows the visualization results of a typical indoor scene, including an office and a conference room. In generally, the semantic segmentation of indoor scenes is difficult, and the whiteboard on the white wall is easily confused with the white wall itself, but our network can still identify it more accurately.

Table 1. Quantitative results of different methods on S3DIS and the classwise metric is IoU (%).

Methods	mIoU(%)	Ceil	Floor	Wall	Beam	Col	Wind	Door	Table	Chair	Sofa	Book	Board	Clut
PointNet [1]	47.6	88.0	88.7	69.3	42.4	23.1	47.5	51.6	54.1	42.0	9.6	38.2	29.4	35.2
RSNet [24]	56.5	92.5	92.8	78.6	32.8	34.4	51.6	68.1	59.7	60.1	16.4	50.2	44.9	52.0
SPG [25]	62.1	89.9	95.1	76.4	62.8	47.1	55.3	68.4	73.5	69.2	63.2	45.9	8.7	52.9
PointCNN [26]	65.4	94.8	97.3	75.8	63.3	51.7	58.4	57.2	71.6	69.1	39.1	61.2	52.2	58.6
Pointweb [3]	66.7	93.5	94.2	80.8	52.4	41.3	64.9	68.1	71.4	67.1	50.3	62.7	62.2	58.5
ShellNet [27]	66.8	90.2	93.6	79.9	60.4	44.1	64.9	52.9	71.6	84.7	53.8	64.6	48.6	59.4
RandLA-Net [4]	70.0	93.1	96.1	80.6	62.4	48.0	64.4	69.4	67.4	76.4	60.0	64.2	65.9	60.1
MuGNet [28]	69.8	92.0	95.7	82.5	64.4	60.1	60.7	69.7	82.6	70.3	64.4	52.1	52.8	60.6
Ours	**70.9**	93.3	96.0	80.6	61.8	46.4	64.4	68.1	69.9	82.0	68.5	63.4	65.4	61.5

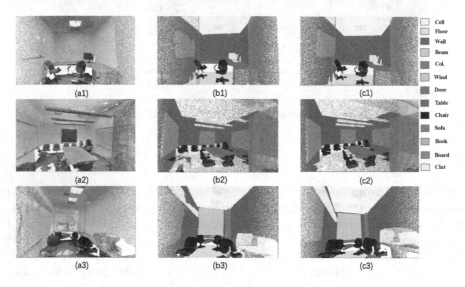

Fig. 4. Visualization examples of three typical indoor scenes on S3DIS. (a) RGB colored input point clouds, (b) Predictions obtained via the proposed EEP-Net, (c) Ground truths.

4.2 Ablation Study

The experimental results on the S3DIS dataset validate the effectiveness of our proposed method, and in order to better understand the network, we evaluate it and conduct the following experiments, which will be performed on Area 5, the location of the S3DIS dataset, for this set of experiments. As shown in Fig. 5, it is easy to see that the segmentation result of (d) is obviously closer to the ground truth than (c), which proves that the performance of EEP-Net is better than that of the network containing only Z-axis rotation invariance Table 2.

Table 2. The mean IoU scores of all ablated networks based on our full EEP-Net.

	mIoU(%)
(1) Rotational invariance for Z-axis only	63.04
(2) Local relative feature + Z-axis rotation invariance	63.38
(3) Rotational invariance of $X - Y - Z$ axes	63.84
(4) Local relative feature + $X - Y - Z$ axis rotation invariance	**64.00**

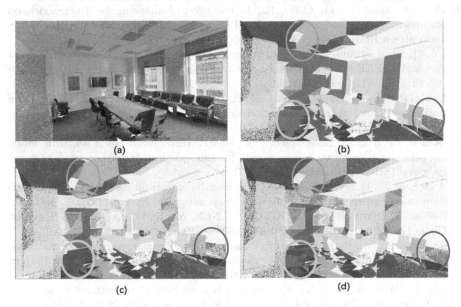

Fig. 5. Visualization example on S3DIS Area 5, (a) RGB color input point cloud, (b) ground truth, (c) network segmentation result with only Z-axis rotation invariance, (d) EEP-Net segmentation result. The circles of the same color are the comparison of segmentation results of the same region.

5   Conclusion

In this paper, to better learn local contextual features of point clouds, we propose a new local feature aggregation module EEP, which works by representing point clouds from Cartesian coordinates to polar coordinates of local regions. To verify the effectiveness of the method, we conduct experiments on the representative dataset S3DIS, and compare with eight methods to verify the advanced nature of our method. And we conduct ablation experiments on Area 5 of S3DIS to verify the effectiveness of EEP-Net.

Acknowledgments. This work was supported by the National Natural Science Foundation of China (nos.U21A20487, U1913202, U1813205), CAS Key Technology Talent Program, Shenzhen Technology Project (nos. JSGG20191129094012321, JCYJ20180507182610734)

References

1. Qi, C., Su, H., Mo, K., Guibas, L.J.: PointNet: Deep learning on point sets for 3D classification and segmentation. In: IEEE/CVF Conference on Computer Vision and Pattern Recognition (CVPR), pp. 77–85 (2017)
2. Qi, C., Yi, L., Su, H., Guibas, L.J.: PointNet++: Deep hierarchical feature learning on point sets in a metric space. In: Conference and Workshop on Neural Information Processing Systems (NIPS) (2017)
3. Zhao, H., Jiang, L., Fu, C.W., Jia, J.: PointWeb: Enhancing local neighborhood features for point cloud processing. In: IEEE/CVF Conference on Computer Vision and Pattern Recognition (CVPR), pp. 5560–5568 (2019)
4. Hu, Q., et al.: RandLA-Net: Efficient semantic segmentation of large-scale point clouds. In: IEEE/CVF Conference on Computer Vision and Pattern Recognition (CVPR), pp. 11105–11114 (2020)
5. Lawin, F.J., Danelljan, M., Tosteberg, P., Bhat, G., Khan, F.S., Felsberg, M.: Deep projective 3D semantic segmentation. In: International Conference on Computer Analysis of Images and Patterns (CAIP) (2017)
6. Boulch, A., Saux, B.L., Audebert, N.: Unstructured point cloud semantic labeling using deep segmentation networks. In: Eurographics Workshop on 3D Object Retrieval (3DOR)@Eurographics (2017)
7. Audebert, N., Le Saux, B., Lefèvre, S.: Semantic segmentation of earth observation data using multimodal and multi-scale deep networks. In: Lai, S.-H., Lepetit, V., Nishino, K., Sato, Y. (eds.) ACCV 2016. LNCS, vol. 10111, pp. 180–196. Springer, Cham (2017). https://doi.org/10.1007/978-3-319-54181-5_12
8. Tatarchenko, M., Park, J., Koltun, V., Zhou, Q.Y.: Tangent convolutions for dense prediction in 3D. In: IEEE/CVF Conference on Computer Vision and Pattern Recognition (CVPR), pp. 3887–3896 (2018)
9. Wu, B., Wan, A., Yue, X., Keutzer, K.: SqueezeSeg: Convolutional neural nets with recurrent CRF for real-time road-object segmentation from 3D Lidar point cloud. In: IEEE International Conference on Robotics and Automation (ICRA), pp. 1887–1893 (2018)
10. Wu, B., Zhou, X., Zhao, S., Yue, X., Keutzer, K.: Squeezesegv 2: Improved model structure and unsupervised domain adaptation for road-object segmentation from a Lidar point cloud. In: International Conference on Robotics and Automation (ICRA), pp. 4376–4382 (2019)
11. Landola, F.N., Moskewicz, M.W., Ashraf, K., Han, S., Dally, W.J., Keutzer, K.: SqueezeNet: AlexNet-level accuracy with 50x fewer parameters and <1mb model size. ArXiv abs/1602.07360 (2016)
12. Milioto, A., Vizzo, I., Behley, J., Stachniss, C.: RangeNet ++: Fast and accurate Lidar semantic segmentation. In: IEEE/RSJ International Conference on Intelligent Robots and Systems (IROS), pp. 4213–4220 (2019)
13. Meng, H.Y., Gao, L., Lai, Y.K., Manocha, D.: VV-Net: Voxel VAE-Net with group convolutions for point cloud segmentation. In: IEEE/CVF International Conference on Computer Vision (ICCV), pp. 8499–8507 (2019)
14. Rethage, D., Wald, J., Sturm, J., Navab, N., Tombari, F.: Fully-convolutional point networks for large-scale point clouds. ArXiv abs/1808.06840 (2018)
15. Huang, J., You, S.: Point cloud labeling using 3D convolutional neural network. In: 23rd International Conference on Pattern Recognition (ICPR), pp. 2670–2675 (2016)

16. Tchapmi, L.P., Choy, C.B., Armeni, I., Gwak, J., Savarese, S.: SEGCloud: semantic segmentation of 3D point clouds. In: International Conference on 3D Vision (3DV), pp. 537–547 (2017)

17. Shelhamer, E., Long, J., Darrell, T.: Fully convolutional networks for semantic segmentation. In: IEEE Transactions on Pattern Analysis and Machine Intelligence (TPAMI) vol. 39(4), pp. 640–651 (2017)

18. Landrieu, L., Simonovsky, M.: Large-scale point cloud semantic segmentation with superpoint graphs. In: IEEE/CVF Conference on Computer Vision and Pattern Recognition (CVPR), pp. 4558–4567 (2018)

19. Landrieu, L., Boussaha, M.: Point Cloud oversegmentation with graph structured deep metric learning. In: IEEE/CVF Conference on Computer Vision and Pattern Recognition (CVPR), pp. 7432–7441 (2019)

20. Wang, L., Huang, Y., Hou, Y., Zhang, S., Shan, J.: Graph attention convolution for point cloud semantic segmentation. In: IEEE/CVF Conference on Computer Vision and Pattern Recognition (CVPR), pp. 10288–10297 (2019)

21. Ye, X., Li, J., Huang, H., Du, L., Zhang, X.: 3D recurrent neural networks with context fusion for point cloud semantic segmentation. In: European Conference on Computer Vision (ECCV), pp. 403–417 (2018)

22. Huang, Q., Wang, W., Neumann, U.: Recurrent slice networks for 3D segmentation of point clouds. In: IEEE/CVF Conference on Computer Vision and Pattern Recognition (CVPR), pp. 2626–2635 (2018)

23. Liu, F., et al.: 3DCNN-DQN-RNN: A deep reinforcement learning framework for semantic parsing of large-scale 3D point clouds. In: IEEE International Conference on Computer Vision (ICCV), pp. 5679–5688 (2017)

24. Huang, Q., Wang, W., Neumann, U.: Recurrent slice networks for 3D segmentation of point clouds. In: IEEE/CVF Conference on Computer Vision and Pattern Recognition (CVPR), pp. 2626–2635 (2018)

25. Landrieu, L., Simonovsky, M.: Large-scale point cloud semantic segmentation with superpoint graphs. In: IEEE/CVF Conference on Computer Vision and Pattern Recognition (CVPR), pp. 4558–4567 (2018)

26. Li, Y., Bu, R., Sun, M., Wu, W., Di, X., Chen, B.: PointCNN: Convolution on x-transformed points. In: Conference and Workshop on Neural Information Processing Systems (NIPS), pp. 820–830 (2018)

27. Zhang, Z., Hua, B.S., Yeung, S.K.: ShellNet: Efficient point cloud convolutional neural networks using concentric shells statistics. In: IEEE/CVF International Conference on Computer Vision (ICCV), pp. 1607–1616 (2019)

28. Xie L., Furuhata T., Shimada K.: Multi-resolution graph neural network for large-scale point cloud segmentation. arXiv preprint arXiv:2009.08924 (2020)

29. Fan, S., Dong, Q., Zhu, F., Lv, Y., Ye, P., Wang, F.: SCF-Net: Learning spatial contextual features for large-scale point cloud segmentation. In: IEEE/CVF Conference on Computer Vision and Pattern Recognition (CVPR), pp. 14499–14508 (2020)

CARR-Net: Leveraging on Subtle Variance of Neighbors for Point Cloud Semantic Segmentation

Mingming Song[✉], Bin Fan, and Hongmin Liu

University of Science and Technology Beijing, Beijing 100083, China
mmsong98@163.com, bin.fan@ieee.org

Abstract. For 3D semantic segmentation task, how to fully explore intrinsic feature of point cloud is worthy to be well considered. We note that neighboring points used for representing local structure of a 3D point are usually very close to the point which means that network is difficult to distinguish different neighbors according to relative relation. This paper proposes a Combination of Absolute and Relative Representations (CARR) module to acquire more discriminative information by combining relative relations after magnifying subtle variance in both geometric and feature space. Subsequently, attention pooling and max pooling are used to aggregate contextual features. With the proposed CARR module, our network can accurately perceive subtle variety of local structures which is important for semantic segmentation. Besides, we use max Euclidean distances of local structures and sub-global module to further improve network's performance. Experiments show that our network performs well on two typical benchmarks, S3DIS and SemanticKITTI. Ablation studies also demonstrate the effectiveness of each component.

Keywords: Point cloud · Semantic segmentation · CARR module

1 Introduction

With the development and popularity of LIDAR device, the acquisition of point cloud data becomes increasingly easy. Compared with images, point cloud is equipped with sufficient geometry information from object surface which can provide important clues for many 3D tasks such as semantic segmentation, object detection and shape classification. That is also the reason why point cloud is widely applied in autonomous driving, robotics, augmented reality, etc.

However, disorder and irregularity of point cloud leads to that direct processing of it is intractable. To solve this problem, many indirect methods [15,21] transforming point cloud to multi-view images or regular grids have been proposed. They utilize well-developed Convolution Neural Networks (CNNs) to achieve specific task. Although these works avoid difficult problem of processing point cloud directly, they suffer from self-occlusion, information loss or computationally inefficient.

S. Yu et al. (Eds.): PRCV 2022, LNCS 13536, pp. 124–136, 2022.
https://doi.org/10.1007/978-3-031-18913-5_10

PointNet [18], the first deep-learning method directly using raw point cloud as input, successfully achieves point permutation invariance by using Multi-Layer Perception (MLP) and a symmetric function - max pooling. PointNet++ [19] adopts a hierarchical architecture that applies PointNet recursively to capture local structure of each point. Subsequently, many works [4,7,12,20,31] with increasing segmentation accuracy have been introduced. Inspired by these works, we propose CARR-Net, a point-based model.

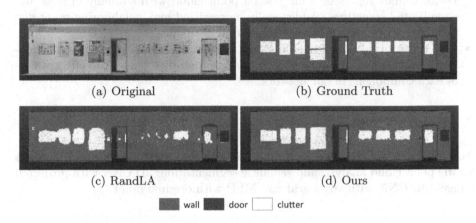

(a) Original   (b) Ground Truth

(c) RandLA   (d) Ours

wall   door   clutter

Fig. 1. It is a hallway in S3DIS Area 5. RandLA-Net [7] cannot rightly classify clutter on the wall while our network recognizes them successfully.

As we all know, the perception of local structures is very critical for network to correctly predict the semantic category of a 3D point. There are tremendous works [9,11,14,23,24,26] adopting different forms of kernel convolution to aggregate contextual information. However, except KPConv [23], other models' performance is not so good. It could be inferred that such complex kernel-based methods fail to fully explore local structures.

Usually, each input point's local structure is represented with relative relation between itself and neighbors. However, such relative relation, in terms of either geometric or high-level feature representation, among neighbors are very close which will prevent the network from acquiring effective and discriminative information from it. We find that normalizing this relative relation can magnify differences among neighbors which further reflect intrinsic local structures. Therefore, we propose to combine original and normalized relative relations, namely absolute and relative representations, to provide the network with more sufficient and effective feature information. Subsequently, contextual features will be aggregated by attention pooling and max pooling. In addition, sub-global module between encoder and decoder and max Euclidean distances of local structures are adopted to further enhance segmentation performance.

Figure 1 compares the segmentation results of our method and a popular learning method in the literature, i.e., RandLA-Net [7]. Our contributions can be summarized as:

- We encode geometric and semantic relative relations as absolute representation of local structures. Since there are only subtle variances among such absolution representations of different neighbors, we further encode the normalized relative representation to magnify the subtle differences among neighbors. By combining these two representations, our network can accurately perceive local structures to improve final segmentation performance.
- We take sub-global information into account since one dimensional global vector cannot represent a large scale point cloud with so many objects and complicated structures. Additionally, normalized max neighboring point distance we adopt can effectively improve performance.
- Experimental results on S3DIS [1] and SemanticKITTI [2] demonstrate superior performances of our approach. Ablation studies reflect the effectiveness of each component in our network.

2   Related Work

According the ways to deal with point cloud, there are three types of methods for 3D point cloud analysis and semantic segmentation: 2D CNN with projected images, 3D CNN with voxel grid and MLP with original point.

Projected Image and Voxel Grid. Some of these models [13,17,25,27,29,30] project point cloud to 2D point image and utilize well-developed 2D Convolution Neural Networks for point cloud analysis while others [5,10,16,22,32] convert point cloud into 3D voxel-grid representation to make use of powerful 3D CNNs.

In addition, many models [3,8,28] adopt mixed inputs to jointly predict segmentation results. Among them, BPNets [8] uses 2D images and 3D voxels while [3,28] use points and voxels. Although they achieve leading results, these methods not only need preprocessing but also have to project results back to the original point cloud which is inconvenient and with information loss. That is the reason why we choose original point cloud as the direct input of the network.

Original Point. PointNet [18] is the first deep-learning method adopting original point cloud as input, which realizes input order invariance with a max pooling function and point-wise feature extraction. Based on it, PointNet++ [19] pays more attention to local feature extraction with a hierarchical structure. Besides, multi-scales features are combined together to deal with non-uniform density of point cloud.

Inspired by 2D CNN, lots of existing works extract local features by irregular convolutions exclusively designed for point cloud [9,11,14,23,24,26]. PCCN [24] achieves a parametric continuous convolution with MLP. KPConv [23] builds a kernel consisting of a series of points regularly distributed in 3D Euclidean space, and the values of kernel points only act on the input points close to them. Although these methods achieve impressive results, they cannot be extended to deal with large-scale point cloud semantic segmentation.

RandLA-Net [7] adopts random sampling and classical encoder-decoder architecture to directly and efficiently process large-scale point cloud. Subsequently, SCF-Net [4] introduces local polar representation and dual-distance attentive pooling to automatically learn effective local features. Although random sampling makes these methods achieve high efficiency, it also sacrifices their accuracy and stability.

BAAF-Net [20] and Point Transformer [31] both adopt Farthest Point Sampling (FPS) and achieve competitive segmentation performance. BAAF-Net fully utilizes geometric and semantic features through a bilateral structure and adaptively fuses multi-resolution features to obtain a comprehensive representation. Point Transformer applies self-attention blocks with positional encoding instead of the classical MLP to construct the whole network.

However, these methods still fail to fully explore intrinsic local structures of point cloud and do not encode global information. We propose CARR module to well perceive contextual information of each input point by combining two types of information representations. Since we aim to process large-scale point cloud, we cannot find an effective global vector to represent the whole point cloud. Hence, we adopt sub-global information instead which can also achieve similar effect.

3 Method

Local and global information of each input point is both vital to the final prediction. How to extract and utilize these information is worthy to be further considered. Our network pays attention to local structures of point cloud and properly adds global information to assist prediction. Details will be elaborated in the following sections.

3.1 CARR Module

For fully perceiving local structures, our CARR module endeavors to excavate the relations between each point and its neighboring points by combining absolute and relative representations. Specifically, we describe a point cloud containing N points from two aspects: 1) the inherent coordinates $\mathcal{P} \in \mathbb{R}^{N \times 3}$ in 3D geometric space; and 2) the semantic features $\mathcal{F} \in \mathbb{R}^{N \times d}$ that the network learns in high dimensional feature space. For a centroid p_i, $\mathcal{N}(p_i)$ is the set of its k nearest neighboring points.

Absolute Representation. As shown in Fig. 2, the absolute representation $\mathcal{G}$ $[\mathcal{G}(p_i), \mathcal{G}(f_i)]$ we build contains differences (Δ), Euclidean distance (euc) and Cosine distance (cos) between the center point p_i and each neighboring point $p_j \in \mathcal{N}(p_i)$. We group them respectively in geometric and feature space.

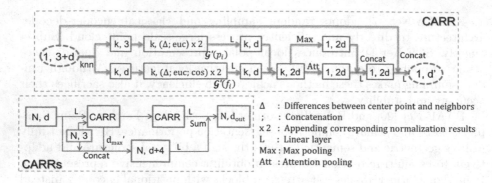

Fig. 2. The details of our CARR module (top) and encoder layer CARRs (bottom).

In particular, absolute representation $\mathcal{G}(p_i)$ in geometric space is defined as:

$$\mathcal{G}(p_i) = (p_i - p_j) \oplus euc(p_i, p_j), \quad \mathcal{G}(p_i) \in \mathbb{R}^{k \times 4}; \tag{1}$$

where p_i and p_j are the x-y-z coordinates of points, $\oplus$ means concatenation, $euc()$ calculates the Euclidean distance between two points and k is the number of neighbors.

In feature space, we append the Cosine distance between features of center point f_i and neighbors f_j to absolute representation $\mathcal{G}(f_i)$ since it can provide extra effective information for the network:

$$\mathcal{G}(f_i) = (f_i - f_j) \oplus euc(f_i, f_j) \oplus cos(f_i, f_j), \quad \mathcal{G}(f_i) \in \mathbb{R}^{k \times (d+2)}; \tag{2}$$

where $f_i, f_j \in \mathbb{R}^d$ and $cos()$ means the Cosine distance between two points.

Combined Representations. Considering the k nearest neighboring points are mostly very close to the center point, their coordinates are proximate and absolute representation $\mathcal{G}(p_i)$ is less discriminative among these neighbors. By normalization of these k neighboring points, we can acquire magnifying-differences relative representation which can provide the network with more information.

While in feature space, features of neighbors are similar sometimes and have significant difference sometimes. Normalization can accordingly magnifying or narrowing this difference. Both absolute and relative representations provide the network with sufficient and complementary contextual information.

Specifically, encoded geometry information $\mathcal{G}'(p_i)$, namely results after combining absolute and relative representations in geometric space, is formulated as:

$$\mathcal{G}'(p_i) = \mathcal{G}(p_i) \oplus Normal(\mathcal{G}(p_i)), \quad \mathcal{G}'(p_i) \in \mathbb{R}^{k \times 8} \tag{3}$$

where $Normal$ means min-max normalization operation for k neighbors.

Accordingly, encoded semantic information is formulated as:

$$\mathcal{G}'(f_i) = \mathcal{G}(f_i) \oplus Normal(\mathcal{G}(f_i)), \quad \mathcal{G}'(f_i) \in \mathbb{R}^{k \times (2d+4)}. \tag{4}$$

Encoded geometry and semantic features, $\mathcal{G}'(p_i), \mathcal{G}'(f_i)$, will be concatenated and processed by attention pooling [7] and max pooling to acquire contextual information of every center point. Attention pooling refers we use the weights which are learned from features itself to aggregate these features. As a result, we can acquire more informative semantic features of the current point by combining its original input features and learned local features.

3.2 CARRs

Each layer in encoder is a residual block with two CARR modules, namely CARRs, as shown in Fig. 2. Different from conventional residual connection, we add coordinate and distance information to residual branch.

Specifically, the max Euclidean distance (d_{max}) to center point among k neighboring points can indirectly reflect the local density of this center point. Together with the point coordinates, it could provide some extra information for the network to distinguish different semantic points. Since the values of d_{max} are all small, we utilize its normalized value d_{max}' for N points in the network.

3.3 Overall Architecture

Our network adopts the standard encoder-decoder architecture and acquire lower-resolution point cloud by farthest point sampling (FPS) [19], as illustrated in Fig. 3. Firstly, we introduce data augmentation during training, including scaling with ratio between 0.8 and 1.2, z-axis rotation, symmetry and jitter operations.

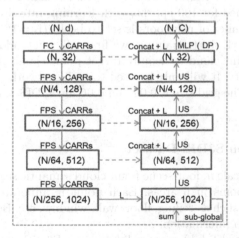

Fig. 3. Overall architecture of our CARR-Net. FPS: Farthest Point Sampling, DP: Dropout.

Secondly, because input point cloud is too large, we cannot find a one dimensional global vector to represent complicated scene with so many different objects. Thus we turn to extract sub-global information. On the basis of current features, max-pooling results of k neighboring points' features will be added, as shown in the bottom right corner of Fig. 3. Since comprising current point's background information, they will help network make correct decisions.

Finally, there are residual connections [6] between corresponding layers of encoder and decoder to speed up network convergence. In every down-sampling stage of encoder, we will build a nearest neighboring index matrix relative to down-sampled point cloud for the input point cloud. During decoder stage, we implement up-sampling operation by these preserved matrices successively to obtain feature representation of the initial points. Subsequently, three consecutive fully-connected layers are used to predict the semantic labels and there is a dropout layer before the last linear layer to reduce overfitting.

4   Experiments

In this section, we first introduce some basic settings of the whole network. Subsequently, we evaluate our CARR-Net on two typical semantic segmentation benchmarks, S3DIS [1] and SemanticKITTI [2]. Finally, we demonstrate the corresponding ablation experiments to prove rationality of our hyper-parameter setting and necessity of some key modules.

4.1   Set up

All experiments are conducted on an NVIDIA RTX 3090 GPU. We use the Adam optimizer with an initial learning rate of 0.01. The batch size is 6 and each epoch has 500, 3000 iterations for S3DIS and SemanticKITTI, respectively. The network is trained for 100 epochs, with learning rate dropped by 5% after each epoch. The number of neighbors is set to be 16 (K = 16).

Before the network starts training, we first will put grid-subsampling operation on original point cloud to acquire target point cloud with more balanced distribution of density. It will only be used to train network and we still test on entire point cloud. The grid size is 0.04 and 0.06 for S3DIS and SemanticKITTI, respectively.

4.2   Evaluation on S3DIS Dataset

S3DIS [1] is a large-scale indoor-scene point cloud semantic segmentation dataset consisting of 272 rooms in 6 areas. Each point is annotated with one of 13 semantic categories, such as ceiling, floor, wall, window, etc. Besides, this dataset provides xyz and rgb information.

We adopt standard 6-fold cross validation on S3DIS dataset to verify our model's effectiveness. Table 1 provides quantitative results of representative methods since 2017 and ours. We can see that our model's mIOU and mAcc both reach state of the art and mIOU surpasses suboptimal method with a large margin. Although OA is not the best, it is just a little bit lower than the best one while 1% higher than the third one. These quantitative numbers demonstrate our model's effectiveness on indoor semantic segmentation dataset.

Table 1. Semantic Segmentation results on S3DIS dataset [1] (6-fold cross validation). **OA**: Overall Accuracy, **mAcc**: mean class Accuracy, **mIOU**: mean Intersection-over-Union.

Year	Method	OA	mAcc	mIOU
2017	PointNet [18]	78.6	66.2	47.6
	PointNet++ [19]	81.0	67.1	54.5
2018	PointCNN [11]	88.1	75.6	65.4
2019	KPConv [23]	-	79.1	70.6
2020	RandLA-Net [7]	88.0	82.0	70.0
2021	SCF-Net [4]	88.4	82.7	71.6
	BAAF-Net [20]	88.9	83.1	72.2
	Point Transformer [31]	**90.2**	81.9	73.5
	CARR-Net (Ours)	89.9	**83.7**	**74.4**

Table 2. Detailed Semantic Segmentation results of our model on each area of S3DIS dataset [1]. **All**: 6-fold cross validation results. **Area x** means Area x is test set while other areas is training set

Test area	mIOU	ceil.	floor	wall	beam	col.	wind.	door	table	chair	sofa	book.	board	clut.
Area 1	77.3	96.3	95.8	81.5	53.5	63.1	82.5	87.2	71.2	85.2	78.3	65.7	72.2	72.0
Area 2	65.2	88.0	96.5	83.2	23.8	66.4	68.1	76.8	58.7	66.1	78.2	53.5	37.9	50.3
Area 3	81.0	95.6	98.3	83.7	71.3	24.2	91.3	90.3	79.7	87.3	89.2	77.2	89.7	75.4
Area 4	68.1	96.0	97.8	81.6	48.9	57.6	48.0	66.5	70.6	80.5	65.9	59.0	47.5	65.0
Area 5	69.0	93.9	98.1	84.0	0.0	33.0	62.1	65.4	82.2	90.1	76.0	76.0	76.9	59.5
Area 6	82.8	96.5	97.7	87.0	82.1	78.6	81.7	90.3	78.0	89.6	71.2	72.8	76.7	73.9
All	74.4	93.9	97.4	83.5	59.9	55.0	68.9	76.7	75.4	78.9	75.7	69.3	68.7	63.7

Moreover, for fully presenting the performance of our model, Table 2 provides our results for each area in the S3DIS dataset, including mIOU and IOUs of each category.

4.3   Evaluation on SemanticKITTI Dataset

We also validate our network on SemanticKITTI [2], an outdoor driving scene point cloud dataset. It consists of 22 sequences and each point is annotated with one of the semantic labels from 13 categories, such as vegetation, road, building and car.

As shown in Table 3, we compare online testing results of our network and some recent published point-based methods. It can be seen that our CARR-Net surpasses other models in term of mIOU and behaves the best in most classes. Besides, Fig. 4 presents some qualitative results of our network on the validation split, sequence 08.

Table 3. Semantic Segmentation results on SemanticKITTI dataset [2]. Red means the best performances of each class and mIOU.

Method	mIOU	car	bicycle	motorcycle	truck	other-vehicle	person	bicyclist	motorcyclist	road	parking	sidewalk	other-ground	building	fence	vegetation	trunk	terrain	pole	traffic-sign
PointNet [18]	14.6	46.3	1.3	0.3	4.6	0.8	0.2	0.2	0.0	61.6	15.8	35.7	1.4	41.4	12.9	31.0	0.1	17.6	2.4	3.7
PointNet++ [19]	20.1	53.7	1.9	0.2	13.8	0.2	0.9	1.0	0.0	72.0	18.7	41.8	5.6	62.3	16.9	46.5	0.9	30.0	6.0	8.9
KPConv [23]	58.8	96.0	30.2	42.5	33.4	44.3	61.5	61.6	11.8	88.8	61.3	72.7	31.6	90.5	64.2	84.8	69.2	69.1	56.4	47.4
RandLA-Net [7]	53.9	94.2	26.0	25.8	61.3	38.9	49.2	48.2	7.2	90.7	60.3	73.7	20.4	86.9	56.3	81.4	40.1	66.8	49.2	47.7
BAAF-Net [20]	59.9	95.4	31.8	35.5	63.4	46.7	49.5	55.7	53.0	90.9	62.2	74.4	23.6	89.8	60.8	82.7	48.7	67.9	53.7	52.0
CARR-Net (Ours)	60.2	95.4	39.8	39.7	56.4	41.3	56.5	56.7	10.3	90.0	64.3	74.7	32.2	91.7	66.1	82.9	66.0	68.2	56.9	55.5

4.4   Ablation Study

To better understand our network, we further evaluate it and conduct the following ablation studies. These experiments are tested on Area 5 of S3DIS dataset [1].

Table 4. Ablation study about different modules of our network.

ID	Model	Parameters	mIOU
I	Only absolute representation	6.8 M	66.1
II	Only relative representation	6.8 M	66.7
III	CARR Module = 1	5.4 M	65.8
IV	Removing d_{max}'	6.9 M	67.8
V	Removing sub-global information	6.9 M	66.2
VI	Removing Cosine distance in $\mathcal{G}(f_i)$	6.9 M	68.3
VII	**Proposed model**	**6.9 M**	**69.0**

CARR Module. Both absolute and relative representations in CARR module are important for our network. We conduct ablation experiments to prove it, and the results are shown by I and II in Table 4. We can see that when only absolute or relative representation is used, network's performance decreases by a large margin which thus demonstrates the necessity of using these two parts together.

The Number of CARR Modules. About the number of CARR modules for each encoder layer, two is the necessary condition of ensuring performance with acceptable computation cost. As shown by III in Table 4, the removal of one CARR module diminishes performance a lot by not being able to provide sufficient local information for the network.

Necessity of d_{max}', sub-global information and Cosine distance in $\mathcal{G}(f_i)$
In Table 4, IV, V and VI present the results after removing d_{max}', sub-global

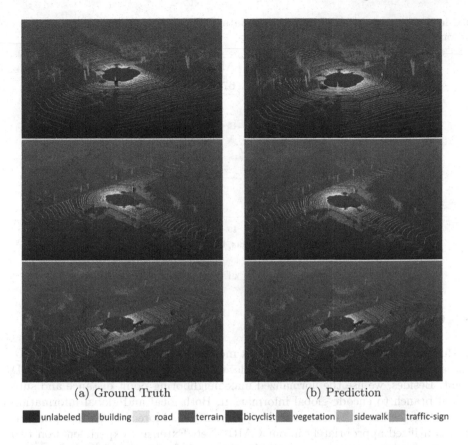

(a) Ground Truth   (b) Prediction

■ unlabeled ■ building □ road ■ terrain ■ bicyclist ■ vegetation □ sidewalk ■ traffic-sign

Fig. 4. Qualitative results of our network on SemanticKITTI [2].

information or Cosine distance in $\mathcal{G}(f_i)$. From the results, we can infer that d_{max}' and Cosine distance provide effective information for the network while sub-global information has greater contribution.

Data Augmentation. We use data augmentation only during training while keep the original input during validation and testing. Quantitative results in Table 5 reveals effectiveness of our strategy.

The Number of Neighbors. K, the number of neighbors, reflects the size of local structures that the network integrates. Increasing the value of k, receptive field and the computation cost will increase accordingly. Considering both efficiency and effectiveness, we choose k = 16. As can been seen from Fig. 5, within affordable time cost, the performance of k = 16 is the best.

Table 5. Comparison of different ways of data augmentation. All-aug means augmentation for training, validation and test sets.

Model	Train-aug	All-aug	No aug
mIOU	69.0	67.4	68.4

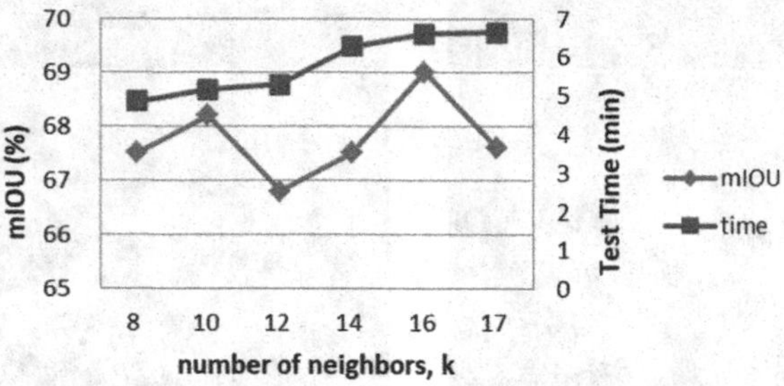

Fig. 5. Test time and mIOU of models with different k.

5   Conclusion

In this paper, we propose a novel CARR module, namely Combination of Absolute and Relative Representations module, to fully perceive local structure of 3D point. Besides, we use the normalized max neighboring point distance and subglobal branch to encode global information. Both local and global information works together to enhance network's performance. Moreover, data augmentation is utilized appropriately in our CARR-Net. Extensive experiments on two benchmarks demonstrate our network's effectiveness on both indoor and outdoor datasets.

Acknowledgement. This work is supported by the National Natural Science Foundation of China (62076026, 61973029, U2013202).

References

1. Armeni, I., et al.: 3D semantic parsing of large-scale indoor spaces. In: Proceedings of the IEEE Conference on Computer Vision and Pattern Recognition, pp. 1534–1543 (2016)
2. Behley, J., et al.: Semantickitti: A dataset for semantic scene understanding of lidar sequences. In: Proceedings of the IEEE/CVF International Conference on Computer Vision, pp. 9297–9307 (2019)
3. Cheng, R., Razani, R., Taghavi, E., Li, E., Liu, B.: 2–s3Net: Attentive feature fusion with adaptive feature selection for sparse semantic segmentation network. In: Proceedings of the IEEE/CVF Conference on Computer Vision and Pattern Recognition, pp. 12547–12556 (2021)

4. Fan, S., Dong, Q., Zhu, F., Lv, Y., Ye, P., Wang, F.Y.: SCF-Net: Learning spatial contextual features for large-scale point cloud segmentation. In: Proceedings of the IEEE/CVF Conference on Computer Vision and Pattern Recognition, pp. 14504–14513 (2021)
5. Graham, B., Engelcke, M., Van Der Maaten, L.: 3D semantic segmentation with submanifold sparse convolutional networks. In: Proceedings of the IEEE Conference on Computer Vision and Pattern Recognition, pp. 9224–9232 (2018)
6. He, K., Zhang, X., Ren, S., Sun, J.: Deep residual learning for image recognition. In: Proceedings of the IEEE Conference on Computer Vision and Pattern Recognition, pp. 770–778 (2016)
7. Hu, Q., et al.: Randla-Net: Efficient semantic segmentation of large-scale point clouds. In: Proceedings of the IEEE/CVF Conference on Computer Vision and Pattern Recognition, pp. 11108–11117 (2020)
8. Hu, W., Zhao, H., Jiang, L., Jia, J., Wong, T.T.: Bidirectional projection network for cross dimension scene understanding. In: Proceedings of the IEEE/CVF Conference on Computer Vision and Pattern Recognition, pp. 14373–14382 (2021)
9. Hua, B.S., Tran, M.K., Yeung, S.K.: Pointwise convolutional neural networks. In: Proceedings of the IEEE Conference on Computer Vision and Pattern Recognition, pp. 984–993 (2018)
10. Le, T., Duan, Y.: PointGrid: A deep network for 3D shape understanding. In: Proceedings of the IEEE Conference on Computer Vision and Pattern Recognition, pp. 9204–9214 (2018)
11. Li, Y., Bu, R., Sun, M., Wu, W., Di, X., Chen, B.: PointCNN: Convolution on X-transformed points. In: Advances in Neural Information Processing Systems, vol. 31 (2018)
12. Liu, Y., Fan, B., Xiang, S., Pan, C.: Relation-shape convolutional neural network for point cloud analysis. In: Proceedings of the IEEE/CVF Conference on Computer Vision and Pattern Recognition, pp. 8895–8904 (2019)
13. Lyu, Y., Huang, X., Zhang, Z.: Learning to segment 3d point clouds in 2d image space. In: Proceedings of the IEEE/CVF Conference on Computer Vision and Pattern Recognition, pp. 12255–12264 (2020)
14. Mao, J., Wang, X., Li, H.: Interpolated convolutional networks for 3d point cloud understanding. In: Proceedings of the IEEE/CVF International Conference on Computer Vision, pp. 1578–1587 (2019)
15. Maturana, D., Scherer, S.: Voxnet: A 3d convolutional neural network for real-time object recognition. In: 2015 IEEE/RSJ International Conference on Intelligent Robots and Systems (IROS), pp. 922–928. IEEE (2015)
16. Meng, H.Y., Gao, L., Lai, Y.K., Manocha, D.: VV-Net: Voxel VAE Net with group convolutions for point cloud segmentation. In: Proceedings of the IEEE/CVF International Conference on Computer Vision, pp. 8500–8508 (2019)
17. Milioto, A., Vizzo, I., Behley, J., Stachniss, C.: RangeNet++: Fast and accurate lidar semantic segmentation. In: 2019 IEEE/RSJ International Conference on Intelligent Robots and Systems (IROS), pp. 4213–4220. IEEE (2019)
18. Qi, C.R., Su, H., Mo, K., Guibas, L.J.: PointNet: Deep learning on point sets for 3D classification and segmentation. In: Proceedings of the IEEE Conference on Computer Vision and Pattern Recognition, pp. 652–660 (2017)
19. Qi, C.R., Yi, L., Su, H., Guibas, L.J.: PointNet++: Deep hierarchical feature learning on point sets in a metric space. In: Advances in Neural Information Processing Systems, 30 (2017)

20. Qiu, S., Anwar, S., Barnes, N.: Semantic segmentation for real point cloud scenes via bilateral augmentation and adaptive fusion. In: Proceedings of the IEEE/CVF Conference on Computer Vision and Pattern Recognition, pp. 1757–1767 (2021)
21. Su, H., Maji, S., Kalogerakis, E., Learned-Miller, E.: Multi-view convolutional neural networks for 3d shape recognition. In: Proceedings of the IEEE International Conference on Computer Vision, pp. 945–953 (2015)
22. Tchapmi, L., Choy, C., Armeni, I., Gwak, J., Savarese, S.: SEGCloud: Semantic segmentation of 3D point clouds. In: 2017 International Conference on 3D Vision (3DV), pp. 537–547. IEEE (2017)
23. Thomas, H., Qi, C.R., Deschaud, J.E., Marcotegui, B., Goulette, F., Guibas, L.J.: KPConv: Flexible and deformable convolution for point clouds. In: Proceedings of the IEEE/CVF International Conference on Computer Vision, pp. 6411–6420 (2019)
24. Wang, S., Suo, S., Ma, W.C., Pokrovsky, A., Urtasun, R.: Deep parametric continuous convolutional neural networks. In: Proceedings of the IEEE Conference on Computer Vision and Pattern Recognition, pp. 2589–2597 (2018)
25. Wu, B., Wan, A., Yue, X., Keutzer, K.: SqueezeSeg: Convolutional neural nets with recurrent CRF for real-time road-object segmentation from 3D lidar point cloud. In: 2018 IEEE International Conference on Robotics and Automation (ICRA), pp. 1887–1893. IEEE (2018)
26. Wu, W., Qi, Z., Fuxin, L.: PointConv: Deep convolutional networks on 3D point clouds. In: Proceedings of the IEEE/CVF Conference on Computer Vision and Pattern Recognition, pp. 9621–9630 (2019)
27. Xu, C., et al.: SqueezeSegV3: spatially-adaptive convolution for efficient point-cloud segmentation. In: Vedaldi, A., Bischof, H., Brox, T., Frahm, J.-M. (eds.) ECCV 2020. LNCS, vol. 12373, pp. 1–19. Springer, Cham (2020). https://doi.org/10.1007/978-3-030-58604-1_1
28. Ye, M., Xu, S., Cao, T., Chen, Q.: DriNet: A dual-representation iterative learning network for point cloud segmentation. In: Proceedings of the IEEE/CVF International Conference on Computer Vision. pp. 7447–7456 (2021)
29. Zhang, C., Luo, W., Urtasun, R.: Efficient convolutions for real-time semantic segmentation of 3D point clouds. In: 2018 International Conference on 3D Vision (3DV), pp. 399–408. IEEE (2018)
30. Zhang, Y., et al.: PolarNet: An improved grid representation for online lidar point clouds semantic segmentation. In: Proceedings of the IEEE/CVF Conference on Computer Vision and Pattern Recognition, pp. 9601–9610 (2020)
31. Zhao, H., Jiang, L., Jia, J., Torr, P.H., Koltun, V.: Point transformer. In: Proceedings of the IEEE/CVF International Conference on Computer Vision, pp. 16259–16268 (2021)
32. Zhu, X., et al.: Cylindrical and asymmetrical 3D convolution networks for lidar segmentation. In: Proceedings of the IEEE/CVF Conference on Computer Vision and Pattern Recognition, pp. 9939–9948 (2021)

3D Meteorological Radar Data Visualization with Point Cloud Completion and Poisson Surface Reconstruction

Xiao Xu and Murong Jiang[✉]

School of Information Science and Engineering, Yunnan University, Kunming, China
jiangmr@ynu.edu.cn

Abstract. 3D visualization of meteorological radar data can not only reflect the basic characteristics of atmospheric motion and clouds spatial distribution, but also help forecasters predict weather changes more efficiently and accurately. The cone information obtained by radar has the features of sparse, discrete, uneven and irregular distribution, which will lead roughly drawn in the process of 3D rendering due to less triangular surfaces. In this paper, a surface drawing method including Point Cloud Completion and improved Poisson Surface reconstruction was proposed to implement high quality radar data surface drawing. Firstly, the skills of Point Cloud was introduced to complete irregular and scattered sparse cloud data, mathematical models were established for different types of echo data, and corresponding completion was investigated to fill the missing spatial data. Secondly, the improved Poisson Surface Reconstruction based on bilateral filtering (BPSR) was used to render the 3D surface data after completion to make 3D visualization more realistic. Experiments showed that the proposed method could well complete and plot irregular meteorological radar data, the data were more denser after processing with the Point Cloud Completion, and the BPSR improved the efficiency and fineness and realized higher reconstruction quality.

Keywords: Point cloud completion · Poisson surface reconstruction · 3D visualization · Meteorological radar data

1 Introduction

Meteorological radar indirectly obtains the distribution of clouds by emitting electromagnetic waves from radar base stations and receiving the reflectivity intensity of echoes from various forms of precipitation in the atmosphere. It is one of the main detection tools used for alerting and forecasting small mesoscale weather systems. The 3D visualization of radar data visually reflects the state of atmospheric motion with observed data, providing a basis for accurate judgment of weather forecasting.

At present, the research on 3D visualization of meteorological radar data is mainly based on data interpolation and surface drawing. The most used data

© The Author(s), under exclusive license to Springer Nature Switzerland AG 2022
S. Yu et al. (Eds.): PRCV 2022, LNCS 13536, pp. 137–150, 2022.
https://doi.org/10.1007/978-3-031-18913-5_11

interpolation algorithms are: the-nearest neighbor method [1], vertical linear interpolation [1], vertical horizontal linear interpolation [1,2], trilinear interpolation [3] and Barnes interpolation[1,4,5], etc. The surface drawing methods are Marching Cubes [6,7], Delaunay Triangular Grids [8], etc. Classical methods like Alpha Shapes [9], Rolling Ball [10], and Poisson Surface Reconstruction [11] are also represented to surface reconstruction. Due to the sparse and uneven distribution of the original radar data, the number of triangular surfaces and vertices drawn directly using the above surface reconstruction algorithms is small, making the constructed 3D surface rougher.

With the introduction of the Point Cloud concept and the rise of Point Cloud processing algorithms represented by PointNet [12], Point Cloud is now widely used in computer vision, unmanned vehicles [13,14] and robotics [15]. There are two kinds of Point Cloud data: dense Point Cloud and sparse Point Cloud. Conventional Point Cloud Completion methods are very suitable for repairing missing data in regular and ordered dense point clouds. But for irregular and scattered sparse point clouds, the above methods cannot repair data quickly.

In this paper, the radar data are converted to Point Cloud data format according to the characteristics of meteorological radar data, and the missing spatial region data are complemented by corresponding Point Cloud Completion algorithms for different types of echo data. After that, the improved Poisson surface reconstruction algorithm is used to draw the 3D surface. The experimental results show that the proposed method not only improves the efficiency and fineness of 3D surface plotting, but also produces smooth and delicate clouds with a strong sense of realism, and also provides a reference solution for the completion of other irregular and scattered sparse point clouds.

The structure of this paper is organized as follows: In Section 2, the proposed method is described in detail, including the construction of Point Cloud extended data, the proposed mathematical model of different precipitation echoes, the completion algorithm and the 3D surface drawing using Poisson surface reconstruction algorithm based on bilateral filtering optimization. In Section 3, the effectiveness of the method is experimentally verified by combining the actual observation data of Doppler meteorological radar in Yunnan Province. Finally, the conclusion is summarized in Section 4.

2   Method Description

The transmitting antenna of the meteorological radar scans one circle along with 14 different elevation angles in certain period, and then arranges the data of different elevation angles together to form a data file, which constitutes the radar body sweep data of that period, where each data point has the corresponding echo reflectivity factor value. Between the cone data layers collected at two adjacent detection elevation angles, there is a gap region with a maximum height of about 20 km, which forms a blind area for radar scanning. If the surface reconstruction is performed directly, we will have a rough and unsmooth surface with reduce the error in forecast. Therefore, the original data needs to be processed first to increase the amount of data in the point set.

2.1   Data Format Conversion

Centered on the base station, the Doppler meteorological radar emits electromagnetic detection pulses to the sky through the antenna at a fixed elevation angle, with a total of 500 data collection points in the transmission direction, each 300 meters apart. The horizontal uniform rotation of the transmitting antenna will produce 512 uniform detection directions. These 500 data acquisition points and 512 detection bearings produce polar data consisting of 25,600 data points (500 × 512). The radar detection schematic for a single detection elevation is shown in Fig. 1

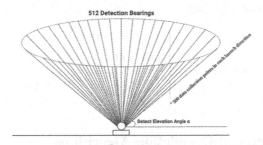

Fig. 1. Radar scan ray diagram of a single detection elevation angle

Fig. 2. Side view of the cone formed by superimposing multiple probe elevation angles

After the coordinate conversion, the reflectivity value of each data point is converted to its corresponding reflectivity intensity RGB color table to display a two-dimensional visual image of the cone data with energy color. After the detection elevation angle scanning is completed, the detection antenna will modify the detection elevation angle again for scanning. The set of cloud cone points formed by the superposition of multiple detection elevation angles is shown in Fig. 2.

Since each point in the Point Cloud data contains only the x, y, z data of the three-dimensional spatial rectangular coordinate system, it is necessary to continue converting each point in the rectangular coordinates to the Point Cloud expansion(pce) data after converting the polar coordinates to rectangular coordinates.

Assuming the radar echo data collected at a certain detection elevation angle is a 1000×1000 matrix and marked as g_α, where α is the detection elevation angle. The value of each element in the matrix is the corresponding reflectivity intensity r_{ij}. The 3D spatial coordinates are centered on the center $(500, 500)$ of matrix g_α, and the corresponding 3D coordinates of this point are $(0, 0, 0)$. With this point as the reference, the pce data of the remaining points are transformed as shown in the following equation.

$$pce(i, j, \alpha) = \begin{cases} x = j - 500 \\ y = 500 - i \\ z = \sqrt{x^2 + y^2} \times sin(\alpha) \\ r = r_{ij} \end{cases} \tag{1}$$

2.2   Echo Models and Completion Algorithms

The reflectivity factor echoes of ordinary precipitation can be broadly classified into three types: cumulus precipitation, stratiform cloud precipitation, and mixed cumulus stratiform cloud precipitation. Stratiform clouds are generally distributed along the horizontal plane. Cumulus clouds generally refer to cumulonimbus clouds, which are associated with heavy precipitation, with cloud bodies like towering hills. Therefore, the completion for stratiform clouds is produced on horizontal completion, and the completion for cumulus clouds is performed on vertical.

Using Inverse Distance Weighted(IDW) to Complete Stratiform Clouds. Stratiform cloud precipitation echoes are more uniform, and the reflectivity factor spatial gradient is larger. The reflectivity factor is generally between 15dBZ and 35dBZ Fig. 3.

We adopted the idea of the inverse distance-weighted averaging method to achieve data completion of stratiform clouds. The method satisfies the following requirements for the assumed distance h between the completion and sampling points:

The smaller h is, the more the completion points will be influenced by the sampled points, and the greater the weight will be. The larger h is, the less the completion points will be influenced by the sampled points and the smaller the weight will be. Assuming the plane coordinates of n points are (x_i, y_i), vertical height is z_i, $i = 1, 2, ..., n$, then the values of the completion points are obtained after IDW average for all sampled points (see Eq. 2).

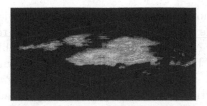

Fig. 3. Basic 3D albedo diagram of a stratiform cloud

$$f(x,y) = \begin{cases} \sum_{j=1}^{n} \dfrac{z_j}{d_j^p \sum_{j=1}^{n} 1/d_j^p} & ,(x,y) \neq (x_i,y_i) \\ z_j & ,(x,y) = (x_i,y_i) \end{cases} \tag{2}$$

$d_j = \sqrt{(x - x_j)^2 + (y - y_j)^2}$ is the horizontal distance from point (x,y) to point (x_j, y_j), $j = 1, 2, ..., n$. p is a constant bigger than 0 which is called the weighted power index. z_j is the reflectance value of the point. The larger p is, the smoother the interpolation result will be. Here, we set $p = 2$. As shown in Fig. 4, the stratiform cloud data were distributed in pieces before the completion. After completion, they were connected into one, and the hierarchy was more clearly defined.

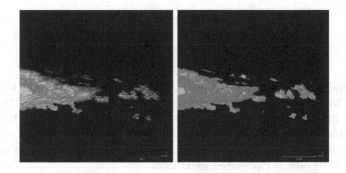

Fig. 4. Comparison of before (left) and after (right) complements of stratus clouds

Using Go-Forward-N Frames (GFN) to Complete Cumulus Clouds

The precipitation echoes of cumulus clouds are characterized by tight structure and undulating echo intensity, and a large spatial gradient of reflectivity factor. The cumulus echoes can be described as a series of fundamental reflectivity echoes of 30dBZ above, with a high reflectivity region in the central region of the echoes and a general trend of decreasing reflectivity from the center to the periphery.

Radar data completion usually inserts a prediction layer between two original layers. So we can compare the process of completion to frame completion of videos. The traditional linear interpolation algorithm assumes that the motion between adjacent frames is a uniform linear motion. However, in contrast to object motion, cloud motion is a different tangential projection presentation of the same thing, and the detection elevation angle of the radar is not uniformly elevated. Therefore, the change of cloud projection is variable speed linear motion at a macroscopic level, but there is some degree of Brownian motion in microscopic.

Assuming the detection elevation angles of Doppler radar be $\alpha_1, \alpha_2, \ldots, \alpha_{14}$ respectively, and each detection elevation angle has a corresponding reflectivity factor matrix $g_1, g_2, \ldots, g_n$, where the value of each point is the reflectivity value of the data collection point. Initialize a screening matrix W with all values as 0. Iterate each element in $g_1, g_2, \ldots, g_n$ in turn, and the reflectance screening weight matrix is calculated as Table 1, and r is the reflectivity value of $g_n[i][j]$.

Table 1. Calculation method of reflectivity screening weight matrix

$W[i][j] = W[i][j] + w$	r
$w = -3$	$r < 5$
$w = 1$	$5 \leq r \leq 15$
$w = 2$	$15 < r \leq 20$
$w = 3$	$20 < r \leq 25$
$w = 4$	$25 < r \leq 30$
$w = 5$	$35 < r \leq 40$
$w = 10$	$r > 40$

The standard deviation of the matrix W is taken as m. When the corresponding weight value of a point is less than m, the linear completion method will be used. When greater than or equal to m, the GFN complementation method will be used. Let a new layer with angle $\theta(\alpha_1 < \theta < \alpha_2)$ be inserted in α_1 and α_2, and the two-dimensional position of the inserted point is (i, j). The reflectance formula of that point is calculated as follows.

A. Linear Completion:

The linear completion method calculates the new reflectance value by calculating the values of the two layers before and after the point to be completed like Eq. 3.

$$r(i, j) = (g_1[i][j] + g_2[i][j]) \times (\frac{\theta - \alpha_1}{\alpha_2 - \alpha_1}) \tag{3}$$

B. GFN:

The GFN method needs to determine the reflectivity value of the point to be complemented based on all the given data. After considering the actual effect of various higher-order curve fitting and the cost of their algorithm, we choose the fourth order curve fitting method. Assuming that a curvilinear relationship exists between the reflectance values at all locations on the 3D space corresponding to the two-dimensional coordinates (i, j): $y = ax^4 + bx^3 + cx^2 + dx + e$. Assuming

n denotes the number of all observed data points on the curve being fitted, find the sum of the distances from each point to the curve y, the sum of squared residuals as Eq. 4.

$$L \equiv \sum_{i=1}^{n} [y_i - (ax_i^4 + bx_i^3 + cx_i^2 + dx_i + e)]^2 \tag{4}$$

In least squares, minimizing the sum of squares of the residuals is necessary. To find the value of each coefficient, we have to find the partial derivative of each coefficient in turn and make the partial derivative $L = 0$. Let $\bar{x} = \sum_{i=1}^{n} x_i$, $\bar{y} = \sum_{i=1}^{n} y_i$, we have

$$
\begin{aligned}
\frac{\partial L}{\partial a} &= a\bar{x}^8 + b\bar{x}^7 + c\bar{x}^6 + d\bar{x}^5 + e\bar{x}^4 - \bar{x}^4\bar{y} \\
\frac{\partial L}{\partial b} &= a\bar{x}^7 + b\bar{x}^6 + c\bar{x}^5 + d\bar{x}^4 + e\bar{x}^3 - \bar{x}^3\bar{y} \\
\frac{\partial L}{\partial c} &= a\bar{x}^6 + b\bar{x}^5 + c\bar{x}^4 + d\bar{x}^3 + e\bar{x}^2 - \bar{x}^2\bar{y} \\
\frac{\partial L}{\partial d} &= a\bar{x}^5 + b\bar{x}^4 + c\bar{x}^3 + d\bar{x}^2 + e\bar{x} - \bar{x}\bar{y} \\
\frac{\partial L}{\partial e} &= a\bar{x}^4 + b\bar{x}^3 + c\bar{x}^2 + d\bar{x} + e - \bar{y}
\end{aligned}
\tag{5}
$$

Thus the problem is also translated into solving the matrix equation:

$$
\begin{bmatrix}
\bar{x}^8 & \bar{x}^7 & \bar{x}^6 & \bar{x}^5 & \bar{x}^4 \\
\bar{x}^7 & \bar{x}^6 & \bar{x}^5 & \bar{x}^4 & \bar{x}^3 \\
\bar{x}^6 & \bar{x}^5 & \bar{x}^4 & \bar{x}^3 & \bar{x}^2 \\
\bar{x}^5 & \bar{x}^4 & \bar{x}^3 & \bar{x}^2 & \bar{x} \\
\bar{x}^4 & \bar{x}^3 & \bar{x}^2 & \bar{x} & 1
\end{bmatrix}
\begin{bmatrix}
a \\ b \\ c \\ d \\ e
\end{bmatrix}
=
\begin{bmatrix}
\bar{x}^4\bar{y} \\ \bar{x}^3\bar{y} \\ \bar{x}^2\bar{y} \\ \bar{x}\bar{y} \\ \bar{y}
\end{bmatrix}
\tag{6}
$$

The values of the coefficients can be obtained by solving the above equations and obtaining the corresponding curve fitting functions. We use GFN to calculate the reflectance data for any hypothetical detection elevation angle in space. Figure 5 shows the calculated detection elevation angles using the GFN, where $0.5°$ and $1.5°$ are the real existing elevation angles, while $1.0°$ is inferred.

Figure 6 shows the comparison before and after the completion of the cumulonimbus. Before the completion, there is an obvious fault between the two cones due to the data. After the completion, the fault has been linked and the cumulonimbus features have been revealed.

2.3   Drawing 3D Surface Using Bilateral-Filtering Poisson Surface Reconstruction Algorithm (BPSR)

In order to facilitate the observation of the effect of Point Cloud completion and to measure the reconstruction quality after Point Cloud completion, a Poisson surface reconstruction algorithm based on bilateral filtering is investigated.

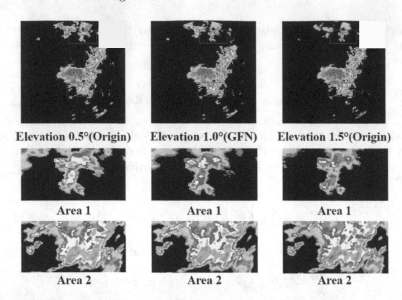

Fig. 5. Generate 1.0° data using GFN algorithm completion

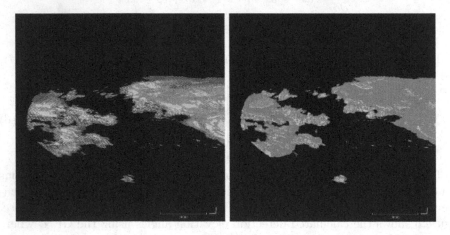

Fig. 6. Comparison of before (left) and after (right) completion of cumulus clouds

Before using the Poisson Surface Reconstruction algorithm, it is necessary to estimate the normal vector of each point in the grid space. We estimate the surface normals by analyzing the eigenvectors and eigenvalues of the covariance matrix generated from the nearest neighbors of the points. For the neighboring points of each p_i in the Point Cloud data, its covariance matrix C is:

$$C = \frac{1}{k} \sum_{i=1}^{k} \cdot (p_i - \bar{p}) \cdot (p_i - \bar{p})^T, \ \ C \cdot v_j = \lambda_j \cdot v_j, \ \ j \in \{0, 1, 2\} \tag{7}$$

The number of K-neighboring points for point p_i is k, which can be determined by the nearest neighbor method or by specifying the radius. $\bar{p}$ denotes the 3D center of mass of the proximity point, λ_j the jth eigenvalue of the covariance matrix, v_j the jth eigenvector of the covariance matrix. Since the dimensions of both p_i and $\bar{p}$ are $(3, 1)$, the dimension of the covariance matrix C is $(3, 3)$.

Bilateral Filtering [16] is a nonlinear filter that achieves edge-preserving and noise-reducing smoothing. Like other filtering principles, bilateral filtering uses a weighted average method in which the intensity of a pixel is represented by a weighted average of the surrounding pixel luminance values based on Gaussian distribution. Bilateral filtering is the best choice that balances these two conditions and is able to accurately estimate the surface normal integral of the vector field, approximating the real surface mesh topology. Let the set of K-neighboring points and the unit normal vector of point p_i be $N_k(p_i)$ and n_i respectively, the expression of the improved Poisson algorithm based on bilateral filtering is:

$$\hat{p}_i = p_i + \lambda n_i \tag{8}$$

$$\lambda = \frac{\Sigma_{p_j \in N_k(p_i)} W_C(||p_j - p_i||) W_S(||\langle n_j, n_i \rangle|| - 1) \langle n_i, p_j - p_i \rangle}{\Sigma_{p_j \in N_k(p_i)} W_C(||p_j - p_i||) W_S(||\langle n_j, n_i \rangle|| - 1)} \tag{9}$$

$||\cdot||$ represents the norm, $\langle \cdot, \cdot \rangle$ represents the inner product, $\hat{p}_i$ is the updated point after bilateral filtering, p_i, p_j are input points, λ is the bilateral filtering factor and n_i, n_j are the normal vector of points. W_C, W_S respectively represent the spatial domain and frequency domain weight functions of bilateral filtering function, which control the flattening degree and feature retention degree of bilateral filtering respectively. They take the form of a Gaussian kernel with standard deviation σ_C, σ_S:

$$W_C(x) = e^{-\frac{x^2}{2\sigma_C^2}}$$
$$W_S(x) = e^{-\frac{y^2}{2\sigma_S^2}} \tag{10}$$

σ_C represents the influence factor of the distance from data point p_i to the neighboring point on p_i. The larger σ_C is, the smoother the point cloud is, but it will be harder to retain the features. σ_S represents the influence factor of the normal deviation of data point p_i and its neighboring points on point p_i. The larger σ_S is, the better the retention effect of features is.

By adjusting parameters σ_C and σ_S, the noise reduction and smooth processing of point cloud data are realized while the characteristic points of meteorological radar data are maintained. In the following experiments, we choose σ_C as the neighboring radius of the point, and σ_S as the standard deviation of the neighboring point.

Summarize the discussion above, the steps of BPSR can be described as:

(S1) Calculate the normal vector for each point using Eq. 7.
(S2) Calculate $\|p_j - p_i\|$ for W_C, $\|\langle n_j, n_i \rangle\| - 1$ for W_S and $\langle n_i, p_j - p_i \rangle$.
(S3) According to Eq. 10, calculate the Gaussian kernel $W_c(x)$ and $W_s(y)$.
(S4) According to Eq. 9, calculate the bilateral filtering factor λ.
(S5) According to Eq. 8, calculate the points after filtering.
(S6) Feed all filtered data points into the Poisson Surface Reconstruction algorithm.

3 Experiments and Analysis

In our experiment, the meteorological radar data were collected by Yunnan Meteorological Station. After preprocessing the initial radar data, the GFN was used for cumulus clouds and the IDW for stratus clouds. BPSR was used to draw the 3D surface of the complemented meteorological radar data.

3.1 Comparison of Meteorological Radar Data Completion

Before using the Point Cloud Completion method, the experimental data were distinctly sparse Point Cloud. Since the points on the left figure were more sparse, the high reflectivity factor hidden underneath can be clearly seen while the right were hard to observe Fig. 7.

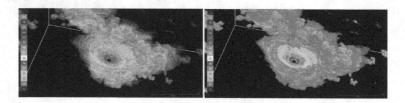

Fig. 7. Comparison of Basic Reflectance Data Before (Left) and After (Right) Completeness

In order to make the comparison results more obvious, we took 35dBZ as the dividing line. We named the data less than 35dBZ as low reflectivity data, and the data more than 35dBZ as high reflectivity data. The left part of Fig. 8 showed the before (top) and after (bottom) comparisons of the low reflectivity data, and the right part showed the before (top) and after (bottom) comparisons of the high reflectivity data. The contrast between sparse and dense was more obvious.

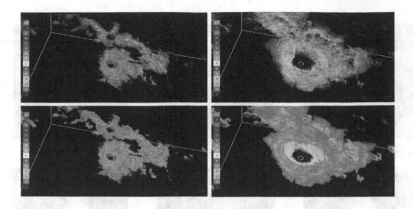

Fig. 8. High Reflectivity Data (Left) and Low Reflectivity Data (Right)

3.2   Comparison of Point Cloud Completion Experiments

To further illustrate the advantages of GFN and BPSR with other classical algorithms for 3D visualization work of meteorological radar data, we combined these two algorithms and compared the experimental results with adaptive-Barnes interpolation algorithm, QVI [17] frame interpolation algorithm, Alpha Shapes, and Rolling Ball method.

Figure 9 showed the complementary results of GFN, adaptive-Barnes [18] and QVI for 1.95° detection elevation angle from left to right. The experiments showed the intermediate frames drawn by the GFN were more detailed, clear and realistic, and there was no echo phenomenon. Table 2 showed the performance comparison of the GFN with the adaptive-Barnes and the QVI.

Figure 10 showed the experimental comparison of the surface reconstruction of the complemented Point Cloud data by BPSR, Gaussian-filter-based Poisson surface reconstruction algorithm, Alpha Shapes and the Rolling Ball from left to right. The experiments showed the 3D surface drawn by BPSR was more complete, fine and smooth, while Alpha Shapes and Rolling Ball both have different degrees of oblique side surface loss. Table 3 showed the performance comparison of the BPSR algorithm with the Alpha Shapes algorithm and Rolling Ball.

Experiments showed the use of GFN combined with BPSR not only greatly improved the speed of Point Cloud Completion and surface drawing of meteorological radar data. At the same time, the quality of surface plotting is substantially improved due to the improvement of fineness brought by GFN and the advantage of 3D reconstruction by BPSR.

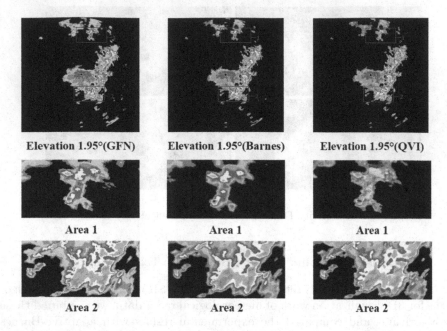

Fig. 9. Comparison of the completion effect of GFN, adaptive-Barnes and QVI

Table 2. Performance Comparison of GFN with Barnes and QVI

Method	Time Consumption (ms)	Clarity	Smoothness	Continuity
GFN	49317	Clearest	Smoothest	Continuous
adaptive-Barnes	86507	Clearer	Smooth	Continuous
QVI	21511	Blurred	Rough	Discontinuous

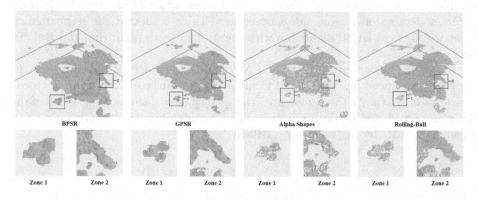

Fig. 10. Comparison of the reconstruction effect of BPSR and other algorithms

Table 3. Performance Comparative of BPSR with other algorithms

Method	Drawing Time (ms)	Vertices	Triangles
BPSR	38182	1,191,787	2,374,222
GPSR	29710	815,949	1,608,460
Rolling Ball	49152	1,875,940	1,941,591
Alpha Shapes	69900	444,155	1,875,940

4 Conclusion

In this paper, according to the characteristics of meteorological radar data, we combine the advantages of Point Cloud Completion technology to investigate the 3D visualization of meteorological data according to IDW, GFN and BPSR.

Firstly, the Doppler radar polar coordinate data are converted to point cloud extended data format by pre-processing means. Secondly, the interpolation problem of cone data is converted into the completion problem of sparse point cloud data, and the models of different types of precipitation echoes are proposed through the discussion of stratiform cloud precipitation echoes and cumulus cloud precipitation echoes. The lateral inverse distance weighted average completion algorithm is used for stratiform cloud precipitation echoes, and the GFN algorithm for cumulus cloud precipitation echoes. Finally, the Poisson surface reconstruction algorithm is used to surface map the meteorological radar data, and the BPSR is proposed by optimizing and improving the Poisson surface reconstruction algorithm using normal constraints and bilateral filtering methods.

The experimental results show that the radar data are denser after processing using the Point Cloud Completion method. The BPSR algorithm gives full play to the advantages of the Poisson surface reconstruction algorithm which also improved the efficiency and fineness and realized higher reconstruction quality.

Acknowledgement. This work is supported by Program for Innovative Research Team in University of Yunnan Province(IRTSTYN) and Professional Degree Postgraduate Practical Innovation Project of Yunnan University(2021Y164).

References

1. Zhang, J., Howard, K., Xia, W., et al.: Comparison of objective analysis schemes for the WSR-88D radar data. In: 31th International Conference on Radar Meteorology, pp. 907–910 (2003)
2. Xiao, Y., Liu, L.: Research on 3D lattice lattice and jigsaw method of new generation weather radar network data. Chin. J. Meteorol. **64**(5), 647–657 (2006)
3. Mohr, C.G., Vaughan, R.L.: An economical procedure for cartesian interpolation and display of reflectivity factor data in three-dimensional space. J. Appl. Meteorol. **18**(5), 661–670 (1979)

4. Barnes, L.: A technique for maximizing details in numerical weather map analysis. J. Appl. Meteor. **3**, 395–409 (1964)
5. Askelson, M.A., Aubagnac, J.-P., Straka, J.M.: An adaptation of the Barnes filter applied to the objective analysis of radar data. Mon. Weather Rev. **128**(9), 3050–3082 (2000)
6. Lorensen, W.E., Cline, H.E.: Marching cubes: a high resolution 3D surface construction algorithm. ACM SIGGRAPH Comput. Graph. **21**(4), 163–169 (1987)
7. MA, J.-C., Jiang, M.-R., Fang, S.-Q.: Three-dimensional reconstruction of cone meteorological data based on improved marching tetrahedra algorithm. Comput. Sci. S2(12), 644–647+654 (2021)
8. Shewchuk, J.R.: Delaunay refinement algorithms for triangular mesh generation. Comput. Geom. Theor. Appl. **47**(1–3), 741–778 (2014)
9. Edelsbrunner, H., Ernst, P.M.: Three-dimensional alpha shapes. ACM Trans. Graph. **13**(1), 43–72 (1994)
10. Gray, P., Bedi, S., Ismail, F.: Rolling ball method for 5-axis surface machining. Comput. Aided Design **35**(4), 347–357 (2003)
11. Kazhdan, M., Bolitho, M., Hoppe, H.: Poisson surface reconstruction. The Japan Institute of Energy (2013)
12. Qi, C. R., Su, H., Mo, K., et al.: PointNet: deep learning on point sets for 3d classification and segmentation. In: IEEE Conference on Computer Vision and Pattern Recognition, pp. 652–660 (2017)
13. Lin J, Zhang F: A fast, complete, point cloud based loop closure for LiDAR odometry and mapping. arXiv preprint arXiv:1909.11811 (2019)
14. Zhang Jian, J.J., Gourley, K., Howard, B.: Maddox: 3D interpolation and mosaicking of radar data fields. The second Southwest Weather Symposium. Tucson (2000)
15. Wang, L., Xiang, Y., Fox, D.: Goal-auxiliary actor-critic for 6d robotic grasping with point clouds. In: IEEE Conference on Computer Vision and Pattern Recognition (2020)
16. Cui, X., Yan, X., Li, S.: Feature-preserving scattered point cloud data denoising. Opt. Precision Eng. **25**(12), 3169–3178 (2017)
17. Xu, X., Li, S., Sun, W., Yin, Q., Yang, M. -H.: Quadratic video interpolation. NeurIPS (2019)
18. Fang, S. Q., Ma, J. C., Jiang, M. R.: Using the moving trapezoid body interpolation to reconstruct 3D meteorological radar image. In: The 2021 2nd International Conference on Computer Vision, Image and Deep Learning(CVIDL2021), Proc of SPIE Vol. 11911, 11911E (2021)

JVLDLoc: A Joint Optimization of Visual-LiDAR Constraints and Direction Priors for Localization in Driving Scenario

Longrui Dong and Gang Zeng[✉]

Key Laboratory of Machine Perception (MoE), School of Intelligence Science and
Technology, Peking University, Beijing 100871, China
{lrdong,zeng}@pku.edu.cn

Abstract. The ability for a moving agent to localize itself in environment is the basic demand for emerging applications, such as autonomous driving, etc. Many existing methods based on multiple sensors still suffer from drift. We propose a scheme that fuses map prior and vanishing points from images, which can establish an energy term that is only constrained on rotation, called the direction projection error. Then we embed these direction priors into a visual-LiDAR SLAM system that integrates camera and LiDAR measurements in a tightly-coupled way at backend. Specifically, our method generates visual reprojection error and point to Implicit Moving Least Square(IMLS) surface of scan constraints, and solves them jointly along with direction projection error at global optimization. Experiments on KITTI, KITTI-360 and Oxford Radar Robotcar show that we achieve lower localization error or Absolute Pose Error (APE) than prior map, which validates our method is effective.

Keywords: Visual-LiDAR SLAM · Sensor fusion · Structure from motion · Vanishing point

1 Introduction

In the fields of computer vision and robotics, Simultaneous localization and mapping (SLAM) is an active research topic, it also plays a vital role in many real world applications. For example, by knowing their precise location, vehicles are able to navigate safely. To fully perceive surrounding scenes, agents are usually equipped with several sensors: camera, LiDAR, GPS/IMU, etc. As we all know, relatively cheaper cameras have been widely set on various kinds of platforms, which makes visual odometry(VO)/visual SLAM(V-SLAM) the main force in

Supplementary Information The online version contains supplementary material available at https://doi.org/10.1007/978-3-031-18913-5_12.

research [4,15]. Due to the characteristics of camera and algorithms' reliance on low-level visual features, V-SLAM tends to fail in challenge conditions: abrupt motion, textureless region, too much occlusion. Light Detection And Ranging sensor(LiDAR), which can cover 360° FoV information, has an advantage over camera that the noise associated with each distance measurement is independent of the distance and the lighting conditions [6]. But LiDAR does not offer texture and is often sparse due to the physical spacing between laser fibers.

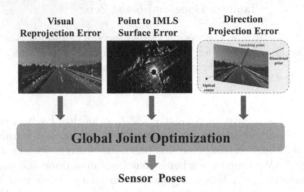

Fig. 1. **JVLDLoc**: a tight-coupling of visual reprojection error, point to Implicit Moving Least Square(IMLS) surface error and direction projection error at global joint optimization.

In order to take advantage of those two types of sensors, fusion of visual and LiDAR data during localization is quite reasonable, which is called visual-LiDAR odometry/SLAM. Some recent work [8,10,19] have explored the way of fusing those two sensors. However, they nearly all fuse visual-LiDAR at a level of loosely coupling. [17,25] use pose graph to fuse different sensors. Although they are very efficient, rich geometric constraints from data are thrown away in optimization.

Unlike [25] which just takes odometry as relative pose factor between adjacent keyframes, we use input trajectory to construct direction priors. They contain scene structure information from images' vanishing points. Since the direction is independent of distance, for the vehicle, as long as there is no road turn, the direction is always in view. As a result, we can establish longer range correspondences among much more keyframes than traditional visual point features [16]. Ideally, the motion of a vehicle on the road plane can be approximated as a two-dimensional movement, in which the rotating part is almost only a twist around an axis perpendicular to the ground. A more accurate rotation estimate can reduce the overall drift of the trajectory [20]. Motivated by them, we extract at most one vanishing point each image, whose corresponding direction is forward. Actually this direction provides only two degrees of freedom constraints to the vehicle's orientation [1]. The main contributions are as follows:

- We come up with a scheme that fuses map prior and image-detected vanishing points, which can establish an energy term that only constrains rotation. That constraint, called the direction projection error, finally helps to mitigate the drift.
- We propose JVLDLoc for localization in driving scenario. Based on graph optimization, it integrates visual reprojection error, point-to-IMLS surface error and direction projection error into one energy function, and directly uses geometric constraints to optimize pose (Fig. 1).

Experiments on KITTI, KITTI-360 and Oxford Radar Robotcar show that we achieve lower localization error or APE than prior map, which validates the effectiveness of our method.

2   Related Work

2.1   Visual-LiDAR SLAM

First we briefly review some of the major visual or LiDAR SLAM in literature. ORB-SLAM [4,16] completely uses ORB features, realizing a full V-SLAM system including loop detection, relocalization, and map fusion. IMLS-SLAM [6] estimates pose by minimizing the distance from the current point to the surface represented by the implicit moving least square method (IMLS). Then we categorize visual-LiDAR SLAM into two major genres according to whether or not to use both multi-modal residuals in the optimization stage.

Loosely Coupled Method. Methods of this type usually extract depth from LiDAR to enhance visual odometry. DEMO [24] integrates the depth information of point clouds into visual SLAM for the first time. LIMO-PL [10] utilizes line features with depths from LiDAR. [23] uses 3D lines from prior LiDAR map to associate with 2D line features from images. DVL-SLAM [19] requires no feature points when using sparse depth from point cloud. However, incorrect pixel-depth pair might damage accuracy.

Tightly Coupled Method. ViLiVO [22] adds the image feature reprojection error and the point cloud matching error to Bundle adjustment(BA). Similiar methods appear in [26] but they further introduce observation error between image feature and point cloud. TVL-SLAM [5] also incorporates visual and lidar measurements in backend optimization. There are also filter based methods for tightly fusion different data [14]. LIO-SAM [17] and LVI-SAM [18] achieve sensor-fusion atop the pose graph instead of including any gemometric constraints.

2.2   Using Vanishing Points as Direction Constraint

The common directions of parallel 3-D lines are known as vanishing points (VPs). Because the VPs offer direction information independent of the present robot proposition [3], Many academics have researched VPs to help improving orientation. [15] apply the orthogonal constraint between multiple VPs, known as the Manhattan world constraint, to calcute the full rotation. [13] on longer need Manhattan world assumption but they will extract all valid VPs from an image while our method indeed only use one VP. [21] also combine VP error in a pose estimator, but it have to generate VPs of three directions before refinement.

3   Notation

$\mathcal{I}_n$, $\mathcal{S}_n$ stands for an image and a point cloud at time t_n. A frame $\mathcal{F}_n$ is the data structure that includes ORB features of $\mathcal{I}_n$ and corresponding processed scan $\mathcal{S}_n$, while $\mathcal{K}_k$ refers to a keyframe. Every 3D point $\mathbf{X} = (X, Y, Z, 1)^T \in \mathbb{R}^4$ in a homogeneous coordinate from visual map, can be observed in the image plane as a pixel coordinate $\mathbf{u} = (u, v, 1)^T \in \mathbb{R}^3$ via a projection function:

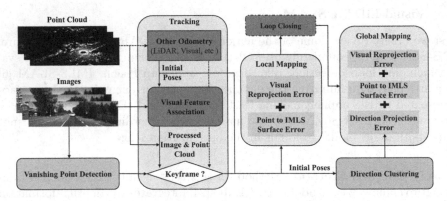

Fig. 2. The Overall diagram of the proposed **JVLDLoc**. Our approach inputs image and point cloud stream and estimates 6DoF poses.

$$\pi(\mathbf{X}) = \frac{1}{Z}\mathbf{K}[\mathbf{I}|\mathbf{0}]\mathbf{X} = \frac{1}{Z}\begin{bmatrix} f_x & 0 & c_x & 0 \\ 0 & f_y & c_y & 0 \\ 0 & 0 & 1 & 0 \end{bmatrix}\begin{bmatrix} X \\ Y \\ Z \\ 1 \end{bmatrix} = \begin{bmatrix} f_x\frac{X}{Z} + c_x \\ f_y\frac{Y}{Z} + c_y \\ 1 \end{bmatrix} = \begin{bmatrix} u \\ v \\ 1 \end{bmatrix} \quad (1)$$

where $K \in \mathbb{R}^{3\times3}$ is camera intrinsic matrix, f_x, f_y, c_x and c_y are intrinsic parameters. We use $T_{wn} \in SE(3)$ to express the transformation from the n_{th} frame's camera coordinate to the world coordinate, T_{nw} is the inverse of T_{wn}. $R_{wn} \in SO(3)$ and $t_{wn} \in \mathbb{R}^3$ are rotation and translation part of T_{wn}.

4   Method

The dataflow of the JVLDLoc is in Fig. 2. The whole system consists of four modules: tracking (Sect. 4.1), local mapping (Sect. 4.2), visual based loop closing(see supplemental material for detail) and global mapping (Sect. 4.3).

4.1   Tracking

We process visual and LiDAR data and compute their features and decide whether to generate a new keyframe. Note that we need to transform point cloud to camera coordinate by given extrinsic: T_{CL}. If there is no initial pose from other odometry, we can still handle it by launching a LiDAR odometry. It is modified from the approach in IMLS-SLAM [6]. The main changes compared to [6] can be found in supplemental material.

Visual Feature Association. Unlike [16], we no longer launch motion-only BA. Instead, we just use odometry poses to construct 2D feature-3D point associations within the visual map. Finally, we incorporate processed image keypoints and point cloud into a frame $\mathcal{F}_n$. Tracking module will treat current $\mathcal{F}_n$ as a new keyframe $\mathcal{K}_n$ if 4 conditions in [16] are satisfied **OR** $\mathcal{F}_n$ has valid supporting direction constraints (described in Sect. 4.3).

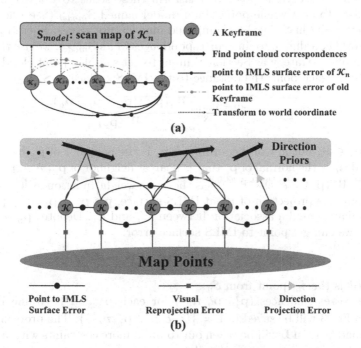

Fig. 3. (a) Scan to map association of one Keyframe in Local and global mapping. We build point to IMLS surface error between $\mathcal{K}_n$ and the keyframe to which the closest point p_c belongs. (b) Global optimization graph structure.

4.2   Local Mapping

A new keyframe $\mathcal{K}_n$ will trigger a visual-LiDAR graph optimization. The corresponding joint energy function consists of visual reprojection error and point to IMLS surface error.

Our backend maintains a covisiblity graph where keyframes that observe same 3D point are connected. Denote keyframe launching local mapping as $\mathcal{K}_n$, sort all the keyframes connected to $\mathcal{K}_n$ at covisiblity graph (abbreviated as $\mathbf{K}_n^{cov}$) including itself by their timestamps: $\mathbf{K}_{local} = \{...\mathcal{K}_i...\mathcal{K}_n\}$. $\mathcal{P}_{local}$ refers to all 3D visual map points seen by $\mathbf{K}_{local}$. Defining $\mathcal{X}_i = \{(\mathrm{x}^j, \mathbf{X}^j)|j = 0, 1...\}$ as the set of correspondences between feature points at keyframe $\mathcal{K}_i$ and 3D visual map points from $\mathcal{P}_{local}$. Then do the following steps:

1) For all keyframes in $\mathbf{K}_{local}$, according to visual correspondences from $\mathcal{X}_k$, we can get visual reprojection error term like [16]: $\mathbf{e}_V(i,j) = \|\mathrm{x}^j_{(.)} - \pi_{(.)}(R_{iw}\mathbf{X}^j + t_{iw})\|_\Sigma^2$.

2) For current keyframe $\mathcal{K}_n$ which has a global frame index f_n, we find the first keyframe whose frame index met $f_n - f_i \leq \mathbf{N}$, where $\mathbf{N}$ is the size of local scan map of each keyframe. Denote this keyframe as $\mathcal{K}_{start}$. Now list all corresponding scan from $\mathcal{K}_{start}$ to $\mathcal{K}_{n-1} : \{\mathcal{S}_{start},...,\mathcal{S}_{n-1}\}$. We use each keyframe's current pose to transform these scans to world frame and accumulate to be a whole point cloud model named $\mathbf{S}_{model}$ (See Fig. 3 (a)).

3) Sort every point in $\mathcal{S}_n$ by their computed nine feature values. Then transform $\mathcal{S}_n$ to world coordinate to find correspondences in its $\mathbf{S}_{model}$. we use the same scan sampling strategy as Section V in [6] to get sampled point cloud $\widetilde{\mathcal{S}}_n$. we compute for each point the distance to the IMLS surface in $\mathbf{S}_{model}$:

$$I^n(\mathbf{p}_x) = \frac{\sum_{\mathbf{P}_i \in \mathbf{S}_{model}} W_i(\mathbf{p}_x)((\mathbf{p}_x - \mathbf{p}_i) \cdot \mathbf{n}_c)}{\sum_{\mathbf{P}_i \in \mathbf{S}_{model}} W_i(\mathbf{p}_x)} \qquad (2)$$

where $\mathbf{p}_x \in \widetilde{\mathcal{S}}_n$ but in world coordinate, $\mathbf{p}_i$ is the neighbor of $\mathbf{p}_x$ from model scan and $\mathbf{n}_c$ is the normal of $\mathbf{p}_c$ that is nearest neighbor of $\mathbf{p}_x$. And $\mathbf{p}_c$ is from $\mathcal{S}_c$ of $\mathcal{K}_c$. $W_i(\mathbf{p}_x) = e^{-\|\mathbf{p}_x - \mathbf{p}_i\|^2/h^2}$ is the same weight function as [6]. Next we can obtain the projection of $\mathbf{p}_x$ at IMLS surface, $\mathbf{p}_y$: $\mathbf{p}_y = \mathbf{p}_x - I^n(\mathbf{p}_x)\mathbf{n}_c$.

4) Now we have found a association between $\mathcal{K}_n$ and $\mathcal{K}_c$. Denote $^c\mathbf{p}_y = T_{cw}\mathbf{p}_y$. Finally, we can get point to IMLS surface error:

$$\mathbf{e}_L(n,j) = \|(T_{cw}T_{nw}^{-1}\mathbf{p}_x^j - {}^c\mathbf{p}_y^j) \cdot \mathbf{n}_c^j\|^2 \qquad (3)$$

where $\mathbf{p}_x^j$ is the j_{th} point from $\widetilde{\mathcal{S}}_n$.

All the correspondences $(\mathbf{p}_x^j, {}^c\mathbf{p}_y^j, \mathbf{n}_c^j)$ for each $\mathbf{p}_x^j$ and keyframe index n and c in Eq. 3 will be saved in $\mathbf{L} = \{(n, c, \mathbf{p}_x^j, {}^c\mathbf{p}_y^j, \mathbf{n}_c^j)\}$. The previous saved correspondences in $\mathbf{L}$ will be taken out to build more costraints within $\mathbf{K}_{local}$, see supplemental material for detail.

5) Our proposed local joint energy function is weighted sum of above two types of constraints:

$$E_{local} = \sum_{i \in \mathbf{K}_{local}} \alpha \sum_{j \in \mathcal{X}_i} \rho(\mathbf{e}_V(i,j)) + \beta \sum_{j \in \widetilde{\mathcal{S}}_n} \mathbf{e}_L(n,j) \qquad (4)$$

where ρ is the robust Huber cost function, α and β are weight hyper parameters to balance those two kinds of measurements. The poses of keyframes in $\mathbf{K}_{local}$ are obtained by minimizing Eq. 4.

4.3   Global Mapping Using Direction Priors

After local mapping of the final keyframe, we will launch the global mapping.

Association of Direction Priors and VPs. We detect the vanishing point $\mathbf{v}$ in each image and get corresponding direction via $\mathbf{d} = \mathbf{R}_{wc}\mathbf{K}^{-1}\mathbf{v}/\|\mathbf{R}_{wc}\mathbf{K}^{-1}\mathbf{v}\|$ [1], where $\mathbf{d} \in \mathbb{R}^3$. Detailed steps and bi-level mean-shift clustering on directions are in supplemental material. After clustering, there is at most one VP per image. Each VP corresponds to a cluster's center which is direction prior $\hat{\mathbf{d}}_w$.

Global Joint Optimization. One can regard global optimization as a special case of local mapping: ALL keyframes in the map are included in $\mathbf{K}_{global}$. We traverse all keyframes in $\mathbf{K}_{global}$ to construct Eq. 3. The global optimization graph is shown in Fig. 3 (b). We express global direction prior $\hat{\mathbf{D}}_w \in \mathbb{R}^4$ in a homogeneous coordinate as follows [1]: $\hat{\mathbf{D}}_w = [\hat{\mathbf{d}}_w, 0]^T$.

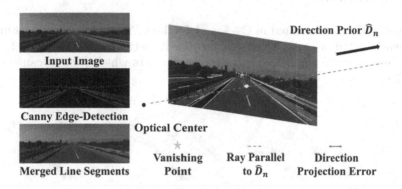

Direction Prior $\hat{D}_n$

Input Image

Canny Edge-Detection

Merged Line Segments

Optical Center

| Vanishing | Ray Parallel | Direction |
| Point | to $\hat{D}_n$ | Projection Error |

Fig. 4. Construction of direction projection error. The left figure show the process of vanishing point detection. A ray parallel to the direction prior passing through the camera optical center intersects the image plane at $\tilde{v}$ as Eq. 5.

The direction prior $\hat{\mathbf{D}}_w$ at world coordinate is transformed by current estimated rotation to camera's coordinate: $\hat{\mathbf{D}}_n$. This direction can be written as a 3D line through a homogeneous point $\mathbf{A}$: $\mathbf{Z}(\lambda) = \mathbf{A} + \lambda\hat{\mathbf{D}}_n$, where $\lambda \in (0, \infty)$. The observation on image of that direction is then equal to the projection of a point at infinity on that 3D line as follows:

$$\tilde{\mathbf{v}} = \lim_{\lambda \to \infty} \pi(\mathbf{Z}(\lambda)) = \lim_{\lambda \to \infty} \pi((\mathbf{A} + \lambda\hat{\mathbf{D}}_n)) = \pi(\hat{\mathbf{D}}_n) \tag{5}$$

The direction projection error is just distance between $\tilde{\mathbf{v}}$ and actual detected VP $\mathbf{v}$ (See Fig. 4):

$$\mathbf{e}_D(n) = \|\mathbf{v} - \tilde{\mathbf{v}}\|_{\Sigma}^2 = \|\mathbf{v} - \pi(\hat{\mathbf{D}}_n)\|_{\Sigma}^2 = \|\mathbf{v} - \pi([\mathbf{R}_{nw}|\mathbf{I}]\hat{\mathbf{D}}_w)\|_{\Sigma}^2 \tag{6}$$

Finally, we take out all keyframes $\mathbf{K}_{global}$ from the global map, the global joint energy function can be written as:

$$\mathbf{E}_{global} = \sum_{n \in \mathbf{K}_{global}} \{\alpha \sum_{j \in \mathcal{X}_n} \rho(\mathbf{e}_V(n,j)) + \beta \sum_{j \in \widetilde{\mathcal{S}}_n} \mathbf{e}_L(n,j) + \gamma \mathbf{e}_D(n)\} \quad (7)$$

where α, β, γ are weights factors to balance these three types of residuals. In practice, we set α to be 1 and set the other two according to the corresponding number of residuals. The poses are optimized by :

$$\{\mathbf{R}_n, \mathbf{t}_n | n \in \mathbf{K}_{global}\} = \arg \min_{\mathbf{R}_n, \mathbf{t}_n} \mathbf{E}_{global} \quad (8)$$

Limited to the length of the paper, please refer to our supplemental material for the jacobin of direction projection error.

5 Experiments

This method is implemented in C++ and Python. All the non-linear optimization mentioned above are Levenberg-Marquardt method in g^2o library [11]. Our experiments involve the following 3 driving datasets which contain camera and LiDAR sensors:

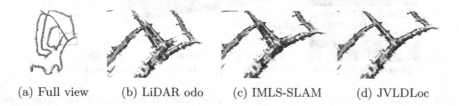

(a) Full view   (b) LiDAR odo   (c) IMLS-SLAM   (d) JVLDLoc

Fig. 5. Mapping result on KITTI 02. (a) is the full view output from JVLDLoc. (b), (c), (d) are the enlargement of the red box region in (a) output from different methods respectively. LiDAR odo means LiDAR Odometry with $\mathbf{N} = 1$. (Color figure online)

Table 1. RMSE(m) of APE for KITTI 00-10. For each sequence, we report RMSE of input pose, JVLDLoc without direction priors and full JVLDLoc respectively.

KITTI odometry	00	01	02	03	04	05	06	07	08	09	10	AVG
ORB-SLAM2 [16]	1.354	10.16	6.899	0.693	0.178	0.783	0.714	0.536	3.542	1.643	1.156	2.515
w.o. direction priors	1.367	3.289	4.669	0.614	0.169	0.705	0.485	0.473	3.354	2.433	0.990	1.686
w. direction priors	1.205	1.999	3.544	0.530	0.151	0.593	0.300	0.441	2.862	1.498	0.818	**1.267**
LiDAR odometry N=1	6.849	35.03	12.74	0.839	0.265	3.379	2.109	0.769	8.123	3.917	1.084	6.828
w.o. direction priors	2.027	5.932	4.414	0.764	0.186	1.286	0.374	0.945	4.602	3.347	1.065	2.268
w. direction priors	1.616	3.097	3.015	0.585	0.175	0.802	0.302	0.521	3.131	1.828	0.933	**1.455**

KITTI Odometry Dataset. [7] may be the most popular dataset for SLAM field, which covers urban city, rural road, highways, roads with vegetation, etc. We compare the algorithm with other state-of-the-art method on 00-10 because they are widely used in other papers.

KITTI-360 Dataset. [12] is still under development, the ground truth does not fully cover each frame of raw data, because they discard some frames collected at very low moving speed. For the convenience of evaluation, we clip two sequences from raw data as test data.

Oxford Radar RobotCar Dataset. [2] is an another fresh dataset. The car is driven to travel 32 times in same scene. We selsect a sequence recorded on datetime 2019-01-10-14-36-48.

5.1   Improvements over Prior Map

To prove that JVLDLoc will reduce global drift, we visualize the output point cloud map with color in Fig. 5. Qualitively, our method greatly improves the global consistency of the map. For more mapping visualization, please turn to supplemental material. We use RMSE of APE [9] to quantify the drift.

Table 1 includes results test on KITTI odometry when fed with diferent prior map. We have set four baselines as input odometry including ORB-SLAM2 [16], our LiDAR odometry under different N which is the number of scans kept as local map. The other two groups of result is shown in supplemental material. Under different quality prior maps, the average accuracy of these 11 sequences can be significantly improved. Especially when input LiDAR odometry with $N-1$, the mean APE is reduced by about 79%. Table 2 is for the other two datasets, which

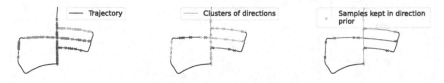

Fig. 6. A visualization of direction priors of KITTI 05 when downsampled under different intervals $V_{interval}$: 2, 15, 300 (from left to right). The number of total direction projectoin error is reduced from 117 to 12.

Table 2. APE for KITTI-360 and Oxford Radar RobotCar. MIN and MAX are the minimum and maximum APE over the entire trajectory.

KITTI-360	12			20		
	MIN	$RMSE$	MAX	MIN	$RMSE$	MAX
ORB-SLAM2 [16]	0.538	1.904	3.289	0.385	2.253	4.812
w.o. direction priors	0.196	1.367	3.934	0.164	0.989	2.952
w. direction priors	**0.057**	**0.891**	**2.828**	**0.129**	**0.786**	**1.980**

Oxford	1		
	MIN	$RMSE$	MAX
Lidar odometry **N**=10	2.592	26.25	53.43
w.o. direction priors	2.158	11.09	**19.01**
w. direction priors	**0.437**	**7.982**	27.08

also prove our method's effect. That is because JVLDLoc directly uses differnent kinds of geometric constraints to optimize pose.

5.2 Effects of Direction Priors

To demonstrate the effects of direction priors itself, we further compare accuracy with and without using the proposed direction priors. APE are still shown in Table 1, Table 2. It can be seen the direction priors are able to further improve localization due to smaller average RMSE on KITTI. For other two datasets, with help of direction priors, maximum of APE strongly decrease on KITTI-360 from the level when there is none direction constraint; The minimum and RMSE have again significantly reduced by 80% and 28% on Oxford Radar RobotCar.

In a word, although the direction priors are not very accurate as they are based on input poses, they still contribute to better localization. We believe the reason is that direction priors impose longer term geometric constraints as the direction is an infinite landmark. Figure 7 presents intuitive trajectory comparisons. Apparently, we can get less drift after long distance under direction priors.

5.3 Comparison to Other Methods on KITTI Odometry Dataset

Besides APE, Table 3 also calculates relative transition error and rotation error for 100, 200,... and 800 meter distances with KITTI's official evaluation code.

Compared to other visual-LiDAR methods, JVLDLoc achieve best relative translation error and APE, which indicates the superiority of our method over others using the same modality of data. LIMO-PL [10] and DVL-SLAM [19] are

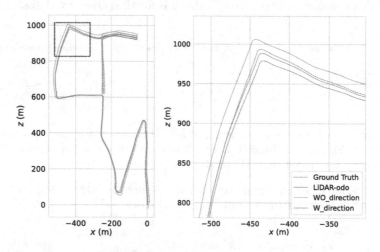

Fig. 7. Trajectory of JVLDLoc (red), JVLDLoc without direction priors (green), LiDAR odometry (blue) on Oxford. The right image is the enlargement of the dotted box on the left image. (Color figure online)

Table 3. Comparison to other methods on KITTI 00–10. t_{rel} and r_{rel} are relative translational error (%) and rotational error ($°/100$ m). Due to page limitations, results on 05–10 are in supplemental material. (NA : Not Available).

Method	00			01			02			03			04			AVG on 00-10		
	t_{rel}	r_{rel}	APE	t_{rel}	r_{rel}	APE	t_{rel}	r_{rel}	APE	t_{rel}	r_{rel}	APE	t_{rel}	r_{rel}	APE	t_{rel}	r_{rel}	APE
IMLS-SLAM [6]	0.50	0.18	3.90	0.82	0.10	2.41	0.53	0.14	7.16	0.68	0.22	0.65	0.33	0.12	0.18	**0.52**	0.14	1.96
LIMO-PL [10]	0.99	NA	NA	1.87	NA	NA	1.38	NA	NA	0.65	NA	NA	0.42	NA	NA	0.94	NA	NA
DVL-SLAM [19]	0.93	NA	NA	1.47	NA	NA	1.11	NA	NA	0.92	NA	NA	0.67	NA	NA	0.98	NA	NA
TVL-SLAM-No calib [5]	0.59	NA	0.84	1.08	NA	6.56	0.74	NA	2.16	0.71	NA	0.75	0.49	NA	0.18	0.62	NA	1.50
TVL-SLAM-VL calib [5]	0.57	NA	0.88	0.86	NA	4.40	0.67	NA	1.87	0.71	NA	0.74	0.45	NA	0.22	0.57	NA	1.19
LIO-SAM [17]	253	31.0	956	2.94	0.60	19.8	268	87.6	212	NA	NA	NA	0.92	0.47	0.30	1.08	0.40	4.16
JVLDLoc input IMLS	0.63	0.15	1.31	0.88	0.06	1.77	0.65	0.11	2.62	0.70	0.14	0.53	0.29	0.10	0.15	0.54	**0.12**	**1.13**

loosely-coupled methods, which cause quite large translation error; TVL-SLAM [5] is a SOTA visual-LiDAR SLAM on KITTI, which also incorporates visual and lidar measurements in backend optimization. TVL-SLAM VL calib refers to their online camera-lidar extrinsics calibration version. Our JVLDLoc can outperform TVL-SLAM VL calib though using raw extrinsics. LIO-SAM [17] is representative method of Lidar-inertial SLAM. We run its open source code with given parameters[1]. Due to the unknown intrinsics of the IMU, LIO-SAM failed on 00, 02, 08, but we can get better acuracy on three metrics for all left sequences.

5.4 Ablation Study

Different Number of Direction Priors. Here we attempt to relax the strength of direction priors by reducing the number of keyframes involved in direction priors. For each direction cluster, downsample at a distance $V_{interval}$ from the distribution of existing VPs. Figure 6 is a visualization of different downsampled direction priors. Figure 8 shows the comparison of APE under different $V_{interval}$.

From those figures, we can concluded that the APE do not suffer drastic expansion due to less direction constraints. Even though there is only about 10 direction constraints retained, we still get quite better accuracy than no direction priors at all. Because the left direction priors can still play some roles. So we argue that as long as there is a few direction constraints over a long distance, the drift will be reduced at a certain level. For each KITTI sequence's relative rotation error and APE RMSE under differnent $V_{interval}$, see supplementary material.

We also explore the influence of different scan map size **N** of each keyframe. The plot and analysis of that result are in supplemental material (page limit).

---

[1] https://github.com/TixiaoShan/LIO-SAM#other-notes.

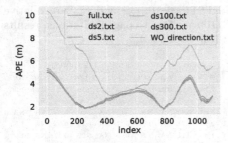 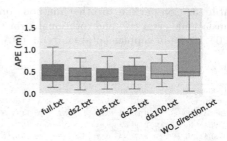

Fig. 8. Left: Comparison of APE on KITTI 01.The x-coordinate is frame index. Right: Box plots of APE on KITTI 07. *full* refers to no downsampling, *WOdirection* refers to no direction priors. Other lines respectively corresponds to different $V_{interval}$. Take *ds2.txt* as an example, it is the APE when $V_{interval} = 2$.

6   Conclusion

This paper present a strategy that combines map prior and VPs from images to create direction projection error, which is an energy term solely bound on rotation. Then, we implement these direction priors into a visual-LiDAR localization system that tightly couples camera and LiDAR measurements. Experiments on three driving datasets prove that our method achieve lower localization drift. Even though our method is effective and outperforms many related work, There are still two flaws. One thing is time efficiency. Our current implementation can not run in real-time. It is a trade-off between performance and time cost. The second thing is that our method relies on an assumption that agent locally moves on an approximate plane. So compared to UAV or handheld devices, the driving scenes are more likely to meet the above assumptions.

Acknowledgements. This work is supported by the National Key Research and Development Program of China (2017YFB1002601), National Natural Science Foundation of China (61632003, 61375022, 61403005), Beijing Advanced Innovation Center for Intelligent Robots and Systems (2018IRS11), and PEK-SenseTime Joint Laboratory of Machine Vision.

References

1. Andrew, A.M.: Multiple view geometry in computer vision. Kybernetes (2001)
2. Barnes, D., Gadd, M., Murcutt, P., Newman, P., Posner, I.: The oxford radar RobotCar dataset: a radar extension to the oxford RobotCar dataset. In: Proceedings of IEEE International Conference on Robotics and Automation (ICRA) (2020). https://doi.org/10.1109/ICRA40945.2020.9196884
3. Bosse, M., Rikoski, R., Leonard, J., Teller, S.: Vanishing points and three-dimensional lines from omni-directional video. Vis. Comput. **19**(6), 417–430 (2003). https://doi.org/10.1007/s00371-003-0205-3

4. Campos, C., Elvira, R., Rodríguez, J.J.G., Montiel, J.M., Tardós, J.D.: ORB-SLAM3: an accurate open-source library for visual, visual-inertial, and multimap slam. IEEE Trans. Robot. **37**(6), 1874–1890 (2021)
5. Chou, C.C., Chou, C.F.: Efficient and accurate tightly-coupled visual-lidar slam. IEEE Trans. Intell. Transp. Syst. **23**, 14509–14523 (2021)
6. Deschaud, J.E.: IMLS-SLAM: scan-to-model matching based on 3d data. In: Proceedings of IEEE International Conference on Robotics and Automation (ICRA), pp. 2480–2485. IEEE (2018)
7. Geiger, A., Lenz, P., Stiller, C., Urtasun, R.: Vision meets robotics: The KITTI dataset. Int. J. Robot. Res. **32**(11), 1231–1237 (2013)
8. Gräter, J., Wilczynski, A., Lauer, M.: LIMO: lidar-monocular visual odometry. In: Proceedings of IEEE International Conference on Intelligent Robots and Systems (IROS), pp. 7872–7879 (2018)
9. Grupp, M.: EVO: Python package for the evaluation of odometry and slam. https://github.com/MichaelGrupp/evo (2017)
10. Huang, S.S., Ma, Z., Mu, T.J., Fu, H., Hu, S.: Lidar-monocular visual odometry using point and line features. In: Proceedings of IEEE International Conference on Robotics and Automation (ICRA), pp. 1091–1097 (2020)
11. Kümmerle, R., Grisetti, G., Strasdat, H., Konolige, K., Burgard, W.: G2o: a general framework for graph optimization. In: Proceedings of IEEE International Conference on Robotics and Automation (ICRA), pp. 3607–3613. IEEE (2011)
12. Liao, Y., Xie, J., Geiger, A.: KITTI-360: a novel dataset and benchmarks for urban scene understanding in 2D and 3D. arXiv:2109.13410 (2021)
13. Lim, H., Jeon, J., Myung, H.: UV-SLAM: unconstrained line-based slam using vanishing points for structural mapping. IEEE Robot. Autom. Lett. **7**, 1518–1528 (2022)
14. Lin, J., Zheng, C., Xu, W., Zhang, F.: R2LIVE: a robust, real-time, LiDAR-inertial-visual tightly-coupled state estimator and mapping. arXiv preprint arXiv:2102.12400 (2021)
15. Liu, J., Meng, Z.: Visual slam with drift-free rotation estimation in Manhattan world. IEEE Robot. Autom. Lett. **5**(4), 6512–6519 (2020)
16. Mur-Artal, R., Tardós, J.D.: ORB-SLAM2: an open-source SLAM system for monocular, stereo, and RGB-D cameras. IEEE Trans. Robot. **33**(5), 1255–1262 (2017)
17. Shan, T., Englot, B., Meyers, D., Wang, W., Ratti, C., Rus, D.: LIO-SAM: Tightly-coupled lidar inertial odometry via smoothing and mapping. In: Proceedings of IEEE International Conference on Intelligent Robots and Systems (IROS), pp. 5135–5142. IEEE (2020)
18. Shan, T., Englot, B., Ratti, C., Rus, D.: LVI-SAM: Tightly-coupled lidar-visual-inertial odometry via smoothing and mapping. In: Proceedings of IEEE International Conference on Robotics and Automation (ICRA), pp. 5692–5698. IEEE (2021)
19. Shin, Y.-S., Park, Y.S., Kim, A.: DVL-SLAM: sparse depth enhanced direct visual-LiDAR SLAM. Auton. Robot. **44**(2), 115–130 (2019). https://doi.org/10.1007/s10514-019-09881-0
20. Sturm, J., Engelhard, N., Endres, F., Burgard, W., Cremers, D.: A benchmark for the evaluation of RGB-D SLAM systems. In: Proceedings of IEEE International Conference on Intelligent Robots and Systems (IROS), pp. 573–580. IEEE (2012)
21. Wang, P., Fang, Z., Zhao, S., Chen, Y., Zhou, M., An, S.: Vanishing point aided lidar-visual-inertial estimator. In: Proceedings of IEEE International Conference on Intelligent Robots and Automation (ICRA), pp. 13120–13126. IEEE (2021)

22. Xiang, Z.Z., Yu, J., Li, J., Su, J.: ViLiVO: Virtual LiDAR-visual odometry for an autonomous vehicle with a multi-camera system. In: Proceedings of IEEE International Conference on Intelligent Robots and Systems (IROS), pp. 2486–2492 (2019)

23. Yu, H., Zhen, W., Yang, W., Zhang, J., Scherer, S.: Monocular camera localization in prior lidar maps with 2D–3D line correspondences. In: Proceedings of IEEE International Conference on Robotics and Systems (IROS), pp. 4588–4594. IEEE (2020)

24. Zhang, J., Kaess, M., Singh, S.: A real-time method for depth enhanced visual odometry. Auton. Robot. **41**(1), 31–43 (2015). https://doi.org/10.1007/s10514-015-9525-1

25. Zhao, S., Zhang, H., Wang, P., Nogueira, L., Scherer, S.: Super odometry: IMU-centric LiDAR-visual-inertial estimator for challenging environments. In: Proceedings of IEEE International Conference on Robotics and Systems (IROS), pp. 8729–8736. IEEE (2021)

26. Zhen, W., Hu, Y., Yu, H., Scherer, S.: LiDAR-enhanced structure-from-motion. In: Proceedings of IEEE International Conference on Intelligent Robots and Automation (ICRA), pp. 6773–6779 (2020)

A Single-Pathway Biomimetic Model for Potential Collision Prediction

Song Zhang[1], Guodong Lei[1], and Xuefeng Liang[1,2($\boxtimes$)]

[1] School of Artificial Intelligence, Xidian University, Xi'an, China
{zhangsong,leiguodong}@stu.xidian.edu.cn, xliang@xidian.edu.cn
[2] Pazhou Lab, Huangpu, China

Abstract. In autonomous driving, predicting the potential collision on road from the first-person view is a very challenging task. Previous study developed a computational model for this task, called LGMD2, which is inspired by a perfect biological visual system, Lobula Giant Movement Detectors, in locusts. LGMD enables locusts to swarm and be free of collision. However, LGMD2 model assumes the moving objects are darker than the background, which rarely happens in real-world scenarios. Meanwhile, its computation structure (ON & OFF pathways) has mutual interference and produces incomplete information. Thus, LGMD2 results in a low prediction accuracy. In this study, we amend the assumption that is more in line with the reality, and propose a novel single-pathway LGMD2 model, SLGMD2. It avoids the interference and generates more complete signal for prediction. To evaluate the effectiveness of SLGMD2, we collect a new first-person view vehicle collision dataset. The experiment on both two public datasets and the newly collected dataset shows state-of-the-art performance of our proposed SLGMD2 model.

Keywords: SLGMD2 · LGMD2 · First-person view · Vehicle collision

1 Introduction

In the era of autonomous driving, it is essential but challenging to predict the potential vehicle collisions on road for the driving control system. Thus, the vision-based potential collision prediction in the first-person view becomes a critical technology. Emerging studies have applied deep learning methods to detect collisions. Liu et al. [16] used generative adversarial neural networks to predict future video frames of potential collisions. Chan et al. [4] introduced

This work was supported in part by the Guangdong Provincial Key Research and Development Programme under Grant 2021B0101410002.

Supplementary Information The online version contains supplementary material available at https://doi.org/10.1007/978-3-031-18913-5_13.

a dynamic spatial attention RNN to detect car accidents. Herzig et al. [12] proposed a spatio-temporal graph action network to represent the relation of multiple moving objects for accident detection. Bao et al. [1] utilized graph convolution and RNN to extract spatio-temporal representation of collisions and leveraged Bayesian neural network to estimate the predictive uncertainty. These methods are supervised learning, which requires a large amount of labeled data for training. However, car accidents are rare events, unlikely to be collected on a large scale. Meanwhile, the end-to-end architecture of deep learning is a black-box model that is difficult to interpret.

In the evolution, animals have developed their highly effective visual systems for predicting potential collisions. Biologists found that locusts have a group of cells [8,9], called Lobula Giant Movement Detectors (LGMDs), which is very sensitive and robust to those quickly looming objects. LGMDs can help locusts avoid collisions during the flight in flocks [15]. It relies on two crucial signals, the angle between the locust's eyes and the approaching target, and the corresponding angular velocity. Inspired by LGMDs, researchers have proposed two computational models: the LGMD1 [18] and the LGMD2 [17]. LGMD1 mimics the wide-field approaching movement-sensitive neurons, and is able to sense all quickly approaching objects. The LGMD2, which is an upgrade version of LGMD1, aims to be more sensitive to the darker looming object in a lighter background [20], representing swooping predators from the sky. Hence, LGMD2 is designed with additional ON and OFF parallel pathways [2]. Both models have been applied to robots [6,7,14,23] and unmanned aerial vehicles [11], and tested in controlled laboratory environments. The results have demonstrated the effectiveness of LGMDs.

However, both models perform much worse on real-world data because of the following two factors: 1. LGMD2 is designed to sense motion signals. The first-person view data consists of two types of motion: 1) the ego-motion caused by the camera, and 2) motions of the foreground moving objects in the scene. The collision motions belong to the 2nd type of motion. However, the input of LGMD2 includes both two types of motions. It introduces massive noise in the processing. 2. The LGMD2 model assumes that the foreground looming objects are darker than the background, therefore has the specific ON and OFF pathways [6]. However, such assumption is rare in real-world driving scenarios, because vehicles may be brighter than the background. It makes the ON and OFF pathways have mutual interference and results in a worse performance.

To address the above two issues, we firstly borrow the instance segmentation method to separate the foreground objects and the background. Only moving foreground objects are used as input signals. Afterwards, the background is marked as black (intensity as 0). This operation changes the assumption of LGMD2 as the foreground objects are always brighter than the background, which is able to eliminate the noisy signals caused by ego-motion. To better utilize the new input signals, we design a single-pathway LGMD2 model, SLGMD2, which merges the ON and OFF pathways to avoid mutual interference. Thus, SLGMD2 can be sensitive to brighter moving objects, and more robust to real-world data. In addition, to evaluate the performance of different collision prediction methods, we collect a new dataset, consisting of 850 first-person view vehicle collision videos and 850 normal (non-collision) videos. The experimental results on two public datasets and the new first-person view vehicle collision dataset demonstrate state-of-the-art performance of our proposed SLGMD2 model.

The main contributions of this work are threefold: 1) we propose a single-pathway LGMD2 model, SLGMD2, which is more robust to the moving objects. Also, we set up a new reliable assumption that the foreground objects are brighter than the background, which is more in line with the reality; 2) the proposed SLGMD2 model achieves state-of-the-art performance on three datasets; 3) we construct a new first-person view collision dataset, including 1700 videos, which boosts the development of first-person view collision prediction methods.

2 Related work

We give an overview of related work on LGMDs and deep learning-based dashcam-mounted collision prediction.

Lobula Giant Moment Detectors (LGMDs): As bio-inspired computational models, LGMDs are detecting looming objects to avoid collision. Based on bio-inspired features of contour change in looming objects, LGMDs is a powerful white-box method. Its clear interpretation is critical for many real-world application, such as autonomous driving. The first computational model of the LGMD1 was proposed by Rind et al. [18]. To enhance the feature of colliding objects, Yue et al. [23] proposed a new excitation enhancing mechanism to filter isolated excitation in robotic scenarios. In order to optimize parameters of LGMD1, Yue et al. [24] introduced genetic algorithms in robot. In UAV application, He et al. [11] combined LGMD1, image moment with deep reinforcement learning for robust mapless navigation. Compared with LGMD1, LGMD2 model has robust selectivity. Fu et al. [17] proposed an LGMD2 model that has ON-OFF pathway. It responses to darker looming objects, which mimics swooping predators from the sky. And Fu et al. [6] utilized LGMD2 to test in three vehicle videos and implement it into a micro-mobile robot.

Deep learning-based collision prediction: Recent works in deep learning boosted the development of collision prediction. Chan et al. [4] introduced the collision prediction task, and they proposed dynamic soft-attention in LSTM model to predict accident. Based on this work, Suzuki et al. [21] applied an adaptive loss function for more earlier collision prediction. In order to improve prediction accuracy, Zeng et al. [25] proposed a multi-task learning method and localized potential dangerous regions. Inspired by self-attention, Herzig et al. [12] proposed a spatio-temporal action graphs to detect collision using scene relationship between objects. Recently, Bao et al. [1] proposed to learn spatio-temporal representation through graph convolution network and recurrent neural network, and introduced Bayesian deep neural network to predict uncertainty of latent representations. However, these deep learning methods are difficult to be interpreted. In addition, they need large scale datasets to train the model to avoid overfitting. Unfortunately, it is extremely dangerous to collect such collision data. Thanks to evolved architecture in nature and explicit biological mechanism, LGMDs does not need large scale datasets.

3   Proposed Method

In this section, we will firstly define the problem of first-person view vehicle collision prediction, and then explain the details of proposed SLGMD2.

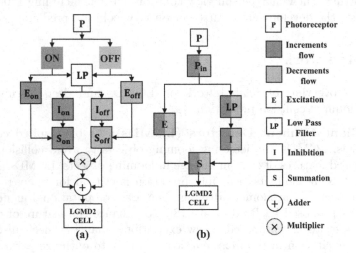

Fig. 1. Structure of (a) original LGMD2 and (b) proposed single-pathway LGMD2.

3.1   Problem Formulation

Given a video's frame x_t captured by dashcam in current time point t, the model is expected to predict the probability $p_t = f(x_t; \theta)$ whether an ego-involved vehicle accident would occur in the future, where θ denotes parameters of model $f(\cdot)$. The valid constraint of predicting time period t ranges from the moment C to the moment T, where C is the time of appearance of the target car, T is the time of the accident. The goal of collision prediction task is to predict the potential collision in the valid time period $C < t < T$ as early as possible. The p_t is ideally expected to be 1 for accident videos and 0 for normal videos (non-collision).

3.2   The Single-Pathway LGMD2

Before explaining our single-pathway LGMD2, let's briefly review the original LGMD2 model. It consists of four kinds of layers, photoreceptor (P), excitation (E), inhibition (I), summation (+), and a LGMD cell, as shown in Fig. 1(a).

The photoreceptor layer computes the temporal derivative of every grayscale pixel to perceive motion information. This information is divided into luminance increments flow (the blue signal in Fig.1(a)) and decrements flow (the orange signal), and passes through parallel ON and OFF pathways that have the excitation, inhibition and summation layers, respectively. In each pathway, luminance flow passes through the excitation layer without temporal latency. Meanwhile, it is fed into a first-order low-pass filter, then, is convolved to form the inhibition signal. Afterwards, the local excitation and inhibition signals compete with each other at the first summation layer. Subsequently, the signals from both ON and OFF pathways interact at the second summation layer. Finally, the LGMD cell integrates the output signals from two pathways. When the collision prediction criterion is met, the original LGMD2 will report a potential collision. The criterion is the cumulative value of output values is greater than the collision threshold, T', in a specified time window.

In experiments, we observe that the signals from both ON and OFF pathways are not perfectly complementary. Therefore, they interfere with each other at the second summation layer, and result in an incomplete signal for the LGMD cell. To avoid the interference between ON and OFF pathways, we propose a single-pathway LGMD2, as shown in Fig. 1(b).

Preprocessing. To set up new assumption for model that foreground objects are brighter than the background, we apply instance segmentation to mask the foreground vehicles, and then set the intensity value of background to be zero. This operation can not only remove the irrelevant background, which let model concentrate on the moving foreground cars instead of the ego-motion, but also set up a new assumption that looming objects are always brighter than the background.

Photoreceptor Layer. The input layer of SLGMD2 is a photoreceptor, which computes the contour change of moving object. Actually, it is the brightness change of moving object between every two successive frames, which is

$$P(x, y, t) = L(x, y, t) - L(x, y, t - 1), \tag{1}$$

where $L(x, y, t)$ represents the video frame at time t, x and y are the horizontal and vertical positions in the camera coordinate. The result is then passed through the single pathway.

The single Pathway. In the SLGMD2 model, the motion information, P_{in}, will not be divided into the brightness increment and decrement flows anymore, but is going to be directly processed, as shown in Fig. 1(b). P_{in} is defined as

$$P_{in}(x, y, t) = P(x, y, t) + \alpha P(x, y, t - 1). \tag{2}$$

To make the motion signal smooth, a small fraction α of residual P is allowed to pass through as well. The excitation layer, E, is motion-dependent [8], hence, P_{in} directly passes through, which is

$$E(x, y, t) = P_{in}(x, y, t). \tag{3}$$

The inhibition layer is size-dependent [8]. In other words, it extracts the change of object size in P_{in}. Thus, P_{in} is firstly processed by a low-pass temporal filter, which is

$$\widehat{I}(x, y, t) = \beta P_{in}(x, y, t) + (1 + \beta)P_{in}(x, y, t - 1), \tag{4}$$

where β is a weight coefficient. Then, $\widehat{I}$ is convolved to generate the size-dependent inhibition signal I. That is

$$I(x, y, t) = -\sum_{i=-1}^{1} \sum_{j=-1}^{1} \widehat{I}(x + i, y + j, t)W(i + 1, j + 1), \tag{5}$$

where W is a 3×3 spatial kernel. When the excitation is greater than the inhibition, the summation S is activated, otherwise, S keeps inactive. It is defined as

$$S(x, y, t) = [E(x, y, t) + I(x, y, t)]^{+}, \tag{6}$$

where x^{+} denotes $max(0, x)$. This single-pathway model is more suitable for the assumption that the looming object is brighter than the background. In addition, it can avoid the interference between ON and OFF pathways.

LGMD Cell. Following the mechanism of pre-synaptic processing in biological visual system, the LGMD cell integrates S value of every pixel in the frame to form the neural potential K, then, K is transformed to the sigmoid membrane potential M as below,

$$\begin{aligned} K(t) &= \sum_{x=1}^{W} \sum_{y=1}^{H} S(x, y, t), \\ M(t) &= \left(1 + e^{-K(t)(W \cdot H)^{-1}}\right)^{-1}, \end{aligned} \tag{7}$$

where W and H denote the width and height of the frame.

Finally, the membrane potential M is exponentially mapped to the output $S_{out}(t)$ of LGMD cell, which is

$$S_{out}(t) = e^{\gamma(M(t) - T_{out})}, \tag{8}$$

where γ is a scale parameter for the firing rate, and T_{out} denotes the output threshold.

3.3   Collision Prediction Criteria

Unlike the prediction criterion of the original LGMD2, we use two criteria for SLGMD2. First, the output of LGMD cell $S_{out}(t)$ must be greater than a threshold T_1. Due to the input noise and computation errors, $S_{out}(t)$ may not be very smooth between adjacent frames. We then use a regression function $f(t)$ to fit values of $S_{out}(t)$ of all frames in a time interval by the least square. Thus, the second criterion requires that the gradient of $f(t)$ must be greater than a threshold T_2. It denotes the speed change of the looming vehicle. When both criteria are met, SLGMD2 will report a potential collision.

$$collision(t) = \begin{cases} True, & \text{if } S_{out}(t) > T_1 \text{ and } \frac{\mathrm{d}f(t)}{\mathrm{d}t} > T_2, \\ False, & otherwise. \end{cases} \tag{9}$$

4   Experiments and Analyses

In this section, we first introduce the datasets used for the experiments and the competing methods, and then give the experimental parameters and evaluation metrics. Finally, the effectiveness of our method is demonstrated by experimental results and correlation analysis.

4.1   Datasets and Competing Methods

To evaluate the effectiveness of our proposed SLGMD2, we utilize three datasets for an impartial comparison, including two public accident benchmarks, i.e., Detection of Traffic Anomaly (DoTA) [22], Car Crash Dataset (CCD) [1], and a new collected FirstPerson view Vehicle Collision (FPVC) dataset. The two public accident datasets are used in ego-involved parts for fair comparison. Because DoTA dataset only contains collision videos (positives), we add varied negatives of new collected FPVC dataset to keep the number of positives and negatives balance. In CCD dataset, we sample one negative video within three consecutive negatives of same scene due to imbalance of positives and negatives. Furthermore, to provide a more diverse and complex dataset, we collected 850 first-person view vehicle collision videos (positives) from Youtube and 850 non-collision videos (negatives) including varied scenes from nuscenes [3], argoverse [5] and apollo [13] datasets, and construct a new dataset, FPVC, for the task of collision prediction. It consists of three typical collision scenarios, head-on crash (268), side crash (333), and rear-end crash (249). Each video lasts from 5 seconds to 15 seconds. We will release this dataset later. Note that we study collision prediction from the first-person view. So, our SLGMD2 is not designed for videos from the third-person view, such as the dashcam accurate dataset (DAD) [4] used in DSA [4] and UString [1].

There also exist a few studies working on the collision prediction as well. However, the method in [16] works in third-person view, meanwhile, requires a still camera. Herzig's approach [12] treats the vehicle collision as a video classification problem, instead of predicting the potential collision. Thus, we only compare with original LGMD2 [6], deep learning methods DSA [4], UString [1] on three datasets.

4.2   Parameter Setting

The parameters of SLGMD2 are set as follows, $\alpha = 0.1$, $\gamma = 4$, $T_{out} = 0.7$, $T_1 = 1.25$, $T_2 = 0.014$,

$$\beta = \begin{bmatrix} 0.16 & 0.22 & 0.16 \\ 0.22 & 0.36 & 0.22 \\ 0.16 & 0.22 & 0.16 \end{bmatrix}, W = \begin{bmatrix} 0.125 & 0.25 & 0.125 \\ 0.25 & 1 & 0.25 \\ 0.125 & 0.25 & 0.125 \end{bmatrix}.$$

Parameter settings of β and W are inspired by locust's cell connection[19]. β represents the multi-frame cumulative inhibition impact in temporal domain. The larger corresponding parameter value, the higher the proportion of current frame's signal, thus inhibition becomes stronger. According to [19], center cell in $3 * 3$ windows has the highest level of inhibition, therefore center cell is set to be the largest, smaller parameters are set to the edge and corner cells. W represents the local cellular interaction in spatial domain. The larger corresponding parameter value, the stronger the inhibition. The order of parameter value setting in W is the same as β. α is the intensity smoothness of the luminance change and is set to 0.1 because an over smoothing will blur the contour variation and degrade performance. γ indicates the firing rate parameter, and T_{out} indicates the output threshold. Increasing of γ and decreasing of T_{out} contribute to larger output values. For T_1 and T_2, over large values will cause a false negative prediction, and over small values will cause a false positive prediction. The feasible values of T_1 and T_2 are 1.25 and 0.014, respectively, which result in a good prediction before the actual accident happening.

We follow the parameter setting in [6], [4] and [1] for original LGMD2, DSA and UString, respectively. And Mask-RCNN [10] is applied to segment vehicles in the videos.

4.3   Evaluation Metrics

Unlike other studies, we define that a valid prediction of true positives (TP) must be made after the time of target appearing in the video (C) and before the time of collision happening (T), $C < t < T$. A prediction is marked as a false positive (FP) if it is made when $t < C$ or $t > T$. For negative samples, we treat them as true negatives (TN) if no prediction is made. On the contrary, we treat them as false negative (FN) if a prediction is made at any time in the videos. To predict the potential collision, we apply *accuracy* and *F1 score* as evaluation metrics,

Table 1. The evaluation results on three datasets.

DataSet	Metric	LGMD2 [6]	DSA [4]	UString [1]	SLGMD2
DoTA [22]	F1-score	0.09	0.30	0.32	**0.35**
	Acc(%)	21.74	41.61	41.72	**46.33**
CCD [1]	F1-score	0.18	0.24	0.24	**0.28**
	Acc(%)	30.09	50.81	51.83	**54.71**
FPVC	F1-score	0.23	0.31	0.29	**0.33**
	Acc(%)	28.88	40.71	40.59	**45.76**

Table 2. Ablation study on three datasets. IS denotes Instance Segmentation.

DataSet	Metric	LGMD2 [6]	IS+LGMD2	SLGMD2-IS	SLGMD2
DoTA [22]	F1-score	0.09	0.17	0.24	**0.35**
	Acc(%)	21.74	29.77	26.71	**46.33**
CCD [1]	F1-score	0.18	0.26	0.27	**0.28**
	Acc(%)	30.09	39.94	32.79	**54.71**
FPVC	F1-score	0.23	0.26	0.32	**0.33**
	Acc(%)	28.88	34.65	37.18	**45.76**

Table 3. The evaluation results on mixed datasets that do not have ego-motion.

Metric	LGMD2 [6]	IS+LGMD2	SLGMD2-IS	SLGMD2
Acc(%)	41.44	43.24	56.76	**63.02**

$$\text{Accuracy} = \frac{TP+TN}{TP+FP+TN+FN},$$
$$F1 = 2 \times \frac{P \times R}{P+R},$$

(10)

where P denotes precision. R denotes recall.

4.4 Experimental Results

Table 1 lists the quantitative comparison among existing state-of-the-art methods and our SLGMD2. One can observe that our proposed SLGMD2 method outperforms all competing methods in terms of two metrics. Note that the prediction of potential collision will not be correct if the target vehicle does not yet appear. However, this kind of invalid predictions often happens in the deep learning methods, DSA and UString. The possible reason might be that DSA and UString methods do the video classification task which let models learn features from videos even before the appearance of target cars. This may make the model overfit the data. On the contrary, SLGMD2 method is based on the bio-inspired feature. Thus, it only predicts potential collision after target vehicle appears and overcomes this problem. Moreover, there are many bypass scenarios in datasets, in which bypass vehicles also show a quick approaching motion. Such scenarios will cause the lower prediction accuracy (Tables 4 and 5).

To evaluate the effectiveness of new assumption and single-pathway architecture, ablation study is carried out on three datasets. Table 2 shows LGMD2 reaches the lowest F1-score and accuracy. The reason could be that the ego-motion gets into the processing as well, which introduces massive noise. This is confirmed in Table 3 tested on foreground-motion only videos in mixed datasets, exclusive of ego-motion. By using instance segmentation, the results of IS+LGMD2 indicate the effectiveness of new assumption that foreground objects are brighter than the background. When both the instance segmentation and single-pathway architecture are applied, SLGMD2 demonstrates a considerable improvement. This is achieved mainly thanks to the single-pathway architecture, which avoids the interference between ON and OFF pathways of original LGMD2. In addition, the vehicle segmentation also helps SLGMD2. When Instance Segmentation is not applied (SLGM2-IS), the performance has a considerable degradation.

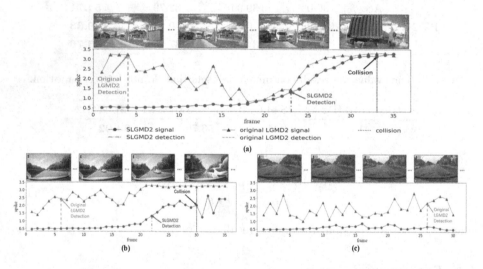

Fig. 2. Three sample videos and the comparison of prediction results. (a) head-on collision, (b) rear-end collision, and (c) non-collision. The triangle curve is the result of original LGMD2. The dot curve is the result of SLGMD2. The red indicates the model predicts a potential collision, on the contrary, the green means that the model does not. The blue and red dashed lines show the timepoints when models predict the potential collision, respectively. The black dashed line shows the timepoint when the actual collision happens. The images on the top are frame samples of videos. The one with red box denotes that the frame triggers the SLGMD2. The one with green box does not. (Color figure online)

Table 4. The prediction accuracies in three types of collision scenarios of FPVC dataset.

Method	Head-on crash	Side crash	Rear-end crash	Average
LGMD2 [6]	20.15	20.12	22.09	20.71
IS+LGMD2	23.88	22.52	21.69	22.71
SLGMD2-IS	23.88	24.62	24.10	24.23
DSA [4]	**27.24**	27.63	25.30	26.82
UString [1]	24.25	24.62	22.09	23.76
SLGMD2	25.37	**29.43**	**26.50**	**27.29**

Table 5. The prediction accuracies in three normal video sets of FPVC dataset.

Method	Nuscenes sets	Argoverse sets	Apollo sets	Average
LGMD2 [6]	26.81	54.19	17.39	37.06
IS+LGMD2	41.70	56.29	**26.09**	46.59
SLGMD2-IS	37.87	55.69	17.39	43.76
DSA [4]	51.49	64.07	17.39	54.59
UString [1]	54.04	67.07	21.74	57.41
SLGMD2	**63.19**	**71.56**	21.74	**64.24**

Figure 2 illustrates the intuitive comparison on three sample videos, which are head-on, rear-end collisions and non-collision scenario. Figure 2 (a) shows a head-on collision. One can see that the original LGMD2 wrongly acts at the very beginning of the video when the opposite vehicle looks pretty tiny. We think it is mainly caused by the ego-motion because the original LGMD2 does not separate the foreground and background. Meanwhile, its result wavily fluctuates, thus, leads to false predictions. On the contrary, SLGMD2 predicts the potential collision about 10 frames before the actual collision. It is because that the result of our SLGMD2 is rather stable and leads to a smoothly monotonic change, which makes our prediction criteria Eq. 9 robust. Figure 2 (b) shows a rear-end collision. The car behind is quickly approaching the car in front. Analogously, the original LGMD2 wrongly acts when the front car is very tiny. And the significant false result continues until the end of the video, regardless of whether two cars are far or close. Instead, the result of SLGMD2 is stable and smooth. We can see an obvious gradient of the result change when two cars are getting close. It makes SLGMD2 act about 8 frames before the actual collision. Figure 2 (c) shows a non-collision scenario. When cars just pass by, the result of original LGMD2 still wavily fluctuates. It gives a false prediction at the 26th frame. We think it is caused by ego-motion and the interference between ON and OFF pathways. Ego-motion causes the over strong output value, and the interference makes the wave fluctuation. By contrast, the result of SLGMD2 is rather smooth. And, no false prediction is reported.

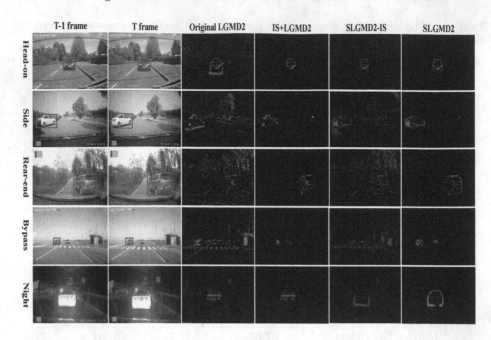

Fig. 3. The visualization of results of summation layers in original LGMD2 and SLGMD2, including 5 different scenarios. The first two columns are two consecutive frames (the vehicles are marked in red boxes). The last four columns show the results of four models respectively. (Color figure online)

To have an insight of the impact of ego-motion and the interference between ON and OFF pathways, we visualize the signals in the summation layer of LGMD2, IS+LGMD2, SLGMD2-IS and SLGMD2 models in Fig. 3. One can see that a lot of background noise exists when the instance segmentation is not applied. The noise severely downgrades the original LGMD2. After applying the instance segmentation, the result of summation layer focuses more on the overlapping part of vehicle between two consecutive frames, but is rather incomplete due to the interference of two pathways. Instead, the result of SLGMD2 shows a much more complete contour of vehicle. It is in line with the biological vision system, which senses the change of the object size. Thus, SLGMD2 performs more robust on this task.

5   Conclusions

This paper proposes a single-pathway LGMD2 model for predicting the potential vehicle collision from the first-person view on road. Compared with the original LGMD2 model, we make a new assumption that the foreground objects are brighter than the background by using the instance segmentation, meanwhile, design a single-pathway architecture that avoids the interference between ON and OFF pathways in original LGMD2. The experiments on two public datasets and a new collected dataset demonstrate the considerable performance improvement. In the future work, we will further study on integrating the motion orientation into our model.

References

1. Bao, W., Yu, Q., Kong, Y.: Uncertainty-based traffic accident anticipation with spatio-temporal relational learning. In: Proceedings of the 28th ACM International Conference on Multimedia (2020)
2. Borst, A., Euler, T.: Seeing things in motion: models, circuits, and mechanisms. Neuron **71**(6), 974–994 (2011)
3. Caesar, H., et al.: nuScenes: a multimodal dataset for autonomous driving. In: Proceedings of the IEEE/CVF Conference on Computer Vision and Pattern Recognition, pp. 11621–11631 (2020)
4. Chan, F.-H., Chen, Y.-T., Xiang, Yu., Sun, M.: Anticipating accidents in dashcam videos. In: Lai, S.-H., Lepetit, V., Nishino, K., Sato, Y. (eds.) ACCV 2016. LNCS, vol. 10114, pp. 136–153. Springer, Cham (2017). https://doi.org/10.1007/978-3-319-54190-7_9
5. Chang, M.F., et al.: Argoverse: 3D tracking and forecasting with rich maps. In: Proceedings of the IEEE/CVF Conference on Computer Vision and Pattern Recognition, pp. 8748–8757 (2019)
6. Fu, Q., Hu, C., Peng, J., Rind, F.C., Yue, S.: A robust collision perception visual neural network with specific selectivity to darker objects. IEEE Trans. Tybernet. **50**(12), 5074–5088 (2019)
7. Fu, Q., Hu, C., Peng, J., Yue, S.: Shaping the collision selectivity in a looming sensitive neuron model with parallel on and off pathways and spike frequency adaptation. Neural Netw. **106**, 127–143 (2018)
8. Gabbiani, F., Krapp, H.G., Koch, C., Laurent, G.: Multiplicative computation in a visual neuron sensitive to looming. Nature **420**(6913), 320–324 (2002)
9. Hatsopoulos, N., Gabbiani, F., Laurent, G.: Elementary computation of object approach by a wide-field visual neuron. Science **270**(5238), 1000–1003 (1995)
10. He, K., Gkioxari, G., Dollár, P., Girshick, R.: Mask r-cnn: In: Proceedings of the IEEE International Conference on Computer Vision, pp. 2961–2969 (2017)
11. He, L., Aouf, N., Whidborne, J.F., Song, B.: Integrated moment-based LGMD and deep reinforcement learning for UAV obstacle avoidance. In: 2020 IEEE International Conference on Robotics and Automation (ICRA), pp. 7491–7497. IEEE (2020)
12. Herzig, R., et al.: Spatio-temporal action graph networks. In: Proceedings of the IEEE/CVF International Conference on Computer Vision Workshops, pp. 2347–2356 (2019)
13. Huang, X., Wang, P., Cheng, X., Zhou, D., Geng, Q., Yang, R.: The ApolloScape open dataset for autonomous driving and its application. IEEE Trans. Pattern Anal. Mach. Intell. **42**(10), 2702–2719 (2019)
14. Jayachandran, D., et al.: A low-power biomimetic collision detector based on an in-memory molybdenum disulfide photodetector. Nature Electron. **3**(10), 646–655 (2020)
15. Kennedy, J.S.: The migration of the desert locust (schistocerca gregaria forsk.). i. the behaviour of swarms. ii. a theory of long-range migrations. In: Philosophical Transactions of the Royal Society of London. Series B, Biological Sciences, pp. 163–290 (1951)

16. Liu, W., Luo, W., Lian, D., Gao, S.: Future frame prediction for anomaly detection-a new baseline. In: Proceedings of the IEEE Conference on Computer Vision and Pattern Recognition, pp. 6536–6545 (2018)
17. Qinbing, Fu, S.Y., Hu, C.: Bio-inspired collision detector with enhanced selectivity for ground robotic vision system. In: Richard, C., Wilson, E.R.H., Smith, W.A.P. (eds.) Proceedings of the British Machine Vision Conference (BMVC), pp. 6.1–6.13. BMVA Press (2016). https://doi.org/10.5244/C.30.6
18. Rind, F.C., Bramwell, D.: Neural network based on the input organization of an identified neuron signaling impending collision. J. Neurophysiol. **75**(3), 967–985 (1996)
19. Rind, F.C., et al.: Two identified looming detectors in the locust: ubiquitous lateral connections among their inputs contribute to selective responses to looming objects. Sci. Rep. **6**(1), 1–16 (2016)
20. Simmons, P.J., Rind, F.C.: Responses to object approach by a wide field visual neurone, the LGMD2 of the locust: characterization and image cues. J. Comp. Physiol. A **180**(3), 203–214 (1997)
21. Suzuki, T., Kataoka, H., Aoki, Y., Satoh, Y.: Anticipating traffic accidents with adaptive loss and large-scale incident DB. In: Proceedings of the IEEE Conference on Computer Vision and Pattern Recognition, pp. 3521–3529 (2018)
22. Yao, Y., Wang, X., Xu, M., Pu, Z., Atkins, E., Crandall, D.: When, where, and what? A new dataset for anomaly detection in driving videos. arXiv preprint arXiv:2004.03044 (2020)
23. Yue, S., Rind, F.C.: A collision detection system for a mobile robot inspired by the locust visual system. In: Proceedings of the 2005 IEEE International Conference on Robotics and Automation, pp. 3832–3837. IEEE (2005)
24. Yue, S., Rind, F.C., Keil, M.S., Cuadri, J., Stafford, R.: A bio-inspired visual collision detection mechanism for cars: optimisation of a model of a locust neuron to a novel environment. Neurocomputing **69**(13–15), 1591–1598 (2006)
25. Zeng, K.H., Chou, S.H., Chan, F.H., Carlos Niebles, J., Sun, M.: Agent-centric risk assessment: accident anticipation and risky region localization. In: Proceedings of the IEEE Conference on Computer Vision and Pattern Recognition, pp. 2222–2230 (2017)

PilotAttnNet: Multi-modal Attention Network for End-to-End Steering Control

Jincan Zhang[1] , Zhenbo Song[1] , Jianfeng Lu[1(✉)] , Xingwei Qu[2] ,
and Zhaoxin Fan[3]

[1] School of Computer Science and Engineering, Nanjing University of Science
and Technology, Nanjing, China
{jczhang,songzb,lujf}@njust.edu.cn
[2] Arcisstr. 21, 80333 Munich, Germany
xingwei.qu@tum.de
[3] School of Information, Renmin University of China, Beijing 100872, China
fanzhaoxin@ruc.edu.cn

Abstract. Vision-based end-to-end steering control is a popular and
challenging task in autonomous driving. Previous methods take single image or image sequence as input and predict the steering control angle by deep neural networks. The image contains rich color and
texture information, but it lacks spatial information. In this work, we
thus incorporate LiDAR data to provide spatial structures, and propose
a novel multi-modal attention model named PilotAttnNet for end-to-end steering angle prediction. We also present a new end-to-end self-driving dataset, Pandora-Driving, which provides synchronized LiDAR
and image sequences, as well as corresponding standard driving behaviors. Our dataset includes rich driving scenarios, such as urban, country, and off-road. Extensive experiments are conducted on both publicly
available LiVi-Set and our Pandora-Driving dataset, showing the great
performance of the proposed method.

Keywords: End-to-end learning · Multi-modal fusion · Steering
control

1 Introduction

Autonomous driving aims to be self-driving without human intervention. Current autonomous driving frameworks can be divided into two main approaches:
modular and end-to-end. The modular approach has good interpretability and is
conducive to the localization and tracking of problems. Nevertheless, this pipeline
is very complex, because many sub-modules and rules are included to handle.
That means the response delay from visual perception to control signal could
be too long. By contrast, the end-to-end approach is a learning-based approach
that directly generates driving commands, including speed control and steering
control from sensor inputs. The end-to-end models decrease the processing time

S. Yu et al. (Eds.): PRCV 2022, LNCS 13536, pp. 179–191, 2022.
https://doi.org/10.1007/978-3-031-18913-5_14

from perception to control, and it is easier to deploy on vehicles. For end-to-end models, steering control is more complicated than speed control due to the significant role it plays in collision avoidance.

Even though the end-to-end steering angle control has recently shown promising results, there are still some challenges with this approach. For example, for vision-based models, when the color of the obstacle is similar to the environment background, collision accidents could happen. The lack of spatial information limits the potential of end-to-end approaches. In this case, LiDAR is a very good choice to provide spatial information. Another observation is that during driving, the driver will pay more attention to objects such as vehicles, pedestrians, and roads and give less attention to backgrounds such as the sky. Similarly, the visual attention mechanism in driving models [5,20] can selectively extract important information, thereby reducing information redundancy and improving the accuracy of efficient driving instruction prediction. The visual attention model predicts a spatial mask of weights corresponding to "where to attend", and this mask can increase model interpretability. To achieve a better end-to-end steering control, we propose a novel multi-modal attention model that takes a color image sequence and corresponding LiDAR data as inputs and generates driving commands directly.

We built a new end-to-end driving dataset that contains more driving scenarios than existing datasets. Our dataset is collected using a camera-LiDAR combined product called Pandora, so we named our dataset as Pandora-Driving. According to the road type, we divide our dataset into two parts: Pandora-DrivingI and Pandora-DrivingII. The proposed method is evaluated on the public LiVi-Set subset and the newly built Pandora-Driving. Experiment results show that our method exceeds the performance of the state of the art models.

Our main contributions are as follows:

(1) We propose a novel end-to-end steering prediction model, PilotAttnNet, which leverages temporal, color images, and corresponding LiDAR information to generate accurate steering control angle values.
(2) We design a multi-modal attentional feature extractor, which is carefully designed to reduce parameter size and computational complexity.
(3) We build a new dataset containing richer scenarios than existing datasets.

2   Related Work

2.1   Driving Model

The modular approach [11,18] detects and classifies the surrounding environment through the sensory inputs and finally generates the corresponding vehicle control commands based on the deterministic rules. This pipeline concentrates on well-defined sub-tasks and independently makes improvements across the whole stack. If useful information is not contained in the current representation, it will not be retrievable for the subsequent modules. As decision-making depends on road and traffic context, the vast variety of driving scenarios and environments makes it incredibly hard to cover all the cases with proper contextualized solutions [8, 9, 21]. What's more, designing ideal rules for various scenarios is a heavy and difficult task.

The end-to-end approach is a behavior reflex approach, which can directly map the visual inputs to the vehicle control commands without human-defined information bottlenecks rules. ALVINN [12] is the first one to use the end-to-end method in autonomous driving and it can only drive well on simple roads with a few obstacles. Nvidia first used CNN to construct an autonomous driving system, they built a PilotNet [4] on self-driving vehicles to predict the steering angle and it performed well on simple highway roads with fewer obstacles. Xu et al. [16] introduced LSTM module into the network to extract the temporal relationship between the images in sequence. Although the color image contains rich color and texture information, it is not sufficient to achieve stable autonomous driving only relying on the color image. In this task, LiDAR is a very good choice to provide spatial information. LiDAR scanners directly produce distance measurements of the environment. Moreover, compared with color cameras, LiDAR scanners are robust under almost all lighting conditions and they can provide rich geometric information and depth information of the scenarios. Most researchers believe that the combination of cameras and LiDAR should obtain a comprehensive semantic understanding of real traffic better. How to use the information provided by LiDAR is crucial in autonomous driving. Chen et al. [7] attempted different lines of techniques to seek powerful range representation, including Point Clouds Mapping and PointNet [13]. As well as the BEV method, Point Clouds Mapping is efficient but loses one dimension, destroying the geometric structure of the point clouds and causing serious information loss.

2.2 Driving Dataset

Existing datasets cover less complex traffic scenarios, which restricts autonomous driving systems from learning different driving strategies. To effectively alleviate the impact of insufficient datasets, a number of platforms have also emerged for automatic driving data generation and vehicle control testing. The platform autonovi-sim [1] supports specific configurations of systems: the changes in time, weather, and participants such as cyclists and pedestrians. The platform APOLLO [17] integrates a large amount of data from virtual traffic. Virtual traffic data use specific, well-defined obstacles and manually created traffic signals. Compared with the real traffic situation, the authenticity and complexity of these data are insufficient. The simulation platforms cannot perfectly simulate complex environments such as weather conditions and road traffic conditions. They also cannot simulate the complex conditions of different vehicles and sensor noise. Some researchers have built a lot of real-life driving datasets, such as LiVi-Set [7] and BDD100K Dataset [19]. The LiVi-Set contains video, point clouds, and corresponding steering angle and speed values. The main driving scenarios included in this dataset are urban roads and highways. The BDD dataset contains only video, GPS, and IMU, and corresponding steering angle values are not collected. The steering angle values are calculated by IMU information, so their accuracy cannot be verified.

We prefer to use the real dataset to make our model more realistic. To make the training effective, we construct our Pandora-Driving dataset. It contains images, camera calibration data, point clouds, and corresponding throttle position, steering angle, and brake position information. It includes multiple driving scenarios, such as urban, country, and off-road. The off-road driving scene is not available in many datasets.

3   Method

3.1   Spatial Information Encoding

As mentioned above, spatial information plays a vital role in autonomous driving. The output of LiDAR is a sparse cloud of unordered points. It is common to preprocess these points into binary 3D occupancy grids and input them into CNNs. However, working toward the 3D occupancy grids (*e.g.* via 3D convolution) can be costly [22], because the number of voxels increases rapidly with spatial precision. PointNet [13] can convert the raw point clouds directly to useful features but the inference delay in the onboard platform is too long. Instead of the raw point clouds, another option is to project the point clouds to a 2D grid in Bird's-Eye View (BEV) [6], or via Polar Grid Mapping (PGM) [14]. BEV projects each point to the ground plane and preserves only points' height information. This projection method is efficient but destroys the geometric structure of the 3D space. By comparison, the PGM method maintains the most information on the 3D structure. That's saying, the approximate point clouds can be recovered from the PGM image. Besides, the PGM representation of LiDAR inputs has been proved to increase end-to-end driving performance [14]. Inspired by this work, we convert the point clouds into a range image via PGM. Then we calculate the object-clustering angle [3] of each valid point to include the instance object information. Afterward, the range image and its corresponding pixel-wise angle map are concatenated together to explicitly encode spatial information. We named them the spatial map.

For each 3D point, the corresponding coordinate on the range image is determined by its horizontal and vertical angle. We define the LiDAR coordinate as the axis of x towards the right, y along the vehicle's forward-moving direction, and z towards the sky. Given a 3D point (x, y, z), the distance to LiDAR origin is computed as follows:

$$D = \sqrt{x^2 + y^2 + z^2} \tag{1}$$

Accordingly, the horizontal and vertical angle is calculated by the following equations.

$$A_h = tan^{-1}(x/y) \tag{2}$$

$$A_v = sin^{-1}(z/D) \tag{3}$$

After getting all points' horizontal and vertical angles, the corresponding coordinate (u, v) on the range image can be obtained. Given the minimum horizontal $min(A_h)$, minimum vertical angle $min(A_v)$, as well as the angle resolution R_h and R_v, the coordinate (u, v) is calculated by:

$$u = round((A_h - min(A_h))/R_h) \tag{4}$$

$$v = round((A_v - min(A_v))/R_v) \tag{5}$$

In the range image, each valid pixel stores the corresponding point distance, which reflects the collision risk around the vehicle. A sample of range image is illustrated in Fig. 3(a). However, in driving scenarios, the raw points do not explicitly describe the instance-level object information. The end-to-end model has to understand high-level semantics from raw input, which imposes additional learning burdens. Consequently, we introduce the object-clustering angle [3] into the end-to-end model to provide implicit semantics. For a valid pixel, the object-clustering angle is calculated with its neighbor pixels in the range image. In Fig. 1, a toy example is given, showing the specific process of the computation. Here A and B as two adjacent valid pixels and OA and OB represent two laser beams. The object-clustering angle β is defined as the angle between AO and AB. Suppose the vertical foot from point B to A is H, then the calculation of β is given by:

$$\beta = tan^{-1}(BH/AH) = tan^{-1}(d_1 sin\omega/(d_2 - d_1 cos\omega)) \tag{6}$$

where ω is the scanning angle between two laser beams, and it can be easily obtained from the range image's resolution settings. d_1 and d_2 are the shorter and longer distance of the two points respectively. In the toy sample, d_1 is the distance of OB and d_2 is the distance of OA. If these two neighboring points A and B given by the range image belong to the same object, β should be larger. Smaller β represents points A and B are more likely to belong to different objects. This insight allows us to define a hyperparameter θ that acts as a threshold on the angle β. This threshold enables us to decide whether to separate any two points in the range image into separate clusters or merge them into one. We can segment instance objects by using θ and β, namely $\beta > \theta$ indicating the same object and $\beta < \theta$ indicating different objects. The pixel-wise angle map and the segmented object map are visualized in Fig. 3(b) and Fig. 3(c). We then use the angle map along with the range image as inputs to the end-to-end model.

3.2   The End-to-End Attentional Driving Model

In the context of end-to-end autonomous driving, given the inputs (*i.e.* images, point clouds, *etc.*) perceived by sensors, our task is to give the corresponding

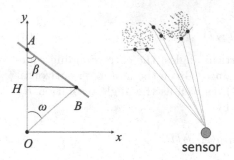

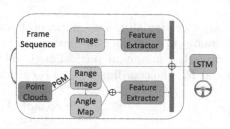

Fig. 1. The schematic of the angle map.

Fig. 2. The framework of PilotAt-tnNet.

steering angle prediction. Due to the continuity of driving behavior, the sequential processing network LSTM is a better choice for this task. Although existing LSTM-based methods have achieved promising results, there are still some drawbacks when handling multi-modal dense inputs. Previous models use CNN for feature extractor, but CNN-based deep features always have redundant. In fact, for human driving, only a few components of the scene call attention, such as the road surface, pedestrians, and vehicles. Recently, the self-attention mechanism has shown great performance in a lot of vision tasks. The attention method could be embedded into the CNN architecture and obtain weighted features according to spatial or channel-wise information. Thus, we employ both spatial attention and channel attention into our end-to-end model.

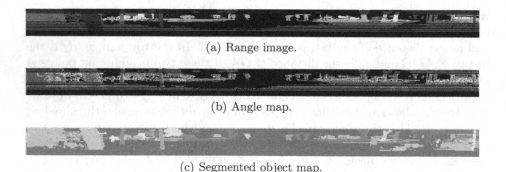

(a) Range image.

(b) Angle map.

(c) Segmented object map.

Fig. 3. The illustration of the range image, angle map, and segmented object map.

Specifically, we insert the CBAM [15] attention module between convolutional blocks of the CNN, forming the attentional feature extractor. We utilize the LSTM module after the attentional feature extractor to integrate the temporal information. We name the proposed network as PilotAttnNet. The whole pipeline is shown in Fig. 2. Considering the low computation capacity of vehicles, we design a lightweight network model as much as possible. As shown in Fig. 4, only three CNN blocks are used in the feature extractor, which would sharply reduce the inference time.

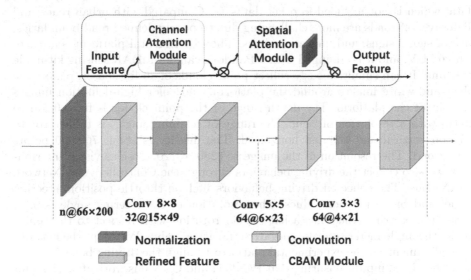

Fig. 4. The network architecture of the feature extractor.

4   Experiments

The prediction of end-to-end autonomous driving can be divided into discrete behavior prediction and continuous behavior prediction. Discrete prediction can be identified as a classification task, which divides the forecasting results into predetermined categories, such as go forward, stop, turn left, turn right, *etc.* Continuous prediction can be identified as a regression task, and the output is the control information of the vehicle such as the steering angle. The latter method can learn from human driving behavior. So, we use continuous prediction to conduct our experiments on real-world datasets.

4.1   Dataset Description

In this work, The LiVi-Set dataset and the proposed Pandora-Driving dataset are used to verify the performance of our method. The LiVi-Set contains point clouds, video, and corresponding driving behaviors. The video is captured by the minor distortion dashboard camera. The driving scenarios in the LiVi-Set dataset are mostly urban roads and highways. They only preprocessed a subset of this dataset [7]. There are some video and driving behavior data misalignments in other raw datasets which have not been preprocessed. We use their prepared dataset with few errors, although the prepared dataset size is small.

The Pandora-Driving dataset contains images, point clouds, and corresponding steering angle values. Our Pandora-Driving covers more frames of data and more complex scenes. Besides urban road data, we also collect some off-road data, which is not included in other datasets. Compared with urban roads and highways, off-roads are more challenging due to poorly defined road boundaries, lack of signal signs, and uneven surfaces. The experimental platform is a Cheetah v6 SUV, and it is equipped with a Pandora camera-LiDAR sensing kit made in China. It can simultaneously collect point clouds of 40 lines laser, panoramic black-and-white images around the platform, and color high-definition images in front of the platform. The depth range of the point clouds is from 0.3 m to 200 m with a resolution of 2 cm. The range of scanning angles is from $-16°$ to $+7°$ on vertical and $360°$ on horizontal. The density is about 700,000 points per second. The resolution of the image is 1280×720. Besides visual information, we also collect the driving behaviors through the Controller Area Network (CAN) bus. The collected driving behaviors include throttle position, steering angle, and brake position values. The resolution of the steering angle is $0.1°$. When the steering wheel has a left (right) rotation with respect to the center angle, the angle meter records a negative (positive) value. We adopt the network time alignment on the experimental platform to align the driving behavior data with the visual inputs, ensuring that Pandora and CAN bus work at 10 HZ. Our dataset contains 20 groups data. The total collection time is more than 100 min, and the total number of images (point clouds) collected is more than 60000 frames. As shown in Fig. 5, we reveal some representative data from Pandora-Driving, including corresponding images, point clouds, and steering angle values in different scenes.

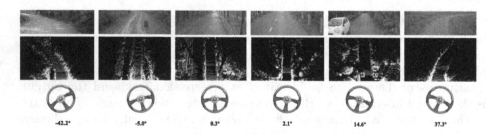

Fig. 5. The representative examples in the Pandora-Driving dataset. For each column, the first line is the RGB image, the second line is the corresponding point clouds, and the last line is the corresponding steering angle.

Compared with the LiVi-Set, our dataset not only has richer scenes but also has higher quality.

4.2   Evaluation Metrics

Many researchers have proposed various different evaluation metrics to evaluate the performance of the end-to-end steering angle prediction model. They can mainly be divided into open-loop evaluation and closed-loop evaluation. In the open-loop evaluation, the decisions of the self-driving model are compared with the recorded decisions of a human driver [5,10]. In contrast, closed-loop evaluation directly evaluates the performance of a driving model in a realistic (real or simulated) driving scenario by giving the model control over the car. The specific metrics in such methods are the percentage of successful trials [8], percentage of autonomy [4], and average distance between infractions [8], *etc.* Such metrics are too crude to accurately evaluate the system. For example, when human intervention is required, we cannot distinguish how far the current system is off the road. In other words, we cannot distinguish the difference between the different predicted steering angles when human intervention is required. The widely adopted accuracy rate [7,10] is one of the most direct and effective evaluation metrics. Therefore, we adopt accuracy as one of the metrics in this work. We need the steering angle tolerance threshold to conveniently calculate the accuracy. Even in the real world, the driver's driving behavior also has a small deviation. In our work, we choose 5° as the steering angle tolerance threshold, while [7] choose 6°. What's more, just using the accuracy lacks details and is not intuitive enough. So, we use the Area Under Curve roc (AUC) as the other evaluation metric.

Since most of the roads are dominated by straight lines, so the most of steering angle values are around 0°. Although our dataset is more complex and balanced than the LiVi-Set, it still cannot fundamentally change this property (Fig. 6). A common idea to solve this double long-tailed distribution data imbalance problem is boosting the importance of some steering angle values which have bigger absolute values and occur rarely. Balanced-MAE [2] can adaptively assign weight to steering angle according to its appearing proportion, which fits our requirement. So, we use balanced-MAE [2] as the loss function.

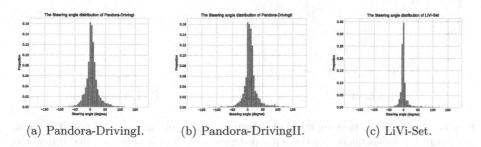

(a) Pandora-DrivingI.   (b) Pandora-DrivingII.   (c) LiVi-Set.

Fig. 6. The comparison of our Pandora-Driving dataset and the LiVi-Set dataset's steering angle distribution range.

4.3   Results

We have done a lot of comparative experiments to verify the effect of our method. Because we want to construct a lightweight model that can be deployed on the onboard platforms, so we use PilotNet [7] as the backbone and balanced-MAE [2] as the loss function for the comparative benchmark.

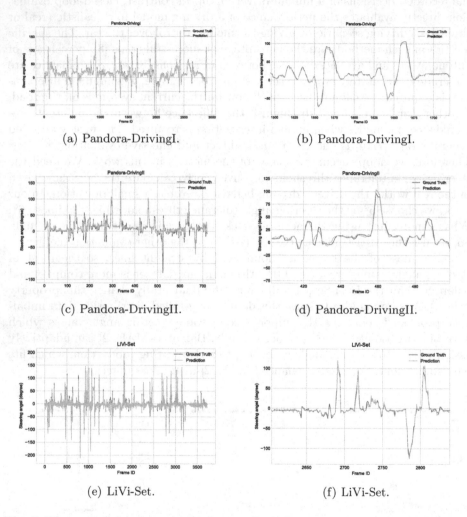

(a) Pandora-DrivingI.   (b) Pandora-DrivingI.

(c) Pandora-DrivingII.   (d) Pandora-DrivingII.

(e) LiVi-Set.   (f) LiVi-Set.

Fig. 7. The predicted steering angle of our method of a continuous sequence. The right sub-figure is a sub-sequence of the left sub-figure such that a more detailed difference can be observed.

Table 1. Performance of different combinations of methods and inputs.

Methods	Metrics	Inputs					
		Image			Image + Spatial Map		
		LiVi-Set	PandoraI	PandoraII	LiVi-Set	PandoraI	PandoraII
PilotNet	Accuracy	69.77%	69.23%	74.17%	74.50%	74.42%	76.39%
	AUC	78.36%	76.47%	82.12%	79.86%	80.15%	81.35%
PilotAttnNet	Accuracy	76.37%	81.11%	79.03%	83.07%	86.43%	83.33%
	AUC	81.48%	84.38%	83.67%	84.94%	86.03%	85.47%

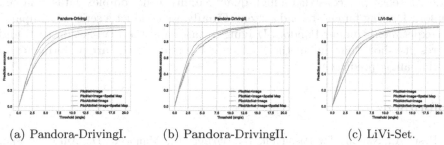

(a) Pandora-DrivingI.   (b) Pandora-DrivingII.   (c) LiVi-Set.

Fig. 8. The prediction accuracy of different combinations of methods and inputs under different tolerance thresholds.

We did comparative experiments by inputting the color image sequence, with or without the corresponding spatial map. All experiments are conducted based on the LiVi-Set and the proposed dataset respectively.

Table 1 respectively shows the steering angle prediction accuracy and AUC of our experiments, where the angle tolerance thresholds are set to 5° and 20° respectively. One line in this table shows the performance of different inputs with the same method in all datasets. One column in this table shows the performance of different methods with the same input in all metrics. It is found that incorporating the spatial map and using the proposed model can both improve the performance on the current task. As can be seen from this table, our method with the color image sequence plus the corresponding spatial map as inputs achieves the best performance in various metrics. To more intuitively show the prediction of this combination, we show the predicted steering angle values of this combination and the ground truth of a continuous sequence in Fig. 7.

In addition, we show the accuracy under different tolerance thresholds in Fig. 8. We can intuitively observe the accuracy of different methods at the same threshold and the accuracy of the same method at different thresholds in this figure respectively. As can be seen from this figure, all the methods have better accuracy performance with the increase of the threshold. The accuracy of our method is the best at different thresholds in both datasets.

5 Conclusion

In this paper, we propose a novel end-to-end steering control model, PilotAttnNet, which inputs image and LiDAR sequences and predicts steering control angle. We first leverage the LiDAR data to encode spatial information as the range image and the angle map. Then, we use self-attention CNN to extract features from spatial information and RGB images. After that, we utilize the LSTM module to integrate the temporal information and generate the steering control angle. Moreover, we construct a high-quality multi-scene complex dataset named Pandora-Driving for end-to-end system. Finally, we conduct a series of comparative experiments on our Pandora-Driving dataset and the LiVi-Set dataset, and the results show that our method achieves the state of the art performance in steering angle prediction.

References

1. Best, A., Narang, S., Pasqualin, L., Barber, D., Manocha, D.: AutonoVi-Sim: autonomous vehicle simulation platform with weather, sensing, and traffic control. In: Proceedings of the IEEE Conference on Computer Vision and Pattern Recognition Workshops, pp. 1048–1056 (2018)
2. Bewley, A., et al.: Learning to drive from simulation without real world labels. In: 2019 International Conference on Robotics and Automation (ICRA), pp. 4818–4824. IEEE (2019)
3. Bogoslavskyi, I., Stachniss, C.: Efficient online segmentation for sparse 3D laser scans. PFG-J. Photogramm. Remote Sens. Geoinf. Sci. **85**(1), 41–52 (2017)
4. Bojarski, M., et al.: End to end learning for self-driving cars. arXiv preprint arXiv:1604.07316 (2016)
5. Bojarski, M., et al.: Explaining how a deep neural network trained with end-to-end learning steers a car. arXiv preprint arXiv:1704.07911 (2017)
6. Chen, X., Ma, H., Wan, J., Li, B., Xia, T.: Multi-view 3D object detection network for autonomous driving. In: Proceedings of the IEEE Conference on Computer Vision and Pattern Recognition, pp. 1907–1915 (2017)
7. Chen, Y., et al.: Lidar-video driving dataset: learning driving policies effectively. In: Proceedings of the IEEE Conference on Computer Vision and Pattern Recognition, pp. 5870–5878 (2018)
8. Dosovitskiy, A., Ros, G., Codevilla, F., Lopez, A., Koltun, V.: Carla: an open urban driving simulator. In: Conference on Robot Learning, pp. 1–16. PMLR (2017)
9. Fan, Z., Zhu, Y., He, Y., Sun, Q., Liu, H., He, J.: Deep learning on monocular object pose detection and tracking: a comprehensive overview. arXiv e-prints, pp. arXiv-2105 (2021)
10. Kim, J., Canny, J.: Interpretable learning for self-driving cars by visualizing causal attention. In: Proceedings of the IEEE International Conference on Computer Vision, pp. 2942–2950 (2017)
11. Krejsa, J., Věchet, S., Hrbáček, J., Schreiber, P.: High level software architecture for autonomous mobile robot. In: Brezina, T., Jablonski, R. (eds.) Recent Advances in Mechatronics, pp. 185–190. Springer, Cham (2010). https://doi.org/10.1007/978-3-642-05022-0_32

12. Pomerleau, D.: An autonomous land vehicle in a neural network. In: Advances in Neural Information Processing Systems, vol. 1 (1998)

13. Qi, C.R., Su, H., Mo, K., Guibas, L.J.: PointNet: deep learning on point sets for 3D classification and segmentation. In: Proceedings of the IEEE Conference on Computer Vision and Pattern Recognition, pp. 652–660 (2017)

14. Sobh, I., et al.: End-to-end multi-modal sensors fusion system for urban automated driving (2018)

15. Woo, S., Park, J., Lee, J.-Y., Kweon, I.S.: CBAM: convolutional block attention module. In: Ferrari, V., Hebert, M., Sminchisescu, C., Weiss, Y. (eds.) ECCV 2018. LNCS, vol. 11211, pp. 3–19. Springer, Cham (2018). https://doi.org/10.1007/978-3-030-01234-2_1

16. Xu, H., Gao, Y., Yu, F., Darrell, T.: End-to-end learning of driving models from large-scale video datasets. In: Proceedings of the IEEE Conference on Computer Vision and Pattern Recognition, pp. 2174–2182 (2017)

17. Xu, K., Xiao, X., Miao, J., Luo, Q.: Data driven prediction architecture for autonomous driving and its application on Apollo platform. In: 2020 IEEE Intelligent Vehicles Symposium (IV), pp. 175–181. IEEE (2020)

18. Yang, S., Mao, X., Yang, S., Liu, Z.: Towards a hybrid software architecture and multi-agent approach for autonomous robot software. Int. J. Adv. Rob. Syst. 14(4), 1729881417716088 (2017)

19. Yu, F., et al.: BDD100K: a diverse driving dataset for heterogeneous multitask learning. In: Proceedings of the IEEE/CVF Conference on Computer Vision and Pattern Recognition, pp. 2636–2645 (2020)

20. Zeiler, M.D., Fergus, R.: Visualizing and understanding convolutional networks. In: Fleet, D., Pajdla, T., Schiele, B., Tuytelaars, T. (eds.) ECCV 2014. LNCS, vol. 8689, pp. 818–833. Springer, Cham (2014). https://doi.org/10.1007/978-3-319-10590-1_53

21. Zeng, W., et al.: End-to-end interpretable neural motion planner. In: Proceedings of the IEEE/CVF Conference on Computer Vision and Pattern Recognition, pp. 8660–8669 (2019)

22. Zhou, Y., Tuzel, O.: VoxelNet: end-to-end learning for point cloud based 3D object detection. In: Proceedings of the IEEE Conference on Computer Vision and Pattern Recognition, pp. 4490–4499 (2018)

Stochastic Navigation Command Matching for Imitation Learning of a Driving Policy

Xiangning Meng, Jianru Xue[✉], Kang Zhao, Gengxin Li, and Mengsen Wu

Institute of Artificial Intelligence and Robotics, College of Artificial Intelligence, Xi'an Jiaotong University, Xi'an, China
jrxue@mail.xjtu.edu.cn

Abstract. Conditional imitation learning provides an efficient framework for autonomous driving, in which a driving policy is learned from human demonstration via mapping from sensor data to vehicle controls, and the navigation command is added to make the driving policy controllable. Navigation command matching is the key to ensuring the controllability of the driving policy model. However, the vehicle control parameters output by the model may not coincide with navigation commands, which means that the model performs incorrect behavior. To address the mismatching problem, we propose a stochastic navigation command matching (SNCM) method. Firstly, we use a multi-branch convolutional neural network to predict actions. Secondly, to generate the probability distributions of actions that are used in SNCM, a memory mechanism is designed. The generated probability distributions are then compared with the prior probability distributions under each navigation command to get matching error. Finally, the loss function weighted by matching and demonstration error is backpropagated to optimize the driving policy model. The significant performance improvement of the proposed method compared with the related works has been verified on the CARLA benchmark.

Keywords: Autonomous driving · Driving policy · Imitation learning

1 Introduction

Driving policy has a pivotal role in autonomous driving system, which builds a bridge from perception to control. Many researches effort within the field of intelligent vehicles have been focused on learning a driving policy. Different from traditional motion planning system [1–4] which realizes autonomous driving from high level to low level (as shown in Fig. 1 left), learning-based method uses a deep neural network to parameterize the driving policy and trains through imitation learning (IL) or reinforcement learning (RL). The learned driving policy model directly maps sensor observations to vehicle controls.

Learning-based methods provide a concise framework for autonomous driving. A series of researches [5–8] for learning driving policy model follow the conditional imitation learning (CIL) [9] which leverages navigation command generated from global

This work is supported by the National Natural Science Foundation of China Projects 62036008.

S. Yu et al. (Eds.): PRCV 2022, LNCS 13536, pp. 192–203, 2022.
https://doi.org/10.1007/978-3-031-18913-5_15

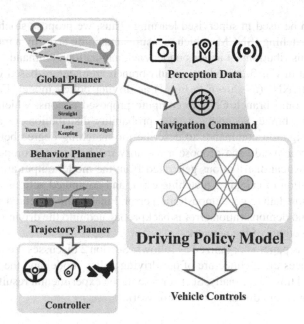

Fig. 1. Overview of the modular pipeline (left) and driving policy model in CIL framework (right). CIL parameterizes driving policy with a neural network and selects the behavior with navigation commands generated from global planner.

route planner to guide motion planning (as shown in Fig. 1 right). The navigation command provides guidance for the vehicle at the intersection and reinforces the controllability of imitation learning. However, during the test of CIL, we find that the vehicle may take wrong actions that are inconsistent with the navigation command in some cases, such as the example shown in Fig. 2. We define this problem as "navigation command mismatch", which most of the existing methods didn't attach importance to as far as we know. Navigation command mismatch may cause the vehicle to spend more time than the optimal global path planning and even make the global planner have to replan the global path.

One possible reason behind the problem of navigation command mismatch in CIL is that it only uses the navigation command as gating function and ignores its strong influence on action generation. The essence of CIL is an end-to-end solution, which may lead learned model only capture weak navigation information. Moreover, CIL only use lowdimensional control parameters as supervision data, effective exploration of the supervision information implied in demonstration data could be used to further improve the performance of the driving policy model. Thus, navigation command matching (NCM) is very important for training an efficient driving policy model.

An NCM model [8] was proposed to generate a smooth reward for reinforcement learning of driving policy model. The model uses conditional probability to measure the matching degree between trajectory (state-action pairs) and navigation commands. Motivated by this work, we further find that relationship between actions and navigation commands could be used in supervised learning. Thus, we propose stochastic navigation command matching (SNCM) which measures matching error by a metric between two probability distributions of actions under each navigation command.

As illustrated in Fig. 3, we adopt a multi-branch architecture-based convolutional neural network (CNN) (as shown in Fig. 4) as driving policy model. Firstly, images are fed into the multi-branch CNN to compute proposed actions, which are steering angle, throttle and brake. Secondly, we use probability distributions of actions under each kind of navigation commands to describe the matching degree between actions and navigation commands and propose a memory mechanism to compute the distributions. The statistical distributions generated from the model output are compared to the prior distribution to calculate matching error, and computed actions are compared with demonstration data to get demonstration error. Finally, the weighted summation of matching error and demonstration error is backpropagated into the driving policy model to optimize the weights of the network.

The rest of this paper is organized as follows. Section 2 discusses the related works. Section 3 introduces the architecture of our driving policy model and the novel SNCM method for model training. Finally, Sect. 4 presents the experimental results, and Sect. 5 concludes the paper and discusses the future work.

Fig. 2. An example of navigation command failure. The navigation command given at the intersection is *Go Straight* (as shown by the green arrow in the figure), but the motion controls output by the driving policy model make the vehicle turn right at the intersection (as shown by the red arrow in the figure). (Color figure online)

2   Related Works

In learning-based autonomous driving, the mainstream method [9–11] adopts camera image as environment observation, and the methods roughly fall into two categories: imitation learning and reinforcement learning. Our work shares the idea of training a vision-based driving policy model by imitation learning.

Imitation learning enables the agent to learn how to perform a given task through the demonstration of human experts [12]. Bojarski *et al.* [10] did pioneering work in applying the imitation method in learning an end-to-end driving policy, and they trained a CNN through human driving data to control the steering wheel angle so that the vehicle can complete lane following task. Pan *et al.* [13] presented a similar IL system to achieve high-speed off-road autonomous driving in the real world. Similar work e.g. [14–16] focused on basic driving tasks like lane-keeping and obstacle-avoiding. Based on previous work, CIL [9] improved traditional policy network with multi decision branches and activated different branches through navigation command. The introduction of navigation command has been proven to improve the controllability of the driving policy model at intersections and improve the performance of autonomous cars in complex urban environments.

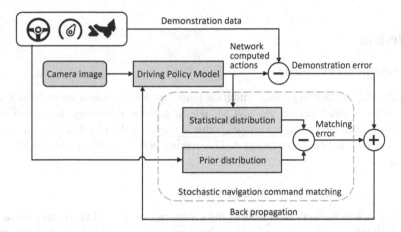

Fig. 3. The process of training driving policy model through stochastic navigation command matching.

As for imitation learning of a driving policy, model optimization uses a loss function. Most studies on driving policy model [7,9,16] adopt mean square error (MSE) between the predicted action value and the ground-truth value as loss functions. Different loss functions are designed along with different factors considered in the driving policy model. Uncertainty-aware imitation learning [6] suggested considering the uncertainty of the model output and proposed an uncertainty-aware loss function, which enabled the vehicle to learn a safer driving policy in unfamiliar scenarios. Li *et al.* [17] proposed a driving approach that splits the driving policy model into a perception module and a driving module. In their approach, softmax categorical cross-entropy and binary cross-entropy are used for perception module training, and MSE is used for driving module training. Conditional affordance learning [18] added the class-weighted categorical cross-entropy and mean average error to its loss function.

Our approach differs from existing methods by introducing NCM into the imitation learning of driving policy model, and we design matching loss to measure the matching degree between generated actions with navigation commands.

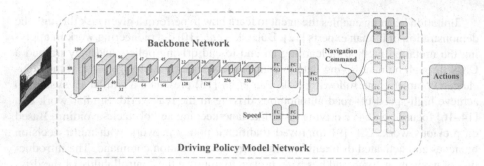

Fig. 4. Network architecture of our driving policy model. Image and speed measurement is fed into the network as input. The four branches follow, and navigation command activates relevant branch which outputs proposed actions.

3   Method

3.1   Problem Formulation

To realize effective driving policy imitation learning, we propose a multi-branch CNN driving policy model trained via SNCM, which generates steering, acceleration and braking commands from camera images, vehicle speeds and navigation commands. Our network architecture is shown in Fig. 4. The driving policy model is built via learning a mapping:

$$\pi(s_t, v_t, c_t, \theta) : s_t \rightarrow a_t \qquad (1)$$

where $s_t \in S$ is the observation state of the environment, $a_t \in A$ represents the actions the car will take, v_t is speed, $c_t \in C$ is the navigation command and θ is the policy parameter. At each time step t, the agent will receive an observation s_t and take an action a_t.

3.2   Backbone Network

As the most popular network architecture for driving policy model, CNN has shown good performance in vision-based autonomous driving. Our backbone network is a CNN, which is composed of four convolutional layers and four max-pooling layers sequentially and alternatively. The first layer has 32 5×5 filters with stride 2 followed by three other layers which have respectively 64, 128 and 256 kernels of size 3×3 and stride 1. Through the backbone network, each input image will result in a feature map. The feature map will be flattened and transformed into a feature vector of size 512 through 2 fully connected layers.

3.3   Navigation Command

In conditional imitation learning [9], navigation commands provide guidance for vehicle's action at intersections, which include:

- *Follow Lane* : lane keeping
- *Turn Left* : turn left at the next intersection
- *Turn Right* : turn right at the next intersection
- *Go Straight* : go straight at the next intersection

In driving policy model, navigation commands are generated from a global path planner and equivalent to the behavioral decision in the modular framework.

3.4   Multi-branch Architecture

To make driving policy model output actions respond to navigation commands, our model adopts a multi-branch structure in policy network. We use gating function $G(c_i)$ to activate the appropriate branch via control command c_i. In each branch, the feature vector f_i acts as input to three fully connected layers. At the output of the network, the activated branch delivers the action a_i, which consists of steering angle, throttle and brake.

3.5   Stochastic Navigation Command Matching

In the course of interaction with environment, at time step t, the agent receives current observation s_t, speed measurement v_t and navigation command c_t, and then learns to perform an action a_t.

Navigation command has a strong influence on steering angle. To qualitatively describe the relationship between them, we obtain the distribution of steering angles for each navigation command according to the data set in [9] and we use them to describe the relationship between navigation commands and steering angles. Therefore, the navigation command not only activates the branch but also guides generating vehicle actions.

We use the standard distribution as benchmark and compare the similarity between the probability distribution of the steering angle output by the model and the standard distribution. The closer the statistical distribution is to the standard distribution, the more actions output by the model matches the navigation commands.

Memory Mechanism. To make statistics on the steering angle output by the model, we need to sample the steering angle under each navigation command. For the supervised training, it is not available to get a large number of prediction results from the model at every moment.

In deep Q-learning [19], a mechanism known as *replay memory* is used for more efficient sampling. We consider applying *replay memory* in steering angle sampling. Specifically, we collect the pair of navigation command and steering angle $\{(c_i, a_i^s)\}_{i=1}^N$ output by the model at each training step, where N is batch size. It is worth noting that we have set four memory units for four different navigation commands (e.g. *Follow Lane, Turn Left, Turn Right, Go Straight*), the sampling result a_i^s will be stored in its corresponding memory unit according to its navigation command c_i (as shown in Fig. 5). Because the memory unit has a capacity limit, it is necessary to check whether the capacity is exceeded after storing the data every time. If it is exceeded, the earliest data stored in the unit will be deleted automatically.

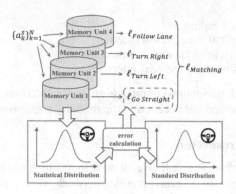

Fig. 5. The process of data storage and matching loss calculation. A batch of steering angles are assigned to memory units according to their corresponding navigation commands respectively, then the memory units update. For each memory unit, a batch of data is sampled to calculate probability distribution. The loss under each navigation command is obtained according to the error between the statistical distribution and prior distribution, and matching loss is the average of them.

Matching Loss. In SNCM, we need to measure the similarity between two distributions. Based on the data set, we get the standard discrete distribution $\mathcal{X} = \{\mathbf{x}^c : c \in C\} = \{(x_1^c, x_2^c, ..., x_n^c) : c \in C\}$ (since we divided the steering angle into 200 units, $n = 200$) of the steering angle under the four navigation commands c ($c \in C, C = \{$*Follow Lane, Turn Left, Turn Right, Go Straight*$\}$). At each training step, we sample in each memory unit separately, and obtain the discrete distribution of steering angle under each navigation command $\mathcal{Y} = \{\mathbf{y}^c : c \in C\} = \{(y_1^c, y_2^c, ..., y_n^c) : c \in C\}$.

We use Bhattacharyya distance to measure the similarity of the two sets of distributions. Bhattacharyya distance is the most common distance metric for measuring the similarity of two probability distributions. For discrete probability distributions, its definition is:

$$D_B(p, q) = -\ln(BC(p, q)) \tag{2}$$

where

$$BC(p, q) = \sum_{x \in X} \sqrt{p(x)q(x)} \tag{3}$$

and p, q are probability distributions of x.

The matching loss calculated by Bhattacharyya distance is:

$$\ell_{matching} = -\frac{1}{|C|} \sum_{c \in C} \ln(\sum_{i=1}^{n} \sqrt{x_i^c \cdot y_i^c}) \tag{4}$$

3.6 Training

We use imitation learning method to train our driving policy network π_θ. The demonstration data $D = \{(o_i, c_i, v_i, a_i)\}_{i=1}^{N}$ consists of observation image o_i, control command c_i, speed v_i and demonstration action a_i.

The complete training process is shown in Fig. 3. Observation o_i and speed v_i are the main input, and we use gating function $G(c_i)$ to activate appropriate branch via navigation command c_i. The parameter optimization of the driving policy network π_θ through imitation learning is to minimize the target loss function ℓ_{π_θ}, which is composed of action loss ℓ_{action} and matching loss $\ell_{matching}$ weighted:

$$\ell_{\pi_\theta} = \ell_{action} + w_\alpha \cdot \ell_{matching} \tag{5}$$

where the action loss is the MSE of the model's predictive value and the ground-truth value:

$$\ell_{action} = \sum_{i=1}^{N} \ell(\pi_\theta(o_i, v_i, G(c_i)), a_i) \tag{6}$$

and the matching loss is calculated according to (4).

4 Experiments

We evaluate our driving policy model in the open-source urban autonomous driving simulator CARLA [20], which provides a dynamic and open environment for research, development and testing of autonomous driving systems. In this section, we verify the effectiveness of our SNCM training in four challenging driving tasks proposed by CARLA.

4.1 Experiment Setting

Dataset. [9] provides an imitation learning dataset which contains more than ten hours of human driving data in CARLA simulator. The dataset mainly consists of RGB images, state measurements, control commands and navigation commands *et al.* We train our driving policy model on the dataset with the form as $D = \{(o_i, c_i, v_i, a_i)\}_{i=1}^{N}$ which is mentioned in Sect. 3.6.

Evaluation Benchmark. The experimental benchmark includes two experimental conditions: training and test, which are different in map and weather settings. The detailed information about the conditions can be seen in Table 1.

Table 1. Summary of experimental condition.

Condition	Map	Weather
Training	Town1	clear noon, clear sunset, hard rain noon, noon after rain
Test	Town2	cloudy noon after rain, soft rain at sunset

The benchmark provides four tasks with increasing difficulty. In each task, the agent car is randomly initialized in a start point and needs to reach a destination point. The tasks include:

- *Straight* : the start point and the destination point are in a straight line;
- *One turn* : there is a turn between the start point and the destination point;
- *Navigation* : there is no special restriction between the start point and the destination point, the path usually includes several turns;
- *Navigation with dynamic obstacles* : same as *Navigation*, but there are dynamic objects in the scenario.

For each combination of a task, a town, and a weather set, the paths are carried out over 25 episodes. In each episode, the target of driving agent is to reach a given goal location. An episode is considered successful if the agent reaches the goal within a time budget, which is set to reach the goal along the optimal path at a speed of 10 km/h.

Implementation Details. Our model was trained using the Adam solver [21] with batch size of 64 samples and an initial learning rate of 0.0001. The capacity of each memory unit is 1000. Training is completed on NVIDIA Titan XP GPUs. Other parameter settings are the same as [9].

4.2 Quantitative Comparison

We compare our SNCM with modular pipeline (MP) [20], reinforcement learning (RL) [20] and conditional imitation learning (CIL) [9] by success rate of autonomous driving tasks on CARLA benchmark. From Table 2, we can observe that our method outperforms all baseline methods with the highest average success rate of about 300 episodes.

Table 2. Average success rate of different methods of all autonomous driving tasks.

Method	Success rate
MP [20]	69.19%
RL [20]	27.44%
CIL [9]	72.19%
SNCM (ours)	**76.13%**

Table 3 reports the quantitative comparisons with baseline methods by the percentage of successful episodes in each task. As we can see, the agent trained via SNCM outperforms the baselines in most tasks, especially in *Straight* and *One Turn* tasks, e.g. 70% of SNCM vs. 50%, 20% and 48% of MP, RL and CIL. Besides, SNCM particularly excels in generalizing to the new town & new weather, the condition where most baselines did not perform well, but the average performance of our method is almost 70% better than the best baseline.

Table 3. Quantitative evaluation on goal-directed navigation tasks, i.e. *Straight* (T1), *One turn* (T2), *Navigation* (T3) and *Navigation with dynamic obstacles* (T4), measured in percentage of successfully completed episodes of the driving tasks. Comparison results include four conditions consisting of different maps and weather settings. The best is in bold.

Method	Training conditions				New town				New weather				New town & weather			
	T1	T2	T3	T4	T1	T2	T3	T4	T1	T2	T3	T4	T1	T2	T3	T4
MP [20]	98	82	80	77	92	61	24	24	**100**	95	**94**	**89**	50	50	47	44
RL [20]	89	34	14	7	74	12	3	2	86	16	2	2	68	20	6	4
CIL [9]	95	89	86	**83**	97	59	40	38	98	90	84	82	80	48	44	42
SNCM (ours)	**100**	**93**	**87**	78	**98**	**63**	**48**	**42**	**100**	**96**	72	62	**100**	**70**	**58**	**50**

4.3 Qualitative Comparison

We do comparison between SNCM and CIL because CIL was chosen as baseline by most driving policy learning methods. In addition, CIL has the most similar training framework and network structure of SNCM. Figure 6 provides some examples of navigation command mismatch that CIL fails and SNCM successfully avoids.

Fig. 6. Comparison between conditional imitation learning (first line) and our stochastic navigation command matching (second line) in some driving cases. The CIL fails with navigation command mismatch while our method successfully completes the driving tasks. Navigation commands of the cases are shown at the top of the images.

4.4 Visualization Results

To understand the input processing of the driving policy model, we extracted and composed the first feature map layer of the CNN to generate a heatmap. The heatmap demonstrates whether the network detects useful features for decision-making.

Figure 7 shows the examples of visualization results in some scenarios. We can observe that the driving policy model trained via SNCM perceives the lane marking and road boundary more clearly, and both static and dynamic targets (e.g. the traffic light and car in the second and third line of Fig. 7) in the environment have more noticeable feature map activations. Contrarily, the model trained without SNCM distracts attention to the background unrelated to the driving task.

Fig. 7. Visualization of the heatmaps. The first row is origin images, the second and third row are the heatmaps of driving policy model trained with and without stochastic navigation command matching.

5   Conclusions

In this paper, we proposed a novel driving policy training method, stochastic navigation command matching (SNCM), utilizing the correlation between the actions and the navigation commands for model optimization. By considering the matching degree between actions and navigation commands, more reasonable actions are proposed by the learned driving policy model. Experimental results show our method can make driving policy model better overcome the navigation command mismatch problem and improve performance in challenging autonomous driving tasks. Matching degree optimization can be migrated into other hierarchical models, future work will explore its application in more complicated hierarchical autonomous driving system.

References

1. Urmson, C., et al.: Autonomous driving in urban environments: boss and the urban challenge. J. Field Robot. **25**(8), 425–466 (2008)
2. Montemerlo, M., et al.: Junior: the Stanford entry in the urban challenge. J. Field Robot. **25**(9), 569–597 (2008)
3. Bohren, J., et al.: Little Ben: the Ben Franklin racing team's entry in the 2007 Darpa urban challenge. J. Field Robot. **25**(9), 598–614 (2008)
4. Bacha, A., et al.: Odin: team VictorTango's entry in the Darpa urban challenge. J. Field Robot. **25**(8), 467–492 (2008)
5. Liang, X., Wang, T., Yang, L., Xing, E.: CIRL: controllable imitative reinforcement learning for vision-based self-driving. In: Ferrari, V., Hebert, M., Sminchisescu, C., Weiss, Y. (eds.) ECCV 2018. LNCS, vol. 11211, pp. 604–620. Springer, Cham (2018). https://doi.org/10.1007/978-3-030-01234-2_36
6. Tai, L., Yun, P., Chen, Y., Liu, C., Ye, H., Liu, M.: Visual-based autonomous driving deployment from a stochastic and uncertainty-aware perspective. In: 2019 IEEE/RSJ International Conference on Intelligent Robots and Systems (IROS), pp. 2622–2628. IEEE (2019)
7. Cultrera, L., Seidenari, L., Becattini, F., Pala, P., Del Bimbo, A.: Explaining autonomous driving by learning end-to-end visual attention. In: Proceedings of the IEEE/CVF Conference on Computer Vision and Pattern Recognition Workshops, pp. 340–341 (2020)

8. Pan, Y., Xue, J., Zhang, P., Ouyang, W., Fang, J., Chen, X.: Navigation command matching for vision-based autonomous driving. In: 2020 IEEE International Conference on Robotics and Automation (ICRA), pp. 4343–4349. IEEE (2020)

9. Codevilla, F., Müller, M., López, A., Koltun, V., Dosovitskiy, A.: End-to-end driving via conditional imitation learning. In: 2018 IEEE International Conference on Robotics and Automation (ICRA), pp. 4693–4700. IEEE (2018)

10. Bojarski, M., et al.: End to end learning for self-driving cars. arXiv preprint arXiv:1604.07316 (2016)

11. Xu, H., Gao, Y., Yu, F., Darrell, T.: End-to-end learning of driving models from large-scale video datasets. In: Proceedings of the IEEE Conference on Computer Vision and Pattern Recognition, pp. 2174–2182 (2017)

12. Osa, T., Pajarinen, J., Neumann, G., Bagnell, J.A., Abbeel, P., Peters, J.: An algorithmic perspective on imitation learning. arXiv preprint arXiv:1811.06711 (2018)

13. Pan, Y., et al.: Agile autonomous driving using end-to-end deep imitation learning. arXiv preprint arXiv:1709.07174 (2017)

14. Muller, U., Ben, J., Cosatto, E., Flepp, B., Cun, Y.L.: Off-road obstacle avoidance through end-to-end learning. In: Advances in Neural Information Processing Systems, pp. 739–746. Citeseer (2006)

15. Song, S., Hu, X., Yu, J., Bai, L., Chen, L.: Learning a deep motion planning model for autonomous driving. In: IEEE Intelligent Vehicles Symposium (IV), pp. 1137–1142. IEEE (2018)

16. Jiang, H., Chang, L., Li, Q., Chen, D.: Deep transfer learning enable end-to-end steering angles prediction for self-driving car. In: IEEE Intelligent Vehicles Symposium (IV), pp. 405–412. IEEE (2020)

17. Li, Z., Motoyoshi, T., Sasaki, K., Ogata, T., Sugano, S.: Rethinking self-driving: multi-task knowledge for better generalization and accident explanation ability. arXiv preprint arXiv:1809.11100 (2018)

18. Sauer, A., Savinov, N., Geiger, A.: Conditional affordance learning for driving in urban environments. In: Conference on Robot Learning, pp. 237–252 (2018)

19. Mnih, V., et al.: Playing Atari with deep reinforcement learning. arXiv preprint arXiv:1312.5602 (2013)

20. Dosovitskiy, A., Ros, G., Codevilla, F., Lopez, A., Koltun, V.: Carla: an open urban driving simulator. In: Conference on Robot Learning, pp. 1–16. PMLR (2017)

21. Kingma, D.P., Ba, J.: Adam: a method for stochastic optimization. arXiv preprint arXiv:1412.6980 (2014)

Recognition, Remote Sensing

Group Activity Representation Learning with Self-supervised Predictive Coding

Longteng Kong[1], Zhaofeng He[1(✉)], Man Zhang[1], and Yunzhi Xue[2]

[1] Beijing University of Posts and Telecommunications, Beijing 100876, China
{konglongteng,zhaofenghe,zhangman}@bupt.edu.cn
[2] Automobile Software Innovation Center, Chongqing 408000, China
xueyunzhi@isauto.ac.cn

Abstract. This paper aims to learn the group activity representation in an unsupervised fashion without manual annotated activity labels. To achieve this, we exploit self-supervised learning based on group predictions and propose a Transformer-based Predictive Coding approach **(TransPC)**, which mines meaningful spatio-temporal features of group activities mere-ly with data itself. Firstly, in TransPC, a Spatial Graph Transformer Encoder (SGT-Encoder) is designed to capture diverse spatial states lied in individual actions and group interactions. Then, a Temporal Causal Transformer Decoder (TCT-Decoder) is used to anticipate future group states with attending to the observed state dynamics. Furthermore, due to the complex group states, we both consider the distinguishability and consistency of predicted states and introduce a jointly learning mechanism to optimize the models, enabling TransPC to learn better group activity representation. Finally, extensive experiments are carried out to evaluate the learnt representation on downstream tasks on Volleyball and Collective Activity datasets, which demonstrate the state-of-the-art performance over existing self-supervised learning approaches with fewer training labels.

Keywords: Group activity recognition · Self-supervised learning · Transformer

1 Introduction

Group activity recognition from videos has attracted more research attention in computer vision [7,15,25,28] due to the significant applications, such as sports tactic analysis and intelligent video surveillance. The core of this task is to model spatial-temporal relations among individuals and generate meaningful group representations. At present, most common tactics to explore individual relations employ supervised/weakly-supervised learning measures, which rely on sufficient manually annotated labels. However, the ground-truth labels are very limited in practical applications, and an unsupervised method is desired for modeling group representations.

S. Yu et al. (Eds.): PRCV 2022, LNCS 13536, pp. 207–219, 2022.
https://doi.org/10.1007/978-3-031-18913-5_16

Fig. 1. Comparison between 'jumping rope' and 'left-setting' which are from UCF101 and Volleyball datasets respectively. In group activity, more complex states in individual actions and group interactions are involved.

Recently, great progress has been made in solving unsupervised learning tasks, including image and video representation [4,11–13,22,27]. Meanwhile, the advances in self-supervised learning for image/video representation have yielded impressive performance, even matching the supervised learning ones. Encouraged by this, in this study, we devote ourselves to model group representation based on self-supervised learning scheme.

Intuitively, the technologies in Self-Supervised Representation Learning (SSRL) for videos can be utilized directly. A typical measure is to design supervised learning pretext tasks for generating supervised signals, e.g. detecting video rotations [16], estimating frame/clip orders [6,19,31], predicting the futures [11,12] and recognizing video playback speed [27,32]. Among them, predicting the future is able to better take advantages of temporal dynamics, which is crucial to understand group activities. Current approaches for this pretext task generally follow the Dense Predictive Coding (DPC) framework [11,12] with contrastive learning. DPC tries to predict correct future temporal states by assigning higher similarity to the true observation, rather than reconstructing the exact future, e.g. raw frames, generating better video representation. Therefore, in DPC, the ability to accurately describe the state transitions is essential.

Indeed, group activities have specific properties, making such self-supervised representation learning difficult. There exist much more complex states not only lied in the actions of individuals, but also in their interactions. For example, as in Fig. 1, in the 'left-setting' activity, individuals have multiple action states, e.g. run, jump, and spike; and the group structures involve diverse interactions among individuals, also vary in a variety of implicit states. Therefore, predicting the future states in a group activity is more challenging than predicting the ones in video action, which generally consists of simple movement hypotheses. As in the 'jumping rope' action, the player mainly performs jump periodically. making the current video SSRL techniques using simple predictors, e.g. RNN, not so effective. Recently, with the progress of transformer network in computer vision, some methods utilize it for future predictions in sequence data, e.g., human actions [9] and pedestrian trajectories [34]. Thanks to the powerful self-attention mechanism for modeling the sequence dependencies, the predictive ability is significantly improved. But unfortunately, they are restricted to normal data sequences and have difficulty in modeling the dynamic group structures. Actually, due to the complex states in group activities, we argue that it is essential for group activity SSRL to better represent the states both lied in individual actions and group interactions, and provide more insurance for state transitions.

In this paper, we refer to the idea of DPC and propose a Transformer-based Predictive Coding approach (TransPC) to learn the representation of group activities. Specifically, we introduce a Spatial Graph Transformer Encoder (SGT-Encoder) for spatial state modeling, which can capture diverse individual action and group interaction states. Given a video sequence, we arrange individuals within the scene into a series of sparse graphs according to their spatial interactions. Based on those sparse graphs, SGT-Encoder updates each node via multi-head attention based message passing with its neighbors, providing better spatial representations of the states. For modeling the temporal transitions of the states, we present a Temporal Causal Transformer Decoder (TCT-Decoder) which can attend to the observed group state dynamics to anticipate the futures. More importantly, in TransPC, we both consider the distinguishability and consistency of predicted states. To achieve this, we optimize the models with contrastive and adversarial learning. Contrastive learning restricts models to pick the correct future states from lots of distractors, while adversarial learning validates the sequence-level coherence of the predictions with the observed state dynamics by a discriminator. Such a joint learning mechanism helps TransPC to better describe the state transitions, and thus generate better group activity representation. In summary, we make the following three contributions:

(1) We propose a Transformer-based Predictive Coding approach, capable of capturing the diverse individual/group states and making rational predictions, and mining meaningful spatio-temporal features of group activities.
(2) We present a joint learning mechanism with contrastive and adversarial losses, taking into account the distinguishability and consistency of predicted states. It enables TransPC to better understand the state transitions in group activities.
(3) We thoroughly evaluate the quality of the learnt representation on group activity recognition task on Volleyball and Collective Activity datasets, and demonstrate state-of-the-art performance over other approaches with fewer training labels.

2   Related Work

Group Activity Recognition (GAR) has received more attention in the last decade, especially with the release of Volleyball dataset [15]. Early attempts tend to model group temporal dynamics using Recurrent Neural Network (RNN). For instance, Ibrahim et al. [15] provide a hierarchical model that consists of two stages to represent the dynamics in individual actions and group activities.

Wang et al. [29] propose a context modeling network to consider the individual, group, and scene level contexts. Kong et al. [18] builds a hierarchical attention framework based on LSTMs, simultaneously attending to the key persons and contexts. Recently, many works concentrate on building the spatio-temporal relations among individuals, significantly improving the recognition performance. Azar et al. [2] present a convolutional relational machine to learn intermediate person relation representation based on video features. Wu et al. [30] propose a relation graph to capture the person relations, where the connections could be learned with graph convolutions. Inspired by the success of the Transformer in NLP and vision tasks, Gavrilyuk et al. [8] introduce an actor-transformer model able to learn relevant information for group activity recognition. Yuan et al. [35] propose a person-specific graph that consists of dynamic relation and dynamic walk modules for better modeling diverse person interactions. Li et al. [20] design a tailored Groupformer to model the spatial-temporal contextual clues based on cross-connected Transformers and clustered attention mechanism. Despite the success of the aforementioned methods, however, they are restricted to supervised learning measures. While, in this paper, we aim at learning group activity representation in self-supervised learning measure.

Self-supervised Learning for Images/Videos has undergone rapid progress in visual representation learning recently. The technologies can be broadly divided into two categories, i.e. pretext task based ones and contrastive learning based ones. For the former, ingenious pretext tasks on video data are designed to generate supervised signals, including predicting sequence orders [6,19,31], estimating playback speed [3,33], etc. For the latter, contrastive learning has been successfully applied to video data, which usually combines predictive coding [22]. A common framework is Dense Predictive Coding [11] which proposes to predict the future representations based on the recent past. Later, [12] improves the method with an additional compressive memory unit, which maps history experience to a set of compressed memories and helps to better anticipate the future, reporting state-of-the-art performance. Recently, based on contrastive learning, additional techniques are combined, e.g. pretext tasks and meta learning [21], which boost the performance. In this paper, we are inspired by the idea of DPC, and focus on group activity representation learning, which is a more challenging issue. Group activities contain more complex states lied in individual actions and group interactions, resulting in the requirement of great efforts to solve this issue.

3   Approach

In this study, we target learning group activity representation from self-supervision, and propose a Transformer-based Predictive Coding approach to mine meaningful spatio-temporal features of group activities by explicitly improving the ability to anticipate future states. The architecture of TransPC is illustrated

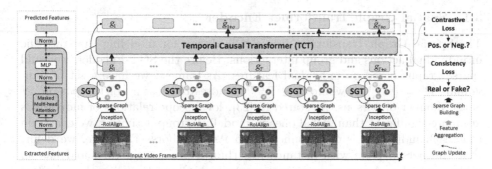

Fig. 2. Overview of proposed TransPC.

in Fig. 2, which mainly involves a Spatial Graph Transformer Encoder (SGT-Encoder) to model the individual/group states, a Temporal Causal Transformer Decoder (TCT-Decoder) to forecast future states, and a joint learning mechanism to train the models. Firstly, a frame sequence is uniformly sampled in order from a given video clip with person detections. We extract features of all frames, and then apply ROIAlign [14] to generate the individual features. Afterward, upon these original individual features at each frame, we build the corresponding graph for the group. Then, we feed each graph to SGT-Encoder for modeling the action/interaction states. SGT-Encoder refines the states by recurrently renovating the graph with self-attention mechanism. After spatial state modeling, the features are aggregated and generates the group state feature at each frame, which are aligned and fed into TCT-Decoder to model the state transitions. Resulting from the causal mechanism, TCT-Decoder is able to attend to the dependencies of the observed states and anticipate the future states.

For training the models, we both employ contrastive and adversarial losses to improve the distinguishability and consistency of predicted states. It should be noted that group activity recognition is a high-level task, which generally builds relations based on person features. As we know, the deep models for video representation, e.g. I3D model, require training on large datasets. Due to the limited scale of existing group activity datasets, it is difficult to train the deep networks for video representation from scratch. In this paper, our target is to learn high-level group relations and make use of the low-level supervisory signals, including I3D model pre-trained model and person detections, to extract person features. Note that our approach does NOT require task-specific annotations (individual action and group activity labels). The relational models, including the encoder and decoder, are trained in self-supervised measure. For inference, the predicted embeddings are aggregated over time into a video level embedding, which is applied for the downstream tasks. In the following, we elaborate on the details of TransPC.

3.1   Spatial Graph Transformer Encoder

The Spatial Graph Transformer Encoder is design for modeling the states lie in individual actions and group interactions. Before the SGT-Encoder, we build sparse graphs based on individual features. At frame t, we have a set of individuals $P^t = \{p_i^t\}_{i=1}^N$, where $p_i \in \mathbb{R}^{1 \times d}$ denotes the feature of the person, N is the number of persons. As stated in [23], local scope relations of individuals are more significant than global ones in modeling group activities, we constrain that each individual is only connected to its neighbors. Therefore, we define that the person pairs with distance less than a pre-defined threshold has an undirected edge. A sparse graph is then reached: $G^t = (P^t, E^t)$ with and edges $E^t = \{(i, j) \mid p_i, p_j$ is connected at time $t\}$. In G^t, each node p_i has its neighbors, denoted as $\mathbb{N}(i, t) = \{p_j^t\}_{j=1}^M$, where M is number of neighbors.

In each frame, SGT-Encoder updates each graph node within its neighbors based on the self-attention mechanism. Assuming the input is a normal data sequence, the self-attention in Transformer can be regarded as message passing on an undirected fully connected graph. For a feature vector h_i of feature set $\{h_i\}_{i=1}^N$ that processed by a Transformer, the corresponding query, key, and value vector can be depicted as $q_i = f_Q(h_i)$, $k_i = f_K(h_i)$, and $v_i = f_V(h_i)$, where f denotes fully connected layer. We define the message passes from node p_j to p_i in the fully connected graph as: $M(i, j) = q_i^T k_j$, and the self-attention operation can be written as:

$$Att(h_i) = softmax \left(\frac{[q_i^T k_j]_{j=1:N}}{\sqrt{d_k}} \right) [v_i]_{i=1}^N, \tag{1}$$

where $\hat{h}_i$ is the updated embedding of h_i, d_k is the scaled dot-product term for numerical stability for attentions, and N is the sequence length.

Apart from the fully connected graph, sparse graph pays close attention to the local scope relations. Therefore, we only apply message passing on each node within its neighbors, rather than all of the nodes. Mathematically, for a sparse graph $G = (P, E)$, the message passing operation for node i can be depicted as:

$$Att(p_i) = softmax \left(\frac{[q_i^T k_j]_{j \mid p_j \in Nei(i)}}{\sqrt{d_k}} \right) [v_i]_{i \mid p_i \in \mathbb{N}(i)}^M, \tag{2}$$

$$\hat{p}_i = p_i + Att(p_i), \tag{3}$$

where $\hat{p}_i$ is the updated individual state. After renovated each node, the group state g_t can be reached by aggregating the nodes in the graph.

3.2   Temporal Causal Transformer Decoder

After the spatial modeling on the observed T frames, SGT-Encoder produces group state sequence $(g_1, g_2, \cdots, g_T)$, which is fed into TCT-Decoder to summary the state evolution and predict the futures progressively. The transition can be written as:

$$\hat{g}_1, \cdots, \hat{g}_T = Decoder(g_1, \cdots, g_T), \tag{4}$$

where $\hat{g}_t$ is the predicted feature corresponding to group state feature g_t with attending to the features $(g_1, g_2, \cdots, g_t)$. Note that the last o frames are predicted in o steps, which are used to select the true embedding in the predictive coding manner. Inspired by popular approaches in generative language modeling, we implement TCT-Decoder using a masked transformer. We start by adding a learnable temporal position encoding to each frame. The group state features are then passed through multiple TCT-Decoder layers, each of which consists of masked multi-head attention, Norm layer and a Multi-Layer Perceptron (MLP), as shown in Fig. 2 (left). The output is then passed through another Norm to obtain the final predicted state features. Aside from the original Transformer [26], TCT-Decoder exploits the causal mask in the multi-head attention, which ensures that the model only attends to the input that proceeds it. Please refer to [1] for more details on the masking implementation.

3.3   Joint Learning Measure

Based on the predicted and extracted features, we apply the joint learning measure to optimize the models. In TransPC, the models, denoted as $\mathcal{G}$, consist of the initialized Inception-v3, SGT-Encoder, and TCT-Decoder. Contrastive Learning generally forces the similarity scores of positive pairs to be higher than those of negatives. The objective function to minimize becomes:

$$\mathcal{L}_{con} = -\mathbb{E}\left[\sum_i \log \frac{e^{\phi(\hat{g}_i{}^T g_i)}}{e^{\phi(\hat{g}_i{}^T g_i)} + \sum_{(j \neq i)} e^{\phi(\hat{g}_i{}^T g_j)}}\right], \tag{5}$$

where i is the temporal index, and $\phi(\cdot)$ is acting as a similarity function. In our case, we simply use dot product between the two vectors. The objective function is essentially a cross-entropy loss of a multi-way classifier, and the goal of optimization is to learn the $\mathcal{G}$ that assigns the highest values for $(\hat{g}_i, g_i)$, i.e. higher similarity between the predicted future states (in the upper red dashed rectangle in Fig. 2) and that from true observations (in the lower red dashed rectangle) originating from the same temporal position. Theoretically, all the predicted states can join the calculation in Eq. 5. Whereas in initial experiments, we found only the last o steps to be equally effective.

Due to the complex states in group activities, the predicted states tend to be less realistic. Inspired by the adversarial training mechanism in GANs [10], we also check the consistency between predicted and observed states from a global perspective of a sequence by introducing a consistency loss. The consistency discriminator $\mathcal{D}$ shares the similar architecture with the TCT-Decoder and output the probability of the input sequence is real with a softmax classification layer. As in Fig. 2, we consider the observed dynamics, denoted as $\mathbf{p_i} = [g_1, \cdots, g_{T+o}]$ as real samples (in the lower blue dashed rectangle), and the predicted ones, denoted as $\hat{\mathbf{p_i}} = [g_1, \cdots, g_{\hat{T}+o}]$ as fake samples (in the upper blue dashed rectangle), where g_t is used for padding to same length to $\mathbf{p_i}$. The quality of the $\mathcal{G}$ is then judged by evaluating how well the fake sample fools $\mathcal{D}$. Formally, we solve the minimax optimization problem:

$$arg \min_{\mathcal{G}} \max_{\mathcal{D}} \mathcal{L}_{adv}(\mathcal{D}, \mathcal{G}) = \mathbb{E}_{\hat{\mathbf{p}}_i}[\log \mathcal{D}(\hat{\mathbf{p}}_i)]$$
$$+ \mathbb{E}_{\mathbf{p}_i}[\log(1 - \mathcal{D}(\{\mathcal{G}(\mathbf{p}_i)\}))], \tag{6}$$

where the distributions $\mathbb{E}(\cdot)$ are over the training sequences. We integrate a contrastive loss $\mathcal{L}_{con}$ and a adversarial loss $\mathcal{L}_{adv}$, and obtain the optimal networks by solving:

$$\mathcal{L} = \lambda_1 arg \min_{\mathcal{G}} \max_{\mathcal{D}} \mathcal{L}_{adv}(\mathcal{D}, \mathcal{G}) + \lambda_2 \mathcal{L}_{con}(\mathcal{G}), \tag{7}$$

where $\mathcal{G}$ tries to minimize the objective against $\mathcal{D}$ which aims to maximize it, and λ_1, λ_2 are trade-off parameters.

4   Experiments

The experiments are carried out on the Volleyball and Collective Activity datasets to evaluate the proposed method. We conduct ablation studies on Volleyball to verify the effectiveness of the different modules in TransPC, and compare it to other state-of-the-art approaches on both datasets. To evaluate the quality of the learned representation, we follow the protocols in DPC [11] that assess the performance on downstream tasks. Specifically, we choose the group activity recognition task and use two evaluation manners: (1) Linear evaluation: freezing the models and only training a linear classifier; and (2) Fine-Tuning: tuning the entire model with supervised learning using part of the training labels.

4.1   Datasets

Volleyball Dataset [15] is released for group activity recognition. It composes of 4,830 clips collected from 55 volleyball games, with 3,493 training clips and 1,337 testing ones. Each sample belongs to one of 8 group activity labels: right-set, right-spike, right-pass, right-winpoint, left-set, left-spike, left-pass and left-winpoint. The dataset also provides the ground truth player bounding boxes and their actions: waiting, setting, digging, failing, spiking, blocking, jumping, moving and standing.

Collective Dataset [5] contains 44 short video sequences, which defines 5 group activities: crossing, waiting, queueing, walking and talking and 6 individual actions: non-action, crossing, waiting, queueing, walking and talking. The group activity label for a frame is defined by the activity in which most people participate, and persons' bounding boxes are annotated every 10 frames. The same evaluation settings in [24]are used in our experiments, where 2/3 of the video sequences are used for training and the rest for inference.

4.2   Implementation Details

We start with the Inception-v3 model with initial weights and extract the person feature $p_i \in \mathbb{R}^{1024}$. We pick out the middle 20 frames as the input to our model on both datasets, where 12 frames are observed ones and 8 frames for future forecasting. During training, we use the Adam [17] optimizer with initial learning rate 0.001, weight decay 0.0001. $\lambda_1 = 1$ and $\lambda_2 = 2$. In both encoder and decoder, we use 4-head attention, 2-layer Transformers. For downstream task evaluation, we take the input frames in the same way as TransPC and extract the context features; then we max-pool the context features to obtain the group-level embedding. We randomly sample 10% from the training data for fine-tuning evaluation, and use all training samples to train a linear classifier. Our experiments are all conducted on 2 GeForce RTX 3090 Ti GPUs.

4.3   Ablations on Volleyball

In this section, we conduct extensive experiments to validate the effectiveness of the counterparts of TransPC by replacing them with other popular strategies, and create several baselines. For spatial encoding, we mainly consider the following strategies: (1) Person Features: We only use the original person features extracted by the backbone model, which is max pooled to form the group state features. (2) Graph Convolution on Person Features (GCN): Based on (1), we apply Graph Convolution on the original person features to capture the person relations, where the GCN follows the settings in [30]. Regarding the decoding, we compare to the LSTM and original Transformer [26].

Table 1. Comparison between our method and the baseline methods in group activity recognition on the Volleyball dataset (Linear: Linear evaluation, FT: Fine-Tuning).

Method	Backbone	Encoder	Decoder	$\mathcal{L}_{con}$	$\mathcal{L}_{adv}$	Linear	FT
B1	Inception-V3	Image features	LSTM	✓	-	67.1%	68.5%
B2	Inception-V3	Person features	LSTM	✓	-	71.3%	72.6 %
B3	Inception-V3	GCN	LSTM	✓	-	73.4%	75.2 %
B4	Inception-V3	GCN	Transformer	✓	-	74.2%	76.8%
B5	Inception-V3	SGT	Transformer	✓	-	75.5%	77.3%
B6	Inception-V3	SGT	TCT	✓	-	76.0%	78.7%
OURS	VGG19	SGT	TCT	✓	✓	78.0 %	80.1%
OURS	Inception-V3	SGT	TCT	✓	✓	**78.4%**	**80.5%**

We show the comparison of different baselines in terms of accuracy in Table 1 using linear evaluation and fine-tuning protocols. As a whole, our model (with Inception-v3 backbone) outperforms the baseline models, indicating the effectiveness of the combination of the SGT-Encoder, TCT-Decoder, and joint learning measure, for better understanding the state transitions. B1 is a variant of

DPC, designed to predict the future video representations based on the recent past using ConvGRU and trained by using noise contrastive loss. $B2$ performs better than $B1$ by a large margin, which proves the necessity in exploiting the person features. $B3$ is able to capture the interactions of persons based on graph convolution, leading to higher accuracy than $B2$, Due to the multi-head attention in Transformer, $B4$ achieves better performance than $B3$. SGT-Decoder shows the advantages in capturing diverse action and interaction states, which can be verified from the comparison between $B5$ to $B4$. The performance gains of our model to $B6$ indicates that the joint training mechanism can guarantee the state transitions in a more reasonable way. In Fig. 3 (left). We evaluate the effects of different lengths of the prediction, observe that the best overall performance is achieved when Length $= 30\%$. We also visualize several examples of the graph generated by our model in Fig. 3 (right). It can be seen that through self-supervised learning, our model (fine-tuned) is able to capture the key message passing among nodes.

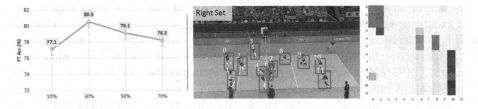

Fig. 3. Accuracies with different percentages of prediction lengths (left). Visualization of learned messages passing intensities in SGT (right).

4.4   Comparison with State-of-the-Art

In this section, we evaluate the group activity recognition performance of TransPC on Volleyball and Collective Activity datasets. We reproduce the state-of-the-art methods using their released codes, including DPC [11], MemDPC [12], OPN [19], and Video-Pace [27], and carefully tune the parameters in the benchmark methods and choose the best accuracies. As analyzed in ablations, we modify the feature extracting stage to use the person features. The comparison results are summarized in Table 2. It can be seen that our proposed approach surpasses the existing ones by a good margin, demonstrating its effectiveness in describing the diverse individual/group state and their transitions, and mining more useful spatio-temporal features of group activities. Moreover, due to complicated group dynamics, temporal supervision is more important, and the predictive coding methods, e.g. MemDPC, deliver preferable result gains compared to the other pretext tasks, including sequence sorting in OPN, playback rate estimating in Video-Pace.

Table 2. Comparison with state-of-the-art on the Volleyball and Collective Activity datasets in terms of the group activity recognition Acc.%.

Method	Backbone	Volleyball		Collective	
		Linear	FT	Linear	FT
OPN [19]	VGG16	70.6%	68.6%	65.7%	67.6%
Video-Pace [27]	S3D-G	69.8%	72.7%	66.8%	68.9 %
DPC [11]	ResNet (2 + 3D)	71.3%	73.5%	67.3 %	69.4%
MemDPC [12]	ResNet (2 + 3D)	73.8%	75.2%	68.7%	70.8%
Actor-Transformer [8]	Inception-V3	-	67.8%	-	64.3%
ARG [30]	Inception-V3	-	80.1%	-	72.3%
OURS	ResNet(2+3D)	78.1%	80.2%	71.5%	73.7%
OURS	Inception-V3	**78.4%**	**80.5%**	**71.8%**	**74.2%**

5   Conclusion

This paper proposes a group self-supervised representation learning approach, i.e. TransPC. We first design the SGT-Encoder to capture the diverse states in individual actions and group interactions by building sparse graphs and pass the messages among nodes via a Transformer. Then, the TCT-Decoder is presented to anticipate future states with attending to the observed dynamics. In addition, we introduce a joint learning measure that makes use of contrastive and adversarial losses to optimize the models, which improves the distinguishability and consistency of predicted states. By better describing the state transitions in group activities, our method can explore more meaningful spatio-temporal features in the self-supervised learning procedure. We extensively evaluate TransPC on the Volleyball and Collective Activity datasets, and the experimental results show its advantage.

Acknowledgement. This work was supported by the National Natural Science Foundation of China (62176025, U21B200389), the Fundamental Research Funds for the Central Universities (2021rc38), and the National Natural Science Foundation of China (62106015).

References

1. Alec, R., Jeff, W., Rewon, C., David, L., Dario, A., Ilya, S.: Language models are unsupervised multitask learners (2019)
2. Azar, S.M., Atigh, M.G., Nickabadi, A., Alahi, A.: Convolutional relational machine for group activity recognition. In: IEEE Conference on Computer Vision and Pattern Recognition, pp. 7892–7901 (2019)
3. Benaim, S., et al.: SpeedNet: Learning the speediness in videos. In: IEEE Conference on Computer Vision and Pattern Recognition, pp. 9919–9928 (2020)

4. Chen, T., Kornblith, S., Norouzi, M., Hinton, G.E.: A simple framework for contrastive learning of visual representations. In: International Conference on Machine Learning, pp. 1597–1607 (2020)
5. Choi, W., Shahid, K., Savarese, S.: What are they doing? : Collective activity classification using spatio-temporal relationship among people. In: IEEE International Conference on Computer Vision Workshops, pp. 1282–1289 (2009)
6. Fernando, B., Bilen, H., Gavves, E., Gould, S.: Self-supervised video representation learning with odd-one-out networks. In: IEEE Conference on Computer Vision and Pattern Recognition, pp. 5729–5738 (2017)
7. Gan, C., Wang, N., Yang, Y., Yeung, D., Hauptmann, A.G.: DevNet: A deep event network for multimedia event detection and evidence recounting. In: IEEE Conference on Computer Vision and Pattern Recognition, pp. 2568–2577 (2015)
8. Gavrilyuk, K., Sanford, R., Javan, M., Snoek, C.G.M.: Actor-transformers for group activity recognition. In: IEEE Conference on Computer Vision and Pattern Recognition, pp. 836–845 (2020)
9. Girdhar, R., Grauman, K.: Anticipative video transformer. https://arxiv.org/abs/2106.02036 (2021)
10. Goodfellow, I., et al.: Generative adversarial nets. pp. 2672–2680 (2014)
11. Han, T., Xie, W., Zisserman, A.: Video representation learning by dense predictive coding. In: IEEE International Conference on Computer Vision Workshops, pp. 1483–1492 (2019)
12. Han, T., Xie, W., Zisserman, A.: Memory-augmented dense predictive coding for video representation learning. In: Vedaldi, A., Bischof, H., Brox, T., Frahm, J. (eds.) European Conference on Computer Vision, pp. 312–329 (2020)
13. He, K., Fan, H., Wu, Y., Xie, S., Girshick, R.B.: Momentum contrast for unsupervised visual representation learning. In: IEEE Conference on Computer Vision and Pattern Recognition, pp. 9726–9735 (2020)
14. He, K., Gkioxari, G., Dollár, P., Girshick, R.B.: Mask R-CNN. In: IEEE International Conference on Computer Vision, pp. 2980–2988 (2017)
15. Ibrahim, M.S., Muralidharan, S., Deng, Z., Vahdat, A., Mori, G.: A hierarchical deep temporal model for group activity recognition. In: IEEE Conference on Computer Vision and Pattern Recognition, pp. 1971–1980 (2016)
16. Jing, L., Yang, X., Liu, J., Tian, Y.: Self-supervised spatiotemporal feature learning via video rotation prediction. arXiv preprint arXiv:1811.11387 (2018)
17. Kingma, D.P., Ba, J.: Adam: A method for stochastic optimization. In: International Conference on Learning Representations (2015)
18. Kong, L., Qin, J., Huang, D., Wang, Y., Gool, L.V.: Hierarchical attention and context modeling for group activity recognition. In: IEEE International Conference on Acoustics, Speech and Signal Processing. pp. 1328–1332 (2018)
19. Lee, H., Huang, J., Singh, M., Yang, M.: Unsupervised representation learning by sorting sequences. In: IEEE International Conference on Computer Vision, pp. 667–676 (2017)
20. Li, S., et al.: GroupFormer: Group activity recognition with clustered spatial-temporal transformer. In: International Conference on Computer Vision, pp. 13648–13657 (2021)
21. Lin, Y., Guo, X., Lu, Y.: Self-supervised video representation learning with meta-contrastive network. In: International Conference on Computer Vision, pp. 8219–8229. IEEE (2021)
22. van den Oord, A., Li, Y., Vinyals, O.: Representation learning with contrastive predictive coding. https://arxiv.org/abs/1807.03748 (2018)

23. Peng, C., Jiang, W., Quanzeng, Y., Haibin, L., Zicheng, L.: TransMot: Spatial-temporal graph transformer for multiple object tracking. In: IEEE Conference on Computer Vision and Pattern Recognition (2021)
24. Qi, M., Qin, J., Li, A., Wang, Y., Luo, J., Gool, L.V.: stagNet: An attentive semantic RNN for group activity recognition. In: European Conference on Computer Vision, pp. 104–120 (2018)
25. Simonyan, K., Zisserman, A.: Two-stream convolutional networks for action recognition in videos. In: Advances in Neural Information Processing Systems, pp. 568–576 (2014)
26. Vaswani, A., et al.: Attention is all you need. In: Advances in Neural Information Processing Systems, pp. 5998–6008 (2017)
27. Wang, J., Jiao, J., Liu, Y.: Self-supervised video representation learning by pace prediction. In: European Conference on Computer Vision, pp. 504–521 (2020)
28. Wang, L., Li, W., Li, W., Gool, L.V.: Appearance-and-relation networks for video classification. In: IEEE Conference on Computer Vision and Pattern Recognition, pp. 1430–1439 (2018)
29. Wang, M., Ni, B., Yang, X.: Recurrent modeling of interaction context for collective activity recognition. In: IEEE Conference on Computer Vision and Pattern Recognition, pp. 7408–7416 (2017)
30. Wu, J., Wang, L., Wang, L., Guo, J., Wu, G.: Learning actor relation graphs for group activity recognition. In: IEEE Conference on Computer Vision and Pattern Recognition, pp. 9964–9974 (2019)
31. Xu, D., Xiao, J., Zhao, Z., Shao, J., Xie, D., Zhuang, Y.: Self-supervised spatiotemporal learning via video clip order prediction. In: IEEE Conference on Computer Vision and Pattern Recognition, pp. 10334–10343 (2019)
32. Yao, Y., Liu, C., Luo, D., Zhou, Y., Ye, Q.: Video playback rate perception for self-supervised spatio-temporal representation learning. In: IEEE Conference on Computer Vision and Pattern Recognition, pp. 6547–6556 (2020)
33. Yao, Y., Liu, C., Luo, D., Zhou, Y., Ye, Q.: Video playback rate perception for self-supervised spatio-temporal representation learning. In: IEEE Conference on Computer Vision and Pattern Recognition, pp. 6547–6556 (2020)
34. Yu, C., Ma, X., Ren, J., Zhao, H., Yi, S.: Spatio-temporal graph transformer networks for pedestrian trajectory prediction. In: European Conference on Computer Vision, pp. 507–523 (2020)
35. Yuan, H., Ni, D., Wang, M.: Spatio-temporal dynamic inference network for group activity recognition. In: International Conference on Computer Vision, pp. 7456–7465. IEEE (2021)

Skeleton-Based Action Quality Assessment via Partially Connected LSTM with Triplet Losses

Xinyu Wang, Jianwei Li[(✉)], and Haiqing Hu

School of Sports Engineering, Beijing Sports University, Beijing, China
jianwei@bsu.edu.cn

Abstract. Human action quality assessment (AQA) recently has attracted increasing attentions in computer vision for its practical applications, such as skill training, physical rehabilitation and scoring sports events. In this paper, we propose a partially connected LSTM with triplet losses to evaluate different skill levels. Compared to human action recognition (HAR), we explain and discuss two characteristics and countermeasures of AQA. To ignore the negative influence of complex joint movements in actions, the skeleton is not regarded as a single graph. The fully connected layer in the LSTM model is replaced by the partially connected layer, using a diagonal matrix which activates the corresponding weights, to explore hierarchical relations in the skeleton graph. Furthermore, to improve the generalization ability of models, we introduce additional functions of triplet loss to the loss function, which make samples with similar skill levels close to each other. We carry out experiments to test our model and compare it with seven LSTM architectures and three GNN architectures on the UMONS-TAICHI dataset and walking gait dataset. Experimental results demonstrate that our model achieves outstanding performance.

Keywords: LSTM · Action quality assessment · Triplet loss · Skeleton sequence

1 Introduction

Automatic action quality assessment has attracted research interest in recent years because of its practical applications, such as skill training [1–3], physical rehabilitation [4, 5] and scoring sports events [6–8]. RGB videos [6, 7, 9, 10] and joint coordinates [4, 11] are widely used for this task. Unlike RGB videos, models based on skeleton data not only reduce the number of parameters but also focus on the human body itself, not environmental noise. Recent advances have provided reliable methods based on skeleton data in HAR. However, there are still many works to complete in AQA.

Compared to HAR, we discover two characteristics of action quality assessment: fine granularity, which makes it a challenging problem, and continuity. The process of

Supported by the Open Projects Program of National Laboratory of Pattern Recognition under Grant No. 202100009, and the Fundamental Research Funds for Central Universities No. 2021TD006.

S. Yu et al. (Eds.): PRCV 2022, LNCS 13536, pp. 220–232, 2022.
https://doi.org/10.1007/978-3-031-18913-5_17

improvement in action is a continuous process. The former has already been referenced in numerous articles [7, 8, 10], but the latter has not.

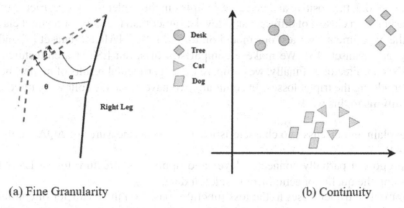

(a) Fine Granularity   (b) Continuity

Fig. 1. Examples of two characteristics with (a) fine granularity and (b) continuity.

Fine Granularity. AQA is a challenging process due to the intricacy of human motion. Human motion can be defined as the movements of joint points, which are split into small and large amounts of movement. In fact, large amount of movement of joint points are usually regarded as the features of motion, such as the joint of the hand in the action "drinking". But experts may focus on small action changes, represented by small amounts of movement or small changes in large amounts of movement. Therefore, it is necessary to make models focus on small differences in the skeleton data. As shown in Fig. 1(a), the dashed lines in red and green represent the final positions of different subjects' right legs. α and θ are large amounts of movement.

Continuity. To better illustrate this characteristic, we will take a classification problem as an example. Say there is a problem classifying "desk", "tree" and "cat". It is obvious that there is no order of preference in these labels. Feature vectors, transformed from the inputs of the same class, form a cluster in feature space. There are long distances between clusters from different classes. But if samples of "dog" are added to this task, the distance between "cat" and "dog" is closer than other distances because of similarities between animals, as shown in Fig. 1 (b). In AQA, labels representing different skill levels are continuous, which shows hierarchical relations. The feature vectors of samples don't distribute randomly in feature space.

In this paper, based on two characteristics of AQA, we propose a partially connected LSTM with triplet losses. Based on the characteristic of fine granularity, we design a partially connected layer to precisely capture the relations among corresponding joints. All nodes on neighboring layers in the original LSTM model are fully connected. In this way, the joints interact with each other, which may have good or bad effects. For example, "standing with feet shoulder width apart" requires models to focus on the subjects' shoulders and feet, which means that the wrist joint is a negative factor. To avoid it, each part is represented by a graph, which constructs a diagonal matrix, activating the model's parameters selectively. Based on the characteristic of continuity, extra information is introduced to the loss function. Extras consists of two triplet loss functions [12], which are used to make the clusters of classes in feature space distributed in order. In the proposed model, the positive and negative samples in the triplet loss are restricted by the distance between classes of different skill levels, rather than the same or distinct classes.

In the experiments, we test our model on the UMONS-TAICHI dataset [3] and the walking gait dataset [13]. We make a comparison of seven LSTM architectures and three GNN architectures. Finally, we compare the experimental results of models before and after adding the triplet losses. In summary, we have made the following three main **contributions** to this work.

- We explain and discuss two characteristics and countermeasures of AQA, compared to HAR.
- We propose a partially connected layer and apply this structure to the LSTM for assessing the quality of action from skeleton data.
- We introduce triplet losses to the loss function, based on the character of continuity, which significantly improve models' performance.

2 Related Work

2.1 Action Quality Assessment

We classify the tasks of AQA based on two factors: certainty of action and annotation type. Actions are decomposed into several certain or uncertain motion units. We all know that each diving consists of various action units, such as somersaults and twists. The final score is made up of the difficulty score and the completion score. Recently, because of the available data from the Olympic projects [6, 7, 9], assessment of uncertain units has been extensively studied. Xu et al. [6] splits video into 9 clips, which were put into 9 different C3D networks, and then used two parallel LSTMs to encode the execution and difficulty scores. Parmar et al. [7] uses related auxiliary tasks, such as counting somersaults and twists, to improve the model's performance.

But in some cases, we just want to know how well that moves, namely the completion score, which helps people do some deeper analysis, such as physical rehabilitation, training skills, and detecting abnormalities. Li et al. [14] figures out the differences between diving actions, which is unsuitable for skill assessment. To avoid the influence of differences, it is required that the actions are composed of a series of units based on fixed rules, such as golf swing [1], rehabilitation exercises [4], and karate kicking [2].

Concerning annotation type, the annotation scores are usually replaced by the features of subjects, such as skill levels, physical conditions, due to the great labor cost of the domain experts' professional annotations. This approach, which skips expert grading, converts this task from grading the videos of actions to classifying the subjects. Szczęsna [2] presents a dataset which consists of recordings of 37 karate athletes at different skill levels. JIGSAWS [15], collected from eight surgeons of varying skill levels, has been widely used as a bench dataset in many studies. But there are problems which need to be considered. If there are two subjects, one expert and one novice, doing the same actions, especially for simple actions, the novice is able to perform as well as the expert, which is a misleading guide to the model.

2.2 Graph-Based Methods

Models [10, 16–18] based on graphs of spatial-temporal joint relations have been developed and explored in HAR and AQA. Graph Convolutional Networks (GCNs) are classified as static [16] or dynamic [10, 17, 18] methods by Chen et al. [19] This paper expands it to include more tasks. Song et al. [18] proposes a spatio-temporal attention LSTM to learn discriminative features adaptively. Pan et al. [10] proposes an action assessment network with two learnable relation graphs: the spatial relation graph and the temporal relation graph. Given the complexity of motion and the lack of data in AQA, our model is proposed to find the right patterns via a static method. Like ST-GCN, static methods achieve good performance [16].

The methods can be categorized by hierarchical relations in graphs. In most methods [16–18], the human skeleton is treated as a single graph. The complexity of human action manifests in the positive or negative influences between joints. It is hard to explain the complex relations between joints with a single graph. So, part-based models are proposed. Our model constructs multiple graphs based on the human structure and assessment rules. Du et al. [20] proposes a hierarchical recurrent neural network, divided into five subnets. Each part of the skeleton based on physical structure is fed to the corresponding subnet. But the more parts are divided from the skeleton, the more subnets are required, which raises the model parameters. The PB-GCN [21] is designed to learn properties from each part and relations between them by performing a convolution on each partition, and then aggregating them. Si et al. [22] extends the part-based model architecture to graph convolutional LSTM, extracting spatial and temporal features. Instead of independent parameters between different parts, our model shares parameters partially.

3 Methods

We propose a partially connected LSTM with triplet losses for AQA. An overview of the proposed approach is given in Fig. 2. The parts with corresponding activation matrixes are fed into a partially connected LSTM. The Hadamard product is used rather than concatenating the output vectors together to create a high-dimensional vector. The final representation of parts is used in the triplet loss. In the following, we present the details of each technical component.

3.1 Joints Graph and Activation Matrix

There are many methods to construct joint graphs, which are proposed to capture more information about action patterns. For instance, traditional one considers a skeleton graph as $G(V, E)$, where V is the set of k joints and E is the set of m bones. To represent the relations between specific joints and ignore the negative influence of other joints, we divide the full set of k joints into subsets $Vs = V_1, \ldots V_n$. Unlike GCN, the bones of the skeleton are ignored in this work. To some extent, the hierarchical relations of a graph replace the edges among the joints.

A set of vertex matrices $Ve = Ve^0, \ldots Ve^n$, with $Ac^n \in R^{k \times k}$, are diagonal matrices. j_m^n, which is the element on the main diagonal of the vertex matrix, is 0 or 1 according

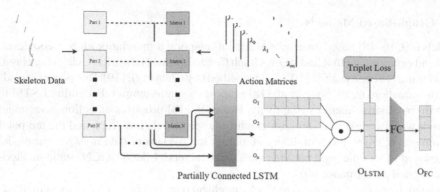

Fig. 2. The architecture of our model.

to whether m-th joint is in the subset V_n or not. Given that the joint is represented by the coordinates (x, y, z), j_m^n is replaced with three corresponding elements.

3.2 Partially Connected Layer

Given the lack of priori information about data, fully and locally connected neural networks are commonly used. Without considering the intrinsic relations between input and output, there are lots of unnecessary connections in the models, which are not conducive to capturing the underlying trend of the data.

Instead of directly multiplying the input vector with the weight matrix, we propose an activation matrix to multiply the weight before the input is put into the model. We can observe that the element in the activation matrix is 1 or 0. According to the basic matrix operation, if the n-th element is 0, the corresponding parameters will be frozen and the nth input node will not participate in the calculation. In this way, the proposed model shares weights partially via activation matrices. Figure 3 shows different processes of calculation in fully and partially connected layers. We can see that the activation matrix activates corresponding parameters in different colors.

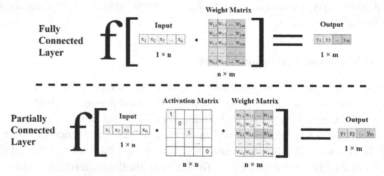

Fig. 3. Fully connected layer and partially connected layer.

3.3 Partially Connected LSTM

To avoid the problem of long-term dependency in RNN, Hochreiter [23] proposed Long Short-Term Memory, which is an advanced RNN architecture. Each standard LSTM unit contains four interacting layers: input gate i_t, forget gate f_t, output gate o_t and internal memory cell state c_t, together with a hidden state h_t.

The activations of the memory cell and three gates are defined as follows

$$
\begin{pmatrix} i_t \\ f_t \\ o_t \\ u_t \end{pmatrix} = \begin{pmatrix} \sigma \\ \sigma \\ \sigma \\ tanh \end{pmatrix} \left(\begin{pmatrix} W_i \\ W_f \\ W_o \\ W_u \end{pmatrix} (x_t) + \begin{pmatrix} U_i \\ U_f \\ U_o \\ U_u \end{pmatrix} (h_{t-1}) + \begin{pmatrix} b_i \\ b_f \\ b_o \\ b_u \end{pmatrix} \right)
\tag{1}
$$

$$
c_t = i_t{}^{\circ}u_t + f_t{}^{\circ}c_{t-1}
\tag{2}
$$

$$
h_t = o_t{}^{\circ}tanh(c_t)
\tag{3}
$$

where two fully connected layers $W(x)$, $U(h)$, are the main components of the LSTM unit. The first is the input layer, which takes input at time step t. The second is the hidden layer, which takes a vector storing the values of the hidden units at time t-1 as input.

The dimensions of the input vector are equal to the order of the activation matrix. The activation matrix multiplies the weight directly to share parameters with coupled features. But for the hidden layer, the size of the weight matrix is decided by the number of features in the hidden state. To solve the problem of dimension mismatch, we decomposed the hidden layer:

$$
\begin{pmatrix} i_t \\ f_t \\ o_t \\ u_t \end{pmatrix} = \begin{pmatrix} \sigma \\ \sigma \\ \sigma \\ tanh \end{pmatrix} \left(WVe^n x_t + U_l Ve^n U_r h_{t-1} + \begin{pmatrix} b_i \\ b_f \\ b_o \\ b_u \end{pmatrix} \right)
\tag{4}
$$

where the weight matrix of the hidden layer is split into two matrices U_l, U_r.

3.4 Triplet Loss

The loss function of cross-entropy is taken as the main component of the function. And extras consist of triplet losses, which have been widely used for ranking [24] and scoring. Given one anchor input X_a, triplet loss [18] is designed to minimize the distance with positive samples X_p and maximize the distance with negative samples X_n at the same time. Our loss function is composed of a set of triplet losses to make better use of hierarchical relationships between samples.

In this work, O_{LSTM}, which is the feature vector of sample X_a, is obtained as:

$$
O_{LSTM} = \prod_{k=1}^{n} aO_k
\tag{5}
$$

where elements corresponding to the same rows and columns of O_k are multiplied together to form O_{LSTM}. While performing each Hadamard product operation, the result is multiplied by a constant a, to avoid output value disappearing.

In the first extra function, a positive sample X_p^1 is taken from a class of the same level, and the distance between the input and negative sample X_n^1 classes is 1. In the second extra function, the negative sample from the first function is changed to a positive sample X_p^2, and as a negative sample X_n^2, a sample is taken from a class of the next two levels. The loss function is defined as:

$$Loss = L_{crossentropy} + L_{triplet}\left(X_a, X_p^1, X_n^1\right) + L_{triplet}\left(X_a, X_n^1, X_n^2\right) \tag{6}$$

4   Experiments

4.1   Evaluation Datasets and Settings

We carry out experiments to test our model in twelve different taijiquan gesture classes on the UMONS-TAICHI dataset and walking gait dataset.

UMONS-TAICHI: It is a dataset of tai chi gestures that includes 13 classes collected from 12 participants at four different skill levels. It is captured by two motion capture systems simultaneously: Qualisys and Microsoft Kinect V2. In this work, we use skeleton data from the Microsoft Kinect V2.

Walking Gait Dataset: It is a dataset of gait that includes normal walking gait and 8 simulated abnormal ones by padding a sole under foot. And we divided different thicknesses into different abnormal levels. Each subject performed 9 walking gaits. Each video in the dataset contains point cloud, skeleton, and frontal silhouette and is acquired in 1200 consecutive frames.

All experiments are carried out with an NVIDIA GeForce GTX 1650 Ti. The neuron size of LSTM cell in the LSTM layer is 128. As shown in Fig. 4, the skeleton is divided into multiple parts based on human structure and assessment rules.

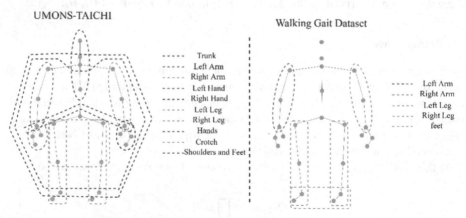

Fig. 4. The parts divided from the human skeleton.

4.2 Data Preprocess

To improve generalization and reduce the risk of over-fitting, models require a large amount of data during the training process. Furthermore, in a small dataset, model performances are excellent and similar, making it difficult to compare and analyze each model. Given the limited size of public dataset for action quality assessment, it is necessary to use data augmentation strategies. According to the different characteristics of the two datasets, we have formulated the following strategies, respectively.

For the UMONS-TAICHI, samples are divided into training and test sets, which are of equal size. Three data augmentation procedures increase the size of the training set to 12 times. First, we select random time steps from the sequence to reduce them to a specific length. Second, we randomly rotate the 3D coordinate in the range of $[-15°, 15°]$, along the x, y axis. The Cartesian coordinates of a vector are mapped to new coordinates by the multiplication of the rotation matrix. Third, apart from the joint of crotch, we randomly add Gaussian noise in data with the $\theta = 0, \sigma = 0.01$.

For the walking gait dataset, each video contains 1200 frames, which is composed of a lot of samples of walking. But the clips of samples are not split from the video. It is totally different from UMONS-TAICHI. If the strategy of video cropping as above is used again, the sample most likely contains a chaotic action sequence. Therefore, the frame sequence but not the frame itself is randomly selected from the video.

Figure 5 shows different data augmentation strategies for the UMONS-TAICHI and the walking gait dataset.

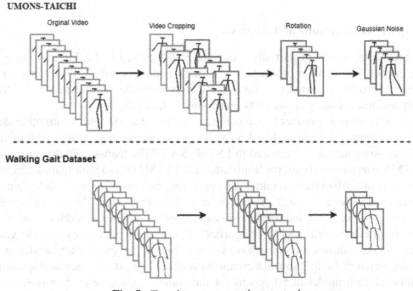

Fig. 5. Two data augmentation strategies

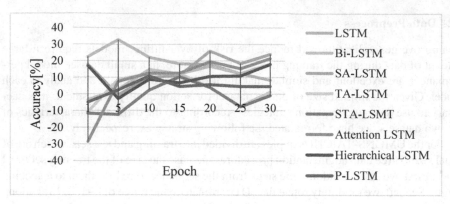

Fig. 6. Training accuracy minus test accuracy.

Table 1. Experimental results of partially connected LSTM on the UMONS-TAICHI (%).

Action		1	2	3	4	5	6	7	8	9	10	11	12
Accuracy	Tr	100	100	100	100	100	100	100	100	100	100	100	100
	Te	62.5	56.3	91.9	93.4	87.2	91.9	94.0	95.1	93.7	80.3	78.9	72.7
Spearman	Tr	100	100	100	100	100	100	100	100	100	100	100	100
	Te	62.9	22.5	94.8	94.0	82.2	92.3	92.3	96.1	95.7	85.2	85.8	66.4

4.3 Experimental Results and Analysis

The experimental results of partially connected LSTM tested in 12 different taijiquan gesture classes. The number of samples of actions 1 and 2 is only 32. We can see that the proposed model is overfitted in Table 1. Partially connected LSTM gets 100% train accuracy and test accuracy is over 90% in actions 3, 4, 6, 7, 8, 9.

In the next set of experiments, we compare our architecture with seven other deep LSTM architectures. LSTM and Bi-LSTM don't pay attention to spatial or temporal relations between actions. Compared to LSTM, SA-LSTM learns spatial patterns and TA-LSTM learns temporal patterns from data. STA-LSTM [18] is a joint spatial-temporal attention network. All of them automatically produces their attention map while training. It is mentioned in Sect. 2 that the right pattern is difficult to learn. Instead of learning attention weights, the attention mechanism calculates them from the hidden state of the decoder. Both hierarchical LSTM and partially LSTM are designed by specific graph structure. Table 2 shows a comparison of the highest accuracy of each model in 30 epochs for action 8. Table 3 shows a comparison of the highest accuracy and spearman correlation of each model in 50 epochs for the walking gait dataset. Figure 6 shows the difference between training accuracy and test accuracy. We discover that models with sub-network learning attention weights automatically perform poorly. Expect our model, the differences between training and test accuracy are all over 10%. Our model has improved the test accuracy to 95.1%, respectively. It turned out that partially LSTM reduces over-fitting by avoiding entering too many features at the same time. On the walking gait dataset, our model obtains accuracy of 70.0%.

Table 2. Experimental results of LSTM architecture on the UMONS-TAICHI (%).

Method	Accuracy	
	Train	Test
LSTM	94.1	89.9
Bi-LSTM	100	89.9
SA-LSTM	88.0	64.0
TA-LSTM	89.7	80.9
STA-LSMT	88.3	82.0
Attention LSTM	99.1	86.5
Hierarchical LSTM	100	93.3
Ours	**100**	**95.5**

Table 3. Experimental results of LSTM architecture on the walking gait dataset (%).

Method	Accuracy		Pearson correlation		Spearman correlation	
	Train	Test	Train	Test	Train	Test
LSTM	50.4	48.8	63.9	68.9	70.5	73.2
Bi-LSTM	60.5	57.1	73.8	80.3	75.5	80.4
SA-LSTM	29.2	30.2	47.4	57.8	51.1	60.8
TA-LSTM	52.2	45.2	68.9	65.8	71.0	67.8
STA-LSMT	25.6	23.4	49.8	41.1	58.4	54.9
Attention LSTM	51.4	47.6	69.9	70.9	71.2	74.1
Hierarchical LSTM	49.0	43.7	65.7	65.7	65.4	68.3
Ours	**70.0**	**68.3**	**89.9**	**89.5**	**90.5**	**90.7**

In the third experiment, we train other advanced methods listed in Table 4 on the UMONS-TAICHI dataset. All graph-based models achieve 100% train accuracy. This shows that the spatial or temporal pattern is beneficial for models to assess the quality of action. However, models exhibit varying degrees of overfitting.

Finally, we evaluate the effect of additional triplet losses by comparing the models' performance. As shown in Table 5, this approach improves the performance of models especially for LSTM architectures.

Table 4. Experimental results of GNN on the UMONS-TAICHI (%).

Method	Train accuracy	Test accuracy
ST-GCN [16]	100	88.8
2S-AGCN [17]	100	91.0
DGNN [25]	100	77.5
Ours	**100**	**95.5**

Table 5. Experimental results of models with triplet loss on the UMONS-TAICHI (%).

Method	No triplet loss		Triplet loss	
	Train	Test	Train	Test
LSTM	94.1	89.9	97.5	93.3
Hierarchical LSTM	100	93.3	100	96.6
Attention LSTM	99.1	86.5	100	97.8
STA-LSTM	88.3	82.0	99.1	88.8
ST-GCN	100	88.8	100	88.8
Ours	**100**	**95.5**	**100**	**97.7**

4.4 Complexity Analysis

This subsection presents the complexity analysis of the runtime and parameters of our model, compared to LSTM and hierarchical LSTM. We recorded the runtimes of three models separately on the train set of the walking gait dataset. All LSTM models are recreated by us. There is no significant difference in time spent between our model and hierarchical LSTM, as shown in Fig. 7.

The complexity of model is related to the number of parameters in the network. Assume that i is the size of the input vector, h is the size of the hidden layer and o is the size of the output vector. Each standard LSTM cell contains 4 dense layers, which has a set of 2 matrices: U and W. U has dimensions $i \times h$ and W has dimensions $h \times h$. Including bias vectors, the number of parameters for LSTM cell, becomes $4 \times (ih + h^2 + h)$. All models are comprised of a single hidden layer and output layer. The number of parameters for LSTM, which is constructed with a hidden layer of a single LSTM cell, becomes $4 \times (ih + h^2 + h) + oh + o$. The hidden layer in hierarchical LSTM is composed of multiple LSTM cells. So, the number of parameters for hierarchical LSTM is $\sum_{k=1}^{n} 4 \times (i^k h + h^2 + h) + oh + h$, decided by the hierarchical relations. So, without increasing the number of parameters, our model makes use of hierarchical relations.

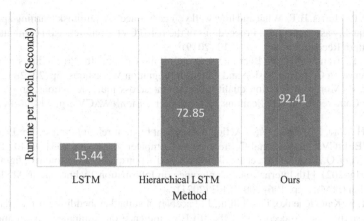

Fig. 7. Runtime per epoch of LSTM models

5 Conclusion

In this paper, we propose a partially connected LSTM with triplet losses for action quality assessment. The Fully connected layer in the LSTM model is replaced by the proposed partially connected layer to explore the hierarchical relations of skeleton graph. Activation matrix is proposed to multiply the weight, which make nodes partially connected. Such an approach can reduce the impact of insignificant features. We introduce two triplet losses to the loss function, which are used to make feature vectors distributed in order. On the UMONS-TAICHI dataset and walking gait dataset, the proposed partially connected LSTM achieves outstanding performance. In future work, we will plan to use the multi-labels fusion method to explore the hierarchical relations in the skeleton to improve the accuracy. We will also focus on employing more advanced models for action quality assessment.

References

1. McNally, W., Vats, K., Pinto, T., et al.: GolfDB: a video database for golf swing sequencing. In: Proceedings of the IEEE/CVF Conference on Computer Vision and Pattern Recognition Workshops (2019)
2. Szczęsna, A., Błaszczyszyn, M., Pawlyta, M.: Optical motion capture dataset of selected techniques in beginner and advanced Kyokushin karate athletes. Sci. Data **8**(1), 1–12 (2021)
3. Tits, M., Laraba, S., Caulier, E., et al.: UMONS-TAICHI: a multimodal motion capture dataset of expertise in Taijiquan gestures. Data Brief **19**, 1214–1221 (2018)
4. Liao, Y., Vakanski, A., Xian, M.: A deep learning framework for assessing physical rehabilitation exercises. IEEE Trans. Neural Syst. Rehabil. Eng. **28**(2), 468–477 (2020)
5. Capecci, M., Ceravolo, M.G., Ferracuti, F., et al.: The KIMORE dataset: KInematic assessment of MOvement and clinical scores for remote monitoring of physical REhabilitation. IEEE Trans. Neural Syst. Rehabil. Eng. **27**(7), 1436–1448 (2019)
6. Xu, C., Fu, Y., Zhang, B., et al.: Learning to score figure skating sport videos. IEEE Trans. Circuits Syst. Video Technol. **30**(12), 4578–4590 (2019)

7. Parmar, P., Morris, B.T.: What and how well you performed? A multitask learning approach to action quality assessment. In: Proceedings of the IEEE/CVF Conference on Computer Vision and Pattern Recognition, pp. 304–313 (2019)
8. Parmar, P., Tran Morris, B.: Learning to score olympic events. In: Proceedings of the IEEE Conference on Computer Vision and pattern Recognition Workshops, pp. 20–28 (2017)
9. Parmar, P., Morris, B.: Action quality assessment across multiple actions. In: 2019 IEEE Winter Conference on Applications of Computer Vision (WACV), pp. 1468–1476. IEEE (2019)
10. Pan, J.H., Gao, J., Zheng, W.S.: Action assessment by joint relation graphs. In: Proceedings of the IEEE/CVF International Conference on Computer Vision, pp. 6331–6340 (2019)
11. Li, H.Y., Lei, Q., Zhang, H.B., et al.: Skeleton based action quality assessment of figure skating videos. In: 2021 11th International Conference on Information Technology in Medicine and Education (ITME), pp. 196–200. IEEE (2021)
12. Schroff, F., Kalenichenko, D., Philbin, J.: FaceNet: a unified embedding for face recognition and clustering. In: Proceedings of the IEEE Conference on Computer Vision and Pattern Recognition, pp. 815–823 (2015)
13. Nguyen, T.N., Huynh, H.H., Meunier, J.: 3D reconstruction with time-of-flight depth camera and multiple mirrors. IEEE Access **6**, 38106–38114 (2018)
14. Li, Z., Huang, Y., Cai, M., et al.: Manipulation-skill assessment from videos with spatial attention network. In: Proceedings of the IEEE/CVF International Conference on Computer 14Vision Workshops (2019)
15. Gao, Y., Vedula, S.S., Reiley, C.E., et al.: JHU-ISI gesture and skill assessment working set (JIGSAWS): a surgical activity dataset for human motion modeling. In: MICCAI Workshop: M2CAI, vol. 3, p. 3 (2014)
16. Yan, S., Xiong, Y., Lin, D.: Spatial temporal graph convolutional networks for skeleton-based action recognition. In Thirty-Second AAAI Conference on Artificial In-telligence (2018)
17. Shi, L., Zhang, Y., Cheng, J., et al.: Two-stream adaptive graph convolutional networks for skeleton-based action recognition. In: Proceedings of the IEEE/CVF Conference on Computer Vision and Pattern Recognition, pp. 12026–12035 (2019)
18. Song, S., Lan, C., Xing, J., et al.: An end-to-end spatio-temporal attention model for human action recognition from skeleton data. In: Proceedings of the AAAI Conference on Artificial Intelligence, vol. 31, no. 1 (2017)
19. Chen, Y., Zhang, Z., Yuan, C., et al.: Channel-wise topology refinement graph convolution for skeleton-based action recognition. In: Proceedings of the IEEE/CVF International Conference on Computer Vision, pp. 13359–13368 (2021)
20. Du, Y., Wang, W., Wang, L.: Hierarchical recurrent neural network for skeleton based action recognition. In: Proceedings of the IEEE Conference on Computer Vision and Pattern Recognition, pp. 1110–1118 (2015)
21. Thakkar, K., Narayanan, P.J.: Part-based graph convolutional network for action recognition. arXiv preprint arXiv:1809.04983 (2018)
22. Si, C., Chen, W., Wang, W., et al.: An attention enhanced graph convolutional LSTM network for skeleton-based action recognition. In: Proceedings of the IEEE/CVF Conference on Computer Vision and Pattern Recognition, pp. 1227–1236 (2019)
23. Hochreiter, S., Schmidhuber, J.: Long short-term memory. Neural Comput. **9**(8), 1735–1780 (1997)
24. Prétet, L., Richard, G., Peeters, G.: Learning to rank music tracks using triplet loss. In: ICASSP 2020-2020 IEEE International Conference on Acoustics, Speech and Signal Processing (ICASSP), pp. 511–515. IEEE (2020)
25. Shi, L., Zhang, Y., Cheng, J., et al.: Skeleton-based action recognition with directed graph neural networks. In: Proceedings of the IEEE/CVF Conference on Computer Vision and Pattern Recognition, pp. 7912–7921 (2019)

Hierarchical Long-Short Transformer for Group Activity Recognition

Yan Zhuang, Zhaofeng He$^{(\boxtimes)}$, Longteng Kong, and Ming Lei

Beijing University of Posts and Telecommunications, Beijing 100876, China
{zhuangyan,zhaofenghe,konglongteng,mlei}@bupt.edu.cn

Abstract. Group activity recognition is a challenging task in computer vision, which needs to comprehensively model the diverse spatio-temporal relations among individuals and generate group representation. In this paper, we propose a novel group activity recognition approach, named *Hierarchical Long-Short Transformer (HLSTrans)*. Based on Transformer, it both considers long- and short-range relationship among individuals via Long-Short Transformer Blocks. Moreover, we build a hierarchical structure in HLSTrans by stacking such blocks to obtain abundant individual relations in multiple scales. By long- and short-range relation modeling in hierarchical mode, HLSTrans is able to enhance the representation of individuals and groups, leading to better recognition performance. We evaluate the proposed HLSTrans on Volleyball and VolleyTactic datasets, and the experimental results demonstrate state-of-the-art performance.

Keywords: Group activity recognition · Transformer · Relation modeling

1 Introduction

Group Activity Recognition (GAR) is a critical issue in video understanding, which has attracted notable research attention in the field of computer vision. The focus of this task is to model complicated spatio-temporal relationship among individuals within the scene, *e.g.* sports games. The existing methods have proposed many techniques for group activity recognition, *e.g.* Recurrent Neural Network (RNN) and Graph Convolutional Networks (GCN), which exhibit excellent ability in capturing the individual relations. With the rise of Transformer, many methods expanded on this and achieved better results [8,12]. However, most of these methods simply used the native Transformer, which leaves a lot of room for improvement.

In fact, there exist more complicated individual relations in group activities, which involve long- and short-range relationship. For example, a movement in volleyball games named passing is always used, as shown in Fig. 1, the player who wants to pass the ball needs to choose whether to pass the ball to the person nearby, or to the person who is far away. Most prior methods

S. Yu et al. (Eds.): PRCV 2022, LNCS 13536, pp. 233–244, 2022.
https://doi.org/10.1007/978-3-031-18913-5_18

Fig. 1. Illustration of passing in volleyball game, where the Setter is both highly correlated with Spiker1 (short-range relation) and Spiker2 (long-range relation).

[8] use fully connected relationship introduced by the native Transformer to model the global dependencies among all individuals, which tend to overlook the local correlation. There are also methods that capture the local context by dividing individuals into different sub-groups, thereby achieving intra-group and inter-group relationships. However, grouping strategies can not take into account long- and short-range relationships simultaneously. Beyond that, these methods restrict relationships between individuals to a single level, unfortunately ignoring multi-scale context, nevertheless, multi-scale characteristics are also particularly important in group activity representations similar to other vision tasks.

To address the aforementioned issues, we propose Hierarchical Long-Short Transformer (HLSTrans), a model capable of mining meaningful representations of group activity. For the former, *i.e.* diverse relation modeling, we present a Long-Short Transformer Block (LSTB), which is able to encode long- and short-range relations among individuals. Inspired by the latest success of local self-attention [11] that restricts the attention in a certain window, we design LSTB by introducing long- and short-distance windows to provide long- and short-range interactions, respectively. For the latter, *i.e.* multi-scale relation modeling, we construct a hierarchical structure using multiple stages to extract multi-scale characteristics, each stage consists of several LSTBs corresponding to a certain scale. Between stages, we design a feature merging layer, responsible for gradually merging neighboring tokens in deeper Transformer layers, and thus generating a pyramid representation. Note that long- and short-range relationships are constructed at each scale, and the pyramid representation explicitly embodies local and global relationships. In summary, we have three contributions in this paper as follows:

- We propose a novel group activity recognition approach, *i.e.* HLSTrans, which takes advantage of local attention to enrich the characteristics of individual and group.
- A Long-Short Transformer Block is introduced to extract the long- short-range relationships within groups. On this basis, we construct a hierarchical structure to generate multi-scale relational context.
- We perform extensive experiments on the Volleyball and Volleytactic datasets. The experiment results show that the proposed HLSTrans achieves the state-of-the-art performance.

2 Related Work

2.1 Group Activity Recognition

Compared with traditional methods, the methods of deep learning [5,10,20,21, 24,26] do not have obvious stages. It is usually a complete end-to-end model that takes raw video as input to model and output activity categories through the model. In [5], a relational layer is introduced to capture the spatial relations of each person in order to generate group representation. [20] deployed a two-level hierarchy of LSTM to recognize the group activities more reliably by minimizing the predicted energy. Among them, feature extraction and activity modeling and recognition are all submerged in deep neural networks. Earlier attempts are analog-based deep convolutional neural networks (CNN) [13], which directly took video as multi-channel input to achieve staged results, but were inferior to traditional methods due to their inability to capture the motion of activities well. Group activity recognition is concerned about high-level semantic information such as relationships among individuals in a scene. The recognition process can generally be divided into object detection, single individual activity modeling and group relationship modeling formed by multiple individuals. Early group activity recognition methods generally used manual local descriptors and graph models to construct high-quality semantic information. However, local descriptors are not robust enough for some individuals to perform similar actions. To improve the recognition performance, many researchers have proposed more distinguished descriptors, such as social character models and hierarchical models. The deep learning-based method draws on the hierarchical idea of traditional methods, and considers the interaction between individual activities and individuals. They usually use sequential deep models such as long short-term memory network (LSTM) to model individuals and groups [15]. Among them, a pooling operation is often used on individual characteristics to obtain group representations of equal length. However, the pooling operation simply takes the extreme values of multiple individual characteristics, which easily leads to the loss of relationship information among individuals. To solve this problem, many researchers use new models to obtain more detailed relational information, such as relational networks based on implicit variables, graph convolutional networks [19]. These models have also become mainstream in the field of group activity recognition.

2.2 Transformer

Transformer first proposed in [2] for sequential machine translation task, and then has been widely used in various natural language processing tasks. The self-attention mechanism is particularly suitable for capturing long-range dependencies. On the basis of Transformer, a series of modifications are designed to address the limitations of the standard Transformer to adapt to new tasks. Transformer is widely used in the field of computer vision. Since the naive application of transformer to images is quadratic, each pixel uses the query-key mechanism to pay attention to all pixels. Therefore, the early method [6,25] only used

self-attention to capture long-range context. [25] designed a non-local attention module to capture long-range dependencies in computer vision task. [6]
adopted a two-dimensional self-attention mechanism to selectively replace the
two-dimensional convolution layer and achieved better results than the original
two-dimensional convolutional layer. DETR [16] simplifies the transformer-based
detection pipeline to a large extent, with stronger performance compared to previous CNN-based detectors. What's more, DETR uses a CNN-based backbone
network to extract low-level characteristics and encoder-decoder transformers
to develop high-level concepts. Although there is no explicitly statement, it is
common to use the attention mechanism to simulate the context of spatial and
temporal scenes. [14] designed a variant of a neural network to model the spatial
dependencies of time-varying. Attention-based spatial-temporal GCN proposed
by [3] captured dynamic correlation from the message passing of the graph to
learn spatial and temporal features. [9] proposed to use a Transformer-based
encoder to build spatial attention and temporal attention, and indexed the temporal attention to the corresponding spatial attention matrix directly. [4] simply
extended the ViT [1] design to video, and proposed several scalable spatial-
temporal self-attention. The previous method captured context in stacked manners [17], or used parallel modules to extract features, and then simply integrated
them [23]. Unlikely, we proposed a novel hierarchical structure that focuses more
on the relationships among individuals and groups.

3   Methodology

3.1   Overview of HLSTrans

The overview of our proposed HLSTrans is illustrated in Fig. 2. Given a video clip
with individual detections, it mainly takes the following phases for group activity recognition. Firstly, a K-frame sequence is uniformly sampled from a given
video clip with person detection. At each frame, we use I3D model to extract the
appearance feature. Following the feature extraction strategy used in (Bagautdinov et al.), we adopt the multi-scale strategy to compute feature maps for each
frame. Then, ROI Align is employed to generate the person feature from the feature map. Afterward, upon these original individual features and positions, we
align the individual descriptors from K frames into a sequence, which consists of
L individuals. With feature sequence, a Feature Merging layer is used to reduce
the length of embeddings (after stage-1) while double their dimensions. Then,
several Long-Short Transformer Blocks from several serial cascaded stages are
used to model the individual relations of multiple scales, each of which involves
long- and short-range attention. Finally, a standard Transformer Block is set up
for producing the final representation for classification task.

3.2   Long-Short Transformer Block

The Transformer network has achieved great success in the field of NLP, such
as machine translation, emotional analysis and text generation. It follows the

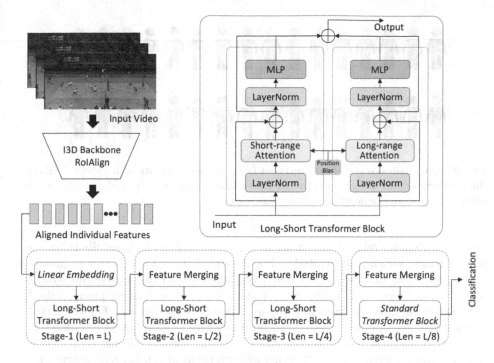

Fig. 2. The architecture of HLSTrans. The input size is L, and the size of feature maps in each stage is shown on the bottom. Stage-i consists of a Feature Merging layer and a Long-Short Transformer Block (except for Stage-1 and Stage-4).

famous encoder decoder structure that is widely used in the RNN sequence-to-sequence model. The core idea of Transformer is to completely replace the recurrence mechanism with multiple attention. For embeddings $\{h_t\}_{t=1}^T$, Transformer self-attention first learns the query matrix $Q = f_Q(\{h_t\}_{t=1}^T)$ of all embeddings from t = 1 to T, the key matrix $K = f_K(\{h_t\}_{t=1}^T)$ and the corresponding value matrix $V = f_V(\{h_t\}_{t=1}^T)$. The formula for calculating attention is:

$$Att\,(Q,\ K,\ V) = Softmax(\frac{QK^T}{\sqrt{d_k}})V, \tag{1}$$

where d_k is the dimension of each query, $1/\sqrt{d_k}$ implements the scalar dot product to the attention of numerical stability. By calculating the self-attention between embeddings at different times, the self-attention mechanism can learn the time dependencies of long-range, compared with RNN that uses a limited vector to memorize historical data. In addition, the attention is decoupled into the query, key, and value meta group, so that the self-attention mechanism can capture more complicated time dependencies.

As mentioned in Sect. 1, the native Transformer is able to model the global sequence dependencies but tend to overlook the local correlations. To capture the

Fig. 3. Short distance attention (top) and Long distance attention (bottom). Embeddings (green cubes) are grouped by red boxes, and the ones with borders of the same color belong to the same group. (Color figure online)

diverse individual relations in group activity, we design the Long-Short Transformer Block, which is illustrated in Fig. 2 (top). It uses Transformer to process more structured data sequences and pays attention to two parts: short-range attention and long-range attention. For the former, each adjacent group embedding is together, as shown in Fig. 3 (top), where group size = 4. For the latter, the features are sampled with a fixed interval. The window size is calculated as input size divide the fixed interval. After grouping the embeddings, both short- and long-range attention use standard self-attention in Eq. (1) to construct the dependencies embedded in each group.

Similar to the standard Transformer, a multi-head mechanism is also used in LSTB. It combines multiple assumptions when calculating attention, allowing the model to jointly process information from different positions. If there are k heads, we have

$$MultiHead(Q, K, V) = f_O\left([head_i]_{i=1}^k\right) \tag{2}$$

$$head_i = Att_i(Q, K, V), \tag{3}$$

where f_O is a fully connected layer, merging k-size outputs; $Att_i(Q, K, V)$ represents the self-attention of head i. Additional position encoding is used to add positional information to Transformer embeddings, introduced in Sect. 3.4. Besides Multi-head Attention, norm layer and feed-forward neural network are followed to abstract the representation. In LSTB, we sum the outputs of short- and long-range attentions as the output of each block.

3.3 Hierarchical Structure

HLSTrans uses hierarchical structure to generate multi-scale group representation. The model consists of four stages, each of which contains a Feature Merging layer and a Long-Short Transformer Block. Note that in Stage-1 and Stage-4, we use the linear embedding and standard attention. To produce a pyramid representation, the number of tokens is reduced by Feature Merging layer as the network goes deeper. The first D-dimensional token concatenates the features of each group of 2 neighbors, and applies a linear layer on the concatenated features. This reduces the number of tokens by a multiple of 2 (downsampling of resolution), and the output dimension becomes to 2D. In Stage-1, the LSTB maintains the number of tokens, $i.e.$ L, and together with the linear embedding. Then we apply feature merging in Stage-2, while the resolution kept at L/2. The merged features are fed into LSTB to model the long- and short range relations. After that, the procedure is repeated once, with output resolution of L/4. Note at the last stage, $i.e.$ Stage-4, we use the standard Transformer block. Since the input length is short enough ($i.e.$ L/8) for modeling the global dependencies. These stages jointly produce a hierarchical representation, with the same feature map resolutions as those of typical convolutional networks, e.g., VGG and ResNet. We apply max-pooling to the output feature sequence to obtain the final group representation and feed it into a softmax classification layer for group activity recognition.

It is worth noting that the hierarchical structure facilitates the effectiveness of long- and short-range relationship modeling. Specifically, because the feature sequence is too long to explore the relationship between distant individual pairs without the help of context. Furthermore, since the windows are not overlapped, some meaningful relationships are easily overlooked if only a single scale is available. In other words, by using a hierarchical structure, the tokens contain more context to connect those embeddings, making multiple long-range attention more accessible.

3.4 Position Bias

Position Bias represents the relative position of the embedded object by increasing the attentional bias of the character-extracted object. The attention map of LSTB with position bias is

$$Attention = Softmax(QK^T/\sqrt{d} + \mathbf{B})V \qquad (4)$$

Among them, Q, K, $V \in R^{G \times D}$ respectively represents query, key and value in the self attention module. $\sqrt{d}$ is a constant normalizer, $\mathbf{B} \in R^{G \times G}$ is the relative matrix. Most previous works fixed the $B_{i,j} = \hat{B}_{\Delta x_{ij}, \Delta y_{ij}}$, where $(\Delta x_{ij}, \Delta y_{ij})$ means the distance between the coordinates from the i to j embedding. Obviously, when $(\Delta x_{ij}, \Delta y_{ij})$ is larger than $\hat{B}$, the group size is limited. Following [22], we use a learnable Position Bias module based MLP to dynamically generate relative position deviation:

$$B_{i,j} = MLP(\Delta x_{ij}, \Delta y_{ij}) \qquad (5)$$

The non-linear transform of MLP is made up of three fully connected layer with layer normalization and ReLU. The input dimension of Position Bias is 2, namely $(\Delta x_{ij}, \Delta y_{ij})$, and intermediate layers' dimension is set as D/4, where D is the embeddings dimension. $B_{i,j}$ is a scalar, encoding the relative position characteristics between the i and j embedding. Due to the learnable mechanism with Transformer model, it can deal with any group size, and do not need to concern about the boundary of $(\Delta x_{ij}, \Delta y_{ij})$.

4　Experiments

In this section, we carry out extensive experiments on the Volleyball and VolleyTactic datasets to evaluate the proposed method by comparing it to other state-of-the-art approaches.

4.1　Datasets

Volleyball dataset is released by [5], which contains 4830 video clips from 55 Volleyball matches. Including 3493 samples for training and 1337 samples for testing. There are 9 kinds of individual action and 8 kinds of group activity. Each video clip belongs to one of eight kinds of group activity, including 'Set', 'Spike', 'Pass' and 'Winpoint', each of these activities are divided into left and right teams, a total of eight. The dataset offers key frames around 40-frame sequences and each sample corresponds to one of the key frames with the athletes' bounding box and tracklet.

VolleyTactic dataset is presented by [12], which contains 4960 video clips from 12 world-class volleyball match videos in YouTube. The matches are randomly split into 8 training and 4 testing, leading to a total of 3,340 training and 1,620 testing clips. The dataset includes 'Receive', 'Offense' and 'Defense'. Receive usually occurs after serve, which is the beginning of a round. Offense is the subject of the game, involves a variety of attack forms, 'Smash', 'Open', 'Switch' and 'Space'. Different from the Volleyball dataset, this one do not annotate personal actions and ground truth bounding boxes, it only use the detections of athletes for identifying tactics.

4.2　Implementation

For both datasets, we adopt 20 frames that uniformly sampled form the video. We adjust the resolution of each frame to 720 × 1280. We start with the initial weights of I3D pre-trained on UCF101 and extract the person feature $p_i \in R^{128}$. For the Group size (G) and Interval I, in the first stage, we set G = 6 and I = 40. In the second stage, G = 12 and I = 10. For the third stage, G = 6 and I = 10. For the last stage, we do not use grouping settings. For network training, we use the batch size of 8 samples. We trained the training model on the Volleyball dataset for 150 iterations. The starting learning rate was set to 5e−4. At the 40th iteration, we trained at a 1e−4 learning rate. At the 80th iteration, we trained at a 5e−5 learning rate. At the 120th iteration, we trained at a 1e−5 learning rate, and this learning rate remained until iterations ended.

4.3 Comparison to Others

We compare our approach with other state-of-the-art group activity recognition methods on the Volleyball dataset, as shown in Table 1. Compared to the top counterpart *i.e.* Actor-Transformer, the proposed method generally performs better in the same protocols (backbone, input). Note that even our baseline methods, *e.g.* w/o LSTB, achieves better scores than Actor-Transformer. HLSTrans achieves better performance than the baselines (w/o LSTB and w/o Hierarchy), indicating its effectiveness of long-short range relationship and multi-scale context modeling. When combining the pose clue, extracted by HRNet, our approach boosts 1.5% in terms of accuracy and achieves the best results.

Table 1. Comparison to state-of-the-art on the Volleyball dataset.

Methods	Backbone	Input	Accuracy
HDTM [15]	AlexNet	RGB	81.9%
CERN [20]	VGG16	RGB	83.3%
stagNet	VGG16	RGB	87.6%
HRN [5]	VGG19	RGB	89.5%
ARG [7]	Inception-v3	RGB	91.5%
CRM [18]	I3D	RGB+Flow	93.0%
Actor-Transformer [8]	I3D	RGB	91.4%
Actor-Transformer [8]	I3D+HRNet	RGB+Pose	93.5%
Ours (HLSTrans w/o LSTB)	I3D	RGB	92.0%
Ours (HLSTrans w/o Hierarchy)	I3D	RGB	92.1%
Ours (HLSTrans)	I3D	RGB	92.4%
Ours (HLSTrans)	I3D+HRNet	RGB+Pose	**93.9%**

Table 2. Comparison to state-of-the-art on the VolleyTactic dataset.

Methods	Backbone	Input	Accuracy
HDTM [15]	AlexNet	RGB	82.03%
HRN [5]	VGG19	RGB	82.59%
ARG [7]	Inception-v3	RGB	80.99%
Actor-Transformer [8]	I3D	RGB	82.96%
Actor-Transformer [8]	I3D+HRNet	RGB+Pose	83.21%
A-GCN+A-TCN [12]	I3D+HRNet	RGB+Pose	87.53%
A-GCN+A-TCN [12]	Inception-v3+HRNet	RGB+Pose	88.27%
Ours (HLSTrans w/o LSTB)	I3D	RGB	86.21%
Ours (HLSTrans w/o Hierarchy)	I3D	RGB	85.83%
Ours (HLSTrans)	I3D	RGB	87.14%
Ours (HLSTrans)	I3D+HRNet	RGB+Pose	**88.50%**

Fig. 4. Visualization of the predicted tactic labels from the VolleyTactic dataset using our model, where each row belongs to a tactic (GT denotes Ground Truth label and PRE denotes PREdicted one).

We further evaluate our approach on the VolleyTactic dataset by reproducing the state-of-the-art methods, including HDTM, HRN, ARG, Actor-Transformer, and A-GCN+ATCN. Following [12], we carefully tune the parameters in the benchmark methods and choose the best accuracies. The comparison results are shown in Table 2. The proposed method surpasses the Actor-Transformer by a large margin (*i.e.* 87.14% vs. 82.96% with RGB and 88.50% vs. 83.21% with RGB+Pose), demonstrating its effectiveness in extending Transformer with long-short and multi-scale relation modeling. When considering pose clue, HLSTrans performs slightly better than A-GCN+A-TCN. A possible reason why the improvement is not obvious is that the advantage of A-TCN in long-range dynamics modeling is fully exhibited in this benchmark compared with Transformer. The baseline (w/o LSTB) achieves better result than the one (w/o Hierarchy), which indicates the superiority of building multi-scale relations representation. In Fig. 4, we visualize our predicted activities with different failure and success scenarios.

5   Conclusion

We proposed a Transformer-based group activity recognition approach, namely HLSTran, which augments long-short range relationship and multi-scale context modeling. We show that individual relationships at different distances play an important role for group activity recognition, and multi-scale feature is of great significance for better expression of group characteristics. Experiments are conducted on Volleyball and VolleyTactic datasets, and the results achieve state-of-the-art performance on both datasets, outperforming previously published results.

Acknowledgement. This work was supported by the National Natural Science Foundation of China (62176025, U21B200389), the Fundamental Research Funds for the Central Universities (2021rc38), and the National Natural Science Foundation of China (62106015).

References

1. Dosovitskiy, A., et al.: An image is worth 16 × 16 words: transformers for image recognition at scale (2020). https://arxiv.org/abs/2010.11929
2. Vaswani, A., et al.: Attention is all you need (2017). https://arxiv.org/abs/1706.03762
3. Yu, C., Ma, X., Ren, J., Zhao, H., Z., Yi, S.: Spatio-temporal graph transformer networks for pedestrian trajectory prediction. In: European Conference on Computer Vision, pp. 507–523 (2020)
4. Bertasius, G., Wang, H., Torresani, L.: Is space-time attention all you need for video understanding? (2021) https://arxiv.org/abs/2102.05095
5. Ibrahim, M.S., Mori, G.: Hierarchical relational networks for group activity recognition and retrieval. In: European Conference on Computer Vision, pp. 721–736 (2018)
6. Bello, I., Zoph, B., Vaswani, A., Shlens, J., Le, Q.V.: Attention augmented convolutional networks. In: IEEE International Conference on Computer Vision, pp. 3286–3295 (2019)
7. Wu, L. Wang, L.W.J.G., Wu, G.: Learning actor relation graphs for group activity recognition. In: IEEE Conference on Computer Vision and Pattern Recognition, pp. 9964–9974 (2019)
8. Gavrilyuk, K., Sanford, R., Javan, M., Snoek, C.G.M.: Actor-transformers for group activity recognition. In: IEEE Computer Vision and Pattern Recognition, pp. 836–845 (2020)
9. Chen, K., Chen, G., Xu, D., Zhang, L., Huang, Y., Knoll, A.: NAST: non-autoregressive spatial-temporal transformer for time series forecasting (2021). https://arxiv.org/abs/2102.05624
10. Li, X., Chuah, M.C.: SBGAR: semantics based group activity recognition. In: IEEE International Conference on Computer Vision, pp. 2876–2885 (2017)
11. Liu, Z., et al.: SWIN transformer: hierarchical vision transformer using shifted windows. In: IEEE International Conference on Computer Vision, pp. 10012–10022 (2021)
12. Kong, L., Pei, D., He, R., Huang, D., Wang, Y.: Spatio-temporal player relation modeling for tactic recognition in sports videos. IEEE Trans. Circ. Syst. Video Technol. **32**(9), 6086–6099 (2022)
13. Ehsanpour, M., Abedin, A., Saleh, F., Shi, J., Reid, I., Rezatofighi, H.: Joint learning of social groups, individuals action and sub-group activities in videos (2020). https://arxiv.org/abs/2007.02632
14. Xu, M., et al.: Spatial-temporal transformer networks for traffic flow forecasting (2020). https://arxiv.org/abs/2001.02908
15. Ibrahim, M.S., Muralidharan, S., Deng, Z., Vahdat, A., Mori, G.: A hierarchical deep temporal model for group activity recognition. In: IEEE Computer Vision and Pattern Recognition, pp. 1971–1980 (2016)

16. Carion, N., Massa, F., Synnaeve, G., Usunier, N., Kirillov, A., Zagoruyko, S.: End-to-end object detection with transformers. In: Vedaldi, A., Bischof, H., Brox, T., Frahm, J.-M. (eds.) ECCV 2020. LNCS, vol. 12346, pp. 213–229. Springer, Cham (2020). https://doi.org/10.1007/978-3-030-58452-8_13

17. Peng, C., Jiang, W., Quanzeng, Y., Haibin, L., Zicheng, L.: TransMOT: spatial-temporal graph transformer for multiple object tracking. In: IEEE Computer Vision and Pattern Recognition (2021)

18. S. M. Azar, M. G. Atigh, A.N., Alahi, A.: Convolutional relational machine for group activity. In: IEEE Conference on Computer Vision and Pattern Recognition, pp. 7892–7901 (2019)

19. Guo, S., Lin, Y., Feng, N., Song, C., Wan, H.: Attention based spatial-temporal graph convolutional networks for traffic flow forecasting. In: AAAI Conference on Artificial Intelligence, pp. 922–929 (2019)

20. Shu, T., Todorovic, S., Zhu, S.C.: CERN: confidence-energy recurrent network for group activity recognition. In: IEEE Computer Vision and Pattern Recognition, pp. 5523–5531 (2017)

21. Bagautdinov, T., Alahi, A., Fleuret, F., Fua, P., Savarese, S.: Social scene understanding: end-to-end multi-person action localization and collective activity recognition. In: IEEE Computer Vision and Pattern Recognition, pp. 4315–4324 (2017)

22. Wang, W., et al.: CrossFormer: a versatile vision transformer based on cross-scale attention (2021). https://arxiv.org/abs/2108.00154

23. Choi, W., Shahid, K., Savarese, S.: What are they doing?: Collective activity classification using spatio-temporal relationship among people. In: IEEE International Conference on Computer Vision, pp. 1282–1289 (2009)

24. Shu, X., Tang, J., Qi, G.-J., Liu, W., Yang, J.: Hierarchical long short-term concurrent memory for human interaction recognition. IEEE Trans. Pattern Anal. Mach. Intell. **43**(3), 1110–1118 (2019)

25. Wang, X., Girshick, R., Gupta, A., He, K.: Non-local neural networks. In: IEEE Computer Vision and Pattern Recognition, pp. 7794–7803 (2018)

26. Deng, Z., Vahdat, A., Hu, H., Mori, G.: Structure inference machines: recurrent neural networks for analyzing relations in group activity recognition. In: IEEE Computer Vision and Pattern Recognition, pp. 4772–4781 (2016)

GNN-Based Structural Dynamics Simulation for Modular Buildings

Jun Zhang[1], Tong Zhang[2], and Ying Wang[1(✉)]

[1] School of Civil and Environmental Engineering, Harbin Institute of Technology, Shenzhen, China
yingwang@hit.edu.cn
[2] Peng Cheng Laboratory, Shenzhen, China

Abstract. Modular buildings are made up of standardized building sections manufactured in a controlled environment. Their advantages include speedy construction process, cost-effectiveness, and higher quality. Further, it provides an opportunity to perform data-driven numerical simulations through a standardized process. Due to its capability of topological generalization, a Graph Neural Network (GNN) based approach is proposed in this study as an innovative structural dynamics simulation tool. The proposed approach can predict the dynamic response of structures with different topologies by changing the relationship matrix. To demonstrate its effectiveness, three spring-mass systems, with 3-DOF, 6-DOF, and 10-DOF, are used as examples of modular buildings. The dynamic response data of the 3-DOF system are used to train a GNN model. After necessary topological adaptation, the model is then used to predict the dynamic response of the 6-DOF system and the 10-DOF system, without any new training process. The results show that the proposed approach can predict the dynamic responses of structures with different topologies with a very low peak mean square error (PMSE), which is less than 0.01. It has the potential to enhance the generalization capabilities of data-driven numerical simulation methods.

Keywords: Modular construction · Structural health monitoring · Graph neural networks · Structural dynamic response prediction · AI for Science

1 Introduction

Modular buildings have become popular in the world due to such advantages as speedy construction process, cost-effectiveness, and higher construction quality. They are normally made up of prefabricated room-sized volumetric units manufactured in the factory [1]. However, if the structural parameters, such as stiffness and/or damping, is uncertain, the dynamic simulation results will not correctly reflect the dynamic response of the real structure [2]. Although physics-based methods are mostly used, data-driven methods received increasing research attention due to their real-time and accurate simulation capabilities, e.g. in structural dynamic simulation and structural health monitoring [3].

J. Zhang and T. Zhang—Contributed equally to this work.

S. Yu et al. (Eds.): PRCV 2022, LNCS 13536, pp. 245–258, 2022.
https://doi.org/10.1007/978-3-031-18913-5_19

To reduce the impact of uncertain parameters on the results of the structural dynamics model, many scholars have resorted to data-driven methods. For example, artificial neural network (ANN) [4, 5] were introduced to learn and predict the response of nonlinear systems. Since then, relevant scholars began to consider using more complex or deeper neural networks to simulate the dynamic response with a strongly nonlinear or actual engineering structure (data are collected from actual engineering structures or experimental structures). Wu and Jahanshahi [6] used the deep convolutional neural network (CNN) model to train and predict the dynamic response of the steel frame structure in the laboratory. Compared with multilayer perceptron (MLP), this prediction result has higher accuracy in both the training set and test set. Zhang et al. [7] established a deep long short-term memory network (LSTM) model by using the field sensing data to simulate the dynamic response of a six-story hotel building under seismic excitations and obtained accurate prediction results. In recent years, considering that the structural response data that can be observed in real life is limited, the method which can greatly reduce the requirement of training data by inputting some known physical information as guidance (physics-guided) has become a hot topic. Yu et al. [8] derived the physics-guided function from the state-space equation and embedded the function into the gate function of the LSTM network. Then, Peng et al. [9] added the physics-guided loss function into the LSTM network, which can further modify the model. The results show that adding physics-guided items to the DL model will improve the training and prediction accuracy to a certain extent. Further, it will greatly reduce the amount of training data. However, there is a challenging problem that most data-driven models cannot solve. That is, once the model is trained with the response of one structure, it cannot predict the dynamic response of other structures unless they are identical. To solve this problem and enhance the generalization ability of the data-driven model, a new type of DL algorithm, Graph Neural Network (GNN) can be used as a structural dynamics simulator.

GNN has a strong data representation ability, so it is often used to store and predict Non-Euclidean data similar to social networks. Recently, it has been applied to the solution of physical problems such as Universal Gravitation [10], Newton's Cradle [11], Fluid-Structure Interaction [12], Robot Control [13], etc. These physical problems have a common feature, that is, the interaction between any two objects is the same. For example, in the universal gravitation field, the gravitation between the balls is only related to the mass of the balls and the distance between them, GNN-based models have shown great performance in the numerical simulation of this phenomenon [10]. Although the interaction in most of the actual structures is not the same, modular buildings can be well simulated by GNN models, because each module in the modular building is an independent structure with the same standardized sections, which provides an opportunity for a standardized data-driven numerical simulation approach. Therefore, a GNN-based approach, which can predict the dynamic response of structures with different topologies by changing the relationship matrix only, is proposed in this study as an innovative structural dynamics simulation tool. A generalized derivation process for the relationship matrix is introduced. Numerical studies on simplified spring-mass systems will be performed to demonstrate the effectiveness of this method in predicting the dynamic response of modular buildings.

This paper is organized as follows. Section 2 introduces the proposed approach, i.e., GNN-based structural dynamics simulation for modular buildings. In Sect. 3, three spring-mass systems, with 3-DOF, 6-DOF, and 10-DOF, are described as numerical examples of modular buildings. Based on the training of the 3-DOF system, the proposed approach is used to predict structural dynamic responses of the 6-DOF and 10-DOF systems. Conclusions will be given in Sect. 4.

2 Methodology

GNN is mainly composed of two parts, one is the graph representation method, and the other is the neural network [10]. Graph representation is a unique data storage and data transmission method of GNN, while the neural network in GNN is to learn unknown mapping relationships. In this section, the GNN-based structural dynamics simulation approach will be introduced.

2.1 Graph Representation Method

Modular buildings, or more general engineering structures, can be simplified as an n-DOF system. The system can be represented as a set of objects and a set of relationships. The objects contain the mass and the response of each DOF. The relationships include the values of stiffness and damping. The objects and the relationships can be written in the form of Eq. (1) and Eq. (2).

$$
Objects: \left\langle \begin{bmatrix} m_1 \\ \vdots \\ m_n \end{bmatrix}, \begin{bmatrix} \mathbf{Y}_1^{\cdot\cdot} \\ \vdots \\ \mathbf{Y}_n^{\cdot\cdot} \end{bmatrix}, \begin{bmatrix} \mathbf{Y}_1^{\cdot} \\ \vdots \\ \mathbf{Y}_n^{\cdot} \end{bmatrix}, \begin{bmatrix} \mathbf{Y}_1 \\ \vdots \\ \mathbf{Y}_n \end{bmatrix} \right\rangle \tag{1}
$$

$$
Relationships: \left\langle \begin{bmatrix} k_{1-} \\ k_{12} \\ k_{21} \\ \vdots \\ k_{n\cdot n-1} \end{bmatrix}, \begin{bmatrix} c_{1-} \\ c_{12} \\ c_{21} \\ \vdots \\ c_{n\cdot n-1} \end{bmatrix} \right\rangle \tag{2}
$$

where m_i is the mass at the ith DOF. $\mathbf{Y}_i^{\cdot\cdot}$, $\mathbf{Y}_i^{\cdot}$ and $\mathbf{Y}_i$ represents the acceleration response, velocity response, and displacement response at the ith DOF, respectively. Since the velocity response of the structure is difficult to obtain directly through measurement, only the acceleration response data and displacement response data will be used to train the GNN model in this study. K_{ij} and c_{ij} represent the stiffness and damping between the ith DOF and the jth DOF respectively. k_{1-} and c_{1-} respectively represent the stiffness and damping between the first DOF and the boundary, e.g., the fixed end in this study.

To establish a connection between objects and relationships, two relationship matrices need to be constructed, as shown in Table 1 and Table 2. Here, r_{ij} represents the relationship between the objects on the ith DOF and the jth DOF. If the objects on the two DOF are not adjacent, then the values in the whole column are equal to 0 in these two matrixes, or this column can be ignored. The order of the subscripts of r_{ij} indicates the sender and receiver relationship between objects. For example, if ith DOF has a relative displacement away jth DOF, then the interaction between ith DOF and jth DOF is about to change due to the motion of ith DOF. In such a case, the ith DOF is called a sender, while the jth DOF is a receiver. The value of r_{ij} column and m_i row in $\mathbf{R}_s$ should be 1. Similarly in the receiver relationship matrix $\mathbf{R}_r$, the value at the position of the m_j row and r_{ij} column should also be 1. If it is neither the sender nor the receiver of the relationship, the value at the corresponding position should be 0.

Table 1. Sender relationship matrix ($\mathbf{R}_s$) for the n-DOF system.

	r_{1-}	r_{12}	$\cdots$	$r_{n,n-1}$
m_1	1	1	$\cdots$	0
m_2	0	0	$\cdots$	0
$\vdots$	$\vdots$	$\vdots$	$\ddots$	$\vdots$
m_n	0	0	$\cdots$	1

Table 2. Receiver relationship matrix ($\mathbf{R}_r$) for the n-DOF system.

	r_{1-}	r_{12}	$\cdots$	$r_{n,n-1}$
m_1	0	0	$\cdots$	0
m_2	0	1	$\cdots$	0
$\vdots$	$\vdots$	$\vdots$	$\ddots$	$\vdots$
m_n	0	0	$\cdots$	0

Based on the above formulations, the structural dynamic equation can be rewritten through the description of objects, relationships, and relationship matrixes. The dynamic response of an n-DOF system can be represented by Eq. (3):

$$\begin{bmatrix} m_1 & \cdots & 0 \\ \vdots & \ddots & \vdots \\ 0 & \cdots & m_n \end{bmatrix} \begin{bmatrix} \ddot{Y}_1 \\ \vdots \\ \ddot{Y}_n \end{bmatrix}$$

$$+ \mathbf{R}_r \cdot \left[k \cdot \left(\mathbf{R}_r^T \cdot \begin{bmatrix} Y_1 \\ \vdots \\ Y_n \end{bmatrix} - \mathbf{R}_r^T \cdot \begin{bmatrix} Y_1 \\ \vdots \\ Y_n \end{bmatrix} \right) + c \cdot \left(\mathbf{R}_s^T \cdot \begin{bmatrix} \dot{Y}_1 \\ \vdots \\ \dot{Y}_n \end{bmatrix} - \mathbf{R}_r^T \cdot \begin{bmatrix} \dot{Y}_1 \\ \vdots \\ \dot{Y}_n \end{bmatrix} \right) \right] = \mathbf{L} \cdot \mathbf{F}$$

$$(3)$$

2.2 GNN Model

The proposed GNN framework is shown in Fig. 1. Based on Sect. 2.1, the relationship matrix is used to perform matrix transformation on the input response data, so the response data can be input into the GNN model in relationship pairs, forming a simple mapping between input and output. The construction of this model depends on two multilayer perceptions, MLP_1 and MLP_2. MLP (Multilayer Perception) is a feedforward artificial neural network model, which maps multiple input data sets to a single output data set. In this study, MLP_1 is selected to compute the interaction force with unknown parameters, and MLP_2 is used to solve the acceleration response. They were constructed through simple parameter adjustment. The details of the MLP network architectures and their parameters are given in Table 3.

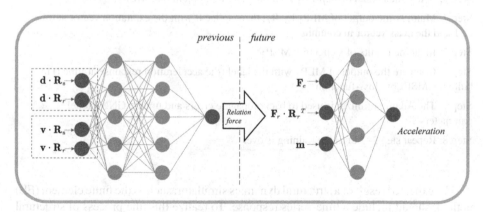

Fig. 1. GNN framework

To train the model, the displacement and acceleration response of the structure at a certain time t will be input into MLP_1 in the form of a relationship pair. The output of MLP_1 is equivalent to the resultant of restoring force and damping force. The resultant force is left multiplied by the relation matrix $\mathbf{R}_r$ and then input into MLP_2 together with the excitation at time t and the mass of each DOF. The output of MLP_2 is the acceleration response of the structure at the time $t + 1$. The detailed process is described in Table 4.

Table 3. GNN network architecture.

MLP$_1$	MLP$_2$
Sequential(	Sequential(
(0): nn.Linear(4, 100),	(0): nn.Linear(3, 100),
(1): ReLU(),	(1): ReLU(),
(2): nn.Linear(100, 100),	(2): nn.Linear(100, 100),
(3): ReLU(),	(3): ReLU(),
(4): nn.Linear(100, 100),	(4): nn.Linear(100, 1),
(5): ReLU(),	)
(6): nn.Linear(100, 1),	
(7): ReLU(),	
)	

Table 4. Procedure for training GNN model.

Training Procedure: Learning and Simulating Structural Dynamic Response at Time t

Step 1: Normalizing data

Step 2: Multiply the response data at time $t-1$ by the transpose of the relational matrix $\mathbf{R}_s$ and $\mathbf{R}_r$ respectively

Step 3: Splice the results of step 1 by column, then, input them into MLP$_1$

Step 4: Multiply the output of MLP$_1$ by $\mathbf{R}_r$, then, splice it with the excitation vector at time $t-1$ and the mass vector in columns

Step 5: Input the results of step 3 into MLP$_2$

Step 6: Compare the output of MLP$_2$ with the label (the acceleration response at time t) to build the MSELoss loss-function

Step 7: The Adam optimizer is used to backpropagate errors and update GNN model parameters

Step 8: Repeat step 2–7 until the training is over

The expected result of a structural dynamics simulator, such as the finite element (FE) method, should include a time-series response. To realize this, the process of structural dynamics simulation using the GNN model uses a set of initial response data as the input. The values of these initial responses are often taken as 0. Based on the acceleration response output from the model, the velocity response and displacement response at the next time step need to be calculated by the numerical integration method. These responses will be input into the GNN model as input data in the next step. The numerical integration method for calculating the velocity response and displacement response from the acceleration response is shown in Eq. (4).

Table 5. Procedure for predicting the structural dynamic response using the GNN model.

Predicting Procedure: Predicted Acceleration Response Time Series
Step 1: Normalizing data
Step 2: Multiply the initial response data by transposing the relational matrix $\mathbf{R}_s$ and $\mathbf{R}_r$ respectively
Step 3: Splice the results of step 1 by column, then, input them into the GNN model
Step 4: The acceleration response output from the GNN model needs to be numerically integrated according to the method shown in Eq. (7), to calculate the initial response data at the next time
Step 5: Repeat step 1–3 until the time series is over

$$\begin{cases} \dot{\mathbf{Y}} = \dot{\mathbf{Y}} + \Delta t \cdot \ddot{\mathbf{Y}} \\ \mathbf{Y} = \mathbf{Y} + \Delta t \cdot \dot{\mathbf{Y}} \end{cases} \tag{4}$$

where Δt represents the time between adjacent sampling time points, which is equal to the reciprocal of sampling frequency f. The specific predicting steps are shown in Table 5.

3 Numerical Studies

3.1 Numerical Examples of Three Spring-Mass Systems

To demonstrate the effectiveness of the GNN-based structural dynamics simulation for modular buildings, three FE models for spring-mass systems with 3-DOF, 6-DOF, and 10-DOF, respectively, were used as numerical examples to generate the data for training and testing the GNN model, shown in Fig. 2. In this study, three points were randomly selected (marked with red boxes) to compare the true values and predicted values of their acceleration response. The basic parameters of the three spring-mass systems were shown in Table 6, where m, c, and k represent the mass, damping, and stiffness corresponding to the DOF in their respective systems.

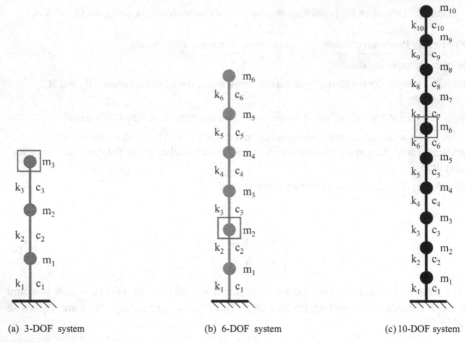

(a) 3-DOF system   (b) 6-DOF system   (c) 10-DOF system

Fig. 2. FE model figure (The model is used to simulate the dynamic response of modular buildings under seismic excitations) (Color figure online)

Two recorded seismic accelerations were selected as the input forces to excite the systems, as shown in Fig. 3. The acceleration response and displacement response of the 3-DOF system under seismic excitation were collected and used for training the GNN model. To balance the efficiency and accuracy, a sampling frequency of 200 Hz was adopted to collect the structural dynamic response.

Table 6. FE model basic parameters.

Parameters	3-DOF	6-DOF	10-DOF
Mass = 2000 kg	m_1	m_1, m_2	m_1, m_2, m_3
Mass = 1500 kg	m_2	m_3, m_4	m_4, m_5, m_6
Mass = 1000 kg	m_3	m_5, m_6	m_7, m_8, m_9, m_{10}
Damping = 2000 N · s/m	c_1-c_3	c_1-c_6	c_1-c_{10}
Stiffness = 20000 N/m	k_1-k_3	k_1-k_6	k_1-k_{10}

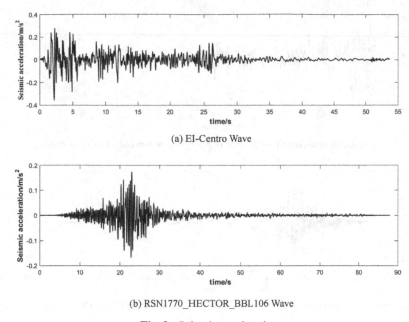

(a) EI-Centro Wave

(b) RSN1770_HECTOR_BBL106 Wave

Fig. 3. Seismic acceleration

Table 7. The first three natural frequencies of the three spring-mass systems (Hz).

3-DOF	6-DOF	10-DOF
0.278	0.153	0.097
0.712	0.411	0.262
1.051	0.654	0.425

The first three natural frequencies of the three spring-mass systems are shown in Table 7. The noiseless acceleration response collected from the DOFs marked by the red boxes in Fig. 2 is shown in Fig. 4. Clear differences can be found at different locations and under different seismic waves.

3.2 Training and Prediction Results

The GNN model was trained with the response data generated from the 3-DOF system under seismic excitation. After necessary topological adaptation, it was used to predict the dynamic response of the 6-DOF system and 10-DOF system. The training data contained five levels of Gaussian noise: 0%, 20%, 50%, 80%, and 100% noise, which was added to the training data by generating random numbers. For example, 50% noise means that a set of training data are multiplied by a set of Gaussian distribution random numbers at each data point, with the mean value 1 and the variance value 0.5. Figure 5 illustrates the difference between the original response data and those with 50% noise.

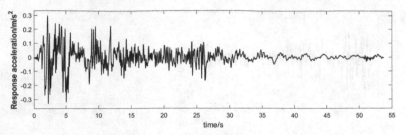

(a) Acceleration response from 3rd DOF of the 3-DOF system under EI-Centro Wave

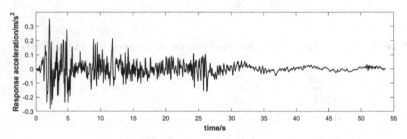

(b) Acceleration response from 2nd DOF of the 6-DOF system under RSN1770_HECTOR_BBL106 Wave

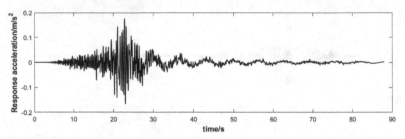

(c) Acceleration response from 6th DOF of the 10-DOF system under EI-Centro Wave

Fig. 4. Seismic acceleration response of partial DOFs of three FE models without noise.

The resulting error of training and prediction can be evaluated by peak mean square error (PMSE) [9]. The PMSE is defined as Eq. (5). $\ddot{Y}_i$ is the predicted value. $\hat{\ddot{Y}}_i$ is the true value. N is the size of the predicted variables. $M = max\left(\hat{\ddot{Y}}_1, \cdots \hat{\ddot{Y}}_i, \cdots \widehat{Y_N}\right)$ is the maximum value of the real variable.

$$PMSE = \frac{\left(\frac{1}{N}\right) \sum_{i=1}^{N} \left(\ddot{Y}_i - \hat{\ddot{Y}}_i\right)^2}{M} \qquad (5)$$

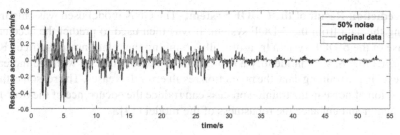

(a) Original acceleration response data and those with 50% noise

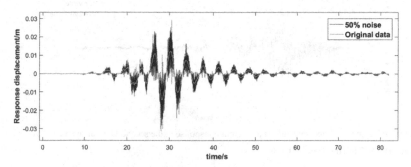

(b) Original displacement response and 50% noise displacement response

Fig. 5. Illustration of the original data and the data with 50% noise

Table 8. PMSE of prediction results using multiple patterns response data train the GNN model.

System	Seism	0% noise	20% noise	50% noise	100% noise
3-DOF	EI	0.0011	0.0011	0.0011	0.0011
	RS	0.0004	0.0004	0.0005	0.0005
6-DOF	EI	0.0026	0.0083	0.0017	0.0014
	RS	0.0006	0.0015	0.0026	0.0021
10-DOF	EI	0.0007	0.0006	0.0006	0.0006
	RS	0.0002	0.0002	0.0003	0.0002

The Training Results (3-DOF). To eliminate the randomness of Gaussian noise, we took the average PMSE value of the three groups as the GNN model training error. The values for 3-DOF system, 6-DOF system, and 10-DOF system are shown in Table 8, where each statistical value represents the error between the predicted value and the true value of the acceleration response corresponding to all DOFs of each system under different conditions. As Table 8 shown, the effects of the noise in the training process of the GNN model are neglectable.

The Prediction Result of the 6-DOF System. The GNN model used was only trained by using the data from the 3-DOF system. It was then used to predict the acceleration response of the 6-DOF system by artificially changing the relationship matrices R_s and R_r. From Table 8, we can identify a strange phenomenon, that is, with the increase of noise level in the training data, the prediction result error decreases. The reason is that the introduction of noise in the training process can reduce the occurrence of the over-fitting phenomenon and enhance the robustness of the model [14].

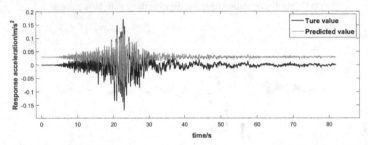

(a) The true value and predicted value of the acceleration response at the second DOF of the 6-DOF system under 100% noise (RSN1770-HECTOR-BBL106)

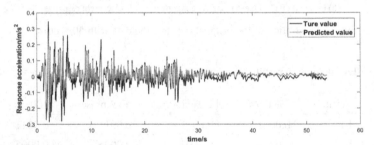

(b) The true value and predicted value of the acceleration response at the second DOF of the 6-DOF system under 100% noise (El-Centro)

Fig. 6. Comparison between the true value and predicted value of the acceleration response at the second DOF of the 6-DOF system under 100% noise. (Color figure online)

To observe the difference between the predicted value and the true value more intuitively, the acceleration response at the 6-DOF system and the 10-DOF system marked by the red box in Fig. 2 are shown in Fig. 6 for comparison. As can be seen, even though the training noise is very large, the difference between the prediction value and the true value is still very small, and the fluctuation trend is almost the same.

The Prediction Result of the 10-DOF System. The 10-DOF system and the 3-DOF system are completely different models. However, based on the prediction results shown in Table 8 and Fig. 7, the error between the prediction value and the true value of response acceleration is surprisingly small, and insensitive to training noise.

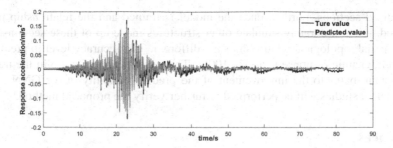

(a) The true value and predicted value of the acceleration response at the sixth DOF of the 10-DOF system under 100% noise (RSN1770-HECTOR-BBL106)

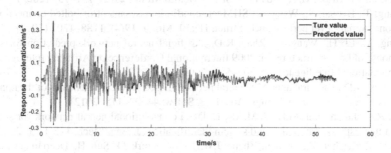

(b) The true value and predicted value of the acceleration response at the sixth DOF of the 10-DOF system under 100% noise (El-Centro)

Fig. 7. Comparison between the true value and predicted value of the acceleration response at the sixth DOF of the 10-DOF system under 100% noise.

To sum up, the GNN model can predict structural dynamic responses with high accuracy and robustness. The simulation results are insensitive to noise. For modular buildings, the GNN model has shown superior generalization ability, which can predict the dynamic responses of structures with standardized sections but different topologies. For other types of engineering structures, this method has the potential to be applied as long as they can be represented with a relationship matrix. From this perspective, the proposed approach has the potential to enhance the generalization capabilities of the data-driven structural dynamics simulation methods.

4 Conclusion

In this study, a GNN-based structural dynamics simulator for modular buildings is proposed. To demonstrate its effectiveness, three FE models for spring-mass systems are used as numerical examples to generate the response data for training and to test the prediction performance. Based on the results, the proposed GNN model can accurately simulate the dynamic response of the simplified model of modular buildings with standardized sections. Further, once the model is trained and the relationship matrix is derived, it can accurately simulate other structures made up of these sections, even if their spatial topological relationships are different. The accuracy level to predict the structural dynamic response is nearly 100%. The introduction of noise in the training process contributes to the improvement of the prediction ability of the GNN model. Experimental studies will be performed to further verify the proposed method.

References

1. Lacey, A.W., Chen, W.S., Hao, H., Bi, K.: Review of bolted inter-module connections in modular steel buildings. J. Build. Eng. **23**(2019), 207–219 (2019)
2. Biswal, S., Chryssanthopoulos, M.K., Wang, Y.: Condition identification of bolted connections using a virtual viscous damper. Struct. Health Monit. **21**(2), 731–752 (2022)
3. Zhang, T., Biswal, S., Wang, Y.: SHMnet: condition assessment of bolted connection with beyond human-level performance. Struct. Health Monit. **19**(4), 1188–1201 (2019)
4. Wang, Y., Li, H., Wang, C., Zhao, R.D.: Artificial neural network prediction for seismic response of bridge structure. In: 2009 International Conference on Artificial Intelligence and Computational Intelligence, pp. 503–506 (2009)
5. Lagaros, N.D., Papadrakakis, M.: Neural network based prediction schemes of the non-linear seismic response of 3D buildings. Adv. Eng. Softw. **44**, 92–115 (2012)
6. Wu, R.T., Jahanshahi, M.R., A.M.ASCE: Deep convolutional neural network for structural dynamic response estimation and system identification. J. Eng. Mech. **145**(1), 1–25 (2019)
7. Zhang, R.Y., Chen, Z., Chen, S., Zheng, J.W., Buyukozturk, O., Sun, H.: Deep long short-term memory networks for nonlinear structural seismic response prediction. Comput. Struct. **220**, 55–68 (2019)
8. Yu, Y., Yao, H.P., Liu, Y.M.: Structural dynamics simulation using a novel physics-guided machine learning method. Eng. Appl. Artif. Intell. **96**, 1–14 (2020)
9. Peng, H., Yan, J.W., Yu, Y., Luo, Y.Z.: Time series estimation based on deep learning for structural dynamic nonlinear prediction. Structures **29**, 1016–1031 (2021)
10. Battaglia, P.W., Pascanu, R., Lai, M., Rezende, D., Kavukcuoglu, K.: Interaction networks for learning about objects. In: Proceedings of the 30th International Conference on Neural Information Processing Systems, pp. 4509–451 NIPS, Barcelona (2016)
11. Li, Y.Z., Wu, J.J., Zhu, J.Y., Tenenbaum, J.B., Torralba, A., Tedrake, R.: Propagation networks for model-based control under partial observation. In: 2019 International Conference on Robotics and Automation (ICRA) (2019)
12. Alvaro, S.G., Godwin, J., Pfaff, T., Ying, R., Leskovec, J., Battaglia, P.W.: Learning to simulate complex physics with graph networks. In: arXiv:2002.09405 (2020)
13. Toussaint, M.A., Allen, K.R., Smith, K.A., Tenenbaum, J.B.: Differentiable physics and stable modes for tool-use and manipulation planning. In: Robotics: Science and Systems (2018)
14. Gao, Y.Q., Mosalam, K.M.: Deep transfer learning for image-based structural damage recognition. Comput.-Aided Civil Infrastruct. Eng. **33**, 748–768 (2018)

Semantic-Augmented Local Decision Aggregation Network for Action Recognition

Congqi Cao[1]($\boxtimes$), Jiakang Li[2], Qinyi Lv[3], Runping Xi[1], and Yanning Zhang[1]

[1] ASGO National Engineering Laboratory, School of Computer Science,
Northwestern Polytechnical University, Xi'an, China
{congqi.cao,ynzhang}@nwpu.edu.cn
[2] China Electronics Technology Group Corporation 54th, Beijing, China
[3] School of Electronics and Information, Northwestern Polytechnical University,
Xi'an, China
lvqinyi@nwpu.edu.cn

Abstract. It is challenging for an intelligent system to recognize the actions recorded in an RGB video due to the large amount of information and wide variations in the RGB video. On the other side, skeleton data focuses on the region of human body but lacks the interaction information with the background, which is complementary to the RGB data. Recently, some works focus on combining the RGB and skeleton data together to boost the performance of action recognition. However, the semantic information between joints is missing in existing works, which is important for action recognition. In this paper, we propose a novel semantic-augmented local decision aggregation network for action recognition. Specifically, we regard the area of body joints as the attention region to extract a local spatio-temporal feature for each body joint. In order to take advantage of the semantic information between joints, we propose a semantic information module, which jointly encodes the spatial and temporal index of body joints to enhance the representation ability of the local features. For better learning ability, instead of aggregating the local features, we first make decisions based on each individual local feature and then aggregate the local decisions for final recognition, which reflects the idea of resemble learning. Extensive experiments demonstrate the effectiveness of our proposed module which improves the performance of action recognition on three commonly used datasets.

Keywords: Action recognition · Attention · Local features · Decision aggregation · Semantic information

---

This work was partly supported by the National Natural Science Foundation of China (61906155, U19B2037), the Young Talent Fund of Association for Science and Technology in Shaanxi, China (20220117), the National Key R&D Program of China (2020AAA0106900), and the Fundamental Research Funds for the Central Universities.

S. Yu et al. (Eds.): PRCV 2022, LNCS 13536, pp. 259–269, 2022.
https://doi.org/10.1007/978-3-031-18913-5_20

1   Introduction

Video action recognition has great application value in video surveillance, human-computer interaction, robot vision, kinematic analysis, and other practical situations, which has attracted extensive research attention. RGB and skeleton are two frequently used data modalities in action recognition. Among them, the RGB data has rich appearance information, which can describe the interaction between people and objects, but it is susceptible to the noise from the background. Compared with the RGB data, the skeleton data abstractly describes human posture and motion, and is insensitive to changes in appearance. However, it lacks the interaction information of the human with the background.

For the RGB data, there are mainly two structures of deep network based methods: one is two-stream convolutional neural network (CNN) [17] and its extensions, which extract spatial features from video frames and temporal features from stacked optical flow images by two separate 2D CNNs. The other is 3D convolutional neural networks [3,20,24], which use 3D convolution to model the spatial and temporal information from video clips jointly. For the skeleton data, Recurrent Neural Networks (RNNs), CNNs, and Graph Convolutional Networks (GCNs) are widely used. RNN based methods utilize RNNs to model the long-term dependency in the skeleton data [7,13]. CNN based methods encode the coordinates of joints as an image and take advantage of CNNs for classification [8,12]. GCN based methods utilize GCN to deal with the structured skeleton data effectively [4,14,23].

In recent years, some works have combined the RGB data and the skeleton data together to improve action recognition performance [1,2,22], such as JDD [2] and LDNet [1]. Both JDD and LDNet regard the body joint areas as the attention areas to obtain the spatio-temporal features for each body joint. However, JDD and LDNet use different aggregation strategies. JDD aggregates all the body joint features to obtain a global feature representation. Then, decision is made based on the aggregated global feature representation. LDNet makes decisions based on each body joint feature respectively, and then fuses the obtained local decisions to get a global decision result, which takes advantage of ensemble learning. However, these methods neglect the semantic information of body joints, which plays an important role in action recognition. For example, two body joints with the same coordinates but different semantics can convey completely different information: for a joint above the head, if this joint is a hand joint, the action is probably *"raising hand"*; if it is a foot joint, the action is probably *"kicking leg"*.

To solve this problem, we propose a semantic information module, which explicitly describes the spatial and temporal index of the body joints, where the spatial index represents the type of the body joint, and the temporal index represents the frame index of the body joint. Unlike previous skeleton-based methods that encode the spatial and temporal indexes of the body joints respectively [25], our proposed module uses one-hot encoding to jointly encode the spatial and temporal indexes to preserve the spatio-temporal information of the skeleton sequence and applies it with the RGB video. Since feature aggregation strategy

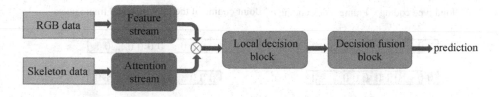

Fig. 1. Framework of the local decision aggregation network.

has some problems, such as the gap between different feature spaces and the high dimension of the global feature representation, we use decision aggregation strategy in this work. We choose LDNet as the backbone network, and add the semantic information module to the local decision block. The contributions of our work mainly include the following aspects:

- In the task of action recognition combining RGB and skeleton data, we introduce a body joint semantic information module, which retains the spatial and temporal structure of skeleton sequence and enhances the representation ability of body joint features.
- Our proposed semantic information module uses one-hot method to jointly encode the spatial and temporal indexes of body joints. Meanwhile, we evaluate two semantic information aggregation strategies.
- We apply the body joint semantic information module with local decision aggregation network, and achieves state-of-the-art performance on subJH-MDB [10], Penn Action [26] and NTU RGB+D [16] datasets.

2   Proposed Approach

In this section, we propose a semantic information module that explicitly encodes the joint type and the frame index. Firstly, we introduce the local decision aggregation network LDNet. Then we introduce the semantic information module. Finally, we introduce the aggregation method of the semantic information module and LDNet.

2.1   LDNet

Following is a brief description of the local decision aggregation network LDNet. As illustrated in Fig. 1, LDNet is composed of two streams. One stream is the feature stream which uses the state-of-the-art lightweight 3D CNN multi-fiber network (MF-Net) to extract the spatio-temporal features. The other stream is the attention stream which regards the body joint areas as the attention areas. LDNet performs bilinear operation on the spatio-temporal feature maps and the attention heatmaps to obtain the spatio-temporal features of each body joint. The local decision block makes decisions based on the spatio-temporal features

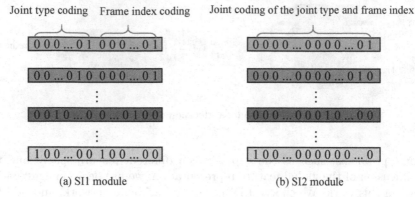

Fig. 2. Illustration of the two semantic information modules. (a) SI1 module. (b) SI2 module.

of each body joint individually with a fully-connected layer and obtains a group of local decisions. The decision fusion block fuses the local decisions to obtain a final decision result.

2.2 Semantic Information Module

The semantic information of body joints is composed of a spatial index and a temporal index. The spatial index can be represented as the joint type, and the temporal index can be represented as the frame index. In this section, we introduce the joint type and the frame index encoding method, and two fusion methods of the joint type and the frame index codings.

We use the following formula to express a skeleton sequence:

$$S = \{p_t^k | t = 1, 2, ..., T; k = 1, 2, ..., J\} \tag{1}$$

where S represents the semantic information set of the skeleton sequence, p_t^k represents the semantic information of the k-th body joint type in the t-th frame. T represents the frame number of the skeleton sequence, and J represents the number of body joints in each frame.

We use the following two strategies to encode the semantic information: one is to encode joint type and frame index respectively, and then fuse the two kinds of coding information; the other is to jointly encode the joint type and frame index.

Encode Joint Type and Frame Index Respectively. In this section, we introduce the first encoding strategy, which can be represented by the symbol SI1. The SI1 module is shown in Fig. 2(a).

Joint Type Coding: We assume that there are J body joints in each video frame, *i.e.*, there are J types of bone points (*e.g.*, head, neck, left shoulder...). For the k-th type of body joint, we define its encoding as:

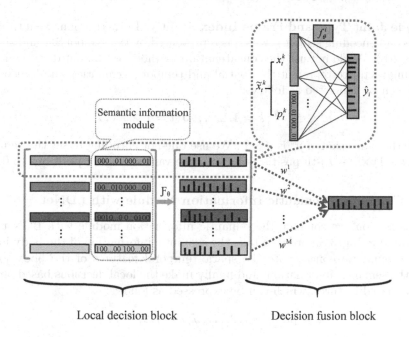

Fig. 3. Combining semantic information module with LDNet.

$$j_k \in R^J; k = 1, 2, \ldots, J \tag{2}$$

where j_k is the coding vector of the k-th body joint type, and its dimension is J. We use one-hot encoding to set the value at the k-th position to 1 and the values at other positions to 0.

Frame Index Coding: Since the input of the network is video clips, there are T frames in each clip. We define the frame index coding of the body joints in the t-th frame as:

$$q_t \in R^T; t = 1, 2, \ldots, T \tag{3}$$

where q_t is the frame index coding vector of the body joints in the t-th frame, and its dimension is T. We also use one-hot encoding to set the value at the t-th position to 1 and the values at other positions to 0.

Fusion of the Joint Type and Frame Index Codings: Then we fuse the joint type and the frame index codings, and the specific fusion encoding is as follows:

$$p_t^k = (j_k \oplus q_t) \in R^{J+T}; k = 1, 2, \ldots, J; t = 1, 2, \ldots, T \tag{4}$$

where p_t^k is obtained by concatenating the encoding vector of j_k and q_t, whose dimension is $J + T$. The symbol $\oplus$ represents the concatenation operation.

Encode Joint Type and Frame Index Jointly. In this section, we introduce the second encoding strategy, which is represented by the symbol SI2 and shown in Fig. 2(b). We do not use the concatenation method for SI2, but directly define a coding vector to represent the spatial and temporal semantics simultaneously, which can be expressed as follows:

$$p_t^k \in R^{J \times T}; k = 1, 2, \ldots, J; t = 1, 2, \ldots, T \tag{5}$$

where the dimension of p_t^k is $J \times T$. We use one-hot encoding to set the value at the $((t-1) \times J + k)$-th position to 1 and the values at other positions to 0.

2.3   Combining Semantic Information Module with LDNet

In this section, we combine the semantic information module with LDNet. As illustrated in Fig. 3, in order to take the semantic information of the body joints into account, we concatenate the spatio-temporal features of the body joints with the semantic information, and finally make the local decisions based on the concatenated features, which can be expressed as follows:

$$X = \{x_t^k | k = 1, 2, \ldots, J; t = 1, 2, \ldots, T\} \tag{6}$$

$$\tilde{X} = \{\tilde{x}_t^k = x_t^k \oplus p_t^k | k = 1, 2, \ldots, J; t = 1, 2, \ldots, T\} \tag{7}$$

where X represents the set of body joint features, x_t^k represents the feature of the k-th body joint type in the t-th frame, $\tilde{X}$ represents the features set of body joints with the semantic information, $\tilde{x}_t^k$ represents the body joint feature with the semantic information in the t-th frame of the k-th type.

3   Experiments

In this section, we first introduce the datasets and implementation details used in the experiments. Then, we verify the effectiveness of the semantic information module. Finally, we compare the proposed method with the state-of-the-art methods on subJHMDB, Penn Action and NTU RGB+D datasets.

3.1   Datasets and Implementation Details

Datasets subJHMDB dataset [10] contains 12 action categories with 316 videos. The length of the video ranges from 16 to 40 frames. In this dataset, 15 human body joints are annotated, and the body joints are all visible.

Penn Action dataset [26] consists of 2326 video samples belonging to 15 action classes. The duration of the videos ranges from 18 to 663 frames. The dataset has 13 annotated body joints for the human in each frame, but some body joints are not visible in the video.

Table 1. Recognition accuracy of different semantic encoding strategies on the sub-JHMDB and Penn Action datasets.

Method	subJHMDB	Penn Action
LDNet(Conv5)+D(NW)	0.839	0.965
LDNet(Conv5)+D(NW)+SI1	**0.845**	**0.970**
LDNet(Conv5)+D(NW)+SI2	0.837	0.957

NTU RGB+D dataset [16] contains 56,880 video sequences belonging to 60 action classes, which provides multi-modality data, including RGB videos, depth maps, skeleton data and infrared sequences. In this paper, we use the RGB and skeleton data, and divide the training set and the test set according to the cross-subject (CS) and cross-view (CV) criteria of the original paper [16].

Implementation Details. We split the videos into 16-frame clips with 8-frames overlap between the consecutive clips as the input of the network. The spatial resolution of the input is 224×224. By averaging the predictions made based on the clip-level features, video-level predictions can be obtained. SGD is used to optimize the parameters. The initial learning rate is set to 0.005 and reduced with a factor of 0.1 after 20, 40, and 60 epochs. We use the open source library PyTorch to implement our model on 2 NVIDIA 1080Ti GPUs.

3.2 Ablation Study

In this section, we verify the effectiveness of the proposed semantic information module on the subJHMDB and Penn Action datasets. In the tables of experimental results, "Conv4" and "Conv5" represent the feature maps after the 4-th block and the 5-th block of MF-Net respectively. Following the setting of LDNet [1], "D(W)" and "D(NW)" respectively represent the weighted average pooling strategy and the average fusion strategy for the decision fusion block. Global supervision is used by default.

Comparison of the Two Encoding Strategies. In this section, we compare the two semantic information encoding strategies on the subJHMDB and Penn Action datasets. The recognition accuracy is shown in Table 1.

From Table 1, it can be seen that when LDNet is combined with SI1 module, the accuracy is boosted from 83.9% to 84.5% on the subJHMDB dataset, and the accuracy is improved from 96.5% to 97.0% on the Penn Action dataset. These experimental results demonstrate the effectiveness of the SI1 module, and prove that the semantic information of body joints can enhance the representation ability of body joint features. When LDNet is combined with SI2 module, the accuracy is reduced from 83.9% to 83.7% on the subJHMDB dataset, and the accuracy is decreased from 96.5% to 95.7% on the Penn Action dataset. The

Table 2. Recognition accuracy of LDNet on the subJHMDB and Penn Action datasets using SI1 module under different settings.

Method	subJHMDB	Penn Action
LDNet(Conv5)+D(NW)	0.839	0.965
LDNet(Conv5)+D(NW)+SI1	0.845	0.970
LDNet(Conv5)+D(W)	0.843	0.973
LDNet(Conv5)+D(W)+SI1	0.848	0.974
LDNet(conv4+5)+D(W)	0.850	0.982
LDNet(Conv4+5)+D(W)+SI1	**0.854**	**0.985**

Table 3. Comparison of the state-of-the-art methods and our proposed method on the subJHMDB dataset.

Method	Accuracy
DT [21]	0.460
P-CNN [5]	0.725
Pose+MD-fusion [9]	0.789
JDD [2]	0.819
Decision aggregation [1]	0.858
Ours	**0.862**

reason for the performance drop is probably because that when the local decision block is combined with the SI2 module, the dimension of the body joint features increases significantly, which leads to severe over-fitting problem.

Verification of the Importance of Semantic Information. In this section, we use the SI1 module to further verify the importance of semantic information. The experimental results on the subJHMDB and Penn Action datasets are shown in Table 2.

From Table 2, we can see that when the network is combined with the SI1 module, the accuracy of the subJHMDB and Penn Action datasets is improved. When the LDNet uses the average fusion strategy, the accuracy increases from 83.9% to 84.5% on the subJHMDB dataset, and the accuracy increases from 96.5% to 97.0% on the Penn Action dataset. When the LDNet uses the weighted average pooling strategy, the accuracy increases from 84.3% to 84.8% on the sub-JHMDB dataset, and the accuracy increases from 97.3% to 97.4% on the Penn Action dataset. If we fuse the local decisions made based on the feature maps both after the 4-th block and the 5-th block, the recognition performance can further increase from 85.0% to 85.4% on the subJHMDB dataset, and increase from 98.2% to 98.5% on the Penn Action dataset. The above experimental results show that the proposed semantic module SI1 can effectively improve the accuracy of action recognition.

Table 4. Comparison of the state-of-the-art methods and our proposed method on the Penn Action dataset.

Method	Accuracy
Action bank [15]	0.839
JDD [2]	0.943
RPAN [6]	0.974
Pose+MD-fusion [9]	0.978
Decision aggregation [1]	0.984
Ours	**0.986**

Table 5. Comparison of the state-of-the-art methods and our proposed method on the NTU RGB+D dataset.

Method	CS	CV
CNN+Motion+Trans [11]	0.832	0.893
Part-aware LSTM [16]	0.629	0.703
STA-LSTM [18]	0.734	0.812
ST-GCN [23]	0.815	0.883
PB-GCN [19]	0.875	0.932
Two-stream CNN/RNN [27]	0.837	0.936
Decision aggregation [1]	0.905	0.942
Ours	**0.912**	**0.948**

Comparison with State-of-the-Art Methods. In this section, we compare our proposed method with the state-of-the-art methods on the subJHMDB, Penn Action, and NTU RGB+D datasets. Note that both the global supervision and the local supervision are used in this section for fair comparison. The experimental results are shown in Table 3, Table 4, and Table 5 respectively.

In Table 3, DT [21] stands for the Dense Trajectory method which extracts features along the trajectories obtained by optical flow field. P-CNN [5] aggregates the appearance and the motion information extracted by a two-stream CNN using each human body part as the input to obtain the global representation. Pose+MD-fusion [9] fuses temporal pose, spatial and motion feature maps for classification. When we combine the proposed semantic module with the decision aggregation based method LDNet, the accuracy increased from 85.8% to 86.2%, achieving the state-of-the-art performance on the subJHMDB dataset.

In Table 4, Action bank [15] is composed of a set of broadly sampled individual action detectors. RPAN [6] utilizes the spatial and temporal evolution of human poses to assist action recognition. Pose+MD-fusion [9] achieves an accuracy of 97.8%. When we combine LDNet [1] with our proposed SI1 module, the accuracy is increased from 98.4% to 98.6%, achieving the state-of-the-art performance on the Penn Action dataset.

In Table 5, CNN+Motion+Trans [11] uses a skeleton transformer module to automatically rearrange and select discriminative body joints. Part-aware LSTM [16] models long-term temporal correlation of the features for each body part. STA-LSTM [18] uses a spatio-temporal attention model to focus on crucial body joints. ST-GCN [23] uses spatio-temporal GCN for action recognition. PS-GCN [19] treats the skeleton as a graph and divides it into four subgraphs to learn a part-based GCN model. Two-stream CNN/RNN [27] combines RNN with CNN in a voting approach. With the proposed method, the accuracy under the CS criterion is increased from 90.5% to 91.2%, and the accuracy under the CV criterion is increased from 94.2% to 94.8%. Our proposed semantic module can effectively utilize the spatial and temporal semantic information of the body joints, and significantly enhance the representation ability of the body joint features, consistently achieving the state-of-the-art performance on the NTU RGB+D dataset.

4   Conclusions

In this paper, we propose a novel skeleton semantic information module, which explicitly utilizes the spatial and temporal index of the body joints to retain the important spatio-temporal sequence information of the skeleton. In addition, we combine the semantic information module with the local decision network. The semantic information module significantly enhances the representation ability of the body joint features, which is conducive to action recognition. Our proposed method achieves the state-of-the-art performance on the subJHMDB, Penn Action and NTU RGB+D datasets.

References

1. Cao, C., Li, J., Xi, R., Zhang, Y.: Club ideas and exertions: aggregating local predictions for action recognition. TCSVT **31**(6), 2247–2259 (2021)
2. Cao, C., Zhang, Y., Zhang, C., Lu, H.: Body joint guided 3-D deep convolutional descriptors for action recognition. IEEE Trans. Cybern. **48**(3), 1095–1108 (2017)
3. Chen, Y., Kalantidis, Y., Li, J., Yan, S., Feng, J.: Multi-fiber networks for video recognition. In: Ferrari, V., Hebert, M., Sminchisescu, C., Weiss, Y. (eds.) ECCV 2018. LNCS, vol. 11205, pp. 364–380. Springer, Cham (2018). https://doi.org/10.1007/978-3-030-01246-5_22
4. Cheng, K., Zhang, Y., Cao, C., Shi, L., Cheng, J., Lu, H.: Decoupling GCN with DropGraph module for skeleton-based action recognition. In: Vedaldi, A., Bischof, H., Brox, T., Frahm, J.-M. (eds.) ECCV 2020. LNCS, vol. 12369, pp. 536–553. Springer, Cham (2020). https://doi.org/10.1007/978-3-030-58586-0_32
5. Chéron, G., Laptev, I., Schmid, C.: P-CNN: pose-based CNN features for action recognition. In: ICCV, pp. 3218–3226 (2015)
6. Du, W., Wang, Y., Qiao, Y.: RPAN: an end-to-end recurrent pose-attention network for action recognition in videos. In: ICCV, pp. 3725–3734 (2017)
7. Du, Y., Wang, W., Wang, L.: Hierarchical recurrent neural network for skeleton based action recognition. In: CVPR, pp. 1110–1118 (2015)

8. Hu, G., Cui, B., Yu, S.: Skeleton-based action recognition with synchronous local and non-local spatio-temporal learning and frequency attention. In: ICME, pp. 1216–1221. IEEE (2019)
9. Huang, Y., Lai, S.-H., Tai, S.-H.: Human action recognition based on temporal pose CNN and multi-dimensional fusion. In: Leal-Taixé, L., Roth, S. (eds.) ECCV 2018. LNCS, vol. 11130, pp. 426–440. Springer, Cham (2019). https://doi.org/10.1007/978-3-030-11012-3_33
10. Jhuang, H., Gall, J., Zuffi, S., Schmid, C., Black, M.J.: Towards understanding action recognition. In: ICCV, pp. 3192–3199 (2013)
11. Li, C., Zhong, Q., Xie, D., Pu, S.: Skeleton-based action recognition with convolutional neural networks. In: ICME Workshops, pp. 597–600. IEEE (2017)
12. Li, C., Zhong, Q., Xie, D., Pu, S.: Co-occurrence feature learning from skeleton data for action recognition and detection with hierarchical aggregation. arXiv preprint arXiv:1804.06055 (2018)
13. Liu, J., Shahroudy, A., Xu, D., Kot, A.C., Wang, G.: Skeleton-based action recognition using spatio-temporal LSTM network with trust gates. TPAMI 40(12), 3007–3021 (2017)
14. Peng, W., Shi, J., Zhao, G.: Spatial temporal graph deconvolutional network for skeleton-based human action recognition. IEEE Sig. Process. Lett. 28, 244–248 (2021)
15. Sadanand, S., Corso, J.J.: Action bank: a high-level representation of activity in video. In: CVPR, pp. 1234–1241. IEEE (2012)
16. Shahroudy, A., Liu, J., Ng, T.T., Wang, G.: NTU RGB+ D: a large scale dataset for 3D human activity analysis. In: CVPR, pp. 1010–1019 (2016)
17. Simonyan, K., Zisserman, A.: Two-stream convolutional networks for action recognition in videos. In: NIPS, pp. 568–576 (2014)
18. Song, S., Lan, C., Xing, J., Zeng, W., Liu, J.: An end-to-end spatio-temporal attention model for human action recognition from skeleton data. arXiv preprint arXiv:1611.06067 (2016)
19. Thakkar, K., Narayanan, P.: Part-based graph convolutional network for action recognition. arXiv preprint arXiv:1809.04983 (2018)
20. Tran, D., Bourdev, L., Fergus, R., Torresani, L., Paluri, M.: Learning spatiotemporal features with 3D convolutional networks. In: ICCV, pp. 4489–4497 (2015)
21. Wang, H., Kläser, A., Schmid, C., Liu, C.L.: Dense trajectories and motion boundary descriptors for action recognition. IJCV 103(1), 60–79 (2013). https://doi.org/10.1007/s11263-012-0594-8
22. Wang, Y., Li, W., Tao, R.: Multi-branch spatial-temporal network for action recognition. IEEE Sig. Process. Lett. 26(10), 1556–1560 (2019)
23. Yan, S., Xiong, Y., Lin, D.: Spatial temporal graph convolutional networks for skeleton-based action recognition. arXiv preprint arXiv:1801.07455 (2018)
24. Yao, Z., Wang, Y., Long, M., Wang, J., Philip, S.Y., Sun, J.: Multi-task learning of generalizable representations for video action recognition. In: ICME, pp. 1–6. IEEE (2020)
25. Zhang, P., Lan, C., Zeng, W., Xing, J., Xue, J., Zheng, N.: Semantics-guided neural networks for efficient skeleton-based human action recognition. In: CVPR, pp. 1112–1121 (2020)
26. Zhang, W., Zhu, M., Derpanis, K.G.: From actemes to action: a strongly-supervised representation for detailed action understanding. In: ICCV, pp. 2248–2255 (2013)
27. Zhao, R., Ali, H., Van der Smagt, P.: Two-stream RNN/CNN for action recognition in 3D videos. In: IROS, pp. 4260–4267 (2017)

Consensus-Guided Keyword Targeting for Video Captioning

Puzhao Ji[1], Bang Yang[1,2], Tong Zhang[2], and Yuexian Zou[1,2(✉)]

[1] ADSPLAB, School of ECE, Peking University, Shenzhen, China
zouyx@pku.edu.cn
[2] Peng Cheng Laboratory, Shenzhen, China

Abstract. Mainstream video captioning models (VCMs) are trained under fully supervised learning that relies heavily on large-scaled high-quality video-caption pairs. Unfortunately, evaluating the corpora of benchmark datasets shows that there are many defects associated with humanly labeled annotations, such as variation of the caption length and quality for one video and word imbalance in captions. Such defects may pose a significant impact on model training. In this study, we propose to lower down the adverse impact of annotations and encourage VCMs to learn high-quality captions and more informative words via Consensus-Guided Keyword Targeting (CGKT) training strategy. Specifically, CGKT firstly aims at re-weighting each training caption using a consensus-based metric named CIDEr. Secondly, CGKT attaches more weights to those informative and uncommonly used words based on their frequency. Extensive experiments on MSVD and MSR-VTT show that the proposed CGKT can easily work with three VCMs to achieve significant CIDEr improvements. Moreover, compared with the conventional cross-entropy objective, our CGKT facilitates the generation of more comprehensive and better-quality captions.

Keywords: Video captioning · Annotation quality · Consensus guidance · Keyword targeting

1 Introduction

Video captioning (VC) aims to automatically describe video content with natural language sentences that can accurately depict the key information of video content, i.e., scenes, actions, and objects. In recent years, mainstream VC methods follow the popular Encoder-Decoder framework under fully supervised manner [1–3], in which the encoder is responsible for video comprehension whereas the decoder is for description generation.

With the emergence of humanly-annotated VC datasets like MSVD [4] and MSR-VTT [5], many VC methods have been proposed and mainly devoted to model design [1, 2, 7–9] or multimodal fusion [3, 10, 11]. Since the mainstream VCMs are trained in a fully supervised fashion, so the quality of annotations

© The Author(s), under exclusive license to Springer Nature Switzerland AG 2022
S. Yu et al. (Eds.): PRCV 2022, LNCS 13536, pp. 270–281, 2022.
https://doi.org/10.1007/978-3-031-18913-5_21

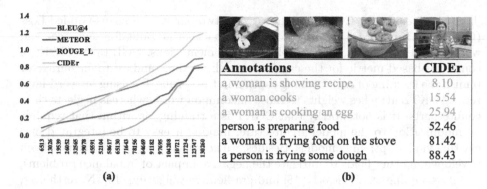

Annotations	CIDEr
a woman is showing recipe	8.10
a woman cooks	15.54
a woman is cooking an egg	25.94
person is preparing food	52.46
a woman is frying food on the stove	81.42
a person is frying some dough	88.43

(a)   (b)

Fig. 1. Illustration of the annotation quality in MSR-VTT dataset. In (a), we quantitatively measure the annotation quality of 130,260 captions in the training split by standard automatic metrics, we find that the sentence quality of the training corpus is uneven and more than 60.6% sentences have lower CIDEr scores than the average; whereas in (b), we mark problems of annotations including oversimplified sentence structure and content mismatch between sentence and video.

have an important influence on the performance of these VCMs. However, the annotation quality of the crowd-sourced VC datasets is rarely explored.

To better understand annotation quality of the VC datasets, we first quantify sentence-level annotation quality via standard automatic metrics, including BLEU@4 [12], METEOR [13], and ROUGE_L [14]. Given that multiple ground-truth (GT) captions are annotated for a video, we follow the leave-one-out procedure, i.e., treating one GT caption as the prediction while the rest as the references, to calculate per-sentence scores. As shown in Fig. 1(a), we quantify the quality of 130,260 captions in the MSR-VTT training set and sort them according to their CIDEr scores. It can be found that the sentence quality of the training corpus is uneven and more than 60.6% sentences have lower CIDEr scores than the average. Figure 1(b) further reveals possible noises in annotations for a specific video in MSR-VTT, like oversimplified sentence structure and content mismatch between sentence and video. Next, we turn our attention to word-level annotation quality. By analyzing word frequency in the MSR-VTT corpus, we found that words with high frequency are common words or functional words (e.g., "person" and "is") while words that correspond to the details within the video content are less frequent (e.g. "frying" and "dough"). Such imbalanced word distribution, however, pose great challenges to model training [16]. All these findings suggest that existing VC datasets suffer from sentence-level uneven quality and word-level imbalance problems, which post adverse impact on the performance of VCMs.

However, the widely adopted training objective, i.e., Cross-Entropy loss treats training samples equally at both sentence and word levels regardless of their uneven quality. Therefore, we propose an improved training objective in this paper, named Consensus-Guided Keyword Targeting (CGKT), to address the uneven sentence quality and imbalanced word distribution problems in VC datasets. Specifically, CGKT is comprised of two parts: Consensus-Guided Loss (CGL) and Keyword Targeting Loss (KTL), which account for sentence- and word-level re-weighting, respectively. In implementations, CGL takes CIDEr, a consensus-based metric for the captioning task, as the standard to encourage or punish the learning of each training caption in the corpus. Focusing on word-level rewards, KTL attaches weights to those uncommon words whereas neglects their counterparts. It is noteworthy that CGKT is a training algorithm that requires no modification to the model architecture, making it easy to be integrated into existing video captioning models. Besides, we note that many methods have been developed in other fields to mitigate the negative impact of imbalance problems, e.g., re-sampling strategies [17,18] and gradient re-weighting [19]. Nevertheless, these methods are dedicated for unstructured class labels and do not perform as well as our proposed CGKT for structural data (i.e., sentences) in the VC task, as we will demonstrate later.

The contributions of this paper are three-fold: (1) We analyze the annotation quality of MSR-VTT and find that various problems exist in the data. (2) To train a better video captioning model, we propose an alternative training objective named Consensus-Guided Keyword Targeting (CGKT) to encourage the model to learn high-quality sentences and keywords. (3) Extensive experiments on MSVD and MSR-VTT datasets show that various baselines trained with our proposed CGKT can achieve up to 8.2% improvement in terms of CIDEr score and describe more distinctive and accurate details of video content.

2   Related Work

2.1   Video Captioning

The early works of VC extract fixed content like the verb, subject, and object, then populate the content into a predefined template [6]. Withing fixed predefined templates and limited hand-crafted grammar rules, these methods are hard to generate flexible and accurate descriptions. Benefit from the raising of deep neural networks, sequence learning based methods [1,24] that adopt an encoder-decoder framework, are widely used to describe video content with flexibility. Recent VC works devoted to the designing of the captioning model [7,8,24], including adding a soft attention mechanism in the encoder to allow the model to focus on significant frames or regions, proposing a module to choose keyframes as inputs to reduce redundant visual information, or using a reconstructor architecture to leverage the backflow from sentence to video while generating caption. In addition, extra semantic information including objects, syntax parts, and latent topics is used to assist in generating captions [3,9,11]. However, all the above methods focus on multimodal feature modeling or syntax structure reasoning and lack analysis and coping methods for uneven quality and imbalance problems in video caption datasets.

2.2   Video Captioning Datasets

MSVD and MSR-VTT are two datasets that are widely used in VC works. MSVD was proposed by Chen et al. [4] in 2011, which is the first open-domain VC dataset. The authors of MSVD used Amazon's Mechanical Turk (AMT) to collect and annotate data. In the data collection stage, crowdsourced annotators were asked to find a clip that contains a single, unambiguous event on YouTube and submit the link of this clip. In the data annotation stage, the author requires crowdsourcing annotators to watch the video and write descriptive sentences in any language within 80 s, and then get the final English annotation sentences through translation. However, the author did not review and filter the sentences annotated by the annotators, which resulted in a large number of sentences of poor quality in the final annotation. Another mainstream VC dataset, MSR-VTT, was proposed by Xu et al. [5] in 2016. It also uses the AMT to collect and annotate data. In the data collection stage, the author searched 20 keywords on video websites to collect video data and asked the annotators to find the clip closest to the keywords within 20 s in the video. MSR-VTT also did not review and filter the sentences annotated by crowdsourced annotators. These two mainstream datasets are used as benchmarks for current VC works [3,9,10,25], but no effort has yet been made to identify and analyze their quality issues.

3   Method

3.1   Encoder-Decoder Framework

As shown in Fig. 2, our model follows the Encoder-Decoder framework and is supervised by CGKT Loss. In the encoding phase, the video V is sampled into frames, which are fed into 2D-CNN and 3D-CNN models to attain RGB feature F_r and motion feature F_m. These multi-modal features are input to the multi-modality fusion module to obtain the input of the decoder F. Then, in the decoding stage, decoder generate description $\hat{Y} = \{\hat{y}_1, \hat{y}_2, ..., \hat{y}_T\}$ where T is the length of caption. θ denotes the parameter to be learned.

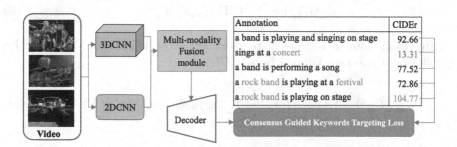

Fig. 2. The framework of our Consensus-Guided Keyword Targeting captioning model. Human annotations in green and red color mean high quality label and poor label respectively. Using CGKT loss, our model will focus on higher quality sentences and more representative words. (Color figure online)

3.2 Consensus-Guided Loss

We introduce Consensus-Guided Loss (CGL) to mitigate the uneven quality problem at the sentence level. The existing video captioning methods treat annotations of different qualities equally, which leads to noisy and biased supervisory signals and weak generalization performance. To mitigate this problem, we adopt the annotation quality score, i.e., CIDEr score as the weight to guide the model to learn more from higher quality annotations.

We denote captioning annotations as $Y^i = \{Y_1^i, Y_2^i, ..., Y_Q^i\}$ in which Q is the caption number of i-th video clip. We take E_q^i as references to measure the quality score $G(Y_q^i)$ of caption Y_q^i before training, in which E_q^i is the set of Y^i except caption Y_q^i. All the video captioning metrics can be used for the calculation of consensus score. We use CIDEr [15] as quality score in CGL.

The n-grams of Y_q^i are denoted as $\omega^{iq} = \{\omega_1^{iq}, \omega_2^{iq}, ..., \omega_M^{iq}\}$ in which M is the number of n-grams belonging to Y_q^i. To compute the i-th annotation's consensus score, we firstly get the Term Frequency Inverse Document Frequency (TF-IDF) of each n-gram in Y_q^i.

$$t(\omega_m^{iq}) = \frac{h(\omega_m^{iq})}{\sum_{\omega_j^{iq} \in \omega^{iq}} h(\omega_j^{iq})} \log(\frac{|\mathcal{V}|}{\sum_{V_p \in \mathcal{V}} \min(1, \sum_l h_{lp}(\omega_m^{iq}))}) \tag{1}$$

where $h(\omega_m^{iq})$ is the number of occurrences of ω_m^{iq} in reference caption Y_q^i, $\mathcal{V}$ is the set of all videos and $h_{lp}(\omega_m^{iq})$ means the number of times n-gram ω_m^{iq} appears in caption Y_l^p. Using the average cosine similarity between target caption and reference caption, we get the n-grams score.

$$\text{CIDEr}_n(Y_q^i, E_q^i) = \frac{1}{Q-1} \sum_{j \neq i} \frac{\mathbf{t^n}(Y_q^i) \cdot \mathbf{t^n}(Y_j^i)}{\|\mathbf{t^n}(Y_q^i)\| \cdot \|\mathbf{t^n}(Y_j^i)\|} \tag{2}$$

where $\mathbf{t^n}(Y_q^i)$ is the weighting vector composed by all n-grams of length n in Y_q^i. Then, we sum up all score for $N = 4$ as final annotation consensus score.

$$G(Y_q^i) = \sum_{n=1}^{N} \text{CIDEr}_n(Y_q^i, E_q^i) \tag{3}$$

After using consensus score G to re-weight every annotation, we can form the following Consensus-Guided Loss (CGL).

$$\mathcal{L}_{cg}(Y_q^i, \hat{Y}) = -G(Y_q^i) \frac{1}{T} \sum_{t=1}^{T} \log p_\theta(\hat{y}_t = y_t^{iq} | \hat{y}_{1:t-1}, F) \tag{4}$$

3.3 Keyword Targeting Loss

The Keyword Targeting Loss (KTL) is designed to alleviate the imbalance problem at the word level. The traditional objective of video captioning trades all word equally which cause captioning model are insensitive to these words that are less frequent but contain more accurate information. To solve this problem, we design KTL to oversample these less frequent words and make the model focus on learning from them. We count the frequency of each words in the dataset and select K words with the lowest frequency as keywords in each annotation. The keywords of caption Y_q^i are denoted as $KW^{iq} = \{y_{t_1}^{iq}, y_{t_2}^{iq}, ..., y_{t_K}^{iq}\}$, and the following is Keyword Targeting Loss. The value of β is 0.02 times of epoch number in training.

$$\mathcal{L}_{kt}(KW^{iq}, \hat{Y}) = -\frac{\beta}{K} \sum_{j=t_1}^{t_K} \log p_\theta(\hat{y}_j = y_j^{iq} | \hat{y}_{1:j-1}, F) \tag{5}$$

3.4   Consensus-Guided Keyword Targeting Captioning Model

We combine CGL $\mathcal{L}_{cg}$ and KTL $\mathcal{L}_{kt}$ to create our Consensus-Guided Keyword Targeting loss.

$$\mathcal{L} = \mathcal{L}_{kt} + \mathcal{L}_{cg} \tag{6}$$

A CGKT captioning model can be formed by replacing objective with CGKT loss without changing the network structure or extracting features again. We implement three CGKT captioning models using the architecture in S2VT [1], AttLSTM [24], and Semantic [20].

Given RGB feature F_r and temporal feature F_m. S2VT model concatenates them and takes single fully connected layer as the Multi-modality Fusion Module. The decoder of S2VT model is implemented with single layer LSTM. p_θ^s is the probability of words in vocabulary generated by S2VT model, W_s and b_s are learnable parameters.

$$p_\theta^s(\hat{y}_t) = \text{LSTM}(W_s[F_r; F_m] + b_s, h_{t-1}^s) \tag{7}$$

For the Semantic model, we use the architecture in [20] as Multi-modality Fusion Module except replacing the objective with CGKT loss. AttLSTM also uses single-layer LSTM as decoder but fuses multi-modality features using an additive attention module at each time step of the decoder. p_θ^a is the probability of words in vocabulary generated by AttLSTM model, v_a, W_a^1, and W_a^2 are learnable parameters.

$$p_\theta^a(\hat{y}_t) = \text{LSTM}(v_a^\top \tanh(W_{a1}\hat{y}_{t-1} + W_{a2}[F_r; F_m]), h_{t-1}^a) \tag{8}$$

4   Experiments

4.1   Datasets and Metrics.

We experiment on two widely used video captioning datasets: MSVD [4] and MSR-VTT [5]. Following the convention [3,9,10], the MSVD is split into 1,200, 100, and 670 videos for training, validation, and testing. Following the official instruction [5], we split MSR-VTT into 6513/497/2990 for training/validation/testing. To evaluate the performance of our method, we employ four commonly used metrics, including BLEU@4 [12], METEOR [13], ROUGE_L [14], and CIDEr [15].

4.2 Implementation Details

We sample 32 frames from video uniformly, and then feed these frames to the ResNeXt model pre-trained on the ImageNet ILSVRC2012 dataset. We take the output of the last *conv* layer of the ResNeXt [22] model as RGB feature which is 2048 dimension. The dynamic temporal feature of 1536 dimension is extracted by ECO [21] model which is pre-trained on the Kinetics400 dataset. For the MSR-VTT dataset, we apply the pre-trained word embedding model Glove to obtain word 300-dim vectors of 20 video categories.

We used are 512 for all the hidden size of LSTM, and our embedding layer dimension size is 300. We employ Adam as our model's optimizer. Following the setting in [20] the initial learning rate is 1e-4 and the learning rate is dropped by 0.316 every 20 epochs for MSR-VTT dataset. We set the keywords number as 5. The batch size is 64 for both MSR-VTT and MSVD. We adopt the model with best performance on validation set to test. The S2VT and AttLSTM use beam search with size 4 for caption generation. Following the [20], Semantic baseline does not use beam search.

Table 1. Performance comparisons with different models and baselines on the test set of MSR-VTT in terms of BLEU@4, METEOR, ROUGE_L, and CIDEr. CE, Res152, IRV2, I3D, Ca, obj, C3D, RL denote Cross Entropy Loss, 152-layer ResNet, InceptionResNet-V2, Inflated 3D, Category embedding vector, object feature detected by Faster RCNN, 3D ConvNets, and Reinforcement learning training strategies respectively.

Method	Feature	BLEU@4	METEOR	ROUGE_L	CIDEr	RL
PickNet [7]	Res152+Ca	38.9	27.2	59.5	42.1	√
RecNet [8]	InceptionV4	39.1	26.6	59.3	42.7	
POS [10]	IRV2+I3D+Ca	41.3	28.7	62.1	53.4	√
RMN [9]	IRV2+I3D+obj	42.5	28.4	61.6	49.6	
SAAT [3]	IRV2+C3D+Ca	39.9	27.7	61.2	51.0	√
HMN [25]	IRV2+C3D+obj	43.5	29.0	62.7	51.5	
S2VT *w/*CE	ResNeXt+ECO+Ca	40.8	27.6	59.7	49.8	
S2VT *w/*CGKT	ResNeXt+ECO+Ca	**41.4**	**27.7**	**60.2**	**52.0**	
AttLSTM *w/*CE	ResNeXt+ECO+Ca	40.6	**27.7**	59.6	49.6	
AttLSTM *w/*CGKT	ResNeXt+ECO+Ca	**41.2**	27.6	**60.3**	**51.7**	
Semantic *w/*CE	ResNeXt+ECO+Ca	**41.3**	27.0	60.0	49.3	
Semantic *w/*CGKT	ResNeXt+ECO+Ca	41.0	**27.1**	**60.1**	**50.8**	

4.3   Quantitative Results

Comparison with the State-of-the-Art. We compare our method with state-of-the-art models on MSR-VTT dataset, including PickNet [7], RecNet [8], POS [10], RMN [9], SAAT [3], and HMN [25]. We adopt S2VT [1], AttLSTM [24], and Semantic [20] with cross-entropy loss as baselines. As shown in Table 1, the CIDEr score of three baselines has been improved by 4.4%, 4.2%, and 3.0% using CGKT loss. Comparing the results between using Cross-Entropy and CGKT as training objectives, we can find that CGKT does alleviate the problem of uneven quality annotations in MSR-VTT. Moreover, CGKT makes the results of S2VT, AttLSTM, and Semantic models close to the SOTA.

Besides, we also compare performance on the test set of MSVD. As shown in Table 2(a), our method outperforms three baselines on BLEU@4, METEOR, ROUGE_L, and CIDEr. And our method achieves an improvement of 8.2%, 1.3%, and 4.0% for three baselines in terms of CIDEr.

Table 2. More performance comparisons results. CE, FL, LS, and ΔC denote cross-entropy loss, focal loss, label smoothing, and relative improvement on CIDEr, respectively.

(a) Performance comparisons with different baselines on MSVD.

Method	BLEU@4	METEOR	ROUGE_L	CIDEr	ΔC
S2VT w/CE	45.8	35.6	70.1	79.2	
S2VT w/CGKT	**49.6**	**36.6**	**71.1**	**85.7**	+8.2%
AttLSTM w/CE	49.5	36.5	**71.1**	88.2	
AttLSTM w/CGKT	**50.6**	**36.7**	71.1	**89.4**	+1.3%
Semantic w/CE	51.0	37.1	71.2	89.4	
Semantic w/CGKT	**51.1**	**37.4**	**71.7**	**93.0**	+4.0%

(b) Performance comparisons with different loss function on MSR-VTT.

Method	BLEU@4	METEOR	ROUGE_L	CIDEr	ΔC
S2VT w/CE	40.8	27.6	59.7	49.8	
S2VT w/FL	40.7	27.8	59.9	50.6	+1.6%
S2VT w/LS	**41.6**	**27.9**	**60.4**	50.8	+2.0%
S2VT w/CGKT	41.4	27.7	60.2	**52.0**	+4.4%

To further prove the effectiveness of our method, we compare our CGKT loss with FocalLoss [19] and LabelSmooth [23]. Following the default setting in [19,23], we set α and γ in FocalLoss to 0.25 and 2, and smoothing parameter to 0.2. As shown in Table 2(b), our CGKT outperforms the other methods on CIDEr. This is reasonable because our method mitigates both sentence-level uneven quality issue and also focus on learning from more representative words, whereas these methods only focus on the word level.

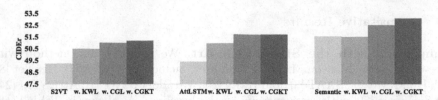

Fig. 3. Performance comparisons between KTL and CGL on three baselines at test set of MSR-VTT.

Ablation Study. To investigate the effectiveness of KTL and CGL, ablation experiments are performed on three models. As shown in Fig. 3, both KTL and CGL can improve the results of baselines, except for Semantic. We consider that this is because Semantic [20] also has the ability to find words with more accurate semantic information using Semantic Detection Network, and extra KTL interferes with it.

The combination of CGL and KTL does not further improve performance on AttLSTM. We think that is because complicated supervisory signals combined with sentence-level and word-level make additive attention hard to learn effective attention weight.

We also studied the effects of different quality scores and keyword numbers, as shown in Table 3, using CIDEr as the quality score is the best choice. But 4 keyword number achieves the best performance than 5 on CIDEr, it can be inferred that since the average length of sentences in MSR-VTT is 9.2, 5 keywords is relatively redundant.

Table 3. The performance of ablated KTL and CGL with various quality score and keyword number on MSR-VTT. B, M, R and C denote BLEU@4, METEOR, ROUGE_L, and CIDEr used as quality score. K@N denotes keyword number is N.

Ablation	Method	BLEU@4	METEOR	ROUGE_L	CIDEr
Quality score	S2VT w/B	39.8	26.8	58.9	46.2
	S2VT w/M	41.2	27.6	60.1	50.4
	S2VT w/R	**41.7**	27.7	**60.2**	51.0
	S2VT w/C	41.3	**27.9**	**60.2**	**51.2**
Keywords num	S2VT w/ K@3	41.5	27.3	60.4	50.7
	S2VT w/K@4	**41.8**	27.9	60.5	**51.6**
	S2VT w/K@5	41.3	27.7	60.0	50.7
	S2VT w/K@6	41.7	**28.0**	**60.6**	51.4

4.4 Qualitative Results

In this section, we investigate what content CGKT encourages the model to learn from video. We provide several examples of video captioning results in Fig. 4. By comparing captions generated by S2VT trained with Cross-Entropy loss and our CGKT loss, we can see that generated captions equipped with our method have a more complete structure and contain more representative words. For example, for the upper left video in Fig. 4, model trained by CGKT generates "knocking on the wall", which is more close to the content of the video.

GT: a girl laying in bed then knocking on the wall then texting
CE: a girl is laying on her bed
CGKT: a girl laying in bed knocking on the wall

GT: boys compete in a wrestling match
CE: two men are wrestling
CGKT: two men are wrestling in a wrestling match

GT: a child explains how to plug a cable into his computer
CE: a man is showing how to use a phone
CGKT: a man is showing how to use a computer

GT: a person playing a football video game kicking and receiving the ball
CE: a man is playing a game
CGKT: a man is playing a football video game

Fig. 4. Qualitative comparison of S2VT using Cross-Entropy and our CGKT as training objectives on the test set of MSVD and MSR-VTT datasets.

5 Conclusion

In this paper, we propose Consensus-Guided Keyword Targeting (CGKT) to alleviate the uneven sentence quality and imbalanced word distribution problems in video captioning datasets. Our approach re-weights training samples according to consensus-based sentence scores and word frequencies and thus encourages the caption model to learn high-quality sentences and keywords. Experiments on MSVD and MSR-VTT demonstrate the effectiveness and versatility of our CGKT, which can be easily integrated into various video captioning models to bring consistent improvements (especially the CIDEr metric) and produce more accurate and detailed descriptions.

Acknowledgements. This paper was partially supported by NSFC (No: 62176008) and Shenzhen Science and Technology Research Program (No: GXWD202012311658 07007-20200814115301001).

References

1. Darrell, T., Venugopalan, S., Rohrbach, M., Donahue, J., Mooney, R., Saenko, K.: Sequence to sequence - video to text. In: Proceedings of the IEEE International Conference on Computer Vision, pp. 4534–4542 (2015)
2. Zhang, Y., Xu, J., Yao, T., Mei, T.: Learning multimodal attention LSTM networks for video captioning. In: Proceedings of the 25th ACM International Conference on Multimedia, pp. 537–545 (2017)
3. Wang, C., Zheng, Q., Tao, D.: Syntax-aware action targeting for video captioning. In: Proceedings of the IEEE Conference on Computer Vision and Pattern Recognition, pp. 13093–13102 (2020)
4. Malkarnenkar, G., et al.: YouTube2Text: recognizing and describing arbitrary activities using semantic hierarchies and zero-shot recognition. In: Proceedings of the IEEE International Conference on Computer Vision, pp. 2712–2719 (2013)
5. Yao, T., Xu, J., Mei, T., Rui, Y.: MSR-VTT: a large video description dataset for bridging video and language. In: Proceedings of the IEEE Conference on Computer Vision and Pattern Recognition, pp. 5288–5296 (2016)
6. Kojima, A., Tamura, T., Fukunaga, K.: Natural language description of human activities from video images based on concept hierarchy of actions. Int. J. Comput. Vis. **50**, 171–184 (2002). https://doi.org/10.1023/A:1020346032608
7. Chen, Y., Wang, S., Zhang, W., Huang, Q.: Less is more: picking informative frames for video captioning. In: Ferrari, V., Hebert, M., Sminchisescu, C., Weiss, Y. (eds.) ECCV 2018. LNCS, vol. 11217, pp. 367–384. Springer, Cham (2018). https://doi.org/10.1007/978-3-030-01261-8_22
8. Zhang, W., Wang, B., Ma, L., Liu, W.: Reconstruction network for video captioning. In: Proceedings of the IEEE Conference on Computer Vision and Pattern Recognition, pp. 7622–7631 (2018)
9. Wang, M., Tan, G., Liu, D., Zha, Z.: Learning to discretely compose reasoning module networks for video captioning. In: Proceedings of the Twenty-Ninth International Joint Conference on Artificial Intelligence, pp. 745–752 (2020)
10. Zhang, W., Jiang, W., Wang, J., Wang, B., Ma, L., Liu, W.: Controllable video captioning with POS sequence guidance based on gated fusion network. In: Proceedings of the IEEE International Conference on Computer Vision, pp. 2641–2650 (2019)
11. Jin, Q., Chen, S., Chen, J., Hauptmann, A.: Video captioning with guidance of multimodal latent topics. In: Proceedings of the 25th ACM International Conference on Multimedia, pp. 1838–1846 (2017)
12. Ward, T., Papineni, K., Roukos, S., Zhu, W.: BLEU: a method for automatic evaluation of machine translation. In: Proceedings of the Annual Meeting of the Association for Computational Linguistics, pp. 311–318 (2002)
13. Denkowski, M.J., Lavie, A.: Meteor universal: language specific translation evaluation for any target language. In: Proceedings of the Ninth Workshop on Statistical Machine Translation, pp. 376–380 (2014)
14. Lin, C.-Y.: ROUGE: a package for automatic evaluation of summaries. In: Proceedings of the ACL Workshop: Text Summarization Branches Out, p. 10 (2004)

15. Zitnick, C.L., Vedantam, R., Parikh, D.: CIDEr: consensus-based image description evaluation. In: Proceedings of the IEEE Conference on Computer Vision and Pattern Recognition, pp. 4566–4575 (2015)
16. Johnson, J.M., Khoshgoftaar, T.M.: Survey on deep learning with class imbalance. J. Big Data **6**(1), 1–54 (2019). https://doi.org/10.1186/s40537-019-0192-5
17. Shi, J., Feng, H., Ouyang, W., Pang, J., Chen, K., Lin, D.: Libra R-CNN: towards balanced learning for object detection. In: Proceedings of the IEEE Conference on Computer Vision and Pattern Recognition, pp. 821–830 (2020)
18. Li, Y., Vasconcelos, N.: REPAIR: removing representation bias by dataset resampling. In: Proceedings of the IEEE Conference on Computer Vision and Pattern Recognition, pp. 9564–9573 (2019)
19. Girshick, R.B., He, K., Lin, T., Goyal, P., Dollar, P.: Focal loss for dense object detection. IEEE Trans. Pattern Anal. Mach. Intell. **42**, 318–327 (2020)
20. Maye, A., Li, J., Chen, H., Ke, L., Hu, X.: A semantics assisted video captioning model trained with scheduled sampling. Front. Robot. AI **7**, 475767 (2020)
21. Zolfaghari, M., Singh, K., Brox, T.: ECO: efficient convolutional network for online video understanding. In: Ferrari, V., Hebert, M., Sminchisescu, C., Weiss, Y. (eds.) ECCV 2018. LNCS, vol. 11206, pp. 713–730. Springer, Cham (2018). https://doi.org/10.1007/978-3-030-01216-8_43
22. Xie, S., Girshick, R.B., Dollár, P., Tu, Z., He, K.: Aggregated residual transformations for deep neural networks. In: IEEE Conference on Computer Vision and Pattern Recognition, pp. 5987–5995 (2017)
23. Ioffe, S., Shlens, J., Szegedy, C., Vanhoucke, V., Wojna, Z.: Rethinking the inception architecture for computer vision. In: Proceedings of the IEEE Conference on Computer Vision and Pattern Recognition, pp. 2818–2826 (2016)
24. Yao, L., et al.: Describing videos by exploiting temporal structure. In: International Conference on Computer Vision, pp. 4507–4515 (2015)
25. Ye, H., Li, G., Qi, Y., Wang, S., Huang, Q., Yang, M.: Hierarchical modular network for video captioning. In: Proceedings of the IEEE Conference on Computer Vision and Pattern Recognition (2022)

Handwritten Mathematical Expression Recognition via GCAttention-Based Encoder and Bidirectional Mutual Learning Transformer

Xiaoxiang Han[1], Qiaohong Liu[2], Ziqi Han[1], Yuanjie Lin[1], and Naiyue Xu[1]

[1] School of Health Science and Engineering, University of Shanghai for Science and Technology, Shanghai 200093, China
[2] School of Medical Instruments, Shanghai University of Medicine and Health Sciences, Shanghai 201318, China
769842320@qq.com

Abstract. Recognition of handwritten mathematical expressions to LaTeX is an image-to-sequence task. Recent research has shown that encoder-decoder models are well suited for this challenge. Many innovative models based on this structure have been proposed, especially on the decoder. Such as attention mechanism and bidirectional mutual learning are used in the decoder. And our model also improves the encoder. We use the multi-scale fusion DenseNet as the encoder and add Global Context Attention. This attention mechanism combines the advantages of force-spatial attention and channel attention. The feature maps of the two scales output by the encoder are used as inputs to the two decoder branches. The decoder uses a two-way mutual learning Transformer, which can understand high-level semantic and contextual information, and can handle long sequences of information well. In order to save memory, the two decoder branches use a set of parameters, and the last two branches are distilled and learned from each other. In this way, not only the bidirectional decoders can learn from each other, but also the two decoder branches can learn from each other, which increases the robustness of the model. Our model achieves 56.80%, 53.34% and 54.62% accuracy on CROHME2014, 2016 and 2019, respectively, and 66.22% accuracy on our own constructed dataset HME100k.

Keywords: Mathematical expression · Handwriting recognition · Multi scale · Global context attention · Transformer · Bidirection mutual learning

1 Introduction

Mathematical formula recognition is an important part of OCR, however, it was not introduced by Anderson in his PhD thesis until the 1960s [1]. He proposed

This work is partially supported by the National Natural Science Foundation of China (Nos. 61801288).

a method of using syntax as a standard segmentation and using a top-down analysis method to identify mathematical formulas. Traditional methods of converting images to LATEX rely on specially designed syntax [16]. However, these grammars require a lot of prior knowledge to define the structure of mathematical expressions, the positional relationship of symbols and the corresponding parsing algorithms in advance, so that complex mathematical expressions cannot be recognized.

Compared with the traditional OCR problem, handwritten mathematical expression recognition is a more complex two-dimensional handwriting recognition problem. Its internal complex two-dimensional spatial structure makes it difficult to analyze, and the traditional method has a poor recognition effect. With the advancement of deep learning, encoder-decoder models have shown fairly effective performance on various tasks such as scene text recognition [4] and image captioning [26]. It also achieves significant performance improvements during HMER processing [5]. Zhang et al. [29] introduced the attention mechanism to undoubtedly increase the accuracy. They propose the Watch, Attend, and Parse (WAP) method, which employs a deep fully convolutional network (FCN) to encode handwritten images and a gated recurrent unit (GRU) with attention mechanism as the decoder to generate serial output. Zhang et al. developed DWAP-MSA [27] to try to use a multi-scale feature encoding to identify symbols of different sizes in handwritten mathematical expressions, so we borrowed this method in model design. LATEX is a markup language designed by humans and therefore has a cleaner and more defined syntactic structure. For example, the two parentheses "(" and ")" must be paired. When dealing with long LATEX sequences, as the distance increases, the dependency information captured between the currency symbol and the previous symbol becomes weaker and weaker, and it is difficult for RNN-based models to capture the relationship between two distant two brackets. And a major limitation of overlay attention is that it only uses historical alignment information without considering future information. Most models in the past only decode left-to-right, ignoring information on the right, so they may not take full advantage of long-range correlations and the grammar specification of mathematical expressions [2,31]. Zhao et al. [31] designed a simple bidirectional Transformer decoder called BTTR, but there is no explicit supervision information for BTTR to learn from the opposite direction, and its decoders in both directions do not learn from each other, which limits its bidirectional learning ability.

2   Related Work

2.1   Image-to-Markup

Deng et al. [6] defined the image-to-markup problem as: transforming a rendered source image into a target rendering markup that fully describes its content and layout. The source, x, consists of an image. The target, y, consists of a sequence of tokens $y_1, y_2, \ldots, y_T$, where T is the length of the output and each y is a token in the markup language.

2.2 CNN

In the past ten years, convolutional neural networks have continued to make efforts in many directions, and have made breakthroughs in speech recognition, face recognition, general object recognition, motion analysis, natural language processing and even brain wave analysis.

In 1962, Hubel and Wiesel's experiments [14] on cats found that the cat's visual cortex processes information in a hierarchical structure, that is to say, it extracts information layer by layer. The simplest information is extracted at the top, and then continuously. For simple information extraction, high-level abstract information is gradually obtained. Yann LeCun [19] was the first to use Convolutional Neural Network (CNN) for handwritten digit recognition and has maintained its dominance in the problem. In 2012, Alexnet [15] introduced a new deep structure and dropout method, which increased the error rate from more than 25% to 15%. It subverts the field of image recognition. In 2014, Karen et al. [20] used CNN to explore the relationship between the depth of the convolutional neural network and its performance. By repeatedly stacking 3×3 small convolution kernels and 2×2 maximum pooling layers, VGGNet successfully constructed 16 19-layer deep convolutional neural network. In the same year, Szegedy et al. [21] proposed GoogLeNet. It does not rely solely on deepening the network structure to improve network performance, but at the same time deepening the network (22 layers), it has made innovations in the network structure. It introduces the Inception structure to replace the traditional operation of simple convolution and activation. In 2015, He et al. [10] proposed ResNet, which made great innovations in the network structure and introduced the residual network structure. With this residual network structure, very deep networks can be designed, providing feasibility for advanced semantic feature extraction and classification. In 2017, Huang et al. [13] proposed DenseNet, which established the connection relationship between different layers, made full use of features, and further alleviated the problem of gradient disappearance. Moreover, its network is narrower and has fewer parameters, which effectively suppresses overfitting and reduces the amount of computation. The Dense block proposed by it solves the problem that the size of each input is different, and it is estimated that there is no need to force the input to be modified into a fixed shape. Due to the many advantages of this network, this paper uses DenseNet with the addition of the GCAttention module as the backbone network for feature extraction, that is, the encoder of our network.

2.3 Global Contextual Attention

The goal of capturing long-range dependencies is a global understanding of the visual scene, which is effective for many computer vision tasks, such as image classification, video classification, object detection, semantic segmentation, etc. Gao et al. [3] proposed a global contextual attention module, which is lightweight and can fully utilize global contextual information. The global context block can be represented as

$$y_i = x_i + w_{v2} ReLU(LN(w_{v1} \sum_{\forall j} \frac{e^{w_k x_j}}{\sum_{\forall m} e^{w_k x_j}} x_j))) \tag{1}$$

2.4 Transformer

Recently transformers [23] have shown good performance on a variety of tasks [7,8], it can avoid recursion, in order to allow parallel computing, and reduce performance degradation due to long-term dependencies. Since the hidden layer nodes of RNNs at time T depend on forward input and intermediate calculation results, this feature limits the parallel computing capability of RNNs.

The core of Transformer is Scaled Dot-Product Attention, which solves the problem that because the network inputs multiple vectors of different sizes, and there may be a certain relationship between the vectors, these relationships cannot be fully utilized. Its formula is as follows:

$$Attention(Q, K, V) = Softmax(\frac{QK^T}{\sqrt{d_k}})V \tag{2}$$

2.5 Mutual Learning

Zhang et al. [30] proposed a deep mutual learning (DML) strategy, in which a group of student networks, learns from and mentor each other throughout the training process. Different from the static pre-defined one-way transition path between teacher and student in distillation model.

Guo et al. [9] proposed an efficient online knowledge extraction method through collaborative learning, called KDCL, which can continuously improve the generalization ability of deep neural networks (DNNs) with different learning capabilities. Different from the two-stage knowledge distillation method, KDCL treats all DNNs as "students" and trains them collaboratively in one stage (knowledge is transferred among any students during collaborative training), thus achieving parallel computing, fast Computing and attractive generalization capabilities.

3 Methodology

3.1 Encoder

Since the size of images of handwritten mathematical expressions is usually random size, a model called Densely Connected Convolutional Network (DenseNet) [13] is used in our encoder. DenseNet is a type of FCN that connects all networks in a feed-forward fashion and enhances feature propagation and reuse by ensuring the maximum information flow between layers in the network, so FCN can handle images of any size.

There are many symbols of different scales in handwritten mathematical expressions, and using pure DenseNet will lose some details. The multi-scale dense network proposed by Gao et al. [12] utilizes information at all scales, which is obviously very expensive. This paper uses a DenseNet with a three-layer structure, and only the last layer of it is upsampled and the output of the second layer is fused. Finally, the encoder outputs the feature degrees of these two scales. This not only obtains multi-scale information, but also saves computational expenses. At the same time, we add a GCAttention layer after each pooling layer to make the network pay more attention to useful features, as shown in Fig. 1.

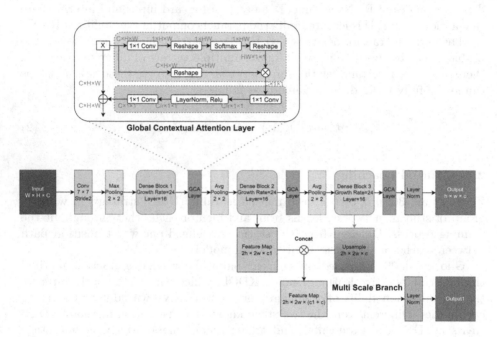

Fig. 1. The structure of the global contextual attention layer and the multi-scale encoder.

3.2   Decoder

We use the standard Transformer [23] as the decoder, and the feature maps output by the encoder are embedded into the decoder respectively. And these branches share a Transformer model to reduce the amount of parameters and computing power as shown in Fig. 2.

To achieve bidirectional training, we add $\langle sos \rangle$ and $\langle eos \rangle$ to the LaTeX sequence as start and end symbols, respectively. For example, a target LaTeX sequence

$$Y = \{Y_1, Y_2, ..., Y_T\} \tag{3}$$

of length T, which is represented as

$$Y_{l2r} = \{\langle sos \rangle, Y_1, Y_2, ..., Y_T, \langle eos \rangle\} \tag{4}$$

from left to right (L2R), is represented as

$$Y_{r2l} = \{\langle eos \rangle, Y_T, Y_{T-1}, ..., Y_1, \langle sos \rangle\} \tag{5}$$

from right to left (R2L).

To quantify the difference in prediction distribution between the two directions and between the two branches, we introduce the Kullback-Leibler (KL) loss [11]. After optimization, this loss can minimize the distance of the probability distribution between different branches. The KL distance in both directions is calculated as follows:

$$\sigma(Z_{i,k}^{l2r}, S) = \frac{\exp(Z_{i,k}^{l2r}/S)}{\sum_{j=1}^{K} \exp(Z_{i,k}^{l2r}/S)} \tag{6}$$

$$L_{KL} = S^2 \sum_{i=1}^{T} \sum_{j=1}^{K} \sigma(Z_{i,k}^{l2r}, S) \log \frac{\sigma(Z_{i,k}^{l2r}, S)}{\sigma(Z_{T+1-i,j}^{r2l}, S)} \tag{7}$$

where σ represents the soft probability of one direction.

3.3 Positional Encoding

Since the Transformer model itself does not have any sense of position for each input vector, we do positional embeddings for both image and word vectors, which can effectively help the model identify areas that need attention. For the positional embedding of word vectors, we directly adopt the method of Transformer's original research [23]. For the positional embedding of word vectors, we directly adopt the method of Transformer's original research. It is defined as follows:

$$PE_{(pos, 2i)} = sin(pos/10000^{2i/d_{model}}) \tag{8}$$

$$PE_{(pos, 2i+1)} = cos(pos/10000^{2i/d_{model}}) \tag{9}$$

where pos is the position and i is the dimension.

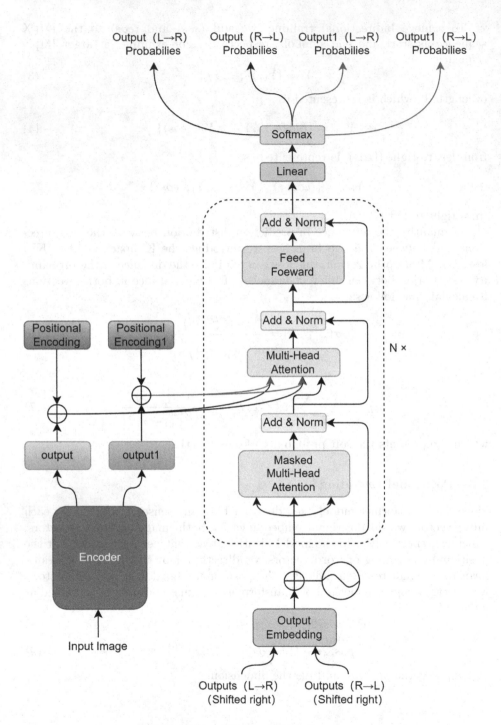

Fig. 2. The structure of the decoder.

Zhao et al. [31] describe a 2D normalized positional encoding for representing image positional features. The sinusoidal positional encoding $P^W_{pos,d/2}$ is first computed in both dimensions and then concatenated. Given a two-dimensional position tuple (x, y) and the same dimension d as the word position encoding, the image position encoding vector $P^I_{x,y,d}$ is represented as:

$$\overline{x} = \frac{x}{H}, \overline{y} = \frac{y}{W} \tag{10}$$

$$P^W_{pos,d/2} = [P^W_{\overline{x},d/2}; P^W_{\overline{y},d/2}] \tag{11}$$

where H and W are height and width of input images. Finally, the weighted summation of the cross-entropy loss and the KL distance of each output is performed.

4 Experiments

4.1 Datasets

We use Competition on Recognition of Online Handwritten Mathematical Expressions (CROHME2014) as our training set. It has 111 types of mathematical symbols and 8836 handwritten mathematical expressions, including numbers, almost all common operators. Then we take three public test datasets, as test sets, they are CROHME 2014, 2016 and 2019 with 986, 1147 and 1199 expressions, respectively.

In addition, we trained and tested on a dataset called HME10k. This dataset collects handwritten mathematical expressions in real handwriting scenarios from students, which is more diverse and richer than the CROHME dataset. But because it is a photo of a real scene, it is inevitable that there are many blurry images that are unrecognizable by humans, which is not helpful for our training, so we remove them. We divided this dataset into two parts, 80,000 training sets and 20,000 test sets.

4.2 Comparison with Prior Works

We compare our method with the previous state-of-the-art as shown in Table 1. All the methods shown in the table only use the 8836 training samples officially provided by CROHME, and do not use data augmentation to ensure the fairness of the performance comparison. These methods include PAL (Wu et al. [24]), PAL-v2 (Wu et al. [25]), WAP (Zhang et al. [29]), PGS (Le at el. [18]), DWAP (WAP with DenseNet as encoder), DWAP-MSA (DWAP with multi-scale attention) (Zhang et al. [27]), DWAP-TD (DWAP with tree decoder) (Zhang et al. [28]), DLA (Le [17]), WS WAP (weakly supervised WAP) (Truong et al. [22]) and BTTR (Zhao et al. [31]).

The results show that our method has a significant improvement in accuracy on CROHME 2014, which is 2.84% higher than BTTR, and at the same time, the accuracy on ≤1 and ≤2 is also improved by 5.25% and 6.57%, respectively.

Table 1. Comparison with prior works (in %). The results in the table are cited from their corresponding papers.

Dataset	Methods	ExpRate	≤1 error	≤2 error
2014	PAL	39.66	56.80	68.51
	WAP	46.55	61.16	65.21
	PGS	48.78	66.13	73.94
	PAL-v2	48.88	64.50	69.78
	DWAP-TD	49.10	64.20	67.8
	DLA	49.85	–	–
	DWAP	50.60	68.05	71.56
	DWAP-MSA	52.80	68.10	72.00
	WS WAP	53.65	–	–
	BTTR	53.96	66.02	70.28
	Ours	**56.80**	**71.27**	**76.85**
2016	PGS	36.27	–	–
	TOKYO	43.94	50.91	53.70
	WAP	44.55	57.10	61.55
	DWAP-TD	48.50	62.30	65.30
	DLA	47.34	–	–
	DWAP	47.43	60.21	63.35
	PAL-v2	49.61	64.08	70.27
	DWAP-MSA	50.10	63.80	67.40
	WS WAP	51.96	64.34	70.10
	BTTR	52.31	63.90	68.61
	Ours	53.34	**67.56**	**74.19**
2019	DWAP	47.70	59.50	63.30
	DWAP-TD	51.40	66.10	69.10
	BTTR	52.96	65.97	69.14
	Ours	**54.62**	**68.97**	**74.64**
HME100K	**Ours**	**66.22**	**77.81**	**81.20**

Table 2. Ablation study on the CROHME 2014 test sets (in %).

Mutual learning	GCAttention	Multi-scale	ExpRate
✗	✗	✗	48.36
✓	✗	✗	53.96
✓	✓	✗	55.22
✓	✓	✓	56.80

Our method also improves ExpRate by 1.03% and 1.66% compared to BTTR on CROHME 2016 and 2019, respectively., which proves the effectiveness of our model.

4.3   Ablation Study

In Table 2, the mutual learning in the first column indicates whether multi-scale and bidirectional mutual learning is used, the multi-scale in the second column indicates whether multi-scale is used in the encoder, and the GCAttention in the third column indicates whether the encoder is added Global contextual attention layer.

First of all, we found that mutual learning has a great impact on the model. Without mutual learning, multi-scale and GCAttention, the accuracy rate is only 48.36%, which is 8.44% different from the highest accuracy rate. Second, we found that under the combined effect of multi-scale and GCAttention, our model also achieved certain results, which improved the accuracy by 2.84% compared to not using them.

4.4   The Program with GUI

Finally, we made a program (Fig. 3) with a GUI for the model trained on the dataset we built, where the user can use the mouse to write a mathematical expression on the drawing board, and then click the *Recognize* button to get the LaTeX expression.

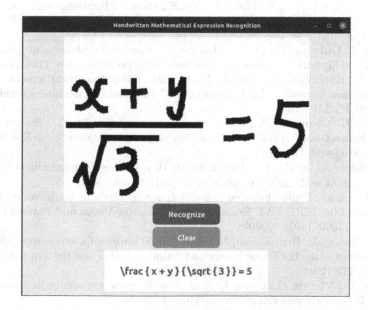

Fig. 3. The program with GUI for HMER.

5 Conclusion

In this paper, we improve the performance of models for recognizing handwritten mathematical expressions by introducing a global contextual attention mechanism and multi-branch mutual learning. We built a dataset ourselves and trained this model on it with good results. However, handwritten mathematical expressions are very complex, and each person's handwriting style is different. Whether it is a single character or the entire expression structure, there are certain differences in what everyone writes. Therefore, in the future we will collect more and more complex data to train our model and improve its robustness.

References

1. Anderson, R.H.: Syntax-directed recognition of hand-printed two-dimensional mathematics. In: Symposium on Interactive Systems for Experimental Applied Mathematics: Proceedings of the Association for Computing Machinery Inc., Symposium, pp. 436–459 (1967)
2. Bian, X., Qin, B., Xin, X., Li, J., Su, X., Wang, Y.: Handwritten mathematical expression recognition via attention aggregation based bi-directional mutual learning. In: Proceedings of the AAAI Conference on Artificial Intelligence, vol. 36, pp. 113–121 (2022)
3. Cao, Y., Xu, J., Lin, S., Wei, F., Hu, H.: GCNet: non-local networks meet squeeze-excitation networks and beyond. In: Proceedings of the IEEE/CVF International Conference on Computer Vision Workshops (2019)
4. Cheng, Z., Bai, F., Xu, Y., Zheng, G., Pu, S., Zhou, S.: Focusing attention: towards accurate text recognition in natural images. In: Proceedings of the IEEE International Conference on Computer Vision, pp. 5076–5084 (2017)
5. Chung, J., Gulcehre, C., Cho, K., Bengio, Y.: Empirical evaluation of gated recurrent neural networks on sequence modeling. arXiv preprint arXiv:1412.3555 (2014)
6. Deng, Y., Kanervisto, A., Ling, J., Rush, A.M.: Image-to-markup generation with coarse-to-fine attention. In: International Conference on Machine Learning, pp. 980–989. PMLR (2017)
7. Devlin, J., Chang, M.W., Lee, K., Toutanova, K.: BERT: pre-training of deep bidirectional transformers for language understanding. arXiv preprint arXiv:1810.04805 (2018)
8. Dosovitskiy, A., et al.: An image is worth 16×16 words: transformers for image recognition at scale. arXiv preprint arXiv:2010.11929 (2020)
9. Guo, Q., et al.: Online knowledge distillation via collaborative learning. In: Proceedings of the IEEE/CVF Conference on Computer Vision and Pattern Recognition, pp. 11020–11029 (2020)
10. He, K., Zhang, X., Ren, S., Sun, J.: Deep residual learning for image recognition. In: Proceedings of the IEEE Conference on Computer Vision and Pattern Recognition, pp. 770–778 (2016)
11. Hinton, G., Vinyals, O., Dean, J., et al.: Distilling the knowledge in a neural network, **2**(7). arXiv preprint arXiv:1503.02531 (2015)
12. Huang, G., Chen, D., Li, T., Wu, F., Van Der Maaten, L., Weinberger, K.Q.: Multi-scale dense networks for resource efficient image classification. arXiv preprint arXiv:1703.09844 (2017)

13. Huang, G., Liu, Z., Van Der Maaten, L., Weinberger, K.Q.: Densely connected convolutional networks. In: Proceedings of the IEEE Conference on Computer Vision and Pattern Recognition, pp. 4700–4708 (2017)
14. Hubel, D.H., Wiesel, T.N.: Receptive fields, binocular interaction and functional architecture in the cat's visual cortex. J. Physiol. **160**(1), 106 (1962)
15. Krizhevsky, A., Sutskever, I., Hinton, G.E.: ImageNet classification with deep convolutional neural networks. In: Advances in Neural Information Processing Systems, vol. 25 (2012)
16. Lavirotte, S., Pottier, L.: Mathematical formula recognition using graph grammar. In: Document Recognition V, vol. 3305, pp. 44–52. SPIE (1998)
17. Le, A.D.: Recognizing handwritten mathematical expressions via paired dual loss attention network and printed mathematical expressions. In: Proceedings of the IEEE/CVF Conference on Computer Vision and Pattern Recognition Workshops, pp. 566–567 (2020)
18. Le, A.D., Indurkhya, B., Nakagawa, M.: Pattern generation strategies for improving recognition of handwritten mathematical expressions. Pattern Recogn. Lett. **128**, 255–262 (2019)
19. LeCun, Y., Bottou, L., Bengio, Y., Haffner, P.: Gradient-based learning applied to document recognition. Proc. IEEE **86**(11), 2278–2324 (1998)
20. Simonyan, K., Zisserman, A.: Very deep convolutional networks for large-scale image recognition. arXiv preprint arXiv:1409.1556 (2014)
21. Szegedy, C., et al.: Going deeper with convolutions. In: Proceedings of the IEEE Conference on Computer Vision and Pattern Recognition, pp. 1–9 (2015)
22. Truong, T.N., Nguyen, C.T., Phan, K.M., Nakagawa, M.: Improvement of end-to-end offline handwritten mathematical expression recognition by weakly supervised learning. In: 2020 17th International Conference on Frontiers in Handwriting Recognition (ICFHR), pp. 181–186. IEEE (2020)
23. Vaswani, A., et al.: Attention is all you need. In: Advances in Neural Information Processing Systems, vol. 30 (2017)
24. Wu, J.-W., Yin, F., Zhang, Y.-M., Zhang, X.-Y., Liu, C.-L.: Image-to-markup generation via paired adversarial learning. In: Berlingerio, M., Bonchi, F., Gärtner, T., Hurley, N., Ifrim, G. (eds.) ECML PKDD 2018. LNCS (LNAI), vol. 11051, pp. 18–34. Springer, Cham (2019). https://doi.org/10.1007/978-3-030-10925-7_2
25. Bian, X., Qin, B., Xin, X., Li, J., Su, X., Wang, Y.: Handwritten mathematical expression recognition via attention aggregation based bi-directional mutual learning. In: Proceedings of the AAAI Conference on Artificial Intelligence, vol. 36, pp. 113–121 (2022)
26. Xu, K., et al.: Show, attend and tell: neural image caption generation with visual attention. In: International Conference on Machine Learning, pp. 2048–2057. PMLR (2015)
27. Zhang, J., Du, J., Dai, L.: Multi-scale attention with dense encoder for handwritten mathematical expression recognition. In: 2018 24th International Conference on Pattern Recognition (ICPR), pp. 2245–2250. IEEE (2018)
28. Zhang, J., Du, J., Yang, Y., Song, Y.Z., Wei, S., Dai, L.: A tree-structured decoder for image-to-markup generation. In: International Conference on Machine Learning, pp. 11076–11085. PMLR (2020)
29. Zhang, J., et al.: Watch, attend and parse: an end-to-end neural network based approach to handwritten mathematical expression recognition. Pattern Recogn. **71**, 196–206 (2017)

30. Zhang, Y., Xiang, T., Hospedales, T.M., Lu, H.: Deep mutual learning. In: Proceedings of the IEEE Conference on Computer Vision and Pattern Recognition, pp. 4320–4328 (2018)
31. Zhao, W., Gao, L., Yan, Z., Peng, S., Du, L., Zhang, Z.: Handwritten mathematical expression recognition with bidirectionally trained transformer. In: Lladós, J., Lopresti, D., Uchida, S. (eds.) ICDAR 2021. LNCS, vol. 12822, pp. 570–584. Springer, Cham (2021). https://doi.org/10.1007/978-3-030-86331-9_37

Semi- and Self-supervised Learning for Scene Text Recognition with Fewer Labels

Cheng Sun, Juntao Cheng, and Cheng Du[✉]

Kingsoft Office AI R&D Department, ZhuHai, GuangDong, China
{suncheng1,chengjuntao1,ducheng}@wps.cn

Abstract. The majority of existing scene recognition methods are trained on synthetic datasets, following which the performance is evaluated on real-world datasets. Real datasets are not used to train scene text recognition models owing to the difficulty and cost of obtaining labels compare to synthetic datasets. With the development of self-supervised learning, many novel methods apply Siamese neural networks and contrastive learning on unlabeled data for pretraining, and subsequently use the trained encoder for downstream tasks. However, a single self-supervised model may not be able to solve all downstream tasks. Therefore, we propose a self-supervised algorithm including data augmentation, loss functions, and an improved semi-supervised learning method to solve the specific downstream field of scene text recognition. We improved the scene text recognition method by using unlabeled data in semi- and self-supervised methods.

Keywords: Self-supervised learning · Constrastive learning · Semi-supervised learning

1 Introduction

A consensus exists in scene text recognition that it is difficult to obtain sufficient real-world data owing to the cost and difficulty of labeling the data. Therefore, the majority of scene text recognition methods are trained on synthetic datasets, and the labeled real-world samples are used as test sets for the model evaluation. This consensus has led to the belief that models that are trained on real-world datasets are not as effective as those that are trained on synthetic datasets. Baek et al. [3] demonstrated that the TRBA [2] model, which uses the self-supervised RotNet [11] algorithm and semi-supervised pseudo-labeling [17] algorithm on a real-world dataset, is more effective than many state-of-the-art scene text recognition models on synthetic datasets. CRNN [23], which is trained on a small number of real datasets using RotNet and pseudo-labels, has also been demonstrated to outperform original models on synthetic datasets.

The process of contrastive learning involves first performing data augmentation on each sample to obtain different views, and then mapping these views to a

S. Yu et al. (Eds.): PRCV 2022, LNCS 13536, pp. 295–307, 2022.
https://doi.org/10.1007/978-3-031-18913-5_23

high-dimensional space. The distance between positive samples is small, whereas the distance between positive and negative samples is large, as illustrated in Fig. 1 (left). Based on this perspective, a series of contrastive learning models have been proposed in recent years, including MoCo [13], SimCLR [5], MoCo v2 [6], BYOL [12], and SimSiam [7]. Dangovski et al. [10] suggested that the use of variable data augmentation to enable the model to predict the same category would be highly ineffective, emphasizing that different data augmentation methods for different downstream tasks may lead to varying results, as indicated in Fig. 1 (middle). Moreover, it was proposed that model should learn the differences in several data augmentation methods to aid in contrastive learning. Peng et al. [22] proposed a novel plug-and-play data augmentation method known as ContrastiveCrop to improve the performance of the contrastive learning network model on the classification network. This method is depicted in Fig. 1 (right).

In this study, we designed a self-supervised model for the specific downstream task of scene text recognition, which includes data augmentation, loss functions, and an improved semi-supervised learning method. The superiority of the model was demonstrated using both synthetic and real datasets. The main contributions of our work can be summarized as follows: 1) Each self-supervised method was pretrained on 4.2M unlabeled data, following which the pretrained encoder was used on synthetic and real datasets to demonstrate the superiority of our self-supervised method. 2) The use of a small amount of real-world data and our pretrained self-supervised method could achieve the same effect as that of a large number of synthetic datasets. Moreover, the ablation experiment revealed that our self-supervised model could significantly improve the accuracy. 3) We improved the semi-supervised pseudo-labeling algorithm to make full use of the 4.2M unlabeled data. The experiment demonstrated that the improved pseudo-labeling algorithm could improve the performance.

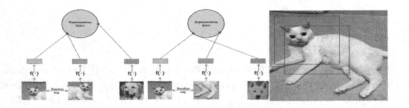

Fig. 1. Use of contrastive learning in image classification tasks.

2   Background and Related Work

2.1   Scene Text Recognition

Two of the most extensive scene text recognition infrastructures, namely CRNN and TRBA, were used in our experiment. As CRNN can achieve fast inference with a simple structure, it is used extensively in the industry. Owing to the attention mechanism and TPS, TRBA is slower but more accurate. The basic processes of the two models, which can be divided into transformation, feature extraction, sequencing, and prediction. We selected these two representative models to verify the proposed contrastive learning model for scene text recognition.

2.2 Datasets

The real-world datasets used in our experiment included 4.2M unlabeled and 276K labeled data. The sources of these datasets and the methods for their collection are described in Table 1.

Street View Text(SVT) [29] contains many low-quality images that were collected from Google Street View.

IIIT5K-Words(IIIT) [18] contains images that were collected from Google Images, including items such as keyword advertisements, house numbers, and movie posters. Most images are horizontally regular.

ICDAR2013(IC13) [16] is a competition dataset that was released by the ICDAR organization in 2013, which is mainly composed of natural scene images.

ICDAR2015(IC15) [15] is a competition dataset that was released by ICDAR in 2015. The dataset was collected by staff wearing Google Glasses. Therefore, many images contain perspective texts.

COCO-Text(COCO) [28] is a dataset that is annotated by Microsoft organizations. As this dataset is often used as an object detection dataset, the texts therein are mostly occlusion, perspective transformation, and illegible images.

RCTW [25] is a competition dataset that was released by the ICDAR organization in 2017. The main scene of this dataset is a street view.

Uber-Text(Uber) [35] consists of street images that were collected from onboard sensors, mainly including house numbers and several street view images.

ArT [8] is a competition dataset that was released by ICDAR in 2019, and it includes the TotalText and CTW1500 datasets. As this dataset was collected to solve the arbitrary shape text problem, the images include substantial perspective transformations and rotations.

LSVT [27] is a competition dataset that was released by ICDAR in 2019. Most of the datasets are street view images.

MLT19 [20] is a competition dataset that was released by ICDAR in 2019. The dataset contains pictures of natural scenes in multiple languages.

ReCTS [34] is a competition dataset that was released by ICDAR in 2019. The images are natural scenes that were captured by phone cameras under uncontrolled conditions. The text mainly consists of irregular images and special fonts.

In addition to the above labeled real datasets, unlabeled data were collected for the semi- and self-supervised learning. The unsupervised datasets mainly included the following:

BOOK32 [14], which was collected from Amazon Books, contains 208K books.

Text-VQA [26] was released by OpenImageV3 based on visual question answering. Each question can be asked once or twice and provides 10 answers, the average length of questions is seven words, and the average length of answers is two words. Most of the images are advertisements in the street view.

ST-VQA [4] contains the COCO-Text, Visual Genome, VizWiz, ICDAR13, ICDAR15, ImageNet and IIIT-STR datasets. As some of these datasets are used as training and validation datasets, such as ICDAR13, ICDAR15, and COCO-Text, these were excluded.

2.3 Self-supervised Learning

Self-supervised learning involves the design a pretext task to learn a representation from unlabeled data, following which the pretrained encoder is used to solve downstream tasks. Most self-supervised learning methods use basic classification for their pretext task, such as RotNet, MoCo, SimSiam, and SimCLR.

RotNet: The data are randomly augmented by a rotation angle of [0, 90, 180, 270] before being input into the network. Subsequently, the encoder extracts features and uses a linear layer to predict the rotation angle. A pretrained encoder that is trained in this manner can fully understand the semantics in the image.

SimSiam: SimSiam effectively avoids the use of a large batch size and negative samples by using the cosine similarity loss with the structural design of the Siamese neural network. SimSiam has demonstrated that momentum encoders can be disabled with a stop gradient of one branch of the Siamese neural network.

Table 1. Number of training sets in public real datasets. The term processed means that duplicates between the datasets were excluded and only English words were collected.

Real labeled dataset	Venue	Year	Processed
SVT	ICCV	2011	231
IIIT	BMVC	2012	1794
IC13	ICDAR	2013	763
IC15	ICDAR	2015	3710
COCO	arXiv	2016	39K
RCTW	ICDAR	2017	8186
Uber	CVPRW	2017	92K
ArT	ICDAR	2019	29K
LSVT	ICDAR	2019	34K
MLT19	ICDAR	2019	46K
ReCTS	ICDAR	2019	23K
Total	–	–	276K
Real unlabeled dataset			
Book32	arXiv	2016	3.7M
Text-VQA	CVPR	2019	463
ST-VQA	ICCV	2019	69K
Total	–	–	4.2M

3   Method

As existing self-supervised methods aim to solve the classification problem, the augmentations used may not aid in downstream tasks, such as scene text recognition. The views may not yield a positive pair when random cropping is performed on the input image. Thus, we propose the adaptation of the augmentation to the specific scene text recognition. Because scene text contains different fonts and sizes, we also consider that the encoder should classify the text angle. For this reason, we add a branch to predict the angle of the input image. Finally, we use a combination of three loss function to aid the encoder in learning more robust representation.

3.1   Architecture

Our self-supervised model structure is designed as illustrated in Fig. 2. First, two different data augmentation methods are first applied to the input data, following which the encoder encodes two different views. Subsequently, average pooling is applied to obtain the width information. The projector (a three-layer multilayer perceptron) is used for decoding to obtain p1 and p2; then, the predictor is used to decode p1 and p2 to obtain z1 and z2. Another branch may use a single linear layer to predict the rotation angle of the input data. Finally, (p1, z2), (p2, z1), and r1 are obtained to calculate the loss. It should be noted that a certain branch of the Siamese neural network will not perform gradient backhaul to prevent the collapse of the model. The remaining important components of the model are introduced in the following.

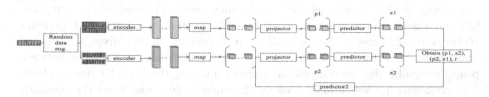

Fig. 2. Proposed self-supervised model.

3.2   Data Augmentation

Inspire by [10], We only use four data augmentation types for the text recognition, namely Blur, Camera, Noise, and Warp [1]. Each data augmentation type includes several specific data augmentation methods. We use the strategy of RandAugment [9]. If input image adopt one specific method, it may feed into next type of data augmentation. Figure 3 depicts the possible results following data augmentation of the input data.

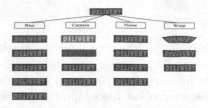

Fig. 3. The images that may be generated by each of the four data augmentation methods that may exist in an image.

3.3   Loss Function

Traditional contrastive learning methods have mainly used the InfoNCE [21] loss as their loss function. For example, in image classification tasks, the views that are generated by different data augmentations of an image are regarded as positive samples, whereas the data of other images are considered as negative samples. The InfoNCE loss is calculated as follows:

$$L_q = -log \frac{exp^{\frac{(q \cdot k_+)}{\tau}}}{\sum_{i=1}^{K} exp^{\frac{q \cdot k_i}{\tau}}} \tag{1}$$

where q is the tensor that is encoded by the encoder, k_+ denotes the positive samples, K is the negative sample in the batch data or memory bank, and τ is the temperature hyper parameter.

Owing to the special considerations of text images, it is difficult to use the InfoNCE loss to distinguish different data augmentations and the same words with different backgrounds. Therefore, the cosine similarity, cross-entropy, and KL divergence loss functions are used in such cases. The cosine similarity loss function calculates the vector space distance between the projector and predictor vector to obtain tensors that are as similar as possible. In KL divergence, p and z are brought closer at the same time, and the distribution distance between p and z should also become closer, thereby making the encoder more robust. The cross-entropy loss function allows the encoder to understand the semantic information of the input image fully and to calculate the different angles of each image. The form of the final loss function is as follows:

$$L = L_{Similarity} + \lambda_1 \cdot L_{KL} + \lambda_2 \cdot L_{Crossentropy} \tag{2}$$

$$L_{Similarity} = \frac{1}{2} \cdot D(p1, z2) + \frac{1}{2} \cdot D(p2, z1) \tag{3}$$

$$L_{KL} = -\frac{1}{N} \cdot \sum_{i=1}^{N} (\frac{p(z)}{\tau}) \cdot log(\frac{p(z)}{p(p)}) \tag{4}$$

$$L_{Crossentropy} = -\frac{1}{N} \cdot \sum_{i=1}^{N} \sum_{c=1}^{M} (y_{ic} \cdot log(p_{ic})) \tag{5}$$

where λ_1 and λ_2 are the hyperparameters of the KL divergence and cross-entropy loss functions during training, D indicates the calculation of the cosine similarity of two tensors, τ is the temperature hyperparameter, and M denotes the four types of text rotation, namely 0, 90, 180, and 270 °C. During the training of our model, λ_1 and λ_2 are initially set to 1 for the cross-entropy loss and KL divergence. After 10 epochs, set $\lambda_1 = 0.5$ and $\lambda_2 = 0.1$.

3.4 Pseudo-labeling

In our work, we referenced the ST++ algorithm [31] and implemented several improvements. The workflow of the algorithm is as follows: 1) The model with improved performance is saved on the validation set. 2) The last k models are used to perform inference on the 4.2M dataset U, and the data for which most of the model inference results are the same are retained as dataset U1. 3) Subsequently, the labeled dataset L, inferred ground-truth labels U1, and remaining unlabeled dataset U2 are used for joint training. As probability values can be obtained following the CTC and attention decoding, we apply a threshold 0.8 of to filter low-confidence data. The final combination of training dataset is guaranteed to be very clean. The improved pseudo-labeling algorithm is depicted in Fig. 4.

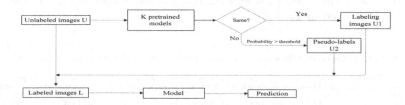

Fig. 4. Improved pseudo-labeling algorithm.

4   Experiments

To verify the effectiveness of our data augmentation, we demonstrated ablation experiments of different type of the data augmentation in Table 2 and Table 3. It can be observed that the proposed data augmentation for scene text recognition effectively improved the performance of the recognition model. For a fair comparison, in the following experiments, the self-supervised methods employed the proposed data augmentation approach to provide a thorough verification of the effectiveness of the proposed model.

4.1   Performance on Real Scene Datasets

We first used the self-supervised methods for pretraining on the 4.2M unlabeled dataset U, subsequently loaded the pretrained encoder weights for fine-tuning

Table 2. The ablation experiment of our data augmentation.

Method	Pretraining data	Training data	Blur	Color	Noise	Warp	Accuracy
CRNN	–	MJ+ST					74.45%
CRNN_ours	U	MJ+ST	✓				74.96%
CRNN_ours	U	MJ+ST		✓			75.22%
CRNN_ours	U	MJ+ST			✓		75.13%
CRNN_ours	U	MJ+ST				✓	74.87%
CRNN_ours	U	MJ+ST	✓	✓	✓	✓	**75.50%**
TRBA	–	MJ+ST					83.77%
TRBA_ours	U	MJ+ST	✓				83.84%
TRBA_ours	U	MJ+ST		✓			83.86%
TRBA_ours	U	MJ+ST			✓		83.89%
TRBA_ours	U	MJ+ST				✓	83.79%
TRBA_ours	U	MJ+ST	✓	✓	✓	✓	**83.93%**

on the 276K real data, and used a model that was trained from scratch for a fair comparison test. The obtained results are presented in Table 4.

We made full use of the unlabeled data to verify the effectiveness of the proposed improved pseudo-labeling algorithm. We conducted tests on CRNN and TRBA using the traditional and improved pseudo-labeling algorithms. The results are presented in Table 5.

Table 3. Performance of self-supervised methods with different data augmentations.

Self supervised method	Data augmentation	Method	Pretraining data	Training data	Total
MoCoV2	Origional paper	CRNN	U	MJ+ST	74.15%
MoCoV2	Our work	CRNN	U	MJ+ST	74.56%
SimSiam	Origional paper	CRNN	U	MJ+ST	74.27%
SimSiam	Our work	CRNN	U	MJ+ST	**74.65%**
MoCoV2	Origional paper	TRBA	U	MJ+ST	82.67%
MoCoV2	Our work	TRBA	U	MJ+ST	83.01%
SimSiam	Origional paper	TRBA	U	MJ+ST	83.17%
SimSiam	Our work	TRBA	U	MJ+ST	**83.75%**

4.2   Performance on Synthetic Datasets

We do the ablation experiment on synthetic dataset, the results are presented in Table 6. We also attempted to use a small amount of labeled data to achieve the same effect on a synthetic dataset to explore the advantages of using a self-supervised algorithm further. The results are displayed in Table 7.

Moreover, we evaluated the accuracy of the trained model on the test set with different numbers of steps, as illustrated in Fig. 5.

Table 4. Comparison of self-supervised models on real datasets. AUG means that the models used data augmentation operations. The data augmentation operations that were used by CRNN were rotation and cropping, whereas those that were used by TRBA were random filtering and cropping.

Method	Pretraining data	Training data	IIIT5 3000	SVT 647	IC13 1015	IC5 2077	SVTP 645	CUTE 288	Total
CRNN	–	Real-L (276K)	82.03%	79.13%	88.77%	59.41%	65.43%	63.19%	75.26%
+MoCoV2	U (4.2M)	Real-L (276K)	82.10%	78.20%	88.11%	60.10%	65.50%	64.66%	77.01%
+RotNet	U (4.2M)	Real-L (276K)	82.53%	77.74%	87.68%	60.42%	65.27%	65.50%	77.07%
+SimSiam	U (4.2M)	Real-L (276K)	81.67%	80.53%	88.47%	60.33%	64.50%	**65.62%**	77.45%
+ours	U (4.2M)	Real-L (276K)	**82.70%**	**80.83%**	**89.26%**	**61.24%**	**66.82%**	63.89%	**78.66%**
CRNN-AUG	–	Real-L (276K)	87.60%	81.92%	88.28%	69.48%	69.46%	74.31%	80.28%
+MoCoV2	U (4.2M)	Real-L (276K)	88.40%	80.48%	88.32%	70.84%	70.69%	77.78%	81.08%
+RotNet	U (4.2M)	Real-L (276K)	88.00%	82.53%	89.16%	70.82%	**71.47%**	81.60%	81.41%
+SimSiam	U (4.2M)	Real-L (276K)	88.47%	80.53%	88.18%	70.63%	71.01%	79.17%	81.11%
+ours	U (4.2M)	Real-L (276K)	**88.67%**	**83.93%**	**90.44%**	70.82%	71.32%	**82.64%**	81.99%
TRBA	–	Real-L (276K)	88.83%	87.64%	93.10%	72.32%	81.24%	**77.78%**	86.18%
+MoCoV2	U (4.2M)	Real-L (276K)	88.28%	87.22%	93.15%	71.57%	78.43%	75.68%	85.78%
+RotNet	U (4.2M)	Real-L (276K)	88.43%	87.94%	93.30%	71.69%	78.60%	76.39%	86.25%
+SimSiam	U (4.2M)	Real-L (276K)	88.87%	**88.72%**	**93.40%**	71.79%	**81.24%**	77.43%	86.31%
+ours	U (4.2M)	Real-L (276K)	**89.23%**	88.41%	**93.40%**	**72.32%**	80.62%	76.39%	**86.99%**
TRBA-AUG	–	Real-L (276K)	93.33%	90.42%	92.81%	79.01%	80.62%	85.42%	87.77%
+MoCoV2	U (4.2M)	Real-L (276K)	92.51%	90.67%	93.01%	77.38%	80.71%	82.58%	86.96%
+RotNet	U (4.2M)	Real-L (276K)	93.13%	89.95%	92.61%	**79.06%**	**82.02%**	88.19%	87.86%
+SimSiam	U (4.2M)	Real-L (276K)	92.73%	**90.73%**	93.10%	77.37%	80.62%	84.72%	87.13%
+ours	U (4.2M)	Real-L (276K)	**93.97%**	90.57%	**94.19%**	78.14%	81.09%	**88.89%**	**88.15%**

Table 5. Performance of different models using pseudo-labels.

	CRNN	CRNN_AUG	TRBA	TRBA_AUG
Train from scratch	75.26%	80.28%	86.18%	87.77%
Traditional PL	78.04%	83.12%	87.96%	89.17%
Improved PL	**78.35%**	**83.30%**	**88.3%**	**89.8%**

Table 6. Performance of different self-supervised models on synthetic datasets.

Method	Pretraining data	Training data	IIIT5 3000	SVT 647	IC13 1015	IC5 2077	SVTP 645	CUTE 288	Total
CRNN	–	MJ+ST (10M)	82.03%	79.13%	88.77%	59.41%	65.43%	63.19%	74.45%
+MoCoV2	U (4.2M)	MJ+ST (10M)	82.10%	78.20%	88.11%	60.10%	65.50%	64.66%	74.56%
+RotNet	U (4.2M)	MJ+ST (10M)	82.53%	77.74%	87.68%	60.42%	65.27%	65.50%	74.62%
+SimSiam	U (4.2M)	MJ+ST (10M)	81.67%	80.53%	88.47%	60.33%	64.50%	**65.62%**	74.65%
+ours	U (4.2M)	MJ+ST (10M)	**82.70%**	**80.83%**	**89.26%**	**61.24%**	**66.82%**	63.89%	**75.50%**
TRBA	–	MJ+ST (10M)	88.83%	87.64%	93.10%	**72.32%**	**81.24%**	**77.78%**	83.77%
+MoCoV2	U (4.2M)	MJ+ST (10M)	88.28%	87.22%	93.15%	71.57%	78.43%	75.68%	83.01%
+RotNet	U (4.2M)	MJ+ST (10M)	88.43%	87.94%	93.30%	71.69%	78.60%	76.39%	83.22%
+SimSiam	U (4.2M)	MJ+ST (10M)	**88.87%**	**88.72%**	**93.40%**	71.79%	**81.24%**	77.43%	83.75%
+ours	U (4.2M)	MJ+ST (10M)	89.23%	88.41%	**93.40%**	72.32%	80.62%	76.39%	**83.93%**

4.3   Comparison with State-of-the-Art Models

We used the pretrained encoder and fine-tuned on the 276K labeled data. Using the improved semi-supervised learning, we obtained the labeled data L, added data U1, and pseudo-labeled data U2 for joint training. The comparison results are presented in Table 8. It was revealed that the use of fewer labeled and numerous unlabeled data yielded excellent results compared to the state-of-the-art methods.

Table 7. Comparison of use of synthetic datasets and small amount of real data plus self-supervised models.

Method	Pretrianing data	Training data	Accuracy
CRNN	–	MJ+ST (10M)	74.45%
CRNN	–	Real-L (81K)	69.66%
CRNN_SSL	U (4.2M)	Real-L (81K)	**75.17%**
TRBA	–	MJ+ST (10M)	83.77%
TRBA	–	Real-L (200K)	82.69%
TRBA_SSL	U (4.2M)	Real-L (200K)	**83.89%**

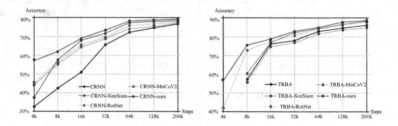

Fig. 5. Accuracy of model with different numbers of steps.

Table 8. Use of 4.2M unlabeled data plus 276K labeled data for comparison with other excellent scene recognition models.

Method	Year	Training data	IIIT5 3000	SVT 647	IC13 1015	IC5 2077	SVTP 645	CUTE 288	Total
Aster [24]	2018	MJ+ST	93.4%	89.5%	91.8%	76.1%	78.5%	79.5%	86.4%
ESIR [32]	2019	MJ+ST	93.3%	90.2%	91.3%	76.9%	79.6%	83.3%	86.8%
DAN [30]	2020	MJ+ST	94.3%	89.2%	93.9%	74.5%	80.0%	84.4%	86.9%
PlugNet [19]	2020	MJ+ST	94.4%	**92.3%**	**95.0%**	**82.2%**	**84.3%**	85.0%	89.8%
GA-SPIN [33]	2021	MJ+ST	95.2%	91.5%	94.8%	79.5%	83.2%	87.5%	89.2%
CRNN-PL-SSL	2022	L+U	90.5%	84.4%	91.0%	72.7%	73.3%	83.7%	83.3%
TRBA-PL-SSL	2022	L+U	**95.3%**	92.1%	94.7%	81.2%	83.0%	**89.2%**	**90.0%**

5 Conclusion

We have introduced an improved self-supervised model based on scene text recognition. The innovations include the model design, data augmentation method, and improvements to the joint loss function and semi-supervised pseudo-labeling algorithm. The superiority of our proposed self-supervised model was demonstrated on both real and synthetic datasets. To explore the effectiveness of the model fully, we used a small amount of real scene datasets and self-supervised models to provide excellent results on synthetic datasets, and the convergence speed of the model was improved significantly.

Acknowledgement. We thank many colleagues at Kingsoft Office AI R&D Department for their help, in particular, Dong Yao, Cheng Du, Ronghua Chen, Juntao Cheng, Junyu Huang, Yushun Zhou for useful discussion and the help on GPU resources.

References

1. Atienza, R.: Data augmentation for scene text recognition. In: Proceedings of the IEEE/CVF International Conference on Computer Vision, pp. 1561–1570 (2021)
2. Baek, J., et al.: What is wrong with scene text recognition model comparisons? dataset and model analysis. In: Proceedings of the IEEE/CVF International Conference on Computer Vision, pp. 4715–4723 (2019)
3. Baek, J., Matsui, Y., Aizawa, K.: What if we only use real datasets for scene text recognition? toward scene text recognition with fewer labels. In: Proceedings of the IEEE/CVF Conference on Computer Vision and Pattern Recognition, pp. 3113–3122 (2021)
4. Biten, A.F., et al.: Scene text visual question answering. In: Proceedings of the IEEE/CVF International Conference on Computer Vision, pp. 4291–4301 (2019)
5. Chen, T., Kornblith, S., Norouzi, M., Hinton, G.: A simple framework for contrastive learning of visual representations. In: International Conference on Machine Learning, pp. 1597–1607. PMLR (2020)
6. Chen, X., Fan, H., Girshick, R., He, K.: Improved baselines with momentum contrastive learning. arXiv preprint arXiv:2003.04297 (2020)
7. Chen, X., He, K.: Exploring simple Siamese representation learning. In: Proceedings of the IEEE/CVF Conference on Computer Vision and Pattern Recognition, pp. 15750–15758 (2021)
8. Chng, C.K., et al.: ICDAR 2019 robust reading challenge on arbitrary-shaped text-rrc-art. In: 2019 International Conference on Document Analysis and Recognition (ICDAR), pp. 1571–1576. IEEE (2019)
9. Cubuk, E.D., Zoph, B., Shlens, J., Le, Q.V.: Randaugment: practical automated data augmentation with a reduced search space. In: Proceedings of the IEEE/CVF Conference on Computer Vision and Pattern Recognition Workshops, pp. 702–703 (2020)
10. Dangovski, R., et al.: Equivariant contrastive learning. arXiv preprint arXiv:2111.00899 (2021)
11. Gidaris, S., Singh, P., Komodakis, N.: Unsupervised representation learning by predicting image rotations. arXiv preprint arXiv:1803.07728 (2018)
12. Grill, J.B.: Bootstrap your own latent-a new approach to self-supervised learning. Adv. Neural Inf. Process. Syst. **33**, 21271–21284 (2020)

13. He, K., Fan, H., Wu, Y., Xie, S., Girshick, R.: Momentum contrast for unsupervised visual representation learning. In: Proceedings of the IEEE/CVF Conference on Computer Vision and Pattern Recognition, pp. 9729–9738 (2020)
14. Iwana, B.K., Rizvi, S.T.R., Ahmed, S., Dengel, A., Uchida, S.: Judging a book by its cover. arXiv preprint arXiv:1610.09204 (2016)
15. Karatzas, D., et al.: ICDAR 2015 competition on robust reading. In: 2015 13th International Conference on Document Analysis and Recognition (ICDAR), pp. 1156–1160. IEEE (2015)
16. Karatzas, D., et al.: ICDAR 2013 robust reading competition. In: 2013 12th International Conference on Document Analysis and Recognition, pp. 1484–1493. IEEE (2013)
17. Lee, D.H., et al.: Pseudo-label: the simple and efficient semi-supervised learning method for deep neural networks. In: Workshop on Challenges in Representation Learning, ICML, vol. 3, p. 896 (2013)
18. Mishra, A., Alahari, K., Jawahar, C.: Scene text recognition using higher order language priors. In: BMVC-British Machine Vision Conference. BMVA (2012)
19. Mou, Y., et al.: PlugNet: degradation aware scene text recognition supervised by a pluggable super-resolution unit. In: Vedaldi, A., Bischof, H., Brox, T., Frahm, J.-M. (eds.) ECCV 2020. LNCS, vol. 12360, pp. 158–174. Springer, Cham (2020). https://doi.org/10.1007/978-3-030-58555-6_10
20. Nayef, N., et al.: ICDAR 2019 robust reading challenge on multi-lingual scene text detection and recognition-RRC-MLT-2019. In: 2019 International Conference on Document Analysis and Recognition (ICDAR), pp. 1582–1587. IEEE (2019)
21. Van den Oord, A., Li, Y., Vinyals, O.: Representation learning with contrastive predictive coding. arXiv e-prints pp. arXiv-1807 (2018)
22. Peng, X., Wang, K., Zhu, Z., You, Y.: Crafting better contrastive views for Siamese representation learning. arXiv preprint arXiv:2202.03278 (2022)
23. Shi, B., Bai, X., Yao, C.: An end-to-end trainable neural network for image-based sequence recognition and its application to scene text recognition. IEEE Trans. Pattern Anal. Mach. Intell. 39(11), 2298–2304 (2016)
24. Shi, B., Yang, M., Wang, X., Lyu, P., Yao, C., Bai, X.: Aster: an attentional scene text recognizer with flexible rectification. IEEE Trans. Pattern Anal. Mach. Intell. 41(9), 2035–2048 (2018)
25. Shi, B., et al.: ICDAR 2017 competition on reading Chinese text in the wild (rctw-17). In: 2017 14th IAPR International Conference on Document Analysis and Recognition (ICDAR), vol. 1, pp. 1429–1434. IEEE (2017)
26. Singh, A., et al.: Towards VQA models that can read. In: Proceedings of the IEEE/CVF Conference on Computer Vision and Pattern Recognition, pp. 8317–8326 (2019)
27. Sun, Y., et al.: ICDAR 2019 competition on large-scale street view text with partial labeling-rrc-lsvt. In: 2019 International Conference on Document Analysis and Recognition (ICDAR), pp. 1557–1562. IEEE (2019)
28. Veit, A., Matera, T., Neumann, L., Matas, J., Belongie, S.: Coco-text: dataset and benchmark for text detection and recognition in natural images. arXiv preprint arXiv:1601.07140 (2016)
29. Wang, K., Babenko, B., Belongie, S.: End-to-end scene text recognition. In: 2011 International Conference on Computer Vision, pp. 1457–1464. IEEE (2011)
30. Wang, T., et al.: Decoupled attention network for text recognition. In: Proceedings of the AAAI Conference on Artificial Intelligence, vol. 34, pp. 12216–12224 (2020)

31. Yang, L., Zhuo, W., Qi, L., Shi, Y., Gao, Y.: St++: make self-training work better for semi-supervised semantic segmentation. arXiv preprint arXiv:2106.05095 (2021)
32. Zhan, F., Lu, S.: Esir: end-to-end scene text recognition via iterative image rectification. In: Proceedings of the IEEE/CVF Conference on Computer Vision and Pattern Recognition, pp. 2059–2068 (2019)
33. Zhang, C., et al.: Spin: structure-preserving inner offset network for scene text recognition. arXiv preprint arXiv:2005.13117 (2020)
34. Zhang, R., et al.: ICDAR 2019 robust reading challenge on reading Chinese text on signboard. In: 2019 International Conference on Document Analysis and Recognition (ICDAR), pp. 1577–1581. IEEE (2019)
35. Zhang, Y., Gueguen, L., Zharkov, I., Zhang, P., Seifert, K., Kadlec, B.: Uber-text: a large-scale dataset for optical character recognition from street-level imagery. In: SUNw: Scene Understanding Workshop-CVPR, vol. 2017, p. 5 (2017)

TMCR: A Twin Matching Networks for Chinese Scene Text Retrieval

Zhiheng Peng[1], Ming Shao[2], and Siyu Xia[1(✉)]

[1] School of Automation, Southeast University, Nanjing, China
xia081@gmail.com
[2] University of Massachusetts Dartmouth, Dartmouth, USA

Abstract. In this paper, we focus on a critical task of retrieving common style in Chinese scene text: given an image of style text, the system returns all the images matching the queried text image. To that, a novel twin Transformer based matching network is proposed, which is featured by the integration of anchor-free detection, text recognition, and similarity matching networks. On the fly, our model retrieves the similarity of text features in the text area and evaluates it through recognition. Our experiments demonstrate that the proposed model outperforms the state-of-the-art in terms of both processing speed and accuracy. Additional experiments show that our model generalizes well on various benchmarks, including a self-constructed Chinese query data set with complex Chinese scenes in the real world.

Keywords: Text retrieval · Chinese scene text · Text detection · Transformer

1 Introduction

Recently, scene text recognition and matching have been widely explored and applied to scenarios such as information security protection, intelligent real-time traffic system [13,24], geographic location, and visual search based on remote sensing technology [3]. It should be noted that most existing works focus on scene text detection in English scenes. However, models for Chinese scenes, e.g., [12, 23] are still under exploration. Dedicated feature extraction for Chinese scenes along with a tailored image-image matching pipeline is demanded. Currently, diverse Chinese fonts and styles usually fail the existing works and lead to inferior performance.

Multi-modal approaches have been popular in Chinese retrieval tasks. However, the current mainstream methods for retrieval of the text content of a specific style, or fuzzy retrieval of partial matching of the retrieved text, often do not yield acceptable results. One way to improve is to leverage the image-image matching results between the query and detected text region to reduce the loss

---

Z. Peng—The first author is a student.

© The Author(s), under exclusive license to Springer Nature Switzerland AG 2022
S. Yu et al. (Eds.): PRCV 2022, LNCS 13536, pp. 308–319, 2022.
https://doi.org/10.1007/978-3-031-18913-5_24

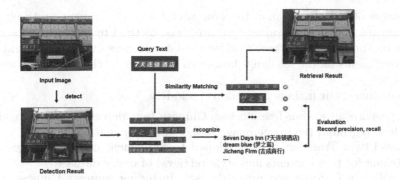

Fig. 1. Example of scene text retrieval process. The upper left is an image to be retrieved, and the upper right is the retrieval result.

due to poor text features and recognition. Integrating image-image matching to the conventional text recognition-based pipeline becomes the key and either of them proved insufficient in Chinese scene text recognition.

Image-image matching has been extensively discussed in various applications, e.g., word semantic similarity analysis, question and answer matching, signature/face verification, handwriting recognition, and one of the most popular approaches is the siamese network. This enables text image matching and could constitute a text similarity network if an appropriate backbone is selected. While convolutional neural networks have been matured in general image recognition, more and more works have been taking Transformer and its variants to replace the spatial convolution layer by the multi-headed self-attention (MHSA) layer [4,16,19]. In particular, stacking Transformer blocks [19] to operate on the linear projection of non-overlapping patches has achieved great success in Vision Transformer (ViT) [5]. Image-to-image matching uses images as the basic inputs while keeping the structure information of the scene text. Therefore, Transformer would be more appropriate for building the siamese network in our problem.

In recent work [20], detection plus well-established recognition module have achieved good performance. While to incorporate the idea of image-to-image matching, the training will shift to siamese network based similarity matching and the recognition module could be used for inference only during the test. The similarity matching could significantly reduced and false pairs and improve the recognition performance.

Motivated by these facts, we explore the use of semantic scenes and spatial contexts for Chinese text retrieval tasks in real and complex Chinese scenes (Fig. 1). First, due to text tilt and characteristics of scene text, an anchor-free method is used to detect the scene text in this paper. Then, the predicted text center is used to determine the text area through the threshold map, followed by the text recognition model. Second, we propose a twin Transformer model for image-image matching based on the detected text region and query text image. The Transformer has been tailored by the multi-head attention mechanism in the process of map-vector-map to allow text feature alignment and text context contents. Finally, we evaluate our proposed method by measuring the mAP metrics on the CSVTR dataset to show the effectiveness of our model and conduct experiments on the self-built dataset to further show the generalization and robustness.

In summary, our main contributions include:

– We propose an anchor-free efficient Chinese text detection and recognition models to ground the image-image based similarity matching.
– A novel twin Transformer is developed to implement effective image-image matching for text contents and style retrieval of query dataset.
– We collect a Chinese text query dataset, including complex Chinese scenes from the real world to reflect the complexity of Chinese text in applications, and verify the performance and generalization of the proposed model.

2   Related Work

At present, the comparison of text retrieval methods is mainly divided into traditional methods and deep learning methods. Traditional methods are to calculate the distance between features. PHOC was first proposed by using characters in [1]. It explores the coding structure after the connection for the prediction and judgment. Earlier text retrieval systems usually used words in the text as index words to represent the text. Wu and Tseng [22] proposed to automatically divide Chinese text into words by classifying each part of speech. Bai et al. [2] uses text and voice queries to handle Chinese text and voice document retrieval problems. They estimate statistical similarity between text/speech queries and text/spoken documents at the phonetic level using syllable-based statistics.

As for deep learning methods, Sadholt et al. [17] and Wilkinson et al. [21] respectively proposed to use neural networks to predict PHOC and DCToW from word images. Gomez et al. [6] instead of using hand-made text representation, proposed to use Levenshtein edit distance [7] between text strings and word images in deep embedding. Wang et al. [20] proposed an end-to-end scene image text retrieval task based on the mask RCNN. The image retrieval process is divided into detection, recognition, and similarity learning.

In recent years, the retrieval of the Chinese text is more oriented towards a cross-modal approach. Mohammadshahi et al. [11] proposed a new method to learn multimodal multilingual embeddings to match images and their associated captions in two languages. They jointly optimize two objective functions that embed both images and captions in the common space, while adjusting the alignment of word embedding. Li et al. [8] introduced a contrastive loss to align image and text representations before the fusion via cross-modal attention (ALBEF). Sun et al. [18] proposed an online proposal matching module incorporated in the whole model, which can spot the keyword regions by sharing parameters.

Different from existing works, for the first time, we introduce the siamese network structure into the process of text retrieval. In addition, the Transformer structure used with siamese network has been improved for multiple attention mechanisms and twinned to enhance the adaptability to text.

3   Methods

As illustrated in Fig. 2, our network consists of three components: (1) detection, (2) recognition, and (3) similarity matching. In particular, a twin Transformer, i.e., Transformer-based siamese network, is proposed and used in similarity matching.

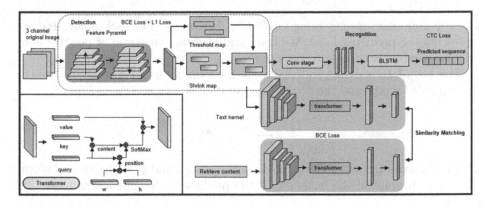

Fig. 2. Illustration of our proposed framework. Entering a scene text image first passes through the text detection process, then is sent to the recognition process and the similarity matching process respectively. The text content retrieval process is realized through the Transformer-based siamese network, and the recognition process is passed. The lower left is the twin Transformer.

3.1   Detection Module

We build our semantic scene context features by refining the context features obtained from the context segmentation decoder based on feature pyramid and multi-scale features. These features are fused by concatenating multi-scale features with context features and then sent to a convolution layer. The concatenation helps suppress saliency distractors by utilizing the scene context information similar to DBnet [9]. The binary maps trained are generated by the threshold map and the region map, and the region map is directly utilized in the model inference process for better efficiency. The threshold and binarization are calculated as:

$$P_{i,j} = \frac{1}{1 + e^{-\beta(Cls_{i,j} - Thed_{i,j})}} \tag{1}$$

where P is the binary graph after our calculation, Cls is the region map of each point after our classification, $Thed$ is the threshold map of the i, j points learned in the network, and β represents the amplification factor.

For the loss of the text detection process, our method is similar to DBnet [9], which contains three parts. The weight is used for learning the threshold map, binarization map, and classification map.

$$L_D = L_c + \gamma_1 L_b + \gamma_2 L_t, \tag{2}$$

where L_c is the loss of the probability map, L_b is the loss of the binarized map, and L_t is the loss of the threshold map. For L_c and L_b, we use the binary cross-entropy loss. For different samples, the balance problem may be different. So the hard negative mining is used.

$$L_c = L_b = \sum_{i \in \chi} (y_i log x_i + (1 - y_i) log (1 - x_i)), \tag{3}$$

where χ indicates samples using OHEM, y_i is true label of each point, and x_i represents the predicted label. We train and generate the ratio of positive and negative samples according to the ratio of 1:3.

The loss of L_t is mainly calculated by the sum of the L1 distances between the expanded image and the actual generated label.

$$L_t = \sum_{i \in \phi} |y_i^* - x_i^*| \tag{4}$$

where ϕ indicate the set of all the pixels of the image, and y_i^* is the ground truth label of each point in the image. x_i^* is the predicted label of each point in the image.

3.2   Recognition Module

As for the recognition component, the structure of CRNN [14] is used to extract features through the convolution layer. At the bottom of the CRNN, the convolution layer automatically extracts feature sequences from each input image. On top of the convolution network, a recurrent network is built to predict each frame of the feature sequence from the convolution layer. The per-frame prediction of the recurrent layer is converted into a sequence of labels using the transcription at the top of the CRNN. The RNN backbone is implemented by bidirectional LSTM to complete the serialization prediction. In brief, at the bottom of the CRNN, the convolution layer automatically extracts a feature sequence from each input image. On top of the convolution network, a recurrent network is constructed to predict each frame of the feature sequence output by the convolution layer.

For the loss of recognition component: similar to the work in [14], we use $\delta = \{I_i, l_i\}$ to represent the training dataset, where I_i is the training image and l_i is the real label sequence. The goal is to minimize the negative log-likelihood of the true conditional probability:

$$L_R = - \sum_{I_i, l_i \in \delta} log(l_i | q_i), \tag{5}$$

where q_i is the sequence produced by the recurrent and convolution layers.

3.3   Similarity Module

A twin Transformer to calculate the similarity of a text line is proposed in this section. It aims at a multi-stage process where the original text line needs to be matched with the input. Extracting the features of the text information under detection, the Transformer-based siamese network can complete the matching process. In addition, an extended Transformer with a multi-head attention mechanism achieves is proposed for the text feature extraction, with which features serialization and contextual information in the text can be extracted and represented by the weight of $\{w, h\}$. Afterward, the text content is added to the location information. Through a softmax layer, the attention activation result of the entire text after serialization is restored to the original scale. The similarity difference between the two fully connected layers is matched.

For the similarity matching process, we use the following BCE loss:

$$L_M = \sum_{i \in \varphi} (o_i log d_i + (1 - o_i) log(1 - d_i)), \tag{6}$$

where φ is the total number of samples, o_i is the category of the i-th sample, and d_i is the predicted value of the i-th sample. As used in other deep models, the BCE loss allows the network and Transformer to learn the feature differences between different text feature instances.

3.4   Loss and Training

The total loss used in our matching model can be represented by following:

$$L = L_D + L_R + L_M, \tag{7}$$

where L_D represents the loss of the detection component, L_R represents the loss in the recognition component, and L_M represents the loss in the similarity matching component. We update this losses in an iterative manner such that each component is optimized towards the query. The training procedure is detailed below:

First, the detection model leverages data enhancement and adaptive processing to improve detection accuracy, which builds better foundations for a twin Transformer based siamese matching network. Second, during the training, we jointly train the detection and recognition models, so that our recognition model can achieve accurate recognition results for our query text fields to a level that can evaluate and train our similarity matching. Third, we further train and enhance the detection model to precisely locate the query text in the target images. Finally, we combine the detection and the similarity matching and send the detected text regions to our similarity matching model to complete the training of similarity matching.

4   Experiments

First, we introduce the dataset used in the experiments and the new dataset we collected. Then, implementation details are provided. Third, we evaluate our methods and compare them with the state-of-the-art scene text retrieval/discovery methods. Finally, we provide ablation studies and validate the potential applications of our method (Fig. 3).

Fig. 3. Examples of experimental results on CSSI. The green box in the images is the output of the scene text retrieval. (Color figure online)

4.1   Dataset and Implementation Details

We use two datasets in our experiments detailed below:

CSVTR Dataset. The Chinese Street View Text Retrieval dataset is recently proposed by [20]. The dataset consists of 23 predefined Chinese query words and 1,667 Chinese scene text images collected from the Google image search engine. Most of the query terms are the names of business premises, such as Seven Days Inn, China Construction Bank, Wallace, Yunhe Soy Milk, etc.

CSSI Dataset (Self-collected). To further demonstrate the effectiveness of our method in the real world, we collect a new dataset, including images captured from the Internet, termed Chinese Scene Street Images (CSSI). Each image in the dataset is annotated with query text. The data set consists of 25 predefined Chinese query words and 7,463 Chinese scene street images. Similar and artistic style images are also included to examine the validity of the model. In order to test the generalization of our model, CSSI also contains a small amount of English text, in addition to the target Chinese text content.

A few practices have been implemented to promote the model training. In preparing the similarity features, the text patch is scaled to 105×105 to address the text features of different directions and scales. To better match the size of the detectors and input text scales, a random scaling operation on the text is performed. During training, we randomly set the slack variables $r1$ and $r2$ in the range of 0.7–1.3. For our changed scale, we have $new_scale = w/h * r1/r2$ for the aspect ratio, and then the scale of random h is 0.75–1.25 of the original scale. The w is determined by new_scale, so as to enhance the adaptability to text deformation. In our experiments, thresholds for the detector and the recognizer are both set to 0.5, which proves very effective in experiments of detection and recognition. When training the similarity model, we train the similarity model through all the targets to be retrieved in the dataset. For the irrelevant text line information that is not in the retrieval target, we do not train it as an irrelevant category, so as to enhance the model for retrieving the feature extraction process for each category. The optimizer used in our training is Adam, the learning rate is set to 0.001, the Epoch is 150, the batch size is 32, the step size is 1, and the $gamma$ of the optimizer is 0.92. For the actual training process, the weights are taken as $\gamma_1 = 1$, $\gamma_2 = 10$. We set β to 50 in the actual experiment process of detection. Experiments are carried out on a computer with a 4.20 GHz Intel I7 CPU, 16GB RAM and an NVIDIA 1080 GPU.

4.2   Comparisons with State-of-the-Art

Table 1. 23* represents 1036 generated images of 23 generated scene text data sets containing query segments. Our* represents the transformer result without adding deformed convolution.

Method	Char num.	mAP
Mafla et al. [10]	1019	4.79
Wang et al. [20]	3755	50.12
Ours	23*(1036)	52.36
Ours*	23*(1036)	53.83

Table 2. Our* represents the model without adding deformed convolution. The results of CSSI datasets are presented.

Method	Char num.	mAP
Ours	25 (3252)	45.27
Ours*	25 (3252)	50.34

We mainly compare with two methods in this section and briefly introduce them here.

- Mafra et al. [10] use a single shot CNN architecture to predict bounding boxes and build compact representations of discovered words. In this way, the nearest neighbor search of the textual representation of the query is performed on the CNN output collected from the entire image database.
- Wang et al. [20] build an end-to-end trainable network to jointly optimize procedures for scene text detection and cross-modal similarity learning. The retrieval task is achieved by performing similarity ranking on detected text instances.

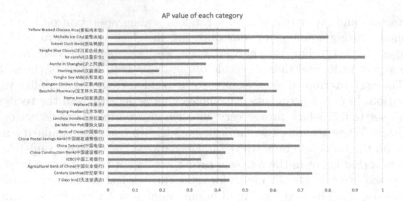

Fig. 4. Experiment on CSVTR, the AP value of each category obtained. The whole model has a certain recognition effect for different categories.

It should be noted that most competitive methods adopted the text-image matching strategy. To make it a fair comparison, a large number of characters are labeled in the competitive methods and applied in the training. This may potentially optimize the output for each query. The method proposed by Mafra et al. needs to make predictions on the character of the word in the prediction box (PHOC). There are more types of characters in the Chinese scene than the 26 characters in English. Therefore, the dimension of PHOC increases sharply with the growth of the number of character types. Wang et al. [20] uses the similarity learning for text similarity vector comparison for the retrieval task. For the similarity ranking of the characters contained in the frame selection after the extraction of the two convolution features, the influence of multiple character types cannot be avoided.

We testify different models and ours under different conditions on CSVTR dataset, and the value of mAP is reported in Table 1. It can be seen that our models outperform the state-of-the-art, especially when the deformable convolution layer is removed from the Transformer. We also show qualitative results based on the CSVTR dataset. From the figure, it can be learned that under different scenarios, the target content can be successfully retrieved. We further provide the AP values for each category achieved by our method in Fig. 4. It can be seen that while the overall performance is good, there is a large variance among different categories. We believe the reason is that the texts from different categories vary significantly, e.g., length of the word, font/color/style, as well as the diverse background. Nonetheless, in simple text-style queries, the results of our model are very appealing.

Table 3. Baseline is the model of using VGGNet [15] for feature extraction only. "DF" represents deformable convolutions, and "Trans" indicates Transformer model. FPS means that our model can predict the number of pictures by an average of 1s in the reasoning stage.

Model	Recall	Precision	F1	AP	FPS
Baseline	0.8136	0.3045	0.4431	18.38	1.37
+DF	0.85 (0.04↑)	0.7265 (0.42↑)	0.7834 (0.34↑)	57.07 (38.7↑)	0.1577
+Trans	0.85 (0.04↑)	0.6489 (0.34↑)	0.7359 (0.29↑)	58.44 (40.1↑)	1.1178
+DF+Trans	0.79 (0.02↓)	0.6423 (0.34↑)	0.7085 (0.26↑)	44.20 (25.82↑)	1.1

4.3 Ablation Study

To demonstrate the effectiveness of a few key components, we conduct the ablation study. We will mainly testify to the usage of Transformer model, deformable convolution. To make it feasible and fair, we use the SOTA CNN model VGGNet [15] as the backbone for the detected text. We also explore the usage of deformable convolution in text feature extraction. Table 3 shows the experimental results under the optimal threshold. It can be seen that adding the Transformer can greatly improve the speed while maintaining better text retrieval performance. The deformable convolutions can greatly speed up the system but may slightly sacrify the performance, compared to Transformer model.

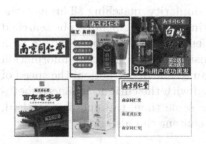

Fig. 5. The upper left is an image with query text. Green boxes in the other images are the output of scene text retrieval. (Color figure online)

Fig. 6. Some experimental results of model generalization.

4.4 Model Generalization

To demonstrate the generalization of our model, we further conduct experiments on our self-collected query dataset CSSI where both Chinese and English text-based retrieval are presented.

First, we conduct a retrieval task on the entire CSSI dataset. Note 3,252 images from 25 categories are used as training data in this experiment and

Table 2 shows our experimental results of AP with and without deformed convolutions in Transformer. In addition, we are curious about the performance of single category query with fewer training samples, which are closer to real-world scenarios. Therefore, we train and compute AP for a single category "KFC" with 67 training samples and 323 images in total. The result is surprisingly good with an AP of 78.52.

Second, it is common that different styles to be presented for the same text, and this becomes extremely challenging in Chinese. Taking the common trademark brand "Tongrentang"with various styles as an example shown in Fig. 5. The figure presents the output of the similarity module with a successful match. It should be noted that the detection and recognition outputs are however very diverse and may be confusing for the regular similarity learning model. However, our twin Transformer framework is more robust and effective in this case.

Last, we study the generalization of our model across different languages in images. We train the model on a total of 1,036 images from the CSVTR dataset that does not include any English text, and then test on a total of 974 images in Chinese and English categories (including 4 categories such as GUCCI, ROLEX, McDonald's, etc.) which are not included in the CSVTR category. As shown in Fig. 6, our model can still work well on English and new text scenes. The mAP values for these categories can reach 24.62.

5   Conclusion

In this paper, we proposed a method for text similarity retrieval, which includes the process of detection, recognition, and similarity matching. Through the traversal of the text content, the image of the input text segment can be searched out. According to the difference of text line features, it is equipped with a twin Transformer structure, comprehensively considering the location information and content information of the text. At the same time of extraction, the speed of the entire process is accelerated, and compared with the current advanced methods, good results have been obtained. At the same time, through this method, the same text content and similar text style content can also be retrieved.

References

1. Almazan, J., Gordo, A., Fornes, A., Valveny, E.: Word spotting and recognition with embedded attributes. IEEE Trans. Pattern Anal. Mach. Intell. **36**(12), 2552–2566 (2014)
2. Bai, B.R., Chen, B., Wang, H.M.: Syllable-based Chinese text/spoken document retrieval using text/speech queries. Int. J. Pattern Recogn. Artif. Intell. **14**(05), 603–616 (2000)
3. Bai, X., Yang, M., Lyu, P., Xu, Y., Luo, J.: Integrating scene text and visual appearance for fine-grained image classification. IEEE Access **6**, 66322–66335 (2017)
4. Bello, I., Zoph, B., Le, Q., Vaswani, A., Shlens, J.: Attention augmented convolutional networks. In: 2019 IEEE/CVF International Conference on Computer Vision (ICCV) (2020)

5. Dosovitskiy, A., Beyer, L., Kolesnikov, A., Weissenborn, D., Houlsby, N.: An image is worth 16×16 words: transformers for image recognition at scale (2020)
6. Gomez, L., Rusinol, M., Karatzas, D.: LSDE: levenshtein space deep embedding for query-by-string word spotting. In: 2017 14th IAPR International Conference on Document Analysis and Recognition (ICDAR) (2017)
7. Levenshtein, V.I.: Binary codes capable of correcting deletions, insertions and reversals. Dokl. Akad. Nauk SSSR **1965** (1966)
8. Li, J., Selvaraju, R.R., Gotmare, A.D., Joty, S., Xiong, C., Hoi, S.: Align before fuse: vision and language representation learning with momentum distillation (2021)
9. Liao, M., Wan, Z., Yao, C., Chen, K., Bai, X.: Real-time scene text detection with differentiable binarization (2019)
10. Mafla, A., Tito, R., Dey, S., Gómez, L., Karatzas, D.: Real-time lexicon-free scene text retrieval. Pattern Recogn. **110**(7553), 107656 (2021)
11. Mohammadshahi, A., Lebret, R., Aberer, K.: Aligning multilingual word embeddings for cross-modal retrieval task (2019)
12. Ren, X., Zhou, Y., Huang, Z., Sun, J., Yang, X., Chen, K.: A novel text structure feature extractor for Chinese scene text detection and recognition. IEEE Access **5**, 3193–3204 (2017). https://doi.org/10.1109/ACCESS.2017.2676158
13. Rong, X., Yi, C., Tian, Y.: Recognizing text-based traffic guide panels with cascaded localization network. In: Hua, G., Jégou, H. (eds.) ECCV 2016. LNCS, vol. 9913, pp. 109–121. Springer, Cham (2016). https://doi.org/10.1007/978-3-319-46604-0_8
14. Shi, B., Bai, X., Yao, C.: An end-to-end trainable neural network for image-based sequence recognition and its application to scene text recognition. IEEE Trans. Pattern Anal. Mach. Intell. **39**(11), 2298–2304 (2016)
15. Simonyan, K., Zisserman, A.: Very deep convolutional networks for large-scale image recognition. Comput. Sci. (2014)
16. Srinivas, A., Lin, T.Y., Parmar, N., Shlens, J., Vaswani, A.: Bottleneck transformers for visual recognition (2021)
17. Sudholt, S., Fink, G.A.: Phocnet: a deep convolutional neural network for word spotting in handwritten documents. IEEE (2017)
18. Sun, Y., Liu, J., Liu, W., Han, J., Ding, E., Liu, J.: Chinese street view text: large-scale Chinese text reading with partially supervised learning (2019)
19. Vaswani, A., et al.: Attention is all you need. arXiv (2017)
20. Wang, H., Bai, X., Yang, M., Zhu, S., Liu, W.: Scene text retrieval via joint text detection and similarity learning (2021)
21. Wilkinson, T., Brun, A.: Semantic and verbatim word spotting using deep neural networks. In: 2016 15th International Conference on Frontiers in Handwriting Recognition (ICFHR) (2016)
22. Wu, Z., Tseng, G.: Chinese text segmentation for text retrieval: achievements and problems. J. Am. Soc. Inf. Sci. **44**, 532–542 (1993)
23. Zheng, T., Wang, X., Yuan, X., Wang, S.: A novel method based on character segmentation for slant Chinese screen-render text detection and recognition. In: 2020 15th IEEE Conference on Industrial Electronics and Applications (ICIEA), pp. 950–954 (2020). https://doi.org/10.1109/ICIEA48937.2020.9248381
24. Zhu, Y., Liao, M., Yang, M., Liu, W.: Cascaded segmentation-detection networks for text-based traffic sign detection. IEEE Trans. Intell. Transp. Syst. **19**(1), 209–219 (2018)

Thai Scene Text Recognition with Character Combination

Chun Li[1,2], Hongjian Zhan[1,2,3], Kun Zhao[4], and Yue Lu[1,2(✉)]

[1] Shanghai Key Laboratory of Multidimensional Information Processing,
Shanghai 200241, China
{ylu,hjzhan}@cee.ecnu.edu.cn
[2] School of Communication and Electronic Engineering, East China Normal
University, Shanghai 200062, China
[3] Chongqing Key Laboratory of Precision Optics, Chongqing Institute of East China
Normal University, Chongqing 401120, China
[4] iFlytek Research, iFlytek Co., Ltd., Hefei, China

Abstract. In recent years, scene text recognition(STR) that recognizing character sequences in natural images is in great demand beyond various fields. However, most STR studies only focus on popular scripts like Chinese or English, too little attention has been paid to minority languages. In this paper, we address problems on Thai STR, and introduce a novel strategy called Thai Character Combination(TCC), which explore original characteristics of Thai text. Unlike most other scripts, characters in Thai text can be written both horizontally and vertically, which brings big challenges to current sequence-based text recognition methods. In order to reduce complexity of structure and alleviate the misalignment problem in attention-based methods, TCC intends to combine Thai characters that stack vertically to independent combined characters. Furthermore, we establish a Thai Scene Text(TST) dataset that collected from multiple scenarios to evaluate the performance of our proposed character modeling strategy. We conduct abundant experiments and analyses to compare the recognition performance of models with and without TCC. The results indicate the effectiveness of the proposed method from multiple perspectives, especially, TCC benefits a lot for long text recognition, and there is a substantial improvement in the recognition accuracy of entire string-level.

Keywords: Scene text recognition · Thai Character Combination · Thai scene text dataset

1 Introduction

In recent years, scene text recognition(STR) has attracted widespread attention in academia and industry due to the huge demand of a large number of

---

C. Li and H. Zhan—These authors contributed equally to this work.

© The Author(s), under exclusive license to Springer Nature Switzerland AG 2022
S. Yu et al. (Eds.): PRCV 2022, LNCS 13536, pp. 320–333, 2022.
https://doi.org/10.1007/978-3-031-18913-5_25

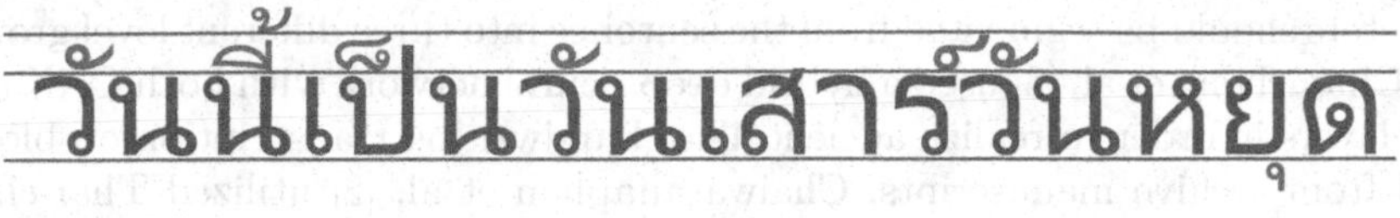

วันนี้เป็นวันเสาร์วันหยุด

Fig. 1. A sample of the Thai text line image. The small parts with brown color are isolated Thai character. There are four layers' characters stacked vertically in Thai texts.

applications, such as automatic driving, product retrieval, card recognition, etc. Unlike optical character recognition(OCR), which focuses on the recognition of documents with clean background, STR aims at reading the context from the real-world images for more operations, so it is suitable for various conditions, including curved and occluded texts. With the advances of deep learning and machine translation, STR models have made breakthroughs in the past decades, they have already achieved high precision on public regular and irregular text recognition benchmarks [1].

Most existing methods of STR can be generally divided into two categories according to whether character segmentation is implemented, namely segmentation-based methods and segmentation-free methods. For segmentation-based methods [11,14,23,24,26,28], natural images are segmented into series of individual characters patches before recognition, and character-level annotations are needed while training, which brings in extra cost. Segmentation-free methods mainly include CTC-based methods and attention-based methods, they focus attention on recognition of sequences, and only need word-level annotations, which are more convenient to acquire. For CTC-based methods [1,7,8,10,16,22], a CTC layer is adopted to decode the sequences. CRNN [22] was a representative CTC-based text recognition method, it naturally handled sequences in arbitrary lengths without segmentation. Attention-based methods [5,12,13,15,17,18,20,25,27] are popular in previous text recognition models, they are always applied on encoder-decoder frameworks, which can learn the dependency among the output characters. For example, SEED [20] consisted of an encoder including CNN backbone for extracting visual features and a decoder including RNN with attention mechanism for predicting the recognition result. Although experiments show that the attention model performs better than the CTC model, the attention model has limited ability to recognize long sequence text images and images in noisy condition, because it is too flexible to predict proper alignments due to the lack of left-to right constraints as used in CTC.

However, these methods place emphasis on the recognition of mainstream languages like English and Chinese, and few works investigate the recognition of minority languages, which is not conducive for communication and cooperation between different areas nowadays. This paper is dedicated to improving performance of Thai scene text recognition.

There is limited literature about Thai recognition and most of them are only focus on single character recognition. Phokharatkul et al. [19] used cavity features and neural network to recognize handprinted Thai characters, and characters should be segmented from the sentence into three different level groups first. Chamchong et al. [3] used a hybrid deep neural network with both CNN and RNN layers in order to realize ancient Thai handwriting transcription on block-based from archive manuscripts. Chaiwatanaphan et al. [2] utilized Thai characters' shape appearance to recognize printed Thai characters in video sequence along a line. Sanguansat et al. [21] applied hidden markov models and n-gram models in the online Thai handwriting character recognition task. To the best of our knowledge, there are only two papers associating with Thai text recognition. Emsawas et al. [6] integrated LSTM and vertical character shifting approach to solve the problem of vertically overlapping characters that occurred in four-level writing system of Thai, as shown in Fig. 1, but this method only worked with completely clean backgrounds and could not be applied to scene text images. ChamchongGM et al. [4] applied CRNN model to Thai text recognition without any consideration about the characteristics of Thai text.

In this paper, we study original characteristics of Thai characters, and propose a Thai Character Combination(TCC) strategy to improve performance of Thai STR. Due to the complex arrangement structure of Thai characters, which brings greater challenges to classification and recognition, we consider making a new combination rule named TCC to combine those single characters stacked vertically to a series of combined characters, and regard them as input labels of our network. In addition, a new dataset called Thai Scene Text(TST) is established to evaluate the performance of recognition models with different character modeling ways. Then we conduct abundant experiments on TST dataset, experimental results have shown effectiveness of the TCC strategy for Thai STR, TCC significantly improves the string accuracy by 6.284%(from 65.040% to 71.424%), and has a great advantage on recognition of long Thai text.

The rest of this paper is organized as follows. In Sect. 2, we introduce the proposed TCC strategy and the basic scene text recognition architecture used in our experiments. In Sect. 3, we describe experimental settings. Besides, experimental results and detailed analyses are presented in Sect. 4. Finally, we conclude this paper and discuss the future work of Thai STR in Sect. 5.

2   Methodology

In this section, we first describe the architecture of our recognition model, it is an end-to-end trainable framework that consists of three stages: feature extraction, sequence modeling and sequence prediction that based on attention mechanism. After that, we introduce characteristics of Thai characters and propose a novel character modeling strategy called Thai Character Combination(TCC) that utilizes the spatial distribution of Thai characters to help improving performance of Thai STR.

2.1   Recognition Architecture

We follow the popular attention-based CNN-LSTM architecture in our experiments. A ResNet module [5] is applied as the feature extractor. In order to improve the modeling ability, we utilize a SE block [9] in each residual block. As for sequence modeling stage, there is a two-layers bi-direction LSTM to capture contextual information within a sequence of Thai characters. The attention mechanism is used to generate features that align to every character of the corresponding output. In the last prediction stage, we choose attention-based decoder to predict Thai texts in images. Finally, a cross entropy function is applied as the network object function. This framework is regarded as a baseline model for following experiments.

2.2 Thai Character Combination

Different from English and most other scripts, Thai characters can be written both horizontally and vertically, as shown in Fig. 1, Thai characters have their own special structure which allows different types of characters to stack vertically. This irregular distribution makes alignment more difficult during decoding process. So we propose a Thai Character Combination(TCC) strategy that eliminates vertical stack between Thai characters to improve the efficiency of recognition. According to the shape and placement of characters, we can visually divide all Thai characters into six categories: shoe characters, main characters, hat characters, tone characters, independent characters, and punctuation characters, as shown in Fig. 2. Just like their names, the shoe character can be superimposed under the main character, as the shoes for the main character. The main character can be put hat character above it and can be placed shoe character below it. As far as the tone character, it is the tone of a word and must be superimposed on the main character or the hat character. The independent character is a type of character that can not wear hats, shoes or tones, therefore, it can only exist independently. The punctuation character is a punctuation mark used to break sentences, similar to functions of punctuation marks in other languages.

shoe	ฺ ุ ู
main	ก ข ฃ ค ฅ ฆ ง จ ฉ ช ซ ฌ ญ ฎ ฏ ฐ ฑ ฒ ณ ด ต ถ ท ธ น ป ผ ฝ พ ฟ ภ ม ย ร ฤ ล ฦ ว ศ ษ ส ห ฬ อ ฮ า
hat	ั ่ ้ ็ ๋ ๊ ์ ิ ี ึ ื ำ
tone	่ ้ ๊ ๋
independent	า ะ . เ แ โ ใ ไ ๆ ฯ ๚ ๛
punctuation	฿ ๏ ๐ ๑ ๒ ๓ ๔ ๕ ๖ ๗ ๘ ๙

Fig. 2. Classification of Thai characters

Based on the above rule of Thai character combination, we combine these six types of characters into Thai combined characters, so that these characters

Before Combination   After Combination

(Each color presents a character in training charset)

(a) Thai character combination strategy.

ณ จิ ทั ริ น์ ภ ลี บุ ณ์ จ ห์ มั ร์ ชิ ติ สี รู บั ที บี
อั ชั ถ โ ยี ช ลิ ซี ที ชี ส์ บิ ลิ นั ห์ ปั ชุ รั ฐ ค์
กุ ฐ์ ติ ฮ ร์ วั ปิ นี ชี่ ตั ร์ อุ ศี ใ ฟ ฏิ อี อิ สี ล่ ที่

(b) Samples of combined Thai characters.

Fig. 3. The diagram of Thai character combination.

Algorithm 1: Thai Character Combination

> **input**   : text labels $X = \{x_1, x_2, ...x_n\}$
> **output**   : combined labels $Y = \{y_1, y_2, ...y_m\}$. $m \leq n$
> **initialize:** Unicode range of Thai characters $P = (3585, 3675)$,Unicode
>   range of main,independent,punctuation characters
> $Q = (3685, 3632) \cup (3634) \cup (3643, 3654) \cup (3663, 3675)$

```
1  for x in X do
2  │  u=ord(x);
      // acquire unicode value of the character x
3  │  if u ∉ P then
4  │  │  output y
5  │  else
6  │  │  if u ∈ Q then
            // Repeated three times, because a combined character
               consists up to four single characters
7  │  │  │  if ord(nextcharacterofx) ∈ Q then
8  │  │  │  │  continue
9  │  │  │  else
10 │  │  │  │  combine the character with x
11 │  │  │  end
12 │  │  else
13 │  │  │  output y
14 │  │  end
15 │  end
16 end
17 Output combined labels Y
```

can only be written horizontally, which reduces complexity of Thai characters' structure. The diagram of TCC is shown in Fig. 3. Figure 3(a) intuitively shows the result of TCC and more combined samples can be found in Fig. 3(b). In addition, we also propose an algorithm based on the Unicode to generate combined Thai character conveniently. The Unicode encoding of Thai ranges from 0E00 to 0E7F, 87 code bits have been allocated, the range is 0E01-0E3A and 0E3F-0E5B, converted to decimal is the range of 3585-3642 and 3647–3675, there are 41 unused reserved code bit. We limit range of Unicode to combine characters only belong to Thai, leaving digits, letters and punctuation keeping independent, especially, we find that a combined character consists of up to four single Thai characters. After running this algorithm, all characters will be arranged horizontally and regularly. The details are described in Algorithm 1.

3 Experimental Setting

In this section, we firstly introduce the new Thai dataset used in this paper, and then describe the implementation details, including data preparing, model configurations and training and evaluation metric.

3.1 Thai STR Datasets

As there is no publicly available Thai dataset for text recognition tasks, we establish a new dataset called Thai Scene Text (TST) dataset to evaluate the performance of models with different character modeling methods. This dataset is collected from various scenarios in Thailand, including maps, cashes, handwritting images, signs, etc., which are very common in daily life. Then we divide TST into training dataset and evaluation dataset in a ratio of 4:1 approximately. Part of images containing in TST are in low qualities, including blurring and occlusion, which brings a big challenge for recognition. Some examples are shown in Fig. 4.

Fig. 4. Some examples of text images in TST, involving cashes, maps, street signs, slogans, etc.

3.2 Data Preparing

Due to the large number of long text images in the dataset, the height of input image is normalized as 64 and the width is calculated with the original aspect ratio, which is up to 1024 by padding zero. The number of Thai character set is 87, after applying the TCC strategy, the number of combined character set is 1239. Since real Thai scene text images not only contain Thai characters, we add 10 digits, 52 case sensitive letters and 32 punctuation characters to the label set to suit more general situations. What's more, like other attention-based methods, three special characters including 'SOS', 'EOS' and 'UNK' are also added to the label set to help model training. Therefore, there are 1366 classifications totally for Thai STR. We set the max length of output sequence N to 150 according to the dataset.

3.3 Model Configurations and Training

The residual network has 29 trainable layers in total. The dimension of all hidden states including the FC layer is set as 256, and the number of output channel of the feature extractor is 512.

We implement our experiments with Pytorch framework, and all experiments are conducted on a workstation with one NVIDIA GeForce RTX 3090 graphics card. The model with two kinds of character modeling ways are both trained and tested on our established TST dataset. We use a batch size of 50 at training time, and the Adadelta optimizer is adopted to update model parameters.

3.4 Evaluation Metric

We evaluate our model under the common text recognition metrics, i.e., character-level accuracy and string-level accuracy. Both of them can be defined by edit distance, which can be calculated by:

$$ED(S_T, S_R) = D_e + S_e + I_e \tag{1}$$

where D_e is the deletion errors, S_e is the substitution errors and I_e is the insertion errors, while S_T, S_R are the ground truth and its corresponding network prediction respectively. The string-level accuracy can be computed by:

$$String_{Acc} = N_A/N \tag{2}$$

where N is the total number of testing images and N_A is the number of images that meet $ED(S_T, S_R) = 0$. For the character-level metric, the accuracy is defined as:

$$Character_{Acc} = 1 - \sum ED(S_T, S_R) / \sum max(len(S_T), len(S_R)). \tag{3}$$

4   Experimental Results and Analyses

In this section, we firstly introduce the general performance of the two character modeling methods. Then we analyze the differences between them in details from multiple perspectives, including single character numbers in combined modality, the text length and training speed. Finally, we visualize some wrong examples to intuitively show the deficiencies of TCC.

4.1   Experimental Results

We conduct experiments to compare performance under two character modeling methods, the recognition results are summarized in Table 1, and TCC exhibits higher efficiency on TST evaluation dataset.

Original Thai label set has 184 characters, including single Thai characters, digits, letters, punctuation characters and three special characters('SOS', 'EOS', 'UNK'). After combining Thai characters stacked vertically to combined characters, we find that the number of set increases to 1366 due to a large number of combinations. Besides, there are lots of long Thai text images in the TST dataset, so it is a challenge to correctly recognize the entire string. Although TCC only improves character accuracy slightly(92.882% to 93.642%), it boosts the string accuracy by 6.284% compared with the baseline model without TCC, which confirms the effectiveness of our proposed modeling strategy. Figure 5 shows several samples of recognition results under two methods. We choose four images with different types as representative samples. As we can see, the first sample is a handwritten text image which has a strong personal style, the second sample is severely blurred so that it's hard for us to distinguish visually, the third one is an occluded image that obscured by smudges, the last one is a poster image with artist font style. We can find that the model with TCC performs well on these situations, while there are some recognition errors occurring without TCC.

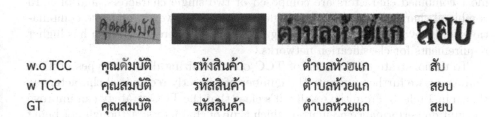

w.o TCC	คุณดัมบัติ	รหังสินค้า	ตำบลห้วยฮแก	สับ
w TCC	คุณสมบัติ	รหัสสินค้า	ตำบลห้วยแก	สยบ
GT	คุณสมบัติ	รหัสสินค้า	ตำบลห้วยแก	สยบ

Fig. 5. Samples of recognition results of the model under two character modeling ways on the TST dataset. 'w.o TCC' means without TCC, 'w TCC' means with TCC, 'GT' means groundtruth. Red color highlights incorrect character predictions. (Color figure online)

Table 1. Number of the character set and recognition results on the TST dataset under two character modeling ways. 'w.o TCC' means the baseline model referred in Sect. 2.1, 'w TCC' means that we implement TCC strategy on the baseline model.

Methods	Charset size	String accuracy(%)	Character accuracy(%)
w.o TCC	184	65.040	92.882
w TCC	1336	**71.424**	**93.642**

Table 2. Distribution of the number of characters, uncombined and combined mean the number of single and combined characters; 2-com,3-com,4-com mean the combined character consists of 2, 3, 4 single characters respectively, '_' means no such type of characters.

Methods	Uncombined	Combined		
		2-com	3-com	4-com
w.o TCC	628589	–	–	–
w TCC	403486	90768	16583	15

4.2   The Effectiveness of TCC

Different Types of Thai Combined Characters. We have mentioned that a combined character consists of up to four single Thai characters in Sect. 2.2. Specially, we count the number of different types of characters in the TST evaluation dataset. As shown in Table 2, the total number of characters dramatically decreases with TCC strategy, since lots of single Thai characters are combined to combined characters. After adopting TCC, uncombined characters still occupy a larger proportion, about 5/6, partly due to the presence of uncombinable characters such as letters, digits and punctuation characters. According to the combination rule, single Thai characters stacked vertically will be combined, most combined characters are composed of two single characters, and only 15 combined characters consist of 4 single characters. However, multiple combinations will inevitably lead to narrowing of character differences, which has higher requirements for classification networks.

To demonstrate the benefits of TCC on recognizing different types of Thai characters, we further compute the number of correctly recognized characters as shown in Table 3. From the results, it's clear that the TCC strategy can improve recognition performance no matter which type of characters. Although not being combined, TCC also has a large advantage on recognition of uncombined characters. It's interesting to note that no 4-com character can be correctly recognized under two modeling methods, nonetheless, we consider it justified because there are too few labels for such characters, only 15 4-com characters exist in the evaluation dataset, and each appears only once, which leads to severe unbalance of labels. By combining characters, TCC simplifies the structure of Thai characters, eliminates stack in vertical direction, leading to improvements of all kinds general Thai characters recognition.

Table 3. Distribution of the number of correctly recognized characters under two character modeling methods, the result under w.o TCC is based on the combination of prediction since it doesn't exist combined characters.

Methods	Uncombined	Combined		
		2-com	3-com	4-com
w.o TCC	389601	82200	14621	0
w TCC	391329	83376	15001	0

Table 4. Performance comparison of different lengths under two character modeling methods.

Method	Text length (number of samples)			
	0–20 (23667)	20–50 (8737)	50–100 (1391)	100–150 (69)
w.o TCC	71.703	55.730	25.018	7.246
w TCC	77.225	62.012	34.867	10.144

Different Length of Text in Images. Text length in the image has big influence on recognition accuracy. Longer text means harder recognition. We divide the test samples into four groups by the text length: [0,20), [20,50), [50,100), [100,150), and compare the string accuracy of different text lengths under two character modeling ways. The results are shown in Table 4. It can be found that with the text length increasing, the accuracy inevitably degrades. But with TCC strategy, the recognition model achieves much better performances on all lengths than single character modeling. When we focus on correct cases for the first three groups, we will find that the TCC strategy outperforms 5.522%, 6.282%, 9.849% respectively, which reveals that TCC has a stronger capability of long text recognition. Although there is a low accuracy of the fourth group, TCC still improves performance by 2.898%, which further proves the effectiveness of TCC especially on long text recognition.

Therefore, we further investigate the problem of length prediction, including the number of images with wrong predicting length and accuracy of correctly predicting text length, as shown in Table 5. From these results, it is clear that the length prediction accuracy outperforms about 2.2% when implementing TCC. We can deduce that TCC is beneficial to conduct alignment based on visual features due to the simplified structure.

Training Speed. We also compare the model convergence speed of TCC and normal single character modeling method. Since the number of characters set increases a lot (from 184 to 1336) after applying TCC strategy, the model training becomes more difficult. The training loss curves of these two character modeling ways are shown in Fig. 6.

We can find that the loss goes down quicker at the beginning without TCC, but from 60K iterations, the gap between two methods is not obvious.

Table 5. Number of length error samples and the corresponding length prediction accuracy under two character modeling methods.

Methods	Error number	Length accuracy(%)
w.o TCC	6915	79.580
w TCC	6190	81.721

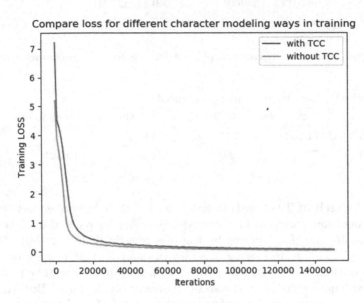

Fig. 6. Training loss under two character modeling ways

Furthermore, there is almost no difference after 80K iterations. So although the recognition model has a little faster convergence speed without TCC, the whole training phases are almost the same.

4.3   Failure Cases Analysis

Some typical failure cases are shown in Fig. 7. As we can see, the error types may not be the same for the two methods, just like the first case, the model with TCC only misidentify one character, while the model without TCC also appears misalignment problem. We have mentioned in Sect. 4.2 that TCC has a better performance on recognition of text length, it can effectively eliminates the alignment errors. For the second case, the character 'rn' is recognized as 'm' because the two adjacent characters are too close. For the third case, a large portion of the last character is cropped, which disturbs the alignment operation during decoding process and finally leads to recognition errors.

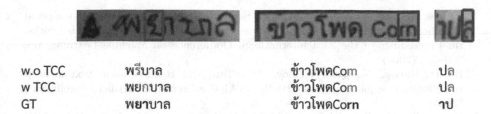

w.o TCC	พรีบาล	ข้าวโพดCom	ปล
w TCC	พยกบาล	ข้าวโพดCom	ปล
GT	พยาบาล	ข้าวโพดCorn	าป

Fig. 7. Failure cases of the recognition model. Red color highlights incorrect character predictions (Color figure online)

5   Conclusion

In this paper, a novel and straightforward character modeling strategy called Thai Character Combination(TCC) is proposed for Thai scene text recognition. TCC targets at characteristic of Thai characters, intends to combine characters stacked vertically to independent combined characters, which simplifies the structure of Thai characters. Additionally, we collect a new Thai Scene Text(TST) dataset to evaluate performance of Thai recognition models. Abundant experiments have shown the effectiveness of TCC, it not only greatly improves the string accuracy compared with the task without TCC, but also alleviates the alignment problem, which benefits for recognizing long Thai text images. We also find that TCC brings in lots of similar combined characters. Next step, we will improve our method from the perspective of model architecture to reduce the recognition errors of similar characters.

References

1. Baek, J., et al.: What is wrong with scene text recognition model comparisons? dataset and model analysis. In: Proceedings of the IEEE/CVF International Conference on Computer Vision, pp. 4715–4723 (2019)
2. Chaiwatanaphan, S., Pluempitiwiriyawej, C., Wangsiripitak, S.: Printed Thai character recognition using shape classification in video sequence along a line. Eng. J. **21**(6), 37–45 (2017)
3. Chamchong, R., Gao, W., McDonnell, M.D.: Thai handwritten recognition on text block-based from Thai archive manuscripts. In: 2019 International Conference on Document Analysis and Recognition (ICDAR), pp. 1346–1351. IEEE (2019)
4. Chamchong, R., Gao, W., McDonnell, M.D.: Thai handwritten recognition on text block-based from Thai archive manuscripts. In: 2019 International Conference on Document Analysis and Recognition, ICDAR 2019, Sydney, Australia, 20–25 September 2019, pp. 1346–1351. IEEE (2019)
5. Cheng, Z., Bai, F., Xu, Y., Zheng, G., Pu, S., Zhou, S.: Focusing attention: towards accurate text recognition in natural images. In: Proceedings of the IEEE International Conference on Computer Vision, pp. 5076–5084 (2017)
6. Emsawas, T., Kijsirikul, B.: Thai printed character recognition using long short-term memory and vertical component shifting. In: Booth, R., Zhang, M.-L. (eds.) PRICAI 2016. LNCS (LNAI), vol. 9810, pp. 106–115. Springer, Cham (2016). https://doi.org/10.1007/978-3-319-42911-3_9

7. Graves, A., Fernández, S., Gomez, F., Schmidhuber, J.: Connectionist temporal classification: labelling unsegmented sequence data with recurrent neural networks. In: Proceedings of the 23rd International Conference on Machine Learning, pp. 369–376 (2006)
8. He, P., Huang, W., Qiao, Y., Loy, C.C., Tang, X.: Reading scene text in deep convolutional sequences. In: Thirtieth AAAI Conference on Artificial Intelligence (2016)
9. Hu, J., Shen, L., Sun, G.: Squeeze-and-excitation networks. In: Proceedings of the IEEE Conference on Computer Vision and Pattern Recognition, pp. 7132–7141 (2018)
10. Hu, W., Cai, X., Hou, J., Yi, S., Lin, Z.: Gtc: guided training of ctc towards efficient and accurate scene text recognition. In: Proceedings of the AAAI Conference on Artificial Intelligence, vol. 34, pp. 11005–11012 (2020)
11. Jaderberg, M., Vedaldi, A., Zisserman, A.: Deep features for text spotting. In: Fleet, D., Pajdla, T., Schiele, B., Tuytelaars, T. (eds.) ECCV 2014. LNCS, vol. 8692, pp. 512–528. Springer, Cham (2014). https://doi.org/10.1007/978-3-319-10593-2_34
12. Lee, J., Park, S., Baek, J., Oh, S.J., Kim, S., Lee, H.: On recognizing texts of arbitrary shapes with 2D self-attention. In: Proceedings of the IEEE/CVF Conference on Computer Vision and Pattern Recognition Workshops, pp. 546–547 (2020)
13. Li, H., Wang, P., Shen, C., Zhang, G.: Show, attend and read: a simple and strong baseline for irregular text recognition. In: Proceedings of the AAAI Conference on Artificial Intelligence, vol. 33, pp. 8610–8617 (2019)
14. Liao, M., et al.: Scene text recognition from two-dimensional perspective. In: Proceedings of the AAAI Conference on Artificial Intelligence, vol. 33, pp. 8714–8721 (2019)
15. Litman, R., Anschel, O., Tsiper, S., Litman, R., Mazor, S., Manmatha, R.: Scatter: selective context attentional scene text recognizer. In: proceedings of the IEEE/CVF Conference on Computer Vision and Pattern Recognition, pp. 11962–11972 (2020)
16. Liu, W., Chen, C., Wong, K.-Y.K., Su, Z., Han, J.: Star-net: a spatial attention residue network for scene text recognition. In: BMVC, vol. 2, p. 7 (2016)
17. Liu, Z., Li, Y., Ren, F., Goh, W.L., Yu, H.: Squeezedtext: a real-time scene text recognition by binary convolutional encoder-decoder network. In: Proceedings of the AAAI Conference on Artificial Intelligence, vol. 32 (2018)
18. Lyu, P., Yang, Z., Leng, X., Wu, X., Li, R., Shen, X.: 2D attentional irregular scene text recognizer. arXiv preprint arXiv:1906.05708 (2019)
19. Phokharatkul, P., Kimpan, C.: Recognition of handprinted Thai characters using the cavity features of character based on neural network. In: IEEE. APCCAS 1998. 1998 IEEE Asia-Pacific Conference on Circuits and Systems. Microelectronics and Integrating Systems. Proceedings (Cat. No. 98EX242), pp. 149–152. IEEE (1998)
20. Qiao, Z., Zhou, Y., Yang, D., Zhou, Y., Wang, W.: Seed: semantics enhanced encoder-decoder framework for scene text recognition. In: Proceedings of the IEEE/CVF Conference on Computer Vision and Pattern Recognition, pp. 13528–13537 (2020)
21. Sanguansat, P., Asdornwised, W., Jitapunkul, S.: Online Thai handwritten character recognition using hidden Markov models and support vector machines. In: IEEE International Symposium on Communications and Information Technology, 2004, ISCIT 2004, vol. 1, pp. 492–497. IEEE (2004)

22. Shi, B., Bai, X., Yao, C.: An end-to-end trainable neural network for image-based sequence recognition and its application to scene text recognition. IEEE Trans. Pattern Anal. Mach. Intell. **39**(11), 2298–2304 (2016)
23. Wang, K., Babenko, B., Belongie, S.: End-to-end scene text recognition. In: 2011 International Conference on Computer Vision, pp. 1457–1464. IEEE (2011)
24. Wang, T., Wu, D.J., Coates, A., Ng, A.Y.: End-to-end text recognition with convolutional neural networks. In Proceedings of the 21st International Conference on Pattern Recognition (ICPR 2012), pp. 3304–3308. IEEE (2012)
25. Wang, T., et al.: Decoupled attention network for text recognition. In: Proceedings of the AAAI Conference on Artificial Intelligence, vol. 34, pp. 12216–12224 (2020)
26. Yao, C., Bai, X., Shi, B., Liu, W.: Strokelets: a learned multi-scale representation for scene text recognition. In: Proceedings of the IEEE Conference on Computer Vision and Pattern Recognition, pp. 4042–4049 (2014)
27. Yue, X., Kuang, Z., Lin, C., Sun, H., Zhang, W.: RobustScanner: dynamically enhancing positional clues for robust text recognition. In: Vedaldi, A., Bischof, H., Brox, T., Frahm, J.-M. (eds.) ECCV 2020. LNCS, vol. 12364, pp. 135–151. Springer, Cham (2020). https://doi.org/10.1007/978-3-030-58529-7_9
28. Zhang, Z., Zhang, C., Shen, W., Yao, C., Liu, W., Bai, X.: Multi-oriented text detection with fully convolutional networks. In: Proceedings of the IEEE Conference on Computer Vision and Pattern Recognition, pp. 4159–4167 (2016)

Automatic Examination Paper Scores Calculation and Grades Analysis Based on OpenCV

Xin-Yu Zhang[1], Zhan-Li Sun[1(✉)], and Mengya Liu[2]

[1] School of Electrical Engineering and Automation,
Anhui University, Hefei 230601, China
`zhlsun2006@126.com`

[2] School of Computer Science and Technology, Anhui University, Hefei 230601, China

Abstract. How to automatically and accurately score the examination paper still remains a challenging task, due to different handwriting habits. In this article, a method based on OpenCV has been proposed that can automatically achieve examination paper scores calculation and grades analysis. Instead of turning pages manually, the paper pages are turned automatically by the device we assembled. When automatically turning the page, the high-speed photographic apparatus can capture images of the examination paper. Then the images are read in python and needed to accept a series of digital processing. After this, the location of the numbers can be located and cut. Moreover, the support vector machine (SVM) is used to construct a handwritten digit recognition system to identify the numbers cut from the images. Experimental results on several samples demonstrate the feasibility and superiority of this method in terms of efficiency.

Keywords: OpenCV · Digital image processing · Handwritten digit recognition

1 Introduction

As one of the important means to select talented people, examination plays a very dominant role in the education field. In China, there are a large number of examinees, and the selection of talents is mainly through examinations. The equality of examination system is related to the superiority of talented people, so scoring requires high accuracy. Of course, it is also important to the right statistical analysis of scores and grades.

Traditional scoring method needs teachers to check one by one carefully, mainly mental arithmetic or using calculators. However, normally the examination papers have a large question quantity and scores are scattered in many areas. Because of this, mental arithmetic is inclined to make mistakes and is also a physical challenge for teachers. Using calculators can assure high accuracy,

S. Yu et al. (Eds.): PRCV 2022, LNCS 13536, pp. 334–345, 2022.
https://doi.org/10.1007/978-3-031-18913-5_26

but this means very slow and troublesome. Sometimes, things like pressing the wrong button may happen and also then lead to mistakes. Both of the methods need to consume lots of manpower and time. What's worse, they can't assure higher accuracy because these two methods have humans involved in the final analysis. In other words, humans can't work with being energetic all the time. That's a non-negligible drawback of the traditional scoring method.

In modern paper scoring, a method is proposed called answer card mode automatic scoring based on Optical Mark Reader (OMR) reading technology. This method is mainly used to score the objective automatically by checking the shading area and the results are read out by a specific optical mark reader. However, in daily life, students sometimes fill in the wrong place or forget to fill in the answer card. At the same time, this method not only needs schools to use specific answer cards, but also needs students to prepare specific pens otherwise the answers can't be identified. In addition, matched optical mark readers are so expensive that this method can't be implemented in every school.

In view of this, the examination scoring system without answer cards is necessary. However, there is no related mature production in the market currently. This kind of automatic examination paper scoring system based on digital image processing is suitable for small and middle size examinations in colleges and universities, and its digital identification technology is a focused area all the time, whether at home or abroad. The kernel of automatic scores calculation is handwritten digit recognition. There are many related studies abroad. STEPNET program divides the problem into easy subproblems and solves the problems by linear divider [1]. The layering convolutional neural network is applied to achieving handwritten numerals recognition with less errors [2]. Of these, the second layer of the neural network screens after activating the first layer. Hybrid orthogonal polynomial is used in [3] to obtain gradient and smooth features. Then adopting embedded image technology, obtained features are classified by support vector machine for different numbers. It turns out that this method owns better robustness for noise distortion and is superior to the convolutional neural network.

There are also a lot of domestic studies on handwritten digit recognition. Reference [4] puts forward an estimation method by combining multiple classifiers based on posterior probability estimation. They also propose a method to obtain handwritten numerals effectively identifying features based on uncorrelated optimal discriminant transformation and Karhunen-Loeve transformation. Based on affinity propagation (AP) and back propagation (BP) neural network, Zhu *et al.* proposed a fast handwritten digit recognition algorithm [6]. Sample redundancy is first eliminated by AP. Then, after reconstructing the sample space, BP neural network is adopted to construct the model. Sample learning applies the University of CaliforniaIrvine database with an accuracy of 96.10%. A kind of scores summator is designed to solve the question of examination paper scores calculation. It uses cameras to sample real-time scores information and do a series of pretreatment [7]. Then the segmented characters are identified by BP neural network and the digital sum is showed in GUI interface.

Although the above methods at home and abroad have achieved good results, it is still challenging to automatically and accurately score examination papers due to different handwriting habits. Nowadays, how to automatically and accurately score the examination paper still remains a challenging task, due to different handwriting habits. To obtain a faster and more convenient machine system and reduce manual errors, this work proposes a method to achieve examination paper scores calculated automatically based on digital image processing. It provides a new path for automatic examination paper scores calculation without specific answer cards.

The rest of the organization of this paper is as follows: the proposed method is introduced in Sect. 2, the experimental results and related discussion are shown in Sect. 3, and the conclusion is finally pointed out in Sect. 4.

2   Methodology

The method includes three stages: image acquisition, image processing and data processing. These three stages are described in the following subsections. Figure 1 shows the flow chart of the whole process.

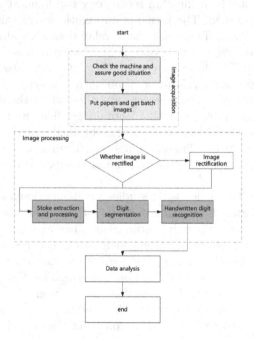

Fig. 1. The flow chart of the whole process.

2.1   Image Acquisition

The device getting the images is called high-speed photographic apparatus, which is an innovative product with a folding design in the office field. It can scan papers at a high speed with HD camera. More importantly, this apparatus can take photos automatically when the pages are turned. Because of this, the most important step of image acquisition is that pages should be turned automatically at a fixed interval. To achieve this, we designed a device comprised of two MG996R steering engines based on Microcontroller Unit. Figure 2 shows high-speed photographic and MG996R steering engine apparatus.

Fig. 2. High-speed photographic and MG996R steering engine apparatus.

Steering engine is a position servo driver, which is applied for control system with varying angles in need. The control signal enters signal modulation chip by the path of receptor to get direct current (DC) offset voltage. There is a reference circuit inside, generating reference signals at a period of 20 ms and a width of 1.5 ms. Comparing obtained DC offset voltage with voltage of potentiometer, the voltage difference can be got to determine the positive and negative rotation of motors.

The steering engine's control signal is PWM signal, namely Pulse Width Modulation signal. It is a technique for getting analog results with digital means. By controlling the switching device of inverter circuit, a series of pulses with same amplitude and different widths are generated, which are used to replace sine waves or other waves in need. Modulating the width of every pulse in certain rules can not only change the inverter circuit's output voltage, but also change the output frequency. The angle of the steering engine can be changed by modulating the pulse width, meaning each angle is corresponding to a certain width. Based on this principle, two MG996R steering engines are programmed respectively to rotate at different angles.

Next is how the device can turn pages automatically. The device is comprised of two MG996R steering engines and high-speed photographic apparatus tied on the platform. MG996R steering engine A rotates at 180°C, while MG996R steering engine B rotates at an angle less than 90°C. Both of the steering engines are welded with a steel wire and steering engine B's steel wire has sticky material on it.

When the examination papers are put on the platform, steering engine B rotates down to the examination papers and its sticky material can take the first page up to a certain position. After this, steering engine B will pause for a little time. In this interval, steering engine A starts to work, rotating 180°C from aboriginal position to the opposite position, driving the first page sticked on the steering engine B's steel wire to the other side. Then, the first page is turned successfully and the high-speed photographic apparatus photos the next image automatically. At the same time, steering engine A rotates 180 °C back to the aboriginal position. Then steering engine B works through rotating down to the examination papers again and up again. Therefore, the key to realizing automatic page turning is that two engines can cooperate well. When repeating these above motions, examination papers are turned automatically and images of examination papers are stored in computers. The basic process is showed in Fig. 3.

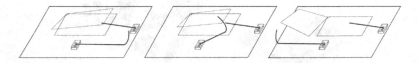

Fig. 3. The basic process.

2.2   Image Processing

Digit Segmentation. When images are obtained, they can be read by OpenCV. First, we need to detect red strokes and extract area of the stroke. The initial image format is Red, Green, Blue (RGB), but this format can't reflect object's concrete color information. So, we need to search for other color spaces to extract the red component. Besides RGB, common color space involves Hue, Saturation, Value (HSV) and lab color space. After comparison, we discover that HSV color space can express color shade, hues and brightness very intuitively, which is very convenient to compare colors.

HSV can be calculated from RGB values using the following functions [5]:

$$
H = \begin{cases}
60 \times \dfrac{G - B}{V - \min(R,G,B)} & , \text{ IF } V = R \\[3mm]
120 + 60 \times \dfrac{B - R}{V - \min(R,G,B)} & , \text{ IF } V = G \\[3mm]
240 + 60 \times \dfrac{R - G}{V - \min(R,G,B)} & , \text{ IF } V = B
\end{cases}
\tag{1}
$$

$$
S = \begin{cases}
1 - \dfrac{\min(R,G,B)}{V} & , \text{ IF } V \neq 0 \\[3mm]
0 & , \text{IF } V = 0
\end{cases}
\tag{2}
$$

$$V = \max(R,G,B) \qquad (3)$$

When the red component of images, namely the red strokes are extracted, some parts may be unclear or have image noise. To extract clear digits, we need to do some filtering processes and morphological operations on the images.

A median filter has a preferable function in removing image noise. It can protect the edge of signal from being vague. For a series of digital signals, the uneven number of data are taken out from certain sample window in image and are sorted out. The data needed to be processed are replaced by the sorted median numbers. After this, we can get images with less image noise, but the strokes are still unclear. To solve the matter, morphological processing of the strokes is important.

Morphological processing is one of the technologies that is widely applied in digital image processing which contains erosion and dilation. Erosion is an operation to contract the selected area, which can eliminate the edge and dot. The size of erosion area is related to the size and shape of structure element. Erosion uses a self-defined structure element, like rectangle or circle, to do some sliding operations like filtering on the binary image. Pixels in binary image are compared with pixels in structure element and the intersection finally obtained is eroded image pixels. Opposite to erosion, dilation is an operation to dilate the selected area. It compares pixels in binary image with pixels in structure element and gets the union as dilated image pixels.

After these operations, we can get clear strokes in binary images. Considering that binary images only have two gray values (0 and 255), we can use specific function boundingRect in OpenCV to segment the strokes. Function boundingRect can calculate the vertical minimum bounding rectangle of contours. Using this function, we can get all the contours containing strokes and segment them into pieces. It should be noted that the strokes segmented contain not only digits but also signs and true marks. In addition, some digits are adherent in strokes because of different writing habits.

Handwritten Digit Recognition. To calculate the scores, digital images need to be. recognized and output the numbers. In this step, we use support vector machine (SVM) to recognize handwritten digit.

SVM is a kind of two-category model and its learning strategy is margin maximization. By selecting feature subset, this method can not only increase the accuracy of image recognition, but also reduce algorithm complexity, accelerating operational speed. The main thought of SVM is sample classification in high dimensional space. Finding a better inner-product function based on practical application is the premise to realize transformation in program.

Here are some conventional kernel functions:

1. Polynomial inner-product kernel function:

$$k(x, x_i) = ((x \times x_i) + 1)^d \qquad (4)$$

2. Linear inner-product kernel function:

$$k(x, x_i) = x \times x_i \tag{5}$$

3. Radial basis function (RBF) inner-product function:

$$k(x, x_i) = exp(-\frac{\|x - x_i\|^2}{\delta^2}) \tag{6}$$

4. Two layer neural network inner-product kernel function:

$$k(x, x_i) = tanh(\eta\langle x, x_i\rangle + \theta) \tag{7}$$

Aforementioned kernel functions have their respective advantages. We need to test continuously and select optimal parameters in practical application. At the same time, we need to find their specific characteristics and accordingly recognize the characters. Characters contain many features, we should decide early to extract which one. Histogram of Oriented Gradient (HOG) feature is more commonly used in image processing technology currently. The key process to extracting HOG feature is to calculate the gradient of the selected area and add them, then we can get histogram in direction of gradient, which can represent this area. By connecting histograms of every area, we can obtain the integral image features. With this, we can train the classifier well by training samples, then put the characters need to be recognized into the classifier and complete the classification.

To assure the accuracy of the classifier, we need to select samples from a large account. In view of this, we decide to use the MNIST dataset (see Fig. 4). MNIST dataset comes from National Institute of Standards and Technology. Training set is written by 250 different people, 50% senior high school students and 50% workers of the Census Bureau. Test set is also the same proportional handwritten digit data. Using this data set, we can offer more data samples to the classifier and enhance the accuracy.

Fig. 4. The MNIST dataset.

2.3 Data Processing

The predictions of SVM are calculated in total and the final result, namely the total scores of the examination paper is saved as excel. In the following, scores are analyzed in several aspects.

a. Grading. Calculate the average score and compare it with every score, we can get the line chart. We rank students' scores in 4 grades and calculate the proportion every grade accounts for.

b. Classification of difficulty degree. Difficulty degree is one of reference standards to appraise the quality of an examination paper. It is not conducive to examinating the students' level if the examination paper is too difficult or too easy. So we need to analyze the examination paper's difficulty degree according to results. Here is the difficulty degree calculation formula:

$$P = 1 - \frac{\bar{x}}{K} \qquad (8)$$

where P represents difficulty degree, $\bar{x}$ represents average of all the students' scores, and K represents the total score of the examination paper. Common difficulty degree standards are shown in the Table 1.

Table 1. Common difficulty degree.

Scale	Difficulty degree
P≤0.15	D
0.15<P≤0.4	C
0.4<P≤0.8	B
P>0.8	A

c. Analysis of distinguishing degree. Distinguishing degree of an examination paper is an indicator to test examinees' ability. Low distinguishing degree is hard to discriminate examinees at different levels. Here is the distinguishing degree calculation formula:

$$D = \frac{x_H - x_L}{N(H - L)} \qquad (9)$$

where D represents distinguishing degree indicator, x_H represents sum of high-scored group examinees' scores, x_L represents sum of low-scored group examinees' scores. High-scored group refers to examinees whose scores rank in the top 25% and low-scored group refers to examinees whose scores rank in the last 25%. H represents the highest score in all the scores, while L represents the lowest score. N represents the overall number of people in high-scored group (or low-scored group), namely 25% of people number in total. Common distinguishing degree standards are shown in the Table 2.

Table 2. Common distinguishing degree.

Scale	Distinguishing degree
D<0.3	C
0.3≤D≤ 0.4	B
D>0.4	A

3   Experimental Results and Discussions

To test the feasibility of the software, we decide to use half of the image of math examination paper first. It should be noted that before extracting the red strokes, the background needs to be removed, in case it disturbs the extraction of strokes, as shown in Fig. 5(a).

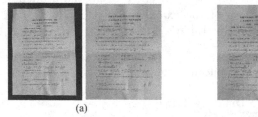   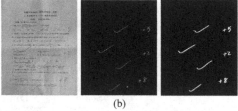

(a)   (b)

Fig. 5. Image process.

In Fig. 5(b), we can see that red strokes are extracted. After morphological process, the strokes become more clear.

We extract the digits and save the images in a certain file folder (see Fig. 6(a)).

Then we use SVM to recognize the digit, to see if the SVM classifier can output results at high accuracy. There is one point we need to pay attention. The input of the SVM classifier needs to be square and the shape of digits we extract most time is the rectangle. So before the recognition, we need to transform the shape of digit images into square (see Fig. 6(b)). As we can see in Fig. 7, the SVM classifier can recognize the digits.

8   Z   5   8   Z   5
1.jpg   2.jpg   3.jpg   1.jpg   2.jpg   3.jpg

(a)   (b)

Fig. 6. Digit extraction.

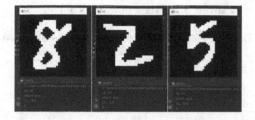

Fig. 7. Handwritten digit recognition.

Although the SVM classifier can recognise digits accurately, we can't appraise the accuracy of this method if we don't have a large number of samples. So we still need to do more experiments. We prepare 30 examination paper samples which are written by 3 people with different handwriting habits (see Fig. 8).

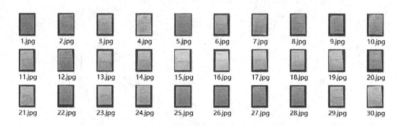

Fig. 8. Examination paper samples.

After automatic scores calculation, we can get the results. The difference values (D-value) between the actual scores and automatically calculated scores are calculated and showed in Table 3. To obviously display, we also visualize them in Fig. 9. As we can see from the Table 3 and Fig. 9, scores of most examination paper samples can be calculated well, that is, D-value is very small, which further proves the effectiveness of the method proposed in this paper. But at the same time, we find that automatically calculated scores of two samples deviate from the actual scores too much, whose D-value is 12 and 16 respectively. To find out the main cause, we pick up these two samples and check the process step by step. As a result, we summarize 3 reasons why the results deviate so much.

Table 3. D-value of every sample.

Calculated score	Actual score	D-value	Calculated score	Actual score	D-value	Calculated score	Actual score	D-value
39	36	−3	32	48	16	31	37	6
29	25	−4	16	17	1	21	22	1
25	19	−6	38	43	5	24	31	7
25	24	−1	48	48	0	20	32	12
27	33	6	35	32	−3	24	26	2
38	38	0	28	25	−3	28	31	3
28	26	−2	19	21	2	9	9	0
27	30	3	20	23	3	19	27	8
29	26	−3	42	41	−1	29	31	2
25	30	5	20	23	3	31	36	5

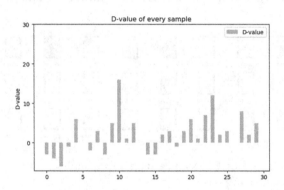

Fig. 9. D-value of every sample.

Firstly, some digits touching with plus sign are cut as a whole, which are showed in Fig. 10(a). Under this circumstance, it's difficult for SVM classifier to recognize the digits accurately. To solve the problem, digits touching with plus sign need to be cut separately.

Secondly, some plus signs are not filtered due to different handwriting habits (see Fig. 10(b)). Commonly, the plus signs are filtered by the characteristics of directional projection graph. However, different handwriting style makes it hard to filter plus signs completely, because not every sign can meet the characteristics we set for a plus sign. Figure 10(b) shows plus signs that can't be filtered by the system. For this reason, unfiltered plus signs are recognized mistakenly as digits, which makes the final result deviate from the actual score too much.

Thirdly, the accuracy of the SVM classifier needs to be improved. In the results, some digits are mistakenly recognised, so the final total score deviates too much from the actual score.

(a)   (b)

Fig. 10. Characters that can't be recognised well.

4   Conclusions

In this article, an automatic model based on OpenCV is proposed, which is used to calculate examination paper scores automatically. Through experiments, we can see that this method is feasible and effective. However, this method still has something that needs to be improved. In handwritten digit recognition stage, signs may be misrecognized as digit. Although the accuracy is high and the automation system is convenient, this problem still prevents the wider application of practical. To apply to practical life better, we plan to focus on alleviating this problem in the future work. We firmly believe that automation is the tide of times and automatic scores calculation can be applied in life widely someday.

References

1. Knerr, S., Personnaz, L., Dreyfus, G.: Handwritten digit recognition by neural networks with single-layer training. IEEE Trans. Neural Networks **3**(6), 962–968 (1992)
2. Kazuya, U., Nobutaka, K., Tetsuya, H., Masahiro, N.: Combination of convolutional neural network architecture and its learning method for rotation-invariant handwritten digit recognition. IEEE Trans. Electr. Electron. Eng. **16**(1), 161–163 (2020)
3. Sadiq, H., Basheera, M., Naser, M., Alsabah, M., Haddad, S.: A robust handwritten numeral recognition using hybrid orthogonal polynomials and moments. Sensors **21**(6), 1999–1999 (2021)
4. Jin, Z., Hu, Z., Yang, J., Liu, K., Sun, J.: Extraction and recognition of handwritten digit valid identified features. Comput. Study Developm. **36**(12), 1484–1489 (1999)
5. Li, Z.: Retinex image enhancement algorithm based on trilateral filtering in HSV color space. Inf. Technol. Inform. **44**(10), 120–122 (2019)
6. Zhu, T., Wei, H., Zhang, K.: Handwritten digit recognition based on AP and BP neural network algorithm. China Sci. Article **9**(4), 479–482 (2014)
7. Wang, J., Suo, Y., Xiao, Z., Zhang, M., Qiao, X.: Design and implementation of handwritten paper scores summator. Mod. Elect. Technol. **38**(8), 22–25 (2015)

Efficient License Plate Recognition via Parallel Position-Aware Attention

Tianxiang Wang[2], Wenzhong Wang[1,2]($\boxtimes$), Chenglong Li[1], and Jin Tang[1,2]

[1] Anhui Provincial Key Laboratory of Multimodal Cognitive Computation,
Hefei, China
[2] School of Computer Science and Technology, Anhui University, Hefei, China
wenzhong@ahu.edu.cn

Abstract. In recent years, Recurrent Neural Networks and Attention Mechanism are used for License Plate Recognition(LPR), and have achieved state-of-the-art performances. However, sequentially generating attention vectors for different characters might lead to attention drift problem and also degrade the recognition efficiency. To address these problems, we propose a novel parallel position-aware attention mechanism for high-performance LPR. Our new attention method focuses more on the positional features of each character in a parallel manner by modeling all characters independently. In order to alleviate the issue of unbalanced problem in existing LPR datasets, we generate a large-scale synthetic dataset via CycleGAN, which includes 500k license plate images and covers all regions in China. Experimental results on the synthesized and public datasets suggest that the proposed approach achieves excellent performance in terms of both accuracy and efficiency.

Keywords: License Plate Recognition · Position attention · CNN

1 Introduction

License Plate Recognition(LPR) aims to recognize the plate numbers from plate images. It is widely used in modern intelligent transportation systems. The latest advances in LPR research regard LPR as a sequence labelling problem, and use Recurrent Neural Networks (RNN) with attention mechanisms to sequentially decode the plate numbers/characters from an encoding of the plate image. Typically, a plate image is converted to a feature vector using Convolutional Neural Networks (CNN), and the feature vector is then fed into a RNN which decodes each character in the plate. In the decoding process, the characters are recognized from left to right. In each step, a spatial attention map is estimated from the previous state of the RNN and the image feature vector. The attention map is used to compute a context vector from the last feature map of the CNN, and the context vector is then classified into one character category.

The sequence labelling approaches implicitly assume the current character depends on the past ones. However, this assumption does not hold in the case

S. Yu et al. (Eds.): PRCV 2022, LNCS 13536, pp. 346–360, 2022.
https://doi.org/10.1007/978-3-031-18913-5_27

of LPR. The character sequence on a license plate is usually contextless [1], and there are little dependencies between the characters. This means that the RNN might not be an appropriate model for LPR, and each plate character should be decoded independently, and furthermore, the sequential attention mechanisms might lead to **attention drift** problem [1]. The attention drift phenomena in LPR is shown in Fig. 1 (first row), the attended locations in the plate image do not align with the location of the characters. The misalignment results in wrong context vector. As shown in Fig. 1, the attention for the third character('G') shifted to the region of the fourth character ('9'), and the model incorrectly classified 'G' as '9'.

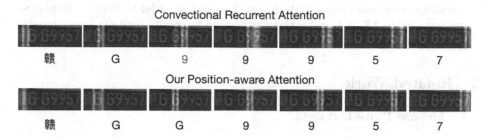

Fig. 1. Attention maps. The character below each panel is the recognition result from the attended feature map. (Above) The attention maps generated by convectional recurrent attention mechanism, exhibiting attention drift problem, and leading to incorrect recognition (the '9' in red). (Below) The attention maps of our position-aware attention model accurately attend to the location of each character, resulting in more accurate recognition. (Color figure online)

In order to mitigate the above problems, we propose a novel model for LPR which is built on a plain CNN model with a *parallel position-aware attention* module. In our model, the attention module outputs K attention maps for K plate characters. Each attention map is used to weight the CNN feature map to get a context vector for each character. The plate characters are then decoded from these context vectors independently. Our model abandons the sequential labelling formulation, by generating attention for each character independently, our model avoids the attention drift problem, and by recognizing characters in a parallel manner, we discard the temporal dependency assumption implicit in the RNN model.

Many current license plate image datasets are collected from a limited number of regions. For example, the CCPD dataset [2] has 290k real license plate images, but more than 95% of which are collected in the same city, with the first two characters in the plates are almost the same. These imbalanced datasets will make the learned model severely biased, and could hardly recognize plates from other regions.

In order to alleviate the imbalance problem, we use CycleGAN [3] to generate a large-scale realistic license plate dataset, which includes 500k plate images, covering all regions in China.

Our contributions can be summarized as follows:

- We propose a parallel position-aware attention mechanism for efficient license plate recognition. In contrast to conventional recurrent attention models, our attention model does not suffer from the attention drift problems. Our model generate attention maps that well align with the location of each character. Furthermore, our attention model is parallel, and it generates an attention map for each character independently, which makes it more computationally efficient than recurrent attention models.
- We propose to synthesize a large number of license plate images, covering all regions of the country, which can effectively alleviate the biased distribution problem in current license plate image datasets. In order to mimic real plates, we use CycleGAN to transfer the synthesized images to realistic ones, thereby reducing the covariate shift between synthetic samples and real samples.

2   Related Work

2.1   License Plate Datasets

Most plate detection and recognition datasets come from one region and they are homogeneous, lacking different plate types like trailers or new energy cars.

CD-HARD [4] dataset covers different situations, but it only has 102 license plates. PKUData [5] contains license plates of various types and different lighting conditions, but the plates are taken from one region, which cannot be used to recognise license plates from other regions. CCPD [2] is currently the largest license plate dataset in China, with 290k which is divided into 7 different subsets based on weather, rotation angle and difficulty of recognition, but more than 95% of this dataset are number plates from one region, so it is not friendly to use this dataset to train for recognition of other regions. The CLPD [6] contains a dataset of 1200 license plates from all over China, but this dataset is only used for evaluate recognition models due to the number of license plates in the dataset.

2.2   License Plate Recognition

There are two major categories of license plate recognition methods, i.e. segmentation-based methods [4,7] and segmentation free methods [2,8–11].

Segmentation-Based Methods first segment or detect the license plate image into several regions, each hopefully containing one single character, and then use Optical Character Recognition (OCR) techniques to recognize each character. In [12], Zhuang et al. modified a semantic segmentation model, DeepLab v2 [13] to segment character in the plate images. However, the segmentation is not guaranteed to precisely segment each character into distinct image regions, and so each region must be fed into a counting module for further processing. Jiao et al. [14] first segment a license plate into several blocks, each containing a single character, and then classify each block using a feed-forward neural network. In [15], Dong et al. use Spatial Transformer Network [16] to partition the plate into different patches, each containing a character, and then classify each patch into a character category using a CNN. Silva et al. [7] modified the YOLO network [17] to detect the license plate characters, and then use OCR to recognize each character. A similar approach was used in [18]. In [19], Björklund et al. regard LPR as an M-class object detection task, where M is the number of all possible plate characters. In this approach, each character is simultaneously located and recognized.

However, the effect of character segmentation or detection is greatly affected by image quality. In many real scenarios, license plate images may have different degrees of degradation, such as blurring, low illumination, overexposure, deformation, weathering, etc., and any segmentation algorithms can hardly segment each character accurately. For this reason, this class of algorithms may not work well in real complex environments where plate images are severely degraded.

Segmentation-Free Methods work by converting a plate image into a feature vector, and then decoding each character from this feature vector. This type of algorithms can be divided into two different categories, i.e. multi-task CNN based methods and sequence labelling methods.

The multi-task CNN approaches view the recognition of each character as a sub-task, and all sub-tasks share a CNN backbone, which is used to extract appropriate image features. Each sub-task uses this feature to identify a specific character in the plate image. For example, the RPNet proposed by Xu et al. [2] combines the feature maps from three different layers of the CNN, resulting in a holistic feature map, and then fed this feature map into seven classifiers, each of which is used to identify a character at a specific location.

However, each character on the license plate occupies only a small compact region, and has almost no dependencies on other characters. Therefore, each character can be recognized from the features of a local area of the image. In the methods mentioned above, each character is identified from a shared global feature map. For any character, this global feature contains a lot of irrelevant information, which increases the difficulty of character recognition.

The sequence labelling methods convert a plate image into a sequence of feature vectors, typically using a CNN, and then decode each character from these feature sequences. Li [20,21] used bi-directional RNNs (BRNN) trained with CTC [9] loss for LPR. The approach in [22] used the Convolutional RNN proposed in [23] for plate recognition. Zou et al. [10] used bi-directional LSTM (BiLSTM) together with an attention model for sequence decoding, where each attention map is sequentially estimated based on previous RNN state. In [6], Zhang proposed a unified recognition model that combines 2D attention mechanism and LSTM recurrent neural network. Zhang [24] proposed a unified framework for license plate detection, tracking, and recognition in videos, in which the plate features are first encoded using a BiLSTM and then decoded using a LSTM network.

Such methods assume inherent temporal dependencies in character sequences, which do not hold for license plates. In models [6,10] that exploit attention mechanisms, this false assumption leads to the attention drift problem, where the features used to decode characters may not align with the character's position in the image.

Our approach is related to the multi-task CNN methods. However, we do not predict each character from the shared global features, we instead propose a position-aware attention to locate each character in the plate image, and use the attended local features to identify each character. Compared to the RNN based methods, we abandon the fault assumption about sequential dependency among plate characters, and thus avoid the attention drift problem.

3 Methods

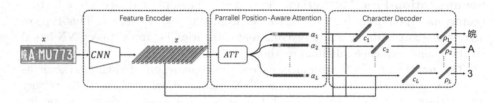

Fig. 2. License plate recognition network. Our network model consists of three modules, namely a feature encoder, a parallel position-aware attention, and a character decoder. The feature encoder is a CNN which converts the image x into a feature sequence z, and the attention module ATT estimates the attention map α_i for each character position $i, i = 1, 2, ...L$, from z. The character decoder calculates a context vector c_i using α_i and z, and then estimate the probability distribution ρ_i of different characters at the position i.

In the discussion below, x denotes a plate image, L is the maximum number of characters in a plate. Let $y = (y_1, y_2, ...y_L)$ denotes the character sequence of a plate, and $y_i \in \{1, ..., n\}$ where n is the cardinality of the character set $A = \{'0','1','2', ...'9','A','B', ...'Y','Z', ...\}$.

In this paper, we only experiment on the Chinese LPs. In Chinese transportation system, the vehicle plate number is a 7- or 8- character string, with the leading one a Chinese character, and the rest a mixture of English letters (omitting 'I' and 'O') and digits(in some cases, suffix with a Chinese character). In order to cope with both 7- and 8- character license plate, we add a special symbol, $< END >$, into the character set A, which is used to indicate the end of a license character string. So $n = 76$ and $L = 9$ in this paper.

The goal of LPR is to infer y from x:

$$y = F(x) \tag{1}$$

We propose an end-to-end neural network shown in Fig. 2 to approximate F. Our model consists of three modules, a feature encoder f, a parallel position-aware attention module g, and a character decoder h. The complex mapping F can then be decomposed into three functions, i.e. f, g, and h:

$$z = f(x)$$
$$\alpha = g(z) \tag{2}$$
$$\rho = h(z, \alpha)$$

where z is the feature encoding of x, α is the position-aware attention map for each character location, and $\rho = (\rho_1, \rho_2, ..., \rho_L)$ with ρ_i the probability distribution of y_i:$\rho_{i,j} \equiv P(y_i = j|x), j = 1, 2...n$.

These three modules are detailed below.

3.1 Feature Encoder

The goal of feature encoder is to convert an image x into a rich feature z: $z = f(x)$. In order to achieve high computational efficiency, we modify a lightweight CNN, i.e. Resnet18 [25], which has relatively few parameters and requires less computation, to realize f. We extract the feature map T from its last convolutional layer, and convert it into a fix-sized feature map T' using *AdaptiveAvgPooling2D*. In this paper, the size $(H \times W \times C)$ of T' is $1 \times 14 \times 512$. We reshape T' into 14×512 and regard T' as a feature sequence $z = (z_1, z_2, ..., z_M)$, where $M = 14$, and $z_i \in R^{512}$. Each feature vector in this sequence covers a local receptive field (RF) in the plate image, as shown in Fig. 3. Hopefully, the character in the RF of z_i can be recognized from z_i.

This is distinct from other multi-task CNN based models, where all characters are predicted from a holistic feature map whose RF covers the whole image.

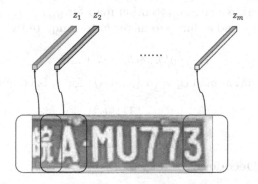

Fig. 3. Sequence of local features. Each feature vector z_i covers a local region of the plate image.

3.2 Parallel Position-Aware Attention

Unlike general text strings, there is almost no temporal correlation between the individual characters of the license plate. Moreover, each character only occupies a very compact local area of the license plate, so each character can be recognized from this local image region without referring to the features of other areas. This has been demonstrated in many segmentation-based LPR algorithms. This means that as long as our model can locate each character and utilize the image features at that location, each character can be recognized independently.

Therefore, we design a position-aware attention module, which computes an attention map for each character position, and uses this attention map to select local features from the image feature encoding z for identifying this character. Since there is no correlation between individual character positions, our attention module estimates each attention map independently. In our attention module, the attention maps of each position can be computed in parallel, so we call it a *parallel position-aware attentions* module.

Unlike previous multi-task CNN models that use global features to classify each character separately, in our model, each character is predicted from features selected using position-aware attention, which are localized and thus reduce the feature interference from other locations.

Different from the sequence labeling methods and the recurrent attention mechanisms, we abandon the temporal dependency assumptions and use a parallel attention mechanism. The attention map of each position is estimated independently and is not disturbed by other positions. This is a more appropriate design for LPR.

The core of our position-aware attention model ATT is a three layer convolutional neural network. The kernel sizes of these layers are $1 \times 1, 1 \times 3, 1 \times 3$, and each layer is followed by a ReLU nonlinearity. The input T and output K are all $1 \times M \times 512$. This network transforms the feature sequence $z = (z_1, z_2, ..., z_M)$ to a *Key* sequence $K = (k_1, k_2, ..., k_M), k_i \in R^{512}, M = 14$.

In order to generate a spatial attention map for $y_i, i = 1...L$, we use a trainable *Query* vector q_i, and a shift parameter b_i to compute the attention score of y_i to position j:

$$e_{ij} = q_i^T k_j + b_i, j = 1...M \tag{3}$$

The spatial attention map $\alpha_i = (\alpha_{i1}, ...\alpha_{iM})$ for y_i is computed by

$$\alpha_{ij} = \frac{exp(e_{ij})}{\sum_{l=1}^{M} exp(e_{il})} \tag{4}$$

3.3 Character Decoder

We use a linear decoder for each target character y_i. Firstly, we compute a *context vector* $c_i \in R^{512}$ for y_i:

$$c_i = \sum_{j=1}^{M} \alpha_{ij} z_j \tag{5}$$

The probability distribution of y_i given x, $P(y_i|x)$, is then decoded from c_i using Softmax regression:

$$\rho_{ij} = \frac{exp(\beta_{ij})}{\sum_{l=1}^{n} exp(\beta_{il})} \tag{6}$$

where $\rho_i = (\rho_{i1}, \rho_{i2}, ..., \rho_{in})$, $\rho_{ij} \equiv P(y_i = j|x)$, and $\beta_{ij} = \theta_{ij}^T c_i$, $\theta_{ij} \in R^{512}$'s are trainable parameters of the Softmax.

After obtaining the probability distribution ρ_i, we can decode the character at position i as $y_i = argmax_j \rho_{ij}$. If the $y_i = <END>$, we discard all characters that follows.

We also use a CTC decoder to decode the feature sequence z into a character sequence. We found that adding CTC decoder improves recognition performance a little bit, although the performance of CTC decoder alone is poor. In our experiments, the CTC decoder is only used to assist in training the model, not for character prediction.

3.4 Loss Function

When training the model, we use the following loss function:

$$L = L_{dec} + \mu L_{ctc} \tag{7}$$

where L_{dec} is the cross-entropy loss for the linear decoder, L_{ctc} is the loss function for the CTC decoder, and μ is empirically set to 0.5.

4 Data Synthesis

Most of the current public license plate datasets are collected from a few regions or a limited number of scenarios. The distribution of license plates in such a dataset is very unbalanced, for example, license plates from some provinces are very rare, or some kinds of license plates (such as truck license plates) are relatively rare. In order to obtain a license plate recognition model with good generalization performance, large-scale and well-distributed license plate image samples are required. However, it is impractical to collect and label such large-scale samples because it requires a lot of labor.

Since the production of license plates is strictly standardized, we can synthesize a large number of license plate image. The image synthesis in this paper is divided into two steps. First, according to the plate specification (size, color and layout of plate), we generate a large number of standard license plate images. The license plate numbers are randomly sampled, so that different characters in the generated plates are almost uniformly distributed. These generated license plate images are not real enough, and are very different from real license plate images. In order to obtain realistic license plate images, we use the synthetic samples and real license plate images to train a CycleGAN [3] model, and convert the synthetic samples into realistic ones using this model. In total, we generated a dataset of about 500,000 license plates covering all regions of mainland China, and containing four major plate styles(e.g. car plate, truck plate, etc.). Some of the samples are shown in Fig. 4.

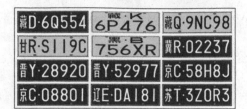 

Fig. 4. Synthesized plate images. (Left) Original unrealistic LPs generated according to license specification. (Right) Realistic images generated from the unrealistic LPs by CycleGAN.

5   Experiments

5.1   DataSets

CCPD [2] is currently the largest license plate dataset, containing more than 290K images. The dataset is divided into 9 groups according to different collecting scenarios and different level of recognition difficulties. Among the nine groups, the CCPD-base contains about 200k images, and the rest ~10 k images.

CLPD [6] consists of 1,200 real license plate images from all over the country, which includes different types of cars. We only use this dataset for testing.

Our Real Dataset. We also collect a new plate image set which consists of 9,737 real plate images, and covers all provincial regions across China.

SynSet. This is the synthesized set of plate images introduced in Sect. 4.

CCPD-SubTest. The CCPD test set is severely imbalanced, in order to evaluate the generalization ability of our algorithm, we search in the set and randomly pick a subset of about 4590 images which covers all provincial regions of mainland China. We use this subset as our new testset.

5.2   Experiment Settings

We conduct three groups of experiments on our algorithm. In the first experiment, we train our model on the CCPD-base [2] dataset, and evaluate on nine different CCPD test sets. In the second experiment, we train our model on the CCPD-base and CCPD-base + SynSet, and evaluate on the CLPD [6] dataset. In the third experiment, we try to adopt the latest algorithms [1,8,26] for scene text recognition to LPR, and compare with our proposed LPR algorithm. We train the models on our real dataset as well as the SynSet, and evaluate on the CCPD-SubTest.

In the experiments below, we train our algorithm using the following hyper-parameters: batch size = 64, optimizer = Adam, and the learning rate = 0.0001.

Due to perspective projection, the area of a license plate in an image is usually not axis-aligned. If an axis-aligned bounding box is used to represent the license plate, there will be a lot of background pixels in the box, which will deteriorate the recognition performance. Therefore, we use the DBNet [27] to detect the four corners of the plate, and then rectify plate to a axis-aligned rectangle. In our experiments, all rectified plate images are resized to the size of $140 \times 440 (H \times W)$.

In real traffic scenarios, license plates may have different degrees of distortion. In order to mimic these deformations, We use the Text-Image-Augmentation (TIA) method proposed in [28], to augment the plate images in training process.

5.3 Experimental Results

1) Results on CCPD: We train our model on the CCPD train set, and test on the nine CCPD test sets. We compare the performance of our algorithm with 6 other algorithms, all train on the same dataset. We use the four plate corner points provided in the dataset to locate the plate and corrected it to the standard plate size by radiometric transformation. The results are shown in Table 1, we can see that we achieve the highest accuracy on Base, Rotate, Tilt, Weather and Challenge subsets. Our method achieves an average accuracy of 99.2% on the CCPD testset. In DB subset, the distance from the LP to the shooting location is relatively far or near which can easily lead to image distortion during correction, so the results are relatively poor.

Also note from the last column that our algorithm is the most efficient, this is because our model is relatively small, yet it achieves the highest AP among all the compared algorithms.

Table 1. Recognition accuracy of different algorithms trained on the CCPD-base dataset and evaluated using nine CCPD testset.

	AP	Base	DB	FN	Rotate	Tilt	Weather	Challenge	Test time (ms)
TE2E [20]	94.4	97.8	94.8	94.5	87.9	92.1	86.8	81.2	310
LPRNet [29]	93.0	97.8	92.2	91.9	79.4	85.8	92.0	69.8	17.8
RPNet [2]	95.5	98.5	96.9	94.3	90.8	92.5	87.9	85.1	11.7
MORAN [30]	98.3	99.5	98.1	98.6	98.1	**98.6**	97.6	86.5	18.2
DAN [31]	96.6	98.9	96.1	96.4	91.9	93.7	95.4	83.1	19.3
Attention Net [6]	98.5	99.6	**98.8**	**98.8**	96.4	97.6	98.5	88.9	24.9
Ours	**99.2**	**99.9**	94.6	97.3	**99.2**	97.7	**99.5**	**94.1**	**11.2**

2) Results on CLPD: We train our model on the CCPD-Base dataset, and test its accuracy with and without recognizing the first region code on the CLPD dataset. We compare the results with [2,6,32]. In order to evaluate the effectiveness of synthesized images, we also train [6] and our model on the joint dataset of CCPD-base and SynSet. The results are shown in Table 2, Our models achieve the best results. It can be verified that synthesized images effectively improve recognition performance. And even without training on SynSet, our model outperforms [6]'s trained with SynSet.

Table 2. Experimental comparison of methods on CLPD.

Criterion	Accuracy	Accuracy w/o region code
Masood *et al.* [8]	–	85.2
Xu *et al.* [2]	66.5	78.9
Zhang (CCPD-base) *et al.* [6]	70.8	86.1
Zhang (CCPD-base + SynSet) *et al.* [6]	76.8	87.6
Ours (CCPD-base)	81.8	93.7
Ours (CCPD-base + SynSet)	**93.0**	**94.75**

Table 3. Recognition accuracy of four different algorithms trained with different datasets and evaluated on CCPD-SubTest.

	SynSet	Our real dataset	SynSet+Our real dataset
Resnet-BiLSTM-Attn [8]	84.532	72.658	92.789
RobustScanner [1]	85.948	73.989	93.573
Scatter [26]	85.098	68.976	93.769
Ours (without CTC Loss)	87.582	77.996	94.27
Ours	**87.734**	**78.279**	**94.728**

3) Results on CCPD-SubTest: We compare three different algorithms for scene text recognition with our model, to see whether the state-of-the-art text recognition models are readily usable for LPR. We also investigate whether the synthesized images can help in model training. We train those models on SynSet, Our Real Dataset and SynSet + Our Real Dataset. All the models are tested on CCPD-SubTest. With the same input, the results are shown in Table 3. According to the results, we find that the models for scene text recognition perform surprisingly well on LPR task. However, our model tailored for LPR achieves the best performances for all the three tests. We also find that CycleGAN-generated plate images significantly improve model performance.

4) Localization Ability of Our Position-Aware Attention Model: In Fig. 5, we select different types of license plates, and visualize the attention maps for each character. The results show that even for different types of license plates, our attention model can locate the position of every character very well, and this process does not require character-level annotation.

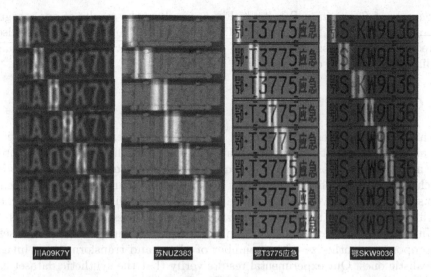

Fig. 5. Visualization of attention weights for each decoding timestep. The results show that the attention model can handle different types of license plates. The recognized results are showed below each panel.

Fig. 6. Recognition results of our model, GT stands for ground truth labels and Pred stands for predicted results.

5) Sample of Recognition Results: In Fig. 6, we show the results of our recognition network on the CCPD dataset. The majority of the plates are recognised correctly, and only a small portion are recognised incorrectly due to poor image quality or incomplete characters.

6   Conclusions

In this paper, we present an efficient algorithm for license plate recognition. We abandon the fault assumption that characters in a license plate are interdependent, and propose a novel *parallel position-aware attention* model, which address the problem of attention drift found in recurrent attention mechanisms, and can effectively attend to the location of each character. Experimental results show that our model out-perform most of the latest LPR algorithms.

In order to mitigate the severe imbalance problem in public LP datasets, we propose to synthesize a large number of plates and transform these images to realistic ones. Our experimental results verify that the synthetic dataset can significantly improve performances of LPR algorithms.

References

1. Yue, X., Kuang, Z., Lin, C., Sun, H., Zhang, W.: Robustscanner: Dynamically enhancing positional clues for robust text recognition. In: Vedaldi, A., Bischof, H., Brox, T., Frahm, J.-M. (eds.) ECCV 2020. LNCS, vol. 12364, pp. 135–151. Springer, Cham (2020). https://doi.org/10.1007/978-3-030-58529-7_9
2. Xu, Z., et al.: Towards end-to-end license plate detection and recognition: A large dataset and baseline. In: Ferrari, V., Hebert, M., Sminchisescu, C., Weiss, Y. (eds.) ECCV 2018. LNCS, vol. 11217, pp. 261–277. Springer, Cham (2018). https://doi.org/10.1007/978-3-030-01261-8_16
3. Zhu, J.-Y., Park, T., Isola, P., Efros, A.A.: Unpaired image-to-image translation using cycle-consistent adversarial networks. In: Proceedings of the IEEE International Conference on Computer Vision (ICCV), pp. 2223–2232 (2017)
4. Silva, S.M., Jung, C.R.: License plate detection and recognition in unconstrained scenarios. In: Ferrari, V., Hebert, M., Sminchisescu, C., Weiss, Y. (eds.) ECCV 2018. LNCS, vol. 11216, pp. 593–609. Springer, Cham (2018). https://doi.org/10.1007/978-3-030-01258-8_36
5. Yuan, Y., Zou, W., Zhao, Y., Wang, X., Hu, X., Komodakis, N.: A robust and efficient approach to license plate detection. Proc. IEEE Trans. Image Process. (TIP) **26**(3), 1102–1114 (2016)
6. Zhang, L., Wang, P., Li, H., Li, Z., Shen, C., Zhang, Y.: A robust attentional framework for license plate recognition in the wild. Proc. IEEE Trans. Intell. Trans. Syst. (TITS) **22**(11), 6967–6976 (2020)
7. Silva, S.M., Jung, C.R.: Real-time brazilian license plate detection and recognition using deep convolutional neural networks. In: 30th SIBGRAPI Conference on Graphics, Patterns and Images (SIBGRAPI), pp. 55–62. IEEE (2017)
8. Baek, J., et al.: What is wrong with scene text recognition model comparisons? dataset and model analysis. In: Proceedings of the IEEE International Conference on Computer Vision (ICCV), pp. 4715–4723 (2019)

9. Graves, A., Fernández, S., Gomez, F., Schmidhuber, J.: Connectionist temporal classification: labelling unsegmented sequence data with recurrent neural networks. In: Proceedings of the 23rd International Conference on Machine Learning (ICML), pp. 369–376 (2006)

10. Zou, Y., et al.: A robust license plate recognition model based on bi-lstm. IEEE Access **8**, 211630–211641 (2020)

11. Wang, J., Huang, H., Qian, X., Cao, J., Dai, Y.: Sequence recognition of Chinese license plates. Neurocomputing **317**, 149–158 (2018)

12. Zhuang, J., Hou, S., Wang, Z., Zha, Z.-J.: Towards human-level license plate recognition. In: Ferrari, V., Hebert, M., Sminchisescu, C., Weiss, Y. (eds.) ECCV 2018. LNCS, vol. 11207, pp. 314–329. Springer, Cham (2018). https://doi.org/10.1007/978-3-030-01219-9_19

13. Chen, L.-C., Papandreou, G., Kokkinos, I., Murphy, K., Yuille, A.L.: Deeplab: semantic image segmentation with deep convolutional nets, atrous convolution, and fully connected crfs. IEEE Trans. Pattern Anal. Mach. Intell. (TPAMI) **40**(4), 834–848 (2017)

14. Jiao, J., Ye, Q., Huang, Q.: A configurable method for multi-style license plate recognition. Pattern Recogn. (PR) **42**(3), 358–369 (2009)

15. Dong, M., He, D., Luo, C., Liu, D., Zeng, W.: A cnn-based approach for automatic license plate recognition in the wild. In: Proceedings of the 28th British Machine Vision Conference (BMVC) (2017)

16. Jaderberg, M., Simonyan, K., Zisserman, A., et al.: Spatial transformer networks. Adv. Neural Inf. Process. Syst. (NIPS) **28**, 2017–2025 (2015)

17. Bochkovskiy, A., Wang, C.-Y., Liao, H.-Y. M.: Yolov4: optimal speed and accuracy of object detection, arXiv preprint arXiv:2004.10934

18. Laroca, R., et al.: A robust real-time automatic license plate recognition based on the yolo detector. In: 2018 International Joint Conference on Neural Networks (IJCNN), pp. 1–10. IEEE (2018)

19. Björklund, T., Fiandrotti, A., Annarumma, M., Francini, G., Magli, E.: Robust license plate recognition using neural networks trained on synthetic images. Pattern Recogn. (PR) **93**, 134–146 (2019)

20. Li, H., Wang, P., Shen, C.: Toward end-to-end car license plate detection and recognition with deep neural networks. Proc. IEEE Trans. Intell. Trans. Syst. (TITS) **20**(3), 1126–1136 (2018)

21. Li, H., Wang, P., You, M., Shen, C.: Reading car license plates using deep neural networks. Image Vis. Comput. (IVC) **72**, 14–23 (2018)

22. Gong, Y., et al.: Unified chinese license plate detection and recognition with high efficiency, arXiv preprint arXiv:2205.03582

23. Shi, B., Bai, X., Yao, C.: An end-to-end trainable neural network for image-based sequence recognition and its application to scene text recognition. IEEE Trans. Pattern Anal. Mach. Intell. (TPAMI) **39**(11), 2298–2304 (2016)

24. Zhang, C., Wang, Q., Li, X.: V-LPDR: towards a unified framework for license plate detection, tracking, and recognition in real-world traffic videos. Neurocomputing **449**, 189–206 (2021)

25. He, K., Zhang, X., Ren, S., Sun, J.: Deep residual learning for image recognition. In: Proceedings of the IEEE Conference on Computer Vision and Pattern Recognition (CVPR), pp. 770–778 (2016)

26. Litman, R., Anschel, O., Tsiper, S., Litman, R., Mazor, S., Manmatha, R.: Scatter: selective context attentional scene text recognizer. In: Proceedings of the IEEE Conference on Computer Vision and Pattern Recognition (CVPR), pp. 11962–11972 (2020)

27. Liao, M., Wan, Z., Yao, C., Chen, K., Bai, X.: Real-time scene text detection with differentiable binarization. In: Proceedings of the AAAI Conference on Artificial Intelligence (AAAI), vol. 34, pp. 11474–11481 (2020)
28. Luo, C., Zhu, Y., Jin, L., Wang, Y.: Learn to augment: joint data augmentation and network optimization for text rxecognition. In: Proceedings of the IEEE Conference on Computer Vision and Pattern Recognition (CVPR), pp. 13746–13755 (2020)
29. Zherzdev, S., Gruzdev, A.: LPRNet: license plate recognition via deep neural networks, arXiv preprint arXiv:1806.10447
30. Luo, C., Jin, L., Sun, Z.: MORAN: a multi-object rectified attention network for scene text recognition. Pattern Recogn. (PR) **90**, 109–118 (2019)
31. Wang, T.: Decoupled attention network for text recognition. In: Proceedings of the AAAI Conference on Artificial Intelligence (AAAI), Vol. 34, pp. 12216–12224 (2020)
32. Masood, S.Z., Shu, G., Dehghan, A., Ortiz, E.G.: License plate detection and recognition using deeply learned convolutional neural networks, arXiv preprint arXiv:1703.07330

Semantic-Aware Non-local Network for Handwritten Mathematical Expression Recognition

Xiang-Hao Liu[1,2], Da-Han Wang[1,2(✉)], Xia Du[1,2], and Shunzhi Zhu[1,2]

[1] School of Computer Science and Information Engineering, Xiaman University of Technology, Xiamen 361024, China
wangdh@xmut.edu.cn

[2] Fujian Key Laboratory of Pattern Recognition and Image Understanding, Xiamen 361024, China

Abstract. Handwritten mathematical expression recognition (HMER) is a challenging task due to its complex two-dimensional structure of mathematical expressions and the high similarity between handwritten texts. Most existing encoder-decoder approaches for HMER mainly depend on local visual features but are seldom studied in explicit global semantic information. Besides, existing works for HMER primarily focus on local information. However, this obtained information is difficult to transmit between distant locations. In this paper, we propose a semantic-aware non-local network to tackle the above problems for HMER. Specifically, we propose to adopt the non-local network to capture long-term dependencies while integrating local and non-local features. Moreover, we customized the FastText language model to our backbone to learn the semantic-aware information. The experimental results illustrate that our design consistently outperforms the state-of-the-art methods on the Competition on Recognition of Online Handwritten Mathematical Expressions (CROHME) 2014 and 2016 datasets.

Keywords: Handwritten mathematical expression recognition · FastText language model · Non-local neural network

1 Introduction

Handwritten mathematical expression recognition (HMER) is one of the critical problems in the document analysis and recognition domain. It has been widely applied in education, finance, and office automation. Despite this success, however, it has been found that HMER is still facing several challenges, i.e., the complex two-dimensional structure, style diversity of handwritten input, and similar handwritten symbols [1].

In recent years, many competitions have been organized at international conferences, such as the Competition on Recognition of Online Handwritten Mathematical Expressions (CROHME) 2014, 2016, and OffRASHME 2020 [2–4]. Many efficient methods are proposed in these competitions to push forward the development of HMER. However, the performance of the state-of-the-art methods is far from satisfactory. For instance, the

S. Yu et al. (Eds.): PRCV 2022, LNCS 13536, pp. 361–371, 2022.
https://doi.org/10.1007/978-3-031-18913-5_28

winner of OffRASHME 2020 only achieved 79.85% without using extra datasets. There is a big room for the improvement of HMER.

In recent years, many attention-based encoder-decoder methods have been proposed. While these methods enable superior performance in HMER, the receptive field of the convolution kernel is local, and it could lead to the attention drift problem when information needs to be passed back and forth between distant locations. Additionally, these methods are sensitive to the long texts and different sizes of symbols in handwritten mathematical expressions (HMEs); hence the existing techniques usually suffer from the attention confusion problems [5–7].

Meanwhile, utilizing semantic information from images that has been proved effective in text/word recognition (such as [8–10]) is always ignored in HMER. In text/word recognition, the semantic information (always is a language model) is integrated with visual information in the path evaluation function and can effectively improve the performance by correcting recognition mistakes in the inference stage. Semantic information is expected to be much effective than grammar-based information in that, grammars are only used for grouping the recognized symbols into a structural output, heavily relying on the performance of symbol recognition.

In this paper, we propose a semantic-aware non-local network that leverages the advantages of the non-local mechanism and semantic information for HMER. Specifically, considering the long texts may raise difficulties for HMER, a non-local module [11] has been used to capture long-term dependencies in mathematical expressions. In this way, our model could alleviate the effect of the attention drift problem caused by the local receptive fields. Moreover, we adopted and customized FastText [12] as our pre-trained language model, such that our framework can effectively generate the corresponding embedding vectors from the mathematical expressions in the training set and gradually learn the semantic information among these expressions. Our design method achieves a superior expression recognition rate of 53.91% and 52.75% on the CROHME 2014 and 2016 [2, 3], respectively.

The rest of this paper is organized as follows. Section 2 briefly introduces the current mainstream methods. Section 3 introduces our proposed method. Section 4 summarizes the training and testing datasets, metrics and highlights the results of the experiments. Section 5 draws the conclusion and our future works.

2 Related Works

2.1 Grammar-Based HMER

The HMER task has been first studied by Anderson in 1970s [13]. The author proposed an idea to transform the images into structured languages and markup symbols. After that, various approaches have been developed and proposed, especially the grammar-based methods. Chan and Yeung [14] tried to use definite clause grammars to develop the HMER. Besides, they proposed a new framework by incorporating some error detection and correction mechanism into a parser. Lavirotte and Pottier [15] proposed a graph-grammar based model that precisely removed ambiguities between grammar rules and the construction of a graph. Yamamoto et al. [16] constructed a framework utilizing

Probabilistic Context-Free Grammars (PCFG) that devised probability based on a "hidden writing area" region representation. MacLean and Labahn [17] introduced a novel system using relational grammars and fuzzy sets.

However, these approaches' performance is significantly dependent on manually defined grammars created by assumption and design decisions. Besides, the recognition is very susceptible to the steps of symbol segmentation, symbol recognition, and classification of spatial relations.

2.2 Encoder-Decoder Based HMER

Deep learning has been successfully applied in many research fields to improve their performance, including HMER. HMER is a sequence to sequence learning problem, its attention-based encoder-decoder structure that has been widely used in a variety of deep learning tasks, such as machine translation [18], speech recognition [19], character recognition [20] and image description [21], etc. Many works in this direction have been proposed [22–24, 27–35].

Zhang et al. [22, 23] noticed the lack of coverage and proposed the encoder-decoder method based on GRU and coverage attention. In their following research, Zhang et al. [24] proposed the WAP-based Dense MSA and replaced the VGG [25] encoder with the DenseNet [26] encoder. They used an extra branch to extract multi-scale features better. Furthermore, Tree Decoder [27] improves the model's capacity by replacing the string decoder with a tree decoder to handle complex formulas. Wu et al. [28] introduced a paired adversarial learning (PAL) method to generate LaTeX of images. In their subsequent study, Wu et al. [29] developed an improved model PAL-v2, which has shown superior performance in dealing with the changes in writing styles by learning semantic invariant features and discriminative features. Li et al. [30] used scale enhancement and randomly lost part of the attention to improve the recognition performance further. Zhao et al. [31] proposed a Transformer-based method for HMER, and the experimental results demonstrated that the analysis of two-dimensional structure is correct and effective. Truong, Thanh-Nghia, et al. [32] integrated an end-to-end network with weakly supervised learning and trained the architecture with the combined loss of the symbol-level BCE loss and the expression-level cross-entropy loss. Based on this idea, Truong, Thanh-Nghia, et al. [33] proposed data generation consisting of decomposing HMEs and interchanging the decomposed sub-HMEs to generate new syntactically valid HME patterns for improving both the HME recognition model and mathematical language model. Bian et al. [34] integrated multi-scale coverage attention with dual-branch bidirectional decoders in a mutual learning manner. Yuan et al. [35] combined syntax information and visual representations to make robust predictions, especially, it incorporates the grammar rules into deep feature learning. The HME100K dataset that they proposed also validates the effectiveness and efficiency of their method.

Compared with above mentioned methods, we utilize not only local but also non-local features to capture long-term dependencies in HMER. Besides, a simple but effective universal language model is applied for capturing the semantic information for HMER.

3 Methodology

In our design, we proposed to adopt the encoder-decoder framework as our core module, such that the encoder-decoder networks can address variable length input and output sequence. Figure 1 shows the network structure of our proposed method, where the black solid arrow lines and the red dashed arrow lines indicate the forward and backward step, respectively. In our framework, the encoder uses the DenseNet to encode the input image to high-level features, and the decoder adopts the GRUs with attention to convert the high-level features into a sequence of LaTeX symbols. More specifically, we incorporate the DenseNet with non-local neural networks to capture long-term dependencies. This approach mitigates the loss of contextual information and fine-grained details of extracted features caused by long texts and different sizes of symbols in handwritten mathematical expressions. Moreover, we use the FastText model to explore the semantic information in mathematical expressions to improve the HMER performance further.

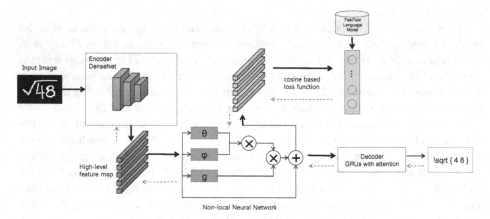

Fig. 1. Structure of the final model

3.1 Non-local Neural Networks

Compared to the traditional grammar-based methods, the performance of the encoder-decoder based model has dramatically improved. However, the receptive field of the convolution kernel is local, and it is difficult for local information to pass between long-term locations at each step, which would lead to attention drift. As a result, problems like deletion, substitution and insertion would occur.

Recent advances in self-attention methods have facilitated investigation of machine translation. In this method, the self-attention module can compute the response at a position in a sequence by relating all positions and taking their weighted average in an embedding space. As a matter of fact, self-attention can be viewed as a form of the non-local mean [36]. In this sense, Wang et al. proposed a non-local network [11] to compute a weighted mean of all pixels in an image which bridges the gap between self-attention for machine translation and the more broad class of non-local filtering operations used in computer vision for image and video problems.

The formula of the non-local operation in deep neural networks is shown as follows:

$$y_i = \frac{1}{C(x)} \sum_{\forall j} f(x_i, x_j) g(x_j) \tag{1}$$

where i is the index of an output position (here is the space) whose response is to be computed and j is the index that enumerates all possible positions. x is the input signal (here is the image features) and y is the output signal of the same size as x. A pairwise function f computes a scalar (representing relationship such as affinity) between i and all j. The unary function g computes a representation of the input signal at the position j. The response is normalized by a factor $C(x)$.

The non-local block operation is a versatile building block that can be combined with convolutional and recurrent layers with ease. Compared with the original convolution operations, the non-local mechanism could expand receptive fields rather than be limited to a local field. This enables us to construct a more complex hierarchy incorporating the non-local and local information.

3.2 FastText Language Model

We choose FastText as our pre-trained language model to generate embedding vectors for all training data, which is based on skip-gram. Given a word vocabulary of size W, each word is recognized by its index $w \in \{1, \ldots, W\}$ and represented by a single embedding vector. These words are put into a feed-forward neural network that aims to predict the context for each word. The embedding vector is optimized by training the network, and the final vector would be close to the words with similar semantics.

Additionally, FastText uses subwords to generate final embedding of each word w. Given the hyper parameters l_{min} and l_{max}, which denotes the subwords' minimum and maximum lengths, respectively. For instance, let $l_{min} = 2$ and $l_{max} = 4$ and the word be "where", the set of subwords is {wh, he, er, re, whe, her, ere, wher, here}. The embedding vectors of all subwords, as well as the word itself, are combined to produce the word representation. Hence, FastText model can learn reliable representation for rare words. With regard to the combination of various mathematical symbols, FastText also has great potential to adapt to the complex two-dimensional structure of mathematical expressions and the similarity of handwritten texts. As a result, the semantic information is integrated with the visual information and can significantly improve the recognition performance in the inference stage.

In the forward step, the encoder encodes the input images to high-level features and then delivers them to the decoder. In the backward step, the model will compute the expression loss and the semantic loss such that the combined loss can be utilized to train the parameters.

Here, the cosine-based loss function is utilized to compute the cosine embedding loss of the predicted semantic information such that the loss function can be used for the word embedding of the transaction label from the pre-trained FastText model. The formula of the semantic loss is shown as follows:

$$loss_{sem} = 1 - cos(S, emb) \tag{2}$$

where S is the predicted semantic information and *emb* is the embedding vectors from pre-trained FastText model.

More precisely, our model learns from the combined loss, which can be calculated as:

$$loss_{combined} = loss_{expression} + \lambda loss_{sem} \tag{3}$$

where $loss_{expression}$ denotes the expression-level cross-entropy loss and λ is a hyper parameter to balance the semantic loss, here we set it to 1.

4 Experiments

To evaluate the effectiveness of our proposed method, we conducted a series of experiments using the publicly available datasets from CROHME [2, 3].

4.1 Datasets

The CROHME 2014 dataset possesses a training set with 8836 math expressions and a testing set with 986 math expressions. The CROHME 2016 possesses testing set with 1147 math expressions. These datasets have 101 math symbol classes in total.

We adopted the Dense WAP we reproduce trained on the CROHME 2014 training set as our baseline in our experiments. The reproduced results are different from [24] as the results we reproduce are 0.2% to 1.0%, which is higher than the Dense WAP using CROHME 2014 and 2016 testing set. Therefore, we use our reproduced results as the baseline.

4.2 Metrics

As in [24], the metrics we use in this paper are the expression recognition rate (ExpRate) and word error rate (WER).

All the CROHME competitions ranked the participating systems by expression recognition rate, representing the percentage of correctly predicted LaTeX sequences.

We also use the WER to evaluate our model because the output of our model is made up of word sequences, and errors such as deletions, substitutions and insertions can be counted to evaluate the performance at the symbol level. The word error rate can be computed as:

$$WER = \frac{Deletions + Substitutions + Insertions}{Total\ word} \tag{4}$$

where *Deletions*, *Substitutions* and *Insertions* indicate the number of deleted symbols, substituted symbols and inserted symbols, respectively, and the *Total word* is the total number of the words in the datasets.

4.3 Results

We conducted the ablation study to evaluate the effects of each module on the CROHME 2014 and 2016 testing sets. The results are shown in Table 1, where "FM" and "NL" denotes "FastText model" and "Non-local", respectively. The $\sqrt{}$ means the use of the method and $\times$ indicates not using it. It can be seen that, compared with the baseline, our method gains an improvement of nearly 3.6 points and 4.2 points on ExpRate on the CROHME 2014 and 2016 testing sets, respectively. Moreover, the overall WERs are also significantly degraded, by about 2 points on the CROHME 2014 and 2016 testing sets.

From Table 1, we can see that in two datasets, the FastText language model and non-local block constantly improves the baseline performance, while the combination of these two methods further improve the performance. These results demonstrate the effectiveness of the language model and the addition of the Non-local block.

Compared with CROHME 2014 testing set, more inequations, equations, and function expressions are involved in CROHME 2016 testing set. Therefore, capturing related semantic information in these expressions is essential for improving the recognition results. Thanks to the semantic module, our model can better understand the symbols with the semantic association. The experimental results demonstrated that our language model is more effective on CROHME 2016 testing set as the use of the FastText model gains an improvement of more than 2 points on ExpRate while it only improves by 0.4 points on the CROHME 2014 testing set.

Table 1. Ablation study on CROHME 2014, 2016 testing sets (%)

Model	FM	NL	ExpRate	WER
CROHME 2014	$\times$	$\times$	50.36	12.90
	$\sqrt{}$	$\times$	50.76	12.40
	$\times$	$\sqrt{}$	52.28	11.63
	$\sqrt{}$	$\sqrt{}$	53.91	10.93
CROHME 2016	$\times$	$\times$	48.56	13.51
	$\sqrt{}$	$\times$	50.88	12.74
	$\times$	$\sqrt{}$	50.48	11.89
	$\sqrt{}$	$\sqrt{}$	52.75	11.40

We compare our model with some typical state-of-the-art methods, and the results on CROHME 2016 testing set are shown in Table 2. It should be noted that the system "MyScript" [3] is not listed because it uses many private datasets. Besides, our model is just a single model without using the ensemble method, to ensure the fairness of performance comparison, we mainly compared our model with the methods that do not use the ensemble method and enhanced datasets.

Table 2. Comparison with other methods on CROHME 2016(%)

Model	ExpRate	≤1 s.error	≤2 s.error	≤3 s.error
Wiris [3]	49.61	60.42	64.69	–
Tokyo [3]	43.94	50.91	53.70	–
Nantes [3]	13.34	21.02	28.33	–
PAL-v2 [29]	48.88	64.50	69.78	–
BTTR [30]	52.31	63.90	68.61	69.40
Tree Decoder [27]	48.5	62.3	65.3	65.9
WS WAP [31]	51.96	64.34	70.10	72.97
Dense WAP [24]	40.1	54.3	57.8	–
ABM [34]	52.92	69.66	78.73	–
SAN [35]	53.6	69.6	76.8	–
Ours	52.75	62.60	68.96	71.14

Image	Dense WAP	Our Model
 $x_1 x_2 x_3 x_4 x_5$	x _ { 1 } x _ { 2 } x _ { 3 } x _ { 4 } \times x _ { 5 }	x _ { 1 } x _ { 2 } x _ { 3 } x _ { 4 } x _ { 5 }
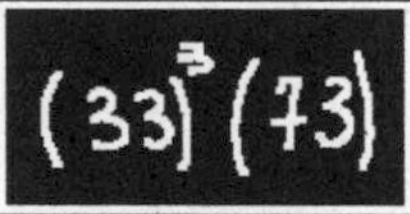 $(33)^3 (73)$	(3 3) ^{ miss } (7 3)	(3 3) ^ { 3 } (7 3)
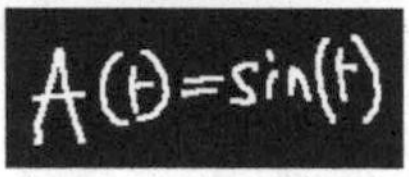 $A(t)=\sin(t)$	A (b) = \sin (t)	A (t) = \sin (t)

Fig. 2. We give several case studies for the "Dense WAP" and "Our Model". Comparing the "Dense WAP" and "Our Model", the under-parsing and over-parsing phenomenon is very distinct in the first and second image, while our model can identify these symbols accurately. Besides, the third image demonstrates that the non-local neural networks and the FastText language model are capable of helping the model to establish the connection between symbols in the first and the second brackets and figure out the semantic relevance between them which proves the effectiveness of our proposed method.

Our model achieves an ExpRate of 53.91% and 52.75% on the CROHME 2014 and CROHME 2016 testing sets, which is a competitive result compared to other participating systems in the competition and some other state-of-the-art methods. Meanwhile, our model is a single model and does not use augmented and synthetic data or the ensemble method. Besides, compared with [35], our model is simpler and can be easily embedded into any encoder-decoder-based framework without requiring additional modification. To sum up, our model is a model with great potential and still has room to be improved (Fig. 2).

5 Conclusion

In this paper, we proposed an end-to-end framework fully utilizing semantic information while capturing long-range dependencies via non-local operations in HMER. Specifically, we proposed to use non-local neural networks to capture long-term dependencies and integrate local and non-local features. Furthermore, the FastText language model is adopted and customized in our method to generate embedding vectors for all the mathematical expressions in training set to improve the performance further. Experimental results on the CROHME 2014 and 2016 datasets demonstrate the effectiveness of the proposed method. Our future work will focus on the better use of semantic information and self-attention mechanism. Moreover, exploring the syntax rules and structure relations in HMER would also be our following work.

Acknowledgement. This work is supported by Industry-University Cooperation Project of Fujian Science and Technology Department (No. 2021H6035), and the Science and Technology Planning Project of Fujian Province (No. 2021J011191, 2020H0023, 2020Y9064), and the Joint Funds of 5th Round of Health and Education Research Program of Fujian Province (No. 2019-WJ-41).

References

1. He, F., Tan, J., Bi, N.: Handwritten mathematical expression recognition: a survey. In: Lu, Y., Vincent, N., Yuen, P.C., Zheng, W.-S., Cheriet, F., Suen, C.Y. (eds.) ICPRAI 2020. LNCS, vol. 12068, pp. 55–66. Springer, Cham (2020). https://doi.org/10.1007/978-3-030-59830-3_5
2. Mouchere, H., et al.: ICFHR 2014 competition on recognition of on-line handwritten mathematical expressions (CROHME 2014). In: International Conference on Frontiers in Handwriting Recognition. IEEE (2014)
3. Mouchère, H., et al.: ICFHR2016 CROHME: competition on recognition of online handwritten mathematical expressions. In: 2016 15th International Conference on Frontiers in Handwriting Recognition (ICFHR). IEEE (2016)
4. Wang, D.-H., et al.: ICFHR 2020 competition on offline recognition and spotting of handwritten mathematical expressions-OffRaSHME. In: 2020 17th International Conference on Frontiers in Handwriting Recognition (ICFHR). IEEE (2020)
5. Cheng, Z., Bai, F., Xu, Y., Zheng, G., Pu, S., Zhou, S.: Focusing attention: towards accurate text recognition in natural images. In: ICCV 2017, pp. 5086–5094 (2017)
6. Dai, Z., Yang, Z., Yang, Y., Carbonell, J., Le, Q.V., Salakhutdinov, R.: Transformer-XL: attentive language models beyond a fixed-length context. In: ACL (1), pp. 2978–2988 (2019)
7. Cheng, J., Dong, L., Lapata, M.: Long short-term memory-networks for machine reading. In: Proceedings of the 2016 Conference on Empirical Methods in Natural Language Processing (2016)
8. Gordo, A., et al.: LEWIS: latent embeddings for word images and their semantics. In: IEEE International Conference on Computer Vision. IEEE (2015)
9. Wilkinson, T., Brun, A.: Semantic and verbatim word spotting using deep neural networks. In: 2016 15th International Conference on Frontiers in Handwriting Recognition (ICFHR). IEEE (2016)
10. Wang, Q.-F., Yin, F., Liu, C.-L.: Handwritten Chinese text recognition by integrating multiple contexts. IEEE Trans. Pattern Anal. Mach. Intell. **34**(8), 1469–1481 (2011)
11. Wang, X., et al.: Non-local neural networks. In: Proceedings of the IEEE Conference on Computer Vision and Pattern Recognition (2018)

12. Bojanowski, P., et al.: Enriching word vectors with subword information. Trans. Assoc. Comput. Linguist. **5**, 135–146 (2017)
13. Anderson, R.H.: Syntax-directed recognition of hand-printed two-dimensional mathematics. In: Symposium on Interactive Systems for Experimental Applied Mathematics: Proceedings of the Association for Computing Machinery Inc. Symposium, pp. 436–459. ACM (1967)
14. Chan, K.F., Yeung, D.Y.: Error detection, error correction and performance evaluation in on-line mathematical expression recognition. Pattern Recogn. **34**(8), 1671–1684 (2001)
15. Lavirotte, S., Pottier, L.: Mathematical formula recognition using graph grammar. Proc. SPIE Int. Soc. Opt. Eng. **3305**, 44–52 (2016)
16. Yamamoto, R., et al.: On-line recognition of handwritten mathematical expressions based on stroke-based stochastic context-free grammar. In: Proceedings of International Workshop on Frontiers in Handwriting Recognition, pp. 249–254, October 2006
17. Maclean, S., Labahn, G.: A new approach for recognizing handwritten mathematics using relational grammars and fuzzy sets. Int. J. Doc. Anal. Recogn. **16**(2), 139–163 (2013)
18. Cho, K., et al.: Learning phrase representations using RNN encoder-decoder for statistical machine translation. Computer Science (2014)
19. Bahdanau, D., et al.: End-to-end attention-based large vocabulary speech recognition. In: 2016 IEEE International Conference on Acoustics, Speech and Signal Processing (ICASSP) (2016)
20. Zhang, J., et al.: Radical analysis network for zero-shot learning in printed Chinese character recognition. In: 2018 IEEE International Conference on Multimedia and Expo (ICME). IEEE (2018)
21. Xu, K., et al.: Show, attend and tell: neural image caption generation with visual attention. Computer Science, pp. 2048–2057 (2015)
22. Zhang, J., Du, J., Dai, L.: A GRU-based encoder-decoder approach with attention for online handwritten mathematical expression recognition. In: 2017 14th IAPR International Conference on Document Analysis and Recognition (ICDAR). IEEE (2018)
23. Zhang, J., et al.: Watch, attend and parse: An end-to-end neural network based approach to handwritten mathematical expression recognition. Pattern Recogn. **71**, 196–206 (2017)
24. Zhang, J., Du, J., Dai, L.: Multi-scale attention with dense encoder for handwritten mathematical expression recognition. In: 2018 24th International Conference on Pattern Recognition (ICPR) (2018)
25. Simonyan, K., Zisserman, A.: Very deep convolutional networks for large-scale image recognition. Computer Science (2014)
26. Huang, G., et al.: Densely connected convolutional networks. In: Proceedings of the IEEE Conference on Computer Vision and Pattern Recognition (2017)
27. Zhang, J., et al.: A tree-structured decoder for image-to-markup generation. In: International Conference on Machine Learning. PMLR (2020)
28. Wu, J.-W., Yin, F., Zhang, YM., Zhang, X.-Y., Liu, C.-L.: Image-to-markup generation via paired adversarial learning. In: Berlingerio, M., Bonchi, F., Gärtner, T., Hurley, N., Ifrim, G. (eds.) ECML PKDD 2018. LNCS, vol. 11051, pp. 18–34. Springer, Cham (2019). https://doi.org/10.1007/978-3-030-10925-7_2
29. Wu, J.-W., et al.: Handwritten mathematical expression recognition via paired adversarial learning. Int. J. Comput. Vis. **128**(10), 2386–2401 (2020)
30. Li, Z., et al.: Improving attention-based handwritten mathematical expression recognition with scale augmentation and drop attention. In: 2020 17th International Conference on Frontiers in Handwriting Recognition (ICFHR). IEEE (2020)
31. Zhao, W., Gao, L., Yan, Z., Peng, S., Du, L., Zhang, Z.: Handwritten mathematical expression recognition with bidirectionally trained transformer. In: Lladós, J., Lopresti, D., Uchida, S. (eds.) ICDAR 2021. LNCS, vol. 12822, pp. 570–584. Springer, Cham (2021). https://doi.org/10.1007/978-3-030-86331-9_37

32. Truong, T.-N., et al.: Improvement of end-to-end offline handwritten mathematical expression recognition by weakly supervised learning. In: 2020 17th International Conference on Frontiers in Handwriting Recognition (ICFHR). IEEE (2020)
33. Truong, T.-N., Nguyen, C.T., Nakagawa, M.: Syntactic data generation for handwritten mathematical expression recognition. Pattern Recogn. Lett. **153**, 83–91 (2022)
34. Bian, X., et al.: Handwritten mathematical expression recognition via attention aggregation based bi-directional mutual learning. arXiv e-prints (2021)
35. Yuan, Y., et al.: Syntax-aware network for handwritten mathematical expression recognition. arXiv preprint arXiv:2203.01601 (2022)
36. Liu, Y.-L., et al.: A robust and fast non-local means algorithm for image denoising. J. Comput. Sci. Technol. **23**(2), 270–279 (2008)

Math Word Problem Generation with Memory Retrieval

Xiaowei Wang[1], Wei Qin[1,2], Zhenzhen Hu[1,2(✉)], Lei Wang[3], Yunshi Lan[4], and Richang Hong[1,2]

[1] Hefei University of Technology, Hefei, China
[2] Institute of Artificial Intelligence Hefei Comprehensive National Science Center, Hefei, China
huzhen.ice@gmail.com
[3] Singapore Management University, Singapore, Singapore
[4] China East Normal University, Shanghai, China

Abstract. The task of math word problem generation (MWPG), which generates a math word problem (MWP) given an equation and several topic words, has increasingly attracted researchers' attention. In this work, we propose a memory retrieval model to better take advantage of the training data. We first record training MWPs into a memory. Later we use the given equation and topic words to retrieve relevant items from the memory. The retrieved results are then used to complement the process of the MWP generation and improve the generation quality. In addition, we also propose a low-resource setting for MWPG, where only a small number of paired MWPs and a large amount of unpaired MWPs are available. Extensive experiments verify the superior performance and effectiveness of our method.

Keywords: Math word problem generation · Memory retrieval · Low-resource

1 Introduction

Math word problems play an important role in mathematics education since they are broadly used to assess and improve students' understanding of mathematical concepts and skills of solving math problems [31–33,35,39]. As shown in Table 1, a MWP consists of a question and a corresponding equation. Students could strengthen their problem-solving skills by learning to identify the underlying math equation under different contexts(i.e., the real-world scenario that the math equation is grounded in) [31]. Many studies [12,13,27] have shown that high-quality MWPs could improve the teaching outcomes. However, manually designing MWPs by experts costs a lot and the quality of the generated MWPs heavily relies on the experts.

In this paper, we focus on the problem of MWPG (math word problem generation) which is to generate a MWP conditioned on both topic words and an equation. Traditional methods usually heuristically generate MWPs based on some pre-defined text templates [5,21,24,37]. However, the diversity of MWPs generated by text templates is not as expected. Recently, some models based on deep neural networks have brought significant improvements in generating MWPs. MaGNET [41], based on a standard encoder-decoder architecture, forces the entities in the generated MWP to correspond to

S. Yu et al. (Eds.): PRCV 2022, LNCS 13536, pp. 372–385, 2022.
https://doi.org/10.1007/978-3-031-18913-5_29

the variables in the input equation. The work in [19] fuses information from equations and commonsense knowledge to facilitate the generation. And the work in [35], based on a large-scale pre-trained language model, introduces an equation consistency constraint, which encourages the generated MWP to contain the same equation as the one used to generate it. However, since the generation process of these methods only conditions on the given topic words and equation, the scenario description of the generated MWP often lacks richness. The underlying equation of the generated MWP usually is not consistent with the input equation. As shown in Fig. 1(a), the generation of *Seq2Seq* lacks some keywords(such as *school* for scenario description and *times* for the input equation).

Table 1. An example of MWP.

MWP:	The school has N_0 boys, and girls are N_1 times of boys. How many students in total?
Topic Words:	boys, girls, students, school
Equation:	$N_0 * N_1 + N_0 \, (80 * 2 + 80)$
Final Answer:	240

To solve this problem, we introduce a memory retrieval(MR) module, which takes full advantage of the training MWPs, into the MWPG framework. Memory retrieval module has been shown to facilitate a number of text generation tasks such as dialogue generation [1,36,38], machine translation [2], and code generation [9,11]. In specific, we record all the training MWPs into a memory in advance. During inference, we utilize the query(i.e., both topic words and equation) to retrieve the memory. According to the similarity between the query and the recorded MWPs, the most related retrieved MWPs are selected to augment the generation condition and improve the quality of the generated MWPs. As shown in Fig. 1(b), the retrieved results, containing the key words school and times, are used to augment the generation condition and improve the quality of the generated MWPs.

In addition, we propose a low-resource MWPG task. The low-resource MWPG means that only a small amount of paired training target data(MWPs with topic words and equation) and a large amount of unpaired target data(MWPs without topic words and equation) are available. On the one hand, a large number of unpaired MWPs are easily collected in the real world; on the other hand, extracting topic words and equations from MWPs costs a lot. Therefore, the low-resource MWPG is a realistic and meaningful setting. We also verify our method on the low-resource MWPG.

We name our proposed model as *MGenMR* (i.e., math word problem generation with memory retrieval). The contributions are as follows:

- To the best of our knowledge, we are the first work that introduces the memory module into math word problem generation task;
- Considering the cost of annotating training data, we propose a challenging and novel MWPG task, i.e., the low-resource MWPG;
- Our proposed method *MGenMR* outperforms all baselines in both the MWPG and the low-resource MWPG. Detailed analysis and discussion verify the effectiveness of the memory retrieval module.

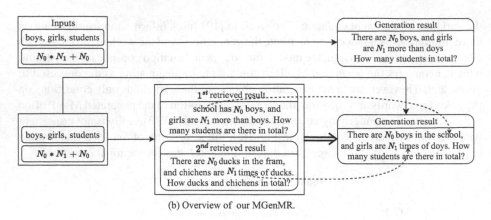

(b) Overview of our MGenMR.

Fig. 1. Illustration about the *Seq2Seq* generation and our *MGenMR*.

2 Related Work

In this section, we briefly review some literatures that are tightly related to our work, namely, Math Word Problem Generation and Memory Retrieval for Text Generation.

2.1 Math Word Problem Generation

Traditional methods usually heuristically generate MWPs based on some pre-defined text templates [5,21,24,37]. However, the diversity of MWPs generated by text templates is not as expected. Recently, some models based on deep neural networks have brought significant improvements in generating MWPs. MaGNET [41], based on a standard encoder-decoder architecture, forces the entities in the generated MWP to correspond to the variables in inputs. The work in [19] fuses information from equations and commonsense knowledge to facilitate the generation. And the work in [35], based on a large-scale pre-trained language model, introduces an equation consistency constraint, which encourages the generated MWP to contain the same equation as the one used to generate it. However, since the generation process of these methods only conditions on the given topic words and equation, the scenario description of the generated MWP often lacks richness. The underlying equation of the generated MWP usually is not consistent with the input equation. Therefore, we introduce a memory retrieval module, which takes full advantage of the training MWPs, into the MWPG framework.

2.2 Memory Retrieval for Text Generation

In the text generation task, normal methods [6,8,25,40] are based on generative model, which is able to store learned knowledge with the form of parameters and has a certain generalization ability. However, in the knowledge-intensive task, it is difficult to remember all the knowledge in the parameters of the generative model. In addition, memory retrieval module can solve a particular task by constructing a knowledge base [7,29], which called memory and will be retrieved during inference to augment the generation conditions. To this end, many works, such as dialogue generation [1,36,38], machine translation [2] and code generation [9,11], had attempted to apply memory retrieval module to text generation task. Our work is inspired by the success of incorporating memory retrieval module with the generative model, showing memory retrieval module is capable of achieving strong performance in MWPG task. Moreover, with the help of memory retrieval module, our proposed MWPG model could take advantage of unpaired MWPs and solve low-resource MWPG task.

3   Problem Setup

3.1   MWPG

Following [35], we formulate MWP generation as a task of multi-view (topic words and an equation) conditional text generation. In specific, we feed the generation network p_Θ with topic words x_i^{tw} and the equation x_i^{eq}, and the output is the generated MWP $\hat{M}_i$. The generated MWP $\hat{M}_i$ is expected to be same with the generation target MWP M_i and consistent with the input equation x_i^{eq} (The detailed evaluation metric will be discussed in Sect. 5). Then, we describe the MWP generation process as:

$$\hat{M}_i = p_\Theta(x_i^{eq}, x_i^{tw}), \tag{1}$$

where $\{M_i, x_i^{eq}, x_i^{tw}\}$ is the ith example in the dataset $\{M_i, x_i^{eq}, x_i^{tw}\}_{i=1}^N$. $M_i = \{m_1, ..., m_T\}$, as the generation target, represents the MWP as a sequence of T tokens. Similarly, $\hat{M}_i = \{\hat{m}_1, ..., \hat{m}_{T'}\}$ represents the generated MWP as a sequence of T' generated tokens.

3.2   Low-Resource MWPG

Compared with the training set of standard MWPG, the training set of low-resource MWPG has a smaller amount of paired data $\{M_i, x_i^{eq}, x_i^{tw}\}_{i=1}^{N_p}$ and an extra large number of unpaired target data $\{M_i'\}_{i=1}^{N_u}$. Fewer training paired samples makes the task more challenging and the extra unpaired target data could help training. The training set of the low-resource MWPG could be described as $\{M_i, x_i^{eq}, x_i^{tw}\}_{i=1}^{N_p} \cup \{M_i'\}_{i=1}^{N_u}$ and $N_p \leq N_u$. The test set and validation set of the low-resource MWPG are as the same as those of the standard MWPG.

4   Proposed Approach

4.1   Overview

Before inference, we **build the MWP memory(MWP-M)** φ. In the standard MWPG, the MWP-M φ records all the MWPs from the train set $\{M_i, x_i^{eq}, x_i^{tw}\}_{i=1}^N$. In the low-resource MWPG, we build the MWP-M φ by recording the MWPs from both the paired training data $\{M_i, x_i^{eq}, x_i^{tw}\}_{i=1}^{N_p}$ and the unpaired training data $\{M_i'\}_{i=1}^{N_u}$.

As illustrated in Fig. 2, our proposed *MGenMR* consists of retrieval module and generation module. In the **retrieval module**, we use the input as a query to retrieve the MWP-M φ. The retrieved results are some most related memory items. **The generation module**, a standard encoder-decoder generation framework, is fed with the original input(topic words and equation) and the retrieved results. Then the generation module outputs the generated MWP $\hat{M}_i$.

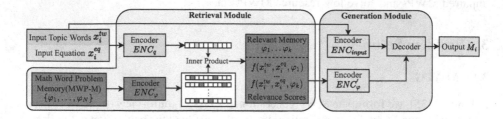

Fig. 2. Framework of our MGenMR.

4.2   Retrieval Module

In this module, we use the input, both the topic words x_i^{tw} and the equation x_i^{eq} as a query to retrieve the MWP-M φ and select the top-k possibly helpful memory items $\{\varphi_j\}_{j=1}^{k}$, according to the relevance score $f(x_i^{tw}, x_i^{eq}, \varphi_j)$. We define the relevance score $f(x_i^{tw}, x_i^{eq}, \varphi_j)$ between the query (x_i^{tw}, x_i^{eq}) and each memory item φ_j as the inner product of their representations:

$$f(x_i^{tw}, x_i^{eq}, \varphi_j) = ENC_q(x_i^{tw}, x_i^{eq})^T ENC_\varphi(\varphi_j) \tag{2}$$

where ENC_q and ENC_φ encode the query and each memory item respectively and are defined as:

$$ENC_q(x_i^{tw}, x_i^{eq}) = \delta(W_q\{Tr_{tw}(x_i^{tw}); GRU(x_i^{eq})\}) \tag{3}$$

$$ENC_\varphi(\varphi_j) = \delta(W_\varphi Tr_\varphi(\varphi_j)) \tag{4}$$

where Tr_{tw} and Tr_φ are the Transformer [30] encoders of the input topic words x_i^{tw} and the MWP-M items φ_j. $\{Tr_{tw}(x_i^{tw}); GRU(x_i^{eq})\}$ means that we concatenate the representation of topic words and the input equation. W_q and W_φ are the matrices of the linear projections, which reduce the dimension of the representations. Function δ could normalize any vector to a unit vector, regulating the range of the relevance score.

4.3   Generation Module

Conditioned on both the original input (x_i^{tw}, x_i^{eq}) and the retrieved results $\{\varphi_j\}_{j=1}^{k}$ from the retrieval module, our generation module, built upon standard encoder-decoder structure, outputs the generated MWP $\hat{M}_i$. Therefore, the generation module could be regarded as a probabilistic model $p(\hat{M}_i | x_i^{tw}, x_i^{eq}, \varphi_1, ..., \varphi_k)$. We use the retrieved memory to augment the input by copying them into generation via the cross attention mechanism [28]. The cross attention mechanism copies related words in the retrieved MWP to the generation outputs.

The encoder encodes the original input (x_i^{tw}, x_i^{eq}) and every retrieved memory item(i.e., MWP) φ_j into representations:

$$v_i^{input} = ENC_{input}(x_i^{tw}, x_i^{eq}) \tag{5}$$

$$v_{\varphi_j} = ENC'_\varphi(\varphi_j) \tag{6}$$

where the function of ENC_{input} and ENC'_φ are similar to ENC_q and ENC_φ defined in Eqs. 3–4 respectively. In Eq. 5, the ENC_{input} encodes the input x_i^{tw} and x_i^{eq} into the representation v_i^{input}. In Eq. 6, the ENC'_φ encodes each retrieved memory item (i.e., MWP) φ_j into the representation v_{φ_j} individually, resulting in a set of contextualized token embeddings $\{v_{\varphi_j h}\}_{h=1}^{l_j}$ where l_j denotes the length of the token sequence φ_j.

The decoder can be regarded as a probabilistic model $p(\hat{M}_i | v_i^{input}, v_{\varphi_1}, ..., v_{\varphi_k})$. Fed with the presentations v_i^{input} and $\{v_{\varphi_j}\}_{j=1}^k$, the decoder generates an output sequence $\hat{M}_i$ in an auto-regressive fashion. At each time step t, the generation decoder attends over both the representation v_i^{input} from the encoders and previously predicted sequence $\hat{m}_{1:t-1}$, outputting a hidden state h_t. The hidden state h_t is then converted to next-token probabilities through a linear projection followed by softmax function, i.e., $P_v = \text{softmax}(W_v h_t + b_v)$. In addition, we also compute a cross attention over the representations of all retrieved memory items:

$$\alpha_{jh} = \frac{exp(h_t^T W_m v_{\varphi_j h})}{\sum_{j=1}^k \sum_{h=1}^{l_j} exp(h_t^T W_m v_{\varphi_j h})} \tag{7}$$

$$c_t = W_c \sum_{j=1}^k \sum_{h=1}^{l_j} \alpha_{jh} v_{\varphi_j h} \tag{8}$$

where $v_{\varphi_j h}$ is the h-th token in the j-th retrieved memory. α_{jh} is the attention score of $v_{\varphi_j h}$, c_t is a weighted combination of memory embeddings, and W_m and W_c are trainable matrices. The next-token probabilities are computed as:

$$p(\hat{m}_t|\cdot) = (1 - \lambda_t) P_v(\hat{m}_t) + \lambda_t \sum_{j=1}^k \sum_{h=1}^{l_j} \alpha_{jh} \mathbb{1}_{v_{\varphi_j h} = \hat{m}_t} \tag{9}$$

where $\mathbb{1}$ is the indicator function and λ_t is a gating variable computed by another feed-forward network $\lambda_t = g(h_t, c_t)$.

4.4 Training

We optimize the parameters Θ of the model using stochastic gradient descent(SGD) on the negative log-likelihood loss function $-\log p(M_i | x_i^{tw}, x_i^{eq}, \varphi_1, ..., \varphi_k)$ where M_i refers to the target MWP. To improve training efficiency, we warm-start the retrieval module by pre-training the two encoders in the retrieval module with a cross-alignment task.

Pre-training the Retrieval Module. We sample all paired training data $\{M_i, x_i^{eq},$ $x_i^{tw}\}_{i=1}^N$ at each training step. Let $X^{input} \in R^{B \times b}$ and $X^M \in R^{B \times b}$ be the representation of the input and MWP through ENC_q and ENC_φ respectively. $S = X^{input}(X^M)^T$ is a $(B \times B)$ matrix of relevance scores, where each row corresponds to the query (i.e., the input) of one training example and each column corresponds to the MWP of one training example. Any (X_i^{input}, X_j^M) pairs should be aligned when $i = j$ and should not otherwise. Therefore, the loss function should maximize the scores along the diagonal of the matrix and minimize the other scores. The loss function can be written as:

$$\mathcal{L}^{(i)} = \frac{-exp(S_{ii})}{exp(S_{ii}) + \sum_{j \neq i} exp(S_{ij})} \tag{10}$$

5   Experiments

We now perform a series of experiments to validate the effectiveness of our *MGenMR*.

5.1   Datasets

Standard MWPG Dataset. We perform experiments on three commonly used MWP solving datasets, i.e., two single-equation MWP datasets Math23K [34], MAWPS [15] and a multiple-equations MWP dataset Dolphine18K [10]. Following the splitting strategy of [16], we split each dataset into train set, validation set and test set. The summary statistics of datasets are shown in Table 2. To transfer those MWP solving datasets into MWPG datasets, we extract equation and topic words for each MWP as the input of the MWPG. We extract at most n_{tp} words with the highest TF-IDF scores as the topic words in our experiments. As shown in Table 1, the equation $N_0 * N_1 + N_0$ and the extracted topic words *boys, girls, students, school* is the input and the MWP is the generation target. For a fair comparison, we follow the settings of baselines [35,41] and set $n_{tp} = 5$, $n_{tp} = 5$ and $n_{tp} = 10$ on Math23K, MAWPS and Dolphin18K respectively. Different from Math23K and MAWPS, Dolphin18K is a multiple-equation MWP dataset. Following [41], we concatenate multiple equations as a single equation.

Table 2. Summary statistics of standard MWPG datasets.

	#train	#val	#test	Total
Math23K	16780	2082	2094	20956
Dolphin18K	7593	847	2110	10550
MAWPS	1865	241	241	2347

Low-Resource MWPG Dataset. We create a low-resource Math23K by extracting a subset of the training data as the paired data and another subset of the training MWPs (without topic words and equation) as the unpaired data. Summary statistics are shown in Table 3. In Math23K$_{1/4}$, only $\frac{1}{4}$ of the standard Math23k training data are used as paired training data$\{M_i, x_i^{eq}, x_i^{tw}\}_{i=1}^{N_p}$. In Math23K$_{4/4}$, $\frac{1}{4}$ of the standard Math23K training data are used as paired training data$\{M_i, x_i^{eq}, x_i^{tw}\}_{i=1}^{N_p}$ and the other $\frac{3}{4}$ of the standard Math23K training data are used as unpaired data $\{M_i'\}_{i=1}^{N_u}$.

Table 3. Summary statistics of low-resource MWPG dataset.

	#train		#val	#test
	Paired	Unpaired		
Math23K$_{1/4}$	4195	0	2082	2094
Math23K$_{4/4}$	4195	12585	2082	2094

5.2 Metrics

We leverage the following three commonly used evaluation metrics: BLEU-4 [22], METEOR [17] and ROUGE [18] to measure the language quality. We implement those three metrics using the package provided by [3]. For mathematical consistency, we use the equation accuracy (ACC-eq) metric that measures whether the generated MWP is mathematically consistent with the input equation.

5.3 Implementation Details

For model details, we build our model using Transformer blocks [30] and bidirectional GRU blocks [4]. The dimension of embedding and encoder/decoder hidden state are set to 512. The number of Transformer blocks is set to 2 for ENC_q and ENC_φ in Eqs. 3–4, 3 for ENC_{input} and ENC_φ' in Eqs. 5–6, and 4 for the decoder in the generation module. The number of GRU blocks is set to 2 for ENC_q in Eq. 3 and ENC_{input} in Eq. 5. We retrieve the top 2 MWP-M sentences. We follow the learning rate schedule, dropout and label smoothing settings described in [30] and use Adam optimizer [14]. In this configuration, the parameter size of the whole model is 53M, which is much smaller than *MCPCC*'s [35] 774M and is similar to *Seq2Seq-tf*'s 52M in Table 4.

For training details, we first train the two encoders in the memory retrieval module. After that, we freeze the two encoders in the memory retrieval module and continue to train the generation module.

5.4 Baselines

Performance Comparison. In Table 4, *Seq2Seq-rnn*, based on the LSTMs with attention [20,41], regards the MWP generation task as a sequence-to-sequence task, which splices the input equation and the input topic words together as a single sequence input. Compared with *Seq2seq-rnn*, *Seq2Seq-rnn-GloVe* uses GloVe [23] instead of random embeddings at initialization and *Seq2Seq-tf* is based on Transformers [30] rather than RNN. We also compare our approach to vanilla GPT-2 [26], either finetuned or not; we denote these models as *GPT* and *GPT-pre*, respectively. Based on *GPT-pre*, *MCPCC* [35] introduces an equation consistency constraint, which encourages the generated MWP to contain the exact same equation as the one used to generate it. In Table 5, *MaGNET* [41], based on a standard seq2seq encoder-decoder architecture, forces the entities in the generated MWP to correspond to the variables in the equation. *KNN*, *Equ2Math* and *Topic2Math* are *MaGNET*'s ablation methods. In the original papers of baselines [35,41], experiments are only performed on part of those three datasets. Therefore, our method is compared with different baselines on different datatsets.

Table 4. Experiment results on the test set of MAWPS and Math23K.

	MAWPS				Math23K			
	BLEU-4	METEOR	ROUGE-L	ACC-eq	BLEU-4	METEOR	ROUGE-L	ACC-eq
Seq2Seq-rnn	0.153	0.175	0.362	0.472	0.196	0.234	0.444	0.390
+GloVe	0.592	0.412	0.705	0.585	0.275	0.277	0.507	0.438
Seq2Seq-tf	0.544	0.387	0.663	0.588	0.301	0.294	0.524	0.509
GPT	0.368	0.294	0.538	0.532	0.282	0.297	0.512	0.477
GPT-pre	0.504	0.391	0.664	0.512	0.325	0.333	0.548	0.498
MCPCC	0.596	0.427	0.715	0.557	0.329	0.328	0.544	0.505
MGenMR	**0.618**	**0.557**	**0.741**	**0.590**	**0.331**	**0.350**	**0.580**	**0.510**

Ablation Study. We perform the ablation method *Seq2Seq** on Math23K to verify the effectiveness of the memory retrieval module. *Seq2Seq** is based on the same encoder-decoder structure with our *MGenMR*, but does not have the memory retrieval module. Since Math23K is the largest dataset of those three datasets, the ablation study is performed on the Math23K.

Low-Resource. In Table 7, the baseline $Seq2Seq^*_{1/4}$ means that we perform the $Seq2Seq^*$ on the Math23K$_{1/4}$ where only the paired training data are available. The baseline $MGenMR_{1/4}$ means that we perform our proposed $MGenMR$ on the Math23K$_{1/4}$. $MGenMR_{4/4}$ means that we perform our proposed $MGenMR$ on the Math23K$_{1/4}$ where both the paired training data and the unpaired training data are available.

5.5   Quantitative Results

Performance Comparison Results. We show the quantitative results of our experiments performed on MAWPS, Math23K and Dolphin18K in the Table 4 and Table 5. As shown in Table 4, our *MGenMR* achieves better language quality and equation consistency than both seq2seq-based methods and GPT-based methods on Math23K and MAWPS. However, the metric ACC-eq of all the methods is not good enough. ACC-eq equals 59.0% and 51.0% on the MAWPS and Math23K respectively. In other words, at least 41.0% and 49.0% of the generated MWPs are unusable, since the equation is not consistent with the input equation.

Table 5. Experiment results on the test set of Dolphin18K.

	BLEU-4	METEOR	ROUGE-L
Equ2Math	0.050	0.135	0.296
KNN	0.120	0.168	0.361
Topic2Math	0.123	0.239	0.422
MaGNET	0.125	0.248	**0.436**
MGenMR	**0.158**	**0.312**	0.407

Table 5 shows our *MGenMR* outperforms the best baseline on Dolphin18K in the metrics of BLEU-4 and METEOR. The quantitative results on Dolphin18K is lower than results on MAWPS and Math23k, since generating MWPs on a multiple-equation MWP dataset is much more difficult. The metric ACC-eq of multiple-equation MWP dataset is difficult to calculate and thus ACC-eq is not used on Dolphin18K.

Ablation Study Results. Table 6 shows the ablation study results on Math23K. Our proposed *MGenMR* achieves better performance than *seq2seq**. Therefore, the retrieved results from the memory could improve the language quality of the generated MWPs and help the generated to be consistent with the input equation.

Table 6. Ablation study results on the test set of Math23K.

	BLEU-4	METEOR	ROUGLE-L	ACC-eq
$Seq2Seq^*$	0.310	0.329	0.526	0.490
MGenMR	0.331	0.350	0.580	0.510

Low-Resource Results. Comparing the $Seq2Seq^*_{1/4}$ with our proposed $MGenMR_{1/4}$ in Table 7, we can conclude that our memory retrieval module could benefit the generation although only a small number of paired data are available. Besides, since $MGenMR_{4/4}$ achieves better performance than $MGenMR_{1/4}$, we can conclude that enlarging the memory with a large number of unpaired data could help to generate better MWPs.

Table 7. Low-resource experiment results on the test set of Math23K.

	BLEU-4	METEOR	ROUGE-L	ACC-eq
$Seq2Seq^*_{1/4}$	0.217	0.267	0.477	0.385
$MGenMR_{1/4}$	0.223	0.272	0.484	0.386
$MGenMR_{4/4}$	0.242	0.282	0.502	0.390

5.6   Qualitative Results

Human Evaluation. In addition, because automatic evaluation metrics are not always consistent with human judgments on the correctness of a math word problem, we conducted human evaluation on our model compared with several baselines mentioned above. We consider three metrics:

- Equation Rel: a problem is relevant to the given equation;
- Topic Word Rel: a problem is relevant to all given topic words;
- Language Flu: a problem is grammatically correct and fluent to read.

For human evaluation, we randomly selected 100 instances from the Math23K test set, and then show the equations and topic words lists with generated MWPs from different models to three human annotators to evaluate the generated problems' quality. For each metrics, we ask the annotators to rate the problems on a 1–3 scale (3 for the best). Results of each human evaluation metric are presented in Table 8. We can see that our *MGenMR* has the highest scores across all the metrics.

Table 8. Human evaluation results.

	Equation Rel	Topic Words Rel	Language Flu
Seq2Seq-rnn	1.71	2.34	2.19
GPT-pre	2.17	2.57	2.55
MCPCC	2.24	2.71	2.60
MGenMR	**2.39**	**2.80**	**2.64**

Case Study. Three MWPs generated by our model are shown in Table 9 along with their ground truth and inputs(equation and topic words). We can see that the generated

Table 9. Examples of MWPs generated by our *MGenMR*.

Equation	N_0 / N_1
Topic words	village, canal
Ground truth	The village needs to dig a N_0 kilometers canal, digging N_1 kilometers every day. How many days can it be dug?
Gen.MWP	The village needs to dig a N_0 kilometers canal. It planned to dig N_1 kilometers every day. How many days will it take to complete the canal?
Equation	$N_0 + N_1$
Topic words	mother, vegetables
Ground truth	My mother spent N_0 yuan to buy vegetables, and there is still N_1 yuan left. How much money did my mother bring?
Gen.MWP	My mother went to the street to buy vegetables, spent N_0 yuan, and there was N_1 yuan left. How much money did mom bring?
Equation:	$N_0 * N_1 + N_2$
Topic words	school, storybooks
Ground truth	The school plans to distribute storybooks to N_0 classes, N_1 for each class, and N_2 for spare. How many storybooks should the school prepare?
Gen.MWP	The school bought N_0 storybooks and bought comics N_2 more than N_1 times the number of storybooks. How many comics did the school buy?

MWPs are reasonable, with respect to equation consistency and topic words relevance. Moreover, the description of the generated MWPs are even richer than the ground truths. For example, new but appropriate words *street* and *comics* are introduced in case 2 and case 3 respectively.

6   Conclusions

In this paper, we propose a novel MWPG framework with memory retrieval. Our model takes full advantage of the training data by recording them into a memory. During inference, the memory items relevant to the inputs are retrieved as additional conditions to facilitate the generation process. Moreover, we introduce a novel and realistic low-resource setting for MWPG. In the low-resource MWPG, our proposed *MGenMR* could exploit the unpaired training MWPs to improve the generation quality. Experiments show our superior performance in standard MWPG and low-resource MWPG.

Acknowledgements. This work was supported by the NSFC NO. 62172138 and 61932009. This work was also partially supported by The University Synergy Innovation Program of Anhui Province NO. GXXT-2021-007.

References

1. Cai, D., et al.: Skeleton-to-response: dialogue generation guided by retrieval memory. In: NAACL (2019)
2. Cai, D., Wang, Y., Li, H., Lam, W., Liu, L.: Neural machine translation with monolingual translation memory. In: ACL, pp. 7307–7318 (2021)
3. Chen, X., et al.: Microsoft coco captions: Data collection and evaluation server. arXiv preprint arXiv:1504.00325 (2015)
4. Cho, K., et al.: Learning phrase representations using rnn encoder-decoder for statistical machine translation. arXiv preprint arXiv:1406.1078 (2014)
5. Deane, P., Sheehan, K.: Automatic item generation via frame semantics: natural language generation of math word problems (2003)
6. Dong, L., et al.: Unified language model pre-training for natural language understanding and generation. In: Advances in Neural Information Processing Systems 32 (2019)
7. Gu, J., Zhao, H., Lin, Z., Li, S., Cai, J., Ling, M.: Scene graph generation with external knowledge and image reconstruction. In: Proceedings of the IEEE/CVF Conference on Computer Vision and Pattern Recognition, pp. 1969–1978 (2019)
8. Han, F.X., Niu, D., Chen, H., Lai, K., He, Y., Xu, Y.: A deep generative approach to search extrapolation and recommendation. In: Proceedings of the 25th ACM SIGKDD International Conference on Knowledge Discovery & Data Mining. pp. 1771–1779 (2019)
9. Hashimoto, T.B., Guu, K., Oren, Y., Liang, P.: A retrieve-and-edit framework for predicting structured outputs. In: NeurIPS (2018)
10. Huang, D., Shi, S., Lin, C.Y., Yin, J., Ma, W.Y.: How well do computers solve math word problems? large-scale dataset construction and evaluation. In: ACL, pp. 887–896 (2016)
11. Huang, S., Wang, J., Xu, J., Cao, D., Yang, M.: Recall and learn: A memory-augmented solver for math word problems. In: Findings of the Association for Computational Linguistics: EMNLP 2021, pp. 786–796. Association for Computational Linguistics, Punta Cana, Dominican Republic (Nov 2021). 10.18653/v1/2021.findings-emnlp.68, https://aclanthology.org/2021.findings-emnlp.68

12. Karpicke, J.D.: Retrieval-based learning: active retrieval promotes meaningful learning. Curr. Dir. Psychol. Sci. **21**, 157–163 (2012)
13. Karpicke, J.D., Roediger, H.L.: The critical importance of retrieval for learning. Science **319**, 966–968 (2008)
14. Kingma, D.P., Ba, J.: Adam: A method for stochastic optimization. arXiv preprint arXiv:1412.6980 (2014)
15. Koncel-Kedziorski, R., Roy, S., Amini, A., Kushman, N., Hajishirzi, H.: MAWPS: A math word problem repository. In: Proceedings of the 2016 Conference of the North American Chapter of the Association for Computational Linguistics: Human Language Technologies. pp. 1152–1157. Association for Computational Linguistics, San Diego, California (Jun 2016). https://doi.org/10.18653/v1/N16-1136,https://aclanthology.org/N16-1136
16. Lan, Y., et al.: Mwptoolkit: an open-source framework for deep learning-based math word problem solvers. arXiv preprint arXiv:2109.00799 (2021)
17. Lavie, A., Agarwal, A.: Meteor: an automatic metric for mt evaluation with high levels of correlation with human judgments. In: Proceedings of the Second Workshop on Statistical Machine Translation, pp. 228–231 (2007)
18. Lin, C.Y.: Rouge: A package for automatic evaluation of summaries. In: Text summarization branches out, pp. 74–81 (2004)
19. Liu, T., Fang, Q., Ding, W., Wu, Z., Liu, Z.: Mathematical word problem generation from commonsense knowledge graph and equations. In: EMNLP (2021)
20. Liu, T., Fang, Q., Ding, W., Li, H., Wu, Z., Liu, Z.: Mathematical word problem generation from commonsense knowledge graph and equations. arXiv preprint arXiv:2010.06196 (2020)
21. Nandhini, K., Balasundaram, S.R.: Math word question generation for training the students with learning difficulties. In: Proceedings of the International Conference & Workshop on Emerging Trends in Technology, pp. 206–211 (2011)
22. Papineni, K., Roukos, S., Ward, T., Zhu, W.J.: Bleu: a method for automatic evaluation of machine translation. In: ACL, pp. 311–318 (2002)
23. Pennington, J., Socher, R., Manning, C.D.: Glove: global vectors for word representation. In: EMNLP, pp. 1532–1543 (2014)
24. Polozov, O., O'Rourke, E., Smith, A.M., Zettlemoyer, L., Gulwani, S., Popovic, Z.: Personalized mathematical word problem generation. In: IJCAI (2015)
25. Qian, Q., Huang, M., Zhao, H., Xu, J., Zhu, X.: Assigning personality/profile to a chatting machine for coherent conversation generation. In: IJCAI, pp. 4279–4285 (2018)
26. Radford, A., et al.: Language models are unsupervised multitask learners. OpenAI Blog **1**, 9 (2019)
27. Rohrer, D., Pashler, H.: Recent research on human learning challenges conventional instructional strategies. Educ. Res. **39**, 406–412 (2010)
28. See, A., Liu, P., Manning, C.: Get to the point: summarization with pointer-generator networks. In: ACL (2017)
29. Song, Z., Hu, Z., Hong, R.: Efficient and self-adaptive rationale knowledge base for visual commonsense reasoning. In: Multimedia Systems, pp. 1–10 (2022)
30. Vaswani, A., et al.: Attention is all you need. NeurIPS 30 (2017)
31. Verschaffel, L., Schukajlow, S., Star, J., Van Dooren, W.: Word problems in mathematics education: a survey. ZDM **52**, 1–16 (2020)
32. Walkington, C.A.: Using adaptive learning technologies to personalize instruction to student interests: the impact of relevant contexts on performance and learning outcomes. J. Educ. Psychol. **105**, 932 (2013)
33. Wang, L., Zhang, D., Gao, L., Song, J., Guo, L., Shen, H.T.: Mathdqn: solving arithmetic word problems via deep reinforcement learning. In: Proceedings of the AAAI Conference on Artificial Intelligence, vol. 32 (2018)

34. Wang, Y., Liu, X., Shi, S.: Deep neural solver for math word problems. In: EMNLP, pp. 845–854 (2017)
35. Wang, Z., Lan, A., Baraniuk, R.: Math word problem generation with mathematical consistency and problem context constraints. In: EMNLP (2021)
36. Weston, J., Dinan, E., Miller, A.H.: Retrieve and refine: Improved sequence generation models for dialogue. In: EMNLP (2018)
37. Williams, S.: Generating mathematical word problems. In: AAAI (2011)
38. Wu, Y., Wei, F., Huang, S., Wang, Y., Li, Z., Zhou, M.: Response generation by context-aware prototype editing. In: AAAI, vol. 33 (2019)
39. Zhang, J., et al.: Teacher-student networks with multiple decoders for solving math word problem. IJCAI (2020)
40. Zhang, Z., Li, J., Zhu, P., Zhao, H., Liu, G.: Modeling multi-turn conversation with deep utterance aggregation. arXiv preprint arXiv:1806.09102 (2018)
41. Zhou, Q., Huang, D.: Towards generating math word problems from equations and topics. In: ICNLG (2019)

Traditional Mongolian Script Standard Compliance Testing Based on Deep Residual Network and Spatial Pyramid Pooling

Chenyang Zhou[1], LiCheng Wu[1(✉)], Wenhui Guo[2], and Dezhi Cao[1]

[1] Minzu University of China, Beijing 100081, China
wulicheng@tsinghua.edu.cn
[2] China Railway Taiyuan Group Co., Ltd., Taiyuan, China

Abstract. Mongolian is a language spoken in Inner Mongolian, China. Traditional Mongolian script standard compliance testing is very important and fundamental work. This paper proposes a classification network for traditional Mongolian script standard compliance testing. The network uses the spatial pyramid pooling mechanism, it can accept images of different sizes in the convolutional neural network. It can effectively solve multi-scale problems of traditional Mongolian words. Experimental results show the SSP-ResNet-18-Single can effectively recognize traditional Mongolian images, and the recognition average accuracy can reach 98.60%. This network achieves good performance in Mongolian word recognition compare with the current mainstream word recognition network. The dataset has been publicly available.

Keywords: Traditional Mongolian script · Deep residual network · Spatial pyramid pooling

1 Introduction

Although traditional Mongolian script was standardized in ISO/IEC 10646 and Unicode in 1999 [1], there are still a large number of non-Unicode traditional Mongolian scripts in China, which has seriously affected the traditional Mongolian information interaction. This happens for two main reasons. One is that the major operating system supports it relatively late. Windows Vista only supported traditional Mongolian scripts in 2007. The other is the lack of standard conformance testing tools. Thus, it is difficult to test the standardization of various traditional Mongolian fonts.

Traditional Mongolian script standard compliance testing is based on the input of the same character code. The character images generated by the standard font are compared with the character images generated by the tested font for consistency. Of course, there may be such cases that are missing, as shown in Fig. 1

© The Author(s), under exclusive license to Springer Nature Switzerland AG 2022
S. Yu et al. (Eds.): PRCV 2022, LNCS 13536, pp. 386–395, 2022.
https://doi.org/10.1007/978-3-031-18913-5_30

Number	Correct form	Character Sequence		Rendered forms in OTFs		
		Unicode	Basic Glyph	Font 1	Font 2	Font 3
1000		U+182A	ဈ			
		U+1822	╗			
		U+1834	ฯ			
		U+1822	╗			
		U+182D	·╗			

Fig. 1. Traditional Mongolian script standard compliance testing.

So the traditional Mongolian script standard compliance testing can be treated as an image classification task. The input character encoding is treated as the label of the image and the traditional Mongolian character images are classified. According to the content of paper [5], we determined the traditional Mongolian script standard compliance testing examples. In this paper, we defined and tested it from three aspects according to the characteristics of traditional Mongolian word formation.

– Task 1. Test of traditional Mongolian encoding character set

It tests a traditional Mongolian letter. Each character is composed of one or two Unicode codes, where the two Unicode codes are composed of letter and control character (see Fig. 2). A total of 52 categories were tested. The specific content of the test is 7 traditional Mongolian punctuation marks, 10 traditional Mongolian numbers and 35 traditional Mongolian nominal characters.

Number	Unicode	Basic Glyph	Rendered Forms
1	U+1820	ᠠ	ᠠ
2	U+1824	ᠤ	
	U+200D	ZWJ	ᠤ
3	U+1826	ᠦ	
	U+200D	ZWJ	ᠦ

Fig. 2. The examples of traditional Mongolian encoding character set.

– Task 2. Test of traditional Mongolian conversion rules set

It tests a short string of traditional Mongolian letters. Each short string is made up of between two and four Unicode codes, where the Unicode codes are composed of letters and control characters (see Fig. 3). A total of 133 categories were tested. The specific content of the test is 63 traditional Mongolian presentation characters and 70 traditional Mongolian mandatory ligature characters.

Number	Unicode	Basic Glyph	Rendered Forms
1	U+182A	᠊ᠣ	᠊ᠣ
	U+1820	᠊ᠡ	
	U+200D	ZWJ	
2	U+182A	᠊ᠣ	᠊ᠣ
	U+1820	᠊ᠡ	

Fig. 3. The examples of traditional Mongolian conversion rules set.

– Task 3. Test of traditional Mongolian resources set

It tests a traditional Mongolian word. Each word is made up of more than three Unicode codes, where the Unicode codes are composed of letters and control characters (see Fig. 4). A total of 64 categories were tested. The specific content of the test is 11 traditional Mongolian feminine words, 11 traditional Mongolian masculine words, 21 traditional Mongolian hyphenated words and 21 traditional Mongolian vowel separated words.

Number	Unicode	Basic Glyph	Rendered Forms
1	U+182A	᠊ᠣ	
	U+1822	᠊ᠢ	
	U+1834	ᠴ	
	U+1822	᠊ᠢ	
	U+182D	᠊ᠭ	

Fig. 4. The examples of traditional Mongolian resources set.

Currently, traditional Mongolian script standard compliance testing can be divided into two categories: letter segmentation recognition and letter image recognition. The method of using letter segmentation recognition needs to divide traditional Mongolian words into letters. Letter image recognition used features of manual design without segmenting traditional Mongolian words. Because Mongolian is an agglutinative language. The length of words is not fixed and the number of words is huge. It is difficult to cover all the word features by manually designed features. Fixed size of the input was required in early researches. These are the reasons that reduce the recognition accuracy. Therefore, we proposed an improved convolutional neural networks method to recognize traditional Mongolian words.

Our contributions can be summarized as follows:

- We provide a new benchmark result on a new dataset.
- We designed a method for traditional Mongolian script standard compliance testing and evaluated it on a printed traditional Mongolian script standard compliance testing dataset. To our best knowledge, this is the first time to explore traditional Mongolian script standard compliance testing.
- We have set up a traditional Mongolian script standard compliance testing dataset and published it on Github.

The rest of the paper is organized as follows: Sect. 2 reviews the related works. Section 3 introduces the network architecture used in this article. Section 4 introduces the experimental results and discusses the experimental results. Finally, a conclusion and future work are presented in Sect. 5.

2   Related Work

In 2012, Wang [2] proposed a method for calculate similarity of glyph features, which is a combination of feature extraction. The global feature is made up of shape context feature. The local features are made up of improved pyramid histogram of oriented gradients (PHOG) feature and wavelet pyramid energy distribution. The similarity distance is calculated by the Chi-square measure. The similarity is judged by comparing the similarity distance with the manually set threshold. The datasets used 200-page 32×32 images from Mongolian Baiti Font by Microsoft corporation and the average accuracy rate of 62.3%. In 2013, Zhao [3] proposed a glyph segmentation method of traditional Mongolian. She found the features which is determining the consistency of printed traditional Mongolian. The features include the number of regional connectivity, the number of horizontal and vertical scan line intersection points and so on. The datasets contains 188 images and the recognition average accuracy reaches 99.3%. In 2015, He et al. [4] analyzed and summarizes the basis of standard conformance test of Mongolian processing software products, from the view of standardization of Mongolian information processing. They identified an automated detection process, but the exact algorithm has not been made public. In 2015, Huslee et al. [5] defined the test points and test examples of traditional Mongolian script standard compliance testing. It relies on a key software system to test and analyze complex text layout engines such as Uniscribe and HarfBuzz that support Mongolian. In 2019, Zhou [6] used AlexNet model for traditional Mongolian script standard compliance testing. And he proposed that the standard compliance testing steps are divided into three parts. The three parts are traditional Mongolian encoding character, traditional Mongolian conversion rules and traditional Mongolian resources. The datasets used 32×32 images of 241 categories from Mongolian Baiti Font by Microsoft corporation and the average accuracy rate of 96.4%. In this work, we proposed a traditional Mongolian words recognition method based on improved convolutional neural networks without segmentation. By adding spatial pyramid pooling mechanism to the network, the model can accept traditional Mongolian words' images of different sizes. It can improve the accuracy of model recognition.

3   Model Architecture

In this section, we will introduce this model from up to bottom. The spatial pyramid pooling mechanism [7] can accept images of different sizes in the convolutional neural network. It can effectively solve multi-scale problems of traditional Mongolian words. As depicted in Fig. 5, the model is proposed by combining deep residual network with spatial pyramid pooling mechanism.

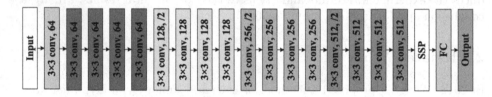

Fig. 5. The model architecture of SPP-ResNet-18.

3.1   Convolutional Layers with Residual Learning

In order to improve the accuracy of the classification of traditional Mongolian script images, the neural network can be deepened to extract higher-dimensional features. However, in practical applications, the learning efficiency of convolutional neural network will not increase as the depth increases. Within a certain depth range, as the number of network can fit more complex function structures, and the overall performance of the model can also be improved, but when the number of convolutional layers increasing to a certain number, as the number of network layers increasing, the accuracy of the model on the test dataset and train dataset will show a downward trend. Researchers found that as the convolutional layers superimposed, the accuracy of the experiment gradually decreased after the neural network converged. The degradation of the network indicates that directly increasing the number of layers of the deep learning network cannot achieve the expected results. Therefore, in order to solve this problem, this paper used the residual module to solve the problem of the decrease in accuracy caused by the deepening of the network. The introduction of the deep residual network module effectively alleviates the vanishing gradient problem of back propagation during high-latitude convolutional neural network training

Figure 6 shows the convolutional layer structure of the deep residual network. Given the input image data, the deep residual network will send the input data to the convolutional layer (Conv), the rectified linear activation function layer (ReLU), and the batch normalization layer (Batch norm) in turn. The processed results are further sent to multiple residual units for training, and the though the batch normalization layer (BN), the spatial pyramid pooling layer (SSP) and several fully connected layer (FC). Finally, the output result is obtained.

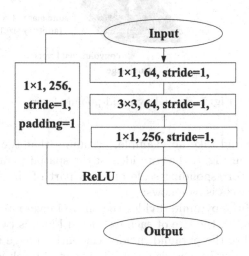

Fig. 6. Basic block structure

The calculation process of the basic block is as follows: Firstly, it uses a 1×1 convolution to reduce the dimensionality. The input dimension in the figure is 256, in order to reduce the amount of calculation, it uses 1×1 convolution to reduce the dimensionality to 64, and the pass 3×3 convolution, so that the 3×3 convolution can be performed on a relatively low-dimensional input to achieve the purpose of improving computational efficiency. Finally, the 1×1 convolution is used to restore the input to the 256 dimensions, so the dimension upgrade will be upgrade and the original dimension will be restored.

3.2   The Spatial Pyramid Pooling Layer

Spatial Pyramid Pooling (SPP) is a pooling layer that removes the fixed-size constraint of the network. We used the spatial pyramid pooling in the deep residual network to replace the original global average pooling, so that the network can accept images of different sizes. Using the idea of the spatial pyramid pooling layer, the neural network can output feature maps in the same dimension, which show different scales obtained by the convolutional layer. This paper used 4 as

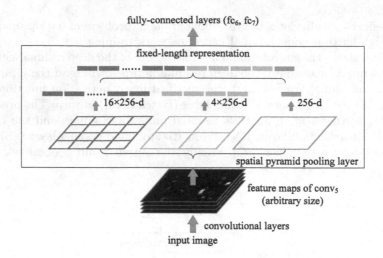

Fig. 7. Spatial pyramid pooling layer

the maximum scale and take an example, assuming that the input image size is (w, h). As shown in Fig. 7, the core idea of the spatial pyramid pooling is to perform pooling of corresponding scale on each part of the feature map. The specific selection process is as follows:

The first level of the pyramid divides the entire image into 16 blocks. In the case of image size(w, h), the size of each extracted block is (w/4, h/4).

The second level of the pyramid divides the entire image into 16 blocks. In the case of image size(w, h), the size of each extracted block is (w/2, h/2).

The third level of the pyramid divides the entire image into a block. In the case of image size(w, h), the size of each extracted block is (w, h).

Through the above selection method, the pooling player can pool out feature maps at the size of 4×4, 2×2 and 1×1, and then connect these feature maps into column vectors to connect to the next fully connected layer, which eliminates the impact of inconsistent input scales.

4   Experiment and Analysis

4.1   Data and Experimental Environment

We implemented our model under the PyTorch framework (version 1.10). All experiments were carried out on dual NVIDIA 3090 GPU and 64GB RAM. The batch size was set to 32 and the number of training epochs is set to 400. We used the stochastic gradient descent (SGD) optimizer to optimized the model and set the learning rate to $1e-3$.

The data of this work, we take samples from 12 traditional Mongolian Baiti fonts. We split into training set, development set and test set by according to 8:1:1. Task1 test set is 52 categories and 92 pictures. Task2 test set is 133 categories and 230 pictures. And Task3 test set is 64 categories and 107 pictures.

4.2   Evaluation Metrics

Traditional Mongolian script standard compliance testing is a multi classification task, so we use *precision*, *recall* and F_1 as the evaluation index. These metrics are calculated as:

$$P_t = \frac{TP_t}{TP_t + FP_t} \tag{1}$$

$$R_t = \frac{TP_t}{TP_t + FN_t} \tag{2}$$

$$Macro - F_1 = \frac{1}{|T|} \sum_{t \in T} \frac{2P_t R_t}{P_t + R_t} \tag{3}$$

where TP is the number of correctly predicted images. FP is the number of images that predicted as true, but in actuality those are negative class. If the prediction is failed, and the positive class is predicted as a false negative(FN). $Macro - F_1$ is also conventional metric used to evaluate classification decisions; unlike $Micro - F_1$ which gives equal weight to all instances in the averaging process, $Macro - F_1$ gives equal weight to each class-lable.

4.3   Results

In this paper, LeNet-5 [8], AlexNet [9], ResNet-18 [10] and MobileNetV3-Large [11] model are used as baselines (Table 1).

Table 1. Task1 - Test of traditional Mongolian encoding character set.

Model	Input size	Params	FLOPs	Acc(%)	P(%)	R(%)	F$_1$(%)
Wang [2]	32×32	–	–	73.65	–	–	–
Zhao [3]	–	–	-	87.64	–	–	–
LeNet-5	32×32	**65.576K**	**0.655M**	95.65	97.76	96.15	95.38
AlexNet	227×227	57.217M	0.713G	95.65	97.12	96.15	95.96
ResNet-18	224×224	11.203M	1.826G	96.74	98.08	97.12	96.92
MobileNetV3-L	224×224	4.269M	0.238G	96.74	98.40	97.12	97.05
SSP-ResNet-18-Single	–	11.736M	0.038G	**97.83**	**98.72**	**98.08**	**97.95**
SSP-ResNet-18-Multi	–	11.736M	0.15G	**97.83**	98.40	**98.08**	97.69

The experiment os divided into two forms: 1) **Single-Size training.** As in previous works, we first consider a network taking a fixed-size input resize from images. The resizing is for the purpose of data augmentation. For an image with a given size, we can pre-compute the bin sizes needed for spatial pyramid pooling. Task1 input size is 32×32 pixels. Task2 input size is 64×32 pixels. Task3 input size is 96×32 pixels. **2) Multi-size Training.** Our network with SPP is expected to be applied on images of any sizes. To address the issue of varying image sizes in training, we consider a set of pre-defined sizes. We use two sizes ($H \times 180$ in addition to 224×224) in this paper (Table 2).

Table 2. Task2 - Test set of traditional Mongolian conversion rules set.

Model	Input size	Params	FLOPs	Acc(%)	P(%)	R(%)	F$_1$(%)
Wang [2]	32×32	–	–	68.76	–	–	–
Zhao [3]	–	–	–	82.65	–	–	–
LeNet-5	32×32	**72.376K**	**0.662M**	94.70	97.35	94.70	92.93
AlexNet	227×227	57.545M	0.713G	95.65	97.10	96.32	95.33
ResNet-18	224×224	11.244M	1.826G	98.26	98.99	98.48	98.38
MobileNetV3-L	224×224	4.371M	0.238G	98.26	98.86	98.11	97.78
SSP-ResNet-18-Single	–	12.596M	0.076G	**98.70**	**99.24**	**98.86**	**98.79**
SSP-ResNet-18-Multi	–	12.596M	1.827G	92.17	95.52	92.42	90.81

Table 3. Task3 - Test of traditional Mongolian resources set.

Model	Input size	Params	FLOPs	Acc(%)	P(%)	R(%)	F$_1$(%)
Wang [2]	32×32	–	–	55.74	–	–	–
Zhao [3]	–	–	–	76.25	–	–	–
LeNet-5	32×32	**66.001K**	**0.656M**	94.74	97.37	94.74	92.98
AlexNet	227×227	57.237M	0.713G	96.49	98.25	96.49	95.32
ResNet-18	224×224	11.206M	1.826G	98.25	99.12	98.25	97.66
MobileNetV3-L	224×224	4.275M	0.238G	97.20	98.25	96.49	96.02
SSP-ResNet-18-Single	–	11.789M	0.112G	**99.07**	**99.42**	**99.12**	**99.06**
SSP-ResNet-18-Multi	–	11.789M	0.112G	98.13	98.54	98.25	97.89

We compare the results from the table (Table 3):

1) The spatial pyramid pooling layer can improve performance. The F1 value of SSP-ResNet model remains the highest among all models. About 1.4% improvement compared with the highest ResNet-18 model in the baseline model in Task3.
2) In the whole model, the introduction of spatial pyramid pooling mechanism can effectively improve the model classification performance. Compared with AlexNet model, our model is improved by about 1.9% in Task 1. Compared with MobileNetV3-L model, our model's classification ability is also significantly enhanced.
3) In the whole model, the introduction of spatial pyramid pooling mechanism can effectively reduce the complexity of the model in all task. It can improve the speed of model inference.

5   Conclusion

In this paper, we used the spatial pyramid pooling mechanism can accept images of different sizes in the convolutional neural network. It can effectively solve multi-scale problems of traditional Mongolian words. We verified the effectiveness of SSP-ResNet-18-Single by exploring the performance of AlexNet, ResNet-18, MobileNetV3-L in the network. Experiments had shown that the performance of this network is better than other networks, and the recognition accuracy can reach 99.06% in Task3. This method also can be used for Mongolian handwriting recognition, and it can also be used for text recognition tasks in other languages.

References

1. Choijinzhab.: Mongolian Encoding, 1st edn. Inner Mongolia University Press, Hohhot (2000). https://www.babelstone.co.uk/Mongolian/MGWBM.html (in Chinese)
2. Wang, Y.: Research of font standard compliance detection technology. Master's thesis. Inner Mongolia University, Hohhot (2012). (in Chinese)
3. Zhao, Y.: The design and implementation of Mongolian information processing products standards compliance testing system. Master's Thesis. Inner Mongolia University, Hohhot (2013). (in Chinese)
4. He, Z., Wang, X., Chen, H.: Research and design of standard conformance test of Mongolian software. Inf. Technol. Standard. z1(14), 47–49 (2015). (in Chinese)
5. Huslee, S., Bai, C.: Standard conformance test of Mongolian complex text layout engine. J. Guangxi Acad. Sci. 34(01), 63–67 (2018). (in Chinese)
6. Zhou, C.: Design of Mongolian standard compliance detection system based on deep learning. Master's thesis. Inner Mongolia University, Hohhot (2019). (in Chinese)
7. He, K., Zhang, X., Ren, S., Sun, J.: Spatial pyramid pooling in deep convolutional networks for visual recognition. IEEE Trans. Pattern Anal. Mach. Intell. 37(9), 1904–1916 (2015)
8. LeCun, Y., et al.: Gradient-based learning applied to document recognition. Proc. IEEE 86(11), 2278–2324 (1998)
9. Krizhevsky, A., Sutskever, I., Hinton, G.E.: Imagenet classification with deep convolutional neural networks. Advances in Neural Information Processing Systems 25 (2012)
10. He, K., et al.: Deep residual learning for image recognition. In: Proceedings of the IEEE Conference on Computer Vision and Pattern Recognition, pp. 770–778 (2016)
11. Howard, A., et al.: Searching for mobilenetv3. In: Proceedings of the IEEE/CVF International Conference on Computer Vision, pp. 1314–1324 (2019)

FOV Recognizer: Telling the Field of View of Movie Shots

Xin Jin[1], Chenyu Fan[1], Biao Wang[1], Yihang Bo[2(✉)], Xinzhe Pan[2], Zihan Jia[2],
Ya Zhuo[2], Runqi Zhang[2], and Shuai Cui[3]

[1] Beijing Electronic Science and Technology Institute, Beijing, China
[2] Beijing Film Academy, Beijing, China
boyihang@bfa.edu.cn
[3] University of California, Davis, USA

Abstract. In film art, the usage of various fields of view in a movie reflects the shooting style of the director or artist. Analyzing which field of view was used by the shot can help us achieve the semi-automatic design and generation of the storyboard. Before achieving the generation of movie shots, the corresponding field of view recognition method and field of view dataset need to help the machine select a suitable field of view. However, although the traditional field of view recognition consumes many resources and time, no one establishes a relevant field of view dataset successfully. To solve this problem, we propose a method for automatically recognizing the field of view in a movie shot. In addition, we create a new field of view dataset by extracting shot images from available movies, including 10041 pictures. Experiments show that the proposed method can accurately achieve the automatic field of view recognition work.

Keywords: Field of view recognition · Movie shot analysis · Field of view recognition method · Field of view dataset

1 Introduction

Field of view is one of the basic elements that make up a movie shot, which refers to the range of the subject in the shot. Generally, directors or artists choose the appropriate field of view according to their understanding of the script; then, they determine the shooting method of each shot. Fields of view are usually divided into five categories: long shot, full shot, medium shot, close-up, and big close-up, based on how much the frame captures the performer's body part fundamentally.

As shown in Fig. 1. Different fields of view can guide the audience's aesthetic psychology and emotional changes. Among them, the long shot is mainly used to display three things: 1. wide-view pictures, such as fields, snowfields, forests, deserts. 2. the large crowd fields of view with very small characters, expressing the scale of things. 3. the environment and the artistic conception of the picture

Supplementary Information The online version contains supplementary material available at https://doi.org/10.1007/978-3-031-18913-5_31.

(Fig. 1(a)). The full shot is often used as the overall angle of a field of view to show the whole body of the character or the whole scene of the shot, which restricts the light, movement direction and position of the subject in the storyboard. Directors often use full shots to maintain a unified visual sense of the scene (Fig. 1(b))). The medium shot shows the picture above the knee of the character or part of the scene. It is a common to use narrative shot. The audience can clearly see the physical movements of the actor's half body and emotional changes in characters, which is convenient for explaining the relationship between characters (Fig. 1(c)). The close-up is used to show the picture above the character's chest or part of the object, which can maximize both the display of the character and the actor's inner activities, facial expressions and micro-expressions (Fig. 1(d)). The big close-up shows the head above the shoulders of the character or the detailed picture of some subjects, which can delicately describe the character and their emotion. The big close-up can also highlight a specific feature (Fig. 1(e)).

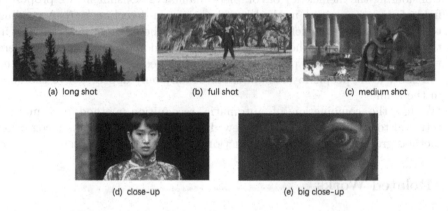

(a) long shot   (b) full shot   (c) medium shot

(d) close-up   (e) big close-up

Fig. 1. Example fields of view of movie shots (in which (a) is from the movie "Cold Mountain", (b) is from the movie "Saved Ginger", (c) is from the movie "Avengers 2", (d) is from the movie "Red Lantern Hanging High", and (e) is from the movie "Batman"). (Color figure online)

It can be said that the design of the movie shots [3] is the first and crucial step in the movie from the script text to the visual presentation. After the directors get the scripts, they will discuss with the artists as soon as possible to draw the storyboard of each shot. This is the generation process from text to image. The storyboard is an important basis for each subsequent film shot [15]. As the foundation of a movie, storyboard determines the final visual presentation effect and style of the entire film. The storyboard also reflects the characters, events, atmosphere, emotions and other content in the script.

At present, the design of the storyboard by artists is still by hand. Although some young artists have begun to use hand-painted boards or related drawing software to improve designing efficiency, it is still unable to meet the production needs of the virtual production method. We urgently need a more intelligent and efficient creation method to complete the step from script to screen generation.

With the continuous progress and development of digital virtual technology, artificial intelligence technology, and machine learning methods, human-machine cooperative film art creation [2] can be a main methods in future film virtual production. In order to use AI technology, it is necessary to establish a corresponding dataset of movie shots for machine training and learning. Currently, although there are a growing number of image datasets for aesthetic metrics, text-to-image generation and emotional metrics, datasets of cinematographic footage exclusively are extremely rare. So, we propose a method to solve this problem. The contributions of our study are three-fold:

1. This paper collects the shots we need from available movies to construct our dataset. We divided these pictures into five fields of view to build a brand new field of view dataset.
2. Considering the inefficiency of complete manual establishment, we propose a field of view recognition method based on human detection [6,7]. According to the definition of the field of view, we retrieve the different fields of view in the movie by detecting the people in the shots and analyzing the parts where the people appear in the pictures. For example, people are fully shown in the full shot, while people in medium shots usually only appear above the knee in the frame.
3. We use the combination of automatic recognition method and manual retrieval to establish our field of view dataset. The field of view recognition method greatly improved the production efficiency of our dataset.

2   Related Works

2.1   Human Detection

Human detection methods are mainly divided into two categories: the top-down method (the order is to determine the position of the person first, and then detect the visible key points of each person) and the bottom-up method (the order is to detect the visible key points first, and then determine their key points. to whom). In recent years, human detection research is mainly divided into single-person detection research [1] and multi-person detection research [10].

In terms of single-person detection, Ke [11] et al. combined the feature maps of two AlexNet models as output in the research of video multi-frame human detection system. The experimental results on the FLIC dataset using a simple data enhancement method showed that compared with the traditional detection algorithm, the accuracy was improved 5%. Compared with single-person detection, multi-person detection also needed to consider the error of matching the body to the human body. The better multi-person detection research was not effective in single-person detection applications. Cao et al. proposed a new bottom-up OpenPose model, which used a non-parametric representation method for key point connections-Part Affinity Fields (PAFs) method to complete the detection from key points to limb connections, then to the construction process of the human skeleton.

2.2 Field of View Recognition Method

The existing field of view recognition methods can be divided into manual identification and computer calculation. The method of manual recognition is that the editor uses the existing experience to observe and subjectively judge the field of view of the shot when editing the video. This method requires the recognition person with professionally editing and directing experiences. The labor cost is high, and the recognition efficiency is low and the probability of error is high. The traditional computer calculation method [9] is to extract the outline of the person through simple feature recognition, calculate the proportion of the outline of the human body in the full frame, and determine the field of view category to which the proportion belongs by setting thresholds for five field of view categories. This method not only lacks the recognition of specific semantic features but also has low error tolerance, poor robustness; this method is not universally applicable to videos of different types and frame ratios.

3 Movie Field of View Dataset(MFOVD)

In order to construct a dataset of cinematographic footage exclusively, we build a dataset named Movie Field of View Dataset(MFOVD) including 10041 images. Our dataset covers excellent films of different eras at home and abroad, as well as winning films of well-known film awards such as the Oscars. Figure 2 shows some of the data in our dataset: Our work is to capture footage from the original films of these films, and classify these shots into five categories: long shot, full shot, medium shot, close and big close-up. The distribution of different categories are as Fig. 3.

The establishment of movie field of view Dataset is mainly aimed at the follow-up training and determining the composition and hierarchical relationship of shots.

4 Field of View Recognition Method

Since our goal is to categorize a movie shot, our first task is to define which category the shot belongs to. The change of the shooting distance has the greatest impact on the effect of the picture, also known as the change of picture's framing range, which leads to the concept of different fields of view. Therefore, we can distinguish the field of view according to the range of characters appeared in the movie shots.

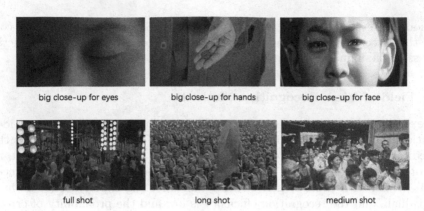

Fig. 2. Examples in the dataset. These samples include both excellent domestic works and award-winning films from abroad, and include different eras and different fields of view.

According to the above definition of the characteristics of different fields of view, for a given frame, our recognition method will determine the framing range of the shot by locating the key points of the characters in the shot [5], and then determine which field of view the shot belongs to.

In the remainder of this subsection, we describe the details of our shot recognition method. As shown in Fig. 5, we use OpenPose to detect 135 key points such as human pose, face, hand, and others [17].

We list the parts corresponding to the 25 key points of human body pose in Table 1.

According to the framing range of different fields of view, we divide the field of view by judging whether the key points representing the part can be located in the shot [4,8]. For example, full shot and long shot should include all 25 body pose key points. The framing range of the close-up is above the chest and below the shoulders, so the lens should not include the key points representing the hips (three points 8, 9, 12), but also include the three key points representing the shoulders (three points 1, 2, 5). The specific classification criteria are shown in Table 2.

The key point judgment of characters in the shot can preliminarily distinguish big close-up, close-up and medium shot [13]. However, the long shot and the full shot should include all 25 key points of the human body posture, so only through the key point detection and judgment cannot accurately distinguish the two kinds of fields of view. From the definition of the characteristics of the long shot and the full shot, the long shot contains more space than the full shot, which also means that the proportion of the characters in the whole shot is smaller.

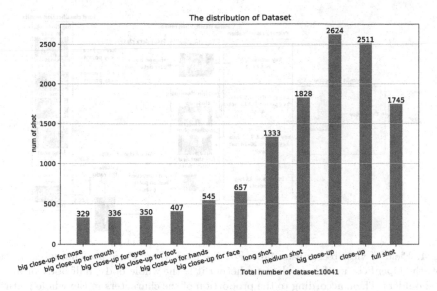

Fig. 3. The distribution of various fields of view in the dataset

Table 1. Representation of key points

Number of points	Representation	Number of points	Representation
1	Neck	13	LKnee
2	Rshoulder	14	LAnkle
3	RElbow	15	REye
4	RWrist	16	LEye
5	LShoulder	17	REar
6	LElbow	18	LEar
7	LWrist	19	LBigToe
8	MidHip	20	LSmallToe
9	RHip	21	LHeel
10	RKnee	22	RBigToe
11	RAnkle	23	RSmallToe
12	LHip	24	RHeel

Therefore, after judging that the shot belongs to one of the long shot and the full shot through the key points, we use self correction human parsing (schp) to obtain the binarized mask image of the shot, and then calculate the proportion of human pixels p_h in the entire shot. For the long shot, there also is a situation where the character in the shot is too small, resulting in inaccurate drawing of the mask map. By obtaining the outline coordinates of the character, we use the

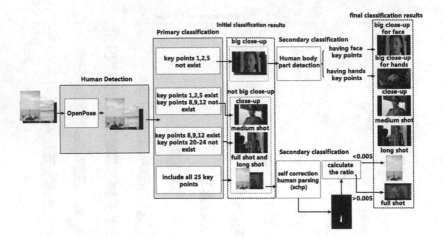

Fig. 4. Field of view recognition flow. For the case where there are characters in the shot, the OpenPose model can detect whether it is the whole body, half body or above the shoulders. Then, according to the proportion of the characters in the whole picture, it can be judged whether it is a full shot, a medium shot or a big close-up.

Table 2. Classification criteria

Field of view	Judgment condition
big close-up	Key points 1,2,5 not exist
close-up	Key points 1,2,5 exist & key points 8,9,12 not exist
medium shot	Key points 8,9,12 exist & key points 20-24 not exist
full shot and long shot	Include all 25 key points

shoelace formula to calculate the area occupied by the character [16], and then calculate the ratio [14]:

$$S_{ch} = \frac{1}{2} | \sum_{i=1}^{n} (x_i y_{i+1} - x_{i+1} y_i) | \tag{1}$$

$$P = \frac{S_{ch}}{H \times W} \tag{2}$$

where H and W represent the height and width of the input shot, S_{ch} represents the area occupied by the character in the shot, and (x_i, y_i) represent the outline coordinates of the character. After extensive experiments, we set the corresponding threshold to 0.005. When the ratio P of the shots occupied by the character is less than this value, the shot is a long shot, otherwise, it is a full shot. The complete process is shown in the Fig. 4.

In addition, in the art of photography, big close-ups are not only big close-ups of the faces of the characters but also big close-ups of legs and hands. After

Fig. 5. Human key points detection by OpenPose

judging that the shot is a big close-up, we will continue to further classify the shot according to the key points of the face and hand located by OpenPose.

5   Experiments

5.1   Recognition on Movie Field of View Dataset(MFOVD)

We use the proposed recognition method to perform recognition work on our Movie Field of View Dataset(MFOVD), and the recognition results are shown in the Fig. 6.

It can be seen that our method can not only accurately identify relatively common shots, but also can identify shots with many characters and big close-ups for local area that are difficult to identify.

We also selected three common classification neural networks for the task of field of view classification on our MFOVD dataset to compare with our method. We divided our Movie Field of View Dataset(MFOVD) into 7531 training images and 2510 testing images. We used three deep neural networks: VGG, ResNet50 and ConvNext, which perform well in classification task, and present experiments trained on the training set and evaluated on the test set. Because images in our dataset were classified into five categories. We uses ACC to measure the accuracy of field of view classification methods. The accuracy of the five-classification indicates whether the predicted field of view of the shot and the real field of

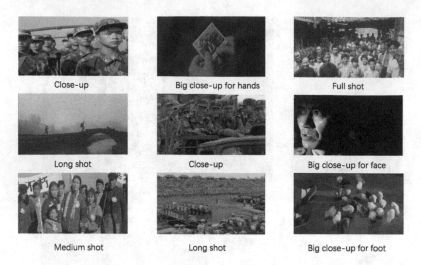

Fig. 6. Examples of recognition results

view of the shot are consistent. The accuracy of five-classification indicates the most basic accuracy of classification; the formula is:

$$ACCURACY = \frac{TP + TN}{P + N} \tag{3}$$

Table 3 shows the accuracy of three classification neural network and our field of view recognition method.

Table 3. The results for field of view classification

	Our Method	VGG	ResNet50	ConvNeXt
ACCURACY	**85.24%**	78.96%	79.12%	82.99%

It can be shown that our method performs better. At the same time, compared with neural networks, our method is more interpretable, and it is also universal to videos of different types and aspect ratios.

5.2 Recognition on a Full Movie

This experiment carried out aims at predicting the field of view distribution of an entire movie. The idea is to show the ability of our method in recognizing fields of view for an unknown movie, where we generate a fingerprint made up of the five predicted values of long shot, full shot, medium shot, close-up and big close-up percentages, respectively.

We selected four complete Antonioni's filmography on feature films, which are Le amiche, L'eclisse, Blow-Up and Zabriskie point. Ground truth values for these movies have been manually annotated second by second by the author of this article [12].

As examples of extracted fingerprints, in Fig. 7 we show the predicted field of view distributions for four movies. We can see that our automatic field of view recognition method has little deviation from the corresponding manual identification. In the face of a complete film, our proposed method still performs well. It can be said that this method can be competent for the task of automatic firld of view recognition.

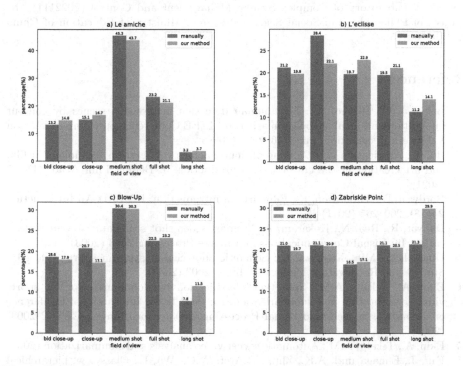

Fig. 7. Field of view distributions (ground-truth in blue, predicted in orange) for movies: a Le amiche, b L'eclisse, c Blow-Up, d Zabriskie point (Color figure online)

6   Conclusion

It is challenging to construct an entirely new dataset in the field of movie shot analysis. By capturing footage from the original films of Oscar, Palme d'Or and other international film festival-winning films, and classifying these shots into five field of views, we get a new dataset called movie field of view dataset(MFOVD). In order to meet the requirements of automatic retrieval and analysis of datasets for fast and accurate field of view calculation, we also propose an automatic field of view recognition method based on the OpenPose model. Through the positioning of relevant key points of OpenPose, it is possible to detect whether it is the whole body, half body or above the shoulders. Then, according to the proportion of the character in the whole picture, it is also possible to judge whether it is a full shot, a medium shot or a close-up. The establishment of datasets by machine and human working simultaneously will greatly improve the efficiency of creating huge datasets.

Acknoledgements. We thank the ACs and reviewers. This work is partially supported by the National Natural Science Foundation of China (62072014 & 62106118), the Beijing Natural Science Foundation (L192040), the Open Fund Project of the State Key Laboratory of Complex System Management and Control (2022111), the Project of Philosophy and Social Science Research, Ministry of Education of China (20YJC760115).

References

1. Beleznai, C., Bischof, H.: Fast human detection in crowded scenes by contour integration and local shape estimation. In: IEEE Conference on Computer Vision & Pattern Recognition, pp. 2246–2253 (2009)
2. Bo, Y.: Application and thinking of man-machine cooperation technology in film and art creation in the era of virtual production. J. Beijing Film Acad. (11), 7 (2021)
3. Bordwell, D., Thompson, K.: Film art: an introduction. Film Art An Introduction **24**(18), 260–265 (2011)
4. Dahyot, R., Rea, N., Kokaram, A.C.: Sport video shot segmentation and classification. In: Visual Communications and Image Processing 2003 (2003)
5. Duan, L.Y., Min, X., Tian, Q.: Semantic shot classification in sports video. In: Storage and Retrieval for Media Databases 2003 (2003)
6. Ekin, A., Tekalp, A.M.: Shot type classification by dominant color for sports video segmentation and summarization. In: 2003 IEEE International Conference on Acoustics, Speech, and Signal Processing, 2003. Proceedings (ICASSP 2003) (2003)
7. Ekin, A., Tekalp, A.M.: Automatic soccer video analysis and summarization (2004)
8. Fan, J., Elmagarmid, A.K., Zhu, X., Aref, W.G., Wu, L.: Classview: hierarchical video shot classification, indexing, and accessing. IEEE Trans. Multimedia **6**(1), 70–86 (2004)
9. Ferrer, M.Z., Barbieri, M., Weda, H.: Automatic classification of field of view in video. In: IEEE International Conference on Multimedia & Expo (2006)
10. Jalal, A., Nadeem, A., Bobasu, S.: Human body parts estimation and detection for physical sports movements. In: International Conference on Communication (2019)
11. Ke, L., Qi, H., Chang, M.C., Lyu, S.: Multi-scale supervised network for human pose estimation. IEEE (2018)
12. Kovács, Bálint, A.: Shot scale distribution: An authorial fingerprint or a cognitive pattern? Projections **8**(2), 50–70(21) (2014)
13. Lienhart, R.W.: Comparison of automatic shot boundary detection algorithms. Proc. SPIE **3656**(1), 290–301 (1999)

14. Lin, Z., Davis, L.S.: Shape-based human detection and segmentation via hierarchical part-template matching. IEEE Trans. Pattern Anal. & Mach. Intell. **32**(4), 604–18 (2010)
15. Mascelli, J.V.: The five C's of cinematography: motion picture filming techniques. The five C's of cinematography: motion picture filming techniques (1998)
16. Uehara, K., Amano, M., Ariki, Y., Kumano, M.: Video shooting navigation system by real-time useful shot discrimination based on video grammar. In: IEEE International Conference on Multimedia & Expo (2004)
17. Yang, L., Song, Q., Wang, Z., Hu, M., Liu, C.: Hier R-CNN: instance-level human parts detection and a new benchmark. IEEE Trans. Image Process. **30**, 39–54 (2021)

Multi-level Temporal Relation Graph for Continuous Sign Language Recognition

Jingjing Guo[1], Wanli Xue[1(✉)], Leming Guo[1], Tiantian Yuan[2],
and Shengyong Chen[1]

[1] School of Computer Science and Engineering, Tianjin University of Technology,
Tianjin 300384, China
xuewanli@email.tjut.edu.cn
[2] Technical College for the Deaf, Tianjin University of Technology,
Tianjin 300384, China

Abstract. Temporal relation modeling is one of the key points to describe gesture changes in continuous sign language recognition. However, there are many similar gestures in sign language, therefore focusing only on global information can exacerbate the recognition ambiguity caused by various gesture combination. To alleviate this problem, we attempt to achieve the balance between the global information and the local information in gesture changes. Therefore, we construct a multi-level temporal relation graph (MLTRG). Specifically, the multi-level temporal relation graph of the video sequence is established according to different time spans, where the graph nodes are the corresponding visual features. Then the feature fusion and propagation of the multi-level temporal relation graph are performed by a graph convolutional network (GCN). Finally, we can reason and balance the global and the local temporal information of gesture changes in continuous sign language videos. We evaluate our method on the large-scale public datasets RWTH-PHOENIX-Weather-2014 and 2014T, the results prove the advantages and effectiveness of our method.

Keywords: Sign language recognition · Temporal relation modeling · Graph convolutional network

1 Introduction

Sign language is a combination of different gestures and facial expressions to convey semantic information between the deaf and the hearing. Video-based continuous sign language recognition (CSLR) [2] has the ability to convert each sign video into a sequence of glosses (a gloss represents a sign with its closest meaning in natural languages [18]). In this regard, CSLR highlights the vast

This work was supported in part by the National Natural Science Foundation of China under Grant 61906135, Grant 62020106004 and Grant 92048301.

potential to alleviate the communication inconvenience for the deaf in the real world. Because of this, CSLR has attracted the attention of experts in organizations.

The CSLR structure of current sign language recognition works contains three components: visual model, contextual model and alignment model [17]. The temporal relation modeling is employed to obtain temporal information of sign video and to enrich the contextual semantic information. Thus the quality of the temporal relation modeling in the contextual model is important.

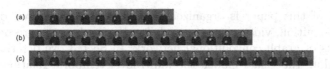

Fig. 1. The video sequences in sub-figures (a), (b), and (c) respectively represent "2", "20", and "22" in German sign language. But when they are combined with other gestures, they can easily lead to ambiguity. E.g, the gesture in (a) combined with the finger bending gesture in (b) represents "20" and the gesture in (b) combined with the gesture of swinging left and right represents "22".

In previous CSLR methods, recurrent neural network (RNN) is a powerful tool for temporal relation modeling. RNN is broadly employed to learn global information of video sequences by recursion. But RNN cannot be parallelized, so Vaswani et al. [21] propose the attention mechanism with the ability to get global information in one step. Li et al. successfully apply transformer [21] to temporal relation modeling and demonstrate that transformer has more validity than RNN in dealing with long-term dependencies [16]. For this reason, Niu et al. apply transformer to extract global temporal information [17].

However, many glosses have very similar gesture movements, this phenomenon is possible to create recognition ambiguities and to bring difficulties to CSLR tasks. Figure 1 illustrates the aforementioned phenomenon due to paying too much focus on global information. A simple inspiration is to allow temporal relation modeling in CSLR to combine both global and local information. While, GCN [11] shows the excellent capability to balance and reason the global-local information [22,24].

In view of the above analysis, we propose a multi-level temporal relation graph (MLTRG) model for CSLR tasks (see Fig. 2). Firstly, visual features of different time spans are established graphical relations by MLTRG. Subsequently, we use GCN to update and to fuse the features of graph nodes, these graph nodes are from different levels of MLTRG. With this, we can reason and balance the global and the local temporal information in gesture movement changes. More importantly, MLTRG can enrich the semantic information between video contexts.

The main contributions of this paper are:

- Propose a temporal relation modeling method MLTRG (Multi-Level Temporal Relation Graph) that takes into account both global and local information for CSLR.
- In the MLTRG, we propose to use GCN to update features of graph nodes. Further, we can reason and balance the global-local relational information via GCN.
- The effectiveness of this method is verified on two large datasets, and the experimental results are significantly improved compared with the baseline.

The rest of this paper is organized as follows: In Sect. 2, we discuss sign language recognition, video contexts modeling in sign language recognition and related works of graph convolutional network. In Sect. 3, we describe our approach, including the visual model, the multi-level temporal relation graph and the alignment model. In Sect. 4 we perform related experiments on two sign language datasets. Finally, a conclusion is drawn in Sect. 5.

2 Related Work

2.1 Sign Language Recognition

The field of computer vision has been intensively studied in the last 20 years for sign language recognition. The pioneering works on sign language recognition have focused on the isolated sign language recognition (ISLR) [27]. However, ISLR mainly focuses on the situation where glosses have been well segmented temporally. This situation may limits the applicability of sign language recognition. Therefore, some works begin to focus on CSLR tasks. Recently, the remarkable progress and great recognition accuracy of CSLR are driven by technologies from deep learning [4].

2.2 Video Contexts Modeling

Recurrent Neural Networks (RNNs) and long short-term memory (LSTM) [4] show superior performance in handling complex dynamic changes of gestures. However, RNN inability to parallelize, this situation makes convergence slow during training and makes the model tend to over-fitting. LSTM, as one of the most representative sequence models, still has shortcomings in dealing with the long-time dependence problem.

In recent years, transformer has demonstrated its outstanding performance in temporal relation modeling. Self-attention in the transformer can establish a direct connection between any elements in the input sequence and handle the input sequence with various length [19]. Because of this, [17] adopts the transformer as the contextual model and achieves great recognition accuracy. Regrettably, self-attention in the transformer pays more attention to the global information, and it also pays more attention to the information transmission between neighboring sequence nodes. Self-attention thus ignores the acquisition of local information.

2.3   Graph Convolutional Network

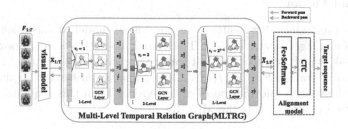

Fig. 2. The pipeline of the proposed method. Feed the frame-wise visual feature sequence $X_{1:T}$ to MLTRG, and the output is $\widetilde{X}_{1:T}$. For the relation graph formed by the frame t at any time and its neighboring feature nodes of different spans, the feature information of graph nodes is merged and renewed through GCN Layer. Employing MLTRG, we can model the temporal relation and balance global-local feature information between different level relation graphs.

Kipf and Welling have been proposed graph convolutional network (GCN) [11]: $X = \sigma(AXW)$. $A \in R^{N \times N}$ represents the adjacency matrix of the graph, $X \in R^{N \times d}$ is the hidden representation of the graph nodes, and $W \in R^{d \times d}$ is the parameter matrix to be learned, σ is the RELU activation function [11, 22] (N is the number of nodes in the graph and d is the dimension of the hidden layer).

In recent years, GCN shows great advantages in dealing with the relation between multiple objects. Notably, [24] proposes a relation reasoning method by building an activity relation graph (ARG) and capture the positional correlation between different actors. Then [24] uses GCN to reason about the relation of the nodes in the ARG. This method can efficiently model the interrelation between different actors to achieve real-life group activity detection.

Additionally, GCN also has been employed extensively on temporal reasoning tasks in the field of action segmentation [22]. Dong Wang et al. construct a multi-layer extended temporal graph. They propose GCN to capture the temporal relation. The dependency relation between video frames also improves the final action segmentation results. It should be noted that its experimental results are better than other methods for several datasets.

Recently, some scholars have applied GCN to ISLR tasks [1]. They create a 3D skeleton node sequence from the pre-extracted skeleton features then input the sequence to ST-GCN [25]. However, this method is based on the skeleton features extracted by the pre-established pose estimation algorithm. Specifically, there are factors such as faulty extraction and incomplete label of the skeleton node features. So the method based on the features of the skeleton node sequence is very noisy.

While the input of the MLTRG is the visual feature of sign videos, so we can avoid the problem caused by incomplete skeleton features. And the MLTRG model can better achieve the balance between the global-local temporal information of sign language gesture changes.

3   Our Approach

3.1   Visual Model

We use the pre-trained ResNet18 [9] as the visual model, it has shown strong capability for image representation. The visual model plays an important role in CSLR task, which extracts a visual feature sequence $X_{1:T} = (x_1, ..., x_T)$ from a sequence of T frames $F_{1:T} = (f_1, f_2, ..., f_T)$. The visual feature sequence $X_{1:T}$ represents the spatial information of a sign video. Then this sequence is fed to the contextual model, that is the MLTRG.

3.2   Multi-level Temporal Relation Graph

We introduce MLTRG as shown in Fig. 2. In summary, MLTRG builds a $L-$level temporal relation graph. Firstly, we input the visual feature sequence $X_{1:T} = (x_1, ..., x_T)$ extracted from the visual medel to MLTRG. In MLTRG, we treat the feature at time step t and its neighboring step as the graph nodes X_t^l at level l, $X_t^l = \{x_{t-\tau_l}^l, x_t^l, x_{t+\tau_l}^l\}$.

Secondly, we construct a temporal relation graph G_t^l upon X_t^l, the edge weights of G_t^l represent the temporal correlation between graph nodes. Notably, when G_t^l is at level $l \in \{1, 2, ..., L\}$, set the expansion factor $\tau_l = 2^{l-1}$. We obtain the local temporal information by the proposed G_t^l, which is composed of the features from the smaller τ_l. As the τ_l increases, we can effectively obtain the global information by the feature fusion and propagation.

Finally, after G_t^l is constructed at each level, the GCN Layer is connected to conduct the aggregation of the feature information. Inside the GCN Layer, we calculate the edge weights of two complementary relational graphs $G_t^{r_1, l}$ and $G_t^{r_2, l}$ respectively, and this process is defined as Eq. (1) and Eq. (2). We collect the edge weights $e_{r_1}(i, j)$ in $G_t^{r_1, l}$ into the adjacency matrix $A_t^{r_1, l}$. The edge weight $e_{r_1}(i, j)$ is calculated by the cosine similarity between the graph nodes X_t^l, and this process is defined as Eq. (1).

$$e_{r_1}(i, j) = \frac{x_i \cdot x_j}{max\left(\|x_i\|_2 \cdot \|x_j\|_2, \epsilon\right)} \tag{1}$$

where x_i, x_j represent any two nodes in the $G_t^{r_1, l}$ and ϵ is employed to avoid the denominator being 0. The key reason for this design is that the frame nodes with similar gloss should have a larger weight.

$G_t^{r_2, l}$ is used to supplement the contextual relation with $G_t^{r_1, l}$. In $G_t^{r_2, l}$, a one-dimensional dilated convolution is applied to X_t^l, which is defined as Eq. (2).

$$A_t^{r_2, l} = Conv\left(X_t^l, W, dilation = \tau_l\right) \tag{2}$$

Based on Eq. (2), the expansion factor $dilation$ of this one-dimensional dilated convolutional layer is equal to the expansion factor τ_l in X_t^l ($dilation = \tau_l$). Where W is the weights of the dilated convolution filter with kernel size is 3.

The output $A_t^{r2,l}$ is a 3×3-dimensional vector and reshaped to the adjacency matrix with size $(3, 3)$.

We use graph convolution to update the representation x_t^l according to its $G_t^{r_1,l}$ and $G_t^{r_2,l}$ at each GCN Layer. The above process is defined as Eq. (3):

$$g_t^l = GCN^{(l)} \left(X_t^l, A_t^{r_1,l}, W_t^{r_1,l} \right) + GCN^{(l)} \left(X_t^l, A_t^{r_2,l}, W_t^{r_2,l} \right)$$
$$x_t^{l+1} = Conv \left(g_t^l, W^l \right) + x_t^l \tag{3}$$
$$\widetilde{X}_t = \widetilde{x}_{[t-\tau_l, t, t+\tau_l]}^L$$

Notably, MLTRG can help our network to handle the recognition difficulties casued by the similar gestures. At the same time, this process helps our network outputs a robust temporal representation. Through, the output feature sequence $\widetilde{X}_{1:T} = (\widetilde{x}_1, \widetilde{x}_2, ..., \widetilde{x}_T)$ of the MLTRG is sent to a fully connected layer (FC) and a softmax layer to get the predicted logits $Z_{1:T} = (z_1, z_2, ..., z_T)$ of sub-gloss states.

3.3 Alignment Model

In CSLR task, each sign video is labeled without any alignment information and without clearly time boundary division for each gesture. Each sentence video of sign language datasets only has its corresponding sentence-level annotation. So in the alignment model, we use the connectionist temporal classification (CTC) [6] to align the sign video sequence to the target label sequence. Constrained by CTC loss, our method generates ordered glosses as the prediction sentence for the given sign videos [23]. And the CTC objective function is defined as Eq. (4):

$$p\left(\boldsymbol{\pi} \mid F_{1:T}\right) = \prod_{t=1}^{T} p\left(\pi_t \mid F_{1:T}\right)$$
$$p\left(y \mid F_{1:T}\right) = \sum_{\pi \in \mathcal{B}^{-1}(y)} p\left(\boldsymbol{\pi} \mid F_{1:T}\right) \tag{4}$$
$$L_{ctc} = -\log p\left(y \mid F_{1:T}\right)$$

To align the sign video sequence $F_{1:T}$ to the ordered ground truth sentence y in temporal dimension, CTC add an extra label "blank". π is a sequence of gloss labels and blank with length T, π_t is the label of π at time t, and $p\left(\pi_t \mid F_{1:T}\right)$ is the emission probability of π_t at time t. $\mathcal{B}$ is used to define the many-to-one mapping process of alignments onto the target sequence y. And $\mathcal{B}^{-1}(y) = \{\pi \mid \mathcal{B}(\pi) = y\}$ denotes the set of all paths that can be mapped into the ground truth sentence y. The many-to-one function can remove the identical and blank predictions in π. Then CTC maximizes the sum of predicted probabilities of all possible alignment paths, and gets the output alignment π at every decoding step [7].

We define the training objective function of the main stream as Eq. (5) (λ_1 is the weight factor of the regularizer, W is the parameters of the whole model):

$$L = L_{ctc} + \lambda_1 \|W\| \tag{5}$$

In testing, beam search algorithm [8] is used to decode. This algorithm chooses the n most probably prefixes at each time step during decoding. In this regard, the beam search algorithm has the ability to reduce the search space [17]. By optimizing the CTC objective function, our method learns to align the gloss with the corresponding according video segment more precisely.

4   Results and Discussion

4.1   Dataset

RWTH-PHOENIX-Weather-2014(PHOENIX2014) [13] is a German sign language dataset, which is recorded by a weather broadcasting and television station. This dataset contains 6841 different sentences with a vocabulary of 1232. There are 5672, 540 and 629 data samples in train, dev and test respectively. The resolution of all videos in the dataset is 210×260 [17]. Although RWTH-PHOENIX-Weather-2014T(PHOENIX2014T) [2] is designed for sign language translation task, it can also be used to evaluate the performance of CSLR task. And the vocabulary size of this dataset is 1085. There are 7096, 519 and 642 samples in train, dev and test respectively. The number of sign language presenters are the same as the PHOENIX2014 dataset, both are 9 [17]. To keep the recognized gloss and ground truth sequences consistent, some words need to be substituted, deleted, or inserted. The word error rate (WER) [20] is used to measure the performance of the sign language recognition task, it is described in Eq.(6).

$$WER = \frac{insertions + deletions + substitutions}{words\ in\ reference} \tag{6}$$

4.2   Experimental Setup

We resize all the frames in the PHOENIX2014 and PHOENIX2014T datasets to 256×256 pixels, and randomly crop to 224×224 pixels during training. At the same time, we use a pre-trained 18-layer 2D ResNet, and remove the fully connected layer. Set the initial learning rate η_i to 1×10^{-4}, and each model has been trained for 60 epochs. The batch size is 1. λ_1 is the weight factor of the regularizer and is empirically set to be 0.0001. For both datasets, the MLTRG model is set to be three layers with the hidden state size of 2048 and $p_{drop} = 50\%$. The graph node number of the temporal relation graph is set to 3. We try to set the value to a larger value of 5 or 7, but the experimental results are not good (WER is around 30). The beam width used in CTC is set to 10 in all test results. And in all experiments, we use an Adam optimizer with $\beta_1 = 0.9$ and $\beta_2 = 0.999$.

4.3   Comparison with SOTA Methods

Table 1. The comparison with other methods on PHOENIX2014 (the lower the better).

Methods	Dev(WER)	Test(WER)
Re-sign [14]	27.1	26.8
Staged-OPt [4]	39.4	38.7
LS-HAN [10]	-	38.3
SF-Net [26]	35.6	34.9
CNN-LSTM-HMM [12]	26.0	26.0
SFD+SGS+SFL+LM [17]	24.9	25.3
Baseline	26.2	26.8
Ours	**26.1**	**25.6**

Table 2. The comparison with other methods on PHOENIX2014T (the lower the better).

Methods	Dev (WER)	Test (WER)
CNN-LSTM-HMM(1-Stream) [12]	24.5	26.5
CNN-LSTM-HMM(2-Stream) [12]	24.5	25.4
CNN-LSTM-HMM(3-Stream) [12]	22.1	24.1
SLT(Gloss) [3]	24.9	24.6
SFD+SGS+SFD [17]	25.1	26.1
Ours	**22.4**	**22.1**

Evaluation on PHOENIX2014: It can be seen from Table 1 that although our method does not achieve the effect of SOTA, it still have a great progress. The CNN-LSTM-HMM [12] uses multiple clue sequences in parallel, including full frames, hands, and mouths. While, our method only uses the visual features of the full-frame and achieve a comparable performance. As Table 1 also shows that our method performs favorably well under the challenging test set that has more samples compared with the dev set. This result also has been shown on PHOENIX2014T. This phenomenon demonstrates that the strong generalization ability of our method is reflected in a large number of samples.

Evaluation on PHOENIX2014T: We compare our method with several state-of-the-art methods, and our method achieves the best result than the others. We analyze that PHOENIX2014T has more training samples than the PHOENIX2014, our method can capture more effectively gesture movement information. At the same time, due to the use of GCN to reason the temporal information, our method can effectively balance the local and the global information and achieve excellent recognition performance.

4.4   Model Validity Experiment

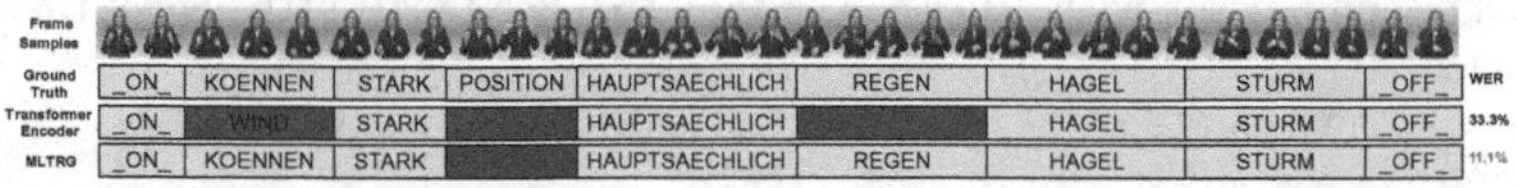

Fig. 3. An example of decoding result. The figure shows the different WER (the lower the better) obtained by using two methods to model the time relation, our WER is marked in red font. It is worth noting that the box with red background denotes the false prediction. (Color figure online)

Table 3. Comparison with methods in contextual model on PHOENIX2014 dataset.

Methods in contextual model	Dev (WER)	Test (WER)
Transformer Encoder	26.5	27.2
MS-TCN	26.5	26.3
MS-TCN++	26.3	26.4
MLTRG	26.1	25.6

Model Analysis: To prove the effectiveness of our proposed MLTRG model, we conduct the following comparative experiments. Replace the MLTRG model with the transformer and MS-TCN [5], MS-TCN++ [15]. Figure 3 shows some visualization results of our MLTRG compared with Transfomer Encoder, our MLTRG achieves better results. When processing visual features of the input sequence, the transformer focuses on all feature nodes of the entire sequence to learn the global information. However, in actual sign language recognition, it is often more likely that adjacent frame nodes have the same gloss. Therefore the combination and split of gesture actions may bring recognition ambiguity in CSLR. This problem can be resolved by achieving the balance between the global information and the local information in gesture changes. The transformer pays more attention to global information that unable to well reason the temporal information. While MLTRG can effectively balance the local-global feature information. In Table 3, MS-TCN uses a simple dilated convolution to capture, and to aggregate the temporal neighborhood information. And MS-TCN++ is improved on the MS-TCN. Compared with the MS-TCN and MS-TCN++, our method also has a better performance.

Parameter Settings: On the one hand, as the number of layers L changes, the temporal relation graph is constructed by a wider range of neighboring frame nodes. Meanwhile, because the parameter L in MLTRG affects the expansion factor τ_l of the composition, we conduct experiments with different settings of L. Figure 4 shows the impact of different layers L and p_{drop} on the final WER performance. We can see from Fig. 4 (left) that when $L=3$, the lowest WER is

25.6/26.1 (test/dev). Further, we analyze the average number of per gloss in the PHOENIX2014 and PHOENIX2014T is about 12.2. When $L=3$ $\tau_l=4$, the span of the frame node that constructs the temporal relation graph is 9, and this is the most suitable value.

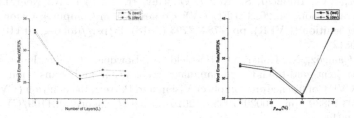

Fig. 4. The impact of different layers L (left) and p_{drop} (right) in MLTRG on WER.

On the other hand, too many video frames may cause frame redundancy, and this phenomenon may affect the final sign language recognition performance. Inspired by [17], to avoid this problem and to improve the model convergence speed. During the training process we randomly discard a settled proportion of frames through uniform sampling. Assuming that there are T frames in the sign video initially, the hyper-parameter ratio is p_{drop}, then $[T \times p_{drop}]$ frames are discarded. During the test process, we select an average of $\frac{1}{p_{drop}}$ frames from the test set and discard them randomly. Figure 4 (right) shows the WER with different dropping rates, and we can clearly see 50% is the most applicable choice. Because discard too many frames may cause a lot of information to be lost. However, if the number of lost frames are too small, this situation may produce information redundancy. So in experimental setting, we set $p_{drop}=50\%$ to enhance the data and speed up the training speed.

5   Conclusions

We provide a new perspective that balances global and local temporal gesture information, namely Multilevel Temporal Relation Graph (MLTRG), to alleviate recognition blur caused by similar gesture movements. In particular, MLTRG is constructed by using the visual information from different time spans, and then the GCN Layer is used for feature fusion and propagation between different levels. Through this process, our method can effectively reason the correlation between global and local movements. Experimental results show that our method can alleviate the recognition ambiguity caused by various gestures in continuous sign language.

References

1. de Amorim, C.C., Macêdo, D., Zanchettin, C.: Spatial-temporal graph convolutional networks for sign language recognition. CoRR abs/1901.11164 (2019), http://arxiv.org/abs/1901.11164
2. Camgoz, N.C., Hadfield, S., Koller, O., Ney, H., Bowden, R.: Neural sign language translation. In: 2018 IEEE/CVF Conference on Computer Vision and Pattern Recognition (CVPR), pp. 7784–7793 (2018). https://doi.org/10.1109/CVPR.2018.00812
3. Cihan Camgöz, N., Koller, O., Hadfield, S., Bowden, R.: Sign language transformers: joint end-to-end sign language recognition and translation. In: 2020 IEEE/CVF Conference on Computer Vision and Pattern Recognition (CVPR). vol. abs/2003.13830, pp. 10020–10030 (2020). https://doi.org/10.1109/CVPR42600.2020.01004
4. Cui, R., Liu, H., Zhang, C.: Recurrent convolutional neural networks for continuous sign language recognition by staged optimization. In: 2017 IEEE Conference on Computer Vision and Pattern Recognition (CVPR), pp. 1610–1618 (2017). https://doi.org/10.1109/CVPR.2017.175
5. Farha, Y.A., Gall, J.: MS-TCN: multi-stage temporal convolutional network for action segmentation. CoRR abs/1903.01945 (2019), http://arxiv.org/abs/1903.01945
6. Graves, A., Fernández, S., Gomez, F., Schmidhuber, J.: Connectionist temporal classification: labelling unsegmented sequence data with recurrent neural networks. In: ICML 2006 - Proceedings of the 23rd International Conference on Machine Learning, vol. 2006, pp. 369–376 (2006). https://doi.org/10.1145/1143844.1143891
7. Graves, A., et al.: A novel connectionist system for unconstrained handwriting recognition. IEEE Trans. Pattern Anal. Mach. Intell. **31**(5), 855–868 (2009). https://doi.org/10.1109/TPAMI.2008.137
8. Hannun, A.Y., Maas, A.L., Jurafsky, D., Ng, A.Y.: First-pass large vocabulary continuous speech recognition using bi-directional recurrent DNNs (2014)
9. He, K., Zhang, X., Ren, S., Sun, J.: Deep residual learning for image recognition. In: 2016 IEEE Conference on Computer Vision and Pattern Recognition (CVPR), pp. 770–778 (2016). https://doi.org/10.1109/CVPR.2016.90
10. Huang, J., Zhou, W., Zhang, Q., Li, H., Li, W.: Video-based sign language recognition without temporal segmentation. CoRR abs/1801.10111 (2018). http://arxiv.org/abs/1801.10111
11. Kipf, T.N., Welling, M.: Semi-supervised classification with graph convolutional networks. CoRR abs/1609.02907 (2016). http://arxiv.org/abs/1609.02907
12. Koller, O., Camgoz, N.C., Ney, H., Bowden, R.: Weakly supervised learning with multi-stream CNN-LSTM-HMMs to discover sequential parallelism in sign language videos. IEEE Trans. Pattern Anal. Mach. Intell. **42**(9), 2306–2320 (2020). https://doi.org/10.1109/TPAMI.2019.2911077
13. Koller, O., Forster, J., Ney, H.: Continuous sign language recognition: towards large vocabulary statistical recognition systems handling multiple signers. Comput. Vis. Image Underst. **141**, 108–125 (2015). https://doi.org/10.1016/j.cviu.2015.09.013
14. Koller, O., Zargaran, S., Ney, H.: Re-sign: re-aligned end-to-end sequence modelling with deep recurrent CNN-HMMs. In: 2017 IEEE Conference on Computer Vision and Pattern Recognition (CVPR), pp. 3416–3424 (2017). https://doi.org/10.1109/CVPR.2017.364

15. Li, S.J., AbuFarha, Y., Liu, Y., Cheng, M.M., Gall, J.: MS-TCN++: multi-stage temporal convolutional network for action segmentation. IEEE Trans. Pattern Anal. Mach. Intell. (2020). https://doi.org/10.1109/TPAMI.2020.3021756

16. Li, S., et al.: Enhancing the locality and breaking the memory bottleneck of transformer on time series forecasting. CoRR abs/1907.00235 (2019). http://arxiv.org/abs/1907.00235

17. Niu, Z., Mak, B.: Stochastic fine-grained labeling of multi-state sign glosses for continuous sign language recognition. In: Vedaldi, A., Bischof, H., Brox, T., Frahm, J.-M. (eds.) ECCV 2020. LNCS, vol. 12361, pp. 172–186. Springer, Cham (2020). https://doi.org/10.1007/978-3-030-58517-4_11

18. Ong, S.C.W., Ranganath, S.: Automatic sign language analysis: a survey and the future beyond lexical meaning. IEEE Trans. Pattern Anal. Mach. Intell. **27**(6), 873–891 (2005). https://doi.org/10.1109/tpami.2005.112

19. Pham, N., Nguyen, T., Niehues, J., Müller, M., Waibel, A.: Very deep self-attention networks for end-to-end speech recognition. CoRR abs/1904.13377 (2019). http://arxiv.org/abs/1904.13377

20. Prabhavalkar, R., et al.: Minimum word error rate training for attention-based sequence-to-sequence models. In: ICASSP 2018 - 2018 IEEE International Conference on Acoustics, Speech and Signal Processing (ICASSP) (2017)

21. Vaswani, A., et al.:Attention is all you need. CoRR abs/1706.03762 (2017). http://arxiv.org/abs/1706.03762

22. Wang, D., Hu, D., Li, X., Dou, D.: Temporal relational modeling with self-supervision for action segmentation. CoRR abs/2012.07508 (2020). https://arxiv.org/abs/2012.07508

23. Wei, C., Zhao, J., Zhou, W., Li, H.: Semantic boundary detection with reinforcement learning for continuous sign language recognition. IEEE Trans. Circ. Syst. Video Technol. **31**, 1138–1149 (2020). https://doi.org/10.1109/TCSVT.2020.2999384

24. Wu, J., Wang, L., Wang, L., Guo, J., Wu, G.: Learning actor relation graphs for group activity recognition. In: 2019 IEEE/CVF Conference on Computer Vision and Pattern Recognition (CVPR), pp. 9956–9966 (2019). https://doi.org/10.1109/CVPR.2019.01020

25. Yan, S., Xiong, Y., Lin, D.: Spatial temporal graph convolutional networks for skeleton-based action recognition. CoRR abs/1801.07455 (2018). http://arxiv.org/abs/1801.07455

26. Yang, Z., Shi, Z., Shen, X., Tai, Y.: SF-Net: structured feature network for continuous sign language recognition. CoRR abs/1908.01341 (2019). http://arxiv.org/abs/1908.01341

27. Yin, F., Chai, X., Chen, X.: Iterative reference driven metric learning for signer independent isolated sign language recognition. In: Leibe, B., Matas, J., Sebe, N., Welling, M. (eds.) ECCV 2016. LNCS, vol. 9911, pp. 434–450. Springer, Cham (2016). https://doi.org/10.1007/978-3-319-46478-7_27

Beyond Vision: A Semantic Reasoning Enhanced Model for Gesture Recognition with Improved Spatiotemporal Capacity

Yizhe Wang, Congqi Cao(✉) (iD), and Yanning Zhang (iD)

National Engineering Laboratory for Integrated Aero-Space-Ground-Ocean Big Data Application Technology, School of Computer Science, Northwestern Polytechnical University, No. 1 Dongxiang Road, Xi'an 710129, China
{congqi.cao,ynzhang}@nwpu.edu.cn

Abstract. Gesture recognition is an imperative and practical problem owing to its great application potential. Although recent works have made great progress in this field, there also exist three non-negligible problems: 1) existing works lack efficient temporal modeling ability; 2) existing works lack effective spatial attention capacity; 3) most works only focus on the visual information, without considering the semantic relationship between different classes. To tackle the first problem, we propose a Long and Short-term Temporal Shift Module (LS-TSM). It extends the original TSM and expands the step size of shift operation to model long-term and short-term temporal information simultaneously. For the second problem, we expect to focus on the spatial area where the change of hand mainly occurs. Therefore, we propose a Spatial Attention Module (SAM) which utilizes the RGB difference between frames to get a spatial attention mask to assign different weights to different spatial positions. As for the last, we propose a Label Relation Module (LRM) which can take full advantage of the relationship among classes based on their labels' semantic information. With the proposed modules, our work achieves the state-of-the-art performance on two commonly used gesture datasets, *i.e.*, EgoGesture and NVGesture datasets. Extensive experiments demonstrate the effectiveness of our proposed modules.

Keywords: Gesture recognition · Temporal modeling · Spatial attention · Semantic relation

1 Introduction

Gesture recognition has drawn an increasing amount of attention, due to its great potential in practical applications. Gestures can be divided into dynamic gestures

This work was partly supported by the National Natural Science Foundation of China (61906155, U19B2037), the Young Talent Fund of Association for Science and Technology in Shaanxi, China (20220117), and the National Key R&D Program of China (2020AAA0106900).

S. Yu et al. (Eds.): PRCV 2022, LNCS 13536, pp. 420–434, 2022.
https://doi.org/10.1007/978-3-031-18913-5_33

and static gestures according to whether they depend on temporal information. Actually, gestures are mostly dynamic. For dynamic gestures, their appearance changes over time, so that the temporal information plays an important role in classifying these gestures. Previous works have attempted to use 3D CNNs [4,16] to capture spatial and temporal information simultaneously. However, 3D CNNs are computationally heavy and time-consuming. Therefore, recent works attempted to use 2D CNNs with extended modules to recognize gestures. TSM [12] proposed a temporal shift module to exchange information between adjacent frames to capture short-term temporal information. However, the long-term temporal information is still dismissed. To solve this problem, some works [11,13] proposed new modules which can capture long-term temporal information. But they usually introduced more parameters. Inspired by TSM [12], we propose to expand the step size of the temporal shift operation, so that we can model long-term temporal information intuitively and effectively.

Meanwhile, for a dynamic gesture, its appearance changes over time. We propose to focus on the area where a gesture mainly occurs. The RGB difference among frames can indicate the motion displacement, which meets our requirement. Previous works utilized RGB difference between adjacent frames to assign more attention to boundary displacement [26], or use it as an additional input [17] to get better performance. But the RGB difference between adjacent frames is usually too small to capture and contains trivial information. The RGB difference between long-distance frames can robustly indicate where the change mainly occurs. Hence, we utilize this information to get a spatial attention map to distribute different weights to different positions for accurate recognition.

Beyond these, there exists semantic relation among gestures, which can help recognize gestures. However, for gesture recognition, most existing works only focus on visual information. Although there exist some methods in multi-label action recognition [2,5,15,21,24] which considered label co-occurrence between different classes, they are based on the statistics of the dataset. It should be noted that the language description of gestures can reflect the semantic relationship among gestures. Zhu et al. [28] proposed to utilize the semantic relation to assist in detecting objects. However, the application of semantic relation in gesture recognition has not been explored yet. Hence, we propose to apply semantic reasoning to gesture recognition. Different from [28] which is an image-level task, gesture recognition is a video-level task. Therefore, in this work, we need to fuse the semantic information with spatiotemporal information instead of simply spatial information. Additionally, for gestures, their labels are always phrases, which are difficult to encode with the word-level encoding method [14] used in [28]. Thus, for better phrase encoding, we utilize a phrase encoding method [19] to encode the labels of gestures.

Based on the aforementioned motivations, we propose our method with three designed modules to solve these problems respectively. The overview of our method is shown in Fig. 1. The contributions are summarized as follows:

- Inspired by the idea of TSM, we propose a Long and Short-term Temporal Shift Module (LS-TSM), which performs two types of temporal shift

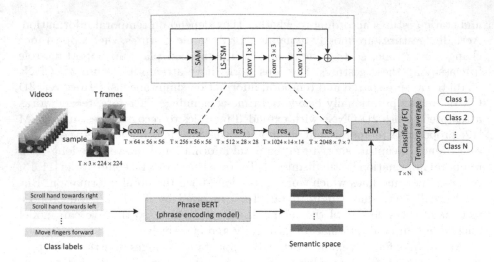

Fig. 1. The overview of the network. ResNet50 [8] is utilized as the backbone. The Long and Short-term Temporal Shift Module (LS-TSM) and Spatial Attention Module (SAM) are inserted into each block to improve spatiotemporal capacity. The Label Relation Module (LRM) is inserted before the fully connected layer to enhance semantic reasoning in the model.

operations of different step sizes, *i.e.*, short-term temporal shift and long-term temporal shift. In this way, we can model the long and short-term temporal information simultaneously.

- To focus on where the gesture mainly occurs, we compute the RGB difference between long-distance frames and propose a Spatial Attention Module (SAM) based on that to assign different weights to different positions.
- We propose a Label Relation Module (LRM) to model the semantic relation among gesture labels and fuse it into the network to enhance the visual features.
- To demonstrate the effectiveness of our work, we evaluate our method on two commonly used gesture datasets, *i.e.*, EgoGesture [27] and NVGesture [7] datasets. Our work has achieved state-of-the-art performance on these datasets.

2   Related Work

2.1   Temporal Information Model

For RGB-based gesture recognition, recent works mainly use the learning-based method. For dynamic gesture recognition, the temporal modeling capacity is highly important. Previous works [4,16] utilized 3D CNNs to model spatial and temporal information. However, 3D CNNs based methods always involve heavy computations and are time-consuming. Therefore, recent works [11,12,23] try to use 2D CNNs with extended modules to tackle this issue. TSM proposed a temporal shift module to transform information between adjacent frames. TEA [11] proposed a motion excitation (ME) module to model short-range motion and a multiple temporal aggregation (MTA) module to model long-range motion. MVFNet [23] introduced a novel multi-view fusion module with separable convolution to exploit spatiotemporal dynamics. Apart from TSM, these works usually introduce more parameters and bring latency. Therefore, in this work, we extend the idea of TSM to model temporal information.

2.2 Attention Mechanism

In gesture recognition, we hope to focus on where the change mainly occurs. Previous works [9,22] proposed some attention modules to this end. CBAM [22] proposed a Convolutional Block Attention Module (CBAM) which infers attention maps along two separate dimensions. Jiang *et al.* [9] proposed a Spatial-wise Attention Module (SAM) and a Temporal-wise Attention Module (TAM) that separately model the temporal relation and spatial relation among contexts. In fact, the motion change can be fitly indicated by the RGB difference among frames, which is more intuitive and easy to compute. Therefore, we utilize it to construct our spatial attention map.

2.3 Semantic Information Model

There exist some related or mutually exclusive information among different classes, which is helpful for recognition. Previous works [2,5,15] in multi-label classification utilized the statistical data in a dataset to model these relations. Bhattacharya *et al.* [2] proposed to formulate human recognition into a sparse linear approximation problem using an over-complete dictionary of descriptors, which are covariance-based and built from labeled training examples. Modiri Assari *et al.* [15] proposed to classify videos using the co-occurrence of concepts extracted from the dataset. In object detection, Zhu *et al.* [28] proposed to use the word embeddings of class labels to fuse semantic information into networks to get better performance. However, in gesture recognition, the semantic relation is always dismissed. Therefore, we apply this method to gesture recognition to improve performance.

3 Method

3.1 The Overview of the Network

The framework of our method is illustrated in Fig. 1. First, given a video V, following the sparse sampling scheme proposed in TSN [18], we divide it into T segments and sample one frame from each segment. Then the sampled frames are fed into the network. Similar to TSM, our model is based on 2D CNNs (*e.g.* ResNet-50 [8]). We insert the proposed Long and Short-term Temporal

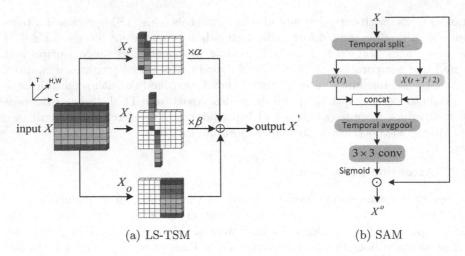

(a) LS-TSM   (b) SAM

Fig. 2. The implementations of the Long and Short-term Temporal Shift Module (LS-TSM) and Spatial Attention Module (SAM).

Shift Module and Spatial Attention Module into each residual block as shown in Fig. 1. Meanwhile, we insert the proposed Label Relation Module (LRM) before the last fully-connected layer of the network to help classification by enhancing the visual feature with the semantic relation information.

3.2   Long and Short-term Temporal Shift Module (LS-TSM)

TSM [12] proposed a temporal shift module that only models short-term temporal information. But for some actions that need long-term temporal information to recognize, this is not sufficient. Extending the idea of TSM, we propose a Long and Short-term Temporal Shift Module (LS-TSM), which aims at modeling the long and short-term temporal information simultaneously, as shown in Fig. 2(a).

Following TSM, we only shift part of the channels. Given an input feature map $X \in R^{T \times C \times H \times W}$, we divide it into three parts along the channel dimension, *i.e.*, the short-term shift part $X_s \in R^{T \times C/8 \times H \times W}$, the long-term shift part $X_l \in R^{T \times C/8 \times H \times W}$, and the others $X_o \in R^{T \times 3C/4 \times H \times W}$.

Short-term Temporal Shift. We select the first 1/8 channels of the input features as X_s to do short-term shifts. In this part, we shift channels among adjacent frames, which is the same as TSM. We select 1/2 channels of X_s to shift forward with step size 1 and select the other 1/2 channels to shift backward with step size 1.

Long-term Temporal Shift. We also select the second 1/8 channels of the input features as X_l to do long-term shift. In the long-term shift part, we shift channels among long-distance frames. We set the step size of temporal shift operation larger, which is $T/2$ in this work. Following this setting, we shift 1/2 channels of X_l forward and 1/2 backward.

Other Channels. For the other channels, we keep them the same as the original input X.

Finally, we fuse the above three parts by a weighted summation as:

$$X' = X_s \times \alpha + X_l \times \beta + X_o \tag{1}$$

where α and β indicate the importance of long and short-term temporal information respectively. Through empirical validation, we find that $\alpha = 1$ and $\beta = 1.5$ work well in practice. X' indicates the output of LS-TSM.

3.3 Spatial Attention Module

In this part, we will introduce our Spatial Attention Module, as shown in Fig. 2(b). Given an input spatiotemporal feature map $X = \{X(1), \ldots X(T)\} \in R^{T \times C \times H \times W}$, we calculate the RGB difference of frame pairs with the time step T/2, *i.e.*, the difference between $X(t)$ and $X(t + T/2)$:

$$D(t) = X(t + T/2) - X(t), t \in \{1, 2, \ldots T/2\} \tag{2}$$

where $D(t) \in R^{1 \times C \times H \times W}$ is the RGB difference between time step t and $t + T/2$, indicating the motion change during this time. We concatenate all $D(t)$ to construct the final motion change matrix D:

$$D = [D(1), \ldots, D(T/2)] \in R^{T/2 \times C \times H \times W} \tag{3}$$

Then we utilize a temporal average pooling to obtain the motion change within the whole video:

$$D_{avg} = Pool(D), D_{avg} \in R^{1 \times C \times H \times W} \tag{4}$$

Next, a 3×3 convolution layer is utilized to perform the channel-wise transformation on D_{avg}. And we apply a sigmoid function to get the mask M:

$$M = \sigma(conv * D_{avg}), M \in R^{1 \times C \times H \times W} \tag{5}$$

Finally, we conduct an element-wise multiplication between the input feature X and mask M.

$$X^o = X \odot M \tag{6}$$

where X^o is the output of SAM. $\odot$ indicates the element-wise multiplication.

Using the proposed SAM discussed above, we can focus on where the motion changes mainly occur.

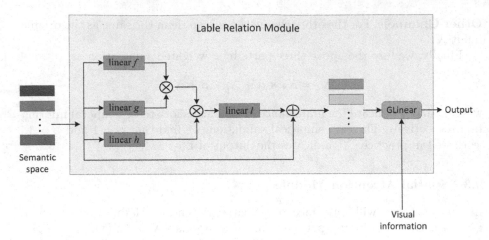

Fig. 3. The structure of the Label Relation Module (LRM).

3.4 Label Relation Module

Different gestures may contain related or mutually exclusive information, which can be reflected in their class labels. Inspired by [28], we propose a Label Relation Module (LRM) to model the semantic relation between gesture classes. The LRM is shown in Fig. 3.

Phrase Encoding Method. If directly applying the method of [28] to gesture recognition, there exists a non-negligible problem. The class labels in object detection are always single words, so Zhu *et al.* used word2vec [14] to encode the class labels. However, the class labels of gestures are usually phrases, which are difficult to encode with word2vec.

Phrase-BERT [19] is a phrase-specific encoding model, which proposed a contrastive fine-tuning objective to enable BERT [6] to encode more powerful phrase embeddings. It achieved impressive performance across a variety of phrase-level similarity tasks. Thus, Phrase-BERT exactly meets our needs. Therefore, when applying the method of [28] to gesture recognition, we utilize the phrase encoding method [19] to encode gesture labels.

Model Label Relation. As explained above, given the class labels of a gesture dataset, we can construct a semantic space by encoding the class labels into a series of word embeddings using the model of Phrase-BERT [19]. We represent the semantic space using a set of d_e dimensional word embeddings $W_e \in R^{N \times d_e}$, where N notes the number of classes. Based on their labels' word embeddings, the gestures' relation can be modeled and fused with the visual information.

First, based on the semantic space discussed above, we build the semantic relation among classes using the self-attention mechanism, as shown in Fig. 3. We transform the semantic space into Q, K, and V by three linear layers f, g, and h. We calculate the self-attention matrix using Q and K. Then the self-attention matrix is multiplied by V.

$$f, g, h : R^{N \times d_e} \mapsto R^{N \times d_k}, Q = f \cdot W_e, K = g \cdot W_e, V = h \cdot W_e \qquad (7)$$

$$Attn = softmax(\frac{QK^T}{\sqrt{d_k}})V \qquad (8)$$

where $Attn \in R^{N \times d_k}$. Then we utilize a linear layer l to align $Attn$ to the dimension of W_e. And a residual connection is introduced to maintain the original semantic information.

$$G_e = l \cdot Attn + W_e, l : R^{N \times d_k} \mapsto R^{N \times d_e} \qquad (9)$$

Through the above self-attention mechanism, we can get a new semantic space that contains class relations. Then we utilize the semantic relation in G_e to enhance the visual vector $v \in R^{d_v}$ for classification by the following operation:

$$Glinear : p = softmax(G_e P v + b) \qquad (10)$$

where $P \in R^{d_e \times d_v}$ is a learnable variable, which aims to fuse the visual and semantic information.

4   Experiment

In this section, we first introduce the two datasets we used and the implementation details. Then we show that our proposed method can dramatically improve the performance of 2D CNNs compared with the vanilla TSM and achieve the state-of-the-art performance on the above two datasets. Finally, we provide detailed ablation studies to indicate the efficacy of the proposed modules.

4.1   Datasets

We evaluate our method on two widely used gesture datasets, *i.e.*, the EgoGesture [27] and NVGesure [7] datasets.

EgoGesture. EgoGesture [27] is a large-scale dataset with 83 classes of static and dynamic gestures. It contains 24,161 gesture samples and 2,953,224 frames collected from 50 subjects. It was designed for egocentric hand gesture recognition which focuses on interaction with wearable devices.

Table 1. Comparison with the state-of-the-art on EgoGesture dataset.

Method	Venue	Frames	Accuracy
C3D [16]	ICCV2015	16-frames	86.88%
C3D+LSTM+RSTTM [3]	ICCV2017	16-frames	89.3%
TSM [12]	ICCV2019	8-frames	92.30%
ResNeXt-101 [10]	FG2019	32-frames	93.75%
MUTU [1]	CVPR2019	64-frames	92.48%
TEA [11]	CVPR2020	16-frames	92.5%
NAS1 [25]	TIP2021	8+16+32-frames	*93.31%*
Ours	–	8-frames	**93.77%**

NVGesture. NVGesture [7] is a dataset composed of 25 gesture types designed for human-computer interaction. These gestures are recorded by multiple sensors and viewpoints. It contains 1,532 dynamic hand gestures performed by 20 subjects.

Although these two datasets both contain multiple types of input, we only use the RGB input in our work. To make a fair comparison, when compared with other works, we only focus on the reported results which only used RGB images as input.

4.2 Implementation Details

Training. We use ResNet50 as our backbone and use the sampling strategy in TSN [18]. We conduct a progressive training strategy as follows. We first train a network with our proposed LS-TSM and SAM. Then we add the LRM in the network and finetune it based on the previous model. The training settings during the two phases are the same. The training settings for EgoGesture [27] are: 100 training epochs, initial learning rate 0.001 (decay by 0.1 at epochs 35&60&80), weight decay 5e–4, batch size 16, and dropout 0.8. For NVGesture [7], the training settings are: 50 epochs, initial learning rate 0.001 (decay by 0.1 at epochs 20&40), weight decay 5e–4, batch size 32, and dropout 0.8. Compared to EgoGesture, NVGesture is much smaller and easy to over-fitting. Therefore, during the first training phase of NVGesture, we finetune it based on the model trained on EgoGesture.

Testing. During testing, following the common setting used in other works [12, 20], we sample multiple clips per video (3 for EgoGesture and 10 for NVGesture). Meanwhile, we scale the short side of the frames to 256 and take 5 crops of 224 × 224 for each frame. Finally, we average the Softmax scores of all clips.

4.3 Comparision with the State of the Art

In this section, we compare our method with state-of-the-art works on EgoGesture [27] and NVGesture [7] datasets to demonstrate the advantage of our work.

Table 2. Comparison with the state-of-the-art on NVGesture dataset.

Method	Venue	Frames	Accuracy
C3D [16]	ICCV2015	16-frames	69.30%
TSM [12]	ICCV2019	16-frames	79.04%
ResNeXt-101 [10]	FG2019	32-frames	78.93%
MUTU [1]	CVPR2019	64-frames	81.33%
NAS1 [25]	TIP2021	8+16+32-frames	*83.61%*
Ours	–	16-frames	**81.73%**

Table 3. Ablation studies on EgoGesture and NVGesture datasets.

Method	Modules			Top-1(EgoGesture)	Top-1(NVGesture)
	LS-TSM	SAM	LRM		
TSM [12]	–	–	–	92.30%	79.04%
Ours	✓			92.79%	79.67%
	✓	✓		93.40%	80.29%
	✓	✓	✓	93.77%	81.73%

To make a fair comparison, we show the results with only RGB frames as input. The comparison of EgoGesture [27] and NVGesture [7] are respectively shown in Table 1 and Table 2. On EgoGesture, we can achieve the state-of-the-art performance. And compared with recent works based on 2D CNNs such as TSM [12] and TEA [11], our method outperforms these methods by a large margin. On NVGesture, our method also achieves the state-of-the-art performance. Although NAS1 [25] achieved a little higher accuracy than our method, it needs three branches with different sampling rate inputs, which involves heavy computation cost. Specifically, our method only involves 25.7M parameters, much smaller compared with NAS1's 127.1M parameters. In conclusion, our method achieves state-of-the-art performance on two commonly-used datasets with concise settings, which demonstrates the efficiency and effectiveness of our method.

4.4   Ablation Study

In this section, we evaluate and analyze our proposed modules on EgoGesture and NVGesture datasets to demonstrate their efficacy. We add our proposed modules to the backbone one by one and report their performance respectively, which is shown in Table 3.

LS-TSM. To determine the values of α and β, we add the LS-TSM with the different value settings to the backbone on EgoGesture [27] dataset, as is shown in Fig. 4. For more concise experiments, we fix the value of α to 1 and only change the value of β. The experimental results show that our model performs best when $\beta = 1.5$.

As shown in the Table 3, when adding the LS-TSM, our model outperforms TSM by 0.49% on EgoGesture and 0.63% on NVGesture. It is worth noting that the gestures in NVGesture are all dynamic gestures, which need more long-term temporal modeling capacity. Meanwhile, we split the gestures in EgoGesture into dynamic gestures and static gestures for more deep analysis. Then we evaluate TSM and our model with LS-TSM on the dynamic gestures and static gestures respectively. The results are shown in Table 4. It can be seen that the improvement on dynamic gestures is more obvious than that on static gestures, which indicates the effectiveness of the proposed LS-TSM.

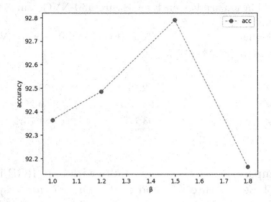

Fig. 4. The ablation study of α and β. The value of α is fixed to 1. The horizontal axis is the value of β. The vertical axis is the accracy under the corresponding values.

Table 4. Performance comparison of the models with and without LS-TSM on dynamic and static gestures.

Method	Modules	
	Dynamic gestures	Static gestures
TSM [12]	91.29%	94.43%
Ours (with LS-TSM)	91.83%	94.87%
Improvement	0.54%	0.44 %

SAM. With the SAM, we can observe that the top-1 accuracies on the two datasets are all improved, *i.e.*, 0.61% for EgoGesture and 0.62% for NVGesture. We draw the class activation maps of TSM and our model with SAM in Fig. 5. It is obvious that with the SAM, the model can pay more attention to the regions where significant change occurs, *i.e.* the movement of hands. Thus it can achieve better performance.

LRM. From Table 3, we can observe that with the LRM, the accuracies on EgoGesture and NVGesture have been improved by 0.37% and 1.44% respectively. The improvement in NVGesture is more obvious than that of EgoGesture. It is probably because there exist more gesture types in EgoGesture, which makes the relation between gestures more complex to model. We visualize the confusion matrices on NVGesture of the models with and without LRM, which is shown in Fig. 6. We can observe that with LRM, the confusion matrix is better distributed on the diagonal. And the accuracies of the two datasets are also consistently improved, which indicates the effectiveness of LRM.

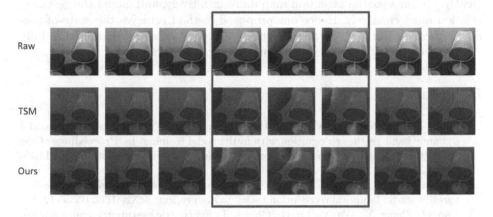

Fig. 5. The class activation maps of TSM and our model with SAM. The first line is the raw frames sampled from a video. The second line is the class activation maps of TSM. The third line is the class activation maps of our model with SAM.

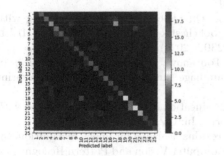
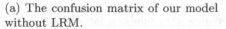
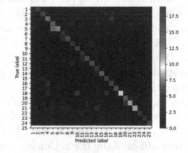

(a) The confusion matrix of our model without LRM.

(b) The confusion matrix of our model with LRM.

Fig. 6. The confusion matrices of the models without and with LRM.

5   Conclusion

In this work, we focus on the three important problems in gesture recognition tasks, *i.e.*, lack of efficient long-term temporal modeling ability, insufficient spatial attention capacity, and the dismission of semantic relation reasoning among gestures. Therefore, we propose three modules, *i.e.*, Long and Short-term Temporal Shift Module, Spatial Attention Module, and Label Relation Module to solve these problems respectively. We evaluate our method on EgoGesture and NVGesture datasets, which are commonly used in gesture recognition. Compared with existing works, our method can model the temporal information more efficiently, obtain a spatial attention map more intuitively, and model the gestures' relation more creatively. Hence our proposed method achieves the state-of-the-art performance on both datasets. Extensive experiments are conducted to fully demonstrate the effectiveness of the proposed modules.

References

1. Abavisani, M., Joze, H.R.V., Patel, V.M.: Improving the performance of unimodal dynamic hand-gesture recognition with multimodal training. In: Proceedings of the IEEE/CVF Conference on Computer Vision and Pattern Recognition, pp. 1165–1174 (2019)
2. Bhattacharya, S., Souly, N., Shah, M.: Covariance of motion and appearance featuresfor spatio temporal recognition tasks. arXiv preprint arXiv:1606.05355 (2016)
3. Cao, C., Zhang, Y., Wu, Y., Lu, H., Cheng, J.: Egocentric gesture recognition using recurrent 3D convolutional neural networks with spatiotemporal transformer modules. In: Proceedings of the IEEE International Conference on Computer Vision, pp. 3763–3771 (2017)
4. Carreira, J., Zisserman, A.: Quo vadis, action recognition? a new model and the kinetics dataset. In: Proceedings of the IEEE Conference on Computer Vision and Pattern Recognition, pp. 6299–6308 (2017)
5. Chen, B., Li, J., Lu, G., Yu, H., Zhang, D.: Label co-occurrence learning with graph convolutional networks for multi-label chest x-ray image classification. IEEE J. Biomed. Health Inform. **24**(8), 2292–2302 (2020)
6. Devlin, J., Chang, M.W., Lee, K., Toutanova, K.: BERT: Pre-training of deep bidirectional transformers for language understanding. arXiv preprint arXiv:1810.04805 (2018)
7. Gupta, P., et al.: Online detection and classification of dynamic hand gestures with recurrent 3D convolutional neural networks. In: CVPR, vol. 1, p. 3 (2016)
8. He, K., Zhang, X., Ren, S., Sun, J.: Deep residual learning for image recognition. In: Proceedings of the IEEE Conference on Computer Vision and Pattern Recognition, pp. 770–778 (2016)
9. Jiang, Q., Wu, X., Kittler, J.: Insight on attention modules for skeleton-based action recognition. In: Ma, H., et al. (eds.) PRCV 2021. LNCS, vol. 13019, pp. 242–255. Springer, Cham (2021). https://doi.org/10.1007/978-3-030-88004-0_20

10. Köpüklü, O., Gunduz, A., Kose, N., Rigoll, G.: Real-time hand gesture detection and classification using convolutional neural networks. In: 2019 14th IEEE International Conference on Automatic Face & Gesture Recognition (FG 2019), pp. 1–8. IEEE (2019)

11. Li, Y., Ji, B., Shi, X., Zhang, J., Kang, B., Wang, L.: TEA: Temporal excitation and aggregation for action recognition. In: Proceedings of the IEEE/CVF Conference on Computer Vision and Pattern Recognition, pp. 909–918 (2020)

12. Lin, J., Gan, C., Han, S.: TSM: temporal shift module for efficient video understanding. In: Proceedings of the IEEE/CVF International Conference on Computer Vision, pp. 7083–7093 (2019)

13. Liu, Z., Wang, L., Wu, W., Qian, C., Lu, T.: TAM: temporal adaptive module for video recognition. In: Proceedings of the IEEE/CVF International Conference on Computer Vision, pp. 13708–13718 (2021)

14. Mikolov, T., Sutskever, I., Chen, K., Corrado, G.S., Dean, J.: Distributed representations of words and phrases and their compositionality. In: Proceedings of the 26th International Conference on Advances in Neural Information Processing Systems, vol. 26 (2013)

15. Modiri Assari, S., Roshan Zamir, A., Shah, M.: Video classification using semantic concept co-occurrences. In: Proceedings of the IEEE Conference on Computer Vision and Pattern Recognition, pp. 2529–2536 (2014)

16. Tran, D., Bourdev, L., Fergus, R., Torresani, L., Paluri, M.: Learning spatiotemporal features with 3d convolutional networks. In: Proceedings of the IEEE International Conference on Computer Vision, pp. 4489–4497 (2015)

17. Wang, L., Tong, Z., Ji, B., Wu, G.: TDN: temporal difference networks for efficient action recognition. In: Proceedings of the IEEE/CVF Conference on Computer Vision and Pattern Recognition, pp. 1895–1904 (2021)

18. Wang, L., et al.: Temporal segment networks: towards good practices for deep action recognition. In: Leibe, B., Matas, J., Sebe, N., Welling, M. (eds.) ECCV 2016. LNCS, vol. 9912, pp. 20–36. Springer, Cham (2016). https://doi.org/10.1007/978-3-319-46484-8_2

19. Wang, S., Thompson, L., Iyyer, M.: Phrase-BERT: improved phrase embeddings from BERT with an application to corpus exploration. arXiv preprint arXiv:2109.06304 (2021)

20. Wang, Z., She, Q., Smolic, A.: Action-Net: multipath excitation for action recognition. In: Proceedings of the IEEE/CVF Conference on Computer Vision and Pattern Recognition, pp. 13214–13223 (2021)

21. Wen, S., et al.: Multilabel image classification via feature/label co-projection. IEEE Trans. Syst. Man Cybernet. Syst. **51**(11), 7250–7259 (2020)

22. Woo, S., Park, J., Lee, J.Y., Kweon, I.S.: CBAM: convolutional block attention module. In: Proceedings of the European Conference on Computer Vision (ECCV), pp. 3–19 (2018)

23. Wu, W., He, D., Lin, T., Li, F., Gan, C., Ding, E.: MvfNet: multi-view fusion network for efficient video recognition. In: Proceedings of the AAAI (2021)

24. Yazici, V.O., Gonzalez-Garcia, A., Ramisa, A., Twardowski, B., Weijer, J.v.d.: Orderless recurrent models for multi-label classification. In: Proceedings of the IEEE/CVF Conference on Computer Vision and Pattern Recognition, pp. 13440–13449 (2020)

25. Yu, Z., et al.: Searching multi-rate and multi-modal temporal enhanced networks for gesture recognition. IEEE Trans. Image Process. **30**, 5626–5640 (2021)

26. Zhang, C., Zou, Y., Chen, G., Gan, L.: PAN: persistent appearance network with an efficient motion cue for fast action recognition. In: Proceedings of the 27th ACM International Conference on Multimedia, pp. 500–509 (2019)
27. Zhang, Y., Cao, C., Cheng, J., Lu, H.: EgoGesture: a new dataset and benchmark for egocentric hand gesture recognition. IEEE Trans. Multimedia **20**(5), 1038–1050 (2018)
28. Zhu, C., Chen, F., Ahmed, U., Shen, Z., Savvides, M.: Semantic relation reasoning for shot-stable few-shot object detection. In: Proceedings of the IEEE/CVF Conference on Computer Vision and Pattern Recognition, pp. 8782–8791 (2021)

SemanticGAN: Facial Image Editing with Semantic to Realize Consistency

Xin Luan[1,2,3], Nan Yang[1,2,3], Huijie Fan[1,2(✉)], and Yandong Tang[1,2]

[1] State Key Laboratory of Robotics, Shenyang Institute of Automation,
Chinese Academy of Sciences, Shenyang 110016, China
[2] Institutes for Robotics and Intelligent Manufacturing, Chinese Academy
of Sciences, Shenyang 110169, China
fanhuijie@sia.cn
[3] University of Chinese Academy of Sciences, Beijing 100049, China

Abstract. Recent work has shown that face editing in the latent space of Generative Adversarial Networks(GANs). However, it is difficult to decouple the attributes in latent space that reduce the inconsistent face editing. In this work, we proposed a simple yet effective method named SemanticGAN to realize consistent face editing. First, we get fine editing on attribute-related regions and note that we mainly consider the accuracy of the edited images possessing the target attributes instead of whether the editing of irrelevant regions is inconsistent. Second, we optimize the attribute-independent regions that ensure the edited face image consistent with the raw image. Specifically, we apply the generated semantic segmentation to distinguish the edited regions and the unedited regions. Extensive qualitative and quantitative results validate our proposed method. Comparisons show that SemanticGAN can achieve a satisfactory image-consistent editing result.

Keywords: Facial image editing · Semantic segmentation · GAN

1 Introduction

Facial editing has made remarkable progress with the development of deep neural networks [18,19]. More and more methods use the GANs to edit faces and generate images that utilize the image-to-image translation [21,27] or embed into the GAN's latent space [22,29,36,37]. Recent studies have shown that the Style-GAN2 contains rich semantic information in latent space and certified realistic editing of high-quality images.

Most GANs based on image editing methods fall into a few categories. Some works rely on image-to-image translation [15], which use the encoder-decoder architecture and take the source image and target image attribute vector as input [5,7,12], e.g. StarGAN [6], AttGAN [13], STGAN [24] and RelGAN [34]. AttGAN first adopts the attribute classification constraints, reconstruction learning, and adversarial learning. STGAN used the difference attribute vector as input and present the selective transfer units with the encoder-decoder. Yue eal proposed

S. Yu et al. (Eds.): PRCV 2022, LNCS 13536, pp. 435–447, 2022.
https://doi.org/10.1007/978-3-031-18913-5_34

HifaFace [9] which is a novel wavelet-based face editing. They observed the generator learns to apply a tricky method to satisfy the constraint of cycle consistency
by hiding signals in the output images. And other works use the latent space of
the GAN's [38], e.g. Image2StyleGAN [1], Image2StyleGAN++ [2], InvertGAN
[42], InterFaceGAN [28] and StyleFlow [3]. Those methods find the disentangled
latent variables suitable for image editing. But these methods can't obtain the
independent editing attributes and generated images are not consistent with the
row image.

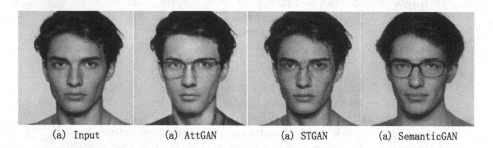

(a) Input   (a) AttGAN   (a) STGAN   (a) SemanticGAN

Fig. 1. The results of adding eyeglasses with different face editing methods.

As shown in Fig. 1, we feed an input face image x into AttGAN and STGAN
[24] and expect it to add eyeglasses on the face. We can find that although the
output of AttGAN does wear eyeglasses, the irrelated region has changed, e.g.,
the face color changed from yellow to white. And the output result of STGAN
with the same result as the input image but the eyeglasses can't see. We can find
the edited facial images are inconsistent with the raw image that the non-editing
attributes/areas changed.

To achieve consistent face editing, we propose a simple yet effective face
editing method called SemanticGAN. We main solve this problem from two
aspects. Firstly, we edit the image directly, and we only consider whether the
editing attributes are successful, regardless of whether the attribute independent regions are consistent. Then, we optimize the attributes vector ensure the
attribute independent regions are consistent.

Specifically, our proposed method builds on a recently proposed StyleGAN
that face images and their semantic segmentation can be generated simultaneously, and a small number of labeled images are required to train it. We embed
images into the latent space of GAN and edit the face image by adding attribute
vectors. We use the generated segmentation to optimize the attributes vector to
be consistent with the input image. Otherwise, the attributes vector can directly
apply to the real images, without any optimization steps.

Our unique contribution that advances the field of face image editing manipulation include:

1) We propose a novel face editing method, named SemanticGAN, for consistency and arbitrary face editing.

2) We design a few-shot semantic segmentation model, which requires only a few annotated data for training and can well obtain the identity with the semantic knowledge of the generator.
3) Both qualitative and quantitative results demonstrate the effectiveness of the proposed framework for improving the consistency of edited face images.

2   Related Works

2.1   Generative Adversarial Networks

Generative Adversarial Networks(GANs) [10,11,26,41] have been widely used for image generation [32,33]. A classic GAN is composed of two parts: a generator and a discriminator. The generator is to synthesize noise to resemble a real image while the discriminator is to determine the authenticity between the real and generated images. Recently GANs have been developed to synthesize faces and generate diverse faces from random noise, e.g., PGGAN [16], BigGAN [4], StyleGAN [18], StyleGAN2 [19] and StyleGAN3 [17] which encode critical information in the intermediate features and latent space for high-quality face image generation. Furthermore, GANs are also widely used in computer vision such as image conversion, image synthesis, super-resolution, image restoration, and style transfer.

2.2   Facial Image Editing

Facial image editing is a rapidly growing field in face image [25,30,39,42]. Thanks to the recent development of GANs, Generally speaking, these methods can be divided into two categories. The first category of methods utilizes image-to-image translation for face editing. StarGAN and AttGAN used target attribute vector as input to the transform model and bring in an attribute classification constraint. STGAN enhances the editing performance of AttGAN by using a different attribute vector as input to generate high-quality face attributes editing. RelGAN proposed a relative-attribute-based method for multi-domain image-to-image translation. ELEGANT [35] proposed to convert the same type of property from one image to another by swapping some parts of the encoding. HiSD [21]realize image-to-image translation by hierarchical style disentanglement for facial image editing. The other category of methods uses the pre-trained GANs, e.g., StyleGAN, StyleGAN2. To achieve facial image editing by changing the latent codes.Yujun Shen et al. proposed semantic face editing by interpreting the latent semantics learned by GANs. StyleFlow proposed conditional exploration of latent spaces of unconditional GANs using conditional normalization flows based on semantic attributes. EditGAN [23] offered a very high-precision editing. However, those methods are unable to give any satisfactory editing results. The first method's synthesis image quality is low, and other methods can't get perfect latent codes. In this paper, we utilize the latent codes of StyleGAN2 to realize facial image editing, and proposed an effective framework to solve inconsistent editing.

3   Proposed Method

In this section, we introduce our proposed editing method named SemanticGAN. Figure 2 gives an overview of our method which mainly contains the following two parts: 1) attribute-related fine editing and 2) attribute-independent optimization.

3.1   Preliminary

Our model is based on StyleGAN2 which extracts the latent codes $z \in Z$ from multivariate normal distributions and maps them to real images. A latent code z is first mapped into a latent code $w \in W$ with a fully connected layer network. And then extended into a W^+ space that controls the generation of images with different styles. The W^+ space is the concatenation of k different w spaces. $W^+ = w^0 \times w^1 \times \ldots \times w^k$. The space can better decouple the model attributes by learning a multi-layer perceptron before the generator. So we embed images into the GAN's latent code W^+ space using an encoder. Thus we can define the encoder and generator $E : x \rightarrow W^+$ and $G_x : W^+ \rightarrow x'$. We followed the previous encoding works and trained an encoder that embeds images into W^+ space. We follow the encoding in style to train the encoder.

$$\mathcal{L}_{\text{per}}(x) = \mathcal{L}_{LPIPS}\left(x, G_x(E(x))\right) + \lambda_1 \|x - G_x(E(x))\|_2 \tag{1}$$

where $\mathcal{L}_{\text{LPIPS}}$ loss is the Learned Perceptual Image Patch Similarity(LPIPS) distance.

$$\mathcal{L}_{ID}(x) = 1 - \langle R(x), R\left(G_x(E(x))\right)\rangle \tag{2}$$

$$\mathcal{L}_{re.g.}(x) = \|E(x) - \bar{W}\|_2 \tag{3}$$

where the E is the latent encoder, R denotes the pre-trained ArcFace [8] feature extraction network, $\langle .,.\rangle$ is cosine-similarity, and $\bar{W}$ is the average of the generator latent.

$$\mathcal{L}(x) = \lambda_2 \mathcal{L}_{\text{per}}(x) + \lambda_3 \mathcal{L}_{ID}(x) + \lambda_4 \mathcal{L}_{re.g.}(x) \tag{4}$$

where λ_1, λ_2, λ_3, and λ_4 are constants defining the loss weight.

3.2   Attribute-Related Fine Editing

We firstly put input image x into the well-trained encoder E that can embed x into W^+ latent space. Then we adopt the vector of editing attributes δW^+ and we have $W_{edit} = W^+ + \delta W^+$ that is put into the generator G. We can get a facial image x' which has the editing attribute. And $x' = G\left(W^+ + \delta W^+\right)$. Notice that we mainly consider the accuracy of edited images possesses the target attributes instead of whether the editing of irrelevant regions is inconsistent. So we design

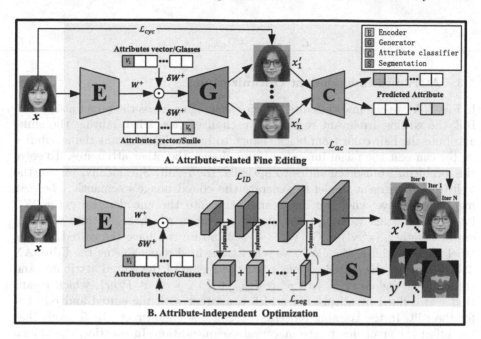

Fig. 2. An overview of our proposed SemanticGAN method. SemanticGAN contains attribute-related fin editing and attribute-independent optimization, where the attribute-related fine editing only focused on the accuracy of the attributes, rather than the none edited areas is changed. The optimization is used the segmentation to select the edited regions and let the non edited areas consistent with the raw segmentation.

an attribute classifier that is composed of convolutional neural networks to detect whether the synthesized facial image contains the corresponding attribute. We train the attribute classifier on the labeled datasets. We apply the well-trained classifier to ensure that the synthesized image x' possesses the target attributes. We apply the classifier loss:

$$\mathcal{L}_{ac} = - \left[\mathbb{I}_{\{|\Delta|=1\}} \left(a_y \log p_y + (1 - a_y) \log (1 - p_y) \right) \right] \tag{5}$$

where $\mathbb{I}$ denotes the indicator function, which is equal to 1 where the condition is satisfied and $\Delta = \mathrm{H}\left(\mathrm{C}\left(\mathrm{x}' \right), a_y \right)$ which H denotes Hamming distance and C is the well trained classifier. We use Δ to determine whether the attribute has been changed (i.e., $|\Delta| = 1$), and p_y is the probability value of the attributes estimated by the classifier C. Ensure the generator G to synthesize facial image x' with the relate attributes.

$$\mathcal{L}_{adv} = \mathbb{E}[\log(\mathrm{D}(x))] + \mathbb{E}\left[\log \left(1 - \mathrm{D}\left(\mathrm{x}' \right) \right) \right] \tag{6}$$

where x is the input image, x' is the synthesized facial image. $\mathcal{L}_{adv}$ encourages the generator G to synthesize a high-quality facial image.

$$\mathcal{L} = \lambda_5 \mathcal{L}_{\text{ac}} + \lambda_6 \mathcal{L}_{\text{adv}} \tag{7}$$

3.3   Attribute-Independent Optimization

In Fig. 2(A) we can find the edited images although possess the target attributes. But the editing irrelevant regions have changed, e.s. when editing the smile attribute the hair color from black change to brown. That means the attributes vector can edit the facial image, but also change the other attributes. To solve this problem, we use semantics to optimize the result. Specifically, we use the well-trained segment model to generate the edited image's semantic label. As mentioned above when we input an image into the encoder, we get a W^+ latent code. Then we adopt the attribute vector, which is put into the generator together. $(x', y') = G'(W^+ + \delta W^+)$. So we can have the edited image's label y'. To optimize the δW^+, we select the edited regions using the EditGAN [23]. We define the edited regions r are the region of the edited attributes and the relevant regions. $r = \{p : p^y \in P_{edit}\} \bigcup \{p : p^{y_{edit}} \in P_{edit}\}$, which means that r is defined by all pixels p which consistent with the edited and relevant for the edit. In the training process, we scale the region r out by 5 pixels that can offset the error due to the inaccurate segmentation. In practice, r acts as a binary pixel-wise mask.

To optimize the attribute independent region and find the appropriate attributes vector δW^+. We use the following loss:

$$\mathcal{L}_{\text{Seg}}(\delta W^+) = L_{LPIPS}(x' \odot (1 - r), x \odot (1 - r)) \\ + L_{L2}(x' \odot (1 - r), x \odot (1 - r)) \tag{8}$$

where L_{LPIPS} is based on the Learned Perceptual Image Patch Similarity(LPIPS) distance, x' is the generated face image and L_{L2} is a regular pixel-wise L2 loss. $\mathcal{L}_{\text{Seg}}(\delta W^+)$ ensures that the synthesized facial image dose not change the unedited region.

$$\mathcal{L}_{ID}(\delta W^+) = \langle R(x'), R(x) \rangle \tag{9}$$

with R denoting the pre-trained ArcFace [8] feature extraction network and $\langle ., . \rangle$ cosine-similarity.

$$\mathcal{L}(\delta W^+) = \lambda_7 \mathcal{L}_{Se.g.} + \lambda_8 \mathcal{L}_{ID} \tag{10}$$

with the hyperparameters λ_7, λ_8.

We define the $D_{x,y}$ is the annotated datasets where x is the real image, and y is the label. Similar to DatasetGAN [40] and Repurpose-GAN [31], to generate segmentation y' alongside images x we train a segmentation branch S which is a sample multi-layer convolutional neural networks. Figure 3 shows the segmentation frame. We input the image into the optimized encoder network which can get a latent code z and then z is fed to the generator. We extract feature maps f_i which dimension is (h_i, w_i, c_i) for $i = 1, 2, 3, \ldots, K$. Each feature map is upsampled to a same dimension, $\hat{f} = U_k(f_k)$ for $k \in 0, \ldots, K$ and U_k is the upsampling functions. Then all the feature maps are concatenated along the channel dimensions. The segment operates on the feature map and predicts the segmentation label for each pixel. It is trained with the cross-entropy loss function.

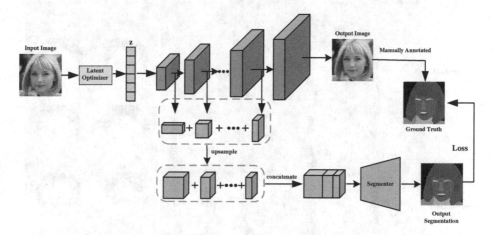

Fig. 3. The framework for few-shot semantic segmentation.

4 Experiments

In this section, we 1) describe the experimental implementation details; 2) show the attributes editing results; 3) show the editing results with SemanticGAN; 4) provide the results of ablation studies.

4.1 Implementation Details

Datasets: We evaluate our model on the CelebA-HQ datasets. The segmentation model and encoder model trained on CelebA-HQ mask datasets [20]. The image resolution is chosen as 1024×1024 in our experiments.

Implementation: We train our segmentation branch using 15 image-mask pairs as labeled training data for a face. The initial learning rate is 0.02 and decreased by half for every 200 epochs. The model is trained by an Adam optimizer with a momentum equal to 0.9. Our experimental environment is based on Lenovo Intelligent Computing Orchestration (LiCO), a software solution that simplifies the use of clustered computing resources for artificial intelligence (AI) model development and training. We implement our method using PyTorch 1.17 library, CUDA 11.0. The models are trained on 32GB Tesla V100 GPUs, respectively.

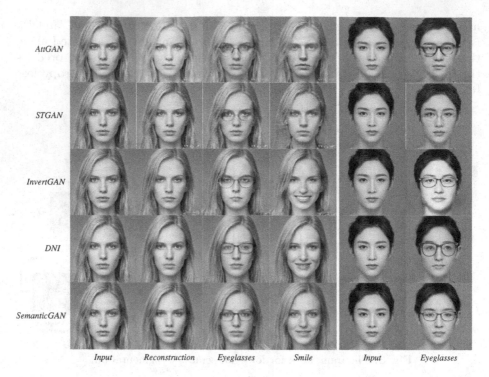

Fig. 4. Comparisons with AttGAN, STGAN, InvertGAN, DNI, and SemanticGAN on real image editing.

4.2   Attribute Face Editing

We compare our method with some recent works: AttGAN, STGAN, InvertGAN, and DNI. Figure 4 shows the results of attribute editing. AttGAN and STGAN used the encoder-decoder architecture, and the image becomes blurred after attribute editing. We can find the reconstruction of AttGAN the skin color and hair color are changed compared to the input image. AttGAN and STGAN can not have the smile attribute and the eyeglasses are not obviously. When editing the smile attribute, the hair is changed. We can find the InvertGAN and DNI successfully edit the eyeglasses and smile attribute and have high image quality compared to AttGAN and STGAN. But InvertGAN changed the age when editing the glasses attribute, and the eyes also changed at the same that DNI edits the glasses. SemanticGAN can edit with the original image details unchanged and we use the generated semantic to optimize the edited image. Table 1 compares the quantitative results of different methods, from which we can see that, considering the values of FID [14], attribute Acc, and ID score, our method outperforms other methods and generates face images that are consistent with row images. Furthermore, we have higher acc value bias and our method has a better ability to edit attributes and ID_score accuracy. The LPIPS of AttGAN is higher than ours but the accuracy of the attributes is only 50.3%.

Table 1. The quantitative results of different methods. ↑ and ↓ denote the higher and the lower the better.

Method	FID↓	Attribute Acc↑	ID_Score↑	LPIPS↑
AttGAN	15.63	50.3	0.65	0.95
STGAN	14.78	84.6	0.67	0.81
InvertGAN	6.20	83.5	0.71	0.82
SemanticGAN	7.46	97.6	0.85	0.89

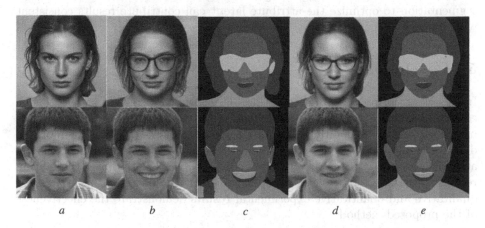

   a   *b*   *c*   *d*   *e*

Fig. 5. The results of SemanticGAN. Left to right for each line denotes: source image, attribute fine editing, the editing segmentation, attribute independent optimization, and final segmentation.

4.3 Editing with SemanticGAN

As shown in Fig. 5, we apply our method to the other images downloaded from the Internet. The process of our model for image editing. Figure 5 (a) is the input image and (b) and (c) are the attribute-related fine editing results and the segmentation. Then we use the segmentation to select the edited region. We optimize the attribute-independent regions. We can obtain the Fig. 5 (d) and (e). We can find see the segmentation changed after the optimization. The final results are consistent with the raw image.

Table 2. Quantitative results for ablation studies.

Method	Attribute Acc↑	ID_Score↑	LPIPS↑
w/o ID_loss	98.2	0.75	0.83
w/o Optimization	99.2	0.68	0.78
SemanticGAN	97.6	0.81	0.89

4.4   Ablation Studies

In this section, we conduct experiments to validate the effectiveness of each component of SemanticGAN. 1) We optimize the latent codes without identity loss. 2) We don't optimize the latent codes. 3) Our full model. Qualitative and quantitative results of these methods are shown in Table 2. We can find after attributes editing, the accuracy of attributes becomes higher and the ID_Score becomes smaller than the without identity loss. It means the identity loss focus on the face identity while neglecting other significant information. We use the segmentation to optimize the attribute latent can contribute results consistent with the raw image.

5   Conclusion

In this work, we propose a novel method named SemanticGAN for facial image editing. SemanticGAN can generate images and their pixel-wise semantic segmentation and the semantic segmentation model requires only a few annotated data for training. We firstly embed the attributes vectors into the latent spaces and focus on the attribute-related fine editing. Then we optimize the editing results so that we can achieve consistent facial image editing results. Extensive qualitative and quantitative experimental results demonstrate the effectiveness of the proposed method.

References

1. Abdal, R., Qin, Y., Wonka, P.: Image2styleGAN: how to embed images into the styleGAN latent space? In: Proceedings of the IEEE/CVF International Conference on Computer Vision, pp. 4432–4441 (2019)
2. Abdal, R., Qin, Y., Wonka, P.: Image2StyleGAN++: how to edit the embedded images? In: Proceedings of the IEEE Computer Society Conference on Computer Vision and Pattern Recognition, pp. 8293–8302 (2020). https://doi.org/10.1109/CVPR42600.2020.00832
3. Abdal, R., Zhu, P., Mitra, N.J., Wonka, P.: StyleFlow: attribute-conditioned exploration of styleGAN-generated images using conditional continuous normalizing flows. ACM Trans. Graph. **40**(3), 1–21 (2021). https://doi.org/10.1145/3447648
4. Brock, A., Donahue, J., Simonyan, K.: Large scale GAN training for high fidelity natural image synthesis. arXiv preprint arXiv:1809.11096 (2018)
5. Chen, X., et al.: CooGAN: a memory-efficient framework for high-resolution facial attribute editing. In: Vedaldi, A., Bischof, H., Brox, T., Frahm, J.-M. (eds.) ECCV 2020. LNCS, vol. 12356, pp. 670–686. Springer, Cham (2020). https://doi.org/10.1007/978-3-030-58621-8_39
6. Choi, Y., Choi, M., Kim, M., Ha, J.W., Kim, S., Choo, J.: StarGAN: unified generative adversarial networks for multi-domain image-to-image translation. In: Proceedings of the IEEE Computer Society Conference on Computer Vision and Pattern Recognition, pp. 8789–8797 (2018). https://doi.org/10.1109/CVPR.2018.00916

7. Chu, W., Tai, Y., Wang, C., Li, J., Huang, F., Ji, R.: SSCGAN: facial attribute editing via style skip connections. In: Vedaldi, A., Bischof, H., Brox, T., Frahm, J.-M. (eds.) ECCV 2020. LNCS, vol. 12360, pp. 414–429. Springer, Cham (2020). https://doi.org/10.1007/978-3-030-58555-6_25

8. Deng, J., Guo, J., Xue, N., Zafeiriou, S.: ArcFace: additive angular margin loss for deep face recognition. In: Proceedings of the IEEE Computer Society Conference on Computer Vision and Pattern Recognition. vol. 2019-June, pp. 4685–4694 (2019). https://doi.org/10.1109/CVPR.2019.00482

9. Gao, Y., et al.: High-fidelity and arbitrary face editing. In: Proceedings of the IEEE/CVF Conference on Computer Vision and Pattern Recognition, pp. 16115–16124 (2021)

10. Goodfellow, I., Pouget-Abadie, J., Mirza, M., Xu, B., Warde-Farley, D., Ozair, S., Courville, A., Bengio, Y.: Generative adversarial networks. Commun. ACM **63**(11), 139–144 (2020). https://doi.org/10.1145/3422622

11. Gulrajani, I., Ahmed, F., Arjovsky, M., Dumoulin, V., Courville, A.: Improved training of wasserstein GANs. Adv. Neural Inf. Proc. Syst. **2017**, 5768–5778 (2017)

12. He, Z., Kan, M., Zhang, J., Shan, S.: PA-GAN: progressive attention generative adversarial network for facial attribute editing. arXiv Preprint arXiv:2007.05892 (2020)

13. He, Z., Zuo, W., Kan, M., Shan, S., Chen, X.: AttGAN: facial attribute editing by only changing what you want. IEEE Trans. Image Process. **28**(11), 5464–5478 (2019). https://doi.org/10.1109/TIP.2019.2916751

14. Heusel, M., Ramsauer, H., Unterthiner, T., Nessler, B., Hochreiter, S.: GANs trained by a two time-scale update rule converge to a local nash equilibrium. In: Advances in Neural Information Processing Systems 30 (2017)

15. Huang, Xun, Liu, Ming-Yu., Belongie, Serge, Kautz, Jan: Multimodal unsupervised image-to-image translation. In: Ferrari, Vittorio, Hebert, Martial, Sminchisescu, Cristian, Weiss, Yair (eds.) ECCV 2018. LNCS, vol. 11207, pp. 179–196. Springer, Cham (2018). https://doi.org/10.1007/978-3-030-01219-9_11

16. Karras, T., Aila, T., Laine, S., Lehtinen, J.: Progressive growing of GANs for improved quality, stability, and variation. arXiv Preprint arXiv:1710.10196 (2017)

17. Karras, T., et al.: Alias-free generative adversarial networks. In: Advances in Neural Information Processing Systems 34 (2021)

18. Karras, T., Laine, S., Aila, T.: A style-based generator architecture for generative adversarial networks. In: Proceedings of the IEEE Computer Society Conference on Computer Vision and Pattern Recognition 2019-June, 4396–4405 (2019). https://doi.org/10.1109/CVPR.2019.00453

19. Karras, T., Laine, S., Aittala, M., Hellsten, J., Lehtinen, J., Aila, T.: Analyzing and improving the image quality of styleGAN. In: Proceedings of the IEEE Computer Society Conference on Computer Vision and Pattern Recognition, pp. 8107–8116 (2020). DOIhttps://doi.org/10.1109/CVPR42600.2020.00813

20. Lee, C.H., Liu, Z., Wu, L., Luo, P.: MaskGAN: towards diverse and interactive facial image manipulation. In: Proceedings of the IEEE/CVF Conference on Computer Vision and Pattern Recognition, pp. 5549–5558 (2020)

21. Li, X., et al.: Image-to-image translation via hierarchical style disentanglement. In: Proceedings of the IEEE Computer Society Conference on Computer Vision and Pattern Recognition, pp. 8635–8644 (2021). https://doi.org/10.1109/CVPR46437.2021.00853, http://arxiv.org/abs/2103.01456

22. Lin, J., Zhang, R., Ganz, F., Han, S., Zhu, J.Y.: Anycost GANs for inter-active image synthesis and editing. In: Proceedings of the IEEE Computer Society Conference on Computer Vision and Pattern Recognition, pp. 14981–14991 (2021). https://doi.org/10.1109/CVPR46437.2021.01474, http://arxiv.org/abs/2103.03243

23. Ling, H., Kreis, K., Li, D., Kim, S.W., Torralba, A., Fidler, S.: EditGAN: high-precision semantic image editing. In: Advances in Neural Information Processing Systems 34 (2021)

24. Liu, M., et al.: STGAN: a unified selective transfer network for arbitrary image attribute editing. In: Proceedings of the IEEE Computer Society Conference on Computer Vision and Pattern Recognition 2019-June, 3668–3677 (2019). https://doi.org/10.1109/CVPR.2019.00379

25. Liu, Z., Luo, P., Wang, X., Tang, X.: Deep learning face attributes in the wild. In: Proceedings of the IEEE International Conference on Computer Vision, ICCV 2015, vol. 2015, pp. 3730–3738 (2015). https://doi.org/10.1109/ICCV.2015.425

26. Mescheder, L., Geiger, A., Nowozin, S.: Which training methods for GANs do actually converge? In: 35th International Conference on Machine Learning, ICML 2018. vol. 8, pp. 5589–5626. PMLR (2018)

27. Richardson, E., et al.: Encoding in style: a styleGAN encoder for image-to-image translation. In: Proceedings of the IEEE Computer Society Conference on Computer Vision and Pattern Recognition, pp. 2287–2296 (2021). https://doi.org/10.1109/CVPR46437.2021.00232

28. Shen, Y., Yang, C., Tang, X., Zhou, B.: InterFaceGAN: interpreting the disen-tangled face representation learned by GANs. IEEE Trans. Pattern Anal. Mach. Intell. (2020). https://doi.org/10.1109/TPAMI.2020.3034267

29. Shen, Y., Zhou, B.: Closed-form factorization of latent semantics in GaNs. In: Proceedings of the IEEE Computer Society Conference on Computer Vision and Pattern Recognition, pp. 1532–1540 (2021). https://doi.org/10.1109/CVPR46437.2021.00158

30. Tan, D.S., Soeseno, J.H., Hua, K.L.: Controllable and identity-aware facial attribute transformation. IEEE Trans. Cybernet. (2021). https://doi.org/10.1109/TCYB.2021.3071172

31. Tritrong, N., Rewatbowornwong, P., Suwajanakorn, S.: Repurposing GANs for one-shot semantic part segmentation. In: Proceedings of the IEEE/CVF Conference on Computer Vision and Pattern Recognition, pp. 4475–4485 (2021)

32. Viazovetskyi, Y., Ivashkin, V., Kashin, E.: StyleGAN2 distillation for feed-forward image manipulation. In: Lecture Notes in Computer Science (including subseries Lecture Notes in Artificial Intelligence and Lecture Notes in Bioinformatics), vol. 12367 LNCS, pp. 170–186. Springer (2020). https://doi.org/10.1007/978-3-030-58542-6_11

33. Wang, Y., Gonzalez-Garcia, A., Van De Weijer, J., Herranz, L.: SDIT: scalable and diverse cross-domain image translation. In: MM 2019 - Proceedings of the 27th ACM International Conference on Multimedia, pp. 1267–1276 (2019). https://doi.org/10.1145/3343031.3351004

34. Wu, P.W., Lin, Y.J., Chang, C.H., Chang, E.Y., Liao, S.W.: RelGAN: multi-domain image-to-image translation via relative attributes. In: Proceedings of the IEEE/CVF international conference on computer vision, pp. 5914–5922 (2019)

35. Xiao, T., Hong, J., Ma, J.: ELEGANT: Exchanging latent encodings with GAN for transferring multiple face attributes. In: Lecture Notes in Computer Science (including subseries Lecture Notes in Artificial Intelligence and Lecture Notes in Bioinformatics), vol. 11214 LNCS, pp. 172–187 (2018). https://doi.org/10.1007/978-3-030-01249-6_11

36. Yang, G., Fei, N., Ding, M., Liu, G., Lu, Z., Xiang, T.: L2M-GAN: learning to manipulate latent space semantics for facial attribute editing. In: Proceedings of the IEEE Computer Society Conference on Computer Vision and Pattern Recognition, pp. 2950–2959 (2021). https://doi.org/10.1109/CVPR46437.2021.00297

37. Yang, N., Zheng, Z., Zhou, M., Guo, X., Qi, L., Wang, T.: A domain-guided noise-optimization-based inversion method for facial image manipulation. IEEE Trans. Image Process. **30**, 6198–6211 (2021). https://doi.org/10.1109/TIP.2021.3089905

38. Yang, N., Zhou, M., Xia, B., Guo, X., Qi, L.: Inversion based on a detached dual-channel domain method for styleGAN2 embedding. IEEE Signal Process. Lett. **28**, 553–557 (2021). https://doi.org/10.1109/LSP.2021.3059371

39. Zhang, K., Su, Y., Guo, X., Qi, L., Zhao, Z.: MU-GAN: facial attribute editing based on multi-attention mechanism. IEEE/CAA J. Autom. Sin. **8**(9), 164–1626 (2020)

40. Zhang, Y., et al.: DatasetGAN: efficient labeled data factory with minimal human effort. In: Proceedings of the IEEE/CVF Conference on Computer Vision and Pattern Recognition, pp. 10145–10155 (2021)

41. Zhao, B., Chang, B., Jie, Z., Sigal, L.: Modular generative adversarial networks. In: Lecture Notes in Computer Science (including subseries Lecture Notes in Artificial Intelligence and Lecture Notes in Bioinformatics), vol. 11218 LNCS, pp. 157–173 (2018). https://doi.org/10.1007/978-3-030-01264-9_10

42. Zhu, J., Shen, Y., Zhao, D., Zhou, B.: In-domain GAN inversion for real image editing. In: Lecture Notes in Computer Science (including subseries Lecture Notes in Artificial Intelligence and Lecture Notes in Bioinformatics) 12362 LNCS, 592–608 (2020). https://doi.org/10.1007/978-3-030-58520-4_35, http://arxiv.org/abs/2004.00049

Least-Squares Estimation of Keypoint Coordinate for Human Pose Estimation

Linhua Xiang[1,3], Jia Li[3,4], and Zengfu Wang[1,2,3(✉)]

[1] University of Science and Technology of China, Hefei, China
xlh1995@mail.ustc.edu.cn, zfwang@ustc.edu.cn
[2] Institute of Intelligent Machines, Chinese Academy of Sciences, Beijing, China
[3] National Engineering Research Center of Speech and Language Information
Processing, Hefei, China
[4] Hefei University of Technology, Hefei, China
jiali@hfut.edu.cn

Abstract. The research on human pose estimation has recently been promoted to a new high degree. As a result, existing methods that are widely used but flawed in theory must be rethought. Most researchers focus on enhancing network structure and data processing details, yet neglect to study encoding-decoding methods for keypoint coordinate. In this paper, we rethink recent encoding-decoding methods and further propose a new, elegant and reliable one. Our method is referred to as *Least-squares Estimation of Keypoint Coordinate* (LSEC), which is a plug-in and can be conveniently used in recent state-of-the-art (SOTA) human pose estimation models. LSEC is mathematically rigorous and unbiased, and it can compensate for the inherent bias introduced by the existing encoding-decoding methods. Besides, LSEC greatly improves the robustness of Gaussian heatmap based human pose estimation methods against adversarial attack by noise. Experiments demonstrate the effective performance and robustness of our proposed method. We will release the source code later.

Keywords: Human pose · Heatmap · Least-squares estimation · Deep learning

1 Introduction

Human pose estimation is an attractive and fundamental research in computer vision that may be applied to a variety of scenarios, including human-computer interaction [26], human action recognition [31], abnormal behavior detection [2], motion retargeting [1], etc. As for the convolutional neural networks (CNNs) dominate in computer vision, the traditional methods have been progressively replaced by deep learning methods. In terms of the deep learning methods, in the last few years, we have witnessed a rapid development from single person pose estimation [14, 24, 30, 32, 36] to multi-person pose estimation [4, 5, 8, 11, 12, 20, 29, 34, 37]

Student paper.

S. Yu et al. (Eds.): PRCV 2022, LNCS 13536, pp. 448–460, 2022.
https://doi.org/10.1007/978-3-031-18913-5_35

then to 3D human pose estimation [7,9,18,33,39]. The foundation for the foregoing accomplishments is 2D human pose estimation, which is the topic of this paper.

2D human pose estimation means that when given a picture, you should locate all the people in this picture, and further locate all the keypoint coordinates we defined beforehand for every person. These keypoints include eyes, ears, shoulders, elbows, knees and other points to describe a person's pose.

We can divide the encoding-decoding methods into three categories in previous work, Direct regression, Gaussian heatmap methods, and Other methods. Direct regression like [30] aims to directly regress the numerical coordinates, which can be trained in an end-to-end manner with less computation and faster speed. However, the location of the keypoint coordinates can heavily influence the fully-connected layer's weights, leading to the decline of spatial generalization ability and lower prediction accuracy [25]. Other methods include methods other than Direct regression and Gaussian heatmap. They have their specific benefits and drawbacks, but do not have a fixed mode and have not become the mainstream approach, e.g., Soft-argmax [22], offset heatmaps [11], SimDR [19], etc. In contrast to the encoding-decoding methods described above, Gaussian heatmap methods [4,5,14,20,24,29,35,37] are now dominant in human pose estimation. The method implicitly transforms the task of inferring numerical keypoint coordinates to finding the peak locations in the 2D Gaussian heatmaps. Therefore, encoding-decoding strategy plays a significant role in Gaussian heatmap methods.

However, the standard and the most widely used encoding-decoding strategy has inevitable quantitative errors. Besides, our experiments revealed that the robustness of the current method is inadequate when the output heatmap encounters adversarial attack by noise, which may not be conducive to defending the adversarial attack against the output heatmap. To overcome those above limitations, we formulate a novel *Least-squares Estimation of Keypoint Coordinate* (LSEC) method for Gaussian heatmap methods in human pose estimation.

In summary, our contributions are as follows:

- We systematically analyse existing encoding-decoding methods based on Gaussian heatmap, accounted for their shortcomings and causes.
- We propose a novel encoding-decoding strategy in 2D human pose estimation named LSEC which make up the gap in other methods, and demonstrated the effective improvement of our method.
- Our LSEC can be used as a plug-in to existing models without any additional modification, and is comparable or even superior to other encoding-decoding methods.
- Extensive experiments have proved the robustness of our proposed method. When the output heatmaps suffer from adversarial attack by noise, performance of other decoding methods will slump sharply while LSEC can still produce acceptable results.

2   Proposed Method

In this paper, the encoding and decoding processes of three methods will be discussed in detail: the most widely used Standard method, DARK [37] (another

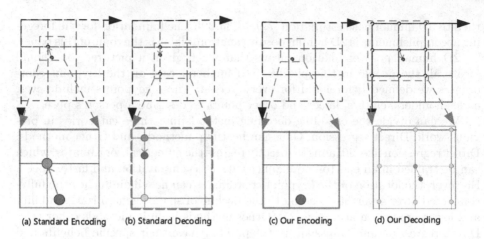

(a) Standard Encoding   (b) Standard Decoding   (c) Our Encoding   (d) Our Decoding

Fig. 1. Illustration of the **Standard method** and our **LSEC** in encoding-decoding. For (a) and (c), red point: groundtruth coordinate, blue point: the encoded coordinate for training label. Notice that the blue and red points of LSEC are overlapping in (c). For (b) and (d), red point: prediction coordinate, blue point: the discrete maximum activation in the output heatmap. yellow point: the points surrounding in the maximum activation to help to estimate the red point. (Color figure online)

method to study the encoding-decoding process), and the proposed LSEC. We will analyse the flaws and the reasons caused by flaws of past methods and propose our solution.

2.1 Encoding

In order to effectively use the groundtruth coordinate, we need an encoding process to map the numerical keypoint coordinates into heatmaps. Specifically, we set the groundtruth coordinate as $\mathbf{g} = (\mathbf{u}, \mathbf{v})$, the downsampling stride as $\mathbf{s}$, the standard variance as σ, floor quantitative function as $\mathbf{Q_f}$, round quantitative function as $\mathbf{Q_r}$, Gaussian function as $\mathbf{G}$.

Standard method generates the Gaussian distribution centered at (u, v) as follows:

$$\mathbf{G}(\mathbf{x}, \mathbf{y}, \mathbf{g}) = \exp(-\frac{(\mathbf{x} - \mathbf{Q_f}(\frac{\mathbf{u}}{\mathbf{s}}))^2 + (\mathbf{y} - \mathbf{Q_f}(\frac{\mathbf{v}}{\mathbf{s}}))^2}{2\sigma^2}), \tag{1}$$

where $|x - \mathbf{Q_f}(\frac{\mathbf{u}}{\mathbf{s}})| \leq \frac{fs-1}{2}$ and $|y - \mathbf{Q_f}(\frac{\mathbf{v}}{\mathbf{s}})| \leq \frac{fs-1}{2}$, fs means Gaussian filter size. Obviously, on account of the employment of quantitative function $\mathbf{Q_f}$, this encoding method is inevitably biased. In practice, the fs of standard method is often chosen empirically like 5,7,9, etc.

LSEC and DARK abandon the quantitative function in the Gaussian function and rewrite the Gaussian distribution through:

$$\mathbf{G}(\mathbf{x}, \mathbf{y}, \mathbf{g}) = \exp(-\frac{(\mathbf{x} - \frac{\mathbf{u}}{\mathbf{s}})^2 + (\mathbf{y} - \frac{\mathbf{v}}{\mathbf{s}})^2}{2\sigma^2}). \tag{2}$$

Theoretically, ours and DARK are both unbiased encoding methods, make up for the error caused by the standard method due to the quantization function in Gaussian distribution function. The difference between ours and DARK is that the latter removes the restriction and applies the Gaussian function to the entire heatmap. Intuitively, removing the restriction is more smooth for the whole heatmap but may confuse our network to pay more attention to unimportant areas.

So we remain $|x - \mathbf{Q_r}(\frac{u}{s})| \leq \mathbf{Q_r}(\frac{fs-1}{2})$ and $|y - \mathbf{Q_r}(\frac{v}{s})| \leq \mathbf{Q_r}(\frac{fs-1}{2})$ to restrict the range of our Gaussian function. The standard method usually uses experiments to design fs manually, consuming time and computation, while we define the fs as:

$$fs = 2(\frac{\sigma - 0.8}{0.3} + 1) + 1 \tag{3}$$

Inspired by [3], obviously, the uniform formula instead of experimental manual design of fs can avoid unnecessary time-cost. Furthermore, we will prove the better effectiveness of our encoding method than the standard method and DARK in Sect. 3.

2.2   Decoding

By reason of the breakage of end-to-end training from an input image to numerical predicted keypoints, it is necessary to take a strategy to decode the output heatmaps to our needed keypoint coordinates. Apparently, we are unable to extract the real maximum activation directly on account of the discrete output heatmaps. As a result, we can only get the maximum activation with discrete position, and the real maximum activation needs to be inferred. Specifically, we define the output heatmaps O, final predicted coordinate location p, the discrete maximum activation O_m and the second discrete maximum activation O_s, the downsampling stride as $\mathbf{s}$. The Standard method usually decodes the keypoint coordinates as:

$$\mathbf{p} = \mathbf{s}(\mathbf{O_m} + \frac{\mathbf{O_m} - \mathbf{O_s}}{4\|\mathbf{O_m} - \mathbf{O_s}\|_2}). \tag{4}$$

Before introducing our LSEC, a visual example can intuitively explain why the standard encoding-decoding method has theoretical drawbacks leading to inaccurate prediction. As shown in Fig. 1, the inherent bias will occur from (a)'s groundtruth coordinate (red point) to (b)'s prediction coordinate (red point). Then the bias will widen further when the prediction back upsampling to origin image's size. In short, the standard encoding-decoding method has inherent precision loss that can't be avoided. DARK uses log-likelihood optimization principle to infer the real maximum activation. However, when output heatmaps facing adversarial attack by noise, DARK has poor robustness (showed later in Sect. 3). To overcome these shortcomings above, the proposed LSEC treats the encoding-decoding process in a different view. We split LSEC into two stages: "Preprocessing Stage" and "Estimation Stage".

Preprocessing Stage. Before introducing our LSEC, keep in mind that our decoding task is to find the real maximum activation (u, v). First, we note the discrete maximum activation coordinate as $O_m = (x_m, y_m)$, so the ratio R of other activation coordinates (x, y) with O_m can be defined as:

$$R = \frac{G(x, y, g)}{G(x_m, y_m, g)}. \tag{5}$$

As we all known, when adapting our encoding method and in the case that our network's prediction is accurate enough, the output heatmap's distribution will be like Eq. 2. So we can use Eq. 2 to translate the Eq. 5 to the following form:

$$-2(x - x_m)u' - 2(y - y_m)v' = b, \tag{6}$$

where $u' = \frac{u}{s}, v' = \frac{v}{s}$, and $b = -2\sigma^2 ln(R) + x_m^2 + y_m^2 - x^2 - y^2$. Then we can rewrite the Eq. 6 using matrix form:

$$\begin{bmatrix} -2(x - x_m) & -2(y - y_m) \end{bmatrix} \begin{bmatrix} u' \\ v' \end{bmatrix} = \begin{bmatrix} b \end{bmatrix}. \tag{7}$$

Then we can select some points $\{(x_i, y_i)|i = 1, 2, ..., n\}$, e.g. the yellow points surrounding in the maximum activation as we showed in Fig. 1(d), and their corresponding $\{b_i|i = 1, 2, ..., n\}$ to expand the Eq. 7 to:

$$\begin{bmatrix} -2(x_1 - x_m) & -2(y_1 - y_m) \\ -2(x_2 - x_m) & -2(y_2 - y_m) \\ \vdots & \vdots \\ -2(x_n - x_m) & -2(y_n - y_m) \end{bmatrix} \begin{bmatrix} u' \\ v' \end{bmatrix} = \begin{bmatrix} b_1 \\ b_2 \\ \vdots \\ b_n \end{bmatrix}. \tag{8}$$

Obviously, Eq. 8 can be treated as:

$$AY = B, \tag{9}$$

where $A \in R^{n,2}$, $B \in R^{n,1}$, $Y = [u', v']^T$. Because A and B can be computed from the output heatmaps, so if we estimate the real maximum activation (u, v), we have to know what Y is.

Estimation Stage. Up to now, we have turned our task into an estimation problem, which means estimating Y based on samples A and B. So according to the least square method, we can treat the estimation problem as:

$$\min_{Y \in R^{2,1}} |AY - B| \iff \min_{Y \in R^{2,1}} ||AY - B||_2^2. \tag{10}$$

Then we can take partial derivative of Eq. 10 with respect to Y:

$$\frac{\partial ||AY - B||_2^2}{\partial Y} = 2A^T AY - 2A^T B = 0. \tag{11}$$

$$Y = (A^T A)^{-1} A^T B. \tag{12}$$

Finally, the prediction coordinate of keypoints estimation (u, v) can be extracted from Eq. 12. We visualize the encoding and decoding process of LSEC in Fig. 1(c)(d). In a word, the standard encoding-decoding method has inherent bias, but our LSEC can be unbiased as long as our output heatmaps are accurate enough.

Table 1. Comparisons on MS COCO 2017 validation set.

Method	Backbone	Input size	AP	AP^{50}	AP^{75}	AP^M	AP^L	AR
SimpleBaseline [34]	ResNet-50	128 × 96	59.3	85.5	67.4	57.8	63.8	66.6
	ResNet-152	384 × 288	74.3	89.6	81.1	70.5	79.7	79.7
Hourglass [24]	4-stage Hourglass	128 × 96	66.2	87.6	75.1	63.8	71.4	72.8
	8-stage Hourglass	256 × 192	66.9	-	-	-	-	-
CPN [5]	ResNet-50	256 × 192	69.6	88.0	76.9	66.1	76.2	76.4
LSEC (ours)	ResNet-50	256 × 192	**70.6**	**88.2**	**77.4**	**67.1**	**77.1**	**77.2**
HRNet [29]	HRNet-W32	256 × 192	74.4	**90.5**	81.9	70.8	81.0	79.8
LSEC (ours)	HRNet-W32	256 × 192	**75.2**	90.1	**82.1**	**71.6**	**82.2**	**80.4**

Table 2. Comparisons on MS COCO 2017 test-dev set.

Method	Backbone	Input size	AP	AP^{50}	AP^{75}	AP^M	AP^L	AR
CPN [5]	ResNet-Inception	384 × 288	72.1	91.4	80.0	68.7	77.2	78.5
PRTR [17]	HRNet-W32	512 × 384	72.1	90.4	79.6	68.1	79.0	79.4
HRNet [29]	HRNet-W32	256 × 192	73.5	92.2	82.0	70.4	79.0	79.0
Posefix [23]	ResNet-152	384 × 288	73.6	90.8	81.0	70.3	79.8	79.0
SimpleBaseline [34]	ResNet-152	384 × 288	73.7	91.9	81.1	70.3	80.0	79.0
TransPose [35]	TransPose-H-A6	256 × 192	75.0	92.2	82.3	71.3	81.1	-
OKS-net [38]	HRNet-W32	384 × 288	75.2	92.7	83.0	71.7	81.2	80.4
HRNet [29]	HRNet-W48	384 × 288	75.5	92.5	83.3	71.9	81.5	80.5
RLE [15]	HRNet-W48	-	75.7	92.3	82.9	72.3	81.3	-
MIPNet [13]	HRNet-W48	384 × 288	75.7	-	-	-	-	-
TokenPose [20]	TokenPose-L/D24	384 × 288	75.9	92.3	83.4	72.2	82.1	80.8
DARK [37]	HRNet-W48	384 × 288	76.2	92.5	83.6	72.5	82.4	81.1
LSEC (ours)	HRNet-W32	256 × 192	74.5	92.1	82.3	71.1	80.4	79.5
LSEC (ours)	HRNet-W48	384 × 288	75.8	92.5	83.1	72.1	81.8	80.3

Table 3. Comparisons on CrowdPose Dataset test set, + employs multi-scale testing, * means using Faster-RCNN rather than YOLO-v3 bounding boxes (our method uses the same YOLO-v3 bounding boxes as HRNet [29]).

Method	Backbone	Input size	GFLOPS	AP	AP_{easy}	AP_{medium}	AP_{hard}
Mask-RCNN [10]	ResNet-50-FPN	-	-	57.2	69.4	57.9	45.8
SimpleBaseline [34]	-	-	-	60.8	71.4	61.2	51.2
AlphaPose [8]	-	-	-	61.0	71.2	61.4	51.1
SPPE [16]	ResNet-50-FPN	-	-	66.0	75.5	66.3	57.4
HRNet [29]	HRNet-W32	256 × 192	7.1	66.4	74.0	67.4	55.6
DoubleHigherNet [27]	DoubleHrNet-w32	-	-	66.8	75.0	67.7	57.5
HigherHRNet$^+$ [6]	HRNet-W48	640	154.3	67.6	75.8	68.1	58.9
MIPNet [13]	ResNet-101	384 × 288	51.9	68.1	74.6	69.2	53.4
MIPNet* [13]	HRNet-W48	384 × 288	46.5	70.0	78.1	71.1	59.4
LSEC (ours)	HRNet-W32	256 × 192	7.1	67.3	69.3	68.5	61.1
LSEC (ours)	HRNet-W48	384 × 288	32.9	69.2	77.8	70.4	58.0

3   Experiments

3.1   Datasets and Evaluation

For experiments, we conducted two benchmark datasets, MS COCO 2017 [21] and CrowdPose Dataset [16]. MS COCO 2017 is a widely used dataset for human pose estimation, which contains over 150,000 people and 1.7 million labeled keypoints. The people labeled in MS COCO 2017 have 17 keypoints (e.g. right eye, left ankle). The various scenarios and complicated human pose make the dataset definitely challenging.

CrowdPose Dataset contains 20,000 images in total and 80,000 human instances, using 14 keypoints definition and full-body bounding boxes. Because the aim is to promote performance in crowded cases, the dataset has a more uniform distribution in Crowd Index [16] compared to MS COCO 2017 and other datasets. The Crowd Index defines the crowding level of an image.

We followed the mainstream method to use average precision (AP) based on object keypoint similarity (OKS) to evaluate the performance of our LSEC.

3.2   Comparison with Other Methods

MS COCO 2017 Dataset. In Table 1, we use HRNet[29] and CPN[5] respectively as our network backbones to evaluate the performance of our LSEC on MS COCO 2017 validation set. For CPN and HRNet with input size of 256×192, promotion of the proposed LSEC is 1.0 and 0.8 AP respectively. As a result, just modifying the encoding and decoding method with no additional cost, LSEC can effectively improve the performance of the current Gaussian heatmap based model.

Table 2 reports the results on the MS COCO 2017 test-dev set. We followed the same detection bounding boxes as Sun et al. [29]. For HRNet-w32 with

256×192 input size, LSEC promote 1.0 AP. Obviously, our method achieves comparable performance with SOTA methods [13,15,20,35,37].

CrowdPose Dataset. As Table 3 shown, LSEC can provide 0.9 AP improvements for HRNet-W32 when input size is 256 × 192. Since MIPNet [13] consumes more 40% GFLOPS (46.5 VS 32.9) than LSEC while employing the HRNet-W48 backbone, we can infer that the proposed LSEC achieves competitive trade-off results compared with SOTA methods on CrowdPose Dataset.

Some visual results are shown in Fig. 2, it is observed that our approach works well in both unconstrained posture and difficult situations.

3.3 Ablation Study

Encoding-Decoding Method. We compared the encoding-decoding methods of standard, DARK, and ours in MS COCO 2017 validation set. To eliminate interference and control variables, we employed the same network structure and training configuration. For encoding methods, from Table 4, we observe that our encoding method can stably achieve better performance no matter what decoding method employed. Why we can outperform DARK is we hold the opinion that it is more necessary for networks to focus on the region of interest (ROI) like the area around a keypoint, rather than make the Gaussian distribution spread in the whole heatmaps. For decoding methods, the standard decoding method is worse than ours in all metrics and our decoding method achieves comparable performance compared with DARK. Table 4 demonstrated the effectiveness of our encoding-decoding method. Besides, according to both Tables 1 and 4, we would like to point out that the proposed LSEC can be plugged into different model backbones and be valid for various scale input sizes.

Robustness to Noise. With the rapid development of artificial intelligence, there are more and more attack methods [28] against neural networks, such as adding noise. So, although overlooked in the past, the robustness against output heatmap noise in adversarial defense is also an important capability for encoding-decoding methods. We specifically considered two kinds of noise, Gaussian and random distributed noise. On account of the value range of our groundtruth heatmaps is within [0,1], so the output heatmaps also tend to be in this range. Therefore, we adopted the following four noise experimental configurations: (1) random distributed noise, range [–0.5, 0.5]; (2) random distributed noise, range [0, 1]; (3) Gaussian noise, range [–0.5, 0.5], $\mu = 0, \sigma = 1$; (4) Gaussian noise, range [0, 1], $\mu = 0.5, \sigma = 1$. After adding the noise to output heatmaps, we normalized the heatmaps, keeping their range [0, 1] like the groundtruth heatmaps.

Referring to the results in Tables 5 and 6, when the output heatmaps suffer from adversarial attack by noise, performance of Standard method and DARK slump sharply, while LSEC can still maintain acceptable performance. Our decoding method surpasses others in all the evaluation metrics, in particular, than 23 AP in Gaussian noise compared with DARK. The experiments demonstrate that other decoding methods perform poorly in different noise, while our method is robust to noise adversarial attack.

Table 4. Evaluation of our encoding-decoding method on the MS COCO 2017 validation set. Model: HRNet-W32; Input size: 128 × 96; Human detector: groundtruth.

Encoding	Decoding	AP	AP^{50}	AP^{75}	AP^M	AP^L	AR
Standard method	Standard method	64.3	90.5	74.4	63.1	66.8	68.4
DARK	Standard method	69.6	91.5	79.1	67.6	72.8	73.0
Ours	Standard method	69.6	**91.6**	**79.3**	**67.9**	72.8	**73.1**
Standard method	DARK	66.7	91.4	76.6	65.3	69.0	70.5
DARK	DARK	72.4	91.5	80.5	70.4	**76.1**	75.8
Ours	DARK	**72.7**	**91.6**	80.5	**70.6**	76.0	75.8
Standard method	**Ours**	65.9	91.4	75.7	64.8	68.3	69.8
DARK	**Ours**	72.1	91.5	80.4	70.0	75.8	75.4
Ours	**Ours**	**72.4**	**91.6**	80.4	**70.4**	**75.9**	**75.6**

Table 5. Evaluation the influence of random distributed noise on the MS COCO 2017 validation set under different decoding methods. All results were obtained by averaging five experimental data. Model: HRNet-W32; Input size: 128 × 96; Human detector: groundtruth.

Method	(1) range [−0.5, 0.5]	(2) range [0, 1]	AP	AP^{50}	AP^{75}	AP^M	AP^L	AR
Standard method			64.3	90.5	74.4	63.1	66.8	68.4
Standard method	✓		41.4	85.1	34.6	41.1	42.4	47.2
DARK	✓		45.5	85.0	44.6	45.1	46.9	51.2
Ours	✓		**54.0**	**88.5**	**61.6**	**52.6**	**56.3**	**58.9**
Standard method		✓	41.4	85.1	34.7	41.1	42.5	47.4
DARK		✓	45.6	85.0	44.6	45.3	46.8	51.3
Ours		✓	**54.1**	**89.1**	**61.1**	**52.9**	**56.1**	**59.0**

Table 6. Evaluation the influence of Gaussian noise on the MS COCO 2017 validation set under different decoding methods. All results were obtained by averaging five experimental data. Model: HRNet-W32; Input size: 128 × 96; Human detector: groundtruth.

Method	(3) range [−0.5, 0.5]	(4) range [0, 1]	AP	AP^{50}	AP^{75}	AP^M	AP^L	AR
Standard method			64.3	90.5	74.4	63.1	66.8	68.4
Standard method	✓		41.1	85.6	32.6	41.2	41.9	47.3
DARK	✓		29.9	77.9	12.4	30.9	29.9	36.4
Ours	✓		**53.4**	**89.1**	**60.4**	**52.5**	**55.4**	**58.6**
Standard method		✓	41.1	85.6	32.6	41.1	41.9	47.2
DARK		✓	29.8	77.5	12.5	30.8	29.9	36.3
Ours		✓	**53.6**	**89.1**	**60.6**	**52.4**	**55.7**	**58.6**

Fig. 2. Some results of our method.

4   Conclusion

In this paper, we rethink and propose a novel and robust encoding-decoding strategy in human pose estimation. The proposed method is referred to as Least Squares Estimation of keypoint Coordinate (LSEC), which is a cost-free plug-in for human pose estimation models based on Gaussian heatmaps. By applying plugged LSEC to existing models, we compensate for the shortcomings of their encoding-decoding methods and significantly increase their performance on the MS COCO 2017 dataset and the CrowdPose Dataset. Furthermore, we attempt to overcome the long-ignored adversarial defense by noise in human pose estimation for the first time. Experimentally, the proposed method proves to be more robust to diversity noise on heatmaps compared to existing encoding-decoding methods.

References

1. Aberman, K., Wu, R., Lischinski, D., Chen, B., Cohen-Or, D.: Learning character-agnostic motion for motion retargeting in 2D. ACM Trans. Graph. (TOG) **38**(4), 1–14 (2019)
2. Ahmed, S.A., Dogra, D.P., Kar, S., Roy, P.P.: Trajectory-based surveillance analysis: a survey. IEEE Trans. Circ. Syst. Video Technol. **29**(7), 1985–1997 (2018)
3. Bradski, G.: The OpenCV Library. Dr. Dobb's Journal of Software Tools (2000)

4. Cao, Z., Simon, T., Wei, S.E., Sheikh, Y.: Realtime multi-person 2D pose estimation using part affinity fields. In: Proceedings of the IEEE Conference on Computer Vision and Pattern Recognition, pp. 7291–7299 (2017)
5. Chen, Y., Wang, Z., Peng, Y., Zhang, Z., Yu, G., Sun, J.: Cascaded pyramid network for multi-person pose estimation. In: Proceedings of the IEEE Conference on Computer Vision and Pattern Recognition, pp. 7103–7112 (2018)
6. Cheng, B., Xiao, B., Wang, J., Shi, H., Huang, T.S., Zhang, L.: HigherHRNet: scale-aware representation learning for bottom-up human pose estimation. In: Proceedings of the IEEE/CVF Conference on Computer Vision and Pattern Recognition, pp. 5386–5395 (2020)
7. Choi, H., Moon, G., Lee, K.M.: Pose2Mesh: Graph convolutional network for 3D human pose and mesh recovery from a 2D human pose. arXiv preprint arXiv:2008.09047 (2020)
8. Fang, H.S., Xie, S., Tai, Y.W., Lu, C.: RMPE: regional multi-person pose estimation. In: Proceedings of the IEEE International Conference on Computer Vision, pp. 2334–2343 (2017)
9. Ge, L., et al.: 3D hand shape and pose estimation from a single RGB image. In: Proceedings of the IEEE Conference on Computer Vision and Pattern Recognition, pp. 10833–10842 (2019)
10. He, K., Gkioxari, G., Dollár, P., Girshick, R.: Mask R-CNN. In: Proceedings of the IEEE International Conference on Computer Vision, pp. 2961–2969 (2017)
11. Huang, J., Zhu, Z., Guo, F., Huang, G.: The devil is in the details: delving into unbiased data processing for human pose estimation. In: Proceedings of the IEEE/CVF Conference on Computer Vision and Pattern Recognition, pp. 5700–5709 (2020)
12. Insafutdinov, E., Pishchulin, L., Andres, B., Andriluka, M., Schiele, B.: DeeperCut: a deeper, stronger, and faster multi-person pose estimation model. In: Leibe, B., Matas, J., Sebe, N., Welling, M. (eds.) ECCV 2016. LNCS, vol. 9910, pp. 34–50. Springer, Cham (2016). https://doi.org/10.1007/978-3-319-46466-4_3
13. Khirodkar, R., Chari, V., Agrawal, A., Tyagi, A.: Multi-instance pose networks: rethinking top-down pose estimation. In: Proceedings of the IEEE/CVF International Conference on Computer Vision (ICCV), pp. 3122–3131 (October 2021)
14. Li, J., Su, W., Wang, Z.: Simple pose: rethinking and improving a bottom-up approach for multi-person pose estimation. In: AAAI, pp. 11354–11361 (2020)
15. Li, J., et al.: Human pose regression with residual log-likelihood estimation. In: Proceedings of the IEEE/CVF International Conference on Computer Vision, pp. 11025–11034 (2021)
16. Li, J., Wang, C., Zhu, H., Mao, Y., Fang, H.S., Lu, C.: CrowdPose: Efficient crowded scenes pose estimation and a new benchmark. arXiv preprint arXiv:1812.00324 (2018)
17. Li, K., Wang, S., Zhang, X., Xu, Y., Xu, W., Tu, Z.: Pose recognition with cascade transformers. In: Proceedings of the IEEE/CVF Conference on Computer Vision and Pattern Recognition, pp. 1944–1953 (2021)
18. Li, S., Chan, A.B.: 3D human pose estimation from monocular images with deep convolutional neural network. In: Cremers, D., Reid, I., Saito, H., Yang, M.-H. (eds.) ACCV 2014. LNCS, vol. 9004, pp. 332–347. Springer, Cham (2015). https://doi.org/10.1007/978-3-319-16808-1_23
19. Li, Y., et al.: Is 2D heatmap representation even necessary for human pose estimation? arXiv preprint arXiv:2107.03332 (2021)
20. Li, Y., et al.: TokenPose: learning keypoint tokens for human pose estimation. In: Proceedings of the IEEE/CVF International Conference on Computer Vision, pp. 11313–11322 (2021)

21. Lin, T.-Y., Maire, M., Belongie, S., Hays, J., Zitnick, C.L.: Microsoft COCO: common objects in context. In: Fleet, D., Pajdla, T., Schiele, B., Tuytelaars, T. (eds.) ECCV 2014. LNCS, vol. 8693, pp. 740–755. Springer, Cham (2014). https://doi.org/10.1007/978-3-319-10602-1_48

22. Luvizon, D.C., Tabia, H., Picard, D.: Human pose regression by combining indirect part detection and contextual information. Comput. Graph. **85**, 15–22 (2019)

23. Moon, G., Chang, J.Y., Lee, K.M.: PoseFix: model-agnostic general human pose refinement network. In: Proceedings of the IEEE/CVF Conference on Computer Vision and Pattern Recognition, pp. 7773–7781 (2019)

24. Newell, A., Yang, K., Deng, J.: Stacked hourglass networks for human pose estimation. In: Leibe, B., Matas, J., Sebe, N., Welling, M. (eds.) ECCV 2016. LNCS, vol. 9912, pp. 483–499. Springer, Cham (2016). https://doi.org/10.1007/978-3-319-46484-8_29

25. Nibali, A., He, Z., Morgan, S., Prendergast, L.: Numerical coordinate regression with convolutional neural networks. arXiv preprint arXiv:1801.07372 (2018)

26. Obdržálek, Š., Kurillo, G., Han, J., Abresch, T., Bajcsy, R.: Real-time human pose detection and tracking for tele-rehabilitation in virtual reality. In: Medicine Meets Virtual Reality, vol. 19, pp. 320–324. IOS Press (2012)

27. Peng, Y., Jiang, Z.: DoubleHigherNet: coarse-to-fine precise heatmap bottom-up dynamic pose computer intelligent estimation. J. Phys. Conf. Ser. **2033**, 012068 (2021)

28. Qiu, S., Liu, Q., Zhou, S., Wu, C.: Review of artificial intelligence adversarial attack and defense technologies. Appl. Sci. **9**(5), 909 (2019)

29. Sun, K., Xiao, B., Liu, D., Wang, J.: Deep high-resolution representation learning for human pose estimation. In: Proceedings of the IEEE Conference on Computer Vision and Pattern Recognition, pp. 5693–5703 (2019)

30. Toshev, A., Szegedy, C.: DeepPose: human pose estimation via deep neural networks. In: Proceedings of the IEEE Conference on Computer Vision and Pattern Recognition, pp. 1653–1660 (2014)

31. Wang, H., Wang, L.: Cross-agent action recognition. IEEE Trans. Circ. Syst. Video Technol. **28**(10), 2908–2919 (2017)

32. Wei, S.E., Ramakrishna, V., Kanade, T., Sheikh, Y.: Convolutional pose machines. In: Proceedings of the IEEE Conference on Computer Vision and Pattern Recognition, pp. 4724–4732 (2016)

33. Wu, S., et al.: Graph-based 3D multi-person pose estimation using multi-view images. In: Proceedings of the IEEE/CVF International Conference on Computer Vision, pp. 11148–11157 (2021)

34. Xiao, B., Wu, H., Wei, Y.: Simple baselines for human pose estimation and tracking. In: Proceedings of the European Conference on Computer Vision (ECCV), pp. 466–481 (2018)

35. Yang, S., Quan, Z., Nie, M., Yang, W.: TransPose: keypoint localization via transformer. In: Proceedings of the IEEE/CVF International Conference on Computer Vision, pp. 11802–11812 (2021)

36. Yang, W., Li, S., Ouyang, W., Li, H., Wang, X.: Learning feature pyramids for human pose estimation. In: Proceedings of the IEEE International Conference on Computer Vision, pp. 1281–1290 (2017)

37. Zhang, F., Zhu, X., Dai, H., Ye, M., Zhu, C.: Distribution-aware coordinate representation for human pose estimation. In: Proceedings of the IEEE/CVF Conference on Computer Vision and Pattern Recognition, pp. 7093–7102 (2020)

38. Zhao, L., Xu, J., Gong, C., Yang, J., Zuo, W., Gao, X.: Learning to acquire the quality of human pose estimation. IEEE Trans. Circ. Syst. Video Technol. **31**(4), 1555–1568 (2020)
39. Zhou, X., Huang, Q., Sun, X., Xue, X., Wei, Y.: Towards 3D human pose estimation in the wild: a weakly-supervised approach. In: Proceedings of the IEEE International Conference on Computer Vision, pp. 398–407 (2017)

Joint Pixel-Level and Feature-Level Unsupervised Domain Adaptation for Surveillance Face Recognition

Huangkai Zhu[1,2], Huayi Yin[1,2], Du Xia[1,2], Da-Han Wang[1,2(✉)], Xianghao Liu[1,2],
and Shunzhi Zhu[1,2]

[1] School of Computer and Information Engineering, Xiamen University of Technology,
Xiamen 361024, China
wangdh@xmut.edu.cn
[2] Fujian Key Laboratory of Pattern Recognition and Image Understanding,
Xiamen 361024, China

Abstract. Face recognition (FR) is one of the most successful image analysis and understanding applications, which has recently received significant attentions. However, despite the remarkable progress in face recognition-related technologies, dependably recognizing surveillance faces is still a big challenge due to different data distributions between commonly used faces and surveillance faces. Although collecting labeled surveillance faces could be direct and helpful, it is infeasible due to privacy and labor cost. In comparison, it is practical to use the unsupervised domain adaptation (UDA) method to regularize the learning of surveillance face representations by utilizing small-scale unlabeled data. In this paper, a joint pixel-level and feature-level UDA framework has been proposed for tacking the above problems. Specifically, we introduce a training method of domain adversarial to align the domain gap in feature space. Additionally, we propose to use a CycleGAN-based image style transformer to capture pixel-level domain shifts. Moreover, we adopt feature identity-consistency loss on the original CycleGAN to alleviate the identity attribute shift caused by unstable image style transfer. The experimental results on the self-built SFace-450 dataset demonstrate that our method consistently outperforms the state-of-the-art FR and UDA methods.

Keywords: Surveillance face recognition · Unsupervised domain adaptation · Image style transform

1 Introduction

Deep learning algorithms presume that training and testing data are drawn from the underlying distribution. In practice, we frequently find that the data in testing domains are distinct from those where the training data is derived [1]. The problem is mirrored in the domain gap between the semi-constrained training set and the unconstrained testing set [2] face recognition (FR). Most state-of-the-art (SOTA) methods are trained on the high-quality photos taken in a semi-constrained environment [3, 4]. However, troubles would occur when we employ these systems in many other scenarios, e.g., surveillance. The large degree of face variation between training and testing scenarios would give rise to sharp degradation in the performance of model.

Generally, the direct way to solve this problem is to collect large-scale labeled surveillance faces for the target task. However, it exhibits privacy issues and labor cost problems. By contrast, it is practical to use unsupervised domain adaptation (UDA) methods to regularize the learning of surveillance face representations [5].

In recent years, many UDA methods have been proposed and enable superior performance in many areas, e.g., object classification, scene segmentation, and person re-identification [1]. Typical UDA is achieved by aligning the distribution of features extracted from the source and target domains [6–9]. It is widely used to reduce the test performance decline due to data covariate shift without accessing the identity of the target domain. In this way, UDA-based methods could significantly reduce the burden of data labeling.

Besides, pixel-level alignment via image style transfer has proven effective in some visual tasks [10] while few works have used it for surveillance face recognition (SFR). The generative pixel-level domain adaptation models, such as CycleGAN [11] and UNIT [12], can perform distribution alignment in raw pixel space by transforming the source data into the target domain style. In this way, the method based on image style transfer addresses the problem that is simply aligning deep features would lead to the failure of modeling low-level appearance variance [10].

In this paper, we proposed a joint pixel-level and feature-level UDA framework that uses training of domain adversarial (DA) and style transformer (ST) modules to learn robust surveillance faces representations. Specifically, considering the domain shift may raise difficulties for SFR, the DA module has been adopted to align the global distribution at the feature level through domain adversarial training. On the other hand, we adopted and customized CycleGAN-based image ST to alleviate the transformed image identity distortion problem. The main objective of this method is to introduce a feature identity-consistency loss for SFR, such that the objective function can retain the identity consistency of the transformed image and the raw in the feature space. Finally, we establish an unconstrained surveillance face dataset SFace-450, evaluate our method's effectiveness on it through ablation studies and compare our proposed method to some other UDA methods.

2   Related Work

2.1   Deep Face Recognition

In these years, deep learning has been successfully applied in many research fields, including FR. DeepFace [13] and DeepID [14] first introduced a convolutional neural network (CNN) for learning face representations. FR is regarded as a classification task, and softmax loss is utilized to learn discriminative features. In the following research, many different loss functions have been explored to improve the discrimination power of the learned feature representations. Facenet [15] utilizes triple loss to learn the mapping from face to Euclidean space. Wen et al. [16] propose center loss to learn the center of deep features for each class and combines it with softmax loss to reduce intra-class variance. Recently, weight and feature normalization [17–20] have been successfully applied to FR, bringing the research focus back to softmax-improved large angular margin learning. Significantly, Arcface [20] reformulates the softmax loss as additive angular margin loss. Besides, the L2 constrain is utilized to help this framework to normalize both features and weights, and reaches the SOTA benchmark in some test sets [21, 22].

2.2 Unsupervised Domain Adaptation

In UDA, users have a dataset of labeled data in the relevant source domain and another of unlabeled data in the target domain for a new task. The objective of the UDA is to improve the target domain's performance to match that of the source domain. Concretely, the typical methods can be divided into two ways: aligning features by minimizing measured distribution difference between two domains [6, 7] or using domain discriminator adversarial training [8, 9] to make the performance of the target domain close to the source domain. Lately, several works have been introduced for the application of UDA. SSPP-DAN [5] inserted a domain classifier after the feature extractor and improved the face recognition accuracy in the target domain through adversarial training. However, [10] pointed out that feature-level domain adaptation is limited to model low-level appearance variance and successfully applied to semantic segmentation tasks by joint pixel and feature space adaptation. Inspired by image translation networks, Shi et al. [2] use auxiliary multi-source unlabeled images to generate stylistically diverse training data to learn robust unconstrained face representation.

3 Methodology

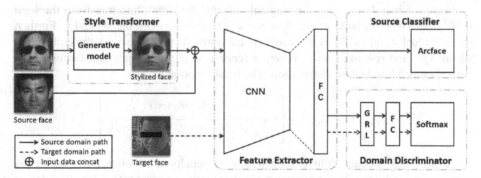

Fig. 1. Outline of the training framework of the feature extractor. In each iteration, Style transformer based on improved CycleGAN is used to directly remap a random subset of labeled training data into the target domain. The adversarial training of binary domain classifier aligns the distribution of source domain and target domain in feature space through gradient reversal layer (GRL).

Our proposed UDA framework is shown in Fig. 1. The labeled source domain face dataset is defined as $X = \{x_i, y_i\}_{i=1}^{N}$, where x_i and y_i denote the ith face image sample and its identity label, respectively. And the unlabeled target domain face dataset is defined as $T = \{t_i\}_{i=1}^{M}$ which is collected by the surveillance cameras, where t_i denotes the ith surveillance face image sample. We denote the CNN-based facial feature extractor as E, and the goal is to generalize the feature extractor E to representations in the surveillance faces that do not appear in the source training data. Specifically, our framework has three simultaneous tasks: (a) Training the improved CycleGAN using labeled source domain images and small-scale unlabeled target domain images, and transforming a part of labeled images to target domain style. (b) Training the facial feature extractor through the labeled original images and partially transformed images. (c) Minimizing the domain gap between source and target via domain adversarial training.

3.1 Training of Feature Extractor

The softmax loss function is widely used in the traditional object classification task, including FR [13, 14]. It can be expressed as follow:

$$\mathcal{L}_{softmax} = -\mathbb{E}_{x_i,y_i \sim X}\left[\log\frac{e^{W_{y_i}^T f_i + b_{y_i}}}{\sum_{j=1}^{n} e^{W_j^T f_i + b_j}}\right], \tag{1}$$

where $f_i = E(x_i)$ represents the feature of the ith sample, belonging to class y_i. W_j represents the jth column of the weight W of the last fully connected layer. The traditional softmax loss function has only separability but no discrimination, and face recognition needs to be generalized to the features of subjects that have not appeared in the training set. Recent works mainly focus on weight and feature normalization and angular margin learning to improve the softmax, such that the objective function is capable of optimizing the metric space with excellent generalization.

Fixes the bias $b_j = 0$ for the original softmax function, then transform the logit as $W_j^T f_i = \|W_j\|\|f_i\|\cos\theta_j$, so that θ_j denotes the angle between the W_j and f_i. Further, the individual weight $\|W_j\|$ is fixed to 1 by L2 normalization. Also, fix the embedding feature $\|f_i\|$ and re-scale it to s. Where s represents the hyperspherical radius of the learned embedding feature distribution. The final function is:

$$\mathcal{L}_{arcface} = -\mathbb{E}_{x_i,y_i \sim X}\left[\log\frac{e^{s(\cos(\theta_{y_i}+m))}}{e^{s(\cos(\theta_{y_i}+m))} + \sum_{j\neq y_i} e^{s\cos\theta_j}}\right]. \tag{2}$$

Arcface [20] sets an additive angular margin penalty m to enhance the intra-class compactness and inter-class discrepancy. In this work, we use Arcface loss function as labeled domain facial feature extractor training.

3.2 Training of Domain Classifier

Although Arcface achieved SOTA on some benchmarks, the faces captured by surveillance cameras have a significant deviation from most public face datasets. This phenomenon usually caused by some differences such as light, blur, background and cross ethnic face. To reduce the gap between the two domains, we introduce a domain classifier D and confuse it with adversarial training to learn domain-invariant features with a binary domain alignment loss. In order to avoid multi-stage training, we adopt the approach of DANN [8], which uses a Gradient Reversal Layer (GRL) instead of adversarial loss. The objective of domain classifier optimization can be formulated as follows:

$$\mathcal{L}_{DA} = \max_{E} \min_{D} \left(-\mathbb{E}_{t \sim T} \left[\log D(E(t)) \right] - \mathbb{E}_{x \sim X} \left[\log(1 - D(E(x))) \right] \right), \tag{3}$$

where D is a binary classifier with multiple linear layers, which is used to predict whether the features extracted by E belong to the target domain or the source domain. The max-min problem in the above formula can be achieved by using GRL. In the back-propagation process, the sign of the gradient is reversed before entering the network E by GRL, and multiplied by a trade-off factor α that is not a fixed value:

$$\alpha = \frac{2}{1 + e^{-\gamma \cdot p}} - 1. \tag{4}$$

The operation mentioned above leads to an adversarial loss relationship between E and D. In our experiments, γ was set to 10 and p linearly changed from 0 to 1 during the training progress. The total loss of the facial feature extraction network is then obtained as:

$$\mathcal{L} = \mathcal{L}_{arcface} + \lambda_{DA} \mathcal{L}_{DA}. \tag{5}$$

3.3   Training of Style Transformer

Typical CycleGAN. Deep Feature-level alignment effectively improves generalization to target domain while it is not robust to low-level modeling. In this sense, we attempt to complement it from an image-to-image data generation perspective. For example, pix2pix [23] draws on the idea of conditional GAN [24] to generate higher-quality images but requires that the training images should be paired. However, there is no mapping relationship between faces across datasets. It is impossible to obtain such paired training data or use semi-supervised methods [1] to solve the problem by pseudo-labeling unlabeled data. Considering the composition of the surveillance dataset, we propose to use CycleGAN to transform face image style, which utilizes cycle-consistency loss to address the problem of unpaired training data.

CycleGAN introduces two pairs of generators and discriminators for image transformation training both forward and backward directions. We denote two fully convolutional generators as $G : X \rightarrow T$ and $F : T \rightarrow X$, and two PatchGAN-based discriminator networks D_X and D_T. To improve the stability of training and generate higher quality images, we replace the negative loglikelihood function with a least-squares loss. Then the objective for learning generators can be written as follow:

$$\mathcal{L}_{GAN} = \mathbb{E}_{x \sim X} \left[(D_T(G(x)) - 1)^2 \right] + \mathbb{E}_{t \sim T} \left[(D_X(F(t)) - 1)^2 \right]. \tag{6}$$

The objective for learning discriminator D_X and D_T can be shown as:

$$\mathcal{L}_{D_T} = \mathbb{E}_{t \sim T} \left[(D_T(t) - 1)^2 \right] + \mathbb{E}_{x \sim X} \left[D_T(G(x))^2 \right], \tag{7}$$

$$\mathcal{L}_{D_X} = \mathbb{E}_{x \sim X}\left[(D_X(x) - 1)^2\right] + \mathbb{E}_{t \sim T}\left[D_X(F(t))^2\right]. \tag{8}$$

The total loss of the discriminator is defined as:

$$\mathcal{L}_D = \mathcal{L}_{D_T} + \mathcal{L}_{D_X}. \tag{9}$$

Besides, to reduce mode collapse problem and preserve the content of raw image during style transfer, CycleGAN introduces a cycle-consistency loss, forcing $F(G(x)) \approx x$ and vice versa:

$$\mathcal{L}_{cyc} = \mathbb{E}_{x \sim X}\left[\|F(G(x)) - x\|_1\right] + \mathbb{E}_{t \sim T}\left[\|G(F(t)) - t\|_1\right]. \tag{10}$$

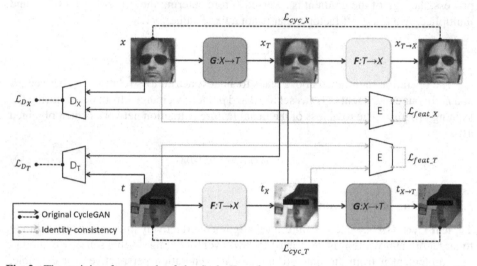

Fig. 2. The training framework of the Style Transformer based on improved CycleGAN. We propose to extract the features of the transformed image and the raw image by feature extractor E, and minimize their differences in the feature space by feature identity-consistency loss.

Improved CycleGAN. Although the forementioned cycle-consistency loss intuitively preserves the content of the image in pixel space, the training of CycleGAN is still easy to overfit to the data. As a result, the face identity before and after transformation are inconsistent in the feature space. Generally speaking, the transformed face should be as close to the raw face in the feature space as possible: $E(G(x)) \approx E(x)$. To mitigate the above problem, a new feature identity-consistency loss $\mathcal{L}_{feat}$ is introduced to preserve the consistency of the face identity in the feature space (Fig. 2). The feature extraction E is used to extract face embedding and the feature identity-consistency loss of the transformed image is constrained by the L1-norm:

$$\mathcal{L}_{feat} = \mathbb{E}_{t \sim T}\left[\|E(F(t)) - E(t)\|_1\right] + \mathbb{E}_{x \sim X}\left[\|E(G(x)) - E(x)\|_1\right] \tag{11}$$

Then the total loss of the improved CycleGAN can be formulated as follows:

$$\mathcal{L} = \mathcal{L}_{GAN} + \lambda_{cyc}\mathcal{L}_{cyc} + \lambda_{feat}\mathcal{L}_{feat} \tag{12}$$

4 Experiment

4.1 Datasets

CASIA-Webface [3] contains 494,414 images of 10,575 celebrities collected on the IMDB website in a semi-automatic way. We use the aligned version by [20] as the labeled domain dataset for facial feature extractor training.

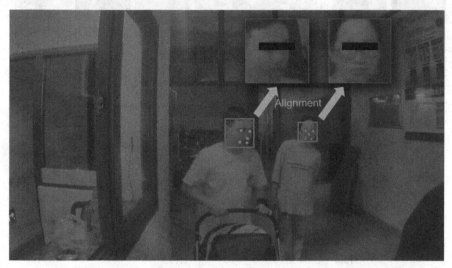

Fig. 3. Shooting conditions of SFace-450 dataset and demonstration of face alignment

SFace-450 is a surveillance face dataset specially established to evaluate our proposed method. It is sampled from the gatehouse surveillance camera of a community in Xiamen, China, and we have obtained permission to use these data for scientific research purposes. We use MTCNN [25] to preprocess the raw surveillance images and retain all the faces with five landmarks detected (Fig. 3 and Fig. 4). Besides, we divide these aligned 13,492 images into three parts: identification, verification, and unlabeled (Table 1). The establishment of the test set mainly refers to the IJB-benchmark protocol [22].

For face identification, the evaluation measurements Rank-n and Average Precision (mAP) [26] are utilized to measure the overall performance of face retrieval. We have manually selected the complex samples as a probe which is quite different from the faces in the gallery (Fig. 4) to avoid the easy saturation performance. Meanwhile, 5,500 images for verification are randomly sampled in the identification dataset. Additionally, we use the paired TAR@FAR to measure verification performance for the pairwise comparison of 32,557 positive and 15,089,693 negative sample pairs. Moreover, 2,173 unlabeled images whose identities do not overlap with the test subset are reserved for UDA training to fairly evaluate the methods.

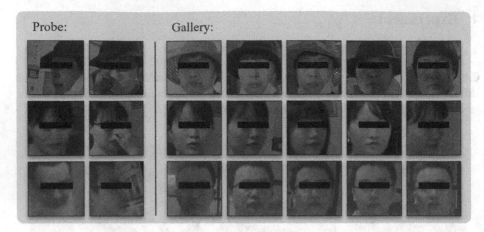

Fig. 4. Examples of face regions from the probe and gallery

Table 1. Specifications of SFace-450 dataset

Sub-set			Images	Subjects
Test	Identification	Probe	1,083	450
		Gallery	10,236	450
	Verification		5,500	450
Train	Unlabeled		2,173	–

4.2 Details of Training

Details of the Feature Extractor. We implemented all the experiments with PyTorch v1.7. All images are resized to 112×112 pixels. A modified Resnet-34 backbone in [20] is used as a feature extractor for all experiments. All models are trained for 40K iterations with a batch size of 512 by default. In the aspect of domain adversarial training, we fed 64 unlabeled images from SFace-450. When using style transformer, 25% of labeled images are converted to the target domain by the generator network. We set momentum to 0.9 and weight decay to $5e - 4$. The initialization learning rate is set to 0.1 and decreased by 0.1 when the training steps reached [16K, 32K]. We set factor λ_{DA} as 0.2 empirically.

Details of the Style Transformer. The training of the style transformer is synchronized with the feature extractor. The batch size is set to 32 images (16 per dataset). Adam optimizer is used for training with $\beta_1 = 0.5$ and $\beta_2 = 0.99$, the learning rate is set to 0.0002. Empirically set $\lambda_{cyc} = 10.0$ and $\lambda_{feat} = 10.0$. Our generator and discriminator models have the same settings as [2], no upsampling and downsampling layers are used for the generator.

4.3 Ablation Experiment

Table 2. Performance (%) on ablation experiment over different modules. All models have trained with Arcface loss by default. "DA", "ST" and "OCG" refer to "Domain Adversarial", "Style Transformer" and "Original CycleGAN", respectively.

Method	Identification				Verification	
	Rank1	Rank-5	Rank10	mAP	1e-3	1e-2
Baseline	63.62	74.42	77.84	39.56	57.17	78.20
+ DA	69.26	80.16	84.40	41.99	67.59	83.99
+ ST(OCG)	67.32	78.86	81.29	42.04	63.87	81.96
+ ST	68.70	79.41	82.46	43.76	64.67	81.99
+ DA + ST(OCG)	69.34	80.26	84.49	44.29	71.21	**86.39**
+ DA + ST	**70.64**	**81.28**	**84.95**	**45.00**	**71.32**	86.03

The ablation experiment to evaluate the effectiveness of the two modules in our proposed UDA framework is shown in Table 2. As the Arcface method was trained only using samples in the source domain for training, we take its results as our baseline. The experiment shows that the pixel-level alignment can effectively complement the feature-level domain adaptation. Obviously, the two modules in our proposed method, namely Style Transformer (ST) and Domain Adversarial (DA), effectively improve various indicators. We randomly extract the deep features of 500 images in both Webface and SFace-450 without/with using DA training strategy, respectively. And the features are visualized using t-SNE (Fig. 5). With the using of DA module, SFace-450-subset is aligned with the distribution of the Webface-subset, even if the identity of the target domain is inaccessible. As for ST module, the introduction of a new feature identity-consistency loss significantly improves the results compared with the original CycleGAN. Although the ST module is weaker than DA in other evaluation metrics, it contributes more to the mAP.

4.4 Quantity Comparison

Through the experiment analysis, we found that transforming all labeled images to the target style would weaken the performance of the feature extractor. From Table 3, it can be observed that the test performance achieves the best when the transformed images account for about 25% of the labeled training data.

4.5 Comparison

We compare our proposed framework with several other UDA methods regarding identification and verification results. It can be seen in Table 4 that our framework outperforms most of these methods, including the DDC [6], DAN [7], and Shi et al. [2] on our SFace-450 benchmark.

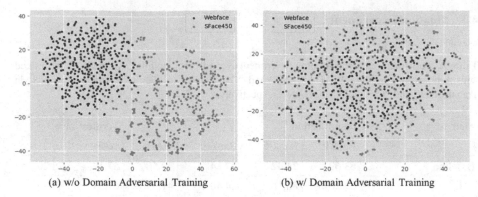

(a) w/o Domain Adversarial Training   (b) w/ Domain Adversarial Training

Fig. 5. t-SNE visualization of the face image embeddings.

Table 3. Performance (%) on quantity comparison.

Transformed number	Identification				Verification	
	Rank1	Rank-5	Rank10	mAP	1e-3	1e-2
16	68.98	79.59	83.84	44.25	69.46	85.15
64	68.61	**81.53**	84.86	44.42	70.06	85.71
96	69.54	80.98	84.12	44.71	70.39	85.66
128	**70.64**	81.28	**84.95**	**45.00**	**71.32**	86.03
192	68.79	79.80	83.65	43.62	70.63	**86.23**
256	67.22	78.62	82.46	41.95	69.05	85.77
512	66.02	76.82	79.87	42.21	67.58	84.72

Table 4. Comparison with state-of-the-art methods on the SFace-450 dataset (%)

Method	Identification				Verification	
	Rank1	Rank-5	Rank10	mAP	1e-3	1e-2
Arcface [20]	63.62	74.42	77.84	39.56	57.17	78.20
DDC [6]	68.49	79.66	83.01	41.54	66.03	83.51
DAN [7]	68.93	79.92	83.66	41.86	67.12	83.57
Shi et al. [2]	69.52	80.42	84.58	43.94	70.50	85.78
Ours (OCG)	69.34	80.26	84.49	44.29	71.21	**86.39**
Ours	**70.64**	**81.28**	**84.95**	**45.00**	**71.32**	86.03

Both DDC and DAN are both based on Maximum Mean Dispersion (MMD) method. Compared with DDC, DAN utilizes multi-kernel MMD for better mean embedding matching and applies it in multiple fully connected (FC) layers. However, to facilitate comparison, DAN we compared our method with only uses the last FC layer in this paper. Besides, we follow all the other settings in [7] for these two methods. In addition, we reproduce the work of Shi et al. using the same settings described in [2]. Moreover, our improved CycleGAN for this framework has improved over using the original one. In brief, with fewer training samples of the unmarked target domain, we achieved 7% and 5.5% improvement on Rank-1 and mAP, respectively.

5 Conclusion

In this paper, we proposed a framework utilizing the joint pixel-level and feature-level UDA method for SFR. Specifically, we introduce a domain adversarial training method to align the domain gap in feature space. Furthermore, we propose to use CycleGAN-based image style transfer to capture pixel-level domain shifts. It is noticed that the feature identity-consistency loss adopted on CycleGAN is helpful to mitigate the identity attribute shift caused by unstable image style transfer. The experimental results demonstrate that pixel-level alignment efficiently complements feature-level adaptation methods by modeling low-level appearance variance. Meanwhile, the surveillance face recognition performance of the feature extractor has greatly improved under the training of our framework and surpasses some UDA methods. Our experiments observed that CycleGAN-based method could only generate the target style with a single-mode. In the future, we will focus on improving the generator to generate diverse-style data rather than single-style data to further generalize face representation.

Acknowledgement. This work is supported by Industry-University Cooperation Project of Fujian Science and Technology Department (No. 2021H6035), and the Science and Technology Planning Project of Fujian Province (No. 2021J011182, 2020H0023, 2020Y9064), and the Joint Funds of 5th Round of Health and Education Research Program of Fujian Province (No. 2019-WJ-41).

References

1. Wang, M., Deng, W.: Deep visual domain adaptation: a survey. Neurocomputing **312**, 135–153 (2018)
2. Shi, Y., Anil, K.J.: Boosting unconstrained face recognition with auxiliary unlabeled data. In: 2021 IEEE/CVF Conference on Computer Vision and Pattern Recognition Workshops (CVPRW), pp. 2789–2798 (2021)
3. Dong, Y., Zhen, L., Liao, S., Li, S.Z.: Learning face representation from scratch. arXiv preprint arXiv:1411.7923 (2014)
4. Cao, Q., et al.: Vggface2: a dataset for recognising faces across pose and age. In: 2018 13th IEEE International Conference on Automatic Face & Gesture Recognition (FG 2018), pp. 67–74. IEEE (2018)
5. Hong, S., Im, W., Ryu, J., Yang, H.S.: SSPP-DAN: Deep domain adaptation network for face recognition with single sample per person. In: 2017 IEEE International Conference on Image Processing (ICIP) (2017)

6. Tzeng, E., et al.: Deep domain confusion: Maximizing for domain invariance. arXiv preprint arXiv:1412.3474 (2014)
7. Long, M., et al.: Learning transferable features with deep adaptation networks. In: ICML, pp. 97–105 (2015)
8. Ganin, Y., Victor L.: Unsupervised domain adaptation by backpropagation. In: ICML, pp. 1180–1189 (2015)
9. Tzeng, E., Hoffman, J., Saenko, K., Darrell, T.: Adversarial discriminative domain adaptation. In: IEEE Conference on Computer Vision and Pattern Recognition (CVPR), pp. 7167–7176 (2017)
10. Hoffman, J., et al.: CyCADA: Cycle-consistent adversarial domain adaptation. In: ICML, pp. 1989–1998 (2018)
11. Zhu, J.Y., et al.: Unpaired image-to-image translation using cycle-consistent adversarial networks. In: 2019 IEEE/CVF International Conference on Computer Vision (ICCV), pp. 2223–2232 (2017)
12. Liu, M.Y., Thomas, B., Jan K.: Unsupervised image-to-image translation networks. In: Advances in Neural Information Processing Systems, pp. 701–709 (2017)
13. Taigman, Y., et al.: Deepface: Closing the gap to human-level performance in face verification. In: IEEE Conference on Computer Vision and Pattern Recognition (CVPR), pp. 1701–1708 (2014)
14. Sun, Y., et al.: Deep learning face representation by joint identification-verification. In: Advances in Neural Information Processing Systems, pp. 1988–1996 (2014)
15. Schroff, F., Dmitry, K., James, P.: Facenet: A unified embedding for face recognition and clustering. In: IEEE Conference on Computer Vision and Pattern Recognition (CVPR), pp. 815–823 (2015)
16. Wen, Y., Zhang, K., Li, Z., Qiao, Y.: A discriminative feature learning approach for deep face recognition. In: Leibe, B., Matas, J., Sebe, N., Welling, M. (eds.) ECCV 2016. LNCS, vol. 9911, pp. 499–515. Springer, Cham (2016). https://doi.org/10.1007/978-3-319-46478-7_31
17. Ranjan, R., Castillo, C.D., Chellppa, R..: L2-constrained softmax loss for discriminative face verification. arXiv preprint arXiv:1703.09507 (2017)
18. Liu, W., et al.: Sphereface: Deep hypersphere embedding for face recognition. In: IEEE Conference on Computer Vision and Pattern Recognition (CVPR), pp. 6738–6746 (2017)
19. Wang, H., et al.: Cosface: Large margin cosine loss for deep face recognition. In: IEEE Conference on Computer Vision and Pattern Recognition (CVPR), pp. 5265–5274 (2018)
20. Deng, J., et al.: Arcface: Additive angular margin loss for deep face recognition. In: IEEE Conference on Computer Vision and Pattern Recognition (CVPR), pp. 4685–4694 (2019)
21. Huang, G.B., et al.: Labeled faces in the wild: a database for studying face recognition in unconstrained environments. In: Workshop on faces in'Real-Life'Images: detection, alignment, and recognition (2008)
22. Whitelam, C., et al.: Iarpa janus benchmark-b face dataset. In: 2017 IEEE/CVF Conference on Computer Vision and Pattern Recognition Workshops (CVPRW), pp. 592–600 (2017)
23. Isola, P., Zhu, J.Y., Zhou, T., Efros, A.A.: Image-to-image translation with conditional adversarial networks. In: IEEE Conference on Computer Vision and Pattern Recognition (CVPR), pp. 5967–5976 (2017)
24. Mirza, M., Simon O.: Conditional generative adversarial nets. arXiv preprint arXiv: 1411.1784 (2014)
25. Zhang, K., et al.: Joint face detection and alignment using multitask cascaded convolutional networks. IEEE Signal Process. Lett. 23(10), 1499–1503 (2016)
26. Ye, M., et al.: Deep learning for person re-identification: a survey and outlook. IEEE TPAMI 44(6), 2872–2893 (2022)

Category-Oriented Adversarial Data Augmentation via Statistic Similarity for Satellite Images

Huan Zhang[1,2], Wei Leng[1,2], Xiaolin Han[1,2], and Weidong Sun[1,2(✉)]

[1] Department of Electronic Engineering, Tsinghua University, Beijing, China
zhanghuan19@mails.tsinghua.edu.cn, lengwei@datall.cn,
hxl15@tsinghua.org.cn, wdsun@tsinghua.edu.cn
[2] Institute for Ocean Engineering, Tsinghua University, Beijing, China

Abstract. Deep learning is one of the essential technologies for remote sensing tasks, which heavily depends on the quantity of training data. However, it is difficult to obtain or label the remotely sensed images in their non-cooperative imaging mode. Data augmentation is a viable solution to this issue, but most of the current data augmentation methods are task specific or dataset specific, which are not as applicable as a generalized solution for the remotely sensed images. In this paper, we propose a category-oriented adversarial data augmentation method using statistic similarity cross categories, which formulates the common appearance-based statistic factors in the object detection into a combination index, to depict the statistic similarity between different categories and to generate new adversarial samples between similar categories with more reliable physical significance. Experimental results demonstrated that, taking the most advanced RT method as a baseline, the total mAP can be increased by 2.0% on the DOTA dataset for the object detection task by using our proposed method.

Keywords: Data augmentation · GAN · Category-oriented · Statistic similarity · Object detection

1 Introduction

Deep learning is one of the essential technologies for the remote sensing tasks, including object detection, image classification, target recognition and etc. It is recognized that, the capabilities of deep learning heavily depend on the quantity of training data. However, it is difficult to obtain or label the remotely sensed images in their non-cooperative imaging mode.

Data augmentation is one of the viable solutions to the above issue, but most of the current data augmentation methods are task specific or dataset specific, which are not as applicable as a generalized solution for the remotely sensed images. Apart from this, for specific task and certain dataset, such as object detection for the sea surface observation using the DOTA dataset [1], some category has more physical significance than the others, such as ship category than the small vehicle category. As these two

S. Yu et al. (Eds.): PRCV 2022, LNCS 13536, pp. 473–483, 2022.
https://doi.org/10.1007/978-3-031-18913-5_37

categories share the same statistical appearance characteristics, like shape, size and space distribution, adversarial generation from the small vehicle to the ship category should be more meaningful. Although very recently, Generative Adversarial Networks (GANs) have been applied to the data augmentation, such as BAGAN [27], DiffAugment [28] and APA [29], the new generated samples are generally lack of physical significance, due to most of them are generated from noise vectors and constrained by some kind of artistic styles. In addition, for the evaluation of GAN-based method, even though various evaluation metrics have been proposed, such as IS [32] and FID [9], the performance of GAN-based data augmentation have never been evaluated as a closed loop of any specific task.

Faced with these problems, a Category-oriented Adversarial Data Augmentation method using statistic similarity, termed as CADA, is proposed in this paper, which formulates the common appearance-based statistic factors in the object detection into a combination index, to depict the statistic similarity between different categories and to generate new adversarial samples between similar categories with more reliable physical significance, which are then fed into object detection for the closed loop evaluation. The novelty and the contributions of this proposed method are as follows:

(1) This is the first time that, the common appearance-based statistic factors in the object detection have been formulated into one combination index, and the statistic similarity between different categories is used to measure the reliability with physical meanings for the new generated samples, in the remote sensing field.
(2) To our best knowledge, this is the first time that GAN has been introduced into data augmentation cross categories, by equipping the physical significance to the new generated samples, and the performance of GAN-based data augmentation is validated in a closed loop task. Compared with that for the entire dataset, this method is more pertinence and can be implemented only for the categories of interest without changing the original annotations.

2 Related Works

2.1 Data Augmentation

Data augmentation methods for deep learning are generally task specific or even dataset specific. As a means of data expansion, in the classification, when trained on MNIST dataset [2], most models utilize scaling, transformation and rotation [3] as a kind of geometric data conversion, and when trained on natural image datasets, most models adopt random flipping and cropping [4] as a kind of data re-editing. When it comes to object detection, cropping, flipping and scaling are generally applied [1]. Apart from these, random erasing, mixup and CutMix have also been proposed [5], to bring some content changes randomly. But most of these methods are limited to the specific task mentioned above.

To avoid this limitation, recent data augmentation methods learn from data directly. Among them, Smart Augmentation generates new data by merging more than two samples from the same category [6]. Bayesian-based approaches generate new data based on the distribution of training sample [7]. Auto Augment searches algorithm space to find the most effective policies [8]. However, most of the methods are limited to classification and are also lack of pertinence to the specific target.

On the other hand, GANs have achieved impressive success for many computer vision tasks, including image generation, image-to-image translation, image completion, super-resolution and etc. [9]. Furthermore, GANs have also been applied to data augmentation, such as BAGAN [27], DiffAugment [28], and APA [29]. However, the new generated samples from the above methods usually are lack of physical significance, due to most of them are generated from the noise vectors. In addition, it is also difficult to evaluate the performance of GAN-based data augmentation methods, even though previous works have proposed various evaluation metrics for GANs, such as IS [32] and FID [9], they have never been evaluated in a closed loop of any specific task.

2.2 Appearance Properties

As one kind of property descriptors of the target object, appearance properties or the visual based properties, have been widely applied in image query, image retrieval [35], visual search [34] and traditional visual tracking [33], etc. Up to now, a series of appearance properties have been devised, such as color descriptors, texture descriptors [35], contour descriptors [30], mixture of Gaussians [33] and etc. While, most of the appearance properties described the feature-level attributes. When it comes to the object in remotely sensed images, these appearance properties may be ineffective, due to the great variation in appearance among the remotely sensed ground surface objects. Facing the problem of data augmentation cross categories, a more reasonable solution is to focus only on the macro attributes of appearance, rather than the details at the feature level.

3 Proposed Method

3.1 Problem Definition and Basic Solutions

In GAN-based data augmentation, the unpaired GANs, such as the CycleGAN and its variants [11], are popular and influential for they don't rely on the source domain and the target domain being in the same low dimensional embedding space or not. Furthermore, unpaired GANs don't require pre-defined sample pairs between source domain and target domain, which brings success in various applications. However, these GANs still suffer from lacking physical significance.

For two similar categories X and Y, the adversarial generation is a two way operation, i.e. from X to Y and from Y to X. Here taking the way that is from X to Y as example, supposing the original sample from the source domain is X, and the new generated sample in the target domain is Y. Facing with the above problems, while maintaining the superiority of unpaired GANs, we can equip them with physical significance by introducing statistic similarity under the following constrains:

(1) The original sample X, which used to generate new adversarial sample Y, should be real images rather than random noise vectors.
(2) The target sample Y, which used to constrain the adversarial generation from the original sample X, should also be real images rather than artistic styles.

(3) To realize a relaxed constrain of the unpaired GANs, the measurement for the similarity between source and target domain should not be feature-level similarity, but a more macro similarity, i.e. the statistic similarity for the appearance of the samples.

On this basis, a Category-oriented Adversarial Data Augmentation method using statistic similarity, the CADA, is proposed in this paper, by which the new generated samples are equipped with physical meanings. Taking ship and vehicle categories discussed above as an example, the overall workflow of our proposed CADA method, is as in Fig. 1.

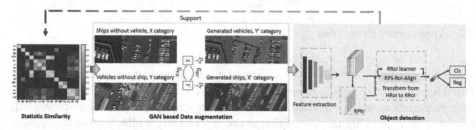

Fig. 1. Workflow of our proposed CADA method.

3.2 Statistic Similarity Evaluation

As we discussed above, similar sensors, similar data acquisition approaches and similar shapes make the targets in different categories possess certain similarity in complexity, scale, appearance and distribution, which can be defined as the statistic similarity. This kind of similarity shouldn't be defined at the feature level, but at a more macro level, the statistic level, which corresponds to the relaxed constrain of unpaired GANs, such as CycleGAN and its variants.

More specifically, statistic similarity $S_{i,j}$ between category i and category j can be formulated using the distance of a newly defined combination index ψ_k as follows:

$$S_{i,j} = e^{-\xi \|\psi_i - \psi_j\|_1}, i, j = 1, \dots, C \tag{1}$$

$$\psi_k = \frac{\sqrt{\rho_k}}{v_k - \frac{1}{1/C \sum v_k}} \times \log\left(\frac{n_k}{N_k}\right), k = 1, \dots, C \tag{2}$$

where, C denotes categories in the dataset, N_k denotes the image number and n_k denotes the target number in category k; ρ_k denotes the averaged target size, v_k denotes the averaged target aspect ratio, $\log\left(\frac{n_k}{N_k}\right)$ means the averaged distribution density in category k; and ξ is simply a scaling factor. We can see that, $S_{i,j} \in (0, 1]$, the bigger the $S_{i,j}$ is, the similar the categories will be; ψ_k can be seen as a descriptor for the statistic appearance of a category, categories with higher statistic similar will have a closer value of ψ_k, such as ψ_k of the two categories of ship (SH) and small vehicle (SV) will be closer than that of ship (SH) and storage tank (ST), in DOTA dataset. We should also mention that, another reason why each statistic factors in Eq.(2) is defined only using statistic property rather than the feature-level ones is that, statistic properties can be pre-acquired before training the network and they keep consistent with the ideology of unpaired GANs.

Taking the DOTA, the most popular object detection dataset in the remote sensing field as an example, ψ_k of the 15 categories are shown as in Fig. 2. From Fig. 2, it can be seen that, if two category i and j possess certain similarity in complexity, scale, appearance and distribution, their ψ_i and ψ_j are also close. And then $S_{i,j}$ becomes large, such as the two categories of the small vehicle (SV) and the ship (SH), and the two categories of the tennis court (TC) and the basketball court (BC). Therefore, $S_{i,j}$ can be utilized to evaluate the statistic similarity between two different categories, and categories which have large statistic similarity can be used in the following adversarial generation.

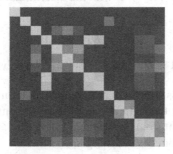

(a) Statistic similarity map between the 15 categories in DOTA dataset.

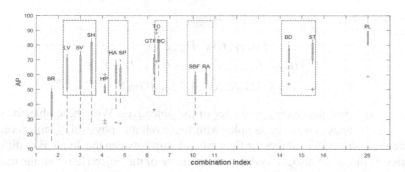

(b) Relation between Ψ_k and object detection accuracy of the 15 categories in DOTA dataset.

Fig. 2. From combination index to statistic similarity.

On the other hand, statistic similarity $S_{i,j}$ between different categories plays a similar role with the confusion matrix of the object detection results, as the most easily confused categories of confusion matrix possess certain similarity in the complexity, scale, appearance or distribution.

3.3 Adversarial Generation Between Similar Categories

Considering that some categories may have more physical significance than other categories for specific purpose, here as an example, the ship category for the sea surface observation is taken as the target category, to achieve data augmentation for it from the other categories.

From the statistic similarity $S_{i,j}$ shown in Fig. 2(a), it can be seen that, the small vehicle category is most similar to the ship category in the DOTA dataset. Therefore, the small vehicle category is selected as the statistic similar category to generate new ship samples. Here, small vehicle category as the source domain is marked as X, and ship category as the target domain is marked as Y. Then, for the given category $\{Y_n\}_{n=1}^N$, $y_n \in Y$, our proposed method will map the most similar samples in the source domain $\{x_m\}_{m=1}^M$, $x_m \in X$ to the target domain Y, using the GAN, i.e. $G_{XY} : X \rightarrow Y$, from the distribution $p_d(x)$ and $p_d(y)$. And certainly, an adversarial generation in backwards from Y to X is also possible. For the mapping $G_{XY} : X \rightarrow Y$ with the discriminator D_Y, the adversarial loss [10] can be formulated as:

$$
\begin{aligned}
&L_{XY}(G_{XY}, D_Y, X, Y) \\
&= E_{y\, p_d(y)}\left[(1 - D_Y(y))^2\right] + E_{x\, p_d(x)}\left[D_Y(G_{XY}(x))^2\right]n
\end{aligned}
\tag{3}
$$

The above adversarial loss tries to match the distribution of G_{XY} to that of the Y, while D_Y tries to distinguish them. In addition, a cycle consistency loss [11] is also applied to mapping an element from one domain to another and backwards, to prevent the mapping G_{XY} and G_{YX} from contradicting each other:

$$
L_{cyc}(G_{XY}) = E_{x \sim p_d(x)}\left[\|G_{YX}(G_{XY}(x)) - x\|_1\right]
\tag{4}
$$

The overall objectives are as the followings:

$$
\begin{aligned}
&L(G_{XY}, G_{YX}, D_X, D_Y) \\
&= L_{XY}(G_{XY}, D_Y, X, Y) + L_{YX}(G_{YX}, D_X, Y, X) \\
&\quad + \lambda L_{cyc}(G_{XY}) + \lambda L_{cyc}(G_{YX})
\end{aligned}
\tag{5}
$$

where, λ is used to balance the importance of the objectives. With these objectives, the mapping encourages generating samples with more reliable physical significance, and the cycle-consistency encourages the tight relationship between the domains of different categories. It should be also noticed that, the premise of the objective is that the training samples have certain structural consistency, including the complexity, scale, appearance and distribution, which is consistent with the statistic similarity.

In Fig. 1, the image samples are cropped into 256×256 blocks and then fed into the network. The network is consisting of 2D CNN with 9 residual blocks for generator [12] and 70×70 PatchGAN for discriminators [13]. After training, the trained network will generate new samples from the source domain to the target domain, so as to realize an effective data augmentation. Through these operations, the new generated samples are equipped with more reliable physical significance, which are then fed into the final task, such as the following task of object detection in the remotely sensed field, for a closed loop evaluation.

3.4 Task of Object Detection

Here, we take object detection as the final task. Up to now, most of the CNN-based object detection methods for remotely sensed images can be divided into directly regression based methods [1], rotated anchors based methods [22] [23] and transformation based methods [15].

Considering the effectiveness and efficiency of these methods, we concentrate on the transformation based methods. And ResNet101 [14] is selected as the backbone, which is pre-trained on the natural image dataset, the ImageNet, to acquire general feature extraction and representation ability. Then, the pre-trained feature extraction network will be transferred to the dataset of remotely sensed images for object detection, with our proposed data augmentation method.

After the feature extraction, we utilize the horizontal anchors, and set the batch size of RPN to 512. Considering the trade-off between the time-consuming and precision, the scale and ratio of the anchor are set to $\{4^2, 8^2, 16^2, 32^2, 64^2\}$ and $\{1/2, 1/1, 2/1\}$ respectively. Then, the rotation-invariant features are extracted using the Rotated Position Sensitive RoI Align [15]. There are 6000 RoIs from the RPN before Non-maximum Suppression (NMS). And fully-connected layers are attached to the output of NMS, similar to the light head RCNN [16], for reducing computation purpose. In the training, a mini-batch is set to 100, and the learning rate is set to 0.0005 with the moment set to 0.9.

4 Experimental Results

Finally, the new generated samples are fed into object detection for the closed loop evaluation on the DOTA dataset [1]. The DOTA dataset is designed for the task of object detection in remote sensing field, which is collected from various sensors and platforms, and consists of 2,806 satellite and aerial images with diverse scales, aspect ratio and arbitrary orientation, ranging from 800×800 to 4000×4000. There are 15 categories and 188,282 instances in this dataset. We should mention that, comparing with the natural image datasets, such as the ImageNet dataset, which have tens of millions of samples, the largest remotely sensed dataset, the scale of DOTA dataset is still quite small. The lack of samples in the remote sensing field, particularly need the technique of data augmentation.

Through the statistic similar categories of DOTA dataset, i.e. the ship category and the small vehicle category, this proposed method can generate new ship samples from small vehicle samples, and vice versa. Figure 3 gives two examples of the original and new generated ship samples from the small vehicle category.

As for the detection of ship objects, the official RoI transformer method (RT) [15] is taken as the baseline method as in [31], training on the selected categories with and without CADA method, to compare the accuracy of object detection. From Table 1 it can be seen that, by using our proposed data augmentation method, the accuracy of ship category can be improved by 2.0% compared with that of the baseline method. And, the final mAP of the RT method trained on the new augmented data, surpasses that with the improvements of network structures.

(a1) Original small vehicle sample

(b1) New generated ship sample from (a1)

(a2) Original small vehicle sample

(b2) New generated ship sample from (a2)

Fig. 3. New generated ship samples from the small vehicle category.

Table 1. Comparison between different methods for the ship category using the same baseline on the DOTA dataset.

Method	mAP
RT [15]	70.8
RT + ACNet [17]	71.1
RT + RON [18]	71.7
RT + SE [19]	72.1
RT + ASPP [20]	72.5
RT + CADA	72.8

To demonstrate the effectiveness of our proposed method, 10 representative object detection methods of Object Detection in Aerial Images (ODAI) challenge are compared on the DOTA dataset, the comparative experimental results are shown in Table 2, in which the best results are shown in bold and suboptimal are in underline. From Table 2, it can be seen that, the accuracy surpasses most of the other methods by using our proposed CADA method, especially for the ship and small vehicle categories.

Table 2. Comparison between different methods for all the categories in the DOTA dataset.

	mAP	PL	BD	BR	GTF	SV	LV	SH	TC	BC	ST	SBF	RA	HA	SP	HC
FR-O [1]	40.7	58.9	59.2	15.8	36.4	23.9	21.1	28.2	69.0	61.3	50.3	33.0	46.1	37.1	41.3	29.0
Retina [21]	47.6	80.0	53.8	31.8	46.7	46.1	39.4	51.8	90.5	59.6	50.2	26.9	54.7	27.9	27.2	27.5
RDFPN [25]	57.9	80.9	65.8	33.8	58.9	55.8	50.9	54.8	90.3	66.3	68.7	48.7	51.8	55.1	51.3	35.9
R2CNN [22]	60.7	**88.5**	71.2	31.7	59.3	51.9	56.2	57.3	90.8	72.8	67.4	56.7	52.8	53.1	51.9	53.6
RRPN [23]	61.0	80.9	65.8	35.3	67.4	59.9	50.9	55.8	90.7	66.9	72.4	55.1	52.2	55.1	53.4	48.2
LR-O [16]	62.0	81.1	77.1	32.3	72.6	48.5	49.4	50.5	89.9	72.6	73.7	**61.4**	58.7	54.8	59.0	48.7
Yang [26]	62.3	81.3	71.4	36.5	67.4	61.2	50.9	56.6	90.7	68.1	72.4	55.1	55.6	62.4	53.4	51.5
DCN [24]	62.5	85.0	75.7	31.6	**73.4**	58.9	46.1	60.7	89.6	75.2	76.8	52.3	**61.7**	47.6	58.7	44.0
RT [15]	69.1	87.2	**82.9**	49.5	59.5	70.7	69.6	67.4	**90.9**	**84.4**	76.0	53.6	58.3	66.5	65.6	54.6
RT + CADA	**70.7**	86.8	75.9	**52.4**	68.6	**73.6**	**77.6**	**72.8**	90.0	78.9	**77.4**	46.3	59.2	**74.9**	**69.6**	**55.8**

5 Conclusion

Facing with the limitation of current data augmentation methods, a category-oriented adversarial data augmentation method using statistic similarity cross categories, termed as CADA, is proposed in this paper, which formulates the common appearance-based statistic factors in the object detection into a combination index, to depict the statistic similarity between different categories and to generate new adversarial samples between similar categories with more reliable physical significance. Experimental results on the DOTA dataset have demonstrated the effectiveness of this proposed method. Subsequent works would focus on the universality of this proposed method across different datasets.

Acknowledgement. This work was supported in part by the National Nature Science Foundation (41971294), China Postdoctoral Science Foundation (2020M680560) and Cross-Media Intelligent Technology Project of BNRist (BNR2019TD01022) of China.

References

1. Xia, G.S., Bai, X., Ding, J., et al.: DOTA: A large-scale dataset for object detection in aerial images. In: IEEE Conference on Computer Vision and Pattern Recognition. CVPR, pp. 3974–3983 (2018)
2. LeCun, Y., Bottou, L., Bengio, Y., et al.: Gradient-based learning applied to document recognition. Proc. IEEE **86**(11), 2278–2324 (1998)

3. Wan, L., Zeiler, M., Zhang, S., et al.: Regularization of Neural Networks using Dropconnect. In: International Conference on Machine Learning. ICLR, pp. 1058–1066 (2013)
4. Zagoruyko, S., Komodakis, N.: Wide Residual Networks. British Machine Vision Conference (2016)
5. Zhong, Z., Zheng, L., Kang, G., et al.: Random erasing data augmentation. In: AAAI Conference on Artificial Intelligence. **34**(07), 13001–13008 (2020)
6. Lemley, J., Bazrafkan, S., Corcoran, P.: Smart augmentation learning an optimal data augmentation strategy. IEEE Access **5**, 5858–5869 (2017)
7. Tran, T., Pham, T., Carneiro, G., et al.: A bayesian data augmentation approach for learning deep models. In: Advances in Neural Information Processing Systems, pp. 2794–2803 (2017)
8. Cubuk, E.D., Zoph, B., Mane, D., et al.: Autoaugment: Learning Augmentation Policies from Data. arXiv preprint arXiv:1805.09501 (2018)
9. Wang, Z., She, Q., Ward, T.E.: Generative adversarial networks in computer vision: a survey and taxonomy. ACM Computing Surveys (CSUR) **54**(2), 1–38 (2021)
10. Goodfellow, I., Pouget-Abadie, J., Mirza, M., et al.: Generative adversarial nets. Advances in Neural Information Processing Systems, NIPS, p. 27 (2014)
11. Zhu, J.Y., Park, T., Isola, P., et al.: Unpaired image-to-image translation using cycle-consistent adversarial networks. In: IEEE International Conference on Computer Vision. ICCV, pp. 2223–2232 (2017)
12. Johnson, J., Alahi, A., Fei-Fei, L.: Perceptual losses for real-time style transfer and super-resolution. In: Leibe, B., Matas, J., Sebe, N., Welling, M. (eds.) ECCV 2016. LNCS, vol. 9906, pp. 694–711. Springer, Cham (2016). https://doi.org/10.1007/978-3-319-46475-6_43
13. Isola, P., Zhu, J.Y., Zhou, T., et al.: Image-to-image translation with conditional adversarial networks. In: IEEE Conference on Computer Vision and Pattern Recognition. CVPR, pp. 1125–1134 (2017)
14. He, K., Zhang, X., Ren, S., et al.: Deep residual learning for image recognition. In: IEEE Conference on Computer Vision and Pattern Recognition. CVPR, pp. 770–778 (2016)
15. Ding, J., Xue, N., Long, Y., et al.: Learning roi transformer for oriented object detection in aerial images. In: IEEE/CVF Conference on Computer Vision and Pattern Recognition. CVPR, pp. 2849–2858 (2019)
16. Li, Z., Peng, C., Yu, G., et al.: Light-head R-CNN: In: Defense of Two-stage Object Detector. arXiv preprint arXiv:1711.07264 (2017)
17. Ding, X., Guo, Y., Ding, G., et al.: Acnet: Strengthening the kernel skeletons for powerful CNN via asymmetric convolution blocks. In: IEEE/CVF International Conference on Computer Vision. ICCV, pp. 1911–1920 (2019)
18. Kong, T., Sun, F., Yao, A., et al.: Ron: reverse connection with objectness prior networks for object detection. In: IEEE Conference on Computer Vision and Pattern Recognition. CVPR, pp. 5936–5944 (2017)
19. Hu, J., Shen, L., Sun, G.: Squeeze-and-excitation networks. In: IEEE Conference on Computer Vision and Pattern Recognition. CVPR, pp. 7132–7141 (2018)
20. Chen, L.C., Papandreou, G., Kokkinos, I., et al.: Deeplab: semantic image segmentation with deep convolutional nets, atrous convolution, and fully connected crfs. IEEE Trans. Pattern Analysis Machine Intelligence **40**(4), 834–848, (2017)
21. Lin, T.Y., Goyal, P., Girshick, R., et al.: Focal loss for dense object detection. IEEE Trans. Pattern Analysis Machine Intelligence pp. 2999–3007 (2017)
22. Jiang, Y., Zhu, X., Wang, X., et al.: R2CNN: rotational region cnn for orientation robust scene text detection. arXiv preprint arXiv:1706.09579 (2017)
23. Ma, J., Shao, W., Ye, H., et al.: Arbitrary-oriented scene text detection via rotation proposals. IEEE Transactions on Multimedia **20**(11), 3111–3122 (2018)
24. Dai, J., Qi, H., Xiong, Y., et al.: Deformable convolutional networks. In: IEEE International Conference on Computer Vision. ICCV, pp. 764–773 (2017)

25. Yang, X., et al.: Automatic ship detection in remote sensing images from google earth of complex scenes based on multiscale rotation dense feature pyramid networks. Remote Sensing **10**(1), 132 (2018)
26. Yang, X., Sun, H., Sun, X., Yan, M., Guo, Z., Fu, K.: Position detection and direction prediction for arbitrary-oriented ships via multiscale rotation region convolutional neural network. IEEE Access **6**, 50839–50849 (2018)
27. Mariani, G., Scheidegger, F., Istrate, R., et al.: Bagan: Data Augmentation with Balancing GAN. arXiv preprint arXiv:1803.09655 (2018)
28. Zhao, S., Liu, Z., Lin, J., et al.: Differentiable augmentation for data-efficient GAN training. Adv. Neural. Inf. Process. Syst. **33**, 7559–7570 (2020)
29. Jiang, L., Dai, B., Wu, W., et al.: Deceive D: Adaptive pseudo augmentation for GAN training with limited data. Advances in Neural Inf. Processing Systems **34**, 2165521667 (2021)
30. Schindler, K., Suter, D.: Object detection by global contour shape. Pattern Recogn. **41**(12), 3736–3748 (2008)
31. Zhang, H., Xu, Z., Han, X., et al.: Refining FFT-based heatmap for the detection of cluster distributed targets in satellite images, British Machine Vision Conference (2021)
32. Shmelkov, K., Schmid, C., Alahari, K.: How good Is my GAN? In: Ferrari, V., Hebert, M., Sminchisescu, C., Weiss, Y. (eds.) ECCV 2018. LNCS, vol. 11206, pp. 218–234. Springer, Cham (2018). https://doi.org/10.1007/978-3-030-01216-8_14
33. Wang, H., Suter, D., Schindler, K.: Effective appearance model and similarity measure for particle filtering and visual tracking. In: European Conference on Computer Vision. Springer, Berlin, Heidelberg, pp. 606–618 (2006). https://doi.org/10.1007/11744078_47
34. Bell, S., Bala, K.: Learning visual similarity for product design with convolutional neural networks. ACM Trans. Graphics (TOG) **34**(4), 1–10 (2015)
35. Siggelkow, S., Schael, M., Burkhardt, H.: SIMBA—search IMages by appearance. In: Joint Pattern Recognition Symposium. Springer, Berlin, Heidelberg, pp. 9-16 (2001). https://doi.org/10.1007/3-540-45404-7_2

A Multi-scale Convolutional Neural Network Based on Multilevel Wavelet Decomposition for Hyperspectral Image Classification

Changlong Yang, Dongmei Song[✉], Bin Wang, and Yunhe Tang

College of Oceanography and Space Informatics, China University of Petroleum (East China),
Qingdao 266580, China
{S20160049,s20160043}@s.upc.edu.cn, {songdongmei,
wangbin007}@upc.edu.cn

Abstract. Deep learning methods have outclassed traditional methods in hyperspectral image classification (HIC). However, due to the limited size of input 3D cube, most HIC networks are shallow in depth, resulting in effectiveness constrained. Multi-scale convolution operation has arisen to alleviate this issue by expanding width of neural networks. Though multi-scale CNN is able to enhance the classification capacity in some extent, there are still some inherent disadvantages, such as heavy computation burden and inadequate multi-scale features extraction. To address these, this paper proposes a multi-scale dense network based on multilevel wavelet decomposition for HIC. The proposed approach characterizes multi-scale features by establishing multiple branches with 2D discrete wavelet transform rather than multi-scale convolution and pooling. Various features are joined with others from adjacent branches by level-wise short cut for supporting classification decision. Otherwise, the dense block is modified to fuse multi-frequency features and fetch underlying scale information with dense connections. The experimental results on Pavia University and University of Houston datasets demonstrate that proposed approach acquires competitive performance with the state-of-the-arts and only requires less computation and time consumptions.

Keywords: Hyperspectral image classification · Multi-scale CNN · Multilevel wavelet decomposition · Dense connection

1 Introduction

Hyperspectral images (HSIs), which contain hundreds of bands with rich spectral information of objects, are extensively applied in vegetation inversion [1], mineral identification [2], precision agriculture [3] and other fields. Hyperspectral image classification (HIC) is one of core tasks of HSIs interpretation. Distinguished from traditional remote sensing imagery classification, hyperspectral tasks focus on the pixel-level classification rather than the scene classification. With the breakthrough of deep learning, neural network methods are generally superior to conventional machine learning methods (i.e.,

S. Yu et al. (Eds.): PRCV 2022, LNCS 13536, pp. 484–496, 2022.
https://doi.org/10.1007/978-3-031-18913-5_38

KNN [4], SVM [5], EMP [6] and MRF [7]), which has been more and more favored in HIC task.

Due to the complex and pervasive spectral mixing phenomenon, methods merely refer to spectral characteristics are prone to misclassify ground objects. Therefore, many networks combined spectral and spatial features for HIC have been proposed. For example, Zhong et al. [8] proposed a spatial-spectral residual network by 3D residual blocks. In [9], the spatial features are extracted by CNN, while spectral features are abstracted by local spatial compression. Then both of them are merged for classification.

In computer vision, the size of input images is up to hundreds of pixels, which can sustain multiple extraction for deep networks. However, the input 3D patches are undersized in length and width, generally no more than 30 × 30 pixels, making spatial-spectral networks hard to go farther. So that nonlinear fitting potential of network is significantly affected. Whereas, inspired by [10], some studies consider to extend the width of the network by multi-scale convolutional layers, consisting of convolutional kernels with different sizes in single layer. For instance, He et al. [11] proposed multi-scale 3D convolution to directly extract mixed spatial-spectral features. In [12], a multi-scale dense block based on 3D convolution was constructed, achieving excellent classification results. Many other researches have indicated that scale information given by multi-scale CNNs is of great benefit to HIC task. In fact, scale characteristics contain semantic information about the pixels as part of a complete object or region and topological information about the relative spatial positions, which can compensate for misclassification caused by spectral mixture to a large extent. However, there are still some problems regarding the current multi-scale CNNs in the following aspects: (1) The multi-scale convolutional kernels increases the computation cost and parameter amount. (2) To reduce the size of images and extract deeper features, the pooling operation is adopted excessively in the network, which inevitably leads to information obliterated. (3) The extraction and utilization of multiscale information is insufficient. The classification networks are more dependent on the posterior layers, thus the multi-scale information mattering to the final decision of such networks, comes more from the deeper features that have been fully abstracted, resulting in insufficient information extraction.

To cope with the above issues, we intend to replace the traditional multi-scale convolution operation by constructing multi-branch structure based on two-dimensional discrete wavelet transform (2D-DWT) [13], which can separate treatment procedure for more effective multiscale feature extraction. 2D-DWT is an image decomposition algorithm that can disassemble a digital image into various scaled components, called wavelet coefficients. The wavelet coefficient is accessed to multi-resolution analysis (MRA), as the frequency-domain description of spatial image that contains global topology information and local texture information, which is widely employed in the fields of image compression [14], denoising [15], restoration [16] and classification [17, 18].

With the backbone of DenseNet [19], this paper proposes a multilevel wavelet based dense network (MLWBDN), which is a multi-scale CNN with multi-branch structure. The 2D-DWT is adopted in each branch for semantic multiscale information separation. Since the decomposed wavelet coefficients theoretically have no loss of spatial information, it is a better compression method than pooling. Meanwhile, this paper also proposes a successively attached dense fusion block (SADFB) modified from dense block to incorporate multi-frequency wavelet features. The multi-scale outputs of branches can exchange information to compensate for the global information lacking of convolution, and these features are eventually joint to classify.

The main contributions in this paper are summarized as follows. (1) A multi-scale deep CNN based on multilevel wavelet decomposition is proposed. Differing the existing multi-scale CNN, the proposed method integrates multilevel wavelet transforms into branches. Thus, feature learning occurs over not only varying low to high frequencies but also multiple scales. In experiments, the proposed model can provide outstanding classification accuracy on HSI datasets even with inadequate training samples. (2) In order to balance the information gain derived from wavelet components and the accompanying parameter and computation obstacle, the SADFB module is proposed for multi-frequency feature fusion. (3) The proposed network has adopted the parameter-free 2D-DWT instead of multi-scale convolution and pooling operations and employed techniques such as feature compression and depth separable convolution. Hence, our network is compact and succinct to reduce running time.

The reminder of the article is organized as follows, Sect. 2 is a brief introduction about 2D discrete wavelet transform and DenseNet. The details of proposed MLWBDN are described in Sect. 3. After that, Sect. 4 systematically elaborates the experimental results and discussions. Finally, Sect. 5 devotes the conclusions of the article.

2 Related Works

2.1 2D Discrete Wavelet Transform

Wavelet transform (WT) is a transformation analysis method inherited and developed from the short-term Fourier transform. Two-dimension discrete wavelet transform is an image analysis method via extending the wavelet transform to 2D, which inherits the multi-resolution analysis capability of wavelet transform and provides a powerful insight into spatial and frequency-domain characteristics of images.

According to 2D-DWT, arbitrary discrete image can be expressed as a linear combination of 2D scale functions and 2D wavelet functions , as shown in Eq. (1) to (3).

$$
f(x, y) = \frac{1}{\sqrt{MN}} \sum_m \sum_n W_\varphi(j_0, m, n) \varphi_{j_0, m, n}(x, y)
$$
$$
+ \frac{1}{\sqrt{MN}} \sum_{j=j_0}^{\infty} \sum_i \sum_m \sum_n W_\psi^i(j, m, n) \psi_{j, m, n}^i(x, y) \tag{1}
$$

$$
W_\varphi(j_0, m, n) = \frac{1}{\sqrt{MN}} \sum_{x=0}^{M-1} \sum_{y=0}^{N-1} f(x, y) \varphi_{j_0, m, n}(x, y) \tag{2}
$$

$$
W_\psi^i(j, m, n) = \frac{1}{\sqrt{MN}} \sum_{x=0}^{M-1} \sum_{y=0}^{N-1} f(x, y) \psi_{j, m, n}^i(x, y), \ i \in \{LH, HL, HH\} \tag{3}
$$

where j denotes scale, $(m.n)$ denotes spatial positions. W_φ and W_ψ^i represent the approximation coefficient and detail coefficient, and $i \in \{LH, HL, HH\}$, stands for different directional components. (M, N) is the size of sub-bands.

Since wavelet coefficients are ordinarily complex for calculation, Mallat et al. [13] put forward the fast wavelet transform (FWT), which simplifies the operations as twice spectral filtering and down-sampling sequentially by rows and columns. In general, 2D-DWT can resolve an image into one approximate component LL and three high-frequency components with halving size, corresponding to horizontal (HL), vertical (LH), and diagonal details (HH). The approximate component can be decomposed again to obtain wavelet coefficients at next scale. The multiple frequency features of different resolutions obtained during multilevel decomposition together constitute the "wavelet fingerprint" of images.

2.2 DenseNet

DenseNet is a classic deep CNN that consists of several dense blocks, as shown in Fig. 1. The network enables feature reuse via dense connection, by which the outputs of all preceding layers are used as inputs into all subsequent layers in the dense block. Dense Blocks contain multiple convolutional layers, called dense layers. Each dense layer accepts the output of all previous layers as its additional input. The principle can be expressed as follows:

$$x_l = H_l([x_0, x_1, ..., x_{l-1}]) \tag{4}$$

where represents output of the ith dense layer, denotes a nonlinear function fitted to the neural network. The output channel of dense layer is fixed to the growth rate K. Assumed that the input channels of dense block is K_0, then input channels of the ith layer will be i[th] . Therefore, as the amount of layer increases, even if K is very small, subsequent dense layers are still given a large amount of input. To reduce parameters, the bottleneck layer with 1×1 convolution can be added before partial dense layer.

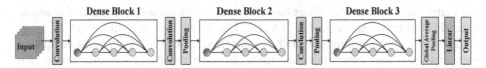

Fig. 1. The structure of DenseNet

3 Proposed Framework

As depicted in Fig. 2, the framework of MLWBDN comprises of three scale branches. The inputs of network are hyperspectral 3D patches after dimensionality reduction by PCA. These samples are firstly decomposed and compressed in multiple frequency feature decomposition block (MFFDB), which contains 2D-DWT operation. Then frequency features can be fused in the successively attached dense fusion block (SADFB). The fused features are fed to the next scale branch for decomposition and fusion. And they will also be sent to participate in the final classification decision through their own classifiers, respectively. The eventual classification result of the network depends on the multi-scale features extracted by different branches. The detailed description of the MLWBDN is given as follows.

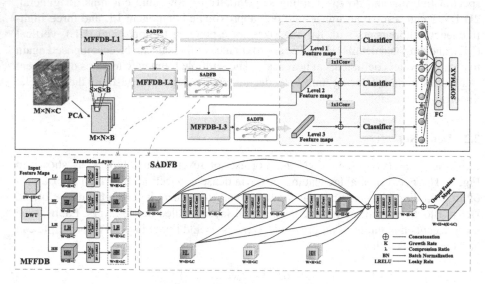

Fig. 2. The structure of MLWBDN-L3

The MFFDB module aims to decompose and compress feature maps which come from the input or previous branch by 2D-DWT. This module can transfer a $2W \times 2H \times C$ feature map into a low-frequency approximation sub-band LL and three high-frequency detail sub-bands HL, LH, and HH. All of sub-bands is halved in spatial domain with size of $W \times H \times C$. Then the four multi-frequency features are each fed into the transition layers to condense the output in spectral domain. The transition layer is composed of 1 $\times$ 1 convolution, and compression ratio λ is set to control the output channel dimension. After this layer, the channel size of {LL, HL, LH, HH} changes from C to λC.

2D-DWT operation produces four components, which brings abundant details but increases the feature channels to four times. In order to balance the information gain and computation burden, this paper proposes the successively attached dense fusion block (SADFB) modified from dense block. The SADFB aims to fuse multi-frequency wavelet features and extract in-depth scale features through densely connected operations, and reduce the parameters through successively attached (SA) strategy. Given that the approximate components retain most of the original image information, the SADFB uses LL only as the initial input, instead of all the components after concatenation. The rest of HL, LH, and HH features is to be added subsequently in the dense connection procedure, as illustrated in Fig. 2 shown. Each dense layer in SADFB consists of a $1 \times 1 \times 4K$ convolutional bottleneck and $3 \times 3 \times K$ convolution layer, where K is the growth rate. Assuming that the size of {LL, HL, LH, HH} obtained after MFFDB is W × H × K_0, the input channels for each dense layer in SADFB and dense block are defined as follows:

$$l_{SAD}^i = K_0 \times i + K \times (i - 1) \tag{5}$$

$$l_{BD}^i = 4K_0 + K \times (i - 1), i = 1, 2, 3, 4 \tag{6}$$

where l_{SAD}^i and respectively denote input the channel of ith layer in SADFB or classic dense block. Comparing Eq. (5) with Eq. (6), the SA strategy alleviates parameter pressure by decreasing channels of wavelet features fed to dense layers. Therefore, the more channels entered, the more pronounced of the effect.

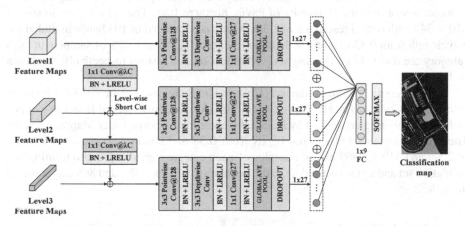

Fig. 3. The multi-branch structure of joint features decision mechanism

Figure 3 shows the tertiary joint feature decision mechanism adopted on the Pavia University dataset. Level1, Level2 and Level3 feature maps extracted by MFFDB and SADFB are fed into the classifiers of their respective scale branches to improve the classification ability. The classifier also employs the depth separable convolution [20] and 1 × 1 convolution to reduce the parameters. Due to the distinct sizes of feature maps from different branches, the global average pooling (GAP) [21] is used to map features into vectors. Otherwise, dropout is employed to enhance model generalization. The vectors generated from three branches are supposed to be concatenated before passing through fully connected layer for incorporating multi-scale decision. It is worth noting that, our network bridges different branches by establishing level-wise short cut before multi-scale features enter their classifier, in order to enhance the information interaction and gradient transmission between features of different scale level.

4 Experimental Results and Discussion

To evaluate the performance of proposed model, this paper has conducted the experiments upon two benchmark datasets, i.e. Pavia University and University of Houston. In order to verify MLWBDNs at different scales, MLWBDN-L1, MLWBDN-L2, MLWBDN-L3 networks are established with incremental branches from 1 to 3, whose performances are compared with state-of-the-art methods such as SSRN [8], M3DCNN [11], and HybridSN [22]. The experiments are conducted in Pytorch with CPU i7-7700K and the GPU GTX1080Ti.

4.1 HIS Datasets

Pavia University dataset (PU) was recorded by Reflective Optics System Imaging Spectrometer sensor over the University of Pavia, northern Italy. The PU image is in size of 640×340 with spatial resolution of $1.3m$, which is composed of 103 bands included the wavelength from 0.43 to $0.86\mu m$. In experiments, 5%, 5% and 90% of samples in each category are divided into training set, validation set and test set respectively, as shown in Table 1.

The University of Houston dataset (UH) was firstly released in the 2013 IEEE GRSS Data Fusion Contest. The HU data was acquired over the University of Houston campus and the neighboring urban area by National Center for Airborne Laser Mapping sensor. The imagery obtains 144 spectral bands from 0.38 to $1.05\mu m$ with spatial resolution of $2.5m$ and 349×1905 pixels. Samples of each category are divided into training set, validation set and test set according to the percentage of 10%, 10% and 80%, as depicted in Table 2.

Table 1. The number of training, validation and test samples for the PU dataset

No.	Class	Train.	Val.	Test
1	Asphalt	332	331	5968
2	Meadows	933	932	16784
3	Gravel	105	105	1889
4	Trees	153	153	2758
5	Metal Sheets	67	67	1211
6	Bare Soil	252	251	4526
7	Bitumen	66	67	1197
8	Bricks	184	184	3314
9	Shadows	47	48	852
-	Total	2139	2138	38499

Table 2. The number of training, validation and test samples for the UH dataset

No.	Class	Train.	Val.	Test
1	Healthy grass	125	125	1001
2	Stressed grass	126	125	1003
3	Synthetic grass	69	70	558
4	Trees	125	124	995
5	Soil	124	124	994
6	Water	32	33	260
7	Residential	127	126	1015
8	Commercial	125	124	995
9	Road	125	125	1002
10	Highway	122	123	982
11	Railway	124	123	988
12	Parking Lot1	123	124	986
13	Parking Lot2	47	47	375
14	Tennis Court	43	43	342
15	Running Track	66	66	528
-	Total	1503	1502	12024

4.2 Experimental Setting

To avoid the fluctuations of classification results due to random sampling, all experiments were repeated by 5 times. The mean of several evaluation indicators are calculated to depict and analyze the performance of aforementioned methods. Since each wavelet decomposition spatially reduces the feature maps in half, the optimal input patch sizes for three MLWBDNs are not exclusive. In our experiments, the patch sizes of MLWBDN-L1, MLWBDN-L2 and MLWBDN-L3 are set to 10×10, 16×16 and 24×24 pixels. The principal component analysis is adopted to reduce spectral dimension of HSIs, after that 15 principal components are retained in MLWBDNs. The Haar wavelet [23] is selected to implement transform. The MLWBDNs employ Adam optimizer with learning rate of 0.001, weight decay of 1e-6 while the training lasts for 300 epochs with cross entropy loss function.

4.3 Results and Discussion

The overall accuracy (OA), the average accuracy (AA) and kappa coefficient are recorded to evaluate the classification performance of models. From the results on PU dataset as shown in Table 3, MLWBDN-L3 has achieved the best OA of 99.80%, which is 2.6% higher than the M3DCNN based on multi-scale 3D convolution, and a little higher than the well-known networks SSRN and HybridSN. It is worth noting that the MLWBDN-L1 and MLWBDN-L2 also have achieved higher OA than M3DCNN and HybridSN, and are slightly inferior to SSRN less than 0.1%. The increasing classification accuracy of three MLWBDNs indicates the effectiveness of multi-scale features joint decision mechanism of the model.

As shown in Table 4, the classification results of the proposed models are superior to the other contrast models on the UH dataset, among which the MLWBDN-L2 outperforms. The performance of MLWBDN-L1 is quite close to MLWBDN-L2, while MLWBDN-L3 is slightly under-performing to the other two. The spatial resolution of the UH data is 2.5 m, which is about twice of PU data, while the image scale corresponding to the adjacent branches in MLWBDN is duple as well. So if the MLWBDN-L3 model achieves the optimal accuracy on the PU dataset, it can be speculated that MLWBDN-L2 is supposed to perform better on the UH dataset, which is consistent with the experimental results.

Table 3. Classification results of the PU dataset

Class	M3DCNN [11]	SSRN[8]	Hybrid SN [22]	MLWBDN-L1	MLWBDN-L2	MLWBDN-L3
1	97.38	99.69	99.70	99.80	**99.85**	99.84
2	98.56	99.94	**99.99**	**99.99**	**99.99**	99.98
3	91.16	98.84	97.35	98.09	98.97	**99.92**
4	97.61	98.98	97.27	**99.08**	98.59	98.95
5	99.88	**99.98**	99.63	99.92	99.70	99.90
6	94.66	99.90	99.92	99.95	**100**	**100**
7	88.51	99.39	99.43	99.83	99.98	**100**
8	96.41	99.47	97.74	98.58	99.04	**99.56**
9	99.19	**99.75**	96.82	99.55	97.35	98.15
OA(%)	97.04	99.72	99.31	99.66	99.67	**99.80**
AA(%)	95.93	99.55	98.65	99.42	99.28	**99.59**
$\kappa \times 100$	96.08	99.62	99.10	99.55	99.56	**99.74**

The quantitative superiority of MLWBDNs is qualitatively manifested as that the classified regions in classification map are smoother and more intact depicted in Figs. 4 and 5. The classification maps of our networks demonstrate that high-level MLWBDN is more suitable for high resolution imagery which is absorbed in bigger objects and larger scale, to yield more complete and smoother classification maps. In contrast, lower-level counterpart pays more attention to the details and small scale for HSIs in low spatial resolution. It turns out that the proposed method can extract features from different levels of detail to carry out multi-resolution analysis, which makes our method more versatile and flexible in practical application scenarios.

Table 4. Classification results of the UH dataset

Class	M3DCNN [11]	SSRN[8]	Hybrid SN [22]	MLWBDN-L1	MLWBDN-L2	MLWBDN-L3
1	97.80	**99.55**	98.84	99.04	98.66	97.98
2	99.05	99.47	99.57	99.40	**99.68**	99.56
3	99.37	**100**	99.87	99.93	99.86	99.64
4	99.19	**99.71**	99.30	99.70	99.54	99.02
5	99.36	99.98	99.98	99.84	**100**	99.98
6	87.42	97.27	96.23	**98.69**	97.85	94.92
7	92.08	97.73	97.03	98.96	**98.96**	98.76
8	85.76	96.49	98.52	98.27	**98.85**	98.75
9	88.63	93.45	95.56	98.16	**98.76**	98.32
10	91.78	98.47	99.36	99.53	99.90	**99.98**
11	90.74	97.99	99.57	99.82	99.76	**99.88**
12	92.46	98.17	**98.84**	98.82	98.52	98.74
13	86.72	95.36	96.37	98.51	**98.61**	97.12
14	97.87	99.94	99.94	**100**	100	100
15	99.11	99.96	99.72	**99.96**	99.92	99.89
OA(%)	93.96	98.22	98.67	99.22	**99.29**	99.03
AA(%)	93.82	98.24	98.58	99.24	**99.26**	98.84
κ × 100	93.47	98.07	98.56	99.15	**99.23**	98.95

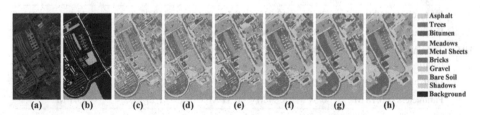

Asphalt
Trees
Bitumen
Meadows
Metal Sheets
Bricks
Gravel
Bare Soil
Shadows
Background

(a)   (b)   (c)   (d)   (e)   (f)   (g)   (h)

Fig. 4. The Classification maps for the UH dataset: (a) Origin image, (b) Ground-truth map, (c) M3DCNN, (d) SSRN, (e) HybridSN, (f) MLWBDN-L1, (g) MLWBDN-L2, (h) MLWBDN-L3

Table 5 lists the time cost and parameter quantities for different deep learning algorithms. The MLWBDN-L1 with single branch structure spends the least amount of time on training and inferring, followed by the HybridSN, which is a little bit faster than MLWBDN-L2 but memory consumed. Overall, with the increase of branch structure, the time consumption is incremental, as well as parameter quantity of MLWBDNs. Nevertheless, benefiting by various reduction strategies, the parameter only reaches 2.41M. So that training cost is acceptable even for MLWBDN-L3.

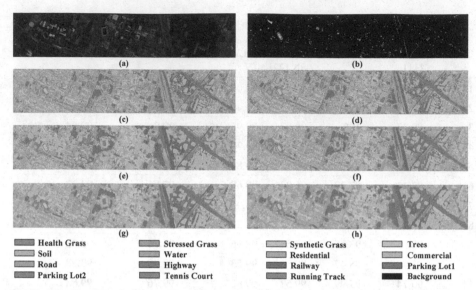

▨ Health Grass	▨ Stressed Grass	▨ Synthetic Grass	▨ Trees
▨ Soil	▨ Water	▨ Residential	▨ Commercial
▨ Road	▨ Highway	▨ Railway	▨ Parking Lot1
▨ Parking Lot2	▨ Tennis Court	▨ Running Track	▨ Background

Fig. 5. The Classification maps for the UH dataset: (a) Origin image, (b) Ground-truth map, (c) M3DCNN, (d) SSRN, (e) HybridSN, (f) MLWBDN-L1, (g) MLWBDN-L2, (h) MLWBDN-L3

Table 5. Cost of time and amount of parameters for different neural networks on two datasets

Methods							
Dataset		M3DCNN [11]	SSRN [8]	Hybrid SN [22]	MLWBDN-L1	MLWBDN-L2	MLWBDN-L3
PU	Training (s/ep)	2.84	3.56	0.84	**0.59**	1.11	1.47
	Inferring (s)	10.9	21.1	13.2	**8.5**	18.2	31.6
	Parameters	0.08 M	0.39 M	4.84M	0.48 M	1.08 M	1.72 M
UH	Training (s/ep)	1.65	4.36	0.58	**0.38**	0.67	0.98
	Inferring (s)	42.8	89.9	42.1	**26.6**	57.2	104.9
	Parameters	0.18 M	0.54 M	4.84 M	0.51 M	1.27 M	2.41 M

5   Conclusion

In this paper, a multi-scale dense convolutional network based on multilevel wavelet decomposition is proposed. The method replaces multi-scale convolution and pooling by 2D-DWT to improve the network capability of multi-scale analysis and reduce the parameters. The SAFDB module is conducted to fuse multi-frequency features and extract underlying scale information via dense connection. Finally, the classification results are obtained by multilevel feature joint decision mechanism. Experimental results demonstrate that the proposed network outperforms the state-of-the-art methods in the scenario of training with only 5% and 10% samples on benchmark datasets.

References

1. Liang, L., et al.: Estimation of crop LAI using hyperspectral vegetation indices and a hybrid inversion method. Remote Sens. Environ. **165**, 123–134 (2015). https://doi.org/10.1016/j.rse.2015.04.032
2. Aslett, Z., Taranik, J.V., Riley, D.N.: Mapping rock forming minerals at Boundary Canyon, Death Valley National Park, California, using aerial SEBASS thermal infrared hyperspectral image data. Int. J. Appl. Earth Obs. Geoinf. **64**, 326–339 (2018)
3. Agilandeeswari, L., Prabukumar, M., et al.: Crop classification for agricultural applications in hyperspectral remote sensing images. Appl. Sci. **12**(3), 1670 (2022)
4. Cariou, C., Chehdi, K.: Unsupervised nearest neighbors clustering with application to hyperspectral Images. IEEE J. Sel. Top. Signal Process. **9**(6), 1105–1116 (2015)
5. Melgani, F., Bruzzone, L.: Classification of hyperspectral remote sensing images with support vector machines. IEEE Trans. Geosci. Remote Sens. **42**(8), 1778–1790 (2004)
6. Benediktsson, J.A., et al.: Classification of hyperspectral data from urban areas based on extended morphological profiles. IEEE Trans. Geosci. Remote Sens. **43**(3), 480–491 (2005)
7. Li, J., Bioucas-Dias, J.M., Plaza, A.: Spectral-spatial hyperspectral image segmentation using subspace multinomial logistic regression and Markov random fields. IEEE Trans. Geosci. Remote Sens. **50**(3), 809–823 (2012)
8. Zhong, Z., Li, J., Luo, Z., Chapman, M.: Spectral-spatial residual network for hyperspectral image classification: A 3-D deep learning framework. IEEE Trans. Geosci. Remote Sens. **56**(2), 847–858 (2018)
9. Zhao, W., Du, S.: Spectral-spatial feature extraction for hyperspectral image classification: a dimension reduction and deep learning approach. IEEE Trans. Geosci. Remote Sens. **54**(8), 4544–4554 (2016)
10. Szegedy, C., Liu, W., Jia, Y., et al.: Going deeper with convolutions. In: 2015 IEEE Conference on Computer Vision and Pattern Recognition (CVPR), pp. 1–9. IEEE (2015)
11. He, M., Li, B., Chen, H.: Multi-scale 3D deep convolutional neural network for hyperspectral image classification. In: 2017 IEEE International Conference on Image Processing (ICIP), pp. 3904–3908. IEEE (2017)
12. Xiao, Y., Xu, Q., Wang, D., Tang, J., Luo, B.: Multi-scale densely 3D CNN for hyperspectral image classification. In: Lin, Z., et al. (eds.) PRCV 2019. LNCS, vol. 11858, pp. 596–606. Springer, Cham (2019). https://doi.org/10.1007/978-3-030-31723-2_51
13. Mallat, S.G.: A theory for multiresolution signal decomposition: the wavelet representation. IEEE Trans. Pattern Anal. Mach. Intell. **11**(7), 674–693 (1989)
14. Lewis, A.S., Knowles, G.: Image compression using the 2-D wavelet transform. IEEE Trans. Image Process. **1**(2), 244–250 (1992)
15. Chen, G., Qian, S.-E.: Denoising of hyperspectral imagery using principal component analysis and wavelet shrinkage. IEEE Trans. Geosci. Remote Sens. **49**(3), 973–980 (2011)
16. Rasti, B., Sveinsson, J.R., Ulfarsson, M.O.: Wavelet-based sparse reduced-rank regression for hyperspectral image restoration. IEEE Trans. Geosci. Remote Sens. **52**(10), 6688–6698 (2014)
17. Williams, T., Li, R.: Advanced image classification using wavelets and convolutional neural networks. In: Proceedings - 2016 15th IEEE International Conference Machine Learning Applications ICMLA 2016, pp. 233–239 (2017)
18. Prabhakar, T.V.N., et al.: Two-dimensional empirical wavelet transform based supervised hyperspectral image classification. ISPRS J. Photogramm. Remote Sens. **133**, 37–45 (2017)
19. Huang, G., Liu, Z., Van Der Maaten, L., Weinberger, K.Q.: Densely connected convolutional networks. In: 2017 IEEE Conference on Computer Vision and Pattern Recognition (CVPR), pp. 2261–2269. IEEE (2017)

20. Chollet, F.: Xception: deep learning with depthwise separable convolutions. In: 2017 IEEE Conference on Computer Vision and Pattern Recognition (CVPR), pp. 1800–1807. IEEE (2017)
21. Lin, M., Chen, Q., Yan, S.: Network in network. In: 2nd International Conference Learning Representation ICLR 2014 - Conference Track Proceedings, pp. 1–10 (2013)
22. Roy, S.K., Krishna, G., Dubey, S.R., Chaudhuri, B.B.: HybridSN: exploring 3-D–2-D CNN feature hierarchy for hyperspectral image classification. IEEE Geosci. Remote Sens. Lett. 17(2), 277–281 (2020)
23. Wang, X.: Moving window-based double haar wavelet transform for image processing. IEEE Trans. Image Process. 15(9), 2771–2779 (2006)

High Spatial Resolution Remote Sensing Imagery Classification Based on Markov Random Field Model Integrating Granularity and Semantic Features

Jun Wang[1] , Qinling Dai[2](✉), Leiguang Wang[3] , Yili Zhao[3], Haoyu Fu[1],
and Yue Zhang[1]

[1] Faculty of Forestry, Southwest Forestry University, Kunming, China
Yu1463412294@swfu.edu.cn
[2] Faculty of Art and Design, Southwest Forestry University, Kunming, China
daiqinling@126.com
[3] Faculty of Big Data and Artificial Intelligence, Southwest Forestry University,
Kunming, China
ylzhao@swfu.edu.cn

Abstract. In remote sensing image classification, it is difficult to distinguish the homogeneity of same land class and the heterogeneity between different land classes. Moreover, high spatial resolution remote sensing images often show the phenomenon of ground object classes fragmentation and salt-and-pepper noise after classification. To improve the above phenomenon, Markov random field (MRF) is a widely used method for remote sensing image classification due to its effective spatial context description. Some MRF-based methods capture more image information by building interaction between pixel granularity and object granularity. Some other MRF-based methods construct representations at different semantic layers on the image to extract the spatial relationship of objects. This paper proposes a new MRF-based method that combines multi-granularity and different semantic layers of information to improve remote sensing image classification. A hierarchical interaction algorithm is proposed that iteratively updates information between different granularity and semantic layers to generate results. The experimental results demonstrate that: on the Gaofen-2 imagery, the proposed model shows a better classification performance than other methods.

Keywords: Markov random field (MRF) · Remote sensing image classification · Multiclass-layer

1 Introduction

Remote sensing image classification is to assign a specific label to each pixel, which is one of the most important research in image processing [1]. A high spatial resolution image provides detailed information to distinguish the tiny terrain category, therefore, it has a wide range of applications in various fields such as agricultural development [2],

© The Author(s), under exclusive license to Springer Nature Switzerland AG 2022
S. Yu et al. (Eds.): PRCV 2022, LNCS 13536, pp. 497–509, 2022.
https://doi.org/10.1007/978-3-031-18913-5_39

forestry investigation [3], and military operations [4]. However, due to the improvement of the spatial resolution of remote sensing images, the types of ground objects present a fragmented distribution. Researchers have proposed many classification methods to solve this problem in recent decades, which can be roughly divided into three categories. The first category is the pixel-based classification method, and the second category is the object-based image analysis (OBIA) method. Among these existing pixel-based methods, the support vector machine (SVM) classifier [5, 6] has excellent generalization ability and robustness in solving problems such as nonlinearity, small sample classification and high-dimensional data, so it is widely used in remote sensing image classification. Random forest (RF) [7] reduces misclassification due to sample limitations because it builds a large number of decision trees to interpret images. Random forests are more reliable as representatives of ensemble learning than single classifiers. However, these pixel-based classification methods all bring salt and pepper noise to the image, which is especially noticeable in high spatial resolution images. Therefore, some scholars have proposed a second method: OBIA [8]. This approach includes the watershed [9], mean shift [10–12], graph-based segmentation with local variations [13], normalized cut (Ncut) [14], Ncut-based Super-Pixel (Ncut-SP) [15, 16], turbopixel [17, 18], etc. These classification methods aim to divide an image into over-segmented regions that are small in size but high in spectral homogeneity, with small inter-class differences within regions, and each region typically represents the most basic land cover category, such as cropland, buildings, etc. In this method, the over-segmentation region is taken as the processing unit. The shape, topology, semantics, spatial context and other characteristics of the image are described and modelled. The OBIA method can fundamentally avoid the occurrence of salt-and-pepper noise. Unfortunately, such methods are more prominent in the generation of over-segmented regions and the uncertainty of object boundaries, which leads to a series of problems such as loss of edge information.

Another method of high-resolution remote sensing image interpretation is the deep learning method based on artificial neural network, which uses end-to-end deep convolutional neural network [19, 20]. However, it requires a large number of training samples and long training time, which greatly restricts the application of this kind of method.

To make full use of the spatial information contained in high-resolution images, some scholars integrate spatial information on multiple semantic layers and extract features to build models. For example, multiclass layer co-occurrence texture extraction with different window sizes [20], multiclass layer morphological filtering [21], multiclass-layer guided filtering [22]. Multiclass-layer features can be combined with other classifiers to achieve excellent performance, such as the combination of SVM and RF with Markov random field (MRF) [23].

Markov random field is a statistical-based probabilistic graphical model. In the framework of the MRF model, the problem of optimal labelling of images is transformed into the maximum posterior probability. Since the model can integrate spatial information and use neighborhood label information to optimize the initial classification results, some MRF models [24, 25] are regarded as post-processing methods for classification. MRF model can not only take into account the spectral difference of modelling objects, but also the spatial connection between them. Due to its stable framework and relatively open model building, many scholars have carried out a lot of research on it. For examples, object-based MRF, multiclass layer MRF, multi granularity MRF [26–29], etc.

The contribution of this paper is to develop a new MRF model for image classification. The model integrates multi-semantic layers information and multi-granularity information to synergistically optimize remote sensing image classification through probability transfer between different features. The rest of the paper is organized as follows. Section 2 presents background on MRF-based methods. The proposed method is presented in Sect. 3. Experimental results and discussions, analyzing the influence are presented in Sect. 4. Conclusions and future directions are given in Sect. 5.

2 Background on MRF-Based Methods

The MRF model is widely used in remote sensing image classification and semantic segmentation due to its unique Markov property. This property connects the ground objects distributed among different pixels, which interprets the image by considering the information of the spatial context, especially for remote sensing images with high spatial resolution. Existing MRF methods typically model interactions between different granularities or construct multiple layers of semantic information to capture spatial information. These two aspects are summarized as follows.

2.1 MRF Model with Different Granularities

MRF models are modeled on the feature field and the label field, as shown in Fig. 1. The classical MRF model is based on pixels [30], because it has regular spatial relationships, and the model is easy to build. Furthermore, pixel-based classification can better retain the detailed information of the image. However, with the number of pixels in high spatial resolution images increasing, the amount of calculation has become larger than before, and it is difficult to capture a wide range of spatial features.

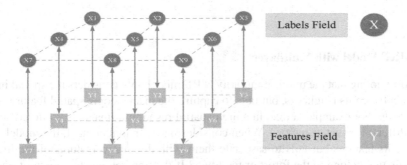

Fig. 1. Features Field and Labels Field of MRF Model.

To improve pixel-based MRF models, modeling objects has changed from being based on pixel granularity to object granularity (OMRF). OMRF model employs the basic segmentation approach to divide the given image into some over segmented regions.

Then, utilize these regions to build the region adjacency graph (RAG) and define the OMRF model on the RAG [27], as shown in Fig. 2. Since a region is composed of many pixels, each region contains low semantic information, the OMRF model reduces the computational complexity of the feature field and the marker field. Moreover, it captures more semantic information about the image and effectively suppresses the phenomenon of salt and pepper noise [31].

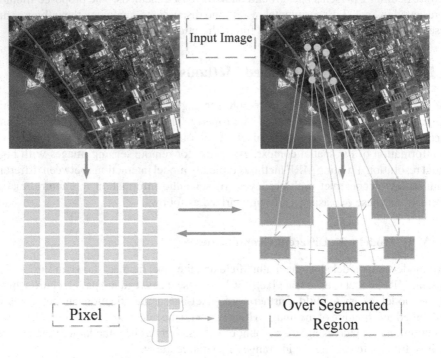

Fig. 2. Information between different granularities of an image.

2.2 MRF Model with Multilayer

It is worth noting that the multi-granularity MRF model only considers the spatial information between its neighbors, but fails to capture the macroscopic spatial features on a larger scale. For example, a tree, in a high spatial resolution image, is scattered across many different pixels or regions. When considering its spatial context, the model only captures its features but fails to associate them with the macro features of the image. Does this tree belong to the forest or the town? If the tree belongs to a town, it will be part of the town, which reduces the salt and pepper noise of the image.

In the label field of the MRF model, each node has a class label which is treated as a random variable that takes values from the set of land cover classes. Objects with the same features obtain different labels inland class sets at different semantic layers, as shown in Fig. 3. The information at different semantic layers could help the model to capture more spatial context, and to realize more information interaction between objects and images. For examples, Multiregion-Resolution MRF Model [29], Object-Based Markov Random Field Model with Auxiliary Label Fields [32], etc.

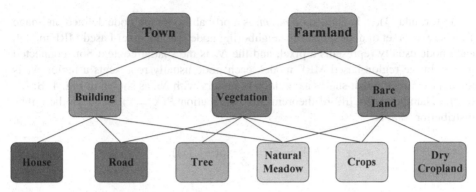

Fig. 3. Representation at Multiple Semantic Layer.

3   Proposed Method

Above the MRF models discussed are either individually modeled at multi-granularity or modeled at multi-semantic layer. Interactions at multi-granularity and multi-semantic scales are not considered in these. In this paper, the MRF-MM model integrates information of multi-granularity and multi-semantic and iteratively updates information in the form of probability. After model convergence to get the final result.

3.1   MRF Model

For a given remote sensing image Y, let M denote a site set with n nodes, $M = \{m_1, m_2, m_3, \ldots, m_n\}$, each node m represents a pixel or a region and n is the number of nodes. The label field $X = \{X_1, X_2, X_3, \ldots, X_n\}$ is defined on M, each random variable X_i $(1 \le i \le n)$ of X denotes the class label of node m_i. X_i takes value from the class set $\omega = \{1, 2, 3, \ldots, k\}$. Here, k is the number of classes. If x_i denotes a realization of $X_i(1 \le i \le n)$, and $x = \{x_1, x_2, \ldots, x_n\}$ is a realization of the label field. For the observed image $Y = \{y_1, y_2, \ldots, y_n\}$, y_i is defined on m_i and x_i is y_i label. In other words, the optimal classification result $\hat{x}$ should be

$$\hat{x} = \underset{x}{\mathrm{argmax}} P(X = x|Y). \tag{1}$$

Based on the Bayesian formula

$$\hat{x} = \underset{x}{\mathrm{argmax}} P(Y|X = x)P(X = x). \tag{2}$$

In the above function, $P(Y|X = x)$ is the likelihood function that measures the occurrence probability of Y conditional on $X = x$, and $P(X = x)$ is a joint probability distribution that captures the spatial interactions between vertexes with Markov property. This property is

$$P(X_i = x_i | x_t, t \in S/s) = P(X_i = x_i | x_t, t \in N_s). \qquad (3)$$

In formula (3), x_i is defined on m_i. m_i is a probability graph node defined on image Y. where N_s is set of nodes spatially neighboring node i. In the pixel-based MRF model, each node usually represents a pixel, and the N_s is the spatial context 8of -connected pixels. In the region-based MRF model, each node usually represents a region N_s is the adjacent region that shares a common boundary with N_i, as shown in Fig. 4. Based on the Hammersley–Clifford theorem, the distribution $P(X = x)$ of obeys the Gibbs distribution, that is

$$P(X = x) = \frac{1}{Z}\exp(-U(x)). \qquad (4)$$

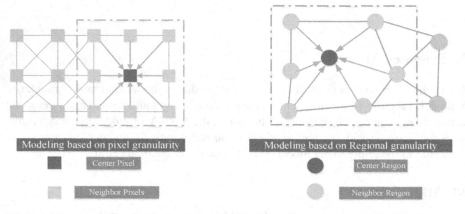

Fig. 4. Markov properties of different granularities.

Here, $Z = \sum_x \exp(-U(x))$ is the normalizing constant and the energy function $U(x)$ equals to the sum of all the clique potential functions. $U(x) = \sum_i \sum_{t \in N_s} \phi(x_i x_t)$. It is defined as

$$\phi(x_i x_t) = \begin{cases} -\beta, \text{ if } (x_i = x_t) \\ \quad \beta, \text{ otherwise} \end{cases}. \qquad (5)$$

3.2 Proposed MRF-MM Model

To combine multiclass layer features and multi-granularity features, this paper develops an MRF-MM model. The model defines the interaction between the two granularities M^1, M^2. Furthermore, two semantic layers ω^1 and ω^2 are respectively defined on each granularity, as shown in Fig. 5. There are four separate modules interacting here, $x^{(M^1, \omega^1)}$,

$x^{(M^2,\omega^1)}$, $x^{(M^1,\omega^2)}$, $x^{(M^2,\omega^2)}$. M^1 is defend on pixel granularities. M^2 is defend on over-segmentation region granularities. ω^1 is a layer with more ground object class and a relatively single semantic information. ω^2 is a layer with fewer ground object class and richer semantic information. $\omega^1 = \{1, 2, 3, \ldots, k_1\}$, $\omega^2 = \{1, 2, 3, \ldots, k_2\}$, $k_1 > k_2$. In the framework of the MRF-MM model unary potential equals to

$$\aleph\left(x^{(M^1,\omega^1)}, x^{(M^2,\omega^1)}, x^{(M^2,\omega^1)}, x^{(M^2,\omega^2)}, y_N^{M^1}, y_N^{M^2}\right)$$

$$= \sum_{n \in NM(1)} \aleph\left(x_N^{M(1),\omega^1}, y_N^{M^1}\right) + \sum_{n \in NM(1)} \aleph\left(x_N^{M(1),\omega^2}, y_N^{M^1}\right) \qquad (6)$$

$$+ \sum_{n \in NM(2)} \aleph\left(x_N^{M(2),\omega^1}, y_N^{M^2}\right) + \sum_{n \in NM(2)} \aleph\left(x_N^{M(2),\omega^2}, y_N^{M^2}\right).$$

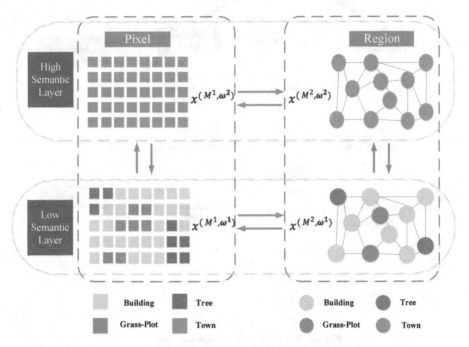

Fig. 5. Framework of the MRF-MM model.

Pairwise potentials are used to capture interactions between different vertices. There are four sub-modules in the MRF-MM model, each module has its potential energy function. In addition, there will also be pairwise potential energy interactions between sub-module. There are three ways of which the potentials interact in the MRF-MM model. 1) The potential energy interaction of a single sub-module itself. 2) The potential energy interaction between two different granularity sub-modules on the same semantic layer. 3) Potential energy interaction between two different semantic layer sub-module at the same granularity. In other words, the pairwise potential, of any sub-module is affected by the other three modules, that is

$$\Psi\left(\mathcal{X}^{M^{(i)},\omega^{(j)}} \mid \mathcal{X}^{M^{(i)},\omega^{(3-j)}},\ \mathcal{X}^{M^{(3-i)},\omega^{(j)}},\ \mathcal{X}^{M^{(3-i)},\omega^{(3-j)}}\right) =$$

$$= \Sigma_{n \in N^{M^{(i)}}} \left\{ \begin{array}{c} \Sigma_{t \in N_t} \Psi_1\left(\mathcal{X}_n^{\mathcal{X}^{M^{(i)},\omega^{(j)}}}, \mathcal{X}_t^{\mathcal{X}^{M^{(i)},\omega^{(j)}}}\right) + \\ \Psi_2\left(\mathcal{X}_n^{\mathcal{X}^{M^{(i)},\omega^{(j)}}}, \mathcal{X}_t^{\mathcal{X}^{M^{(i)},\omega^{(3-j)}}}\right) + \Psi_3\left(\mathcal{X}_n^{\mathcal{X}^{M^{(i)},\omega^{(j)}}}, \mathcal{X}_t^{\mathcal{X}^{M^{(3-i)},\omega^{(3-j)}}}\right) \end{array} \right\}. \tag{7}$$

In formula (7), $i, j = \{1, 2\}$. N_i is the neighborhood of the i node, Ψ is pairwise potential. The workflow diagram is shown in Fig. 6.

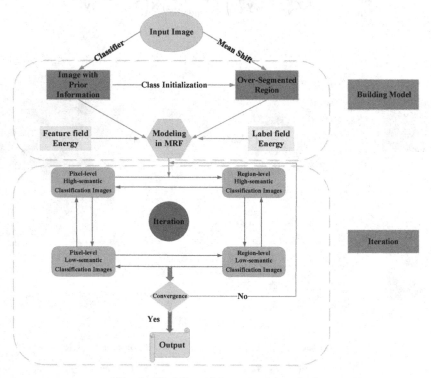

Fig. 6. Workflow of the proposed method.

4 Experimental Results

In this paper, a new improved model MRF-MM based on MRF model was proposed. To experimentally test the effectiveness of MRF-MM, we evaluate it from three aspects: experimental data, classification results and parameter testing.

4.1 Data

The tested image is obtained by the Gaofen-2 sensor, which has 3.2-m spatial resolution and sizes 1000 × 650. Experiments intercept some of them to test the effectiveness of the model. The experimental area is located in China. Both images and ground truth are from Gao fen Image Dataset (GID) data sets [33].

4.2 Classification Experiment

To evaluate the effectiveness of the proposed method, performances of five other methods are also considered. That is the support vector machine (SVM), iterative condition model (ICM), multi-semantic layer MRF (MRF-MR) model based on single granularity, multi-granularity MRF (MRF-MG) model based on single semantic layer and the U-Net model in deep learning. The experimental results are shown in Fig. 7.

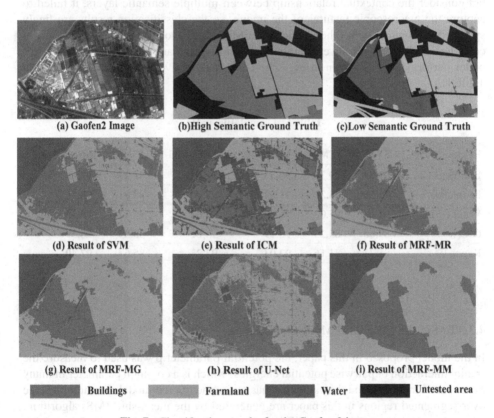

Fig. 7. Classification results for the Gaofen-2 image.

The experimental data is divided into three classes: farmland, buildings, and water. The experimental area is located in the countryside, the buildings are not clustered, and the roof colors of the buildings are different. The color of the roofs of some buildings is closer to the farmland and water, so the phenomenon of salt and pepper noise is particularly serious in classifiers such as SVM. In the imagery, a part of the water flows through the building group to the farmland. Due to the high spatial resolution of the image, this water around the building group will exist independently of the building group, as shown in Fig. 7-e and 7-g. However, from the high-semantic perspective of the imagery, this water should be part of the building group. Different types of crops are grown in the farmland, so the spectral reflectance varies greatly. In addition, some of the bare lands in the farmland have a color close to the roof of the building. The perception range of pixel-based MRF models is limited, so this class will be scattered in the farmland in the form of speckles. The MRF-MG model of multi-granularity modeling reduces the occurrence of this phenomenon as shown in Fig. 7-g, but it did not consider the contextual relationship between multiple semantic layers, it failed to capture the macroscopic features of the image, so the classification results are finely speckled. Compared with other models, the MRF-MM model proposed in this paper considers multi-semantic layer features and multi-granularity features, and achieves better performance, as shown in Fig. 7-i. Their quantitative indexes are discussed in Table 1.

Table 1. Quantitative index

Indexes	SVM	ICM	MRF-MR	MRF-MG	U-Net	MRF-MM
Buildings (%)	83.63	79.34	90.33	92.33	83.23	**97.66**
Farmland (%)	85.56	78.23	91.52	91.06	82.01	**98.46**
Water (%)	94.23	95.02	96.89	97.63	96.17	**99.53**
OA (%)	89.06	85.23	93.19	94.01	88.53	**98.39**
Kappa (%)	85.73	81.16	92.03	93.23	85.63	**97.40**

4.3 Test of the MRF-MM Model Parameters

In the model proposed in this paper, the potential parameter β was used to measure the spatial interaction of pairwise potential energies, which is a common parameter in many MRF-based methods, and the value of β has an impact on the model. Furthermore, the over-segmented regions in this paper are generated by the mean-shift (MS) algorithm, where the minimum region areas (MRA) have great effect on the accuracy of the model. To discuss the effects of parameters β and MRA, the model was tested multiple times in this study. As shown in Fig. 8, the MRF-MM model is quite robust against β and MRA.

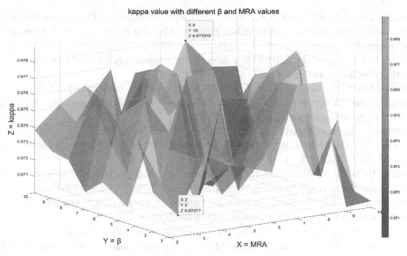

Fig. 8. Kappa value of model with different β and MRA values from 2 to 10.

5 Conclusion

This paper proposed a new MRF-MM model for remote sensing image classification, the model considers both multi-granularity information and multi-semantic layer information. The advantage of model is that develops a framework for probabilistic interactions. Within the framework, the information of granularity and semantic layer is transferred to each other in the form of probability, and each modeled object gets the maximum class probability after iteration. Compared with other methods, the model has strong applicability which can achieve significant robustness on different imagery. The choice of parameters has tiny effect on the accuracy of the model, which can achieve better classification results under different parameters.

In this paper, we only considered pixel-level 8-neighbors and adjacent regions with common edges in the spatial context. In many high spatial resolution remote sensing images, the spatial relationship between ground objects is relatively extensive, not limited to 8 neighbors. Subsequent research will study the method of multi-spatial neighbor MRF-MM model on remote sensing image classification.

References

1. Wang, L., Huang, X., Zheng, C., Zhang, Y.: A Markov random field integrating spectral dissimilarity and class co-occurrence dependency for remote sensing image classification optimization. ISPRS J. Photogrammetry Remote Sensing. **128**, 223–239 (2017)
2. Goel, P.K., Prasher, S.O., Patel, R.M., Landry, J.-A., Bonnell, R., Viau, A.A.: Classification of hyperspectral data by decision trees and artificial neural networks to identify weed stress and nitrogen status of corn. Comput. Electron. Agric. **39**(2), 67–93 (2003)
3. Li, R., et al.: Classifying forest types over a mountainous area in southwest china with landsat data composites and multiple environmental factors. Forests **13**(1), 135 (2022)

4. Benediktsson, J.A., Palmason, J.A., Sveinsson, J.R.: Classification of hyperspectral data from urban areas based on extended morphological profiles. IEEE Trans. Geosci. Remote Sens. **43**(3), 480–491 (2005)
5. Chang, C.-C., Lin, C.-J.: LIBSVM: a library for support vector machines. ACM Trans. Intelligent Systems Technol. (TIST). **2**(3), 1–27 (2011)
6. Muñoz-Marí, J., Bovolo, F., Gómez-Chova, L., Bruzzone, L., Camp-Valls, G.: Semisupervised one-class support vector machines for classification of remote sensing data. IEEE Trans. Geosci. Remote Sens. **48**(8), 3188–3197 (2010)
7. Breiman, L.: Random forests. Machine Learning. **45**(1), 5-32 (2001)
8. Blaschke, T.: Object based image analysis for remote sensing. ISPRS J. Photogramm. Remote. Sens. **65**(1), 2–16 (2010)
9. Vincent, L., Soille, P.: Watersheds in digital spaces: an efficient algorithm based on immersion simulations. IEEE Trans. Pattern Anal. Mach. Intell. **13**(06), 583–598 (1991)
10. Comaniciu, D., Meer, P.: Mean shift: a robust approach toward feature space analysis. IEEE Trans. Pattern Anal. Mach. Intell. **24**(5), 603–619 (2002)
11. Huang, X., Zhang, L., Li, P.: An adaptive multiscale information fusion approach for feature extraction and classification of IKONOS multispectral imagery over urban areas. IEEE Geosci. Remote Sens. Lett. **4**(4), 654–658 (2007)
12. Wang, L., Liu, G., Dai, Q.: Optimization of segmentation algorithms through mean-shift filtering preprocessing. IEEE Geosci. Remote Sens. Lett. **11**(3), 622–626 (2013)
13. Felzenszwalb, P.F., Huttenlocher, D.P.: Efficient graph-based image segmentation. Int. J. Comput. Vision **59**(2), 167–181 (2004)
14. Shi, J., Malik, J.: Normalized cuts and image segmentation. IEEE Trans. Pattern Anal. Mach. Intell. **22**(8), 888–905 (2000)
15. Mori, G., Ren, X., Efros, A.A., Malik, J.: Recovering human body configurations: Combining segmentation and recognition. In: Proceedings of the 2004 IEEE Computer Society Conference on Computer Vision and Pattern Recognition. CVPR, IEEE, p. II (2004)
16. Ren, X., Malik, J.: Learning a classification model for segmentation. In: IEEE International Conference on Computer Vision, p. 10. IEEE Computer Society (2003)
17. Levinshtein, A., Stere, A., Kutulakos, K.N., Fleet, D.J., Dickinson, S.J., Siddiqi, K.: Turbopixels: Fast superpixels using geometric flows. IEEE Trans. Pattern Anal. Mach. Intell. **31**(12), 2290–2297 (2009)
18. Xiang, S., Pan, C., Nie, F., Zhang, C.: Turbopixel segmentation using eigen-images. IEEE Trans. Image Process. **19**(11), 3024–3034 (2010)
19. Long, J., Shelhamer, E., Darrell, T.: Fully convolutional networks for semantic segmentation. In: Proceedings of the IEEE Conference on Computer Vision and Pattern Recognition, pp. 3431–3440 (2015)
20. Chen, Y., Jiang, H., Li, C., Jia, X., Ghamisi, P.: Deep feature extraction and classification of hyperspectral images based on convolutional neural networks. IEEE Trans. Geosci. Remote Sens. **54**(10), 6232–6251 (2016)
21. Benediktsson, J.A., Pesaresi, M., Amason, K.: Classification and feature extraction for remote sensing images from urban areas based on morphological transformations. IEEE Trans. Geosci. Remote Sens. **41**(9), 1940–1949 (2003)
22. Li, N., Huo, H., Fang, T.: A novel texture-preceded segmentation algorithm for high-resolution imagery. IEEE Trans. Geosci. Remote Sens. **48**(7), 2818–2828 (2010)
23. Dai, Q., Luo, B., Zheng, C., Wang, L.: Regional multiscale Markov random field for remote sensing image classification. J. Remote Sensing (Chinese) **24**(03), 245–253 (2020)
24. Malfait, M., Roose, D.: Wavelet-based image denoising using a Markov random field a priori model. IEEE Trans. Image Process. **6**(4), 549–565 (1997)
25. Chang, Y.-C.: Statistical Models for MRF Image Restoration and Segmentation. Purdue University (2000)

26. Wang, L., Dai, Q., Xu, Q.: Constructing hierarchical segmentation tree for feature extraction and land cover classification of high resolution MS imagery. IEEE J. Selected Topics Appl. Earth Observations Remote Sensing **8**(5), 1946–1961 (2015)
27. Zheng, C., Wang, L.: Semantic segmentation of remote sensing imagery using object-based Markov random field model with regional penalties. IEEE J. Selected Topics Applied Earth Observations Remote Sensing **8**(5), 1924–1935 (2014)
28. Zheng, C., Pan, X., Chen, X., Yang, X., Xin, X., Su, L.: An object-based Markov random field model with anisotropic penalty for semantic segmentation of high spatial resolution remote sensing imagery. Remote Sensing **11**(23), 2878 (2019)
29. Zheng, C., Wang, L., Chen, R., Chen, X.: Image segmentation using multiregion-resolution MRF model. IEEE Geosci. Remote Sens. Lett. **10**(4), 816–820 (2012)
30. Li, S.: Random Field Modeling in Image Analysis. Springer (2001)
31. Zheng, C., Wang, L., Zhao, H., Chen, X.: Urban area detection from high-spatial resolution remote sensing imagery using Markov random field-based region growing. J. Appl. Remote Sens. **8**(1), 083566 (2014)
32. Zheng, C., Zhang, Y., Wang, L.: Semantic segmentation of remote sensing imagery using an object-based Markov random field model with auxiliary label fields. IEEE Trans. Geosci. Remote Sens. **55**(5), 3015–3028 (2017)
33. Tong, X.-Y., et al.: Land-cover classification with high-resolution remote sensing images using transferable deep models. Remote Sens. Environ. **237**, 111322 (2020)

Feature Difference Enhancement Fusion for Remote Sensing Image Change Detection

Renjie Hu, Gensheng Pei, Pai Peng, Tao Chen, and Yazhou Yao[✉]

Nanjing University of Science and Technology, Nanjing 210094, China
{hrjsulv,peigsh,taochen,yazhou.yao}@njust.edu.cn

Abstract. Remote sensing image change detection identifies pixel-wise differences between bitemporal images. It is of great significance for geographic monitoring. However, existing approaches still lack efficiency when dealing with the change features. The most general manner is to introduce attention mechanisms in different time streams to strengthen the features and then superimpose them together to complete the fusion of the features. These methods can not effectively excavate and apply the relationship between different temporal features. To alleviate this problem, we introduce a feature difference enhancement fusion module based on pixel position offset in the time dimension (time-position offset). We will learn the offset of the pixel changes in the corresponding areas between the bitemporal features, which will be used to guide the enhancement of the difference between the change-related areas and the change-irrelated areas in a single feature map. Meanwhile, we propose a general and straightforward change detection framework composed of the basic ResNet18 as the encoder and a simple MLP structure as the decoder, instead of the complex structures like UNet or FPN. Extensive experiments on three datasets, including LEVIR-CD, LEVIR-CD+, and S2Looking datasets, demonstrate the effectiveness of our method.

Keywords: Change detection · Deep learning · Difference enhancement

1 Introduction

Remote sensing is one of the most popular research directions in computer vision [5, 7, 27, 28, 31, 37, 43, 44], and change detection (CD) is one of the hot topics in remote sensing (RS). Recently, with the development of deep convolutional networks [18, 19, 21, 33, 39, 45], the performance and stability of change detection methods have been greatly improved.

The process of CD is to identify the changed and unchanged areas on the pixel level between the co-registered bitemporal images [23]. Presently, CD has been widely used in various fields such as urbanization detection [13], disaster assessment [30], environmental monitoring [9], etc. Therefore, automated remote

S. Yu et al. (Eds.): PRCV 2022, LNCS 13536, pp. 510–523, 2022.
https://doi.org/10.1007/978-3-031-18913-5_40

sensing change detection technology has received increasing attention due to the advancement of practical applications.

Nowadays, CD tasks still remain challenging mainly due to the two aspects in terms of data: 1) complex scenes in high-resolution RS images; 2) imaging conditions vary a lot between the co-registered bitemporal images. Therefore, the ability to identify the real changed regions from complex environments and change-irrelevant information is critical to the performance of CD methods [15].

In recent years, deep convolutional neural networks (CNN) have been widely used in the analysis of RS images due to the powerful ability of feature expression [6,16,25,29,34,36,42]. More and more works of CD are trying to apply CNN-based structures such as ResNet [12] and HRNet [24] to extract multi-level semantic features to highlight the change of interest [26,35,38,41]. Both the performance and robustness of CD methods have significantly been improved in sophisticated scenes. But for now, the performance of CNN-based CD methods still mainly depends on the quality of change features they learned [4,19,32,40]. Consequently, the learning ability of change features and the way of fusing the bitemporal features extracted from the CNN-based backbones are the critical factors for the detection results.

The existing works on processing features extracted from bitemporal RS images mainly include the following three types: 1) They directly superimpose the bitemporal features together through concatenation or addition [8]. It is evident that such a simple feature stacking method is challenging to mine effective change of interest, especially in the face of sophisticated imaging conditions or environments. 2) They introduce attention mechanisms to the bitemporal features before fusing them, which is beneficial to model the global information, increase the perceptual field and realize feature enhancement. The final output features truly have more vital semantic expressions but fail to explore the relationship between co-registered images at the time dimension efficiently. 3) They still introduce an attention mechanism for the change features that have been fused and strengthen the change features in the channel or space dimension [3]. For the latter two methods, the application of the attention mechanisms has brought a certain degree of improvement, but it costs extensive computing resources and requires a more significant amount of parameters. Meanwhile, they cannot fully exploit the relationship of the co-registered bitemporal images.

In our work, to alleviate these problems, we introduce a feature difference enhancement fusion module (DEFM) based on the time-position offset of the pixels in the bitemporal images. For actual CD tasks, the formation of the change results from the shift of pixels in some areas of the co-registered images. However, due to the varying imaging conditions and the transformation of the background, the pixels of change-irrelevant regions will also shift to a certain extent. Therefore, we have to distinguish the pixel offset between the change-related and change-irrelated areas, which will directly affect the performance of the models. To this end, we introduce a learnable time-position offset in our work, and the features will be enhanced under the guidance of the offset. Due to the strong representation ability of convolutional neural networks, the changes that we care about tend to learn a more robust and prominent time-position offset compared with the irrelevant changes generated by imaging conditions or the background. Then, based on the original feature, we employ the learned time-position offset to warp the original feature map, which will further enhance and expand the difference of change-related areas and change-irrelated areas. Namely, we expand the difference between the inter-classes (changed and unchanged) in a single feature map and strengthen the representation of the changed areas. Finally, we fuse the enhanced feature with the original feature of another time period to generate a more significant change feature map. In summary, the contributions of the paper are as follows:

(1) We introduce a feature difference enhancement fusion module (DEFM) based on a learn-able time-position offset, which contributes to enhancing and expanding the difference of classes (changed and unchanged) in a single feature map.
(2) We propose a concise and effective CD method, a pure CNN-based method with the encoder-decoder structure. We use an original ResNet18 structure as the encoder to extract bitemporal features. Then the multi-level features extracted will be input into DEFM and finally get handled by the decoder based on a simple MLP structure. Through the whole pipeline, we do not introduce any attention mechanisms and complex structures like UNet or FPN.
(3) To present the effectiveness of our method, we have conduct extensive experiments on three CD datasets: LEVIR-CD [3], LEVIR-CD+ [22], and S2Looking [22] datasets. Meanwhile, we have compared our method with the existing state-of-the-art (SOTA) methods and finally validated the significance of the proposed method.

2   Related Work

2.1   Traditional Change Detection Methods

There are two main types of CD techniques in the RS domain: traditional methods and deep learning-based methods. Traditional methods are based on manual feature extraction represented by change vector analysis (CVA) [20], and principal component analysis (PCA) [11]. CVA is a method of pre-classification change detection. CVA works after the image is subjected to radiation correction and strict preprocessing of geometric registration. And then, the magnitude of the change is measured by the magnitude of the bitemporal vectors to determine the separation threshold and identify the changed and unchanged areas. PCA is a mathematical dimensionality reduction method converting a series of linearly related variables into a set of linearly unrelated variables, which is also called principal components, and then uses the transformed variables to demonstrate the features at a lower dimension [11].

2.2   Deep Learning Based Change Detection Methods

Deep learning-based CD methods can be divided mainly into two categories: 1) Single-stream neural network: The architecture of the single-stream neural network is an image-level fusion method. Usually, the two RS images of different times are cascaded or added in the channel dimension as a single input to the CNN architecture, such as the modified version of UNet++ [48]. Zheng et al. proposed Clnet [47], which designed a cross-layer block to fuse the multi-scale features and multi-level context information. 2) Siamese neural network: Also known as a dual-stream network, it is a method based on feature-level fusion. The model architecture mainly relies on two weight-shared encoders to extract bitemporal features from co-registered RS images. And then, feature fusion is performed to determine the final changed areas by means of measurement or classification. Compared with the single-stream neural network architectures, the current mainstream works tend to favor the siamese neural network. Although the bitemporal features are generated by a weight-shared siamese neural network, the generated feature maps will still produce significant differences in irrelevant changed regions. So far, how to effectively fuse the generated bitemporal features is still a problem worth exploring. Presently, the methods of fusing the bitemporal features mainly rely on directly superimposing including addition, subtraction, and concatenation, such as FC-Siam-Conc [8], FC-Siam-Diff [8]; on the other way, the attention mechanisms will be introduced to strengthen the bitemporal features before or after the stage of feature fusion. Zhang et al. [46] proposed a CD network based on object-level detectors guided by a bi-correlated attention module, using location-correlated and channel-correlated attention modules to achieve feature-level fusion. Although these hierarchical fusion methods based on attention mechanisms succeed in improving the performance of the networks, they need to consume a lot of computing resources and have a large number of parameters. More importantly, most attention-based methods can not explore and utilize the relationship or the difference between the features of different time streams. The main work of this paper is devoted to alleviating the problem.

3   Method

In this section, we will introduce the specific implementation of the proposed method in detail. The first subsection will show the overall change detection framework. The second subsection will elaborate on the implementation of the feature difference enhancement fusion module (DEFM) based on the time-position offset (TPO).

3.1   Overall Structure of Proposed CD Architecture

In the task of change detection, a pair of remote sensing images of different phases I_{t1} and I_{t2} with the shape of $W \times H \times C$ tend to be the original input.

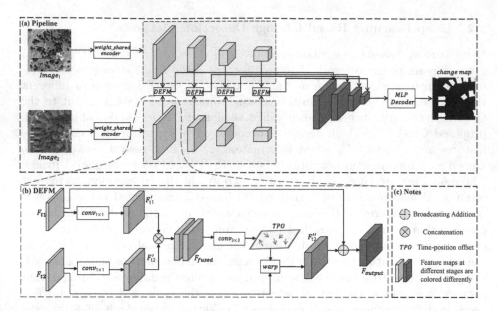

Fig. 1. (a). The pipeline of our method. (b). The feature difference enhancement fusion module (DEFM). (c). Some notes about some modules of the pipeline.

Our work focuses on studies of binary change detection, so the ultimate goal is to generate a binary change prediction map M, where 0 and 1 respectively represent the labels of unchanged and changed regions.

The general CD architecture is shown in Fig. 1, which is based on a standard encoder-decoder structure. The pipeline mainly consists of three parts: a weight-shared feature extractor, a feature difference enhancement fusion module (DEFM), and a simple MLP-based decoder. Firstly, the co-registered bitemporal images will be input into the weight-shared encoders to generate the bitemporal feature maps F_{t1}^i, $F_{t2}^i \in R^{C_i \times H_i \times C_i}$, where $i \in \{1, 2, 3, 4\}$, $W \times H$ represents the size of the feature map and C represents the number of channels. After that, the two feature maps will be input into the DEFM to generate the final enhanced change feature map F_{output}^i as the output. Finally, the output change feature map will be decoded by a simple MLP-based decoder to calculate the probability of the change of each pixel and output the final change result images.

3.2   Difference Enhancement Fusion Module (DEFM)

The key to the CD tasks is distinguishing between the change-related areas and change-irrelated areas, where the former is the part we need to pay attention to. Therefore, in our work, we hope to learn a time-position offset by exploiting the difference between the corresponding pixel positions of the bitemporal features. And then, we will expand the difference between change-related and change-irrelated regions within a single feature map under the guidance of the learned time-position offset. In the learning process of the network, the changes we care about often have more substantial offsets than changes caused by imaging conditions or the complex background. The enhanced features can better highlight the changed areas and improve the regions we are interested in, and then they will be fused to generate a change feature map with a better semantic expression. DEFM is mainly composed of two parts: learning the time-position offset and enhancing the difference with the guide of the learned offset.

As shown in Fig. 1, the specific process of DEFM is exhibited. Firstly, the bitemporal feature maps F_{t1} and F_{t2} output from each level are compressed into a unified channel depth with two 1×1 convolutional layers and generate two feature maps F'_{t1} and F'_{t2}. Then we concatenate them together to get the fused feature map F_{fused} as the input for the next stage. The process is described as:

$$F_{fused} = concat\left(conv_{1\times 1}\left(F_{t2}\right), conv_{1\times 1}\left(F_{t1}\right)\right), \tag{1}$$

where $conv_{1\times 1}\left(F_{t1}\right)$ and $conv_{1\times 1}\left(F_{t2}\right)$ is the feature map F'_{t1} and F'_{t2} mentioned above. It is worth noting that the processing of different features is sequential at the stage of concatenation because the time-position offset we want to learn is a directional vector. In this way, we can achieve a better result when enhancing the feature differences. Then, the concatenated feature map is input into a convolutional layer with the kernel size of 3×3, and the output of the stage is the time-position offset we want to learn, which can be described as $\triangle_{tp}$ and the stage can be formulated as:

$$\triangle_{tp} = conv_{3\times 3}\left(F_{fused}\right), \tag{2}$$

where $conv_{3\times 3}\left(\cdot\right)$ compresses the channels of the concatenated feature map into 2. The time-position offset $\triangle_{tp}$ aims to learn the displacement deviation of each pixel in the co-registered bitemporal images so that a straightforward semantic expression can describe the strength of the offset vector well, and it is also convenient for subsequent difference enhancement operations. So far, we completed the calculation of the time-position offset and got the key quantity $\triangle_{tp}$.

Then we warp the original feature map F_{t2} at the time of T_2 into the feature map F''_{t2} where the difference of inter-classes has been enhanced under the guidance of time-position offset $\triangle_{tp}$. The details of the process are as follows: According to the coordinates of each point in the time-position offset, we assign the pixels of the corresponding coordinates in the feature map F_{t2} to the related positions. However, the coordinates of each point may not correspond precisely between F_{t2} and $\triangle_{tp}$, and we can use the differentiable bi-linear sampling mechanism proposed in [14] to generate the approximate value from the 4-neighbors of the points in F_{t2} [17]. Finally, we can obtain the difference-enhanced feature map F''_{t2}. The process can be formulated as:

$$F''_{t2} = warp\left(F_{t2}, \triangle_{tp}\right). \tag{3}$$

The detailed operation of each point p_{t2} in feature map F_{t2} can be described as:

$$F''_{t2}\left(p_{new}\right) = F_{t2}\left(p_{t2}\right) = \sum_{p\in N(p_{t2})} w_p F_{t2}\left(p\right), \tag{4}$$

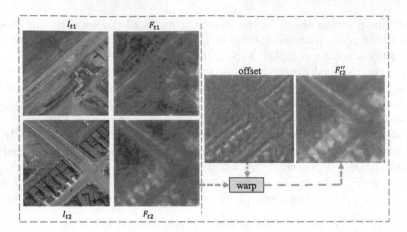

Fig. 2. The change of the feature maps in DEFM. I_{t1} and I_{t2} are the origin bitemporal images, F_{t1} and F_{t2} are the feature maps extracted from the weight-shared encoder, offset is the learned time-position offset, $F_{t2}^{''}$ is the feature map that the difference between classes has been enhanced.

where $p \in N\,(p_{t2})$ represent the four adjacent points of any points p_{t2} in the feature map F_{t2} and w_p is the bi-linear kernel weights generated by $\triangle_{tp}$. The operation has the property of alignment, which is beneficial to the enhancement of the difference of $F_{t2}^{''}$. At the end of DEFM, we add the difference-enhanced feature map $F_{t2}^{''}$ with the original feature map F_{t1} at the time of T_1 to generate the final change feature map F_{output} as the output of the module. The process can be described as:

$$F_{output} = add\left(F_{t2}^{''}, F_{t1}\right). \tag{5}$$

Finally, F_{output} will be decoded by a brief MLP-based decoder. It is worth noting that we only enhance the difference within F_{t2} in our method. As described in the concatenation operation above, the time-position offset we learned is a directional vector. The pixel position offset of the T_2 to T_1 is chosen in our method. A further comparative study has been done in our ablation experiments.

In the works of CD tasks, more methods prefer to introduce the attention mechanisms when dealing with the bitemporal features extracted from the weight-shared encoder. It is inevitable to ignore the relationship or difference of the features in the time dimension. However, DEFM based on time-position offset has alleviated the problem to a large extent. We fully learn the time-position offset of the corresponding pixels in two different feature maps. And we enhance the difference of inter-classes (changed and unchanged) under the guidance of the offset. Our method works because the learned time-position offset has a more substantial offset for the changed regions than the change-independent regions. It can more clearly highlight the real changed regions inside a single feature map. The feature maps through the module are demonstrated in Fig. 2. It is evident that the changed areas in F''_{t2} are more highlighted, and the outline is more precise. Numerically, the real changed areas have a larger change probability corresponding to the conspicuous part.

4   Experiments

4.1   Experimental Setup

Datasets. We offer a brief view of the three datasets (LEVIR-CD dataset [3], LEVIR-CD+ dataset [22] and S2Looking dataset [22]) in Table 1 we experimented on. During the experiments, for the constraint of GPU memory capacity, we cut all the images of three datasets into patches of 256×256 with no overlap following [2]. The LEVIR-CD dataset is a public building change detection dataset. After cropping, we obtain 7,120/1,024/2,048 pairs of patches for training/validation/test respectively. The LEVIR-CD+ dataset does not divide the test set. Then after cropping, we obtain 10,192/5,568 pairs of patches for training/validation. As for the S2Looking dataset, it has 5,000 pairs of bitemporal RS images, but it owns only 65,920 change instances. Compared with the other two datasets, the change detection of the S2Looking dataset is relatively more difficult. After cropping, we obtain 56,000/8,000/16,000 pairs of patches for training/validation/test respectively.

Table 1. A brief introduction of the three datasets.

Name	Pairs	Size	Resolution	Change instances	Change pixels
LEVIR-CD	634	1024×1024	0.5	31,333	30,913,975
LEVIR-CD+	985	1024×1024	0.5	48,455	47,802,614
S2looking	5,000	1024×1024	0.5–0.8	65,920	69,611,520

Evaluation Metircs. Our experiments introduce F1-score (F1) and Intersection over Union (IoU) as the main evaluation indices [7]. They can be calculated as follows:

$$F1 = 2 \times \frac{precision \times recall}{precision + recall}, \tag{6}$$

$$IoU = \frac{TP}{TP + FP + FN}, \tag{7}$$

where precision (P) and recall (R) are difined as follows:

$$precision = \frac{TP}{TP + FP}, \tag{8}$$

$$recall = \frac{TP}{TP + FN}, \tag{9}$$

where TP, FN, and FP represent the number of true positive, false negative, and false positive respectively.

Table 2. The comparison results on three datasets.

Method	LEVIR-CD				LEVIR-CD+				S2Looking			
	P	R	F1	IoU	P	R	F1	IoU	P	R	F1	IoU
FC-EF	86.91	80.17	83.40	71.53	61.30	72.61	66.48	49.79	81.36	8.95	7.65	8.77
FC-Siam-Diff	89.53	83.31	86.31	75.92	74.97	72.04	73.48	58.07	**83.29**	15.76	13.19	15.28
FC-Siam-Conc	91.99	76.77	83.69	71.96	66.24	81.22	72.97	57.44	68.27	18.52	13.54	17.05
SNUNet	89.18	87.17	88.16	78.83	79.51	81.42	80.45	67.29	74.14	48.84	58.89	41.73
STANet	83.81	**91.00**	87.26	77.40	74.62	**84.54**	79.31	65.66	38.75	**56.49**	45.97	29.84
CDNet	90.50	84.60	87.55	77.70	**88.96**	73.45	80.46	67.31	67.48	54.93	60.56	43.43
BIT	89.24	89.37	89.31	80.68	82.74	82.85	82.80	70.64	72.64	53.85	61.85	44.77
Ours	**92.88**	88.70	**90.74**	**83.05**	88.74	83.63	**86.11**	**75.61**	72.53	54.53	**62.25**	**45.19**

Implementation Details. The proposed method is implemented on PyTorch and MMSegmentation. Our model is trained on a single NVIDIA Tesla V100 GPU (16 GB memory). We crop images of all the three datasets into patches of 256×256 as the input to the model. Then we apply regular data augmentation to the input patches such as random crop, flip and resize. We employ the AdamW optimizer with the learning rate of 6e-5 and the poly schedule to optimize the model. Uniformly, we set the batch sizes to 16 and train the model with 160k iterations. We evaluate the models saved without any test time augmentation techniques when testing.

4.2   Experimental Results

In the comparative experiments, we compared the performance with some classic methods, including FC-EF [8], FC-Siam-Diff [8] and FC-Siam-Conc [8] which are classical pure convolutional CD methods and four SOTA methods including SNUNet [10], STANet [3], CDNet [1] and BIT [2]. The results are demonstrated in Table 2.

As is shown in Table 2, our method is verified to have a better performance on the three datasets. Compared with BIT, our method outperforms by 1.43/3.31/0.4 points of F1-score on the three datasets respectively. Especially in the LEVIR-CD+ dataset, the proposed method improves by 3.31 and 4.97 points of F1-score and IoU than BIT. It is worth noting that our method takes the basic ResNet18 structure as the encoder and a simple MLP-based structure as the decoder. We abandon any complicated structures like UNet, FPN, or attention mechanisms. Obviously, the proposed DEFM plays a key role in the improvement of the results.

To show the performance of the proposed method more vividly, we demonstrate the result maps of our method and compare them with the results of BIT on the three all datasets. As is shown in Fig. 3, our method provides better results with a lower probability of false and missing detection than BIT.

Table 3. The comparison of the three methods (Output, Diff, Ours).

	F1	△
Diff	90.54	−0.20
Output	90.57	−0.14
Ours	90.74	-

Table 4. The comparison of the three methods (Method1, Method2, Ours).

	F1	△
Method1	89.98	−0.76
Method2	90.45	−0.29
Ours	90.74	-

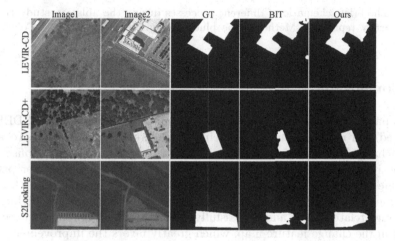

Fig. 3. The results of proposed method compared with ground truth (GT) and BIT. (Color figure online)

4.3   Ablation Studies

In this subsection, we conduct a series of ablation experiments on the LEVIR-CD dataset to verify the effectiveness of our method. The ablation experiments are mainly divided into two directions. Firstly, we perform ablation studies on how to deal with the difference-enhanced feature map. They include directly outputting the enhanced feature map to the decoder module (Output), subtracting the enhanced feature map with the original feature map of T_1 and taking the absolute value (Diff), and adding the enhanced map with the original map of T_1 together (Ours). The results are displayed in Table 3.

Then, in the proposed method, we only enhance the difference of the feature map of T_2 with the time-position offset. During the second ablation study, we warp both bitemporal feature maps with the same time-position offset to enhance the difference between the changed and unchanged areas. We subtract or add them together as the input to the decoder module. The process is briefly illustrated in Fig. 4. We mark the operation of the red dotted arrow as Method1, which subtracts both enhanced maps and takes the absolute value and the blue one as Method2, which adds them together. The comparison results are shown in Table 4.

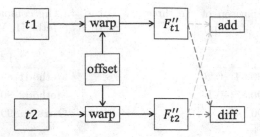

Fig. 4. The brief schematic of different processes during the ablation study (the red dotted arrow represents Method1, the blue one represents Method2). (Color figure online)

5   Conclusion

In this paper, a concise and practical change detection module named DEFM is proposed. Our method aims at enhancing the difference of inter-classes (changed and unchanged) in a single feature map with a learned time-position offset. The time-position offset is a directional vector describing the shift of per pixel at the same areas between co-registered images, and it is learnable. With extensive experiments, DEFM has been confirmed to be adequate in highlighting the change-related areas and successfully expanding the difference between two classes in the change feature map, which greatly favors the improvement of the results. Meanwhile, our method improves by 1.43/3.31/0.4 points of F1-score on the LEVIR-CD/LEVIR-CD+/S2Looking datasets compared to the previous SOTA (BIT).

Acknowledgments. This work was supported by the pre-research project of the Equipment Development Department of the Central Military Commission (No. 31514020205).

References

1. Chen, H., Li, W., Shi, Z.: Adversarial instance augmentation for building change detection in remote sensing images. IEEE Trans. Geosci. Remote Sens. **60**, 1–16 (2021)
2. Chen, H., Qi, Z., Shi, Z.: Remote sensing image change detection with transformers. IEEE Trans. Geosci. Remote Sens. (2021)
3. Chen, H., Shi, Z.: A spatial-temporal attention-based method and a new dataset for remote sensing image change detection. Remote Sens. **12**(10), 1662 (2020)
4. Chen, P., Zhang, B., Hong, D., Chen, Z., Yang, X., Li, B.: FCCDN: Feature constraint network for VHR image change detection. ISPRS J. Photogramm. Remote. Sens. **187**, 101–119 (2022)
5. Chen, T., Wang, S.H., Wang, Q., Zhang, Z., Xie, G.S., Tang, Z.: Enhanced feature alignment for unsupervised domain adaptation of semantic segmentation. IEEE Trans. Multimedia (TMM) **24**, 1042–1054 (2022)

6. Chen, T., Xie, G., Yao, Y., Wang, Q., Shen, F., Tang, Z., Zhang, J.: Semantically meaningful class prototype learning for one-shot image segmentation. IEEE Trans. Multimedia (TMM) **24**, 968–980 (2022)
7. Chen, T., Yao, Y., Zhang, L., Wang, Q., Xie, G., Shen, F.: Saliency guided inter-and intra-class relation constraints for weakly supervised semantic segmentation. IEEE Trans. Multimedia (TMM) (2022). https://doi.org/10.1109/TMM.2022.3157481
8. Daudt, R.C., Le Saux, B., Boulch, A.: Fully convolutional siamese networks for change detection. In: 2018 25th IEEE International Conference on Image Processing (ICIP), pp. 4063–4067. IEEE (2018)
9. De Bem, P.P., de Carvalho Junior, O.A., Fontes Guimarães, R., Trancoso Gomes, R.A.: Change detection of deforestation in the Brazilian amazon using Landsat data and convolutional neural networks. Remote Sens. **12**(6), 901 (2020)
10. Fang, S., Li, K., Shao, J., Li, Z.: SNUNet-CD: a densely connected siamese network for change detection of VHR images. IEEE Geosci. Remote Sens. Lett. **19**, 1–5 (2021)
11. Fung, T., LeDrew, E.: Application of principal components analysis to change detection. Photogramm. Eng. Remote. Sens. **53**(12), 1649–1658 (1987)
12. He, K., Zhang, X., Ren, S., Sun, J.: Deep residual learning for image recognition. In: Proceedings of the IEEE conference on computer vision and pattern recognition, pp. 770–778 (2016)
13. Huang, X., Zhang, L., Zhu, T.: Building change detection from multitemporal high-resolution remotely sensed images based on a morphological building index. IEEE J. Selected Topic Appl. Earth Obs. Remote Sens. **7**(1), 105–115 (2013)
14. Jaderberg, M., Simonyan, K., Zisserman, A., et al.: Spatial transformer networks. In: Advances in neural information processing systems 28 (2015)
15. Khelifi, L., Mignotte, M.: Deep learning for change detection in remote sensing images: comprehensive review and meta-analysis. IEEE Access **8**, 126385–126400 (2020)
16. LeCun, Y., Bengio, Y., Hinton, G.: Deep learning. Nature **521**(7553), 436–444 (2015)
17. Li, X., You, A., Zhu, Z., Zhao, H., Yang, M., Yang, K., Tan, S., Tong, Y.: Semantic flow for fast and accurate scene parsing. In: Vedaldi, A., Bischof, H., Brox, T., Frahm, J.-M. (eds.) ECCV 2020. LNCS, vol. 12346, pp. 775–793. Springer, Cham (2020). https://doi.org/10.1007/978-3-030-58452-8_45
18. Liu, H., et al.: Exploiting web images for fine-grained visual recognition by eliminating open-set noise and utilizing hard examples. IEEE Trans. Multimedia (TMM) **24**, 546–557 (2022)
19. Liu, H., Zhang, H., Lu, J., Tang, Z.: Exploiting web images for fine-grained visual recognition via dynamic loss correction and global sample selection. IEEE Trans. Multimedia (TMM) **24**, 1105–1115 (2022)
20. Malila, W.A.: Change vector analysis: an approach for detecting forest changes with Landsat. In: LARS symposia, p. 385 (1980)
21. Pei, G., Shen, F., Yao, Y., Xie, G.S., Tang, Z., Tang, J.: Hierarchical feature alignment network for unsupervised video object segmentation. In: Proceedings of the European Conference on Computer Vision (ECCV) (2022)
22. Shen, L., et al.: S2Looking: a satellite side-looking dataset for building change detection. Remote Sens. **13**(24), 5094 (2021)
23. Singh, A.: Review article digital change detection techniques using remotely-sensed data. Int. J. Remote Sens. **10**(6), 989–1003 (1989)

24. Sun, K., Xiao, B., Liu, D., Wang, J.: Deep high-resolution representation learning for human pose estimation. In: Proceedings of the IEEE/CVF Conference on Computer Vision and Pattern Recognition, pp. 5693–5703 (2019)
25. Sun, Z., Hua, X.S., Yao, Y., Wei, X.S., Hu, G., Zhang, J.: CRSSC: salvage reusable samples from noisy data for robust learning. In: Proceedings of the ACM International Conference on Multimedia (ACMMM), pp. 92–101 (2020)
26. Sun, Z., Liu, H., Wang, Q., Zhou, T., Wu, Q., Tang, Z.: Co-LDL: a co-training-based label distribution learning method for tackling label noise. IEEE Trans. Multimedia (TMM) 24, 1093–1104 (2022)
27. Sun, Z., et al.: PNP: robust learning from noisy labels by probabilistic noise prediction. In: Proceedings of the IEEE Conference on Computer Vision and Pattern Recognition (CVPR), pp. 5311–5320 (2022)
28. Sun, Z., et al.: Webly supervised fine-grained recognition: Benchmark datasets and an approach. In: Proceedings of the IEEE International Conference on Computer Vision (ICCV), pp. 10602–10611 (2021)
29. Sun, Z., Yao, Y., Wei, X., Shen, F., Liu, H., Hua, X.S.: Boosting robust learning via leveraging reusable samples in noisy web data. IEEE Trans. Multimedia (TMM) (2022). https://doi.org/10.1109/TMM.2022.3158001
30. Xu, J.Z., Lu, W., Li, Z., Khaitan, P., Zaytseva, V.: Building damage detection in satellite imagery using convolutional neural networks. arXiv preprint arXiv:1910.06444 (2019)
31. Yao, Y., et al.: Non-salient region object mining for weakly supervised semantic segmentation. In: Proceedings of the IEEE Conference on Computer Vision and Pattern Recognition (CVPR), pp. 2623–2632 (2021)
32. Yao, Y., Hua, X.S., Shen, F., Zhang, J., Tang, Z.: A domain robust approach for image dataset construction. In: Proceedings of the ACM International Conference on Multimedia (ACMMM), pp. 212–216 (2016)
33. Yao, Y., Hua, X., Gao, G., Sun, Z., Li, Z., Zhang, J.: Bridging the web data and fine-grained visual recognition via alleviating label noise and domain mismatch. In: Proceedings of the ACM International Conference on Multimedia (ACMMM), pp. 1735–1744 (2020)
34. Yao, Y., et al.: Exploiting web images for multi-output classification: from category to subcategories. IEEE Trans. Neural Netw. Learn. Syst. (TNNLS) 31(7), 2348–2360 (2020)
35. Yao, Y., Shen, F., Zhang, J., Liu, L., Tang, Z., Shao, L.: Extracting multiple visual senses for web learning. IEEE Trans. Multimedia (TMM) 21(1), 184–196 (2019)
36. Yao, Y., Shen, F., Zhang, J., Liu, L., Tang, Z., Shao, L.: Extracting privileged information for enhancing classifier learning. IEEE Trans. Image Proc. (TIP) 28(1), 436–450 (2019)
37. Yao, Y., et al.: Jo-SRC: a contrastive approach for combating noisy labels. In: Proceedings of the IEEE Conference on Computer Vision and Pattern Recognition (CVPR), pp. 5192–5201 (2021)
38. Yao, Y., Zhang, J., Shen, F., Hua, X., Xu, J., Tang, Z.: Exploiting web images for dataset construction: a domain robust approach. IEEE Trans. Multimedia (TMM) 19(8), 1771–1784 (2017)
39. Yao, Y., Zhang, J., Shen, F., Liu, L., Zhu, F., Zhang, D., Shen, H.T.: Towards automatic construction of diverse, high-quality image datasets. IEEE Trans. Knowl. Data Eng. (TKDE) 32(6), 1199–1211 (2020)
40. Yao, Y., Zhang, J., Shen, F., Yang, W., Huang, P., Tang, Z.: Discovering and distinguishing multiple visual senses for polysemous words. In: Proceedings of the AAAI Conference on Artificial Intelligence (AAAI), pp. 523–530 (2018)

41. Zhang, C., Lin, G., Wang, Q., Shen, F., Yao, Y., Tang, Z.: Guided by meta-set: a data-driven method for fine-grained visual recognition. IEEE Trans. Multimedia (TMM) (2022). https://doi.org/10.1109/TMM.2022.3181439

42. Zhang, C., Wang, Q., Xie, G., Wu, Q., Shen, F., Tang, Z.: Robust learning from noisy web images via data purification for fine-grained recognition. IEEE Trans. Multimedia (TMM) **24**, 1198–1209 (2022)

43. Zhang, C., et al.: Web-supervised network with softly update-drop training for fine-grained visual classification. In: Proceedings of the AAAI Conference on Artificial Intelligence (AAAI), pp. 12781–12788 (2020)

44. Zhang, C., Yao, Y., Shu, X., Li, Z., Tang, Z., Wu, Q.: Data-driven meta-set based fine-grained visual recognition. In: Proceedings of the ACM International Conference on Multimedia (ACMMM), pp. 2372–2381 (2020)

45. Zhang, C., et al.: Extracting useful knowledge from noisy web images via data purification for fine-grained recognition. In: Proceedings of the ACM International Conference on Multimedia (ACMMM), pp. 4063–4072 (2021)

46. Zhang, L., Hu, X., Zhang, M., Shu, Z., Zhou, H.: Object-level change detection with a dual correlation attention-guided detector. ISPRS J. Photogramm. Remote. Sens. **177**, 147–160 (2021)

47. Zheng, Z., Wan, Y., Zhang, Y., Xiang, S., Peng, D., Zhang, B.: CLNet: cross-layer convolutional neural network for change detection in optical remote sensing imagery. ISPRS J. Photogramm. Remote. Sens. **175**, 247–267 (2021)

48. Zhou, Z., Rahman Siddiquee, M.M., Tajbakhsh, N., Liang, J.: UNet++: a nested U-Net architecture for medical image segmentation. In: Stoyanov, D., et al. (eds.) DLMIA/ML-CDS -2018. LNCS, vol. 11045, pp. 3–11. Springer, Cham (2018). https://doi.org/10.1007/978-3-030-00889-5_1

WAFormer: Ship Detection in SAR Images Based on Window-Aware Swin-Transformer

Zhicheng Wang[1,3], Lingfeng Wang[2(✉)], Wuqi Wang[3], Shanshan Tian[3], and Zhiwei Zhang[3]

[1] School of Artificial Intelligence, University of Chinese Academy of Sciences, Beijing 100049, China
[2] College of Information Science and Technology, Beijing University of Chemical Technology, Beijing 100029, China
`lfwang@mail.buct.edu.cn`
[3] Institute of Automation, Chinese Academy of Sciences, Beijing 100190, China

Abstract. The research work of synthetic aperture radar (SAR) image target detection based on deep learning has made great progress. However, most of them apply the methods applicable to optical images directly to SAR images, ignoring the characteristics of targets in SAR images. For instance, the size of target in SAR images is usually small and volatile. Meanwhile, the target distribution is relatively sparse and the detection is affected by the complex background noise. In this paper, we propose an improved backbone network, called WAFormer, for ship targets detection in SAR images, based on the latest Swin-Transformer. WAFormer improves the local window attention mechanism of Swin-Transformer by introducing the new window settings. Our model can be more suitable to match the shape of the target, so that it obtains more accurate detection in SAR images. Experimental results show that the WAFormer achieves 74.4% mAP on the Official-SSDD SAR dataset, surpassing Swin-Transformer by +1.0, especially for large targets.

Keywords: Synthetic-Aperture Radar (SAR) · Ship detection · Transformer · Window attention

1 Introduction

As an active microwave remote sensing device, synthetic aperture radar (SAR) is capable generate all-day, all-weather and high-resolution earth observations. SAR images are of great importance in reconnaissance and surveillance missions in the military and civilian domains. SAR images target detection can be applied in many tasks, such as environmental monitoring, battlefield reconnaissance, geographic survey and ocean monitoring.

Deep learning technology has achieved excellent results in solving optical images detection and recognition tasks, and has attracted more and more scholars to use deep learning technology in SAR images interpretation tasks [1–4].

© The Author(s), under exclusive license to Springer Nature Switzerland AG 2022
S. Yu et al. (Eds.): PRCV 2022, LNCS 13536, pp. 524–536, 2022.
https://doi.org/10.1007/978-3-031-18913-5_41

But the complex imaging mechanism of SAR images is different from optical image, leads to the fact that algorithms perform well on optical images may not be perfectly adapted to SAR images. In general, the challenges of applying deep learning to study the tasks of SAR images target detection are mainly as follows: (1) As shown in Table 1 and Fig. 1 statistics from Official-SSDD [5,6] and HRSID [7], two mainstream SAR image dataset, the size of sparse targets is generally small and the scale varies greatly, it undoubtedly increases the difficulty of SAR images target detection. (2) SAR images are often accompanied by cluttered noise and complex backgrounds such as docks, islands and reefs, resulting in lots of false detection or missed detection. (3) The difference between different datasets is large, lead to the generalization of the model trained on a single dataset is weak.

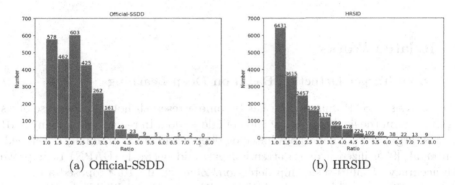

(a) Official-SSDD   (b) HRSID

Fig. 1. Distribution of the ratio of the long side to the short side of the target bounding box.

As above, we aim to extract precise target features from complex SAR images to solve the problem of small target detection and multi-scale target detection. We propose an improved Transformer backbone based on Swin-Transformer [8] which called WAFormer. The backbone redesign the window attention module considering the size and shape of the SAR images targets. The improved window can better capture targets of various sizes and directions and distinguish them from the background. WAFormer achieves higher box AP than Swin-Transformer and other classic convolutional neural network (CNN) method with lower FLOPS than Swin-Transformer. Meanwhile we prove the Transformer method is suitable for SAR images target detection.

The main contributions of this paper are as follows:

(1) We redesign the Transformer window attention module with the size variable window. The resizable window make feature extraction more suitable for SAR images targets of various postures.

(2) To enhance connections between non-overlapping windows in abovementioned window attention module, we improve the original shift window mechanism in Swin-Transformer to make it more reasonable.

(3) In order to alleviate the computational redundancy problem caused by the new window attention, we introduce a channel splitting mechanism to calculate the window attention of different direction at the same time.

Table 1. Statistical results of multi-scale ships in Official-SSDD and HRSID.

Dataset	Size of ships (number)			Special size (pixels)	
	Small	Medium	Large	Smallest	Largest
Official-SSDD	1624	895	68	4 * 4	384 * 308
HRSID	9242	14776	321	3 * 1	800 * 653

2   Related Works

2.1   SAR Target Detection Based on Deep Learning

The analysis of SAR images data has become a research hot spot because of its significance in the field of military and civil detection. In recent years, many SAR images target detection methods based on deep learning are gradually developed. Cui et al. [9] utilized a dense attention pyramid network (DAPN) to improve the accuracy of multi-scale ship detection. Zhao et al. [10] proposed an attention receptive pyramid network (ARPN) with receptive fields block (RFB) and convolutional block attention module (CBAM) to improve the performance of detecting multi-scale ships. Cui et al. [11] proposed an anchor-free method which introduces spatial shuffle-group enhance (SSE) attention module to CenterNet to achieve better performance than some classic CNN methods. Fu et al. [12] are also based on anchor-free strategy, proposed a feature balancing and refinement network (FBR-Net) to achieve the state-of-the-art performance among the general anchor-free methods. Guo et al. [13] presented CenterNet++ consists of feature refinement module, feature pyramids fusion module, and head enhancement module to improve the effectiveness and robustness. Tang et al. [14] proposed a scale-aware feature pyramid network comprises a scale-adaptive feature extraction module and a learnable anchor assignment strategy to address the problem of feature misalignment and targets' appearance variation. Xu et al. [15] improved YOLOv5 to present Lite-YOLOv5, a lightweight onboard SAR ship detector with decreasing FLOPS and without sacrificing accuracy. Xia et al. [16] proposed a visual transformer framework based on contextual joint-representation learning by combining the global information of Transformer and the local feature representation of CNN.

2.2   Vision Transformer

Transformer [17] is the framework of encoder-decoder with attention mechanism for natural language processing (NLP). With Transformer's impressive performance in NLP, a growing number of computer vision research work based on Transformer has emerged. ViT [18] presented a pure Transformer architecture for vision by inputting the patches sequences splitted from an image to Transformer. But when the training data is not sufficient ViT will not generalize well. Also based on convolution-free Transformers, DeiT [19] introduced distillation strategy into Transformer to achieve competitive performance. DEtection TRansformer (DETR) [20] realized an end to end detector including a transformer encoder-decoder architecture and a global loss calculated in the parallel decoder. PVT [21] introduced pyramid structure to Transformer to generate an excellent vision Transformer backbone with lower computation than ViT. But these methods based on global attention have high computational complexity. Swin-Transformer [8] presented a general vision Transformer backbone which innovatively designed the shifted windows based on hierarchical architecture. The non-overlapping local windows attention mechanism and cross-window connection not only reduces the computational complexity, but also realizes the state-of-the-art of multiple visual tasks. CSwin [22] proposed a cross-shaped window consists of horizontal and vertical stripes split from feature in a parallel manner, meanwhile introduced Locally-enhanced Positional Encoding (LePE) to achieve better position encoding ability. However, local window attention is not friendly to big target detection. Our method optimizes this disadvantage inspired by Swin-Transformer and CSwin to optimize this disadvantage.

3   Method

3.1   Motivation

Swin-Transformer [8] is currently state-of-the-art vision Transformer backbone with higher accuracy and lower cost than others. The excellent feature extraction capability and advantages for small target detection of the window attention mechanism inspired us to apply it to SAR images target detection. Nevertheless, due to characteristics of small and diverse target size, sparse distribution and different postures, Swin-Transformer can not be directly applied to SAR images. Thus we redesign the window with variable size and apply it to the original Swin structure, formed the improved backbone for ship target detection in SAR images, called WAFormer.

3.2   Overview

The overall architecture of WAFormer is shown in Fig. 2. Because the proposed method is based on Swin-Transformer, so that the overall structure of the network tends to be similar. Taking an image as input, same to Swin-Transformer, followed with the patch partition module to split the image into evenly divided patches. Then applying a linear embedding layer project the patch tokens to C dimension. The setting of patch size and the number of tokens, and the design of the hierarchical representation are both same to Swin-Transformer, so that we also have $\frac{H}{2^{i+1}} \times \frac{W}{2^{i+1}}$ tokens in the ith stage with decreased resolution and increased channels. The difference is that we replace the original Swin-Transformer block with our WAFormer block. The WAFormer block will be described in detail as follows.

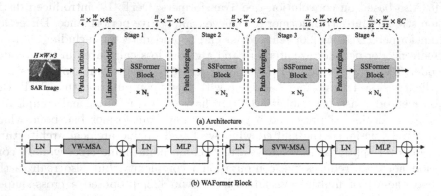

(a) Architecture

(b) WAFormer Block

Fig. 2. (a) The overall architecture of our proposed WAFormer; (b) an effective Transformer block for ship detection in SAR images described in Sect. 3.4). VW-MSA and SVW-MSA are multi-head attention modules with vertical/horizontal and shifted windowing configurations, respectively.

3.3 Variable Size Window Self-attention

Variable Size Window. Based on the local window attention mechanism, we propose a variable size window more suitable for ship target in SAR images. Firstly, in order to allow multi-scale input, the image is padded. Then the padded feature is partitioned into non-overlapping windows. The window size is set as $M \times N$ mean that each window contains $M \times N$ patches. As shown in Fig. 1, statistics indicate that the ratio of long and short sides of the bounding box of SAR images is mostly in the range of 4:1. While the aspect ratio of the window of Swin-Transformer is 1:1 which can not cover all targets and will truncate some targets. Thus we set the window size according to this ratio range as shown in Fig. 3. Specifically, from "Stage 1" to "Stage 4", we empirically set the long and short sides of the window to $\frac{224}{7*2^{i-1}}$ (i = 1, 2, 3, 4) and [7, 4, 2, 1]. Meanwhile, we set horizontal and vertical windows to capture the targets of different postures. Inspired by CSWin [22], we introduce the channel split method to calculate horizontal and vertical window attention at the same time to reduce costs.

Shifted Window. Since our window is no longer a fixed size, the original shifted window is not applicable. To increase the connection between non-overlapping windows, we replace the original shift step with $\left(\left\lfloor \frac{short\text{-}side}{2} \right\rfloor, \left\lfloor \frac{short\text{-}side}{2} \right\rfloor\right)$ to displace the regularly partitioned windows. In other words, the shift size becomes half of the short side of the window, which is proved to be effective by experiments.

Convolution Position Encoding. It is well known that position encoding is of great significance to the Transformer model [17,26,27]. However, we abandoned absolute position encoding and chose to utilize relative position encoding. Because we notice that the absolute position encoding does not lead to performance improvement. Inspired by LePE of CSWin, we also utilize a learnable additive positional encoding by performing convolution operation on *value* V of the window. We calculate the attention for a window according to the following formula:

$$Attention(Q, K, V) = SoftMax(QK^T/\sqrt{d})V + Conv(V) \tag{1}$$

Experiments show that this position encoding can effectively improve the accuracy.

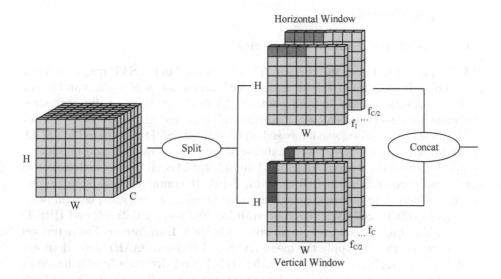

Fig. 3. The illustration of the variable size window with channel splitting manner

Computation Complexity Analysis. Omitting SoftMax, the computation complexity of a variable size window attention module based on an SAR image of $h \times w$ patches is:

$$\Omega(VW\text{-}MSA) = 4hwC^2 + 2MNhwC \tag{2}$$

where hw denote the patch num, it can be seen that our computational complexity is also linear with hw when MN set as we design.

3.4   WAFormer Block

Our network is built on WAFormer block, with other layers kept same with Swin-Transformer. A WAFormer block contains a pair of regular and shifted variable size window attention modules. This block is defined as:

$$
\begin{aligned}
\hat{X}^l &= VW\text{-}MSA(LN(X^{l-1})) + X^{l-1}, \\
X^l &= MLP(LN(\hat{X}^l) + \hat{X}^l), \\
\hat{X}^{l+1} &= SVW\text{-}MSA(LN(X^l)) + X^l, \\
X^{l+1} &= MLP(LN(\hat{X}^{l+1}) + \hat{X}^{l+1}),
\end{aligned}
\tag{3}
$$

where VW - MSA and SVW - MSA respectively denote the regular and shifted variable size window attention modules; $\hat{X}^l$ and X^{l+1} denote the output feature of the (S)VW - MSA module and the MLP module for block l.

4   Experiments

4.1   Dataset and Evaluation Metrics

SSDD [6] is the first open dataset which is widely used in the SAR remote sensing community. It includes 1160 SAR images with about 500×500 pixels and under 1–15 m resolutions. The dataset contains 2456 ship targets of different sizes and materials, good and bad sea condition, offshore and inshore scenes. Official-SSDD [5] is an optimized version based on the initial SSDD. Compared to SSDD, Official-SSDD revises labels, formulates stricter using standards and provides a comprehensive data analysis. HRSID [7] includes 5604 SAR images with 800×800 pixels and three resolutions(0.5 m, 1 m, 3 m). It contains 16951 ship targets covering different resolutions, polarization, sea condition, sea area, coastal port. We choose Official-SSDD as the main training and testing dataset, and HRSID as the validation dataset for comparison with Swin-Transformer. For detection evaluation metrics, we apply the mean Average Precision (mAP), detection rate at IOU $= 0.5$ (AP_{50}) and IOU $= 0.75$ (AP_{75}), and detection performance of target detection on small, medium, large targets (AP_S, AP_M, AP_L). The FLOPS and parameters of model used are also calculated and compared.

4.2   Implementation Details

We implement our proposed network on the PyTorch framework and MMDetection [23] toolbox. Multi-scale training [20,24] and data augmentation techniques [19] are adopted while the largest size is set as 1333×800 refer to Swin-Transformer. The experiments run at a NVIDIA GeForce RTX 3090 GPU and the batch size is set as 4 limited by the compute capability. The initial learning rate and training epoch are set as 0.0001 and 300. We use AdamW [25] optimizer and cosine decay learning rate scheduler with 5 epochs of linear warm-up. The weight decay is set as 0.05.

4.3 Comparison Results

We compare our proposed WAFormer backbone with Swin-Transformer using Mask R-CNN [28] object detection framework. Meanwhile, we also choose 5 classic object detection methods including YOLOv3 [29], SSD-512 [30], RetinaNet [31], Faster R-CNN [32], Mask R-CNN using ResNet-50 [33] as backbone. Figure 4 shows the visual results on Official-SSDD of WAFormer and Swin-Transformer with Mask R-CNN framework compared with other classic methods. It can be seen that the detection performance of our method is better than Swin-Transformer, and the confidence of the detection box is higher than that of other methods.

Table 2. Detection results on Official-SSDD test set.

Method	Image size	mAP	AP_{50}	AP_{75}	AP_S	AP_M	AP_L
YOLOv3	1024^2	65.7	96.1	78.1	66.3	65.3	67.7
SSD-512	512^2	70.1	96.3	84.4	70.1	71.1	74.4
RetinaNet	1024^2	73.8	98.3	88.8	73.2	76.4	**80.3**
Faster R-CNN	1024^2	73.1	96.7	88.1	71.6	**78.2**	76.9
Mask R-CNN R-50	1024^2	73.5	96.8	87.8	72.0	**78.2**	75.0
Mask R-CNN Swin	1024^2	73.4	97.7	89.6	73.3	74.7	62.9
Mask R-CNN WAFormer	1024^2	**74.4**	**98.6**	**90.4**	**73.7**	77.9	71.8

Table 3. Parameter size and FLOPs of methods in experiment.

Method	Image size	#Params	FLOPs
YOLOv3	1024^2	61.52M	198.5G
SSD-512	512^2	24.39M	87.12G
RetinaNet	1024^2	36.1M	209.13G
Faster R-CNN	1024^2	41.12M	211.28G
Mask R-CNN R-50	1024^2	43.75M	262.76G
Mask R-CNN Swin	1024^2	47.37M	267.01G
Mask R-CNN WAFormer	1024^2	41.31M	250.55G

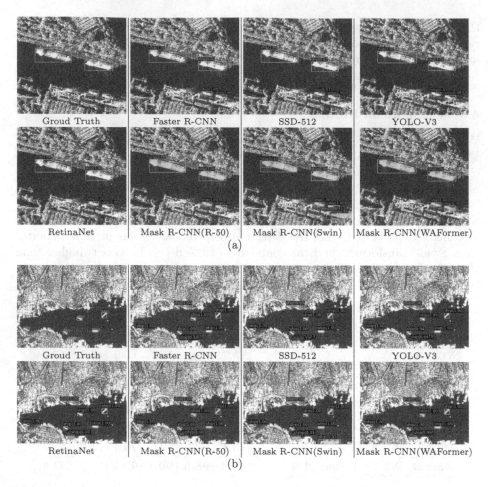

Fig. 4. Visual results of methods involved on Official-SSDD. R-50 namely ResNet-50 and Swin namely Swin-Tranformer.

Table 2 shows the performance comparisons of WAFormer with Swin-Transformer and other methods. Our WAFormer architecture achieves the highest detection accuracy among all the methods involved in the comparison. Specifically, our method achieves 74.4% mAP surpassing Swin-Transformer by +1.0, while the AP_{50} and AP_{75} are also bring advantages of +0.9 and +0.8 respectively. Meanwhile, we achieve the best result at AP_S and competitive result at AP_M with 73.7% and 77.9% respectively. The results demonstrate that our method brings improvements for solving small and multi-scale targets detection of SAR images. Table 3 shows the parameters and FLOPs of these methods. When using Mask R-CNN detection framework, our WAFormer realize less parameters and FLOPs than Swin-Transformer. Our method achieves the best results with a lighter architecture. This further shows the effectiveness and superiority of WAFormer for target detection in SAR images.

To validate the universality of our method over Swin-Transformer in SAR images target detection, we retrain and test WAFormer and Swin-Transformer with Mask R-CNN framework on HRSID. Table 4 shows that we still have advantage compared with Swin-Transformer.

Table 4. Detection results on HRSID test set.

Method	Image size	mAP	AP_{50}	AP_{75}	AP_S	AP_M	AP_L
Mask R-CNN Swin	1024^2	64.3	87.0	75.3	65.3	67.4	38.5
Mask R-CNN WAFormer	1024^2	**65.1**	**87.2**	**75.5**	**65.8**	**68.2**	**44.2**

4.4 Related Configuration Adjustment

Window Size and Shift Size. To achieve the optimal performance, we conducted different configuration experiments on the size and the shift size of the window. Table 5 shows the results of different configuration. The results show that the highest accuracy is achieved when the long side and short side are of the window set as [32, 16, 8, 4] and [7, 4, 2, 1]. And when the shift size is set as $\left(\lfloor \frac{short\text{-}side}{2} \rfloor, \lfloor \frac{short\text{-}side}{2} \rfloor\right)$, the shifted window can bring optimal performance.

Table 5. The performance of different configuration on size of the window and step size of the shifted window. The long side and short side denote the size of the window.

Long side	Short side	Shift size	mAP	AP_{50}	AP_{75}	AP_S	AP_M	AP_L
[56, 28, 14, 7]	[8, 4, 2, 1]	$\left(\lfloor \frac{short\text{-}side}{2} \rfloor, \lfloor \frac{short\text{-}side}{2} \rfloor\right)$	73.4	97.7	90.5	73.3	74.6	71.0
[56, 28, 14, 7]	[7, 4, 2, 1]	$\left(\lfloor \frac{short\text{-}side}{2} \rfloor, \lfloor \frac{short\text{-}side}{2} \rfloor\right)$	73.5	97.7	89.3	73.0	76.5	68.8
[32, 16, 8, 4]	[8, 4, 2, 1]	$\left(\lfloor \frac{short\text{-}side}{2} \rfloor, \lfloor \frac{short\text{-}side}{2} \rfloor\right)$	73.9	98.6	89.1	73.4	76.6	**77.7**
[32, 16, 8, 4]	[7, 4, 2, 1]	$\left(\lfloor \frac{short\text{-}side}{2} \rfloor, \lfloor \frac{short\text{-}side}{2} \rfloor\right)$	**74.4**	**98.7**	90.4	**73.8**	77.4	71.0
[16, 8, 4, 2]	[8, 4, 2, 1]	$\left(\lfloor \frac{short\text{-}side}{2} \rfloor, \lfloor \frac{short\text{-}side}{2} \rfloor\right)$	73.7	98.5	**90.7**	73.2	75.8	70.0
[16, 8, 4, 2]	[7, 4, 2, 1]	$\left(\lfloor \frac{short\text{-}side}{2} \rfloor, \lfloor \frac{short\text{-}side}{2} \rfloor\right)$	73.3	97.7	89.8	72.6	76.1	65.9
[32, 16, 8, 4]	[7, 4, 2, 1]	$\left(\lfloor \frac{long\text{-}side}{2} \rfloor, \lfloor \frac{short\text{-}side}{2} \rfloor\right)$	73.6	98.6	90.4	72.7	76.8	73.8
[32, 16, 8, 4]	[7, 4, 2, 1]	$\left(\lfloor \frac{long\text{-}side}{2} \rfloor, \lfloor \frac{long\text{-}side}{2} \rfloor\right)$	73.9	98.6	89.4	73.0	**77.5**	66.7

Convolution Position Encoding. To validate the effect of convolutional relative position encoding, we also conducted relevant experiments. We calculate the origin attention without the convolution position encoding, the attention with additive and multiplicative convolutional position encoding, respectively. The results show in Table 6, the results show that the additive convolutional position encoding is beneficial to improve the accuracy.

Table 6. The performance of different position encoding. mul conv rel pos.: multiplicative convolutional position encoding, add conv rel pos.: additive convolutional position encoding

Position encoding	mAP	AP_{50}	AP_{75}	AP_S	AP_M	AP_L
No pos.	73.3	97.8	90.3	72.5	76.5	71.3
Mul conv rel pos.	73.6	**98.6**	89.4	72.5	**77.9**	**77.7**
Add conv rel pos.	**74.4**	**98.6**	**90.4**	**73.7**	**77.9**	71.8

5   Conclusion

In this paper, according to the characteristics of the SAR images, we propose a backbone focus on target size based on Swin-Transformer. Our method improves the target detection performance in SAR images while reducing the cost. Experiments show the targeted improvements have played an effective role in solving the problem of difficult detection of small and multi-scale targets in SAR images. At the same time, our size variable window is also applicable to other datasets, since it is designed according to the dataset. However, it can be found that our large target detection results are not excellent. We consider this may be a shortcoming of window attention mechanism. In future work, we plan to increase the number of large windows in the shallow layer, and introduce the channel attention mechanism to increase the information interaction between channels.

References

1. Jiao, J., et al.: A densely connected end-to-end neural network for multiscale and multiscene SAR ship detection. IEEE Access **6**, 20881–20892 (2018)
2. Chang, Y.-L., Anagaw, A., Chang, L., Wang, Y.C., Hsiao, C.-Y., Lee, W.-H.: Ship detection based on YOLOv2 for SAR imagery. Remote Sens. **11**(7), 786 (2019)
3. Zhang, T., Zhang, X.: High-speed ship detection in SAR images based on a grid convolutional neural network. Remote Sens. **11**(10), 1206 (2019)
4. An, Q., Pan, Z., Liu, L., You, H.: DRBox-v2: an improved detector with rotatable boxes for target detection in SAR images. IEEE Trans. Geosci. Remote Sens. **57**(11), 8333–8349 (2019)
5. Zhang, T., et al.: SAR ship detection dataset (SSDD): official release and comprehensive data analysis. Remote Sens. **13**(18), 3690 (2021)
6. Li, J., Qu, C., Shao, J.: Ship detection in SAR images based on an improved faster R-CNN. In: 2017 SAR in Big Data Era: Models, Methods and Applications (BIGSARDATA), pp. 1–6. IEEE (2017)
7. Wei, S., Zeng, X., Qu, Q., Wang, M., Su, H., Shi, J.: HRSID: a high-resolution SAR images dataset for ship detection and instance segmentation. IEEE Access **8**, 120234–120254 (2020)
8. Liu, Z., et al.: Swin transformer: hierarchical vision transformer using shifted windows. In: Proceedings of the IEEE/CVF International Conference on Computer Vision, pp. 10012–10022 (2021)

9. Cui, Z., Li, Q., Cao, Z., Liu, N.: Dense attention pyramid networks for multi-scale ship detection in SAR images. IEEE Trans. Geosci. Remote Sens. **57**(11), 8983–8997 (2019)

10. Zhao, Y., Zhao, L., Xiong, B., Kuang, G.: Attention receptive pyramid network for ship detection in SAR images. IEEE J. Sel. Top. Appl. Earth Observations Remote Sens. **13**, 2738–2756 (2020)

11. Cui, Z., Wang, X., Liu, N., Cao, Z., Yang, J.: Ship detection in large-scale SAR images via spatial shuffle-group enhance attention. IEEE Trans. Geosci. Remote Sens. **59**(1), 379–391 (2020)

12. Fu, J., Sun, X., Wang, Z., Fu, K.: An anchor-free method based on feature balancing and refinement network for multiscale ship detection in SAR images. IEEE Trans. Geosci. Remote Sens. **59**(2), 1331–1344 (2020)

13. Guo, H., Yang, X., Wang, N., Gao, X.: A CenterNet++ model for ship detection in SAR images. Pattern Recogn. **112**, 107787 (2021)

14. Tang, L., Tang, W., Qu, X., Han, Y., Wang, W., Zhao, B.: A scale-aware pyramid network for multi-scale object detection in SAR images. Remote Sens. **14**(4), 973 (2022)

15. Xu, X., Zhang, X., Zhang, T.: Lite-YOLOv5: a lightweight deep learning detector for on-board ship detection in large-scene sentinel-1 SAR images. Remote Sens. **14**(4), 1018 (2022)

16. Xia, R., et al.: CRTransSar: a visual transformer based on contextual joint representation learning for SAR ship detection. Remote Sens. **14**(6), 1488 (2022)

17. Vaswani, A., et al.: Attention is all you need. In: Advances in Neural Information Processing Systems, vol. 30 (2017)

18. Dosovitskiy, A., et al.: An image is worth 16 × 16 words: Transformers for image recognition at scale. arXiv preprint arXiv:2010.11929 (2020)

19. Touvron, H., Cord, M., Douze, M., Massa, F., Sablayrolles, A., Jégou, H.: Training data-efficient image transformers and distillation through attention. In: International Conference on Machine Learning, pp. 10347–10357. PMLR (2021)

20. Carion, N., Massa, F., Synnaeve, G., Usunier, N., Kirillov, A., Zagoruyko, S.: End-to-end object detection with transformers. In: Vedaldi, A., Bischof, H., Brox, T., Frahm, J.-M. (eds.) ECCV 2020. LNCS, vol. 12346, pp. 213–229. Springer, Cham (2020). https://doi.org/10.1007/978-3-030-58452-8_13

21. Wang, W., et al.: Pyramid vision transformer: a versatile backbone for dense prediction without convolutions. In: Proceedings of the IEEE/CVF International Conference on Computer Vision, pp. 568–578 (2021)

22. Dong, X., et al.: CSWin transformer: A general vision transformer backbone with cross-shaped windows. arXiv preprint arXiv:2107.00652 (2021)

23. Chen, K., et al.: MMDetection: Open MMLab detection toolbox and benchmark. arXiv preprint arXiv:1906.07155 (2019)

24. Sun, P., et al.: Sparse R-CNN: end-to-end object detection with learnable proposals. In: Proceedings of the IEEE/CVF Conference on Computer Vision and Pattern Recognition, pp. 14454–14463 (2021)

25. Kingma, D.P., Ba, J.: Adam: A method for stochastic optimization. arXiv preprint arXiv:1412.6980 (2014)

26. Gehring, J., Auli, M., Grangier, D., Yarats, D., Dauphin, Y.N.: Convolutional sequence to sequence learning. In: International Conference on Machine Learning, pp. 1243–1252. PMLR (2017)

27. Shaw, P., Uszkoreit, J., Vaswani, A.: Self-attention with relative position representations. arXiv preprint arXiv:1803.02155 (2018)

28. He, K., Gkioxari, G., Dollár, P., Girshick, R.: Mask R-CNN. In: Proceedings of the IEEE International Conference on Computer Vision, pp. 2961–2969 (2017)
29. Redmon, J., Farhadi, A.: YOLOv3: An incremental improvement. arXiv preprint arXiv:1804.02767 (2018)
30. Liu, W., et al.: SSD: single shot multibox detector. In: Leibe, B., Matas, J., Sebe, N., Welling, M. (eds.) ECCV 2016. LNCS, vol. 9905, pp. 21–37. Springer, Cham (2016). https://doi.org/10.1007/978-3-319-46448-0_2
31. Lin, T.-Y., Goyal, P., Girshick, R., He, K., Dollár, P.: Focal loss for dense object detection. In: Proceedings of the IEEE International Conference on Computer Vision, pp. 2980–2988 (2017)
32. Girshick, R.: Fast R-CNN. In: Proceedings of the IEEE International Conference on Computer Vision, pp. 1440–1448 (2015)
33. He, K., Zhang, X., Ren, S., Sun, J.: Deep residual learning for image recognition. In: Proceedings of the IEEE Conference on Computer Vision and Pattern Recognition, pp. 770–778 (2016)

EllipseIoU: A General Metric for Aerial Object Detection

Xinbo Yang[1], Chenglong Li[2,3], Rui Ruan[4(✉)], Lei Liu[1],
Wang Chao[1], and Bin Luo[1]

[1] School of Computer Science and Technology, Anhui University, Hefei, China
[2] School of Artificial Intelligence, Anhui University, Hefei, China
[3] Anhui Provincial Key Laboratory of Multimodal Cognitive Computation,
Hefei, China
[4] School of Internet, Anhui University, Hefei, China
rr_ahu@126.com

Abstract. Existing works in object detection usually adopt different
Intersection over Union (IoU) metrics to define the similarity between
predicted box and target box, which greatly boost the detection performance. For the task of aerial object detection, since the predicted
and target boxes are with different sizes, aspect ratios and orientations,
existing IoU metrics can not measure their similarity well. In this work,
we propose a new and generic metric for robust aerial object detection,
called EllipseIoU, which incorporates the *ellipse distance* between the
predicted box and the target box. In particular, we find the inner ellipse
from the box, and then calculate the ellipse distance between predicted
and target boxes based on the distances of focal points. We prove that
the proposed ellipse distance well measures the relations of sizes, aspect
ratios and orientations between predicted and target boxes. Moreover,
we also incorporate the relation of short axis length between two boxes
to measure the relation of sizes. Based on the ellipse distance, we design
the EllipseIoU metric by combining with the IoU metric and integrate it
into detectors for performance boosting of aerial object detection. Experimental results on public datasets show that the detector with EllipseIoU
significantly improve the baseline without impact on the efficiency and
achieves state-of-the-art performance.

Keywords: Aerial object detection · Intersection over Union (IoU)

1 Introduction

Aerial object detection, as an important branch in object detection, become a
popular topic in the computer vision community recently. It has a wide range
of applications, such as resource detection, urban planning, and ship detection.
Different from natural images, aerial images are collected from remote sensing
platforms. And objects in these aerial images are usually with various orientation
and large aspect ratio, which bring a big challenge for aerial object detection.

© The Author(s), under exclusive license to Springer Nature Switzerland AG 2022
S. Yu et al. (Eds.): PRCV 2022, LNCS 13536, pp. 537–550, 2022.
https://doi.org/10.1007/978-3-031-18913-5_42

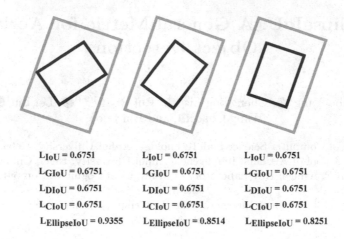

$L_{IoU} = 0.6751$ $L_{IoU} = 0.6751$ $L_{IoU} = 0.6751$

$L_{GIoU} = 0.6751$ $L_{GIoU} = 0.6751$ $L_{GIoU} = 0.6751$

$L_{DIoU} = 0.6751$ $L_{DIoU} = 0.6751$ $L_{DIoU} = 0.6751$

$L_{CIoU} = 0.6751$ $L_{CIoU} = 0.6751$ $L_{CIoU} = 0.6751$

$L_{EllipseIoU} = 0.9355$ $L_{EllipseIoU} = 0.8514$ $L_{EllipseIoU} = 0.8251$

Fig. 1. Illustration of the advantages of the EllipseIoU loss. If a bounding box contains another one, traditional IoU metrics have the same value in different scenarios. However, the proposed EllipseIoU loss can produce different values for these situations, which ultimately accelerate the training convergence speed and improve the detection performance.

Researchers put forward improvement in this field by using a oriented-rectangle bounding box, which includes coordinates of the center point, width, height and rotation angle. Qi et al. [6] designs detector optimization as a sample label assignment to improve training performance of the detector. While X. Yang et al. [11,22] replaces the angle regression task by an angle classification task to avoid large loss of angle prediction. R3Det [13] proposes a feature refinement module based on RetinaNet [3] to overcome the inconsistency problem of features between proposal box and target box when the object is rotated. These methods have achieved good results on public remote sensing datasets such as DOTA [9], HRSC2016 [4] and etc., but the accuracy of the prediction box is still insufficient. The main reason is that the existing bounding box losses are Insensitive to the orientation and aspect ratio of objects, which leads to an inappropriate distance measure between the predicted box and target box. This suggests that it is critical to design an appropriate loss for aerial object detection.

Intersection over Union(IoU) is defined as ratio between Area of intersection and Area of Union from two boxes. In the field of horizontal object detection, researchers found that computing the IoU loss [16] using the IoU between the predicted and target boxes is better than using the L1-loss directly at training time. However, if the two boxes do not intersect, the similarity cannot be reflected because the IoU is zero. Therefore, researchers have proposed Generalized IoU (GIoU) loss [8], which pays attention not only to overlapping areas, but also to other non-overlapping areas, in order to better reflect the similarity between two boxes that do not intersect. To solve the problem of GIoU and IoU when a box completely contains another box, some methods based on the center point distance are proposed, such as DIoU loss and CIoU loss [19]. Although these IoU

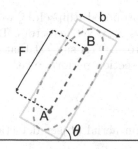

bounding box
the inner ellipse
focal point: A, B
short side length: b
focal length: F
(the distance from A to B)

Fig. 2. For objects in aerial images, we can accurately describe its location, size and orientation information according to the short axis length and the properties of the inner ellipse focus line.

losses have good applications in the field of horizontal object detection, they are hard to be applied in the field of aerial oriented object detection. These losses, designed for horizontal bounding boxes, do not need to consider the inconsistency of angles between rotating bounding boxes. Especially in the extreme case of complete inclusion and zero intersection area, these IoU losses cannot filter boxes with similar angles and sizes, which can be seen in Fig. 1.

To solve this problem, we propose a new metric based on the *ellipse distance* in this work, called EllipseIoU, for aerial object detection. As shown in Fig. 2, we use the inner ellipse of the target box and its focal points in the ellipse to describe its properties in terms of center location, size and rotation. Specifically, we define a distance of two pairs of focal points, which come from predicted box and target box respectively. It reflects distance in terms of location, size and orientation between two boxes. Besides, the aspect ratio correlation coefficient is used to make it more sensitive to narrow and long targets. Therefore, we measure a distance of short-axis length between two boxes to jointly measure the similarity between the sizes. Based on these properties, we define the ellipse distance to measure the difference between the predicted box and the target box.

In summary, our contributions are as follows.

- We investigate and analyze the shortcomings of existing IoU-based metrics, which will drop efficacy for some situations in aerial object detection, such as box inclusion, orientation and large aspect ratio.
- We propose a new ellipse distance to effectively measure the difference between boxes, especially for objects with huge aspect ratio and arbitrary rotation. The ellipse distance makes full use of the properties of the inner ellipse of the box to describe the information of its location, size and orientation and thus well represent the distance relation with another box.
- We design a general metric called EllipseIoU measure by combining the ellipse distance and the IoU metric to adapt the characteristic of bounding box regression in aerial object detection. Our EllipseIoU not only discusses the overlap ratio of predicted box and target box, but also considers their dissimilarity in terms of size, aspect ratio and orientation of box.

– To demonstrate the effectiveness of the proposed EllipseIoU, we integrate it as EllipseIoU Loss into RetinaNet [3] and S2A-Net detectors. The extensive experiments on public datasets HRSC2016, DOTA suggest that the designed loss function significantly improve the detection performance.

2   Related Work

In this section, we perform a brief review on aerial object detection and IoU-based metrics.

2.1   Aerial Object Detection

Deep learning methods have dominated this research field in recent years, which mainly benefit from the powerful representation ability of CNN, and have significantly improved the performance. Unlike objects in natural images, objects in aerial images are usually distributed with orientations. Therefore, aerial object detection usually uses oriented bounding boxes to represent the target. To enhance the feature discrimination of rotating objects, J. Ma et al. [5] propose a new strategy called RRPN, which is used to improve the rotation anchor point and rotation region proposal in any direction, and re-integrated at the feature level by using RRoI Pooling layer. X. Yan et al. [15] design a feature fusion structure from the perspective of feature fusion and anchor sampling, and design a multi-dimensional attention network to reduce the adverse effects caused by background noise. X. Yan et al. [21] also noticed the need for a new metric scheme that is more suitable for rotating boxes in the field of remote sensing object detection, and proposed GWD from a statistical point of view. Although the advanced network can make the feature extraction of rotating objects more discriminative, there is still a problem that the direction is difficult to detect. Gliding-vertex [10] avoids the boundary problem of direction by predicting the sliding value of horizontal box and its vertex. DAL [6] consider the inconsistency of box features before and after the detection, and uses the regression results to divide the samples, which achieves better performance.

2.2   IoU-Based Metrics

Intersection over Union(IoU) [16] is an important indicator in object detection. It is calculated by the ratio of the intersection and union between the predicted box and target box.

$$IoU = \frac{|A \cap B|}{|A \cup B|}$$

where A is the predicted box, B is the target box.

IoU is not only used to evaluate the detection results, but also to constrain bounding box regression. Unlike L1-norm, which is generally used for fine-tuning of bounding boxes, IoU loss directly constrains the network through the IoU back-propagation gradient. However, the IoU metrics have two serious shortcomings, which can be summarized as follows:

- If two boxes do not intersect, the gradient back-propagation cannot be used because the IoU is zero.
- When two boxes are contained, the existing IoU metrics can not distinguish boxes with different orientations, as shown in Fig. 1.

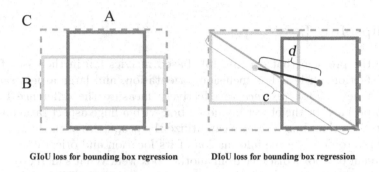

GIoU loss for bounding box regression   DIoU loss for bounding box regression

Fig. 3. GIoU and DIoU

Generalized IoU(GIoU) [8] is another distance measure, which focuses on both overlapping and non-overlapping regions. GIoU ranges from -1 to 1, where -1 indicates that the two boxes do not intersect and are infinitely far away, and 1 indicates that the two boxes completely overlap. As shown in Fig. 3, it makes the closer box selected when there is no intersecting area.

$$GIoU = IoU - \frac{|C - (A \cap B)|}{|C|}$$

where A is the predicted box, B is the target box, C is the minimum closure area of A and B.

Distance IoU(DIoU)[19] is proposed by considering the distance of the center point of the boxes, which could guide the center of the prediction box to approach the center of the target box quickly.

$$DIoU = IoU - \frac{\rho^2(b, b_{gt})}{c^2}$$

where b and b_{gt} represent the center of the predicted box and target box respectively, ρ is euclidean distance between those two center points, c is the diagonal distance of the minimum closure box of those two boxes.

Complete IoU(CIoU) [19] is further proposed on the basis of DIoU considering the shape of object.

$$CIoU = IoU - \left[\frac{\rho^2(b, b_{gt})}{c^2} + \alpha v\right]$$

where α is weight function, v is the similarity in shape.

Although these IoU losses have good applications in the field of horizontal object detection, but they are hard to be applied in the field of aerial oriented object detection, because these losses do not consider the inconsistency of angles between rotating bounding boxes. Especially in the extreme case of complete inclusion and zero intersection area, these IoU losses cannot filter boxes with similar angles and sizes, which can be seen in Fig. 1.

3   EllipseIoU Loss

To solve the problem that existing IoU-based metrics fail in the case of aerial object detection, such as box inclusion, orientation, and large aspect ratio, we propose a new *ellipse distance* to effectively measure the difference between boxes. Especially for the object bounding box with a huge aspect ratio and arbitrary rotation, the ellipse distance can utilize the properties of the bounding box inner ellipse to describe the information of its location and orientation. Thus it can represent one box's distance from another box well. What's more, by combining the ellipse distance with the IoU metric, we propose the EllipseIoU measure to solve the problem of bounding-box regression in aerial object detection, which not only discusses the overlapping ratio of the predicted box and target box but also considers their dissimilarity in terms of aspect ratio and orientation.

In this section, we first introduce the proposed ellipse distance and EllipseIoU. Then, we describe the design of EllipseIoU loss. At last, we discuss the difference between the proposed ellipse metric and several IoU-based metrics.

Fig. 4. An example of a heat map of a ship is like an ellipse state.

3.1 EllipseIoU

We found that the heat map of a rectangular bounding box presents an ellipse-like state in Fig. 4, and inspired by this, we begin to think about representing a rectangular bounding box with its inner ellipse.

In mathematics like Fig. 2, the focal line and short axis(or long axis) can be used to determine the whole ellipse, including size, location, and orientation. So we could accurately represent the bounding box through focal line and short axis information. Therefore, if we can measure the difference between the focal lines, we can use this to judge the degree of difference between the boxes.

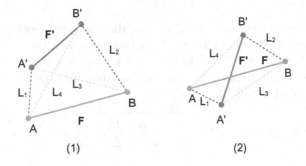

Fig. 5. The group lines with the smallest sum is named as L_1, L_2, and the other group lines is called as L_3, L_4. (1) two focal lines are separated, and (2) two focal lines are intersected.

When we have a predicted box and the target box, we can also have two inner ellipses and their two focal lines with four endpoints. We divide four auxiliary lines between these endpoints into two groups like the form in Fig. 5. The paired group (A' to A, B' to B) and the exchange group (A' to B, B' to A). The two lines with the shorter group sum are called L_1 and L_2 respectively, and the other two lines are called L_3 and L_4. Then, we obtain the following formula:

$$L_1^2 + L_2^2 = L_3^2 + L_4^2 - 2F \cdot F' \cdot cos\theta$$

where θ is the corresponding acute angle between the two focal lines.

Next, we deduce a new proportional formula called focal mixing distance project:

$$\frac{L_1^2 + L_2^2}{L_3^2 + L_4^2} = \frac{L_3^2 + L_4^2 - 2F \cdot F' \cdot cos\theta}{L_3^2 + L_4^2}$$
$$= \frac{L_1^2 + L_2^2}{L_1^2 + L_2^2 + 2F \cdot F' \cdot cos\theta}$$

From the above formula, we analyze that if this focal mixing distance project converges to 0, we need to optimize the following three points at the same time.

First, as the corresponding point approaches gradually, the lengths of L_1 and L_2 tend to zero. Second, θ gradually decreases to 0, and $\cos\theta$ approaches 1. Third, the length of the focal line approach gradually, and L_3, L_4, and F' approach to F. In addition, this distance is more sensitive to narrow and long bounding boxes by measuring the similarity of two focal lines and comprehensively considering the location and orientation.

In order to determine an ellipse, the length of the short axis is also needed. Therefore, we introduce the short axis difference to measure the similarity between the short axes of two ellipses, which is formulated as follows.

$$\frac{(b - b')^2}{b^2}$$

Combining the original IoU, focal mixing distance and short axis difference, we propose EllipseIoU to measure the bounding box with orientation, which is formulated as follows. And We add the aspect ratio factor into the EllipseIoU formula to make it more sensitive to narrow and rotating object bounding boxes, which is formulated as follows.

$$EllipseIoU = IoU - \sqrt{\left[\frac{w - h}{w} * \frac{L_1^2 + L_2^2}{L_3^2 + L_4^2} + \frac{(b - b')^2}{b^2}\right]}$$

Compared with other IoU, we decompose the focal line and short axis of the inner ellipse, and comprehensively consider its location, size, and orientation. Next, we will apply it to the loss constraint to guide bounding box regression.

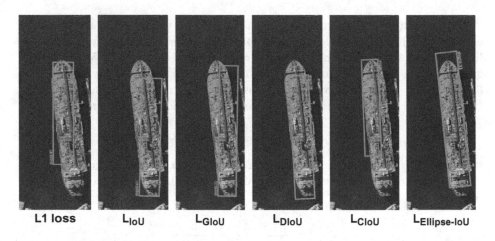

| L1 loss | L_{IoU} | L_{GIoU} | L_{DIoU} | L_{CIoU} | $L_{Ellipse\text{-}IoU}$ |

Fig. 6. Obb-Retinanet on HRSC2016 dataset results show that our EllipseIoU predicts more accurate bounding box on rotated and narrow object.

3.2   EllipseIoU Loss

In this section, we integrate proposed EllipseIoU as EllipseIoU loss into RetinaNet and S2A-Net detectors to carry out aerial object detection, which is formulated as follows.

$$L_{EllipseIoU} = 1 - EllipseIoU$$

$$= 1 - IoU + \sqrt{\left[\frac{w - h}{w} * \frac{L_1^2 + L_2^2}{L_3^2 + L_4^2} + \frac{(b - b')^2}{b^2}\right]} \tag{1}$$

Our focal mixing distance implicitly contains angle information, which can improve the defect that the existing IoU method is insensitive to angle, as shown in Fig. 1.

These advantages will enable the detector using EllipseIoU Loss (such as RetinaNet modified for the oriented bounding box) to converge faster during the training stage (especially at the beginning of training), and improve the performance of the detector on the oriented bounding box, as shown in Fig. 7.

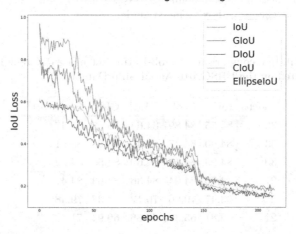

Fig. 7. Comparing the changes of different IoU-based losses with Obb-RetinaNet on HRSC2016 dataset, our proposed EllipseIoU Loss will converge faster during the training process, to finally achieve better training results.

3.3   Discussion on Several IoU-Based Metrics

In Fig. 8, we show the loss results of different IoU-based metrics when the predicted bounding box and the target box have no intersect part. We set up two boxes of the same shape and size with no intersection between them. In this way, the effect of the angle on the loss is simulated when the prediction box and the target box are far apart in the early stage of training. When angle of two boxes changes, IoU loss remains unchanged, GIoU and DIoU even obtain different values with angle changing, but they do not conform to the correct trend of angle change.

However, with the change of the angle between the directions of the two boxes, the loss curve shows our proposed EllipseIoU loss is sensitive to angle changes and can correctly indicate the change trend of the angle. Therefore, our proposed EllipseIoU loss could guide network to regress more accurate rotated bounding box, and achieve better aerial object detection performance.

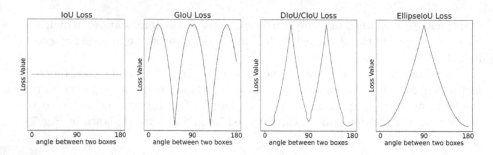

Fig. 8. The trend of two disjoint bounding boxes with the same size under different IoU losses with the change of box included angle.

Table 1. Quantitative comparison of Obb-RetinaNet using different IoU-losses. The results are reported on the HRSC2016 Aerial Ship DataSet

epochs	IoU	GIoU	DIoU	CIoU	EllipseIoU
36	84.55	84.89	84.64	85.08	85.47
33	84.90	84.47	83.40	84.68	85.01
30	84.96	84.15	84.69	84.50	84.92
27	84.00	84.04	84.36	84.03	84.47
24	63.47	70.96	70.12	72.37	79.48
21	60.81	65.30	69.66	69.93	71.42

In Fig. 7 and Table 1, we present the convergence process of different classic IoU-based loss on Obb-RetinaNet detector. It can be seen that the convergence speed of EllipseIoU loss is more efficient than other losses, while detector with EllipseIoU loss takes less time to reach the stable at the beginning of training. The results of different IoU loss on the horizontal box dataset PascalVOC show that the metric we designed can also achieve similar training effects in horizontal box detection in Table 2.

Table 2. The results of different IoU LOSS on horizontal box dataset PascalVOC with RetinaNet detector.

Pascal VOC	Baseline	IoU	GIoU	DIoU	CIoU	EllipseIoU
mAP	72.58	73.25	73.50	73.35	73.73	73.84

4   Experimental Results

In this section, we evaluate our EllipseIoU on two public aerial object detection datasets including HRSC2016 [4] and DOTA [9], based on the classical aerial object detector Obb-RetinaNet and S2A-Net.

4.1   Datasets

- HRSC2016 dataset contains images from two scenarios including ships on the sea and ships close inshore, which contains 1061 images. All the images are collected from six famous harbors, with image sizes ranging from 300×300 to 1,500×900.
- DOTA dataset for object detection on aerial image. It contains 2,806 aerial images from different sensors and platforms. The image size ranges from approximately 800×800 to 4,000×4,000 pixels, and includes various objects with different sizes, directions, and shapes.

Fig. 9. Visualization of detection results on DOTA with EllipseIoU Loss.

4.2   Results on DOTA and HRSC2016 Dataset

We use the orientated detector Obb-Retinanet and S2A-Net as baseline, which employs ResNet with Feature Pyramid Network(FPN) as backbone. Compared with baseline, we only change the final predicted box regression loss from original loss into our EllipseIoU loss. As shown in Table 3, our method has achieved an outstanding better performance than baseline and other methods. It can be seen from the Fig. 6 that our method achieves more accurate detection results

Table 3. Performance evaluation on HRSC2016 and DOTA dataset.

Methods	Backbone	HRSC2016	DOTA
R2CNN [12]	R101	73.07	60.67
FR-O [9]	R101	–	52.93
R-DFPN [14]	R101	–	62.01
RRPN [5]	R101	79.08	61.01
R2PN [18]	VGG16	79.60	–
RoI Trans. [2]	R101	86.20	69.56
CAD-Net [17]	R101	–	69.90
DRN [7]	H104	–	70.70
R3Det [13]	R152	89.26	73.74
PIoU [1]	R101	80.32	60.50
DAL [6]	R101	89.77	71.78
Obb-Retinanet	R50	73.29	72.72
Obb-Retinanet+EllipseIoU loss	R50	85.47	73.72
Obb-Retinanet+EllipseIoU loss	R101	85.58	73.83
Obb-Retinanet+EllipseIoU loss	x101	86.61	74.68
S2A-Net	R50	90.17	74.12
S2A-Net+EllipseIoU loss	R50	90.23	74.57
S2A-Net+EllipseIoU loss	R101	90.28	74.97
S2A-Net+EllipseIoU loss	x101	90.36	75.46

5   Conclusion

In this paper, we propose EllipseIoU to effectively guide aerial object detector training, especially for objects with big aspect ratio and arbitrary rotation. EllipseIoU can make full use of the properties of the inner ellipse of bounding box to describe the information of its location, size and orientation and thus have a good ability to guide the training process. Extensive experiments on two datasets demonstrate the effectiveness of the proposed EllipseIoU. In the future, we will explore applying ellipse distance in anchor label assignment or sampling strategy.s

References

1. Chen, Z., et al.: PIoU loss: towards accurate oriented object detection in complex environments. In: Vedaldi, A., Bischof, H., Brox, T., Frahm, J.-M. (eds.) ECCV 2020. LNCS, vol. 12350, pp. 195–211. Springer, Cham (2020). https://doi.org/10.1007/978-3-030-58558-7_12
2. Ding, J., Xue, N., Long, Y., Xia, G.S., Lu, Q.: Learning roi transformer for oriented object detection in aerial images. In: 2019 IEEE/CVF Conference on Computer Vision and Pattern Recognition (CVPR) (2020)
3. Lin, T.Y., Goyal, P., Girshick, R., He, K., Dollár, P.: Focal loss for dense object detection. IEEE Trans. Pattern Anal. Mach. Intell. **42**, 2999–3007 (2017)
4. Liu, Z., Yuan, L., Weng, L., Yang, Y.: A High Resolution Optical Satellite Image Dataset for Ship Recognition and Some New Baselines, vol. 2, pp. 324–331 (2017)
5. Ma, J., et al.: Arbitrary-oriented scene text detection via rotation proposals. IEEE Trans. Multimedia **20**(11), 3111–3122 (2018)
6. Ming, Q., Zhou, Z., Miao, L., Zhang, H., Li., L.: Dynamic anchor learning for arbitrary-oriented object detection, vol. 1(2), p. 6. arXiv preprint arXiv:2012.04150 (2021)
7. Pan, X., et al.: Dynamic refinement network for oriented and densely packed object detection. In: Proceedings of the IEEE/CVF Conference on Computer Vision and Pattern Recognition, p. 11207–11216 (2020)
8. Rezatofighi, H., Tsoi, N., Gwak, J., Sadeghian, A., Reid, I., Savarese, S.: Generalized intersection over union: a metric and a loss for bounding box regression. In: Proceedings of the IEEE/CVF Conference on Computer Vision and Pattern Recognition, pp. 658–666 (2019)
9. Xia, G.-S.: Dota: a large-scale dataset for object detection in aerial images. In: Proceedings of the IEEE Conference on Computer Vision and Pattern Recognition, pp. 3974–3983 (2018)
10. Yongchao, X., et al.: Gliding vertex on the horizontal bounding box for multi-oriented object detection. IEEE Trans. Pattern Anal. Mach. Intell. **43**(4), 1452–1459 (2020)
11. Yang, X., Yan, J., He, T.: On the arbitrary-oriented object detection: classification based approaches revisited. arXiv preprint arXiv:2003.05597 (2020)
12. Yang, X.: R2cnn++: multi-dimensional attention based rotation invariant detector with robust anchor strategy (2018)
13. Yang, X., Liu, Q., Yan, J., Li, A., Zhang, Z., Yu, G.: R3det: refined single-stage detector with feature refinement for rotating object, vol.2(4). arXiv preprint arXiv:1908.05612 (2019)
14. Yang, X., et al.: Automatic ship detection in remote sensing images from google earth of complex scenes based on multiscale rotation dense feature pyramid networks. Remote Sens. **10**(1), 132 (2018)
15. Yang, X.: Scrdet: Towards more robust detection for small, cluttered and rotated objects. pp. 8232–8241 (2019)
16. Yu, J., Jiang, Y., Wang, Z., Cao, Z., Huang, T., Unitbox: an advanced object detection network. In: Proceedings of the 24th ACM international conference on Multimedia, pp. 516–520
17. Zhang, G., Shijian, L., Zhang, W.: Cad-net: A context-aware detection network for objects in remote sensing imagery. IEEE Trans. Geosci. Remote Sens. **57**(12), 10015–10024 (2019)

18. Zhang, Z., Guo, W., Zhu, S., Wenxian, Yu.: Toward arbitrary-oriented ship detection with rotated region proposal and discrimination networks. IEEE Geosci. Remote Sens. Lett. **15**(11), 1745–1749 (2018)
19. Zheng, Z., Wang, P., Liu, W., Li, J., Ye, R., Ren, D.: Distance-iou loss: faster and better learning for bounding box regression. In :Proceedings of the AAAI Conference on Artificial Intelligence, vol. 34, pp. 12993–13000 (2020)
20. Zhu, H., Chen, X., Dai, W., Fu, K., Ye, Q., Jiao, J.: Orientation robust object detection in aerial images using deep convolutional neural network. In: 2015 IEEE International Conference on Image Processing (ICIP), pp. 3735–3739. IEEE (2015)
21. Yang, X., Yan, J., Ming, Q., Wang, W., Zhang, X., Tian, Q.: Rethinking rotated object detection with gaussian wasserstein distance loss. In: International Conference on Machine Learning, pp. 11830–11841. PMLR (2021)
22. Yang, X., Hou, L., Zhou, Y., Wang, W., Yan, J.: Dense label encoding for boundary discontinuity free rotation detection. In: Proceedings of the IEEE/CVF Conference on Computer Vision and Pattern Recognition, pp. 15819–15829 (2021)

Transmission Tower Detection Algorithm Based on Feature-Enhanced Convolutional Network in Remote Sensing Image

Zhengpeng Zhang[1]([⊠]), Xinyu Xie[1], Chenggen Song[2], Dong Dai[1], and Lijing Bu[1]

[1] The College of Automation and Electronic Information, Xiangtan University, Xiangtan, China
zhangzhengpeng@xtu.edu.cn
[2] Piesat Information Technology Co., Ltd., Beijing, China

Abstract. Transmission tower object detection from aerial image is an important task of power transmission fundamental infrastructure monitoring. However, the geometric variations, large-scale variation, complex background features and truss structure of transmission tower in aerial remote sensing images bring huge challenges to object detection. In this work, we propose a feature enhanced convolution network method (DSA-YOLOv3) to improve the performance of transmission tower detection in aerial images by modifying YOLOv3. The four layer feature extraction and fusion in darknet53 deep residual network is designed to enhance the feature expression ability of the network. Secondly, the DSA enhanced feature extraction module (the module consists of deformable convolution, SPP module, and attention module, which is named DSA module) is proposed. We use deformable convolution to improve the network's generalization ability due to the geometric variations of transmission tower in aerial image. Considering the large-scale variation of the transmission towers, we use the SPP module to increase the effective receptive field of the network. Then an attention module is used to eliminate the interference for the mixed characteristics of target and background environment, which is caused by truss structure of the transmission tower. Finally, we use CIoU as the loss function and DIoU as the non-maximum suppression judgment condition to improve the discrimination of highly overlapping targets. The proposed method was used in the transmission tower data sets to experiment. Experimental results demonstrate that the proposed method's AP, recall rate, and precision are 93.52%, 87.55%, and 96.16%, respectively. Compared with the original YOLOv3, the indexes of our method improved by 3.72%, 2.32%, and 5.91%, respectively.

Keywords: Remote sensing image · Feature fusion · Deformable convolution · Attention mechanism · Transmission tower detection

S. Yu et al. (Eds.): PRCV 2022, LNCS 13536, pp. 551–564, 2022.
https://doi.org/10.1007/978-3-031-18913-5_43

1 Introduction

With the rapid development of China's economy, the production level of industry and people's living standards continue to improve, a variety of electricity-using devices are widely used in people's lives, and the huge energy consumption has prompted the rapid development of China's power industry. China's power supply is mainly distributed in the western region and the northwestern region (coal power), the central region (hydropower), and the plain region in the northwest (wind power). From the distribution situation, China's electric energy load areas are mainly in the eastern and southern regions, which leads to the problem of uneven distribution of electric energy in China. In order to meet the demand for electricity in various regions of the country, people realize long-distance power transmission by establishing cross-region and cross-country interconnected power grids. Transmission towers are important infrastructure for carrying power grids and play an extremely important role in the process of power transportation, and the operational status of transmission towers determines the safe and stable operation of the entire power grid.

With the rapid development of remote sensing technology, remote sensing images have an important role in people's production life, and are widely used in mapping, urban dynamic monitoring, earth resource investigation, geological disaster investigation and rescue, military reconnaissance, and also have an important role in the field of power transmission [1–3]. It provides great help for the detection of power transmission towers. The traditional remote sensing image target detection mainly uses sliding windows to screen the region of interest and extracts features using algorithms such as HOG [4], SIFT [5], SURF [6], and finally uses SVM [7] and Adaboost [8] to classify the features.

Since the emergence of R-CNN [9], target detection has gradually entered the era of deep learning. Wenbin Yin et al. based on the improved R-CNN framework and successfully applied it to remote sensing image aircraft target recognition with good results [10]. Keming He et al. proposed SPP-Net [11] by introducing image pyramids, which effectively avoids the influence of image scale on convolution calculation. This method enables multi-layer convolutional computation at different scales and preserves shallow detail features. Jintao Shi et al. achieved remarkable results based on Faster-RCNN for grid foreign object detection [12]. Yang Zhi et al. used a target detection algorithm based on SAR images for transmission towers with YOLOv2 and VGG model cascade, firstly using YOLOv2 to identify transmission towers in the whole scene, and then using VGG to eliminate false positives in the identification results [13], which improved the detection accuracy but significantly decreased the detection speed. Bonnie Liang et al. based on YOLOv3's high-resolution SAR images for transmission pole tower target detection, changed the input of the original network to 960x960 adapted to the size of the target, combined with the idea of Focal loss [14] to improve the loss function [15], which improved the false detection and missed detection of YOLOv3 with the problem of long iteration time. Wenyan Wei et al. used Faster R-CNN algorithm for transmission tower detection, using VGG16 as a feature extraction network and migration learning [16], which improved the detection accuracy and shortened the training time but the detection time did not improve.

In summary, the current commonly used target detection algorithms for detecting transmission towers on remote sensing images have problems of low accuracy and poor results. In addition, the current algorithms are mainly for the detection of transmission towers on SAR images and ground shot images, and there is less research on the detection of transmission towers on high-resolution remote sensing images. Therefore, this paper proposes an algorithm for transmission tower detection based on feature-enhanced convolutional network for remote sensing images.

Finally, because the current publicly available large datasets such as DOTA [17] and VEDAI [18] mainly contain common targets such as cars, ships, airplanes, and ball fields, this paper produces a transmission pole tower dataset from aerial remote sensing images, which has important practical application value for the subsequent research and development of transmission pole tower detection.

2 Dataset Production

2.1 Data Collection

Transmission towers are sparsely distributed and used for long-distance power transmission; they are mainly distributed in transmission stations and mountainous areas. The data set in this paper uses aerial remote sensing images. It is mainly aimed at the image collection of pipeline facilities in the Sino-Russian border, Jiangsu Province, Guangzhou Province and other regions. The image with the original pixel size of about 30,000 * 20000 is cropped at an overlap rate of 50% using a Python program to ensure the integrity of the transmission tower. The aerial remote sensing images related to the transmission towers this time have 1110 scenes with a resolution of 0.5 m. The detailed parameters are shown in Table 1. The data set mainly intercepts image data of transmission towers with different backgrounds, shapes and directions. The data set has 4509 images. An example of a transmission tower is shown in Fig. 1.

From Fig. 1, it can be seen that the transmission towers in the high-resolution remote sensing images show the following characteristics:

Transmission towers are tower-like features, and the shape of the towers in the remote sensing image varies significantly due to the angle of the shot, as shown in Fig. 1(a), Fig. 1(c), and Fig. 1(d).

The spatial structure of the transmission tower is a truss structure, causing the target and the background to present a mixed feature phenomenon of the target containing the background, as in Fig. 1(a) and Fig. 1(d).

The background is complex due to the topographical variability of transmission tower locations, resulting in different target backgrounds in the remote sensing images, Fig. 1(a) is a water area, Fig. 1(b) is a mountain, Fig. 1(c) is woodland and Fig. 1(d) is farmland, where Fig. 1(c) is bare ground, influenced by shooting angle, lighting, etc. At this point, the tower target and background are confused.

In conclusion, aiming at of difficult detection of remote sensing image transmission towers under complex background interference, this paper proposes a detection method based on a feature-enhanced convolutional network based on the existing target detection network.

Table 1. Parameters of aerial remote sensing image data

Data sources	Shooting time	Image width	Resolution	Scenery
Sino-Russian border	September, October, November, and December 2019	About 30000 × 20000	0.5 m	105
Jiangsu Province	January and March 2018, August 2019	About 30000 × 20000	0.5 m	406
Guangzhou Province	January 2021	About 30000 × 20000	0.5 m	599

(a) water   (b) mountains   (c) woodland   (d) farmland

Fig. 1. Example of transmission tower with different backgrounds and shapes.

2.2 Dataset Production

In this paper, the PASCAL VOC [19] format standard was used to produce the transmission tower dataset. LabelImg software was used for manual annotation. The annotation process: firstly, the transmission towers in the images were identified manually as transmission tower targets; then the transmission tower targets were selected using a minimum outer rectangle to ensure data accuracy.

2.3 Dataset Expansion

Due to the limited high-resolution remote sensing image data, I use online data augmentation, which is a random combination of operations such as translation, zooming, rotation, and color change, to expand the targets of transmission towers of different scales and shapes. This improves the generalization ability of the model and avoids the problem of model training over-fitting.

2.4 YOLOv3 Algorithm Principle

In YOLO target detection algorithm YOLOv3 [20] inherits the advantages of YOLOv1 and YOLOv2 algorithms and combines the feature pyramid module and other algorithm advantages to improve the overall detection accuracy of YOLO especially for small targets.

The YOLOv3 target detection algorithm is mainly composed of three modules, which are the feature extraction module (Darknet53), the feature fusion module (feature pyramid), and the detection module (YOLOv3 detection).

YOLOv3 uses 3*3 convolution with a step size of 2 to downsample the feature map and 1 * 1 convolution to adjust the number of channels to reduce the loss of small target feature information, thus realizing Darknet-53 of the full convolutional network. 32 times downsampling is performed on the input image in the feature extraction process, and when the input image size is 416 * 416, the output three feature layers are 13 * 13, 26 * 26, and 52 * 52, respectively. Drawing on the idea of feature pyramid, three different sizes of anchor frames are assigned to the feature maps at each of the three scales, and target detection is performed based on global features, thus realizing an end-to-end target detection algorithm.

Among them, YOLOv3 is by far the most balanced target detection network in terms of speed and accuracy, and its performance is particularly outstanding in the target detection task.

The loss function of the YOLOv3 algorithm is composed of three parts, loss in predicting the center position (x, y) of the target frame, loss in predicting the width and height adjustment of the target frame, loss in confidence and in category [20].

2.5 Algorithms in This Paper

As can be seen from Fig. 1, the geometry of the transmission tower target in the high-resolution image varies greatly and the background information is complex, and its location and contour information are richer and play an important guiding role in the process of target detection. The shallow network in the convolutional network is mainly responsible for extracting the contour and size information of the target and the deep network is mainly responsible for extracting the semantic information of the target. By analyzing the geometric features of transmission towers in the dataset, the DSA-YOLOv3 detection algorithm is proposed to be suitable for the task of detecting tower-like features of such spatial truss structures as transmission towers. The algorithm first extracts the shallow feature layer output from the second residual block (res2 in Fig. 4), performs feature fusion between adjacent feature layers, and then performs detection on the new multi-scale feature map. Secondly, an enhanced feature extraction module (DSA) is added behind the 13 * 13 feature layer, which enhances the feature expression capability of the network and increases the proportion of transmission tower feature information without increasing the computational power of the network, thus improving the overall detection accuracy of the network.

Adding a Shallow Feature Layer. The shallow detail information of transmission tower targets plays an important guiding role in remote sensing image target detection, in order to be able to better utilize the shallow detail information of transmission towers in remote sensing images. Now the original image in the feature extraction network is downsampled by quadruple to extract the feature map. And the three feature outputs of the original Darknet53 feature extraction network are changed to four feature outputs, which are 13 * 13, 26 * 26, 52 * 52 and 104 * 104, respectively.

Feature Fusion. Such targets as transmission towers belong to tower-like features, whose geometric shapes vary greatly in the images due to the shooting angle, the types and sizes of towers are extremely different, and they belong to spatial truss structures with more complex backgrounds. In view of this, before the feature pyramid features are fused, the features under the large, medium and small scales are fused first, to enrich the feature information of each part and enhance the expression ability of the feature extraction network. Then the four output features from the Darknet53 feature extraction network are feature fused, as shown in Fig. 2, where the red arrows represent the downsampling of shallow subscale features, representing feature fusion.

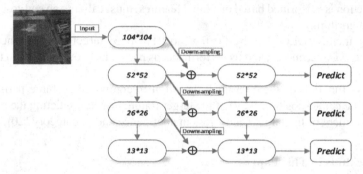

Fig. 2. Feature fusion.

Enhanced Feature Extraction Module (DSA). The module mainly consists of deformable convolution [21], SPP module [11], and attention module [22]. Due to the large geometric differences and complex background information of transmission towers, detection is difficult. Therefore, deformable convolution and SPP modules are introduced.

First, in the actual sampling process, the geometry of the transmission pole tower cannot be a regular figure, and using ordinary convolution will cause some sampling points to be invalid or even extract the information of the background, while using deformable convolution will be able to contain the target well and extract the useful target feature information.

Secondly, due to the different transmission distances, there will be transmission towers of different voltage levels. Low-voltage transmission towers are suitable for short-distance transmission, so the geometry of low-voltage transmission towers is smaller, while high-voltage transmission towers are used to be long-distance transmission, so the geometry of high-voltage transmission towers is larger. As the targets of transmission towers with large geometric differences may exist in the same image, the image is continuously downsampled in the process of feature extraction, which will cause the features of small targets to disappear. So the fusion of different sensory field features of the SPP module makes the feature information of transmission towers richer, which can better solve the problem of small target miss detection in the process of target detection.

Finally, in order to balance the weight adjustment of deformable convolution on each position this paper introduces a light weight attention module (CBAM, Convolutional Block Attention Module) [22], CBAM can increase the weight proportion of the target by giving certain attention mechanism in channel and spatial dimensions. The first operation is to apply the channel attention mechanism to the input features and multiply them with the original features, and then the channel attention result is applied to the spatial attention mechanism and multiplied with the channel attention mechanism result to get the result features. Based on the analytical design, the DSA feature enhancement module is proposed in this paper, as shown in Fig. 3.

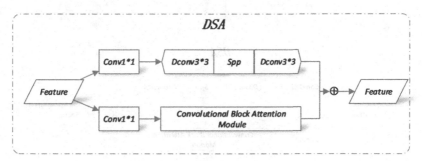

Fig. 3. Structure diagram of DSA feature enhancement module.

In this paper, the DSA enhanced feature extraction module is set between the 13 * 13 feature layer and the feature pyramid after fusion. Then, use two parallel branches to compress the 13 * 13 feature layer using 1 * 1 convolution for channel compression, one of which performs 3 * 3 deformable convolution as well as SPP module, and the other branch applies the attention mechanism. The features of the two branches are fused to output the final network structure is shown in Fig. 4.

Loss Function Optimization. Based on the problem that iou does not accurately describe the overlap between the target frame and the real frame, literature [23] introduced the euclidean distance information of the center coordinates of the predicted frame and the real frame and the aspect ratio penalty term on the basis of iou and converged faster with better performance. In order to obtain a more accurate and suitable external rectangular frame for the transmission tower target, this experiment replaces the original iou with the ciou that can better measure the overlap relationship between the prediction frame and the target frame based on YOLOv3. The overall loss function after being improved to CIoU is shown in Eq. 1. Among them, α represents the weight function, as shown in Eq. 2, and ϑ is used to measure the similarity of the aspect ratio, as shown in Eq. 3. I_{ij}^{obj} means: whether the j-th anchor box of the i-th grid is responsible for this target object, if it is responsible, $I_{ij}^{obj} = 1$, otherwise it is 0; w, h are the width and height of the prediction box; b and b^{gt} represent the center points of the prediction frame and the target frame respectively, and ρ represents the Euclidean distance between the center point of the calculated target frame and the real frame. c represents the diagonal distance of the smallest rectangle that can cover both the prediction box and the target box at the

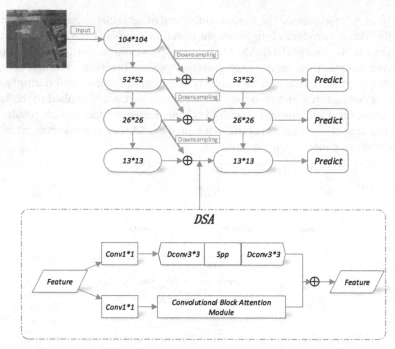

Fig. 4. Structure diagram of this paper.

same time. $\widehat{C}_i^j$ represents the target frame and the the IoU of the real frame, C_i^j is the prediction confidence obtained by the predicted value through the Sigmoid function; $\widehat{P}_i^j$ indicates whether there is a j-th type of target in the predicted target frame i, and P_i^j is the target probability obtained by the predicted value through the Sigmoid function.

$$
\begin{aligned}
\text{Loss} =\ & \lambda_{\text{coord}} \sum_{i=0}^{S^2} \sum_{j=0}^{B} I_{ij}^{obj} \left(2 - w_i^j * h_i^j\right) * \left[1 - \text{IoU} + \frac{\rho^2\left(b, b^{gt}\right)}{c^2} + \alpha\vartheta\right] \\
& -\sum_{i=0}^{S^2} \sum_{j=0}^{B} I_{ij}^{obj} \left[\widehat{C}_i^j \log\left(C_i^j\right) + \left(1 - \widehat{C}_i^j\right) \log\left(1 - C_i^j\right)\right] \\
& -\lambda_{\text{coord}} \sum_{i=0}^{S^2} \sum_{j=0}^{B} I_{ij}^{noobj} \left[\widehat{C}_i^j \log\left(C_i^j\right) + \left(1 - \widehat{C}_i^j\right) \log\left(1 - C_i^j\right)\right] \\
& -\sum_{i=0}^{S^2} I_{ij}^{obj} \sum_{c \in \text{class}} \left[\widehat{P}_i^j \log\left(P_i^j\right) + \left(1 - \widehat{P}_i^j\right) \log\left(1 - P_i^j\right)\right]
\end{aligned}
\tag{1}
$$

$$
\alpha = \frac{\vartheta}{(1 - IoU) + \vartheta}
\tag{2}
$$

$$\vartheta = \frac{4}{\pi^2} \left(\arctan \frac{\omega^{gt}}{h^{gt}} - \arctan \frac{\omega}{h} \right)^2 \tag{3}$$

Non-maximum Suppression Optimization. In the original YOLOv3 non-maximal suppression, the IoU metric is used to suppress redundant detection frames, but since only overlapping regions are considered, it often results in incorrect suppression, especially when the prediction frames contain each other. Therefore, DIoU [23] can be used as a criterion for NMS, solving the problem that traditional NMS algorithms have a large degree of missed and false detection of targets especially in scenarios with highly overlapping targets. The improved non-extreme value suppression improves the accuracy of the YOLOv3 target detection algorithm for transmission towers detection.

3 Experiments and Results Analysis

3.1 Experimental Setup

This experiment is based on Pytorch 1.2 deep learning framework; programming language Python 3.6; platform configuration: Intel(R) Xeon(R) W-2123 CPU@3.60GHz 3.60GHz, RAM: 24.0GB, GPU: NVIDIA GeForce RTX2070 SUPER (8GB).

The datasets are divided into training set and validation set with the ratio of 0.9 and 0.1 for 3661 and 406 images, respectively, which are trained and validated on the training and validation sets in the transmission pole tower dataset, which are randomly assigned. To ensure the accuracy of the experiment a total of 442 test datasets were recreated from images unrelated to the dataset.

The training parameters were set: the maximum iteration epoch was 100, the Adam optimizer was chosen, the first 50 epoch batch size was set to 8 images (according to the computer performance), the initial learning rate was 1e-4, and the second 50 generations batch size was set to 4 with a learning rate of 1e-5. After adjusting to the appropriate parameters, the loss converged smoothly.

Effectiveness is evaluated using object-based evaluation metrics, i.e., mean accuracy (AP), F1 measure (F1), recall (Recall), and precision (Precision).

3.2 Analysis of Results

The algorithm in this paper was compared and tested with the original YOLOv3 algorithm, and the improved algorithm was evaluated in the algorithm in the verification set of remote sensing image transmission towers in this paper, where the number of transmission towers in the verification set is 458, and the results of each algorithm are shown in Table 2.

Algorithm A in Table 2 is to add SPP module and attention module. Algorithm B is to add feature fusion module, SPP module and attention mechanism module. Algorithm C is to add feature fusion module, SPP module, attention mechanism module, CIoU loss function, non-maximal value suppression conditioned on DIoU, Algorithm DSA-YOLOv3: for the algorithm in this paper, on the basis of Algorithm C deformable convolution is added.

Table 2. Results of each algorithm.

Algorithms	AP	F1	Recall	Precision
YOLOv3	89.80%	87%	85.23	90.25%
Faster-RCNN	80.94%	78%	84.50%	72.47%
A	91.22%	88%	81.22%	96.37%
B	92.65%	90%	85.93%	94.98%
C	93.09%	91%	86.46%	95.88%
DSA-YOLOv3	93.52%	92%	87.55%	96.16%

As can be seen from Table 2, compared with the YOLOv3 algorithm, Algorithm A reduces the recall rate by 4.01% but improves the precision by 6.12%. Moreover, the average detection accuracy reached 91.22%. It can be seen that the expanded perceptual field operation and attention mechanism provide some help for the target detection of transmission towers. Algorithm B is based on Algorithm A with the addition of the feature fusion module. It can be seen that the overall performance of the algorithm is improved after feature enrichment, with 2.85%, 0.70% and 4.73% improvement in average precision, recall and precision, respectively.

Algorithm C outperforms the other two algorithms in all aspects. Compared with A, the recall rate increases by 5.24%, the precision decreases by 0.49%, the average precision increases by 1.87%, and the average precision increases to 93.09%. Compared with YOLO, the recall rate increases by 1.23%, the precision increases by 5.63%, and the average precision increases by 3.29%.

DSA-YOLOv3 is the algorithm of this paper, and after adding deformable convolution, it improves the generalization ability of the model, and has improved performance in all aspects compared with YOLOv3. The correct number of transmission towers in the test sample is 458, and the DSA-YOLOv3 can correctly detect 431. As can be seen from Table 2, compared with Faster R-CNN, the recall rate of DSA-YOLOv3 algorithm is 3.05% higher, the precision is 23.69% higher, the average precision increases by 12.58%. Compared with the original YOLOv3 algorithm, the algorithm in this paper increases the recall rate by 2.32%, the precision by 5.91%, the average precision by 3.72%, and the average precision is increased to 93.52%.

It can be seen from the results of the comparative experiment that the transmission tower detection method based on the DSA-YOLOv3 can better adapt to the detection of transmission towers. Part of the experimental results is shown in Figs. 5, 6 and 7.

From Fig. 5(a) (b), it can be seen that the background information accounts for a relatively large proportion of the transmission tower targets; secondly, objects with similar spatial structure also lead to false detection by the YOLOv3 algorithm, while the algorithm in this paper effectively reduces the false detection rate of transmission towers in remote sensing images.

(a) Original algorithm

(b) Algorithms in this article

Fig. 5. Example of false detection comparison.

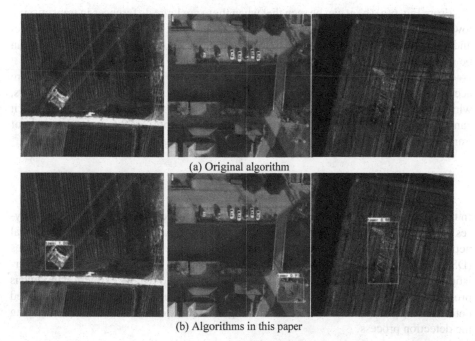

(a) Original algorithm

(b) Algorithms in this paper

Fig. 6. Comparison example of missed detection.

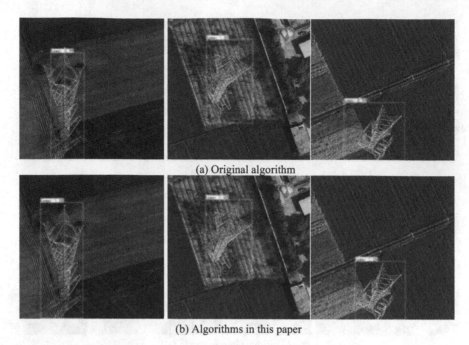

(a) Original algorithm

(b) Algorithms in this paper

Fig. 7. Example of target frame positioning comparison.

From Fig. 6(a) (b), it can be seen that when there are large differences in transmission tower geometry, interference from complex backgrounds and mixed features of target and background, the problem of missed detection caused by the above phenomena can be solved by the algorithm of this paper.

From Fig. 7(a) (b), it can be seen that the algorithm in this paper provides more accurate minimum external rectangular box in the detection of transmission towers, which provides more accurate data for the positioning of towers. From the above it can be seen that the improved algorithm has a certain improvement on the detection of transmission poles in high resolution remote sensing images.

4   Conclusion

In this paper, we study the target detection algorithm for remote sensing images, analyses the transmission pole tower dataset, and proposes a feature-enhanced convolutional network-based algorithm for transmission pole tower detection in remote sensing images (DSA-YOLOv3). The YOLOv3 target detection algorithm is improved for the characteristics of transmission poles in images, and a DSA-enhanced feature extraction module is proposed. The improved algorithm effectively reduces the problem of false and missed detection and provides a more accurate rectangular frame for transmission towers during the detection process.

The experimental results show that the AP of the DSA-YOLOv3 is 93.52%, the recall rate is 87.55%, and the precision is 96.16% on the transmission tower data set. Comparing the method proposed in this paper to the original YOLOv3, the performance improvement for the AP was 3.72%, the recall rate was 2.32%, and the precision was 5.91%. It shows the feasibility of the deep learning algorithm in the detecting high-resolution remote sensing image transmission towers, and the production of this data set has specific reference significance for the subsequent in-depth research of remote sensing image transmission tower detection.

The following research direction is based on multi-source, multi-temporal remote sensing target detection. Improving the generalization ability and universality of the network is the next research direction.

References

1. Shengyin, S.: Application of satellite remote sensing image technology in electric power survey. Jiangxi Build. Mater. **01**, 61–62 (2020)
2. Xi, L., Xiangyu, X.: Estimation method of night time images'electric power consumption based on Boston matrix. Geomat. Inform. Sci. Wuhan Univ. **43**(12), 1994–2002 (2018)
3. Rujun, D.: Research on inspection method of hidden danger of tansmission line Tower foundation based on remote sensing satellinte image. North China Electric Power University (Beijing) (2020)
4. Dalal, N., Triggs, B.: Histograms of oriented gradients for human detection. In: Proceedings of 2005 IEEE Computer Society Conference on Computer Vision and Pattern Recognition, San Diego, CA, vol. 1, pp. 886–893. IEEE (2005)
5. Lowe, D.: Distinctive image features from scale-invariant keypoints. Int. J. Comput. Vision **60**(2), 91–110 (2004)
6. Bay, H., Ess, A., Tuytelaars, T., et al.: Speeded-up robust features (SURF). Comput. Vis. Image Underst. **110**(3), 346–359 (2008)
7. Zhaoxia, Y., Zhengrong, Z., Chao, T., et al.: Hyperspectral image classification based on the combination of spatial-spectral feature and sparse representation. Acta Gewdaetica et Cartographica Sinica **44**(7), 75–781 (2015)
8. Li, S., Hong, T., Shidong, W., et al.: River extraction from the high resolution remote sensing Image based on spatially correlated pixels template and adboost algorithm. Acta Geodlactica et Cartographica Sinica **42**(3), 344–350 (2013)
9. Girshick, R., Donahue, J., Darell, T.: Ricth feature hierarchies for accurate object detection and semantic segmentation In: Proceedings of 27th IEEE Conference on Computer Vision and Pattern Recognition, pp. 580–587. IEEE Press, Piscataway (2014)
10. Wenbin, Y., Chenbo, W., Cui, Y., et al.: A method of aitrcraft recoginition in remote sensing images. Bull. Surv. Mapp. **03**, 34–37 (2017)
11. Kaiming, H., Xiangyu, Z., Shaoqing, R., et al.: Spatial pyramid pooling in deep convolutional networks for visual recognition]. IEEE Trans. Pattern Anal. Mach. Intell. **37**(9), 1904–1916 (2015)
12. Jintao, S.: Research on foreign matter monitoring of power grid with faster R-CNN based on sample expansion. Power Grid Technol. **44**(01), 44–51 (2020)
13. Zhi, Y., Wenhao, O., Xiangze, F., et al.: Smart identification of transmission tower based on high-resolution SAR image and deep learning. Electr. Measur. Instrument. **57**(04), 71–77 (2020)
14. Lin, T.Y., Goyal, P., Girshick, R., et al.: Focal loss for Dense Object Detection. IEEE Trans. Pattern Anal. Mach. Intell. (2017)

15. Yiqing L.: Research on target detection in high resolution SAR image based on deep learning convolutional neural network. Changsha University of Technology (2019)
16. Xia, G.S., Bai, X., Ding, J., et al.: DOTA: a largescale dataset for object detection in aerial images. In: Proceedings of the IEEE Conference on Computer Vision and Pattern Recognition, Salt Lake City, pp. 3974–3983. IEEE (2018)
17. Razakarivony, S., Jurie, F.: Vehicle detection in aerial imagery: a small target detection benchmark. J. Vis. Commun. Image Represent. **34**, 187–203 (2016)
18. Everingham, M., Gool, L.V., Williams, C.K.I., et al.: The pascal visual object classes (VOC) challenge. Int. J. Comput. Vision, 3485–3492 (2010)
19. Redmon, J., Farhadi, A.: YOLOv3: an incremental improvement: arXiv:1804.02767v 1[R/OL]. Cornell University, Ithaca, NY, US: (2018)
20. Zhou, J., Tian, Y., Yuan, C., et al.: Improved uav opium poppy detection using an updated yolov3 model. Sensors **19**(22), 4851 (2019)
21. Jifeng, D., Haozhi, Q., Yuwen, X., et al.: Deformable convolutional networks. In: Proceedings of the IEEE International Conference on Computer Vision, pp. 764–773 (2017)
22. Woo, S., Park, J., Lee, J.Y., et al.: CBAM: convolutional block attention module. Springer, Cham (2018)
23. Zhaohui, Z., Ping, W., Wei, L., et al.: Distance-IoU loss: faster and better learning for bounding box regression. arxiv:1911.08287 (2019)

Vision Analysis and Understanding

Mining Diverse Clues with Transformers for Person Re-identification

Xiaolin Song[✉], Jin Feng, Tianming Du, and Honggang Zhang

Beijing University of Posts and Telecommunications, Beijing, China
{sxlshirley,fengjin2012,dtm,zhhg}@bupt.edu.cn

Abstract. Person Re-identification (ReID) is a challenging task due to the inherently large intra-class variation and subtle inter-class differences. Early works mainly tackle this problem by learning a discriminative pedestrian feature representation. Recently, vision transformer (ViT) has shown outstanding performance in many tasks, where the self-attention mechanism plays a key role that links every patch tokens with the class token. Intuitively, the class token could serve as a good global feature that captures local details naturally. Experiments demonstrate that the vanilla ViT can achieve impressive performance when directly applied to the ReID problem. Nevertheless, the class token may pay much attention to most salient patches while ignoring less salient but informative ones and missing some potential clues. To reduce this limitation, we propose a novel network MDCTNet to mine divers clues for person re-identification with transformers. Based on the cascaded architecture of transformer encoder, a Patch Suppression Module (PSM) is incorporated into the last several transformer layers, which aims to progressively discard some most salient patch tokens and make less salient ones passed to the next layer. Thus, the model is enforced to mine more potential useful clues in the remained patches and the resulting pedestrian representation can be more robust. Extensive experiments on three mainstream datasets including Market1501, DukeMTMC-ReID and MSMT17 validate the effectiveness of our method.

Keywords: Person re-identification · Vision transformer · Self-attention mechanism

1 Introduction

Person re-identification (ReID) is a challenging task which is widely used in many computer vision applications, such as surveillance security and criminal investigation. It aims to retrieve a probe pedestrian among all gallery images captured from different cameras. Benefited from progresses of deep neutral networks, the performance of person ReID has reached a new level. Since pedestrian images are captured in different scenes from disjoint views, the main challenges lie in the large intra-class and small inter-class variation caused by different pedestrian poses, occlusion patterns, clothes, background clutters, view angles, etc. A common solution is to extract a discriminative global feature from the whole human body [7,15,18,31], which aims to capture the most salient information among all different identities. However, some non-salient or infrequent

© The Author(s), under exclusive license to Springer Nature Switzerland AG 2022
S. Yu et al. (Eds.): PRCV 2022, LNCS 13536, pp. 567–577, 2022.
https://doi.org/10.1007/978-3-031-18913-5_44

detailed information can be easily ignored, which makes the global feature be not robust enough. A typically strategy to tackle this problem is to learn some local features to enhance the representation [17,19,22,26–28]. Although achieve good performance, these methods often suffer from noises and extra computation from external models, the complex network architecture, the over-fitting problem, etc., which limit the performance.

Most recently, vision transformer (ViT) [5] achieves huge success in image classification, which improves that applying the transformer directly to a sequence of image patches can capture the important regions and facilitate classification. Extended works [6,30] on other computer vision tasks confirm ViT's strong ability of learning discriminative feature representation. Intuitively, ViT seems to suit the person ReID problem perfectly with its innate multi-head self-attention mechanism, where the class token could serve as a good global feature since it naturally captures information of each local patch token. In this paper, we firstly construct a baseline ReID framework using ViT [5] as backbone and the class token as the pedestrian representation. Though applying ViT on person ReID directly achieves impressive results, the class token may capture "easiest" salient local features but ignore potential informative ones.

To reduce the limitations and mine more diverse clues for re-identification of pedestrian identities, we propose a novel network MDCTNet that extracts potential salient pedestrian features with transformers, where the class token is enforced to pay attention to potential salient patch tokens by discarding some most salient tokens progressively when data flows through the last several transformer layers. The Patch Suppression Module (PSM) is proposed to let the less salient patch tokens with relatively smaller attention weights pass to the next transformer layers and some most salient ones with larger attention weights be suppressed. The remained patches will stand out to catch the attention of the class token instead of being suppressed by those most salient ones. Then, we can get several hidden class tokens with different potential clues and combining them with the final class token will obtain a more discriminative and robust pedestrian representation. We evaluate our methods extensively on three popular person ReID datasets including Market1501 [29], DukeMTMC-reID [14] and MSMT17 [23]. Our methods improves the results of the baseline work and shows favorable performance against the state-of-the-art approaches.

2   Related Work

Person ReID: Many studies for Person ReID [7,15,18,31] focus on building a CNN model to extract the global feature of the whole pedestrian image. To further enhance the feature representation, recent studies give insight into local features learning. Stripe-based methods [19,22,27] divide input images or feature maps horizontally into stripes to capture more human-part-based local information. They suffer from the problem of body parts misalignment and performance gains often come with over-fitting and information redundancy problems. Moreover, some other works try to exact more semantic local features guided by external cues. Pose-guided methods [17,26,28] represent a pedestrian by the combination of body part features, where the body part regions are detected using off-the-shell pose estimators. Mask-guided methods [9,13,16] exploit masks generated by semantic segmentation algorithms to refine the feature representation. However, the information acquired from extra models inevitably contains noises and needs additional computation consumption. Besides, attention-based methods [2,3,8,20,24] resort to attention mechanism to highlight informative regions, which tend to rely on the "easiest" salient features and ignore potential salient ones. SCSN[4] attempts to handle this problem by mining potential useful features with a complex multi-stage learning mechanism. In a novel way, we propose to mine diverse clues to represent pedestrian identities discriminatively based on the popular vision transformer.

Vision Transformer: The original transformer is proposed in the field of natural language processing and machine translation, where the multi-head self-attention and feed-forward MLP layer are stacked to capture the long-term correlation between words. Inspired by that, there are more and more explorations for the usage of transformer structures in computer vision tasks. DETR [1] proposes a fully end-to-end detector, where transformer is appended inside the detection head. STTR [10] and LSTR [11] employ transformers in disparity estimation and lane shape prediction respectively. Recently, ViT [5] proposes the first work to apply a pure transformer-based image classification model to a sequence of image patches and achieves the state of the art performance. After that, SETR [30] adopts ViT as the encoder for image segmentation. TransReID [6] firstly extends ViT to object ReID task, which embeds side information into transformer and proposes JPM module to capture more local features. Our method is also built upon ViT [5]. Without exploiting any side information, we make some modifications to improve the vanilla ViT's ability of mining more diverse details and capturing subtle differences.

3 Proposed Method

In this section, we briefly review the architecture of ViT in Sect. 3.1 and show how to exploit ViT to tackle Person ReID problem in Sect. 3.2. The overall framework of our proposed MDCTNet is presented and introduced in detail in Sect. 3.3.

3.1 Vision Transformer as Feature Extractor

We briefly review the literature of ViT and construct a transformer-based feature extractor step-by-step.

Image Patches. Following ViT, we reshape the given 2D pedestrian image $x \in R^{H \times W \times C}$ into a sequence of flattened 2D patches $x_p \in R^{N \times (P^2 \cdot C)}$, where H, W and C are the height, width and the number of channels of the image, (P, P) $(P = 16$ in this paper) is the resolution of each image patch, $N = HW/P^2$ is the resulting number of patches. Alternatively, we also construct a hybrid model (denoted as ResViT), where images patches are directly formed from features maps of ResNet50. Since the transformer uses constant latent vector size D through all of its layers, the image patches x_p are flattened into D dimensions with a trainable linear projection.

Position Embedding. The position embedding (denoted as E_{pos}) is added to the patch embedding to retain the positional information. Following ViT, we emoploy the standard learnable 1D position embedding. For better training, we load the position embedding parameters of ViT which has been pre-trained on ImageNet. Specifically, to handle the resolution mismatch of images of the person ReID dataset and ones of ViT, we perform 2D interpolation before loading.

Class Token. Following ViT, a learnable embedding (denoted as class token x_{cls}) is appended to the embedded image patches. The class token is exploited as the representation of the global feature of the given image.

Patch Embedding. In Eq. 1, the resulting sequence of embedding vectors z_0 is called the patch embedding, which serves as the input to the transformer encoder.

$$z_0 = [x_{cls}; x_p^1 \mathbf{E}; x_p^2 \mathbf{E}; \cdots ; x_p^N \mathbf{E}] + \mathbf{E}_{pos}, \tag{1}$$

where $E \in R^{(P^2 \dot{C})*D}$ is the patch embedding projection.

Transformer Encoder. The transformer encoder contains L transformer layers of multi-head self-attention (MSA) and multi-layer perceptron (MLP) blocks. Layernorm (LN) is applied before every block. We show the architecture of one transformer layer in Fig. 1 (b). The output of the l_{th} layer z_l can be obtained as follows:

$$z_l' = MSA(LN(z_{l-1})) + z_{l-1}, \qquad l = 1 \cdots L,$$

$$z_l = MLP(LN(z_l')) + z_l', \qquad l = 1 \cdots L,$$

where z_l can be writttened as follows:

$$z_l = [z_l^0; z_l^1, z_l^2, \cdots, z_l^N],$$

where z_l^0 represents the class token of the l_{th} layer. We denote the class token of the L_{th} (last) transformer layer as z_L^0. The final output of ViT is $f = LN(z_L^0)$, which serves as the final global feature representation of the input image.

3.2   Person ReID with Transformers

In this section, we construct our baseline person ReID network (denoted as ViT-baseline and ResViT-baseline), which employs ViT (ResViT alternatively) as backbone feature extractor. Given a pedestrian image, we firstly pass the image to the feature extractor and treat the final output f as the global feature representation of the pedestrian. Following most mainstream deep ReID methods, we employ ID loss for classification and Triplet loss for metric learning in training phases.

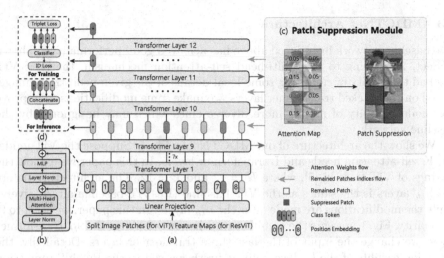

Fig. 1. Overview of our proposed MDCTNet: (a) For ViT, we firstly split the input image into flattened patches. For ResViT, We treat the feature map from ResNet50 as image patches. Then, We linearly embed each patch, add position embedding, and feed the resulting sequence of vectors to the first transformer layer. The token flows in first n transformer layers are the same as the vanilla ViT[5]. For clarity, we present the architecture when $n = 9$. After the 9_{th} layer, the current layer's attention weights will be firstly passed to PSM that decides which patches will be suppressed. Then, the remained tokens will be passed to the next layer. (b) Architecture of a transformer layer. (c) Patch Suppression Module (PSM). (d) Training and inference strategy.

ID loss indicates the identity loss based on a Softmax Classifier, where the person ReID task is regarded as a multi-class classification problem and the number of classes is corresponding to the number of training identities. The f will be firstly passed to a softmax classifier and then output ID prediction logits of the image. We denote p_i as the ID prediction of class i, y as the ground-truth ID label and C as the number of identities. ID loss is formulated as:

$$L_{ID} = \sum_{i=1}^{C} -q_i log(p_i) \begin{cases} q_i = 0, y \neq i \\ q_i = 1, y = i \end{cases}, \tag{2}$$

Triplet loss is used to enhance the ranking performance. For a triplet set $\{a, p, n\}$, we employ the soft-margin version of triplet loss as follows:

$$L_{Tri} = log[1 + exp(||f_a - f_p||_2^2 - ||f_a - f_n||_2^2)], \tag{3}$$

These two losses will guide the model to learn discriminative pedestrian feature representation. The final loss of our model can be written as:

$$L = L_{ID} + L_{Tri}, \tag{4}$$

3.3   MDCTNet Architecture

The baseline network introduced above has achieved good performance as shown in Sect. 2. Owning to the multi-head self-attention mechanism, the pure ViT has had the ability of capturing some local details of the given pedestrian image. Based on the stacked transformer layers, we make some modifications to improve the model's ability of mining more diverse clues which may be ignored by the baseline network.

We show the architecture of our MDCTNet in Fig. 1. Suppose the ViT model has K self-attention heads and L transformer layers. In this paper we exploit the settings of ViT-Base in [5], where $K = 12$ and $L = 12$. The architecture before the n_{th} layers is the sames as the ViT-baseline (ResViT-baseline alternatively) while the modifications are made after the n_{th} layers. In this paper, we set n to 9. For clarity, Fig. 1 presents the architecture when $n = 9$. After the 9_{th} transformer layer, we change the input of the last three transformer layers. Detailedly, the attention weights of the l_{th} layer will be firstly passed to the Patch Suppression Module (PSM). According to the attention weights, the PSM will decide which patch tokens will be remained and which ones will be discarded. After filtering by PSM, the remained patch tokens combined with the class token z_l^0 will be passed to the $(l + 1)_{th}$ layer. Below, we introduce the PSM in detail.

Patch Suppression Module. In Fig. 1 (c), we present the process flow of our PSM. The input of PSM is the attention weights from the l_{th} ($l >= n$) transformer layer and the output is the remained patch token indices. The attention weights of the l_{th} layer can be written as follows:

$$A_l = [A_l^1, A_l^2, A_l^3, \cdots, A_l^K], \tag{5}$$

We firstly average the attention weights of the K self-attention heads as follows:

$$a_l = \frac{1}{K} \sum_{i=1}^{K} A_l^i, \tag{6}$$

The average attention weights a_l can be written as:

$$a_l = [a_l^0, a_l^1, a_l^2, \cdots, a_l^N]$$

$$a_l^i = [a_l^{i_0}, a_l^{i_1}, a_l^{i_2}, \cdots, a_l^{i_N}], i = 0, 1, \cdots, N,$$

where N is the current number of image patches. In this paper, we extract $[a_l^{0_1}, a_l^{0_2}, \cdots, a_l^{0_N}]$, which is the attention weights linked with the class token. With the N attention weights, we can obtain a global attention map as shown in Fig. 1 (c). PSM chooses the indices of patches with the maximum S attention weight values to suppress and the index set of remained N' patches is returned ($N' = N - S$, S is set to 32 in this paper). The returned index set is denoted as $\{ind_1, ind_2, \cdots, ind_{N'}\}$. According to the returned indices, we extract the corresponding patch tokens in z_l. Then we concatenate the class token z_l^0 with the extracted patch tokens as follows:

$$z_l' = [z_l^0; z_l^{ind_1}, z_l^{ind_2}, \cdots, z_l^{ind_{N'}}], N' = N - S, \tag{7}$$

where z_l' is the input to the $(l+1)_{th}$ transformer while the suppressed patch tokens are discarded.

Training and Inference. As shown in Fig. 1 (d), We use the output class tokens of the last 4 transformer layers for training and inference. For training, these four class tokens are used as four independent feature representations to compute the ID loss and Triplet loss separately use Eq. 4. For inference, these class tokens will be concatenated together firstly, which is denoted as $f = LN([z_{L-3}^0, z_{L-2}^0, z_{L-1}^0, z_L^0])$. The resulting f will serve as the final feature representation for the given pedestrian image.

4   Experiments

4.1   Datasets

We evaluate our proposed method on three widely-used person ReID datasets: Market1501 [29], DukeMTMC-reID [14] and MSMT17 [23]. The detailed statistics are summarized in Table 1. According to the scale and diversity, MSMT17 is the most challenging one. Following previous works, we use Rank1 accuracy and mAP for evaluation.

Table 1. Statistics of datasets used in this paper

Dataset	#ID	#Image	#Cam
Market1501 [29]	1501	32668	6
DukeMTMC-reID [14]	1404	36441	8
MSMT17 [23]	4101	126441	15

4.2   Implementation Details

We resize all images to 384×128 in all experiments. Both ViT and the hybrid ResViT are pre-trained on ImageNet. For data augmentation, we deploy random horizontal flipping and random erasing on the training set. SGD is employed with the weight decay of $1e-4$. The batch size is set to 48 per GPU with 4 images per ID. All experiments are performed with Pytorch toolbox. No re-ranking tricks are employed.

4.3   Ablation Study

To validate the effectiveness of our method, we conduct some ablation experiments on MSMT17, which is one of the most challenging Person ReID datasets. Table 2 shows the results. The ResNet50-baseline is a baseline ReID network that uses ResNet50 as backbone and Eq. 4 for training. Comparing ResNet50-baseline with ViT-basline, we find that the vanilla ViT serves a satisfactory feature extractor. Furthermore, we establish the ResViT-baseline with the hybrid model ResViT as backbone. It can be seen that the performance has been improved further. This demonstrates that ViT can effectively refine the features extracted by CNN and make the model concentrate on discriminative patches. Then, we consturct our MDCTNet with both ViT and ResViT as backbone (denoted as MDCTNet-ViT and MDCTNet-ResViT respectively). We can see that MDCTNet-ViT outperforms ViT-baseline by 2.2% in Rank1 and 3.5% in mAP while MDCTNet-ResViT exceeds ResViT-basline by 0.5% in Rank1 and 1.5% in mAP. In conclusion, our MDCTNet can effectively mine diverse clues and generate a more discriminative and robust pedestrian feature representation.

Table 2. Ablation study on MSMT17 dataset

Method	Rank1 (%)	mAP (%)
ResNet50-baseline	76.7	52.0
ViT-baseline	78.8	57.7
ResViT-baseline	86.1	67.2
MDCTNet-ViT	81.0	61.2
MDCTNet-ResViT	86.6	68.7

4.4   Comparison with State-of-the-Arts

In Table 3, we compare our MDCTNet with state-of-the-art methods on Market1501, DukeMTMC-reID and MSMT17. When comparing with the most related work TransReID in Rank1, our MDCTNet outperforms TransReID by 0.4% on MSMT17 and 0.6% on DukeMTMC-ReID while getting the same 95.2% on Market1501. Despite performing a little poorly in mAP, our MDCTNet gets a comparable performance with TransReID in general. Notice that we never exploit any side information like camera IDs exploited in TransReID. Comparing with previous methods except TransReID, it can be seen that our MDCTNet achieves competitive performance on Market1501 and the best performance on DukeMTMC-ReID and MSMT17.

Table 3. Comparisons with the state-of-the-arts

Methods	Market1501		DukeMTMC-ReID		MSMT17	
	Rank1 (%)	mAP (%)	Rank1 (%)	mAP (%)	Rank1 (%)	mAP (%)
CBN [33]	91.3	77.3	82.5	67.3	72.8	42.9
OSNet [32]	94.8	84.9	88.6	73.5	78.7	52.9
MGN [22]	95.7	86.9	88.7	78.4	76.9	52.1
RGA-SC [25]	96.1	88.4	–	–	80.3	57.5
ABDNet [3]	95.6	88.3	89.0	78.6	82.3	60.8
PGFA [12]	91.2	76.8	82.6	65.5	–	–
HOReID [21]	94.2	84.9	86.9	75.6	–	–
SCSN [4]	95.7	88.5	91.0	79.0	83.8	58.5
TransReID [6]	95.2	89.5	90.7	82.6	86.2	69.4
MDCTNet (ours)	95.2	88.5	91.3	80.7	86.6	68.7

5   Conclusion

In this paper, we propose a novel network MDCTNet to mine diverse clues for person re-identification with transformers. When data flows through stacked transformer layers, we progressively discard some most relatively salient patch tokens and make the class token to mine clues in remained less salient patch tokens. As a result, we can get several class tokens with different local information, which are concatenated to obtain a more robust feature representation with divers clues. Extensive experiments show that our approach achieves competitive performance against the state-of-the-arts person ReID methods. In future work, we plan to employ our MDCTNet on other tasks and explore more adaptive robust feature extraction strategy with transformers.

References

1. Carion, N., Massa, F., Synnaeve, G., Usunier, N., Kirillov, A., Zagoruyko, S.: End-to-end object detection with transformers. In: Vedaldi, A., Bischof, H., Brox, T., Frahm, J.-M. (eds.) ECCV 2020. LNCS, vol. 12346, pp. 213–229. Springer, Cham (2020). https://doi.org/10.1007/978-3-030-58452-8_13
2. Chen, B., Deng, W., Hu, J.: Mixed high-order attention network for person re-identification. In: ICCV (2019)
3. Chen, T., et al.: Abd-net: Attentive but diverse person re-identification. In: ICCV (2019)
4. Chen, X., et al.: Salience-guided cascaded suppression network for person re-identification. In: CVPR (2020)
5. Dosovitskiy, A., et al.: An image is worth 16 × 16 words: Transformers for image recognition at scale. In: International Conference on Learning Representations (2021)
6. He, S., Luo, H., Wang, P., Wang, F., Li, H., Jiang, W.: Transreid: Transformer-based object re-identification. arXiv preprint arXiv:2102.04378 (2021)

7. Hermans, A., Beyer, L., Leibe, B.: In defense of the triplet loss for person re-identification. arXiv preprint arXiv:1703.07737 (2017)

8. Hou, R., Ma, B., Chang, H., Gu, X., Shan, S., Chen, X.: Interaction-and-aggregation network for person re-identification. In: CVPR (2019)

9. Kalayeh, M.M., Basaran, E., Gökmen, M., Kamasak, M.E., Shah, M.: Human semantic parsing for person re-identification. In: Proceedings of the IEEE Conference on Computer Vision and Pattern Recognition, pp. 1062–1071 (2018)

10. Li, Z., et al.: Revisiting stereo depth estimation from a sequence-to-sequence perspective with transformers. arXiv preprint arXiv:2011.02910 (2020)

11. Liu, R., Yuan, Z., Liu, T., Xiong, Z.: End-to-end lane shape prediction with transformers. In: (WACV) (2021)

12. Miao, J., Wu, Y., Liu, P., Ding, Y., Yang, Y.: Pose-guided feature alignment for occluded person re-identification. In: ICCV (2019)

13. Qi, L., Huo, J., Wang, L., Shi, Y., Gao, Y.: Maskreid: A mask based deep ranking neural network for person re-identification. arXiv preprint arXiv:1804.03864 (2018)

14. Ristani, E., Solera, F., Zou, R., Cucchiara, R., Tomasi, C.: Performance measures and a data set for multi-target, multi-camera tracking. In: Hua, G., Jégou, H. (eds.) ECCV 2016. LNCS, vol. 9914, pp. 17–35. Springer, Cham (2016). https://doi.org/10.1007/978-3-319-48881-3_2

15. Ristani, E., Tomasi, C.: Features for multi-target multi-camera tracking and re-identification. In: CVPR, pp. 6036–6046 (2018)

16. Song, C., Huang, Y., Ouyang, W., Wang, L.: Mask-guided contrastive attention model for person re-identification. In: Proceedings of the IEEE Conference on Computer Vision and Pattern Recognition, pp. 1179–1188 (2018)

17. Su, C., Li, J., Zhang, S., Xing, J., Gao, W., Tian, Q.: Pose-driven deep convolutional model for person re-identification. In: ICCV (2017)

18. Sun, Y., Zheng, L., Deng, W., Wang, S.: Svdnet for pedestrian retrieval. In: ICCV (2017)

19. Sun, Y., Zheng, L., Yang, Y., Tian, Q., Wang, S.: Beyond part models: Person retrieval with refined part pooling (and a strong convolutional baseline). In: Ferrari, V., Hebert, M., Sminchisescu, C., Weiss, Y. (eds.) ECCV 2018. LNCS, vol. 11208, pp. 501–518. Springer, Cham (2018). https://doi.org/10.1007/978-3-030-01225-0_30

20. Tay, C.P., Roy, S., Yap, K.H.: Aanet: Attribute attention network for person re-identifications. In: CVPR (2019)

21. Wang, G., et al.: High-order information matters: Learning relation and topology for occluded person re-identification. In: CVPR (2020)

22. Wang, G., Yuan, Y., Chen, X., Li, J., Zhou, X.: Learning discriminative features with multiple granularities for person re-identification. In: Proceedings of the 26th ACM international conference on Multimedia (2018)

23. Wei, L., Zhang, S., Gao, W., Tian, Q.: Person transfer gan to bridge domain gap for person re-identification. In: CVPR (2018)

24. Xu, J., Zhao, R., Zhu, F., Wang, H., Ouyang, W.: Attention-aware compositional network for person re-identification. In: CVPR (2018)

25. Zhang, Z., Lan, C., Zeng, W., Jin, X., Chen, Z.: Relation-aware global attention for person re-identification. In: CVPR (2020)

26. Zhao, H., et al.: Spindle net: Person re-identification with human body region guided feature decomposition and fusion. In: CVPR (2017)

27. Zheng, F., et al.: Pyramidal person re-identification via multi-loss dynamic training. In: CVPR (2019)

28. Zheng, L., Huang, Y., Lu, H., Yang, Y.: Pose-invariant embedding for deep person re-identification. IEEE Trans. Image Process. **28**, 4500–4509 (2019)
29. Zheng, L., Shen, L., Tian, L., Wang, S., Wang, J., Tian, Q.: Scalable person re-identification: A benchmark. In: ICCV (2015)
30. Zheng, S., et al.: Rethinking semantic segmentation from a sequence-to-sequence perspective with transformers. In: CVPR (2021)
31. Zheng, Z., Zheng, L., Yang, Y.: A discriminatively learned cnn embedding for person reidentification. ACM Trans. Multimedia Comput. Commun. Appli. **14**, 1–20 (2018)
32. Zhou, K., Yang, Y., Cavallaro, A., Xiang, T.: Omni-scale feature learning for person re-identification. In: ICCV (2019)
33. Zhuang, Z., et al.: Rethinking the distribution gap of person re-identification with camera-based batch normalization. In: Vedaldi, A., Bischof, H., Brox, T., Frahm, J.-M. (eds.) ECCV 2020. LNCS, vol. 12357, pp. 140–157. Springer, Cham (2020). https://doi.org/10.1007/978-3-030-58610-2_9

Mutual Learning Inspired Prediction Network for Video Anomaly Detection

Yuan Zhang[1]([✉]) [iD], Xin Fang[2] [iD], Fan Li[2] [iD], and Lu Yu[1] [iD]

[1] Zhejiang University, Hangzhou, China
12031110@zju.edu.cn
[2] Xi'an Jiaotong University, Xi'an, China
lifan@mail.xjtu.edu.cn

Abstract. Video anomaly detection has made great achievements in security work. A basic assumption is that the abnormal is the outlier of the normal. However, most existing methods only focus on minimizing the reconstruction or prediction error of normal samples while ignoring to maximize that of abnormal samples. The completeness of the training data and the similarity between certain normal and abnormal samples can cause the network overfitting to normal samples and generalizing to abnormal samples. To address the two problems, we propose Mutual Learning Inspired Prediction Network. Specifically, it consists of two student generators and one discriminator to predict the future frame, together with our proposed Boundary Perception-Based Mimicry Loss and Self-Supervised Weighted Loss. The proposed Boundary Perception-Based Mimicry Loss guides the generators to learn the predicted frame from each, which can help to increase the diversity of training data and prevent interference at the same time. The proposed Self-Supervised Weighted Loss constraints the confusion samples in training data with a small weight, which can clarify the modeling goal of the network and enlarge the distance between normal and abnormal samples. Experiments on four mainstream datasets demonstrate the effectiveness of our proposed method.

Keywords: Anomaly detection · Surveillance video · Future frame prediction · Mutual learning

1 Introduction

Anomaly detection is an essential task in artificial intelligence technology, which has diverse applications in surveillance video [16], Medical industry [13], etc. However, because of the unbounded and rare characters of anomalies, it is laborious and time-consuming to harvest enough abnormal data. Compared with the abundant quantity of normal events, extremely unbalanced data makes it infeasible to realize anomaly detection with a binary classification task. Thus, an intuitive approach for anomaly detection is to model the external or potential pattern for normal data [3]. Only normal data is given during training, and abnormal data is aimed to be discovered in the testing data set.

S. Yu et al. (Eds.): PRCV 2022, LNCS 13536, pp. 578–593, 2022.
https://doi.org/10.1007/978-3-031-18913-5_45

The reconstruction-based anomaly detection method is widely researched. Researchers leverage Convolutional Neural Networks (CNN) [8, 22, 24] or Auto-Encoder (AE) [23, 26] to model the distribution of normal samples in training and classify the irregular samples as abnormal in testing. Hasan et al. [7] proposed to utilize a fully convolutional Auto-Encoder (CAE) to reconstruct the scene. Dhole et al. [4] used a Winner-Take-All convolutional Auto-Encoder (WTA-AE) because of its competitive classifying ability. To deal with the complex background and noise, Chalapathy et al. [2] proposed a Robust Convolutional AE (RCAE) to enhance its robustness to noise. Xu et al. [27] proposed Stacked Denoising Auto-Encoders (SDAE) to learn the appearance and motion features as well as a joint representation for anomaly detection in complex scenes. Although these reconstruction-based solutions well extract the spatial features of video frames and have a satisfactory performance in the testing phase, they only focus on the distribution of single spatio-temporal blocks and ignore the continuous spatio-temporal sequences.

Further, prediction-based methods for anomaly detection have been proposed to solve the problem, and show their effectiveness in handling this problem. Luo et al. [18] proposed a Temporally-Coherent Sparse Coding (TSC) mapped with a stacked Recurrent Neural Network (sRNN) to detect the abnormal according to prediction errors, which is constrained by the temporal coherence of surveillance video. Villegas et al. [25] proposed to decompose the motion and content in videos by building a model combined with a Long Short-Term Memory Network (LSTM) and AE. They utilize the dual branches to analyze the content and motion information of the video. Besides, researchers apply both reconstruction and prediction strategies to anomaly detection. Zhao et al. [28] proposed a Spatio-Temporal Encoder (STAE) with three-dimensional convolution for spatio-temporal feature extraction, aiming to realize both reconstruction and prediction. Liu et al. [14] proposed a future frame prediction framework with Generative Adversarial Networks (GAN) and imposed optical flow constraints to predict the motion trend of videos accurately.

However, most reconstruction or prediction-based anomaly detection methods are equipped with a training set entirely composed of normal samples [19]. They only constraint networks to minimize the reconstruction or prediction errors of normal patterns while ignoring to maximize those of abnormal samples. Consequently, it's challenging for networks to polarize the errors of normal and abnormal samples when the training set only consists of normal samples. In this case, the accuracy of anomaly detection is usually affected by the following two negative effects: i) Overfitting to normal samples. When the diversity of normal samples in the training set is incomplete, normal samples may be classified as abnormal in the test due to overfitting. ii) Generalization of abnormal samples. When normal samples have similar distributions to abnormal, abnormal samples may be classified as normal in the test due to generalization.

To address the above two problems, we propose a Mutual Learning Inspired Prediction Network which consists of two student generators with the same structure but different initializations and one discriminator. The two generators predict the future frame from the input video clips and learn from each other. The discriminator identifies the true/false of the predicted image and the ground truth. To avoid overfitting to the normal, we propose a Boundary Perception-Based Mimicry Loss to guide the generators to learn the predicted frames from each other. Different initializations will cause generators to obtain different local optima, and the fitted normal sample characteristics will also be diverse. Having two generators with different initializations learn from each other can indirectly increase the diversity of learning samples during training. To prevent generalization to the abnormal, we propose a Self-Supervised Weighted Loss to assign different weights on different training samples. The training weights of samples with similar distributions to the abnormal are reduced, so the generalization to the abnormal samples is suppressed. The experimental results on four mainstream data sets prove the high effectiveness of our method.

The rest of our paper is organized as follows: In Sect. 2, we first introduce the proposed Mutual Learning Inspired Prediction Network for anomaly detection in detail. In Sect. 3, we present our experimental results and comparison with state-of-arts. Finally, we conclude this paper in Sect. 4.

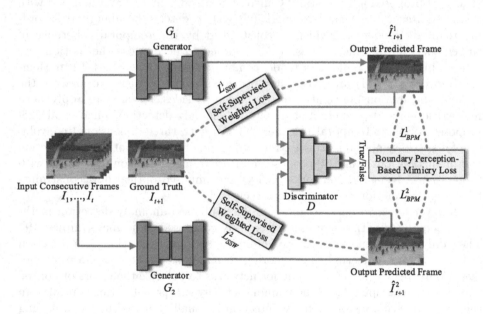

Fig. 1. The structure of our proposed Mutual Learning Inspired Prediction Network.

2   Mutual Learning Inspired Prediction Network

The structure of our proposed Mutual Learning Inspired Prediction Network is shown in Fig. 1, which is composed of two generators (G_1 and G_2) and one discriminator (D). Each generator consists of encoding and decoding parts, in which we utilize t consecutive frames ($I_1, I_2, ..., I_t$) as the input. Then they extract the features of t consecutive frames in the encoder and generate the predicted frames ($\hat{I}_{t+1}^1$ and $\hat{I}_{t+1}^2$) in the decoder, respectively. To reduce the interference of background on the prediction, we add the attention mechanism to each generator to let them focus on the behaviors. For the discriminator, the input is the ground truth (I_{t+1}) and the predicted frames, and the output is the discrimination result of the different patches of each frame, which is different from the ordinary discriminator to distinguish the entire frame and can identify more details. Because the generator and the discriminator are constrained by each other, we also add the attention mechanism to the discriminator, which helps the generator pay more attention to the behavior during the prediction.

In order to prevent the network from overfitting to normal samples, we design a Boundary Perception-Based Mimicry Loss (L_{BPM}^1 and L_{BPM}^2) for each generator to guide them to learn from each other and increase the diversity of normal samples during training. Moreover, in order to prevent the network from generalizing to normal samples, we also design a Self-Supervised Weighted Loss (L_{SSW}^1 and L_{SSW}^2) for each generator to figure out the normal samples that have similar distributions to the abnormal and assign them with smaller weights, which can prevent the generator to model the pattern similar to the abnormal samples.

2.1 Framework

For each generator in mutual learning, their network structure is exactly the same, but the initialization of the parameters is different, so the prediction frames generated by each generator are diverse. Therefore, they can provide each other with additional "ground truth", which helps to increase the posterior entropy and indirectly increases the diversity of normal samples during the training process.

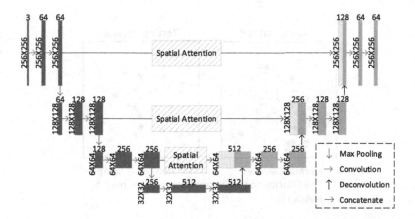

Fig. 2. The network architecture of our prediction generator (the modified U-Net).

The generator usually used for future frame prediction is the slightly modified U-Net [14], which extracts the features of input frames with a gradually decreasing spatial resolution encoder and predicts the future frame with a gradually increasing spatial resolution decoder. However, this kind of generator pays equal attention to every pixel of the predicted frame, which is in a sense neglecting the target behavior because the generator will waste a lot of training on predicting the complex background. To solve this problem, we modify the U-Net with the spatial attention mechanism. The architecture in detail of our prediction generator is shown in Fig. 2. We keep the output resolution of each two convolution layers unchanged and add spatial attention before the concatenation for each layer. The kernel sizes of all convolution and deconvolution and that of max-pooling layers are unchanged, which are set to 3×3 and 2×2, respectively. The kernel size of spatial attention is set to 7×7.

The patch discriminator [9] is utilized in our framework in order to preserve more details. We slightly modify the discriminator by adding the spatial attention mechanism to the penultimate convolutional layer, which aims to let the discriminator focus on the behavior in different patches of the video frames when discriminating.

2.2 Boundary Perception-Based Mimicry Loss

Our proposed Boundary Perception-Based Mimicry Loss is designed to solve the problem of the overfitting of the network to normal samples. According to the basic assumption of anomaly detection, abnormal samples are regarded as the complementary set of normal samples, which is divided by the fitting curve learned by the network. If the prediction training for normal samples is biased, then there will be problems in the prediction of abnormal samples during the test.

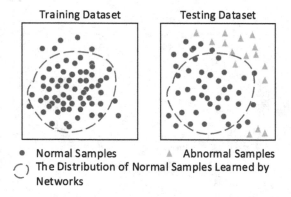

Fig. 3. The schematic diagram of the problem of network overfitting to normal samples due to the incompleteness of the training data.

As shown in Fig. 3, we can find that the insufficient diversity of normal samples in the training set will cause more normal samples to be distinguished as abnormal in the test phase. Therefore, we design a Boundary Perception-Based Mimicry Loss for our proposed to increase the diversity of the training data. We consider that those predicted frames with large differences generated by different generators are more worth learning, which can bring larger posterior entropy and more knowledge. We not only let the student generators learn the predicted frames from each other but also assign the learning object. We let the generators learn the appearance information and motion information of the predicted frame from each other, including intensity, gradient, and optical flow information. As the prediction results of the two generators tend to be the same, the diversity of normal samples in the network increases.

2.3 Self-supervised Weighted Loss

Our proposed Self-Supervised Weighted Loss is designed to guide the prediction frames closer to the ground truth and solve the problem of generalization of the network to abnormal samples. During the research, we found that some normal samples may be similar to the abnormal. For example, some fighting postures may be similar to greeting postures, it's hard to accurately distinguish the abnormal behaviors under this condition.

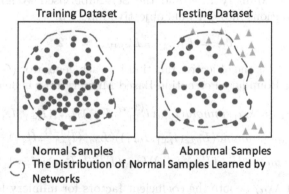

Fig. 4. The schematic diagram of the network generalization abnormal samples due to the similar distribution of some normal samples and abnormal samples.

As shown in Fig. 4, those normal samples that have similar distributions to the abnormal can cause the network to have a certain prediction ability for abnormal samples, which will cause the network to misjudge the abnormal samples as normal during the test. Therefore, we utilize One-Class Support Vector Machine (OCSVM) to classify the training samples into prototypical normal samples and confusion samples. Prototypical normal samples indicate that their normal characteristics are significant and the abnormal characteristics are not included. Confusion samples represent those samples that cannot be distinguished from abnormal samples. Then we assign high weights on the former and low weights on the latter to avoid the confusion caused by the similar distributions between boundary samples and abnormal samples. Consequently, the smaller weights of confusion samples will help the network learn more information about regular patterns and less information about irregular patterns, which can help to polarize the prediction errors between normal and abnormal samples during testing.

2.4   Objective Function

Mathematically, we denote the randomly picked consecutive t frames of a video clip as $I_1, I_2, ..., I_t$, which we stack and use as the input of the two generators G_1 and G_2 to predict the future frame, the generators have the same structure of U-Net [14] but the different initializations. The initialization functions used by the two generators are the same, but the parameters are different due to their random generations each time. We denote the predicted frame for G_1 and G_2 as $\hat{I}_{t+1}^1$ and $\hat{I}_{t+1}^2$, respectively. The real future frame used as ground truth is represented as I_{t+1}. The discriminator is represented as D, the output scalar of which corresponds to a patch of an input image [14]. (BPM Loss, L_{BPM}^1 and L_{BPM}^2 for G_1 and G_2, respectively) and Self-Supervised Weighted Loss (SSW Loss, L_{SSW}^1 and L_{SSW}^2 for G_1 and G_2, respectively). We combine the Boundary Perception-Based Mimicry Loss and the Self-Supervised Weighted Loss with different contributions into our final objective function:

$$L_{G_i} = L_{BPM}^i + L_{SSW}^i, i = 1, 2 \tag{1}$$

where $L_{G_i}, i = 1, 2$ is the objective function for each generator (G_1 and G_2). The loss function for Boundary Perception-Based Mimicry Loss is defined as follows:

$$
\begin{aligned}
L_{BPM}^i = {} & \lambda_{MI} sigmoid(L_{int}(\hat{I}_{t+1}^{(3-i)}, I_{t+1})) L_{int}(\hat{I}_{t+1}^i, \hat{I}_{t+1}^{(3-i)}) \\
& + \lambda_{MG}(sigmoid(L_{gdx}(\hat{I}_{t+1}^i, I_{t+1}))(L_{gdx}(\hat{I}_{t+1}^{(3-i)}, \hat{I}_{t+1}^i) \\
& + sigmoid(L_{gdy}(\hat{I}_{t+1}^i, I_{t+1})) L_{gdy}(\hat{I}_{t+1}^{(3-i)}, \hat{I}_{t+1}^i)), i = 1, 2 \tag{2}
\end{aligned}
$$

where λ_{MI} and λ_{MG} denote the coefficient factors for mimicry loss in intensity and gradient. $L_{int}(\hat{I}, I) = \left\| \hat{I} - I \right\|_2^2$ represents the intensity loss between image $\hat{I}$ and I. The horizontal gradient loss is represented as $L_{gdx}(\hat{I}, I)$ and the vertical gradient loss is represented as $L_{gdy}(\hat{I}, I)$.

The proposed Self-Supervised Weighted Loss is defined as follows:

$$
\begin{aligned}
L_{SSW}^i = {} & \lambda_{OP} L_{OP}^i + \lambda_G L_G^i + \omega(\lambda_{WI} L_{int}(\hat{I}_{t+1}^i, I_{t+1}) \\
& + \lambda_{WG}(L_{gx}(\hat{I}_{t+1}^i, I_{t+1}) + L_{gy}(\hat{I}_{t+1}^i, I_{t+1}))), i = 1, 2 \tag{3}
\end{aligned}
$$

where $L_{OP}^i = \left\| f(\hat{I}_{t+1}^i, I_t) - f(I_{t+1}, I_t) \right\|_1$ represents the optical flow loss for G_i. I_t denotes the previous frame of I_{t+1}, $f(\cdot)$ represents obtaining the optical flow of two images. The adversarial loss for G_i is represented as

$L_G^i = \sum_{p,q} \frac{1}{2} L_{MSE}(D(\hat{I}_{t+1}^1)_{p,q} - 1)$. To calculate ω, we set the error rate of OCSVM with ε. Since the training dataset is consist of normal samples, we consider that the samples that are classified as abnormal by OCSVM are confusion samples that have similar properties to the abnormal. Therefore, we apply the correctly classified samples with small weight and the incorrectly classified samples with large weight, which is calculated as follows:

$$\omega = \begin{cases} 1, \text{abnormal} \\ \frac{1}{2\varepsilon}, \text{normal} \end{cases} \tag{4}$$

Finally, the loss functions for the discriminator is:

$$L_D^i = \sum_{p,q} \frac{1}{2} L_{MSE}(D(I_{t+1})_{p,q} - 1)$$

$$+ \sum_{p,q} \frac{1}{2} L_{MSE}(D(\hat{I}_{t+1}^i)_{p,q} - 0) \tag{5}$$

where $L_D^i, i = 1, 2$ represents the different loss functions for the discriminator D.

During training, we first normalize the intensity of pixels of input frames into range $[-1, 1]$ and resize each frame to the size of 256×256. We pick a random video clip of 5 sequential frames, in which we set $t = 4$ (4 sequential frames are utilized as input and the 5-th frame is set as the ground truth) [21]. We utilize Adam [11] based Stochastic Gradient Descent to optimize the parameters of networks. We set each generator with the same structure but different initializations and independent optimizers. The learning rate of generators is 0.0001 for gray scale datasets and 0.0002 for color scale datasets. The learning rate of the discriminator is set to 0.00001 and 0.00002 for gray scale datasets and color scale datasets, respectively. The error rate ε for calculating weight ω and the coefficient factors of $\lambda_{MI}, \lambda_{MG}, \lambda_{OP}, \lambda_G, \lambda_{WI}$, and λ_{WG} are different according to different datasets.

2.5 Anomaly Detection on Testing Data

Since anomaly detection assumes that abnormal samples do not conform to the regular pattern of normal samples, we utilize the prediction error between the predicted frame $\hat{I}$ and the corresponding ground truth I to distinguish the abnormal from normal. A mainstream measurement for image quality assessment is to estimate the Peak Signal to Noise Ratio (PSNR) [21] between the predicted frame and its corresponding ground truth, which is defined as follows:

$$PSNR(I, \hat{I}) = 10\log_{10} \frac{[\max_{\hat{I}}]^2}{\frac{1}{N}\sum_{i=0}^{N}(I_i - \hat{I}_i)^2} \tag{6}$$

where $[\max_{\hat{I}}]$ denotes the maximum value of the predicted frame $\hat{I}$, N represents the number of pixels, and i represents the index of $\hat{I}$ and I. Higher PSNR for the t-th frame indicates that it is more likely to be normal. After calculating the PSNR score of each testing video frame, we normalize the PSNR score into the regular score which is in the range of $[0, 1]$ using the following equation:

$$S(t) = \frac{PSNR(I_t, \hat{I}_t) - \min_t PSNR(I_t, \hat{I}_t)}{\max_t PSNR(I_t, \hat{I}_t) - \min_t PSNR(I_t, \hat{I}_t)} \qquad (7)$$

Table 1. The comparison of the AUC of different methods on different datasets.

Method	Ped1	Ped2	Avenue	ShanghaiTech
MPPCA [10]	59.0%	69.3%	N/A	N/A
MPPC+SFA [20]	66.8%	61.3%	N/A	N/A
MDT [20]	81.8%	82.9%	N/A	N/A
Conv-AE [7]	75.0%	85.0%	80.0%	60.9%
ConvLSTM-AE [17]	75.5%	88.1%	77.0%	N/A
Stacked RNN [18]	N/A	92.2%	81.7%	68.0%
Frame-Pred [14]	83.1%	95.4%	85.1%	72.8%
RC-GAN [12]	80.9%	93.5%	82.1%	69.1%
Spatiotemporal [4]	81.3%	73.6%	73.5%	N/A
LSA [1]	N/A	95.4%	N/A	72.5%
MemAE [6]	N/A	84.1%	83.3%	71.2%
sRNN-AE [16]	N/A	92.2%	83.5%	69.6%
Ours	**83.9%**	**96.0%**	**85.9%**	**73.1%**

where $\min_t PSNR(I_t, \hat{I}_t)$ and $\max_t PSNR(I_t, \hat{I}_t)$ denote the minimum and the maximum PSNR values between the t-th predicted frame $\hat{I}_t$ and the corresponding ground truth I_t. After getting the regular score $S(t)$, we can distinguish the normal and abnormal frames by setting a threshold for $S(t)$.

Differentiating normal and abnormal samples with different thresholds will result in different detection accuracies. Therefore, we draw the results of different thresholds into Receiver Operating Characteristic (ROC) curves during the testing process and use Area Under Curve (AUC) as the final test accuracy. Since we use two generators that learn from each other to predict the future frame, we can finally get two AUCs. However, because mutual learning will make the abilities of the two generators converge, the final AUCs will also tend to be similar. Therefore, we choose the generator that performs relatively better for testing.

3 Experiment

In this Section, we evaluate our proposed approach and the main components on four mainstream datasets. We first introduce the datasets in Sect. 3.1. Then we arrive at the evaluation metrics in Sect. 3.2 and compare our approach with the state-of-arts on the introduced four datasets in Sect. 3.3. At last, the running time will be shown in Sect. 3.4.

3.1   Dataset

The datasets we utilize in our experiments are presented as follows:

CUHK Avenue [15] dataset contains 16 training videos and 21 testing videos, a total of 30652 frames. There are 47 abnormal events, including throwing objects, loitering, and running. The size of a person may vary depending on the position and angle of the camera.

UCSD [20] dataset consists of UCSD Pedestrian 1 (Ped1) dataset and UCSD Pedestrian 2 (Ped2) dataset. Ped1 dataset contains 34 training video samples and 36 test video samples. There are 40 abnormal events, all of which are related to vehicles such as bicycles and cars. Ped2 dataset contains 16 training video samples and 12 test video samples. It contains 2550 training frames and 2010 test frames with a resolution of 240 × 360, which mainly includes human walking scenes and abnormal events such as vehicles, bicycles, wheelchairs, and skateboarders crossing the pedestrian area.

ShanghaiTech [18] dataset contains 330 training videos and 107 testing videos. There are 130 abnormal events which consist of 13 scenes and various anomaly types.

3.2   Evaluation Metrics

In most of the literature on anomaly detection, a common evaluation metric is to calculate the Receiver Operating Characteristic (ROC) curve by changing the score threshold dividing normal and anomaly. The introduction about the ROC curve and related concepts are as follows:

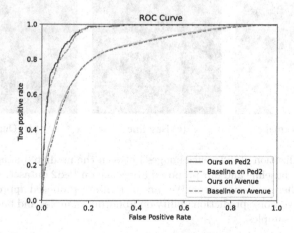

Fig. 5. The ROC curves of our approach and baseline on the Ped2 and Avenue dataset.

True Positive Rate (TPR): The rate that abnormal samples are correctly judged as abnormal.

False Positive Rate (FPR): The rate that normal samples are incorrectly judged as abnormal.

Receiver Operating Characteristic (ROC): Using different prediction score thresholds to classify normal and abnormal and calculate TPR and FPR, establishing a coordinate system with TPR as the horizontal axis and FPR as the vertical axis, then the ROC curve can be drawn.

Area Under Curve (AUC): The area under the ROC curve.

Therefore, we utilize the ROC curve to evaluate the performance of our approach and calculate the AUC to compare the state-of-arts. An expected approach with powerful detection capability should achieve the value of AUC closer to one.

3.3   Comparison with Existing Methods

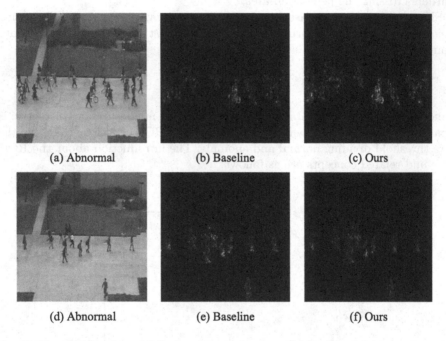

Fig. 6. The visualization of difference images between the predicted image and ground truth obtained by baseline and our proposed approach on Ped2 dataset, where brighter pixel presents higher prediction error. We can see that our proposed approach can guide the network to have worse prediction ability on abnormal samples and better prediction ability on normal samples.

The comparison between our approach and existing methods is shown in this Section. The AUC of each method is presented in Table 1. We can see that our approach has a better performance than the listed existing methods (a better average performance on all datasets, not just on one dataset). It shows the effectiveness of our proposed approach. Besides, the ROC curves of our approach and baseline [14] on the Ped2 and Avenue dataset are presented in Fig. 5, it can reflect the relationship between sensitivity and specificity. The area under the curve of our proposed approach is closer to 1 than that of the baseline [14], which denotes our approach is more effective than the baseline [14].

To better improve the effectiveness of our proposed approach on future frame prediction and anomaly detection, we visualize the results of the experiments of our approach and the baseline [14]. Figure 6 shows the visualization of difference images between the predicted image and ground truth on the Ped2 dataset. The value of each pixel of the difference image is normalized to [0, 255] and the brighter area represents the larger distance between the predicted frame and the ground truth. Through figures (a), (b), and (c), we can find that the difference image of our approach is brighter than that of the baseline [14], which means that our approach can predict the abnormal behaviors with a larger prediction error. Through figures (d), (e), and (f), we can see that for normal behavior, our framework has a better prediction ability than the baseline [14] because the difference image of ours is much darker than that of the baseline [14]. Therefore, our proposed approach can realize the polarizing of the prediction errors between normal and abnormal samples, which can lead to a more accurate anomaly detection result.

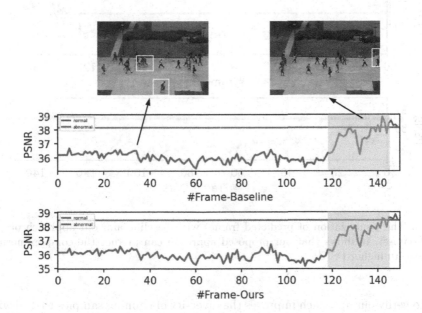

Fig. 7. The visualization of predicted frames with Baseline and our approach on the Ped2 dataset. The red box represents abnormal behavior. We can find that in the transition phase between abnormal behavior and normal behavior, our proposed approach can more effectively cut the PSNR of abnormal frames, thereby reducing the confusion caused by boundary samples. (Color figure online)

To show the effect of our approach in dealing with the boundary samples more intuitively, we visualize the PSNR of a predicted video utilizing different methods on the Ped2 dataset, which is shown in Fig. 7, the higher PSNR represents the more accurate prediction. Intuitively, when abnormal behavior transitions to normal behavior, there is always a stage in which the distributions of normal and abnormal behavior are very similar. As shown in the two grayscale images in Fig. 7, when the abnormal behavior of cycling is about to leave sight, it's even hard to distinguish the abnormal by naked eyes. Our approach tries to avoid confusion by weakening the weight of these boundary samples, and we can see that compared to the baseline [14], our approach can better suppress the increase of PSNR in boundary samples transiting from abnormal to normal and alleviate the confusion.

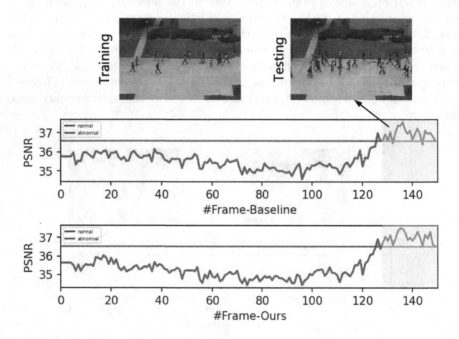

Fig. 8. The visualization of predicted frames with baseline and our approach on the Ped2 dataset. It shows that our proposed approach can predict the complex normal scenes with higher PSNR.

To verify our approach improves the diversity of training samples to deal with the complex normal scene in testing, we visualize the PSNR of the predicted video as well as the normal scene in training and testing. Because of the lack of diversity of training samples, the prediction network may not perform well in complex normal behavior. As shown in Fig. 8, we can find that our approach can increase the value of PSNR, which means lower prediction error, in the complex normal scene compared to the baseline [14].

3.4   Running time

Table 2. The running time of our approach and compared methods on Ped1, Ped2, and Avenue datasets.

Dataset	Ped1	Ped2	Avenue
Frame-Pred [14]	**42.792 fps**	37.822 fps	22.566 fps
Online	37.037 fps	40.000 fps	N/A
DDGAN-Loss [5]	16.861 fps	14.913 fps	10.212
Ours	40.628 fps	**44.974 fps**	**24.926 fps**

The inference time of on Ped1, Ped2, and Avenue datasets with our approach and existing methods are presented in Table 2. Obviously, our framework is much faster than those of other algorithms on anomaly detection (about 4.7 fps higher than baseline [14] in Ped1 and Avenue dataset, about 4.2 fps higher than Online in Ped1 and Ped2 dataset, and 22.8 fps higher than DDGAN-Loss [5] on Ped1, Ped2, and Avenue dataset), which means that our proposed approach is more effective and more efficient than others.

4   Conclusion

Normal samples may have similar distributions to abnormal samples, which may cause the network to have a certain generalization ability to abnormal samples. Besides, the lack of diversity of training data may cause the overfitting of network to normal samples. Consequently, it is not enough to merely improve the prediction ability of the network to the normal samples in the training set. In this paper, we proposed a mutual learning inspired prediction network with anti-aliasing for anomaly detection. Specifically, our proposed classifier based weighting method for anti-aliasing can figure out the confusion boundary samples in training data and weaken their weights during training, which can alleviate the generalization of prediction network to abnormal samples, then the proposed mutual learning inspired prediction framework can increase the diversity of prototypical normal samples and avoid the overfitting of network to normal samples. In this way, we can polarize the prediction errors between normal and abnormal samples and increase the accuracy of anomaly detection. Experiments on four datasets prove the effectiveness and efficiency of our approach for anomaly detection.

References

1. Abati, D., Porrello, A., Calderara, S., Cucchiara, R.: Latent space autoregression for novelty detection. In: 2019 IEEE/CVF Conference on Computer Vision and Pattern Recognition (CVPR) (2020)

2. Chalapathy, R., Menon, A.K., Chawla, S.: Robust, deep and inductive anomaly detection. In: Ceci, M., Hollmén, J., Todorovski, L., Vens, C., Džeroski, S. (eds.) ECML PKDD 2017. LNCS (LNAI), vol. 10534, pp. 36–51. Springer, Cham (2017). https://doi.org/10.1007/978-3-319-71249-9_3

3. Chandola, V., Banerjee, A., Kumar, V.: Anomaly detection: a survey. ACM Comput. Surv. **41**(3) (2009). https://doi.org/10.1145/1541880.1541882

4. Dhole, H., Sutaone, M., Vyas, V.: Anomaly detection using convolutional spatiotemporal autoencoder. In: 2019 10th International Conference on Computing, Communication and Networking Technologies (ICCCNT) (2019)

5. Fan, S., Meng, F.: Video prediction and anomaly detection algorithm based on dual discriminator. In: 2020 5th International Conference on Computational Intelligence and Applications (ICCIA), pp. 123–127 (2020). https://doi.org/10.1109/ICCIA49625.2020.00031

6. Gong, D., et al.: Memorizing normality to detect anomaly: memory-augmented deep autoencoder for unsupervised anomaly detection. In: 2019 IEEE/CVF International Conference on Computer Vision (ICCV) (2020)

7. Hasan, M., Choi, J., Neumann, J., Roy-Chowdhury, A.K., Davis, L.S.: Learning temporal regularity in video sequences. CoRR abs/1604.04574 (2016). http://arxiv.org/abs/1604.04574

8. Ionescu, R.T., Smeureanu, S., Popescu, M., Alexe, B.: Detecting abnormal events in video using narrowed normality clusters. In: 2019 IEEE Winter Conference on Applications of Computer Vision (WACV), pp. 1951–1960 (2019). https://doi.org/10.1109/WACV.2019.00212

9. Isola, P., Zhu, J.Y., Zhou, T., Efros, A.A.: Image-to-image translation with conditional adversarial networks. In: IEEE Conference on Computer Vision and Pattern Recognition (2016)

10. Kim, J., Grauman, K.: Observe locally, infer globally: a space-time MRF for detecting abnormal activities with incremental updates. In: 2009 IEEE Computer Society Conference on Computer Vision and Pattern Recognition (CVPR 2009), Miami, Florida, USA, 20–25 June 2009 (2009)

11. Kingma, D., Ba, J.: Adam: a method for stochastic optimization. Computer Science (2014)

12. Kwon, Y.H., Park, M.G.: Predicting future frames using retrospective cycle GAN. In: IEEE Computer Vision and Pattern Recognition (CVPR) (2019)

13. Liang, Z., Wang, H., Ding, X., Mu, T.: Industrial time series determinative anomaly detection based on constraint hypergraph. Knowl.-Based Syst. **233**, 107548 (2021). https://doi.org/10.1016/j.knosys.2021.107548. https://www.sciencedirect.com/science/article/pii/S0950705121008108

14. Liu, W., Luo, W., Lian, D., Gao, S.: Future frame prediction for anomaly detection - a new baseline. In: 2018 IEEE/CVF Conference on Computer Vision and Pattern Recognition, pp. 6536–6545 (2018). https://doi.org/10.1109/CVPR.2018.00684

15. Lu, C., Shi, J., Jia, J.: Abnormal event detection at 150 FPS in MATLAB. In: IEEE International Conference on Computer Vision (2014)

16. Luo, W., et al.: Video anomaly detection with sparse coding inspired deep neural networks. IEEE Trans. Pattern Anal. Mach. Intell. **43**(03), 1070–1084 (2021). https://doi.org/10.1109/TPAMI.2019.2944377

17. Luo, W., Liu, W., Gao, S.: Remembering history with convolutional lstm for anomaly detection. In: 2017 IEEE International Conference on Multimedia and Expo (ICME), pp. 439–444 (2017). https://doi.org/10.1109/ICME.2017.8019325

18. Luo, W., Liu, W., Gao, S.: A revisit of sparse coding based anomaly detection in stacked RNN framework. In: 2017 IEEE International Conference on Computer Vision (ICCV), pp. 341–349 (2017). https://doi.org/10.1109/ICCV.2017.45

19. Lv, F., Liang, T., Zhao, J., Zhuo, Z., Wu, J., Yang, G.: Latent Gaussian process for anomaly detection in categorical data. Knowl.-Based Syst. **220**, 106896 (2021). https://doi.org/10.1016/j.knosys.2021.106896. https://www.sciencedirect.com/science/article/pii/S0950705121001593

20. Mahadevan, V., Li, W.X., Bhalodia, V., Vasconcelos, N.: Anomaly detection in crowded scenes. In: Computer Vision and Pattern Recognition (2010)

21. Mathieu, M., Couprie, C., Lecun, Y.: Deep multi-scale video prediction beyond mean square error. In: ICLR (2016)

22. Nazaré, T.S., de Mello, R.F., Ponti, M.A.: Are pre-trained CNNs good feature extractors for anomaly detection in surveillance videos? CoRR abs/1811.08495 (2018). http://arxiv.org/abs/1811.08495

23. Qiao, M., Wang, T., Li, J., Li, C., Lin, Z., Snoussi, H.: Abnormal event detection based on deep autoencoder fusing optical flow. In: 2017 36th Chinese Control Conference (CCC), pp. 11098–11103 (2017). https://doi.org/10.23919/ChiCC.2017.8029129

24. Sabokrou, M., Fayyaz, M., Fathy, M., Moayed, Z., Klette, R.: Deep-anomaly: fully convolutional neural network for fast anomaly detection in crowded scenes. Comput. Vis. Image Underst. **172**, 88–97 (2018). https://doi.org/10.1016/j.cviu.2018.02.006. https://www.sciencedirect.com/science/article/pii/S1077314218300249

25. Villegas, R., Yang, J., Hong, S., Lin, X., Lee, H.: Decomposing motion and content for natural video sequence prediction. CoRR abs/1706.08033 (2017). http://arxiv.org/abs/1706.08033

26. Wang, X., Du, Y., Lin, S., Cui, P., Shen, Y., Yang, Y.: adVAE: a self-adversarial variational autoencoder with gaussian anomaly prior knowledge for anomaly detection. Knowl.-Based Syst. **190**, 105187 (2020). https://doi.org/10.1016/j.knosys.2019.105187. https://www.sciencedirect.com/science/article/pii/S0950705119305283

27. Xu, D., Ricci, E., Yan, Y., Song, J., Sebe, N.: Learning deep representations of appearance and motion for anomalous event detection. In: Proceedings of the British Machine Vision Conference (BMVC), pp. 8.1–8.12. BMVA Press, September 2015. https://doi.org/10.5244/C.29.8

28. Zhao, Y., Deng, B., Shen, C., Liu, Y., Lu, H., Hua, X.S.: Spatio-temporal autoencoder for video anomaly detection. In: Proceedings of the 25th ACM International Conference on Multimedia, MM 201717, pp. 1933–1941. Association for Computing Machinery, New York (2017). https://doi.org/10.1145/3123266.3123451

Weakly Supervised Video Anomaly Detection with Temporal and Abnormal Information

Ruoyan Pi, Xiangteng He, and Yuxin Peng[✉]

Wangxuan Institute of Computer Technology, Peking University, Beijing, China
pengyuxin@pku.edu.cn

Abstract. Weakly supervised video anomaly detection is to distinguish anomalies from normal scenes and events in videos, under the setting that we only know whether there are abnormal events in a video, but the specific occurrence time of abnormal events is unknown. It is generally modeled as a MIL (multiple instance learning) problem, where video-level labels are provided to train an anomaly detector to obtain frame-level labels for videos. However, most existing methods generally overlook temporal information in abnormal videos (positive bags), and only use one sample (snippet) in the positive bag to train. The positive bag may include more useful information with high possibility. Therefore, we propose the Weakly Supervised Video Anomaly Detection Approach with Temporal and Positive Features, which consider both the temporal information and more positive samples for video anomaly detection. Its contributions can be summarized as follows: (1) we consider more temporal information and introduced the attention mechanism in our network, we use both local and global snippets' features to enhance the temporal representation ability of these features. (2) We use more positive (abnormal) samples and its features in bags to train our model, so that more complementary and relevant information will make our model more robust and effective. (3) We consider not only the differences between normal samples and abnormal samples but also between abnormal samples and abnormal samples, which can help our proposed approach to excavate positive (abnormal) samples' information more efficiently and adequately. Experimental results demonstrate the effectiveness of our proposed methods in the UCF-Crime and ShanghaiTech dataset.

Keywords: Video anomaly detection · Weakly supervision · Multiple instance learning · Temporal features

1 Introduction

Video anomaly detection is a task to locate abnormal events in videos temporally. It is an important problem in the field of computer vision, for it has great potential in many fields of real life. Using the video information captured by the surveillance camera, this task can detect unconventional or abnormal behaviors and events in the video (violation of traffic rules, fighting, violence, sensitive information, etc.). The model of video anomaly detection will involve many aspects of computer vision, including action recognition, scene classification, object detection, video semantic segmentation, skeleton detection, behavior detection and other tasks. Although it has been researched for many years, there are still many problems to be solved in this task: (1) The frequency of abnormal events is very low, which makes it difficult to collect and label data; (2) The scarcity of abnormal events leads to the fact that the positive samples in training are far less than the negative samples; And the lack of positive samples also makes it more difficult to learn abnormal features; (3) In real scenes, both normal and abnormal events are diverse and complex. There are many types normal events in the real world video, while abnormal events also have many kinds. In addition, we cannot exhaust the abnormal situations, all abnormal events and behaviors should be attributed to abnormalities, The abnormal situation in the test may be something the model has never seen. Therefore, it is really difficult to distinguish normal and abnormal events.

In some previous work, video anomaly detection was regarded as an unsupervised (or semi supervised) task because of these difficulties. Many previous methods first learn a common pattern and assume that any pattern that violates the common pattern should be abnormal. Actually, unsupervised video anomaly detection can be defined in different statistical models. Includes linear fitting such as PCA, and non-linear fitting such as deep generation models. The existing models are roughly divided into three categories, reconstructed model, predicted model and generated model. The commonly used datasets include UMN [2], UCSD Ped [3], CUHK Avenue [4], ShanghaiTech [5] and so on.

But, the problems still exist, whether the normal situation in datasets can cover the normal situation in the real situation? The answer is definitely no. Moreover, with the development of computer vision, deep learning technology and hardware, the ability of feature representation is becoming stronger and stronger and models are becoming more and more generalized, so some abnormal events may be regarded as normal because of the powerful generalization ability of these models. Besides, the datasets [2–5] these unsupervised methods used are mostly pedestrian walking on the sidewalk under the surveillance video, and the anomalies often are abnormal motion (such as fast motion). However, these datasets are very different from the risks expected to be solved in the real situation. So weakly supervised problem are proposed as MIL (multiple instance learning) problem. Weak supervision means that during training, we only know whether there are or no abnormal events in a video, and the specific time of abnormal events is unknown. MIL is often used in weakly supervised learning problem. Instead of sample-level labels, it use bag-level labels (a bag is consist of several samples) to train the model, which significantly reduces the cost of manually labeling data. Compared with unsupervised methods, weakly supervised methods are able to produce more reliable results and obtaining the video-level labels is also kind of realistic in the real situation.

Recent methods usually divide the video into several equal length snippets (segments), extract features from each snippet, and then use these features and video-level labels for training to obtain snippet-level scores to judge whether it is an abnormal sample. However, video is continuous, no one knows which part of the video will have problems (abnormal), so equal length segmentation may just separate the abnormal events, or the abnormal events may span multiple snippets, so the temporal information of adjacent snippets should be taken into consideration. Therefore, we use each snippet's feature of video to interact with both adjacent and long-distance snippets' features, and design a method to strengthen this relationship. Besides, because of the diversity of anomalies, we also think that there are several types of anomalies in videos (although we only need to judge whether they belong to anomalies). There is no doubt that the features should be at a large distance between the normal features and abnormal features, but they should also be dissimilar between anomaly features from different types of anomalies. So, we propose a novel N-pair loss to improve this problem. What's more, the MIL method usually takes only the sample with the highest anomaly score in a positive bag and the sample with the highest anomaly score in the negative bag for training. This also ignores the possibility that the abnormal events or behaviors may span multiple segments or have more than one anomaly in a video (bag). Therefore, if the anomaly score of a snippet feature in the positive bag is very close to the highest one, though it is not the highest, or the features are relatively similar, we have reason to improve the MIL and use more snippets and its features in the positive bags in the training. Experiments show that our TAI method achieves the state-of-the-art results on ShanghaiTech and UCF-Crime dataset. In summary, our contributions are as follows:

- Aiming at the lack of using insufficient temporal information in the existing methods, we introduce the attention mechanism in our method. We use both local and global snippets features to enhance the temporal representation ability of features, which help our method to get a more effective classifier that can give us more convincing scores.
- We utilize more samples and its features in the videos, so that we use more positive and relevant information to train our model than previous methods.
- We consider not only the differences between abnormal and normal samples, but also the difference between abnormal samples, so that we can use abnormal and normal samples more substantially and efficiently.

2   Related Work

2.1   Unsupervised Video Anomaly Detection

The existing methods can be roughly divided into three categories, reconstructed methods, predicted methods and generated methods. Giorno et al. [12] introduced the a unsupervised framework for large video anomaly detection problem, a sliding window and a classifier are used to detect anomalies in videos. Ionescu et al. [13] inherited the idea of the previous one, this paper applied unmasking to measure the anomalies. Wang et al. [14] solved the problem by using an auto-encoder to predict what will happen next, and then compare the predicted features with the actual features. The greater the difference, the greater the possibility of abnormality. Many works also choose to propose a framework as a generator to generate or predict future frames and compare with real frames. Liu et al. [15] proposed to add constraint on intensity, gradient and motion to generate new frames. Ye et al. [16] proposed a framework based on GAN, which use a coding module to predict what will happen next and an error refinement module to distinguish whether the actual frames is abnormal. Datasets using by unsupervised video anomaly detection include UMN [2], UCSD Ped [3], CUHK Avenue [4], ShanghaiTech [5] and so on.

2.2 Weakly-Supervised Video Anomaly Detection

Sultani et al. [1] proposed the UCF-crime data set, and introduced the weakly supervised multi instance learning method to the video anomaly detection. They use a C3D framework to extract spatio-temporal features and generate anomaly score, so that they can use the score to distinguish normal and anomaly frames. He et al. [6] proposes a graph-based MIL framework with anchor dictionary learning. They use weakly supervised setting UCSD Ped [3] dataset. Zhong et al. [7] provided a new viewpoint that weakly supervised learning task is a supervised learning task under noisy labels, so they proposed a graph convolutional network to correct noisy labels.

With the development of deep learning technology and the introduction of attention mechanism, more high-performance models have been proposed. Wan et al. [10] proposed an anomaly detection framework called Anomaly Regression Net. They design a dynamic MIL loss and a center loss to improve the MIL, which makes the scores' difference got from abnormal and normal bags respectively larger and got both from normal bags less. Wu et al. [8] proposed a new dataset called XD-Violence, which use not only vision information, but also audio information to help model to distinguish the normal and abnormal instances. Feng et al. [11] proposed a MIL-based pseudo label generator and a self-guided attention task-specific encoder to detect the anomalies. Tian et al. [9] proposed robust temporal feature magnitude learning to distinguish the abnormal and normal instances, which also improved the MIL by including more information from positive bags and negative bags. In weakly supervised video anomaly detection, datasets include ShanghaiTech [5], UCF-Crime [1], XD-Violence [8] and UCSD-Peds [3].

2.3 Multiple Instance Learning

MIL is often used to solve weakly supervised learning problem. In Multi-Instance Learning, the data is labeled. But the target of the labels is not sample-level, but bag-level. One or several samples together are called a bag, and each bag has its own label. When the label of a bag is negative, the labels of all samples in the bag is negative. When a bag is marked as positive, at least one sample in the bag is marked as positive. In Multiple Instance Learning, our goal is to learn a classifier, so that we can distinguish new input exact samples (not bags) is positive or negative samples. In video tasks, MIL takes a video as a bag and snippets in the videos as instances or samples [1,19,20].

2.4   Pair-Based Loss in Deep Metric Learning

We choose to use pair-based loss in deep metric learning to help the model to notice the difference between abnormal samples. Metric learning is a method of spatial mapping, which can learn an embedded space. In this space, all data are transformed into one feature, and the features' distance between the similar samples is smaller than distance between dissimilar samples, so as to distinguish the data.

In deep learning, many metric learning methods use paired samples for loss calculation. This kind of method is called pair-based deep metric learning. Here are some pair-based loss: Contrastive loss [18] takes a pair of embedding vectors as input, and aims to make them similar if they are of the same class and make them dissimilar otherwise. Triplet loss [21] associates each anchor with a positive and a negative data point. N-pair loss [22] and Lifted Structure loss [23] reflect hardness of data.

3   Approach

The purpose of anomaly detection is to detect the anomalies in the videos in frame-level or snippet-level. In the weakly supervised video anomaly detection, we have a video sequence X and its video-level labels Y where $y = 1$ means the bags, that is the whole video, is a positive bag, which means in this video, something abnormal exists, while $y = 0$ means that there is no abnormal events or situation in the video. Then, in order to localize where is abnormal in the video temporally, we divided the entire video into several snippets with equal lengths, denoted as $X = (X_1; X_2; ...; X_T)$, and a snippet is a exact sample. So this is a MIL problem.

Then, we use a pretrained network to extract features for every snippets. Following previous WSVAD methods [9,11], We use I3D [25] to extract features from videos. I3D is a video action recognition model, which is a two stream model based on 3D convolution and uses two convolution (2D) models pre-trained through Imagenet, one for RGB data processing and the other for optical flow data processing. Some previous work [1,11] will also use C3D [36] to extract the task-agnostic features, however, the performance is often lower. C3D used CNN with few layers to train on small datasets, instead of using those successful pre-training models on Imagenet such as I3D, which cause the represent ability of features extracted from C3D is not as good as those from I3D.

After that, T snippets (samples) are changed into T features, and a video (bag) is a T-tuple features, that is $(x_1; x_2; ...; x_T)$. However, these features are

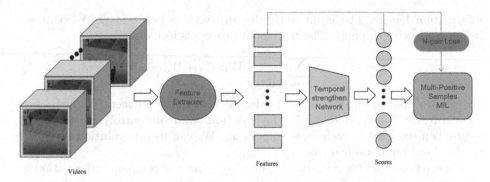

Fig. 1. Framework of our method. First, we divided a video into T snippets, and then use pre-trained model to extract features for every snippets here. After that, we use a temporal strengthen network to obtain the anomaly scores for every features. Finally, we use multiple positive samples MIL and a novel N-pair loss to get the final classifier.

task-agnostic, our work is to make these features fit for the WSVAD task and get abnormal scores for every snippets.

To detect the snippet-level anomalies in videos, we propose a method called TAI (Temporal strengthen network and Multi-Positive Features MIL), which are consists of 3 parts:

- We consider more temporal information. We propose a temporal strengthen network, which use both local and global snippets' features to enhance the temporal representation ability of features
- We improve the MIL method, which results in that more snippets and its features in the positive bag participate in the training.
- We consider not only the difference between abnormal and normal samples, but also the difference between abnormal samples. And based on this, we propose a novel n-pair loss.

The framework of our method is shown in Fig. 1.

3.1   Temporal Strengthen Network

After extracting the features $(x_1; x_2; ...; x_T)$, we use a $S()$ function to obtain the anomaly scores $(s_1; s_2; ...; s_T)$ for every features. There is no doubt that scores of normal videos are expected to be smaller than anomalous videos, and abnormal videos are expected to be higher. To use the temporal information for every snippets, the first thing we should think about is that the adjacent snippets of the anchor snippet. These adjacent snippets and their features will contribute in distinguishing whether the anchor snippet is an abnormal sample. So we should use m-nearest snippets and its feature to strengthen the feature, so that we are able to get a more convincing score for that snippet. So formally, we design a temporal strengthen function $F()$ to extract high-level temporal information locally. The input is the feature vectors $(x_1; x_2; ...; x_T)$ extracted from consecutive snippets. The regression process is formulated as:

$$x_i = \sum_{j=-m,...,m,j\neq 0,j\neq T} W_j x_{i+j} + W_0 x_i + b \tag{1}$$

So, we are able to choose the m to decide how many adjacent snippets and its features will be considered in the function. And m controls the temporal strengthen modeled in each local snippet x_i. We can use convolution layers to get the local temporal features.

However, besides the adjacent feature, long-distance temporal information is also useful in this task. Because an abnormal event may be continuous happening for a very long time or one abnormal event happen for a while and after some time, it happens again. So, we should also pay attention to long-distance temporal information.

But because the receptive field of convolution kernel is local, it takes many layers to associate the regions of different parts of the whole image, which will cause a lot of computation. So, in order to process long-distance temporal information, we add attention layer in our temporal information strengthen network. There are some works about attention mechanism in vision area, such as NLNet [27] and SENet [26]. However, NLNet learns location independent attention map for each location, resulting in a lot of computational waste, while SENet uses the global context to recalibrate the weights of different channels to adjust the channel dependence, but feature fusion using weight recalibration cannot make full use of the global context. So, we choose to use GCNet [28] to combine the global temporal information in our model. Global context block (GCNet) can not only establish effective long-distance dependence like NL block, but also save computation like SE block. GC block can be formulated as:

$$z_i = x_i + W_{v2}\text{RELU}(\text{LN}(W_{v1} \sum_{j=1}^{N_p} \frac{exp(W_k x_j)}{\sum_{m=1}^{N_p} exp(W_k x_m)} x_j)) \tag{2}$$

$\alpha = \frac{exp(W_k x_j)}{\sum_{m=1}^{N_p} exp(W_k x_m)}$ is the weight for global attention pooling, and $\delta() = W_{v2}\text{RELU}(\text{LN}(W_{v1}()))$ denotes the bottleneck transform.

In our method, we use a function $C()$ to represent the context block from GCNet to get the long-distance temporal information, and function $F()$ is used to represent the convolution layers to get the adjacent temporal information. After that, we concatenate 2 features (one is local temporal feature and another is global temporal feature), and use 3 fully connected layers, activated by a Sigmoid function, to obtain the anomaly scores, which use $\theta()$ to represent. The total process of this part can be formulated as:

$$S(x) = \theta(F(x), C(x)) \tag{3}$$

The structure of our temporal information strengthen network is shown in Fig. 2.

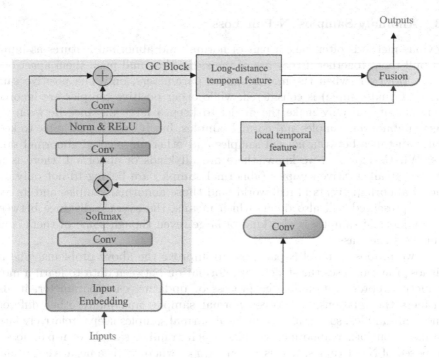

Fig. 2. Structure of our temporal information strengthen network (TISN). We use the task-agnostic feature extracted from I3D as input, then enhance the temporal information by not only local but global temporal information. GC block is used to get long-distance (global) temporal information and several convolution layers are used to get local temporal information.

3.2 Multi-positive Sample MIL

The MIL method usually takes only the snippet features with the highest anomaly score in the positive bag and the features with the highest anomaly score in the negative bag for training. This is a big weakness because it may ignore a lot of useful information in a positive bag, as the abnormal events or behaviors may span multiple segments (snippets) or have more than one anomaly (positive sample) in a video (bag). So we propose a improved MIL called multi-positive sample MIL to use more positive samples in a positive bag.

Given a video V with T snippets, the anomaly score is predicted through a mapping function $S()$. We use top-k scores and its features to optimize the network. if $k = 1$, our multi-positive sample MIL is equal to MIL. Given a batch $(V^1, V^2, ..., V^n)$, we will get $n \times T$ features and scores in the first part, and then, in multi-positive sample MIL, we have $n \times k$ positive samples and its features and scores. Using that and our n-pair loss in next part, we can get the classifier.

3.3   Anomaly Samples' N-Pair Loss

Previous methods often take a pair of normal and abnormal features as input, and pull them together if they are of the same class and push them apart otherwise. However, when the model update parameters, only one positive sample (abnormal sample) is considered, while other positive samples are ignored. Therefore, it can only make the model to keep a large distance between the selected abnormal samples and normal samples, but it cannot guarantee to keep a large distance between normal samples and other un-selected abnormal samples. What's more, as we know, there are all kinds of abnormal, there is no doubt that all positive samples (abnormal sample) are belong to not only one kind of abnormal events in real world, and those abnormal samples and its features represented will also differ, which means, the average distance between those abnormal samples is also kind of large, even though some of them come from the same class.

So we propose a novel N-pair Loss to improve the above problems. The N-pair loss function uses the structural information between data to learn a more distinctive representation. In the process of updating each parameter, it also considers the relationship between normal samples and many other different abnormal samples, so it is able to make abnormal samples keep a relatively large distance from other abnormal samples. Each training sample of n-pair loss is composed of $N+1$ tuples, that is $x^-, x_1, ..., x_N$, where x^- is a negative (normal) sample's feature relative to others, and others are positive samples' features, and D is the distance function of two features, N is the feature standardization function:

$$
\begin{aligned}
L(x^-, x_1, ..., x_N; D) = log(1 + \sum_{1}^{N} exp(D(N(x^-) - N(x_i)))) \\
+ \lambda[t - log(1 + \sum_{i,j} exp(D(N(x_i) - N(x_j))))]_+
\end{aligned}
\tag{4}
$$

The first part presents the difference of more negative samples and selected positive sample. And the second part contributes in pull away the average distance of abnormal samples and abnormal samples. t is a threshold value. The greater m means we want the distance between abnormal samples is greater, and λ means how much attention we will pay to the distance between different anomaly.

4   Experiment

4.1   Datasets and Metrics

We conduct experiments on ShanghaiTech dataset [5] and UCF-Crime dataset [1]. ShanghaiTech is a medium-scale dataset that contains 437 campus surveillance videos. It has 13 scenes with complex light conditions and camera angles. It contains 130 abnormal events and over 270, 000 training frames. Moreover, pixel level ground truth of abnormal events is also annotated in the dataset. However, all the training videos of this dataset are normal. In line with the weakly supervised setting, we followed Zhong et al. [7]'s work to split dataset into 238 training videos and 199 testing videos. UCF-Crime is a large-scale data set of real-world surveillance videos, including 13 kinds of abnormal events and 1900 long and untrimmed videos, of which 1610 videos are training videos with video-level labels and the rest are test videos with frame-level labels.

As for metrics, following previous works (Zhong et al. [7], Wan et al. [10]), we also use the Area Under the Curve (AUC) of the frame-level ROC (Receiver Operating Characteristic) as our metric for both ShanghaiTech and UCF-Crime.

4.2 Implementation Details

Following [1], Each video is divided into 32 video snippets, which means, $T = 32$. Scores obtained by our temporal strengthen network ranges from 0 to 1, The closer the score is to 0, the more the model tends to believe that the input snippet is a normal sample, and it is a abnormal sample otherwise. As for our backbone, following previous WSVAD methods [9,11], We choose to use $mixed_{5c}$ layer of the pre-trained I3D[25] to extract 2048D snippet features. Therefore, for each video, we have a 32×2048 feature matrix. In our temporal strengthen network, we first use 3 Conv1D layers to extract the local information of the snippet, and then use a context block to extract the long-distance temporal information of the snippet. Finally, we use 3 full connection layers, which have 256, 32 and 1 nodes respectively. First two full connection layer is followed by ReLU functions, while the last one is followed by Sigmoid functions. And, we make $m = 3$ in Eq. 1. Besides, dropout with 70% are implemented after each fully connect layer. And in our multi-positive samples MIL, we use top-3 scores and its features, and we use them in a batch to calculate the N-pair loss.

We train the model for a total of 10000 iterations on Nvidia GTX-1080Ti. And for both ShanghaiTech and UCF-Crime, we set the learning rate to 0.001. We use PyTorch to implement the methods.

4.3 Results on ShanghaiTech

The AUC results on ShanghaiTech are shown in Table 1. Compared with previous state-of-the-art unsupervised learning methods and weakly supervised approaches, our method TAI achieves a good performance. Our model achieves 96.92% AUC on this dataset. Our method is 6.7% AUC higher than SSMT [32], the SOTA unsupervised method, at the cost of adding several hundreds of video level tags. And TAI also get an improvement of 2.09% AUC comparing with current SOTA weakly supervised method MIST, which also use I3D-RGB features. The result shows that scores learning from features is more representative and differentiated. Our model is able to capture temporal information well and is more effective cause we use more positive samples and consider the difference between anomalies.

Table 1. Comparison of AUC performance with other unsupervised and weakly-supervised methods on ShanghaiTech.

Supervised	Method	Feature	AUC (%)
Unsupervised	CAC [33]		79.30
	AMMC [34]		73.70
	SSMT [32]		90.20
Weakly-Supervised	GCN [7]	C3D-RGB	76.44
	GCN [7]	TSN-Flow	84.13
	GCN [7]	TSN-RGB	84.44
	AR-Net [31]	I3D RGB	85.38
	AR-Net [31]	I3D RGB + Flow	91.24
	MIST [11]	I3D RGB	<u>94.83</u>
	CLAWS [35]	C3D RGB	89.67
	Ours	**I3D RGB**	**96.92**

4.4 Results on UCF-Crime

The AUC results on UCF-Crime are shown in Table 2. Compared with previous state-of-the-art unsupervised learning methods and weakly supervised approaches, our method TAI achieves the best performance. Our model achieves 85.73% AUC on this dataset. Our method TAI outperforms previous unsupervised and weakly supervised learning approaches. TAI achieves a performance improvement of 3.43% AUC comparing with MIST [11], and 1.7% AUC comparing with RTFM [9], with the same I3D-RGB features. These demonstrates that scores our model learns from I3D-RGB features is more representative and differentiated. More positive samples and difference between anomalies make our model perform better.

Table 2. Comparison of AUC performance with other unsupervised and weakly-supervised methods on UCF-Crime.

Supervised	Method	Feature	AUC (%)
Unsupervised	Conv-AE [29]		50.60
	GODS [30]		70.46
	BODS [30]		68.26
Weakly-Supervised	MIL-Rank [1]	C3D-RGB	75.41
	GCN [7]	C3D-RGB	81.08
	GCN [7]	TSN-Flow	78.08
	GCN [7]	TSN-RGB	82.12
	MIST [11]	C3D RGB	81.40
	MIST [11]	I3D RGB	82.30
	RTFM [9]	C3D RGB	83.28
	RTFM [9]	I3D RGB	<u>84.03</u>
	CLAWS [35]	C3D RGB	83.03
	Ours	**I3D RGB**	**85.73**

4.5 Ablation Studies

We perform the ablation study on ShanghaiTech and UCF Crime with I3D features, as shown in Table 3. The temporal information strengthen function $S()$ is TF, multi-positive samples MIL is MMIL, and NPL represents the new n-pair loss we propose. The baseline achieves only 92.22% AUC on ShanghaiTech and 80.89% AUC on UCF Crime. After adding TF, the AUC performance is boosted to 95.82% on ShanghaiTech and 84.05% on UCF, This indicates that TF module is useful and effective, it contributes to get more representative scores. When only adding the MMIL part, the AUC substantially increases to 93.7% on ShanghaiTech and 81.5% on UCF- Crime, respectively, indicating that our improvement for the original MIL method is also useful, it can help the classifier to be more differentiated. Additionally, combining TF and MMIL, the AUC increases to 96.63% on ShanghaiTech and 84.72% on UCF- Crime. Then, adding the NPL part the full model TAI can achieve the best performance of 96.92% and 85.73% on the two datasets. The result is shown in Table 3. We can see in the result that compared with the other 2 part, TF part contributes most. But MMIL and NPL are still useful and beneficial for utilizing and capturing more effective anomalous information. All of them improve the performance of video anomaly detection.

Table 3. Ablation studies on ShanghaiTech and UCF-Crime.

Baseline	TF	MMIL	NPL	AUC (%)-SH	AUC (%)-UCF
√				92.22	80.89
√	√			95.82	84.05
√		√		93.7	81.5
√	√	√		96.63	84.72
√	√	√	√	96.92	85.73

4.6 Qualitative Analyse

Figure 3 presents some qualitative results on ShanghaiTech and UCF-Crime datasets. We visualize the anomaly score curves (blue) and ground truth label curves (red). Generally, we can see that our TAI can generate frame-level labels successfully, it is able to detect a very long time abnormal events (Fig. 2(b)(c)), and it also can detect more than one abnormal events in videos (Fig. 2(a)). Besides, We can also see that our approach is valid in complex surveillance videos in the video (d) in Fig. 2.

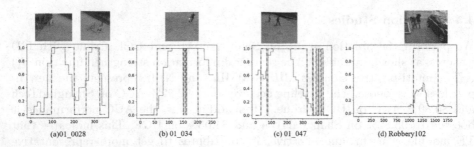

Fig. 3. Visualization of abnormal score curves (blue) and ground truth scores curves (red). The x-axis represents the number of frames, and the y-axis represents the abnormal scores. Videos (a), (b) and (c) are from the ShanghaiTech dataset, and video (d) are from UCF-Crime dataset. (Color figure online)

5   Conclusion

We introduced a novel method, that enables top-k MIL approaches for weakly supervised video anomaly detection. We put more temporal information into MIL, by using adjacent snippets' features to enhance the representation ability of features. Besides, We use more snippets and its features in the positive bags in the training. At last, We consider difference between anomalies and propose a n-pair loss to pull away the average distance between each abnormal samples. Scores our model learns from features consider more temporal information so that it is more representative and differentiated, our model is also more effective by using more positive samples in training process and considering difference between anomaly features. Finally, experimental results demonstrate the effectiveness of our proposed methods in the UCF-Crime and ShanghaiTech dataset.

Acknowledgments. This work was supported by the grants from the National Natural Science Foundation of China (61925201, 62132001, U21B2025) and the National Key R&D Program of China (2021YFF0901502).

References

1. Sultani, W., Chen, C., Shah, M.: Real-world anomaly detection in surveillance videos. In: IEEE Conference on Computer Vision and Pattern Recognition (CVPR), pp. 6479–6488 (2018)
2. Unusual crowd activity dataset of University of Minnesota. http://mha.cs.umn.edu/Movies/Crowd-Activity-All.avi
3. Li, W., Mahadevan, V., Vasconcelos, N.: Anomaly detection and localization in crowded scenes (PAMI). IEEE Trans. Pattern Anal. Mach. Intell. **36**(1), 18–32 (2013)
4. Lu, C., Shi, J., Jia, J.: Abnormal event detection at 150 FPS in MATLAB. In: IEEE International Conference on Computer Vision (ICCV), pp. 2720–2727 (2013)
5. Liu, W., Lian, D., Luo, W., Gao, S.: Future frame prediction for anomaly detection - a new baseline. In: IEEE International Conference on Computer Vision (ICCV) (2018)

6. He, C., Shao, J., Sun, J.: An anomaly-introduced learning method for abnormal event detection. Multimedia Tools Appl. **77**(22), 29573–29588 (2017). https://doi.org/10.1007/s11042-017-5255-z

7. Zhong, J., Li, N., Kong, W., Liu, S., Li, T.H., Li, G.: Graph convolutional label noise cleaner: train a plug-and-play action classifier for anomaly detection. In: IEEE Conference on Computer Vision and Pattern Recognition (CVPR), pp. 1237–1246 (2019)

8. Wu, P., et al.: Not only look, but also listen: learning multimodal violence detection under weak supervision. In: Vedaldi, A., Bischof, H., Brox, T., Frahm, J.-M. (eds.) ECCV 2020. LNCS, vol. 12375, pp. 322–339. Springer, Cham (2020). https://doi.org/10.1007/978-3-030-58577-8_20

9. Tian, Y., Pang, G., Chen, Y., Singh, R., Verjans, J.W., Carneiro, G.: Weakly-supervised video anomaly detection with robust temporal feature magnitude learning. In: IEEE International Conference on Computer Vision (ICCV) (2021)

10. Wan, B., Fang, Y., Xia, X., Mei, J.: Weakly supervised video anomaly detection via center-guided discriminative learning. In: IEEE International Conference on Multimedia and Expo (ICME), pp. 1–6 (2020)

11. Feng, J.-C., Hong, F.-T., Zheng, W.-S.: MIST: multiple instance self-training framework for video anomaly detection. In: IEEE Conference on Computer Vision and Pattern Recognition (CVPR), pp. 14009–14018 (2021)

12. Del Giorno, A., Bagnell, J.A., Hebert, M.: A discriminative framework for anomaly detection in large videos. In: Leibe, B., Matas, J., Sebe, N., Welling, M. (eds.) ECCV 2016. LNCS, vol. 9909, pp. 334–349. Springer, Cham (2016). https://doi.org/10.1007/978-3-319-46454-1_21

13. Ionescu, R., Smeureanu, S., Alexe, B., Popescu, M.: Unmasking the abnormal events in video. In: IEEE International Conference on Computer Vision (ICCV) (2017)

14. Wang, S., Zeng, Y., Liu, Q., Zhu, C., Zhu, E., Yin, J.: Detecting abnormality without knowing normality: a two-stage approach for unsupervised video abnormal event detection. In: ACM International Conference on Multimedia (ACM MM) (2018)

15. Liu, W., Lian, D., Luo, W., Gao, S.: Future frame prediction for anomaly detection - a new baseline. In: 2018 IEEE Conference on Computer Vision and Pattern Recognition (CVPR) (2018)

16. Ye, M., Peng, X., Gan, W., Wu, W., Qiao, Y.: AnoPCN: video anomaly detection via deep predictive coding network. In: ACM International Conference on Multimedia (ACM MM), pp. 1805–1813 (2019)

17. Zhong, J., Li, N., Kong, W., Liu, S., Li, T.H., Li, G.: Graph convolutional label noise cleaner: train a plug-and-play action classifier for anomaly detection. In: 2018 IEEE Conference on Computer Vision and Pattern Recognition (CVPR), pp. 1237–1246 (2019)

18. Bromley, J., Guyon, I., Lecun, Y., Sckinger, E., Shah, R.: Signature verification using a "Siamese" time delay neural network. In: Neural Information Processing Systems (NeurIPS) (1994)

19. Hong, F., Huang, X., Li, W., Zheng, W.: Mini-Net: multiple instance ranking network for video highlight detection. arXiv preprint arXiv:2007.09833 (2020)

20. Nguyen, P., Liu, T., Prasad, G., Han, B.: Weakly supervised action localization by sparse temporal pooling network. In: IEEE Conference on Computer Vision and Pattern Recognition (CVPR) (2018)

21. Schroff, F., Kalenichenko, D., Philbin, J.: FaceNet: a unified embedding for face recognition and clustering. In: IEEE Conference on Computer Vision and Pattern Recognition (CVPR) (2015)

22. Sohn, K.: Improved deep metric learning with multiclass n-pair loss objective. In: Neural Information Processing Systems (NeurIPS) (2016)

23. Song, H., Xiang, Y., Jegelka, S., Savarese, S.: Deep metric learning via lifted structured feature embedding. In: IEEE Conference on Computer Vision and Pattern Recognition (CVPR) (2016)

24. Liu, W., Luo, W., Li, Z., Zhao, P., Gao, S., et al.: Margin learning embedded prediction for video anomaly detection with a few anomalies. In: International Joint Conference on Artificial Intelligence (IJCAI) (2019)

25. Carreira, J., Zisserman, A.: Quo vadis, action recognition? A new model and the kinetics dataset. In: IEEE Conference on Computer Vision and Pattern Recognition (CVPR), pp. 6299–6308 (2017)

26. Hu, J., Shen, L., Sun, G.: Squeeze-and-excitation networks. In: IEEE Conference on Computer Vision and Pattern Recognition (CVPR) (2018)

27. Wang, X., Girshick, R., Gupta, A., He, K.: Non-local neural networks. In: IEEE Conference on Computer Vision and Pattern Recognition (CVPR) (2018)

28. Cao, Y., Xu, J., Lin, S., et al.: GCNet: non-local networks meet squeeze-excitation networks and beyond. In: 2019 IEEE/CVF International Conference on Computer Vision Workshop (ICCVW). IEEE (2020)

29. Hasan, M., Choi, J., Neumann, J., Roy-Chowdhury, A.K., Davis, L.S.: Learning temporal regularity in video sequences. In: IEEE Conference on Computer Vision and Pattern Recognition (CVPR), pp. 733–742 (2016)

30. Wang, J., Cherian, A.: GODS: generalized one-class discriminative subspaces for anomaly detection. In: IEEE International Conference on Computer Vision (CVPR), pp. 8201–8211 (2019)

31. Wan, B., Fang, Y., Xia, X., Mei, J.: Weakly supervised video anomaly detection via center-guided discriminative learning. In: IEEE International Conference on Multimedia and Expo (ICME), pp. 1–6 (2020)

32. Georgescu, M.-I., Barbalau, A., Ionescu, R.T., Khan, F.S., Popescu, M., Shah, M.: Anomaly detection in video via self-supervised and multi-task learning. In: IEEE Conference on Computer Vision and Pattern Recognition (CVPR), pp. 12742–12752 (2021)

33. Wang, Z., Zou, Y., Zhang, Z.: Cluster attention contrast for video anomaly detection. In: ACM International Conference on Multimedia (ACM MM), pp. 2463–2471 (2020)

34. Cai, R., Zhang, H., Liu, W., Gao, S., Hao, Z.: Appearance-motion memory consistency network for video anomaly detection. In: Association for the Advancement of Artificial Intelligence (AAAI), pp. 938–946 (2021)

35. Zaheer, M.Z., Mahmood, A., Astrid, M., Lee, S.-I.: CLAWS: clustering assisted weakly supervised learning with normalcy suppression for anomalous event detection. In: Vedaldi, A., Bischof, H., Brox, T., Frahm, J.-M. (eds.) ECCV 2020. LNCS, vol. 12367, pp. 358–376. Springer, Cham (2020). https://doi.org/10.1007/978-3-030-58542-6_22

36. Tran, D., Bourdev, L., Fergus, R., Torresani, L., Paluri, M.: Learning spatiotemporal features with 3d convolutional networks. In: IEEE international conference on Computer Vision (ICCV), pp. 4489–4497 (2015)

Towards Class Interpretable Vision Transformer with Multi-Class-Tokens

Bowen Dong[1], Pan Zhou[2], Shuicheng Yan[2], and Wangmeng Zuo[1($\boxtimes$)]

[1] Harbin Institute of Technology, Harbin, China
wmzuo@hit.edu.cn
[2] National University of Singapore, Singapore, Singapore

Abstract. For multi-label classification tasks, vision transformers exist two fundamental issues. First, ViT cannot provide a clear per-class saliency region for multi-label classification tasks. This greatly restricts the interpretability of ViT for multi-label classification. Second, when processing images with multiple categories, the single feature vector, i.e., class token, of ViT gathers features of foreground regions from different categories. In this way, the class token indeed interfuses features of multiple objects and could not well distinguish the key feature of multiple objects, thus restricting the network performance. To alleviate these issues, we present a Multi-Class-Tokens-based vision transformer for multi-label image classification. MCT-ViT assigns each class token to a specific category, and generates a corresponding class-level attention map by cross attention module, thus providing a per-class saliency region (distinguishable feature). Since those token patches having high attention scores with a specific class token are the saliency regions corresponding to a certain class, improving the interpretability and also boosting the performance of tasks where detecting and identifying multiple categories are needed. Besides, we use a novel non-parametric scoring method instead of the fully connected classifier in ViT. Specifically, since each class token actually performs binary classification, we can directly compute its ℓ_2 norm to obtain a classification score of the corresponding category for classification. Experimental results on multi-label classification show that our MCT-ViT achieves superior performance over the state-of-the-art on popular benchmark datasets while enjoying per-class interpretability without extra training.

Keywords: Vision transformer · Visual interpretability · Multi-class classification

1 Introduction

Vision transformers (ViTs) [7] have achieved impressive performance in image classification tasks [14,20,21,23,26], attracting growing attention in the computer vision community. Different from previous CNNs which rely on stacking

Supplementary Information The online version contains supplementary material available at https://doi.org/10.1007/978-3-031-18913-5_47.

S. Yu et al. (Eds.): PRCV 2022, LNCS 13536, pp. 609–622, 2022.
https://doi.org/10.1007/978-3-031-18913-5_47

convolution layers to construct long-range interaction of features, ViT uses self-attention layer [22] and can directly achieve the global and long range feature interaction. To further improve the performance and generalization capability of ViTs, previous works exploit strong regularization with data augmentation [20], improve locality [14,26], or introduce multi-scale features with a pyramid network structure [23].

Motivations. Most ViTs utilize a single class token to gather semantic information from the given input images and calculate classification scores. In this way, for single-label classification, the attention map between this class token and all patch tokens can be used to discriminate the foreground and background regions, which help find per-class saliency region. However, for multi-label classification tasks, such an attention map cannot provide a clear per-class saliency region description, since the class token could contain features from multiple objects and the score in the attention map cannot tell which category the specific foreground region belongs to explicitly. Consequently, ViTs does not enjoy the visual interpretability for multi-label classification scenarios, which is particularly important in many tasks, e.g. objection detection and segmentation, and medical pathology detection.

Besides, single class token in ViT is designed for single-label classification task and may not perform well on multi-label classification. This is because for single-label classification, using single class token is capable to distinguish an object from foreground region via attention mechanism or average pooling. This ensures that single class token can gather one certain kind of semantically discriminative information, resulting in relatively clean feature representation of input images and satisfactory classification performance. However, for the images in PASCAL VOC [8], MS-COCO [15] or NUS-WIDE [5] which often contain multiple objects, using a single class token will mix up different semantic information from multiple objects, and leads to more noisy feature representation (information from multiple categories are mixed up). This could lead to performance degeneration in ViTs.

Contributions. To alleviate the above issues, we propose an effective Multi-Class-Tokens based ViT (MCT-ViT) to boost the interpretability and performance of conventional ViTs for multi-label image classification. We replace the single class token used in conventional ViT by multiple learnable class tokens, where each token corresponds to a specific category. Specifically, for the backbone, we directly employ the conventional ViT but replace its single class token with multiple ones. After obtaining the patch tokens and class tokens in the last layer, we design an effective cross attention block which 1) computes the attention between each class token and all the patch tokens in the last layer, and 2) updates each class token via combining all patch tokens in an attention manner. Then to perform multi-label classification, we only need to perform binary classification by using each class token. To this end, here we propose a non-parametric scoring method instead of a fully connected classifier in conventional ViTs. That is, we directly compute ℓ_2 norm of each class token and view it as the final classification score of the corresponding class. As a result, our cross attention block relieve the resultant computation burden in constructing attention between class tokens and all patch tokens from $O((N + K)^2C)$ to $O(NKC)$, where N, K, C means number of patch tokens, number of classes and feature dimension, respectively. Besides the efficiency, another advantage of MCT-ViT is that for a specific class token, its corresponding attention map with all the patch tokens explicitly demonstrates the localization information of this category. So our method can endow ViTs with heatmap based per-class visual interpretability without extra training or propagation steps.

Extensive experimental results show that on multiple label classification tasks, our MCT-ViT achieves much better performance over state-of-the-arts on widely adopted benchmark datasets; on single label classification tasks, our MCT-ViT achieves slightly better or comparable performance. In summary, our contributions can be summarized as follows:

1) We propose a multi-class-tokens based ViT (MCT-ViT), which uses a set of learnable per-class tokens and a cross attention block for multi-label classification. Given a class, MCT-ViT can provide its corresponding saliency region by computing the attention score of the corresponding class token and the patch tokens, greatly improving the interpretability in conventional ViTs.
2) We propose a non-parametric scoring method for multi-label classification in MCT-ViT. For each class token, we compute its ℓ_2 norm to measure the probability whether current image belongs to the corresponding class or not. In this way, compared with ViTs, we do not extra parameters since multiple class tokens in MCT-ViT has the same parameter in fully-connected classifier in ViTs.
3) Experimental results show MCT-ViT performs favorably against state-of-the-arts for multi-label classification.

2 Related Work

2.1 Vision Transformer

Vision Transformer (ViT). Inspired by [22], Dosovitskiy et al. [7] proposed ViT to construct long-range interaction explicitly on images. In ViT, the backbone is constructed by stacking multiple multi-head self attention layers and feed forward network layers. The vanilla ViT suffers from low performance without large-scale pretraining and lack of locality modeling. Touvron et al. [20] proposed a specially designed combination of regularization hyper-parameters and data augmentation to make data-efficient training of ViT possible. To further improve the recognition ability of transformers, overlapped patch embedding [25], locality Attention or MLP [14,16], pyramid architecture [16,23] and deeper backbones [21] are introduced to enhance the vision transformers.

Meanwhile, in ViT, a single class token [20] or the global average pooling feature [16] is used as the global representation of an image for final image classification in the last fully connected layer. However, this global representation is not sufficient to represent an image with multiple objects from different categories. In this work, we propose to utilize multiple class tokens to handle different

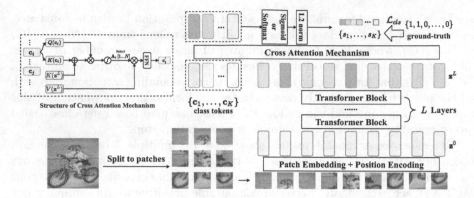

Fig. 1. Illustration of our proposed *multi-class-tokens based ViT* (MCT-ViT) as well as the structure of cross attention mechanism. First we follow conventional ViT to construct patch embedding $\mathbf{z}^0$ and extract feature $\mathbf{z}^L$ with L stacked transformer blocks. Then, we introduce K learnable class tokens to calculate the attention between each $\mathbf{c}_i$ and all patch tokens $\mathbf{z}^L$ and update each $\mathbf{c}_i$ using $\mathbf{z}^L$. Finally, we introduce ℓ_2 normalization of each updated class token as the non-parametric scoring function to generate the final score of each category.

semantic features by a divide-and-conquer strategy. By assigning a class token to each class, the proposed multi-class-tokens scheme is able to provide better per-class visual interpretability for ViTs and also better performance for multi-label classification tasks.

2.2   Heatmap-Based Visual Interpretability

Heatmap-based visual interpretability is to generate per-class heatmap that indicates local relevance of each class with given input image. Recent studies attempt to utilize heatmaps generated from gradient or other attributes to provide better visual interpretability of their models. Research on visual interpretability of CNNs can generally be divided into three groups. The first group is based on saliency, *e.g.*, Class Activation Map [27]. These works introduce some specially designed layers such as global average pooling with a fully connected layer to generate a class-specific saliency heatmap for each class in the image. The second group achieves better visual interpretability via exploiting gradient [18]. For example, GradCAM [18] uses the gradient of a specific category on the classifier, and backpropagates the gradient to the rectified convolutional feature maps of interest, and then generates a coarse heatmap for this category. Thirdly, there are also some propagation based works that calculate the relevance between two neighboring layers progressively to generate heatmaps. For example, LRP [1,9,11,13] calculates the relevance between any two closing layers from predicted classes to input images by utilizing the deep taylor decomposition principle.

Heatmap based visual interpretability of ViTs has also been studied. Zhang *et al.* [26] proposed a gradient-based class-aware tree-traversal method, aiming

Table 1. GFLOPS comparison between self attention and cross attention in multi-class-tokens. Note that we set class number $K = 1000$, token number $N = 196$ and feature dimension $C = 384$.

Methods	Self attention	Cross attention
GFLOPS	1.65	**0.23**

to find the most valuable traversal from leaf patch to root patch by selecting the one with the biggest contribution to the classification score progressively. Chefer *et al.* [2] proposed a relevance propagation based method, which assigns local relevance based on the deep taylor decomposition principle and then propogates corresponding relevance scores through pretrained transformer layers. In this work, we try to improve visual interpretability of ViTs based on saliency. The proposed multi-class-tokens scheme can provide ViTs with per-class visual interpretability without extra training or extra propogation steps.

3 Proposed Method

3.1 Overview of Proposed Approach

A basic hypothesis of feature representation learning is that a well-trained ViT backbone can extract features for each patch token with corresponding semantic information, and patch tokens belonging to the same object tend to be similar. Therefore given a query vector for each category, we can calculate the similarity between this vector and each patch token via the attention mechanism, and then gather all patch tokens with similarity into a single token by weighted sum. This divide-and-conquer strategy can mitigate the confusing effect due to direct sum of tokens with different semantic information while keeping a simple but effective structure. Based on this hypothesis, we present a multi-class-tokens module and plug it onto the ViT backbone.

The core component in our model, i.e., the multi-class-tokens based cross attention, is shown in Fig. 1. Such an attention can be plugged into most of ViTs, and the derived ViT variants are call *multi-class-tokens based ViT* (MCT-ViT) in this work. In the following, we focus on introducing multi-class-tokens based attention. Given an input image $\mathbf{I}$, we first follow the conventional ViT [7,20] to convert the image into patch embeddings $\mathbf{z}^0 = \mathbf{x}$ without the traditional class token $\mathbf{c}$. Note that positional encoding is also added in patch embeddings. Then, such $\mathbf{z}^0$ is fed into L stacked transformer blocks like [7,20] to calculate the updated patch tokens $\mathbf{z}^L$, and these transformer blocks can be viewed as the backbone network of the transformer. Next, we utilize the cross attention mechanism to compute the similarity between K different class tokens C and patch tokens $\mathbf{z}^L$ separately and update each class token $\mathbf{c}_i$ using weighted sum of $\mathbf{z}^L$. We will provide details of our proposed modules in the following paragraphs, respectively.

3.2   Multi-Class-Tokens and Cross Attention

Instead of using only one class token $\mathbf{c}$ to gather overall semantic information from images, we introduce a set of class tokens $C = \{\mathbf{c}_1, \mathbf{c}_2, ..., \mathbf{c}_K\}$, where K is the class number in the dataset. To avoid the large computation cost from cross attention between C and $\mathbf{z}$, meanwhile gathering high-level semantic features explicitly, we only plug multi-class-tokens C as well as cross attention mechanism after the last transformer block. Then the initial patch embedding $\mathbf{z}^0$ is expressed as $\mathbf{z}^0 = [\mathbf{x}]$ and we build cross attention between C and $\mathbf{z}^L$.

To construct the attention between each $\mathbf{c}_i$ and all updated patch tokens $\mathbf{z}^L$, a simple solution is to first concatenate C and $\mathbf{z}^L$, and then update class tokens using a basic transformer block. However, the computation cost of basic MHSA is too large when $K > N$. In addition, the feature interaction among different class tokens can not lead to better performance [20]. To tackle this issue, we introduce a simple cross attention mechanism. Following [22], we also utilize a multi-head strategy in cross attention to capture semantic information from different views. Here we define the number of heads as H. Consider three projection functions of the h-th head Q_h, K_h, V_h where $h \in \{1, ..., H\}$. For each i-th class token $\mathbf{c}_i$ and all patch tokens $\mathbf{z}^L$, we calculate the scaled inner product between $Q_h(\mathbf{c}_i)$ and $K_h([\mathbf{c}_i, \mathbf{z}^L])$ and then generate the corresponding attention map $\mathbf{A}_{i,h}$, which is shown as Eq. (1).

$$\mathbf{A}_{i,h} = \text{Softmax}\left(\frac{Q_h(\mathbf{c}_i)K_h([\mathbf{c}_i, \mathbf{z}^L]^T)}{\sqrt{D}}\right) \tag{1}$$

Since only $\mathbf{z}^L$ contains the semantic information of images, we obtain the updated class token $\mathbf{u}_{i,h}^c$ by Eq. (2).

$$\mathbf{u}_{i,h}^c = \mathbf{A}_{i,h}[1, ..., N]V_h(\mathbf{z}^L) \tag{2}$$

Finally, we concatenate all $\mathbf{u}_{i,h}^c$ into a single vector and use a linear projection function $O(\mathbf{W}_o, \mathbf{b}_o)$ to fuse semantic information in different channels and obtain another token $\mathbf{u}_i^c$.

$$\mathbf{u}_i^c = \mathbf{W}_o \text{concat}(\{\mathbf{u}_{i,1}^c, ..., \mathbf{u}_{i,H}^c\}) + \mathbf{b}_o \tag{3}$$

Compared to vanilla self-attention, using cross attention can significantly reduce the overall computation cost, especially when the number of categories is extremely large (e.g., 1000), our cross attention is $8\times$ faster than conventional self-attention, which is shown in Table 1.

Following transformer block [22], we also add a two-layer FFN after the cross attention mechanism to further extract the feature for each class token and obtain the final updated class token $\mathbf{c}_i'$, which is shown as Eq. (4).

$$\mathbf{c}_i' = \mathbf{W}_2\sigma(\mathbf{W}_1\mathbf{u}_i^c + \mathbf{b}_1) + \mathbf{b}_2 \tag{4}$$

We execute this procedure for each $\mathbf{c}_i$ and do not introduce any constraint among class tokens. Therefore, compared to applying conventional MHSA into our framework, the computation complexity is reduced from $O((K + N)^2 C)$ to $O(KNC)$ (the number of heads H is omitted for simplicity), where N, K, C means number of patch tokens, number of classes and feature dimension, respectively.

Moreover, compared to using only one class token to capture features of multiple objects from different categories, in multi-class-tokens, each class token only focuses on gathering features of a certain category. This design makes sure that the representation in each class token is more clear than before, which improves the performance as demonstrated by the experimental results in Sect. 4.

3.3 Non-parametric Scoring Function

Based on the hypothesis about feature representation in ViT, in case of multiple categories in the images, the length of corresponding updated class tokens $\mathbf{c}_i'$ would be very large. This indicates that the signals from existing categories are stronger than non-existing categories, which can be an explicit measurement for image classification. Therefore, instead of using weight and bias of the fully connected layer to calculate the classification score for each category, we simply calculate the ℓ_2 normalization of each updated class token $\mathbf{c}_i'$ as Eq. (5).

$$s_i = \sqrt{\sum\nolimits_{j=1}^{D} (\mathbf{c}_{i,j}')^2} \tag{5}$$

A larger ℓ_2 normalization that the class token obtains would indicate the higher signal of the corresponding category. Therefore we can use overall classification scores $\mathbf{s} = s_1, ..., s_K$ to recognize each category in images.

The above ℓ_2 normalization approach has two merits. First, ℓ_2 normalization is a non-parametric scoring approach, which indicates this module does not necessarily introduce extra parameters. Actually, the parameter number of $\{c'\}$ equals to the parameters of the classifier for conventional ViT, which means our MC-ViT does not increase additional parameters compared to conventional ViT. Second, using ℓ_2 normalization encourages each $\mathbf{c}_i$ to learn corresponding prior of each category i directly, thus $\mathbf{c}_i$ can generate reasonable attention with $\mathbf{z}^L$ on corresponding foreground regions.

Loss Function $\mathcal{L}_{cls}$. During training on single-label classification tasks (*e.g.*, ImageNet [6]), we simply apply cross-entropy loss between the probability of classification $\mathbf{p} = \text{Softmax}(\mathbf{s})$ and the label y to optimize overall framework. For multi-label classification tasks (*e.g.*, MS-COCO [15]), we calculate the per-class classification score $\mathbf{s}$ by Sigmoid function and scale the scores by $2\mathbf{s} - 1$ to $(0, 1)$. Then we use binary cross-entropy loss to measure $\mathcal{L}_{cls}$ of the multi-class-tokens mechanism.

3.4 Heatmap Based Per-class Interpretability

With our multi-class-tokens mechanism, each class token $\mathbf{c}_i$ generates an attention map $\mathbf{A}_i$, which can be used to build the heatmap based visual interpretability map $\mathbf{V}_i$. When the number of heads $H = 1$ in the cross-attention mechanism,

Table 2. Comparison of our method (where AGHF means ADD-GCN head fusion) and other state-of-the-art methods on Pascal VOC 2007 dataset. The best results are marked in bold. Our method achieves the best mAP among all methods.

Method	mAP
ResNet-101 [10]	90.8
ML-GCN [4]	94.0
SSGRL [3]	95.0
ADD-GCN [24]	96.0
T-ResNet [19]	95.8
Ours (DeiT-S)	95.8
Ours w/AGHF (DeiT-S)	96.3
Ours w/AGHF (CaiT-S-24)	**96.6**

for each updated class token c_i', we simply compute the corresponding attention map $\mathbf{A}_i$ as the visual interpretability map $\mathbf{E}_i$. Moreover, when multi-head attention mechanism is applied, for each category i, we select the attention map $\mathbf{A}_{i,h}$ with the highest ℓ_2 normalization score $s_{i,h} = \ell_2\mathrm{norm}(c_{i,h}')$ from the h-th head, where h means the index of the head and $h \in \{1, ..., H\}$. Compared to previous methods, our method does not introduce extra training or propagation steps, which is time-efficient and convenient. We will demonstrate corresponding visualization results of different categories in one specific image to show visual interpretability of our method.

4   Experiments

4.1   Datasets

PASCAL VOC [8]. This dataset contains 9,963 images collected from 20 object classes, with 5,011 and 4,952 images for *trainval* set and *test* set respectively. Here we use image-level labels as supervision for multi-label classification tasks. For fairness, we use *trainval* set to train and report evaluation results on *test* set.

MS-COCO [15]. It is a large-scale object detection dataset with 80 different categories, containing 83K images and 41K images in *train* set and *val* set, respectively. Here we use image-level labels as supervision for multi-label classification tasks. For fair comparison, we use *train* set for training networks and report evaluation results on *val* set.

Besides, we evaluate our method on other datasets (*e.g.*, NUS-WIDE [5]), which is introduced in the supplementary material.

4.2   Implementation Details

When constructing our multi-class-tokens and cross attention mechanism, we follow the transformer block [22] to initialize all projection functions and FFN, and set the class tokens number K as the number of categories in the dataset. We initialize all class tokens before pretraining and finetuning. For the channel dimension D and the head number H, we simply keep them the same as the backbone network, *e.g.*, we set $H = 6$ and $D = 384$ when we use DeiT-S as our backbone network. To constrain the overall computation cost we set the number of cross attention blocks as 1. For comparison with DeiT baseline [20], we use DeiT-S with patch size of $P = 16$ as our backbone. And for comparison with previous state-of-the-art multi-label classification methods, we use DeiT-S and CaiT-S-24 [21] with patch size of $P = 16$ as our backbone, and we additionally introduce head of [24] to compute a fusion score with our multi-class-tokens mechanism to evaluate the compatibility of MCT-ViT with previous methods.

During multi-label classification experiments, we use AdamW [17] with the learning rate of 1e−4. For PASCAL VOC we use batch size of 16 and for MS-COCO we use batch size of 64. The overall training framework contains 80 epochs and warmup strategy is applied during the first 20 epochs. Input images are scaled to 448×448 during VOC and COCO training and evaluation for fair comparison with previous methods. We follow the same data augmentation methods during all training procedures. All programs are implemented by PyTorch toolkit, and all experiments are conducted on NVIDIA A100 GPUs.

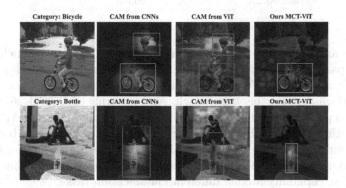

Fig. 2. Visualization of CAMs from ResNet-101 and ViT as well as the attention of our methods. The green boxes mean correct localization while the red boxes mean wrong or coarse localization. The localization ability of our method is better. (Color figure online)

4.3 Comparison Results

Furthermore, we combine our multi-class-tokens method with ADD-GCN [24] to construct a fusion score model and make comparison with previous state-of-the-art methods. During training, all parameters in our networks are finetuned. Evaluation results of our method are shown in Table 2 and Table 3. It can be seen that our proposed method with DeiT-S backbone [20] achieves 96.3% mAP on PASCAL VOC 2007 dataset and 85.4% mAP on COCO 2014 dataset, which is competitive with performance of ADD-GCN but our method only uses half parameters compared to ADD-GCN with ResNet-101. When replacing DeiT-S

Table 3. Comparison of our method (where AGHF means ADD-GCN head fusion) and other state-of-the-art methods on MS-COCO 2014 dataset. The best results are marked in bold. Our method achieves competitive results.

Methods	mAP	OF1	CF1
ResNet-101 [10]	79.7	78.4	74.3
ML-GCN [4]	83.0	80.3	78.0
SSGRL [3]	83.8	79.7	76.8
ADD-GCN [24]	85.2	82.0	80.1
C-Tran [12]	85.1	81.7	79.9
T-ResNet [19]	86.6	81.8	**81.4**
Ours w/AGHF (DeiT-S)	85.4	81.4	78.1
Ours w/AGHF (CaiT-S-24)	**87.2**	**83.6**	80.3

Table 4. Multi-label classification performance (mAP) on VOC 2007 dataset of our method, where MCT means multi-class-tokens, and AGHF means ADD-GCN head fusion.

ViT	ADD-GCN	MCT-ViT	MCT-ViT w/AGHF
93.0%	93.2%	95.8%	96.3%

by a larger and deeper backbone network (*e.g.*, CaiT-S-24 [21]) such that the number of parameters is the same with previous methods, our method achieves 96.6% mAP on PASCAL VOC 2007 dataset, which is the state-of-the-art classification performance on this benchmark. And in terms of COCO 2014 dataset, compared to previous methods, our method achieves the highest mAP and OF1 scores and the second highest CF1 score, as shown in Table 3. Above results show that our method has great potential to achieve favorable multi-label classification performance on different datasets. This proves our method has sufficient generalization capability among different classification tasks.

4.4   Ablation Study

Effect of Multi-Class-Tokens. To demonstrate the effect of our multi-class-tokens in multi-label classification tasks, we compare the performance among the standard ViT, MCT-ViT and MCT-ViT with ADD-GCN fusion, note that all methods conduct end-to-end finetune with the same DeiT-S backbone as well as the same pretrained parameters. Table 4 demonstrates the performance of each method on VOC 2007 dataset, MCT-ViT outperforms the standard ViT by 2.8% in terms of mAP. This result indicates that our multi-class-tokens can improve the overall multi-label performance of vision transformer. Note that introducing ADD-GCN fusion module can further improve the classification by 0.5% mAP, while pure ADD-GCN only reaches 93.2% mAP.

To further evaluate the ability of visual interpretability, We also visualize the per-class saliency map of CAM (ResNet-101), CAM (ViT) and our MCT-ViT.

Table 5. We introduce multi-class-tokens based attention into various transformers to verify its compatibility on ImageNet. Compared to baselines, backbones with our method achieve the same or better performance on single-label classification benchmarks. Evaluation results demonstrate the compatibility of our method with different backbones.

Methods	Top-1 Acc
DeiT-Ti [20]	72.2
DeiT-S [21]	80.8
PVT-T [23]	75.1
CaiT-XXS-36 [21]	79.1
Ours (DeiT-Ti)	75.5 (+3.2%)
Ours (DeiT-S)	81.0 (+0.2%)
Ours (PVT-T)	76.9 (+1.8%)
Ours (CaiT-XXS-36)	79.4 (+0.3%)

Table 6. Multi-label classification performance of our method with different backbones, our MCT-ViT and MCT-Swin-T perform better.

Backbone	mAP (ViT)	mAP (MCT-ViT)
DeiT-S	93.0%	95.8%
Swin-T	92.9%	94.5%

As illustrated in Fig. 2, CAM (ResNet-101) faces wrong localization issue (*e.g.*, the red box in row 1 column 2) and coarse localization issue (*e.g.*, the red box in row 2 column 2). And similarly, CAM (ViT) performs bad due to training with additional single class token. On the contrary, MCT-ViT can generate more precise per-class interpretability.

Backbone Compatibility. Recently, some modern vision transformers (e.g., Swin Transformer) have replaced single class token by global average pooling like previous CNN [10]. To evaluate the compatibility of our multi-class-tokens, we also conduct the comparison between Swin-Tiny and MCT-Swin-Tiny. As illustrated in Table 6, both MCT-ViT and MCT-Swin-Tiny outperform the corresponding baseline methods by 2.6% and 1.6%, respectively. This result demonstrates the compatibility of multi-class-tokens.

Generalization to Single-Label Pretraining. Furthermore, we also analyze our MCT-ViT in single-label pretraining on ImageNet [6] dataset. In this setting, our multi-class-tokens method should achieve at least the same evaluation performance with corresponding baseline networks since only one class token can gather semantic information from object regions, such that it is equal to the conventional class token in the transformer. During experiments, we select DeiT-Ti/S (standard ViT), PVT-T (multi-scale and locality ViT) and CaiT-XXS-36 (deeper ViT) for comparison. Experimental results are shown in Table 5. It is clear that our methods with DeiT-S and CaiT-XXS-36 achieve the same performance with corresponding baselines. And our method with DeiT-Ti and PVT-T outperforms their baselines by 3.3% and 1.8% in terms of Top-1 accuracy. These results support that our multi-class-tokens method has sufficient compatibility for different backbone in single-label classification tasks.

Visual Interpretability Analysis. Here we analyse the visual interpretability maps $\mathbf{E}$ generated by our method on VOC 2007 dataset. The input images and corresponding visual interpretability maps are shown as Fig. 3. We can easily find that, for each existing category i, the highest attention signal of $\mathbf{E}_i$ falls into the region of the corresponding category i. For non-existing categories, these visual interpretability maps tend to converge to the same small regions, which always belong to the background of images. Furthermore, we also visualize the ℓ_2 normalization values of each token in $\mathbf{z}^L$ for this image, and it can be seen that these background regions own the smallest ℓ_2 normalization values on $\mathbf{z}^L$, which means the classification scores of non-existing categories tend to be small. Besides, as shown in Fig. 4, when the multi-head strategy is applied, different categories tend to activate different heads. And for an existing category i, if the head h is activated for this category, all the other heads tend to leave attention to background regions like the case in non-existing categories. Above observations well prove that our method can generate effective visual interpretability maps.

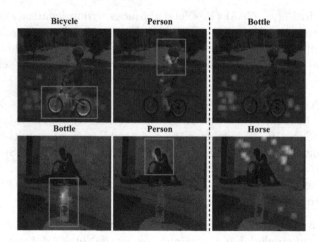

Fig. 3. Visualization of interpretability of existing categories (shown in red) and non-existing categories (shown in green). Discriminative parts of existing categories are emphasized by red boxes. (Color figure online)

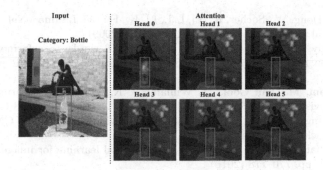

Fig. 4. Visual interpretability maps of existing categories on different heads. Heads with correct activation are shown as red and others are shown as green. We also emphasize the discriminative part by red boxes. This visualization shows that only one head can generate correct attention for each category, which proves effectiveness and rationality of our visual interpretability design. (Color figure online)

5 Conclusion

In this paper, we present a simple and effective multi-class-tokens mechanism to improve the multi-label classification performance and per-class visual interpretability of ViTs. We replace the conventional single class token by a set of class tokens with each extracting features of a corresponding category from patch tokens via a cross attention module. We also introduce a non-parametric scoring method that calculates ℓ_2 normalization of each updated class token as the classification score for each category instead of using the conventional linear classifier. Meanwhile the per-class visual interpretability map can be extracted from attention maps in our cross attention mechanism explicitly. Experimental results show that ViTs with our proposed method perform favorably against state-of-the-art multi-label classification methods. Our method can also provide reasonable visual interpretability results without extra computation.

References

1. Binder, A., Montavon, G., Lapuschkin, S., Müller, K.R., Samek, W.: Layer-wise relevance propagation for neural networks with local renormalization layers. In: ICANN (2016)
2. Chefer, H., Gur, S., Wolf, L.: Transformer interpretability beyond attention visualization. In: CVPR (2021)
3. Chen, T., Xu, M., Hui, X., Wu, H., Lin, L.: Learning semantic-specific graph representation for multi-label image recognition. arXiv preprint arXiv:1908.07325 (2019)
4. Chen, Z.M., Wei, X.S., Wang, P., Guo, Y.: Multi-label image recognition with graph convolutional networks. In: CVPR (2019)
5. Chua, T.S., Tang, J., Hong, R., Li, H., Luo, Z., Zheng, Y.T.: NUS-WIDE: a real-world web image database from National University of Singapore. In: Proceedings of the ACM Conference on Image and Video Retrieval (CIVR 2009) (2009)

6. Deng, J., Dong, W., Socher, R., Li, L.J., Li, K., Fei-Fei, L.: ImageNet: a large-scale hierarchical image database. In: CVPR. IEEE (2009)

7. Dosovitskiy, A., et al.: An image is worth 16x16 words: transformers for image recognition at scale. In: International Conference on Learning Representations (2021)

8. Everingham, M., Van Gool, L., Williams, C.K., Winn, J., Zisserman, A.: The PASCAL visual object classes (VOC) challenge. IJCV **88**, 303–338 (2010)

9. Gu, J., Yang, Y., Tresp, V.: Understanding individual decisions of CNNs via contrastive backpropagation. In: ACCV (2018)

10. He, K., Zhang, X., Ren, S., Sun, J.: Deep residual learning for image recognition. In: CVPR, pp. 770–778 (2016)

11. Iwana, B., Kuroki, R., Uchida, S.: Explaining convolutional neural networks using softmax gradient layer-wise relevance propagation. In: ICCVW (2019)

12. Jack, L., Tianlu, W., Vicente, O., Yanjun, Q.: General multi-label image classification with transformers. In: CVPR (2021)

13. Lapuschkin, S., Binder, A., Montavon, G., Klauschen, F., Müller, K.R., Samek, W.: On pixel-wise explanations for non-linear classifier decisions by layer-wise relevance propagation. PLoS ONE **10**, e0130140 (2015)

14. Li, Y., Zhang, K., Cao, J., Timofte, R., Gool, L.V.: LocalViT: bringing locality to vision transformers (2021)

15. Lin, T.-Y., et al.: Microsoft COCO: common objects in context. In: Fleet, D., Pajdla, T., Schiele, B., Tuytelaars, T. (eds.) ECCV 2014. LNCS, vol. 8693, pp. 740–755. Springer, Cham (2014). https://doi.org/10.1007/978-3-319-10602-1_48

16. Liu, Z., et al.: Swin transformer: hierarchical vision transformer using shifted windows. In: ICCV (2021)

17. Loshchilov, I., Hutter, F.: Decoupled weight decay regularization. In: International Conference on Learning Representations (2019)

18. Selvaraju, R.R., Cogswell, M., Das, A., Vedantam, R., Parikh, D., Batra, D.: Grad-CAM: visual explanations from deep networks via gradient-based localization. Int. J. Comput. Vis. **11**, 1213 (2019)

19. Tal, R., Hussam, L., Asaf, N., Emanuel, B.B., Gilad, S., Itamar, F.: TResNet: high performance GPU-dedicated architecture. In: WACV (2021)

20. Touvron, H., Cord, M., Douze, M., Massa, F., Sablayrolles, A., Jégou, H.: Training data-efficient image transformers and distillation through attention. In: ICML (2021)

21. Touvron, H., Cord, M., Sablayrolles, A., Synnaeve, G., Jégou, H.: Going deeper with image transformers (2021)

22. Vaswani, A., et al.: Attention is all you need. In: NeurIPS, pp. 5998–6008 (2017)

23. Wang, W., et al.: Pyramid vision transformer: a versatile backbone for dense prediction without convolutions (2021)

24. Ye, J., He, J., Peng, X., Wu, W., Qiao, Yu.: Attention-driven dynamic graph convolutional network for multi-label image recognition. In: Vedaldi, A., Bischof, H., Brox, T., Frahm, J.-M. (eds.) ECCV 2020. LNCS, vol. 12366, pp. 649–665. Springer, Cham (2020). https://doi.org/10.1007/978-3-030-58589-1_39

25. Yuan, L., et al.: Tokens-to-Token ViT: training vision transformers from scratch on imagenet. arXiv preprint arXiv:2101.11986 (2021)

26. Zhang, Z., Zhang, H., Zhao, L., Chen, T., Pfister, T.: Aggregating nested transformers (2022)

27. Zhou, B., Khosla, A., Lapedriza, A., Oliva, A., Torralba, A.: Learning deep features for discriminative localization. In: CVPR (2016)

Multimodal Violent Video Recognition Based on Mutual Distillation

Yimeng Shang$^{(\boxtimes)}$, Xiaoyu Wu, and Rui Liu

Communication University of China, 1 Dingfuzhuang East Street, Chaoyang District,
Beijing, China
ym_s@cuc.edu.cn

Abstract. Violent video recognition is a challenging task in the field of computer
vision and multimodal methods have always been an important part of it. Due to
containing sensitive content, it is not easy to collect violent videos and resulting in
a lack of big public datasets. Existing methods of learning violent video representations are limited by small datasets and lack efficient multimodal fusion models.
According to the situation, firstly, we propose to effectively transfer information
from large datasets to small violent datasets based on mutual distillation with the
self-supervised pretrained model for the vital RGB feature. Secondly, the multi-
modal attention fusion network (MAF-Net) is proposed to fuse the obtained RGB
feature with flow and audio feature to recognize violent videos with multi-modal
information. Thirdly, we build a new violent dataset, named Violent Clip Dataset
(VCD), which is on a large scale and contains complete audio information. We
performed experiments on the public VSD dataset and the self-built VCD dataset.
Experimental results demonstrate that the proposed method outperforms existing
state-of-the-art methods on both datasets.

Keywords: Violence recognition · Mutual distillation · Multimodal information
fusion

1 Introduction

In recent years, with the development of communication, there is a greatly increasing
number of videos spreading faster and more widely. Extremely exciting and bloody
images in violent videos will cause psychological trauma to viewers and the negative
effect is more difficult to underestimate.

Automatic recognition of violent videos has become a very important branch of
computer vision, and many scholars have carried out relevant research on this issue.
There are two main ways of violent video recognition: Hand-crafted features are used
to detect violent behaviors in the early stage. With the development of deep learning
algorithms, they have become the mainstream approach for violence recognition [1–5].
Models trained from large-scale datasets usually have strong generalization and good
effect. Violent events include various scenes and types. Violent datasets also play a
crucial role in deep learning methods of violence recognition, as its distribution, size,

© The Author(s), under exclusive license to Springer Nature Switzerland AG 2022
S. Yu et al. (Eds.): PRCV 2022, LNCS 13536, pp. 623–637, 2022.
https://doi.org/10.1007/978-3-031-18913-5_48

modalities and other conditions all affect the overall learning process. Commonly used violent datasets, such as Hockey [6], Movies Fight [6], RLVS [7], RWF2000 [8], are not large enough to cover the full sample space. To the best of our knowledge, the existing methods are trained on small violent video datasets for the recognizing task. For deep neural networks driven by big data, public violent datasets are not large enough to learn good representation and are not conducive to the development of violence recognizing task.

We propose two solutions to this problem: First, we construct a Violent Clip Dataset (VCD), larger than existing violent video datasets. Secondly, considering that it is difficult to collect violent data due to its particularity and sensitivity, how can we combine violent video recognition task with big-dataset information? Knowledge distillation is an effective way of transferring knowledge. And mutual distillation [9] does not depend on a strong teacher network. We consider migrating information from a large dataset to a small violent dataset by the mutual distillation task for the apparent feature. Compared with traditional supervised learning, self-supervised learning obtains more general features from large-scale data itself without any human-annotated labels. Therefore, we consider the pretrained model obtained from self-supervised learning as a network in mutual distillation.

In addition, violent elements like guns, fighting and explosions are reflected in appearance, motion and audio information in violent scenes. Multimodal methods have always been an important part in the field of violent video recognition. [10, 11] combine RGB and optical flow with a two-stream structure. [12–14] adopt audio information as auxiliary information. However, many datasets, such as CCTV-Fights [6], Hockey [18], RWF2000 [22], do not provide audio data. Meanwhile, existing fusing methods of violent feature are too simple to consider the association between different modalities. In this paper, we introduce the attention interaction module to strengthen the association between different modalities and add a channel attention module to enhance the single-modal features. Multiple attention modules are combined to form Multimodal Attention Fusion Network (MAF-Net).

To sum up, our work mainly includes the following three aspects:

- We combine the classification task with mutual distillation task for RGB, so that the general apparent information learned on big datasets are effectively in combination with violent data and the big-dataset information is effectively transferred to the violent video recognition task.
- We propose the MAF-Net to fuse the obtained RGB feature with optical flow and audio feature, integrating multimodal information for violent video recognition with considering cross-modal association.
- We perform experiments on VSD2015 and on our self-built VCD dataset. Both datasets contain audio information.

The structure of this paper is as follows: The second section introduces related work, including violent video recognition, self-supervised learning, knowledge distillation. The third part introduces our overall model including mutual distillation process and MAF-Net. The fourth section presents the experimental results. The fifth section is the summary.

2 Related Work

2.1 Violent Video Recognition

Violent videos are mainly collected from three categories: films(with audio), daily videos(with part of audio) and surveillance videos(without audio). Datasets commonly used for violent video recognition are described on Table 1.

Table 1. Commonly-used public violent video datasets

Name	Year	Size	Audio(Y/N)
Hockey[6]	2011	1000 clips	No
Movies Fight[6]	2011	200 clips	Yes
Violent-Flows[16]	2012	246 clips	No
VSD[17]	2015	1317 videos	Yes
UCF-Crime[18]	2018	1900 videos	No
CCTV-Fights[15]	2019	1000 videos	No
RLVS[7]	2019	1000 videos	Part
RWF2000[8]	2019	2000 videos	No
XD-Violence[19]	2020	4754 videos	Yes

As shown in Table 1, most existing violent datasets are small and only Movies Fight, VSD, XD-Violence contain complete audio information. XD-Violence is the only existing large-scale dataset containing visual and audio information. But XD-Violence is mainly for violence detecting task and samples in its testing set are tagged with frame-level labels, while we need video-level labels for the violence recognizing task.

Current violence-recognizing methods are trained on small datasets. [10, 20] proposed intelligent models based on different CNN (MobileNet et al.) and LSTM on RLVS, RWF-2000, VSD, Hockey or Movies Fight dataset. [12] proposed a violent scene detecting method and it concatenated two-streams ConvNet to long short-term memory (LSTM) on VSD. [21] proposed the idea of simultaneously merging two networks on Hockey and Movies Fight. Perez et al. [15] presented a novel concept by proposing a pipeline relied on the two-stream architectures, 3D CNN architectures and local interest points, on the CCTV-Fights dataset. A unique approach for violence detection using modified 3D Convolutional Neural Network was proposed in [22], which used Hockey and Movies Fight. Xu et al. [23] presented a novel strategy of P3D-LSTM for deep learning-based violent video classification assisted by spatial-temporal cues, on Hockey Fight, Violent-Flows and a self-built dataset. [5] proposed a data-efficient video transformer on RLVS. As above mentioned, most of the existing methods conduct end-to-end training networks with labels on small datasets. Compared to the complexity of violent action and scenes, public violent video datasets cover limited sample space and are not big enough to learn good and generalized representation for deep neural networks.

2.2 Self-supervised Learning

Self-supervised Learning is a subset of unsupervised learning that does not require labels. Its general pipeline contains pretrain (pretext task) and finetune(downstream task): pretext tasks are used to mine data own supervised information from large-scale unlabeled datasets; then transfer the learned parameters to downstream tasks by fine-tuning [24]. Pretext tasks are pre-designed according to the characteristics of downstream tasks. Contrastive learning is a common method of pretext tasks for self-supervised learning, which aims at both image and video tasks. Videos contain more information than image, such as temporal information, optical flow information and audio information, as free supervisory signals. Multimodal contrastive learning is the most common video self-supervised method. AVTS [25], AVID [26], and CrissCross [27] define positive and negative sample pairs according to audio and visual correlation. MMV [28] maps motion, apparent, and audio features into the same space for comparison using temporal co-occurrence. Compared with supervised learning, multimodal contrastive learning makes full use of videos themselves to mine internal high-level semantic information without labels, and achieves good results in downstream tasks such as action recognition and video retrieval. Currently there are no specific pretext tasks for violent video recognition.

2.3 Knowledge Distillation

Knowledge distillation is a teacher-student training structure [29], which transfers the knowledge of the teacher model to the student model through distillation training, containing model compression and model enhancement. For model compression, big teacher network guide small student network on the same labeled dataset to obtain a simple and efficient network model. Model enhancement emphasizes taking advantage of other resources (such as unlabeled or cross-modal data) or optimization strategies of knowledge distillation (such as mutual distillation) to improve the performance of a complex student model. Mutual learning [9] is an online distillation of knowledge, in which the teacher and student models are trained and updated simultaneously. Experiments show that in this peer-teaching-based training, each student performs better than training alone.

3   Methods

For the input video, we propose to train a network in the mutual distillation method with the self-supervised pretrained model to extract better RGB feature. And we propose the MAF-Net to fuse it with the other modalities to get the final predicted violent score. An overview of our framework is present in Fig. 1. It includes two main parts: mutual distillation(MD) for violent RGB feature and the MAF-Net. And we will introduce MD and the MAF-Net in details in 3.1 and 3.2.

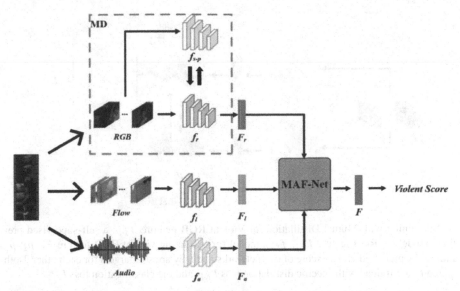

Fig. 1. Our Framework. $f_{s\text{-}p}$: a self-supervised pretrained network. f_r, f_l, f_a: networks to extract RGB, flow and audio feature. F_r, F_l, F_a: RGB, flow and audio feature. F: the final fused future. $f_{s\text{-}p}$ and f_r are both trained with a method of mutual distillation(MD) to get better RGB feature. Then we propose the MAF-Net to fuse the obtained RGB feature, flow feature and audio feature and get the final feature F. We calculate predicted violent score based on F.

3.1 Mutual Distillation for Violent RGB Feature

For traditional knowledge distillation methods [29], the large teacher network remains fixed during the learning process and only transfers unidirectional knowledge to the small student network. It is difficult to obtain feedback from the learning state of the small network to optimize the training process. In order to overcome the limitation and make full use of the general features learned by the self-supervised pretrained network on large datasets, our teacher model is trained together with the student network and updated according to the output of student network. The overall structure diagram of our distillation method for violent RGB feature consists of two parts: (1) training with mutual distillation (2) evaluation.

Training with Mutual Distillation. As shown in Fig. 2, feature extractor $f_{s\text{-}p}$ is pretrained with self-supervised methods on large-scale datasets, such as Kinetics400 [30], AudioSet [31] and so on. It contains general feature learned from big datasets without labels. Considering a small violent video dataset of N samples $D = \{d_i\}^N_{i=1}$, we feed the RGB sequence of the same video d_i into $f_{s\text{-}p}$ and f_r each time. $f_{s\text{-}p}$ and f_r are both updated during training time. The total loss function for each network contains two parts: the first part is the supervised classification loss L_s, calculating the cross entropy according to the classification result got from each network and the label of violent videos (whether it is violent or not); the second part is the distillation loss L_{KD}, using KL divergence to measure the difference between the prediction probability distributions of

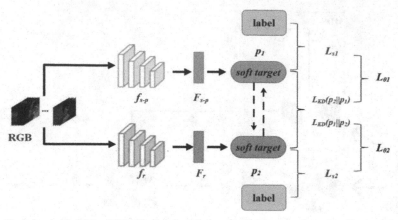

Fig. 2. Training with Mutual Distillation for Violent RGB Feature. $f_{s\text{-}p}$: a self-supervised pre-trained model for RGB feature $F_{s\text{-}p}$. f_r: a model for extracting violent RGB feature F_r. p_1, p_2 stand for the predicted violent score of two networks and they are soft targets for each other. Both $f_{s\text{-}p}$ and f_r are trained with specific distillation loss L_{KD} and the classification loss L_s.

the two networks. We calculate the total loss according to the following formulas, taking f_r as an example:

$$p_i(z_i, T) = \frac{\exp\left(\frac{z_i}{T}\right)}{\sum_{j=0}^{k} \exp\left(\frac{z_j}{T}\right)} \tag{1}$$

$$L_s(y, p_2) = \sum_{i=0}^{k} - y_i \log(p_{2i}(z_i, T = 1)) \tag{2}$$

$$L_{KD}(p_1 \| p_2) = \sum_{i=0}^{k} - p_{1i}(z_i, T) \log(p_{2i}(z_i, T)) \tag{3}$$

$$L_{\theta 2} = \alpha L_s(y, p_2) + (1 - \alpha) L_{KD}(p_1 \| p_2) \tag{4}$$

z_i is the ith-class original output prediction. T is the temperature to control the softening degree of the output probability. $p_i(z_i, T)$ is the ith-class soft target. y stands for labels. $L_{\theta 2}$ is the total loss for f_r. α in the formula (4) is a proportional hyper-parameter, which will be adjusted according to the effect in the experiment. Both $f_{s\text{-}p}$ and f_r are trained with L_θ so that the network can not only learn how to distinguish different categories, but also improve its generalization ability by referring to the probability estimation of another network. As a whole, the $f_{s\text{-}p}$ network obtained by the self-supervised method provides f_r with the general information learned from big datasets in the way of knowledge distillation, which is not available in the supervised training only on small violent datasets. Due to the existence of task-related supervision loss, the model is constantly optimized for better results. We describe the training details in Sect. 4.2.

Evaluation. As shown in Fig. 3, we take the input videos into the trained network f_r to get the RGB feature F_r and the classification result based on RGB.

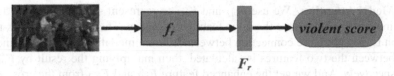

Fig. 3. Framework of the evaluation for RGB feature.

3.2 MAF-Net

Appearance features are the most important features in violent video. We use the TSM-50 [28] as f_r, trained by mutual distillation to extract RGB features of violent videos. Optical flow map is obtained by computing the relative motion information of adjacent frames. In the process of extracting motion features, we choose the ResNet50 network with the Time displacement Module (TSM) [32] for optical flow feature extraction from optical flow maps. PANNs [33] has a strong ability for extracting audio features. We choose pretrained PANNs as our audio feature extraction network. After obtaining F_r, F_l and F_a features, we propose an efficient and lightweight multimodal attention fusion network (MAF-Net) based on attention mechanism, as shown in the Fig. 4.

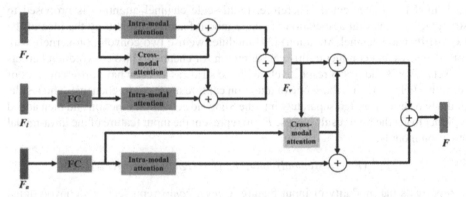

Fig. 4. Architecture of the MAF-Net. F_v: new visual feature obtained from F_r and F_l. FC: the full connection layer. MAF-Net includes FC, intra-modal and cross-modal attention modules. F_r(RGB feature), F_l(flow feature) and F_a(audio feature) are fed into it to get the final feature F.

The fusion network is composed of spatial mapping and two kinds of attention modules, including cross-modal and intra-modal attention.

Spatial Mapping. The spatial mapping maps different feature spaces to the same dimension to eliminate the influence of inter-modal heterogeneity. It is usually used to map each modal feature to a third feature space with full connection layers followed by activation function. However, the full connection layer has a large number of parameters. In order to reduce the amount of calculation, we cancel the mapping process of apparent feature. The optical flow feature F_l and audio feature F_a are mapped with the full connection layer(FC) to the apparent feature F_r space. Then the mapped features are fused using attention modules.

Cross-Modal Attention. We use F_{m1} and F_{m2} to represent spatially mapped feature of two modalities. They have the same feature dimension. The purpose of cross-modal attention is to capture the connection between different modalities. Firstly, cosine similarity between the two features is calculated, then multiplying the result by F_{m1} and F_{m2} respectively. And we get the enhanced feature F_{m1} and F_{m2} from the cross-modal attention:

$$att_{m1}^c = cos(F_{m1}, F_{m2}) \cdot F_{m1} \tag{5}$$

$$att_{m2}^c = cos(F_{m1}, F_{m2}) \cdot F_{m2} \tag{6}$$

$$att_{m1,m2}^c = cos(F_{m1}, F_{m2}) \cdot (F_{m1} + F_{m2}) \tag{7}$$

m_1 and m_2 represent different modalities. The enhanced feature derived from cross-modal attention of two modalities is obtained. And the formula (7) represents the sum result of them.

Intra-Modal Attention. The complementary information between modalities is well supplemented after cross-modal enhancement. But the information enhancement within each modality is neglected. Therefore, multi-scale channel attention is proposed to strengthen the internal association of single-modal feature. Inspired by the idea of the ECA (Efficient Channel Attention) [34] module, we use two convolution kernels with different sizes and conduct multi-scale attention for channels. Two convolution kernels are set as 3×3 and 5×5 respectively with the stride as 1. They have different sizes of receptive fields, making the scope of attention capture more comprehensive. The results of the two kernels are fed separately into the Sigmoid activation function and then added together to get the final result. We use F_m to represent the input feature of the intra-modal attention module:

$$att_m^I(F_m) = sigmoid(conv_1(F_m)) + sigmoid(conv_2(F_m)) \tag{8}$$

m represents the modality of input feature. $Conv_1$, $conv_2$ represent two convolutional operations with different kernel size.

As shown in Fig. 4, F_l and F_a are mapped with the full connection layer to the RGB feature F_r space. Then attention modules are used to fuse the mapped features. We obtain the visual feature F_V by fusing the visual feature F_r and optical flow feature F_l:

$$F_V = att_r^I(F_r) + att_{r,l}^c(F_r, FC(F_l)) + att_l^I(F_l) \tag{9}$$

$FC(\cdot)$ represents a full connection layer followed by activation function. And the final feature F is calculated by F_V and F_a:

$$F = att_A^I(FC(F_a)) + att_{A,V}^c(F_V, FC(F_a)) \tag{10}$$

After getting the final feature F, it is then fed into a classifier to obtain the final violence score of the video. And we calculate the cross-entropy loss between the final violence score and ground truth to optimize the network.

4 Experiments

4.1 Datasets and Metrics

We conduct experiments and evaluate the proposed method on violent video datasets. As shown in Table 1, XD-Violence, Movies Fight and VSD offer complete audio data. Other datasets, such as [8, 15, 16, 18], do not provide audio data; meanwhile, quite a few audio videos in [7] are silent. XD-Violence is the largest public violent dataset offering visual and audio data at the same time. But samples in the testing set are tagged with frame-level labels, while our methods need video-level labels. And Movies Fight is too small. Therefore, we evaluate the proposed method on the VSD [17] and the self-built dataset VCD. Both datasets contain complete audio information.

The VSD [17] comes from 37 Hollywood movies and 30 YouTube video clips. Each video is about 8–12 s. There is a serious imbalance on the distribution of the original dataset. We augment violent videos of the training set with four methods: mirror, rotation, brightness adjustment and immediate cropping. For audio, we apply the same audio with original data to augmented data. The data imbalance in the test set leads to the failure of the accuracy as the evaluation metric. To solve this problem, we use the average precision (AP) of the violence class:

$$AP = \frac{1}{P}\sum_{i=1}^{N} L_i \frac{P_i}{i} \tag{11}$$

where P is the number of ground-truth violent video, N is the total number of testing video, $L_i = 1$ when the ith video clip is violent, otherwise $L_i = 0$. The prediction scores of the testing videos are arranged in descending order, and P_i videos are predicted correctly in the first i predicted samples.

Violent Clip Dataset (VCD) includes 7279 videos. Each video is about 3–10 s with a violent or non-violent label. The distribution of VCD is shown in Table 2. As there is not an imbalance on the distribution of the dataset, we use accuracy as the evaluation metric for VCD.

Table 2. Distribution of the VCD dataset

	Violent	Nonviolent
Training set	2977	2902
Testing set	700	700

4.2 Experiments on Mutual Distillation for Violent RGB Feature

Experimental Setup. We introduce a self-supervised model trained on a large dataset using multimodal contrastive learning without labels as $f_{s\text{-}p}$. We consider two kinds: the Crisscross model [27] the MMV model [28]. Both models achieve great performance on downstream tasks. Crisscross uses the pretrained 18-layer R(2+1)D [35] as the RGB backbone and is trained on the AudioSet (1.8M) [31]. MMV uses TSM [32] with a ResNet50 backbone trained on the HowTo100M [36] and the train split of AudioSet [31]. We choose the same f_r backbone as $f_{s\text{-}p}$, setting 18-layer R(2+1)D and TSM as two backbones. Raw videos are decoded at a frame rate 16 fps and video clips composed of 32 frames of size 224 × 224, covering around 2 s. The SGD optimizer is used with initial learning rate of 10^{-2} decayed by a factor 0.1 every 30 epochs for a total of 120 epochs. α is set as 0.83, with the ratio of distillation loss to classification loss is 1:6.

Results. We conduct experiments to validate the effectiveness of our mutual learning method on two datasets, using two different backbones for RGB. We use two methods to train the network: trained alone or mutual learning with the other.

Table 3. Mutual learning results. We group results of two training methods by dataset and backbone. Evaluation metrics for two datasets are different.

Dataset	Backbone	Training method	Results
Evaluation metrics: AP			
VSD	R(2+1)D-18	Trained alone	0.2781
		Mutual learning	**0.2974**
	TSM-50	Trained alone	0.2802
		Mutual learning	**0.3097**
Evaluation metrics: Accuracy			
VCD	R(2+1)D-18	Trained alone	0.8506
		Mutual learning	**0.8842**
	TSM-50	Trained alone	0.8714
		Mutual learning	**0.9025**

Table 3 shows that our method performs better than training the network separately based on two different backbones. The pretrained model contains general information learned from big datasets with the self-supervised method. Training both networks with combining mutual learning and classification tasks can effectively transfer the large dataset information to violent video recognition task and improve the performance. It combines general information from big datasets well with characteristics of violent videos. Each network is guided primarily by traditional supervised learning loss, which guarantees performance generally improved. Since two networks start from different initial conditions, they estimate different probability of the most likely class, thus providing additional knowledge and realizing knowledge transfer.

Ablation Study on Different α. Table 4 shows accuracy of TSM-50 with different α values (α in Eq. (4)) used during training on the VCD dataset.

Table 4. Ablation study on VCD datasets with TSM-50. We present the results of different α.

α	0.5	0.75	0.8	0.83	0.875	0.9
Accuracy	0.8826	0.8852	0.8937	**0.9025**	0.8984	0.8902

It performs reasonably well when α is in $0.8 \sim 0.875$, showing that the combination of external information of big datasets is beneficial. When α is too small (e.g., 0.5) or too large (e.g., 0.9), the accuracy drops. These results support our motivation of combing two kinds of information and show that we have to find a balance between the distillation loss and supervised loss.

4.3 Experiments on Multimodal Feature Fusion

Experimental Setup. The dense optical flow is uniformly sampled in the time domain to obtain the stacked sequence, which is then randomly cropped to 224×224. Finally, the sequence is input into a ResNet50 network with TSM block [32] to obtain 2048-dimensional motion feature. For audio feature extraction, the audio signal is filtered by hamming window with a size of 1024 and a jump distance of 320. Then a logarithmic mel-spectrogram with a size of 100×64 is obtained by a short-time Fourier transform. Finally, the original audio and spectrogram are fed into PANNs [33] network in parallel to generate 2048-dimensional audio features. For feature fusion, on VSD, we set 50 epochs with a batch size of 64 and he SGD optimizer is used with initial learning rate of 0.0003 decayed by a factor 0.1 every 30 epochs. On VCD, we set 30 epochs with a batch size of 64 and he SGD optimizer is used with initial learning rate of 0.0005 decayed by a factor 0.1 every 15 epochs. The weight decay rate of the SGD optimizer is 1×10^{-5} and momentum term is 0.9 on two datasets.

Results. We fuse multimodal information with different methods, including concatenate, add, score fusion and our MAF-Net method. We conduct experiments on VSD and VCD dataset.

As shown in Table 5 and Table 6, the following phenomena can be observed: Compared with considering RGB single modality, fusing multimodal information improves the performance. Audio feature often play an auxiliary role to visual features. And it is best to consider all three modalities. Compared with simple fusion methods, including feature concatenation, addition and score fusion, MAF-Net shows the best performance on both datasets.

Table 5. Multimodal feature fusion results on VSD dataset. For modality, 'R' refers to RGB, 'F' is optical flow and 'A' is audio.

Modality	Fusion methods	AP
R	-	0.3097
R+A	concatenate	0.4023
	add	0.4044
	score	0.3901
R+F	concatenate	0.3442
	add	0.3453
	score	0.3390
R+A+F	concatenate	0.4534
	add	0.4594
	score	0.4237
R+A+F	**MAF-Net**	**0.4809**

Table 6. Multimodal feature fusion results on VCD datasets. For modality, 'R' refers to RGB, 'F' is optical flow and 'A' is audio.

Modality	Fusion methods	Accuracy
R	-	0.9025
R+A	concatenate	0.9415
	add	0.94
	score	0.9329
R+F	concatenate	0.9281
	add	0.9225
	score	0.9195
R+A+F	concatenate	0.9716
	add	0.971
	score	0.9504
R+A+F	**MAF-Net**	**0.9728**

4.4 Comparison with Others

We compare our final results with other violent video recognition methods on two datasets.

Table 7. Comparison with other approaches on the VSD dataset.

Methods	AP
Autoencoder Mapping[37]	0.3154
Multi-Task[38]	0.3242
Semantic Correspondence[39]	0.3930
Multimodal and Multi-Task[40]	0.3976
VMRN[41]	0.4178
MA-Net[42]	0.4525
Ours	**0.4809**

Table 8. Comparison with other approaches on the VCD dataset.

Methods	Accuracy (%)
DMRN[43]	95.5%
VMRN[41]	96.2%
MA-Net[42]	96.2%
Ours	**97.3%**

In Table 7 and Table 8, we show performance of other methods on VSD and VCD for violent video recognition. Our method significantly outperforms all previous methods on both datasets.

References

1. Mohammadi, H., Nazerfard, E.: SSHA: Video Violence Recognition and Localization using a Semi-Supervised Hard Attention Model (2022)
2. Ding, C., Fan, S., Ming, Z., et al.: Violence detection in video by using 3D convolutional neural networks. In: International Symposium on Visual Computing. Springer, Cham (2014). https://doi.org/10.1007/978-3-319-14364-4_53
3. Samuel, D., Fnil, E., Manogaran, G., et al.: Real time violence detection framework for football stadium comprising of big data analysis and deep learning through bidirectional LSTM. Computer Networks 151(MAR.14), 191–200 (2019)
4. Hanson, A., Pnvr, K., Krishnagopal, S., et al.: Bidirectional Convolutional LSTM for the Detection of Violence in Videos. Springer, Cham (2018). https://doi.org/10.1007/978-3-030-11012-3_24
5. Abdali, A.R.: Data Efficient Video Transformer for Violence Detection. In: 2021 IEEE International Conference on Communication, Networks and Satellite (COMNETSAT). IEEE (2021)
6. Nievas, E.B., Suarez, O.D., Gloria Bueno García, et al.: Violence detection in video using computer vision techniques. In: International Conference on Computer Analysis of Images and Patterns. Springer, Berlin, Heidelberg (2011). https://doi.org/10.1007/978-3-642-23678-5_39

7. Elesawy, M., Hussein, M., Mina, A.E.M.: https://www.kaggle.com/mohamedmustafa/real-life-violence-situations-dataset
8. Cheng, M., Cai, K., Li, M.: RWF-2000: an open large scale video database for violence detection. In: 2020 25th International Conference on Pattern Recognition (ICPR). IEEE, pp. 4183–4190 (2021)
9. Zhang, Y., Xiang, T., Hospedales, T.M., et al.: Deep Mutual Learning (2017)
10. Islam, Z., Rukonuzzaman, M., Ahmed, R., et al.: Efficient Two-Stream Network for Violence Detection Using Separable Convolutional LSTM (2021)
11. Xu, Q., See, J., Lin, W.: Localization guided fight action detection in surveillance videos. In: 2019 IEEE International Conference on Multimedia and Expo (ICME). IEEE, pp. 568–573 (2019)
12. Dai, Q., Zhao, R.W., Wu, Z., et al.: Fudan-Huawei at MediaEval 2015: Detecting Violent Scenes and Affective Impact in Movies with Deep Learning (2015)
13. Peixoto, B., Lavi, B., Martin, J.P.P., et al.: Toward subjective violence detection in videos. In: ICASSP 2019–2019 IEEE International Conference on Acoustics, Speech and Signal Processing (ICASSP). IEEE, pp. 8276–8280 (2019)
14. Pang, W.F., He, Q.H., Hu, Y., et al.: Violence detection in videos based on fusing visual and audio information. In: ICASSP 2021–2021 IEEE International Conference on Acoustics, Speech and Signal Processing (ICASSP). IEEE, pp. 2260–2264 (2021)
15. Perez, M., Kot, A.C., Rocha, A.: Detection of real-world fights in surveillance videos. In: IEEE International Conference on Acoustics, Speech, and Signal Processing (ICASSP). IEEE (2019)
16. Hassner, T., Itcher, Y., Kliper-Gross, O.: Violent flows: real-time detection of violent crowd behavior. In: Computer Vision & Pattern Recognition Workshops. IEEE (2012)
17. Demarty, C.H., et al.: VSD: A public dataset for the detection of violent scenes in movies: design, annotation, analysis and evaluation. Multimedia Tools Appl. **74**(17), 7379–7404 (2015)
18. Sultani, W., Chen, C., Shah, M.: Real-world anomaly detection in surveillance videos. In: Proceedings of the IEEE Conference on Computer Vision and Pattern Recognition, pp. 6479–6488 (2018)
19. Wu, P., Liu, J., Shi, Y., et al.: Not only look, but also listen: Learning multimodal violence detection under weak supervision. In: European Conference on Computer Vision. Springer, Cham, pp. 322–339 (2020). https://doi.org/10.1007/978-3-030-58577-8_20
20. Halder, R., Chatterjee, R.: CNN-BiLSTM model for violence detection in smart surveillance. SN Computer Sci. 1(4), 1–9 (2020)
21. Sargana, A.B.: Fast learning through deep multi-net CNN model for violence recognition in video surveillance. The Computer Journal (2020)
22. Song, W., Zhang, D., Zhao, X., et al.: A novel violent video detection scheme based on modified 3d convolutional neural networks. IEEE Access, pp. 39172–39179 (2019)
23. Xu, X., Wu, X., Wang, G., et al.: Violent video classification based on spatial-temporal cues using deep learning. In: 2018 11th International Symposium on Computational Intelligence and Design (ISCID) (2018)
24. Jing, L., Tian, Y.: Self-supervised visual feature learning with deep neural networks: a survey. IEEE Trans. Pattern Analysis Machine Intell. **43**(11), 4037–4058 (2020)
25. Alwassel, H., Mahajan, D., Torresani, L., et al.: Self-Supervised Learning by Cross-Modal Audio-Video Clustering (2019)
26. Morgado, P., Vasconcelos, N., Misra, I.: Audio-Visual Instance Discrimination with Cross-Modal Agreement (2020)
27. Sarkar, P., Etemad, A.: Self-Supervised Audio-Visual Representation Learning with Relaxed Cross-Modal Temporal Synchronicity (2021)

28. Alayrac, J.B., Recasens, A., Schneider, R., et al.: Self-Supervised MultiModal Versatile Networks (2020)
29. Hinton, G., Vinyals, O., Dean, J.: Distilling the knowledge in a neural network. Computer Science **14**(7), 38–39 (2015)
30. Kay, W., Carreira, J., Simonyan, K., et al.: The Kinetics Human Action Video Dataset (2017)
31. Gemmeke, J.F., Ellis, D., Freedman, D., et al.: AudioSet: an ontology and human-labeled dataset for audio events. In: IEEE International Conference on Acoustics. IEEE (2017)
32. Lin, J., Gan, C., Han, S.: TSM: Temporal Shift Module for Efficient Video Understanding (2018)
33. Kong, Q., Cao, Y., Iqbal, T., et al.: Panns: Large-scale pretrained audio neural networks for audio pattern recognition. IEEE/ACM Trans. Audio, Speech, Language Process. **28**, 2880–2894 (2020)
34. Wang, Q., Wu, B., Zhu, P., et al.: ECA-Net: Efficient channel attention for deep convolutional neural networks. In: 2020 IEEE/CVF Conference on Computer Vision and Pattern Recognition (CVPR). IEEE (2020)
35. Du, T., Wang, H., Torresani, L., et al.: A closer look at spatiotemporal convolutions for action recognition. In: 2018 IEEE/CVF Conference on Computer Vision and Pattern Recognition (CVPR). IEEE (2018)
36. Miech, A., Zhukov, D., Alayrac, J.B., et al.: HowTo100M: learning a text-video embedding by watching hundred million narrated video clips. In: 2019 IEEE/CVF International Conference on Computer Vision (ICCV) (2019)
37. Liu, H.: Violence recognition based on auditory-visual fusion of autoencoder mapping. Electronics 10(21), 2654 (2021)
38. Zheng, Z., Zhong, W., Ye, L., et al.: Violent scene detection of film videos based on multi-task learning of temporal-spatial features. In: 2021 IEEE 4th International Conference on Multimedia Information Processing and Retrieval (MIPR). IEEE, pp. 360–365 (2021)
39. Gu, C., Wu, X., Wang, S.: Violent video detection based on semantic correspondence. IEEE Access **8**, 85958–85967 (2020)
40. Wu, X., Gu, C., Wang, S.: Multi-modal feature fusion and multi-task learning for special video classification. Opt. Precis. Eng. **28**(5), 10 (2020)
41. Gu, C.: Research on Violent Video Recognition based on Multi-Modal Feature and Multi-Task Learning, pp. 1–53. Library of Communication University of China, Beijing (2021)
42. Liu, R., Wu, X.: Multimodal attention network for violence detection. In: 2022 2nd International Conference on Consumer Electronics and Computer Engineering (ICCECE), pp. 503–506 (2022). https://doi.org/10.1109/ICCECE54139.2022.9712676
43. Tian, Y., Shi, J., Li, B., Duan, Z., Xu, C.: Audio-visual event localization in unconstrained videos. In: Ferrari, V., Hebert, M., Sminchisescu, C., Weiss, Y. (eds.) ECCV 2018. LNCS, vol. 11206, pp. 252–268. Springer, Cham (2018). https://doi.org/10.1007/978-3-030-01216-8_16

YFormer: A New Transformer Architecture for Video-Query Based Video Moment Retrieval

Shuwei Huo⬮, Yuan Zhou(✉)⬮, and Haiyang Wang⬮

School of Electrical and Information Engineering, Tianjin University, Tianjin, China
{huosw,zhouyuan,wanghaiyang}@tju.edu.cn

Abstract. Video-query based video moment retrieval (VQ-VMR) aims to localize the segment in a long reference video that semantically corresponds to a short query video. This task faces the problem of matching long and short videos feature, which requires extracting dependencies of long-term sequences. To address this problem, we developed a new transformer architecture, termed YFormer, for VQ-VMR task. Specific to this work, a Spatio-temporal Feature Extractor based on self-attention is proposed to build fine-grained semantic embedding for each frame, and a Semantic Relevance Matcher based on cross-attention is proposed to extract cross-correlation between the query and reference videos. The token-based prediction head and pool-based head are developed to localize the start and end boundaries of the result. These prediction heads for video moment localization facilitate a complete end-to-end retrieval process. We reorganize the videos in ActivityNet dataset to build a video moment retrieval dataset and conduct extensive experiments on this benchmark. Our model achieves favorable performance compared to those state-of-the-art methods.

Keywords: Video moment retrieval · Video query · Transformer

1 Introduction

Video retrieval aims to search for target videos that are semantically relevant to the given query information from a large-scale video database [13, 20, 25]. Traditional studies have focused mainly on searching for an entire video. However, a video usually contains complex scenes, and the actions and instances in the scenes shift frequently over time. As a result, only some video moments match the

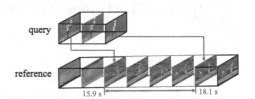

Fig. 1. Illustration of VQ-VMR task. VQ-VMR aims to detect the segment in the reference video that semantically corresponds to the given query video.

ⓒ The Author(s), under exclusive license to Springer Nature Switzerland AG 2022
S. Yu et al. (Eds.): PRCV 2022, LNCS 13536, pp. 638–650, 2022.
https://doi.org/10.1007/978-3-031-18913-5_49

query, whereas the rest may be redundant to the end-users. Therefore, video moment retrieval, *i.e.*, the retrieval of specific moments from a long untrimmed video, is essential in real-world applications, such as video surveillance [3,21] and navigation [19,30].

Existing video moment retrieval methods are mainly based on natural language queries [18,24, 33]. The current dominant approach is to encode text and video into a joint embedding space to measure cross-modal similarities, which achieves good retrieval performance and promotes the progress of related applications. However, in many scenarios, a query may not take the form of natural language text. Consider a common scenario: when an online video recommendation sys-

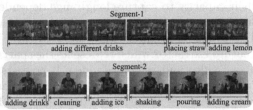

Fig. 2. An example to illustrate the temporal difference among semantically similar video segments. The two segments both describe a scene of "mixing drinks", but the elemental actions ("adding ice", "shaking", and etc.) in each segment are sequenced differently.

tem estimates that a user is interested in a certain video scene, the system should recommend other video moments involving similar content to the user. It is worth stressing that, in this case, the query itself is a video rather than a text. Thus, we should design a model that uses the video clip of interest as the query to localize semantically matched moments from untrimmed videos. To this end, video-query based video moment retrieval (VQ-VMR) is of important practical value and exciting prospects.

The VQ-VMR is illustrated as Fig. 1. Given a short query video and an untrimmed reference video, VQ-VMR model aims to localize a segment of the reference video that semantically corresponds to the given query video. VQ-VMR is a challenging task because of the following reasons: First, the videos usually contain extensive information and various visual representation, and videos expressing the same semantic concept may exhibit distinct visual representations (as shown in Fig. 1). Second, although the semantics of the two videos may be similar, the order and duration of each action element in the video may be different. Figure 2 provides a specific example demonstrating above challenge. The two segments in Fig. 2 both describe a scene of "mixing drinks", but the elemental actions ("adding ice", "shaking", etc.) in each segment are sequenced differently. Third, accurately localizing the temporal boundaries from the reference video is also challenging. Previous methods estimate the boundary likelihood of each frame, and use hand-designed strategies (such as thresholding and non-maximum suppression) to localize the boundary. However, the frame on the boundary is often visually similar to its neighbors, therefore it is difficult to identify which frame is on the boundary.

To address the aforementioned problems, we develop a new network that utilizes multiple attention-based models for video feature representation and inter-video cross-correlations. This network is inspired by the fundamental principle of transformer architecture [28], which transforms one sequence into another one using attention-based encoders and decoders. Transformer-based models have shown favorable performance in representing sequential data because of their capacity to capture long-range dependencies. In this work, we leverage the transformer to build a new architecture, termed YFormer, for VQ-VMR task. The proposed architecture consists of three components: 1) a Spatio-Temporal Feature Extractor which represents the spatial and temporal features of the input query video and reference video. It consists of 3D convolutional networks and self-attention modules; 2) a Semantic Relevance Matcher, which receives the output features from the Spatio-Temporal Feature Extractor, and models the semantic relevance between the query video and reference; and 3) a prediction head for the final prediction of the temporal boundaries of target video moment. The main contributions of this work are summarized as follows.

1) We make a pioneering attempt in inheriting the existing success of transformers to VQ-VMR. Thus, we develop a new transformer architecture, YFormer, for semantic relevance measurement. The self-attention of the transformer is used to build fine-grained semantic embedding for each frame, and the cross-attention of transformer extracts cross-correlation between the query video and reference videos.
2) The token-based and pool-based prediction heads facilitate a complete end-to-end retrieval process. By contrast, other video moment localization networks only produce for each frame the probabilities that the query video matches the frame, and require manual post-processing to generate the final matched video moment.
3) We conducted extensive experiments on the standard ActivityNet [17] dataset, and experimental results show that our model achieves favorable performance compared to those of the state-of-the-art methods. We also demonstrate the effectiveness of each module in our model by ablation studies.

2   Related Work

2.1   Transformer in Computer Vision

The transformer was originally developed by Vaswani et al.. [29] for machine translation tasks, and has since become a prevailing architecture in the field of natural language processing (NLP). Based on the success of transformers in NLP, researchers have proposed several transformer-based network architectures for various computer vision tasks, such as image classification [8], object detection [4], and object re-identification [15]. The success of transformers in image understanding and processing has led to an investigation of transformer-based architectures [16,23] for video recognition tasks. While previous transformer-based investigations are mainly focused on semantic representation for a single video, there remains a technology gap in using transformers to model semantic relevance between a pair of videos, which is essential in video moment retrieval.

In this paper, we make a pioneering attempt in inheriting the existing success of transformers to video moment retrieval. Thus, we build a new transformer encoder-decoder architecture for semantic relevance measurement.

2.2 Video Moment Retrieval

Video moment retrieval focuses on localizing the video moment that is semantically similar with a given query in a long and untrimmed reference video.

Existing video moment retrieval methods are primarily based on natural language queries. Early work was mostly developed for constrained video scenes, including fixed spatial prepositions [27], ordering constraints [1] and so on. In the deep learning era, moment retrieval in wide-ranging video scenes was studied. The general approach involves representing the query text and reference video in a joint feature space to measure cross-modal similarities [12,34]. Recent works have introduced state-of-the-art operations (e.g., attention [22,32] and graph [33]) to capture the inter actions between videos and texts. To localize the boundaries more accurately, a reinforcement learning (RL) strategy has been adopted to progressively refine the predicted boundaries [14,26,31].

In addition to natural language queries, VQ-VMR is also a promising approach of considerable practical value. Existing research related to this task is still inadequate. Feng et al. [10] made a preliminary attempt towards VQ-VMR by proposing a cross-gated bilinear matching model to match reference video and query video. Their subsequent work [11] extended the localization task to a spatial-temporal level. Chen et al. [6] propose a graph feature pyramid network with dense prediction to encode scene relations and localize target moments.

3   YFormer for Video Moment Retireval

As shown in Fig. 3, our proposed YFormer model consists of three components as follows: 1) **Spatio-Temporal Feature Extractor** (STFE), that extracts the feature of input videos 2) **Semantic Relevance Matcher** (SRM), which models the semantic relevance between the query video and reference; 3) **Prediction head**, that predicts the start- and end-time of the target video moment.

We developed two kinds of YFormer architectures, their main differences lie in the inputs of SRM and the architecture of prediction head. We name them as "**YFormer-token**" and "**YFormer-pool**", according to their prediction head. Detailed description of each component is provided below.

3.1   Spatio-Temporal Feature Extractor

Two STFEs, i.e., STFE-Q and STFE-R, are designed to extract the features of the input query video and reference video, respectively. The STFE consists of a C3D network and L_e stacked multi-head self-attention (MHSA) and FFN layers [29].

The C3D is used to extract a spatial features of the input video. In our implementation, we chunk all videos into short overlapping segments of 16 frames and use a C3D network model pretrained on the Kinetics dataset [5] to extract a feature vector of d-dim from each chunk. We send query and reference videos into the C3D network to obtain two feature sequences $\mathbf{v}^q = [\mathbf{v}_1^q, \mathbf{v}_2^q, ..., \mathbf{v}_{T_q}^q] \in \mathbb{R}^{T_q \times d}$ and $\mathbf{v}^r = [\mathbf{v}_1^r, \mathbf{v}_2^r, ..., \mathbf{v}_{T_q}^r] \in \mathbb{R}^{T_r \times d}$, where T_q and T_r denotes the number of chunks of query and reference videos, respectively.

The 3D convolutional network simply provides a sequence of local features and does not incorporate the overall context of the video. Therefore, we subsequently use self-attention modules interactions among local features for a more high-level representation. In our work, we utilize $L_e = 4$ stacked transformer encoders, each encoder performs the multi-head self-attention and FFN operations on input sequence $\mathbf{X}$, express as,

$$\mathbf{X}^{sa} = \text{FFN}\left(\sum\nolimits_{i=1}^{h} A_i(\mathbf{X})(\mathbf{X}\mathbf{W}_i^v)\mathbf{W}_H^i\right), \tag{1}$$

where $A_i(\mathbf{X}) = \text{softmax}((\mathbf{X}\mathbf{W}_i^q)(\mathbf{X}\mathbf{W}_i^k)^T/\sqrt{d})$ is attention matrix, $\mathbf{W}_i^q, \mathbf{W}_i^k, \mathbf{W}_i^v \in \mathbb{R}^{d \times \frac{d}{h}}, \mathbf{W}_i^H \in \mathbb{R}^{\frac{d}{h} \times d}$ are trainable parameter matrices, h is the number of head. FFN is a 2-layer fully-connected network with ReLU activation.

The C3D feature sequences $\mathbf{v}^q$ and $\mathbf{v}^r$ are sent to the stacked encoders. The encoders produce two new sequences $\mathbf{E}_Q = [\mathbf{e}_1^q, \mathbf{e}_2^q, ..., \mathbf{e}_{T_q}^q] \in \mathbb{R}^{T_q \times d}$ and $\mathbf{E}_R = [\mathbf{e}_1^r, \mathbf{e}_2^r, ..., \mathbf{e}_{T_r}^r] \in \mathbb{R}^{T_r \times d}$.

3.2 Semantic Relevance Matcher

The STFE builds frame-wise semantic representations of query and the reference video separately. The Semantic Relevance Matcher (SRM) interacts the features of the query and reference videos. As shown in Fig. 4, a SRM module consists of $L_d = 4$ stacked units. In each unit, the multi-head cross-attention and FFN operations are performed on two input sequence $\mathbf{X}$ and $\mathbf{Y}$, expressed as,

$$\mathbf{X}^{ca} = \text{SRMunit}(\mathbf{X}, \mathbf{Y}) = \text{FFN}\left(\sum\nolimits_{i=1}^{h} A_i(\mathbf{X}, \mathbf{Y})(\mathbf{Y}\mathbf{W}_i^v)\mathbf{W}_i^H\right), \tag{2}$$

where $A_i(\mathbf{X}, \mathbf{Y}) = \text{softmax}((\mathbf{X}\mathbf{W}_i^q)(\mathbf{Y}\mathbf{W}_i^k)^T/\sqrt{d})$ is attention matrix, $\mathbf{W}_i^q, \mathbf{W}_i^k, \mathbf{W}_i^v \in \mathbb{R}^{d \times \frac{d}{h}}, \mathbf{W}_i^H \in \mathbb{R}^{\frac{d}{h} \times d}$ are trainable parameter matrices, h is the number of head. FFN is a 2-layer fully-connected network with ReLU activation. The SRM($\mathbf{X}, \mathbf{Y}$) includes L_d stacked SRMunit(). The first unit receives the direct input $\mathbf{X}$ and $\mathbf{Y}$ produces a new sequence $\mathbf{X}^{ca}$. Then the output sequence $\mathbf{X}^{ca}$ and the input sequence $\mathbf{Y}$ are fed into the subsequent unit. The output of the last unit is the final output of the entire SRM(). The input data of the SRM in "YFormer-token" and "YFormer-pool" are slightly different.

YFormer-Token: Vision transformers typically add an extra learnable token to the sequence of the embedded patches [8]. In our work, we propose a localization token representing the information of both query and reference videos. This token

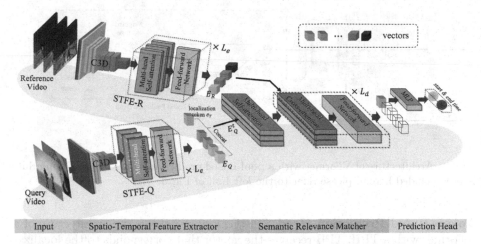

Fig. 3. Framework of the proposed YFormers model with token-based prediction head. YFormer consists of 1) a Spatio-Temporal Feature Extractor (STFE), that generate compact representations of from the input query video and reference video, respectively; 2) Semantic Relevance Matcher (SRM), which receives the output features from STFE, and models the semantic relevance between the query video and reference; and a Prediction head, that predicts temporal range.

design originated from BERT [7]. The localization token is represented by $\mathbf{e}_T$ (a d-dimensional learnable vector), which is first concatenated with the output of STFE-Q (i.e., $\mathbf{E}_Q$), obtaining a new sequence $\mathbf{E}_Q^t$ as Eq. (3),

$$\mathbf{E}_Q^t = [\mathbf{e}_T, \mathbf{E}_Q] = [\mathbf{e}_T, \mathbf{e}_1^q, \mathbf{e}_2^q, ..., \mathbf{e}_{T_q}^q]. \tag{3}$$

Subsequently, $\mathbf{E}_Q^t$ and $\mathbf{E}_R$ are fed into the SRM to generate a fused feature sequence:

$$\mathbf{D}^{tk} = \mathrm{SRM}(\mathbf{E}_Q^t, \mathbf{E}_R). \tag{4}$$

The $\mathbf{D}^{tk} \in \mathbb{R}^{(T_q+1)\times d}$ is a sequence representing the semantic relevance between query and reference videos.

YFormer-Pool: As shown in Fig. 4, this YFormer-pool doesn't require extra tokens, the output of two STFE modules are directly passed to the SRM. The SRM produces a relevance embedding sequence through,

$$\mathbf{D}^{pl} = [\mathbf{D}_1^{pl}, \mathbf{D}_2^{pl}, ..., \mathbf{D}_{T_r}^{pl}] = \mathrm{SRM}(\mathbf{E}_R, \mathbf{E}_Q). \tag{5}$$

3.3 Prediction Heads

Prediction head receives the output feature sequence of the decoder and generates the final localization result. We design two types of prediction heads: a token-based prediction head (TPH) and pool-based prediction head (PPH).

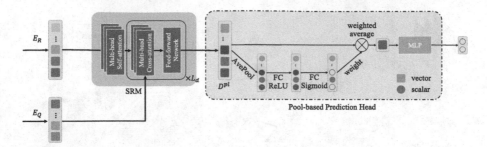

Fig. 4. Architecture of YFormer with a pool-based prediction head. The STFE module is not included herein, please refer to the left half of Fig. 3.

Token-Based Prediction Head (TPH): Figure 3 shows the architecture of a YFormer with a TPH. TPH receives the vector that corresponds to the localization token from sequence $\mathbf{D}^{tk}$, *i.e.*, $\mathbf{D}_0^{tk}$ in Eq. (4), then generate the localization result through a 3-layer perceptron with ReLU activation function and hidden dimension d: $[t_s, t_e] = \mathrm{MLP}(\mathbf{D}_0^{tk})$.

Pool-Based Prediction Head (PPH): Figure 4 shows the architecture of a YFormer with a pool-based prediction head. YFormer-pool receives all feature vectors $\mathbf{D}^{pl} = [\mathbf{D}_1^{pl}, \mathbf{D}_2^{pl}, ..., \mathbf{D}_{T_r}^{pl}]$ produced by decoder (see Eq. (5)). The feature vectors are fused using a new adaptive weighted average pooling operation, which sequentially performs the following computations on $\mathbf{D}^{pl}$:

- 1) average pooling on each vector of $\mathbf{D}^{pl}$, obtaining a vector $\mathbf{a} \in \mathbb{R}^{T_r}$;
- 2) the passing of $\mathbf{a}$ into 2-layer fully-connected network, and obtaining the adaptive weight array $\mathbf{w} \in \mathbb{R}^{T_r}$;
- 3) aggregating the feature vectors in $\mathbf{D}^{pl}$ using adaptive weights through $\mathbf{D}^{\mathrm{agg}} = \sum_i \mathbf{w}(i)\mathbf{D}_i^{pl} / \sum_i \mathbf{w}(i)$.

Subsequently, similar to YFormer-token, the fused feature vector $\mathbf{D}^{\mathrm{agg}}$ is fed into a 3-layer perceptron, to generate the final localization result, *i.e.*., $[t_s, t_e] = \mathrm{MLP}(\mathbf{D}^{\mathrm{agg}})$.

3.4   Losses

In the training phrase, we employ temporal Intersection-over-Union (tIoU) loss and L_1 loss. Assuming that our model estimates the temporal range of the target video moment as $[t_s, t_e]$, while the ground-truth is $[t_s^g, t_e^g]$, the tIoU loss and L_1 loss are defined as,

$$\mathcal{L}_{tiou} = 1 - \frac{\max\{0, \min\{t_e^g, t_e\} - \min\{t_s^g, t_s\}\}}{\max\{t_e^g, t_e\} - \max\{t_s^g, t_s\}}, \ \mathcal{L}_{l1} = |t_s^g - t_s| + |t_e^g - t_e|, \quad (6)$$

The total loss is a weighted sum of $\mathcal{L}_{tiou}$ and $\mathcal{L}_{l1}$, expressed as

$$\mathcal{L} = \lambda_1 \mathcal{L}_{tiou} + \lambda_2 \mathcal{L}_{l1}. \quad (7)$$

where λ_1 and λ_2 are balance weights.

4 Experiments

We conduct several experiments to demonstrate the effectiveness of the proposed YFormer model. This section describes the experimental configurations and reports the evaluation results.

4.1 Experiment Setup

Dataset. The dataset used for VQ-VMR is collected in [10] from ActivityNet [9], which is a large-scale action localization dataset with segment-level action annotations. The new collected dataset has 9,400 untrimmed videos, and each video contains only one action instance. The dataset is split into three disjoint sets including the training, validation and testing sets. There are 7,593 videos of 160 classes in the training set, 978 videos of 20 classes in the validation set and 829 videos of 20 classes in the testing set.

To ease training, we use the C3D features released by ActivityNet Challenge 2016. The features are extracted using a publicly available pre-trained C3D model with a temporal resolution of 16 frames. The values in the second fully-connected layer are projected to 500 dimensions via principal component analysis.

Implementation Details. We train all our models using Adam optimizer for 100,000 steps. The learning rate is initially set to 1×10^{-4}, and reduced by 10 after 75,000 training steps. The batch size is set to 256. In both YFormer-token and YFormer-pool model, the dimension of feature vector d is set to 512; the head number of multi-head attention, $i.e.$, h, is set to 8. In the loss function, the balance weights λ_1 and λ_2 are set to 2 and 5, respectively.

Evaluation Metrics. Following [10], we use the average top-1 mAP computed with tIoU thresholds $\{0.5, 0.6, .07, 0.8, 0.9\}$ to evaluate the performances of our proposed model and other state-of-the-art methods.

Compared Methods. Only a few methods have been designed specifically for the VQ-VMR task. To obtain extensive comparison, we apply several models designed for similar tasks to the VQ-VMR task, and compare their performances against the proposed YFormer. We compare our method with: 1) VQ-VMR methods, including Frame-level baseline [10], Video-level baseline [10], CGBM [10], and GDP [6]; 2) action proposal method, SST [2]; and 3) state-of-the-art language-query based video moment retrieval (LQ-VMR) methods, including 2D-TAN [34] and MABAN [26]. To adapt the LQ-VMR models to VQ-VMR task, we add a C3D network to each model for query video feature extraction.

4.2 Quantitative Results

Table 1 lists the evaluation results of the existing methods and compared against the proposed YFormer. It reveals that both proposed models perform better than the state-of-the-art algorithms compared. Specifically, YFormer outperforms existing methods in terms of tIoU losses; in fact, when tIoU is less than 0.8, and YFormer achieves a 29.1% average mAP which is 1.3% higher than the best result obtained by the previous methods.

Table 1. Evaluation of our and compared methods on ActivityNet dataset.

Method	mAP					
	0.5	0.6	0.7	0.8	0.9	Average
Random	15.5	11.0	5.2	2.7	1.1	7.1
Frame-level [10]	18.8	13.9	9.6	5.0	2.3	9.9
Video-level [10]	24.3	17.4	12.0	5.9	2.2	12.4
SST [2]	33.2	24.7	17.2	7.8	2.7	17.1
CGBM [10]	43.5	35.1	27.3	16.2	6.5	25.7
GDP [6]	44.0	35.4	27.7	20.0	**12.1**	27.8
2D-TAN [34]	39.6	33.9	26.0	18.5	6.0	24.8
MABAN [26]	37.5	28.9	20.2	12.0	4.5	20.6
YFormer-token (ours)	**47.0**	**39.5**	**29.7**	20.6	8.6	**29.1**
YFormer-pool (ours)	44.3	36.3	29.4	**21.7**	**12.1**	28.8

4.3   Qualitative Results

To validate the performance of our YFormer model qualitatively, we provide some qualitative examples of moment retrieval using our approach. Retrieving desired video moment from the given examples is relatively difficult: in the first examples, the query and reference videos are of great visual difference; and in the second example, the target video moment in the reference video is visually resembles other parts in this video. As shown in Fig. 5, our YFormer model manages these difficult examples effectively, that is, it accurately localizes boundaries of the target video moments.

Table 2. Effects of the main YFormer model components. The experiments are carried out on the ActivityNet dataset using mAP scores. The value in parentheses indicate the mAP difference between a model without a particular component and the corresponding complete model. "w/o Att": no self-attention module in STFE; "w/o SRM": no SRM module.

Model	mAP					
	0.5	0.6	0.7	0.8	0.9	Average
YFormer-token	47.0	39.5	29.7	20.6	8.6	29.1
YFormer-token w/o Att	41.7	36.4	27.3	19.2	7.5	$26.4_{(-2.7)}$
YFormer-pool	44.3	36.3	29.4	21.7	12.1	28.8
YFormer-pool w/o Att	40.9	33.5	26.1	19.9	10.6	$26.2_{(-2.6)}$
YFormer w/o SRM	38.3	31.0	23.4	16.4	5.80	$23.0_{(-6.1)}$

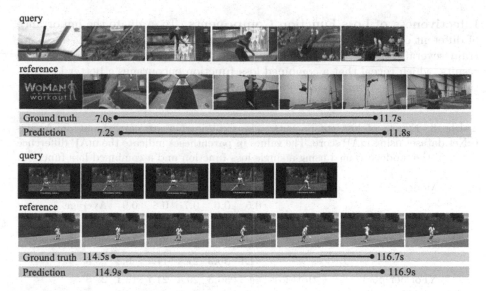

Fig. 5. Qualitative examples of the proposed YFormer model. The proposed method consistently generates accurate boundaries of the target video moments.

4.4   Ablation Study

In this section, we explore how the main components (*i.e.*, STFE, SRM module and losses) of our YFormer influence the final model performance.

Effectiveness of the STFE. We validate the effectiveness of the attention mechanism by testing the architectures without self-attention modules and comparing their localization performance with that of the complete architecture. As listed in Table 2, the average mAP scores reduce by 2.7% (YFormer-token) and 2.6% (YFormer-pool) when the self-attention modules are removed from the YFormer, which demonstrates that the transformer attention mechanism can help C3D network to produce better frame-wise video representation.

Effectiveness of the SRM. Similar to the experiment for STFE, we test a YFormer model using other feature matching models and compare its localization performance with that of the complete YFormer model to validate the effectiveness of the decoder. In our experiments, we replace the proposed SRM module with a fully-connected layer based on the designs in [12]. The comparison results are listed in Table 2. The results reveal that when the proposed SRM is replaced by a simple model, the average mAP score decreases by 6.1%, which suggests that the proposed SRM is highly effective in capturing semantic relevance between videos.

Effectiveness of Loss Function Components. To evaluate the importance of different components of the loss function (namely, tIoU loss and L_1 loss), we train several models turning the components on and off. Table 3 presents the results, which reveal that a combined loss function encourages a better localization performance than the individual losses.

Table 3. Effects of loss components. The experiments are carried out on ActivityNet dataset using mAP score. The values in parentheses indicate the mAP difference between the models trained using a single loss function and a combined loss function.

Model	Loss	mAP					
		0.5	0.6	0.7	0.8	0.9	Average
YFormer-token	L_1 + tIoU loss	47.0	39.5	29.7	20.6	8.6	29.1
	tIoU loss	44.1	38.5	29.2	20.2	8.4	$28.1_{(-1.0)}$
	L_1 loss	41.1	35.3	27.4	17.7	6.8	$25.6_{(-3.5)}$
YFormer-pool	L_1 + tIoU loss	44.3	36.3	29.4	21.7	12.1	28.8
	tIoU loss	41.9	35.1	27.5	20.3	11.2	$27.2_{(-1.6)}$
	L_1 loss	39.5	33.0	25.2	18.5	9.3	$25.1_{(-3.7)}$

5   Conclusion

Video-query based video moment retrieval (VQ-VMR) aims to detect the segment in a long untrimmed video that semantically corresponds to the given query video. This task faces the problem of semantic matching between the long and short videos feature, which requires extracting dependencies of long-term sequences. In this paper, we develop YFormer model, a new transformer-like architecture for VQ-VMR task. Transformer-based models have shown a favorable performance in representing sequential data because of their capacity to capture long-range dependencies. The proposed YFormer model consists of three well-designed modules: a Spatio-Temporal Feature Extractor, a Semantic Relevance Matcher, and a prediction head to predict the localization results in an end-to-end manner. Experimental results on the standard dataset show that our proposed YFormer model achieves significant performance gain over state-of-the-art methods. We also demonstrate the effectiveness of each module in our model by ablation studies.

References

1. Bojanowski, P., et al.: Weakly-supervised alignment of video with text, pp. 4462–4470 (2015)
2. Buch, S., Escorcia, V., Shen, C., Ghanem, B., Niebles, J.C.: SST: single-stream temporal action proposals. In: IEEE Conference on Computer Vision and Pattern Recognition (CVPR) (2017)

3. Cao, D., Yu, Z., Zhang, H., Fang, J., Nie, L., Tian, Q.: Video-based cross-modal recipe retrieval. In: Proceedings of the 27th ACM International Conference on Multimedia, MM 2019, pp. 1685–1693. Association for Computing Machinery, New York, NY, USA (2019). https://doi.org/10.1145/3343031.3351067

4. Carion, N., Massa, F., Synnaeve, G., Usunier, N., Kirillov, A., Zagoruyko, S.: End-to-end object detection with transformers. In: Vedaldi, A., Bischof, H., Brox, T., Frahm, J.-M. (eds.) ECCV 2020. LNCS, vol. 12346, pp. 213–229. Springer, Cham (2020). https://doi.org/10.1007/978-3-030-58452-8_13

5. Carreira, J., Zisserman, A.: Quo Vadis, action recognition? a new model and the kinetics dataset. In: 2017 IEEE Conference on Computer Vision and Pattern Recognition (CVPR), pp. 4724–4733 (2017). https://doi.org/10.1109/CVPR.2017.502

6. Chen, L., Lu, C., Tang, S., Xiao, J., Li, X.: Rethinking the bottom-up framework for query-based video localization. Proc. AAAI Conf. Artif. Intell. **34**(7), 10551–10558 (2020)

7. Devlin, J., Chang, M.W., Lee, K., Toutanova, K.: BERT: pre-training of deep bidirectional transformers for language understanding. In: Conference of the North American Chapter of the Association for Computational Linguistics (2019)

8. Dosovitskiy, A., et al.: An image is worth 16×16 words: transformers for image recognition at scale. arXiv preprint arXiv:2010.11929 (2020)

9. Heilbron, F.C., Victor Escorcia, B.G., Niebles, J.C.: ActivityNet: a large-scale video benchmark for human activity understanding. In: Proceedings of the IEEE Conference on Computer Vision and Pattern Recognition, pp. 961–970 (2015)

10. Feng, Y., Ma, L., Liu, W., Zhang, T., Luo, J.: Video re-localization. In: European Conference on Computer Vision (2018)

11. Feng, Y., Ma, L., Liu, W., Luo, J.: Spatio-temporal video re-localization by warp LSTM. In: Proceedings of the IEEE/CVF Conference on Computer Vision and Pattern Recognition, pp. 1288–1297 (2019)

12. Gao, J., Sun, C., Yang, Z., Nevatia, R.: TALL: temporal activity localization via language query, pp. 5277–5285 (2017)

13. Habibian, A., Mensink, T., Snoek, C.: Composite concept discovery for zero-shot video event detection. In: Proceedings of International Conference on Multimedia Retrieval (2014)

14. Hahn, M., Kadav, A., Rehg, J.M., Graf, H.: Tripping through time: efficient localization of activities in videos. arXiv abs/1904.09936 (2020)

15. He, S., Luo, H., Wang, P., Wang, F., Li, H., Jiang, W.: TransReID: transformer-based object re-identification. arXiv preprint arXiv:2102.04378 (2021)

16. He, X., Pan, Y., Tang, M., Lv, Y.: Self-supervised video retrieval transformer network. arXiv abs/2104.07993 (2021)

17. Heilbron, F.C., Escorcia, V., Ghanem, B., Niebles, J.C.: ActivityNet: a large-scale video benchmark for human activity understanding. In: IEEE Conference on Computer Vision and Pattern Recognition (CVPR) (2015)

18. Hendricks, L.A., Wang, O., Shechtman, E., Sivic, J., Darrell, T., Russell, B.C.: Localizing moments in video with natural language, pp. 5804–5813 (2017)

19. Huang, H., et al.: Transferable representation learning in vision-and-language navigation. In: Proceedings of the IEEE/CVF International Conference on Computer Vision (ICCV), October 2019

20. Kordopatis-Zilos, G., Papadopoulos, S., Patras, I., Kompatsiaris, I.: FIVR: fine-grained incident video retrieval. IEEE Trans. Multimedia **21**(10), 2638–2652 (2019). https://doi.org/10.1109/TMM.2019.2905741

21. Liu, M., Wang, X., Nie, L., He, X., Chen, B., Chua, T.S.: Attentive moment retrieval in videos. In: The 41st International ACM SIGIR Conference on Research & Development in Information Retrieval, SIGIR 2018, pp. 15–24. Association for Computing Machinery, New York, NY, USA (2018). https://doi.org/10.1145/3209978.3210003

22. Liu, M., Wang, X., Nie, L., Tian, Q., Chen, B., Chua, T.S.: Cross-modal moment localization in videos. In: Proceedings of the 26th ACM International Conference on Multimedia, MM 2018, pp. 843–851. Association for Computing Machinery, New York, NY, USA (2018)

23. Liu, Z., et al.: Video Swin transformer. CoRR abs/2106.13230 (2021). https://arxiv.org/abs/2106.13230

24. Mithun, N.C., Paul, S., Roy-Chowdhury, A.K.: Weakly supervised video moment retrieval from text queries, pp. 11584–11593 (2019)

25. Song, J., Zhang, H., Li, X., Gao, L., Wang, M., Hong, R.: Self-supervised video hashing with hierarchical binary auto-encoder. IEEE Trans. Image Process. **27**(7), 3210–3221 (2018). https://doi.org/10.1109/TIP.2018.2814344

26. Sun, X., Wang, H., He, B.: MABAN: multi-agent boundary-aware network for natural language moment retrieval. IEEE Trans. Image Process. **30**, 5589–5599 (2021)

27. Tellex, S., Roy, D.: Towards surveillance video search by natural language query. In: CIVR 2009 (2009)

28. Vaswani, A., et al.: Attention is all you need. In: Proceedings of the IEEE/CVF Conference on Computer Vision and Pattern Recognition (CVPR). Curran Associates Inc., Red Hook, NY, USA (2017)

29. Vaswani, A., et al.: Attention is all you need. arXiv abs/1706.03762 (2017)

30. Wang, X., et al.: Reinforced cross-modal matching and self-supervised imitation learning for vision-language navigation. In: Proceedings of the IEEE/CVF Conference on Computer Vision and Pattern Recognition (CVPR), June 2019

31. Wu, J.Y., Li, G., Liu, S., Lin, L.: Tree-structured policy based progressive reinforcement learning for temporally language grounding in video. arXiv abs/2001.06680 (2020)

32. Yuan, Y., Mei, T., Zhu, W.: To find where you talk: temporal sentence localization in video with attention based location regression, July 2019

33. Zeng, Y., Cao, D., Wei, X., Liu, M., Zhao, Z., Qin, Z.: Multi-modal relational graph for cross-modal video moment retrieval. In: Proceedings of the IEEE/CVF Conference on Computer Vision and Pattern Recognition (CVPR), pp. 2215–2224, June 2021

34. Zhang, S., Peng, H., Fu, J., Luo, J.: Learning 2D temporal adjacent networks for moment localization with natural language. In: American Association for Artificial Intelligence (AAAI) (2020)

Hightlight Video Detection in Figure Skating

Shun Fan[ID], Yuantai Wei[ID], Jingfei Xia[ID], and Feng Zheng[✉][ID]

Department of Computer Science and Engineering, Southern University of Science
and Technology, Shenzhen 518055, People's Republic of China
jingfeix@alumni.cmu.edu, zfeng02@gmail.com

Abstract. Figure skating is an ornamental competitive sport with fancy
technical moves. In particular, highlight videos in figure skating, which
contain these elegant moves, have always been a favorite part of the vast
audience. However, research in highlight video detection has not yielded
much success. Previous researches mainly focus on detecting the falling
action in the video rather than numerous technical moves. Therefore, we
propose a segmentation method for the whole video to use Tube self-
Attention for highlights detection. In particular, we have added a new
module outside the existing network, which enables the editing and integration of the highlight moments of athletes in a single competition to
produce highlight videos. Additionally, since few datasets have explored
highlight actions in figure skating, we design a new dataset HS-FS (Highlight Shot in Figure Skating), which can be used to train the Tube Self-
Attention model to satisfy highlight detection. Experiments show that
the training accuracy obtained on the new dataset is 99.35% during training. Visualizations have demonstrated that our proposed methods could
identify the highlight moment in figure skating videos.

Keywords: Highlight detection · Highlight video clip · Figure skating
video

1 Introduction

With the emergence of video platforms, the number of sports-related video works
on the Internet has also gradually increased. The audience for sports videos is
also gradually increasing. In the case of sports videos, viewers are significantly
more interested in highlighting video clips from matches. The production of highlight videos has a significant commercial value, but the extraction of the highlights
takes much effort. Therefore, it is becoming essential to automate the extraction of
highlights from the video [16,17,25]. However, figure skating has not been extensively studied on the detection and automatic extraction of highlight scenes. Most
research derived from figure skating-type competitions has been on scoring and
action recognition tasks. However, the detection of highlight videos for figure skating has a wide range of application and research significance. In terms of commercial value, highlight videos can help the publisher increase the audience's interest.

S. Yu et al. (Eds.): PRCV 2022, LNCS 13536, pp. 651–664, 2022.
https://doi.org/10.1007/978-3-031-18913-5_50

In addition, highlight videos are also effective in helping skaters understand their strengths in that competition, allowing athletes to recognize their performance and participation status better and help them fully understand their strengths. Also, the athletes can watch moments of excellence from competitors or other participants in the competition, which can help them better understand other participants' strengths. Highlight video detection will also help score figure skating: highlight video detection will facilitate the construction of relevant datasets, and immediate highlight video detection will help provide a better reference for sports video scoring. The resulting temporal scoring is more in line with the results. The judges are scoring figure skating in the same way.

To detect highlight shots in figure skating video, one idea is to split figure skating videos into several slices and score each clip time by time. Higher scores stand for highlight parts in the video. There are lots of work about scoring Figure Skating [14,19,23,24], but they just to scoring the overall feature data and that there is no mature temporal scoring model. These studies are related to action scoring, whereas the dataset corresponding to the relevant actions and scoring for figure skating was too sparse. Recently, some work have proposed a study on the recognition of falling movements of figure skaters [21]. This paper proposes a well-trained action evaluation model in action quality assessment (AQA): Tube Self-Attention Network (TSA-Net). This model is capable of identifying divers' movements and detecting falls in figure skaters. We realized that falls and moments of excellence have large body movements.

Based on TSA-Net, we built a new structure to use the TSA-Net model for highlight video detection. We adjusted the target tracking module so that the model can be used directly for the provided. The model can perform faster feature extraction from the original video. This adjustment solves the problem that the original model did not provide a corresponding visual object tracking (VOT) part of the model. In order to replace the original tracking model, we used openpose to get the tracking markers of the athletes. Using the trained model for highlight video extraction allows the viewer to freely choose the confidence interval needed to get highlight videos with different degrees of feasibility. Moreover, we found that few dataset is suitable for highlight video detection during our experiment. Therefore, we collected a new dataset HS-FS, which stands for Highlight Shoot in Figure Skating that used in our task. Extensive experiments and ablation studies show the effectiveness of our methods.

The main contributions of this paper are as follows:

- A new visual object tracking labeling method is proposed to help data extraction and replace the original tracking model.
- A pipeline method is proposed to complete the highlight video detection and extract the complete video.
- The generation of bright spot videos uses credibility as a marker, and confidence intervals can be freely selected to help users generate videos with different requirements and standards.
- A dataset "HS-FS" is proposed for training highlight video recognition.

2   Related Works

2.1   Action Quality Assessment

Action Quality Assessment (AQA) was proposed before 2016, and several methods like SVR, LSTM was introduced on this task. Most of the existing AQA methods focus on two fields: surgical maneuver assessment and sports video analysis [10,12,13,19,24]. In focusing on sports video analysis, there are mainly two parts: pose-based [10,12] and non-pose methods. Pose-based mainly extracts bone features and then inputs them into the network. Non-pose mainly extracts feature information through DNN models such as I3D or C3D [20], but it requires incredibly high computational costs. With the rise of attention base network and transformer in NLP, some network with attention also developed to solve the AQA tasks.

The Tube Self-Attention Network, in short TSA-Net, is designed for the AQA task. It takes the difference in feature map into consideration, such as foreground and background information. It cost little computing resource, with high flexibility and have the SOTA performance. The Tube module can efficiently generate rich spatiotemporal contextual information by employing sparse feature interactions [21]. Unlike the previous models, the TSA model selected here can effectively perform feature extraction and aggregation and be well qualified for the task of highlight video recognition. Inspire by its excellent performance and efficiency, we adopt TSA mechanism for prediction.

2.2   Figure Skating

Scoring figure skating competitions is a challenging task. A single player match last for 3 to 4 min, which means the input sequence is long. The PCS scores need both visual and audio information, which needs the model to adopt multi-modal input. There are several work and dataset related to figure skating. Xia et al. [23] designed the Skating-Mixer model, combined the video and audio parts of the figure skating scoring competition, and proposed a complete dataset FS1000. Nakano et al. [9] study in the highlight video segmentation of figure skating. The purpose of marking highlight videos is achieved by using 1D-CNN to predict the physiological response of the human eye to suppress the blink frequency at wonderful moments naturally.

There are also several datasets that are related to figure skating. Xu et al. [24] proposes Fis-V data set, but this data set is relatively small in scale and only the women's single competition is included. Liu et al. [8] research in the direction of action recognition, and the FSD-10 dataset is proposed. The dataset contains ISU figure skating contests videos from 2017 to 2019, with a total length of 17 h. For each segment of the competition, they manually do temporal action segmentation on frames, and mark the technical scores of each segmented elements (PCS not included), and also extract the skaters pose data for further training.

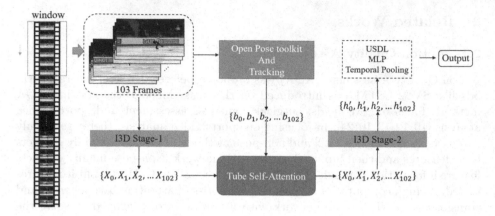

Fig. 1. Structure of the exciting moments generation model (TSA-Net is an existing structure, from the paper [21]).

2.3   Temporal Action Segmentation

Action Segmentation are related to high-level video understanding. The result of the segmentation can be further used in several applications, such as robotics, surveillance, VQA task and sports video scoring. There exist several datasets for this task, most of which labels people's daily action name and the related video segmented part [5,7]. This task has strong relation with temporal information. Colin Lea introduced Temporal Convolutional Networks for Action Segmentation and Detection in 2017, which is capable for capturing data over segment duration and is faster to train than LSTM-based networks. [6] After the transformer and attention is widely used in computer vision area, Yi *et al.* propose ASFormer, introduce the transformer to TAS task, and reach the SOTA benchmark on Breakfast dataset. [26] Junyong Park use Dilation Passing and Reconstruction Network to deal with long range dependencies of long videos. [11] TAS task have several similarity with AQA task, which inspire part of AQA approaches.

3   Approach

3.1   Overview

In order to extract highlights from single-person videos of figure skating, this work uses TSA-Net [21] as the classification network. This work uses a pipeline model to combine the classification model and the generated highlight video model, and the structure is shown in the Fig. 1.

The pipeline model reads the entire video frame by frame and divides it into groups of 103 frames. The bit rate of the video is 25 FPS (which means that each group is $4s + 3$ frames). The difference between the first frame of each group is $k = 25$ frames, and the meaning of k represents whether the subsequent segment is a highlight video after 1s. The feature extraction for each set of videos uses the openpose toolkit [1, 2, 18, 22]. By extracting the character's bones in the image, then wrap all the bone points with the smallest rectangle. The JSON file of the athlete tracking identification box that meets the model input requirements is obtained through this method. The extraction effect of obtaining the tracking identification frame is shown in the Fig. 2:

Fig. 2. Visualization of tracking results of sit spin movements in figure skating competitions.

3.2   Video Segmentation

The duration of a single figure skating competition is between 2 min 10 s and 3 min 20 s, which is a large amount of computation for feature extraction. To have a good performance requires splitting the entire video into smaller pieces. There are several ways to split the video: a certain number of frames into multiple parts and sliding windows. The advantages of cutting video into small parts by the constant frames are that the amount of data for the recognition task can be reduced, and the video segmentation iterations are more manageable than sliding windows. However, the disadvantages of this task are apparent: firstly, a straightforward video segmentation may split an entire scoring action into two or more parts and lead to recognition failure. Secondly, this method has only a single detection for each frame, which can easily make errors in judgment.

The sliding window is a perfect solution to these problems. Firstly, the sliding window maintains a fixed size window. Then move the window in the direction of time with a constant number of frames. So that all the video clips can be combined, thus avoiding the situation where some of the action is divided into two parts and not recognized. Each time point of the video can have numerous possible probability results. These results can represent the athlete's performance in that frame. Based on these advantages of sliding windows, this work chose this method.

3.3   Tube Self-Attention

When extracting feature information from the video, the network needs to focus more on the time-domain details in the video and less on the spatial factors of each frame in the video. In this context, target tracking to obtain the region of the athlete's position can increase the speed with which the model can obtain the primary spatial information. In contrast, the image information obtained through the Tube approach can significantly reduce the computational effort when combined with the time-domain information. The feature matrix X of each frame is generated by I3D-stage1 in the pre-training of the I3D model. The feature matrix X and the target tracking result B got feature matrix Ω through the Spatial-temporal tube generation method. The new feature matrix X' is obtained by self-attention of Ω and X. Then, transfer X' to I3D-Stage2 to obtain H. Afterwards, H is put into the network head MLP block by pooling to obtain the predicted score.

3.4   Frame Scoring

The prediction scores for all periods are generated via the tube self-Attention. This score represents the probability that the video is a highlight moment. However, these clips have numerous duplications. So that there are different scores for each frame. For these scores from different video clips, a value is assigned to each frame in the video by removing the highest and lowest probabilities and averaging them. A threshold filters the consecutive frames to generate the target video.

4   Experiments

4.1   Dataset

The datasets used in this work are FS1000, HS-FS, and FR-FS. The complete single-player game video for detecting the effect of highlight video clips is available in FS1000. On the other hand, the HS-FS dataset provides highlight video clips used to train the model.

Each video in this dataset is a short video of 4 s, resulting from cropping in the highlight video officially provided by ISU. The FR-FS dataset is a dataset for figure skating fall detection proposed in the paper TSA-Net [21].

HS-FS (Highlight Shoot in Figure Skating). Although there are already some excellent datasets [8,23,24] for figure skating scoring, they are all used for scoring long competitions and are not very helpful for identifying and critiquing short movements. On the other hand, the FR-FS dataset focuses mainly on the landing movements of figure skaters. Therefore, this thesis proposes a dataset that marks the highlight videos of figure skating singles competitions. The videos in this dataset are all taken from the official ISU highlights on the YouTube platform. Two hundred videos are included in the whole dataset, each of which is a highlight video. For training, the entire dataset was divided into two parts and later randomly combined with the FR-FS [21] dataset as the training set.

Design Training Set. The dataset size for model training is 155 videos for Train Set and 145 videos for Test Set. These videos are randomly selected from datasets: HS-FS and FR-FS. There are three categories of videos in the training and detection datasets, respectively: highlight videos, fall videos, and general videos.

The reason for designing the training set is that highlight videos are generally complex movements or movements with more scores. Such movements generally have significant changes in body movements. This change is reflected in the time domain as a significant change in action. However, the fall video also generally appears at the end or midway of the more challenging movement. Therefore, we chose to include the fall video as part of the training set to improve the robustness of the model, resulting in better training results.

Feature Extraction. In the data preprocessing, this work uses the openpose toolkit to export the JSON file of the skeleton point by drawing the human skeleton for each frame of the picture. Because in the figure skating video, there will be situations where athletes and spectators appear in the same picture. For this foreground where multiple human bodies are detected, we use the biggest bone frame by calculating the size of the detected human bones (In a game, the focus is always on the athlete, so the athlete's skeletal frame will be the largest). On this basis, the final filtered points are output to the file.

Regarding the question of drawing a block diagram, the method we use is to select the two farthest points and connect the line as the diagonal of the box. Then draw a circle with this as the center, and then select another diagonal line on the circle according to the interval of each rotation of $1°$ until the drawn frame can include all the bone points.

In addition, we also use the function of drawing the smallest box in OpenCV: $cv2.minAreaRect()$ to draw the contrasting frame and select the frame with the smallest area in the two frames. In this way, the optimal selection area is ensured to reduce the computational cost of subsequent calculations.

4.2 Implementation Details

The working platform of this work is based on the Pytorch toolbox [15]. The openpose toolbox [1,2,18,22] is used in data feature extraction. The training of the classification model is based on the architecture provided in TSA-Net Models [21]. The pre-trained feature extractor of I3D [3] is trained on the Kinetics dataset [4], provided by the article TSA-Net [21]. The system environment where the program runs is Intel(R) Xeon(R) CPU E5-2680 v4 @ 2.40 GHz. All models are trained on multiple NVIDIA TITAN V GPUs.

The detection of highlight videos for figure skating needs to involve long-period model detection and movement recognition, and action evaluation of the characters. However, identifying and scoring athletes on a movement-by-movement basis requires more training, a higher quality data set, and more graphics power. Before starting the work, we planned to use C3D, I3D, and other networks to score this task as an AQA task after reviewing the previous literature on the subject, scoring the figure skating video in real-time, and then editing the higher scores.

Before starting the work, we planned to use the C3D and I3D models to score the action as an AQA task after reviewing previous literature on the subject, scoring the figure skating video in real-time, and then editing the higher scoring parts. Nevertheless, after learning about the TSA-Net model, we realized that the model provided by this deep learning network could detect the more significant movements of the athletes exceptionally well. This model was used in the thesis to detect falls of figure skaters, which are remarkably similar to the highlighting movements during figure skating. The action of the falls is characterized by significant stance changes and a certain amount of movement jams, as opposed to exciting moments of high action and excellent fluidity. Furthermore, challenging movements often mean more significant body movements. The high similarity of the detection target made me realize that this would be an excellent choice.

Moreover, TSA-Net proposes the method of Tube self-Attention, which can significantly reduce the space and time required for training the model while the model provides high judgment accuracy. These advantages of the TSA-Net model led me to finally choose to use this model as the primary model for the exciting moment generation task.

Due to the length of the figure skating videos, it is impractical to implement them all into the model for evaluation. The choice was made to use a pipeline approach, detecting a small video section at a time and then shifting the window used for detection backward in time.

In implementing this part of the model, we set up a window of size 103 frames to represent all the content that needs to be examined. After the detection area has been selected, the method calls the existing model, passing in all the images in the current window and the features of the corresponding boxes. Afterward, the model gives the probability of whether the clip is a highlight video or not. Afterward, the window is moved by 25 frames (1 s in the video). And so on, until the back end of the window reaches the end of the video. The predictions for all the video clips are saved as a list and output as a result.

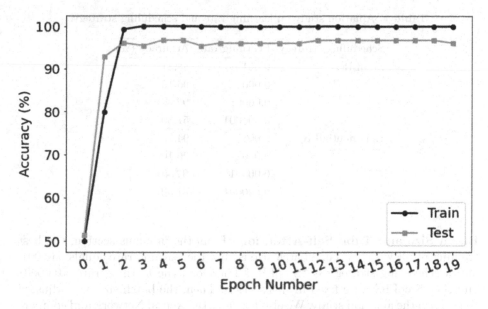

Fig. 3. The relationship between training accuracy and Epoch.

4.3 Results During Training

The training of the model is based on an expansion of the content of the FR-FS dataset. The training set is divided into two parts, Train Set and Test Set. Both sections contain highlights from moments, down moments, and general moments. The highlight videos in these data were obtained from ISU's intercepts of the excellent videos available on the YouTube platform, as mentioned in the previous sub-section. All three components of the dataset used in training account for approximately 33% of the total. The final training result show as Fig. 3.

4.4 Ablation Study

Learning Rate and Scheduling Strategy. The ablation study was carried out by adjusting the learning rate and the scheduling strategy, respectively, while controlling the batch size as 2. There are two scheduling strategies to choose from, namely "StepLR" and "ExponentialLR". The "StepLR" method is an equal interval dynamic adjustment method, which means the learning rate is decayed by the gamma parameter (0.5) every five epochs. The "ExponentialLR" method is a dynamic adjustment of the current learning rate according to gamma for each epoch, equivalent to an exponential operation with gamma as the base and epoch as the power, where the gamma is 0.9.

The best result (97.40%) is obtained when the learning rate equals 0.00001 by comparing the different Scheduling Strategies (Table 1).

Table 1. Ablation study on learning rate and scheduling strategy.

Scheduling strategy	Learning rate	Accuracy (%)
StepLR	0.001	88.31
	0.0001	96.10
	0.00001	**97.40**
	0.000001	51.30
ExponentialLR	0.001	94.16
	0.0001	96.10
	0.00001	**97.40**
	0.000001	51.30

Batch Size and Tube Self-Attention. From the previous section, the best training result with the same batch size is that the learning rate equals 0.00001, and a scheduling strategy is "StepLR". Therefore, the learning rate = 0.00001 and the "StepLR" were fixed in this section. Then, the batch size was adjusted to perform the ablation study. We also consider the Neural Network and compare different situations: with Tube Self-Attention or not.

In all cases, the case with Tube Self-Attention was better than the case which does not have. The best training results for both network structures were achieved when batch size = 8 (Table 2).

Table 2. Ablation study on Tube Self-Attention Model.

Structure	Batch Size			
	2	3	4	8
Using Tube Self-Attention	97.40	99.35	99.35	**99.35**
Not use Tube Self-Attention	94.81	98.05	98.70	98.70

Result on Different Dataset. This part is the Ablation Study of the Dataset. Compare these two datasets based on different Neural NetWork structures (Table 3).

Training on the HS-FS dataset has better results for different network structures than training on FR-FS.

Table 3. Ablation study on different Dataset.

DataSet	With Tube Self-Attention	No Tube Self-Attention
FR-FS	98.56	66.35
HS-FS	99.35	98.75

4.5   Results in the Singles Figure Skating Competition

In testing how well the model worked, we chose a random selection of single matches from the FS1000 dataset as the input raw video for generating the highlight videos. The resultant video of the task output is measured and scored. One of the match videos is used as an example, and the possibilities for each period are plotted as Fig. 4. All the possibilities corresponding to the time are filtered to obtain the video clips that meet the required threshold.

The time points were checked against the scenes in the original video. It Can be seen from the diagram that the selected clips are more in line with the exciting moments.

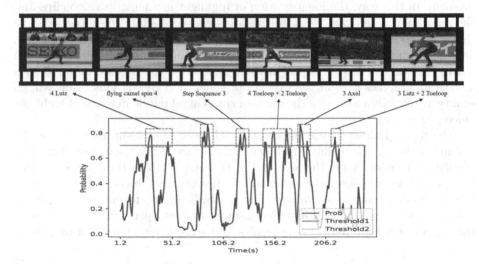

Fig. 4. The relationship between time and the probability of highlights, where Threshold 1 is 0.7 and Threshold 2 is 0.8.

As the definition of a highlight moment is a very subjective rating, we have chosen to use a manual rating for this final generated video on whether it is a highlight video or not. We searched for 50 participants for this evaluation (These participants were all students from the University of Southern Technology). The participants' knowledge of figure skating was as follows: 30 had little knowledge of figure skating, and the remaining 20 participants had experienced watching figure skating and knew the scoring system. For the evaluation, three match-generated highlight videos are provided, with two videos generated for each match according to a threshold of 0.7 and 0.8.

The results of the manual judging were as follows:

For videos generated with 0.8 as the threshold, 78% of participants thought they matched the highlight videos. 10% thought most segments were highlight videos, but some did not highlight moments. 8% thought they were somewhat of a highlight compilation but not very convincing. The remaining 4% thought these did not belong to highlight videos.

For videos generated with 0.8 as the threshold, 92% considered them to be highlight video compilations. 6% considered the usual clips to be present in the generated videos. 2% did not consider them to be countable as highlight videos.

5   Conclusion

In this paper, we perform a scan recognition of the entire video in the form of a sliding window by adapting the original VOT module in TSA-Net to use the model as the classification core for solving the highlight video generation problem. In this way, the identification of highlight moments in video clips and the generation of the final video integration were successfully accomplished. The choice of model makes recognition in this task more efficient and, in addition, detection using the pre-trained model does not require high GPU power, which means that this method of highlight video generation can be used on a PC with a separate graphics card at the expense of generation speed. This result will go some way towards addressing the needs of the general public in terms of highlight video generation.

The method chose to use the official ISU video of close-up moments as the training dataset. The results from the training are quite good, but there is a significant problem with the size of the training set: the total video volume is only 298 video clips as training input. However, no high-quality highlight video dataset is currently available for this task. In the future, efforts will be made to expand the highlight video dataset and to optimize TSA-Net, with the expectation that the training results and recognition speed will be further improved.

References

1. Cao, Z., Hidalgo Martinez, G., Simon, T., Wei, S., Sheikh, Y.A.: OpenPose: real-time multi-person 2D pose estimation using part affinity fields. IEEE Trans. Pattern Anal. Mach. Intell. **43**, 172–186 (2019)
2. Cao, Z., Simon, T., Wei, S.E., Sheikh, Y.: Realtime multi-person 2D pose estimation using part affinity fields. In: CVPR (2017)
3. Carreira, J., Zisserman, A.: Quo Vadis, action recognition? A new model and the kinetics dataset. In: Proceedings of the IEEE Conference on Computer Vision and Pattern Recognition, pp. 6299–6308 (2017)
4. Kay, W., et al.: The kinetics human action video dataset. arXiv preprint arXiv:1705.06950 (2017)
5. Kuehne, H., Arslan, A., Serre, T.: The language of actions: recovering the syntax and semantics of goal-directed human activities. In: Proceedings of the IEEE Conference on Computer Vision and Pattern Recognition, pp. 780–787 (2014)
6. Lea, C., Flynn, M.D., Vidal, R., Reiter, A., Hager, G.D.: Temporal convolutional networks for action segmentation and detection. In: Proceedings of the IEEE Conference on Computer Vision and Pattern Recognition, pp. 156–165 (2017)

7. Li, Y., Ye, Z., Rehg, J.M.: Delving into egocentric actions. In: Proceedings of the IEEE Conference on Computer Vision and Pattern Recognition, pp. 287–295 (2015)
8. Liu, S., et al.: FSD-10: a dataset for competitive sports content analysis. arXiv preprint arXiv:2002.03312 (2020)
9. Nakano, T., Sakata, A., Kishimoto, A.: Estimating blink probability for highlight detection in figure skating videos. arXiv preprint arXiv:2007.01089 (2020)
10. Pan, J.H., Gao, J., Zheng, W.S.: Action assessment by joint relation graphs. In: Proceedings of the IEEE/CVF International Conference on Computer Vision (ICCV), October 2019
11. Park, J., Kim, D., Huh, S., Jo, S.: Maximization and restoration: action segmentation through dilation passing and temporal reconstruction. Pattern Recognit. **129**, 108764 (2022)
12. Parmar, P., Morris, B.: Action quality assessment across multiple actions. In: 2019 IEEE Winter Conference on Applications of Computer Vision (WACV), pp. 1468–1476. IEEE (2019)
13. Parmar, P., Morris, B.T.: What and how well you performed? A multitask learning approach to action quality assessment. In: Proceedings of the IEEE/CVF Conference on Computer Vision and Pattern Recognition (CVPR), June 2019
14. Parmar, P., Tran Morris, B.: Learning to score Olympic events. In: Proceedings of the IEEE Conference on Computer Vision and Pattern Recognition Workshops, pp. 20–28 (2017)
15. Paszke, A., et al.: Automatic differentiation in PyTorch (2017)
16. Ping, Q., Chen, C.: Video highlights detection and summarization with lag-calibration based on concept-emotion mapping of crowd-sourced time-sync comments. arXiv preprint arXiv:1708.02210 (2017)
17. Rochan, M., Krishna Reddy, M.K., Ye, L., Wang, Y.: Adaptive video highlight detection by learning from user history. In: Vedaldi, A., Bischof, H., Brox, T., Frahm, J.-M. (eds.) ECCV 2020. LNCS, vol. 12366, pp. 261–278. Springer, Cham (2020). https://doi.org/10.1007/978-3-030-58589-1_16
18. Simon, T., Joo, H., Matthews, I., Sheikh, Y.: Hand keypoint detection in single images using multiview bootstrapping. In: CVPR (2017)
19. Tang, Y., et al.: Uncertainty-aware score distribution learning for action quality assessment. In: Proceedings of the IEEE/CVF Conference on Computer Vision and Pattern Recognition (CVPR), June 2020
20. Tran, D., Bourdev, L., Fergus, R., Torresani, L., Paluri, M.: Learning spatiotemporal features with 3d convolutional networks. In: Proceedings of the IEEE International Conference on Computer Vision, pp. 4489–4497 (2015)
21. Wang, S., Yang, D., Zhai, P., Chen, C., Zhang, L.: TSA-Net: tube self-attention network for action quality assessment. In: Proceedings of the 29th ACM International Conference on Multimedia, pp. 4902–4910 (2021)
22. Wei, S.E., Ramakrishna, V., Kanade, T., Sheikh, Y.: Convolutional pose machines. In: CVPR (2016)
23. Xia, J., et al.: Audio-visual MLP for scoring sport (2022). https://doi.org/10.48550/ARXIV.2203.03990, https://arxiv.org/abs/2203.03990
24. Xu, C., Fu, Y., Zhang, B., Chen, Z., Jiang, Y.G., Xue, X.: Learning to score figure skating sport videos. IEEE Trans. Circuits Syst. Video Technol. **30**(12), 4578–4590 (2019)

25. Xu, M., Wang, H., Ni, B., Zhu, R., Sun, Z., Wang, C.: Cross-category video highlight detection via set-based learning. In: Proceedings of the IEEE/CVF International Conference on Computer Vision (ICCV), pp. 7970–7979, October 2021
26. Yi, F., Wen, H., Jiang, T.: AsFormer: transformer for action segmentation. arXiv preprint arXiv:2110.08568 (2021)

Memory Enhanced Spatial-Temporal Graph Convolutional Autoencoder for Human-Related Video Anomaly Detection

Sibo Luo, Shangshang Wang, Yuan Wu, and Cheng Jin$^{(\boxtimes)}$

School of Computer Science, Fudan University, Shanghai, China
{sbluo20,shangshangwang20,wuyuan,jc}@fudan.edu.cn

Abstract. Human-related video anomaly detection is a challenging problem due to unclear definitions of anomalies and insufficient training data. Pose-based methods have attracted widespread attention by exploiting highly structured skeleton data that are robust to background noise and illumination changes. However, existing methods use recurrent neural network to extract temporal information while ignoring the spatial dependencies between skeleton joints, which are crucial to reason behaviors. Additionally, commonly-used methods are expected to produce larger reconstruction errors for anomalies than normal samples to achieve anomaly detection. But in practice, due to the strong generalization ability of these models, they fail to obtain significant reconstruction errors for abnormal samples, resulting in missing anomalies. In this paper, we propose a novel framework Memory Enhanced Spatial-Temporal Graph Convolutional Autoencoder(Mem-STGCAE) to address these problems. We use spatial-temporal graph convolution as an encoder to capture discriminative features in spatial and temporal domains. We enhance the autoencoder with a memory module that records normal patterns. The encoded representation is used as a query to retrieve the most relevant patterns. Thus, the decoder reconstructs anomalies using normal patterns, resulting in significant reconstruction errors. Different from traditional autoencoders, two branches of decoder are introduced to reconstruct past and predict future pose sequences respectively. Extensive experiments on two challenging video anomaly datasets, ShanghaiTech and IITB-Corridor, show that our proposed network outperforms other state-of-the-art methods.

Keywords: Anomaly detection · Spatial-temporal graph convolution · Memory networks · Skeleton

1 Introduction

Human-related video anomaly detection aims to discover unexpected events, which has been a challenging task in video analysis. It defines anomalies as

© The Author(s), under exclusive license to Springer Nature Switzerland AG 2022
S. Yu et al. (Eds.): PRCV 2022, LNCS 13536, pp. 665–677, 2022.
https://doi.org/10.1007/978-3-031-18913-5_51

unpredictable behaviors that are different from existing patterns or break the regularity of the movement. For example, chasing among normally walking people is often seen as an abnormal behavior. Since anomalies are rare and difficult to collect, the anomaly detection task is often formulated as an unsupervised learning problem.

Most current methods utilize appearance features which are extracted from whole frames [1,5,7,8,22] or localized on image patches [18,20,23]. However, appearance features are high-dimensional data containing lots of noisy cues that obscure important information about the abnormal event. Furthermore, appearance features are also affected by illumination changes and camera shake, limiting the performance of such methods.

In recent years, pose estimation algorithms have made significant progress. Compact and strongly structured pose features have gradually attracted the attention of researchers [6,9,11,14,15,17]. Compared with appearance-based features, pose features contain rich semantics and descriptions of human behaviors, making them more suitable for human-related video anomaly detection. Morais et al. [14] decomposed the motion of human skeletons into global and local components and used a message-passing encoder-decoder LSTM architecture to reconstruct and predict pose sequences. Although LSTMs can capture temporal dynamics, the fully connected operator within LSTM will destroy the spatial relationships between joints. The limitation of their model is that it neglects the spatial patterns of the skeleton, which is critical for understanding and reasoning behavior. Additionally, reconstruction-based methods are expected to produce larger reconstruction errors for abnormal behaviors than normal ones after training on normal data. However, this assumption does not always hold in practice. It has been observed that sometimes the model generalizes so well that it also reconstructs anomalous behavior well, leading to missing anomalies.

To mitigate the aforementioned limitations, we propose a novel framework Memory Enhanced Spatial-Temporal Graph Convolutional Autoencoder (Mem-STGCAE) for human-related video anomaly detection. As shown in Fig. 2, the architecture mainly consists of an encoder, a memory module, and two decoders. We propose to take advantage of GCNs [24] for analyzing structured data, which skeletons belong. We utilize spatial-temporal graph convolutional encoder to extract human action representations of pose sequences. Unlike the single-encoder-single-decoder architecture used in typical autoencoders [19], the network contains both reconstruction and prediction branches, respectively. The dual-decoder structure jointly forces the encoder to learn compact representations for reconstructing and predicting. The reconstruction and prediction errors are then calculated as anomaly scores for detecting anomalies. Inspired by [4], we use a memory module to enhance the autoencoder. The memory module records various patterns of normal data as memory items. The encoded representation is not fed directly into the decoder, but used it as a query to retrieve the most relevant memory items. With the trained memory module, only the normal patterns can be retrieved for reconstruction and prediction. Therefore, normal samples can naturally be well reconstructed and predicted. Instead, the encoding of the abnormal input will be represented by the retrieved normal patterns, resulting in a significant reconstruction and prediction error on anomalies.

The main contributions of this work are summarized as follows: 1. We utilize the spatial-temporal graph convolutional encoder to strengthen the behavior representation by learning spatial-temporal features and adopt the dual-decoder to reconstruct the past and predict the future simultaneously. 2. We introduce the memory module to record the various patterns of normal data. The encoded representation used for reconstruction and prediction will be replaced by the retrieved normal patterns, resulting in significant errors on anomalies. 3. Experimental results show that our approach outperforms other state-of-the-art methods on two challenging video anomaly datasets, ShangahaiTech [7] and IITB-Corridor [17] (Fig. 1).

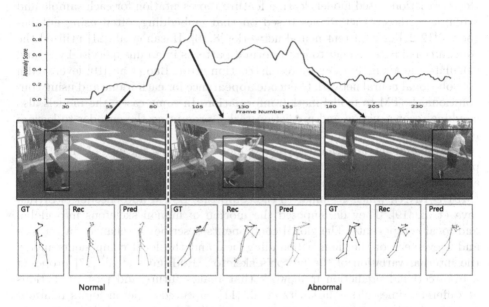

Fig. 1. An illustration of how the proposed approach captures abnormal events. The top row is the frame-level anomaly score curve obtained by computing the error between the generated pose and the ground truth. In the middle row, the jumping behavior in the right frames is identified as an anomalous event in the pavement. The last row compares the ground truth (red) with the reconstructed pose (blue) and the predicted pose (yellow) in normal or abnormal patterns. (Color figure online)

2   Related Work

2.1   Video Anomaly Detection

Video anomaly detection has attracted great interest from computer vision researchers in recent years. Traditional methods used hand-crafted features, such as 3D gradient [13], Histogram of Oriented Gradient (HOG) [2] and Histogram of Flow (HOF) [3]. However, these traditional methods are not ideal when dealing with complex anomalous patterns in large-scale video anomaly detection datasets.

In recent years, a series of works tackle the problem using deep learning based models. Generative-based methods mainly use variational autoencoders or GANs to model the distribution of the normal data. Jain et al. [6] proposed a conditional variational autoencoder based framework to make stochastic future pose trajectory predictions by the hybrid training strategy comprising of self-supervised and unsupervised learning. Liu et al. [7] used an adversarial neural network with gradient features and optical flow features to predict future frames. Although optical flow can capture motion information by describing pixel changes between adjacent frames, extracting optical flow requires huge computation and time. Reconstruction-based models learn a feature representation for each sample and attempt to reconstruct frames based on that embedding, often using autoencoders [12,21] or recurrent neural networks [8,10]. Hasan et al. [21] utilized the convolutional autoencoder to learn normal patterns in an unsupervised way and calculate the anomaly score by reconstruction error. Luo et al. [10] leveraged a convolutional neural network to encode appearance for each frame and using convolutional LSTM to model motion information. In some cases, the models also combine reconstruction and prediction tasks, prompting the encoder to learn a more rich representation [12,14,25].

Pose-based methods have attracted more attention because of their interpretability and robustness to complex backgrounds. Morais et al. [14] proposed a model called Message-Passing Encoder-Decoder Recurrent Neural Network (MPED-RNN), which is similar to the composite LSTM autoencoder of Srivastava et al. [19]. They decomposed the motion of human skeletons into global and local components. The global components describe the changes in the size and movement of the human bounding box and the local components model the internal variation of the person's skeleton. Rodrigues et al. [17] proposed a bi-directional prediction framework that makes future and past predictions at different timescales. Markovitz et al. [11] captured skeleton joints relationships by graph convolutional network and applied deep embedded clustering to anomaly detection. However, their method is inflexible and demands empirically determining the number of clusters in different scenes. Moreover, Pang et al. [15] applied the Transformer framework to capture the dependencies between arbitrary pairwise pose components from diverse perspectives.

2.2 Graph Convolutional Networks

In order to effectively extract features from structured graph data, Graph Convolutional Networks have been developed and explored extensively. The implementation of graph convolutional neural networks can be summarized into two categories: spatial GCNs and spectral GCNs. Spectral GCNs transform graph signals and apply spectral filters on spectral domains. For spatial GCNs, the methods directly construct a convolution filter on the spatial domain for feature extraction. In this work, inspired by [11], we exploit the spatial-temporal GCNs [24] to learn inherent spatial-temporal representations from pose sequences.

2.3 Memory Networks

Memory networks have attracted increasing interest in solving different problems. For the anomaly detection task, Gong et al. [4] propose a Memory-augmented Autoencoder for anomaly detection in order to suppress the generalization capability of AE. Park et al. [16] present a more compact and separate memory that can be updated during testing. In this work, we also exploit the memory module to restrain the reconstruction and prediction capability on anomalies by recording various patterns of normal data in the memory.

3   Method

In this section, we describe the details of the proposed model. The overall architecture of the proposed Mem-STGCAE is illustrated in Fig. 2. Firstly, we obtained the pose trajectories from the videos by pose estimation and tracking algorithm. Then we extract features from both spatial and temporal dimensions by spatial-temporal graph convolutional encoder. Instead of directly feed to decoders, we use the encoded representation as a query to retrieve normal patterns in the memory items. Finally, we feed the memory-enhanced representation to the decoder which has two branches that make past reconstruction and future prediction, respectively. The reconstructed and predicted pose sequences are compared with past and future pose sequences to calculate the anomaly scores for detecting anomalies.

3.1   Preprocessing

We use human pose trajectory as the input, represented by spatial-temporal graph. The spatial-temporal graph $G = (V, E)$ is constructed on a pose sequence with N joints and T frames. In the graph, the node set $V = \{v_{ti} \mid t = 1, \ldots, T, i = 1, \ldots, N\}$ includes all the joints in a pose sequence, and the edge set E contains the intra-body and inter-frame edges of naturally connected human body joints. The edges between joints are represented by an adjacency matrix $\mathbf{A} \in R^{N \times N}$ where initially $\mathbf{A_{i,j}} = 1$ if an edge directs from v_i to v_j and 0 otherwise. As the input, the feature vector on a node at time t consists of coordinate vectors of body joints, which is represented as $F_{v_t} = \{(x_t^i, y_t^i) \mid i = 1, \ldots, N\}$. We follow the prepossessing operation in [14] to decompose the original pose into local component and global component. Then the width and height of the skeleton's bounding box are utilized to normalize the local component $f^{l,i} = (x^{l,i}, y^{l,i})$.

$$x^g = \frac{\max(x^i) + \min(x^i)}{2}; \quad y^g = \frac{\max(y^i) + \min(y^i)}{2} \\ w = \max(x^i) - \min(x^i); \quad h = \max(y^i) - \min(y^i) \tag{1}$$

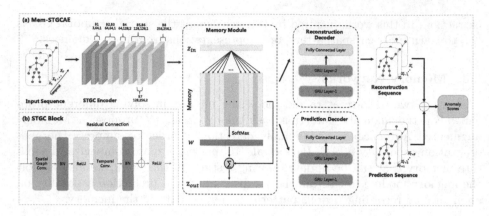

Fig. 2. Architecture overview. Mem-STGCAE owns a single-encoder-dual-decoder architecture with a memory module. STGC Encoder is stacked by multiple layers of STGC Block with different numbers of input channels, output channels, and strides. The memory module is followed by two branches of decoder for reconstructing and predicting pose sequences respectively. Reconstruction and prediction errors are then calculated as anomaly scores for detecting anomalies.

$$x^{l,i} = \frac{x^i - x^g}{w}; \quad y^{l,i} = \frac{y^i - y^g}{h} \tag{2}$$

Finally, the sequence of the normalized local component $F^l = \left\{ \left(x_t^{l,i}, y_t^{l,i} \right) \mid t = 1, \ldots, T, i = 1, \ldots, N \right\}$ is taken as the input of Mem-STGCAE.

3.2 Network Architecture

Spatial-Temporal Graph Convolutional Encoder. We employ the spatial-temporal graph to model the structured information between joints in both the spatial and temporal dimensions. We adopt the same implementation of spatial graph convolution as in [24], formulated as follows:

$$GCN\left(F^l\right) = \sigma\left(\Lambda^{-\frac{1}{2}} \hat{A} \Lambda^{-\frac{1}{2}} F^l \mathbf{W}\right) \tag{3}$$

where $\Lambda \in R^{N \times N}$ is the degree matrix of $\hat{A} = A + I$. I is an identity matrix describing self-connection of joints. $\mathbf{W}$ is the matrix of trainable parameters formed by stacking the weight vectors of multiple output channels C'. σ is a non-linear activation function.

The spatial graph convolution transforms the input tensor F^l with a shape of $C \times T \times N$ into the output tensor with a shape of $C' \times T \times N$. Then the convolution for the temporal dimension performs the $K_t \times 1$ convolution on the $C' \times T \times N$ feature maps. As shown in Fig. 2(b), the STGC block consists of a spatial GCN and a temporal GCN, each of them followed by a batch normalization layer and a ReLU layer. Residual connection is adopted to stabilize the training.

The Spatial-Temporal Graph Convolutional Encoder is composed of 8 layers of STGC block. The numbers of output channels for each block are 64, 64, 64, 128, 128, 128, 256, and 256. The strides of the 4-th and the 7-th temporal convolution layers are set to 2 as pooling layer. Finally, a global pooling was performed to get the encoded representation z for each sequence and then feed it into memory module.

Memory Module. The proposed memory module consists of a memory bank for recording the prototypical encoded patterns and an attention-based addressing operator for accessing the memory. The memory bank is designed as a matrix $\mathbf{M} \in R^{N \times C}$ which contains N items of dimension C recording various patterns of normal data. Similar to [4], we adopt an attention-based addressing scheme that computes attention weights w based on the similarity of the memory items m_i and the query z. Each weight w_i is computed as follows:

$$w_i = \frac{\exp\left(\frac{\mathbf{z}\mathbf{m}_i^\top}{\|\mathbf{z}\|\|\mathbf{m}_i\|}\right)}{\sum_{j=1}^{N} \exp\left(\frac{\mathbf{z}\mathbf{m}_j^\top}{\|\mathbf{z}\|\|\mathbf{m}_j\|}\right)} \tag{4}$$

For each query z, we represent the query by a sum of similar memory items in the memory and obtain the aggregated feature $\hat{\mathbf{z}}$ as follows.

$$\hat{\mathbf{z}} = \mathbf{w}\mathbf{M} = \sum_{i=1}^{N} w_i \mathbf{m}_i \tag{5}$$

The aggregated features are subsequently used to reconstruct and predict pose sequences.

Reconstruction and Prediction Decoders. In this work, we use the dual-decoders architecture to conduct different tasks, reconstruct and predict pose sequences. The two branches of the decoder have the same architecture and adopt two-layers Gated Recurrent Units (GRU) for its fewer parameters and similar performance to LSTM. The dual-decoder structure jointly enforces the encoder to learn compact representations. Specifically, we use the training strategy proposed by [19] to make the decoder fully dependent on the hidden state passed by the encoder. We use the fully-connected layers to project the hidden states to local component $\hat{F}^l$. Finally, the two outputs of decoder are concatenated to generate perceptual feature $\hat{F}^p$ in the original image space.

3.3   Loss Function

To train our network, we use a combined loss by a weighted sum:

$$L_{total} = \lambda_l L_l + \lambda_p L_p + \lambda_m L_m \tag{6}$$

where $\lambda_l, \lambda_p, \lambda_m$ are corresponding weights to the losses. The local component loss L_l and perceptual loss L_p defined by

$$L_* = \frac{1}{T} \sum_{t=1}^{T} \left\| \hat{F}_t^* - F_t^* \right\|_2^2 + \frac{1}{P} \sum_{t=T}^{T+P} \left\| \hat{F}_t^* - F_t^* \right\|_2^2 \tag{7}$$

where $*$ represents l or p, T and P denotes the reconstruction and prediction length, respectively. The perceptual loss L_p constrains the model to produce the normal sequences in the image coordinate system. Furthermore, we impose the pose motion loss that enforces temporal consistency and improves the quality of reconstructed and predicted motions.

$$L_{motion} = \frac{1}{T} \sum_{t=1}^{T} \left\| \delta\hat{F}_t^p - \delta F_t^p \right\|_1 + \frac{1}{P} \sum_{t=T}^{T+P} \left\| \delta\hat{F}_t^p - \delta F_t^p \right\|_1 \tag{8}$$

where $\delta\hat{F}_t^p = \left| \hat{F}_t^p - F_{t-1}^p \right|$ denotes the motion between adjacent frames.

3.4   Anomaly Detection

In this section, we present the details for anomaly detection on the testing data. To calculate the anomaly score of each frame in the video, the process is divided into the following several steps:

1. Extract segments: Similar to the training phase, we take a sliding window of size T and stride 1 to extract the testing pose sequences
2. Calculate pose anomaly score: We use the perceptual feature $\hat{F}^p$ to calculate reconstruction and prediction errors as anomaly scores. The errors are calculated as:

$$error_n^* = \left\| \hat{F}_{n,t}^{p,*} - F_{n,t}^{p,*} \right\|_2^2 \tag{9}$$

where $*$ represents rec or $pred$, $\hat{F}_{n,t}^p$ denotes the pose instance n at frame t.
3. Calculate frame anomaly score: Since each frame may contain multiple pose instances, we choose the instance with the largest error. Finally, we combine the reconstruction and prediction errors of the t frame as frame-level anomaly score for detecting anomalies:

$$score_t = \max_{n \in S_t} \left(error_n^{rec} \right) + \max_{n \in S_t} \left(error_n^{pred} \right) \tag{10}$$

where S_t stands for the set of pose instances appearing in the frame t.

4   Experiments

4.1   Datasets

We conduct extensive experiments on two challenging video anomaly detection datasets, ShanghaiTech [7] and IITB-Corridor [17], to demonstrate the effectiveness of the proposed model. Since the pose-based approach pays more attention to human-related anomalies, we also test our method on HR-ShanghaiTech [14] and HR-Corridor proposed by [6]. The training set of these datasets contains only normal events, while the test set contains normal and abnormal events.

ShanghaiTech Campus Dataset. It contains 130 abnormal events and over 270,000 training frames in 13 scenes with complex light conditions and camera angles, making it challenging for current video anomaly detection methods. Anomalies in the dataset include behaviors such as riding a bike, pushing and loitering.

IITB-Corridor Dataset. The dataset is captured in IIT Bombay campus under a single-camera setup. It contains over 300,000 training frames and 181,567 testing frames where the normal activities are usually walking and standing. It consists of group activities such as fighting, and chasing as well as single person activities such as loitering and cycling.

4.2 Implementation Details

In our experiments, we divide the input pose sequence into fixed-length clips by sliding window with size 12 and stride 6. In addition, we apply the Adam optimizer with $\beta_1 = 0.9$ and $\beta_2 = 0.999$. The initial learning rate is 0.001 and adjusted by the cosine annealing method. The batch size is 256 and trained on ShanghaiTech and IITB-Corridor for 30 and 50 epochs, respectively.

Table 1. Frame-level AUC performance comparisons with other methods on two challenging datasets, ShanghaiTech and IITB-Corridor. HR is the subset of the dataset, which only contains human-related samples.

Methods	ShanghaiTech	HR-ShanghaiTech	IITB-Corridor	HR-IITB-Corridor
Conv-AE [12]	70.40	69.80	–	–
Frame-Pred [7]	72.80	72.70	64.65	–
Normal graph [9]	76.50	74.10	–	–
GEPC [11]	75.20	75.60	–	–
Multi-timescale [17]	76.03	77.04	67.12	–
MPED-RNN [14]	73.40	75.40	64.27	68.07
PoseCVAE [6]	74.90	75.70	67.34	70.60
Ours	**77.80**	**78.72**	**69.30**	**75.63**

4.3 Evaluation

Following the work [14], we use frame-level ROC AUC for performance evaluation. We compare our method with other approaches on two popular video anomaly detection datasets, ShanghaiTech and IITB-Corridor, and the results are shown in Table 1. The methods [7,12] in the first two rows are appearance-based methods and the latter methods [6,9,11,14,17] are pose-based. We achieve state-of-the-art performance on both two datasets, including Human-Related (HR) and original datasets. Furthermore, to better analyze the anomaly detection results, we visualize the anomaly score curve on ShanghaiTech video clips. As shown in Fig. 3, the anomaly scores increase immediately when some anomalies appear in the video frame.

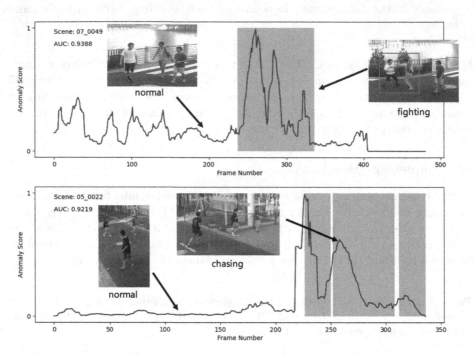

Fig. 3. Anomaly score curves under two scenes in the ShanghaiTech dataset. Red regions represent ground truth anomalous frames. The sampled video frames display the normal or abnormal events. (Color figure online)

4.4   Ablation Studies

We conducted ablation experiments to demonstrate the effectiveness of each proposed module in Mem-STGCAE. We use LSTM Autoencoder with GRU cell as the baseline. STGCAE replaces the baseline encoder with spatial-temporal graph convolutional, and the decoder has a similar structure. Mem-STGCAE enhances the autoencoder by adding a memory module between the encoder and decoder of STGCAE. The results in Table 2 demonstrate that STGCAE outperforms the baselines thanks to the spatial information of the skeleton. Furthermore, the memory-enhanced STGCAE significantly improves the performance by 2.05% compared to STGCAE, proving that the memory module is necessary and can effectively improve the performance. In addition, the combination of reconstructing and predicting branches outperforms either of the two branches, demonstrating that the dual decoder structure is useful for detecting abnormalities.

Table 2. Ablation study about the components of Mem-STGCAE on ShanghaiTech. Rec: reconstruction only, Pred prediction only, and Rec+Pred: the fusion of reconstruction and prediction.

Variants	ShanghaiTech		
	Rec.	Pred.	Rec. + Pred.
LSTM AE	73.61	73.72	73.90
STGCAE	75.46	75.62	75.75
Mem-STGCAE	**76.47**	**76.56**	**77.80**

5 Conclusions

In this paper, we developed a framework with spatial-temporal graph convolution to encode spatial and temporal representations and two branches of decoder to reconstruct and predict pose sequences. Furthermore, we apply the memory module to augment the autoencoder for the first time in pose-based approaches. Experimental results on the ShanghaiTech dataset and IITB-Corridor dataset show that the proposed framework outperforms other state-of-the-art models. In the future work, we plan to combine pose features with appearance and detect abnormal events of human-object interactions.

Acknowledgement. This work was supported by National Natural Science Foundation of China under Grant No. 61732004.

References

1. Chong, Y.S., Tay, Y.H.: Abnormal event detection in videos using spatiotemporal autoencoder. In: Cong, F., Leung, A., Wei, Q. (eds.) ISNN 2017. LNCS, vol. 10262, pp. 189–196. Springer, Cham (2017). https://doi.org/10.1007/978-3-319-59081-3_23
2. Dalal, N., Triggs, B.: Histograms of oriented gradients for human detection. In: 2005 IEEE Computer Society Conference on Computer Vision and Pattern Recognition (CVPR 2005), vol. 1, pp. 886–893. IEEE (2005)
3. Dalal, N., Triggs, B., Schmid, C.: Human detection using oriented histograms of flow and appearance. In: Leonardis, A., Bischof, H., Pinz, A. (eds.) ECCV 2006. LNCS, vol. 3952, pp. 428–441. Springer, Heidelberg (2006). https://doi.org/10.1007/11744047_33
4. Gong, D., et al.: Memorizing normality to detect anomaly: memory-augmented deep autoencoder for unsupervised anomaly detection. In: Proceedings of the IEEE/CVF International Conference on Computer Vision, pp. 1705–1714 (2019)

5. Hasan, M., Choi, J., Neumann, J., Roy-Chowdhury, A.K., Davis, L.S.: Learning temporal regularity in video sequences. In: Proceedings of the IEEE Conference on Computer Vision and Pattern Recognition, pp. 733–742 (2016)
6. Jain, Y., Sharma, A.K., Velmurugan, R., Banerjee, B.: PoseCVAE: anomalous human activity detection. In: 2020 25th International Conference on Pattern Recognition (ICPR), pp. 2927–2934. IEEE (2021)
7. Liu, W., Luo, W., Lian, D., Gao, S.: Future frame prediction for anomaly detection-a new baseline. In: Proceedings of the IEEE Conference on Computer Vision and Pattern Recognition, pp. 6536–6545 (2018)
8. Luo, W., Liu, W., Gao, S.: A revisit of sparse coding based anomaly detection in stacked RNN framework. In: Proceedings of the IEEE International Conference on Computer Vision, pp. 341–349 (2017)
9. Luo, W., Liu, W., Gao, S.: Normal graph: spatial temporal graph convolutional networks based prediction network for skeleton based video anomaly detection. Neurocomputing **444**, 332–337 (2021)
10. Luo, W., Liu, W., Gao, S.: Remembering history with convolutional LSTM for anomaly detection. In: 2017 IEEE International Conference on Multimedia and Expo (ICME), pp. 439–444. IEEE (2017)
11. Markovitz, A., Sharir, G., Friedman, I., Zelnik-Manor, L., Avidan, S.: Graph embedded pose clustering for anomaly detection. In: Proceedings of the IEEE/CVF Conference on Computer Vision and Pattern Recognition, pp. 10539–10547 (2020)
12. Medel, J.R., Savakis, A.: Anomaly detection in video using predictive convolutional long short-term memory networks. arXiv preprint arXiv:1612.00390 (2016)
13. Mehran, R., Oyama, A., Shah, M.: Abnormal crowd behavior detection using social force model. In: 2009 IEEE Conference on Computer Vision and Pattern Recognition, pp. 935–942. IEEE (2009)
14. Morais, R., Le, V., Tran, T., Saha, B., Mansour, M., Venkatesh, S.: Learning regularity in skeleton trajectories for anomaly detection in videos. In: Proceedings of the IEEE/CVF Conference on Computer Vision and Pattern Recognition, pp. 11996–12004 (2019)
15. Pang, W., He, Q., Li, Y.: Predicting skeleton trajectories using a skeleton-transformer for video anomaly detection. Multimedia Syst. **28**, 1481–1494 (2022)
16. Park, H., Noh, J., Ham, B.: Learning memory-guided normality for anomaly detection. In: Proceedings of the IEEE/CVF Conference on Computer Vision and Pattern Recognition, pp. 14372–14381 (2020)
17. Rodrigues, R., Bhargava, N., Velmurugan, R., Chaudhuri, S.: Multi-timescale trajectory prediction for abnormal human activity detection. In: Proceedings of the IEEE/CVF Winter Conference on Applications of Computer Vision, pp. 2626–2634 (2020)
18. Sabokrou, M., Fayyaz, M., Fathy, M., Klette, R.: Deep-cascade: cascading 3D deep neural networks for fast anomaly detection and localization in crowded scenes. IEEE Trans. Image Process. **26**(4), 1992–2004 (2017)
19. Srivastava, N., Mansimov, E., Salakhudinov, R.: Unsupervised learning of video representations using LSTMs. In: International Conference on Machine Learning, pp. 843–852. PMLR (2015)
20. Wang, T., et al.: Generative neural networks for anomaly detection in crowded scenes. IEEE Trans. Inf. Forensics Secur. **14**(5), 1390–1399 (2018)
21. Xie, J., Girshick, R., Farhadi, A.: Unsupervised deep embedding for clustering analysis. In: International Conference on Machine Learning, pp. 478–487. PMLR (2016)

22. Dan, X., Yan, Y., Ricci, E., Sebe, N.: Detecting anomalous events in videos by learning deep representations of appearance and motion. Comput. Vis. Image Underst. **156**, 117–127 (2017)
23. Xu, D., Ricci, E., Yan, Y., Song, J., Sebe, N.: Learning deep representations of appearance and motion for anomalous event detection. arXiv preprint arXiv:1510.01553 (2015)
24. Yan, S., Xiong, Y., Lin, D.: Spatial temporal graph convolutional networks for skeleton-based action recognition. In: Thirty-Second AAAI Conference on Artificial Intelligence (2018)
25. Zhao, Y., Deng, B., Shen, C., Liu, Y., Lu, H., Hua, X.-S.: Spatio-temporal autoencoder for video anomaly detection. In: Proceedings of the 25th ACM International Conference on Multimedia, pp. 1933–1941 (2017)

Background Suppressed and Motion Enhanced Network for Weakly Supervised Video Anomaly Detection

Yang Liu[1,2]([⊠]), Wanxiao Yang[2], Hangyou Yu[2], Lin Feng[1,2], Yuqiu Kong[1,2], and Shenglan Liu[1,2]

[1] School of Innovation and Entrepreneurship, Dalian University of Technology, Dalian 116024, China
{ly,fenglin,yqkong,liusl}@dlut.edu.cn
[2] Faculty of Electronic Information and Electrical Engineering, Dalian University of Technology, Dalian 116024, China
{yang224425,yuhangyou01}@mail.dlut.edu.cn

Abstract. Weakly supervised video anomaly detection (VAD) is a significant and challenging task in the surveillance video analysis field, locating anomalous motion frames using only video-level label information. In general, weakly supervised VAD mainly faces two obstacles. Firstly, the greatly changed background always causes false detection. Secondly, the motion changes are implicit in real-world surveillance videos caused by unsuitable focal distance, illumination, etc. This paper proposes a background suppressed and motion enhanced network (BSMEN) for Weakly Supervised VAD to solve the problems. The BSMEN utilizes the multi-head self-attention mechanism to construct a triple branch framework to suppress the influence from the background and enhance the motion significance in the VAD process. Moreover, a motion discrimination sequence extraction (MDSE) module is devised to locate the anomaly motion frames more accurately in the BSMEN. Extensive experiments on two mainstream VAD evaluation datasets validate that BSMEN outperforms state-of-the-art weakly supervised VAD methods.

Keywords: Video anomaly detection · Weakly supervised · Background suppressed · Motion enhanced

1 Introduction

Video anomaly detection (VAD) aims to temporally or spatially Video anomaly detection (VAD) aims to temporally or spatially localize anomalous events in videos. Although great efforts have been paid to video anomaly detection for many years, it is still very complex and challenging. The main reason is that

This research is supported in part by the grants from the National Natural Science Foundation of China (No. 62006037, No. 61972074, No. 62172073), and in part by the National Key Research and Development Program of China (No. 2021YFB3301904).

(a) redundant background   (b) changing background

(c) unsuitable illumination   (d) unsuitable focal distance

Fig. 1. (a) represents redundant background frames in the video. (b) represents background changes caused by traffic flow. (c) represents implicit anomalous frames of fights caused by low illumination. (d) represents implicit anomalous frames of clothes stealing caused by unsuitable focal distance. The above scenes will bring obstacles for the weakly supervised VAD tasks. Hence, it is necessary to suppress the influence from the background and enhance the significance of the motions in the VAD process.

anomalous events are rare, diverse, and inexhaustible, dramatically complicating distinguishing abnormal events from normal events in video surveillance analysis. Currently, video anomaly detection is mainly utilized in surveillance video analysis, such as fall detection, traffic accident detection, violence detection, etc. VAD with intelligent technologies can significantly reduce the burden of manual observation and analysis of surveillance videos.

Obtaining temporal and spatial anomaly annotations for a large number of videos is quite challenging and stressful. Therefore, previous works mainly focus on unsupervised video anomaly detection, which is usually trained on normal unlabeled videos. Another category of video anomaly detection is weakly supervised VAD with easily available video-level labels. Compared with unsupervised VAD, weakly supervised VAD has video-level labels and can be trained on anomalous videos, but the consequent problem is that it is challenging to locate anomalies in anomalous videos. In general, video anomaly detection is mainly based on analyzing changes in appearance and motion [16]. However, the background in the videos always brings considerable influence to the analysis of the motion changes, such as the sudden changes in the background will always cause false detection, as shown in Fig. 1(b). In addition, considering the impact of the unsuitable illumination and focal distance, existing VAD methods based on deep learning cannot focus on the anomalous region well but tend to treat some background information as anomalies instead. An illustration of these problems is shown in Fig. 1. Hence, it is necessary to suppress the influence from the background and enhance the significance of the motions in the VAD process. This paper proposes a background suppressed and motion enhanced network (BSMEN) for Weakly Supervised VAD. The BSMEN utilizes the multi-head attention mechanism to construct a triple branch framework to suppress the influence from the background and enhance the motion significance in the VAD process. The BSMEN models the background and the motions separately to suppress background information and improve motion significance in the anomalous score calculation.

Unlike most existing methods that apply attention-based weights on the features of the frames in videos, the BSMEN devises a motion discrimination sequence extraction (MDSE) module to generate the motion discrimination sequence (MDS) to represent the original anomalies probability of each frame [17]. Based on MDS, the attention-based weights in BSMEN can be directly applied to the final anomaly evaluation scores.

In summary, the contributions of this paper are three folds:

1. We propose a background suppressed and motion enhanced network (BSMEN) by utilizing the multi-head self-attention mechanism, which can effectively eliminate the influence from the background and enhance the significance of the motion in the VAD process.
2. Devises a motion discrimination sequence extraction (MDSE) to generate the motion discrimination sequence, based on which the anomaly evaluation scores can be calculated more precisely, and the anomalous events can be located more accurately.
3. Extensive evaluation results demonstrate that our approach outperforms the state-of-the-art methods on two benchmark datasets.

2   Related Work

2.1   Unsupervised Video Anomaly Detection

Generally, deep learning based methods for video anomaly detection (VAD) can be divided into two categories: unsupervised and weakly supervised anomaly detection methods [8]. Unsupervised deep learning based video anomaly detection methods realize anomalies localization through extracting the pattern changes of the motions. By extracting the patterns, unsupervised VAD methods can be divided into two main types: reconstruction-based and prediction-based methods. Reconstruction-based methods [3,6,14] mainly train an autoencoder-based network to extract the changing patterns based on the assumption that anomalous behavior cannot be well reconstructed. During the test, the patterns with significant reconstruction errors are considered anomalous behaviors. Based on the belief that anomalous behaviors are unpredictable, prediction-based methods [10,12,23] predict future frames based on the current and the past frames. During the test, the patterns with significant prediction errors are considered anomalous behaviors. There are also hybrid approaches [13] for video anomaly detection. In addition, [5] introduces a memory module to record the prototype patterns of the motions. For a given input, the encoded result is utilized as a query to retrieve the most similar item in the memory module.

2.2 Weakly Supervised Video Anomaly Detection

Weakly supervised VAD is a task of anomaly detection under video labels. Compared with unsupervised methods, easily available video-level labels are utilized in the training process to enhance the localization accuracy for the anomalies. Researchers make great efforts from different perspectives to take full advantage of the video-level labels. Sultani et al. [18] introduce a new large-scale video dataset with video-level labels and propose a deep multiple instance ranking framework for weakly supervised VAD. Zhu et al. [27] observe that motion information is essential for video anomaly detection and introduce an attention mechanism based temporal multiple instance learning model to generate motion-aware features. Liu et al. [11] find that the background information would weaken model learning of anomaly patterns. Thus, they offer the bounding box annotation of UCF-Crime dataset to explore background bias for video anomaly detection. Zhong et al. [26] treat the weakly supervised VAD as a supervised learning task under noisy labels and apply a graph convolutional neural network to clean noise labels. However, the iterative optimization between noise label cleaner and action classifier is slow and inefficient.

3 Background Suppressed and Motion Enhanced Network (BSMEN)

To detect anomalous events in the videos efficiently, this paper proposes a background suppressed and motion enhanced network (BSMEN, as shown in Fig. 2) to suppress the influence from the background and enhance significant features of the motions. The BSMEN adopts a self-attention based triple branch module to enhance the significance of the motions. To further explicitly locate the anomalies, the BSMEN generates a motion discrimination sequence (MDS) to represent the original anomalies probability of each frame. Based on MDS, the final anomaly scores can effectively suppress the influence from the background and enhance significant features.

3.1 Motion Discrimination Sequence Extraction (MDSE)

Unlike most existing attention-based methods that apply significant weight to the features, the BSMEN uses the weight on the initial anomalous probabilities

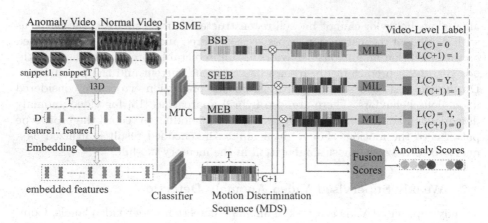

Fig. 2. Overview of the BSMEN framework. BSB, SFEB, and MEB represent the background suppression branch, the salient feature extraction branch, and the motion enhancement branch, respectively.

and devises the motion discrimination sequence extraction module to generate a motion discrimination sequence to support the calculation of the final anomaly scores.

Given an untrimmed video V, divide it into non-overlapping segments $\{v_1, v_2, \cdots, v_T\}$. In the training process, the anomalous video is denoted as positive bag B_a, and its corresponding video-level label is $Y = 1$. The normal video is defined as negative bag B_n, and its corresponding video-level label is $Y = 0$. This paper utilizes the I3D feature extractor to extract the original feature representations of the non-overlapping segments like previous works [2], which are represented as $\{F_1, F_2, \cdots, F_T\}$. Since different videos have different time lengths, we follow the previous setting [18] in the training process and divide each training video into the same number of segments. Stack all segment features to represent the video features $F \in \mathbb{R}^{T \times D}$.

Since the original features extracted from the pre-trained model without fine-tuning cannot be well adapted to the task. We utilize an embedding layer to map the features to a task-specific feature space. The specific implementation is to sequentially utilize the Conv1D, the ReLU activation, and the dropout functions. Thus, the embedding layer can be described as follows:

$$X = Dropout(ReLU(Conv1D(F))) \tag{1}$$

The embedded video feature is fed into a classification network to obtain the motion discrimination sequence. The sequence can distinguish simple normal motions and anomalies but cannot identify semantically ambiguous movements well. Therefore, the network utilizes a fully connected network to map the embedded video feature to the category space and generate the initial MDS. The output

$MDS \in \mathbb{R}^{T \times (C+1)}$ resents the anomalous probability of each segment over time. MDS is expressed as follows:

$$MDS = FC(X) \tag{2}$$

3.2 Background Suppressed and Motion Enhanced Module (BSMEM)

In addition, to accurately detect anomalous motion frames and suppress the influence from the background, the BSMEN adopts the background suppressed and motion enhanced nodule (BSMEM, shown in Fig. 2) to realize this goal. BSMEM adopts three branches based on the self-attention mechanism to separate the video's background, original features, and motions and designs a multi-resolution temporal convolution module (MTC) to enhance the separation effect. The summary of the MTC is shown in Fig. 3.

The BSMEM comprises three parallel branches to realize the separation of the background, the original features, and the significant motions. The branches are the background suppression branch (BSB), significant feature extraction branch (SFEB), and motion enhancement branch (MEB), respectively. The BSB branch can extract background information from the motions and suppress the influence of the background in the final anomalies evaluation. The SFEB can extract important information from both the motions and background. The MEB can effectively extract significant motion information. To effectively utilize the three branches, We expand a video-level background label to generate a new video-level label of $y = \{0,1\} \in \{0,1\}^{C+1}$, where the C dimension represents the original video-level label and the $C + 1$ dimension represents the background label, in this paper $C = 1$.

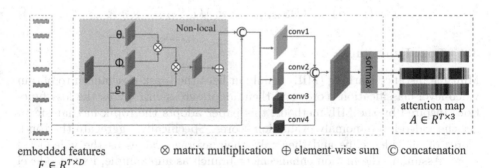

embedded features $F \in R^{T \times D}$ $\otimes$ matrix multiplication $\oplus$ element-wise sum $\copyright$ concatenation

Fig. 3. Structure of the multi-resolution temporal convolution module.

Global information and local information are both important in anomaly detection. Therefore, we utilize the self-attention mechanism [20] to obtain the global information and multi-scale dilated convolution pyramids to obtain the local information at different scales. The specific implementation of MTC is as follows. The multi-scale dilated convolution pyramid consists of conv1, conv2, conv3, and conv4 with different kernel sizes and dilation rates. Firstly, the embedded video feature X is fed into a self-attention based non-local neural network on obtaining the video feature $\tilde{x}$ with global information. Then, input embedded video feature X and video feature $\tilde{x}$ into multi-scale dilated convolution pyramids, respectively, and concatenate the results over channels to formulate fusion feature $\bar{x}$. Finally, we utilize a convolutional layer and softmax normalization to calculate the probability of each segment containing the background, significant feature, and significant motion information. The output is expressed as attention map $A = (A_{MEB}, A_{SFEB}, A_{BSB}) \in \mathbb{R}^{T \times 3}$. We represent the Attention Map as follows, where $A_{MEB} \in \mathbb{R}^{T \times 1}$, and A_{SFEB} and A_{BSB} are the same size.

Based on the above-obtained attention maps, three motion discrimination sequences can be calculated according to the attention mechanism, denoted as MDS_{MEB}, MDS_{SFEB}, and MDS_{BSB}, respectively. Formally, $MDS_{MEB} \in \mathbb{R}^{T \times (C+1)}$ is expressed as follows.

$$MDS_{MEB} = MDS \times A_{MEB} \qquad (3)$$

MDS_{SFEB} and MDS_{BSB} can be obtained in the same way. MDS_{MEB} focuses on significant motions and suppresses the influence of the other information. MDS_{SFEB} only pays attention to semantically ambiguous frames and ignores easily distinguishable action frames, MDS_{BSB} only pays attention to background information. MDS_{MEB}, MDS_{SFEB} and MDS_{BSB} are equivalent to the classification score of each segment over time in the training process. In the inference stage, given the test video, we combine MDS_{MEB} and MDS_{SFEB} as the anomaly score, which can be described as follows: α is a hyperparameter utilized to connect the MDS_{MEB} and MDS_{SFEB}.

$$s = (1 - \alpha) \times MDS_{MEB} + \alpha \times MDS_{SFEB}, s \in \mathbb{R}^T \qquad (4)$$

3.3   Loss Function

Multiple instance learning (MIL) mainly utilizes the top-k mechanism to obtain video-level classification scores and then adopts cross-entropy as the loss function. Inspired by the MIL methods, this paper adopts the top-k mechanism to get the video-level anomaly evaluation scores. Specifically, aggregate the top-k scores of all video clips and then take their average values as the video-level score. Assuming the motion enhancement branch as an example, its video-level score s^{MEB} is as follows,

$$s^{MEB} = \frac{1}{k_{MEB}} \max_{\Omega_k(MDS_{MEB}) \subseteq \Omega(MDS_{MEB})} \sum_{i \in \Omega_k(MDS_{MEB})} MDS_{MEB}(i) \qquad (5)$$

Classification Loss. The cross-entropy loss $\mathcal{L}_{cls}^{MEB}$ of the motion enhancement branch (MEB) is formulated as follows:

$$\mathcal{L}_{cls}^{MEB} = \sum_{i=1}^{C+1} y_i^{MEB} \log s_i^{MEB} \tag{6}$$

The $\mathcal{L}_{cls}^{SFEB}$ and $\mathcal{L}_{cls}^{BSB}$ are calculated similarly. We manually design video-level labels $y^{MEB} = [L(C) = Y, L(C+1) = 0]$ to enhance the significant motions. Then, we set the video-level labels of the SFEB as $y^{SFEB} = [L(C) = Y, L(C + 1) = 1]$ and the BSB as $y^{BSB} = [L(C) = 0, L(C + 1) = 1]$. MDS_{SFEB} and MDS_{BSB} are more concerned with the semantically ambiguous motions and background information, respectively, rather than motion information.

We express the total classification loss as follows,

$$\mathcal{L}_{cls} = \mathcal{L}_{cls}^{MEB} + \mathcal{L}_{cls}^{SFEB} + \mathcal{L}_{cls}^{BSB} \tag{7}$$

Feature Separation Loss. We introduce a feature separation loss adapted from the hinge-loss formulation to distinguish the background information, significant features, and enhanced motions. X_{MEB}, X_{SFEB} and X_{BSB} represent video-level motion enhanced feature, extracted significant feature, and background feature, respectively. For simplicity, X_{MEB} is described as follows,

$$X_{MEB} = \frac{1}{k_{MEB}} \max_{\Omega_k(X) \subseteq \Omega(X)} \sum_{i \in \Omega_k(X)} x_i \tag{8}$$

To make the video features more distinguishable for motions and background, we introduce the feature separation loss $\mathcal{L}_{fs}$ at feature norm space. Feature separation loss can be obtained from these features. Formally, feature separation loss is formulated as follows:

$$\mathcal{L}_{fs}^{MEB} = \max(0, margin- \parallel X_{MEB} \parallel^2 + \parallel X_{SFEB} \parallel^2) \tag{9}$$

$$\mathcal{L}_{fs}^{SFEB} = \max(0, margin- \parallel X_{SFEB} \parallel^2 + \parallel X_{BSB} \parallel^2) \tag{10}$$

$$\mathcal{L}_{fs}^{BSB} = \parallel X_{BSB} \parallel^2 \tag{11}$$

$$\mathcal{L}_{fs} = (\mathcal{L}_{fs}^{MEB} + \mathcal{L}_{fs}^{SFEB} + \mathcal{L}_{fs}^{BSB})^2 \tag{12}$$

$\parallel \cdot \parallel^2$ is the feature norm function, and margin is a hyperparameter representing the degree of feature norm separation. The total loss function can be formulated as follows. λ is a hyperparameters.

$$\mathcal{L} = \mathcal{L}_{cls} + \lambda \cdot \mathcal{L}_{fs} \tag{13}$$

4   Experiments

4.1   Datasets

UCF-Crime. UCF-Crime [18] dataset is a large-scale dataset of 128 h of videos. It consists of 1900 long untrimmed surveillance videos which cover 13 real world anomalies, namely abuse, arrest, arson, assault, road accident, burglary, explosion, fighting, robbery, shooting, stealing, shoplifting, and vandalism. The training set consists of 810 anomalous videos and 800 normal videos, and the testing set consists of 140 anomalous videos and 150 normal videos.

ShanghaiTech. ShanghaiTech [12] contains 13 different scenes from fixed angles of the street surveillance videos. It contains 330 training videos and 107 testing ones with 130 anomalous events, including skateboarders, bikers, and people fighting. The original training set only has normal videos for unsupervised anomaly detection. To adapt to the weakly supervised methods, Zhong et al. [26] reorganized the videos into 238 training videos and 199 testing videos. We follow the setting utilized in [26] to conduct experiments on ShanghaiTech dataset.

4.2   Evaluation Metric

In the field of anomaly detection, a popular evaluation criterion is the Area Under the Curve (AUC) [9] of Receiver Operating Characteristic (ROC) [28]. The ROC curve is created by plotting the true positive rate against the false positive rate at various threshold settings. The Area Under the Curve (AUC) is a performance metric for a ROC curve. The higher the AUC value, the more accurate the detection. We apply frame-level Area Under the Curve (AUC) as the evaluation metric.

4.3   Implementation Details

Following [18], a video is divided into 32 ($T = 32$) non-overlapping snippets. Snippet feature is extracted from I3D pretrained networks on Kinetics-400 dataset. The features $f \in \mathbb{R}^{2048}$ are extracted from the $Mixed_5c$ layer of the I3D network. We utilize the Adam optimizer [7] with the learning rate of 10^{-4} and a weight decay of 5×10^{-4}. Batch size is set to 32, containing 16 normal and 16 anomalous videos. In our experiments, k_{MEB}, k_{SFEB}, k_{BSB} and *margin* are set to 3, 10, 10 and 50, respectively. α is set to 0.1 for ShanghaiTech and 0 for UCF-Crime dataset. λ is set to 5×10^{-5} since feature separation loss has a higher magnitude compared with other loss terms. All experiments are performed on an NVIDIA GeForce RTX 2080 Ti GPU using PyTorch.

4.4   Comparison with State-of-the-Art Methods

We conducted experiments on UCF-Crime dataset and ShanghaiTech dataset to validate the effectiveness of our proposed method. The frame-level AUC results on UCF-Crime and ShanghaiTech datasets are shown in Table 1.

Table 1. Quantitative comparisons with existing methods on UCF-Crime and Shang-haiTech.

Supervision	Publish	Method	Feature	UCF-Crime	Shanghai-Tech
Unsupervised	ICCV 2019	Mem-AE [5]	–	–	71.2
	CVPR 2020	MNAD [15]	–	–	70.5
	CM MM 2020	VEC [22]	–	–	74.8
	AAAI 2021	AMCM [1]	–	–	73.7
	ICCV2021	HF2-VAD [13]	–	–	76.2
Weakly supervised	CVPR 2018	Sultani et al. [18]	C3D RGB	75.41	–
	ICIP 2019	Zhang et al. [25]	C3D RGB	78.66	82.50
	–	Motion-aware [27]	PWC-Flow	79.00	–
	CVPR 2019	GCN-anomaly [26]	TSN RGB	82.12	84.44
	ICME 2020	AR-Net [19]	I3D RGB+Flow	–	91.24
	ECCV 2020	Wu et al. [21]	I3D RGB	82.44	–
	ECCV 2020	CLAWS [24]	C3D RGB	83.03	89.67
	CVPR 2021	MIST [4]	I3D RGB	82.30	94.83
	–	Ours	I3D RGB	**83.63**	**96.34**

The BSMEN can effectively suppress the influence from the background and enhance the significance of the motions in VAD through a triple branch framework. The evaluation results on the UCF-Crime dataset show that our model significantly improves the AUC score compared with the benchmark model by Sultani et al. [18]. Furthermore, our method outperforms the supervised method of Liu et al. [11], which explores background bias for anomaly detection. The AUC score improves from 82.00 to 83.63, with a relative gain of 1.63%. Our method also outperforms CLAWS [24], which utilizes normalcy suppression for anomaly detection. The AUC score increases from 83.03 to 83.63, and the relative gain is 0.60%.

For the ShanghaiTech dataset, which contains scenes from fixed-angle street videos, motion changes are always implicit in these scenes. The BSMEN can effectively enhance the significance of the motions in the VAD process, which pays more attention to the motion. As is shown in Table 1, our model achieves remarkable improvement compared to previous methods. Notably, compared to MIST [4], the AUC score of our model significantly improves from 94.83 to 96.34 with a relative gain of 1.53%. These results verify that our proposed method is more effective than previous work on both benchmarks. The qualitative results of our approach are shown in Fig. 4.

4.5 Ablation Studies

In this section, we further explore the impact of three branches in BSMEN to evaluate the effectiveness of background suppression and motion enhancement. For simplicity, the ablation experiments are conducted on the UCF-Crime

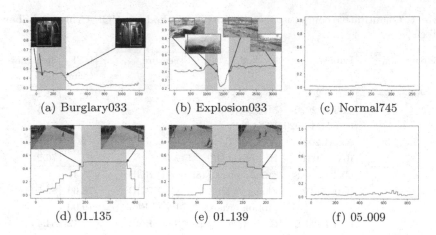

(a) Burglary033   (b) Explosion033   (c) Normal745

(d) 01_135   (e) 01_139   (f) 05_009

Fig. 4. Qualitative results of our method on UCF-Crime dataset (anomaly videos: Burglary033, Explosion33, normal videos: Normal745) and ShanghaiTech dataset (anomaly videos: 1_135, 01_139, normal videos: 05_009). The colored window shows the ground truth of the anomalous event region. The horizontal axis represents frame number, and the vertical axis represents anomaly detection score.

Table 2. Ablation studies on UCF-Crime.

SFEB	MEB	BSB	AUC
–	–	–	0.8042
–	✓	✓	0.8257
✓	–	✓	0.5185
✓	✓	–	0.4998
✓	✓	✓	0.8363

dataset. The results in Table 2 demonstrate that the designed three branches are effective and indispensable.

We do not employ background suppressed and motion enhanced module at first, only adopt the embedding layer and the classifier as the benchmark. The AUC score is 80.42. Since the motion enhanced branch and significant feature extraction branch are needed to obtain the score, we utilize the method of removing one branch and keeping the rest branches for the ablation experiment. From the results in Table 2, removing the SFEB will weaken the final result, but the effect is insignificant. However, losing the MEB will seriously impair the final result. This indicates that action information is vital for anomaly detection. The absence of the BSB also severely weakens the final result since the method is designed based on background separation. In general, with the facilitation of BSMEN, the AUC score improves from 80.42 to 83.63, with a relative gain of 3.21%.

5   Conclusions

In this paper, we propose a BSMEN framework by adopting the multi-head self-attention mechanism to construct a triple branch framework to suppress the influence from the background and enhance the motion significance in the VAD process. Moreover, to locate the anomaly motion frames more accurately, a motion discrimination sequence extraction module is devised in the BSMEN, which facilitates the BSMEM to apply significant weights directly on the anomalous scores and improves the detection accuracy. Remarkably, our method makes significant improvements on two benchmark datasets.

References

1. Cai, R., Zhang, H., Liu, W., Gao, S., Hao, Z.: Appearance-motion memory consistency network for video anomaly detection. In: Proceedings of the AAAI Conference on Artificial Intelligence, vol. 35, pp. 938–946 (2021)
2. Carreira, J., Zisserman, A.: Quo vadis, action recognition? a new model and the kinetics dataset. In: proceedings of the IEEE Conference on Computer Vision and Pattern Recognition, pp. 6299–6308 (2017)
3. Chong, Y.S., Tay, Y.H.: Abnormal event detection in videos using spatiotemporal autoencoder. In: Cong, F., Leung, A., Wei, Q. (eds.) ISNN 2017. LNCS, vol. 10262, pp. 189–196. Springer, Cham (2017). https://doi.org/10.1007/978-3-319-59081-3_23
4. Feng, J.C., Hong, F.T., Zheng, W.S.: Mist: Multiple instance self-training framework for video anomaly detection. In: Proceedings of the IEEE/CVF Conference on Computer Vision and Pattern Recognition, pp. 14009–14018 (2021)
5. Gong, D., et al.: Memorizing normality to detect anomaly: memory-augmented deep autoencoder for unsupervised anomaly detection. In: Proceedings of the IEEE/CVF International Conference on Computer Vision, pp. 1705–1714 (2019)
6. Hasan, M., Choi, J., Neumann, J., Roy-Chowdhury, A.K., Davis, L.S.: Learning temporal regularity in video sequences. In: Proceedings of the IEEE Conference on Computer Vision and Pattern Recognition, pp. 733–742 (2016)
7. Kingma, D.P., Ba, J.: Adam: a method for stochastic optimization. arXiv preprint arXiv:1412.6980 (2014)
8. Kiran, B.R., Thomas, D.M., Parakkal, R.: An overview of deep learning based methods for unsupervised and semi-supervised anomaly detection in videos. J. Imaging 4(2), 36 (2018)
9. Li, W., Mahadevan, V., Vasconcelos, N.: Anomaly detection and localization in crowded scenes. IEEE Trans. Pattern Anal. Mach. Intell. 36(1), 18–32 (2013)
10. Liu, B., Chen, Y., Liu, S., Kim, H.S.: Deep learning in latent space for video prediction and compression. In: Proceedings of the IEEE/CVF Conference on Computer Vision and Pattern Recognition, pp. 701–710 (2021)
11. Liu, K., Ma, H.: Exploring background-bias for anomaly detection in surveillance videos. In: Proceedings of the 27th ACM International Conference on Multimedia, pp. 1490–1499 (2019)
12. Liu, W., Luo, W., Lian, D., Gao, S.: Future frame prediction for anomaly detection-a new baseline. In: Proceedings of the IEEE Conference on Computer Vision and Pattern Recognition, pp. 6536–6545 (2018)

13. Liu, Z., Nie, Y., Long, C., Zhang, Q., Li, G.: A hybrid video anomaly detection framework via memory-augmented flow reconstruction and flow-guided frame prediction. In: Proceedings of the IEEE/CVF International Conference on Computer Vision, pp. 13588–13597 (2021)
14. Nguyen, T.N., Meunier, J.: Anomaly detection in video sequence with appearance-motion correspondence. In: Proceedings of the IEEE/CVF International Conference on Computer Vision, pp. 1273–1283 (2019)
15. Park, H., Noh, J., Ham, B.: Learning memory-guided normality for anomaly detection. In: Proceedings of the IEEE/CVF Conference on Computer Vision and Pattern Recognition, pp. 14372–14381 (2020)
16. Ramachandra, B., Jones, M., Vatsavai, R.R.: A survey of single-scene video anomaly detection. IEEE Trans. Pattern Anal. Mach. Intell. **44**, 2293–2312 (2020)
17. Shou, Z., Gao, H., Zhang, L., Miyazawa, K., Chang, S.-F.: Autoloc: Weakly-supervised temporal action localization in untrimmed videos. In: Ferrari, V., Hebert, M., Sminchisescu, C., Weiss, Y. (eds.) ECCV 2018. LNCS, vol. 11220, pp. 162–179. Springer, Cham (2018). https://doi.org/10.1007/978-3-030-01270-0_10
18. Sultani, W., Chen, C., Shah, M.: Real-world anomaly detection in surveillance videos. In: Proceedings of the IEEE Conference on Computer Vision and Pattern Recognition, pp. 6479–6488 (2018)
19. Wan, B., Fang, Y., Xia, X., Mei, J.: Weakly supervised video anomaly detection via center-guided discriminative learning. In: 2020 IEEE International Conference on Multimedia and Expo (ICME), pp. 1–6. IEEE (2020)
20. Wang, X., Girshick, R., Gupta, A., He, K.: Non-local neural networks. In: Proceedings of the IEEE Conference on Computer Vision and Pattern Recognition, pp. 7794–7803 (2018)
21. Wu, P., et al.: Not only look, but also listen: learning multimodal violence detection under weak supervision. In: Vedaldi, A., Bischof, H., Brox, T., Frahm, J.-M. (eds.) ECCV 2020. LNCS, vol. 12375, pp. 322–339. Springer, Cham (2020). https://doi.org/10.1007/978-3-030-58577-8_20
22. Yu, G., et al.: Cloze test helps: Effective video anomaly detection via learning to complete video events. In: Proceedings of the 28th ACM International Conference on Multimedia, pp. 583–591 (2020)
23. Yu, J., Lee, Y., Yow, K.C., Jeon, M., Pedrycz, W.: Abnormal event detection and localization via adversarial event prediction. IEEE Trans. Neural Netw. Learn. Syst. **33**, 3572–3586 (2021)
24. Zaheer, M.Z., Mahmood, A., Astrid, M., Lee, S.-I.: CLAWS: Clustering assisted weakly supervised learning with normalcy suppression for anomalous event detection. In: Vedaldi, A., Bischof, H., Brox, T., Frahm, J.-M. (eds.) ECCV 2020. LNCS, vol. 12367, pp. 358–376. Springer, Cham (2020). https://doi.org/10.1007/978-3-030-58542-6_22
25. Zhang, J., Qing, L., Miao, J.: Temporal convolutional network with complementary inner bag loss for weakly supervised anomaly detection. In: 2019 IEEE International Conference on Image Processing (ICIP), pp. 4030–4034. IEEE (2019)
26. Zhong, J.X., Li, N., Kong, W., Liu, S., Li, T.H., Li, G.: Graph convolutional label noise cleaner: Train a plug-and-play action classifier for anomaly detection. In: Proceedings of the IEEE/CVF Conference on Computer Vision and Pattern Recognition, pp. 1237–1246 (2019)
27. Zhu, Y., Newsam, S.: Motion-aware feature for improved video anomaly detection. arXiv preprint arXiv:1907.10211 (2019)
28. Zweig, M.H., Campbell, G.: Receiver-operating characteristic (roc) plots: a fundamental evaluation tool in clinical medicine. Clin. Chem. **39**(4), 561–577 (1993)

Dirt Detection and Segmentation Network for Autonomous Washing Robots

Shangbin Guan[1,2] and Gang Peng[1,2(✉)]

[1] Key Laboratory of Image Processing and Intelligent Control,
Ministry of Education, Wuhan, China
[2] School of Artificial Intelligence and Automation, Huazhong University of Science
and Technology, Wuhan, China
penggang@hust.edu.cn

Abstract. In the field of industrial, robots are becoming a modern method to perform automatic washing on large industrial components while detecting dirt. Therefore, the detection and segmentation of dirt have a great impact on optimizing the effects and improving quality of washing by modern washing robots. We propose DDSN (Dirt Detection and Segmentation Network) in this paper which improves the SVDD (Support Vector Data Description), using neural networks to obtain the optimal kernel function of SVDD, so that training images with no dirt can be mapped to the smallest hypersphere in the feature space. In dirt detection and segmentation, the distance between the test images and the centers of the corresponding hypersphere is defined as the feature value, and the dirt scores of the pixels can be obtained. Before training of dirt dataset, we use a larger anomaly detection dataset named MVTecAD which is also the one-class classification to pretrain the feature extraction network, which makes up for the lack of samples in the dirt dataset and speeds up the convergence of the model. Afterwards, we transfer the feature extraction network to training the dirt dataset of large industrial components. The results show that the methods proposed in this paper performs well in detection and segmentation of both MVTecAD dataset and dirt dataset of large industrial components.

Keywords: Robot vision · Dirt detection · Dirt segmentation

1 Introduction

In the field of large industrial components washing such as car components, industrial product components, high-speed train bogies and other components, the working conditions are quite poor. The method of manual washing is not only relatively large in labor costs, but also low in labor efficiency. At the same time, it also threatens the physical and mental health of workers and even causes occupational diseases. A typical way of using robots for washing is to first use robots to carry a high-pressure water gun for washing. However, after cleaning, there are usually parts of components which have not been cleaned, or there are areas that have not been cleaned, for the reason that the cleaning equipment does not have dirt detection. Therefore, the method above has poor cleaning consistency, and it is difficult to clean the dirt in the dead corners, threaded holes, and other small places. What's more, it not only wastes a lot of water and the cleaning quality is hard to ensure. With the development of more advanced cleaning robots, dirt detection has been introduced [1] and has become an increasingly important research topic. With the help of dirt detection, the washing robots perform better in finding the location of dirt, so that it is no longer blind [2] when performing washing tasks, which solves the problem of wasting water, in addition, it solves the problem of dirt dead corners by washing robots without dirt detection.

However, a great number of methods proposed before use rectangular frames to mark the dirt objects when performing detecting tasks, which can only obtain the approximate position information of the dirt in the image samples. If we wanted to obtain more accurate location of dirt, dirt segmentation of components is of vital importance. Therefore, a methods of dirt detection and segmentation network for large industrial components based on improved deep SVDD is proposed in this paper, which can achieve more accurate positioning and segmentation at the pixel level. In summary, the main contributions of this paper are:

- The main idea of the method proposed in this paper is to generate the minimum enclosing hypersphere in the feature space by training the image samples with no dirt in the training set, so only a few binary masks of negative samples in the test set need to be produced, which greatly reduces the work of dataset making;
- Before training the large industrial components dirt dataset, we first use the MVTecAD anomaly dataset to pre-train the feature extraction network, which makes up for the lack of samples in the dirt dataset of large industrial components, and the method proposed in this paper shows good performance of detection and segmentation on both datasets;
- We extend Deep SVDD to image blocks, which not only solves the problem of difficulty in selecting the SVDD kernel function, but also realizes the segmentation of dirt at the pixel level, which improves the accuracy of the washing robots to locate dirt.

2   Relate Works

When it comes to dirt detection, the more common method is to use some object detection methods like YOLOv3 [3] and Faster-RCNN [4], which are commonly used in multi-class classification. Richard Bormann et al. [5] improved the YOLOv3 and proposed DirtNet in his paper, which make the cleaning robots perform well in Dirt Detection. Daniel Canedo [6] proposes a vision system based on the YOLOv5 [7] framework for detecting dirty spots on the floor, and proves it is able to use synthetic data for the training step and effectively detect dirt on real dataset. Another method used to apply traditional object detection algorithms like [8–11], which have to learn the appearance of either the different types of dirt or the pattern of the floor or background. These methods asked each new floor or background must be input to the system. What's more, although it would allow to detect any dirt on known surfaces it has to overcome the problem of correct alignment of the clean pattern with the measurements.

However, dirt detection is a one-classification problem [12] which is used to detect whether there is dirt in the obtained images or not, and if dirt is found in it, a pixel-wise segmentation will be performed on it. What's more, the methods like YOLO and Faster-RCNN can only obtain the dirt positions of dirt marking by rectangular candidate frame, which is not accurate enough.

There are two common one-classification algorithms named SVM(Support Vector Machines) and SVDD (Support Vector Data Description). The principle of SVM is to constructs a hyperplane or set of hyperplanes in a high- or infinite-dimensional space, which can be used for classification [13]. Similar to SVM, SVDD is also a one-classification algorithm, which is to constructs a hyper-sphere which contains the training data in the kernel space by the given kernel function to realize the distinction between positive samples and negative samples [14]. Zhou [15] mentioned that when performing one-classification, we hope that the samples is linearly separable in the feature space, and the kernel function implicitly defines this space. Therefore, the selections of kernel function are significant to the performance of SVM and SVDD. If the kernel function is selected improperly, the samples may be mapped to an improper space, so that the performance will be reduced obviously. Hofmann et al. [16] compared several kernel functions in machine learning by their principles and performance, and analyzed the application conditions. However, the kernel function is still hard to select, if the selection is not good, the performance of models will be extremely poor. Therefore, Ruff et al. [17] proposed Deep SVDD, using neural network to obtain the optimal kernel function of the classification model without manual selection. Moreover, on the basis of [17], Ruff et al. [18] applied Deep-SVDD with the semi-supervised one-classification for detection, and achieved a better result. SVDD is often used for one-classification detection, besides, Jihun et al. [19] proposed patch SVDD anomaly detection method with self-supervised learning and hierarchical encoder, which also performed well in anomaly detection of MVTecAD dataset [20,21]. Philipp Liznerski et al. [22] present an explainable deep one-class classification method, Fully Convolutional Data Description (FCDD), where the mapped samples are themselves also an explanation heatmap. Similar to anomaly detection, for dirt detection tasks, the color and shape of dirt have randomness and uncertainty [2,23], especially in large industrial components, where samples are usually clean which is collected after washing, so we can use clean(positive) samples for training to form a clean feature space model. In the test set, we compare dirt samples to match the distribution of the trained feature space model, and the feature space distribution between the trained model and dirt points is significantly different, so the location of dirt is found by the difference.

In this paper, we obtain the kernel function of SVDD through neural network and propose a deep-SVDD-based dirt detection and segmentation for large industrial components, which solves the difficult problem of selection of kernel function, and perform segmentation of dirt at the pixel level. However, due to the small scale of dirt samples of large industrial components, and there are fewer public datasets related to dirt detection, we pretrain the anomaly detection MVTecAD dataset, which is related to dirt detection and segmentation. The pretrained feature extraction network is transferred to the dirt detection of large industrial components and then train the hypersphere of SVDD for classification, so that the training of the dirt samples has better initial performance, and it makes the model converge faster and reduces the demand for numbers of samples. At the same time, the improved Deep SVDD network model designed in this paper solves the one-classification problem, compared with some common multi-class object detection algorithms such as YOLO and Faster-RCNN, it has fewer network layers and parameters, faster model training, so it can performance well with limited equipment computing resources in industry, in addition to the detection of dirt objects, the model designed in this paper also performs pixel-level segmentation of the dirt of large industrial components samples, so as to find the location of dirt on the components accurately.

3   Method

3.1   SVDD (Support Vector Data Description)

According to SVDD [14], suppose there is a set of positive training data $x \in R^{n \times d}$, where n is the number of samples and d is the feature dimension. First, the data is mapped from the original space to the feature space through the nonlinear transformation function $\Phi : x \to F$, and then a hypersphere with the smallest volume is found in the feature space. Before constructing such a minimum-volume hypersphere, the goal that SVDD needs to optimize is:

$$\min_{a,R,\xi} R^2 + C \sum_{i=1}^{n} \xi_i \tag{1}$$

which makes

$$\|\Phi(x_i) - a\|^2 \leq R^2 + \xi_i, \xi_i \geq 0, \ \forall i = 1, 2, \cdots, n \tag{2}$$

where R is the radius of the hypersphere, a is the center of the hypersphere, ξ is the relaxation factor, and C is a penalty parameter that weighs the volume of the hypersphere and the error rate. Combined with the methods of Lagrangian multiplier, the formula for obtaining the center and radius of the hypersphere is:

$$a = \sum_{i=1}^{n} \alpha_i \Phi(x_i) \tag{3}$$

$$R = \sqrt{K\left(x_v, x_v\right) - 2\sum_{i=1}^{n} \alpha_i K\left(x_v, x_i\right) + \sum_{i=1}^{n}\sum_{j=1}^{n} \alpha_i\alpha_j K\left(x_i, x_j\right)} \qquad (4)$$

where α_i is the Lagrangian coefficient corresponding to the sample x_i. Among all training samples, the sample which Lagrangian coefficient satisfies $0 < \alpha_i < C$ is called a support vector. The sample set belonging to the support vector in the training dataset is SV, where $x_v \in SV$, $K\left(x_i, x_j\right)$ is the kernel function, which is equivalent to the inner product of the feature space samples, that is

$$K\left(x_i, x_j\right) = <\Phi\left(x_i\right), \Phi\left(x_j\right)> \qquad (5)$$

For the sample $x_t est$ in the test set, the distance from it to the center of the hypersphere is:

$$D = \sqrt{K\left(x_{test}, x_{test}\right) - 2\sum_{i=1}^{n} \alpha_i K\left(x_{test}, x_i\right) + \sum_{i=1}^{n}\sum_{j=1}^{n} \alpha_i\alpha_j K\left(x_i, x_j\right)} \qquad (6)$$

If $d \leq R$, it means that the test sample is on or inside the hypersphere so it is a positive sample; otherwise, it is a negative sample.

For the kernel functions above mentioned, the commonly used kernel functions include Gaussian kernel function [24], linear kernel function, Laplacian kernel function, polynomial kernel function, etc. For the same set of binary data containing positive and negative samples, the distribution of the kernel function (3D, 2D) and classification effects are shown from Fig. 1 to Fig. 4.

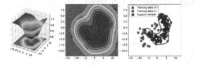

Fig. 1. Gaussian kernel function.

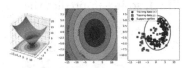

Fig. 2. Linear kernel function.

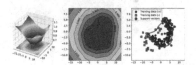

Fig. 3. Laplace kernel function.

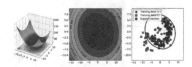

Fig. 4. Polynomial kernel function.

By comparing the effects on classifying the same set of 2D data, it can be seen that the Gaussian kernel function performs significantly better on this dataset, and it is obvious that the choice of the kernel function is particularly important. However, in different datasets, the performance of the kernel function is not always the same, and the selection of the kernel function has a great influence on the performance in classification. In order to select the optimal kernel function, we uses neural networks to fit the kernel function named Deep SVDD [17] in this paper.

3.2 Deep SVDD

In Deep SVDD, a feature extraction network is trained to map the entire training data to a smallest hypersphere in the feature space. Use the following loss function to train the mapping function f_θ of the extraction network to minimize the Euclidean distance between the feature and the center of the hypersphere:

$$L_{SVDD} = \sum_i \|f_\theta(x_i) - c\|_2 \tag{7}$$

where x is the input of images. During the test process, the distance between the input representation in feature space and the center of hypersphere is used as the characteristic value for anomaly or dirt detection. c is the center of the hypersphere, which can be calculated by Eq. 8

$$c = \frac{1}{n}\sum_i^n f_\theta(x_i) \tag{8}$$

3.3 DDSN (Dirt Detection and Segmentation Network)

Dorsch et al. [25] trained an encoder like feature extraction network and classifier pair to predict the target position of 9 blocks in the 3×3 grid, as shown in Fig. 5. The trained encoder has extracted useful features for position prediction, and then the extracted features are input into the classifier of the fully connected layer(FC), so it can predict the object position in the 3×3 grid.

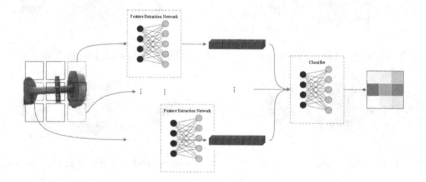

Fig. 5. Process of Doersch's method.

We extend the Deep SVDD to blocks in this paper, and the feature extraction network performs feature extraction on each block of the image in the dataset instead of the entire image, as shown in Fig. 6. There are several advantages to checking block by block. First of all, each location has a prediction result, so we can locate the location of the dirt at pixel level. Second, its inspection improves overall inspection performance.

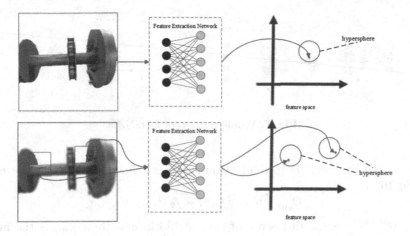

Fig. 6. Comparison of Deep SVDD and DDSN (ours).

The advantages of extension of Deep SVDD to block checking are obvious. The feature extraction network uses L_{SVDD} for training, where x is replaced by block b. The dirt score is defined as the Euclidean distance between the feature of dirt sample and the center of the hypersphere training before. Unfortunately, for images with high complexity, the performance of detection and segmentation is poor. However, some image blocks belong to the background, while other blocks contain dirt, which have highly intra-class variation. Therefore, it is not appropriate to use a single center c for all different blocks, and multi-center for every block is introduced. The feature extraction network is trained to use the following loss function to minimize the Euclidean distance between the features and the corresponding centers of the hypersphere:

$$L_{DDSN} = \sum_i \|f_\theta(b_i) - c_i\|_2 \tag{9}$$

where c_i is the corresponding center of the hypersphere which belongs to block b_i.

For a given training images, DDSN first resizes the 1024×1024 images to 256×256, divides the images into several blocks of size 8×8 and set the stride as 2. After that, every block is mapped to the corresponding hypersphere in the feature space, the 8×8 block moves in stride size of 2. For a given test images, DDSN also preprocesses like the training images, and then uses the trained feature extraction network to extract their features. The Euclidean distance to the corresponding center of the hypersphere in the feature space becomes the dirt score of each block. The generated dirt map locates the dirt (indicated by red). Figure 7 shows the whole process of DDSN.

After training the feature extraction network, the feature extraction network is used to perform dirt detection and segmentation. Given a test image x, for each 8×8 block b with stride 2, the Euclidean distance to t the corresponding

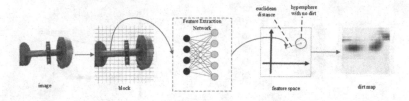

Fig. 7. Whole process of DDSN.

center of the hypersphere in the feature space is defined as its dirt score using the Eq. 10

$$D_{cur}^{block}(b) = \| f_\theta(b) - f_\theta(b_{clean}) \|_2 \tag{10}$$

where $D_{cur}^{block}(b)$ is the dirt score of current block, and the b_{clean} is the image corresponding block of training image, which is clean with no dirt.

Then the dirt score calculated by block is assigned to each pixel. Therefore, pixels receive the average dirt scores of each block which passes by the pixel, so we can obtain the dirt score of pixel using the Eq. 11

$$D_{cur}^{pixel}(p) = \sum_i D_i^{block}(b_i)/n \tag{11}$$

where $D_{cur}^{pixel}(P)$ is the dirt score of current pixel, and the $D_i^{block}(b_i)$ is dirt scores of each block which passes by the current pixel, and n is the number of $D_i^{block}(b_i)$. With the calculation of each pixel, DDSN can generate dirt maps, which can perform dirt detection and segmentation at pixel level.

For the whole images, the maximum dirt score of pixels in the image is its dirt score, as shown in Eq. 12

$$D^{image}(x) = \max_i D_i^{pixel}(p_i) \tag{12}$$

where $D^{image}(x)$ is the dirt score of the whole image x, and the $D_i^{pixel}(p_i)$ is the dirt scores of every pixel in the image x.

4   Evaluation

4.1   Experiment Setup

We firstly train DDSN on the MVTecAD dataset, the images of size 700×700(Metal Nut), 800×800(Pill), 840×840(Tile), 900×900(Bottle) or 1024×1024(11 other categories) are all resized to the network input of size 256×256. We set the learning rate as 1e-4, using Adam optimizer, and set epoch as 500 for each category. And that, we train DDSN on the dirt dataset of large industrial components, the images of size 1024×1024(wheel) are also resized to the network input of size 256×256, and we set the learning rate as 3.33e-5, using Adam optimizer as well, and we set epoch as 2000 for the dirt dataset.

4.2   Experimental Result on MVTecAD Dataset

During the experiment, we first evaluate the MVTecAD dataset with more samples. The detection and segmentation results of the 15 categories are as Fig. 8 shown.

The images are the anomaly samples in test set noted by the mask in the ground-truth folder, and anomaly maps are the result image generated by the detection and segmentation of the method proposed in this paper, which is depicted as a red outline and a darker heat map indicates a higher anomaly score.

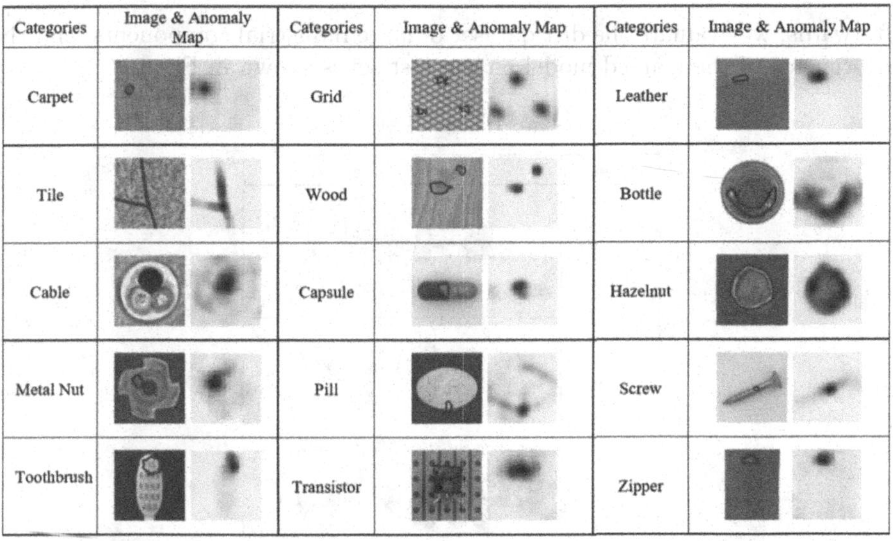

Categories	Image & Anomaly Map	Categories	Image & Anomaly Map	Categories	Image & Anomaly Map
Carpet		Grid		Leather	
Tile		Wood		Bottle	
Cable		Capsule		Hazelnut	
Metal Nut		Pill		Screw	
Toothbrush		Transistor		Zipper	

Fig. 8. Anomaly detection and segmentation on MVTecAD dataset.

The comparison of segmentation performance of the method proposed in this paper with Random Encoder [25] and FCDD [22] on the MVTecAD dataset is shown in Table 1, The evaluation method is AUC. Figure 9 shows the ROC curve of DDSN on MVTecAD dataset, and the AUC is 0.9403.

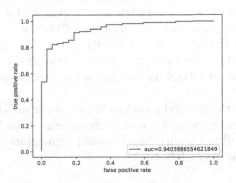

Fig. 9. ROC curve on MVTecAD dataset.

Table 1. Anomaly segmentation (MVTecAD dataset).

Method	AUC
Random Encoder	0.8641
FCDD heading	0.7918
DDSN (ours)	0.9403

4.3   Experimental Result on Dirt Dataset

Afterwards, we evaluate the dirt dataset of large industrial components, and the performance of the trained model on the test set is shown in Fig. 10.

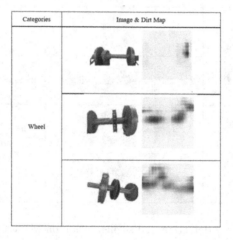

Fig. 10. Dirt detection and segmentation on dirt dataset.

The images are the image of the samples with dirt in the test set noted by the mask in ground-truth folder, and the dirt maps are the result image generated by the detection and segmentation of the method proposed in this paper, which is depicted as a red outline and a darker heat map indicates a higher dirt score. The comparison of segmentation performance of the method proposed in this paper with Random Encoder [25] and FCDD [22] on the dirt dataset collected in the laboratory is shown in Table 2. The evaluation method is AUC. Figure 11 shows the ROC curve of DDSN on dirt dataset of large industrial components, and the AUC is 0.9071.

It is obvious that the method proposed in this paper not only has a good performance in the anomaly detection and segmentation of the MVTecAD dataset, but also performs well in the dirt detection and segmentation of large industrial components collected in the laboratory.

Table 2. Dirt segmentation (dirt dataset of large industrial components).

Method	AUC
Random Encoder	0.6124
FCDD heading	0.6501
DDSN (ours)	0.9071

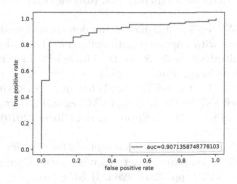

Fig. 11. ROC curve on dirt dataset of large industrial components.

5 Conclusion

In this paper, we improved Deep SVDD to fit the kernel function to obtain the minimum enclosing hypersphere in the feature space of the training images with no dirt in block, so that the model can find out the difference between the hypersphere with no dirt and the test images to achieve dirt detection and pixel-wise segmentation. What's more, for the reason that DDSN only needs the images with no dirt while training, it can obviously reduce the workload of dataset making. In addition, before training the dirt dataset of large industrial components, we first train the MVTecAD industrial anomaly dataset to make up for the insufficiency of the dirt dataset. The experimental results show that DDSN not only does well in detection and segmentation on the MVTecAD dataset, it also shows excellent performance on the dirt dataset of large industrial components, which realizes dirt detection and pixel-wise segmentation in both datasets.

References

1. Richard, B., et al.: Autonomous dirt detection for cleaning in office environments. In: International Conference on Robotics and Automation, pp. 1260–1267. IEEE (2013)
2. Jürgen, H., et al.: A probabilistic approach to high-confidence cleaning guarantees for low-cost cleaning robots. In: International Conference on Robotics and Automation (ICRA), pp. 5600–5605. IEEE (2014)

3. Redmon, J., et al.: You only look once: unified, real-time object detection. In: Proceedings of the IEEE Conference on Computer Vision and Pattern Recognition (CVPR), pp. 779–788 (2016)
4. Shaoqing, R., et al.: Faster r-cnn: towards real-time object detection with region proposal networks. In: Advances in Neural Information Processing Systems, vol. 28 (2015)
5. Richard, B., et al.: DirtNet: visual dirt detection for autonomous cleaning robots. In: 2020 IEEE International Conference on Robotics and Automation (ICRA), pp. 1977–1983 (2020)
6. Daniel, C., et al.: A deep learning-based dirt detection computer vision system for floor-cleaning robots with improved data collection. Technologies 9(4), 94 (2021)
7. Glenn, J., et al.: ultralytics/yolov5: v5. 0-YOLOv5-P6 1280 models. AWS, Supervise. ly and YouTube integrations 10 (2021)
8. Deng, J., Berg, A.C., Li, K., Fei-Fei, L.: What does classifying more than 10,000 image categories tell Us? In: Daniilidis, K., Maragos, P., Paragios, N. (eds.) ECCV 2010. LNCS, vol. 6315, pp. 71–84. Springer, Heidelberg (2010). https://doi.org/10.1007/978-3-642-15555-0_6
9. Stefan, H., et al.: Dominant orientation templates for real-time detection of textureless objects. In: IEEE Computer Society Conference on Computer Vision and Pattern Recognition (CVPR), pp. 2257–2264. IEEE (2010)
10. Alvaro, C., et al.: The MOPED framework: object recognition and pose estimation for manipulation. Int. J. Rob. Res. 30(10), 1284–1306 (2011)
11. Jan, F., et al.: A framework for object training and 6 DoF pose estimation. In: 7th German Conference on Robotics, pp. 1–6. VDE (2012)
12. Vert, R., et al.: Consistency and convergence rates of one-class SVMs and related algorithms. J. Mach. Learn. Res. 7(5), 817–854 (2006)
13. Platt, J.C. Sequential Minimal Optimization: A Fast Algorithm for Training Support Vector Machines (1998)
14. Tax, D.M.J., Duin, R.P.W.: Support vector data description. Mach. Learn. 54(1), 45–66 (2004)
15. Zhou, Z., et al.: Machine learning, 1st edn. Tsinghua University Press, Beijing (2016)
16. Hofmann, T., et al.: Kernel methods in machine learning. Ann. Stat. 36(3), 1171–1220 (2008)
17. Ruff, L., et al.: Deep one-class classification. In: International Conference on Machine Learning pp. 4393–4402. PMLR (2018)
18. Ruff, L., et al.: Deep semi-supervised anomaly detection. arXiv preprint arXiv:1906.02694 (2019)
19. Jihun, Y., et al.: Patch svdd: patch-level svdd for anomaly detection and segmentation. In: Proceedings of the Asian Conference on Computer Vision (2020)
20. Paul, B., et al.: MVTec AD-a comprehensive real-world dataset for unsupervised anomaly detection. In: Proceedings of the IEEE/CVF Conference on Computer Vision and Pattern Recognition, pp. 9592–9600 (2019)
21. Bergmann, P., Batzner, K., Fauser, M., Sattlegger, D., Steger, C.: The MVTec anomaly detection dataset: a comprehensive real-world dataset for unsupervised anomaly detection. Int. J. Comput. Vision 129(4), 1038–1059 (2021). https://doi.org/10.1007/s11263-020-01400-4
22. Philipp, L., et al.: Explainable deep one-class classification. arXiv preprint arXiv:2007.01760 (2020)

23. Grünauer, A., Halmetschlager-Funek, G., Prankl, J., Vincze, M.: The power of GMMs: unsupervised dirt spot detection for industrial floor cleaning robots. In: Gao, Y., Fallah, S., Jin, Y., Lekakou, C. (eds.) TAROS 2017. LNCS (LNAI), vol. 10454, pp. 436–449. Springer, Cham (2017). https://doi.org/10.1007/978-3-319-64107-2_34
24. Hansi, J., et al.: Fast incremental SVDD learning algorithm with the Gaussian kernel. In: AAAI Conference on Artificial Intelligence, vol. 33(01), pp. 3991–3998 (2019)
25. Carl, D., et al.: Unsupervised visual representation learning by context prediction. In: Proceedings of the IEEE International Conference on Computer Vision, pp. 1422–1430 (2015)

Finding Beautiful and Happy Images for Mental Health and Well-Being Applications

Ruitao Xie[1,2], Connor Qiu[3], and Guoping Qiu[4,5,6(✉)]

[1] Shenzhen Institutes of Advanced Technology, Chinese Academy of Sciences,
Shenzhen 518055, China
rt.xie@siat.ac.cn
[2] University of Chinese Academy of Sciences, Beijing 100049, China
[3] School of Public Health, Faculty of Medicine, Imperial College London,
London SW7 2AZ, UK
c.qiu@imperial.ac.uk
[4] Shenzhen University, Shenzhen, China
[5] Pengcheng National Lab, Shenzhen, China
[6] University of Nottingham, Nottingham, UK
guoping.qiu@nottingham.ac.uk

Abstract. This paper explores how artificial intelligence (AI) technology can contribute to achieve progress on **good health and well-being**, one of the United Nations' 17 Sustainable Development Goals. It is estimated that one in ten of the global population lived with a mental disorder. Inspired by studies showing that engaging and viewing beautiful natural images can make people feel happier and less stressful, lead to higher emotional well-being, and can even have therapeutic values, we explore how AI can help to promote mental health by developing automatic algorithms for finding beautiful and happy images. We first construct a large image database consisting of nearly 20K very high resolution colour photographs of natural scenes where each image is labelled with beautifulness and happiness scores by about 10 observers. Statistics of the database shows that there is a good correlation between the beautifulness and happiness scores which provides anecdotal evidence to corroborate that engaging beautiful natural images can potentially benefit mental well-being. Building on this unique database, the very first of its kind, we have developed a deep learning based model for automatically predicting the beautifulness and happiness scores of natural images. Experimental results are presented to show that it is possible to develop AI algorithms to automatically assess an image's beautifulness and happiness values which can in turn be used to develop applications for promoting mental health and well-being.

Supported by Guangdong Key Laboratory of Intelligent Information Processing, Shenzhen, China, Shenzhen Institute for Artificial Intelligence and Robotics for Society, Shenzhen, China, and Shenzhen Key Laboratory of Digital Creative Technology, Shenzhen, China.

S. Yu et al. (Eds.): PRCV 2022, LNCS 13536, pp. 704–717, 2022.
https://doi.org/10.1007/978-3-031-18913-5_54

Keywords: AI for Good · Mental health · Technological nature · Beautiful image · Happy images

1 Introduction

This paper explores how artificial intelligence (AI) technology can contribute to achieve progress on **Good Health and Well-being**, one of the United Nations' 17 Sustainable Development Goals (SDGs). According to the latest available data[1], it was estimated that 792 million people, i.e., more than one in ten of the global population (10.7%) lived with a mental health disorder. The COVID-19 pandemic is exacerbating the mental health problem across the world. Developing AI solutions to improve mental health is therefore one of the most meaningful ways to achieve **AI for Good** .

Engaging and viewing beautiful natural images can make people feel happier and less stressful [1], lead to higher emotional well-being [2], and can even have therapeutic values [3,4]. However, in these previous studies, the subjectively *beautiful* images had to be chosen manually which means that it is very difficult to obtain large amount of such images to tailor the tastes of different users to benefit the mass. We therefore ask the question whether it is possible to develop AI solutions to automatically search for beautiful natural images that can make people feel happy and relaxing, thus enabling the development of applications for promoting mental health and well-being. The subject matters of this study is highly interdisciplinary and even the definitions of *beautiful* and *happy* images are very subjective concepts. These factors have made our attempt, the very first of its kind, to develop AI solutions to automatically search for beautiful and happy images with the expressed goal of promoting mental health, extremely challenging. Despite the difficulties, we have nevertheless developed a possible solution and make the following contributions.

Firstly, we contribute a large high quality Beautiful Natural Image Database (BNID) consisting of 20,996 very high resolution natural images. Each image in the BNID is labelled with a *beautifulness* score and a *happiness* score obtained from ratings by about 10 human observers. This is the first ever such database designed for developing automatic algorithms to search for beautiful and happy images for mental health applications. To ensure high image quality and diversity, the data was obtained by manually and algorithmically sieving through an initial set of 500,000 images down to a subset of 20,996, which were then rated by more than 200 human observers. Nearly 420,000 ratings were then obtained in this database, which have been made publicly available[2] for research purposes. We present statistics to show that in general there is a good positive correlation between the images beautifulness and happiness scores. For large majority of the cases, a beautiful image is also a happy image, and vice versus. We also show that

---

[1] https://ourworldindata.org/mental-health.
[2] https://drive.google.com/drive/folders/1qJ56Cvd5K4TR7NKBsW0kvu0iYu5LpUJx?usp=sharing.

observers personal attributes and the ratings they gave exhibits some interesting patterns such as more optimistic persons will give higher beautifulness and happiness scores, the more pro-society the observers are, the higher scores they will give the images, and the better mood the observers are in, their scores are higher. Our BNID is the largest database providing anecdotal evidences which corroborate previous findings that beautiful natural images positively correlate with higher emotional well-being.

Secondly, we present a deep learning based system for automatically predicting images beautifulness scores and happiness scores. We employ content-based image retrieval to first find a similar image with manually annotated scores to provide a reference to improve prediction accuracy. Instead of predicting the beautifulness or happiness independently, we exploit the correlations between beautifulness and happiness by making use of an image's happiness score to assist the prediction of the beautifulness score, and vice versus, by making use of an image's beautifulness score to assist the prediction of happiness score. We present experimental results to show that it is possible to automatically predict the beautifulness and happiness scores of natural images, which in turn can be used to automatically search for beautiful and happy images to be used for the purpose of developing applications aiming for improving mental well-being.

It is worth mentioning that the contribution of this paper is an initial attempt to explore how computer vision and pattern recognition algorithms can be used to automatically find beautiful and happy images for mental heath and well-being applications. The emphasis is on AI for Good rather than on developing the most advanced machine learning algorithms.

2   Related Work

The *beautifulness* of an image is related to image aesthetics assessment (IAA) [5]. Image aesthetic is very subjective and to complicate things further, a piece of work with a high aesthetic value can incur negative emotion. The *happiness* of an image is related to affective image quality assessment [6]. In this paper, we are only interested in image aesthetics that invokes positive emotions. The emotions evoked by a picture can be modelled in either positive or negative categorical emotion states [7]. Experiencing the aesthetics of beautiful pictures has been shown to invoke positive emotions and promote physical and physiological well-being [8,9]. Positive emotion categories such as amusement, contentment, and excitement are finer grained versions of *happiness* [10].

Early IAA algorithms mainly used hand-crafted features for rating image aesthetics. The advancement of deep learning has witnessed rapid increase in works based on deep neural networks. Wang et al. [11] leveraged popular neural networks for predicting image aesthetics. Jin et al. [12] proposed a new neural network to extract the local and global features for image aesthetics assessment.

Similar to IAA, early image emotion assessment (IEA) algorithms also used hand crafted features. Multi-level region based CNN has been developed for image emotion classification in [13]. For more comprehensive review and recent advances in the field IEA, readers are referred to recent surveys in [14].

In fields outside computational sciences, researchers have long recognised the benefits of engaging with beautiful natural environments and studied how they can induce aesthetic and affective responses in humans [15]. In fact, studies have shown that humans can engage with the so called *technological nature* [16], electronic display of natural environments, to gain emotional, psychological and physiological benefits.

Research has shown that engaging and viewing beautiful natural images can make the viewers feel happier and less stressful [1], which in turn leads to higher emotional well-being [2], pro-social behaviours [8], higher levels of life satisfaction and a better spiritual outlook [17]. In addition to relieving stress, viewing beautiful natural images can also elicit improvements in the recovery process following acute mental stress [8,18], reduce perception of pain [3], significantly reduce pro re nata medication incidents, help reducing mental health patients' anxiety and agitation in healthcare settings [19], and can be a cost-effective treatment strategy for individuals with substance use disorder [4].

3   A Beautiful Natural Image Database (BNID)

3.1   Collecting the Images

We started by collecting about 500,000 landscape images from the web. Considering aspect ratio can interfere with aesthetic rating, we only selected those images with an aspect ratio of about 4:3. As images of low resolution will affect the reliability of rating, only those with resolutions nearly or exceeding 1800 × 1200 were kept. After first round of data cleaning, about 70,000 very high quality landscape images were left. Content diversity and variety are important in order to have a high quality database. We calculated the color histograms of each image and compared the similarity between two images based on the distance of their color histograms. If the distance is below a preset threshold, we randomly throw away one of them. Through this round of data cleaning, 20,996 images were left for collecting beautifulness and happiness labels.

3.2   Collecting Beatutifulness and Happiness Scores

In order to collect beautifulness and happiness scores, we built a website and recruited more than 200 volunteers. We followed a common practice in the psychology literature [8] and adopted a 7-point scoring scale for both beautifulness and happiness scores. We used very simple and general language to instruct the participants to score the images. For collecting the beautifulness score, we presented the image to the raters along with the text: *This image is beautiful, strongly agree = 7, strongly disagree = 1*. The raters are free to choose any one of the 7 scores. For collecting the happiness score, we presented the viewers with the image and the text: *This image makes me feel happy, strongly agree = 7, strongly disagree = 1*. Again, the raters can choose any one of the 7 scores.

Apart from these simple instructions, the raters have not received any training, they rated the images in their own environment and in their own time. To ensure reliability, the raters had to stay on one image for at least 3 s before moving to the next one. The raters participated in the exercise anonymously but we have asked them to fill in a questionnaire consisted of questions such as their gender, knowledge about photography, the lighting conditions of the viewing environment, and some personal attributes such as their mood when rating the images, their personality, general attitude towards society and their environments.

3.3   Analysis of Beautifulness and Happiness Scores

It will be interesting to see how the images beautifulness scores relate to their happiness scores. Figure 1 shows the relation between beautifulness and happiness scores and their distributions. It is seen that the distributions both have a bell shape. The beautifulness scores and happiness scores are highly correlated.

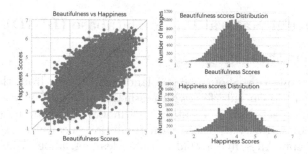

Fig. 1. Left: Scatter plot between happiness and beautifulness scores. Right: Beautifulness and happiness score distributions

Table 1 shows the beautifulness-happiness difference distribution. It is seen that for the majority of the images, their beautifulness and happiness scores only differ between 0 and 0.5. These statistics show that in majority of the cases, there is a strong positive correlation between an image's beauty and the positive emotion (happiness) it invokes, and that a beautiful image is also a happy image, and vice versus. It is important to note that all image in the BNID are natural landscape images, these relations may not hold for arbitrary contents. Indeed, all conclusions in this paper are based on such image types.

Table 1. Beautifulness-happiness difference distribution

Diff. interval	<0.25	<0.5	<0.75	<1
No of images	30.62%	54.05%	75.71%	86.95%

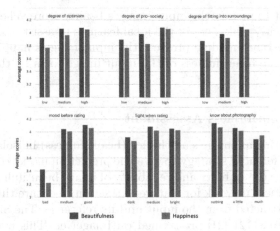

Fig. 2. Observers personal attributes and other factors versus raters' average beautifulness and happiness scores.

How raters' personal attributes and the viewing environment affect their ratings is of interest. Figure 2 show how raters' degrees of optimism, pro-society,
fitting with the surrounding environments, their mood before started the rating
exercise, their knowledge of photography, and the lighting condition of the viewing environment affect their scores. It is very interesting to observe that more
optimistic persons will give higher beautifulness and happiness scores, the more
pro-society the raters are, the higher scores they will give the images, the better
the raters can fit in with their surroundings, the higher the scores they will rate
the images, and the better mood the raters are in, their scores are higher. In
terms of the viewing environment, a lighter environment tend to make raters
give higher scores. Not surprisingly, the more knowledge the raters had about
photography, the lower scores they gave. This is because they may judge the
photos from the rules of photography rather than the beauty of the images.

These results supports findings from previous studies that engaging with
beautiful natural images can gain emotional and well-being benefits [1–4, 8, 18,
19]. In order to enable the public to benefit from such beautiful natural images,
we need to be able to automatically find large amount of such images to engage
the public to help improve the mental well-being.

4   Beautifulness and Happiness Assessment

We begin by describing our method for image beautifulness assessment which
can be easily extended to image happiness assessment. The overall image beautifulness assessment framework is shown in Fig. 3 which consists of 4 major
components. The retrieval module uses content-based image retrieval (CBIR)
[20] to retrieve a reference image that is similar to the input. The global comparison module consists of a Siamese network that takes the input image and its

reference as input to predict the input image's beauty score. The local comparison module explicitly makes use of the local features to assist beauty prediction. The emotion-assistance module predicts the input image's happiness value and its relation with the beautifulness of the input image to assist the prediction of its beauty value.

4.1   Image Beautifulness Assessment

Instead of evaluating an image's aesthetics (beautifulness) in isolation, we introduce a content-referenced strategy to give the prediction model contextual information to enhance the stability and reliability of image beautifulness assessment. We exploit a Siamese network for feature extraction to ensure that the same set of features are extracted from the input and its reference. The Siamese network is based on Densenet121 [21] pre-trained on ImageNet. This network architecture integrates features of different layers and can better integrate semantic and structural information to construct powerful representative features to facilitate beauty score prediction.

Local information is also important for image aesthetics assessment [22]. Various local information will have different effects on image beauty, the aesthetics of the central area will largely determine the image's beauty. To leverage local information to achieve better beautifulness assessment performances, we introduce a module to estimate the relative aesthetic score between the input image and its reference image.

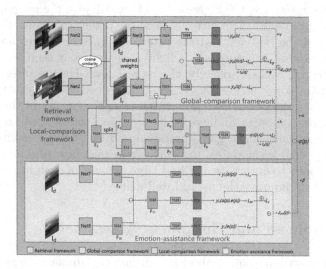

Fig. 3. The overall framework of our proposed algorithm for image beautifulness assessment. In all modules, the yellow boxes refer to the networks used, the brown and green boxes represent the features, in which the numbers indicate the channels of features, and the blue boxes represent the classifiers composed of fully connected layers. p is the input image and q is the paired reference image for comparison. (Color figure online)

As discussed previously and demonstrated in Sect. 3, the beautifulness and happiness scores of an image are highly correlated. In order to make full use of the happiness information of the images, we propose a collaborative beautifulness and happiness assessment solution. As shown in the emotion assistance module in Fig. 3, we use two parallel networks to regress the beautifulness score and the happiness score respectively. The feature map F_9 represents aesthetic related image features while F_{10} contains happiness related features. The feature map F_{11} which is obtained by subtracting F_{10} from F_9 mixes the beautifulness and happiness features and is used to estimate the difference between the beauty and happiness scores of the image. A one-layer classifier is used to predict the beautifulness and happiness scores respectively whilst a two-layer classifier is used to predict the difference between the scores. Similarly, DenseNet121 pre-trained on ImageNet is used to implement the feature extraction here.

Beautifulness and happiness scores are content dependent. It is more meaningful and reliable to compare two images with similar contents. We use content based image retrieval (CBIR) [20] to find a similar image from the training set as a reference image to help build better and more reliable image beautifulness assessors. The retrieval process leveraged the features extraction module of Densenet161 [21] pre-trained on the Places365 dataset [23] used for scene classification. The feature maps of input image p and reference image q extracted from the pre-trained Densenet161 are used to derive two feature vectors v_p and v_q using the average pooling operator. The distance between v_p and v_q are then used to find the most similar image from the reference image set as the input image's reference.

4.2 Loss Functions

Training of the overall framework is divided into 3 stages corresponding to the training of the global, local and emotion-assistance modules. As shown in Eqs. (1) to (3), we use mean square errors to design the loss functions.

$$\mathcal{L}_g = (y_g(p) - t_a(p))^2 + (y_g(q) - t_a(q))^2$$
$$+ (y_g(p,q) - (t_a(p) - t_a(q)))^2 \tag{1}$$
$$\mathcal{L}_l = (y_l(p,q) - (t_a(p) - t_a(q))^2 \tag{2}$$
$$\mathcal{L}_c = (y_c[a(p)] - t_a(p))^2 + (y_c[e(p)] - t_e(p))^2$$
$$+ (y_c[a(p), e(p)] - (t_a(p) - t_e(p)))^2 \tag{3}$$

where $t_a(p)$ and $t_e(p)$ respectively represent the ground truth of the beautifulness and happiness scores of the input image p, and $t_a(q)$ is the beautifulness ground truth of the reference image q, $y_g(p)$ and $y_g(q)$ are respectively the predicted beauty scores of the input image p and reference image q by the global comparison module, $y_g(p,q)$ and $y_l(p,q)$ are respectively the predicted relative beautifulness values between images p and q by the global comparison and the local comparison modules, $y_c[a(p)]$ and $y_c[e(p)]$ are respectively the predicted beautifulness score and happiness score of image p, and $y_c[a(p), e(p)]$ is the predicted difference between beautifulness and happiness of image p.

4.3   Final Score

Empirically, we found that by combining predictions from the content-referenced module and the emotion assisted module gives the best results. The final beautifulness score of image p, $z(p)$ is estimated as follows

$$z(p) = z_{cr}(p) + z_{ea}(p) \tag{4}$$

where $z_{cr}(p)$ and $z_{ea}(p)$ are respectively the beautifulness scores of image p estimated by the content-referenced module and the emotion assisted module, $z_{cr}(p)$ and $z_{ea}(p)$ are calculated as follows

$$z_{cr}(p) = y_g(p) + y_g(p, q) + y_l(p, q) + 2t_a(q) \tag{5}$$
$$z_{ea}(p) = y_c[e(p)] + y_c[a(p), e(p)] \tag{6}$$

4.4   Extension to Image Happiness Prediction

We can easily extend the framework in Fig. 3 to predict images' happiness score. All we have to do is to substitute beautifulness by happiness and happiness by beautifulness in Fig. 3 and in Eqs. (1) to (6). As we shall show in the experimental section, this is indeed the case.

5   Experiments

In order to ensure data quality for effectively verifying our automatic assessment algorithms, we removed noisy ratings from the data by first removing outlier scores of each image and then deleting images that have too few valid ratings after outlier removal. After this round of data cleaning, 14644 images were used in our experiments. We randomly sample 2218 images with beautifulness scores between 3.8 and 4.2 as the reference images, in which 1663 are used during training and 555 are used in testing. The remaining 12426 are used as input images in which 9320 randomly sample are used for training and the other 3106 are used for testing. To reduce over fitting, we perform data augmentation by resize the images by some random factors and flipping horizontally with a probability of 0.5.

Evaluation Metrics. We divide images in the database into two classes. Those with scores exceed or equal to 4 are classified as good and the others are defined as bad. We calculate the accuracy (ACC) based on binary classification (good or bad) and use it as one of the evaluation criteria. Furthermore, we take the mean square error (MSE) between the ground truth and the predicted results as another evaluation metric. Spearman's rank correlation coefficient ($SRCC$) and linear correlation coefficient (LCC) are also computed between the predicted and ground truth scores.

5.1 Image Beautifulness Assessment Results

As a comparison baseline, we fine tune a Densenet121 end-to-end, input an image and output its corresponding beautiful score as is done in the vast majority of existing deep learning based approaches.

Table 2. Results of beautifulness prediction

Metrics	ACC	MSE	$SRCC$	LCC
Baseline	73.79%	0.7602	0.6331	0.6361
Content reference without emotion assistance				
wo/local	75.34%	0.7165	0.6525	0.6540
w/local	75.82%	0.7024	0.6597	0.6631
wo/retrieval	74.66%	0.7241	0.6449	0.6486
Content reference plus emotion assistance				
w/emotion (single)	76.14%	0.6886	0.6663	0.6705
w/emotion (Full)	**77.33%**	**0.6547**	**0.6871**	**0.6903**
Improvement	4.80%	13.88%	8.53%	8.52%

Overall Results. The second last line in Table 2, w/emotion (Full), shows our full system's beautifulness score prediction result. We can see that with a complete content reference module and a complete emotion assisted module, accuracy (ACC) performance has reached to 77.33%, achieving a 4.80% improvement over the baseline. For the mean square error (MSE) metric, our approach has achieved a 13.88% improvement over the base line. In the cases of Spearman's rank correlation coefficient ($SRCC$) and linear correlation coefficient (LCC) performances, the method has improved 8.53% and 8.52% respectively over baseline. Figure 4 shows some example images and the predicted beautifulness scores by our method. As can be seen, for those images that are obviously beautiful, the predicted scores are high, and those obvious unattractive looking, the predicted scores are low. These examples clearly demonstrate the excellent ability of our method in assessing images' beauty values.

Fig. 4. Predicted beautifulness scores. The number below are predicted scores and ground truth scores (inside bracket)

Content Referencing and CBIR. In this paper, we introduce content reference and content-based image retrieval (CBIR) into image beautifulness assessment as shown in our overall framework in Fig. 3. Here we study the roles they
play. We first investigate the roles of global and local features. As shown in
Table 2, explicitly making use of local features can indeed help improve the system's ability in better predicting the beautifulness scores. It is seen that including
local features (w/local) is better than using global feature only (wo/local). To
investigate the soundness of content reference and the importance of retrieving
similar images based on CBIR, we perform experiments by randomly choosing
reference images from the reference set. As seen in Table 2, even use randomly
chosen reference image, the results are better than the baseline, demonstrating
the usefulness of using content reference. Compared to results based on CBIR
(indicated by "w/local" in the Table 2), using randomly chosen reference image
performs worse which is entirely expected.

Happiness Helps Beautifulness Prediction. Table 2 also lists results when
the emotion assisted module is included in the full system. The result labelled
as "w/emotion (single) means when the happiness score of the input image is
estimated by a single network (the Net8-F_{10}-$FC7$ path in Fig. 3) and replacing
$Z_{ea}(p)$ with $y_c(e(p))$. It is seen that happiness can indeed assist the prediction of
beautifulness. The full result is when the complete emotion assistance module,
where we not only learn the happiness score of the input image, but also its relation with the beautifulness is also explicitly modelled. This result shows that
modelling happiness and beautifulness together through extracting happiness
and beautifulness features and then mixing them together for learning the relation between the two can help improve performances. This further demonstrate
the intrinsic relation between the two.

As mentioned previously and as can be expected that not all images' beauty
scores are positively related with their happiness scores. There are cases where
the gap between the scores can be large. It is for this reason, we introduce a
network branch that models the difference between the beautifulness and happiness of the image in our emotion-assistance module (see the middle blocks in
the emotion assistance module). Figure 5 shows some example images and the
predicted beautifulness-happiness difference of the images. We can see that large
difference values are predicted for those images which are good-looking but with
dark tone (a dark tone is more likely to make the viewers feeling sad), or those
images look bright (generally a bright tone can cheer people up) but with normal looking and not so beautiful contents. These examples also demonstrate the
ability of our system in modelling the gap between an image's beautifulness and
happiness scores.

Fig. 5. Example image and their predicted beautifulness-happiness difference. The numbers below each image represent predicted *beautifulness - happiness*. A positive means the image's beauty score is higher than happiness score whilst a negative means the image's happiness is higher than beautifulness.

5.2 Image Happiness Assessment Results

By swapping places between beautifulness and happiness, we can easily turn the scheme in Fig. 3 to predict image happiness score. For the happiness assessment experiments, we also take the similar data split strategy and as a result, 9329 and 1654 images are randomly selected as the input and reference images respectively for training. The numbers of input and reference images in the test set are 3110 and 551 respectively. The emotion assessment algorithm implementation is the same as beautifulness prediction shown above (only swapping positions between beautifulness and happiness). The results of happiness assessment are presented in Table 3. As we can see, the content reference and aesthetics assistance methods also bring improvement in image happiness assessment. Figure 6 shows some example images with their predicted happiness scores which further demonstrate the reliability of our proposed algorithms for happiness prediction.

Table 3. Happiness prediction results

Metrics	*ACC*	*MSE*	*SRCC*	*LCC*
Baseline	77.62%	0.6643	0.7026	0.6963
Content reference without beautifulness assistance				
wo/local	79.26%	0.6494	0.7119	0.7108
w/local	79.45%	0.6421	0.7159	0.7141
wo/retrieval	78.78%	0.6535	0.7059	0.7085
Content reference plus beautifulness assistance				
w/beauty (single)	79.81%	0.6355	0.7265	0.7264
w/beauty (Full)	**80.42%**	**0.5895**	**0.7450**	**0.7455**
Improvement	3.60%	11.26%	6.03%	7.07%

1. 87 (1. 63)   2. 86 (2. 50)   3. 30 (3. 56)

4. 70 (4. 56)   5. 25 (5. 33)   5. 76 (5. 33)

Fig. 6. Predicted happiness scores. The number below are predicted scores and ground truth scores (inside bracket)

6   Concluding Remarks

Aiming at exploiting artificial intelligence to help improve mental health, this paper has attempted for the first time to study image beautifulness and happiness under a unified computational framework. We have constructed the first ever very high quality large natural image database in which each image is labelled with a beautifulness score and a happiness score. We show that natural landscape images beautifulness scores are highly correlated with their happiness scores, and that these scores supports previous findings that beautiful natural images can benefit emotional well-being. Building on this database, we have developed a deep learning system for automatically predicting the beautifulness and happiness scores of natural images. Such system can be used to search for beautiful and happy images for the purpose of developing applications that promote mental health and well-being.

References

1. Van den Berg, M.M.H.E., et al.: Autonomic nervous system responses to viewing green and built settings: differentiating between sympathetic and parasympathetic activity. Int. J. Environ. Res. Public Health **12**(12), 15860–15874 (2015)
2. Zhang, J.W., Howell, R.T., Iyer, R.: Engagement with natural beauty moderates the positive relation between connectedness with nature and psychological well-being. J. Environ. Psychol. **38**, 55–63 (2014)
3. Vincent, E.A.: Therapeutic benefits of nature images on health. Clemson University (2009)
4. Reynolds, L., et al.: Virtual nature as an intervention for reducing stress and improving mood in people with substance use disorder. J. Addict. **2020**, 1–7 (2020)
5. Reber, R., Schwarz, N., Winkielman, P.: Processing fluency and aesthetic pleasure: Is beauty in the perceiver's processing experience? Pers. Soc. Psychol. Rev. **8**(4), 364–382 (2004)
6. Machajdik, J., Hanbury, A.: Affective image classification using features inspired by psychology and art theory. In: Proceedings of the 18th ACM International Conference on Multimedia, pp. 83–92 (2010)

7. Achlioptas, P., et al.: Artemis: affective language for visual art. In: Proceedings of the IEEE/CVF Conference on Computer Vision and Pattern Recognition, pp. 11569–11579 (2021)
8. Zhang, J.W., et al.: An occasion for unselfing: beautiful nature leads to prosociality. J. Environ. Psychol. **37**, 61–72 (2014)
9. Mastandrea, S., Fagioli, S., Biasi, V.: Art and psychological well-being: linking the brain to the aesthetic emotion. Front. Psychol. **10**, 739 (2019)
10. Diener, E., Scollon, C.N., Lucas, R.E.: The evolving concept of subjective well-being: the multifaceted nature of happiness. In: Diener, E. (eds.) Assessing Well-Being. Social Indicators Research Series, vol. 39. Springer, Dordrecht (2009). https://doi.org/10.1007/978-90-481-2354-4_4
11. Wang, Z., et al.: Brain-inspired deep networks for image aesthetics assessment. arXiv preprint arXiv:1601.04155 (2016)
12. Jin, X., et al.: ILGNet: inception modules with connected local and global features for efficient image aesthetic quality classification using domain adaptation. IET Comput. Vision **13**(2), 206–212 (2019)
13. Rao, T., et al.: Multi-level region-based convolutional neural network for image emotion classification. Neurocomputing **333**, 429–439 (2019)
14. Zhao, S., et al.: Computational emotion analysis from images: recent advances and future directions. Hum. Percept. Visual Inf. **21**, 85–113 (2022)
15. Ulrich, R.S.: Aesthetic and affective response to natural environment. In: Behavior and the Natural Environment, pp. 85–125. Springer, Boston (1983). https://doi.org/10.1007/978-1-4613-3539-9_4
16. Kahn, P.H., Jr., Severson, R.L., Ruckert, J.H.: The human relation with nature and technological nature. Curr. Dir. Psychol. Sci. **18**(1), 37–42 (2009)
17. Diessner, R., Solom, R.D., Frost, N.K., et al.: Engagement with beauty: appreciating natural, artistic, and moral beauty. J. Psychol. **142**(3), 303–332 (2008)
18. Brown, D.K., Barton, J.L., Gladwell, V.F.: Viewing nature scenes positively affects recovery of autonomic function following acute-mental stress. Environ. Sci. Technol. **47**(11), 5562–5569 (2013)
19. Nanda, U., Eisen, S., Zadeh, R.S., et al.: Effect of visual art on patient anxiety and agitation in a mental health facility and implications for the business case. J. Psychiatr. Ment. Health Nurs. **18**(5), 386–393 (2011)
20. Dubey, S.R.: A decade survey of content based image retrieval using deep learning. IEEE Trans. Circuits Syst. Video Technol. **32**(5), 2687–2704 (2021)
21. Huang, G., et al.: Densely connected convolutional networks. In: Proceedings of the IEEE Conference on Computer Vision and Pattern Recognition, pp. 4700–4708 (2017)
22. Lu, X., et al.: Rapid: rating pictorial aesthetics using deep learning. In: Proceedings of the 22nd ACM International Conference on Multimedia, pp. 457–466 (2014)
23. Zhou, et al.: Places: a 10 million image database for scene recognition. IEEE Trans. Pattern Anal. Mach. Intell. **40**(6), 1452–1464 (2017)

Query-UAP: Query-Efficient Universal Adversarial Perturbation for Large-Scale Person Re-Identification Attack

Huiwang Liu and Ya Li[✉]

Guangzhou University, Guangzhou 510006, China
liuhuiwang@e.gzhu.edu.cn, liya@gzhu.edu.cn

Abstract. The performance of person re-identification (ReID) has improved significantly with the development of deep learning. And we find that even the state-of-the-art ReID models are vulnerable to universal adversarial perturbation (UAP) attack under white-box attack. However, the white-box setting that the adversary has full access to model is not suitable for practical application. This situation inspires us to explore the UAP attack in more realistic black-box setting. In this paper, we propose a novel query-based black-box UAP attack algorithm for large-scale ReID attacking, which adopts the coordinate-wise gradient estimation method combined with importance sampling for gradient estimation. In particular, the UAP attack can be more easily applied to large-scale attacks, compared with the commonly used image-specific attack in the literature. What's more, in order to speed up the convergence of attack, we propose a coordinate-wise MI-FGSM with spatial momentum prior to update UAP. Meanwhile, our UAP updating method avoids the undesirable spread of inaccurate gradient estimation in iterations. Extensive experiments show that, at a very low average number of queries per image, the attack success rate and visual quality of the adversarial samples generated by our attack algorithm are very close to white-box attack. For example, when attacking AP-Net, one of the best ReID models at present, only an average of 297 queries per image can significantly reduce the mAP from 0.89 to 0.03 under Market1501. The code is available at https://github.com/HWliiu/QueryUAPReidAttack.

Keywords: Universal adversarial perturbation (UAP) · Query-efficient attack · Black-box attack · Person re-identificatio (ReID)

1 Introduction

Person re-identification (ReID) is viewed as a image retrieval task. The objective is to rank a gallery of images by order of similarity to a query image. With the development of deep learning, the performance of ReID has improved significantly [3,5,11,28]. However, deep learning based ReID models have found to inherit the vulnerability from deep neural networks (DNNs) like close-set classification task. Despite recent researches have paid more attention to the attack

S. Yu et al. (Eds.): PRCV 2022, LNCS 13536, pp. 718–731, 2022.
https://doi.org/10.1007/978-3-031-18913-5_55

on classification task, the attack on ReID, an open-set task that test data may not exist in the training set, has not attracted enough attention.

In the literature, most of recent emerged attack methods on ReID are designed to be used in the white-box attack [1,2,22,29,31], where the adversary has full access to the attacked models. In most practical scenarios, however, this kind of access is not available. The black-box setting, where only input query image and the network output are known, is considered more realistic. In this circumstance, we cann't directly obtain the gradients of the loss function of the attacked model. One solution in black-box setting is trainning and attacking a substitute model, and then generating the adversarial examples using it to attack other models. This kind of approach is also known as transfer-based attack. The attack effect is restricted by the transferability of substitute model. Attack failure often occurs in cross model attack. Unfortunately, most of the current researches use this approach to achieve black-box attack [1,2,7,22]. Another solution is estimating the gradients by query of DNNs for generating the adversarial examples, which called query-based attack, and the performance of it outperforms above one. But this solution is criticized by large query quantities. To the best of our knowledge, only one paper (QAIR [14]) so far focuses on query-based image retrieval task. However, their approach requires generating adversarial samples for each image. When extended to attack thousands of images, the number of queries made by their method is too large to be acceptable.

To address the problem of large-scale black-box attack in ReID, we propose a Query-UAP attack method. UAP attack refers to the attack with universal adversarial perturbation (UAP) [20], which fools a given model using a shared perturbation. Our approach combines query-based black-box attack with UAP attack. Our goal is generating UAP for query images so as to modify similarities between gallery images and query images. We hope that our metirc attack can push the most similar image farthest. Meanwhile we have three requirements: reducing total number of queries for attack on the entire dataset, improving success rate of the attack, and maintaining high visual quality of the adversarial samples.

We achieve our requirements by the following strategies. **First**, to improve the success rate of attack and maintain visual quality of the adversarial sample, we use a more accurate coordinate-wise gradient estimation method. **Second**, to reduce the total number of queries for attacking on the entire dataset, we exploit importance sampling. When querying each image, we only obtain the gradients of a small fraction of pixels guided by importance instead of all. **Third**, considering the good performance of MI-FGSM, we propose a coordinate-wise attack algorithm based on it to update the UAP. **Finally**, to avoid the undesirable spread of inaccurate gradient estimation in iterations, we propose a spatial momentum prior to correct the gradient update direction, and the stability of directions updating is guaranteed not only in temporal dimension, but also in spatial dimension.

In summary, we make the following contributions:

- We propose a new query efficient black-box attack method for ReID, and we improve the gradient estimation approach exploiting importance sampling to make the number of queries acceptable.
- To accelerate the convergence of the attack but ensure the stability of gradient directions, we propose a coordinate-wise MI-FGSM attack algorithm, which integrates the spatial momentum prior term into the process of updating in spatio-temporal dimension.
- Comprehensive experiments demonstrate the effectiveness of our method from not only the boost of success rate but also the improvement of visual quality.

2   Related Work

There are a large number of black-box attack algorithms proposed for classification task, mainly including transfer-based and query-based attack. For transfer-based approach, several recent studies take a different perspective to improve the transferability of adversarial samples. For example, by exploring the ensemble of multiple substitute models for training [15,17,26], or by augmenting the training data [9,24,25], or by using more advanced gradient update strategies [8,16,23]. Query-based approach is first proposed in [4]. Subsequently, in order to improve the efficiency of queries, several approaches combine query-based attack with transfer-based attack [6,27], or with meta-learning techniques [10,19], which reduces the number of queries to some extent.

However, these methods are all designed for the attack classification task, and may not be suitable for the ReID attack task with open-set. Currently there are few black-box attack algorithms for ReID task, and almost all are transfer-based approaches. These algorithms can be separated into image-specific and image-agnostic attack.

Image-specific attack generate adversarial samples optimized for each image individually. Opposite Direction Feature Attack (ODFA) [31] makes an early attempt in the image retrieval (or ReID) attack task, where they push clean samples in the feature space in opposite direction to generate adversarial samples. Bai et al. [1] propose the Adversarial Metric Attack (AMA) attack algorithm to generate adversarial samples by maximizing the mean square error between the clean and adversarial sample features. Wang et al. [22] propose a learning-to-mis-rank formulation to perturb the ranking of the system output and use generative adversarial network (GAN) to generate adversarial samples. However, these methods are designed for white-box attack, and the attack success rate is not high when migrating to other black-box target models. Li et al. [14] make the first attempt on query-efficient attack against image retrieval (QAIR) under the black-box setting. Unfortunately, their approach still generates the own adversarial samples for each sample, and is not applicable to the scenario of large-scale adversarial sample attack.

Image-agnostic perturbations are also known as universal adversarial perturbation (UAP), which generate a shared perturbation to attack the entire dataset.

Ding *et al.* [7] apply the UAP to the ReID attack task, and propose a model-insensitive mechanism for cross-model attack. However, their approach is still a transfer-based attack, and it depends on the transferability of the adversarial samples. Li *et al.* [13] proposed the image retrieval universal adversarial perturbations (IR-UAP) attack method, but their method is not a real black-box attack. This is because they train a distillation model with the same structure, and conduct white-box attack on it to generate UAP, which under the assumption that the structure information of the attacked model is known.

Our approach different from above, which suffer from low success rate on transfer-based approaches or inefficient on query-based approaches. Our approach combines query-based attack with image-agnostic attack, which maintains a high attack success while significantly reducing the total queries.

3 Methodology

3.1 Problem Definition

Let f_θ be a metric learning model with parameter θ for ReID system. Denote f_θ projects image x to the feature space as $f_\theta(x)$. Given a query image q and gallery G, the system returns top-k similar images by their features similarity to q. The formula is defined as follows:

$$RList^k(q, f_\theta) = \{g_1, g_2, \ldots, g_i, \ldots, g_k \mid g_i \in G\}$$
$$s.t.\ \mathcal{S}\big(f_\theta(q), f_\theta(g_i)\big) \geq \mathcal{S}\big(f_\theta(q), f_\theta(g_j)\big),\ i,j \in \{1, \cdots, k\} \text{ and } i < j \qquad (1)$$

where $\mathcal{S}(\cdot, \cdot)$ refers the metric to feature similarity between two images. In this paper, we use the cosine similarity function.

For ReID attack, our goal is to find a small universal perturbation δ added to all query images, so that the images returned by the ReID system are as dissimilar as possible to the query image q. The attack goal is formalized as follows:

$$RList^k(q + \delta, f_\theta) = \{g_1, g_2, \ldots, g_i, \ldots, g_k \mid g_i \in G\}$$
$$s.t.\ \mathcal{S}\big(f_\theta(q), f_\theta(g_i)\big) < \mathcal{S}\big(f_\theta(q), f_\theta(g_j)\big),\ i,j \in \{1, \cdots, k\} \text{ and } i < j, \qquad (2)$$
$$s.t.\ \|\delta\|_\infty \leq \epsilon$$

where ϵ is the maximum allowed perturbation, $\|\cdot\|_\infty$ denotes the infinity norm.

In this paper, we mainly focus on query-based black-box attack. It is assumed that we don't know the structure of the attacked model, and cannot access the model parameters, so we have no way to obtain the model gradient through back-propagation. Considering a more practical scenario, the query image labels are unknown, either. We assume that the information available is the input query images and their features of the model.

3.2 Loss Function

It is worth mentioning that the ReID task is an open-set problem without explicit decision boundary. So the loss function used in the classification task cannot be applied directly. Recently, adversarial triplet loss [22] and average precision(AP) loss [7] are proposed to disrupt the sorted list of system outputs. However, these complex loss functions relying on label-based triplet sampling cannot be adapted to our label-free assumption. We directly use the cosine similarity as our loss function due to the only information we can use is image features. And we generate the UAP by minimizing the cosine similarity. The loss function is defined as follows:

$$\mathcal{L}\big(f_\theta\left(q+\delta\right), f_\theta\left(q\right)\big) = \frac{f_\theta(q+\delta) \cdot f_\theta(q)}{\|f_\theta(q+\delta)\|_2^2 \cdot \|f_\theta(q)\|_2^2} \quad s.t. \ \|\delta\|_\infty \le \epsilon \qquad (3)$$

where δ is the UAP and ϵ is the maximum allowed perturbation. Our experiments demonstrate that this simple loss function is sufficient to generate strong adversarial samples.

3.3 Query-UAP Attack

Through experiments we find that, the accuracy of most state-of-the-art ReID models are degraded drastically by a few gradient iterations of updating the UAP in the white-box setting. *This phenomenon inspires us to explore whether a small number of queries in the black-box setting could achieve similar results.* To this end, we propose a novel query-based UAP black-box attack algorithm, as described in Algorithm 1.

The whole pipeline of the algorithm is as follows. Given a query image q and initial perturbation δ, we can obtain the features of q and its adversarial example $q + \delta$ by one query firstly. Then, we sample some pixels by importance sampling strategy. And next, for each sampling point, we need a query to calculate its gradient and update the perturbation according to the gradient. If n points are sampled, n queries are required. We use finite differentiation method to estimate the gradients, and use the proposed coordinate-wise MI-FGSM with spatial momentum prior to update the perturbation. Repeat the above steps until all image queries are complete. The experimental results show that our method not only achieves the approximate attack effect as the white-box attack, but also controls the number of queries in an acceptable range.

Pixels Importance Sampling. In order to reduce the number of queries, we update the UAP by calculating the gradient of only a few pixels[1] selected by importance sampling in each image. For ReID problem, the regions of person in the images are remarkable for recognition. Meanwhile, we should not ignore the non-person regions completely, some belongings may also be important for identification, such as backpack, umbrella etc. Since the images for ReID task have

---

[1] The pixels mentioned here are channel distinguished, that is, pixels at the same spatial position on different channels are regarded as different pixels.

Algorithm 1: Query-UAP attack for person re-identification.

Input: Dataset $\mathcal{Q}$, target model f_θ, number of epochs T

Output: Universal adversarial perturbation δ

1 Initialize $\delta \leftarrow U(-\epsilon, \epsilon)$

2 **while** *epochs* $\leq T$ **do**

3   **for** *each sample* $q \in \mathcal{Q}$ **do**

4   Calculate the features of the original sample $f_\theta(q)$

5   Calculate the features of the adversarial examples $f_\theta(q + \delta)$

6   Sampling n pixels $\mathcal{P}_{c,i,j}$ with Eq. (4).

7   **for** *each coordinate* $e_{c,i,j} \in \mathcal{P}_{c,i,j}$ **do**

8   Calculate the gradient of the coordinate $g_{c,i,j}$ with Eq .(5).

9   Update the universal adversarial perturbation δ with Eq. (6) and Eq. (7).

10   **end**

11   **end**

12 **end**

---

a uniform pattern, we can easily get an accurate person segmentation model, and use this to guide the sampling process of important pixels. The process is formulated as follows:

$$\mathcal{M}_{c,i,j} = s_\theta(q)$$
$$\mathcal{W}_{c,i,j} = \gamma \mathcal{M}_{c,i,j} + (1 - \gamma)(1 - \mathcal{M}_{c,i,j}) \tag{4}$$
$$\mathcal{P}_{c,i,j} = \text{multinomial}(\mathcal{W}_{c,i,j}, n)$$

where s_θ is the person segmentation model, $\mathcal{M}_{c,i,j}$ is the segmented person image, (c, i, j) represents the coordinate with channel and spatial position information. The original segmentation result is single channel, we extend it to multi-channel. γ is a parameter that controls the importance of person and non-person regions ($\gamma \in [0, 1]$, we set $\gamma = 0.95$), so $\mathcal{W}_{c,i,j}$ can be viewed as the sampling weights. Next, we can obtain n pixels $\mathcal{P}_{c,i,j}$ for gradient estimation by multinomial probability distribution sampling.

Gradient Estimation. We use the coordinate-wise finite differentiation gradient estimation method to obtain the gradients of sampled coordinates. Although the coordinate-wise gradient estimation algorithm is criticized for the large number of queries it generates, our query-based UAP only calculates gradients for a small number of pixels in each picture. Furthermore, as the gradients computed by our method are more precise, the total number of queries required to successfully attack the whole dataset stays minimal. We define the gradient g of UAP at coordinate (c, i, j) as follows:

$$
\begin{aligned}
g_{c,i,j} &= \frac{\partial \mathcal{L}\big(f_\theta(q + \delta), f_\theta(q)\big)}{\partial \delta_{c,i,j}} \\
&= \frac{\mathcal{L}\big(f_\theta(q + \delta + h \cdot e_{c,i,j}), f_\theta(q)\big) - \mathcal{L}\big(f_\theta(q + \delta), f_\theta(q)\big)}{h}
\end{aligned}
\tag{5}
$$

where h is a small constant (we set $h = 0.01$), and $e_{c,i,j}$ is a standard basis vector, only the value at the coordinate (c, i, j) is 1 and otherwise is 0. Note that $f_\theta(q)$ and $f_\theta(q + \delta)$ are only queried once for each image. For $f_\theta(q + \delta + h \cdot e_{c,i,j})$ we need to query n times for each image to obtain the gradients of n coordinate points.

Coordinate-wise MI-FGSM. To speed up the convergence of the attack, we use the MI-FGSM [8] algorithm to update the UAP, and modify it to adapt to the coordinate-wise update. Unlike the traditional MI-FGSM algorithm that updates momentum and perturbation in all coordinates at a time, our coordinate-wise MI-FSGM only updates the sampled n coordinates each time. It is worth noting that this update of our coordinate-wise is similar to ZOO [4], but the difference is that ZOO uses it for an optimization-based attack, while we use it for a more efficient gradient sign attack. The formula is as follows:

$$
\begin{aligned}
g_{c,i,j}^{t+1} &= \mu \cdot m_{c,i,j}^t + \frac{g_{c,i,j}^t}{\|g_{c,i,j}^t\|_1} \\
\delta_{c,i,j}^{t+1} &= \prod\nolimits_{\mathcal{B}_\infty(\delta,\epsilon)} \left(\delta_{c,i,j}^t - \alpha \cdot \text{sign}(g_{c,i,j}^{t+1}) \right) \\
m_{c,i,j}^{t+1} &= g_{c,i,j}^{t+1}
\end{aligned}
\tag{6}
$$

where μ is the decay factor, m is the momentum, t is the number of iterations. $\prod_{\mathcal{B}_\infty(\delta,\epsilon)}$ denotes the projection operation, which makes $l_\infty(\delta) \le \epsilon$, and α is the step size.

Spatial Momentum Prior. Furthermore, to avoid the undesirable effect of inaccurate gradient estimation for some pixels, we use a spatial momentum prior to correct the gradient update direction. This idea is inspired by [12], which find that the similarities exist between the gradients of adjacent coordinates, and they obtain the gradient prior information by upsampling. Our approach is different from theirs, we perform a Gaussian filter operation on the momentum at each gradient update. We consider the filtered momentum as our gradient prior, which provides a more stable direction for the gradient update. Our approach is more controllable and yields better visual quality than the upsampling approach which produces conspicuous blocky perturbations. We rewrite the first term in Eq. (6) as follows:

$$
\begin{aligned}
g_{c,i,j}^{t+1} &= \mu \cdot (W * m)_{c,i,j}^t + \frac{g_{c,i,j}^t}{\|g_{c,i,j}^t\|_1} \\
W_{u,v \in [-\frac{k}{2}, \frac{k}{2}]} &= \frac{1}{2\pi\sigma^2} \exp\left(-\frac{u^2 + v^2}{2\sigma^2} \right)
\end{aligned}
\tag{7}
$$

where W is Gaussian kernel, $*$ denotes convolution operation, k is the kernel size, u, v are the coordinates of the kernel and σ is standard deviation. Since the prior will accumulate over many iterations, we set the kernel size and sigma to a smaller value ($k = 3$ and $\sigma = 0.4$). It is worth noting that, in contrast to the traditional MI-FGSM algorithm, our method considers not only the updated direction of the stable gradient in the temporal dimension, but also the correlation in the spatial dimension.

4   Experiment

4.1   Experimental Settings

Datasets. We evaluate our approach on Market-1501 [30] and DukeMTMC [21], which are two commonly used person ReID datasets. Market-1501 dataset consists of 32,217 images of 1501 pedestrians captured by 6 cameras, of which, 12,936 images of 751 pedestrians are used for training and 3,368 images of another 750 pedestrians are used as the query set. DukeMTMC dataset was collected from 8 different cameras, and contains 16,522 training images from 702 individuals and 2,228 query images from another 702 individuals.

Implementation Details. Considering the more challenging cases, our attack algorithm uses only 160 unlabeled images as training samples. To reduce the fluctuation of the results, we fixed the first 160 images of the training set as the dataset $\mathcal{D}$. The size of the input image is 256×128, we set epochs $T{=}1$, pixels numbers sampled for each sample $n = 6144$ ($64 \times 32 \times 3$). We set decay factor $\mu = 1$, and step size $\alpha = 10/255$. If not specified, we set perturbation budget $\epsilon = 10/255$ in all experiments. Additionally, we use mean average precision (mAP) as an evaluation metric.

4.2   Comparison with State of the Arts

We compare our Query-UAP with several state-of-the-art black-box attack, including TI-DIM [9], MUAP [7] and Bandits [12]. These methods include both image-specific and image-agnostic approaches, as well as transfer-based and query-based approaches.

We compare our approach with these four different types of attacks. For transfer-based image-specific attack, we use the TI-DIM [9] as our baseline, and set all parameters as in the original paper, except that the loss function is replaced by the cosine similarity function and the perturbation budget is set to the same as ours. For transfer-based image-agnostic attack, we compare with MUAP [7], and use the open source code provided in their paper directly. It should be noted that due to the backbones of our comparison models are mostly based on ResNet50 improvements, for a fair comparison, we uniformly use InceptionV3 as agent model in transfer-based attack. For query-based image-specific attack, we use Bandits [12] as our baseline, although QAIR [14] seems more

Table 1. The mAP of black-box attack against different backbones. * denotes white-box attack. **T** denotes transfer-based, **Q** denotes query-based, **S** denotes image-specific and **A** denotes image-agnostic.

mAP		Market1501					DukeMTMC				
Backbone		Inc-v3	Res-50	ResIBNa	SeResXt	Vit	Inc-v3	Res-50	ResIBNa	SeResXt	Vit
Before attack		0.77	0.86	0.87	0.87	0.87	0.68	0.76	0.79	0.78	0.79
TS	TI-DIM [9]	0.01*	0.24	0.42	0.33	0.47	0.01*	0.12	0.28	0.19	0.33
TA	MUAP [7]	0.05*	0.33	0.47	0.39	0.57	0.07*	0.22	0.41	0.30	0.48
QS	Bandits [12]	0.18	0.22	0.54	0.41	0.52	0.23	0.10	0.39	0.24	0.43
QA	BanditsUAP [12]	0.14	0.09	0.33	0.28	0.28	0.16	**0.07**	0.28	0.17	0.31
	QueryUAP(ours)	**0.05**	**0.06**	**0.17**	**0.22**	**0.24**	**0.07**	0.10	**0.25**	**0.15**	**0.23**

appropriate as the only paper focusing on query-based image retrieval so far, it is pity that its source code has not been released. We use cosine similarity as loss function and set a fixed number of 500 queries per image. For query-based image-agnostic attack, we modify the Bandits algorithm to the UAP version, and set the total number of queries to $1,000,000^2$ times the same as ours.

Attacking Different Backbones. To compare the effectiveness of our attack method with other models with different backbones, we train five ReID models with different backbones using all the tricks of BoT [18], which includes InceptionV3, ResNet50, ResNet50IBNa, SeResNeXt50, and Vit. The results of the attack are shown in Table 1. It can be seen that our method consistently outperforms other methods with different backbone networks. For example, compared to the Bandits UAP, our method improves the mAP term by ranging from 0.03 to 0.16. In addition, based on the observation of the results we have some findings. **First**, the robustness of different backbone networks varies widely. For example, InceptionV3 and ResNet50 are more vulnerable than other backbones. It is worth noting that even small differences in network structure will bring great differences in robustness, *e.g.*, ResNet50IBNa is more robust than ResNet50. Nevertheless, our attack method is still very effective. **Second**, compared with the transfer-based attack method, the query-based attack method is more effective. Experiments have confirmed our suspicion that the attack ability of transfer-based attack method is limited by the transferability of the substitute model. We think that due to the great differences in the structure between

---

2 Our method uses 160 images, epochs set to one, 6144 queries per image, plus each image requires two additional queries, the total number of queries is $160 \times 6146 \times 1 \approx 1,000,000$, which average of 297 queries per image in Market1501 and 449 queries per image in DukeMTMC. For Bandits UAP, we use the same images, each image query 6145 times, epochs set to one, plus each image requires one additional query, the total number of queries is $160 \times 6146 \times 1 \approx 1,000,000$.

Table 2. The mAP of black-box attack against different state-of-the-art ReID models. *
denotes white-box attack. **T** denotes transfer-based, **Q** denotes query-based, **S** denotes
image-specific and **A** denotes image-agnostic.

mAP	Market1501					DukeMTMC				
Reid model	ABD	AGW	AP	OSNet	TrsReid	ABD	AGW	AP	OSNet	TrsReid
Before attack	0.87	0.88	0.89	0.83	0.89	0.77	0.79	0.80	0.72	0.82
TS TI-DIM [9]	0.29	0.28	0.31	0.37	0.46	0.17	0.19	0.22	0.25	0.31
TA MUAP [7]	0.37	0.41	0.32	0.30	0.52	0.28	0.30	0.35	0.34	0.48
QS Bandits [12]	0.26	0.25	0.24	0.35	0.53	0.15	0.16	0.20	0.37	0.42
QA BanditsUAP [12]	0.19	0.17	0.07	0.21	0.31	**0.13**	**0.09**	**0.13**	0.23	0.32
QueryUAP(ours)	**0.15**	**0.07**	**0.03**	**0.16**	**0.25**	0.14	0.19	0.15	**0.14**	**0.26**

different models, it is difficult to successfully attack all other models with the
adversarial samples generated by one model. The experimental results show that
this is true. Our method generates UAP for each model individually, which is
more reliable compared to transfer-based attack. **Third**, the UAP attack is more
suitable for query-based ReID attack. In Table 1, we can see that Bandits UAP
significantly beats the Bandits algorithm for a comparable average number of
queries per image. Our approach adopts this form of query-based UAP attack
and defeats Bandits UAP.

Attacking State-of-the-Art ReID Models. We also compare the performance of our attack algorithm on the state-of-the-art ReID models, these models include ABD-Net [5], AGW-Net [28], AP-Net [3], OSNet [32] and TransReID
[11]. The results are shown in Table 2. It can be seen that even if we attack the
most advanced models, our attack method is still effective. For instance, even
for TransReID, one of the most advanced and robust models, our approach is
still able to reduce its mAP term to 0.26 with few queries. Notably, it seems
that our method does not have a significant advantage over Bandits UAP in the
DukeMTMC dataset, but as shown in Fig. 1, our method generates higher visual
quality of the adversarial samples and obtains comparable attack performance.
So our method is still more practical. Furthermore, besides the findings mentioned above, we have some additional new findings. **First**, lightweight models
are not necessarily more vulnerable. It's intuitive that lightweight models should
be more vulnerable to attacks, however, in our experiments the lightweight
OSNet is more robust than the AGW-Net and AP-Net. **Second**, Transform-
based networks are more robust than CNN-based. We can see that Vit in Table 1
and TransReID in Table 2 show greater robustness in all these attack methods
compared to other CNN-based networks. Nevertheless, our attack method can
still generate adversarial samples with sufficient threat.

Table 3. Effectiveness of our spatial momentum prior. smp denotes spatial momentum prior.

mAP	Market1501					DukeMTMC				
Backbone	Inc-v3	Res-50	ResIBNa	SeResXt	Vit	Inc-v3	Res-50	ResIBNa	SeResXt	Vit
VanillaUAP(white-box)	**0.04**	**0.03**	**0.11**	**0.16**	**0.21**	**0.06**	**0.04**	**0.18**	**0.10**	**0.20**
QueryUAP(w/o smp)	0.09	0.07	0.24	0.27	0.31	0.14	0.19	0.38	0.24	0.27
QueryUAP(w/ smp)	0.05	0.06	0.17	0.22	0.24	0.07	0.10	0.25	0.15	0.23

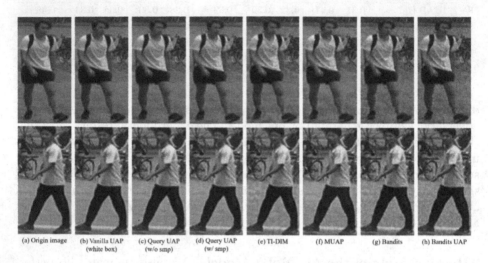

(a) Origin image   (b) Vanilla UAP (white box)   (c) Query UAP (w/o smp)   (d) Query UAP (w/ smp)   (e) TI-DIM   (f) MUAP   (g) Bandits   (h) Bandits UAP

Fig. 1. The visualization of the adversarial examples generate for InceptionV3. All the perturbation budget satisfy $\|\delta\|_\infty \leqslant 10/255$, and smp denotes spatial momentum prior.

4.3 Ablation Study

The Effectiveness of Spatial Momentum Prior. To verify the effectiveness of our proposed spatial momentum prior approach, we compare the effect of the attack with and without the spatial momentum prior, and also compare with the white-box attack trained with the same input images and same iterations. The results are shown in Table 3. It can be seen that our method with spatial momentum prior can achieve a consistent improvement in all backbones, and approach the performance of white-box attack. *e.g.*, even in the worst case, the difference is only 0.07 in term of mAP over the white-box attack. In addition, we also visualized the adversarial samples generated by our method in Fig. 1. It can be seen that the visual quality of our adversarial samples is also very close to the white-box attack.

Number of Queries. We further explore the impact of the number of queries on the attack results, and the results are shown in Fig. 2, it can be seen that our method can be further improved as the number of queries increases, which sufficiently demonstrates the high practicality of our method.

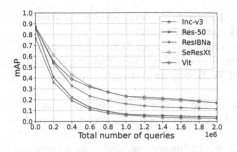 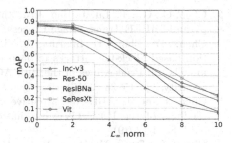

Fig. 2. Compare the total number of queries for the attack Market1501

Fig. 3. Compare the size of perturbation ϵ for the attack Market1501

Comparisons of Different. ϵ In addition, we also explore the effect of different perturbation sizes on the experimental results, and the results are shown in Fig. 3. It can be seen that the perturbation size has a relatively large effect on the results, but as shown in Fig. 1, even with the same perturbation budget, the adversarial samples generated by our method still obtain higher visual quality.

5 Conclusion

In this paper, we propose a novel query-based UAP black-box attack algorithm, which is well suitable to the task of large-scale ReID attack. Extensive experiments have shown the effectiveness of our algorithm. In addition, our algorithm achieves a balance between attack success rate, number of queries and visual quality of the adversarial samples. Meanwhile, our experiments also reveal the vulnerability of the state-of-the-art ReID models, and we also hope that our findings will drive the construction of more robust ReID models with an aim to resist more unknown attacks.

Acknowledgement. This work was supported in part by National Natural Science Foundation of China (No. 61906049, No. 62072127, No. 62002076), in part by Natural Science Foundation of Guangdong Province (No. 2020A1515010423, No. 2021A1515011859), in part by Science and Technology Program of Guangzhou, China (No. 202002030131), in part by Guangdong basic and applied basic research fund joint fund Youth Fund (No. 2019A1515110213).

References

1. Bai, S., Li, Y., Zhou, Y., Li, Q., Torr, P.H.: Adversarial metric attack and defense for person re-identification. IEEE Trans. Pattern Anal. Mach. Intell. **43**(6), 2119–2126 (2020)
2. Bouniot, Q., Audigier, R., Loesch, A.: Vulnerability of person re-identification models to metric adversarial attacks. In: Proceedings of the IEEE/CVF Conference on Computer Vision and Pattern Recognition Workshops, pp. 794–795 (2020)

3. Chen, G., Gu, T., Lu, J., Bao, J.A., Zhou, J.: Person re-identification via attention pyramid. IEEE Trans. Image Process. **30**, 7663–7676 (2021)
4. Chen, P.Y., Zhang, H., Sharma, Y., Yi, J., Hsieh, C.J.: Zoo: Zeroth order optimization based black-box attacks to deep neural networks without training substitute models. In: Proceedings of the 10th ACM Workshop on Artificial Intelligence and Security, pp. 15–26 (2017)
5. Chen, T., et al.: ABD-Net: attentive but diverse person re-identification. In: Proceedings of the IEEE/CVF International Conference on Computer Vision, pp. 8351–8361 (2019)
6. Cheng, S., Dong, Y., Pang, T., Su, H., Zhu, J.: Improving black-box adversarial attacks with a transfer-based prior. In: Advances in Neural Information Processing Systems, vol. 32 (2019)
7. Ding, W., Wei, X., Ji, R., Hong, X., Tian, Q., Gong, Y.: Beyond universal person re-identification attack. IEEE Trans. Inf. Forensics Secur. **16**, 3442–3455 (2021)
8. Dong, Y., et al.: Boosting adversarial attacks with momentum. In: Proceedings of the IEEE conference on Computer Vision and Pattern Recognition, pp. 9185–9193 (2018)
9. Dong, Y., Pang, T., Su, H., Zhu, J.: Evading defenses to transferable adversarial examples by translation-invariant attacks. In: Proceedings of the IEEE/CVF Conference on Computer Vision and Pattern Recognition, pp. 4312–4321 (2019)
10. Du, J., Zhang, H., Zhou, J.T., Yang, Y., Feng, J.: Query-efficient meta attack to deep neural networks. In: International Conference on Learning Representations (2019)
11. He, S., Luo, H., Wang, P., Wang, F., Li, H., Jiang, W.: TransReID: transformer-based object re-identification. In: Proceedings of the IEEE/CVF International Conference on Computer Vision, pp. 15013–15022 (2021)
12. Ilyas, A., Engstrom, L., Madry, A.: Prior convictions: black-box adversarial attacks with bandits and priors. arXiv preprint arXiv:1807.07978 (2018)
13. Li, J., Ji, R., Liu, H., Hong, X., Gao, Y., Tian, Q.: Universal perturbation attack against image retrieval. In: Proceedings of the IEEE/CVF International Conference on Computer Vision, pp. 4899–4908 (2019)
14. Li, X., et al.: QAIR: practical query-efficient black-box attacks for image retrieval. In: Proceedings of the IEEE/CVF Conference on Computer Vision and Pattern Recognition, pp. 3330–3339 (2021)
15. Li, Y., Bai, S., Zhou, Y., Xie, C., Zhang, Z., Yuille, A.: Learning transferable adversarial examples via ghost networks. In: Proceedings of the AAAI Conference on Artificial Intelligence, vol. 34, pp. 11458–11465 (2020)
16. Lin, J., Song, C., He, K., Wang, L., Hopcroft, J.E.: Nesterov accelerated gradient and scale invariance for adversarial attacks. In: International Conference on Learning Representations (2019)
17. Liu, Y., Chen, X., Liu, C., Song, D.: Delving into transferable adversarial examples and black-box attacks. arXiv preprint arXiv:1611.02770 (2016)
18. Luo, H., et al.: A strong baseline and batch normalization neck for deep person re-identification. IEEE Trans. Multimedia **22**(10), 2597–2609 (2019)
19. Ma, C., Chen, L., Yong, J.H.: Simulating unknown target models for query-efficient black-box attacks. In: Proceedings of the IEEE/CVF Conference on Computer Vision and Pattern Recognition, pp. 11835–11844 (2021)
20. Moosavi-Dezfooli, S.M., Fawzi, A., Fawzi, O., Frossard, P.: Universal adversarial perturbations. In: Proceedings of the IEEE Conference on Computer Vision and Pattern Recognition, pp. 1765–1773 (2017)

21. Ristani, E., Solera, F., Zou, R.S., Cucchiara, R., Tomasi, C.: Performance measures and a data set for multi-target, multi-camera tracking. In: ECCV Workshops (2) (2016)

22. Wang, H., Wang, G., Li, Y., Zhang, D., Lin, L.: Transferable, controllable, and inconspicuous adversarial attacks on person re-identification with deep misranking. In: Proceedings of the IEEE/CVF Conference on Computer Vision and Pattern Recognition, pp. 342–351 (2020)

23. Wang, X., He, K.: Enhancing the transferability of adversarial attacks through variance tuning. In: Proceedings of the IEEE/CVF Conference on Computer Vision and Pattern Recognition, pp. 1924–1933 (2021)

24. Wang, X., He, X., Wang, J., He, K.: Admix: enhancing the transferability of adversarial attacks. In: Proceedings of the IEEE/CVF International Conference on Computer Vision, pp. 16158–16167 (2021)

25. Xie, C., et al.: Improving transferability of adversarial examples with input diversity. In: Proceedings of the IEEE/CVF Conference on Computer Vision and Pattern Recognition, pp. 2730–2739 (2019)

26. Xiong, Y., Lin, J., Zhang, M., Hopcroft, J.E., He, K.: Stochastic variance reduced ensemble adversarial attack for boosting the adversarial transferability. In: Proceedings of the IEEE/CVF Conference on Computer Vision and Pattern Recognition, pp. 14983–14992 (2022)

27. Yang, J., Jiang, Y., Huang, X., Ni, B., Zhao, C.: Learning black-box attackers with transferable priors and query feedback. Adv. Neural. Inf. Process. Syst. **33**, 12288–12299 (2020)

28. Ye, M., Shen, J., Lin, G., Xiang, T., Shao, L., Hoi, S.C.: Deep learning for person re-identification: a survey and outlook. IEEE Trans. Pattern Anal. Mach. Intell. **44**, 2872–2893 (2021)

29. Zhao, G., Zhang, M., Liu, J., Wen, J.R.: Unsupervised adversarial attacks on deep feature-based retrieval with GAN. arXiv preprint arXiv:1907.05793 (2019)

30. Zheng, L., Shen, L., Tian, L., Wang, S., Wang, J., Tian, Q.: Scalable person re-identification: a benchmark. In: Proceedings of the IEEE International Conference on Computer Vision, pp. 1116–1124 (2015)

31. Zheng, Z., Zheng, L., Yang, Y., Wu, F.: Query attack via opposite-direction feature: towards robust image retrieval. arXiv preprint arXiv:1809.02681 (2018)

32. Zhou, K., Yang, Y., Cavallaro, A., Xiang, T.: OMNI-scale feature learning for person re-identification. In: Proceedings of the IEEE/CVF International Conference on Computer Vision, pp. 3702–3712 (2019)

Robust Person Re-identification with Adversarial Examples Detection and Perturbation Extraction

Qizheng Chen, Ya Li[✉], and Yuming Ma

Guangzhou University, Guangzhou 510006, China
{chenqizheng,mym}@e.gzhu.edu.cn, liya@gzhu.edu.cn

Abstract. Person re-identification (ReID) systems, those based on deep neural networks, have been shown their vulnerability to adversarial examples, i.e. images that only added slight perturbations. In previous defense methods, those input transformations based are easy to reduce the recognition accuracy, while those adversarial examples detection based only prevent the possible adversarial samples from entering the system rather than really improving the system's robustness. In this paper, we aim to construct a robust person ReID model, which not only can defend against the adversarial attack, but also maintains the recognition accuracy. We combine the advantages of adversarial example detection and adversarial training in the model implementation. On the one hand, we propose a novel adversarial examples detection method based on perturbation information. This method not only has high detection accuracy, but also can purify the adversarial examples through a simple perturbation removal operation. On the other hand, we propose an adversarial example generation method for the matching problem, and use the adversarial examples generated by this method to extract the perturbation. That is, we train a perturbation extractor in a way like adversarial training. Experiments show the effectiveness of our method. For example, when facing Deep Mis-Ranking attack, the strongest attacker at present, our model's accuracy is greatly improved from 36.68% to 73.97% compared to previous state-of-the-art defense model. In addition, our defense method can be deployed as a plug-and-play defense solution to protect ReID systems.

Keywords: Person re-identification · Adversarial examples detection · Adversarial defense · Perturbation extract

1 Introduction

Person re-identification (ReID) [13, 16, 18, 24, 27, 30] is a hot topic in the field of computer vision and artificial intelligence, which is viewed as a matching task, aiming to match person by distance or similarity in images taken across non-overlapping cameras. With the widespread of deep learning, ReID has made

S. Yu et al. (Eds.): PRCV 2022, LNCS 13536, pp. 732–744, 2022.
https://doi.org/10.1007/978-3-031-18913-5_56

great progress, especially in recognition accuracy. However, since Szegedy *et al.* [19] found deep neural networks (DNNs) are vulnerable to adversarial examples in classification, researchers recently have found that DNN based ReID also inherited this vulnerability: if the query images are added only a slight perturbation, that is imperceptible to the human eye, can fool the ReID models and make them fail to correctly recognize a person. Nevertheless, few researches ([1,21,26]) focus on defense these adversarial attacks in the field of ReID as far as we know. Therefore, it is necessary to construct a robust person ReID model.

The existing methods have their disadvantages. Adversarial training is considered as one of the most effective defense methods, which adds the adversarial examples generated by one or more attack models into the training set to retrain the systems, and paper [1] tries to apply adversarial training to ReID defense. What's more, attacks to ReID are often defined as metric attacks, which is different from classification attacks. Therefore, for better defense, the adversarial examples generated by attacking classification models cannot be directly applied to ReID. We need to improve the adversarial examples generation method to make adversarial training more effective for matching task.

Another kind of defense method is based on input transformations, such as JPEG compression [7], random resizing and padding [22], and other processing [15,17] to remove the perturbations and obtain the clean images of input. These methods perform the same operation on all input images. In most practical scenarios, a large number of inputs are normal examples without any perturbation. Such unified standard operation brings the decline of recognition accuracy. An intuitive way to improve these methods is detecting adversarial examples before input processing.

In the literature, there are defense methods based on adversarial examples detection [12,14,21]. However, the existing methods adopt the detect-discard methodology, that is, if the input image is detected as adversarial example it will be discarded without further processing. Obviously, the anti-attack ability of the system comes from strict input constrain, rather than the robustness of the system itself. We think that this treatment does not really achieve the robustness of the system, which deviates from our goal.

In this paper, we aim to construct a robust person ReID model, which can not only defend against the adversarial attack, but also maintain the recognition accuracy. We combine the advantages of adversarial example detection and adversarial training in the model implementation. On the one hand, we follow the idea of purification and make improvements. In order to maintaining the recognition accuracy, we only purify the possible adversarial example, not all inputs. And our detection method is based on perturbations information which is different from all the existing ones. The difference is that the training process of the classification model that distinguish the adversarial example from the normal example. The general approach is to train directly on the mixed dataset of original images and their adversarial examples. Our method is to train on the dataset after extracting the perturbation. This idea is inspired by the observation that the remarkable difference in feature space between adversarial examples and the original image lies in the presence or absence of adversarial perturbations, that is, the perturbed part plays a decisive role in distinguishing. Therefore, it is necessary to extract perturbation first. We train a perturbation extractor in the way like adversarial training. And the adversarial example detector utilizes the extracted perturbations to discriminate adversarial examples. In the next purification operation, we only remove the perturbation of images identified as the adversarial examples, and then feed them to the ReID system.

On the other hand, we improve the adversarial example generation method used for the training of perturbation extractor. In terms of methodology, we aims to improve the overall defense generalization by improving the attack ability of adversarial examples using in perturbation extractor. In order to make the adversarial example adaptive to the matching task, we propose an iterative adversarial example generation method, named iterative metric gradient attack (**IMGA**). The proposed method implements metric attack by iterative injecting the gradients computed by triplet loss [3] into images. It is worth mentioning that our method is different from the method proposed in paper [1]. **IMGA** increases the distance between images with the same ID and reduces the distance between images with different IDs by attacking triplet loss. While paper [1] uses existing methods like FGSM, I-FGSM, etc. to generate adversarial examples by increasing the feature distance of images with the same ID.

The main contributions of our work are:

- We propose a novel adversarial examples detection method based on perturbation information. This method not only has high detection accuracy, but also can purify the adversarial examples through a simple perturbation removal operation.
- We propose an adversarial example generation method for the matching problem, and use the adversarial examples generated by this method to extract the perturbation.
- Experiments show the effectiveness of our method, which can not only defend against the adversarial attack, but also maintain the recognition accuracy. When facing Deep Mis-Ranking attack, the strongest attack at present, our model's accuracy is greatly improved from 36.68% to 73.97% compared to the previous state-of-the-art.

2   Related Work

2.1   Adversarial Attack

Person ReID is generally regarded as a distance metric problem. Thus the adversarial attack methods proposed for classification problems are not suitable for ReID. Metric attacks are proposed in the security research of metric tasks, such as ReID, by attacking metric distances to mislead metric task retrieval failures. Self metric attack (SMA) [2] obtains adversarial examples by attacking the feature distance between the original image and the image with added noise. Opposite-direction feature attack (ODFA) [28] utilizes feature-level adversarial gradient to generate adversarial examples that push features in opposite directions. Bai *et al.* [1] propose the adversarial metric attack attack algorithm to generate adversarial examples by maximizing the mean square error between the clean and adversarial example features. Wang *et al.* [20] propose a learning-to-mis-rank formulation to perturb the ranking of the system output and use a generative adversarial network (GAN) to generate adversarial examples.

2.2 Adversarial Defense

At present, adversarial training is one of the most effective methods to defend against adversarial attacks, which exposes the model to adversarial examples during training to obtain immunity against them. Bai *et al.* [1] apply adversarial training to ReID defense. Another method to defend against adversarial attacks is input transformations. For example, Guo *et al.* [7] use JPEG compression to remove high-frequency components to reduce the impact of adversarial perturbations. A compressed sensing approach called Total variation minimization (TVM) is proposed in [7] to remove the small localized changes caused by adversarial perturbations. Xie *et al.* [22] introduce the process of random resizing and padding (RRP) to mitigate adversarial effects by combining random resizing and random padding. Shen et al. [17] propose a new perspective of defending against adversarial examples, which eliminates the adversarial perturbations using a trained network based on the generative adversarial nets (APE-GAN). A defense approach that removes perturbations using an trained purifier was proposed in [15], this method is named NRP. Another method to provide defense for deep neural networks is adversarial detection. Gong *et al.* [5] propose a binary classifier, a simple yet effective and robust way to separate adversarial from the original clean images. An adversarial example detection process via local intrinsic dimensionality (LID) is shown in [14]. Lee *et al.* [12] model the natural examples' distribution by a multivariate Gaussian, and the Mahalanobis distance (MD) of an example to this Gaussian is used for adversarial detection. Wang *et al.* [21] leverage the three relations of query-support affinity, support-support affinity and cross-expert affinity to form the context feature for each query example, and detect adversarial attacks against ReID systems by checking context inconsistency.

3   Proposed Method

Our defense aims to combine the advantages of adversarial detection and adversarial training in a defense framework, named person ReID safeguard framework (PSF). We hope this framework can effectively improve the robustness of the ReID system against adversarial attacks and maintain accuracy on clean images. The whole pipeline of PSF: for the input image, we first utilize a **perturbation extractor** to extract adversarial perturbations from input images, and then use an **adversarial example detector** determines whether the image is an adversarial example according to the extracted perturbations. If the image is judged

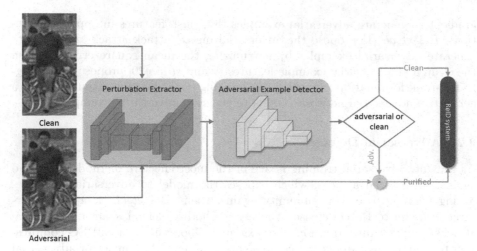

Fig. 1. The pipeline of PSF. First extract the perturbations from input images. Second detect with the extracted perturbations whether the input image is an adversarial example. If it is an adversarial example, the image is purified by removing perturbations and then is fed to the ReID system; otherwise, the image is directly fed to the ReID system.

to be an adversarial example, purify it first and then feed it to the ReID system; otherwise, the image is directly fed to the ReID system (see Fig. 1).

In the training stage, we first utilize the proposed adversarial example generation method to generate adversarial examples x_{adv}. Then we train the perturbation extractor E_θ to learn extracting adversarial perturbations from x_{adv} (see Fig. 2). After E_θ training is completed, then the parameters of E_θ is fixed, we train the adversarial example detector D_θ which utilize the perturbations extracted by E_θ to decide whether the images belong to the adversarial example.

3.1 Networks Architecture

Here, we outline the architecture of the perturbation extractor and adversarial example detector.

Perturbation Extractor (E_θ): Our extractor architecture is inspired by [8,15]. It is composed of a convolutional layer followed by leak-relu [23] and multiple "residual blocks". Each residual block consists of 2 convolutional layers with a leaky-relu between the convolutional layers. Finally, there is a convolutional layer whose output has the same dimension as the input.

Adversarial Example Detector (D_θ): Our detector architecture is also based on ResNet50 [8] which has 48 convolutional layers along with 1 max-pool and 1 average-pool layer.

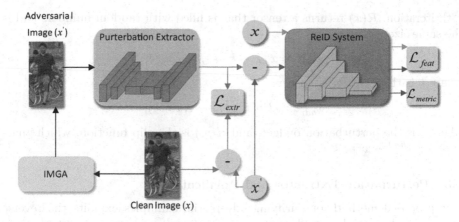

Fig. 2. The training process of the perturbation extractor. The perturbation extractor learns to extract perturbations from the adversarial examples generated by IMGA and combines the reverse process of adversarial example synthesis to achieve the purpose of purifying the image.

3.2 Adversarial Examples Generation

To improve the generalization ability of perturbation extractor, we improve the adversarial example generation method to be suitable for matching task and use it in the training stage. Inspired by I-FGSM, we propose an iterative gradient-based adversarial example generation method named iterative metric gradient attack (IMGA) that adopts triplet loss [9] (see Eq. 1) to compute gradient which is more suitable for matching task.

$$\mathcal{L}_{tri}(X) = \sum_{i=1}^{P} \sum_{a=1}^{K} [m + \max_{p=1...K} D(T(x_a^i), T(x_p^i))$$
$$- \min_{\substack{j=1...P \\ n=1...K \\ j \neq i}} D(T(x_a^i), T(x_n^j))]_+, \tag{1}$$

for a mini-batch X, sampling P person identities and K images of each person. A data point x_j^i corresponds to the j-th image of the i-th person in the batch. $D(x, y)$ is a distance metric function, $T(\cdot)$ represents the embedding feature output by the target ReID model T_θ. In other words, for each sample a in the batch, we can select the hardest positive and the hardest negative samples within the batch by computing the triplet loss.

IMGA is defined as iterative optimization as follows:

$$x_{adv}^{(0)} = \mathcal{R}(x), \tag{2}$$
$$grad^n = \nabla_{X_{adv}^n} \mathcal{L}_{tri}(X_{adv}^n), \tag{3}$$

where x is the attacked image in the batch, x_{adv}^n is the adversarial example generated in the n-th iteration, $grad^n$ is the gradient value generated in the

n-th iteration. $\mathcal{R}(x)$ returns a tensor that is filled with random numbers and is the same size with x.

$$x_{adv}^{n+1} = x_{adv}^n + k \cdot sign(grad^n), \tag{4}$$

where k is the iteration step size.

$$x_{adv}^{n+1} = clip(x_{adv}^{n+1}, x - \epsilon, x + \epsilon), \tag{5}$$

where ϵ is the perturbation budget, and $clip()$ is the clip function, which guarantees $\| x^{n+1} - x \|_\infty < \epsilon$.

3.3 Perturbation Extractor and Purification

Our proposed method for purifying adversarial examples exploits the reverse process of adversarial example synthesis, i.e., removing adversarial perturbations from adversarial examples to obtain purified image (see Eq. 6).

$$x_{pur} = x_{adv} - E(x_{adv}), \tag{6}$$

where $E(\cdot)$ is the perturbation extractor.

In order to extract adversarial perturbations from images and achieve a better purification effect, we propose a hybrid loss function to train the perturbation extractor. This loss function consists of three terms that we will explain below:

Extracted Loss: Adversarial examples are generated by adding adversarial perturbations to the original image, and we hope that the perturbation extractor E can extract these perturbations from the adversarial examples. Therefore, we apply the l_2 loss in the image pixel space,

$$\mathcal{L}_{extr} = \| E(x_{adv}) - (x_{adv} - x) \|_2, \tag{7}$$

where x represent the original input images and x_{adv} represent the corresponding adversarial examples of x.

Feature Loss: To further purify the image, we narrow the distance between adversarial examples and clean examples in the embedding feature space of the ReID model T_θ by calculating the following loss:

$$\mathcal{L}_{feat} = \| T(x_{pur}) - T(x) \|_1 . \tag{8}$$

where, $\|\cdot\|$ is the mean absolute error (MAE).

Metric Loss: The adversarial examples generated with IMGA are the result of increasing the triplet loss (Sect. 3.2). Correspondingly, when learning to purify images, we need to decrease the triplet loss via adding a loss term:

$$\mathcal{L}_{metric} = \mathcal{L}_{tri}(x_{pur}), \tag{9}$$

where $\mathcal{L}_{tri}(\cdot)$ is defined in Eq. 1. The hybrid training loss for E_θ is the combination of the extracted loss and the metric loss, as well as the loss defined on feature space:

$$\mathcal{L}_{E_\theta} = \lambda_1 \cdot \mathcal{L}_{extr} + \lambda_2 \cdot \mathcal{L}_{feat} + \lambda_3 \cdot \mathcal{L}_{metric} \tag{10}$$

Table 1. Performance of normally trained models on origin examples of Market1501.

Dataset	ResNet50		DenseNet121		OSNet	
	mAP	Rank-1	mAP	Rank-1	mAP	Rank-1
Market-1501	76.54%	91.09%	77.73%	90.97%	82.01%	93.97%

3.4 Adversarial Example Detector

Like popular adversarial example detectors, the proposed adversarial example detector D_θ learns a decision boundary between clean images and adversarial examples. However, a key difference is that our proposed adversarial example detector utilizes the extracted perturbations to discriminate adversarial examples, since the perturbed part of the image brings greater discrimination. The detector is trained using a binary cross-entropy loss:

$$\mathcal{L}_{dect} = \mathbb{E}_x \left[logD(E(x)) \right] + \mathbb{E}_{x_{adv}} \left[1 - logD(E(x_{adv})) \right]. \tag{11}$$

4 Experiments

4.1 Experimental Settings

Dataset. The Market-1501 dataset [25] is a widely used for person ReID. Market-1501 contains 1501 identities captured by six different cameras. The dataset is divided into two parts: 750 identities are used for training, and the remaining 751 identities are used for testing.

Training Details. Training is done on two RTX 2080Ti GPUs and batch size is set to 64. Learning rates for extractor is set to 10^{-4}, and for detector is set to 10^{-6}, with the value of $\lambda_1 = 10^{-3}$, $\lambda_2 = 1$, and $\lambda_3 = 10^{-4}$.

Attacks Implementation. We conduct experiments on the metric learning version of three state-of-the-art attacks (FGSM [6], I-FGSM [11] and MI-FGSM [4]) developed by [2], two state-of-the-art adversarial attack approaches (SMA [2], Deep Mis-Ranking [20]) specifically designed against ReID systems. The perturbation budget ϵ for FGSM, I-FGSM, MI-FGSM, SMA is 8, while the perturbation budget ϵ for Deep Mis-Ranking is 16 for verification in larger perturbations. And iterative attacks run 40 iterations using step size 1/255.

Evaluation Criteria of ReID. Following existing works, rank-k precision and mean average precision (mAP) are adopted as the evaluation metrics. Rank-k denotes the average accuracy of the top k returned result corresponding to each query image. The mAP denotes the mean of average accuracy, the query results are sorted according to the similarity, and the closer the correct result is to the top of the list, the higher the score.

Person ReID Models. We train two ReID models using ResNet50 [8] and DenseNet121 [10] as backbone networks, and adopted pretrained ImageNet

Table 2. Robustness of different defense methods against state-of-the-art white-box attacks. Proposed purification method significantly improves the mAP and rank-1 (the higher is better).

ReID models	Defenses	Attacks							
		I-FGSM		MI-FGSM		SMA		Deep Mis-Ranking	
		mAP	Rank-1	mAP	Rank-1	mAP	Rank-1	mAP	Rank-1
OSNet	No defense	0.81%	0.98%	0.78%	1.04%	0.62%	0.85%	0.50%	0.18%
	AT	38.51%	66.95%	37.31%	65.97%	34.99%	62.95%	23.14%	44.12%
	RRP	26.98%	42.43%	21.85%	35.01%	39.69%	56.29%	21.24%	31.56%
	APE-GAN	29.54%	45.04%	22.74%	36.22%	46.38%	61.76%	38.37%	53.09%
	NRP	33.35%	50.71%	24.71%	38.95%	48.52%	64.90%	36.68%	49.79%
	Ours	**78.17%**	**92.19%**	**80.59%**	**92.99%**	**79.14%**	**92.55%**	**73.97%**	**89.49%**
DenseNet121	No defense	0.44%	0.33%	0.40%	0.24%	0.47%	0.18%	1.69%	1.37%
	AT	35.67%	65.97%	33.58%	63.72%	35.76%	66.48%	11.86%	23.25%
	RRP	21.60%	30.88%	15.01%	21.76%	31.34%	41.86%	3.09%	2.49%
	APE-GAN	22.40%	31.24%	12.99%	17.90%	34.72%	44.57%	4.92%	4.75%
	NRP	24.37%	33.58%	14.04%	19.98%	38.26%	48.75%	9.55%	10.24%
	Ours	**70.91%**	**85.57%**	**74.85%**	**88.81%**	**71.48%**	**86.07%**	**42.61%**	**55.34%**

parameters for network initialization. We also do experiments on the ReID-specific model OSNet [30]. The above ReID models are trained using the code and hyperparameters provided by the torchreid [29], and the performance on the original examples is shown in Table 1.

4.2 Robustness of Purification

To measure the defense capability, we compare the proposed purification method with adversarially trained model (AT) and state-of-the-art input transformation defense methods (i.e., RRP, APE-GAN, and NRP) against I-FGSM, MI-FGSM, SMA, and Deep Mis-Ranking. For AT, we adopt the adversarial examples generated by FGSM for training. For a fair comparison, we retrain APE-GAN and NRP on Market-1501.

As shown in Table 2, our purification method significantly outperforms state-of-the-art methods in protecting ReID systems from attacks. Specifically, the proposed purification method enhances the average mAP of OSNet and DenseNet121 under four attacks, respectively, from 0.77% to 77.97% and from 0.75% to 64.9%. Thus, it is proved that our purification method can greatly discount the attack effect of adversarial examples.

Table 3. ACC and AUC(%) of state-of-the-art adversarial detection methods vs. ours method against adversarial attacks

Detectors	FGSM		I-FGSM		MI-FGSM		SMA	
	ACC	AUC	ACC	AUC	ACC	AUC	ACC	AUC
LID	91.25%	96.82%	92.45%	97.60%	94.73%	98.70%	92.74%	97.54%
MD	98.53%	99.72%	97.56%	99.64%	98.85%	99.88%	96.21%	99.19%
Ours	**99.45%**	**100.00%**	**99.96%**	**99.94%**	**99.57%**	**99.97%**	**98.83%**	**99.58%**
	Deep Mis-ranking							
	ACC				AUC			
MEAAD (Voting)	91.7%				91.7%			
MEAAD (Detector)	**98.5%**				**99.80%**			
Ours	96.29%				99.52%			

4.3 Adversarial Detection

We also compare the proposed adversarial detection strategy with state-of-the-art adversarial detection methods to verify the effectiveness. We compare our detection method with MD and LID on four attacks with small perturbation settings (FGSM, I-FGSM, MI-FGSM, SMA) and with state-of-the-art ReID-specific adversarial example detection methods (MEAAD (Voting), MEAAD (Detector)) [21] on ReID-specific attack with larger perturbations (Deep Mis-Ranking). One metric used to evaluate detection performance is classification accuracy, or called detection accuracy (ACC), where the ratio of positive images to negative images is 1:1. Moreover, we flexibly adjust the threshold to decide whether it is an adversarial example and get the receiver operating characteristic (ROC) curve, and we calculate the area under the ROC curve (AUC) as another detection performance metric. We follow the standard training and testing splits for Market-1501.

As shown in Table 3, although our detection method falls short of MEAAD (Detector) on Deep Mis-Ranking attack, it achieves leading accuracy in most cases. In conclusion, our proposed detector guarantees the discriminative accuracy of adversarial examples and clean examples.

4.4 Ablation Experiments

We also summarize the following points through ablation experiments: **(i)** Training with adversarial examples generated by IMGA can improve the robustness of PSF, and **(ii)** PSF performance slightly degrades without $\mathcal{L}_{extr}$ or $\mathcal{L}_{metric}$.

Robustness of IMGA. Figure 3a compares the purification performance of PSF trained with IMGA to other SOTA attack method I-FGSM.

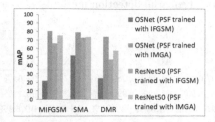 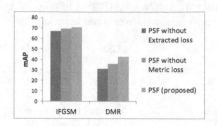

(a) Comparison of purification performance of PSF trained with IMGA and
I-FGSM generative adversarial examples.
The PSF trained with IMGA significantly
improves the defense performance. Tests
are performed on two ReID models (OS-
Net and ResNet50).

(b) PSF trained without $\mathcal{L}_{extr}$ or $\mathcal{L}_{metric}$
performs decreasingly indicating the im-
portance of these two losses. Tests are
performed on DenseNet121.

Fig. 3. Ablation experiments.

Contribution of $\mathcal{L}_{extr}$ and $\mathcal{L}_{metric}$. Figure 3b investigates the contribution
of $\mathcal{L}_{extr}$ and $\mathcal{L}_{metric}$ to the purification effect, and the following conclusion is
drawn: training without $\mathcal{L}_{extr}$ or $\mathcal{L}_{metric}$ will reduce the recognition accuracy
after purification.

5   Conclusion

We propose a robust ReID defense framework which consists of a perturbation
extractor and an adversarial example detector. The detector utilizes perturbations extracted by the extractor and achieves great detection performance
against five different attacks. We utilize the detector to distinguish adversarial
examples from clean images and only purify the possible adversarial examples
to maintain recognition accuracy. We purify the adversarial examples with a
simple perturbation removal operation, and our proposed purification method
can significantly improve the identification performance of the ReID model under
adversarial attacks. To have a better robustness of the extractor, we also improve
the adversarial example generation method to be suitable for matching task and
use it in the training process. Finally, we hope that our work can facilitate the
development of ReID defense applications.

Acknowledgement. This work was supported in part by National Natural Science Foundation of China (No. 61906049, No. 62072127, No. 62002076), in part
by Natural Science Foundation of Guangdong Province (No. 2020A1515010423, No.
2021A1515011859), in part by Science and Technology Program of Guangzhou, China
(No. 202002030131), in part by Guangdong basic and applied basic research fund joint
fund Youth Fund (No. 2019A1515110213).

References

1. Bai, S., Li, Y., Zhou, Y., Li, Q., Torr, P.H.: Adversarial metric attack and defense for person re-identification. IEEE Trans. Pattern Anal. Mach. Intell. **43**(6), 2119–2126 (2020)
2. Bouniot, Q., Audigier, R., Loesch, A.: Vulnerability of person re-identification models to metric adversarial attacks. In: Proceedings of the IEEE/CVF Conference on Computer Vision and Pattern Recognition Workshops, pp. 794–795 (2020)
3. Ding, S., Lin, L., Wang, G., Chao, H.: Deep feature learning with relative distance comparison for person re-identification. Pattern Recogn. **48**(10), 2993–3003 (2015)
4. Dong, Y., et al.: Boosting adversarial attacks with momentum. In: Proceedings of the IEEE Conference on Computer Vision and Pattern Recognition, pp. 9185–9193 (2018)
5. Gong, Z., Wang, W., Ku, W.S.: Adversarial and clean data are not twins. arXiv preprint arXiv:1704.04960 (2017)
6. Goodfellow, I.J., Shlens, J., Szegedy, C.: Explaining and harnessing adversarial examples. arXiv preprint arXiv:1412.6572 (2014)
7. Guo, C., Rana, M., Cisse, M., Van Der Maaten, L.: Countering adversarial images using input transformations. arXiv preprint arXiv:1711.00117 (2017)
8. He, K., Zhang, X., Ren, S., Sun, J.: Deep residual learning for image recognition. In: Proceedings of the IEEE Conference on Computer Vision and Pattern Recognition, pp. 770–778 (2016)
9. Hermans, A., Beyer, L., Leibe, B.: In defense of the triplet loss for person re-identification. arXiv preprint arXiv:1703.07737 (2017)
10. Huang, G., Liu, Z., Van Der Maaten, L., Weinberger, K.Q.: Densely connected convolutional networks. In: Proceedings of the IEEE Conference on Computer Vision and Pattern Recognition, pp. 4700–4708 (2017)
11. Kurakin, A., Goodfellow, I.J., Bengio, S.: Adversarial examples in the physical world. arXiv preprint arXiv:1607.02533 (2016)
12. Lee, K., Lee, K., Lee, H., Shin, J.: A simple unified framework for detecting out-of-distribution samples and adversarial attacks. Adv. Neural Inf. Process. Syst. **31**, 7167–7177 (2018)
13. Li, W., Zhu, X., Gong, S.: Harmonious attention network for person re-identification. In: Proceedings of the IEEE Conference on Computer Vision and Pattern Recognition, pp. 2285–2294 (2018)
14. Ma, X., et al.: Characterizing adversarial subspaces using local intrinsic dimensionality. arXiv preprint arXiv:1801.02613 (2018)
15. Naseer, M., Khan, S., Hayat, M., Khan, F.S., Porikli, F.: A self-supervised approach for adversarial robustness. In: Proceedings of the IEEE/CVF Conference on Computer Vision and Pattern Recognition, pp. 262–271 (2020)
16. Qian, X., Fu, Y., Jiang, Y.G., Xiang, T., Xue, X.: Multi-scale deep learning architectures for person re-identification. In: Proceedings of the IEEE International Conference on Computer Vision, pp. 5399–5408 (2017)
17. Shen, S., Jin, G., Gao, K., Zhang, Y.: APE-GAN: adversarial perturbation elimination with GAN. arXiv preprint arXiv:1707.05474 (2017)
18. Sun, Y., Zheng, L., Yang, Y., Tian, Q., Wang, S.: Beyond part models: person retrieval with refined part pooling (and a strong convolutional baseline). In: Proceedings of the European Conference on Computer Vision (ECCV), pp. 480–496 (2018)

19. Szegedy, C., et al.: Intriguing properties of neural networks. arXiv preprint arXiv:1312.6199 (2013)
20. Wang, H., Wang, G., Li, Y., Zhang, D., Lin, L.: Transferable, controllable, and inconspicuous adversarial attacks on person re-identification with deep Misranking. In: Proceedings of the IEEE/CVF Conference on Computer Vision and Pattern Recognition, pp. 342–351 (2020)
21. Wang, X., Li, S., Liu, M., Wang, Y., Roy-Chowdhury, A.K.: Multi-expert adversarial attack detection in person re-identification using context inconsistency. In: Proceedings of the IEEE/CVF International Conference on Computer Vision, pp. 15097–15107 (2021)
22. Xie, C., Wang, J., Zhang, Z., Ren, Z., Yuille, A.: Mitigating adversarial effects through randomization. arXiv preprint arXiv:1711.01991 (2017)
23. Xu, B., Wang, N., Chen, T., Li, M.: Empirical evaluation of rectified activations in convolutional network. arXiv preprint arXiv:1505.00853 (2015)
24. Zhang, X., et al.: AlignedReID: surpassing human-level performance in person re-identification. arXiv preprint arXiv:1711.08184 (2017)
25. Zheng, L., Shen, L., Tian, L., Wang, S., Wang, J., Tian, Q.: Scalable person re-identification: a benchmark. In: Proceedings of the IEEE International Conference on Computer Vision, pp. 1116–1124 (2015)
26. Zheng, Y., Velipasalar, S.: Part-based feature squeezing to detect adversarial examples in person re-identification networks. In: 2021 IEEE International Conference on Image Processing (ICIP), pp. 844–848. IEEE (2021)
27. Zheng, Z., Zheng, L., Yang, Y.: Unlabeled samples generated by GAN improve the person re-identification baseline in vitro. In: Proceedings of the IEEE International Conference on Computer Vision, pp. 3754–3762 (2017)
28. Zheng, Z., Zheng, L., Yang, Y., Wu, F.: Query attack via opposite-direction feature: Towards robust image retrieval. arXiv preprint arXiv:1809.02681 (2018)
29. Zhou, K., Xiang, T.: TorchReID: a library for deep learning person re-identification in PyTorch. arXiv preprint arXiv:1910.10093 (2019)
30. Zhou, K., Yang, Y., Cavallaro, A., Xiang, T.: Omni-scale feature learning for person re-identification. In: ICCV (2019)

Self-supervised and Template-Enhanced Unknown-Defect Detection

Tingting Li[1,2], Yaqiao Liao[1,2], Xu Wang[1(✉)], Guowen Kuang[1], Zhibin Chen[2], and Jinfeng Yang[1]

[1] Institute of Applied Artificial Intelligence of the Guangdong-Hong Kong-Macao Greater Bay Area, Shenzhen Polytechnic, Shenzhen 518055, China
wangxu@szpt.edu.cn
[2] School of Electronics and Information Engineering, University of Science and Technology Liaoning, Anshan 114045, China
zhibinchen1969@ustl.edu.cn

Abstract. Surface defect detection has great significance to the manufacturing industry. It is also a challenging task because of the large variation of unknown defects and limited available datasets. In this paper, we propose a self-supervised generative approach for unknow-defect detection. The training process only involves masked defect-free samples, and additional template information is used to achieve a more robust performance of GAN-based image reconstruction. We design a fusion module based on an attention mechanism, which aligns features of an image with mask or defect to template image for better image reconstruction and defect-localization. The reconstructed defect-free image with uncertainty heatmap is generated by a subsequent decoder. Our proposed method outperforms the baseline method in defect description on a bottle cap dataset from the real industrial process.

Keywords: Unknown defect detection · Template · Self-supervised learning

1 Introduction

The surface defect detection is an important part of the manufacturing process, and many methods have been developed to solve this problem. Traditional machine vision [1] and deep neural networks (DNN) [2] are the two main kinds of detect detection methods at present. The defect detection methods based on traditional machine vision [3] include template matching [4], statistical method [5], low-rank decomposition [6], frequency domain analysis [7], sparse representation [8], support vector [9] and so on. Recently, the defect detection methods based on DNN can be classified into three categories: supervised [10], unsupervised [11], and semi-supervised learning [12,13]. For now, it is found that the performance of defect detection [14] methods based on DNN is much better than those based on traditional machine vision.

© The Author(s), under exclusive license to Springer Nature Switzerland AG 2022
S. Yu et al. (Eds.): PRCV 2022, LNCS 13536, pp. 745–757, 2022.
https://doi.org/10.1007/978-3-031-18913-5_57

However, the surface defect detection methods based on DNN [15], especially supervised learning [16], require a large number of defect samples for training, while the defect samples are hard to be obtained and the datasets are very rare. It is difficult for these methods to detect unknown defects. Furthermore, defect detection performance is always affected by many factors, such as environment lighting, camera conditions, and so on. To deal with the above practical problems, some methods have already been proposed recently, for example, self-supervised learning [17], data augmentation [18] and so on. Unfortunately, the performance of these methods is lower than their supervised-based competitors.

This paper proposes a self-supervised method to detect unknown defects, which uses the template as an auxiliary input to enhance performance. The template is a defect-free product image, and it can provide complementary information for the embedding representation of the input masked/defective image in training and testing. The fushion module is designed to integrate the information of the template and the input image based on the attention mechanism [19]. We summarize our contributions as follows:

- We use additional template information to improve performance of image reconstruction in the generative model.
- We design an attention-based fusion module, which aligns features between input image and template image.
- We extend generative model to surface defect detection, which is especially capable of detecting unknown defects.

The structure of this paper is as follows. Section 2 briefly introduces related work, and the proposed method is given in detail in Sect. 3. Then, the results of the proposed method are shown in Sect. 4. Finally, conclusion and future research are discussed in Sect. 5.

2   Related Work

In practical production process, there are various kinds of defects with different shapes or sizes. Thus, it is quite difficult to predict and identify all the defects in the actual process. Because the datasets are hard to be obtained and the defective samples are usually very rare, the usage of the supervised learning [20] methods are hindered. Compared with the supervised learning, the unsupervised detection methods [21] pay more attention to unknown defect detection, and it can solve the problem more effectively without the need of the defective samples for training.

Self-supervised learning is one kind of unsupervised learning. In contrast to supervised learning, self-supervised learning is trained on unlabeled data. Many popular methods, such as Auto-Encoders [22] and Generative Adversarial Networks (GAN) [23] can be considered for self-supervised learning. In 2021, Mask Auto-Encoder (MAE) [24] was proposed, which trains the neural networks by adding masks to the samples in the dataset. MAE can be used to train the pre-trained model that can effectively extracts features, and it soon becomes one of the most popular self-supervised learning methods. Recently, many self-supervised defect detection methods have been proposed. X Tao et al. proposed a metal surface defect detection method by using cascaded auto-encoders [25] to reconstruct images. Also, Z Zhao et al. proposed a defect detection method based on the combination of GAN [26] and Local Binary Pattern (LBP) algorithm [27] in 2018. In 2021, a self-supervised method was proposed to detect and localize the abnormalities [1].

Compared with existing self-supervised defect detection methods as mentioned above, the method proposed in this paper not only leverages self-supervised learning [1], but also utilizes the template to enhance the performance. The template is a defect-free sample image, and a fusion module is designed to integrate the information of the template into the reconstruction, which improves the reconstruction quality and detection performance at last. The template, the corresponding neural network branch, and the fusion module can be seen as a fixed part of the whole neural network, or some kind of prior knowledge. Furthermore, the proposed method detects the unknown defects and their locations by estimating the pixels' uncertainty of the reconstructed image to reduce disturbances of the edges. According to [28], the uncertainty is usually larger on the edge than that at the center of the object.

3   Approach

3.1   Framework

The framework of the proposed surface defect detection method is shown in Fig. 1. At first, the input image x_i with the size of 256×256 is imported into the encoder, and the encoder outputs the 2048-dimensions feature map F_1 with the size of 8×8. The feature map F_2 corresponding to the template is also obtained by the same encoder. Secondly, these two feature maps are fused by the fusion module (the green module in the middle of Fig. 1), by which the feature maps F_1 and F_2 are fused and compressed into a 512-dimensional feature vector F_{fuse}. Thirdly, F_{fuse} is input into the decoder, and the decoder generates the corresponding reconstructed image $\mu(x_i)$ (shown in right side of Fig. 1) and uncertainty heatmap $\log \sigma^2(x_i)$, i.e. the logrithm function of $\sigma^2(x_i)$. Finally, the loss can be calculated by the difference between the reconstructed defect-free image $\mu(x_i)$ and the input image x_i. To realize self-supervised learning, there is a pre-processing step to add a noisy mask to the input image x_i for training. One example of the input image before and after patching the mask is shown in Fig. 2. This figure is better viewed in color. To improve the robustness of the defect detection, random rotation and scaling are also applied to the input image before patching mask.

The encoder makes use of ResNet101 to extract more detailed information/features from the input image x_i. To generate high-resolution images, StyleGAN [29] is chosen as the decoder. The corresponding discriminator of the decoder (StyleGAN) is ResNet50 [30].

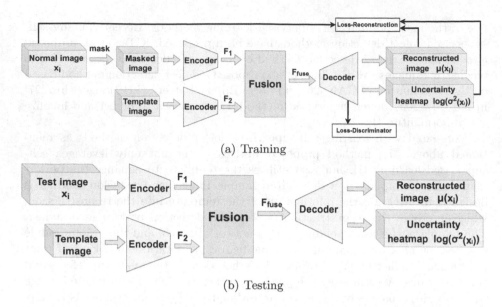

(a) Training

(b) Testing

Fig. 1. Overall architecture of generative approach for unknown defect detection. Training and testing process are shown in (a) and (b) respectively. They share the same backbone, i.e. the encoder, fusion module and the decoder, except that the normal image is patched with masks before being fed into the encoder in the training process. (Color figure online)

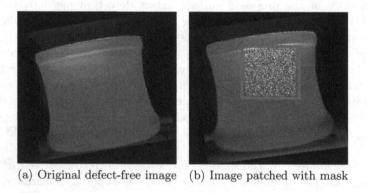

(a) Original defect-free image   (b) Image patched with mask

Fig. 2. Example of patching masks to defect-free images. The original input image and its corresponding masked image are shown in the left and right figures, respectively.

3.2 Feature Fusion Module

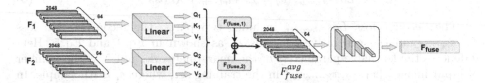

Fig. 3. Feature fusion module.

To enhance the quality of reconstructed image $\mu(x_i)$, the template's information is fused with the input image x_i in the fusion module (Fig. 3). At First, the template and the input image x_i go through the encoder (ResNet101) to obtain the feature maps F_1 and F_2. Then, they are fused by the attention scheme according to Transformer [31,32]. The formulas are as follows.

$$F_{(fuse,1)}(Q_1, K_2, V_2) = softmax(\frac{Q_1 K_2^T}{\sqrt{d_k}})V_2 \tag{1}$$

$$F_{(fuse,2)}(Q_2, K_1, V_1) = softmax(\frac{Q_2 K_1^T}{\sqrt{d_k}})V_1 \tag{2}$$

$$F_{fuse}^{avg} = \frac{F_{(fuse,1)} + F_{(fuse,2)}}{2} \tag{3}$$

Here $V_i, Q_i, K_i (i = 1, 2)$ represents value, query and key calculated from feature map F_i, respectively. $i = 1$ means the input image, while $i = 2$ represents the template. After pooling and convolution, F_{fuse}^{avg} turns into the output vector F_{fuse}. In this way, the information of input image and template is fused.

3.3 Loss Function

Based on the above analysis, two losses are involved in the training.

Decoder Loss. The goal of the decoder is to generate the corresponding high-quality defect-free image with respect to the input image.

$$Loss_{recon}(\theta, x_i) = \frac{1}{NM} \sum_{i=1}^{N} \sum_{k=1}^{M} \{\frac{(x_{i,k} - \mu_k(x_i))^2}{\sigma_k^2(x_i)} + \log \sigma_k^2(x_i)\} \tag{4}$$

$$Loss_G(x_i) = \log(1 + e^{-D(\mu(x_i))}) \tag{5}$$

$$Loss_{decoder}(\theta) = Loss_{recon} + \lambda Loss_G \tag{6}$$

The decoder loss $Loss_{decoder}$ includes two parts, the reconstruction loss $Loss_{recon}$ and the generative loss $Loss_G$, as shown in Eq. 4 and Eq. 5. Here θ denotes the learnable parameters of the neural network, and N is the number of input images $\{x_1, x_2, x_3.....x_N\}$ in the training set, where x_i is ith sample. In Eq. 4, $\sigma_k^2(x_i)$ is the value of the uncertainty heatmap $\sigma(x_i)$ at kth pixel, which is used to estimate the probability of the defect at kth pixel [28]. M is the amount of pixels, and $\{\sigma_1^2, \sigma_2^2, \sigma_3^2.....\sigma_M^2\}$ are variances. $\mu_k(x_i)$ represents the kth pixel of reconstructed image $\mu(x_i)$ corresponding to input image x_i. $\dfrac{(x_{i,k} - \mu_k(x_i))^2}{\sigma_k^2(x_i)}$ is the weighted differences between the ith input image x_i and its corresponding reconstructed image $\mu(x_i)$ at the kth pixel. In Eq. 5. The value of λ is 1.0 in the training.

Discriminant Loss. The goal of the discriminator is to improve the quality of the reconstructed image. The formula of the discriminant loss is as follows.

$$Loss_D(x_i) = E_{x_i \sim p_{data}}[\log D(\mu(x_i))] + E_{x_i \sim p_G}[\log(1 - D(\mu(x_i)))] \tag{7}$$

where D and G stand for discriminator and decoder respectively.

3.4   Defect Detection

The decoder of the proposed defect detection method generates defect-free reconstructed image $\mu(x_i)$ of the input image x_i with an uncertainty heatmap. For every input image x_i, the differences between x_i and its corresponding reconstructed image $\mu_{(x_i)}$ are divieded by $\sigma^2(x_i)$. Also, a threshold is chosen. $\dfrac{|x_{i,k} - \mu_k(x_i)|}{\tan(\alpha|\sigma_k(x_i)|)}$ is an uncertain heatmap. The tangent algorithm is used to improve the eigenvalue of image uncertainty and reduce the influence of edge. α is the dynamic coefficient. Since the maximum value of each variance diagram is different, different coefficients are taken here.

$$\alpha = \frac{\pi}{2\sigma_k(x_i)_{max}} \tag{8}$$

4   Experiments

4.1   Dataset

The collected cap samples are the plastic bottle caps of a popular yogurt drink, and the method proposed in this paper aims to detect the unknown defect for this product in practical production.

Table 1. Bottle cap dataset. The dataset contains a total of 2168 non-defective images and 282 defective images, and the non-defective pictures are divided into training set (710 images) and test set (1458 pictures). Defective images are all used in the testing process.

Cap-dataset	Positive	Negative
Training dataset	710	0
Test dataset	1458	282

The cap dataset contains 2168 defect-free images and 282 defective images, as shown in Table 1. The size of each image in the dataset is 1280×960, which will be resized into 256×256 for training. Among the 2168 defect-free samples, 710 samples are selected as the training data set. The remaining 1458 defect-free samples are collected recently after training, which is combined with 282 defective samples as the test set. These cap samples are collected and labeled by our team, and the cap dataset will be opened to the public soon.

In this experiment, UAE [28] is trained on the cap dataset for comparison, as it is a relatively new work in abnormality detection by using the uncertainty estimation and generative method. Also, UAE is trained on the training set following its original training way, without patching masks.

The appointed hyper-parameter *threshold* is used to decide whether there exist defects at each pixel. In the experiment, the *threshold* is chosen separately for UAE and our method to compare the best performance of each method.

4.2 Training Parameters

The proposed method is trained on the NVIDIA A100-SXM4-40GB server. The initial value of the learning rate for the encoder and the decoder is 10^{-5}, while the initial value of the discriminator's learning rate is 10^{-2}. Then, in order to make the training converge, the learning rate decay is used in the proposed method [33]. The learning rates of the encoder, generator, and discriminator decrease by a factor of 0.1 for every 100 iteration.

Also, this method uses the mask method [24] to realize self-supervised learning, and it only requires defect-free samples in training. The size of the mask is randomly selected between 32×32 and 128×128, with a random position.

4.3 Results

The detection results of UAE [28] and the proposed methods are shown in Table 2.

Table 2. Experimental results. TP represents the number of defective samples that are detected successfully. FN represents the number of defective samples that are not detected. FP and TN denote the number of defect-free samples that are decided as defective and defect-free, respectively.

—	TP	FN	FP	TN	Accuracy	Precision	Recall
UAE	155	129	35	1421	0.9057	0.8158	0.5458
Ours	206	76	334	1124	0.7644	0.3815	**0.7305**

From Table 2, it can be found that the proposed method can reach higher recall score, which is important in practical production to reduce the miss rate of unqualified production.

To make the difference between the two methods' performance more obviously, some results of UAE and the proposed methods with the same input images are shown in Fig. 4 and 5, respectively. In Fig. 4 and 5, x (the first column) represents the input image, and $\mu(x)$ (the second column) denotes the reconstructed image. $|\mu(x) - x|$ (the third column) is the difference between the input image and the reconstructed image. Also, $\sigma(x)$ (the forth column) is the variance (i.e. uncertainty heatmap), which is used to filter out the reconstructed difference caused by the edge of the object.

Comparing the first 3 lines of Fig. 4 and 5, although both methods can successfully detect the cap with defects, it is obvious that the proposed method can generate a cleaner reconstructed image, which can make the stains more distinctive in the weighted difference heatmap, the last column of Fig. 4 and 5. Please pay attention to the green boxes. Referring to the last 2 lines of Fig. 4 and 5, the outputs of UAE are worse than ours, as the missing part (marked by red boxes in Fig. 4 and Fig. 5) can not be fully reconstructed. On the other side, The proposed method can reconstruct the missing part by using the information provided by the input template, which is the key to enhancing the performance. Although the quality of the reconstructed image does not affect the result of cap defect detection, it is important in the defect detection for more complex objects, such as IC chips and circuits. The training of defect detection for chips will be put into operation, and it is not presented in the paper due to the time limit.

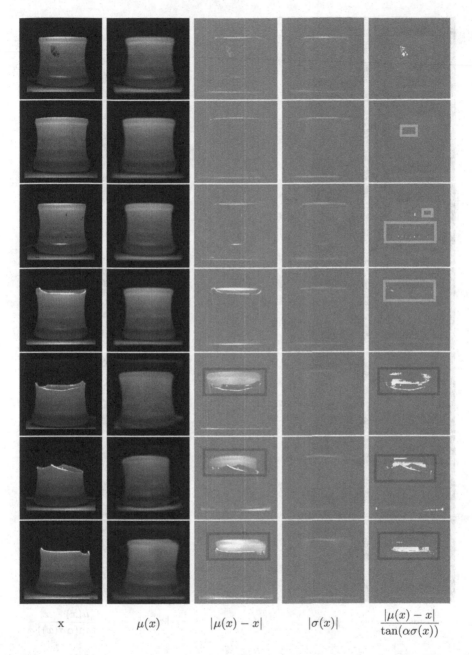

$$\text{x} \qquad \mu(x) \qquad |\mu(x) - x| \qquad |\sigma(x)| \qquad \frac{|\mu(x) - x|}{\tan(\alpha\sigma(x))}$$

Fig. 4. Cap Result-UAE method. x is the input image. $\mu(x)$ is the reconstructed positive sample. On the far right is the uncertainty heat map, which is the image of the defect area.

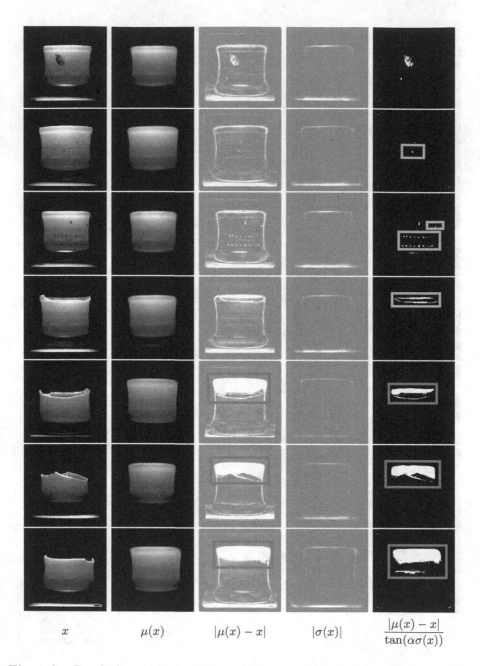

$$x \qquad \mu(x) \qquad |\mu(x) - x| \qquad |\sigma(x)| \qquad \frac{|\mu(x) - x|}{\tan(\alpha\sigma(x))}$$

Fig. 5. Cap Result-Our method. x is the input image. $\mu(x)$ is the reconstructed positive sample. On the far right is the uncertainty heat map, which is the image of the defect area.

5   Conclusion

In this paper, a template enhanced self-supervised defect detection method was proposed. To enhance the performance, a fusion module was designed to fuse the information of the template into the reconstructed image, where the template could be considered as auxiliary information or knowledge. The effectiveness of the proposed method was demonstrated by the experiments in Sect. 4. This method can be applied to production defect detection conveniently, and it has great practical value. One future work will focus on that whether the proposed method can learn to use a template in the same way as human workers, who use a 'golden map' (i.e. templates) to decide the existence of defects on the product surface. Also, this proposed method will be applied to the surface defect detection of more complex objects, such as electronic chips or Integrated Circuits. Furthermore, it will be checked whether this method could easily switch to defect detection for other products by changing the template to the corresponding image.

References

1. Li, C.-L., Sohn, K., Yoon, J., Pfister, T.: CutPaste: self-supervised learning for anomaly detection and localization. In: Proceedings of the IEEE/CVF Conference on Computer Vision and Pattern Recognition (CVPR), pp. 9664–9674, June 2021
2. Schmidhuber, J.: Deep learning in neural networks: an overview. Neural Netw. **61**, 85–117 (2015). https://doi.org/10.1016/j.neunet.2014.09.003
3. Lv, C.-K., Shen, F., Zhang, Z.-T., Zhang, F.: Review of image anomaly detection. Acta Automatica Sin. **47**, 1–27 (2021). https://doi.org/10.16383/j.aas.c200956
4. Korman, S., Reichman, D., Tsur, G., Avidan, S.: Fast-match: fast affine template matching. In: Proceedings of the IEEE Conference on Computer Vision and Pattern Recognition, pp. 2331–2338, June 2013
5. Veracini, T., Matteoli, S., Diani, M., Corsini, G.: Fully unsupervised learning of Gaussian mixtures for anomaly detection in hyperspectral imagery. In: 2009 Ninth International Conference on Intelligent Systems Design and Applications, pp. 596–601 (2009). https://doi.org/10.1109/ISDA.2009.220
6. Li, C., Liu, C., Gao, G., Liu, Z., Wang, Y.: Robust low-rank decomposition of multi-channel feature matrices for fabric defect detection. Multimed. Tools Appl. **78**(6), 7321–7339 (2019). https://doi.org/10.1007/s11042-018-6483-6
7. Tsai, D.-M., Hsieh, C.-Y.: Automated surface inspection for directional textures. Image Vis. Comput. **18**(1), 49–62 (1999). https://doi.org/10.1016/S0262-8856(99)00009-8
8. Boracchi, G., Carrera, D., Wohlberg, B.: Novelty detection in images by sparse representations. In: 2014 IEEE Symposium on Intelligent Embedded Systems (IES), pp. 47–54. IEEE (2014). https://doi.org/10.1109/INTELES.2014.7008985
9. Amraee, S., Vafaei, A., Jamshidi, K., Adibi, P.: Abnormal event detection in crowded scenes using one-class SVM. SIViP **12**(6), 1115–1123 (2018). https://doi.org/10.1007/s11760-018-1267-z
10. Gobert, C., Reutzel, E.W., Petrich, J., Nassar, A.R., Phoha, S.: Application of supervised machine learning for defect detection during metallic powder bed fusion additive manufacturing using high resolution imaging. Addit. Manuf. **21**, 517–528 (2018). https://doi.org/10.1016/j.addma.2018.04.005

11. Mujeeb, A., Dai, W., Erdt, M., Sourin, A.: Unsupervised surface defect detection using deep autoencoders and data augmentation. In: 2018 International Conference on Cyberworlds (CW), pp. 391–398 (2018). https://doi.org/10.1109/CW.2018.00076
12. Zhang, G., Pan, Y., Zhang, L.: Semi-supervised learning with GAN for automatic defect detection from images. Autom. Constr. **128**, 103764 (2021). https://doi.org/10.1016/j.autcon.2021.103764
13. Božič, J., Tabernik, D., Skočaj, D.: Mixed supervision for surface-defect detection: from weakly to fully supervised learning. Comput. Ind. **129**, 103459 (2021). https://doi.org/10.1016/j.compind.2021.103459
14. Zavrtanik, V., Kristan, M., Skočaj, D.: DRAEM-a discriminatively trained reconstruction embedding for surface anomaly detection. In: Proceedings of the IEEE/CVF International Conference on Computer Vision, pp. 8330–8339 (2021)
15. Montavon, G., Samek, W., Müller, K.-R.: Methods for interpreting and understanding deep neural networks. Digit. Sig. Process. **73**, 1–15 (2018). https://doi.org/10.1016/j.dsp.2017.10.011
16. Khosla, P., et al.: Supervised contrastive learning. In: Advances in Neural Information Processing Systems, vol. 33, pp. 18661–18673 (2020)
17. Liu, X., et al.: Self-supervised learning: generative or contrastive. IEEE Trans. Knowl. Data Eng. (2021). https://doi.org/10.1109/TKDE.2021.3090866
18. Li, B., Wu, F., Lim, S.-N., Belongie, S., Weinberger, K.Q.: On feature normalization and data augmentation. In: Proceedings of the IEEE/CVF Conference on Computer Vision and Pattern Recognition, pp. 12383–12392 (2021)
19. Vig, J.: A multiscale visualization of attention in the transformer model. In: Proceedings of the 57th Annual Meeting of the Association for Computational Linguistics: System Demonstrations (2019)
20. Zhu, X.J.: Semi-supervised learning literature survey (2005)
21. Barlow, H.B.: Unsupervised learning. Neural Comput. **1**(3), 295–311 (1989). https://doi.org/10.1162/neco.1989.1.3.295
22. Wang, W., Huang, Y., Wang, Y., Wang, L.: Generalized autoencoder: a neural network framework for dimensionality reduction. In: Proceedings of the IEEE Conference on Computer Vision and Pattern Recognition Workshops, pp. 490–497, June 2014
23. Creswell, A., White, T., Dumoulin, V., Arulkumaran, K., Sengupta, B., Bharath, A.A.: Generative adversarial networks: an overview. IEEE Sig. Process. Mag. **35**(1), 53–65 (2018). https://doi.org/10.1109/MSP.2017.2765202
24. He, K., Chen, X., Xie, S., Li, Y., Dollár, P., Girshick, R.: Masked autoencoders are scalable vision learners. In: Proceedings of the IEEE/CVF Conference on Computer Vision and Pattern Recognition, pp. 16000–16009 (2022). https://doi.org/10.48550/arXiv.2111.06377
25. Tao, X., Zhang, D., Ma, W., Liu, X., De, X.: Automatic metallic surface defect detection and recognition with convolutional neural networks. Appl. Sci. **8**(9), 1575 (2018). https://doi.org/10.3390/app8091575
26. Zhao, Z., Li, B., Dong, R., Zhao, P.: A surface defect detection method based on positive samples. In: Geng, X., Kang, B.-H. (eds.) PRICAI 2018. LNCS (LNAI), vol. 11013, pp. 473–481. Springer, Cham (2018). https://doi.org/10.1007/978-3-319-97310-4_54
27. Ye, N., Ding, J., Wang, D., Wang, H., Xu, Z.: Detection of wood texture defects based on LBP feature extraction. In: The 2nd China Classification Technology and Application Academic Conference (2007)

28. Mao, Y., Xue, F.-F., Wang, R., Zhang, J., Zheng, W.-S., Liu, H.: Abnormality detection in chest X-ray images using uncertainty prediction autoencoders. In: Martel, A.L., et al. (eds.) MICCAI 2020. LNCS, vol. 12266, pp. 529–538. Springer, Cham (2020). https://doi.org/10.1007/978-3-030-59725-2_51. https://doi.org/10.17632/rscbjbr9sj.3
29. Karras, T., Laine, S., Aila, T.: A style-based generator architecture for generative adversarial networks. In: Proceedings of the IEEE/CVF Conference on Computer Vision and Pattern Recognition, pp. 4401–4410 (2019)
30. He, K., Zhang, X., Ren, S., Sun, J.: Deep residual learning for image recognition. In: Proceedings of the IEEE Conference on Computer Vision and Pattern Recognition, pp. 770–778 (2016)
31. Vaswani, A., et al.: Attention is all you need. In: Advances in Neural Information Processing Systems, vol. 30 (2017)
32. Zhou, X., Duan, X., Yu, H., Zhang, M.: Neural machine translation based on multi-layer information fusion. J. Xiamen Univ. Nat. Sci. Ed. 58(2), 149–157 (2019)
33. Fenf, Y., Li, Y.: Overview of deep learning optimizer methods and learning rate decay. Hans J. Data Min. 8, 186 (2018). https://doi.org/10.12677/HJDM.2018.84020

JoinTW: A Joint Image-to-Image Translation and Watermarking Method

Xiaohan Zhao, Yunhong Wang, Ruijie Yang, and Yuanfang Guo[✉]

Laboratory of Intelligent Recognition and Image Processing, School of Computer Science and Engineering, Beihang University, Beijing 100191, China
{xhzhao,yhwang,rjyang,andyguo}@buaa.edu.cn

Abstract. The image-to-image translation tasks have been widely explored in recent years due to the rapid development of deep neural networks. Unfortunately, the misuse of image-to-image translation techniques may induce disastrous consequences. Although the existing proactive watermarking methods can give decent performances in tracing the manipulated images, they can be escaped by malicious users because they can only embed the watermarks after the generation of the deep manipulated images. Under such circumstances, we are motivated to propose a joint image-to-image translation and watermarking (JoinTW) framework with the correspondingly designed loss functions. Our JoinTW embeds the watermark as a fingerprint during the image-to-image translation process without being noticed or escaped, which enables the potential regulators to directly trace the producing source of the translated images once misuses happen. Experiments have demonstrated that our JoinTW can effectively embed watermarks without obvious degradations to the perceptual qualities of the generated images, as well as ensure the robustness of the watermark against various post-processing operations.

Keywords: Image-to-image translation · Digital watermarking · Proactive forensic · Joint image-to-image translation and watermarking

1 Introduction

Image-to-image translation [15, 29, 31, 39, 41], which is generally defined as translating one representation of an image to another, has been widely studied in recent years. The explosive development of deep neural networks (DNNs) gives rise to extraordinary breakthroughs in image-to-image translation tasks, and makes the traceability of the generated images extremely difficult.

Given sufficient data, DNNs can easily perform artistic style transfer [14, 22], human face manipulation [8, 21, 30], etc., by learning the mappings between different image domains. Therefore, the misuse of these techniques will undoubtedly induce various pernicious consequences, ranging from fraudulent forgeries

This work was supported in part by the National Natural Science Foundation of China under Grant 61802391, and in part by the Fundamental Research Funds for Central Universities. The corresponding author is Yuanfang Guo.

S. Yu et al. (Eds.): PRCV 2022, LNCS 13536, pp. 758–772, 2022.
https://doi.org/10.1007/978-3-031-18913-5_58

to misinformation in political journalism. Numerous passive forensic (detection) methods have been proposed to prevent the malicious applications of deep forgeries, most of which are designed to detect the artifacts in the fake images [24,40]. However, these techniques tend to show a high dependency to the datasets and might fail to identify the fake images generated by the unseen forgery methods in the future. Thus, researchers are also studying proactive forensic solutions [19,23,34,42]. Different from passive detection methods, proactive forensic techniques usually preprocess the images when their integrities can still be guaranteed. A typical type of proactive methods is watermarking, i.e., the proactive watermarking techniques will embed an invisible watermark into the original image, such that the watermark can be extracted for verification, traitor tracing, etc., when necessary.

Although the existing proactive watermarking methods have achieved impressive results in the robustness and concealment of watermarks, these methods can actually be escaped by malicious users, because they can only embed the watermark after the generation of the deep manipulated images. Thus, we are motivated to propose a special proactive approach to facilitate the traceabilities of the generated images, by combining the process of image-to-image translation models with watermarking. It is worth noting that our approach aims to embed the watermark as a fingerprint during the image-to-image translation process without being noticed or escaped, which enables the potential regulators to directly trace the producing source of the translated images once misuses happen. Specifically, we propose a Joint Image-to-image Translation and Watermarking framework (JoinTW) with a correspondingly designed loss function, to achieve embedding the image watermark during the process of image-to-image translation. Inspired by [23], we further co-adapt the adversarial training into our method to strengthen the watermark robustness against various distortions. Experiments have shown that our method can effectively embed watermarks without significant performance degradations on the generated images and can also ensure the watermark robustness against various post-processing distortions.

We summarize our contributions as follows:

- We propose a novel proactive forensic method for image-to-image translation models to facilitate the traceability of the deep generated (forged) images, by proposing a joint image-to-image translation and watermarking framework, which embeds the watermark during the image-to-image translation process.
- We propose a new generator architecture for image-to-image translation and the corresponding loss functions to constrain the embedding and extraction of watermarks while guaranteeing the visual quality of the generated images.
- We verify the effectiveness of our method based on U-Net employed in pix2pix [16], which is one of the most widely applied backbone network in image-to-image translation tasks. Therefore, our method can be transferred conveniently to various generative architectures based on U-Net, which enhances the potential applications of our method.

2   Related Work

Image-to-Image Translation. Image-to-image translation tasks are generally described as predicting pixels frompixels based on sufficient data [3,5,15,17,21, 31,32,39,41]. These tasks have been traditionally formulated as diverse pixel classification or regression problems, and handled with separate mechanisms. Pix2pix [16] was proposed as the first general framework for the image-to-image translation problems, and it was adopted by numerous subsequent solutions [6,28,36,37,41,43]. Considering that pix2pix is a basic framework with various subsequent applications, we select it as our backbone network. Accordingly, our solution can be easily transferred to other models, which adopt pix2pix as their backbone network.

Digital Watermarking. Digital watermarking [1,2,33] is the process of hiding information into cover messages (such as images), while inducing negligible distortions on the original cover messages, such that the embedded watermark can still survive under various distortions. Traditional watermarking techniques usually possess hand-crafted procedures based on transformations in the spatial or frequency domains, such as least significant bits modifications [12,13], Fourier transform based watermarking methods [4,9], etc. Recently, deep learning-based methods [7,10,18,23,34,42] have been developed based on DNN encoders and decoders, and achieved remarkable results in both visual quality and watermark robustness. Hence, we cautiously design an encoder and decoder based on convolutional neural networks, to embed and extract watermarks while retaining the original image-to-image translation performance.

3   Proposed Work

3.1   Problem Statement

For a typical image-to-image translation task, X, Y are two different image domains, which contains paired images. We denote $x \in X$ as a source image and $y \in Y$ as a target image. It is well known that a typical conditional generative model, i.e., conditional GAN, can learn a mapping from the observed image x and random noise vector z to y, which can be illustrated as $G : \{x, z\} \to y$. Similar to the unconditional GANs, the generator G is trained to fool the discriminator D, and D is supposed to distinguish the real images from the images generated by G. G and D will eventually reach the Nash equilibrium via a zero-sum game. In this paper, we construct a special generator, named Watermark Embedding Generator (WEG), which simultaneously embeds image watermarks and performs image-to-image translation task. We denote the watermarked image generated from WEG with respect to x as y', and the image watermark to be embedded as w. Then, the joint image-to-image translation and watermarking task can be expressed as $WEG(x, w) = y' \wedge Dec(y') = w'$, where Dec represents the watermark extractor and w' is the extracted image watermark.

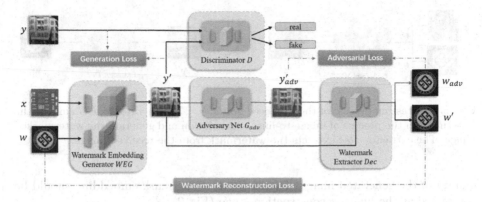

Fig. 1. The training process of the proposed JoinTW. The entire framework consists of four major components, including the generator WEG, the discriminator D, the adversarial network G_{adv}, and the watermark extractor Dec. The generator WEG simultaneously performs the image-to-image translation and embeds the watermark. The extractor Dec extracts the watermark from the generated watermarked images and the adversary net G_{adv} is utilized in the adversarial training phase (represented with green arrows).

3.2 Method Overview

Our overall architecture is depicted in Fig. 1. We construct a new generator WEG, which contains a CNN-based watermark encoder sub-module denoted as Enc, by modifying the U-Net based generator in pix2pix [16]. A source image x and a watermark image w are randomly selected as inputs. Then, the image y' is generated with watermark information embedded. The generated image y' is then fed into two branches, i.e., the standard discriminator D and a CNN-based watermark extractor Dec. D learns to discriminate between the true image y and generated image y'. Dec serves to extract the watermark w' from y' by constraining the difference between w and w' to be small. In addition, we adopt adversarial training to further strengthen the watermark robustness against different distortions. In the adversarial training phase, a distorted image y'_{adv} is obtained by feeding y' into G_{adv}. Then, for each iteration, y'_{adv} and y' will be subsequently fed into Dec to perform watermark extraction twice. The two calculated losses will be jointly utilized in the back-propagation process.

Considering that the U-Net based generator in pix2pix is widely adopted in many image-to-image translation techniques, we construct WEG based on the architecture of U-Net, which is depicted in Fig. 3. During the process of generation, x is fed into the encoder part of WEG to obtain a high dimensional representation in the latent space, which is upsampled and rendered in the decoder part after the bottleneck layer. If the watermark embedding is performed at the image feature encoding stage, the latent representation of the input image may be conceivably damaged, which tends to yield a degradation on the visual

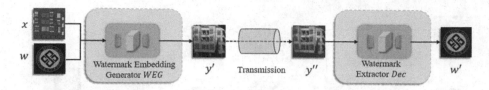

Fig. 2. The testing process of the proposed JoinTW. The generator WEG embeds the watermark in the process of image-to-image translation and generate the watermarked image. The extractor Dec extracts the watermark from the received image.

quality of the generated image. Therefore, the watermark embedding should be completed at the image reconstruction stage (Fig. 2).

It is generally believed that the high dimensional latent spaces possess more semantic features, and the low dimensional latent spaces contain the majority of the low-level information such as texture and color features. Since the preservation of the high-level semantic features usually plays a particularly significant role in image-to-image translation tasks, we suggest to embed the watermark at the top layers of the image reconstruction stage in U-Net.

Let $x, y, y' \in [0, 1]^{C \times H \times W}$, $w, w' \in [0, 1]^{C \times H' \times W'}$, and the output of the ith layer in the reconstruction stage of U-Net as $f^i \in \mathbb{R}^{C^i \times H^i \times W^i}$. Note that H', W' are respectively smaller than H and W to avoid the interactive interferences between the features of the to-be-embedded watermark and the input image. A CNN-based watermark encoder Enc is designed to be a sub-module of WEG to extract the features of the watermark w, and the details of Enc are displayed in Table 1.

To achieve the watermark embedding, a fusion operation is designed. Specifically, the output of Enc, $p^i \in \mathbb{R}^{C^{i'} \times H^i \times W^i}$, is firstly concatenated with f^i to generate a combined feature representation $q^i \in \mathbb{R}^{(C^{i'} + C^i) \times H^i \times W^i}$. Then, this representation is transformed to $r^i \in \mathbb{R}^{C^i \times H^i \times W^i}$ by applying an 1×1 conv layer. At last, r^i is fed back into the $(i+1)^{th}$ layer to perform the latter processings and then generate the output image y', which is the translated result with the watermark w embedded.

3.3   The Watermark Extractor

The watermark extractor Dec is designed to extract w' from y', where the divergence between w and w' is supposed to be as small as possible. To achieve this, a convolutional network is constructed to decouple the features of the watermark and the cover image content, and reconstruct the watermark. Note that the number of convolutional blocks in this network will greatly affects the quality of the extracted watermark, i.e., if the number of layers is too small or too large, the quality of the extracted watermark will substantially decrease.

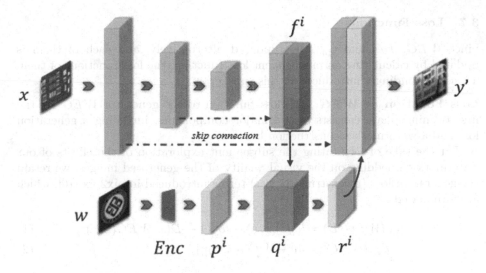

Fig. 3. The architecture of the generator WEG.

3.4 Watermark Embedding Generator

3.5 The Adversary Net

The robustness of watermarks, which is highly proportional to the surviving ability of the watermarks against various post-processing operations or malicious manipulations, is a vital property in digital watermarking. Inspired by the distortion-agnostic watermarking scheme in [23], which utilizes adversarial training and an adversarial net to drastically improve the robustness of watermarks, we adopt its adversarial network G_{adv} to enhance the robustness of our watermarks. Note that the output of WEG, y', is fed into G_{adv} to generate a distorted version of y', i.e., $y'_{adv} \in [0,1]^{C \times H \times W}$.

3.6 Training Details

Specifically, we divide the training process into two phases. The first phase focuses on the image-to-image translation process, with D, Dec, WEG alternatively updating their parameters. Then, G_{adv} is added in the second phase for adversarial training, and D, Dec, G_{adv}, WEG are optimized sequentially. We modify the loss functions of the generator WEG and the watermark decoder Dec by adding an adversarial loss term respectively in the second (adversarial training) phase. Note that the adversary net G_{adv} is only utilized in the training process.

3.7   Loss Functions

Since WEG, Dec and G_{adv} are updated alternatively, and each of them is updated by calculating an independent loss function, the loss functions of them are correspondingly introduced in this subsection.

Loss Function of WEG. The loss function of the generator WEG for the first training phase consists of two major components, including a generation loss and a watermark reconstruction loss.

For the sake of facilitating the subsequent exploration of the effects of our watermark embedding on the visual quality of the generated images, we retain the generation loss (reconstruction loss) terms introduced in pix2pix [16], which are formulated as

$$\mathcal{L}_{cGAN}(WEG, D) = log D(x, y) + log(1 - D(x, WEG(x, z))), \tag{1}$$
$$\mathcal{L}_{L1}(WEG) = ||y - WEG(x, z)||_1. \tag{2}$$

On the other hand, since the embedded image watermarks should be extracted as complete as possible, we utilize the L2 distance to model the distortions between the extracted (reconstructed) and original watermarks, as

$$\mathcal{L}_{wm}(WEG) = ||w - w'||_2. \tag{3}$$

With the generation loss and the watermark reconstruction loss, the loss function of WEG becomes

$$WEG^* = \arg \min_{WEG} \max_{D} \mathcal{L}_{cGAN}(WEG, D) + \lambda \mathcal{L}_{L1}(WEG) + \beta \mathcal{L}_{wm}(WEG), \tag{4}$$

where λ and β serve as the hyper-parameters. It is worth noting that β controls the embedding strength of the watermark. In general, a large β usually induced a lower visual quality of the generated image, while an inadequate weight tend to damage the embedding strength of the watermark and thus leading to a worse performance when extracting the watermarks.

In the adversarial training phase, we modify the above watermark reconstruction loss by adding another constraint, which constrains the watermark to be correctly decoded against diagnostic distortions. Besides, a new image distortion constraint is added to prevent excessive distortions from being generated by the adversary net G_{adv}. These two losses described above is formally defined as

$$\mathcal{L}_{wm}^{adv}(WEG) = ||w - w'||_2 + ||w - w_{adv}||_2, \tag{5}$$
$$\mathcal{L}_{img}^{adv}(WEG) = ||y' - y'_{adv}||_2. \tag{6}$$

Then, the complete optimization objective of WEG in the adversarial training phase is formulated as

$$WEG_{adv}^* = \arg \min_{WEG} \max_{D} \mathcal{L}_{cGAN}(WEG, D) + \lambda \mathcal{L}_{L1}(WEG)$$
$$+ \beta \mathcal{L}_{wm}^{adv}(WEG) + \gamma \mathcal{L}_{img}^{adv}(WEG). \tag{7}$$

Loss Function of Dec. The training objective of Dec in the first phase is defined by constraining the watermark reconstruction distortions, as

$$\mathcal{L}(Dec) = ||w - w'||_2. \tag{8}$$

Besides of constraining the different between w and w', the loss function of Dec in the second training phase (adversarial training) also contains a penalty term for measuring the difference between w_{adv} and w. It is formulated as

$$\mathcal{L}_{adv}(Dec) = ||w - w'||_2 + ||w - w_{adv}||_2. \tag{9}$$

Loss Function of G_{adv}. For updating the adversary net in the adversarial training stage, we minimize an adversarial training loss defined as

$$\mathcal{L}_{adv}(G_{adv}) = \alpha_1 ||y' - y'_{adv}||_2 - \alpha_2 ||w - w_{adv}||_2, \tag{10}$$

where α_1 controls the strength of the distortion strengths generated by G_{adv} and α_2 controls the importance of the watermark reconstruction loss.

4   Experimental Results

4.1   Datasets

Image-to-Image Translation Dataset. We evaluate our method on the CMP Facades dataset [35], which contains more than 500 pairs of architectural labels and real photos. The image-to-image translation task remains the same as that in [16], where the pix2pix model learns a mapping from architectural labels to photos. The 256×256 images are employed in both the training and testing process, and the translated images are generated with the same resolution.

Image Watermark Dataset. We collected 55 emblems from different universities to serve as an image watermark dataset. 50 out of 55 are employed as the training set and 5/55 are employed as the testing set. These emblems are preprocessed into 64×64 resolution images with a black background and a white foreground.

4.2   Training Details

The inputs and outputs of the models are images with 3 channels, in all the experiments in this paper. The batch size is set to 1, which is also employed in [16]. The Adam optimizer [20] is adopted, with a learning rate of 0.0002 and the momentum parameters $\beta_1 = 0.5$ and $\beta_2 = 0.999$. The network configurations of WEG (Enc), Dec, and G_{adv}, are displayed in Table 1. The U-Net part of the generator WEG and the discriminator D are not listed in Table 1, because their detailed architectures are identical to that in pix2pix. A randomly selected watermark is embedded at each iteration during the training/testing stage. Note that the experiments in this paper are performed by placing the fusion operation at the last layer of U-Net.

Table 1. Network configurations of WEG, Dec, and G_{adv}.

Name	Operation	Channel	Filter size	Stride	Padding
$WEG(Enc)$	Conv2dTranspose	16	5×5	2	2 (Output = 1)
Dec	Conv2d	16	5×5	1	2
	Conv2d	16	5×5	1	2
	Conv2d	16	5×5	1	2
	Conv2d	16	5×5	1	2
	Conv2d	16	5×5	1	2
	Conv2d	12	5×5	1	2
	AvgPool2D	–	2×2	2	–
	Conv2d	6	5×5	1	2
	AvgPool2D	–	2×2	2	–
	Conv2d	3	5×5	1	2
G_{adv}	Conv2d	16	5×5	1	2
	Conv2d	3	5×5	1	2

4.3 Visual Quality Study of the Generated Images

In this experiment, pix2pix is implemented by ourselves as the baseline to quantitatively evaluate the quality of the generated images (from the proposed JoinTW and the baseline) with various metrics. Meanwhile, we analyze the impact of adopting the watermark embedding into the image-to-image translation process on image qualities. The results are presented in Table 2 and the qualitative results of generated images are displayed in Fig. 4. The results presented are based on embedding 64×64 watermarks into 256×256 images.

Table 2. Quantitative evaluation results.

	SSIM [38]	FID [11]	NIQE [26]	PIQE [27]	BRISQUE [25]
Pix2pix	0.256	154.035	61.405	5.495	**0.506**
JoinTW	**0.261**	**148.879**	**51.314**	**4.643**	0.496

Structural Similarity (SSIM). SSIM [38] is a frequently used metric for image quality assessment. It measures the similarity between two images, where a higher scores indicates a better visual quality. When the two images are completely identical, the SSIM score reaches 1. Here, the ground-truth images in the dataset are employed as the reference images. We calculate the SSIM scores for pix2pix and JoinTW generated images respectively. Unfortunately, both groups give low scores. In our opinion, the unsatisfactory SSIM scores are induced by the existence of certain differences between the generated images and their corresponding ground truths, though the visual quality of the generated results are

original image x ground truth y pix2pix   JoinTW

Fig. 4. Qualitative results of the generated images.

decent (as shown in Fig. 4). Still, we can observe that the visual qualities of the images generated from JoinTW and pix2pix are very close, which reveals that our joint watermarking and translation scheme gives little degradations to the image-to-image translation performances.

Fréchet Inception Distance (FID). FID [11] is commonly used to evaluate the visual quality of GAN-generated images, where a lower score indicates a better image quality. FID is calculated between the ground-truths and the images generated from JoinTW and pix2pix, respectively. According to Table 2 and Fig. 4, JoinTW performs slightly better than pix2pix, which also indicates that our watermarking mechanism does not hurt the performances of image-to-image translation model.

NIQE, PIQE and BRISQUE. Three no-reference image quality assessment methods, NIQE [26], PIQE [27], and BRISQUE [25], are employed to directly evaluate the qualities of the images generated from JoinTW and pix2pix. In general, the performances of JoinTW and pix2pix are highly similar, where JoinTW performing slightly better in terms of both NIQE and PIQE, and slightly inferior when using BRISQUE. These results again reveals that our proposed method can maintain the quality of the generated images while embedding the watermarks.

Ground Truth   Extracted Watermark

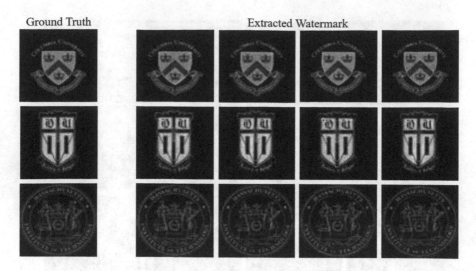

Fig. 5. Qualitative results of the watermarks.

4.4 Qualities of the Extracted Watermarks

We analyze the extracted image watermarks qualitatively and quantitatively. Qualitatively, watermarks are extracted with high integrity and university emblems can be identified, as shown in Fig. 5. By employing the preprocessed watermark images as ground truths, we utilize SSIM and MSE to quantitatively evaluate the qualities of the extracted watermarks. The average MSE metric score is 0.000722 and the average SSIM score is 0.943, which strongly proves that our proposed work is reasonable and effective in jointly performing watermark embedding and image-to-image translation.

4.5 Watermark Robustness Under Agnostic Distortions

To evaluate the robustness of our embedded watermarks against different distortions conditions, we firstly generate the watermarked images in the testing stage. Then, these generated images are process by various post-processing techniques. At last, the image watermarks are extracted from these post-processed images and compared to the ground truth watermarks in terms of the MSE metric. Meanwhile, a baseline group of watermarks is obtained without the adversarial training step. Its extracted watermarks are also assessed under the same post-processing conditions. The quantitative results are shown in Table 3 and some of the extracted watermarks are displayed in Fig. 5. Note that the mixed distortion stands for the combination of brightness, hue, contrast, and saturation adjustments.

According to the experimental results, the image watermarks, which are extracted by our proposed framework, can maintain a high quality even against unseen distortions. It proves that our proposed watermarking method can ensure high robustness.

Table 3. Quantitative evaluation results.

Distortion	Brightness			Hue		
Amplitude	0.1	0.2	0.3	0.1	0.2	0.3
JoinTW w/adv	0.003363	0.003865	0.005417	0.006093	0.017695	0.027104
JoinTW w/o adv	0.007615	0.007504	0.008727	0.012950	0.024439	0.034831
Distortion	Contrast			Saturation		
Amplitude	0.1	0.2	0.3	0.1	0.2	0.3
JoinTW w/adv	0.003366	0.003656	0.003461	0.003681	0.003726	0.004184
JoinTW w/o adv	0.007279	0.007627	0.008371	0.007306	0.007837	0.008060
Distortion	Mix			Gaussian noise (mean = 0.0, variance = 1.0)		
Amplitude	0.1	0.2	0.3	5.0	10.0	15.0
JoinTW w/adv	0.006274	0.014602	0.025605	0.003636	0.004099	0.005197
JoinTW w/o adv	0.013166	0.024261	0.028879	0.007632	0.008744	0.010433
Distortion	Gaussian blur					
Amplitude	0.1	0.2	0.3	0.4	0.5	0.6
JoinTW w/adv	0.003463	0.003977	0.004723	0.006390	0.008879	0.011834
JoinTW w/o adv	0.007221	0.007250	0.007727	0.008884	0.010861	0.013045

5 Conclusions

In this paper, we propose a proactive forensic method for the image-to-image translation tasks to facilitate the traceabilities of the generated images, by jointly performing image-to-image translation and image watermarking. Specifically, we propose a joint image-to-image translation and watermarking framework (JoinTW) as well as the corresponding loss functions, and boost the robustness of watermark by adopting an adversarial training technique. Experiments demonstrate that our proposed JoinTW can successfully and effectively embed the watermark during the image-to-image translation process and the embedded watermark possesses strong robustness against various seen and unseen distortions. Note that our proposed mechanism can actually be conveniently transferred to other image reconstruction models, which are constructed based on U-Net architecture.

References

1. Barni, M.: Steganography in digital media: principles, algorithms, and applications. IEEE Sig. Process. Mag. **28**(5), 142–144 (2011)
2. Barni, M., Bartolini, F., Cox, I.J., Hernández, J., Pérez-González, F.: Digital watermarking for copyright protection: a communications perspective. IEEE Commun. Mag. **39**(8), 90–91 (2001)
3. Bhattacharjee, D., Kim, S., Vizier, G., Salzmann, M.: DUNIT: detection-based unsupervised image-to-image translation. In: IEEE/CVF Conference on Computer Vision and Pattern Recognition, pp. 4786–4795 (2020)

4. Cayre, F., Fontaine, C., Furon, T.: Watermarking security: theory and practice. IEEE Trans. Sig. Process. **53**(10), 3976–3987 (2005)
5. Chen, Y., Xu, X., Jia, J.: Domain adaptive image-to-image translation. In: IEEE/CVF Conference on Computer Vision and Pattern Recognition, pp. 5273–5282 (2020)
6. Dou, H., Chen, C., Hu, X., Jia, L., Peng, S.: Asymmetric CycleGAN for image-to-image translations with uneven complexities. Neurocomputing **415**, 114–122 (2020)
7. Fang, H., et al.: Deep template-based watermarking. IEEE Trans. Circ. Syst. Video Technol. **31**(4), 1436–1451 (2021)
8. Gao, Y., et al.: High-fidelity and arbitrary face editing. In: IEEE Conference on Computer Vision and Pattern Recognition, pp. 16115–16124 (2021)
9. Hamidi, M., Haziti, M.E., Cherifi, H., Aboutajdine, D.: A blind robust image watermarking approach exploiting the DFT magnitude. In: IEEE/ACS International Conference of Computer Systems and Applications, pp. 1–6 (2015)
10. Hayes, J., Danezis, G.: Generating steganographic images via adversarial training. In: Guyon, I., et al. (eds.) Advances in Neural Information Processing Systems 30: Annual Conference on Neural Information Processing Systems, pp. 1954–1963 (2017)
11. Heusel, M., Ramsauer, H., Unterthiner, T., Nessler, B., Hochreiter, S.: GANs trained by a two time-scale update rule converge to a local Nash equilibrium. In: Guyon, I., et al. (eds.) Advances in Neural Information Processing Systems 30: Annual Conference on Neural Information Processing Systems, pp. 6626–6637 (2017)
12. Holub, V., Fridrich, J.J.: Designing steganographic distortion using directional filters. In: IEEE International Workshop on Information Forensics and Security, pp. 234–239 (2012)
13. Holub, V., Fridrich, J.J., Denemark, T.: Universal distortion function for steganography in an arbitrary domain. EURASIP J. Inf. Secur. **2014**, 1 (2014). https://doi.org/10.1186/1687-417X-2014-1
14. Huang, X., Belongie, S.J.: Arbitrary style transfer in real-time with adaptive instance normalization. In: IEEE International Conference on Computer Vision, pp. 1510–1519 (2017)
15. Iizuka, S., Simo-Serra, E., Ishikawa, H.: Let there be color!: Joint end-to-end learning of global and local image priors for automatic image colorization with simultaneous classification. ACM Trans. Graph. **35**(4), 110:1–110:11 (2016)
16. Isola, P., Zhu, J., Zhou, T., Efros, A.A.: Image-to-image translation with conditional adversarial networks. In: IEEE Conference on Computer Vision and Pattern Recognition, pp. 5967–5976 (2017)
17. Jeong, S., Kim, Y., Lee, E., Sohn, K.: Memory-guided unsupervised image-to-image translation. In: IEEE Conference on Computer Vision and Pattern Recognition, pp. 6558–6567 (2021)
18. Jing, J., Deng, X., Xu, M., Wang, J., Guan, Z.: HiNet: deep image hiding by invertible network. In: IEEE/CVF International Conference on Computer Vision, pp. 4713–4722 (2021)
19. Kim, S., Jeong, Y., Kim, J., Kim, J., Lee, H.T., Seo, J.H.: IronMask: modular architecture for protecting deep face template. In: IEEE Conference on Computer Vision and Pattern Recognition, pp. 16125–16134 (2021)
20. Kingma, D.P., Ba, J.: Adam: a method for stochastic optimization. In: International Conference on Learning Representations (2015)

21. Li, X., et al.: Image-to-image translation via hierarchical style disentanglement. In: IEEE Conference on Computer Vision and Pattern Recognition, pp. 8639–8648 (2021)
22. Lin, T., et al.: Drafting and revision: Laplacian pyramid network for fast high-quality artistic style transfer. In: IEEE/CVF Conference on Computer Vision and Pattern Recognition, pp. 5141–5150 (2021)
23. Luo, X., Zhan, R., Chang, H., Yang, F., Milanfar, P.: Distortion agnostic deep watermarking. In: IEEE/CVF Conference on Computer Vision and Pattern Recognition, pp. 13545–13554 (2020)
24. Marra, F., Gragnaniello, D., Verdoliva, L., Poggi, G.: Do GANs leave artificial fingerprints? In: IEEE Conference on Multimedia Information Processing and Retrieval, pp. 506–511 (2019)
25. Mittal, A., Moorthy, A.K., Bovik, A.C.: No-reference image quality assessment in the spatial domain. IEEE Trans. Image Process. **21**(12), 4695–4708 (2012)
26. Mittal, A., Soundararajan, R., Bovik, A.C.: Making a "completely blind" image quality analyzer. IEEE Sig. Process. Lett. **20**(3), 209–212 (2013)
27. Venkatanath, N., Praneeth, D., Bh, M.C., Channappayya, S.S., Medasani, S.S.: Blind image quality evaluation using perception based features. In: National Conference on Communications, pp. 1–6 (2015)
28. Park, T., Liu, M., Wang, T., Zhu, J.: Semantic image synthesis with spatially-adaptive normalization. In: IEEE/CVF Conference on Computer Vision and Pattern Recognition, pp. 2337–2346 (2019)
29. Richardson, E., et al.: Encoding in style: a StyleGAN encoder for image-to-image translation. In: IEEE Conference on Computer Vision and Pattern Recognition, pp. 2287–2296 (2021)
30. Shafaei, A., Little, J.J., Schmidt, M.: AutoRetouch: automatic professional face retouching. In: IEEE Winter Conference on Applications of Computer Vision, pp. 989–997 (2021)
31. Shaham, T.R., Gharbi, M., Zhang, R., Shechtman, E., Michaeli, T.: Spatially-adaptive pixelwise networks for fast image translation. In: IEEE/CVF Conference on Computer Vision and Pattern Recognition, pp. 14882–14891 (2021)
32. Shelhamer, E., Long, J., Darrell, T.: Fully convolutional networks for semantic segmentation. IEEE Trans. Pattern Anal. Mach. Intell. **39**(4), 640–651 (2017)
33. Singh, P., Chadha, R.S.: A survey of digital watermarking techniques, applications and attacks. Int. J. Eng. Innov. Technol. **2**(9), 165–175 (2013)
34. Tancik, M., Mildenhall, B., Ng, R.: StegaStamp: invisible hyperlinks in physical photographs. In: IEEE/CVF Conference on Computer Vision and Pattern Recognition, pp. 2114–2123 (2020)
35. Tyleček, R., Šára, R.: Spatial pattern templates for recognition of objects with regular structure. In: Weickert, J., Hein, M., Schiele, B. (eds.) GCPR 2013. LNCS, vol. 8142, pp. 364–374. Springer, Heidelberg (2013). https://doi.org/10.1007/978-3-642-40602-7_39
36. Wang, T., Liu, M., Zhu, J., Tao, A., Kautz, J., Catanzaro, B.: High-resolution image synthesis and semantic manipulation with conditional GANs. In: IEEE Conference on Computer Vision and Pattern Recognition, pp. 8798–8807 (2018)
37. Wang, T., et al.: Video-to-video synthesis. In: Advances in Neural Information Processing Systems 31: Annual Conference on Neural Information Processing Systems, pp. 1152–1164 (2018)
38. Wang, Z., Bovik, A.C., Sheikh, H.R., Simoncelli, E.P.: Image quality assessment: from error visibility to structural similarity. IEEE Trans. Image Process. **13**(4), 600–612 (2004)

39. Xie, S., Tu, Z.: Holistically-nested edge detection. In: IEEE International Conference on Computer Vision, pp. 1395–1403 (2015)
40. Yu, N., Davis, L., Fritz, M.: Attributing fake images to GANs: learning and analyzing GAN fingerprints. In: IEEE/CVF International Conference on Computer Vision, pp. 7555–7565 (2019)
41. Zhao, Y., Wu, R., Dong, H.: Unpaired image-to-image translation using adversarial consistency loss. In: Vedaldi, A., Bischof, H., Brox, T., Frahm, J.-M. (eds.) ECCV 2020. LNCS, vol. 12354, pp. 800–815. Springer, Cham (2020). https://doi.org/10.1007/978-3-030-58545-7_46
42. Zhong, X., Huang, P., Mastorakis, S., Shih, F.Y.: An automated and robust image watermarking scheme based on deep neural networks. IEEE Trans. Multim. **23**, 1951–1961 (2021)
43. Zhu, J., Park, T., Isola, P., Efros, A.A.: Unpaired image-to-image translation using cycle-consistent adversarial networks. In: IEEE International Conference on Computer Vision, pp. 2242–2251 (2017)

Author Index

Printed in the United States
by Baker & Taylor Publisher Services